UNIVERSITY CASEBOOK SERIES

EDITORIAL BOARD

ROBERT C. CLARK
DIRECTING EDITOR
Dean & Royall Professor of Law
Harvard University

DANIEL A. FARBER
Henry J. Fletcher Professor of Law
University of Minnesota

OWEN M. FISS
Sterling Professor of Law
Yale University

GERALD GUNTHER
William Nelson Cromwell Professor of Law, Emeritus
Stanford University

THOMAS H. JACKSON
President
University of Rochester

HERMA HILL KAY
Dean & Barbara Nachtrieb Armstrong Professor of Law
University of California, Berkeley

HAROLD HONGJU KOH
Gerard C. & Bernice Latrobe Smith Professor of International Law
Yale Law School

DAVID W. LEEBRON
Dean & Lucy G. Moses Professor of Law
Columbia University

SAUL LEVMORE
William B. Graham Professor of Law
University of Chicago

ROBERT L. RABIN
A. Calder Mackay Professor of Law
Stanford University

CAROL M. ROSE
Gordon Bradford Tweedy Professor of Law & Organization
Yale University

DAVID L. SHAPIRO
William Nelson Cromwell Professor of Law
Harvard University

PROCESSES OF DISPUTE RESOLUTION:

The Role of Lawyers

THIRD EDITION

by

ALAN SCOTT RAU
Robert F. Windfohr & Anne Burnett Windfohr Professor of Law
The University of Texas at Austin School of Law

EDWARD F. SHERMAN
Professor of Law
Tulane University School of Law

SCOTT R. PEPPET
Associate Professor of Law
University of Colorado School of Law

Chapter VI, "International Dispute Resolution: Cross–Cultural Dimensions
and Structuring Appropriate Processes" was contributed by Professor
Harold I. Abramson, Touro Law School

This edition is the successor to John S. Murray, Alan Scott Rau, & Edward
F. Sherman, Processes of Dispute Resolution: The Role of Lawyers, first
published in 1989 (2nd Edition 1996)

NEW YORK, NEW YORK

FOUNDATION PRESS

2002

Foundation Press, a division of West Group, has created this publication to provide you with accurate and authoritative information concerning the subject matter covered. However, this publication was not necessarily prepared by persons licensed to practice law in a particular jurisdiction. Foundation Press is not engaged in rendering legal or other professional advice, and this publication is not a substitute for the advice of an attorney. If you require legal or other expert advice, you should seek the services of a competent attorney or other professional.

COPYRIGHT © 1989, 1996 FOUNDATION PRESS
COPYRIGHT © 2002 By FOUNDATION PRESS
                      395 Hudson Street
                      New York, NY 10014
                      Phone Toll Free 1–877–888–1330
                      Fax (212) 367–6799
                      fdpress.com
All Rights Reserved
Printed in the United States of America
ISBN 1–58778–011–9

PREFACE TO THE THIRD EDITION

The Alternative Dispute Resolution field has come of age since the first edition of this text was published thirteen years ago. We no longer need to persuade lawyers, law school professors, and law students that ADR is an appropriate subject for study or a useful topic for practicing lawyers and judges.

Alternative methods of dispute resolution have become part of the processing of a wide range of disputes in our society. Hundreds of thousands of disputes are voluntarily submitted to mediation each year through community dispute resolution centers, other non-profit institutions, and a growing host of entrepreneurial providers. In a sizable number of state and federal courts, dispute resolution procedures are invoked as part of the litigation process. Private companies and governmental agencies have adopted "system designs" incorporating ADR procedures to prevent, or to resolve, the inevitable disputes that arise in their operations. Delivery of mediation services has moved to videoconferencing and cyberspace, as experimentation with different forms continues. Arbitration has expanded from such traditional fields as labor and construction to a wide range of contractual services such as investments, banking, health care, and employment. It is obvious that lawyers today must have a grounding in ADR in order to provide adequate advice and representation in many areas of the law.

Most law schools now offer courses in ADR. Still, stereotypes persist, and habits that developed over many decades change slowly. Within the first few months of law school, law students are often socialized to believe that the most prestigious role for a lawyer finds its principal outlet in the courtroom. Litigation is the standard; negotiation, mediation and arbitration are invisible processes. Our aim in this book is to bring litigation into perspective—to encourage students to see it as a system of dispute resolution, one with its own virtues and failings, but not an inevitable or the only process for resolving legal disputes We want students to see that the many alternative processes of dispute resolution are not distinct from litigation, nor mutually exclusive, but usefully complementary processes. The contemporary lawyer needs to develop an ability to work effectively with all available processes, separately, in series, and even simultaneously.

The reasons for the great expansion of ADR in the last couple of decades are varied. They stem in part from the inadequacies of litigation as a dispute resolution mechanism. Parties have expressed dissatisfaction with a court system that imposes heavy costs in terms of time and money and that

iii

lacks flexibility in providing solutions. But there are other important dimensions of ADR than an anti-litigation bias that account for its new popularity, such as its potential for reducing the adversariness of the trial system and accomplishing a more satisfactory resolution of disputes. We will examine in this book both the philosophical well-springs of the ADR movement and the countervailing objections of its critics.

As the title to this book indicates, our focus is on process. At times, this is theoretical and policy-oriented. We think an understanding of the underlying philosophy, history, strengths, and weaknesses of each alternative dispute resolution process is necessary for a lawyer to appreciate how and when it can be used in helping clients resolve their disputes. But we place equal importance on practical application. Thus, we attempt to provide a comprehensive overview of the legal procedures and doctrines that a lawyer will need to know in order to use the techniques effectively. These legal aspects are sometimes highly technical—as in the litigation procedures that influence negotiated settlement, the law governing arbitration practice, and the formalities of court-administered ADR—and we believe these materials provide a solid introduction to their use. We have included extensive citations to cases and other sources so that these materials will also be a helpful reference book for students once they are in practice.

We place particular stress on the role of "the law" in each alternative process, on the lawyer's role in choosing processes and implementing strategies, and on the lawyering skills needed to use the processes effectively. The skills component to the course can be substantial, depending on the specific objectives of the instructor. We believe that the more students practice ADR skills and become comfortable with ADR procedures, the better equipped they will be to serve their clients' interests.

We have organized these materials to make them flexible for the varied ADR-related courses currently being offered in law schools. We strongly recommend that a skills component, with stress on the lawyer's role as an advocate for his or her client, be blended into the course through the many simulation exercises provided in the Teacher's Manual. We are also continuing, in this edition, our practice of publishing separate smaller books aimed at specific processes: Negotiation (chapter II), Mediation (chapters III and IV) and Arbitration (chapter V).

A note on form: We have substantially edited most cases and selections to delete unnecessary material. Deletions of text due to our editing are indicated by spaced asterisks. Citations in the text, and footnotes from the text, have usually been omitted without indication. Where footnotes to selections do appear, however, we have retained the number they have in the original material. A reader desiring to use the opinion as a research tool can, of course, go the official case reporters.

We have benefited from the helpful comments and critiques of many colleagues and students who have used the prior editions of this book. We are also extremely grateful to those whose conscientious and able research and administrative assistance made completion of this book possible—in particu-

PREFACE TO THE THIRD EDITION **v**

lar Christina Garcia, Chris Piazzola, Sandy Schmeider, Shawn Stigler, Mary Pace, Jonae Harrison, Janice Sayas, Pat Smith and Pat Floyd.

A.S.R.
E.F.S.
S.R.P

DECEMBER, 2001

*

ACKNOWLEDGMENTS*

The following authors and publishers gave us permission to reprint excerpts from copyrighted material; we gratefully acknowledge their assistance.

CHAPTER I

PEANUTS cartoon reprinted by permission of United Features Syndicate, Inc.

Llewellyn, The Bramble Bush: On Our Law and Its Study 12 (1960). Reprinted by permission of Oceana Publications, Inc.

Miller & Sarat, Grievances, Claims, and Disputes: Assessing the Adversary Culture, 15 Law & Soc'y Rev. 525, 526-27, 531-33, 536-46, 561-64 (1980-81). Reprinted by permission of the Law and Society Association.

Galanter, Reading the Landscape of Disputes: What We Know and Don't Know (And Think We Know) About Our Allegedly contentious and Litigious Society, 31 UCLA L. Rev. 4, 13-14 (1983). Originally published in 31 UCLA L. Rev. 4, copyright © 1983, The Regents of the University of California. All rights reserved.

Auerbach, Justice Without Law? 10, 12-13, 78 (1983). From Justice Without Law? by Jerold S. Auerbach. Copyright © 1983 by Oxford University Press, Inc. Reprinted by permission.

Trubek, Sarat, Felstiner, Kritzer & Grossman, The Costs of Ordinary Litigation, 31 UCLA L. Rev. 72, 84, 89, 122 (1983). Originally published in 31 UCLA L. Rev. 4. copyright © 1983, The Regents of the University of California. All rights reserved.

Newman, Rethinking Fairness: Perspectives on the Litigation Process, 94 Yale L.J. 1643, 1644-45 (1985). Reprinted by permission of The Yale Law Journal Company and William S. Hein Company from The Yale Law Journal, Vol. 94, pages 1643-1659.

Gulliver, Disputes and Negotiations: A Cross-Cultural Perspective 13 (1979).

Brazil, The Attorney as Victim: Towards More Candor About the Psychological Price Tag of Litigation Practice, 3 J. Legal Prof. 107, 109-10, 114-117 (1978-79).

vii

viii ACKNOWLEDGMENTS

Fuller, The Forms and Limits of Adjudication, 92 Harv. L. Rev.. 353, 364-71, 382-85, 393-400, 403 (1978). Copyright © 1978 by the Harvard Law Review Association. Reprinted with permission.

The Role of Courts in American Society: Final Report of Council on the Role of Courts, 102-114, 120-21 (Jethro K. Lieberman ed. 1984).

Fuller, Collective Bargaining and the Arbitrator, Proceedings of the 15th Annual Meeting, National Academy of Arbitrators 8, 39-41 (1962). Reprinted with permission. Chapter 2, pages 8, 29-33, and 37-48 and 34-41 from Collective Bargaining and the Arbitrator's Role (Proceedings of the 15th Annual Meeting National Academy of Arbitrators), by Lon L. Fuller. Copyright © 1962, by The Bureau of National Affairs, Inc. Washington, D.C. 20037.

Chayes, The Role of the Judge in Public Law Litigation, 89 Harv. L. Rev. 1281, 1298-99 (1976). Copyright © 1976 by the Harvard Law Review Association.

Fiss, Against Settlement, 93 Yale L.J. 1073, 1075-78, 1082-90 (1984). Reprinted by permission of The Yale Law Journal Company and William S. Hein Company from The Yale Law Journal, Vol. 93, pages 1073-1090.

Edwards, Alternate Dispute Resolution: Panacea or Anathema , 99 Harv. L. Rev.. 668, 678-79 (1986). Copyright © 1986 by the Harvard Law Review Association.

Galanter, The Day After the Litigation Explosion, 46 Maryland L. Rev. 3, 32-37 (1986).

Burger, Isn't There a Better Way?, March 1982, ABA Journal, The Lawyers Magazine, 274-75 (1982).

Friendly, Some Kind of Hearing, 123 U. Pa. L. Rev. 1267, 1287-90 (1975).

Terry Leap, Tenure, Discrimination, and the Courts 16-17 (1993).

CHAPTER II

Cartoon, used by permission of United Media.

Lax & Sebenius, The Manager as Negotiator 90-102 (1986). From The Manager as Negotiator by David Lax and James Sebenius. Used by permission of Simon and Schuster.

Bazerman & Gillespie, Betting on the Future: The Virtues of Contingent Contracts, Harvard Business Review 155, 156-160 (Sept.-Oct. 1999). Copyright © 1999 by the Harvard Business Review.

Falk, The Art of Contract Negotiation, 3 Marquette Sports L.J. 1, 12-14 (1992). Copyright © 1992 by the Marquette Sports Law Journal. Reprinted by permission of the Marquette Sports Law Journal.

Wetlaufer, The Limits of Integrative Bargaining, 85 Georgetown L.J. 369, 374-375 (1996).

Menkel-Meadow, The Transformation of Disputes by Lawyers: What the Dispute Paradigm Does and Does Not Tell Us, J. of Disp. Res. 25, 31-33 (1985). Copyright © 1985 by the Journal of Dispute Resolution. Reprinted by permission of the Journal of Dispute Resolution.

Lax & Sebenius, The Power of Alternatives or the Limits of Negotiation, 1 Neg. J. 163, 169-170 (1985). Reprinted by permission of Plenum Publishing Corp.

Fisher, Ury & Patton, Getting to Yes 3-4 (2d ed. 1991). Excerpts from GETTING TO YES 2/e by Roger Fisher, William Ury and Bruce Patton. Copyright © 1981, 1991 by Roger Fisher and William Ury. Reprinted by permission of Houghton Mifflin Company. All rights reserved.

Gifford, A Context-Based Theory of Strategy Selection in Legal Negotiation, originally published in 46 Ohio St. L.J. 41, 48-52 (1985). Used by permission of the Ohio State Law Journal.

Goodpaster, A Primer on Competitive Bargaining, J. Disp. Res. 325, 346-348 (1996). Reprinted by permission of the Journal of Dispute Resolution.

Schelling, The Strategy of Conflict 22-28 (1960). Reprinted by permission of the publisher from "An Essay on Bargaining" in THE STRATEGY OF CONFLICT by Thomas C. Schelling, pp. 22-28, Cambridge, Mass.: Harvard University Press, Copyright © 1960, 1980 by the President and Fellows of Harvard College, Copyright © renewed 1988 by Thomas C. Schelling.

Fisher, Ury & Patton, Getting to Yes 7-9 (2d ed. 1991). Excerpts from GETTING TO YES 2/e by Roger Fisher, William Ury and Bruce Patton. Copyright © 1981, 1991 by Roger Fisher and William Ury. Reprinted by permission of Houghton Mifflin Company. All rights reserved.

Edwards & White, The Lawyer as Negotiator 115-116 (1977). Reprinted from The Lawyer as Negotiator, Edwards & White, Copyright © 1977, with permission of the West Group.

Lax & Sebenius, The Manager as Negotiator 132-134 (1986). From The Manager as Negotiator by David Lax and James Sebenius. Used by permission of Simon and Schuster.

Fisher, Beyond Yes, 1 Neg. J. 67, 67 (1985). Reprinted by permission of Plenum Publishing Corp.

Fisher, Ury & Patton, Getting to Yes 40-50 (2d ed. 1991). Excerpts from GETTING TO YES 2/e by Roger Fisher, William Ury and Bruce Patton. Copyright © 1981, 1991 by Roger Fisher and William Ury. Reprinted by permission of Houghton Mifflin Company. All rights reserved.

Menkel-Meadow, When Winning Isn't Everything: The Lawyer as Problem-Solver, 28 Hofstra L. Rev. 905, 915-918 (2000). Used by permission of the Hofstra Law Review Association.

Raiffa, Post-Settlement Settlements, 1 Neg. J. 9-12 (1985). Reprinted by permission of Plenum Publishing Corp.

Fisher, Comment, 34 J. of Legal Educ. 120, 121 (1984). Reprinted by permission of the Journal of Legal Education.

Bazerman, Gibbons, Thompson & Valley, Can Negotiators Outperform Game Theory?, in Halpern & Stern (eds.), Debating Rationality: Nonrational Aspects of Organizational Decision Making 78 (1998). Reprinted by permission of the ILR Press.

Korobkin, A Positive Theory of Legal Negotiation, 88 Georgetown L.J. 1789, 1821-1829 (2000).

Thompson & Nadler, Judgmental Biases in Conflict Resolution and How to Overcome Them, in Deutsch & Coleman (eds.), The Handbook of Conflict Resolution: Theory and Practice 213, 224-225 (2000).

Mnookin & Ross, Barriers to Conflict Resolution: Introduction, in Arrow et al. (eds), Barriers to Conflict Resolution 7-8 (1995).

Luce & Raiffa, Games and Decisions 95 (1957).

Lax & Sebenius, The Manager as Negotiator 157-160 (1986). From The Manager as Negotiator by David Lax and James Sebenius. Used by permission of Simon and Schuster.

Pruitt, Strategic Choice in Negotiation, 27 Am. Behavioral Sci. 167-194 (1983).

Shell, Bargaining for Advantage: Negotiation Strategies for Reasonable People 12-14 (1999). Used by permission of Penguin Putnam Inc.

Morris, Sim & Girotto, Time of Decision, Ethical Obligation, and Causal Illusion: Temporal Cues and Social Heuristics in the Prisoner's Dilemma, in Kramer & Messick (eds.), Negotiation as a Social Process 210-213 (1995).

Heumann & Hyman, Negotiation Methods and Litigation Settlement Methods in New Jersey: "You Can't Always Get What You Want," 12 Ohio St. J. Disp. Resol. 253, 262-265 (1997). Reprinted by permission of the Ohio State Journal of Dispute Resolution.

Mnookin, Peppet & Tulumello, Beyond Winning: Negotiating to Create Value in Deals and Disputes 321-322 (2000). Reprinted by permission of the publishers from BEYOND WINNING: NEGOTIATING TO CREATE VALUE IN DEALS AND DISPUTES, by Robert H. Mnookin, Scott R. Peppet, and Andrew S. Tulumello, Cambridge, Mass.: Harvard University Press, Copyright © 2000 by Robert Mnookin, Scott R. Peppet and Andrew S. Tulumello.

Condlin, Bargaining in the Dark: The Normative Incoherence of Lawyer Dispute Bargaining Role, 51 Md. L. Rev. 1, 71-72 (1992).

Birke & Fox, Psychological Principles in Negotiating Civil Settlements, 4 Harv. Neg. L. Rev. 1, 7-12, 14-20, 42-47, 48-51 (1999).

Thompson & Nadler, Judgmental Biases in Conflict Resolution and How to Overcome Them, in Deutsch & Coleman (eds.), The Handbook of Conflict Resolution: Theory and Practice 213, 214-219 (2000).

Kahneman & Tversky, Conflict Resolution: A Cognitive Perspective, in Arrow et al. (eds), Barriers to Conflict Resolution 47 (1995).

Ross, Reactive Devaluation in Negotiation and Conflict Resolution, in Arrow et al. (eds), Barriers to Conflict Resolution 34-40 (1995).

Allred, Anger and Retaliation in Conflict: The Role of Attribution, in Deutsch & Coleman (eds.), The Handbook of Conflict Resolution: Theory and Practice 236, 243-244 (2000).

Adler, Rosen & Silverstein, Emotions in Negotiation: How to Manage Fear and Anger, 14 Neg. J. 161, 167-177 (1998). Reprinted by permission of Plenum Publishing Corp.

Tjosvold & Huston, Social Face and Resistance to Compromise in Bargaining, 104 J. of Soc. Psychol. 57, 59 (1978). Reprinted by permission of Heldref Publications and the Journal of Social Psychology.

Heumann & Hyman, Negotiation Methods and Litigation Settlement Methods in New Jersey: "You Can't Always Get What You Want," 12 Ohio St. J. Disp. Resol. 253, 262-265 (1997). Reprinted by permission of the Ohio State Journal of Dispute Resolution.

Gifford, Legal Negotiation: Theory and Applications 21 (1989). Reprinted from Legal Negotiation: Theory and Applications, Gifford, 1989 with permission of the West Group.

Mnookin, Peppet & Tulumello, The Tension Between Empathy and Assertiveness, 12 Neg. J. 217, 218-226 (1996). Reprinted by permission of Plenum Publishing Corp.

Allred, Distinguishing Best and Strategic Practices: A Framework for Managing the Dilemma Between Creating and Claiming Value, Neg. J. 387, 388-390 (2000). Reprinted by permission of Plenum Publishing Corp.

Stone, Patton & Heen, Difficult Conversations 37-40, 167-168 (1999). Copyright © 1999 by Douglas Stone, Bruce Patton and Sheila Heen. Used by permission of Penguin Putnam Inc.

Nyerges, Ten Commandments for a Negotiator, 3 Neg. J. 21 (1987). Reprinted by permission of Plenum Publishing Corp.

Menkel-Meadow, Teaching about Gender and Negotiation: Sex, Truths, and Videotape, Neg. J. 357, 358-359, 364 (2000). Reprinted by permission of Plenum Publishing Corp.

Rhode, Gender and Professional Roles, 63 Fordham L. Rev. 39, 42-43 (1994).

Rack, Negotiated Justice: Gender and Ethnic Minority Bargaining Patterns in the Metro Court Study, 20 Hamline J. Pub. L. & Pol. 211, 222-236 (1999).

Watson, Gender Versus Power as a Predictor of Negotiation Behavior and Outcomes, 10 Neg. J. 117, 119 (1994). Reprinted by permission of Plenum Publishing Corp.

Rubin & Sander, Culture, Negotiation, and The Eye of the Beholder, 7 Neg. J. 249 (1991). Reprinted by permission of Plenum Publishing Corp.

Lewicki & Litterer, Negotiation 166-169 (1985).

Ayres, Further Evidence of Discrimination in New Car Negotiations and Estimates of Its Cause, 94 Mich. L. Rev. 109, 120 (1995).

Adler & Silverstein, When David Meets Goliath: Dealing With Power Differentials in Negotiations, 5 Harv. Neg. L. Rev. 1, 29-48 (2000).

Farnsworth, Precontractual Liability and Preliminary Agreements: Fair Dealing and Failed Negotiations, 87 Colum. L. Rev. 217, 239-242 (1987). This article originally appeared at Colum. L. Rev. 217 (1987). Reprinted by permission.

Longan, Ethics in Settlement Negotiations: Forward, 52 Mercer L. Rev. 807, 810-829 (2001).

Crystal, The Lawyer's Duty to Disclose Material Facts in Contract or Settlement Negotiations, 87 Kentucky L.J. 1055, 1059-1074 (1998-99).

Rosenberger, Laissez-"Fair": An Argument for the Status Quo Ethical Constraints on Lawyers as Negotiators, 13 Ohio St. J. on Dis. Resol. 611, 638 (1998).

White, Machiavelli and the Bar: Ethical Limitations on Lying in Negotiation, Am. B. Found. Research J. 921, 927-938 (1980).

Applbaum, Ethics for Adversaries: The Morality of Roles in Public and Professional Life 5-6 (1990).

Raiffa, The Art and Science of Negotiation 142-144 (1982). Reprinted by permission of the publisher from THE ART AND SCIENCE OF NEGOTIATION: HOW TO RESOLVE CONFLICTS AND GET THE BEST OUT OF BARGAINING by Howard Raiffa, pp. 142-144, Cambridge Mass.: The Belknap Press of Harvard University Press, Copyright © 1982 by the President and Fellows of Harvard College.

Gordon, Private Settlement as Alternative Adjudication: A Rationale for Negotiation Ethics, 18 U. Mich. J. L. Ref. 503, 530 (1985).

Steele, Deceptive Negotiating and High-Toned Morality, 39 Vand. L. Rev. 1387, 1402 (1986).

Alfini, Settlement Ethics and Lawyering in ADR Proceedings: A Proposal to Revise Rule 4.1, 19 N. Ill. U. L. Rev. 255, 270-271 (1999).

Perschbacher, Regulating Lawyers' Negotiations, 27 Ariz. L. Rev. 75, 133-136 (1985).

Rubin, A Causerie on Lawyers' Ethics in Negotiation, 35 La.L.Rev. 577, 591-592 (1975).

Mnookin, Peppet & Tulumello, Beyond Winning: Negotiating to Create Value in Deals and Disputes 286-293 (2000). Reprinted by permission of the publishers from BEYOND WINNING: NEGOTIATING TO CREATE VALUE IN DEALS AND DISPUTES, by Robert H. Mnookin, Scott R. Peppet, and Andrew S. Tulumello, Cambridge, Mass.: Harvard University Press, Copyright © 2000 by Robert Mnookin, Scott R. Peppet and Andrew S. Tulumello.

Fisher, A Code of Negotiation Practices for Lawyers, 1 Neg. J. 105-110 (1995). Reprinted by permission of Plenum Publishing Corp.

Epstein, Post-Settlement Malpractice: Undoing the Done Deal, 46 Cath. U. L. Rev. 453, 453-460, 463-464, 472-474 (1997).

Kramer, Consent Decrees and the Rights of Third Parties, 87 Mich. L. Rev. 321, 324-331 (1988).

Kull, Restitution as a Remedy for Breach of Contract, 67 S. Cal. L. Rev. 1465, 1512-1514 (1994).

Sherman, From Loser Pays to Modified Offer-of-Judgment Rules: Reconciling Incentives to Settle with Access to Justice, 76 Tex. L. Rev. 1863, 1863-1877 (1998). Copyright © 1998 by the Texas Law Review Association. Used by permission.

Michaels, Rule 408: A Litigation Mine Field, 19 Litig. 34, 34-38, 71 (Fall 1992).

Brazil, Settling Civil Disputes 44-46 (1985). Published by the American Bar Association.

Panel Discussion, Comments by Judge Hubert L. Will, The Role of the Judge in the Settlement Process (Federal Judicial Center 1983).

Panel Discussion, Comments by Judge Alvin B. Rubin, The Role of the Judge in the Settlement Process (Federal Judicial Center 1983).

Schuck, The Role of Judges in Settling Complex Cases: The Agent Orange Example, 53 U. Chi. L. Rev. 337, 344-348 (1986). Reprinted by permission of the University of Chicago Law Review.

Sherman, Court-Mandated Alternative Dispute Resolution: What Form of Participation Should be Required?, 46 SMU L. Rev. 2079, 2094-2096, 2103-2108 (1993).

CHAPTER III

Cartoon, "Would I be a wimp to suggest mediation?," by John Chase, published with artist's permission.

Northrop, The Mediational Approval Theory of Law in American Realism, 44 Va. L. Rev. 347, 349 (1958).

Folberg & Taylor, Mediation: A Comprehensive Guide to Resolving Conflicts Without Litigation, 39-34 (1994).

Shaw, Divorce Mediation: Some Keys to the Process, 9 Mediation Q. 27 (1985). Reprinted with permission from Jossey-Bass, Inc.

Odom , The Mediation Hearing: A Primer, in Joseph E. Palenski & Harold M. Launer, Mediation: Context and Challenges 12 (1986). Courtesy of Charles C. Thomas, Publisher, Springfield, Illinois.

Moore, The Caucus: Private Meetings That Promote Settlement, 16 Mediation Q. 87, 89 (1987).

Silbey & Merry, Mediator Settlement Strategies, 8 Law & Policy 7, 12-19 (1986). Reprinted with permission from Basil Blackwell Limited.

Moore, The Mediation Process, 204-206, 212-216 (1986). Reprinted with permission from Jossey-Bass, Inc.

Mnookin & Kornhauser, Bargaining in the Shadow of the Law: The Case for Divorce, 88 Yale L.J. 950, 968 (1979). Reprinted by permission of The Yale Law Journal Company and William S. Hein Company from The Yale Law Journal, Vol. 88, pages 950-997.

Erlanger, Chambliss, & Melli, Participation and Flexibility in Informal Processes: Cautions from the Divorce Context, 21 Law & Soc'y Rev. 585, 598-600 (1987). Reprinted by permission of the Law and Society Association.

Marlow, The Rule of Law in Divorce Mediation, 9 Mediations Q. 5, 10-13 (1985). Reprinted with permission from Jossey-Bass, Inc.

Stulberg & Montgomery, Design Requirements for Mediator Developments Programs, 15 Hofstra L.Rev. 499, 504 (1987). Reprinted with permission of the Hofstra Law Review.

Riskin, Mediation and Lawyers, 43 Ohio St. L.J. 29, 34-5, 37-41 (1982). Originally published in 43 Ohio St. L.J. 29 (1982). Copyright © 1982 by The Ohio State University.

Rogers & Salem, A Student's Guide to Resolving Conflicts Without Litigation 19–20 (1987). Reprinted with permission of Matthew Bender.

McEwan & Maiman, Mediations in Small Claims Court: Achieving Compliance Through Consent, 18 Law & Soc'y Rev. 11, 40-47 (1984). Reprinted by permission of the Law and Society Association.

Vidmar, Assessing the Effects of the Case Characteristics and Settlement Forum on Dispute Outcomes and Compliance, 21 Law & Soc'y Rev. 155, 162-63 (1987). Reprinted by permission of the Law and Society Association.

Fuller, Mediation-Its Forms and Functions, 44 S. Cal. L. Rev. 305, 308, 325-26 (1971). Reprinted with permission of the Southern California Law Review.

Posner, American Bar Association Section of Dispute Resolution, 11th Annual Frank E.A. Sander Program: The 21st Century Lawyer: Problem Solver or Case Processor? (July 8, 2000).

Haynes, Mediation and Therapy: An Alternative View, 10 Mediation Q. 21, 22-30 (1992).

Freund, The Neutral Negotiator: Why and How Mediation Can Work to Resolve Dollar Disputes, 18-48 (Prentice Hall Law & Business, 1994).

Contuzzi, Should Parties Tell Mediators Their Bottom Line?, 6 Dispute Resolution Mag. 30, 31-32 (Spring 2000).

Purnell, The Attorney as Mediator-Inherent Conflict of Interest? 32 UCLA L. Rev. 986, 1008-1011 (1985).

Bush, Using Process Observations to Teach Alternative Dispute Resolution: Alternatives to Simulation, 37 J. Legal Educ. 46, 52 (1987).

Grillo, The Mediation Alternative: Process Dangers for Women, 100 Yale L.J. 1545-92 (1991). Reprinted by permission of The Yale Law Journal Company and William S. Hein Company from The Yale Law Journal, Vol. 100, pages 1545-1610.

Woods, Mediation: A Backlash to Women's Progress on Family Law Issues, 19 Clearinghouse Rev. 431, 435 (1985).

Rosenberg, In Defense of Mediation, 33 Ariz. L. Rev. 467, 467-8 (1991).

Riskin, Mediator Orientations, Strategies and Techniques, 12 Alternatives 111, 111-112 (1994).

Stulberg, Facilitative Versus Evaluative Mediator Orientations: Piercing the "Grid" Lock, 24 Florida State U. L. Rev. 985, 991-995 (1997). Reprinted by permission of The Florida State University College of Law, Law Review.

Baruch Bush & Folger, The Promise of Mediation: Responding to Conflict Through Empowerment and Recognition 5-12 (1994).

Menkel-Meadow, The Many Ways of Mediation: The Transformation of Traditions, Ideologies, Paradigms, and Practices, 11 Negotiation J. 217, 235-38 (1995). Reprinted by permission of Plenum Publishing Corp.

Cooley, Mediation Advocacy 91-95, 116-123 (1996).

Dougherty & Rendon, Models, Styles and Process of Family Mediation, Alternative Resolutions 22, 25 (June 2001). Reprinted by permission.

McEwen & Rogers, Bring Lawyers Into Divorce Mediation, Disp. Resolution Mag. 8-10 (1994). Reprinted by permission.

Stern, Mediation: An Old Dog with Some New Tricks, 24 Litigation 31, 35 (Summer 1998).

Galton, Mediation of Medical Negligence Claims, 28 Cap. U. L. Rev. 31 (2000).

Allen & Mohr, Your Role in a Client's Mediation, California Bar Journal (Sept. 1999).

Krivas, A Winning Formula for Mediation, www:L//mediate.com/articles.krivas6.cfm (May 4, 2001).

Rogers, Lawyers-Mediators Wanting Ethical Guidance Must Look Beyond Attorney Ethics Standards, 66 U.S. Law Week 2307-2308 (November 25, 1997). Reproduced with permission from The United States Law Week, Vol.66, No. 20, pp2307-2308 (Nov. 25, 1997). Copyright © 1997 by The Bureau of National Affairs, Inc. (800-372-1033) <http://www.bna.com>.

American Bar Association, Model Rules of Professional Conduct. Copyright © by the American Bar Association.

Freedman & Prigoff, Confidentiality in Mediation: The Need for Protection, 2 Ohio St. J. Dispute Res. 37, 39 (1986).

Kirkpatrick, Should Mediators Have a Confidentiality Privilege? 9 Mediation Q. 85, 94-6 (1985). Reprinted with permission of Josey-Bass, Inc.

Deason, Enforcing Mediated Settlement Agreements: Contract Law Collides with Confidentiality, 35 U.C. Davis L.Rev. 33 (2001).

Green , A Heretical View of a Mediation Privilege, 2 Ohio St. J. Dispute Res. 1, 29-30 (1986).

Sherman, A Process Model and Agenda for Civil Justice Reforms in the States, 46 Stan. L. Rev. 1553, 1580-82 (1994).

ABA, The ABA Standards of Practice for Lawyer Mediators in Family Disputes, Sec. II.A.

Sherman, Introduction to Symposium on Standards of Professional Conduct in Alternative Dispute Resolution, 1995 J. of Dispute Resolution 95. Reprinted by permission from the Journal of Dispute Resolution and the Curators of the University of Missouri-Columbia. For more information, contact: Editor-in-Chief, Journal of Dispute Resolution, University of Missouri School of Law, Columbia, Missouri, 65211.

CHAPTER IV

Adler, Hensler, & Nelson, Simple Justice: How Litigants Fare in the Pittsburgh Court Arbitration Program 9-14, 87-94 (1983). RAND, MR-3071-ICJ.

Olson, An Alternative for Large Case Dispute Resolution, 6 Litigation 22 (Winter 1980). Copyright © 1987 American Bar Association. Reprinted with permission from Vol. 6, No. 2, Litigation. All rights reserved.

Gold, A New Approach in ADR: A Mini-Trial at Trial, 24 The Brief 77, 78 (Summer 1985). Copyright © 1995. Reprinted by permission of the American Bar Association.

Lambros, Summary Jury Trial-An Alternative Method of Resolving Disputes, 69 Judicature 286, 286-90 (1986).

Plapinger & Stienstra, ADR and the Settlement in the Federal District Courts: A Sourcebook for Judges and Lawyers, Alternative Dispute Resolution: The Litigators Handbook, eds. Nancy F. Atlas, Stephen K. Huber, & E. Wendy Trachte-Huber, 399, 406-15 (ABA Section of Litigation 2000).

Sander & Goldberg, Fitting the Forum to the Fuss: A User-Friendly Guide to Selecting and ADR Procedure, 10 Negotiation J. 49, 51-2, 54-60 (1994). Reprinted by permission of Plenum Publishing Corp.

CHAPTER V

Drawing by Lorenz; copyright © 1991 The New Yorker Magazine, Inc.

Landes & Posner, Adjudication as a Private Good, 8 J. Legal Stud. 235, 235-40, 245-47 (1979). Copyright © 1979 by the University of Chicago. All rights reserved.

Fuller , Collective Bargaining and the Arbitrator, 1963 Wisc.L.Rev. 3, 11-12, 17.

Sperber, Overlooking Negotiating Tools, 20 Les Nouvelles 81 (June 1985).

Galanter, Justice in Many Rooms: Courts, Private Ordering, and Indigenous Law, 19 J. Pluralism & Unofficial L. 1, 17-18, 25 (1981).

Mentschikoff, The Significance of Arbitration-A Preliminary Inquiry, 17 Law & Contemporary Problems 698, 709 (1952). Copyright © 1952 Duke University School of Law.

Craver , The Judicial Enforcement of Public Sector Interest Arbitration, 21 B.C.L.Rev., 557, 558 n.8 (1980). Reprinted by permission of Boston College, Office of the Law Reviews.

Jones, Three Centuries of Commercial Arbitration on New York: A Brief Survey, 1956 Wash. U.L.Q. 193, 209-10, 218-19.

Mentschikoff, Commercial Arbitration, 61 Colum. L. Rev. 846, 848-54 (1961). Copyright © 1961 by the Directors of the Columbia Law Review Association Inc. All rights reserved. This article originally appeared at 61 Colum. L. Rev. 846 (1961). Reprinted by permission.

Craig, Park, & Paulsson, International Chamber of Commerce Arbitration 638, 29-30, 744 (3rd Ed. 2000).

Tang, Arbitration—A Method Used in China to Settle Foreign Trade and Economic Disputes, 4 Pace L. Rev. 519, 533-34 (1984).

Hays, Labor Arbitration: A Dissenting View 112-13 (1966).

Getman, Labor Arbitration and Dispute Resolution, 88 Yale L.J. 916, 928-30 (1979). Reprinted by permission of The Yale Law Journal Company and William S. Hein Company from The Yale Law Journal, Vol. 88, pages 916-949.

Moller, Rolph, & Ebener, Private Dispute Resolution in the Banking Industry 12-13 (RAND 1993). RAND, MR-259-ICJ.

Terry, The Technical and Conceptual Flaws of Medical Malpractice Arbitration, 30 St. Louis U.L.J. 571, 572-73, 586 (1986). Reprinted with permission.

Henderson, Contractual Problems in the Enforcement of Agreements to Arbitrate Medical Malpractice, 58 Va.L.Rev. 947, 994 (1972). Reprinted by permission of Fred B. Rothman & Co.

St. Antoine, Judicial Review of Labor Arbitration Awards: A Second Look at Enterprise Wheel and its Progeny, 75 Mich. L. Rev. 1137, 1140, 1142 (1977).

Rau , Contracting Out of the Arbitration Act, 8 American Review of International Arbitration 225 (1997).

Rau, On Integrity in Private Judging, 14 Arbitration International 115, 146-150, 230-31 (1998).

Rau, Integrity of Private Judging 38 So. Tex. L. Rev. 485, 526-27 (1997). Reprinted by permission of South Texas College School of Law.

Hart & Sacks, The Legal Process 310 (1994).

Stein, The Selection of Arbitrators, N.Y.U Eighth Annual Conference on Labor 291, 293 (1955).

Raffaele, Lawyers in Labor Arbitration, 37 Arb.J. No.3 (Sept. 1982).

Roth, When to Ignore the Rules of Evidence in Arbitration, 9 Litigation 20 (Winter 1983). Copyright © 1983 American Bar Association. Reprinted with permission from Vol. 9, No.2, Litigation. All rights reserved.

Allison, The Context, Properties, and Constitutionality of Nonconsensual Arbitration,1990 Journal of Dispute Resolution 1, 6, 15. Reprinted by permission from the Journal of Dispute Resolution and the Curators of the University of Missouri-Columbia. For more information, contact: Editor-in Chief, Journal of Dispute Resolution, University of Missouri School of Law, Columbia, Missouri 65211.

Summers, Public Sector Bargaining: Problems of Governmental Decision-making, 44 U Cinn. L. Rev. 672 (1975). Reprinted with permission.

Raiffa, The Art and Science of Negotiation 118 (1982). Reprinted by permission of the publisher from THE ART AND SCIENCE OF NEGOTIATION: HOW TO RESOLVE CONFLICTS AND GET THE BEST OUT OF BARGAINING by Howard Raiffa, The Belknap Press of Harvard University Press, Copyright © 1982 by the President and Fellows of Harvard College.

Fuller, Collective Bargaining and the Arbitrator, Proceedings, Fifteenth Annual Meeting, National Academy of Arbitrators 8, 29-33, 37-48 (1962). Reprinted with permission. Chapter 2, pages 8, 29-33, and 37-48 and 34-41 from Collective Bargaining and the Arbitrator's Role (Proceedings of the 15th Annual Meeting National Academy of Arbitrators), by Lon L. Fuller. Copyright © 1962, by The Bureau of National Affairs, Inc. Washington, D.C. 20037.

Panel Discussion, Proceedings, 33rd Annual Meeting, National Academy of Arbitrators 232 (1981). Reprinted with permission, Chapter 7, pages 224-239 from Decision Thinking of Arbitrators and Judges, (Proceedings of the 33rd Annual Meeting National Academy of Arbitrators) by Rolf Valtin. Copyright © 1981, by The Bureau of National Affairs, Inc. Washington, DC 20037.

Folberg & Taylor, Mediations 277-78 (1984). Reprinted by permission of Jossey-Bass, Inc.

Christensen, Private Justice: California's General Reference Procedure, 1982 American Bar Foundation Research J. 79, 81-82, 103.

Note, The California Rent-A-Judge Experiment: Constitutional and Policy Considerations of Pay-As-You-Go Courts, 94 Harv. L. Rev.. 1592, 1601-02, 1607-08 (1981). Copyright © 1981 by the Harvard law Review Association.

CHAPTER VI

Salacuse, Making Global Deals 58-70 (1991). Used by permission of Times Books, a division of Random House, Inc.

Corne, The Complex Art of Negotiation Between Cultures, Arb. J. 46, 48 (December 1992). Permission given by American Arbitration Association.

Gans, Saving Time and Money in Cross-Border Commercial Disputes, Disp. Resol. J. 52-54 (January 1997). Permission given by American Arbitration Association.

Bühring-Uhle, Arbitration and Mediation in International Business 88, 141-143, 371, 389-391 (1996). With kind permission from Kluwer Law International.

Bond, How to Draft an Arbitration Clause, J. of Intl. Arb. 65, 66, 72, 74-75, 76, 78 (June 1989). With kind permission from Kluwer Law International.

Abramson, Protocols for International Arbitrators Who Dare to Settle Cases, 10 Am. Rev. of Intl. Arb. 1,2, 8-15 (1999).

*

SUMMARY OF CONTENTS

PREFACE iii
ACKNOWLEDGMENTS vii
TABLE OF CASES xxxvii

CHAPTER I. Lawyers, Litigation and Process 1

A. Introduction 1
B. Courts and Litigation 11
  1. The Dimensions of Litigation 11
  2. The Limits of the Judicial Process 15
  3. The Case for the Judicial Process 33
C. The Choice of Process 49
  1. Lawyers and the Choice of Process 49
  2. Problem: Sheridan v. Hopewell College 70

CHAPTER II. Negotiation 78

A. The Structure of Negotiation 79
  1. One Issue 79
  2. Multiple Issues 83
  3. The Role of Information 96
B. Strategy 109
  1. Positional Bargaining 109
  2. Problem–Solving 126
  3. Choosing an Approach 142
C. Psychological and Social Aspects of Bargaining 157
  1. Psychological Barriers to Conflict Resolution 158
  2. Interpersonal Style and Skill 179
  3. Gender, Race, Culture and Stereotyping 189
D. Professional and Legal Framework for Negotiation 202
  1. Constraints on Negotiation Behavior 202
  2. Judicial Promotion of Settlement 296

CHAPTER III. Mediation 327

A. The Sources of Contemporary Mediation 327
  1. Labor Mediation 329
  2. Family Law Mediation 330
  3. Community Mediation 332
  4. Settlement Promotion 333
  5. Cooperative Problem–Solving 334
  6. Evaluative Mediation 335
  7. Public Policy Dispute Resolution 335
  8. Systems Design 336

xxi

9. Cybermediation	337
B. The Mediation Process	337
1. Format of the "Classical" Mediation	340
C. The Role of the Mediator	375
1. Mediator Advantages	377
2. Mediator Control of the Process	380
3. Providing Information	402
4. Dealing with Power Imbalances	405
5. Issues of Fairness of Settlement and Discriminatory Impacts on Women and Minority Participants	406
6. Mediator Approaches and Orientations	414
D. The Role of the Party's Attorney	431
1. Duty to Advise Clients About ADR	431
2. Pre–Mediation Advice and Preparation	433
3. Representing the Client in Mediation	438
4. Post–Mediation Representation	452
5. Attorney as Mediator	452
E. Confidentiality in Mediation	461
1. Evidentiary Exclusion for Compromise Discussions	463
2. Mediation Privilege	467
F. Enforceability of Mediation Agreements	514
1. Written Agreements: Completeness, Ambiguity, and Parol Evidence	518
2. Enforcing Mediated Settlement Agreement Repudiated Before Entry of Judgment	527
G. Regulating Professional Conduct in Mediation and Alternative Dispute Resolution	532
1. Standards of Professional Conduct	532
2. Liability or Immunity of Mediators & ADR Neutrals	539

CHAPTER IV. Court–Annexed ADR Processes — 545

A. A Range of Processes	545
1. Mediation	547
2. Judicial Settlement Conference	548
3. Early Neutral Evaluation (ENE)	549
4. Court–Annexed Arbitration	550
5. Mini–Trial	559
6. Summary Jury Trial	564
B. Administering Court–Annexed ADR	579
1. Referral of Cases to ADR	586
2. Selecting the Process	587
3. Selecting the Neutral(s)	593
4. Who Pays for Court–Annexed ADR?	594
5. Appellate ADR	595

SUMMARY OF CONTENTS **xxiii**

CHAPTER V. Arbitration 597

A. The Process of Private Adjudication 597
    1. Introduction 597
    2. Arbitration and Dispute Resolution 600
    3. Arbitration and the Application of "Rules" 611
    4. "Rights" Arbitration and "Interest" Arbitration 613
B. Some Frequent Uses of Arbitration 620
    1. Commercial Arbitration 620
    2. International Commercial Arbitration 626
    3. Labor Arbitration 633
    4. Arbitration of Consumer Disputes 642
C. Arbitration and the Courts 653
    1. Introduction 653
    2. The Federal Arbitration Act and State Law 655
    3. The Agreement to Arbitrate 684
    4. Judicial Supervision and Review 729
D. The Arbitration Proceeding 834
    1. The Decision–Makers 835
    2. Conduct of the Proceeding 854
E. Variations on a Theme 876
    1. Compulsory Arbitration 876
    2. Final–Offer Arbitration 888
    3. "Med–Arb" 892
    4. "Rent a Judge" 900

CHAPTER VI. International Dispute Resolution: Cross–Cultural Dimensions and Structuring Appropriate Processes 906

A. Demystifying Cross–Cultural Dimensions 906
    1. Cross–Cultural Differences 907
    2. Cultural Conceptual Framework 911
    3. Developing Cultural Sensitivity 917
B. International ADR Clauses for Business Disputes 927
    1. Distinctive Issues When Mediating International Business Disputes 929
    2. International Adjudicatory Options 938
    3. Institutional or Ad Hoc Administration of Processes 941
    4. Adopting or Adapting Off–The–Shelf Procedural Rules 942
    5. Combining Settlement Processes with Arbitration 952
    6. Public Dispute Resolution Systems for Commercial Disputes 958

APPENDICES 963
FURTHER REFERENCES 1007
INDEX 1019

*

TABLE OF CONTENTS

PREFACE	iii
ACKNOWLEDGMENTS	vii
TABLE OF CASES	xxxvii

CHAPTER I. Lawyers, Litigation and Process 1

A. Introduction	1
Richard E. Miller and Austin Sarat, Grievances, Claims, and Disputes: Assessing the Adversary Culture	2
Notes and Questions	10
B. Courts and Litigation	11
1. The Dimensions of Litigation	11
Jerold S. Auerbach, Justice Without Law?	11
Notes and Questions	12
David M. Trubek, Austin Sarat, William L.F. Felstiner, Herbert M. Kritzer & Joel B. Grossman, The Costs of Ordinary Litigation	13
Notes and Questions	13
2. The Limits of the Judicial Process	15
Notes and Questions	16
Wayne D. Brazil, The Attorney as Victim: Towards More Candor About the Psychological Price Tag of Litigation Practice	20
Lon Fuller, The Forms and Limits of Adjudication	22
The Role of Courts in American Society: Final Report of Council on the Role of Courts	26
Notes and Questions	31
3. The Case for the Judicial Process	33
Owen M. Fiss, Against Settlement	33
Notes and Questions	39
Marc Galanter, The Day After the Litigation Explosion	41
Notes and Questions	43
C. The Choice of Process	49
1. Lawyers and the Choice of Process	49
Robert Kagan, Do Lawyers Cause Adversarial Legalism? A Preliminary Inquiry	50
Notes and Questions	54
Walters v. National Association of Radiation Survivors	55
Notes and Questions	67
2. Problem: Sheridan v. Hopewell College	70

CHAPTER II. Negotiation 78

A. The Structure of Negotiation	79
1. One Issue	79
2. Multiple Issues	83
a. Pareto Optimality	84

TABLE OF CONTENTS

A. The Structure of Negotiation—Continued
    b. Sources of Value 86
        David Lax and James Sebenius, The Manager as Negotiator   87
        Max H. Bazerman and James J. Gillespie, Betting on the
           Future: The Virtues of Contingent Contracts 91
        Notes and Questions 93
   3. The Role of Information 96
    a. Interests, Resources and Preferences 97
        Carrie Menkel–Meadow, The Transformation of Disputes by
           Lawyers: What the Dispute Paradigm Does and Does Not
           Tell Us 97
        Notes and Questions 99
    b. Alternatives: Using Litigation Analysis 100
        Notes and Questions 105
B. Strategy 109
   1. Positional Bargaining 109
    Roger Fisher, William Ury and Bruce Patton, Getting to Yes 109
    a. Hard Positional Bargaining 110
        Donald G. Gifford, A Context–Based Theory of Strategy
           Selection in Legal Negotiation 110
        Gary Goodpaster, A Primer on Competitive Bargaining 112
        Thomas C. Schelling, An Essay on Bargaining 114
        Notes and Questions 117
    b. Soft Positional Bargaining 118
    c. The First Offer Problem 119
        Harry Edwards and James J. White, The Lawyer as Negoti-
           ator 120
        David Lax & James Sebenius, The Manager as Negotiator ... 121
        Notes and Questions 123
   2. Problem–Solving 126
    a. The Basics of a Problem–Solving Approach 126
        Roger Fisher, William Ury and Bruce Patton, Getting to Yes 126
        Carrie J. Menkel–Meadow, When Winning Isn't Everything:
           The Lawyer as Problem–Solver 128
        Howard Raiffa, Post–Settlement Settlements 130
        Notes and Questions 131
    b. Fairness and Norms 133
        Max H. Bazerman, Robert Gibbons, Leigh Thompson, and
           Kathleen L. Valley, Can Negotiators Outperform Game
           Theory? 134
        Russell Korobkin, A Positive Theory of Legal Negotiation 135
        Leigh Thompson and Janice Nadler, Judgmental Biases In
           Conflict Resolution and How to Overcome Them 139
        Notes and Questions 140
   3. Choosing an Approach 142
    a. The Negotiator's Dilemma 142
        Robert H. Mnookin and Lee Ross, Barriers to Conflict Reso-
           lution: Introduction 142
        Notes and Questions 144
    b. Self–Interest and the Prisoner's Dilemma Analogy 145
        Notes and Questions 147
    c. Will Problem–Solving Sacrifice My Client's Interests? 153

B. Strategy—Continued

Milton Heumann and Jonathan M. Hyman, Negotiation Methods and Litigation Settlement Methods in New Jersey: "You Can't Always Get What You Want" 154

Robert Mnookin, Scott Peppet & Andrew Tulumello, Beyond Winning: Negotiating to Create Value in Deals and Disputes 155

Notes and Questions 156

C. Psychological and Social Aspects of Bargaining 157

1. Psychological Barriers to Conflict Resolution 158
   a. Cognition, Perception and Recall 158

   Richard Birke and Craig R. Fox, Psychological Principles in Negotiating Civil Settlements 158

   Notes and Questions 168

   b. The Role of Emotion 173

   Keith G. Allred, Anger and Retaliation in Conflict: The Role of Attribution 173

   Robert S. Adler, Benson Rosen, and Elliot M. Silverstein, Emotions in Negotiation: How to Manage Fear and Anger 175

   Notes and Questions 177

2. Interpersonal Style and Skill 179

   Donald G. Gifford, Legal Negotiation: Theory and Applications 179

   Robert H. Mnookin, Scott R. Peppet and Andrew S. Tulumello, The Tension Between Empathy and Assertiveness 180

   Keith G. Allred, Distinguishing Best and Strategic Practices: A Framework for Managing the Dilemma Between Creating and Claiming Value 182

   Douglas Stone, Bruce Patton and Sheila Heen, Difficult Conversations 185

   Notes and Questions 186

3. Gender, Race, Culture and Stereotyping 189

   Christine Rack, Negotiated Justice: Gender and Ethnic Minority Bargaining Patterns in the Metro Court Study 191

   Carol Watson, Gender Versus Power as a Predictor of Negotiation Behavior and Outcomes 194

   Jeffrey Z. Rubin and Frank E.A. Sander, Culture, Negotiation, and The Eye of The Beholder 196

   Notes and Questions 198

D. Professional and Legal Framework for Negotiation 202

1. Constraints on Negotiation Behavior 202
   a. Fraud, Duress and Other Limits on Bargaining 202

   Robert S. Adler & Elliot M. Silverstein, When David Meets Goliath: Dealing With Power Differentials in Negotiations 202

   Notes and Questions 206

   b. A Lawyer's Professional Obligations In Settlement Negotiations 210

   Patrick Emery Longan, Ethics In Settlement Negotiations: Foreward 210

   Nathan M. Crystal, The Lawyer's Duty to Disclose Material Facts in Contract or Settlement Negotiations 217

   Arthur Isak Applbaum, Ethics for Adversaries: The Morality of Roles in Public and Professional Life 220

xxviii TABLE OF CONTENTS

D. Professional and Legal Framework for Negotiation—Continued

Walter W. Steele, Jr., Deceptive Negotiating and High-Toned Morality ... 221

Notes and Questions ... 222

(1) Alternatives ... 229

Robert B. Gordon, Private Settlement as Alternative Adjudication: A Rationale for Negotiation Ethics ... 229

Walter Steele, Jr., Deceptive Negotiating and High-Toned Morality ... 229

James J. Alfini, Settlement Ethics and Lawyering in ADR Proceedings: A Proposal to Revise Rule 4.1 ... 230

ABA Litigation Section, Ethical Guidelines for Civil Settlement Negotiations ... 230

Alvin B. Rubin, A Causerie On Lawyers' Ethics In Negotiation ... 231

Discussion Draft Of The Model Rules Of Professional Conduct ... 231

Rex R. Perschbacher, Regulating Lawyers' Negotiations 232

Notes and Questions ... 234

(2) Dealing With Ethical Dilemmas ... 236

Robert H. Mnookin, Scott R. Peppet & Andrew S. Tulumello, Beyond Winning: Negotiating to Create Value in Deals and Disputes ... 236

Notes and Questions ... 241

c. Malpractice ... 245

Lynn A. Epstein, Post–Settlement Malpractice: Undoing the Done Deal ... 245

Notes and Questions ... 249

d. Stability of Settlements ... 254

Larry Kramer, Consent Decrees and the Rights of Third Parties ... 255

Notes and Questions ... 258

e. Judicial Sanctions ... 260

Hadges & Kunstler v. Yonkers Racing Corp. ... 261

Notes and Questions ... 269

f. Fee and Cost–Shifting and Offers of Judgment ... 270

Edward F. Sherman, From Loser Pays to Modified Offer-of-Judgment Rules: Reconciling Incentives to Settle With Access to Justice ... 270

Notes and Questions ... 278

g. Confidentiality ... 279

Jane Michaels, Rule 408: A Litigation Mine Field ... 279

Notes and Questions ... 287

Young v. State Farm Mutual Automobile Insurance Company ... 288

Notes and Questions ... 294

2. Judicial Promotion of Settlement ... 296

a. The Proper Role of the Judge ... 297

Wayne D. Brazil, Settling Civil Disputes ... 297

Notes and Questions ... 299

Peter H. Schuck, The Role of Judges in Settling Complex Cases: The Agent Orange Example ... 301

TABLE OF CONTENTS   **xxix**

D. Professional and Legal Framework for Negotiation—Continued
  Notes and Questions 304
  b. Form of Participation Required 304
    Edward F. Sherman, Court–Mandated Alternative Dispute
      Resolution: What Form of Participation Should Be Re-
      quired? 305
    Notes and Questions 309
  c. Obligation to Attend 311
    Edward F. Sherman, Court–Mandated Alternative Dispute
      Resolution: What Form of Participation Should Be Re-
      quired? 311
    G. Heileman Brewing Co. v. Joseph Oat Corp. 315
    Notes and Questions 325

CHAPTER   III.   Mediation 327

A. The Sources of Contemporary Mediation 327
  1. Labor Mediation 329
  2. Family Law Mediation 330
  3. Community Mediation 332
  4. Settlement Promotion 333
  5. Cooperative Problem–Solving 334
  6. Evaluative Mediation 335
  7. Public Policy Dispute Resolution 335
  8. Systems Design 336
  9. Cybermediation 337
B. The Mediation Process 337
  1. Format of the ''Classical'' Mediation 340
    a. Introductory Remarks by Mediator(s) 340
      Jay Folberg & Alison Taylor, Mediaton: A Comprehensive
        Guide to Resolving Conflicts Without Litigation 341
      Notes and Questions 345
    b. Statement of the Problem by the Parties 345
    c. Information Gathering 347
    d. Problem Identification 349
      Susan S. Silbey & Sally E. Merry, Mediator Settlement
        Strategies 349
      Notes and Questions 356
    e. Problem Solving: Generating Options and Bargaining 358
      Christopher W. Moore, The Mediation Process 358
      Lenard Marlow, The Rule of Law in Divorce Mediation ... 365
      Notes and Questions 368
    f. Writing of Agreement 370
      The Significance of Consent in Compliance with Mediation
        Agreements 370
      Craig A. McEwen & Richard M. Maiman, Mediation in
        Small Claims Court: Achieving Compliance Through Con-
        sent 372
      Notes and Questions 374
C. The Role of the Mediator 375
  1. Mediator Advantages 377

TABLE OF CONTENTS

C. The Role of the Mediator—Continued
   Richard A. Posner, Mediation — 377
  2. Mediator Control of the Process — 380
    John M. Haynes, Mediation and Therapy: An Alternative View — 380
    Notes and Questions — 387
    James C. Freund, The Neutral Negotiator: Why and How Mediation Can Work to Resolve Dollar Disputes — 387
    Notes and Questions — 399
  3. Providing Information — 402
    Sandra E. Purnell, The Attorney as Mediator–Inherent Conflict of Interest? — 403
  4. Dealing with Power Imbalances — 405
  5. Issues of Fairness of Settlement and Discriminatory Impacts on Women and Minority Participants — 406
    Trina Grillo, The Mediation Alternative: Process Dangers for Women — 407
    Notes and Questions — 412
  6. Mediator Approaches and Orientations — 414
    Leonard L. Riskin, Mediator Orientations, Strategies and Techniques — 415
    Notes and Questions — 419
    Robert A. Baruch Bush & Joseph P. Folger, The Promise of Mediation: Responding to Conflict Through Empowerment and Recognition — 423
    Notes and Questions — 427

D. The Role of the Party's Attorney — 431
  1. Duty to Advise Clients About ADR — 431
    a. Advice in Advance Planning Situations — 431
    b. Advising A Client Contemplating Litigation — 432
    c. Considerations Favoring Use of Mediation — 433
  2. Pre–Mediation Advice and Preparation — 433
    John W. Cooley, Mediation Advocacy — 434
  3. Representing the Client in Mediation — 438
    a. Degree of Participation — 438
      (1) Attorney as Non–Participant — 438
      (2) Attorney as Silent Advisor — 439
      (3) Attorney as Co–Participant — 439
      (4) Attorney as Dominant or Sole Participant — 439
      Craig McEwen & Nancy Rogers, Bring the Lawyers Into Divorce Mediation — 440
    b. Attorney's Opening Statement — 442
      David M. Stern, Mediation: An Old Dog with Some New Tricks — 442
      Eric Galton, Mediation of Medical Negligence Claims — 443
    c. Use of the Caucus — 444
      John W. Cooley, Mediation Advocacy — 444
      Notes and Questions — 450
    d. Impasse — 451
      Elizabeth Allen & Donald D. Mohr, Your Role in a Client's Mediation — 451
      Jeffrey Krivas, A Winning Formula for Mediation — 451

TABLE OF CONTENTS   **xxxi**

D. The Role of the Party's Attorney—Continued
  4. Post–Mediation Representation ----- 452
  5. Attorney as Mediator ----- 452
    Leonard L. Riskin, Mediation and Lawyers ----- 454
    Lance J. Rogers, Lawyer–Mediators Wanting Ethical Guidance
      Must Look Beyond Attorney Ethics Standards ----- 456
    Notes and Questions ----- 459
E. Confidentiality in Mediation ----- 461
  Lawrence R. Freedman & Michael L. Prigoff, Confidentiality in
    Mediation: The Need for Protection ----- 461
  1. Evidentiary Exclusion for Compromise Discussions ----- 463
    Notes and Questions ----- 465
  2. Mediation Privilege ----- 467
    a. Judicially Created Privilege ----- 467
      Sheldone v. Pennsylvania Turnpike Commission ----- 469
      Notes and Questions ----- 476
      Fenton v. Howard ----- 477
      Notes and Questions ----- 479
    b. Statutory Mediation Privilege ----- 481
      Ellen E. Deason, Enforcing Mediated Settlement Agree-
        ments: Contract Law Collides with Confidentiality ----- 481
      Three Statutory Approaches ----- 486
      Colo.Rev.Stat. § 13–22–307 (Supp.1995) ----- 486
      Mass.Ann.Laws ch. 233, § 23C ----- 487
      Texas Civil Practice and Remedies Code, Title 7, ch. 154 ----- 487
      Notes and Questions ----- 488
    c. Carving Out Exceptions from Mediation Confidentiality ----- 492
      (1) Exception for Evidence of the Mediated Agreement ----- 493
        Vernon v. Acton ----- 493
        Notes and Questions ----- 499
      (2) Exception for Testimony Relevant to Sanctions Sought
        for Improper Participation in Mediation ----- 500
        Foxgate Homeowners' Association, Inc. v. Bramalea Cal-
          ifornia, Inc. ----- 500
        Notes and Questions ----- 509
    d. Contractual Agreements of Confidentiality ----- 510
      Simrin v. Simrin ----- 511
      Notes and Questions ----- 513
F. Enforceability of Mediation Agreements ----- 514
  1. Written Agreements: Completeness, Ambiguity, and Parol Evi-
    dence ----- 518
    Hardman v. Dault ----- 518
    Notes and Questions ----- 520
    Cain v. Saunders ----- 521
    Notes and Questions ----- 527
  2. Enforcing Mediated Settlement Agreement Repudiated Before
    Entry of Judgment ----- 527
G. Regulating Professional Conduct in Mediation and Alternative
  Dispute Resolution ----- 532
  1. Standards of Professional Conduct ----- 532
    Edward F. Sherman, Introduction to Symposium on Standards
      of Professional Conduct in Alternative Dispute Resolution 532

xxxii TABLE OF CONTENTS

G. Regulating Professional Conduct in Mediation and Alternative
    Dispute Resolution—Continued

        Notes and Questions ---- 535

    2. Liability or Immunity of Mediators & ADR Neutrals ---- 539

        Wagshal v. Foster ---- 539

        Notes and Questions ---- 543

CHAPTER IV. Court–Annexed ADR Processes ---- 545

A. A Range of Processes ---- 545

    1. Mediation ---- 547

    2. Judicial Settlement Conference ---- 548

    3. Early Neutral Evaluation (ENE) ---- 549

    4. Court–Annexed Arbitration ---- 550

        *Jane W. Adler, Deborah R. Hensler, & Charles Nelson, Simple
           Justice: How Litigants Fare In The Pittsburgh Court Arbitra-
           tion Program* ---- 551

        Notes and Questions ---- 554

    5. Mini–Trial ---- 559

        *Ronald L. Olson, An Alternative for Large Case Dispute Resolu-
           tion* ---- 559

        Notes and Questions ---- 562

    6. Summary Jury Trial ---- 564

        *Thomas D. Lambros, Summary Jury Trial—An Alternative
           Method of Resolving Disputes* ---- 565

        Notes and Questions ---- 568

        Judicial Power to Require Participation in Summary Jury Trial ---- 572

        Strandell v. Jackson County ---- 572

        Arabian American Oil Co. v. Scarfone ---- 575

        Notes and Questions ---- 577

B. Administering Court–Annexed ADR ---- 579

    *Elizabeth Plapinger & Donna Stienstra, ADR and Settlement in
        the Federal District Courts: A Sourcebook for Judges and Law-
        yers* ---- 579

    1. Referral of Cases to ADR ---- 586

    2. Selecting the Process ---- 587

        *Frank E.A. Sander & Stephen B. Goldberg, Fitting the Forum
           to the Fuss: A User–Friendly Guide to Selecting an ADR
           Procedure* ---- 588

    3. Selecting the Neutral(s) ---- 593

    4. Who Pays for Court–Annexed ADR? ---- 594

    5. Appellate ADR ---- 595

CHAPTER V. Arbitration ---- 597

A. The Process of Private Adjudication ---- 597

    1. Introduction ---- 597

        *William M. Landes & Richard A. Posner, Adjudication as a
           Private Good* ---- 597

    2. Arbitration and Dispute Resolution ---- 600

TABLE OF CONTENTS

A. The Process of Private Adjudication—Continued
   Lon Fuller, Collective Bargaining and the Arbitrator 601
   Notes and Questions 602
   William M. Landes & Richard A. Posner, Adjudication as a Private Good 605
   In The Matter of the Arbitration Between Mikel and Scharf 606
   Notes and Questions 610
   3. Arbitration and the Application of "Rules" 611
   4. "Rights" Arbitration and "Interest" Arbitration 613
   Notes and Questions 617

B. Some Frequent Uses of Arbitration 620
   1. Commercial Arbitration 620
   William C. Jones, Three Centuries of Commercial Arbitration in New York: A Brief Survey 620
   Soia Mentschikoff, Commercial Arbitration 621
   Notes and Questions 625
   2. International Commercial Arbitration 626
   Notes and Questions 628
   3. Labor Arbitration 633
   United Steelworkers of America v. Warrior & Gulf Navigation Co. 634
   Notes and Questions 641
   4. Arbitration of Consumer Disputes 642
   Notes and Questions 648

C. Arbitration and the Courts 653
   1. Introduction 653
   2. The Federal Arbitration Act and State Law 655
      a. Preemption of State Law 655
      Southland Corporation v. Keating 656
      Notes and Questions 665
      b. Preemption and Choice of Law: The Problem of Multi–Party Disputes 670
      Volt Information Sciences, Inc. v. Board of Trustees of the Leland Stanford Junior University 674
      Notes and Questions 682
   3. The Agreement to Arbitrate 684
      a. Arbitration Clauses and Contract Formation 684
      Notes and Questions 686
      b. The "Separability" of the Arbitration Clause 690
      Prima Paint Corp. v. Flood & Conklin Mfg. Co. 690
      Notes and Questions 695
      c. Contracts of Adhesion and Unconscionability 699
      Broemmer v. Abortion Services of Phoenix, Ltd. 699
      Notes and Questions 704
      d. "Arbitrability" 711
      AT & T Technologies, Inc. v. Communications Workers of America 712
      Notes and Questions 718
      Notes and Questions 728
   4. Judicial Supervision and Review 729
      a. Judicial Review of Arbitral Awards 730

C. Arbitration and the Courts—Continued

United Paperworkers International Union v. Misco, Inc. 731
Notes and Questions ... 740
Alan Rau, Contracting Out of the Arbitration Act ... 746
Notes and Questions ... 755
Alan Rau, On Integrity in Private Judging ... 758
Notes and Questions ... 762

    b. "Public Policy" and Arbitrability ... 766
Mitsubishi Motors Corp. v. Soler Chrysler–Plymouth, Inc. 766
Notes and Questions ... 777
Note: Investor/Broker Disputes Under the Securities Acts ... 783
Note: Employment Disputes and the Statutory Rights of Employees ... 787
Notes and Questions ... 791
Armendariz v. Foundation Health Psychcare Services, Inc. ... 796
Notes and Questions ... 815

    c. Limitations on Remedies in Arbitration ... 824
Mastrobuono v. Shearson Lehman Hutton, Inc. ... 824
Notes and Questions ... 830

D. The Arbitration Proceeding ... 834

1. The Decision–Makers ... 835
    a. Selection of Arbitrators ... 835
Notes and Questions ... 839
    b. Arbitral Impartiality ... 842
Commonwealth Coatings Corp. v. Continental Casualty Co. ... 842
Notes and Questions ... 846

2. Conduct of the Proceeding ... 854
    a. Introduction ... 854
    b. The Role of Lawyers ... 855
    c. Evidence ... 857
Notes and Questions ... 859
    d. Discovery ... 862
Notes and Questions ... 866
    e. Interim Measures ... 870
Teradyne, Inc. v. Mostek Corp. ... 870
Notes and Questions ... 874

E. Variations on a Theme ... 876

1. Compulsory Arbitration ... 876
John Allison, The Context, Properties, and Constitutionality of Nonconsensual Arbitration ... 876
Note: Data Compensation Disputes Under "FIFRA" ... 877
Notes and Questions ... 880
Note: Mandatory Arbitration in Public Employment ... 884
Notes and Questions ... 886
Note: Mandatory Arbitration and Public Regulation ... 887

2. Final–Offer Arbitration ... 888
Notes and Questions ... 890

3. "Med–Arb" ... 892
Lon Fuller, Collective Bargaining And The Arbitrator ... 893
Notes and Questions ... 898

4. "Rent a Judge" ... 900

E. Variations on a Theme—Continued
 Barlow F. Christensen, Private Justice: California's General Reference Procedure 901
 Notes and Questions 902

CHAPTER VI. International Dispute Resolution: Cross–Cultural Dimensions and Structuring Appropriate Processes 906

A. Demystifying Cross–Cultural Dimensions 906
 1. Cross–Cultural Differences 907
  a. What Is Culture? 907
  b. Difficulties In Identifying Cultural Behavior 909
 2. Cultural Conceptual Framework 911
  Jeswald W. Salacuse, Making Global Deals 913
 3. Developing Cultural Sensitivity 917
  Notes and Questions 921
B. International ADR Clauses for Business Disputes 927
 1. Distinctive Issues When Mediating International Business Disputes 929
  a. Benefits of International Mediation 929
   Walter G. Gans, Saving Time And Money In Cross–Border Commercial Disputes 930
  b. Convening a Mediation Session 932
  c. Selecting a Mediator 934
  d. Style of Mediation 935
  e. Confidentiality of Mediation Process 935
  f. Enforcing Settlement Agreements 936
  g. Back–Up Adjudicatory Process 938
 2. International Adjudicatory Options 938
  Christian Buhring–Uhle, Arbitration And Mediation In International Business 938
  Notes and Questions 940
 3. Institutional or Ad Hoc Administration of Processes 941
 4. Adopting or Adapting Off–The–Shelf Procedural Rules 942
  a. Mediation 943
  b. Arbitration 943
   Stephen R. Bond, "How To Draft An Arbitration Clause" 945
  Notes and Questions 947
 5. Combining Settlement Processes with Arbitration 952
  a. Set–Arb–Set–Arb 952
   Christian Buhring–Uhle, Arbitration and Mediation in International Business 953
  b. Arb–Set–Arb 954
   Harold Abramson, Protocols For International Arbitrators Who Dare To Settle Cases 955
  Notes and Questions 957
 6. Public Dispute Resolution Systems for Commercial Disputes 958
  a. World Trade Organization (WTO) 959

xxxvi TABLE OF CONTENTS

B. International ADR Clauses for Business Disputes—Continued
b. NAFTA (North American Free Trade Agreement) 959
Notes and Questions 961

APPENDICES 963
FURTHER REFERENCES 1007
INDEX 1019

TABLE OF CASES

Principal cases are in bold type. Non-principal cases are in roman type. References are to Pages.

Adler v. Adams, No. 675-73C (W.D.Wash. 1979), 465

Advanced Micro Devices, Inc. v. Intel Corp., 36 Cal.Rptr.2d 581, 885 P.2d 994 (Cal. 1994), 833

Advest, Inc. v. McCarthy, 914 F.2d 6 (1st Cir.1990), 756

Aero Spark Plug Co. v. B.G. Corp., 130 F.2d 290 (2nd Cir.1942), 780

Aetna Cas. & Sur. Co. v. Grabbert, 590 A.2d 88 (R.I.1991), 850

Agur v. Agur, 32 A.D.2d 16, 298 N.Y.S.2d 772 (N.Y.A.D. 2 Dept.1969), 780

Air Crash Near Cali, Colombia on Dec. 20, 1995, In re, 959 F.Supp. 1529 (S.D.Fla. 1997), 471

A.L.A. Schechter Poultry Corporation v. United States, 295 U.S. 495, 55 S.Ct. 837, 79 L.Ed. 1570 (1935), 880

Alexander v. Gardner–Denver Co., 415 U.S. 36, 94 S.Ct. 1011, 39 L.Ed.2d 147 (1974), 749, 787, 788, 790, 791, 792, 793, 794, 796

Alford v. Dean Witter Reynolds, Inc., 939 F.2d 229 (5th Cir.1991), 792

Allied–Bruce Terminix Companies, Inc. v. Dobson, 513 U.S. 265, 115 S.Ct. 834, 130 L.Ed.2d 753 (1995), 668

Alpex Computer Corp. v. Nintendo Co., Ltd., 770 F.Supp. 161 (S.D.N.Y.1991), 281

Al's Formal Wear of Houston, Inc. v. Sun, 869 S.W.2d 442 (Tex.App.-Hous. (1 Dist.) 1993), 690

Alvarez v. Reiser, 958 S.W.2d 232 (Tex.App.-Eastland 1997), 531

American Almond Products Co. v. Consolidated Pecan Sales Co., 144 F.2d 448 (2nd Cir.1944), 861

American Centennial Ins. Co. v. National Cas. Co., 951 F.2d 107 (6th Cir.1991), 673

American Homestar of Lancaster, Inc., In re, 50 S.W.3d 480 (Tex.2001), 782

American Physicians Service Group, Inc. v. Port Lavaca Clinic Associates, 843 S.W.2d 675 (Tex.App.-Corpus Christi 1992), 690

American Postal Workers Union, AFL–CIO v. United States Postal Service, 789 F.2d 1 (D.C.Cir.1986), 744

American Safety Equipment Corp. v. J.P. Maguire & Co., 391 F.2d 821 (2nd Cir.1968), 778

Americorp Securities, Inc. v. Sager, 239 A.D.2d 115, 656 N.Y.S.2d 762 (N.Y.A.D. 1 Dept.1997), 832

Ames, Matter of Marriage of, 860 S.W.2d 590 (Tex.App.-Amarillo 1993), 528, 529, 530, 531

AMF Inc. v. Brunswick Corp., 621 F.Supp. 456 (S.D.N.Y.1985), 752

Amgen Inc. v. Kidney Center of Delaware County, Ltd., 879 F.Supp. 878 (N.D.Ill. 1995), 869

Anderson v. Elliott, 555 A.2d 1042 (Me.1989), 651

Application of (see name of party)

Arabian American Oil Co. v. Scarfone, 119 F.R.D. 448 (M.D.Fla.1988), **575,** 577, 578

Arbitration Between Astoria Medical Group v. Health Ins. Plan of Greater New York, 227 N.Y.S.2d 401, 182 N.E.2d 85 (N.Y. 1962), 850

Arbitration Between Brill and Muller Bros., Inc., 40 Misc.2d 683, 243 N.Y.S.2d 905 (N.Y.Sup.1962), 860

Arbitration Between Chevron Transport Corp. and Astro Vencedor Compania Naviera, S. A., 300 F.Supp. 179 (S.D.N.Y. 1969), 863

Arbitration Between Egyptian Co. and Hamlet Shipping Co., Matter of, 1982 A.M.C. 874 (S.D.N.Y.1981), 671

Arbitration Between Marlene Industries Corp. v. Carnac Textiles, Inc., 408 N.Y.S.2d 410, 380 N.E.2d 239 (N.Y.1978), 685, 687, 689

Arbitration Between Mikel and Scharf, 105 Misc.2d 548, 432 N.Y.S.2d 602 (N.Y.Sup.1980), **606**

Arbitration Between Oinoussian S. S. Corp. of Panama and Sabre Shipping Corp., 224 F.Supp. 807 (S.D.N.Y.1963), 861

Arbitration Between Silverman and Benmor Coats, Inc., 473 N.Y.S.2d 774, 461 N.E.2d 1261 (N.Y.1984), 611

Arbitration Between Singer Co. and Tappan Co., 403 F.Supp. 322 (D.N.J.1975), 718

Arbitration Between Staklinski and Pyramid Elec. Co., 188 N.Y.S.2d 541, 160 N.E.2d 78 (N.Y.1959), 833

xxxvii

TABLE OF CASES

Arbitration of Torano and Motor Vehicle Acc. Indemnification Corp., 258 N.Y.S.2d 418, 206 N.E.2d 353 (N.Y.1965), 757

Arenson v. Casson Beckman Rutley & Co., [1975] 3 All E.R. 901 (H.L.1975), 854

Armendariz v. Foundation Health Psychcare Services, Inc., 99 Cal. Rptr.2d 745, 6 P.3d 669 (Cal.2000), **796,** 815, 816

AT & T Technologies, Inc. v. Communications Workers of America, 475 U.S. 643, 106 S.Ct. 1415, 89 L.Ed.2d 648 (1986), **712,** 719

Avedon Engineering, Inc. v. Seatex, 126 F.3d 1279 (10th Cir.1997), 689

Avitzur v. Avitzur, 459 N.Y.S.2d 572, 446 N.E.2d 136 (N.Y.1983), 610

Baar v. Tigerman, 140 Cal.App.3d 979, 189 Cal.Rptr. 834 (Cal.App. 2 Dist.1983), 854

Badie v. Bank of America, 79 Cal.Rptr.2d 273 (Cal.App. 1 Dist.1998), 707

Baesler v. Continental Grain Co., 900 F.2d 1193 (8th Cir.1990), 673

Ballas v. Mann, 3 Misc.2d 445, 82 N.Y.S.2d 426 (N.Y.Sup.1948), 836

Baravati v. Josephthal, Lyon & Ross, Inc., 28 F.3d 704 (7th Cir.1994), 855

Barbier v. Shearson Lehman Hutton Inc., 948 F.2d 117 (2nd Cir.1991), 831

Barrentine v. Arkansas–Best Freight System, Inc., 450 U.S. 728, 101 S.Ct. 1437, 67 L.Ed.2d 641 (1981), 788

Beckham v. William Bayley Co., 655 F.Supp. 288 (N.D.Tex.1987), 720

Belton v. Fibreboard Corp., 724 F.2d 500 (5th Cir.1984), 465

Bennett v. La Pere, 112 F.R.D. 136 (D.R.I. 1986), 294, 295

Bercovitch v. Baldwin School, Inc., 133 F.3d 141 (1st Cir.1998), 792

Bergstrom v. Sears, Roebuck and Co., 532 F.Supp. 923 (D.Minn.1982), 515

Bernhardt v. Polygraphic Co. of America, 350 U.S. 198, 76 S.Ct. 273, 100 L.Ed. 199 (1956), 655

Bigge Crane & Rigging Co. v. Docutel Corp., 371 F.Supp. 240 (E.D.N.Y.1973), 865, 866

Blonder–Tongue Laboratories, Inc. v. University of Illinois Foundation, 402 U.S. 313, 91 S.Ct. 1434, 28 L.Ed.2d 788 (1971), 781

Blue Cross of California v. Superior Court, 78 Cal.Rptr.2d 779 (Cal.App. 2 Dist.1998), 711

Bondy's Ford, Inc. v. Sterling Truck Corp., 147 F.Supp.2d 1283 (M.D.Ala.2001), 697

Booth v. Mary Carter Paint Co., 202 So.2d 8 (Fla.App. 2 Dist.1967), 228

Boston Medical Center v. Service Employees Intern. Union, 113 F.Supp.2d 169 (D.Mass.2000), 763

Bottaro v. Hatton Associates, 96 F.R.D. 158 (E.D.N.Y.1982), 294, 295

Bowen v. United States Postal Service, 459 U.S. 212, 103 S.Ct. 588, 74 L.Ed.2d 402 (1983), 637

Bowles Financial Group, Inc. v. Stifel, Nicolaus & Co., Inc., 22 F.3d 1010 (10th Cir. 1994), 861

Bowmer v. Bowmer, 428 N.Y.S.2d 902, 406 N.E.2d 760 (N.Y.1980), 722

Boyd v. Homes of Legend, Inc., 981 F.Supp. 1423 (M.D.Ala.1997), 782

Brandeis Intsel Ltd. v. Calabrian Chemicals Corp., 656 F.Supp. 160 (S.D.N.Y.1987), 765

Branzburg v. Hayes, 408 U.S. 665, 92 S.Ct. 2646, 33 L.Ed.2d 626 (1972), 467

Bratt Enterprises, Inc. v. Noble Intern., Ltd., 99 F.Supp.2d 874 (S.D.Ohio 2000), 697

Brazell v. American Color Graphics, 2000 WL 364997 (S.D.N.Y.2000), 868

Breuer Elec. Mfg. Co. v. Toronado Systems of America, Inc., 687 F.2d 182 (7th Cir. 1982), 465

Bridas Sociedad Anonima Petrolera Industrial Y Commercial v. International Standard Elec. Corp., 128 Misc.2d 669, 490 N.Y.S.2d 711 (N.Y.Sup.1985), 726

Brocklesby v. United States, 767 F.2d 1288 (9th Cir.1985), 466

Broemmer v. Abortion Services of Phoenix, Ltd., 173 Ariz. 148, 840 P.2d 1013 (Ariz.1992), **699,** 704, 705

Brothers Jurewicz, Inc. v. Atari, Inc., 296 N.W.2d 422 (Minn.1980), 726

Broughton v. Cigna Healthplans of California, 90 Cal.Rptr.2d 334, 988 P.2d 67 (Cal. 1999), 783

Brower v. Gateway 2000, Inc., 246 A.D.2d 246, 676 N.Y.S.2d 569 (N.Y.A.D. 1 Dept. 1998), 709

Brown v. Board of Educ. of Topeka, Kan., 349 U.S. 294, 75 S.Ct. 753, 99 L.Ed. 1083 (1955), 40

Brown v. Richard A. Murphy, Inc., 261 Mont. 275, 862 P.2d 406 (Mont.1993), 254

Burton v. Bush, 614 F.2d 389 (4th Cir.1980), 865

Bush v. Paragon Property, Inc., 165 Or.App. 700, 997 P.2d 882 (Or.App.2000), 667

Cabinetree of Wisconsin, Inc. v. Kraftmaid Cabinetry, Inc., 50 F.3d 388 (7th Cir. 1995), 727

Cadle Co. v. Castle, 913 S.W.2d 627 (Tex. App.-Dallas 1995), 530, 531

Cain v. Saunders, 2001 WL 499167 (Ala. Civ.App.2001), **521,** 527

Cancanon v. Smith Barney, Harris, Upham & Co., 805 F.2d 998 (11th Cir.1986), 698

Cargill Rice, Inc. v. Empresa Nicaraguense Dealimentos Basicos, 25 F.3d 223 (4th Cir. 1994), 841

Carr v. Runyan, 89 F.3d 327 (7th Cir.1996), 483, 499

TABLE OF CASES **xxxix**

Carro v. Parade of Toys, Inc., 950 F.Supp. 449 (D.Puerto Rico 1996), 751

Cary v. Cary, 894 S.W.2d 111 (Tex.App.-Hous. (1 Dist.) 1995), 528, 529

Caudle v. AAA, 230 F.3d 920 (7th Cir.2000), 711

Cavac Compania Anonima Venezolana de Administracion y Comercio v. Board for Validation of German Bonds in the United States, 189 F.Supp. 205 (S.D.N.Y.1960), 728

Central Soya Co. Inc. v. Epstein Fisheries, Inc., 676 F.2d 939 (7th Cir.1982), 465

CFTC v. Schor, 478 U.S. 833, 106 S.Ct. 3245, 92 L.Ed.2d 675 (1986), 881

Chelsea Square Textiles, Inc. v. Bombay Dyeing and Mfg. Co., Ltd., 189 F.3d 289 (2nd Cir.1999), 687

Christensen v. Dewor Developments, 191 Cal. Rptr. 8, 661 P.2d 1088 (Cal.1983), 728

Chrysler Corp. v. Pitsirelos, 721 So.2d 710 (Fla.1998), 883

Chrysler Motors Corp. v. International Union, Allied Indus. Workers of America, AFL–CIO, 2 F.3d 760 (7th Cir.1993), 742

Cincinnati Gas & Elec. Co. v. General Elec. Co., 117 F.R.D. 597 (S.D.Ohio 1987), 570, 571

Cipollone v. Liggett Group, Inc., 785 F.2d 1108 (3rd Cir.1986), 465

Circuit City Stores, Inc. v. Adams, 532 U.S. 105, 121 S.Ct. 1302, 149 L.Ed.2d 234 (2001), 670

C. Itoh & Co. (America) Inc. v. Jordan Intern. Co., 552 F.2d 1228 (7th Cir.1977), 688

City of (see name of city)

Clark v. Bear Stearns & Co., Inc., 966 F.2d 1318 (9th Cir.1992), 795

Cline v. H.E. Butt Grocery Co., 79 F.Supp.2d 730 (S.D.Tex.1999), 697

Coady v. Ashcraft & Gerel, 996 F.Supp. 95 (D.Mass.1998), 750

Coca–Cola Bottling Co. of New York, Inc. v. Soft Drink and Brewery Workers, 242 F.3d 52 (2nd Cir.2001), 670

Coddington Enterprises, Inc. v. Werries, 54 F.Supp.2d 935 (W.D.Mo.1999), 816

Cohen v. Wedbush, Noble, Cooke, Inc., 841 F.2d 282 (9th Cir.1988), 706

Cole v. Burns Intern. Sec. Services, 105 F.3d 1465 (D.C.Cir.1997), 822, 839

Comins v. Sharkansky, 38 Mass.App.Ct. 37, 644 N.E.2d 646 (Mass.App.Ct.1995), 853

Commerce & Industry Ins. Co. v. Bayer Corp., 433 Mass. 388, 742 N.E.2d 567 (Mass.2001), 687

Commercial Solvents Corp v. Louisiana Liquid Fertilizer Co, 20 F.R.D. 359 (S.D.N.Y. 1957), 869

Commonwealth Coatings Corp. v. Continental Cas. Co., 393 U.S. 145, 89 S.Ct. 337, 21 L.Ed.2d 301 (1968), **842,** 846

Comprehensive Accounting Corp. v. Rudell, 760 F.2d 138 (7th Cir.1985), 724

COMSAT Corp. v. National Science Foundation, 190 F.3d 269 (4th Cir.1999), 868

Congregation B'Nai Sholom v. Martin, 382 Mich. 659, 173 N.W.2d 504 (Mich.1969), 610

Connecticut General Life Ins. Co. v. Sun Life Assur. Co. of Canada, 210 F.3d 771 (7th Cir.2000), 672

Connecticut Light & Power Co. v. Local 420, Intern. Broth. of Elec. Workers, AFL–CIO, 718 F.2d 14 (2nd Cir.1983), 741

Consolidated Coal Co. v. Local 1643, United Mine Workers of America, 48 F.3d 125 (4th Cir.1995), 849

Consolidated Pac. Engineering, Inc. v. Greater Anchorage Area Borough, 563 P.2d 252 (Alaska 1977), 671

Consolidation Coal Co. v. United Mine Workers of America, Dist. 12, Local Union 1545, 213 F.3d 404 (7th Cir.2000), 741

Container Technology Corp. v. J. Gadsden Pty., Ltd., 781 P.2d 119 (Colo.App.1989), 756

Cooper v. Ateliers de la Motobecane, S.A., 456 N.Y.S.2d 728, 442 N.E.2d 1239 (N.Y. 1982), 875

Coopertex, Inc. v. Rue De Reves, Inc., 1990 WL 6548 (S.D.N.Y.1990), 833

Corey v. New York Stock Exchange, 691 F.2d 1205 (6th Cir.1982), 853

Coulter v. Carewell Corp. of Oklahoma, 21 P.3d 1078 (Okla.Civ.App. Div. 2 2001), 520, 521

Daniel v. Ryan's Family Steak Houses, Inc., 211 F.3d 306 (6th Cir.2000), 823

David Co. v. Jim W. Miller Const., Inc., 444 N.W.2d 836 (Minn.1989), 834

David Nassif Associates v. United States, 644 F.2d 4 (Ct.Cl.1981), 618

David Nassif Associates v. United States, 557 F.2d 249 (Ct.Cl.1977), 618

Davis v. Blue Cross of Northern California, 158 Cal.Rptr. 828, 600 P.2d 1060 (Cal. 1979), 728

Davis v. Gaona, 260 Ga. 450, 396 S.E.2d 218 (Ga.1990), 556

DDI Seamless Cylinder Intern., Inc. v. General Fire Extinguisher Corp., 14 F.3d 1163 (7th Cir.1994), 842

Dean Witter Reynolds, Inc. v. Ness, 677 F.Supp. 866 (D.S.C.1988), 723

Dean Witter Reynolds, Inc. v. Trimble, 166 Misc.2d 40, 631 N.Y.S.2d 215 (N.Y.Sup. 1995), 832

Dearborn Fire Fighters Union v. City of Dearborn, 394 Mich. 229, 231 N.W.2d 226 (Mich.1975), 885, 886

Decker v. Lindsay, 824 S.W.2d 247 (Tex.App.-Hous. (1 Dist.) 1992), 547

Deiulemar Compagnia Di Navigazione S.p.A. v. M/V Allegra, 198 F.3d 473 (4th Cir. 1999), 866

TABLE OF CASES

Delta Air Lines, Inc. v. Air Line Pilots Ass'n, Intern., 861 F.2d 665 (11th Cir.1988), 763

DeValk Lincoln Mercury, Inc. v. Ford Motor Co., 811 F.2d 326 (7th Cir.1987), 752

Diapulse Corp. of America v. Carba, Ltd., 626 F.2d 1108 (2nd Cir.1980), 756

DiCrisci v. Lyndon Guar. Bank of New York, 807 F.Supp. 947 (W.D.N.Y.1992), 831

Diematic Mfg. Corp. v. Packaging Industries, Inc., 381 F.Supp. 1057 (S.D.N.Y.1974), 781

Doctor's Associates, Inc. v. Casarotto, 517 U.S. 681, 116 S.Ct. 1652, 134 L.Ed.2d 902 (1996), 689

Doe v. Roe, 93 Misc.2d 201, 400 N.Y.S.2d 668 (N.Y.Sup.1977), 511

Dow Corning Corp., In re, 211 B.R. 545 (Bkrtcy.E.D.Mich.1997), 571

D.R. by M.R. v. East Brunswick Bd. of Educ., 838 F.Supp. 184 (D.N.J.1993), 452

Drukker Communications, Inc. v. N.L.R.B., 700 F.2d 727 (D.C.Cir.1983), 477

Eastern Associated Coal Corp. v. United Mine Workers of America, Dist. 17, 531 U.S. 57, 121 S.Ct. 462, 148 L.Ed.2d 354 (2000), 762, 818

Edmund E. Garrison, Inc. v. International Union of Operating Engineers, 283 F.Supp. 771 (S.D.N.Y.1968), 850

E.E.O.C. v. Frank's Nursery & Crafts, Inc., 177 F.3d 448 (6th Cir.1999), 820

E.E.O.C. v. Kidder, Peabody & Co., Inc., 156 F.3d 298 (2nd Cir.1998), 820

E.E.O.C. v. Waffle House, Inc., 193 F.3d 805 (4th Cir.1999), 820

Egol v. Egol, 118 A.D.2d 76, 503 N.Y.S.2d 726 (N.Y.A.D. 1 Dept.1986), 722

E.I. DuPont de Nemours and Co. v. Grasselli Employees Independent Ass'n of East Chicago, Inc., 790 F.2d 611 (7th Cir.1986), 761

Engalla v. Permanente Medical Group, Inc., 64 Cal.Rptr.2d 843, 938 P.2d 903 (Cal. 1997), 647

Ericksen, Arbuthnot, McCarthy, Kearney & Walsh, Inc. v. 100 Oak Street, 197 Cal. Rptr. 581, 673 P.2d 251 (Cal.1983), 695, 696

Erie v. Tompkins, 304 U.S. 64, 58 S.Ct. 817, 82 L.Ed. 1188, 11 O.O. 246 (1938), 492, 655

Exercycle Corp. v. Maratta, 214 N.Y.S.2d 353, 174 N.E.2d 463 (N.Y.1961), 697

Exum, United States v., 748 F.Supp. 512 (N.D.Ohio 1990), 571

Faherty v. Faherty, 97 N.J. 99, 477 A.2d 1257 (N.J.1984), 779

Farkas v. Receivable Financing Corp., 806 F.Supp. 84 (E.D.Va.1992), 860

Fenton v. Howard, 118 Ariz. 119, 575 P.2d 318 (Ariz.1978), **477**, 480

Fields–D'Arpino v. Restaurant Associates, Inc., 39 F.Supp.2d 412 (S.D.N.Y.1999), 461

Firelock Inc. v. District Court of 20th Judicial Dist., 776 P.2d 1090 (Colo.1989), 556

First Options of Chicago, Inc. v. Kaplan, 514 U.S. 938, 115 S.Ct. 1920, 131 L.Ed.2d 985 (1995), 720, 724, 747

Flint Warm Air Supply Co., Inc. v. York Intern. Corp., 115 F.Supp.2d 820 (E.D.Mich.2000), 667

Folb v. Motion Picture Indus. Pension & Health Plans, 16 F.Supp.2d 1164 (C.D.Cal.1998), 471

Foreca, S.A. v. GRD Development Co., Inc., 758 S.W.2d 744 (Tex.1988), 520

Forsythe Intern., S.A. v. Gibbs Oil Co. of Texas, 915 F.2d 1017 (5th Cir.1990), 854

Foxgate Homeowners' Ass'n, Inc. v. Bramalea California, Inc., 108 Cal.Rptr.2d 642, 25 P.3d 1117 (Cal.2001), **500,** 509, 510

Fraser v. Merrill Lynch Pierce, Fenner & Smith, Inc., 817 F.2d 250 (4th Cir.1987), 727

Fudickar v. Guardian Mut. Life Ins. Co., 62 N.Y. 392 (N.Y.1875), 753

Fulgence v. J. Ray McDermott & Co., 662 F.2d 1207 (5th Cir.1981), 515

Gabriel v. Gabriel, 654 N.E.2d 894 (Ind.App. 1995), 499

Garden Grove Community Church v. Pittsburgh–Des Moines Steel Co., 140 Cal. App.3d 251, 191 Cal.Rptr. 15 (Cal.App. 4 Dist.1983), 673

Garrity v. Lyle Stuart, Inc., 386 N.Y.S.2d 831, 353 N.E.2d 793 (N.Y.1976), 830, 831, 832

Garstang v. Superior Court, 46 Cal.Rptr.2d 84 (Cal.App. 2 Dist.1995), 480

Geiger v. Ryan's Family Steak Houses, Inc., 134 F.Supp.2d 985 (S.D.Ind.2001), 823

Geldermann, Inc. v. CFTC, 836 F.2d 310 (7th Cir.1987), 881

General Acc. Ins. Co. v. Poller, 321 N.J.Super. 252, 728 A.2d 845 (N.J.Super.A.D.1999), 887

General Motors Corp. v. Abrams, 897 F.2d 34 (2nd Cir.1990), 650

General Motors Corp. v. Simmons, 558 S.W.2d 855 (Tex.1977), 295

Genesco, Inc. v. T. Kakiuchi & Co., Ltd., 815 F.2d 840 (2nd Cir.1987), 721

George Watts & Son, Inc. v. Tiffany and Co., 248 F.3d 577 (7th Cir.2001), 818

Georgia Power Co. v. Cimarron Coal Corp., 526 F.2d 101 (6th Cir.1975), 614

G. Heileman Brewing Co. v. Joseph Oat Corp., 871 F.2d 648 (7th Cir.1989), **315,** 326, 578

Gilling v. Eastern Airlines, Inc., 680 F.Supp. 169 (D.N.J.1988), 557

TABLE OF CASES xli

Gilmer v. Interstate/Johnson Lane Corp., 500 U.S. 20, 111 S.Ct. 1647, 114 L.Ed.2d 26 (1991), 789, 790, 791, 792, 819

Glauber v. Glauber, 192 A.D.2d 94, 600 N.Y.S.2d 740 (N.Y.A.D. 2 Dept.1993), 779

Government of the United Kingdom v. Boeing Co., 998 F.2d 68 (2nd Cir.1993), 673, 683

Graham v. Scissor–Tail, Inc., 171 Cal.Rptr. 604, 623 P.2d 165 (Cal.1981), 704, 852

Graphic Arts Intern. Union, Local 97–B v. Haddon Craftsmen, Inc., 489 F.Supp. 1088 (M.D.Pa.1979), 741

Gray v. Eskimo Pie Corp., 244 F.Supp. 785 (D.Del.1965), 208

Grayson v. Wofsey, Rosen, Kweskin and Kuriansky, 231 Conn. 168, 646 A.2d 195 (Conn.1994), 253

Green Tree Financial Corp.–Alabama v. Randolph, 531 U.S. 79, 121 S.Ct. 513, 148 L.Ed.2d 373 (2000), 815

Groton, Town of v. United Steelworkers of America, 254 Conn. 35, 757 A.2d 501 (Conn.2000), 765

GTE North, Inc., In re, 113 Lab.Arb. 665 (1999), 744

GTFM, LLC v. TKN Sales, Inc., 2000 WL 364871 (S.D.N.Y.2000), 882

Guinness–Harp Corp. v. Jos. Schlitz Brewing Co., 613 F.2d 468 (2nd Cir.1980), 874

Hacker v. Smith Barney, Harris Upham & Co., Inc., 131 Misc.2d 757, 501 N.Y.S.2d 977 (N.Y.City Civ.Ct.1986), 689

Hadges & Kunstler v. Yonkers Racing Corp., 48 F.3d 1320 (2nd Cir.1995), **261,** 269

Haertl Wolff Parker, Inc. v. Howard S. Wright Const. Co., a Div. of Wright Schuchart, Inc., 1989 WL 151765 (D.Or.1989), 752

Halligan v. Piper Jaffray, Inc., 148 F.3d 197 (2nd Cir.1998), 817, 818

Hampton v. ITT Corp., 829 F.Supp. 202 (S.D.Tex.1993), 669

Hanes Corp. v. Millard, 531 F.2d 585, 174 U.S.App.D.C. 253 (D.C.Cir.1976), 729

Harbour Assurance Co (UK) Ltd. v. Kansa General International Assurance Co. Ltd., [1993] Q.B. 701 (C.A.1993), 765

Hardman v. Dault, 2 S.W.3d 378 (Tex.App.-San Antonio 1999), **518,** 520

Harrison v. Nissan Motor Corp., 111 F.3d 343 (3rd Cir.1997), 651

Harvey Aluminum v. United Steelworkers of America, AFL–CIO, 263 F.Supp. 488 (C.D.Cal.1967), 858

Haynsworth v. The Corporation, 121 F.3d 956 (5th Cir.1997), 777

Helen Whiting, Inc. v. Trojan Textile Corporation, 307 N.Y. 360, 121 N.E.2d 367 (N.Y.1954), 686

Herrington v. Union Planters Bank, N.A., 113 F.Supp.2d 1026 (S.D.Miss.2000), 708

Hickman v. Taylor, 329 U.S. 495, 67 S.Ct. 385, 91 L.Ed. 451 (1947), 465

Hikers Industries, Inc. v. William Stuart Industries (Far East) Ltd., 640 F.Supp. 175 (S.D.N.Y.1986), 683

Hill v. Gateway 2000, Inc., 105 F.3d 1147 (7th Cir.1997), 708, 709, 741

Hill v. Norfolk and Western Ry. Co., 814 F.2d 1192 (7th Cir.1987), 740

Hillsdale PBA Local 207 v. Borough of Hillsdale, 263 N.J.Super. 163, 622 A.2d 872 (N.J.Super.A.D.1993), 886

Hoffman v. Red Owl Stores, Inc., 26 Wis.2d 683, 133 N.W.2d 267 (Wis.1965), 208

Honda Motor Co., Ltd. v. Oberg, 512 U.S. 415, 114 S.Ct. 2331, 129 L.Ed.2d 336 (1994), 831

House Grain Co. v. Obst, 659 S.W.2d 903 (Tex.App.-Corpus Christi 1983), 757

Hume v. M & C Management, 129 F.R.D. 506 (N.D.Ohio 1990), 571, 577, 578

Hunt v. Mobil Oil Corp., 654 F.Supp. 1487 (S.D.N.Y.1987), 836, 863

Hyundai America, Inc. v. Meissner & Wurst GmbH & Co., 26 F.Supp.2d 1217 (N.D.Cal.1998), 673

ILC Peripherals Leasing Corp. v. International Business Machines Corp., 458 F.Supp. 423 (N.D.Cal.1978), 779

Independent Lift Truck Builders Union v. Hyster Co., 2 F.3d 233 (7th Cir.1993), 719

In re (see name of party)

Instructional Television Corp. v. National Broadcasting Co., Inc., 45 A.D.2d 1004, 357 N.Y.S.2d 915 (N.Y.A.D. 2 Dept.1974), 720

Integrity Ins. Co. v. American Centennial Ins. Co., 885 F.Supp. 69 (S.D.N.Y.1995), 868

International Components Corp. v. Klaiber, 54 A.D.2d 550, 387 N.Y.S.2d 253 (N.Y.A.D. 1 Dept.1976), 866

International Produce, Inc. v. A/S Rosshavet, 638 F.2d 548 (2nd Cir.1981), 848, 849

International Union of Operating Engineers, Local No. 450 v. Mid–Valley, Inc., 347 F.Supp. 1104 (S.D.Tex.1972), 832

Interpool Ltd. v. Through Transport Mut. Ins. Ass'n Ltd., 635 F.Supp. 1503 (S.D.Fla.1985), 690

Jack Greenberg, Inc. v. Velleman Corp., 1985 U.S. Dist. Lexis 17132 *5 n.1 (E.D.Pa. 1985), 686

Jaffee v. Redmond, 518 U.S. 1, 116 S.Ct. 1923, 135 L.Ed.2d 337 (1996), 470, 471, 476

Jansen v. Packaging Corp. of America, 123 F.3d 490 (7th Cir.1997), 47

Jeereddi A. Prasad, M.D., Inc. v. Investors Associates, Inc., 82 F.Supp.2d 365 (D.N.J. 2000), 666

TABLE OF CASES

Jefferson County v. Barton–Douglas Contractors, Inc., 282 N.W.2d 155 (Iowa 1979), 674

J.E. Liss & Co. v. Levin, 201 F.3d 848 (7th Cir.2000), 726

John McShain, Inc. v. Cessna Aircraft Co., 563 F.2d 632 (3rd Cir.1977), 466

Johnson v. Georgia Highway Exp., Inc., 488 F.2d 714 (5th Cir.1974), 594

Johnson v. West Suburban Bank, 225 F.3d 366 (3rd Cir.2000), 710

John Wiley & Sons, Inc. v. Livingston, 376 U.S. 543, 84 S.Ct. 909, 11 L.Ed.2d 898 (1964), 725

Jones v. Fujitsu Network Communications, Inc., 81 F.Supp.2d 688 (N.D.Tex.1999), 792

Joseph Martin, Jr., Delicatessen, Inc. v. Schumacher, 436 N.Y.S.2d 247, 417 N.E.2d 541 (N.Y.1981), 617

Kabia v. Koch, 186 Misc.2d 363, 713 N.Y.S.2d 250 (N.Y.City Civ.Ct.2000), 853

Kelley v. Benchmark Homes, Inc., 250 Neb. 367, 550 N.W.2d 640 (Neb.1996), 752

Kelley v. Michaels, 830 F.Supp. 577 (N.D.Okla.1993), 830

Kelley Drye & Warren v. Murray Industries, Inc., 623 F.Supp. 522 (D.N.J.1985), 884

Kimbrough v. Holiday Inn, 478 F.Supp. 566 (E.D.Pa.1979), 556

Kingsbridge Center of Israel v. Turk, 98 A.D.2d 664, 469 N.Y.S.2d 732 (N.Y.A.D. 1 Dept.1983), 611

Klocek v. Gateway, Inc., 104 F.Supp.2d 1332 (D.Kan.2000), 709

Knepp, In re, 229 B.R. 821 (Bkrtcy.N.D.Ala. 1999), 710

Knorr Brake Corp. v. Harbil, Inc., 556 F.Supp. 489 (N.D.Ill.1983), 727

Kodak Min. Co. v. Carrs Fork Corp., 669 S.W.2d 917 (Ky.1984), 655

Kotam Electronics, Inc. v. JBL Consumer Products, Inc., 93 F.3d 724 (11th Cir. 1996), 778

Kothe v. Smith, 771 F.2d 667 (2nd Cir.1985), 297

Koveleskie v. SBC Capital Markets, Inc., 167 F.3d 361 (7th Cir.1999), 792

Kroger Company and United Food and Commercial Workers, In re, 85 Lab.Arb. 1198 (1985), 638

Kukla v. National Distillers Products Co., 483 F.2d 619 (6th Cir.1973), 515

Kulukundis Shipping Co., S/A v. Amtorg Trading Corporation, 126 F.2d 978 (2nd Cir.1942), 654

Kunda v. Muhlenberg College, 621 F.2d 532 (3rd Cir.1980), 70

Kurtz v. Kurtz, 538 So.2d 892 (Fla.App. 4 Dist.1989), 547

Lapidus v. Arlen Beach Condominium Ass'n, Inc., 394 So.2d 1102 (Fla.App. 3 Dist. 1981), 726

Lapine Technology Corp. v. Kyocera Corp., 130 F.3d 884 (9th Cir.1997), 747, 751, 754

Lawson v. Brown's Day Care Center, Inc., 776 A.2d 390 (Vt.2001), 510

Lear, Inc. v. Adkins, 395 U.S. 653, 89 S.Ct. 1902, 23 L.Ed.2d 610 (1969), 780

L.H. Lacy Co. v. City of Lubbock, 559 S.W.2d 348 (Tex.1977), 654

Lipcon v. Underwriters at Lloyd's, London, 148 F.3d 1285 (11th Cir.1998), 777

Lipschutz v. Gutwirth, 304 N.Y. 58, 106 N.E.2d 8 (N.Y.1952), 841

Litton Bionetics, Inc. v. Glen Const. Co., Inc., 292 Md. 34, 437 A.2d 208 (Md.1981), 671, 672, 719

Litton Financial Printing Div. v. N.L.R.B., 501 U.S. 190, 111 S.Ct. 2215, 115 L.Ed.2d 177 (1991), 719

LiVolsi, In re, 85 N.J. 576, 428 A.2d 1268 (N.J.1981), 652

Local 58, Intern. Broth. of Elec. Workers v. Southeastern Michigan Chapter, Nat. Elec. Contractors Ass'n, Inc., 43 F.3d 1026 (6th Cir.1995), 757

Loew's Inc. v. Krug (Cal.Super.1953), 756

Lopez, United States v., 514 U.S. 549, 115 S.Ct. 1624, 131 L.Ed.2d 626 (1995), 668, 669

Los Angeles Community College District, In re, 112 Lab.Arb. 733 (1999), 744

Lundgren v. Freeman, 307 F.2d 104 (9th Cir.1962), 853

Lyeth v. Chrysler Corp., 929 F.2d 891 (2nd Cir.1991), 883

Lyons v. Wickhorst, 231 Cal.Rptr. 738, 727 P.2d 1019 (Cal.1986), 556

Manion v. Nagin, 255 F.3d 535 (8th Cir. 2001), 876

Manss–Owens Co. v. H.S. Owens & Son, 129 Va. 183, 105 S.E. 543 (Va.1921), 517

Mantas v. Fifth Court of Appeals, 925 S.W.2d 656 (Tex.1996), 531

Marra v. Papandreou, 216 F.3d 1119 (D.C.Cir.2000), 699

Marriage of (see name of party)

Marsh v. First United StatesA Bank, N.A., 103 F.Supp.2d 909 (N.D.Tex.2000), 708

Martin v. Black, 909 S.W.2d 192 (Tex.App.-Hous. (14 Dist.) 1995), 529, 530

Martin v. Wilks, 490 U.S. 755, 109 S.Ct. 2180, 104 L.Ed.2d 835 (1989), 258

Mastrobuono v. Shearson Lehman Hutton, Inc., 514 U.S. 52, 115 S.Ct. 1212, 131 L.Ed.2d 76 (1995), **824,** 830, 831, 832

Matter of (see name of party)

McBro Planning and Development Co. v. Triangle Elec. Const. Co., Inc., 741 F.3d 342 (11th Cir.1984), 684

McCarthy v. Providential Corp., 1994 WL 387852 (N.D.Cal.1994), 711

TABLE OF CASES

xliii

McDonald v. City of West Branch, Mich., 466 U.S. 284, 104 S.Ct. 1799, 80 L.Ed.2d 302 (1984), 788, 793, 794

McGuire, Cornwell & Blakey v. Grider, 765 F.Supp. 1048 (D.Colo.1991), 652

McHale v. Alcon Surgical, Inc., 1992 WL 99658 (E.D.Pa.1992), 557

MCI Telecommunications Corp. v. Exalon Industries, Inc., 138 F.3d 426 (1st Cir.1998), 723

McKay v. Ashland Oil, Inc., 120 F.R.D. 43 (E.D.Ky.1988), 577

McLaughlin v. Superior Court, 140 Cal. App.3d 473, 189 Cal.Rptr. 479 (Cal.App. 1 Dist.1983), 514

McNulty v. Prudential–Bache Securities, Inc., 871 F.Supp. 567 (E.D.N.Y.1994), 792

Meadows Indem. Co. Ltd. v. Nutmeg Ins. Co., 157 F.R.D. 42 (M.D.Tenn.1994), 864

Mediterranean Enterprises, Inc. v. Ssangyong Corp., 708 F.2d 1458 (9th Cir.1983), 721

Merit Ins. Co. v. Leatherby Ins. Co., 714 F.2d 673 (7th Cir.1983), 848

Merrill Lynch, Pierce, Fenner & Smith, Inc. v. Dutton, 844 F.2d 726 (10th Cir.1988), 874

Merrill Lynch, Pierce, Fenner, and Smith, Inc. v. Longoria, 783 S.W.2d 229 (Tex. App.-Corpus Christi 1989), 690

Merrill Lynch, Pierce, Fenner & Smith, Inc. v. Ware, 414 U.S. 117, 94 S.Ct. 383, 38 L.Ed.2d 348 (1973), 666

Metro Industrial Painting Corp. v. Terminal Const. Co., 287 F.2d 382 (2nd Cir.1961), 668

Metropolitan Property and Cas. Ins. Co. v. J.C. Penney Cas. Ins. Co., 780 F.Supp. 885 (D.Conn.1991), 850

Meyers v. Contra Costa County Dept. of Social Services, 812 F.2d 1154 (9th Cir. 1987), 544

Meyers v. Univest Home Loan, Inc., 1993 WL 307747 (N.D.Cal.1993), 709

Miller v. Miller, 423 Pa.Super. 162, 620 A.2d 1161 (Pa.Super.1993), 779

Miller Brewing Co. v. Brewery Workers Local Union No. 9, 739 F.2d 1159 (7th Cir. 1984), 741

Mitsubishi Motors Corp. v. Soler Chrysler–Plymouth, Inc., 473 U.S. 614, 105 S.Ct. 3346, 87 L.Ed.2d 444 (1985), 627, 718, **766,** 777, 778, 779, 782, 783, 784, 790, 817

Monroe County, In re, 113 Lab.Arb. 933 (1999), 891

Moock, Application of, 99 A.D.2d 1003, 473 N.Y.S.2d 793 (N.Y.A.D. 1 Dept.1984), 866

Moore v. Fragatos, 116 Mich.App. 179, 321 N.W.2d 781 (Mich.App.1982), 706

Moore v. Gunning, 328 So.2d 462 (Fla.App. 4 Dist.1976), 515

Morgan v. Smith Barney, Harris Upham & Co., 729 F.2d 1163 (8th Cir.1984), 722

Morrison, United States v., 529 U.S. 598, 120 S.Ct. 1740, 146 L.Ed.2d 658 (2000), 669

Moses H. Cone Memorial Hosp. v. Mercury Const. Corp., 460 U.S. 1, 103 S.Ct. 927, 74 L.Ed.2d 765 (1983), 673, 683, 718

Motor Vehicle Acc. Indemnification Corp. v. McCabe, 19 A.D.2d 349, 243 N.Y.S.2d 495 (N.Y.A.D. 1 Dept.1963), 868

Motor Vehicle Mfrs. Ass'n of United States, Inc. v. New York, 551 N.Y.S.2d 470, 550 N.E.2d 919 (N.Y.1990), 883

Muhammad v. Strassburger, McKenna, Messer, Shilobod and Gutnick, 526 Pa. 541, 587 A.2d 1346 (Pa.1991), 253

Munson v. Straits of Dover, S.S. Co., 102 F. 926 (2nd Cir.1900), 654

Nagel v. ADM Investor Services Inc., 65 F.Supp.2d 740 (N.D.Ill.1999), 603

National Ass'n of Radiation Survivors v. Derwinski, 782 F.Supp. 1392 (N.D.Cal.1992), 67

National Broadcasting Co., Inc. v. Bear Stearns & Co., Inc., 165 F.3d 184 (2nd Cir.1999), 863

NCR Corp. v. CBS Liquor Control, Inc., 874 F.Supp. 168 (S.D.Ohio 1993), 729

Nestel v. Nestel, 38 A.D.2d 942, 331 N.Y.S.2d 241 (N.Y.A.D. 2 Dept.1972), 780

New Bedford Defense Products Division v. Local No. 1113, 258 F.2d 522 (1st Cir. 1958), 718

New England Merchants Nat. Bank v. Hughes, 556 F.Supp. 712 (E.D.Pa.1983), 556

Nghiem v. NEC Electronic, Inc., 25 F.3d 1437 (9th Cir.1994), 778

Nguyen v. City of Cleveland, 121 F.Supp.2d 643 (N.D.Ohio 2000), 792

Nicolet Instrument Corp. v. Lindquist & Vennum, 34 F.3d 453 (7th Cir.1994), 252

NLO, Inc., In re, 5 F.3d 154 (6th Cir.1993), 577, 578

N.L.R.B. v. Acme Industrial Co., 385 U.S. 432, 87 S.Ct. 565, 17 L.Ed.2d 495 (1967), 870

N.L.R.B. v. Columbus Printing Pressmen and Assistants' Union No. 252, 543 F.2d 1161 (5th Cir.1976), 620

N.L.R.B. v. General Elec. Co., 418 F.2d 736 (2nd Cir.1969), 209

N.L.R.B. v. Joseph Macaluso, Inc., 618 F.2d 51 (9th Cir.1980), 476, 477, 480

Nodak Rural Elect. Coop. and Int'l Bro. of Elect. Workers, In re, 78 Lab.Arb. 1119 (1982), 619

North American Foreign Trading Corp. v. Rosen, 58 A.D.2d 527, 395 N.Y.S.2d 194 (N.Y.A.D. 1 Dept.1977), 864

Northern Pipeline Const. Co. v. Marathon Pipe Line Co., 458 U.S. 50, 102 S.Ct. 2858, 73 L.Ed.2d 598 (1982), 878

Northrop Corp. v. Triad Intern. Marketing S.A., 811 F.2d 1265 (9th Cir.1987), 764

NOS Communications, Inc. v. Robertson, 936 F.Supp. 761 (D.Colo.1996), 832

TABLE OF CASES

Novak, In re, 932 F.2d 1397 (11th Cir.1991), 326

Nuclear Elec. Ins. Ltd. v. Central Power and Light Co., 926 F.Supp. 428 (S.D.N.Y. 1996), 696

Nueces County v. De Pena, 953 S.W.2d 835 (Tex.App.-Corpus Christi 1997), 548

Olam v. Congress Mortg. Co., 68 F.Supp.2d 1110 (N.D.Cal.1999), 509, 510

Olde Discount Corp. v. Dartley, N.Y.L.J. Dec.12 (1997), 832

Olde Discount Corp. v. Tupman, 1 F.3d 202 (3rd Cir.1993), 668, 820

Olshan Demolishing Co. v. Angleton Independent School Dist., 684 S.W.2d 179 (Tex. App.-Hous. (14 Dist.) 1984), 655

OPE Intern. LP v. Chet Morrison Contractors, Inc., 258 F.3d 443 (5th Cir.2001), 667

Orr Const. Co., United States v., 560 F.2d 765 (7th Cir.1977), 499

PaineWebber, Inc. v. Agron, 49 F.3d 347 (8th Cir.1995), 819

Parsons & Whittemore Overseas Co., Inc. v. Societe Generale De L'Industrie Du Papier (RAKTA), 508 F.2d 969 (2nd Cir.1974), 765

Party Yards, Inc. v. Templeton, 751 So.2d 121 (Fla.App. 5 Dist.2000), 764

Patterson v. ITT Consumer Financial Corp., 18 Cal.Rptr.2d 563 (Cal.App. 1 Dist.1993), 707

Patton v. Garrett, 116 N.C. 847, 21 S.E. 679 (N.C.1895), 745

Penn v. Ryan's Family Steakhouses, Inc., 95 F.Supp.2d 940 (N.D.Ind.2000), 823

Performance Unlimited, Inc. v. Questar Publishers, Inc., 52 F.3d 1373 (6th Cir.1995), 874

Perini Corp. v. Great Bay Hotel & Casino, Inc., 129 N.J. 479, 610 A.2d 364 (N.J. 1992), 746

Perry v. Thomas, 482 U.S. 483, 107 S.Ct. 2520, 96 L.Ed.2d 426 (1987), 666, 710

Pickell v. Guaranty Nat. Life Ins. Co., 917 S.W.2d 439 (Tex.App.-Hous. (14 Dist.) 1996), 529

Pierre v. General Acc. Ins., 100 A.D.2d 705, 474 N.Y.S.2d 622 (N.Y.A.D. 3 Dept.1984), 858

Pietrelli v. Peacock, 16 Cal.Rptr.2d 688 (Cal. App. 1 Dist.1993), 645

Pittsburgh Post-Gazette and Pittsburgh Typographical Union, In re, 113 Lab.Arb. 957 (1999), 639

Plum Creek Timber Company v. Hillman, 95 Wash.App. 1061 (Wash.App. Div. 1 1999), 483

Polin v. Kellwood Co., 103 F.Supp.2d 238 (S.D.N.Y.2000), 839

Pollard v. Merkel, 1999 WL 72209 (Tex.App.-Dallas 1999), 532

Poly Software Intern., Inc. v. Su, 880 F.Supp. 1487 (D.Utah 1995), 460

Portland General Elec. Co. v. United States Bank Trust Nat. Ass'n, 38 F.Supp.2d 1202 (D.Or.1999), 853

PPG Industries, Inc. v. Pilkington plc, 825 F.Supp. 1465 (D.Ariz.1993), 777

PPG Industries, Inc. v. Stauffer Chemical Co., 637 F.Supp. 85 (D.D.C.1986), 880, 881

Prande v. Bell, 105 Md.App. 636, 660 A.2d 1055 (Md.App.1995), 251

Prendergast v. Nelson, 199 Neb. 97, 256 N.W.2d 657 (Neb.1977), 645

Prestressed Concrete, Inc. v. Adolfson & Peterson, Inc., 308 Minn. 20, 240 N.W.2d 551 (Minn.1976), 674

Prima Paint Corp. v. Flood & Conklin Mfg. Co., 388 U.S. 395, 87 S.Ct. 1801, 18 L.Ed.2d 1270 (1967), **690,** 696, 697, 698, 721, 764

Progressive Cas. Ins. Co. v. C.A. Reaseguradora Nacional De Venezuela, 991 F.2d 42 (2nd Cir.1993), 689

Prudential–Bache Securities, Inc. v. Stevenson, 706 F.Supp. 533 (S.D.Tex.1989), 727

Prudential Ins. Co. of America v. Shammas, 865 F.Supp. 429 (W.D.Mich.1993), 690

Prudential Securities Inc. v. Laurita, 1997 WL 109438 (S.D.N.Y.1997), 726

Publishers' Ass'n of N.Y. and N.Y. Typographical Union, In re, 36 Lab.Arb. 706 (1961), 839, 840

Pueblo of Laguna v. Cillessen & Son, Inc., 101 N.M. 341, 682 P.2d 197 (N.M.1984), 673

Quincy, Illinois and International Association of Machinists, In re City of, 81 Lab.Arb. 352 (1982), 618

Ramonas v. Kerelis, 102 Ill.App.2d 262, 243 N.E.2d 711 (Ill.App. 1 Dist.1968), 724

Rangel, In re, 45 S.W.3d 783 (Tex.App.-Waco 2001), 706

Raymond Lloyd Co. v. District Court for Twentieth Judicial Dist., 732 P.2d 612 (Colo.1987), 300

Raytheon Co. v. Automated Business Systems, Inc., 882 F.2d 6 (1st Cir.1989), 830

RCM Technologies, Inc. v. Brignik Technology, Inc., 137 F.Supp.2d 550 (D.N.J.2001), 721

Regents of University of California v. Sumner, 50 Cal.Rptr.2d 200 (Cal.App. 1 Dist. 1996), 483

Reichenbach v. Smith, 528 F.2d 1072 (5th Cir.1976), 466

Reno v. Haler, 734 N.E.2d 1095 (Ind.App. 2000), 499

Republic of Nicaragua v. Standard Fruit Co., 937 F.2d 469 (9th Cir.1991), 697

TABLE OF CASES

xlv

Republic of the Philippines v. Westinghouse Elec. Corp., 714 F.Supp. 1362 (D.N.J. 1989), 697

Rhodes v. Consumers' Buyline, Inc., 868 F.Supp. 368 (D.Mass.1993), 696

Richards v. Lloyd's of London, 135 F.3d 1289 (9th Cir.1998), 778

Ridder v. City of Springfield, 109 F.3d 288 (6th Cir.1997), 261

Rinaker v. Superior Court, 74 Cal.Rptr.2d 464 (Cal.App. 3 Dist.1998), 509

Robbins v. Day, 954 F.2d 679 (11th Cir.1992), 756

Robinson v. Warner, 370 F.Supp. 828 (D.R.I. 1974), 683

Rodriguez de Quijas v. Shearson/American Exp., Inc., 490 U.S. 477, 109 S.Ct. 1917, 104 L.Ed.2d 526 (1989), 784, 790

Rojo v. Kliger, 276 Cal.Rptr. 130, 801 P.2d 373 (Cal.1990), 800

Rosenberg v. Merrill Lynch, Pierce, Fenner & Smith, Inc., 170 F.3d 1 (1st Cir.1999), 792

Rosenthal v. Great Western Fin. Securities Corp., 58 Cal.Rptr.2d 875, 926 P.2d 1061 (Cal.1996), 666

Ruckelshaus v. Monsanto Co., 467 U.S. 986, 104 S.Ct. 2862, 81 L.Ed.2d 815 (1984), 877

Saari v. Smith Barney, Harris Upham & Co., Inc., 968 F.2d 877 (9th Cir.1992), 792

Saika v. Gold, 56 Cal.Rptr.2d 922 (Cal.App. 4 Dist.1996), 813

Salomon Inc. Shareholders' Derivative Litigation 91 Civ. 5500 (RRP):, In re, 68 F.3d 554 (2nd Cir.1995), 836

Salt Lake City v. International Ass'n of Firefighters, 563 P.2d 786 (Utah 1977), 885

S.A. Mineracao Da Trindade–Samitri v. Utah Intern., Inc., 745 F.2d 190 (2nd Cir.1984), 721

S and T Mfg. Co., Inc. v. County of Hillsborough, 815 F.2d 676 (Fed.Cir.1987), 499

Sanford Const. Co. v. Rosenblatt, 25 Ohio Misc. 99, 266 N.E.2d 267 (Ohio Mun. 1970), 726

San Jose Peace Officer's Assn. v. City of San Jose, 78 Cal.App.3d 935, 144 Cal.Rptr. 638 (Cal.App. 1 Dist.1978), 884

Sargent v. Paine Webber Jackson & Curtis, Inc., 882 F.2d 529 (D.C.Cir.1989), 756

Saturn Distribution Corp. v. Williams, 905 F.2d 719 (4th Cir.1990), 667

Scherk v. Alberto–Culver Co., 417 U.S. 506, 94 S.Ct. 2449, 41 L.Ed.2d 270 (1974), 627, 699

Schmidt v. Midwest Family Mut. Ins. Co., 426 N.W.2d 870 (Minn.1988), 670

Schneider v. Kreiner, 83 Ohio St.3d 203, 699 N.E.2d 83 (Ohio 1998), 484

Schneider Moving & Storage Co. v. Robbins, 466 U.S. 364, 104 S.Ct. 1844, 80 L.Ed.2d 366 (1984), 718

School Board of the City of Detroit and Detroit Federation of Teachers, In re, 93 Lab.Arb. 648 (1989), 618

Schoonmaker v. Cummings and Lockwood, 252 Conn. 416, 747 A.2d 1017 (Conn. 2000), 780

Schubtex, Inc. v. Allen Snyder, Inc., 424 N.Y.S.2d 133, 399 N.E.2d 1154 (N.Y. 1979), 687

Schulze and Burch Biscuit Co. v. Tree Top, Inc., 831 F.2d 709 (7th Cir.1987), 687

Seck v. Hamrang, 657 F.Supp. 1074 (S.D.N.Y. 1987), 556

Securities Industry Ass'n v. Lewis, 751 F.Supp. 205 (S.D.Fla.1990), 667

Security Life Ins. Co. of America v. Duncanson & Holt, 228 F.3d 865 (8th Cir.2000), 864, 869

Seifert v. United States Home Corp., 750 So.2d 633 (Fla.1999), 723

795 Fifth Ave. Corp. v. Trusthouse Forte (Pierre) Management, Inc., 131 Misc.2d 291, 499 N.Y.S.2d 857 (N.Y.Sup.1986), 728

Shearson/American Exp., Inc. v. McMahon, 482 U.S. 220, 107 S.Ct. 2332, 96 L.Ed.2d 185 (1987), 783, 784, 785, 786, 790

Sheldone v. Pennsylvania Turnpike Com'n, 104 F.Supp.2d 511 (W.D.Pa. 2000), **469,** 476

Simrin v. Simrin, 233 Cal.App.2d 90, 43 Cal.Rptr. 376 (Cal.App. 5 Dist.1965), **511,** 513, 514

Sisters of Visitation v. Cochran Plastering Co., Inc., 775 So.2d 759 (Ala.2000), 668, 669

Smith, Application of, 381 Pa. 223, 112 A.2d 625 (Pa.1955), 555

Smith v. Smith, 154 F.R.D. 661 (N.D.Tex. 1994), 492

Smith Barney Shearson Inc. v. Sacharow, 666 N.Y.S.2d 990, 689 N.E.2d 884 (N.Y.1997), 726

Snyder–Falkinham v. Stockburger, 249 Va. 376, 457 S.E.2d 36 (Va.1995), 452

Southern United Fire Ins. Co. v. Knight, 736 So.2d 582 (Ala.1999), 668

Southland Corp. v. Keating, 465 U.S. 1, 104 S.Ct. 852, 79 L.Ed.2d 1 (1984), **656,** 666, 674, 689

Sperry Intern. Trade, Inc. v. Government of Israel, 532 F.Supp. 901 (S.D.N.Y.1982), 874

State ex rel. v. _____ (see opposing party and relator)

Stateside Machinery Co., Ltd. v. Alperin, 591 F.2d 234 (3rd Cir.1979), 721

Stefano Berizzi Co. v. Krausz, 239 N.Y. 315, 146 N.E. 436 (N.Y.1925), 861

Stevens/Leinweber/Sullens, Inc. v. Holm Development and Management, Inc., 165 Ariz. 25, 795 P.2d 1308 (Ariz.App. Div. 1 1990), 697, 698, 816

Stifel, Nicolaus & Co. Inc. v. Freeman, 924 F.2d 157 (8th Cir.1991), 727, 728

xlvi   TABLE OF CASES

Stinson v. America's Home Place, Inc., 108 F.Supp.2d 1278 (M.D.Ala.2000), 836

Stone, In re, 986 F.2d 898 (5th Cir.1993), 547

Strandell v. Jackson County, 838 F.2d 884 (7th Cir.1987), **572,** 577, 578

Strange v. Gulf & South American S. S. Co., Inc., 495 F.2d 1235 (5th Cir.1974), 515

Stroehmann Bakeries, Inc. v. Local 776 Intern. Broth. of Teamsters, 762 F.Supp. 1187 (M.D.Pa.1991), 764

Stroh Container Co. v. Delphi Industries, Inc., 783 F.2d 743 (8th Cir.1986), 603, 745

Strotz v. Dean Witter Reynolds, Inc., 223 Cal.App.3d 208, 272 Cal.Rptr. 680 (Cal. App. 4 Dist.1990), 698

Stylemaster, Inc. and Production Workers Union of Chicago, In re, 79 Lab.Arb. 762 (1982), 638

Sunkist Soft Drinks, Inc. v. Sunkist Growers, Inc., 10 F.3d 753 (11th Cir.1993), 850

Sun Printing & Publishing Ass'n v. Remington Paper & Power Co., 235 N.Y. 338, 139 N.E. 470 (N.Y.1923), 618

Supak & Sons Mfg. Co., Inc. v. Pervel Industries, Inc., 593 F.2d 135 (4th Cir.1979), 686

Sweet Dreams Unlimited, Inc. v. Dial–A–Mattress Intern., Ltd., 1 F.3d 639 (7th Cir. 1993), 721

Tamari v. Bache & Co. (Lebanon) S.A.L., 637 F.Supp. 1333 (N.D.Ill.1986), 795

Tang v. State of R.I. Dept. of Elderly Affairs, 904 F.Supp. 69 (D.R.I.1995), 796

Tarasoff v. Regents of University of California, 131 Cal.Rptr. 14, 551 P.2d 334 (Cal. 1976), 42

Tate v. Saratoga Savings & Loan Assn., 216 Cal.App.3d 843, 265 Cal.Rptr. 440 (Cal. App. 6 Dist.1989), 850

Tech–Bilt, Inc. v. Woodward–Clyde & Associates, 213 Cal.Rptr. 256, 698 P.2d 159 (Cal. 1985), 229

Telecredit, Inc., of Los Angeles v. TRW, Inc. (1977), 562

Teradyne, Inc. v. Mostek Corp., 797 F.2d 43 (1st Cir.1986), **870,** 874

Texaco, Inc. v. American Trading Transp. Co., Inc., 644 F.2d 1152 (5th Cir.1981), 750

Texas Dept. of Transp. v. Pirtle, 977 S.W.2d 657 (Tex.App.-Fort Worth 1998), 548

Texas Parks and Wildlife Dept. v. Davis, 988 S.W.2d 370 (Tex.App.-Austin 1999), 548

Textile Workers Union v. Lincoln Mills, 353 U.S. 448, 77 S.Ct. 912, 1 L.Ed.2d 972 (1957), 634

Thermos Co. v. Starbucks Corp., 1998 WL 299469 (N.D.Ill.1998), 499

Thiele v. Merrill Lynch, Pierce, Fenner & Smith, 59 F.Supp.2d 1060 (S.D.Cal.1999), 792

Thomas v. Resort Health Related Facility, 539 F.Supp. 630 (E.D.N.Y.1982), 464

Thomas v. Union Carbide Agr. Products Co., 473 U.S. 568, 105 S.Ct. 3325, 87 L.Ed.2d 409 (1985), 878, 881, 882

Three Valleys Mun. Water Dist. v. E.F. Hutton & Co., Inc., 925 F.2d 1136 (9th Cir. 1991), 698

Toon v. Wackenhut Corrections Corp., 250 F.3d 950 (5th Cir.2001), 510

Town of (see name of town)

Tracer Research Corp. v. National Environmental Services Co., 42 F.3d 1292 (9th Cir.1994), 721, 750

Trafalgar Shipping Co. v. International Mill. Co., 401 F.2d 568 (2nd Cir.1968), 720, 725

Twin City Rapid Transit Co., 7 Lab.Arb. 845 (1947), 616, 617

Twitty v. Minnesota Mining & Mfg. Co., 16 Pa. D. & C.4th 458 (Pa.Com.Pl.1993), 577

290 Park Avenue v. Fergus Motors, 275 A.D. 565, 90 N.Y.S.2d 613 (N.Y.A.D. 1 Dept. 1949), 862

Unionmutual Stock Life Ins. Co. of America v. Beneficial Life Ins. Co., 774 F.2d 524 (1st Cir.1985), 697

United Offshore Co. v. Southern Deepwater Pipeline Co., 899 F.2d 405 (5th Cir.1990), 720

United Paperworkers Intern. Union, AFL–CIO v. Misco, Inc., 484 U.S. 29, 108 S.Ct. 364, 98 L.Ed.2d 286 (1987), 670, **731,** 741, 744

United States v. _____ (see opposing party)

United States Department of Labor and American Federation of Gov't Employees, In re, 98 Lab.Arb. 1129 (1992), 863

United States E.E.O.C. v. Air Line Pilots Ass'n, 489 F.Supp. 1003 (D.Minn.1980), 464

United States, In re, 149 F.3d 332 (5th Cir. 1998), 547

United States Postal Service v. National Ass'n of Letter Carriers, AFL–CIO, 64 F.Supp.2d 633 (S.D.Tex.1999), 742

United Steelworkers of America v. American Mfg. Co., 363 U.S. 564, 80 S.Ct. 1343, 4 L.Ed.2d 1403 (1960), 636

United Steelworkers of America v. Warrior & Gulf Nav. Co., 363 U.S. 574, 80 S.Ct. 1347, 4 L.Ed.2d 1409 (1960), **634,** 636, 637, 718, 720

University of Miami v. Echarte, 618 So.2d 189 (Fla.1993), 650

Vaca v. Sipes, 386 U.S. 171, 87 S.Ct. 903, 17 L.Ed.2d 842 (1967), 637

Vandenberg v. Superior Court, 88 Cal. Rptr.2d 366, 982 P.2d 229 (Cal.1999), 795

Vernon v. Acton, 732 N.E.2d 805 (Ind. 2000), **493,** 499

Virginia Carolina Tools, Inc. v. International Tool Supply, Inc., 984 F.2d 113 (4th Cir. 1993), 725

TABLE OF CASES

Volt Information Sciences, Inc. v. Board of Trustees of Leland Stanford Junior University, 489 U.S. 468, 109 S.Ct. 1248, 103 L.Ed.2d 488 (1989), **674,** 682, 689, 690, 750, 831, 832

Wagshal v. Foster, 28 F.3d 1249 (D.C.Cir. 1994), **539**

Walker v. J.C. Bradford & Co., 938 F.2d 575 (5th Cir.1991), 727

Walters v. National Ass'n of Radiation Survivors, 473 U.S. 305, 105 S.Ct. 3180, 87 L.Ed.2d 220 (1985), **55,** 67, 68

Warwick, City of v. Warwick Regular Firemen's Ass'n, 106 R.I. 109, 256 A.2d 206 (R.I.1969), 886

Wasyl, Inc. v. First Boston Corp., 813 F.2d 1579 (9th Cir.1987), 853

Waterspring, S.A. v. Trans Marketing Houston Inc., 717 F.Supp. 181 (S.D.N.Y.1989), 841

Weinrott v. Carp, 344 N.Y.S.2d 848, 298 N.E.2d 42 (N.Y.1973), 721

Westinghouse Elec. Corp. v. New York City Transit Authority, 603 N.Y.S.2d 404, 623 N.E.2d 531 (N.Y.1993), 852

Wheeler v. St. Joseph Hospital, 63 Cal.App.3d 345, 133 Cal.Rptr. 775 (Cal.App. 4 Dist. 1976), 705, 706

Wickard v. Filburn, 317 U.S. 111, 63 S.Ct. 82, 87 L.Ed. 122 (1942), 669

Wilkinson v. Vaughn, 419 S.W.2d 1 (Mo. 1967), 518

Wilko v. Swan, 346 U.S. 427, 74 S.Ct. 182, 98 L.Ed. 168 (1953), 745, 749, 783, 784

Williams v. Katten, Muchin & Zavis, 837 F.Supp. 1430 (N.D.Ill.1993), 792

Willoughby Roofing & Supply Co., Inc. v. Kajima Intern., Inc., 598 F.Supp. 353 (N.D.Ala.1984), 830

Wilmington v. J.I. Case Co., 793 F.2d 909 (8th Cir.1986), 789

Wilmington Hospitality, L.L.C. v. New Castle County, 2001 WL 291948 (Del.Ch.2001), 500

Wilson v. Waverlee Homes, Inc., 954 F.Supp. 1530 (M.D.Ala.1997), 782

Witkowski v. Welch, 173 F.3d 192 (3rd Cir. 1999), 795

W.K. Webster & Co. v. American President Lines, Ltd., 32 F.3d 665 (2nd Cir.1994), 837

Wolitarsky v. Blue Cross of California, 61 Cal.Rptr.2d 629 (Cal.App. 2 Dist.1997), 696

Wolsey, Ltd. v. Foodmaker, Inc., 144 F.3d 1205 (9th Cir.1998), 752

Woods v. Holy Cross Hospital, 591 F.2d 1164 (5th Cir.1979), 556

Wright v. Circuit City Stores, Inc., 82 F.Supp.2d 1279 (N.D.Ala.2000), 817

Wright v. Universal Maritime Service Corp., 525 U.S. 70, 119 S.Ct. 391, 142 L.Ed.2d 361 (1998), 791

WWOR–TV, Inc. v. Local 209, NABET-CWA, 166 F.3d 1203 (2nd Cir.1998), 899

Yasuda Fire & Marine Ins. Co. of Europe, Ltd v. Continental Cas. Co., 37 F.3d 345 (7th Cir.1994), 874

Yorkaire, Inc. v. Sheet Metal Workers Intern. Ass'n, 758 F.Supp. 248 (E.D.Pa.1990), 724

Young v. State Farm Mut. Auto. Ins. Co., 169 F.R.D. 72 (S.D.W.Va.1996), **288,** 294, 463, 465

Zenger–Miller, Inc. v. Training Team, GmbH, 757 F.Supp. 1062 (N.D.Cal.1991), 750

Zwitserse Maatschappij Van Levensverzekering En Lijfrente v. ABN Intern. Capital Markets Corp., 996 F.2d 1478 (2nd Cir. 1993), 727

*

PROCESSES OF DISPUTE RESOLUTION:

The Role of Lawyers

*

CHAPTER I

Lawyers, Litigation and Process

A. Introduction

"What, then, is this law business about? It is about the fact that our society is honeycombed with disputes. Disputes actual and potential; disputes to be settled and disputes to be prevented; both appealing to law, both making up the business of the law. But obviously those which most violently call for attention are the actual disputes, and to these our first attention must be directed. Actual disputes call for somebody to do something about them. First, so that there may be peace, for the disputants; for other persons whose ears and toes disputants are disturbing. And secondly, so that the dispute may really be put at rest, which means, so that a solution may be achieved which, at least in the main, is bearable to the parties and not disgusting to the lookers-on. This doing of something about disputes, this doing of it reasonably, is the business of law. And the people who have the doing in charge, whether they be judges or sheriffs or clerks or jailers or lawyers, are officials of the law. *What these officials do about disputes is, to my mind, the law itself.*[1]"

This book is about the ways in which those "in charge" of "doing something about disputes" help to resolve those disputes. In particular, it is about the choices that lawyers make in helping to "put at rest" the disputes in which their clients have become involved.

Lawyers make choices about the appropriate process for resolving disputes even as they handle the most routine cases—in writing a letter suggesting possible settlement options for a divorce case, filing a lawsuit for a personal injury claimant, requesting arbitration under the provisions of a supply contract, filing a request for a waiver of a local zoning restriction, or asking a former school board member to mediate a dispute between a parent group and the elementary school principal. Often, however, such

---

1. Karl Llewellyn, The Bramble Bush: On Our Law and Its Study 12 (1960).

"choices" are made instinctively and without a great deal of reflection. Legal education—beginning with the traditional first-year curriculum and continuing through many advanced courses and extracurricular programs—may well have socialized the attorney into accepting litigation as the default process, that is, the normal, routine way in which client problems are to be resolved. The dominance of the "case book" and the hallowed "case method," while reflecting the importance of court decisions within the common law system, conveys the impression that a court is the inevitable forum for resolving disputes between individuals. Legal training may well focus intensively on the intricacies of the litigation process—but it will rarely address the strengths and weaknesses of litigation as only one among many processes available to resolve disputes.

During the last few decades, however, increased concern has been expressed by both the professionals who are engaged in litigation and the public at large about our judicial system. Litigation has been criticized as being too slow and costly and as failing ultimately to provide a resolution of disputes that is fair and that the parties will respect—as being, in short, "formal, tricky, divisive, time-consuming, and distorting."[2] Clients have begun to demand attention to process issues, and many now expect their lawyers to be familiar with the full range of alternative processes available for dispute resolution. And lawyers, trying to respond to this challenge, have begun to treat process as an important variable in the dispute resolution equation. This book seeks to give lawyers greater awareness of the process choices they make, and to expand their understanding of, and ability to use, a wide range of available dispute resolution processes.

We will be looking more closely at the litigation process in the next section. Our first step, however, is to develop some background understanding of conflict and the lawyer's role in its resolution. The typical lawyer probably gives very little thought to the nature of conflict—for example, how a dispute arises, or how and why a person decides to come to an attorney for help with a particular dispute. The lawyer is likely to take the dispute as a "given," turning immediately to the processing of the dispute in order to arrive at a satisfactory resolution. Yet any human problem will have traversed a long route and gone through a complex transformation before arriving at the lawyer's office. Understanding the social context out of which a dispute has arisen may help us in choosing and applying the appropriate process.

Richard E. Miller and Austin Sarat, Grievances, Claims, and Disputes: Assessing the Adversary Culture

15 Law & Soc'y Rev. 525, 526–27, 531–33, 536–46, 561–64 (1980–81).

One of the most important characteristics of dispute processing is the degree to which it emphasizes or requires adversariness. The comparison of

---

2. Lieberman & Henry, Lessons from the Alternative Dispute Resolution Move- ment, 53 U.Chi.L.Rev. 424, 427 (1986).

mediation and other techniques is frequently structured as a comparison between conciliation and contention. Criticism is often directed against legal professionals and legal processes for unnecessarily intensifying hostility between disputants. * * * [T]his intensification occurs because lawyers treat disputes through the adversarial forms prescribed by the legal order and thus remove them from their natural context.

Many theoretical statements about dispute processing reflect this concern for its adversarial elements. Theories of dispute transformation examine techniques for "heating up" or "cooling down" disputes. Dispute processing researchers typically favor methods of resolution which minimize adversarial elements; informality and reconciliation are preferred over formality and coercion. Dispute processing research has thus acquired its own ideology, which, apart from its intrinsic merits, further obscures the social context of disputing. It denies, implicitly, that disputes and disputing are normal components of human association.

Disputes begin as *grievances*. A grievance is an individual's belief that he or she (or a group or organization) is entitled to a resource which someone else may grant or deny. People respond to such beliefs in various ways. They may, for example, choose to "lump it" so as to avoid potential conflict. They may redefine the problem and redirect blame elsewhere. They may register a *claim* to communicate their sense of entitlement to the most proximate source of redress, the party perceived to be responsible. As Nader and Todd suggest,

> The grievance or preconflict stage refers to a circumstance or condition which one person ... perceives to be unjust, and the grounds for resentment or complaint.... The grievance situation ... may erupt into conflict, or it may wane. The path it will take is usually up to the offended party. His grievance may be escalated by confrontation; or escalation may be avoided by curtailing further social interaction....

Consumers, for example, make claims when they ask retailers to repair or replace defective goods. Claims can be rejected, accepted, or they can result in a compromise offer.

If the other party accepts the claim in full and actually delivers the resource in question in a routine manner ("Yes, we'll repair your new car; just bring it in"), there is no dispute. Outright rejection of a claim ("The car was not defective; it broke down because of your misuse") establishes an unambiguous dispute; there are now two (or more) parties with conflicting claims to the same resource. A compromise offer ("We'll supply the parts if you will pay for the labor") is a partial rejection of the claim, which initiates negotiation, however brief, and thus constitutes a dispute. * * * *A dispute exists when a claim based on a grievance is rejected either in whole or in part*. It becomes a civil legal dispute when it involves rights or resources which could be granted or denied by a court.

* * *

The manner and rate at which disputes are generated is sometimes taken as an indicator of societal "health." This view is most characteristic of the work of historians writing about World War II. They presented a picture of American society as a stable balance between conflict and calm, a society in which all disputes were resolved within a framework of consensus. Some may question the validity of that picture as a description of *any* period in American life, but the experience of the last two decades has certainly undermined both the social basis upon which the balance of conflict and calm may have existed and its viability as an ideology or a system of legitimizing beliefs. We increasingly hear the voices of those who perceive and fear the growth of an "adversary society", a society of assertive, aggressive, rights-conscious, litigious people ready and eager to challenge each other and those in authority. Images of our allegedly unprecedented assertiveness, or the ingenious ways which we have found to fight each other, flow through the popular culture, from *New Yorker* cartoons about children threatening to sue their parents for forcing them to drink their milk to palimony suits against celebrities.

There is, of course, another view of contemporary American society, a view which suggests that we are in fact, relatively uncontentious and even passive. Americans are said to be reluctant to admit that their lives are troubled and conditioned to accept circumstances and treatment which are far from ideal. Since our institutions respond slowly, inefficiently, and reluctantly, we learn not to complain, not to pursue our grievances or claim our rights. Even when we do, we find that appropriate institutions do not exist. As our society becomes ever more complex and expansive, it becomes easier to avoid conflict or to ignore it merely by moving on. People unable or unwilling to assert their rights or defend their interests may be easily victimized by self-interested organizations seeking to perpetuate a social and economic status quo. Proponents of this view typically question the adequacy of existing political, social, and economic arrangements to achieve justice.

It is ultimately both an empirical question and a matter of definition as to whether ours is a society of rights consciousness and conflict, or one of acquiescence and equilibrium.

* * *

DESCRIBING THE STRUCTURE OF CONFLICT: GRIEVING, CLAIMING, AND DISPUTING

Grieving

Disputes emerge out of grievances. Consequently we look first to the incidence of grievances to establish the baseline potential for disputes. There is, however, a conceptual problem. Grievances are composed of concrete events or circumstances which are relatively objective, but they are also composed of subjective perceptions, definitions, and beliefs that an event or circumstance is unwarranted or inappropriate. Individuals may react differently to the same experience. One buyer of a defective good may find it unacceptable and remediable; another may regard the bad purchase as "inevitable" and "lump it" or write it off to experience. According to our definition the first individual has a grievance; the second does not. Grievance rates reflect both the occurrence of certain events and a willingness by the participants to label those events in a particular way. * * *

Claiming

Given the perception that some event or circumstance is unacceptable and remediable, we can ask how assertive those who experience grievances are in seeking a remedy. Possible responses, as previously mentioned, range from avoidance, through repair without direct confrontation, registering a claim, to a demand for monetary compensation. Unless a claim is made, a dispute cannot occur. Other responses, such as avoidance, may be accompanied by feelings of bitterness or resentment which could lead to later conflict.

* * *

The Role of Lawyers and Courts

The language of rights and remedies is preeminently the language of law. One might logically ask where, in all of this, the law and legal institutions play a role. There is relatively little empirical work on the role of lawyers and courts in disputing. An assessment of the role of law, legal institutions, and legal services in the development of, or response to, conflict requires us to confront the problem of baselines.

[The authors then analyze the results of a telephone survey of approximately 1000 randomly-selected households in each of five federal judicial districts. In this survey grievances involving less than $1000 were screened out.]

Examining [Figures 1A and 1B], we find that relatively few disputants use a lawyer's services at all. Lawyers were used by less than one-fourth of those engaged in the disputes we studied. There are, however, two significant exceptions to the pattern. The role of lawyers is much more pronounced in post-divorce and tort problems. In the former, the involvement of lawyers is a function of the fact that many of these problems, e.g., adjustment in visitation arrangements or in alimony, *require* court action. In the latter, the contingent fee system facilitates and encourages lawyer use.

Few disputants (11.2 percent) report taking their dispute to court. Excluding post-divorce disputes, where court action is often required, that number is approximately 9 percent. These findings do not mean that courts or lawyers play a trivial role in middle-range disputes. Claims are made, avoided, or processed at least in part according to each party's understanding of its own legal position and that of its opponent; that understanding reflects both the advice that lawyers provide and the rights and remedies which courts have in the past recognized or imposed.

Figure 1A. A Dispute Pyramid: The General Pattern
No. per 1000 Grievances

Court Filings	50
Lawyers	103
Disputes	449
Claims	718
Grievances	1000

Figure 1B. Dispute Pyramids: Three Deviant Patterns
No. per 1000 Grievances

	Tort	Discrimination	Post-Divorce
Court Filings	38	8	451
Lawyers	116	29	588
Disputes	201	216	765
Claims	857	294	879
Grievances	1000	1000	1000

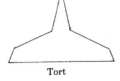 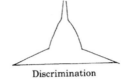 

Tort   Discrimination   Post-Divorce

... Courts
... Lawyers
... Disputes
... Claims
... Grievances

Summary

We can visualize the process of dispute generation through the metaphor of a pyramid (see Figure 1A). At the base are grievances, and the width of the pyramid shows the proportions that make the successive transitions to claims, disputes, lawyer use, and litigation. Figure 1B presents three contrasting patterns—the disputing pyramids for torts, post-divorce, and discrimination grievances.

Torts show a clear pattern. Most of those with grievances make claims (85.7 percent), and most claims are not formally resisted (76.5 percent result in immediate agreement). As a result, disputes are relatively rare (23.5 percent of claims). Where they occur, however, lawyers are available, accessible, and are, in fact, often employed (57.9 percent). Moreover, the same can be said for the employment of courts (at least in comparison with other problems). The overall picture is of a remedy system that minimizes formal conflict but uses the courts when necessary in those relatively rare cases in which conflict is unavoidable.

The pattern for discrimination grievances is quite different. Seven of ten grievants make no claim for redress. Those who do are very likely to have their claim resisted, and most claimants receive nothing. Only a little more than one in ten disputants is aided by a lawyer, and only four in a hundred disputes lead to litigation. The impression is one of perceived rights which are rarely fully asserted. When they are, they are strongly resisted and pursued without much assistance from lawyers or courts. Of course, we do not know how many of these or any other grievances would be found meritorious in a court of law. Nonetheless, as perceived grievances, they are a source of underlying tension and potential social conflict.

Post-divorce problems engender high rates of grievances, claims, and disputes, and are characterized by frequent use of lawyers and courts. As a result, almost half of all grievances lead to court involvement. While the court's activity in many, possibly most, of these cases is more administrative than adjudicative, this is, at least formally, the most disputatious and litigious grievance type we have measured.

Dispute pyramids could be drawn for the other types of problems, but they would all be quite similar: high rates of claims (80 to 95 percent of grievances), high rates of disputes (75 to 85 percent of claims), fairly low proportions using a lawyer (10 to 20 percent of disputants), and low litigation rates (3 to 5 percent of disputants). Indeed, the most striking finding in these descriptive data is again the general uniformity of rates at each stage of the disputing process across very different types of middle-range grievances.

* * *

We have found that, when measured against a baseline of perceived injustices or grievances, disputing is fairly common. But we are in no position, absent historical or comparative data, to determine just how substantial or significant it is. Our own belief is that where there are grievances there ought to be claims and that where there are claims, conflict is not necessarily an undesirable or unhealthy result. Those who fear conflict or who advocate acquiescence in the face of grievances fear threats to the social status quo. They bear a substantial burden in showing how people benefit from lumping or enduring injurious experiences or the denial of rights or how the status quo is served in the longer run as frustrations increase and legitimacy decreases. Indeed, it may be that the most significant aspect of our data, at least to those interested in arguments about the adversary culture, is the relatively low grievance rate for most of the transactions or relationships which we studied. Either those transactions are routinely efficient and satisfactory or people are reluctant to perceive or acknowledge trouble as it occurs. The incidence of social conflict ultimately hinges both on the rates at which injurious experiences are inflicted upon people and on what people define as acceptable performance of obligations or tolerate as acceptable conditions of life. The fact that almost 60 percent of our respondents report no recent middle-range grievance indicates a relatively low level of "injury" and/or a relatively high level of satisfaction or acquiescence.

Levels of "real" and perceived injuries, and the way people respond to them, are not self-generating. Economic, social, and political forces shape the context in which problems are perceived and conflicts generated, just as they affect the kind and amount of problems which occur. Thus we found, for example, that grievance rates were affected not only by the risk factors of particular transactions, statuses, and relationships, but also by educational levels and legal contacts. Particular concerns and not others come to be seen as worthwhile; particular responses and not others are legitimated; and those who declare trouble or who participate in conflict are differentially rewarded or stigmatized.

We wonder whether a survey of discrimination problems conducted twenty or thirty years ago would have found, as we did, that female-headed households reported a higher incidence of such problems or that blacks with such grievances were more likely to make a claim for redress. Not only have social and economic changes increased the number of women at risk of discrimination in employment or housing, but concomitant political and cultural changes have brought both increased sensitivity to and legislative condemnation of such discrimination. We have no basis on which to speculate about changes, if any, in blacks' "sensitivity" to racial discrimination, but social and political developments clearly have both reflected and enhanced the willingness and ability of blacks to resist such behavior.

Sex discrimination is a classic example of a movement from unperceived injurious experiences (unPIES) to perceived injurious experiences (PIES), which Felstiner *et al.* argue lies at the heart of the process through which new grievances emerge and new types of disputes arise. With each newly recognized injurious experience comes a strengthened or reinforced sense of harm and entitlement, both of which prepare the way for higher rates of grievances and conflict. Such cultural labeling is often matched by the use of official declarations, particularly the declaration of legal rights, as a device to regulate grievance perception and the response to grievances. The political forces that lead to declaration of legal rights may also result in the establishment of specialized remedy systems. Such systems may arise from other sources as well, such as an economic incentive to share risks. In any case, it is possible that the balance of rights declared and remedies provided is important in cueing responses to middle-range problems.

Problems differ in terms of the availability and kind of *institutionalization of remedy systems*. By institutionalization of remedy systems we mean the extent to which there are well-known, regularized, readily available mechanisms, techniques, or procedures for dealing with a problem. Take, for example, automobile accident and discrimination problems. The remedy system for auto accidents is highly institutionalized. There are routinized, well-known, and widely available procedures for dealing with such problems. The problem itself is one which has been recognized and acknowledged in the society for a long time and the principles—at least, the legal principles—involved are relatively settled. The result is a high claim rate, a low dispute rate, and considerable success for claimants.

The same cannot be said for discrimination problems. Neither a clear and widely accepted definition of discriminatory behavior which creates an entitlement to redress nor notions about appropriate kinds of redress have yet evolved. Existing legislated definitions are not well understood by the public, and those definitions are themselves in flux. Furthermore, remedy systems are less well developed and certainly less accessible. One simply doesn't pick up the phone and call one's insurance agent about a discrimination problem, and the principles governing redress are both rather unsettled and highly controversial. Under these circumstances, it is not surprising that, while quite a few households report some discrimination grievance, only three in ten of these asked for any redress of their grievance.

[The authors had earlier suggested other possible explanations for the low level of "claiming" for discrimination grievances:

Perhaps a lack of assertiveness has more to do with the substance of the problem itself. In discrimination situations it seems easier for those who believe that they have been unfairly denied a job or home just to keep on looking. Securing a job or home is likely to be much more pressing and important than filing a claim for something which is made undesirable by the very act that generates the grievance. "I need a job, and who would want to work there anyway" would not be an inexplicable response. * * *

Furthermore, there may be some stigma attached to the grievance itself or to the act of assertion. Victims, for example, may blame themselves for the unfair treatment. In discrimination grievances, especially, victory may turn into defeat. Those who are assertive, even if vindicated, are branded as troublemakers. Furthermore, grievants may be uncertain about the fit between their own perceptions and definitions of grievances and those embodied in statutes or otherwise recognized in their community. Indeed, both the law and popular expectations in this area of relatively new rights appear unsettled. Many who experience discrimination problems are, as a result, uncertain whether their grievance constitutes a sustainable claim.]

The institutionalization of remedies affects grievance perception, claiming, and disputing in two ways: first, by legitimizing action, and second, by shaping the objective probabilities of success should action be taken. The institutionalization of remedies alone suggests that the frequency and importance of a problem, as well as the appropriateness of action taken in response to it, is recognized. Where remedies are institutionalized, the probability of successful action can be more accurately assessed and prospective action thereby more clearly shaped and considered. Higher levels of institutionalization, everything else being equal, would be associated with higher rates of grievance perception and claiming, lower rates of disputes, and higher rates of success in recovery for meritorious claims.

Disputing is minimized where remedies are most and least institutionalized. Conflict can be avoided where automatic remedies are provided for felt grievances or where the demand for redress is discouraged by making it uncertain and hard to obtain. It is easier, on the whole, for societies to declare rights than to provide remedies; indeed, the development of remedies almost inevitably lags substantially behind the recognition of rights. The inability to vindicate rights discourages their expression and thus helps avoid a precondition for overtly adversarial relations. At the same time, of course, the gap between rights and remedies contributes to feelings of frustration and alienation which breed adversity between individuals and institutions. It is this tension which drives the development of remedy

CHAPTER I LAWYERS, LITIGATION & PROCESS

systems. Where rights are not realized or realizable over a long period of time and among a substantial portion of the population, where raised expectations are disappointed, interpersonal conflict is discouraged at the price of social and political strain. The balance of rights recognized and remedies provided is, in our view, important to an understanding of the generation of disputes and adversarial behavior.

NOTES AND QUESTIONS

1. Whether an individual even perceives that he has been "injured" may depend on his background and circumstances. A cancer victim previously exposed to asbestos may fail to perceive that he is ill; a consumer may fail to appreciate that a product is dangerous or not working as it is intended to. And among those experiences which *are* perceived as "injurious" "some may be seen as deserved punishment, some as the result of assumed risk or fickle fate"; only a limited number will be seen as a violation of some right or entitlement for which another person is responsible (that is, the subject of a "grievance"):

> [C]haracterization of an event as a grievance will depend on the cognitive repertoire with which society supplies the injured person and his idiosyncratic adaptation of it. He may, for example, be liberally supplied with ideological lenses to focus blame or to diffuse it. * * *
>
> The perception of grievances requires cognitive resources. Thus Best and Andreasen found that both higher income and white households perceive more problems with the goods they buy and complain more both to sellers and to third parties than do poor or black households. It seems unlikely that this reflects differences in the quality of goods purchased. Similarly, Curran reports that better educated respondents experience more problems of infringement of their constitutional rights.

Galanter, Reading the Landscape of Disputes: What We Know and Don't Know (And Think We Know) About Our Allegedly Contentious and Litigious Society, 31 U.C.L.A.L.Rev. 4, 13–14 (1983). See also Best & Andreasen, Consumer Response to Unsatisfactory Purchases: A Survey of Perceiving Defects, Voicing Complaints, and Obtaining Redress, 11 Law & Soc'y Rev. 701 (1977); Felstiner, Abel, & Sarat, The Emergence and Transformation of Disputes: Naming, Blaming, Claiming . . ., 15 Law & Soc'y Rev. 631 (1980–81).

Finally, even perceived grievances may not become the subject of complaints or claims. Despite much talk about our "litigious" society, many Americans seem reluctant to voice grievances. To do so, after all, may require them to acknowledge—both to themselves and to others—that they have been bettered by others or that they have allowed themselves to be victimized. See, e.g., Kristin Bumiller, The Civil Rights Society: The Social Construction of Victims 109 (1988) ("people who have experienced discriminatory treatment" feel that asserting their legal rights "would force them to justify their worthiness against a more powerful opponent"; they "reluctantly employ the label of discrimination because they shun the role of the victim"); Abel, The Real Tort Crisis—Too Few Claims, 48 Ohio St.L.J. 443 (1987).

Should the legal profession play any role in this process by which grievances and claims are generated? How does the relationship between "sensitivity" to grievances and disputes affect a lawyer's practice? His relationship with the client?

2. The Miller and Sarat data suggest that lawyers may play a less significant role in processing disputes than is commonly thought. Even where a grievance has crystallized into a "dispute," it may be brought to a lawyer's office less than a quarter of the time. Even in tort cases or in post-divorce conflicts, a sizable minority of disputants may choose not to seek legal help. What might account for this choice? Do disputants have an effective alternative?

3. Miller and Sarat state: "Claims are made, avoided, or processed at least in part according to each party's understanding of its own legal position and that of its opponent; that understanding reflects both the advice that lawyers provide and the rights and remedies which courts have in the past recognized or imposed." The notion that dispute resolution may take place "in the shadow of the law" is central to the lawyer's role in negotiation as well as in the other dispute resolution processes that we will be considering here. The authors imply, however, that the advice of lawyers may in some way be different from the rights and remedies expressed by courts. Why might this be true? It has been suggested that lawyers in consumer disputes often see their major role to be that of "gatekeepers" to the legal system: The individual client may be "cooled out"—discouraged from pressing claims that the lawyer feels may not be in the client's best interests to pursue, or that the lawyer *himself* for one reason or another would rather not pursue. See Macaulay, Lawyers and Consumer Protection Laws, 14 Law & Soc'y Rev. 115 (1979).

B.   COURTS AND LITIGATION

1.   THE DIMENSIONS OF LITIGATION

Jerold S. Auerbach, Justice Without Law?

10, 12–13 (1983).

Americans prefer to stand apart, separated from their ancestors, contemporaries, and descendents. Individualism means freedom—above all, the freedom to compete, acquire, possess, and bequeath. It is precisely this freedom that our legal system so carefully cultivates and protects. In a society where the dominant ethic is competitive individualism, regulated by the loose ground rules of the Darwinian struggle (with special protection reserved for crippled corporate giants), social cohesion is an enduring problem. Even as litigiousness expresses, and accentuates, the pursuit of individual advantage, the rule of law helps to hold such a fractured society together. At the least (usually it is also the most), people can agree upon how they will disagree. In a restless, mobile society of strangers, the staple scene of Western movies is perpetually reenacted: an American, at the first sign of danger, reaches for his (hired) gun and files a lawsuit. Yet contradictions abound. Our individualistic society encourages the assertion of legal rights as an entitlement of citizenship, but distributes them according to the ability to pay. Conflict is channeled into adversary proceedings with two combatants in every legal ring; but beyond the implicit assumption that every fight and any winner is good for society, the social good is ignored. Litigation is the all-purpose remedy that American society provides to its aggrieved members. But as rights are asserted, combat is encouraged; as the rule of law binds society, legal contentiousness increases social fragmentation.

* * *

The consuming American reverence for legal symbols and institutions slights the manifold ways in which law not only reinforces, but imposes, an atomistic, combative vision of reality. "Sue Thy Neighbor" is the appropriate modern American inversion of the Biblical admonition. So a newspaper photograph shows an angry woman, her face contorted with rage, who points menacingly at a cowering man, whose hands are raised in retreat and surrender. A judge looks on impassively, an American flag at his side. "If thy neighbor offend thee," the caption reads, "don't turn the other cheek. Slap him with a summons. And take him to Small Claims Court." It is only a blurb for a television special report, but the line between soap opera and reality is hopelessly blurred. Viewers are promised "a free course in self-defense," evidently a requirement for life among neighbors. (With neighbors like these, of course, enemies are superfluous.) Armed with the sword of litigation, Americans can wage ceaseless warfare against each other—and themselves.

NOTES AND QUESTIONS

1. Auerbach's image of a rights-obsessed, combative, litigious American society is certainly a familiar one in popular culture. After having spent some time in law school, does this ring true to you? Or does it strike you as something of a caricature? Does the picture he draws seem consistent with the data collected by Miller and Sarat on disputing patterns in America?

2. The rhetoric of the preceding excerpt may obscure one crucial fact: Even where disputants do have recourse to the courts, "full-blown" adjudication remains extremely rare. In the early 1980s the Civil Litigation Research Project (CLRP), sponsored jointly by the U.S. Department of Justice and the University of Wisconsin, compiled data about civil litigation in state and federal courts in five federal judicial districts. The following excerpt is based on data published in the Project's Final Report.

David M. Trubek, Austin Sarat, William L.F. Felstiner, Herbert M. Kritzer & Joel B. Grossman, The Costs of Ordinary Litigation

31 U.C.L.A. L.Rev. 72, 89, 122 (1983).

What happens in ordinary litigation? There is a popular image that litigation involves extensive pretrial activity and protracted trials. Our data suggest the contrary. Trials are rare, pretrial activity modest, and most cases terminate through settlement negotiations.

Less than 8% of the cases in our sample went to trial. In another 22.5%, the judge dismissed the complaint or rendered judgment on the merits without a trial. The most frequent mode of termination is voluntary agreement between the parties, which occurred in over 50% of the cases. Our data suggest civil judges and juries provide final, authoritative third party dispute processing in less than a third of the cases. More often, the courts serve as the background for bargaining between the parties. Bargaining occurs "in the shadow of the law," but is conducted primarily, if not exclusively, by the parties and their lawyers.

* * *

One of the most striking aspects of our study of litigation was that bargaining and settlement are the prevalent and, for plaintiffs, perhaps the most cost-effective activity that occurs when cases are filed. This will come as no surprise to litigators, but it is remarkable how seldom this fact is taken into account in discussions of the litigation crisis, costs of litigation, and the need for "alternatives to litigation."

Much of the literature advocating alternatives to litigation naively assumes that what occurs in courts is adjudication, in the classical sense. Since "adjudication" by definition uses judicial time heavily, the literature deduces that increased litigation will increase court budgets dramatically. Since adjudication presents an imposed, rather than a bargained or mediated solution, many observers believe it to be ineffective for the resolution of certain kinds of disputes. Finally, if adjudication is expensive and intrusive, then what is needed, so it is argued, are cheaper, more flexible "alternatives." But if in the world of ordinary litigation judges rarely reach formal decisions on the merits, the parties negotiate, albeit "in the shadow of the law," judges actively intervene to encourage settlement, and settlement is the rule, not the exception, then perhaps the whole reform debate falls wide of the mark. Perhaps the right approach is not to reach for wholly new institutional alternatives to a hypothetical process of adjudication, but to understand the non-adjudicative dimensions of litigation, to see how and why they work, and to seek to make this dimension of the litigation process even more central and effective.

NOTES AND QUESTIONS

1. A similar picture appears in a more recent study drawn from business litigation in the state courts of Rhode Island. In civil cases "in which there was at least one business entity on each side," less than 3% of the cases even reached the opening of trial—suggesting strongly that "business litigation in state court is overwhelmingly resolved in the shadow of the law, rather than through the formal legal process." The authors of the study also argue that economic trends may help to explain litigation rates—and in particular that

> less litigation will be observed in expanding industries than in stagnant or contracting ones. As firms fight over a shrinking economic pie, short-term gains and the bottom line will be emphasized sometimes at the cost of healthy long-term relationships. * * * Expanding conditions mean that the short-term value of winning a case in court will likely be less than either the potential profits from a future relationship with the party or simply the return on resources invested elsewhere. Our data provide modest support for the hypothesis.

Ross E. Cheit & Jacob E. Gersen, When Businesses Sue Each Other: An Empirical Study of State Court Litigation, 25 Law & Social Inquiry 789, 797, 807 (2000).

2. Would you expect that we would see different rates of settlement in cases involving different areas of law? The CLRP data indicate that while the "trial rate" for torts cases was 10%, by contrast 25% of domestic relations cases, and 15% of civil rights and discrimination cases, were "tried." Of course, "the higher 'trial rate' in domestic relations reflects the requirement of a formal resolution in divorce cases; while the court record may show an event that is labeled as a trial, it is typically nothing more than the ratification of a settlement agreed upon by the parties." Kritzer, Adjudication to Settlement: Shading in the Grey, 70 Judicature 161, 164 (1986).

3. The CLRP data also suggest that even where a lawsuit has been filed, the lawyers involved are likely to devote as much or more time to settlement than to actually "trying" the case in the traditional sense. When asked how they allocated their time in the cases being studied, lawyers reported spending 15% of their time on "settlement discussions." In addition, we can assume that a substantial proportion of their time nominally devoted to other activities, such as conferring with the client (16%), investigating the facts (12.8%), and engaging in legal research (10.1%), must have been directly aimed at reaching a settlement.

These results underscore even further the complementary relationship between litigation and negotiation: The CLRP study suggests that just as negotiation is an integral part of the dynamic of the litigation process, conversely, litigation may be just one stage—one strategic move—in the ongoing process of negotiation. Professor Marc Galanter has coined the term "litigotiation" to refer to this "single process of disputing in the vicinity of official tribunals"—"the strategic pursuit of a settlement through mobilizing the court process." Galanter, Worlds of Deals: Using Negotiation to Teach about Legal Process, 34 J.Legal Educ. 168 (1984). As a practical matter, then, in our system a lawsuit may be little more than a rather pointed way of opening negotiations—one way of bringing the other party to the bargaining table, where the real work of dispute resolution takes place.

4. A careful study of the much-publicized "litigation explosion" acknowledges that there has been an increase over the last century in the per capita filings of civil cases in both state and federal courts. However, "there is no evidence to suggest an increase in the portion of cases that runs the whole course. * * * [T]he percentage of cases reaching trial has diminished." On the other hand, for the small minority of cases that *do* run the full course, adjudication is likely to be "more protracted, more elaborate, more exhaustive, and more expensive." Galanter, Reading the Landscape of Disputes: What We Know and Don't Know (And Think We Know) About Our Allegedly Contentious and Litigious Society, 31 U.C.L.A. L.Rev. 4, 43–44 (1983). Perhaps of even greater interest is a comparison of American litigation rates with rates in other countries. The evidence suggests that the rate at which Americans use the civil courts "is in the same range as England, Ontario, Australia, Denmark, [and] New Zealand," although far higher than in Japan, Spain, and Italy. Id. at 55. The inclusion of Spain and Italy—societies that are not usually considered models of harmony and lack of contentiousness—may suggest the danger of facile "cultural" generalizations about litigation patterns.

5. The words "adjudication" and "litigation" are often casually used as if they were interchangeable, and you may see examples of this confusion in material quoted throughout this book. "Adjudication" refers to the process by which final, authoritative decisions are rendered by a neutral third party who enters the controversy without previous knowledge of the dispute. The third party's solution may, if necessary, be enforced by recourse to governmental sanctions; he may (but need not) have the authority to resolve the dispute according to a set of objective norms and following an elaborate procedure for the presentation of arguments and proof. In this sense, arbitration—a private process that we will discuss in detail in Chapter V— shares with the official court system some of the characteristics of dispute settlement through "adjudication." In "litigation," by contrast, the parties invoke the official court mechanism; as we have already seen, however, "litigation" need not lead to any final third-party decision. The dominance of negotiation and settlement has focused attention on what Trubek calls the "non-adjudicative dimensions of litigation." In addition, a number of mechanisms which aim at resolving disputes short of trial—such as the mini-trial, court-administered arbitration, or the summary jury trial—are closely connected to and may be considered part of the litigation process. These mechanisms are discussed in Chapter IV.

2. THE LIMITS OF THE JUDICIAL PROCESS

The high prestige and symbolic importance that Americans attach to the formal court system have never been incompatible with an intense awareness of the limitations and inadequacies of the litigation process. In 1850 Abraham Lincoln wrote in notes for a law lecture, "Discourage litigation. Persuade your neighbors to compromise whenever you can. Point

16 CHAPTER I LAWYERS, LITIGATION & PROCESS

out to them how the nominal winner is often a real loser—in fees, expenses, in waste of time.''

Recent attention to the shortcomings of litigation also begins with complaints about the frequent delay and expense of legal proceedings, as does this excerpt from a speech by Judge Jon Newman of the Second Circuit:

> Whether we have too many cases or too few, or even, miraculously, precisely the right number, there can be little doubt that the system is not working very well. Too many cases take too much time to be resolved and impose too much cost upon litigants and taxpayers alike. No one should have to wait five years for a case to come to trial, but many litigants in this country face this reality. Legal expenses should not exceed damage awards, yet in the asbestos litigation morass, for example, those expenses total $1.56 for every $1 provided to a victim. If long delays and high litigation costs were aberrational, systemic change could safely be avoided. But we know the problem is more serious. Even if the modern defenders of our current litigation level are right, systemwide averages should not obscure the long delays and high costs imposed upon hundreds or thousands who use or participate in the litigation process and the losses endured by those who are deterred from seeking redress in court.[3]

Moreover, the impact of delay and expense in litigation is not equally allocated. In a personal injury case, delay before trial will affect a plaintiff with mounting medical bills and without substantial resources far more than it will affect the defendant. And particularly where legal services are not available on a contingent fee basis, the costs of litigation may have made the courts inaccessible to large sections of the poor and middle class. As former President Derek Bok of Harvard has commented, ''There is far too much law for those who can afford it and far too little for those who cannot.''[4]

NOTES AND QUESTIONS

1. The portion of suits that are ''pursued through the full possibilities of contest'' has indeed continued to decline—but Professor Galanter has suggested that there may be other explanations for this besides a decrease in the ''appetite for litigious combat'': ''[I]t may be that more contest can be packed into earlier stages; or that increased transaction costs mean that parties can afford less contest than they would prefer.'' Galanter, The Life and Times of the Big Six: Or, The Federal Courts Since the Good Old Days, 1988 Wisc. L. Rev. 921, 951. Might this indicate that settlement is not always an unmitigated virtue—and that it might often be instead mere acquiescence in a lesser evil?

---

3. Newman, Rethinking Fairness: Perspectives on the Litigation Process, 94 Yale L.J. 1643, 1644–45 (1985).

4. Bok, Law and its Discontents: A Critical Look At Our Legal System, 38 Record of the Ass'n of the Bar of the City of New York 12, 13 (1983).

2. The New York City Health Code requires window guards for apartments with children under the age of ten. The board of a co-operative apartment building in New York voted to charge the cost of installation to the individual residents who needed such guards, rather than having the cost shared by everyone in the building; however the owner of a ninth-floor loft apartment, whose child was a month old, refused to pay. The co-op's law firm devoted a number of hours to settlement attempts and when this failed, the co-op brought a lawsuit against the owner. The New York Civil Court ruled in favor of the co-op; this was reversed, but on further appeal to the Appellate Division, the original ruling was reinstated. The contract by which the owner had acquired the apartment provided that the losing party in any litigation was to be responsible for the winner's attorneys' fees, and so further litigation then ensued concerning responsibility for the co-op's legal fees. Throughout all the stages of this suit the board paid its attorneys a total of $73,547, but it was ultimately held that it could recover only $30,000 of this from the owner of the apartment. In addition, the owner had paid around $30,000 to *his own* attorneys. It had originally cost $909 to purchase and install child-proof window guards across the 32 windows of the apartment in question. A full account appears in Lambert, "Ever Hear the One About the Lawyers and Window Bars?," Wall St. J., March 23, 1994, p. A1; see also Owners Corp. v. Diacou, N.Y.L.J., Feb. 23, 1994, p. 21.

What could possibly account for this behavior?

3. The CLRP study suggests that by contrast to such aberrant cases, the typical lawsuit is in fact

> a "paying" proposition for the parties. The average plaintiff will recover some portion of the amount claimed, and the amount recovered will significantly exceed the money and the value of time spent on the case. Even the defendants can be said to have "gained" from the litigation, at least in the sense that their litigation expenditures are less than the amount by which plaintiff's claim was reduced during litigation.

However, while it may be true that litigation typically "pays" in the sense of yielding net monetary benefits, the study left open the question whether "these gains are wiped out by negative non-monetary features of the litigation experience." Trubek et al., 31 U.C.L.A.L.Rev. at 84.

4. One study has estimated that the total expenditure nationwide for tort litigation in state and federal courts in 1985 was between $29 billion and $36 billion. Of this amount, plaintiffs received "about $14 to $16 billion in net compensation, after deducting all their litigation costs." James S. Kakalik & Nicholas M. Pace, Costs and Compensation Paid in Tort Litigation vi–ix (Rand 1986).

5. The more burdensome the prospect of litigation, of course, the more likely it becomes that the judicial process will be invoked strategically— that is, for purposes that have little or nothing to do with obtaining a favorable judgment.

18 CHAPTER I LAWYERS, LITIGATION & PROCESS

In 1983 Seward Johnson, an heir to the Johnson & Johnson fortune, died and left virtually all his $400 million estate to his third wife, who had once worked in the Johnson household as a maid. His children hired Alexander Forger, of the New York firm of Milbank, Tweed, Hadley & McCloy, to challenge the will, and the ensuing will contest became "the largest, costliest, ugliest, [and] most spectacular" in American history:

> [I]t was dubious that Milbank could knock out one will, let alone the long line of them Seward had signed over the years. Forger must have known from the outset that the children could never actually win their case; the object had to be settlement. But for that to work, Milbank needed a scorched-earth brand of litigator, someone who could make life so miserable for [the widow and the executor of the estate] that they would eventually have to surrender. The more wretched they could be made to be, the higher the price they'd pay.

David Margolick, Undue Influence: The Epic Battle for the Johnson & Johnson Fortune 12, 198 (1993).

6. A recent survey of business attorneys and nonlawyer executives indicated that virtually all the executives (96%) and inside counsel (91%) thought that less than half of suits involving a business are "resolved at an appropriate cost"; 86% and 79% respectively thought that less than of half of suits involving a business are "resolved within an appropriate amount of time." In addition, only 28% of executives and 38% of inside counsel believed that the legal system correctly determines the truth more than half the time (the comparable figure for outside counsel was only 40%). "Indeed many respondents laughed cynically when the proposition was posed to them." John Lande, Failing Faith in Litigation? A Survey of Business Lawyers' and Executives' Opinions, 3 Harv. Neg. L. Rev. 1, 29, 35–36 (1998).

The delay and expense associated with litigation are largely a function of the limited resources that we are willing to allocate to the judiciary, and of our highly stylized and structured trial procedure. There are other shortcomings of the judicial process, however, which may be less contingent and more fundamental.

In resolving a dispute a court is likely to rely on the use of objective, abstract "rules." Not even the most conscientious fact-finder can come away from a trial with more than the most limited, partial view of any given situation; out of the complexity and messiness of a dispute, out of an infinite variety of elements, the court will select just what seems relevant to enable it to place the dispute into one of several pre-existing "categories" (for example, "this is an action based on anticipatory repudiation of an executory contract"). The appropriate rule to govern the category is then neatly applied. Courts will only rarely be willing to use more person-oriented norms of conduct. Only exceptionally, for example, will a court feel able to consider (at least openly) the personal characteristics of the disputants, the human texture of their relationship, what may be in their long-term interest, or what they themselves may perceive as critical to their own dispute. In this process, the disputants themselves participate only secondarily. The lawyers and judge are the principal actors; the parties themselves speak and act only within court-imposed restrictions.

One consequence is that the court's solution may not be particularly well-adapted to the parties' needs. It is certainly not likely to be as appropriate or efficient as something that the parties familiar with the situation might have worked out for themselves. A related point is that the range of remedies available to a court is traditionally limited. A court will reduce most claims to the payment of money or the transfer of goods; it necessarily avoids person-or relationship-oriented relief. It may not, for example, call for an apology, expression of regret, or acknowledgment of fault, although this might be the relief that would most satisfy a hurt or angry plaintiff. "Claims for personal injury are treated as if the issue is how to put a dollar price on pain and suffering, while claims essentially based on insult and psychic hurt are not dealt with well, if they are recognized at all."[5] Nor, in a commercial dispute, is a court in any position to try to "salvage" the deal by calling for the restructuring or renegotiation of the transaction for the future.

In addition, a court's decision is "binary" in character:

[T]he "verdict of the court has an either/or character; the decision is based upon a single, definite conception of what has actually taken place and upon a single interpretation of the legal norms." This implies that adjudication operates largely in terms of black and white: This is the rule, that is not; this rule is superior to or more compelling than that one and therefore the latter is overridden; these facts are more probably correct, those are less probably, and therefore the latter are rejected; this disputant is in the right, the other is in the wrong.[6]

Even in jury trials "in the great majority of the cases, perhaps 80% to 85%, the verdict is a clear victory for one side and a clear loss for the other."[7]

The result is not only to limit the court's creativity in the matter of remedies. Often, the "either/or" nature of adjudication may also polarize the parties and drive them still further apart. The dynamic of litigation brings with it a need for self-justification and for the strategic escalation of struggle; being caught up in the process is likely to be an intense, emotionally charged experience which can generate considerable antagonism. The

---

5. Wagatsuma & Rosett, The Implications of Apology: Law and Culture in Japan and the United States, 20 Law & Soc'y Rev. 461, 494 (1986); see also Note, Healing Angry Wounds: The Role of Apology and Mediation in Disputes Between Physicians and Patients, 1987 J. of Dispute Res. 111.

6. P.H. Gulliver, Disputes and Negotiations: A Cross–Cultural Perspective 13 (1979).

7. Samuel Gross & Kent Syverud, Don't Try: Civil Jury Verdicts in a System Geared to Settlement, 44 U.C.L.A. L. Rev. 1, 46–47 (1996). The authors term a "loser" a litigant "who does less well than she could have by accepting an available settlement offer from the opposing side (and a 'winner' is someone who does better by that standard) considering both the judgment and the cost of obtaining it."

parties may finally lose sight altogether of the problem that gave rise to the dispute in the first place. Nor is it only the behavior and attitude of the disputants that may be affected; as the following excerpt suggests, the process may affect their representatives as well.

Wayne D. Brazil, The Attorney as Victim: Towards More Candor About the Psychological Price Tag of Litigation Practice

3 J. of the Legal Profession 107, 109–10, 114–117 (1978–79).

Some form of manipulation is a very real component of the professional lives of most litigators every day. The targets of the litigator's manipula -tory efforts include people, data, documents, precedents, institutions— virtually everything that can be moved to serve some purpose. The potential human subjects of the litigator's manipulations are almost countless: clients, witnesses, opposing counsel, judges, clerks, jurors, expert consultants, court reporters, even colleagues.

* * *

It is commonly believed by many litigators that to simply turn over all the relevant data to a consultant expert is to flirt with disaster: namely, the possibility that your expert will reach a negative conclusion about the role of your client. To reduce the chances of such an eventuality, many litigators carefully control the flow of information to their consultants. They first forward the data that would support a positive conclusion. Their hope is that the expert will form a positive opinion, will identify with the attorney's client, and will develop an ego investment in the positive conclusion that the attorney wants reached. Thereafter, the attorney may feed the expert some negative data about the client's conduct in order to prepare the expert to withstand cross-examination. By the time the expert receives the bulk of the negative information (at least so goes the litigator's theory of manipulation), he has so heavily identified with the client's position and has invested so much of his own professional ego in his positive opinion that all his impulses are in the direction of defending rather than reevaluating that opinion. Thus the lawyer hopes to capitalize on the expert's relatively predictable reactions to cognitive dissonance.

* * *

I believe that "money" and "winning" are the primary motivations of a high percentage of the litigators who are most comfortable with their work and the current system of dispute resolution. The people who seem least disturbed by litigation and best adapted to its pressures are not people to whom justice and esthetics are the paramount values, but are people who thrive on competition and doing battle, who are thoroughly engaged by gamesmanship, who love the taste of victory, and to whom the power and status that accompany wealth in our culture are very important. * * *

I find some support for these generalizations in the ways many litigators measure their professional success. For too many attorneys, success is not primarily seen as a function of how close to a just result was achieved for their clients. Indeed, some attorneys have retreated so far back into mystical (and self-serving) veneration for the adversary process that they insist that justice is whatever result the system produces and that they would violate their role if they even tried to determine what a "fair" result would be. Instead of measuring success by fairness of result, the adversary system encourages its participants to estimate their achievements by determining how much more they got for their client than his just deserts, by how much better they did for their client than other attorneys might have done and than opposing counsel did for her client, and by how much money they made. The system, in short, is seen as rewarding competitors and winners, not humanists, esthetes or moralists. And the pressures the system imposes track the reward it offers. Since rewards go to the competitors and the winners, the pressures are to compete and to win. Woe to the peaceful. Woe to those to whom constant competition is not comfortable and to whom victory is less important than justice. They are the ones who will be most distorted and strained by a litigation practice.

Most of my suggestions about the psychic implications of the manipulative and exploitative behavior of litigators originate in my own experiences. * * * Every time I manipulated a person or a precedent, tried to exploit an opponent's weakness, or failed to disclose some clearly important information (case, argument, or evidence), I felt not only dishonest, but also in some measure distorted, alienated from the kind of human being our culture has taught me to respect and to strive to be. When I wanted to be open, candid, and cooperative I felt pressure to be closed, self-conscious, and contrived. I emerged from encounters with other lawyers where I had hidden some weakness in my own case or postured for some tactical advantage feeling lessened, cheapened, degraded, and shaken. Even when my tactics were completely "successful," I felt discomfort, dissatisfaction, and unhappiness. I did not like myself in this role and did not respect the product of my professional endeavors. * * *

My manipulations and concealments not only eroded my self-respect, but also subtly discolored my feelings about others. The human subjects of my manipulatory tactics were converted in my eyes, by the process of manipulation itself, into something different from me, something less complex and sacred, something more like the inanimate objects in my environment that I move around more or less at will to satisfy myself. Manipulation, in short, bred objectification. If the people I manipulated were not fully reduced to inanimacy, they at least tended to become children in my clouded psychological vision—children in the old pejorative sense of only partial people, people not to be related to as equals. This kind of objectification of others probably leads to objectification of self and, thus, to the final closing of the circle of alienation. It must be very difficult to regularly view others as incomplete and manipulable without gradually coming to view oneself that way.

* * *

What assurance can an attorney who lives in a manipulation-oriented world for eight to ten hours a day have that she will be able to shift to another interpersonal gear in the evenings and on weekends? My experiences and my observations of other attorneys suggest that there is a very real danger that the modes of behavior that begin as adaptations to a special professional setting will gradually expand to fill virtually all of the lawyer's interpersonal space. Subtly, we may come to view all people as proper subjects for manipulation and become suspicious that all people will manipulate us if the opportunity and need arises. If manipulation and suspicion extend into our personal lives, they inevitably will bring with them their psychological baggage: a tendency to objectify and devalue others which invites a general cynicism and sense of alienation from the entire social fabric. The product of all this is hardly attractive: a person distorted and alone, unhappy with himself, suspicious of and separated from others.

Recent discussions of adjudication frequently sound other themes as well. One such theme suggests that there may be "functional" limits on the types of disputes that courts can appropriately handle—that is, that there are types of disputes that are inherently unsuited to resolution through the judicial process. What are these limits, and what effect might they have on a lawyer's choice of process for resolving a client's dispute? These questions are explored in the following excerpts.

Lon Fuller, The Forms and Limits of Adjudication

92 Harv. L. Rev. 353, 364–71, 393–400, 403 (1978).

* * * This whole analysis will derive from one simple proposition, namely, that the distinguishing characteristic of adjudication lies in the fact that it confers on the affected party a peculiar form of participation in the decision, that of presenting proofs and reasoned arguments for a decision in his favor. Whatever heightens the significance of this participation lifts adjudication toward its optimum expression. Whatever destroys the meaning of that participation destroys the integrity of adjudication itself.

* * *

When I am entering into a contract with another person I may present proofs and arguments to him, but there is generally no formal assurance that I will be given this opportunity or that he will listen to my arguments if I make them. (Perhaps the only exception to this generalization lies in the somewhat anomalous legal obligation to "bargain in good faith" in labor relations.) During an election I may actively campaign for one side and may present what I consider to be "reasoned arguments" to the electorate. If I am an effective campaigner this participation in the decision ultimately reached may greatly outweigh in importance the casting of my single vote. At the same time, it is only the latter form of participation that is the subject of an affirmative institutional guarantee. The protection accorded my right to present arguments to the electorate is almost entirely indirect and negative. The way will be clear for me, but I shall have to pave it myself. * * * The voter who goes to sleep before his television set is surely not subject to the same condemnation as the judge who sleeps through the arguments of counsel.

Adjudication is, then, a device which gives formal and institutional expression to the influence of reasoned argument in human affairs. As such it assumes a burden of rationality not borne by any other form of social ordering. A decision which is the product of reasoned argument must be prepared itself to meet the test of reason. We demand of an adjudicative decision a kind of rationality we do not expect of the results of contract or of voting. This higher responsibility toward rationality is at once the strength *and the weakness* of adjudication as a form of social ordering.

* * *

Now if we ask ourselves what kinds of questions are commonly decided by judges and arbitrators, the answer may well be, "Claims of right." Indeed, in the older literature * * * courts were often distinguished from administrative or executive agencies on the ground that it is the function of courts to "declare rights." If, then, we seek to define "the limits of adjudication," a tempting answer would be that the proper province of courts is limited to cases where rights are asserted. * * *

Is this a significant way of describing "the limits of adjudication"? I do not think so. In fact, what purports here to be a distinct assertion is merely an implication of the fact that adjudication is a form of decision that defines the affected party's participation as that of offering proofs and reasoned arguments. It is not so much that adjudicators decide only issues presented by claims of right or accusations. The point is rather that *whatever* is submitted to them for decision, tends to be converted into a claim of right or an accusation of fault or guilt. This conversion is effected by the institutional framework within which both the litigant and the adjudicator function.

* * *

I have suggested that it is not a significant description of the limits of adjudication to say that its proper province lies where rights are asserted or accusations of fault are made, for such a statement involves a circle of reasoning. If, however, we regard a formal definition of rights and wrongs as a nearly inevitable product of the adjudicative process, we can arrive at what is perhaps the most significant of all limitations on the proper province of adjudication. Adjudication is not a proper form of social order-ing in those areas where the effectiveness of human association would be destroyed if it were organized about formally defined "rights" and "wrongs." Courts have, for example, rather regularly refused to enforce agreements between husband and wife affecting the internal organization of family life. There are other and wider areas where the intrusion of "the machinery of the law" is equally inappropriate. An adjudicative board might well undertake to allocate one thousand tons of coal among three claimants; it could hardly conduct even the simplest coal-mining enterprise by the forms of adjudication. Wherever successful human association depends upon spontaneous and informal collaboration, shifting its forms with the task at hand, there adjudication is out of place except as it may declare certain ground rules applicable to a wide variety of activities.

* * * [T]he point I should like to stress is that the incapacity of a given area of human activity to endure a pervasive delimitation of rights and wrongs is also a measure of its incapacity to respond to a too exigent rationality, a rationality that demands an immediate and explicit reason for every step taken. Back of both of these incapacities lies the fundamental truth that certain kinds of human relations are not appropriate raw material for a process of decision that is institutionally committed to acting on the basis of reasoned argument.

THE LIMITS OF ADJUDICATION

Attention is now directed to the question, what kinds of tasks are inherently unsuited to adjudication? The test here will be that used throughout. If a given task is assigned to adjudicative treatment, will it be possible to preserve the meaning of the affected party's participation through proofs and arguments?

* * *

Some months ago a wealthy lady by the name of Timken died in New York leaving a valuable, but somewhat miscellaneous, collection of paintings to the Metropolitan Museum and the National Gallery "in equal shares," her will indicating no particular apportionment. When the will was probated the judge remarked something to the effect that the parties seemed to be confronted with a real problem. The attorney for one of the museums spoke up and said, "We are good friends. We will work it out somehow or other." What makes this problem of effecting an equal division of the paintings a polycentric task? It lies in the fact that the disposition of any single painting has implications for the proper disposition of every other painting. If it gets the Renoir, the Gallery may be less eager for the Cezanne but all the more eager for the Bellows, etc. If the proper apportionment were set for argument, there would be no clear issue to which either side could direct its proofs and contentions. Any judge assigned to hear such an argument would be tempted to assume the role of mediator or to adopt the classical solution: Let the older brother (here the Metropolitan) divide the estate into what he regards as equal shares, let the younger brother (the National Gallery) take his pick.

As a second illustration suppose in a socialist regime it were decided to have all wages and prices set by courts which would proceed after the usual forms of adjudication. It is, I assume, obvious that here is a task that could not successfully be undertaken by the adjudicative method. The point that comes first to mind is that courts move too slowly to keep up with a rapidly changing economic scene. The more fundamental point is that the forms of adjudication cannot encompass and take into account the complex repercussions that may result from any change in prices or wages. A rise in the price of aluminum may affect in varying degrees the demand for, and therefore the proper price of, thirty kinds of steel, twenty kinds of plastics, an infinitude of woods, other metals, etc. Each of these separate effects may have its own complex repercussions in the economy. In such a case it is simply impossible to afford each affected party a meaningful participation through proofs and arguments. * * *

We may visualize this kind of situation by thinking of a spider web. A pull on one strand will distribute tensions after a complicated pattern throughout the web as a whole. Doubling the original pull will, in all likelihood, not simply double each of the resulting tensions but will rather create a different complicated pattern of tensions. This would certainly occur, for example, if the doubled pull caused one or more of the weaker strands to snap. This is a "polycentric" situation because it is "many centered"—each crossing of strands is a distinct center for distributing tensions.

Suppose again, it were decided to assign players on a football team to their positions by a process of adjudication. I assume that we would agree that this is also an unwise application of adjudication. It is not merely a matter of eleven different men being possibly affected; each shift of any one player might have a different set of repercussions on the remaining players: putting Jones in as quarterback would have one set of carryover effects, putting him in as left end, another. Here, again, we are dealing with a situation of interacting points of influence and therefore with a polycentric problem beyond the proper limits of adjudication.

* * *

It should be carefully noted that multiplicity of affected persons is not an invariable characteristic of polycentric problems. This is sufficiently illustrated in the case of Mrs. Timken's will. * * * This insistence on a clear conception of polycentricity may seem to be laboring a point, but clarity of analysis is essential if confusion is to be avoided. For example, if a reward of $1000 is offered for the capture of a criminal and six claimants assert a right to the award, hearing the six-sided controversy may be an awkward affair. The problem does not, however, present any significant polycentric element as that term is here used.

Now, if it is important to see clearly what a polycentric problem is, it is equally important to realize that the distinction involved is often a matter of degree. There are polycentric elements in almost all problems submitted to adjudication. * * * It is not, then, a question of distinguishing black

The Role of Courts in American Society: Final Report of Council on the Role of Courts

102–114, 120–21 (Jethro K. Lieberman ed. 1984).

Which types of cases are and which are not fit for courts? We note at the outset that we can give no definitive answer to the question. Indeed, we believe that there is no single answer; rather, a number of criteria dictate various axes of inclusion and exclusion. What follows are meant as suggestions, not prescriptions. At best we can offer a series of observations that should help organize the inquiry.

* * *

These criteria can be grouped loosely in two categories; functional criteria and prudential criteria. Because no mathematical exactitude is possible, we state these criteria in the form of questions whose answers can be given only as a matter of degree.

FUNCTIONAL CRITERIA

By functional criteria we mean those factors that make a court peculiarly suited (or unsuited) to hear the matter in controversy. Here we are asking whether the court, as a particular type of governmental institution, is competent to hear and determine the dispute.

1. Objectivity

Does the dispute demand detached objectivity, in both reality and appearance? As we have seen, independence and impartiality are hallmarks of courts, and party participation in giving proof and making arguments are basic attributes of the judicial process that courts employ. In combination, the politics, psychology, and process are calculated to assure close, balanced, and open-minded scrutiny to contested claims. These in turn give integrity and respect to judicial decisions. When it is important for a decision to have the kind of integrity that the nature of the court and its process impart, the court is the proper forum. This criterion of objectivity surely applies in life-and-death cases, in constitutional claims, and in cases where liberty is at stake. It may or may not apply in cases turning on a dispute over a sum of money.

2. Necessity for Authoritative Standards

Can authoritative and ascertainable standards be applied to the facts of the dispute to produce a principled resolution? Courts are not as well suited as other institutions to adjudicate disputes in the absence of an ascertainable and authoritative standard. This inability is evident in disputes that present issues involving multiple criteria that cannot be weighed and ranked on an objective scale (e.g., selecting the position of players on a football team, picking the winner of a beauty contest).

To speak of authoritative and ascertainable standards is to speak in terms of degree, not mathematical precision. An authoritative standard can but need not be "black letter law." It may be a legal standard, as in a statute, or a private standard, as in a contract. It may be written, as in the commands of a constitution, or it may be found in the logic of common law decision or in the culture or traditions of a people. Likewise, to be ascertainable means to be capable of being discerned, possibly after some struggle. Of course an ascertainable standard may be one that is precisely spelled out, as in a statute of limitations that tells exactly after which date an action may no longer be pursued. But vague constitutional language like "due process of law" is, for all its frequent opaqueness, no less a standard that a court can apply. If some authoritative and ascertainable standard can be applied to a dispute to produce a principled resolution, the dispute likely belongs in court.

Nevertheless, not every "standard" capable of being applied by some person is proper for application in court. Thus courts are reluctant to intervene in questions of academic scholarship, not because professors do not use standards to evaluate student performance, but because the standards are not capable of easy or formulistic expression for application by an outsider. Compare, for example, a mathematics examination with an examination testing the student's knowledge of French literature. The math exam may call for answers that are ascertainable according to an authoritative standard; i.e., only one correct answer is possible for each question and any person knowledgeable in mathematics could state beforehand a precise formula for uncovering it. If a professor were to give a student a bad grade in the face of correct answers, a court could arguably intervene. But the French examination would pose an intractable difficulty: assuming that it did not call for such exact answers as a poet's birthdate, a court would have no standard to apply.

* * *

PRUDENTIAL CRITERIA

By prudential criteria, we mean those factors that make a court more or less suited than other institutions to hearing and resolving a dispute, given that on any view the court is competent to adjudicate the issue in controversy.

1. Costs

In a dispute over a monetary claim, is the cost of judicial resolution disproportionately large in relation to the amount at stake? When the dispute involves only money and the cost of determining the controversy is out of proportion to the amount at stake, some process of deciding that is less expensive and less time-consuming than adjudication should be sought * * *.

2. Particularized Consideration

Does the type of case typically present only repetitive kinds of factual or administrative questions not calling for particularized consideration of legal issues in each case? The deliberateness and individuated assessment associated with the judicial process may be of little use and may even be extraneous when courts are called upon to process en mass types of cases that pose only routine and repetitive issues. * * * In short, cases that do not require particularized consideration do not routinely call for courts. Examples are found in the administration of estates, in the determination and payment of various forms of public benefits, and in the routine disposition of traffic cases in lower courts.

3. Preference of the Parties

Would a sounder resolution of the controversy likely be achieved through a process giving effect to the parties' preferences rather than through the imposition of a third-party judgment? When the best solution is closely tied to giving effect to the parties' own preferences and utilities, bargaining rather than adjudication is desirable. A clear example is the case Fuller posed of the apportionment of paintings by a will * * *.

* * *

4. Vitality of Another Institution

Would judicial resolution of the matter at hand likely impair the vitality of an existing institution with means of dealing with the matter? When a decision would closely affect the continued vitality of another valued institution—a family, a school, a private political party—a court should supplant the traditional decision maker only in compelling cases. As one court put it in hearing a dispute over academic standards: "(I)n matters of scholarship, the school authorities are uniquely qualified by training and experience to judge the qualifications of a student, and efficiency of instruction depends in no small degree upon the school faculty's freedom from interference from other noneducational tribunals."

* * *

This rule can be illuminated further by considering a few cases in which courts have been invited to intrude on that great bastion of private autonomy, the family. Traditionally, courts have refused to adjudicate disputes and grant legal relief between members of an intact family. Thus, in McGuire v. McGuire [157 Neb. 226, 59 N.W.2d 336 (1953)] the court refused to order a husband, financially able to do so, to provide more adequately for his elderly wife, who was compelled to live in meager circumstances in a rundown house without indoor plumbing. The court based its refusal to intervene on the observation that the couple were still living together as husband and wife. Although the wife's claim would have been cognizable had she been separated from her husband, her demand for support here was not properly resolvable in a judicial forum because it was "a matter of concern to the household." * * *

A few years ago, Justice Rehnquist issued a broad warning against adjudication of claims that "can only disrupt ongoing relations" because "the very crystallization of the parties' differences in the adversary process may threaten the future of the institutional relationship." Others, while acknowledging the importance of preserving the family, have advocated a more particularized analysis in each case. They would balance the likely harm that judicial intrusion into family matters would cause against the damage resulting from refusal to redress an individual family member's claim.

* * *

5. Immediate Resolution of a Specialized Problem

Is the controversy one that arises in a specialized area when an immediate, on-the-spot decision that must be final is necessary? Even though a dispute is justiciable and serious, courts are not the best forum when the decision calls for an expert, on-the-scene determination and when delaying matters to get a more careful and accurate judgment from the courts will destroy the values that immediate finality would assure. A clear example of this type of case is the athletic contest during which it is claimed that an official made an erroneous call.

* * *

CASES IN WHICH COURTS SHOULD PLAY A BACKUP ROLE

1. Child Custody Cases

Courts now determine custody disputes. Does an analysis of the factors favoring and disfavoring judicial handling of the disputes support the conclusion that courts are the right place for these disputes to be resolved?

a. Factors Favoring Court Determination

(i) When parents disagree about the custody of a minor child, an institution enjoying high public confidence must resolve the disagreement.

(ii) Society has a deep interest in protecting children; it is essential to assure that injury to them is kept to a minimum. Courts can insist that the proceedings protect the child.

(iii) Some believe that the judicial process, with its emphasis on decency and dignity, may impart these qualities to the outcome.

b. Factors Opposing Court Determination

(i) In child custody disputes, "the actual determination of what is in fact in the child's best interest is ordinarily quite indeterminate." Because the standard of decision is so amorphous, courts are not able to apply it in a judicious way.

(ii) Determining the best interest of the child in part requires predicting future behavior patterns and interpersonal relationships, work in which courts do not excel.

30 CHAPTER I LAWYERS, LITIGATION & PROCESS

(iii) Because the parties' own preferences and utilities are so crucial to the best possible outcome, the court's process is not especially useful. In these cases, consensual agreements may yield greater permanency than imposed arrangements.

(iv) Adversary adjudication intensifies frictions and exposes private affairs to no useful end in reaching the decision.

c.   How the Courts May Be of Use

The foregoing list of pros and cons suggests that the court is not the proper institution to *make* the decision but is the proper forum to help *guide* the parties to reach their own decision. Obviously if the parents have reached no agreement, a dispute remains that urgently requires settlement. It seems far better to enlist the court than an administrative agency in the search for private agreement: The court process will ensure a modicum of decorum and decency along the way, and the court's imprimatur will be more convincing than a bureaucrat's. Courts thus have an important backup role to play in related-party cases, not "because judges can deftly resolve domestic controversies, but [because] . . . the very threat of their being called upon to do so can expedite negotiated settlement."

* * *

CASES NOT SUITABLE FOR COURTS

An ingenious enough lawyer can fashion any quarrel into the form of a legal dispute—or so it might seem. But few would argue that the courts should be open to hear any matter; problems that have not been shaped into disputes resting on a claim of legal entitlement ought not be aired in court. A matter may be of pressing moral concern, and proponents may make moral claims to remedial action by other institutions. Unless the moral claim is rooted in a legal entitlement, however, it is unsuited to judicial resolution. * * *

A second type of case that might be deemed unsuitable for the courts, no matter which view of courts' role is adopted, is that which raises issues that policy-makers would prefer to leave to the unfettered discretion of the individual. In fact, this category of cases—simple examples of which are claims based on breach of promise to marry or alienation of affection—is more properly seen as embracing matters that legislators on policy grounds would prefer not to see raised legally at all than as cases that jurisprudentially courts are unequipped to handle. Another example is the difference between fault and no-fault regimes in divorce law. If fault is an issue, then the question must be adjudicated—was the defendant guilty of adultery or abusive behavior or some other conduct that the law lays down as grounds for divorce? But cause is not a universal necessity: the legislature may decide, as many legislatures have decided, that a couple may divorce without assigning causes, leaving only disputes over the estate and custody of the children to be resolved in court. Diverting factual issues to other forums or denying the issues justiciability is one way of avoiding the difficulties that especially arise when adjudication must touch ongoing relations.

NOTES AND QUESTIONS

1. Exactly what does Brazil appear to mean by "manipulation"? And just what is wrong with it?

2. Just how may "problems" be "shaped into disputes resting on a claim of legal entitlement"? How would Professor Fuller have responded to such a question?

3. The problem of Mrs. Timken's will and its unsuitability for adjudication were explored further in another article by Professor Fuller, Collective Bargaining and the Arbitrator, Proceedings, 15th Annual Meeting, Nat. Academy of Arbitrators 8 (1962). Professor Fuller suggested that the typical cases falling neatly within the competence of the adjudicative process tend to be cases that call for a decision of "yes or no," or "more or less." By contrast, the available solutions in the Timken case "are scattered in an irregular pattern across a checkerboard of possibilities." To try to effect an "equal division" of the paintings within the framework of the adjudicative process would run into the difficulty that "meaningful participation by the litigants through proofs and arguments would become virtually impossible. There is no single solution, or simple set of solutions, towards which the parties meeting in open court could address themselves. If an optimum solution had to be reached through adjudicative procedures, the court would have had to set forth an almost endless series of possible divisions and direct the parties to deal with each in turn."

Professor Fuller also cautioned that he was not asserting

that an agency called a "court" should never under any circumstances undertake to solve a "polycentric" problem. Confronted by a dire emergency, or by a clear constitutional direction, a court may feel itself compelled to do the best it can with this sort of problem. All I am urging is that this sort of problem cannot be solved within the procedural restraints normally surrounding judicial office. Courts do in fact discharge functions that are not adjudicative in the usual sense of the word, as in supervising equity receiverships or in setting up procedures for admission to the bar. What I ask is clear thinking about the limits of the adjudicative process and about the value of those limits in the perspective of government as a whole. Thus, what I have said is relevant to the question whether courts should undertake to rewrite the boundaries of election districts to make them more representative of the distribution of population. It does not, however, preemptively decide that question.

Id. at 39–41.

4. Do you agree that courts assume "a burden of rationality not borne by any other form of social ordering"? What appears to be meant here by "rationality"? As we proceed through these materials, you might consider in what sense "rationality" plays a more limited role in other dispute-resolution processes such as negotiation, mediation, and arbitration.

5. Does Professor Fuller's exclusive focus on "polycentricity" lessen the usefulness of his analysis in evaluating the appropriateness of adjudication? In what ways might the functional and prudential criteria suggested by the Report of the Council on the Role of Courts be more helpful? Does the choice of the members of a college golf team involve "polycentricity"? Is this choice any more suitable for adjudication than is the choice of the members of the football or baseball team? See Eisenberg, Participation, Responsiveness, and the Consultative Process: An Essay for Lon Fuller, 92 Harv.L.Rev. 410 (1978).

6. One way that a court may handle polycentric problems is to encourage parties to negotiate a resolution acceptable to them. The degree of judicial involvement in negotiation will vary from judge to judge, as well as across different subject areas. To a large extent, however, the litigation system relies on the negotiating ability and judgment of lawyers to provide fair, efficient, and durable solutions to disputes.

Consider, for example, the case of Mrs. Timken: The substantive law of wills, and the threat that a court may step in and itself resolve the dispute between the two museums, is likely to assure that negotiation and a satisfactory settlement take place. Compare also the discussion of the "backup" role of courts in child custody cases in the Report of the Council on the Role of Courts. This also seems to be the prevailing way in which ongoing remedies are worked out in the "public law" or "institutional reform" litigation that places so much strain on the Fuller model of adjudication. In these complex cases, which typically challenge the operation and organization of public schools, mental hospitals, or prisons, the litigation system provides a framework within which the parties can bargain:

> The court will ask the parties to agree on an order or it will ask one party to prepare a draft. * * * The draftsman understands that his proposed decree will be subject to comment and objection by the other side and that it must be approved by the court. He is therefore likely to submit it to his opponents in advance to see whether differences cannot be resolved. Even if the court itself should prepare the initial draft of the order, some form of negotiation will almost inevitably ensue upon submission of the draft to the parties for comment.

> The negotiating process ought to minimize the need for judicial resolution of remedial issues. Each party recognizes that it must make some response to the demands of the other party, for issues left unresolved will be submitted to the court, a recourse that is always chancy and may result in a solution less acceptable than might be reached by horse-trading. * * * Indeed, relief by way of order after a determination on the merits tends to converge with relief through a consent decree or voluntary settlement. And this in turn mitigates a major theoretical objection to affirmative relief—the danger of intruding on an elaborate and organic network of interparty relationships.

Chayes, The Role of the Judge in Public Law Litigation, 89 Harv.L.Rev. 1281, 1298–99 (1976).

3. THE CASE FOR THE JUDICIAL PROCESS

Owen M. Fiss, Against Settlement

93 Yale L.J. 1073, 1075–78, 1082–90 (1984).

In a recent report to the Harvard Overseers, Derek Bok called for a new direction in legal education.[1] He decried "the familiar tilt in the law curriculum toward preparing students for legal combat," and asked instead that law schools train their students "for the gentler arts of reconciliation and accommodation." He sought to turn our attention from the courts to "new voluntary mechanisms" for resolving disputes. In doing so, Bok echoed themes that have long been associated with the Chief Justice,[4] and that have become a rallying point for the organized bar and the source of a new movement in the law. This movement is the subject of a new professional journal, a newly formed section of the American Association of Law Schools, and several well-funded institutes. It has even-received its own acronym—ADR (Alternative Dispute Resolution).

The movement promises to reduce the amount of litigation initiated, and accordingly the bulk of its proposals are devoted to negotiation and mediation prior to suit. But the interest in the so-called "gentler arts" has not been so confined. It extends to ongoing litigation as well, and the advocates of ADR have sought new ways to facilitate and perhaps even pressure parties into settling pending cases.

[Professor Fiss discusses amendments to Rule 16 and Rule 68 of the Federal Rules of Civil Procedure intended to "sharpen the incentives for settlement." See Appendix A, infra.]

The advocates of ADR are led to support such measures and to exalt the idea of settlement more generally because they view adjudication as a process to resolve disputes. They act as though courts arose to resolve quarrels between neighbors who had reached an impasse and turned to a stranger for help. Courts are seen as an institutionalization of the stranger and adjudication is viewed as the process by which the stranger exercises power. The very fact that the neighbors have turned to someone else to resolve their dispute signifies a breakdown in their social relations; the advocates of ADR acknowledge this, but nonetheless hope that the neighbors will be able to reach agreement before the stranger renders judgment. Settlement is that agreement. It is a truce more than a true reconciliation,

---

1. Bok, A Flawed System, Harv. Mag., May–June 1983, *reprinted in* N.Y.St.B.J., Oct. 1983, at 8, N.Y.St.B.J., Nov. 1983, at 31, *excerpted in* 33 J.Legal Educ. 570 (1983).

4. See, e.g., Burger, Isn't There a Better Way?, 68 A.B.A.J. 274 (1982); Burger, Agenda for 2000 A.D.—A Need for Systematic Anticipation, 70 F.R.D. 83, 93–96 (1976).

34 CHAPTER I LAWYERS, LITIGATION & PROCESS

but it seems preferable to judgment because it rests on the consent of both parties and avoids the cost of a lengthy trial.

* * *

In my view, however, this account of adjudication and the case for settlement rest on questionable premises. I do not believe that settlement as a generic practice is preferable to judgment or should be institutionalized on a wholesale and indiscriminate basis. It should be treated instead as a highly problematic technique for streamlining dockets. Settlement is for me the civil analogue of plea bargaining: Consent is often coerced; the bargain may be struck by someone without authority; the absence of a trial and judgment renders subsequent judicial involvement troublesome; and although dockets are trimmed, justice may not be done. Like plea bargaining, settlement is a capitulation to the conditions of mass society and should be neither encouraged nor praised.

By viewing the lawsuit as a quarrel between two neighbors, the dispute-resolution story that underlies ADR implicitly asks us to assume a rough equality between the contending parties. It treats settlement as the anticipation of the outcome of trial and assumes that the terms of settlement are simply a product of the parties' predictions of that outcome. In truth, however, settlement is also a function of the resources available to each party to finance the litigation, and those resources are frequently distributed unequally. Many lawsuits do not involve a property dispute between two neighbors, or between AT & T and the government (to update the story), but rather concern a struggle between a member of a racial minority and a municipal police department over alleged brutality, or a claim by a worker against a large corporation over work-related injuries. In these cases, the distribution of financial resources, or the ability of one party to pass along its costs, will invariably infect the bargaining process, and the settlement will be at odds with a conception of justice that seeks to make the wealth of the parties irrelevant.

The disparities in resources between the parties can influence the settlement in three ways. First, the poorer party may be less able to amass and analyze the information needed to predict the outcome of the litigation, and thus be disadvantaged in the bargaining process. Second, he may need the damages he seeks immediately and thus be induced to settle as a way of accelerating payment, even though he realizes he would get less now than he might if he awaited judgment. All plaintiffs want their damages immediately, but an indigent plaintiff may be exploited by a rich defendant because his need is so great that the defendant can force him to accept a sum that is less than the ordinary present value of the judgment. Third, the poorer party might be forced to settle because he does not have the resources to finance the litigation, to cover either his own projected expenses, such as his lawyer's time, or the expenses his opponent can impose through the manipulation of procedural mechanisms such as discovery. It might seem that settlement benefits the plaintiff by allowing him to avoid the costs of litigation, but this is not so. The defendant can anticipate the plaintiff's costs if the case were to be tried fully and decrease his offer by that amount. The indigent plaintiff is a victim of the costs of litigation even if he settles.

* * *

Of course, imbalances of power can distort judgment as well: Resources influence the quality of presentation, which in turn has an important bearing on who wins the terms of victory. We count, however, on the guiding presence of the judge, who can employ a number of measures to lessen the impact of distributional inequalities. He can, for example, supplement the parties' presentations by asking questions, calling his own witnesses, and inviting other persons and institutions to participate as amici. These measures are likely to make only a small contribution toward moderating the influence of distributional inequalities, but should not be ignored for that reason. Not even these small steps are possible with settlement. There is, moreover, a critical difference between a process like settlement, which is based on bargaining and accepts inequalities of wealth as an integral and legitimate component of the process, and a process like judgment, which knowingly struggles against those inequalities. Judgment aspires to an autonomy from distributional inequalities, and it gathers much of its appeal from this aspiration.

* * *

THE LACK OF A FOUNDATION FOR CONTINUING JUDICIAL IN-VOLVEMENT

The dispute-resolution story trivializes the remedial dimensions of lawsuits and mistakenly assumes judgment to be the end of the process. It supposes that the judge's duty is to declare which neighbor is right and which wrong, and that this declaration will end the judge's involvement (save in that most exceptional situation where it is also necessary for him to issue a writ directing the sheriff to execute the declaration). Under these assumptions, settlement appears as an almost perfect substitute for judgment, for it too can declare the parties' rights. Often, however, judgment is not the end of a lawsuit but only the beginning. The involvement of the court may continue almost indefinitely. In these cases, settlement cannot provide an adequate basis for that necessary continuing involvement, and thus is no substitute for judgment.

The parties may sometimes be locked in combat with one another and view the lawsuit as only one phase in a long continuing struggle. The entry of judgment will then not end the struggle, but rather change its terms and the balance of power. One of the parties will invariably return to the court and again ask for its assistance, not so much because conditions have changed, but because the conditions that preceded the lawsuit have unfortunately not changed. This often occurs in domestic-relations cases, where the divorce decree represents only the opening salvo in an endless series of skirmishes over custody and support.

The structural reform cases that play such a prominent role on the federal docket provide another occasion for continuing judicial involvement.

CHAPTER I LAWYERS, LITIGATION & PROCESS

In these cases, courts seek to safeguard public values by restructuring large-scale bureaucratic organizations. The task is enormous, and our knowledge of how to restructure on-going bureaucratic organizations is limited. As a consequence, courts must oversee and manage the remedial process for a long time—maybe forever. This, I fear, is true of most school desegregation cases, some of which have been pending for twenty or thirty years. It is also true of antitrust cases that seek divestiture or reorganization of an industry.

The drive for settlement knows no bounds and can result in a consent decree even in the kinds of cases I have just mentioned, that is, even when a court finds itself embroiled in a continuing struggle between the parties or must reform a bureaucratic organization. The parties may be ignorant of the difficulties ahead or optimistic about the future, or they may simply believe that they can get more favorable terms through a bargained-for agreement. Soon, however, the inevitable happens: One party returns to court and asks the judge to modify the decree, either to make it more effective or less stringent. But the judge is at a loss: He has no basis for assessing the request. He cannot, to use Cardozo's somewhat melodramatic formula, easily decide whether the "dangers, once substantial, have become attenuated to a shadow," because, by definition he never knew the dangers.

* * *

Settlement also impedes vigorous enforcement, which sometimes requires use of the contempt power. As a formal matter, contempt is available to punish violations of a consent decree. But courts hesitate to use that power to enforce decrees that rest solely on consent, especially when enforcement is aimed at high public officials, as became evident in the Willowbrook deinstitutionalization case[33] and the recent Chicago desegregation case. Courts do not see a mere bargain between the parties as a sufficient foundation for the exercise of their coercive powers.

* * * Of course, a plaintiff is free to drop a lawsuit altogether (provided that the interests of certain other persons are not compromised), and a defendant can offer something in return, but that bargained-for arrangement more closely resembles a contract than an injunction. It raises a question which has already been answered whenever an injunction is issued, namely, whether the judicial power should be used to enforce it. Even assuming that the consent is freely given and authoritative, the bargain is at best contractual and does not contain the kind of enforcement commitment already embodied in a decree that is the product of a trial and the judgment of a court.

---

33. New York State Ass'n for Retarded Children, Inc. v. Carey, 631 F.2d 162, 163–64 (2d Cir.1980) (court unwilling to hold governor in contempt of consent decree when legislature refused to provide funding for committee established by court to oversee implementation of decree). The First Cir-

cuit explicitly acknowledged limitations on the power of courts to enforce consent decrees in Brewster v. Dukakis, 687 F.2d 495, 501 (1st Cir.1982), and Massachusetts Ass'n for Retarded Citizens, Inc. v. King, 668 F.2d 602, 610 (1st Cir.1981).

JUSTICE RATHER THAN PEACE

The dispute-resolution story makes settlement appear as a perfect substitute for judgment, as we just saw, by trivializing the remedial dimensions of a lawsuit, and also by reducing the social function of the lawsuit to one of resolving private disputes: In that story, settlement appears to achieve exactly the same purpose as judgment—peace between the parties—but at considerably less expense to society. The two quarreling neighbors turn to a court in order to resolve their dispute, and society makes courts available because it wants to aid in the achievement of their private ends or to secure the peace.

In my view, however, the purpose of adjudication should be understood in broader terms. Adjudication uses public resources, and employs not strangers chosen by the parties but public officials chosen by a process in which the public participates. These officials, like members of the legislative and executive branches, possess a power that has been defined and conferred by public law, not by private agreement. Their job is not to maximize the ends of private parties, nor simply to secure the peace, but to explicate and give force to the values embodied in authoritative texts such as the Constitution and statutes: to interpret those values and to bring reality into accord with them. This duty is not discharged when the parties settle.

* * * To be against settlement is not to urge that parties be "forced" to litigate, since that would interfere with their autonomy and distort the adjudicative process; the parties will be inclined to make the court believe that their bargain is justice. To be against settlement is only to suggest that when the parties settle, society gets less than what appears, and for a price it does not know it is paying. Parties might settle while leaving justice undone. The settlement of a school suit might secure the peace, but not racial equality. Although the parties are prepared to live under the terms they bargained for, and although such peaceful coexistence may be a necessary precondition of justice,[35] and itself a state of affairs to be valued, it is not justice itself. To settle for something means to accept less than some ideal.

* * *

THE REAL DIVIDE

To all this, one can readily imagine a simple response by way of confession and avoidance: We are not talking about those lawsuits. Advocates of ADR might insist that my account of adjudication, in contrast to the one implied by the dispute-resolution story, focuses on a rather narrow

---

35. Some observers have argued that compliance is more likely to result from a consent decree than from an adjudicated decree. See O. Fiss & D. Rendleman, Injunctions 1004 (2d ed. 1984). But increased compliance may well be due to the fact that a consent decree asks less of the defendant, rather than from its creating a more amicable relationship between the parties. See McEwen & Maiman, Mediation in Small Claims Court: Achieving Compliance Through Consent, 18 Law & Soc'y Rev. 11 (1984).

category of lawsuits. They could argue that while settlement may have only the most limited appeal with respect to those cases, I have not spoken to the "typical" case. My response is twofold.

First, even as a purely quantitative matter, I doubt that the number of cases I am referring to is trivial. My universe includes those cases in which there are significant distributional inequalities; those in which it is difficult to generate authoritative consent because organizations or social groups are parties or because the power to settle is vested in autonomous agents; those in which the court must continue to supervise the parties after judgment; and those in which justice needs to be done, or to put it more modestly, where there is a genuine social need for an authoritative interpretation of law. I imagine that the number of cases that satisfy one of these four criteria is considerable; in contrast to the kind of case portrayed in the dispute-resolution story, they probably dominate the docket of a modern court system.

Second, it demands a certain kind of myopia to be concerned only with the number of cases, as though all cases are equal simply because the clerk of the court assigns each a single docket number. All cases are not equal. The Los Angeles desegregation case, to take one example, is not equal to the allegedly more typical suit involving a property dispute or an automobile accident. The desegregation suit consumes more resources, affects more people, and provokes far greater challenges to the judicial power. The settlement movement must introduce a qualitative perspective; it must speak to these more "significant" cases, and demonstrate the propriety of settling them. Otherwise it will soon be seen as an irrelevance, dealing with trivia rather than responding to the very conditions that give the movement its greatest sway and saliency.

* * *

In fact, most ADR advocates make no effort to distinguish between different types of cases or to suggest that "the gentler arts of reconciliation and accommodation" might be particularly appropriate for one type of case but not for another. They lump all cases together. This suggests that what divides me from the partisans of ADR is not that we are concerned with different universes of cases, that Derek Bok, for example, focuses on boundary quarrels while I see only desegregation suits. I suspect instead that what divides us is much deeper and stems from our understanding of the purpose of the civil law suit and its place in society. It is a difference in outlook.

Someone like Bok sees adjudication in essentially private terms. The purpose of lawsuits and the civil courts is to resolve disputes, and the amount of litigation we encounter is evidence of the needlessly combative and quarrelsome character of Americans. Or as Bok put it, using a more diplomatic idiom: "At bottom, ours is a society built on individualism, competition, and success." I, on the other hand, see adjudication in more public terms: Civil litigation is an institutional arrangement for using state power to bring a recalcitrant reality closer to our chosen ideals. We turn to the courts because we need to, not because of some quirk in our personalities. We train our students in the tougher arts so that they may help secure all that the law promises, not because we want them to become gladiators or because we take a special pleasure in combat.

To conceive of the civil lawsuit in public terms as America does might be unique. I am willing to assume that no other country—including Japan, Bok's new paragon[43]—has a case like *Brown v. Board of Education* in which the judicial power is used to eradicate the caste structure. I am willing to assume that no other country conceives of law and uses law in quite the way we do. But this should be a source of pride rather than shame. What is unique is not the problem, that we live short of our ideals, but that we alone among the nations of the world seem willing to do something about it. Adjudication American-style is not a reflection of our combativeness but rather a tribute to our inventiveness and perhaps even more to our commitment.

NOTES AND QUESTIONS

1. When, if at all, is it appropriate to rely on "private," non-official processes to resolve disputes in which "public" values are implicated? When should the diversion of such disputes from the court system be discouraged? Despite Professor Fiss's suggestion to the contrary, it would be highly unlikely that anyone interested in dispute resolution today would "lump all" such cases together. Can we find techniques or approaches that might moderate any tension between the need to articulate and uphold societal values and the potential advantages of alternative processes? These are all questions that will recur constantly throughout these materials: You should not lose sight of them as you proceed to consider the variety of the available means of dispute resolution.

2. Judge Harry Edwards tells the story of a seminar conducted by the Carter Center at Emory University, which brought together people on both sides of the tobacco controversy. As described by former First Lady Rosalynn Carter, "when those people got together, I won't say they hated each other, but they were enemies. But in the end, they were bringing up ideas about how they could work together." Judge Edwards comments:

> This result is praiseworthy—mutual understanding and good feeling among disputants obviously facilitates intelligent dispute resolution— but there are some disputes that cannot be resolved simply by mutual agreement and good faith. It is a fact of political life that many

---

43. As to the validity of the comparisons and a more subtle explanation of the determinants of litigiousness, see Haley, The Myth of the Reluctant Litigant, 4 J. Japanese Stud. 359, 389 (1978) ("Few misconceptions about Japan have been more widespread or as pernicious as the myth of the special reluctance of the Japanese to litigate."); see also Galanter, Reading the Landscape of Disputes: What We Know and Don't Know (And Think We Know) About Our Allegedly Contentious and Litigious Society, 31 U.C.L.A.L.Rev. 4, 57–79 (1983) (paucity of lawyers in Japan due to restrictions on number of attorneys admitted to practice rather than to non-litigiousness).

disputes reflect sharply contrasting views about fundamental public values that can never be eliminated by techniques that encourage disputants to "understand" each other. Indeed, many disputants understand their opponents all too well. Those who view tobacco as an unacceptable health risk, for example, can never fully reconcile their differences with the tobacco industry, and we should not assume otherwise. One essential function of law is to reflect the public resolution of such irreconcilable differences; lawmakers are forced to choose among these differing visions of the public good. A potential danger of ADR is that disputants who seek only understanding and reconciliation may treat as irrelevant the choices made by our lawmakers and may, as a result, ignore public values reflected in rules of law.

Edwards, Alternative Dispute Resolution: Panacea or Anathema, 99 Harv. L.Rev. 668, 678–79 (1986).

3. Does it follow from the views expressed by Professor Fiss that all cases of "imbalances of power" (such as consumer claims) and all cases implicating public values (such as racial discrimination) must reach court judgment? For example, does the critical importance of *Brown v. Board of Education* mandate that all discrimination disputes need judicial attention? Once a body of law has become well-developed and the applicable principles clearly defined, might not other processes be as good or better in resolving specific recurring problems?

4. Is it likely that a settlement arrived at through the participation and with the consent of the parties may often appear more satisfying to them than the result of adjudication? In what ways—other than in the sense that (in Fiss's grudging terms) it helps them to "secure the peace" at an acceptable cost? These too are questions that you should return to continually as we proceed through the following chapters.

5. More generally, where does the average plaintiff or defendant fit into a view of dispute resolution (such as that advanced by Professor Fiss) that rests so completely on the public interest? Surely the community's need for the open development and enforcement of public values should not "trump" in all cases the individual's choice of process? Cf. Carrie Menkel–Meadow, Whose Dispute Is It Anyway?: A Philosophical and Democratic Defense of Settlement (In Some Cases), 83 Georgetown L.J. 2663, 2669 (1995): "I fear, but am not sure, that this debate can be reduced to those who care more about the people actually engaged in disputes versus those who care more about institutional and structural arrangements."

6. The influence of the judicial process radiates far beyond the impact of litigation—actual or threatened—on the parties immediately involved. Beyond the effect on the individual disputants, one must consider what has been called the "general effects" of public adjudication that result from the communication to *others* of information about litigation. These effects are the subject of the following excerpt.

Marc Galanter, The Day After the Litigation Explosion

46 Maryland L.Rev. 3, 32–37 (1986).

Special effects [arising from litigation] are changes in the behavior of the specific actors involved in a particular lawsuit—like the Princeton club [an all-male college eating club votes to admit women in response to the filing of a sex discrimination suit against the college] or the University of Georgia [dismissed English professor who refused to pass failing athletes receives $2.75 million verdict] or the plaintiffs who sued them. We can, in theory at least, isolate various kinds of effects on the subsequent activity of such actors. An actor may be deprived of resources for future violations. This is *incapacitation*. Or the result of litigation may be increased *surveillance* which renders future offending behavior less likely. The Georgia case dramatically illustrates this surveillance effect. Or the offending actor may be deterred by fear of being caught again. This is *special deterrence*. Or, the experience of being exposed to the law may change the actor's view that it is right to exclude women or pass failing athletes or whatever. This is *reformation*.

In addition to these special effects on the parties before the court, there may be effects on wider audiences that we may call general effects. Litigation against one actor may lead others to reassess the risks and advantages of similar activity. We see this displayed in our Cape Cod [bar owner, fearing law suits, teaches employees how to recognize intoxicated customers] and Madison Parks [city removes asphalt from children's play areas in parks because liability insurance settlements are high] examples. This is *general deterrence*. It neither presumes nor requires any change in the moral evaluation of the acts in question, nor does it involve any change in opportunities to commit them. It stipulates that behavior will be affected by acquisition of more information about the costs and benefits that are likely to attach to the act—information about the certainty, celerity, and severity of "punishment," for example. Thus the actor can hold to what Hart called the "external point of view," treating law as a fact to be taken into account rather than a normative framework that he is committed to uphold or be guided by. The information that induces the changed estimate of costs and benefits need not be accurate. What a court has done may be inaccurately perceived; indeed, the court may have inaccurately depicted what it has done.

On the other hand, communication of the existence of a law or its application by a court may change the moral evaluation by others of a specific item of conduct. To the extent that this involves not the calculation or the probability of being visited by certain costs and benefits, but a change in moral estimation, we may call this general effect *enculturation*. There is suggestive evidence to indicate that at least some segments of the population are subject to such effects. Less dramatically, perceiving the application of law may maintain or intensify existing evaluations of conduct, an effect that Gibbs calls *normative validation*.

In addition to these effects on the underlying behavior, litigation may produce effects on the level of disputing behavior. It may encourage or discourage the parties to a case from making (or resisting) other claims. And generally it may encourage claimants and lawyers to pursue claims of a given type. It may provide symbols for rallying a group, broadcasting awareness of grievance and dramatizing challenge to the status quo. On the other hand, grievances may lose legitimacy, claims may be discouraged, and organizational capacity dissipated. The effects may be labeled *mobilization* and *demobilization.*

While supposition about the effects of litigation is abundant, serious studies of these effects are relatively rare. During the 1960s political scientists (chiefly) accumulated a body of findings on the impact of decisions of the United States Supreme Court (mostly) and other appellate courts, exploring the extent to which these decisions elicited compliance from the lower courts, school boards, police and other agencies they were designed to regulate. A critical survey of this literature concluded that:

> [T]he decisions of the Court, far from producing uniform impact or automatic compliance, have varying effects—from instances in which no action follows upon them to wide degrees of compliance (usually underreported), resistance, and evasion. These varying effects include increases in the level of political activity and activity within the judicial system itself and changes in governmental structure.... Important social interests, both economic and noneconomic, may be dislocated or legitimated, and the court's decisions also often perform an agenda-setting function for other political actors.

A new generation of "impact" research has widened its concerns from the United States Supreme Court to other courts, from public to private law, and from a focus on compliance with doctrinal pronouncements to ascertainment of a wider range of effects. Recent work includes studies tracing out the effects of specific tort cases. Thus Wiley found that a decision of the Supreme Court of Washington holding liable an ophthalmologist for failing to test a young patient for glaucoma did bring about an increase in the amount of testing for glaucoma in young patients. And Givelber, Bowers and Blitch found that a California decision [Tarasoff v. Regents of University of California, 17 Cal.3d 425, 131 Cal.Rptr. 14, 551 P.2d 334 (1976)], holding that therapists had a duty to exercise reasonable care to protect third parties from violence by their patients, had important effects nationwide. Eighteen months after its highly publicized original ruling that a therapist has a duty to warn the potential victim, the court, upon reconsideration, nullified its earlier opinion and modified the duty to one of exercising reasonable care to protect potential victims. The researchers found that the case was widely known by therapists throughout the nation, that observation of its ruling was felt to be obligatory by most even though technically it bound only those in California and "by and large the case appears to be misunderstood as involving and requiring the warning of potential victims" [i.e., in accordance with the withdrawn original opinion]—and to have influenced therapist responses to threatening behavior toward giving warnings, initiating involuntary hospitalizations and taking notes. The story is wonderfully complex. What happens is remote from a calculated intervention by the court designed to bring about these effects; and the therapists' response is more than a calculating re-estimation of costs and benefits.

In contrast to these studies focusing on the radiating effects of a single decision, other researchers have examined the way that an array of judicial decisions impinges on decision making by private actors. Thus a study of large manufacturers found that:

> [E]xcept for firms subject to the maximally intrusive regulation of such agencies as the Food and Drug and the General Aviation administrations, product liability is the most significant influence on product safety efforts. Product liability, however, conveys an indistinct signal. The long lags between the design decision and the final judgment on product liability claims (frequently five or more years), the inconsistent behavior of juries, and the rapid change in judicial doctrine in the area, all tended to muffle the signal.

* * *

A study of small manufacturers of agricultural implements in California found that 22% had dropped product lines out of fear of product liability suits.

I am not claiming that these effects are optimal or that the benefits they product outweigh all the costs or that existing litigation patterns represent the best way to achieve these benefits. But we should recognize that benefits are present and that any assessment of the social value of litigation must take account of them and must involve an attempt to estimate the *net* effects of present litigation patterns and the proposed or likely alternatives. These examples should also remind us that these effects are not ascertainable by supposition or by deduction.

NOTES AND QUESTIONS

1. Professor Galanter suggests that when courts decide cases by authoritatively stating generally applicable "rules," they strongly influence the primary conduct of all actors in our society. The courts convey information and warnings that are intended to bring private conduct into compliance with norms of appropriate behavior. In addition, the communication by courts of rules of decision plays a part in the process by which disputes are managed. Information disseminated in the form of "legal precedents" is used every day by individuals and their lawyers in routine decisions concerning which claims they should assert, and under what circumstances they should settle those claims. The pattern of decided cases thus helps provide a "blueprint" for settlement, a background against which settlement negotiations can take place. We will discuss this function later when we consider in some detail the dynamics of settlement. See also Galanter,

CHAPTER I LAWYERS, LITIGATION & PROCESS

Justice in Many Rooms: Courts, Private Ordering, and Indigenous Law, 19 J.Legal Pluralism & Unofficial L. 1, 6–16 (1981).

2. Some information conveyed by courts is undoubtedly redundant, in the sense that even without it the parties to a litigated case would already be quite able to predict the outcome with some clarity. But if too many suits are settled—if too many important cases are taken out of the judicial system—is it possible that this function of courts in facilitating the settlement process might be impaired? "[I]n a world where all cases settle, it may not even be possible to base settlements on the merits because lawyers may not be able to make reliable estimates of expected trial outcomes. If similar cases never go to trial, predictions of expected trial outcomes will have no factual grounding. * * * [T]here is nothing to cast a shadow in which the parties can bargain." Alexander, Do the Merits Matter? A Study of Settlements in Securities Class Actions, 43 Stan.L.Rev. 497, 567 (1991). What might be the ultimate effects of the resulting uncertainty? Might one consequence—paradoxically—be a decrease in the rate of settlement? See Richard Posner, Economic Analysis of Law 541–42 (4th ed. 1992); cf. Coleman & Silver, Justice in Settlements, 4 Soc.Phil. & Pol. 102 (1986).

3. It has been suggested that one substantial obstacle to the ability of litigation to generate information for future disputants is the "increased variability of judges and juries," which "reduces the value of a litigation outcome as an accurate guide to the resolution of later cases. If federal juries increasingly vary in their evaluation of similar evidence, or federal judges increasingly vary in their evaluation of legal issues, then the presumptive value of the information lost on account of settlement is reduced accordingly." Bundy, The Policy in Favor of Settlement in an Adversary System, 44 Hastings L.J. 1, 54 (1992). What might account for such "increased variability"?

The "Alternative Dispute Resolution" Movement

The notion that use of the official court system is only one among an abundant variety of ways of solving disputes has flourished in recent years. There has been an outpouring of scholarly work, creative proposals, and practical experimentation. The "ADR movement" referred to by Fiss is one reflection of that idea—an idea that is, in fact, one impetus for this book. Indeed by 1990, as Laura Nader has written, ADR had "become a major industry. * * * In some ways it was a rebellion against law and lawyers—often by lawyers themselves."[1]

Although Fiss speaks of the ADR "movement" as if it were unified and homogeneous, that is hardly the case. The proponents of alternatives to litigation are of diverse backgrounds—from "elite" lawyers like corporate counsel and luminaries such as former President Bok of Harvard and former Chief Justice Burger, to the sponsors of neighborhood "community justice centers." And in addition, each advocate of ADR is likely to have his

---

1. Laura Nader, Controlling Processes in the Practice of Law: Hierarchy and Pacification in the Movement to Re–Form Dispute Ideology, 9 Ohio St. J. on Disp. Resol. 1 (1993).

or her own agenda. Encouragement of non-judicial means of dispute resolution may reflect different goals and the desire to promote widely differing values.

Thus one can identify in the ADR literature a "cool" theme—a theme that emphasizes "efficient institutional management: clearing dockets, reducing delay, eliminating expense, unburdening the courts."[2] For example, in a 1997 survey of corporate counsel of "Fortune 1000" companies, 90% of the respondents identified ADR as a "critical cost control technique."[3] And at the same time, one can identify a "warm" theme—in which the search is for higher *quality* solutions than may be available in the courts. The stress here may be on generating solutions that are more responsive than is litigation to the underlying needs and interests of the parties: "Freed from formal legal categories and procedures," alternative processes "could get at the heart of problems and actually solve them."[4] Or the focus may be on replacing adversary conflict with "reconciliation" of the parties—on finding processes that can restore mutual understanding and preserve ongoing relationships.[5] ADR processes may appear "more humanely 'real,' democratic, participatory, and cathartic than more formalized processes."[6]

Consider, for example, the "informality" that is often associated with processes like mediation and arbitration. "Informality" can hardly be an ultimate value in itself. "Informal" procedure may be valued by some who see in it merely a loosening of the rules, restrictions, and rituals of the judicial process. They praise it, then, for its potential for speedier and less expensive decisionmaking. But for others, "informality" may be understood primarily to involve "a more relaxed flow of procedure, to make parties more comfortable and decrease enmity and disaffection costs."[7] Under this

---

2. Marc Galanter, The Emergence of the Judge as a Mediator in Civil Cases 2 (1985).

3. See Rinat Fried, "Corporations Backing ADR, Study Says," The Recorder, April 29, 1997 at p. 4; David Lipsky & Ronald Seeber, In Search of Control: The Corporate Embrace of ADR, 1 U. Pa. J. Lab. & Employment L. 133 (1998) (the "competitive market pressure faced by American corporations" has led many to examine the costs associated with their legal affairs; some respondents "told us that the transaction costs associated with settling a dispute, including the costs of inside and outside legal counsel, * * * were often two to three time the amounts of the settlements themselves.")

4. Silbey & Sarat, Dispute Processing in Law and Legal Scholarship: From Institutional Critique to the Reconstruction of the Juridical Subject, 66 Denver U.L.Rev. 437, 453 (1989) (characterizing views of "quality proponents" of ADR).

5. See, e.g., Smith, A Warmer Way of Disputing: Mediation and Conciliation, 26 Am.J.Comp.L. (Supp.) 205 (1978) ("Therapy and catharsis, rather than an attempt to arrive at some 'truth,' becomes the goal of dispute settlement"); McThenia & Shaffer, For Reconciliation, 94 Yale L.J. 1660 (1985) ("[T]he religious tradition seeks not *resolution* (which connotes the sort of doctrinal integrity in the law that seems to us to be Fiss's highest priority) but *reconciliation* of brother to brother, sister to sister, sister to brother, child to parent, neighbor to neighbor, buyer to seller, defendant to plaintiff, *and judge to both*.").

6. Carrie Menkel–Meadow, Whose Dispute Is It Anyway?: A Philosophical and Democratic Defense of Settlement (In Some Cases), 83 Geo. L.J. 2663, 2692 (1995).

7. Bush, Dispute Resolution Alternatives and the Goals of Civil Justice: Jurisdictional Principles for Process Choice, 1984 Wisc.L.Rev. 893, 1006 n. 251.

CHAPTER I LAWYERS, LITIGATION & PROCESS

view it may be valued because of its beneficial effects on the relationship, and on the level of trust, respect, and understanding between the parties. "Conversation and cooperation replace conflict; informality empowers."[8]

The goals that the various proponents of ADR seek to advance are not only diverse; in some cases they may actually be in conflict. Judge Harry Edwards has warned that

> Inexpensive, expeditious, and informal adjudication is not always synonymous with *fair* and *just* adjudication. The decisionmakers may not understand the values at stake and parties to disputes do not always possess equal power and resources. Sometimes because of this inequality and sometimes because of deficiencies in informal processes lacking procedural protections, the use of alternative mechanisms will produce nothing more than inexpensive and ill-informed decisions. And these decisions may merely legitimate decisions made by the existing power structure within society.[9]

Consider, for example, the case for "alternatives" made by former Chief Justice Burger:

> One reason our courts have become overburdened is that Americans are increasingly turning to the courts for relief from a range of personal distresses and anxieties.

> Remedies for personal wrongs that once were considered the responsibility of institutions other than the courts are now boldly asserted as legal "entitlements." The courts have been expected to fill the void created by the decline of church, family, and neighborhood unity.

> Possibly the increased litigiousness that court dockets reflect simply mirrors what is happening worldwide. The press, television, and radio for hours every day tell us of events in Asia, Africa, Europe, and Latin America where there is seething political, social, and economic turmoil. It is not surprising that our anxieties are aggravated.[10]

---

8. Resnik, Many Doors? Closing Doors? Alternative Dispute Resolution and Adjudication, 10 Ohio St.J.Disp.Res. 211, 249–50 (1995) (characterizing claims that alternative processes are "more congenial than adjudication"; by contrast adjudication "is seen as a process that often brings out the worst in its participants, either because it distorts their abilities to pursue self-interest or because it defines self-interest in such a fashion that requires inflicting losses, rather than maximizing gains").

9. Edwards, Alternative Dispute Resolution: Panacea or Anathema, 99 Harv.L.Rev. 668, 679 (1986). See also Lazerson, In the Halls of Justice, the Only Justice is in the Halls, in 1 Richard Abel (ed.), The Politics of Informal Justice 119 (1982) ("informaliza-

tion" of New York City Housing Court—through introduction of hearing officers who encouraged "conciliation" in order to reduce court backlog—eroded the legal position of tenants in substandard housing); Anita Bernstein, Complaints, 32 McGeorge L. Rev. 37, 48 (2000) ("When he encounters ADR that he doesn't want, our complainant has reached another minefield: a consensus that certain types of grievances do not warrant the full attention of the law, even though longstanding legal rules cover them and even though a person has cried out to the law for justice").

10. Burger, Isn't There a Better Way?, ABA Journal, March 1982, pp. 274–275 (1982).

B. Courts and Litigation

What seems to be the underlying message that is being conveyed here? It has been suggested that in some cases, the recent discovery of alternatives to courts may be a reaction to an increased consciousness of legal rights and an explosion of claims to "entitlements" on the part of consumers, users of substandard housing, victims of sexual and racial discrimination or of domestic violence, and other disadvantaged groups. The encouragement of alternatives may not proceed entirely from the desire to ensure these groups broader access to inexpensive and meaningful dispute resolution—it may proceed instead from a desire to relieve the courts from the pressures and problems posed by these cases, enabling judges to deal more efficiently with more "traditional" types of judicial business. "Elite lawyers want to conserve judicial resources for the resolution of business and commercial disputes and are willing to see other matters removed from courts if not from the legal field itself."[11] From this point of view ADR can indeed be seen (as Professor Fiss suggests) as subordinating legal rights and public values to accommodative bargaining, and justice to the single-minded objective of settling disputes. It has even been claimed that for some proponents, an enthusiastic support of non-judicial processes may be nothing more than "another form of the deregulation movement, one that permits private actors with powerful economic interests to pursue self-interest free of community norms."[12]

Many of the recent experiments with ADR have been designed to be separate from and independent of the courts. But an increasingly important phenomenon is the use of ADR processes that are closely linked to the judicial system. One impetus for such a development was the Civil Justice Reform Act of 1990, which required every federal district court to implement "a civil justice expense and delay reduction plan"; in drawing up such plans courts were instructed to consider a number of case management principles aimed at reducing cost and delay—including notably "authorization to refer appropriate cases to alternative dispute resolution programs that * * * the court may make available, including mediation, minitrial, and summary jury trial."[13] An even more significant piece of legislation is

---

11. Silbey & Sarat, supra n. 4 at 446.

12. McThenia & Shaffer, For Reconciliation, 94 Yale L.J. 1660, 1665 n. 33 (1985) (suggestion of Milner Ball). See also Provine, Justice a la Carte: On the Privatization of Dispute Resolution, 12B Studies in Law, Politics, and Society 345 (1992) ("the recent transformation of dispute resolution is part of a broader political movement to reduce the scope and power of government as a provider of services").

In Jansen v. Packaging Corp. of America, 123 F.3d 490 (7th Cir.1997), the court affirmed a grant of summary judgment in favor of an employer on an employee's Title VII retaliation claim. In Judge Coffey's concurring opinion, he "join[ed] with thousands of American citizens who are of the opinion that employers today are over-regulated and saddled with an increasingly burdensome, indeed an overwhelming, amount of litigation, including Title VII litigation (much of which, as we realize, often is without merit)." "Indeed," he went on, "the rising tide of employment-related litigation has prompted many firms to require * * * that employees agree to accept arbitration and forego their right to sue in court over employment-related disputes." 123 F.3d at 541; see Chapter V, Section C.4.b infra.

13. 28 U.S.C.A. §§ 471, 473(a)(6). A district-by-district survey of ADR programs operating in federal courts is Elizabeth Plapinger & Donna Stienstra, ADR and Settle-the Alternative Dispute Resolution Act of 1998: ADR, Congress found, "has the potential" to provide "greater satisfaction of the parties, innovative methods of resolving disputes, and greater efficiency in achieving settlements"—as well as to reduce "the large backlog of cases now pending" in some federal courts, thus allowing courts "to process their remaining cases more efficiently." As a consequence each federal district court was instructed to provide litigants in all civil cases with "at least one alternative dispute resolution process," and was to "require" that litigants "consider the use of an alternative dispute resolution process at an appropriate stage in the litigation."[14]

Courts have in other ways, too, become more frequently and more visibly involved in the direct promotion of settlement. Recent amendments to the Federal Rules of Civil Procedure encourage judges at pretrial conferences to raise and take action on such subjects as "settlement and the use of special procedures to assist in resolving the dispute"; judges may also require that a party or its representative be present or available by telephone "in order to consider possible settlement of the dispute."[15] And in many jurisdictions courts have the authority, either at the request of a party or on their own initiative, to order the parties to engage in an ADR procedure prior to trial.[16] Some years ago a survey revealed that state courts have instituted ADR (mostly mediation) programs in all but seven states.[17] In short, judges have begun to "make ADR their own—either by sponsoring or by running it."[18]

These developments are explored in considerable detail in the chapters that follow. They have given rise to some concern that the ADR movement may now be in the process of being "captured" or "co-opted" by the very legal system to which it was supposed to be an "alternative." To some purists, the virtues of alternative processes may be lost where the parties have been coerced into participating.[19] And in the view of a number of critics, the growing institutionalization of ADR programs has inevitably led to their being "legalized"—with the danger that they may become "just

---

ment in the Federal District Courts: A Sourcebook for Judges & Lawyers (1996) ("In marked contrast to five years ago when only a few courts had court-based programs for mediation, over half of the ninety-four districts now offer—and in several instances, require—mediation"; "arbitration is the second most frequently authorized ADR program, but falls well short of mediation in the number of courts that have implemented it").

14. Public Law 105–315, 112 Stat. 2993; see 28 U.S.C. § 652.

15. FRCP Rule 16(c).

16. E.g., V.T.C.A., Civ.Prac. & Rem. Code § 154.021. The federal ADR Act of 1998 also provides that a district court may "elect

to require the use of [ADR] in certain cases" but, in the absence of the parties' consent, may do so only with respect to mediation and early neutral evaluation. 28 U.S.C. § 652(a).

17. See Richard Reuben, "The Lawyer Turns Peacemaker," ABA J., Aug.1996, at pp. 54, 56.

18. Resnik, Failing Faith: Adjudicatory Procedure in Decline, 53 U.Chi.L.Rev. 494, 536 (1986).

19. E.g., Katz, Compulsory Alternative Dispute Resolution and Voluntarism: Two–Headed Monster or Two Sides of the Coin?, 1993 J.Disp.Res. 1 ("voluntariness is consistent with the underlying philosophy of ADR").

C. THE CHOICE OF PROCESS

1. LAWYERS AND THE CHOICE OF PROCESS

As we have seen, the overwhelming majority of disputes—even when a lawsuit has been filed—terminate short of a trial. It may seem something of a paradox, then, to suggest that for the average member of the bar, awareness and acceptance of non-judicial processes of dispute resolution have been slow in coming. Even now, it seems, thinking about alternative processes—and making conscious choices among them—have not yet become habits that have penetrated very deeply into the everyday practice of law.

Some of the lingering indifference to ADR on the part of the bar might be attributed simply to unfamiliarity with the potential for alternative processes, and with the form they might take. This at least has certainly begun to change—as new generations of law students filter through the system, and as many more lawyers have the occasion to participate in court-mandated processes. In addition, some lack of enthusiasm can often be explained by simple self-interest. "Self-interest" is at least partly a matter of economics: Lawyers, especially those paid by the hour, are able to extract substantial fees from prolonged conflict, and may have an incentive to shape disputes in such a way as to maximize their benefits from them. Economic changes such as intensified business conflict—and above all heightened competition in an increasingly entrepreneurial legal profession—may also play a role in dampening interest in non-adversarial settlement.[1] And "self-interest" can have other, less tangible, aspects: Alternative processes often function in such a way as to transfer greater power and control over disputing to the parties themselves, or to other professionals (such as mediators) who may be involved in helping to resolve the dispute. To many lawyers, this may seem to threaten the attorney's exclusive control over dispute resolution—a feeling of dominance that only the judicial process can provide.

Still another explanation might be found in the education of attorneys. We have all gone through the most rigorous and stressful training, focusing almost exclusively on the virtues of "legal analysis" and argumentation—of "thinking like a lawyer." Carefully defining the issues, marshalling the

---

20. E.g., Menkel–Meadow, Pursuing Settlement in an Adversary Culture: A Tale of Innovation Co-opted or "The Law of ADR," 19 Fla.St.U.L.Rev. 1, 17 (1991).

1. See Bryant Garth, From Civil Litigation to Private Justice: Legal Practice at War with the Profession and Its Values, 59 Brooklyn L. Rev. 931, 938–45 (1993) (referring to a variety of "scorched earth litigation" tactics and other tactical innovations in high-stakes disputes, attributable to a search for competitive advantage within the profession).

CHAPTER I LAWYERS, LITIGATION & PROCESS

arguments and counterarguments, manipulating the precedents—all in the interest of "zealous advocacy" in the assertion of one's legal "rights"—are made to seem the essence of the lawyer's craft. Having survived such a process, lawyers are likely to have an investment in the belief that this is the "natural" way for disputes in our society to be resolved. The role models and legendary cult figures held up to the admiration of law students are likely to be those who have proven themselves "toughest" as "hired guns" in the service of their clients' advantage. (You can readily think of examples.). This process of socialization reinforces the thrust of the curriculum, with its emphasis on formal court adjudication. The result, as suggested by the following excerpt, is that litigation and the adversary system tend to dominate the "mental landscape" of the lawyer and obscure other possibilities that may be in the background. "Lawyer and client are apt to agree that adversary combat in a judicial arena is the normal, socially acceptable, and psychologically satisfying method of resolving disputes."[2]

Robert Kagan, Do Lawyers Cause Adversarial Legalism? A Preliminary Inquiry

19 Law and Social Inquiry 1, 5, 25–26, 37–39, 61–62 (1994)

In a society pervaded by the threat of legal action, lawyers for business corporations, school boards, and other organizations undoubtedly prevent litigation simply by spreading the word about potential liabilities. In their everyday practice, corporate lawyers attempt in many ways to forfend litigation, drafting imaginative contractual provisions for resolving conflict in case business earnings decline or debts go unpaid. Many attorneys decline to advance claims or defenses that seem to them unjustified in law or in equity. Other lawyers, emphasizing the costliness of the adversarial process, push clients intent on moral vindication to accept financial compromise.

Some American lawyers go further, systematically trying to *reduce* the overall volume of adversarial legalism. Bar associations dominated by elite lawyers often have fought against "ambulance chasing" or increased litigation in hopes of enhancing the image of the profession. In some corporations, the general counsel has insisted on using private mediation firms, rather than litigation, to resolve entire categories of disputes; the leading mediation firms are run and staffed by lawyers and former judges. * * *

Consequently, one might argue that even if some members of the American legal profession consciously and on their own account work to amplify adversarial legalism, there are even more members of the profession who work to dampen it. * * *

---

2. Stephen Goldberg et al., Dispute Resolution 422 (2nd ed. 1992). See also Bush, Dispute Resolution Alternatives and the Goals of Civil Justice: Jurisdictional Principles for Process Choice, 1984 Wisc. L. Rev. 893, 995–1004.

C. THE CHOICE OF PROCESS **51**

Perhaps, but probably not. The dampeners undoubtedly reduce adversarial legalism below the level that would exist if they had instead become amplifiers. But the relative number of lawyers in each camp does not resolve the question. The burglary rate can go up even if most people try to deter burglary. Relatively small numbers of determined people can have a big impact. The fact remains that adversarial legalism, by most measures, has increased in the last quarter-century. The issue is whether the actions of lawyers—not all lawyers, but lawyers—have played a role in that net increase, even though many of their professional brothers and sisters may have prevented the increase from being greater.

* * * *

Law Professors and the Culture of Adversarial Legalism

* * * Comparative observers often note that when contrasted with legal education in England and Western Europe, current day American law schools promote a remarkably activist, instrumentalist image of law and the role of lawyers and judges. * * * [W]hile English legal academics defer to barristers and judges in shaping law and legal culture, American law professors actively seek to shape legal culture, and through it society, and have had a significant degree of success: "American law schools have been the source of the dominant general theory of law in America—*'instrumentalism'*—[which] conceives of law essentially as a pragmatic instrument of social improvement." Instrumentalism is embraced by many politically conservative as well as liberal professors, most prominently by adherents of the influential "law and economics" movement, who seek law reforms designed to enhance economic efficiency.

Whereas British law students are expected to learn the rules of rules as laid down in rather dogmatic textbooks, and Continental students are expected to learn and accept the theoretical underpinnings of their legal systems, American law students are taught to challenge or at least to question their country's law. They spend more time studying the most disputed cases than basic black letter doctrine. They are urged to analyze the merits of legal doctrines and judicial opinions in terms of the fairness, economic efficiency, or equality of their social consequences. They are prodded to formulate legal arguments that would support their gut feelings about what the results should be. The law reviews they edit bulge with articles calling for new legal rights and changes in old ones, along with essays stressing the indeterminacy of legal rules.

American law students are taught by their professors that judges often are incompetent or as apt to be influenced, by their political attitudes and allegiances as by the letter of the law. [And "[l]aw is treated as more malleable, open to parties' novel legal and policy arguments. In civil cases, lay jurors still play a large and normatively important role in the United States, which magnifies the importance of skillful legal advocacy and reduces legal certainty."] The legal system, many American law professors implicitly suggest, is a field of political struggle, shaped by the play of creative lawyering and argumentation (at best) and by raw economic and

52 CHAPTER I LAWYERS, LITIGATION & PROCESS

political power (at worst). So the lawyer's job is to pick her way through that uncertain mine field, striving for justice as best she can when she sees an opening, whether as lawyer or judge. Not surprisingly, that is the view of the system that American lawyers convey to their clients.

* * *

Constructing Lawyers' Ethics

In constructing rules of ethics for practitioners, a legal profession has a range of choices. It can stress the lawyer's duty to her client alone, zealously protecting and advocating the client's interests regardless of the costs or injustices to the rest of the world. Or legal ethics can enjoin attorneys to temper pursuit of clients' interests with concern for legitimate interests of third parties and society at large. The American legal profession long has stressed the ethic of zealous advocacy, in contrast to the legal professions of England and Western European nations, where the ethical rules of conduct set greater limits on the lawyer's duty to protect client loyalty and confidentiality in deference to larger societal and third party interests. * * *

Thus American lawyers have fought for rules of evidence that provide a broader and more absolute lawyer-client privilege than exists in most other countries. In contrast to most other legal professions, the American bar has endorsed contingency fees, justifying them on grounds that they facilitate litigation by the nonwealthy. American legal ethics endorse lawyers' practice of pretrial coaching of witnesses; German legal ethics strongly discourage it.

The American legal profession's endorsement of the lawyer's duty of zealous advocacy—as opposed to her duty to serve as "officer of the court"—encourages a more entrepreneurial form of legal practice than prevails in Europe. It authorizes lawyers to advance novel legal claims and claims and arguments, challenging or stretching existing, doctrine, and asserting that it is the court's job, not the lawyer's, to separate the wheat from the chaff.[130]

The adversarial ethic disseminated by the profession also has validated American trial lawyers' competition to develop ever more aggressive and costly techniques of litigation-dramatic "day-in-the-life" videos to illustrate the adverse effects of accidents; calculatedly burdensome pretrial discovery demands in high-stakes cases; extended voir dire of prospective jurors. Finally, the ethic of zealous advocacy encourages an aggressive style bounds of existing legal rules and institutions * * *.

---

130. [Mark J. Osiel, Lawyers as Monopolists and Entrepreneurs: Review of *Lawyers in Society,* 103 Harv. L. Rev. 2009, 2060 (1990)] argues, "The stringency of their ethical guidelines on matters of client loyalty impelled American lawyers toward the imaginative discovery of doctrinal ambiguity where such ambiguity would otherwise have remained merely latent. In particular, the view of legal expertise as the skillful exploitation of doctrinal uncertainty would not have become so central to the self-understanding of American attorney's had their ethical guidelines encouraged them to view themselves, like many lawyers elsewhere in the West primarily as 'officers of society.' "

Most attorneys, sociolegal studies indicate, serve as stolid gatekeepers for the courts. Hence, most day-to-day, non-law-reform litigation, we can safely assume, is stimulated not by lawyers but by clients or complainants. But surely that is not *always* the case. * * *

Well, how much legal contestation is lawyer-induced (as opposed to client-induced)? 10%? 15%? 20%? 2%? We don't know. Legal and scholars have had little to say on the subject, perhaps for fear of providing support to conservative lawyer bashers. But a great deal of anecdotal evidence, and limited systematic evidence, suggests that there is a significant amount of what we might call superaggressive lawyering, exacerbating the costs and delays of "adversarial legalism as practice." Quantitative measures are elusive. * * *

* * *

What if all the lawyers—or at least those who consciously work to extend and preserve adversarial legalism, or engage in superaggressive litigation—were suddenly banished to a reservation in central Nevada? It is hard to believe that the resulting change in the legal order would be truly massive in the long run. The social divisions, economic conflicts, political fragmentation, and popular beliefs that generate adversarial legalism surely would not disappear.

On the other hand, suppose American lawyers—not just a few but most of them—reconfigured legal ethics to discourage superaggressive litigation; and argued that social insurance was preferable to tort law for compensating injury; and insisted that judges should urge legislatures to reform the laws rather than doing it themselves; and lobbied for the creation of cheaper, less adversarial dispute-resolution forums; and fostered administrative law and conceptions of due process that sought to improve rather than subvert administrative authority? After all, that is not so different from the stance taken by the legal profession in other rich democracies. If the bulk of the legal profession did these things, it almost certainly would have some effect—probably a considerable effect—on the level of adversarial legalism. For what lawyers think and say, the legal culture they generate and the behaviors they exhibit, surely influence what clients, interest groups, legislators, journalists, and the general public think appropriate to demand of the legal order.

* * *

In the 1960s, the comedian Lenny Bruce used to say that in New York City, even the Gentiles were Jewish. In the law-saturated United States of today, he might say that even the laymen are lawyers. Or at least every politician, governmental official, and corporate executive, law-trained or not, thinks like a lawyer to a considerable extent. So if American lawyers are not the only force working to recreate adversarial legalism, it may be partly because they have trained their fellow citizens to do it too.

NOTES AND QUESTIONS

1. Lawyers are increasingly coming into contact on a daily basis with non-judicial processes. But it should hardly be surprising, in light of the previous discussion, that even when they do so they may have a tendency to view these processes through the optic of litigation—that is, they may expect their experience to mirror or mimic what happens in court. We will see later that this is particularly noticeable in the attitude of some lawyers to negotiation and arbitration. These processes may be approached as if they were merely variants or extensions of the judicial, adversarial model which to so many lawyers is the paradigm of disputing. See, e.g., Susan Sturm, From Gladiators to Problem–Solvers: Connecting Conversations About Women, the Academy, and the Legal Profession, 4 Duke J. of Gender L. & Pol'y 119, 121–22 (1997) ("Even in more informal settings such as negotiations or in-house advising, lawyering often proceeds within the gladiator model"—a model that "celebrates analytical rigor, toughness, and quick thinking").

It is perhaps symptomatic of this attitude that a recent continuing legal education program promises to help attorneys to learn how they can "win at ADR." (JAMS/Endispute Workshop, "Effective Negotiation and Winning at ADR," [Boston, May 15, 1995]).

2. The United States has many more lawyers than any other country—the number of lawyers per capita in the United States is roughly four times as great as it is in England, and ten times as great as it is in France. In contrast, the number of judges is relatively small, and the American ratio of lawyers to judges is one of the highest anywhere. Marc Galanter, Reading the Landscape of Disputes: What We Know and Don't Know (And Think We Know) About Our Allegedly Contentious and Litigious Society, 31 U.C.L.A. L.Rev. 4, 52, 55 (1983). In addition, we have seen in recent years an extraordinary growth in the number of large law firms: In 1993 the largest firm had 1662 lawyers, and 184 firms were larger than the largest law firm in 1968 (which then had "only" 169 lawyers). See Ronald Gilson & Robert Mnookin, Disputing through Agents: Cooperation and Conflict Between Lawyers in Litigation, 94 Colum. L. Rev. 509, 538 (1994).

How might these facts be relevant to Professor Kagan's discussion? See also John Setear, The Barrister and the Bomb: The Dynamics of Cooperation, Nuclear Deterrence, and Discovery Abuse, 69 B.U. L. Rev. 569 (1989).

3. One empirical study of family and neighbor disputes in a small American city concluded that by the time a conflict has become serious enough to warrant an outsider's intervention, disputants simply "do not want what alternatives have to offer." At that point, they want "vindication, protection of his or her rights * * * an advocate to help in the battle, or a third party who will uncover the 'truth' and declare the other party wrong." "It is in precisely those cases which have developed to the point where they seem so unavoidable and principled that the grievant can justify going to an outside agency that she/he is least likely to be enthusiastic about the offer of an alternative dispute resolution process which removes the advocate and eliminates the third party who would make a definitive decision about right and wrong." Sally Engle Merry & Susan Silbey, What Do Plaintiffs Want? Reexamine the Concept of Dispute, 9 Justice System J. 151, 153–54 (1984). More generally, as Professor Kagan suggests, cultural attitudes concerning the centrality of the adversary process may routinely mold the assumptions of *clients* with respect to how disputes should normally be resolved, as well as the assumptions of lawyers. So the behavior of a lawyer may in fact often be a response to the desire or expectation of the *client* for a "valiant champion"—or, perhaps, an attempt to live up to what the lawyer *assumes* the client expects. See Riskin, Mediation and Lawyers, 43 Ohio St. L.J. 29, 49 (1982).

Is there any way to break out of this vicious circle? Can we envisage that there may be clients, or areas of the law, where an attorney's experience and talent in non-litigation processes may constitute a competitive advantage—even, indeed, a "marketing tool"? See Bryant Garth, From Civil Litigation to Private Justice: Legal Practice at War With the Profession and Its Values, 59 Brooklyn L. Rev. 931, 950–53 (1993).

4. The assumptions behind the "adversary model" are tested, in a rather unique context, by the Supreme Court's decision in the *Walters* case, which follows.

Walters v. National Association of Radiation Survivors

Supreme Court of the United States, 1985.
473 U.S. 305, 105 S.Ct. 3180, 87 L.Ed.2d 220.

■ JUSTICE REHNQUIST delivered the opinion of the Court.

* * *

Congress has by statute established an administrative system for granting service connected death or disability benefits to veterans. The amount of the benefit award is not based upon need, but upon service connection—that is, whether the disability is causally related to an injury sustained in the service—and the degree of incapacity caused by the disability. A detailed system has been established by statute and Veterans Administration (VA) regulation for determining a veteran's entitlement, with final authority resting with an administrative body known as the Board of Veterans' Appeals (BVA). Judicial review of VA decisions is precluded by statute. The controversy in this case centers on the opportunity for a benefit applicant or recipient to obtain legal counsel to aid in the presentation of his claim to the VA. [38 U.S.C. § 3404(c) limited to $10 the fee that may be paid an attorney or agent who represents a veteran seeking benefits for service-connected death or disability, and § 3405 imposed criminal penalties on anyone charging fees in excess of this $10 limitation.]

Appellees here are two veterans' organizations, three individual veterans, and a veteran's widow. The two veterans' organizations are the National Association of Radiation Survivors, an organization principally concerned with obtaining compensation for its members for injuries result-

56   CHAPTER I Lawyers, Litigation & Process

ing from atomic bomb tests, and Swords to Plowshares Veterans Rights Organization, an organization particularly devoted to the concerns of Vietnam veterans. * * *

Appellees contended in the District Court that the fee limitation provision of § 3404 denied them any realistic opportunity to obtain legal representation in presenting their claims to the VA and hence violated their rights under the Due Process Clause of the Fifth Amendment and under the First Amendment. The District Court agreed with the appellees on both of these grounds, and entered a nationwide "preliminary injunction" barring appellants from enforcing the fee limitation. To understand fully the posture in which the case reaches us it is necessary to discuss the administrative scheme in some detail.

Congress began providing veterans pensions in early 1789, and after every conflict in which the Nation has been involved Congress has, in the words of Abraham Lincoln, "provided for him who has borne the battle, and his widow and his orphan." The VA was created by Congress in 1930, and since that time has been responsible for administering the congressional program for veterans benefits. In 1978, the year covered by the report of the Legal Services Corporation to Congress that was introduced into evidence in the District Court, approximately 800,000 claims for service-connected disability or death and pensions were decided by the 58 regional offices of the VA. Slightly more than half of these were claims for service-connected disability or death, and the remainder were pension claims. Of the 800,000 total claims in 1978, more than 400,000 were allowed, and some 379,000 were denied. Sixty-six thousand of these denials were contested at the regional level; about a quarter of these contests were dropped, 15% prevailed on reconsideration at the local level, and the remaining 36,000 were appealed to the BVA. At that level some 4,500, or 12%, prevailed, and another 13% won a remand for further proceedings. Although these figures are from 1978, the statistics in evidence indicate that the figures remain fairly constant from year to year.

As might be expected in a system which processes such a large number of claims each year, the process prescribed by Congress for obtaining disability benefits does not contemplate the adversary mode of dispute resolution utilized by courts in this country. It is commenced by the submission of a claim form to the local veterans agency, which form is provided by the VA either upon request or upon receipt of notice of the death of a veteran. Upon application a claim generally is first reviewed by a three-person "rating board" of the VA regional office—consisting of a medical specialist, a legal specialist, and an "occupational specialist." A claimant is "entitled to a hearing at any time on any issue involved in a claim...." Proceedings in front of the rating board "are ex parte in nature"; no Government official appears in opposition. The principal issues are the extent of the claimant's disability and whether it is service-connected. The panel is required by regulation "to assist a claimant in developing the facts pertinent to his claim," and to consider any evidence offered by the claimant. In deciding the claim the panel generally will request the applicant's Armed Service and medical records, and will order a medical examination by a VA hospital. Moreover, the board is directed by regulation to resolve all reasonable doubts in favor of the claimant.

After reviewing the evidence the board renders a decision either denying the claim or assigning a disability "rating" pursuant to detailed regulations developed for assessing various disabilities. Money benefits are calculated based on the rating. The claimant is notified of the board's decision and its reasons, and the claimant may then initiate an appeal by filing a "notice of disagreement" with the local agency. If the local agency adheres to its original decision it must then provide the claimant with a "statement of the case"—a written description of the facts and applicable law upon which the panel based its determination—so that the claimant may adequately present his appeal to the BVA. Hearings in front of the BVA are subject to the same rules as local agency hearings—they are ex parte, there is no formal questioning or cross-examination, and no formal rules of evidence apply. The BVA's decision is not subject to judicial review.

The process is designed to function throughout with a high degree of informality and solicitude for the claimant. There is no statute of limitations, and a denial of benefits has no formal res judicata effect; a claimant may resubmit as long as he presents new facts not previously forwarded. Although there are time limits for submitting a notice of disagreement and although a claimant may prejudice his opportunity to challenge factual or legal decisions by failing to challenge them in that notice, the time limit is quite liberal—up to one year—and the VA boards are instructed to read any submission in the light most favorable to the claimant. Perhaps more importantly for present purposes, however, various veterans' organizations across the country make available trained service agents, free of charge, to assist claimants in developing and presenting their claims. These service representatives are contemplated by the VA statute, and they are recognized as an important part of the administrative scheme. Appellees' counsel agreed at argument that a representative is available for any claimant who requests one, regardless of the claimant's affiliation with any particular veterans' group.[4]

* * *

In reaching its conclusions the court relied heavily on the problems presented by what it described as "complex cases"—a class of cases also focused on in the depositions. Though never expressly defined by the District Court, these cases apparently include those in which a disability is slow-developing and therefore difficult to find service-connected, such as the claims associated with exposure to radiation or harmful chemicals, as well as other cases identified by the deponents as involving difficult matters of medical judgment. Nowhere in the opinion of the District Court is there any estimate of what percentage of the annual VA caseload of 800,000 these

---

4. The VA statistics show that 86% of all claimants are represented by service representatives, 12% proceed pro se, and 2% are represented by lawyers. Counsel agreed at argument that the 12% who proceed pro se do so by their own choice.

cases comprise, nor is there any more precise description of the class. There is no question but what the three named plaintiffs and the plaintiff veteran's widow asserted such claims, and in addition there are declarations in the record from 12 other claimants who were asserting such claims. The evidence contained in the record, however, suggests that the sum total of such claims is extremely small; in 1982, for example, roughly 2% of the BVA caseload consisted of "agent orange" or "radiation" claims, and what evidence there is suggests that the percentage of such claims in the regional offices was even less—perhaps as little as 3 in 1,000.

With respect to the service representatives, the court again found the representation unsatisfactory. Although admitting that this was not due to any "lack of dedication," the court found that a heavy caseload and the lack of legal training combined to prevent service representatives from adequately researching a claim. Facts are not developed, and "it is standard practice for service organization representatives to submit merely a one to two page handwritten brief."

Based on the inability of the VA and service organizations to provide the full range of services that a retained attorney might, the court concluded that appellees had demonstrated a "high risk of erroneous deprivation" from the process as administered. The court then found that the Government had "failed to demonstrate that it would suffer any harm if the statutory fee limitation ... were lifted." The only Government interest suggested was the "paternalistic" assertion that the fee limitation is necessary to ensure that claimants do not turn substantial portions of their benefits over to unscrupulous lawyers. The court suggested that there were "less drastic means" to confront this problem.

* * *

Appellees' first claim, accepted by the District Court, is that the statutory fee limitation, as it bears on the administrative scheme in operation, deprives a rejected claimant or recipient of "life, liberty or property, without due process of law," by depriving him of representation by expert legal counsel. Our decisions establish that "due process" is a flexible concept—that the processes required by the Clause with respect to the termination of a protected interest will vary depending upon the importance attached to the interest and the particular circumstances under which the deprivation may occur. See *Mathews* [*v. Eldridge*, 424 U.S. 319 (1976)] at 334. In defining the process necessary to ensure "fundamental fairness" we have recognized that the Clause does not require that "the procedures used to guard against an erroneous deprivation ... be so comprehensive as to preclude any possibility of error," and in addition we have emphasized that the marginal gains from affording an additional procedural safeguard often may be outweighed by the societal cost of providing such a safeguard.

These general principles are reflected in the test set out in *Mathews,* which test the District Court purported to follow, and which requires a court to consider the private interest that will be affected by the official

C. The Choice of Process — 59

action, the risk of an erroneous deprivation of such interest through the procedures used, the probable value of additional or substitute procedural safeguards, and the government's interest in adhering to the existing system. In applying this test we must keep in mind, in addition to the deference owed to Congress, the fact that the very nature of the due process inquiry indicates that the fundamental fairness of a particular procedure does not turn on the result obtained in any individual case; rather, "procedural due process rules are shaped by the risk of error inherent in the truth-finding process as applied to the generality of cases, not the rare exceptions."

The government interest, which has been articulated in congressional debates since the fee limitation was first enacted in 1862 during the Civil War, has been this: that the system for administering benefits should be managed in a sufficiently informal way that there should be no need for the employment of an attorney to obtain benefits to which a claimant was entitled, so that the claimant would receive the entirety of the award without having to divide it with a lawyer. This purpose is reinforced by a similar absolute prohibition on compensation of any service organization representative.

* * *

There can be little doubt that invalidation of the fee limitation would seriously frustrate the oft-repeated congressional purpose for enacting it. Attorneys would be freely employable by claimants to veterans' benefits, and the claimant would as a result end up paying part of the award, or its equivalent, to an attorney. But this would not be the only consequence of striking down the fee limitation that would be deleterious to the congressional plan.

A necessary concomitant of Congress' desire that a veteran not need a representative to assist him in making his claim was that the system should be as informal and nonadversarial as possible. This is not to say that complicated factual inquiries may be rendered simple by the expedient of informality, but surely Congress desired that the proceedings be as informal and nonadversarial as possible. The regular introduction of lawyers into the proceedings would be quite unlikely to further this goal. Describing the prospective impact of lawyers in probation revocation proceedings, we said in *Gagnon v. Scarpelli*, 411 U.S. 778, 787–788 (1973):

> The introduction of counsel into a revocation proceeding will alter significantly the nature of the proceeding. If counsel is provided for the probationer or parolee, the State in turn will normally provide its own counsel; lawyers, by training and disposition, are advocates and bound by professional duty to present all available evidence and arguments in support of their clients' positions and to contest with vigor all adverse evidence and views. The role of the hearing body itself . . . may become more akin to that of a judge at a trial, and less attuned to the rehabilitative needs of the individual. . . . Certainly, the decisionmaking process will be prolonged, and the financial cost to the State—for

60 CHAPTER I Lawyers, Litigation & Process

appointed counsel, ... a longer record, and the possibility of judicial review—will not be insubstantial.

* * *

Knowledgeable and thoughtful observers have made the same point in other language:

> To be sure, counsel can often perform useful functions even in welfare cases or other instances of mass justice; they may bring out facts ignored by or unknown to the authorities, or help to work out satisfactory compromises. But this is only one side of the coin. Under our adversary system the role of counsel is not to make sure the truth is ascertained but to advance his client's cause by any ethical means. Within the limits of professional propriety, causing delay and sowing confusion not only are his right but may be his duty. The appearance of counsel for the citizen is likely to lead the government to provide one—or at least to cause the government's representative to act like one. The result may be to turn what might have been a short conference leading to an amicable result into a protracted controversy.

> These problems concerning counsel and confrontation inevitably bring up the question whether we would not do better to abandon the adversary system in certain areas of mass justice.... While such an experiment would be a sharp break with our tradition of adversary process, that tradition ... was not formulated for a situation in which many thousands of hearings must be provided each month.

Friendly, "Some Kind of Hearing," 123 U.Pa.L.Rev. 1267, 1287–1290 (1975).

Thus, even apart from the frustration of Congress' principal goal of wanting the veteran to get the entirety of the award, the destruction of the fee limitation would bid fair to complicate a proceeding which Congress wished to keep as simple as possible. It is scarcely open to doubt that if claimants were permitted to retain compensated attorneys the day might come when it could be said that an attorney might indeed be necessary to present a claim properly in a system rendered more adversary and more complex by the very presence of lawyer representation. It is only a small step beyond that to the situation in which the claimant who has a factually simple and obviously deserving claim may nonetheless feel impelled to retain an attorney simply because so many other claimants retain attorneys. And this additional complexity will undoubtedly engender greater administrative costs, with the end result being that less Government money reaches its intended beneficiaries.

We accordingly conclude that under the *Mathews v. Eldridge* analysis great weight must be accorded to the Government interest at stake here. The flexibility of our approach in due process cases is intended in part to allow room for other forms of dispute resolution; with respect to the individual interests at stake here, legislatures are to be allowed considerable leeway to formulate such processes without being forced to conform to a rigid constitutional code of procedural necessities. It would take an extraor-

dinarily strong showing of probability of error under the present system—
and the probability that the presence of attorneys would sharply diminish
that possibility—to warrant a holding that the fee limitation denies claimants due process of law. We have no hesitation in deciding that no such
showing was made out on the record before the District Court.

* * *

Passing the problems with quantifying the likelihood of an erroneous
deprivation, however, under *Mathews* we must also ask what value the
proposed additional procedure may have in reducing such error. In this
case we are fortunate to have statistics that bear directly on this question,
which statistics were addressed by the District Court. These unchallenged
statistics chronicle the success rates before the BVA depending on the type
of representation of the claimant, and are summarized in the following
figures taken from the record.

**ULTIMATE SUCCESS RATES BEFORE THE BOARD OF VETER-
ANS APPEALS BY MODE OF REPRESENTATION**

American Legion	16.2%
American Red Cross	16.8%
Disabled American Veterans	16.6%
Veterans of Foreign Wars	16.7%
Other nonattorney	15.8%
No representation	15.2%
Attorney/Agent	18.3%

The District Court opined that these statistics were not helpful,
because in its view lawyers were retained so infrequently that no body of
lawyers with an expertise in VA practice had developed, and lawyers who
represented veterans regularly might do better than lawyers who represented them only pro bono on a sporadic basis. * * *

We think the District Court's analysis of this issue totally unconvincing, and quite lacking in the deference which ought to be shown by any
federal court in evaluating the constitutionality of an Act of Congress. We
have the most serious doubt whether a competent lawyer taking a veteran's
case on a pro bono basis would give less than his best effort, and we see no
reason why experience in developing facts as to causation in the numerous
other areas of the law where it is relevant would not be readily transferable
to proceedings before the VA. * * *

The District Court also concluded, apparently independently of its ill-
founded analysis of the claim statistics, (1) that the VA processes are
procedurally, factually, and legally complex, and (2) that the VA system
presently does not work as designed, particularly in terms of the representation afforded by VA personnel and service representatives, and that these
representatives are "unable to perform all of the services which might be
performed by a claimant's own paid attorney." Unfortunately the court's
findings on "complexity" are based almost entirely on a description of the
plan for administering benefits in the abstract, together with references to
"complex" cases involving exposure to radiation or agent orange, or post-

62   CHAPTER I LAWYERS, LITIGATION & PROCESS

traumatic stress syndrome. The court did not attempt to state even approximately how often procedural or substantive complexities arise in the run-of-the-mill case, or even in the unusual case.

* * *

The District Court's treatment of the likely usefulness of attorneys is on the same plane with its efforts to quantify the likelihood of error under the present system. The court states several times in its opinion that lawyers could provide more services than claimants presently receive—a fact which may freely be conceded—but does not suggest how the availability of these services would reduce the likelihood of error in the run-of-the-mill case. Simple factual questions are capable of resolution in a nonadversarial context, and it is less than crystal clear why *lawyers* must be available to identify possible errors in *medical* judgment. The availability of particular lawyers' services in so-called "complex" cases might be more of a factor in preventing error in such cases, but on this record we simply do not know how those cases should be defined or what percentage of all of the cases before the VA they make up. Even if the showing in the District Court had been much more favorable, appellees still would confront the constitutional hurdle posed by the principle enunciated in cases such as *Mathews* to the effect that a process must be judged by the generality of cases to which it applies, and therefore a process which is sufficient for the large majority of a group of claims is by constitutional definition sufficient for all of them. But here appellees have failed to make the very difficult factual showing necessary.

* * *

We have in previous cases, of course, held not only that the Constitution permits retention of an attorney, but also that on occasion it requires the Government to provide the services of an attorney. The Sixth Amendment affords representation by counsel in all criminal proceedings * * *.

In cases such as *Gagnon v. Scarpelli,* 411 U.S. 778 (1973), we observed that counsel can aid in identifying legal questions and presenting arguments, and that one charged with probation violation may have a right to counsel because of the liberty interest involved. * * *

But where, as here, the only interest protected by the Due Process Clause is a property interest in the continued receipt of Government benefits, which interest is conferred and terminated in a nonadversary proceeding, these precedents are of only tangential relevance. Appellees rely on *Goldberg v. Kelly,* 397 U.S. 254 (1970), in which the Court held that a welfare recipient subject to possible termination of benefits was entitled to be represented by an attorney. The Court said that "counsel can help delineate the issues, present the factual contentions in an orderly manner, conduct cross-examination, and generally safeguard the interests of the recipient." But in defining the process required the Court also observed that "the crucial factor in this context ... is that termination of aid pending resolution of a controversy over eligibility may deprive an *eligible* recipient of the very means by which to live while he waits.... His need to concentrate upon finding the means for daily subsistence, in turn, adversely affects his ability to seek redress from the welfare bureaucracy."

We think that the benefits at stake in VA proceedings, which are not granted on the basis of need, are more akin to the Social Security benefits involved in *Mathews* than they are to the welfare payments upon which the recipients in *Goldberg* depended for their daily subsistence. * * *

This case is further distinguishable from our prior decisions because the process here is not designed to operate adversarially. While counsel may well be needed to respond to opposing counsel or other forms of adversary in a trial-type proceeding, where as here no such adversary appears, and in addition a claimant or recipient is provided with substitute safeguards such as a competent representative, a decisionmaker whose duty it is to aid the claimant, and significant concessions with respect to the claimant's burden of proof, the need for counsel is considerably diminished. We have expressed similar concerns in other cases holding that counsel is not required in various proceedings that do not approximate trials, but instead are more informal and nonadversary. See *Parham v. J.R.*, 442 U.S., at 608–609; *Goss v. Lopez*, 419 U.S. 565, 583 (1975). *Wolff v. McDonnell*, 418 U.S., at 570.

* * *

■ JUSTICE O'CONNOR, with whom JUSTICE BLACKMUN joins, concurring.

I join the Court's opinion and its judgment because I agree that * * * the District Court abused its discretion in issuing a nationwide preliminary injunction against enforcement of the $10 fee limitation in 38 U.S.C. § 3404(c). I also agree that the record before us is insufficient to evaluate the claims of any individuals or identifiable groups. I write separately to note that such claims remain open on remand.

* * *

[I]t is my understanding that the Court, in reversing the lower court's preliminary injunction, does not determine the merits of the respondents' individual "as applied" claims. The complaint indicates that respondents challenged the fee limitation both on its face and as applied to them, and sought a ruling that they were entitled to a rehearing of claims processed without assistance of an attorney. Respondent Albert Maxwell, for example, alleges that his service representative retired and failed to notify him that he had dropped his case. Mr. Maxwell's records indicate that he suffers from the after effects of malaria contracted in the Bataan death march as well as from multiple myelomas allegedly a result of exposure to radiation when he was a prisoner of war detailed to remove atomic debris in Japan. Maxwell contends that his claims have failed because of lack of expert assistance in developing the medical and historical facts of his case. * * *

The merits of these claims are difficult to evaluate on the record of affidavits and depositions developed at the preliminary injunction stage. Though the Court concludes that denial of expert representation is not "per se unconstitutional," given the availability of service representatives to assist the veteran and the Veterans' Administration boards' emphasis on nonadversarial procedures, "[o]n remand, the District Court is free to and should consider any individual claims that [the procedures] did not meet the standards we have described in this opinion."

■ JUSTICE STEVENS, with whom JUSTICE BRENNAN and JUSTICE MARSHALL join, dissenting.

The Court does not appreciate the value of individual liberty. It may well be true that in the vast majority of cases a veteran does not need to employ a lawyer, and that the system of processing veterans benefit claims, by and large, functions fairly and effectively without the participation of retained counsel. Everyone agrees, however, that there are at least some complicated cases in which the services of a lawyer would be useful to the veteran and, indeed, would simplify the work of the agency by helping to organize the relevant facts and to identify the controlling issues. What is the reason for denying the veteran the right to counsel of his choice in such cases? The Court gives us two answers: First, the paternalistic interest in protecting the veteran from the consequences of his own improvidence; and second, the bureaucratic interest in minimizing the cost of administering the benefit program. I agree that both interests are legitimate, but neither provides an adequate justification for the restraint on liberty imposed by the $10–fee limitation.

* * *

The first fee limitation—$5 per claim—was enacted in 1862. That limitation was repealed two years later and replaced by the $10–fee limitation, which has survived ever since. The limitation was designed to protect the veteran from extortion or improvident bargains with unscrupulous lawyers. Obviously, it was believed that the number of scoundrels practicing law was large enough to justify a legislative prohibition against charging excessive fees.

At the time the $10–fee limitation was enacted, Congress presumably considered that fee reasonable. The legal work involved in preparing a veteran's claim consisted of little more than filling out an appropriate form, and, in terms of the average serviceman's base pay, a $10 fee then was roughly the equivalent of a $580 fee today. At its inception, therefore, the fee limitation had neither the purpose nor the effect of precluding the employment of reputable counsel by veterans. Indeed, the statute then, as now, expressly contemplated that claims for veterans' benefits could be processed by "agents or attorneys."

The fact that the statute was aimed at unscrupulous attorneys is confirmed by the provision for criminal penalties. Instead of just making an agreement to pay a greater fee unenforceable—as an anticipatory pledge of an interest in future pension benefits is unenforceable—the Act contains a flat prohibition against the direct or indirect collection of a greater fee, and provides that an attorney who charges more than $10 may be imprisoned for up to two years at hard labor. Thus, an unscrupulous moneylender or merchant who might try to take advantage of an improvident veteran might have difficulty collecting his bill, but the unscrupulous lawyer might go to jail.

* * * In today's market, the reasonable fee for even the briefest conference would surely exceed $10. Thus, the law that was enacted in 1864 to protect veterans from unscrupulous lawyers—those who charge excessive fees—effectively denies today's veteran access to all lawyers who charge reasonable fees for their services.

The Court's opinion blends its discussion of the paternalistic interest in protecting veterans from unscrupulous lawyers and the bureaucratic interest in minimizing the cost of administration in a way that implies that each interest reinforces the other. Actually the two interests are quite different and merit separate analysis.

In my opinion, the bureaucratic interest in minimizing the cost of administration is nothing but a red herring. Congress has not prohibited lawyers from participating in the processing of claims for benefits and there is no reason why it should. The complexity of the agency procedures can be regulated by limiting the number of hearings, the time for argument, the length of written submissions, and in other ways, but there is no reason to believe that the *agency's* cost of administration will be increased because a claimant is represented by counsel instead of appearing *pro se*. The informality that the Court emphasizes is desirable because it no doubt enables many veterans, or their lay representatives, to handle their claims without the assistance of counsel. But there is no reason to assume that lawyers would add confusion rather than clarity to the proceedings. As a profession, lawyers are skilled communicators dedicated to the service of their clients. Only if it is assumed that the average lawyer is incompetent or unscrupulous can one rationally conclude that the efficiency of the agency's work would be undermined by allowing counsel to participate whenever a veteran is willing to pay for his services. I categorically reject any such assumption.

* * *

The paternalistic interest in protecting the veteran from his own improvidence would unquestionably justify a rule that simply prevented lawyers from overcharging their clients. Most appropriately, such a rule might require agency approval, or perhaps judicial review, of counsel fees. It might also establish a reasonable ceiling, subject to exceptions for especially complicated cases. In fact, I assume that the $10–fee limitation was justified by this interest when it was first enacted in 1864. But time has brought changes in the value of the dollar, in the character of the legal profession, in agency procedures, and in the ability of the veteran to proceed without the assistance of counsel.

* * *

It is evident from what I have written that I regard the fee limitation as unwise and an insult to the legal profession. It does not follow, however, that it is unconstitutional. The Court correctly notes that the presumption of constitutionality that attaches to every Act of Congress requires the challenger to bear the burden of demonstrating its invalidity.

* * *

The Court recognizes that the Veterans' Administration's procedures must provide claimants with due process of law, but then concludes that the constitutional requirement is satisfied because the appellees have not proved that the "probability of error under the present system" is unacceptable. In short, if 80 or 90 percent of the cases are correctly decided, why worry about those individuals whose claims have been erroneously rejected and who might have prevailed if they had been represented by counsel?

The fundamental error in the Court's analysis is its assumption that the individual's right to employ counsel of his choice in a contest with his sovereign is a kind of second-class interest that can be assigned a material value and balanced on a utilitarian scale of costs and benefits. It is true that the veteran's right to benefits is a property right and that in fashioning the procedures for administering the benefit program, the Government may appropriately weigh the value of additional procedural safeguards against their pecuniary costs. It may, for example, properly decide not to provide free counsel to claimants. But we are not considering a procedural right that would involve any cost to the Government. We are concerned with the individual's right to spend his own money to obtain the advice and assistance of independent counsel in advancing his claim against the Government.

In all criminal proceedings, that right is expressly protected by the Sixth Amendment. As I have indicated, in civil disputes with the Government I believe that right is also protected by the Due Process Clause of the Fifth Amendment and by the First Amendment. If the Government, in the guise of a paternalistic interest in protecting the citizen from his own improvidence, can deny him access to independent counsel of his choice, it can change the character of our free society. Even though a dispute with the sovereign may only involve property rights, or as in this case a statutory entitlement, the citizen's right of access to the independent, private bar is itself an aspect of liberty that is of critical importance in our democracy. Just as I disagree with the present Court's crabbed view of the concept of "liberty," so do I reject its apparent unawareness of the function of the independent lawyer as a guardian of our freedom.[24]

In my view, regardless of the nature of the dispute between the sovereign and the citizen—whether it be a criminal trial, a proceeding to terminate parental rights, a claim for social security benefits, a dispute over welfare benefits, or a pension claim asserted by the widow of a soldier who

---

24. That function was, however, well understood by Jack Cade and his followers, characters who are often forgotten and whose most famous line is often misunderstood. Dick's statement ("The first thing we do, let's kill all the lawyers") was spoken by a rebel, not a friend of liberty. See W. Shakespeare, King Henry VI, pt. II, Act IV, scene 2, line 72. As a careful reading of that text will reveal, Shakespeare insightfully realized that disposing of lawyers is a step in the direction of a totalitarian form of government.

was killed on the battlefield—the citizen's right to consult an independent lawyer and to retain that lawyer to speak on his or her behalf is an aspect of liberty that is priceless. It should not be bargained away on the notion that a totalitarian appraisal of the mass of claims processed by the Veterans' Administration does not identify an especially high probability of error.

NOTES AND QUESTIONS

1. Precisely what does Justice Rehnquist mean when he describes the VA's claim procedure as "nonadversarial"?

2. Following the Supreme Court's decision, the plaintiffs in *Walters* amended their complaint to challenge the constitutionality of the fee limit "as applied to claimants with service-connected disability or death compensation claims based on exposure to ionizing radiation." See the concurring opinion of Justice O'Connor. A motion for class certification was granted, 111 F.R.D. 595 (N.D.Cal.1986). The district court ultimately found that the $10 fee limitation was a violation of the plaintiffs' rights under the due process clause and the First Amendment, because it deprived them "of a meaningful opportunity to present their claims to the VA and to petition the government":

> [P]reparation of ionizing radiation [IR] claims involves a wide variety of tasks for which attorneys are trained and particularly well suited. * * * Attorneys are skilled and experienced in working with experts in support of legal claims [and are] trained to be and are effective at framing the legally relevant issues for experts and at understanding the legal standards by which those issues will be judged. This training would contribute substantially to the work of medical and scientific experts in IR claims.

> * * * Attorneys are more likely to detect and respond to procedural violations by the VA and to ensure that the claimant effectively takes advantage of procedural protections such as the right to a hearing. Attorneys are better able to track down the relevant regulations, manual provisions and internal documents of the VA in order to muster support for their clients' IR claims and to interpret the myriad of complex regulations and rules relating to IR cases. Moreover, attorneys, because of their training, can more competently prepare briefs and appellate papers, conduct legal research, apply the law to the facts, and bring legal challenges to mistaken agency interpretations of regulations and statutes.

National Ass'n of Radiation Survivors v. Derwinski, 782 F.Supp. 1392, 1406 (N.D.Cal.1992). The Ninth Circuit, however, reversed, 994 F.2d 583 (9th Cir.1992) (accepting the government's argument that "the proper inquiry is whether lawyers are necessary to make the process fair, not whether lawyers are better able to pursue claims than non-lawyers").

68 CHAPTER I LAWYERS, LITIGATION & PROCESS

3. After the Supreme Court's decision in *Walters,* significant changes were made with respect to the adjudication of benefits claims before the VA (now the Department of Veterans Affairs). Under the Veterans' Judicial Review Act of 1988, decisions of the BVA may now be reviewed by a newly-created Article I court, the Court of Veterans' Appeals; further review on issues of law is possible by appeal to the Court of Appeals for the Federal Circuit. An attorney is still not permitted to charge a claimant any fee at all for services rendered "before the date on which the [BVA] first makes a final decision" on a claim. (By prohibiting an attorney from charging for services "until the VA affirms its decision to deny a claim, the [Act] intends to preserve as much of the informal and efficient means of claim adjudication as possible," H.R.Rep. 100–963, 1988 U.S.C.C.A.N. 5782, 5810–11). However, claimants may now agree to pay a lawyer for services rendered *after* that date—for example, in an appeal to the Court of Veterans' Appeals or in seeking to reopen a claim for further proceedings based on new evidence. Any fee agreement is subject to review by the BVA, which may order a reduction in a fee found to be "excessive or unreasonable." If the agreement provides for a contingent fee to be paid directly by the Department to the attorney out of any past-due benefits awarded, the fee may not exceed 20% of such benefits. See 38 U.S.C.A. § 5904(c), (d), § 7252, § 7263, § 7292.

4. The new Court of Veterans' Appeals has consistently overturned more than 60% of the BVA decisions it reviews. In many of these cases, substantial recovery in the form of retroactive benefits is at stake, and in most successful appeals prosecuted by a lawyer, attorneys' fees are awarded. Nevertheless more than two-thirds of the nearly 20,000 veterans who have appealed to the Court have proceeded pro se. "Nobody knows how many others have chosen not to appeal or file a reopened claim due to lack of representation." The probable explanation for this dearth of willing lawyers "is an unfortunate legacy of the longstanding limit on attorney fees. This is an entirely new area of law for the private bar and the upfront costs of becoming proficient can seem daunting." See Barton Stichman, Veterans Benefits Law: A Wide–Open Area of Practice, 17 No. 5 GPSolo 47 (July/Aug. 2000); see also Lawrence Hagel & Michael Horan, Five Years Under the Veterans' Judicial Review Act, 46 Maine L. Rev. 43 (1994).

5. Does the *Walters* case suggest that there is a necessary trade-off between an "efficiency" interest in the mass processing of claims and an interest in the quality of decision in the individual case? Does it suggest that the efficiency interest is necessarily impaired by an "adversarial" procedure and the presence of lawyers? Do you agree with these propositions? Are the concerns expressed by Professor Fiss relevant in helping to draw a proper balance between the two interests?

6. Compare Justice Rehnquist's observations on the "informal" and "nonadversarial" nature of VA proceedings with these excerpts from an article by Professor Lon Fuller:

> What generally occurs in practice is that at some early point [in adjudication] a familiar pattern will seem to emerge from the evidence;

an accustomed label is wanting for the case and, without awaiting further proofs, this label is promptly assigned to it. It is a mistake to suppose that this premature cataloguing must necessarily result from impatience, prejudice or mental sloth. Often it proceeds from a very understandable desire to bring the hearing into some order and coherence, for without some tentative theory of the case there is no standard of relevance by which testimony may be measured. But what starts as a preliminary diagnosis designed to direct the inquiry tends, quickly and imperceptibly, to become a fixed conclusion, as all that confirms the diagnosis makes a strong imprint on the mind, while all that runs counter to it is received with diverted attention.

An adversary presentation seems the only effective means for combatting this natural human tendency to judge too swiftly in terms of the familiar that which is not yet fully known. The arguments of counsel hold the case, as it were, in suspension between two opposing interpretations of it. While the proper classification of the case is thus kept unresolved, there is time to explore all of its peculiarities and nuances.
* * *

These, then, are the reasons for believing that partisan advocacy plays a vital and essential role in one of the most fundamental procedures of a democratic society. * * * Viewed in this light, the role of the lawyer as a partisan advocate appears not as a regrettable necessity, but as an indispensable part of a larger ordering of affairs. The institution of advocacy is not a concession to the frailties of human nature, but an expression of human insight in the design of a social framework within which man's capacity for impartial judgment can attain its fullest realization.

Fuller, The Forms and Limits of Adjudication, 92 Harv.L.Rev. 353, 382–85 (1978).

7. One commentator has suggested that *lawyers* too may have an independent interest in having their "day in court," whether or not their clients need one. He argues that "lack of trial experience in a legal and ethical system premised on adjudication threatens the effective functioning" of litigators. For example, a movement towards increased reliance on settlement of litigation might impair attorney competence in forensic skills—and it might lead lawyers to seriously underestimate their chances of success at trial, out of a "fear of the unknown" or an unconscious attempt to avoid "embarrassment" from a "public display" of untested trial skills. All this may have a "demoralizing" impact on litigators. And litigators may also become "demoralized" because their "role and function are tied to the process and results of adjudication since the cardinal tenets of legal ethics are most often justified in terms of the function of the adversary system of adjudication": If adjudication becomes less frequent, "the value and justifications for lawyers become more attenuated," bringing "a lessening of the lawyer's ability to believe in the value of her own role."

Does any of this ring true? Or is it in effect an argument that we should burn down some perfectly good houses "in order to give the fire depart-

70 CHAPTER I LAWYERS, LITIGATION & PROCESS

ment the opportunity to improve its fire fighting skills"? See McMunigal, The Costs of Settlement: The Impact of Scarcity of Adjudication on Litigating Lawyers, 37 U.C.L.A. L.Rev. 833 (1990).

2. PROBLEM: SHERIDAN V. HOPEWELL COLLEGE[1]

You are practicing law in a large Dallas law firm. On several occasions in the past you have handled some litigation on behalf of your alma mater, Hopewell College. Hopewell is a small well-regarded liberal arts college located in the small North Texas town of Mt. Pleasant. The school was founded by the Lutheran Church in 1897 and is now coeducational (women were admitted for the first time in 1959).

You have just received a copy of a complaint in a lawsuit filed against the College by a former instructor in its Physical Education Department, Mary Kate Sheridan. The complaint alleges discrimination on the basis of sex in violation of Title VII of the Civil Rights Act, and names Hopewell, the College's President, and various other school officials as defendants. Hopewell's in-house counsel has very little trial experience and has been used mostly for routine legal problems. Your firm has therefore been asked to handle the defense of this suit.

After reviewing the complaint, you discussed the matter briefly with the College's counsel and have been able to obtain a certain amount of background information about the case. You gather that Sheridan was hired as an instructor in the Phys. Ed. Department eight years ago; she taught Modern Dance and Tap Dance, and was apparently a popular teacher. In her fifth and sixth years the Department put her name forward for promotion to Assistant Professor; despite favorable recommendations by the Faculty Personnel Committee, the President and the College Board of Trustees refused to promote her. Again the following year the Department recommended her for both promotion and tenure; again the FPC voted to approve the recommendation, and again the President and the Board refused. Last spring she was given a "terminal" contract for the current school year. (An "up or out" decision is required after seven years of teaching under the rules of both Hopewell and the American Association of University Professors.) Sheridan appealed to the elected "Faculty Board of Appeals," which unanimously voted that she be given tenure; this recommendation also was rejected. She filed suit against the College shortly after receiving a "right to sue" letter from the Equal Employment Opportunity Commission.

Ms. Sheridan received a Bachelor's degree 17 years ago, but has no higher degree. The Hopewell "faculty handbook" requires that before receiving tenure, a faculty member must hold a "terminal degree" (in Physical Education, this is a Master's) or its "scholarly equivalent." At Hopewell this requirement has traditionally been honored in the breach—

---

1. This problem draws on George La-Noue & Barbara Lee, Academics in Court: The Consequences of Faculty Discrimination Litigation (1987). See also Kunda v. Muhlenberg College, 621 F.2d 532 (3d Cir.1980).

the head of the Phys. Ed. Department, a full professor, has only a Bachelor's degree. However, the appointment six years ago of President Davies, who came to the job with a firm commitment to "upgrade the quality of the faculty," has led to the degree requirement being rigorously enforced.

Sheridan's complaint asks for $600,000 in compensatory and punitive damages, attorneys' fees, and reinstatement to her job with the rank of Associate Professor with tenure.

President Davies is concerned. The College has no liability insurance that will cover this kind of discrimination claim. Davies assures you that this is the first such complaint that has ever been made against the College. However, he has heard disquieting stories about the impact of discrimination suits on other educational institutions—in terms of the burden of litigation on the time and energy of school officials, of the divisiveness and harm to institutional morale, and of the difficulty thereafter in raising funds and recruiting talented new faculty:

> Administrators at large institutions who employ full-time counsel may regard litigation as simply another cost of doing business; that is, legal expenses may be considered a sunk cost. Nevertheless, institutions of higher learning rarely emerge from wrongful discharge and employment discrimination litigation unscathed. A race, sex, national origin, or other discrimination charge against a college or university is almost certain to generate media exposure. Students may hold public demonstrations to protest the termination, especially if the case involves a popular professor. Charges of racism, sexism, religious bias, or blatant disregard for a faculty member's career are likely to tarnish the liberal image of the institution and may make it more difficult for the school to attract high-quality students and faculty or to generate philanthropic support and research funds. University administrators who are named in an employment discrimination suit almost always have their personal integrity called into question and run the risk of suffering irreparable damage to their professional reputations. Faculty members in the department or college where the suit originated may split into factions, some of whom support the faculty member while others support the administration. Many cases involve comparisons between the qualifications of faculty who were promoted or tenured and those who were not. Counsel for the plaintiff may attempt to belittle the research and teaching accomplishments of the faculty who have been selected for comparison. When such attacks are made public, either through the press or during a grievance hearing or trial, the damage to interpersonal relationships in a department may be irreparable.[2]

At the same time, of course, the costs—social and psychological as well as financial—that such lawsuits can impose on the plaintiff faculty member can also be traumatic. You understand, by the way, that Sheridan would very much like to stay at Hopewell. She was born and raised in Mt.

---

2. Terry Leap, Tenure, Discrimination, and the Courts 16–17 (1993).

72   CHAPTER I   LAWYERS, LITIGATION & PROCESS

Pleasant, and her two young children are now in the local public schools. She continues to perform in her own physical fitness program that she developed some years ago and that is shown twice a week on the local television station. College officials have made a point of telling you that this show, along with sporadic employment as a substitute high-school teacher and manager of a health spa, has been her only source of income following her divorce.

Davies has asked your firm for a memorandum on the legal issues raised by Sheridan's claim. He has also asked you for advice as to what process should be used to resolve the problem in the best interests of the College. What do you tell him?

Your first reaction may be to focus on the relevant law invoked in the complaint: What elements does the plaintiff have to establish to make a prima facie case under Title VII? Where are the burdens of proof and of producing evidence? What remedies do courts impose for violations of Title VII? You will also of course want to ask a number of questions concerning the facts relevant to the merits of the claim: You may want to ask, for example, whether Sheridan's failure to achieve promotion or tenure might be due to reasons other than discrimination such as inadequate performance as an instructor. (The faculty "Board of Appeal" did note that it had "uncovered no statement about Mary Kate's contribution to the College that was less than enthusiastic." But of course, adverse tenure decisions may frequently be based on any number of other considerations including the College's future plans for the department, the number of tenured faculty already in the department, and the financial constraints both on the department and the College as a whole.) You would certainly also want to inquire into the College's practices with respect to promotion and tenure of male faculty. It appears that Davies has been adamant about uniformly requiring a "terminal" degree for tenure candidates, and that over the past five years no faculty member at Hopewell has been given tenure without such a degree. However, Sheridan claims that she had never been warned that any Master's degree requirement would be insisted on in her case—although male candidates had been advised of the requirement and encouraged to make progress towards the higher degree. You also understand that two male instructors who did not have a Master's were promoted to Assistant Professor without tenure four years ago, even though the faculty handbook states that a Master's is "normally" required even for promotion to that rank.

In addition to these issues of fact and law, it is clear that sustained attention will have to be given to the *process* by which you expect to help Hopewell resolve this problem. You will probably think of the litigation process first—if only because the opposing lawyer has already announced his intention to use the court system. In addition, you have to recognize that both Ms. Sheridan and the College might want or need vindication, in the form of an authoritative public decision that they are "in the right." But is litigation an inevitable process? Is it the best process for the College? What other processes might be useful, and how might opposing counsel be induced to participate in these processes? How do you evaluate and compare processes in terms of the best interests of the client?

Litigation is far from being the only process available in a situation like this. By filing a lawsuit, Sheridan's attorney has certainly gotten the College's attention. But he has hardly foreclosed the opportunity for negotiation and private settlement. You may have many opportunities to negotiate a voluntary settlement of the dispute, even though the suit has been filed—and indeed, this opportunity will persist even as discovery in the suit proceeds and even as the "trial" gets under way. Although lawyers are expected to understand and use the negotiation process, they usually have very little formal instruction in this part of their work. It is inevitable then that there will be wide variations in the skill which different lawyers bring to bear in negotiation and the energy with which they pursue a negotiated settlement. Chapter II here provides a basic introduction to this subject.

You might also wish to explore other, alternative processes that might be appropriate in the Sheridan case. Some processes would bring in third parties to help the College and Ms. Sheridan reach a settlement of their dispute short of trial and with some privacy—such third parties might even have some special familiarity with the particular culture and problems of higher education. However, you are not entirely clear how such suitable persons might be chosen—or just what their role would be in the dispute: Is the third party expected merely to help facilitate the parties' own voluntary settlement by helping them bargain and communicate with each other? Or is she expected to render a "decision?" If the latter, is this decision intended to be binding on the parties or merely advisory? May the power of the state be harnessed to support this decision, and does the third party enjoy other sources of influence and authority? Is she expected to proceed by articulating and applying general "rules," or in a more ad hoc manner through compromise or persuasion?

Because of the importance of this process factor in choosing among dispute resolution mechanisms, the presence of a third party is used here as a natural organizing theme for these materials. After our brief look at litigation in this chapter, and a consideration of the negotiation process in Chapter II, we will proceed to consider a variety of processes in which the participation of third parties becomes increasingly dominant and authoritative. The materials in Chapter III describe the process of mediation and analyze how lawyers might resort to it in order to resolve disputes; in Chapter IV we will primarily consider processes that are court-administered or court-ordered. Still another alternative is a process like arbitration, in which a third party typically "hears" a case and issues a final and binding decision, while still insuring a greater measure of privacy in the resolution of the dispute than litigation can promise. Arbitration is the subject of Chapter V of this book.

Of course, lawyers seldom use just one process to try to resolve a single dispute. They may combine two or more and work them simultaneously, playing one against the other, or they may try them in succession. The

74 CHAPTER I LAWYERS, LITIGATION & PROCESS

dynamics of this interactive use of process is a substantial part of a lawyer's practice and therefore an important focus of these materials. An equally important point is that processes like "negotiation," "mediation," and "arbitration" are ideal types; we use them primarily for purposes of organization. There are no sharp or clear distinctions between them, and the various techniques of dispute resolution represent points on a continuum rather than essentially distinct methods. There exist in fact any number of hybrid processes that reflect unique combinations of the primary forms—and only the limited creativity of the lawyers involved imposes any restrictions on the fashioning of new hybrid combinations. Moreover, our organization is not meant to imply that there is any fixed or rigid form which a particular process must inevitably take. The way a process works in practice will depend on the context and the personalities involved. Some "mediators" may be so active in devising solutions and so forceful in imposing them on the parties that it may in fact be hard to distinguish them from arbitrators.

The lawyer's search throughout is for the "appropriate process" to use in resolving the client's problem, and this, of course, becomes an important theme in these materials. There are many variables that will affect the choice of process; particular case factors, for example, may make a dispute more or less suitable for resolution by a particular process. One of the most important case-related factors centers on the relationship between the disputing parties: Is the relationship an ongoing one, which looms large in the life of both parties? Is there an expectation of frequent or valuable interaction in the future? This may be true, for example, not only in family and neighborhood disputes, but in employment, collective bargaining, and many business disputes as well. In such cases, the value of the continuing relationship may furnish an incentive for both parties to participate in an alternative dispute resolution process even though it lacks the coercive effects of the court system. Stated in another way, the prospect of damage to an ongoing relationship may constitute one sanction for failing to participate in the process or to comply with the result reached.

That a dispute arises in the context of a continuing relationship may have implications for the choice of process. When the potential benefits from future contacts (and the costs from disruption or termination) are great, a process that seeks to restore and maintain satisfying patterns of personal interaction seems called for. Such a process might be structured in such a way as to help the parties to reduce the causes of future conflict by helping them to deal with and work at the "real," underlying problems in their relationship. Merely getting the parties to understand and to talk directly to each other in an "atmosphere of mutual recognition and empathy"[3] may go a long way in this respect. Adjudication, by contrast,

---

3. Bush, Dispute Resolution Alternatives and the Goals of Civil Justice: Jurisdictional Principles for Process Choice, 1984 Wisc.L.Rev. 893, 982.

seems ill-suited to the task, since it can easily sour future relations by escalating conflict and focusing on symptoms rather than on underlying causes. Indeed in many cultures the very invocation of formal legal "rights" in the adversarial contest of litigation may be seen as a violation of the social norms governing a relationship.[4]

As Professor Auerbach has observed:

Whether disputants ignore their differences, negotiate, submit to mediation or arbitration, or retain lawyers to litigate is a matter of significant choice. How people dispute is, after all, a function of how (and whether) they relate. In relationships that are intimate, caring, and mutual, disputants will behave quite differently from their counterparts who are strangers or competitors. Selfishness and aggression are not merely functions of individual personality; they are socially sanctioned—or discouraged. So is the decision to define a disputant as an adversary, and to struggle until there is a clear winner and loser; or, alternatively, to resolve conflict in a way that will preserve, rather than destroy, a relationship. In some cultures, the patterns of interaction suggest that those who participate in litigation may be psychologically deviant. Among Scandinavian fishermen and the Zapotec of Mexico, in Bavarian villages and certain African tribes, among the Sinai Bedouin and in Israeli *kibbutzim* * * *, the importance of enduring relations has made peace, harmony, and mediation preferable to conflict, victory, and litigation. But in the United States, a nation of competitive individuals and strangers, litigation is encouraged; here, the burden of psychological deviance falls upon those who find adversary relations to be a destructive form of human behavior.[5]

It is probably illusory to hope to be able to match particular processes of dispute resolution to particular types of disputes—to "fit the forum to the fuss"[6]—in any systematic way. Considerations are so diverse, and factual situations so fluid, that the choice may ultimately have to be made in a more intuitive fashion. But one threshold question might be, *from whose perspective* are we to engage in this task of evaluating processes?

---

4. See, e.g., Merry, Book Review, 100 Harv.L.Rev. 2057, 2061 (1987) (if murder occurred between two Nuer tribesmen and their kinsmen lived nearby and expected to see one another in the future, "they would mediate the dispute and pay bloodwealth in cattle"; however, if they lived further apart "they would refuse to pay damages and transform their relationship into a feud."). See also Robert Ellickson, Order without Law: How Neighbors Settle Disputes 62–64 (1991) (for the ranchers and farmers of Shasta County, California, the " 'natural working order' calls for two neighbors to work out their problems between themselves"; only de-

viants—termed "bad apples" or "odd ducks"—would turn to an attorney for help on a problem with a neighbor). Cf. Yngvesson, Re–Examining Continuing Relations and the Law, 1985 Wisc.L.Rev. 623 (courts and other official forums often resorted to in order to redefine and reshape terms of an ongoing relationship over the "long run").

5. Jerold S. Auerbach, Justice Without Law? 78 (1983).

6. See Sander & Goldberg, Fitting the Forum to the Fuss: A User–Friendly Guide to Selecting an ADR Procedure, Negotiation J., Jan. 1994 at p. 49.

CHAPTER I LAWYERS, LITIGATION & PROCESS

Lawyers frequently tend to assume that all that matters for their clients is the size of the settlement and the speed of resolution—in this respect they regard "the psychology of client satisfaction as self-evident."[7] The underlying assumption is that the client has no serious independent concern with just *how* the problem has been resolved. But are these assumptions correct? A number of recent studies suggest that "non-outcome concerns"—like the ability to personally participate in the process or to have some "control over the processing or handling of the case," the opportunity to "express oneself and to have one's views considered by someone in power"—may be at least as important as the actual result in determining a disputant's satisfaction with a dispute-resolution process.[8] Other studies report a higher level of satisfaction and sense of fairness among those whose disputes were resolved in mediation as compared to those whose cases were litigated.[9] But on the other hand—even if we can identify such preferences—is disputant satisfaction truly a reliable indication of the quality of a dispute resolution process? After all, are not expressed "preferences" often a product of ignorance, of lack of awareness of alternatives, or of simple rationalization? "[A]n inexperienced litigant's preference for harmony may reflect ignorance of the pleasures of vindication and justice," or may reflect the fact that a litigant who has been the victim of injustice "may, as a means of reducing her unhappiness, have lost her taste for justice precisely because it seems unattainable."[10]

A related question is whether the choice of process is to be an entirely private matter: Are we to engage in this evaluation exclusively from the viewpoint of the lawyer with a client sitting in front of him? Or from that of the social engineer or philosopher-king, whose primary concern is the impact on the broader society? What role is there for public intervention and oversight of the decision on the basis of external social values? As Professor Menkel–Meadow has asked in a recent article, "Whose dispute is

---

7. Tyler, A Psychological Perspective on the Settlement of Mass Tort Claims, 53 Law & Contem.Probs. 199 (1990).

8. See E. Allan Lind & Tom R. Tyler, The Social Psychology of Procedural Justice 85–86, 94–106, 215–17 (1988); Lind et al., In the Eye of the Beholder: Tort Litigants' Evaluations of their Experiences in the Civil Justice System, 24 Law & Soc'y Rev. 953 (1990) (in small-dollar tort litigation, trial and arbitration were both perceived as fairer than judicial settlement conferences or bilateral settlement; "it is noteworthy that there was no substantial relationship between procedural fairness judgments and objective measures of outcome"); Lind et al., Decision Control and Process Control Effects on Procedural Fairness Judgments, 13 J.Applied Soc.Psych. 338 (1983) (judgments of procedural fairness are less influenced by control over the likely *outcome* of the dispute than by control over the *process;* the "general im-

plication [is] that procedural evaluations are less outcome-oriented and more process-and structure-oriented than had previously been thought").

9. See the review of the literature in Galanter & Cahill, "Most Cases Settle": Judicial Promotion and Regulation of Settlements, 46 Stan.L.Rev. 1339, 1355–57 (1994).

10. Bundy, The Policy in Favor of Settlement in an Adversary System, 44 Hastings L.J. 1, 16–17 (1992). See also Michele Hermann et al., University of New Mexico Center for the Study and Resolution of Disputes, The MetroCourt Project Final Report xi (1993). This study found that minority women reported the highest level of satisfaction with mediation—"[d]espite their tendency to achieve lower monetary awards as claimants and to pay more as respondents" compared with nonminorities.

it anyway?"[11] Should we aspire to replace our courthouses with "dispute resolution centers" where a "screening clerk" would "channel" parties to the process he considers "most appropriate" for the case?[12] Or could this "screening" function more appropriately be performed in the lawyer's office? These too are questions that you should be prepared to consider as we proceed through these materials.

[11] See Menkel–Meadow, Whose Dispute Is It Anyway?: A Philosophical and Democratic Defense of Settlement (In Some Cases), 83 Georgetown L.J. 2663, 2669 (1995).

[12] Cf. Sander, Varieties of Dispute Processing, 70 F.R.D. 111, 131 (1976); see also Ericka B. Gray, Multi–Door Courthouses (State Justice Institute 1993).

CHAPTER II

NEGOTIATION

We all negotiate every day. You may be buying or selling a car, working out the lease on an apartment or the closing terms for purchasing a house, starting or ending a business partnership, asking for a raise, or dealing with a contractor working on your home who is late or significantly over his bid price. You may negotiate with friends, family, or a spouse about seemingly simple personal issues like what movie to see, who should take the trash out, whether to spend holidays with your in-laws, or where to take a vacation. Any time your interests differ from or conflict with another person's and you actively attempt to persuade them or to resolve your differences, you are negotiating.[1] We have all been practicing the art of negotiation since we first learned as infants that crying induced someone to pick us up or to give us milk.

Attorneys also negotiate constantly. In transactions or "deal-making," a lawyer may bargain over the structure of a corporate merger, try to hammer out the details of a client's executive compensation agreement, or negotiate the terms of a real estate purchase and sale. In dispute resolution, an attorney may sit down with opposing counsel to discuss a divorce or separation agreement, debate the meaning of a disputed contract clause, plea bargain a client's criminal matter, contest the distribution of an estate, or seek payment for a client who has initiated a personal injury suit.

---

1. Lax and Sebenius define negotiation as "a process of potentially opportunistic interaction in which two or more parties, with some apparent conflict, seek to do better through jointly decided action than they could do otherwise." Lax and Sebenius, The Manager as Negotiator 11 (1986). Abhinay Muthoo defines bargaining as occurring in a situation where parties "can mutually benefit from reaching agreement on an outcome from a set of possible outcomes (that contains two or more elements), but have conflicting interests over the set of outcomes." Muthoo, Bargaining Theory with Applications 1–2 (1999). Melissa Nelken says, "Anytime you deal with someone else, seeking to reach agreement on some matter, you are involved in a negotiation." Nelken, Understanding Negotiation 1 (2001).

As we have already seen, the vast majority of disputes that involve legal issues—disputes that *could* be tried in a court of law—are settled through informal negotiation. Understanding the negotiation process and how best to approach bargaining opportunities is thus critically important for attorneys.

In this chapter we focus on the use of negotiation to resolve legal disputes. The chapter is divided into four parts. In Section A we first explore the basic structure of negotiation—the economic underpinnings of both single and multiple issue bargaining. This section investigates the distributive aspects of negotiation—who gets how much of whatever is in dispute—and the integrative or value-creating opportunities bargaining can present—how the two parties can "expand the pie" by finding mutually-beneficial trades. Section B then considers the problem of strategy—given that many disputes present both distributive issues and integrative opportunities, how should you negotiate? Should you bargain hard and press for every possible concession? Or work towards a fair resolution that satisfies both parties' interests? What are the advantages and disadvantages of different strategies? Section C explores several factors that can complicate legal negotiation. We examine certain cognitive and social psychological biases or heuristics that can act as a barrier to conflict resolution, and consider their implications for decision-making in the negotiation context. We also discuss the interpersonal skills needed to negotiate effectively, and the role of race, gender and cultural differences in negotiation. Finally, Section D considers the ethical and legal framework for settlement negotiations, including the ways in which litigation processes affect negotiation, the law governing negotiation behavior, and the judge's role in settlement discussions.

A. THE STRUCTURE OF NEGOTIATION

1. ONE ISSUE

It is easiest to analyze the structure of a simple negotiation between two parties with only one issue in dispute. Two neighbors might be negotiating over where to put the fence between their properties—each wants it to be farther onto the other's land. You might be trying to persuade a plumber to come fix your leaking kitchen sink—he wants to do the job tomorrow morning, you want him to come out to your apartment tonight. Often money is the issue in dispute and each party has the same goal: to maximize their own return by receiving more or paying less. If you are buying a used laptop computer from a stranger, bargaining with a mechanic over the price of his repairs to your car, or trying to secure a discount on your rent—and both sides focus solely on the single issue of money—then you want to pay less and the other side wants you to pay more. This sort of negotiation is often called "zero-sum," because a gain for one party means an equivalent loss for the other.

Imagine the following situation. Tammy Tompkins has brought a lawsuit against Dr. Sander alleging that the doctor negligently caused the death of Tammy's mother, Lyla.[2] Lyla died a year ago at age sixty-seven from complications related to a rare immunological disease called Pemphigus. This disease causes the body's immune system to malfunction and to begin to attack the afflicted patient's skin and tissues. If left untreated it causes painful skin lesions, hemorrhaging and deterioration of vital organ function. It also leaves its victim exposed to infection and all manner of diseases. In severe cases it can lead to death.

Lyla lived in a rural town in the Midwest and was caught completely by surprise when she became ill. She had no idea that she had Pemphigus. After unsuccessfully trying various remedies for Lyla's early symptoms, her local primary care physician referred her to Dr. Sander, an "expert" on skin disorders who practiced at a larger nearby hospital. Although Lyla visited Dr. Sander several times over a three-month period, he never diagnosed her accurately as having Pemphigus. Instead, he thought she was suffering from severe allergies. Lyla's medical records show that he prescribed several different steroids for Lyla in hopes of alleviating whatever allergic reaction was causing her such distress.

Just four months after her initial visit to Dr. Sander, Lyla died from a massive stroke. At first Tammy and the rest of Lyla's family assumed that the stroke was a random event, and they made no connection between the "allergies" that Lyla had complained about and her death. One day, however, Tammy mentioned Lyla's symptoms to a friend's father who was an immunologist. After hearing the list of Lyla's problems, this physician was sure that Lyla must have had Pemphigus, and he was shocked that Dr. Sander hadn't considered that possibility. At his urging, Tammy hired a lawyer who began investigating her mother's case.

The initial complaint that Tammy's lawyer filed in state court asked for $1 million from Dr. Sander (and his insurance company) for Lyla's death. Tammy alleges that Dr. Sander's negligent misdiagnosis caused her mother's premature death by delaying treatment and aggravating her condition through the prescription of steroids (which raised her blood pressure and made her symptoms worse, not better). The stroke, according to Tammy, was a direct result of this improper medical care. To date, Dr.

---

2. For a discussion of the law and economics of medical malpractice, see Bovbjerg, Medical Malpractice: Research and Reform, 79 Va.L.Rev. 2155 (1993); Frankel, Medical Malpractice Law and Health Care Cost Containment: Lessons for Reformers from the Clash of Cultures, 103 Yale L.J. 1297 (1994); Liang, Medical Malpractice: Do Physicians Have Knowledge of Legal Standards and Assess Cases as Juries Do?, 3 U.Chi.L.Sch. Roundtable 59 (1996); Silver, One Hundred Years of Harmful Error: The Historical Jurisprudence of Medical Malpractice, 1992 Wis. L.Rev. 1193.

Several legal scholars have written about medical malpractice and informal dispute resolution. See Farber and White, A Comparison of Formal and Informal Dispute Resolution in Medical Malpractice, 23 J.Leg.Stud. 777 (1994); Wheeler, Medical Malpractice Dispute Resolution: A Prescription for the New Millenium, 28 Cap.U.L.Rev. 249 (2000); Dauer, Marcus & Payne, Prometheus and the Litigators: A Mediation Odyssey, 21 J.Leg.Med. 159 (2000).

A. THE STRUCTURE OF NEGOTIATION — 81

Sander has agreed to pay $30,000, which he says is a "good faith gesture" to settle the claim.

These wildly divergent initial positions are just part of the story. In addition to these initial offers or demands, each party also generally has (or should have) a *reservation value*—the point at which that party is indifferent between staying in the negotiation and walking away. Here, the reservation values are the minimum amount Tammy will accept to settle the claim and the maximum amount that Dr. Sander will pay. For example, if Tammy will accept $250,000 to drop her lawsuit, that is her reservation value. If offered less she will walk away rather than settle.

Although sometimes negotiators arbitrarily invent a "bottom line," reservation values should be tied to the parties' Best Alternative To a Negotiated Agreement (or *BATNA*), a term invented by Roger Fisher, William Ury and Bruce Patton. See Fisher, Ury and Patton, Getting to Yes 100 (2d ed., 1991). The set of a negotiator's alternatives is made up of all those actions that the negotiator can take away from the table if no agreement is reached. The BATNA is the best alternative in that set. For example, if you are choosing whether to leave your current job and accept an offer from another employer, the set of alternatives open to you consists of all of the offers you have so far received. Your BATNA is the offer that you would most likely take if you leave your current position—it is, in your estimation, the best of those available to you.

Your reservation price is not the same thing as your BATNA, but they are related. For example, imagine that your best alternative to your current job is to work for a competing company in another city. The competing company has offered you $100,000 per year, which is a substantial increase from your present salary. If you can't negotiate a raise from your current boss, you will take this job offer—it is your best alternative *away from the table* in your negotiation with your boss. What is your reservation value? In other words, how will you know when to walk away from your negotiations with your boss? You need to translate your BATNA into a reservation value that you can keep in mind while you negotiate. To do so, you must factor in any intangible costs associated with that BATNA. For example, perhaps staying in your current home and not being forced to transfer locations is worth something to you—for simplicity's sake, imagine that it is worth $10,000 to you *not* to have to move. If that is the only variable that affects your evaluation of your BATNA, then your reservation value in your negotiation with your boss is $90,000—so long as your boss offers $90,000 or greater, you would prefer to stay in your current job rather than walk to your BATNA.

The bargaining range is determined by these reservation values. In our medical example, imagine that Dr. Sander would be willing to pay up to $750,000 to settle Tammy's claim.[3] Because the parties' reservation values overlap, there is a *zone of possible agreement* (or ZOPA for short) in this negotiation. We can illustrate this ZOPA using a simple diagram. (See Figure 1.)

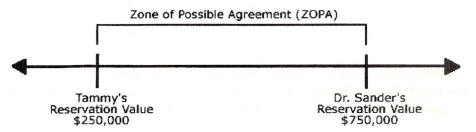

3. In litigation, both parties usually share the same alternative to negotiating a resolution of their dispute: proceeding to court. Theoretically, then, their reservation values should be fairly close, adjusted for risk preferences and transaction costs. We discuss how one analyzes a litigation alternative in section A(3)(b), below. In addition, we consider the subjective nature of analyzing one's BATNA or reservation value and the ways in which one's perspective or biases may influence this analysis.

Assuming that Tammy and Dr. Sander focus solely on the single issue of money, they face a zero-sum negotiation in which all that they must decide is how to distribute the $500,000 ZOPA, or *surplus*, between them. Any settlement between their reservation values is better for each than refusing to settle, but of course not all agreements within the ZOPA are equally good for one party or the other. For example, if they ultimately settled for $700,000, Tammy would claim most of the surplus—she would get the better deal. If they settled for $300,000, Dr. Sander would claim the majority of the surplus. If they split the difference between their reservation values and reached agreement at $500,000, they would divide the surplus equally. They must negotiate over this *distributive issue* to resolve their dispute.

Of course, Tammy is unlikely to know the most that Dr. Sander will pay, and he is unlikely to tell her. Similarly, he will not know that Tammy would accept an offer of as little as $250,000. We will discuss strategy in Section B, but for now we can assume from their extreme initial positions— $1 million versus $30,000—that each is trying to claim as much value as he or she can in this distributive bargaining situation.

2. MULTIPLE ISSUES

Although the one-issue case is convenient as a starting point, many negotiations—perhaps most—involve more than one issue. If you are buying a house, most of the bargaining may focus on the sale price. But timing may be contested as well—you might prefer to close the deal quickly because your apartment lease is expiring, while the seller wants to delay until he closes on the new house he has purchased in another city. You might also bargain over the amount of the down payment, mortgage contingencies, who should pay for various improvements or repairs, or what fixtures to include in the sale. All of these variables may be in play simultaneously as you and the seller attempt to reach a deal.

If each issue is considered in isolation, the addition of these multiple variables merely complicates the distributive bargaining. You now not only want to secure the lowest possible price but also to push the seller as far as possible on timing, fixtures, financing and the other issues on the table. Viewed separately, each new issue is simply another item to be bargained over.

Considered in combination, however, multiple issues can dramatically alter a negotiation by introducing the possibility of trade-offs *between* issues. For example, timing might be extremely important to you but only moderately important to the seller—he can stay with a friend for a few weeks quite easily if you move the closing date forward. Conversely, having a larger cash deposit might be extremely valuable to him—because he wants to ensure that you won't walk away from the deal—but relatively easy for you to provide because you have the cash on hand. You and the seller might be better off if your agreement takes advantage of these different priorities by providing for an early closing date in exchange for a large cash deposit. Each of you then captures value on the issue you care about, in return for sacrificing on an issue that is less important to you.

The possibility of such trade-offs between issues can transform a multiple issue negotiation from a zero-sum situation—in which when I gain, you lose—to a positive-sum bargain in which both parties can be made better off through trades. In economic terms, a negotiated agreement is *efficient* if the parties have captured all of the possible gains from trade. Finding such efficiencies is often called integrative, "win-win," positive-sum, joint gains, or value-creating negotiation. Regardless of the label we affix, the point is simple but powerful. In a multiple issue negotiation, the parties can "expand the pie," not merely slice it up.

a. PARETO OPTIMALITY

Returning to the example of Tammy and Dr. Sander, we can illustrate the concept of efficiency using a two-dimensional graph. Figure 2 shows Tammy's utility—the benefit she would receive from a given negotiated solution—on the vertical axis and Dr. Sander's utility on the horizontal axis.

Imagine that Solution I represents a simple compromise: Dr. Sander pays Tammy $500,000. Both Tammy and the defendant get some satisfaction from this agreement. It is certainly better for each than no agreement at all. But now add a second issue to the negotiation: whether Dr. Sander will agree to attend training about Pemphigus so that he will be less likely to make such a mistake in the future. Tammy and her family might get great benefit from knowing that Dr. Sander will attend such a training.

Imagine that Solution A represents a payment of $500,000 *plus* an agreement from Dr. Sander to attend a training session. This solution is better for Tammy than Solution I: she receives the same financial compensation plus the intangible benefits of having done something to help future patients. And Solution A is just as good for Dr. Sander as Solution I— imagine that the training is free and that the costs in terms of his time and effort are balanced equally by the benefit he receives from learning more about this disease. So long as Dr. Sander is not envious of Tammy's improved position, he will be indifferent between Solution A and Solution I.

Figure 2

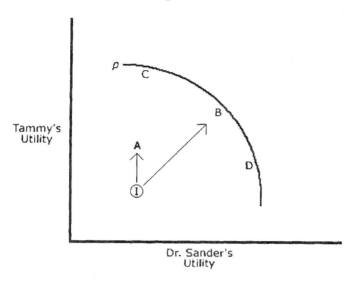

Because Solution A is better for one party—Tammy—without being worse for another, we say that Solution A is *Pareto superior* to Solution I.[4]

Now consider incorporating a related issue into the negotiation: rather than merely attending a training session, what if Dr. Sander were to agree to implement a hospital-wide education campaign to inform his colleagues about Pemphigus? This campaign would cost Dr. Sander time, money and energy. Tammy and her family, however, would value this campaign even more than they value Dr. Sander attending an educational training session. This seems like a straight distributive issue—she wants him to do the campaign, he doesn't want to incur the costs.

But what if Tammy were willing to sacrifice on one issue—dollars—to trade for the educational campaign? Assume that the intangible, emotional benefit to Tammy of implementing such a program is worth $50,000. In other words, she would accept up to $50,000 less in return for an agreement that includes such programs. Similarly, assume that the cost to Dr. Sander of implementing an educational campaign is roughly $20,000. Clearly, the value of such measures to Tammy is significantly greater than the cost to Dr. Sander. Assuming they started from Solution I—the simple compromise at $500,000—*both would be better off* by moving to Solution B—an agreement that includes $475,000, the training and an educational campaign.[5] All else being equal, both would prefer Solution B to Solution I.

---

4. Vilfredo Pareto was a 19th century economist who is credited with proposing this definition of efficiency.

5. Tammy would be better off because she receives the equivalent of $525,000 in value ($475,000 plus the educational programs that she values at $50,000). Dr. Sand-

CHAPTER II NEGOTIATION

These parties might find a variety of other issues that they could also work into value-creating trades. They might jointly contribute to a national Pemphigus foundation. Tammy might be involved with Dr. Sander's educational campaign. Over time, Tammy might find it extremely beneficial to receive recent articles and information about Pemphigus from medical journals and sources. It might be easy for Dr. Sander to provide her with such reference materials, and extremely difficult or costly for her to gain access to them on her own. Finally, an apology might also create value in this negotiation. It may be relatively easy for Dr. Sander to apologize, and it may be of great benefit to Tammy and her family.[6]

If Solutions C and D in Figure 2 represent some of these other value-creating agreements that Tammy and Dr. Sander could explore, then Line p—connecting Solutions C, B and D—represents what economists call the *Pareto frontier* or the *efficiency frontier*. See Raiffa, The Art and Science of Negotiation 139 (1982). This frontier is made up of all of the *Pareto optimal* solutions in a negotiation. A solution is Pareto optimal if there is no other solution that can make one party better off without making the other party worse off. In other words, the parties have exploited all of the achievable joint gains—there are no solutions Pareto superior to a Pareto optimal one.

Two points about the efficiency frontier deserve mention. First, the frontier is finite—there is only so much value that the parties can create in a given interaction. Second, as between possible agreements *along* the frontier—as between Solutions B, C, or D, for example—the parties face a distributive negotiation. Although each solution on the frontier is efficient or value-creating vis-à-vis other, less efficient solutions (such as I or A), each solution on the frontier will be better for one party or the other. Both parties, for example, would prefer Solution C to Solution A, but choosing Solution *B* over Solution C would make Dr. Sander better off but Tammy worse off. Thus, even in multiple issue negotiations where the parties can exploit joint gains, certain distributive issues remain.

b. SOURCES OF VALUE

In a real negotiation, of course, neither party is likely to know all of the possible solutions nor the priorities and preferences that suggest trade-offs between different agreements. In our Section B on "Strategy" we turn to the strategies and tactics that negotiators can use to try to find efficient outcomes and expand the pie—*how* to engage in value-creating or integrative negotiation. First, however, we explore the sources of value-creating solutions—*what* value-creating trades are economically based on.

Shared interests or preferences are the first and most intuitive source of value-creating agreements. If we both like pizza, it makes sense to

---

er would be better off because he pays only $495,000 instead of $500,000 ($475,000 plus the educational programs that cost him only $20,000).

6. For a discussion of apology in litigation, see Cohen, Apology and Organizations: Exploring an Example from Medical Practice, 27 Fordham Urban L.J. 1447 (2000); Cohen, Advising Clients to Apologize, 72 S.Cal.L.Rev. 1009 (1999).

choose that for dinner rather than to go to a burger joint. We will both be better off. Similarly, both parties may wish to benefit a third party—if two divorcing parents both care deeply about the well-being of their children, they will want to craft custodial and visitation arrangements that are in their kids' best interests. Creating workable terms on this issue will make both better off than they would be if conflict permeated their future relationship. Conversely, two parties may be able to maximize their joint utility at the expense of a third party: disputants might share an interest in minimizing the tax consequences of their settlement agreement, for example (at the expense of the government). If two parties can find such non-competitive similarities, they can create value. See Mnookin, Peppet, and Tulumello, Beyond Winning: Negotiating to Create Value in Deals and Disputes 16 (2000).

In addition to shared interests, *differences* between the parties are a major source of value-creating trades. Although the parties' stated positions may seem to conflict, sometimes their interests are merely different, not opposed. In the 1920s, Mary Parker Follett, a pioneer in conflict and management studies, described a now classic example:

> [W]hen two desires are integrated, that means that a solution has been found in which both desires have found a place, that neither has had to sacrifice anything. Let us take some very simple illustration. In the Harvard Library one day, in one of the smaller rooms, someone wanted the window open, I wanted it shut. We opened the window in the next room, where no one was sitting. This was not a compromise, because there was no curtailing of desire; we both got what we really wanted. For I did not want a closed room, I simply did not want the North wind to blow directly on me; likewise the other occupant did not want that particular window open, he merely wanted more air in the room.

Follett, Constructive Conflict (1925), in Graham (ed.), Follett: Prophet of Management 69 (1995). See also Kolb, The Love for Three Oranges, or What Did We Miss about Ms Follett in the Library?, 11 Neg.J. (1995).

The following two excerpts explore the ways in which differences can generate integrative bargaining solutions.

David Lax and James Sebenius, The Manager as Negotiator

90–102 (1986).

Gain from negotiation often exists because negotiators *differ* from one another. Since they are not identical—in tastes, forecasts, endowments, capabilities, or in other ways—they each have something to offer that is relatively less valuable to them than to those with whom they are bargaining. * * *

* * *

That differences lie at the heart of many joint gains follows readily from the fact that two utterly identical individuals may have no basis for any negotiation: neither has or wants anything that the other does not. If differences are admitted among many dimensions, however, negotiation opens up the prospect of joint gains. For example, gains may arise from differences in interests, in possessions, in forecasts, in aversion to risk, in attitudes toward the passage of time, in capabilities, in access to technology, and in other areas.

Since joint gains often derive from such differences, a primary orientation of managers, negotiators, and mediators should be toward discovering and dovetailing them. In line with this observation, this section will argue on behalf of two broad prescriptions:

1. When contemplating the potential gains from agreement, begin with a careful inventory of all the ways that the parties differ from one another—not how they are alike.

2. The basic principle underlying the realization of joint gains from differences is to match what one side finds or expects to be relatively costless with what the other finds or expects to be most valuable, and vice versa.

* * *

DIFFERENCES OF INTEREST IMPLY EXCHANGES

If a vegetarian with some meat bargains with a carnivore who owns some vegetables, it is precisely the *difference* in their known preferences that can facilitate reaching an agreement. No one would counsel the vegetarian to persuade the carnivore of the zucchini's succulent taste. More complicated negotiations may concern several items. Although the parties may have opposing preferences on the settlement of each issue, they may feel most strongly about different issues. An overall agreement can reflect these different preferences by resolving the issues of relatively greater importance to one side more in favor of that side. A package or "horse trade" can be constructed this way so that, as a whole, all prefer it to no agreement.

* * * This theory applies not only to trading discrete things but also to constructing agreements that respond to different underlying interests. One party may primarily fear the precedential effects of a settlement; another may care about the particulars of the current question; thus, both might profit by contriving a unique-looking agreement on the immediate issue. One side may be keen on a political "victory"; the other may want quiet accommodation for a particular constituency. Whether the differences are between vegetables and meat, form and substance, ideology and practice, reputation and results, or the intrinsic versus the instrumental qualities of a settlement, cleverly crafted agreements can often dovetail differences into joint gains.

From an economic viewpoint, then, differences in relative valuation can lead to the possibility of gain from exchange and thus can improve the likelihood of reaching agreement. This contention is consistent with the proposition of the noted analyst of social behavior, George Homans: "The more the items at stake can be divided into goods valued more by one party than they cost to the first, the greater the chances of a successful outcome."

* * *

[Consider the example of a] midwestern utility that wanted to build a dam. The company had become embroiled in a dispute with farmers about downstream water flow and with conservationists worried about the effects of water diversion on the downstream habitat of the endangered whooping crane. After years of wrangling, the utility offered to guarantee downstream waterflow and to pay $7.5 million to purchase additional water rights or otherwise to protect the whooping crane habitat. Although both the utility and the conservationists saw the offer on the issue of financial compensation as generous, the utility was surprised that the conservationists rejected it.

After much more discussion, the utility came to understand that the conservationists' personal control over the money might make it appear as if they were being paid off and reduce their credibility with conservationist groups. An acceptable settlement had to unbundle the issue of financial compensation in a way that separated compensation and control. So, the parties created a $7.5 million trust fund to protect the whooping crane with a strict covenant that limited its trustees' control over the fund. To reach agreement, the parties needed to learn a great deal about the others' real interests. They had to identify differentially valued interests that were unnecessarily bundled. Then, they needed to invent ways to modify the issues and unbundled the interests to permit joint gains.

* * *

PROBABILITY DIFFERENCE SUGGEST CONTINGENT ARRANGEMENTS

At the heart of the sale of an investment property may be the buyer's belief that its price will rise and the seller's conviction that it will drop. The deal is facilitated by differences in belief about what will happen. * * *

Probability assessments of uncertain events derive from the combination of prior beliefs and observed evidence; discrepancies in either of these factors may form the basis for contingent agreements. We have already observed that value differences can lead to horse trades. Analogously, for probabilities, Mark Twain noted that "it is difference of opinion that makes horse races." Two classes of situations suggest themselves in which contingent agreements based on different expectations may produce joint gains.

Issues Subject to Different Odds. In the first case, outcomes of the event under discussion may be uncertain and subject to different probability estimates. * * * For example, an engineering firm had completed plans for a plant designed to burn garbage, to produce steam, and to convert it into electricity. The firm was negotiating with a medium-sized southern city over the sale of this electricity to the city. The city wanted to pay a lower price; the company insisted on a much higher one. As the discussions proceeded and then stalled, it became clear that the city representatives expected an oil glut and hence a drop in the price of the fuel most important to its electrical generation. The company believed that an oil price rise was much more likely. After protracted talks, the two sides could not agree on a set price for the sale of the plant's electricity to the city. Finally, however, they agreed to tie that price to the future cost of oil. Thus, the city expected to pay a lower price while the company expected to receive a higher price. While they also negotiated an upper and lower cap on the range of acceptable fluctuations, both sides could live with either outcome, and the plant went forward.

* * *

Different Assessments of the Attractiveness of Proposed Procedures. Contingent agreements may be employed in a second common class of situations where the parties believe that they can positively affect the chances for favorable outcome of an uncertain event. Consider the voluntary submission of a dispute to arbitration. Firmly believing the persuasiveness of its position and highly confident in the quality of its representation before the tribunal, each side may feel that its chances of obtaining the desired outcome are very good. * * *

* * *

DIFFERENCES IN RISK AVERSION LEAD TO RISK–SHARING SCHEMES

Suppose that two people agree on the probabilities of an uncertain prospect. Even so, they may still react differently to taking the risks involved. In such cases, they may devise a variety of ways to share the risk. In general, such mechanisms should shift more of the risk to the party who is less risk-averse than the other. For example, suppose that Mr. Broussard, a single, fairly wealthy, middle-aged accountant, and Ms. Armitage, a younger, less-well-off lawyer with significant family responsibilities, are planning to buy and operate a business together. The younger, more risk-averse Ms. Armitage may prefer to take a larger but fixed salary while Mr. Broussard may prefer a smaller set salary but much larger share of any profits. Though they may expect the same total amount of money to be paid in compensation, both parties are better off than had they, say, both chosen either fixed salaries or larger contingent payments.

* * *

DIFFERENCES IN TIME PREFERENCES SUGGEST ALTERED PAYMENT PATTERNS

People may value the same event quite differently, depending on when it occurs. If one side is relatively less impatient than the other, mechanisms for optimally sharing the consequences over time may be devised.

* * * Consider a highly stylized example. Suppose that Ms. Kanwate has a 10 percent discount rate, that Mr. Hurree's rate is 20 percent, and that each party cares about the present value of income.[8] Ms. Kanwate will receive $100 next year; Mr. Hurree is slated to receive $100 the year afterward. Thus the present value of her income is about $91 and his is $69.[9] The two could engineer a variety of profitable trades to dovetail this difference. Because Mr. Hurree values early income relatively more than does Mr. Kanwate, though, he should get the first year's $100. If, in the second year, Ms. Kanwate gets $100 plus $20 from him, the present value of her income rises from $91 in the original division to $99. The present value of Mr. Hurree's income stream (+ $100 in a year,—$20 in two years) remains at about $69. If he gave $10 to Ms. Kanwate in the second period, she could have the same present value as in the original division ($91), while the present value of his income would be $76 instead of the original $69. Any outcome in which he gets the first $100 and she gets between $110 and $120 in the second period is as good as or better than the original division for both parties.

Max H. Bazerman and James J. Gillespie, Betting on the Future: The Virtues of Contingent Contracts

Harvard Bus.Rev. 155, 156–160 (Sept.–Oct. 1999).

It used to be assumed that differences were always a source of contention in negotiations, limiting the parties' ability to reach an agreement. But in recent years, negotiation scholars have shown that differences are often constructive. They provide the basis for tradeoffs that can pave the way to mutually beneficial agreements. When the differences have to do with uncertain future events that are critically important to both parties, however, trade-offs become very difficult to make. By making the differences the basis for a bet that offers potential gains to both parties, contingent contracts enable negotiators to avoid long, costly, and often futile arguments. * * *

Consider how a contingent contract might have changed the course of one of the century's most famous (and fruitless) antitrust cases. In 1969, the U.S. Department of Justice filed suit against IBM, alleging monopolistic behavior. More than a decade later, the case was still bogged down in litigation. Some 65 million pages of documents had been produced, and

8. The "future value" of a present amount of money reflects the compounding of interest forward over time. The "present value" of a future amount of money reverses this process, "discounting" it back to the present amount that, if compounded forward at the same interest (or discount) rate, would just equal the future amount.

9. That is, because Ms. Kanwate has alternative investment possibilities that re-

turn 10 percent, her getting $100 in a year is equivalent to placing $91 now in the alternative investment and taking out the $100 it will produce a year later. Similarly, for Mr. Hurree, getting $100 in two years is equivalent to putting $69 now in an investment that returns 20 percent and, two years hence, drawing the $100 produced by the investment.

92   CHAPTER II NEGOTIATION

each side had spent millions of dollars in legal expenses. The DOJ finally dropped the case in 1982, when it was clear that IBM's once-dominant share of the computer market was eroding rapidly.

During the case's 13 years, IBM and the DOJ had essentially been arguing over differences in expectations. IBM assumed that its market share would decrease in coming years as competition in the lucrative computer market increased. The DOJ assumed that IBM, as a monopolist, would hold its dominant market share for the foreseeable future. Because neither felt the other's view was valid, neither would compromise.

A contingent contract would have been an efficient and rational way to settle this dispute. IBM and the government might have agreed, for example, that if by 1975 IBM still held at least 70% of the market—its share in 1969—it would pay a set fine and divest itself of certain businesses. If, however, its market share had dropped to 50% or lower, the government would not pursue antitrust actions. If its share fell somewhere between 50% and 70%, another contingency plan would be executed.

Constructing such a contract would not have been easy. There were, after all, an infinite number of feasible permutations, and many details would have had to have been hammered out. But it would have been far more rational—and far cheaper—to have lawyers from both sides devote a few weeks to arguing over how to structure a contingent contract than it was for them to spend years filing motions, taking depositions, and reviewing documents. We would suggest, parenthetically, that a similar course might have been taken in the dispute between Microsoft and the U.S. government.

* * *

While we believe that contingent contracts are valuable in many kinds of business negotiations, they're not right in every situation. [Negotiators] should keep three points in mind:

First, contingent contracts require *continuing interaction* between the parties. After all, the final outcome of the contract will not be determined until sometime after the initial agreement is signed. Therefore, negotiators need to consider the nature of their future relationship with the other party. If the parties are seeking a spot transaction, or if there's outright ill will between the two, they should probably not enter into a contingent contract.

Second, negotiators need to think about the *enforceability* of a contract. Under a contingent contract, it is probable that one or more of the parties will not receive its full value up front. In some cases, the deferred value may represent a significant portion of the overall value. What if the loser of the bet refuses to pay up? What should the winner do? There are many ways to solve such issues—placing the money in escrow, for instance. Our main message is, don't bet if you can't collect.

Third, contingent contracts require *transparency*. The future event the parties bet on must be one that both sides can observe and measure and

A. THE STRUCTURE OF NEGOTIATION **93**

that neither side can covertly manipulate. Vague bets set the stage for different interpretations later. The terms of the bet should be clearly delineated by the contract.

NOTES AND QUESTIONS

1. George Bernard Shaw stated the basic principle behind trading on differences when he said, "It is unwise to do unto others as you would have them do unto you. Their tastes may not be the same." Although negotiators often assume that reaching agreement requires uncovering *similarities*, mining differences for mutually-beneficial trades is often most rewarding. As a thought experiment, consider the ways in which you might create value through trading on differences in the following examples. For each example, identify whether you would be trading on differences in resources or capabilities, relative valuations, predictions about the future (probabilities), risk preferences, or timing preferences.

  a. You are buying a used car from a dealer but worry that the new clutch the dealer installed may be a lemon. The dealer has mechanics in his shop that could easily repair the clutch if it breaks. What might you do to create value in this negotiation?

  b. You are negotiating an executive compensation agreement for a client who is becoming Chief Financial Officer at BigCorp. Your client fears that a change in corporate control is imminent if BigCorp. gets taken over by a competitor, and in that event he might lose he new job. He initially demands a $1 million signing bonus to protect himself against that imminent possibility. BigCorp.'s lawyer refuses, insisting that the company is not a likely takeover candidate. What might you do?

  c. You represent a client in a negotiation over the division of a family estate. Your client has one sibling, and they are the only two heirs. There are five items in dispute: a beautiful antique grandfather clock (worth $120,000), a small painting by Picasso ($50,000), a photo album with rare pictures of the sibling's now deceased parents and grandparents (worth $200), a small silver brooch often worn by their mother (worth $6,500), and a baby grand piano (value unknown). The siblings live far from each other and will be unable, and unwilling, to share the items over time. Assuming that the two siblings have intangible interests—such as emotional attachment—in addition to their desire for financial gain, how will you ensure that the estate division is most efficient, in the sense that it allocates the five items to create the most value possible? Will an efficient division necessarily be "fair?"[7]

---

7. For an innovative and useful discussion of decision-making procedures that can be useful in crafting efficient outcomes in such circumstances, see Brams and Taylor, The Win–Win Solution (1999).

2. In addition to exploiting shared interests and the categories of differences that Lax and Sebenius describe, negotiators can create value by generating *economies of scale*. If two people carpool to work it is significantly cheaper than if they drive separately. Similarly, it is less expensive for a couple to live together—and share a stereo, appliances, heat, etc.—than to maintain separate residences. As we consume together, the individual cost of consumption drops. Finding such efficiencies is another way to create value in negotiations. See Lax and Sebenius, The Manager as Negotiator 90–102 (1986); Mnookin, Peppet and Tulumello, Beyond Winning: Negotiating To Create Value in Deals and Disputes 16 (2000).

3. Value-creating trades are the foundation of most economic exchange. You can easily discover opportunities for such trades. Try this simple exercise with another student in your class or with a friend or neighbor. Take two minutes together—time yourselves—and try to find ways that you could trade to make one or both of you better off. Perhaps you each subscribe to a magazine that the other would like to read? After finishing reading your magazine you could swap each month to get a chance to enjoy the other's subscription. Maybe you know how to ski and she knows how to set up a computer? You could take your friend for a daylong skiing lesson in exchange for her setting up your printer and explaining how to back up your computer files. Look for trades in goods, capabilities or services, timing, or risk-preferences. Also look for shared interests and for economies of scale.

4. Finding value-creating opportunities can require in-depth understanding of the economics and trade-offs in a given context. Experienced negotiators sometimes don't even realize they are "expanding the pie"—they just know how the various issues connect in their context and where trades are typically found. The following description from David Falk, a sports agent and attorney, illustrates that finding trade-offs can be central to a negotiator's task:

> * * * Every deal has trade-offs; they are the essence of the bargaining process. You can call it bargaining, negotiating, or horse-trading. There are some basic trade-offs I use when I am negotiating a deal. The first is the length of the contract. You must understand the needs and goals of your client. Does he want security? Does he want to maximize the amount of dollars protected in case he fails to reach an expected level of performance? Or does he want flexibility, so if the market changes substantially in the first two or three years of his contract, he has the ability to renegotiate as a free agent? * * * [Consider] the case of Stanley Roberts, * * * the twenty-third pick in the 1991 [NBA] draft. * * * Most general managers thought that he was overweight, was not a very hard worker, and therefore was a risky pick. Roberts averaged ten points and six rebounds a game as a rookie. But he was a center, and centers are extremely hard to obtain in the NBA. As a result, at the conclusion of his one-year contract, four or five teams bid for him. He signed a contract averaging in excess of $3 million a year. Had he come out of school and signed a great contract

for the twenty-third pick, let's say $1 million a year, but locked himself up for five years, he would have cost himself a tremendous amount of money. Because he was in a position to get only a one-year deal, it ended up working to his benefit. The decision whether to sign long-term or short-term is a critical one that demands full discussion with your client. You cannot make judgments *for* your client. You have to make judgments *with* your client. You have to point out the benefits of security and the detriments of locking him in for a long period of time and having to renegotiate a contract when you do not have a lot of leverage.

The second trade-off is guarantees. In basketball, eighty-three percent of all contracts are guaranteed for either skill or injury. This means that if the club terminates the contract, it remains obligated to pay the player. In football, a very small percentage of contracts are guaranteed. Since guarantees provide security, teams will often pay a player more dollars if he will take fewer guarantees. Conversely, teams may propose that the player sacrifice dollars in order to get the entire contract guaranteed.

The third trade-off is current cash dollars versus deferred money.
* * *

* * *

Another area of trade-offs is incentive bonuses. * * * [W]hen you are negotiating a contract and you are apart in your positions, one area available to you to close the deal is incentive bonuses. * * * When you have "maxed out" guaranteed cash, but you have not closed the deal, bonuses are a creative trade-off in closing the gap.

Falk, The Art of Contract Negotiation, 3 Marquette Sports L.J. 1, 12–14 (1992).

5. Some commentators have tried to clarify what exactly constitutes win-win or integrative bargaining and what distinguishes it from distributive negotiation. Gerald Wetlaufer makes the following distinctions between what he calls Form I, II and III value creation:

For purposes of clarification, I will distinguish three forms of value creation, only one of which constitutes an opportunity for integrative or win-win bargaining. The first of these forms is found where the pie can be made larger only in the sense that is true of all bargaining including bargaining that is merely distributive. In such circumstances, there is a zone of agreement * * * within which both parties will be better off than they would have been in the absence of the agreement. Thus, in this minimal sense, purely distributive bargaining can be said to "create value" or "expand the pie." I shall call this "Form I" value creation. * * *

* * * Form II value creation is possible when there is one issue (e.g., the amount of money to be paid for some product), and one party cares more about that issue than does the other. This is a situation in which, assuming there is a range of possible agreements that would leave both parties better off, there is an opportunity for Form I value creation in that the aggregate benefits to the parties will vary depending on whether or not they can reach agreement. Also, and this is what distinguishes Form II value creation, this is a situation in which the aggregate benefits to the parties, the size of the pie, will vary across the range of possible agreements. Thus, the total value created by the agreement will be relatively large if most of that over which the parties are negotiating (e.g., surplus as measured in dollars) is captured by the party who cares more about that issue. Similarly, the total value created by the agreement will be relatively small if most of the surplus is captured by the party who cares less about that issue.

An opportunity for Form II value creation is not an opportunity for integrative bargaining because the possible agreements are arrayed along a single continuum such that any possible agreement is, in its relationship to any other, better for one party but worse for the other. One cannot move from any one possible agreement to any other possible agreement in such a way that both parties are made better off by the move. Nor can one even move from one possible agreement to another in such a way that one party is better off and the other is no worse off. Thus Form II value creation, like Form I, does not involve integrative bargaining.

Only what I shall call "Form III" value creation offers an opportunity for integrative or win-win bargaining. Unlike Forms I and II, Form III value creation involves that kind of pie-expansion or value creation in which the parties can reach a range of different agreements, in which the size of the pie will vary across the range of possible agreements (also true of Form II), but in which some of those agreements leave both parties better off than do others. If there are some possible agreements that both parties would regard as better than others, then the size of the pie created by the agreements depends both upon the parties' ability to reach some agreement (Form I value creation) and upon their wit and ability to arrive at one of the better agreements. It is in this sense that a situation presenting an opportunity for Form III value creation is a non-zero sum game and an opportunity for integrative or win-win bargaining.

Wetlaufer, The Limits of Integrative Bargaining, 85 Georgetown L.J. 369, 374–375 (1996).

Review the discussion of possible trades in Tammy and Dr. Sander's negotiation. Are those Form I, II, or III value creation, according to Wetlaufer's scheme? What about the example earlier in this section having to do with the purchase of a house—and trades based on closing date and the down payment amount? Does Wetlaufer's distinction make a difference? Why or why not?

3. THE ROLE OF INFORMATION

As this discussion of single-issue and multiple-issue bargaining shows, information plays a critical role in both distributive and integrative negoti-

A. The Structure of Negotiation

ation. To create value, each side must know its own interests, preferences and priorities—as well as something about the other side's—to be able to find trades. To approach distributive issues, each party must at least know its own best alternative and reservation value *and* try to estimate the other side's.

In legal disputes, attorneys are often at the table negotiating on behalf of their clients, who may or may not be present for the actual bargaining. A lawyer, therefore, must prepare herself for a negotiation by uncovering the information she will need to conduct that negotiation successfully. What information should an attorney search for in advance of a negotiation? What does she need to know to be able to create value-creating trades? To resolve distributive issues? How much of that information should she try to learn from her client before (and during) her negotiation, and how much will she have to find elsewhere? And what will she need to tell her client both before and during the negotiation?

Here we explore the role of information and the lawyer's role as gatherer and organizer of that information. To begin, we consider the information that a lawyer must learn in order to find integrative solutions to a client's problem. We then turn to the problem of estimating the value of a client's best alternative in a legal dispute.

a. INTERESTS, RESOURCES AND PREFERENCES

If a lawyer is "in the middle" between her client and the other side, that lawyer must be prepared to find value-creating trades if such trades are possible. This requires that an attorney discover her client's interests, resources and preferences in order to be able to base deals upon them. Are lawyers well suited to this task? In the following excerpt, noted bargaining scholar Carrie Menkel–Meadow argues that they are not. Instead, she claims, lawyers are more prone to "narrowing" a dispute—not broadening it to find creative, integrative solutions.

Carrie Menkel–Meadow, The Transformation of Disputes by Lawyers: What the Dispute Paradigm Does and Does Not Tell Us

J. of Disp.Res. 25, 31–33 (1985).

The literature on lawyer transformation of disputes is rather accusatory. In general, if the *who* of dispute processing is a lawyer one may assume that the lawyer will make the dispute worse, much as medical treatment may make the illness worse. Lawyers are said to exacerbate disputes by increasing the demands and conflicts and narrow disputes by translating into limited legal categories what might have been broader and more general. * * *

For Mather & Yngvesson, the principal transformation of disputes occurs in their *rephrasing*, that is, "some kind of reformulation into a public discourse." Thus, the grievant tells a story of felt or perceived wrong to a third party (the lawyer) and the lawyer transforms the dispute by imposing "categories" on "events and relationships" which redefine the subject matter of the dispute in ways "which make it amenable to conventional management procedures." This process of "narrowing" disputes occurs at various stages in lawyer-client interactions * * * First, the lawyer may begin to narrow the dispute in the initial client interview. By asking questions which derive from the lawyer's repertoire of what is likely to be legally relevant, the lawyer defines the situation from the very beginning. Rather than permitting the client to tell a story freely to define what the dispute consists of, the lawyer begins to categorize the case as a "tort," "contract," or "property" dispute so that questions may be asked for legal saliency. This may narrow the context of a dispute which has more complicated fact patterns and may involve some mix of legal and non-legal categories of dispute. A classic example of such a mixed dispute is a landlord-tenant case in which relationship issues and political issues (such as in rent control areas) intermingle with strictly legal issues of rent obligation, maintenance obligation, and nuisance. Thus, during the initial contact the lawyer narrows what is "wrong" by trying to place the dispute in a legal context which the lawyer feels he can handle.

Even if the client is allowed to tell his lawyer a broader story, the lawyer will narrow or rephrase the story in his efforts to seek remediation. Beginning with an effort to negotiate with the other side, the lawyer will construct a story which is recognizable to the other lawyer so that he can demand a stock remedial solution. In recent social, psychological, and legal literature this process has been called the telling of "stock stories." The "stock stories" can be likened to a legal cause of action with prescribed elements which must be pleaded in a particular way in the legal system to state a "claim for which relief can be granted." If pre-litigation negotiation fails and the lawyer begins to craft a lawsuit, the dispute will be further narrowed by the special language requirements of the substantive law, pleading rules, and the rules of procedure. * * *

Once negotiation commences the dispute is further narrowed, the issues become stylized, and statements of what is disputed become ritualized because of the very process and constraints of litigation. In negotiation, lawyers begin to demand what they will ask the court to do if the case goes to trial. Lawyers are told to plan "minimum disposition," "target," and "reservation" points that are based on an analysis of what would happen if the case went to trial. Because a court resolution of the problem will result in a binary win/loss ruling, lawyers begin to conceive of the negotiation process as simply an earlier version of court adjudication. Thus, lawyers seek to persuade each other, using many of the same principles and normative entreaties that they will use in court, that they are right and ought to prevail now, before either party suffers further monetary or temporal loss. The remedies lawyers seek from each other may be sharply limited to what they think would be possible in a court case considering the court's remedial powers. Thus, most negotiations, like most lawsuits, are converted into linear, zero-sum games about money, where money serves as the proxy for a host of other needs and potential solutions such as apologies or substitute goods. Negotiated solutions become compromises in which each side concedes something to the other to avoid the harshness of a binary solution. The compromise, which by definition forces each side to give up something, may be unnecessary and fail to meet the real needs of the parties. * * *

* * *

In counseling clients lawyers may tell them what remedies are legally possible (money or an injunction) and thus preclude inquiry into alternatives which the client might prefer or which might be easier to obtain from the other party. [S]ome disputants prefer an acknowledgement that wrong has been done to them to receiving money. Once lawyers are engaged and the legal system, even if only informally, has been mobilized, the adversarial structure * * * forces polarization and routinization of demands and stifles a host of possible solutions.

NOTES AND QUESTIONS

1. Do you agree with Menkel–Meadow's assessment that a lawyer can disserve his client by narrowing a dispute and focusing too much on the categories of information with which the lawyer is already familiar and comfortable? Assuming this tendency exists, what are its advantages? Disadvantages?

2. It seems reasonable to assume that many lawyers *do* focus on the legal aspects of a dispute—on the information that might prove or disprove a client's legal claim, for example, instead of on the client's broader interests, needs, concerns and priorities. This is, of course, important: as we'll see below, part of a lawyer's job is determining whether a client has a case and how strong that case may be. At the same time, lawyers and clients will almost certainly be better served if a lawyer also prepares to search for value-creating trades when he goes to negotiate with the other side. What information does he need to do so?

Consider the example of Tammy and Dr. Sander. Imagine that you are Tammy's lawyer and that you have not yet begun to negotiate with Dr. Sander's attorney. You are about to meet with Tammy to discuss the upcoming negotiation. You know that the settlement amount in dollars is most likely going to be the primary distributive issue to be negotiated. At the same time, you are concerned that you could miss value-creating opportunities if you and Dr. Sander's attorney merely spend your time trading offers and counteroffers. You have even thought about the possibility that Tammy might be interested in some creative options like asking Dr. Sander to educate his peers or to apologize to Tammy and her family. Yet you aren't sure whether Tammy would go along with such a trade, nor how valuable it would be to her.

In preparation for a meeting with Tammy, make a list of the information you would like to learn from her. Then add to that a list of the questions that you can imagine asking her to learn that information.

Review the Lax and Sebenius excerpt in Section A(2)(b) above. Are your questions likely to prepare you to find value-creating trades based on the parties' differences, as Lax and Sebenius discuss?

3. Not all disputes are created equal. Some offer a wide variety of integrative opportunities, even if at first glance they appear to be primarily distributive. Disputes in which the parties have had (or could have) an ongoing relationship, there are various intangible interests at stake in addition to money, there are interests that extend over time, and there are many issues on the table are more likely to present value-creating opportunities. Other disputes—such as a very simple personal injury case in which the plaintiff and defendant have no long-term relationship and few interests on the table other than receiving or avoiding compensation—are more like the single-issue distributive example that we explored earlier.

Think about the following types of disputes: (1) divorce litigation; (2) personal injury litigation; (3) medical malpractice; (4) family estate litigation; (5) disputes over commercial contracts; (6) intellectual property litigation over copyright infringement; (7) dissolution of a business partnership or joint venture; (8) employee discrimination litigation; (9) securities class actions; (10) a mass tort class action against the maker of an allegedly defective product.

Which of these are likely to be primarily distributive? Which will have integrative possibilities (and what might those be)? If there is a spectrum—with ''mostly distributive'' at one end and ''mostly integrative'' at the other—where do these types of disputes fall upon it? See Mnookin, Peppet and Tulumello, Beyond Winning: How to Create Value in Deals and Disputes 43 (2000).

b. ALTERNATIVES: USING LITIGATION ANALYSIS

We have seen that searching for value-creating trades requires information about interests, resources, preferences and priorities, that clients are most often likely to possess such information, and that lawyers must therefore prepare carefully *with* their clients to enable themselves to find such trades. We have also seen, however, that a negotiator must know the value of her best alternative to a negotiated agreement so that she knows when and whether to walk away from the negotiating table. Such information allows you to compare any proposed settlement agreement against the value of your BATNA.

Parties in a legal dispute generally share the same best alternative: proceeding to court. In the words of Professors Mnookin and Kornhauser, they ''bargain in the shadow of the law.'' See Mnookin and Kornhauser, Bargaining in the Shadow of the Law: The Case of Divorce, 88 Yale L.J. 950 (1979). Their private negotiations are—and should be—shaped by the public rights, duties and norms that a court would apply if their bargaining fails. If Tammy or Dr. Sander doesn't like the deal they arrive at through negotiation, either could walk away and continue with their litigation. This should, in theory, make matters simple. If both sides have the same

A. The Structure of Negotiation 101

BATNA, then the parties should be able to determine what going to court would be worth and settle for that amount, thereby saving the transaction costs (in time, money, aggravation, etc.) that they would spend fighting it out before a judge.[8]

Reality is rarely so simple.

First, the lawyers might face a great deal of *uncertainty* about what the court outcome would be. Perhaps the facts in dispute are still unclear, either because discovery has not yet occurred or because it has failed to reveal a "smoking gun" that makes one side's story a slam-dunk. Perhaps the substantive law governing their dispute is novel or unsettled. Perhaps the judge presiding over their litigation is difficult to read or seems equivocal. Regardless, sometimes litigants are extremely uncertain about what outcome they face if they walk away from their negotiation.

Second, there can be *strategic temptations* to exaggerate, argue about, or try to influence the other side's perception of the value of continuing litigation. Each lawyer may posture and advocate to try to influence the other side's perceptions of its legal case. After all, if I can persuade you that your case is weak, then you may be willing to pay more or accept less. At the same time, my attempts to do so may undermine our ability to work constructively together to resolve our clients' differences. "Our case is a sure winner; your case is lousy." "Your client will never get a penny out of a jury for such a flimsy claim." "Do you *really* want to put your client on the stand?" The lawyers (or the parties) in litigation may be unable to discuss the likely court outcome without escalating their dispute and derailing their negotiations.

Third, lawyers and clients often struggle with *communication problems* when discussing the litigation alternative. When the lawyer says "you have a strong case," the client may think it's a sure winner. The lawyer, however, may only mean that there is a better than average chance of success—a fifty-fifty situation. Studies show that lawyers and clients experience difficulty communicating about such probabilities.[9] Such communication failures can lead to unmatched expectations and poor decision-making. For example, a lawyer may not understand why her client is holding out for more rather than accepting the other side's settlement offer, while the client simultaneously wonders why the lawyer is "suddenly" sounding so pessimistic about the case and pressuring him to agree to such a poor offer. They may fail to realize that their initial communications about the value of the litigation alternative left them with widely divergent understandings about expectations of success.

---

8. See Gross and Syverud, Getting to No: A Study of Settlement Negotiations and the Selection of Cases for Trial, 90 Mich. L.Rev. 319 (1991); Priest and Klein, The Selection of Disputes for Litigation, 13 J.Leg. Stud 1 (1984); Mnookin and Kornhauser, Bargaining in the Shadow of the Law: The Case of Divorce, 88 Yale L.J. 950, 973–77 (1979).

9. See e.g. Lerman, Lying to Clients, 138 U.Pa.L.Rev. 659, 734 (1990).

Litigation analysis can be a useful tool for a lawyer struggling with such complications.[10] By breaking down a client's legal dispute, analyzing the uncertainties and attempting to quantify—as much as possible—the value of the dispute's component parts, an attorney can sometimes make more precise and accurate estimations of the value of proceeding with litigation *and* more skillfully communicate those estimations to her client or the other side.

To illustrate, begin with the simple example of a coin toss. I am about to flip a dollar coin. If it lands heads, you win the dollar. If it lands tails, you win nothing. If I were to charge you some fixed amount to allow you to play my coin-toss game, and if you were risk neutral, what would you be willing to pay to take this bet?

The answer is any amount up to or equal to fifty cents. Although the outcome of any given coin toss is uncertain, we know that there is a fifty percent probability of heads and a fifty percent probability of tails. We also know the payoff associated with each possibility: you win one dollar if it lands heads, and nothing if tails. The *expected value* of this coin toss—the average value of betting on the toss many times—is thus fifty cents. This does not mean, of course, that you will win fifty cents on any given toss: it's an all or nothing game. Nevertheless, the law of averages tells us that if we toss the coin one hundred times, it will likely come up heads fifty of those one hundred. To compute the expected value of the coin toss you must merely multiply the probabilities by their associated outcomes and then add the results. (E.g., (.50 x $1.00) + (.50 x $0) = $.50)

Litigation analysis offers a similar way to model the decision of whether to settle or litigate. Assuming no transaction costs, the expected value of proceeding with a lawsuit equals the value of winning (say, $100,000) multiplied by the probability of winning (say, 30 percent) plus the value of losing ($0) multiplied by the probability of losing. In this simple example, of course, the expected value is $30,000. A risk-neutral plaintiff should take any settlement offer greater than $30,000 rather than gamble on going to court.

You can arrange this information in a decision tree—a graphical representation of a decision showing its *ultimate issues* and *influencing factors*. In dispute settlement, ultimate issues are those on which the outcome of the legal case turns. For example, will the jury find that the defendant was negligent? Influencing factors are uncertainties that will impact a given ultimate issue. For example, whether the jury finds the

---

10. Commentators use various terms to describe the process of breaking down and attempting to quantify the decision to sue or settle, including decision analysis, litigation risk analysis, BATNA-analysis, strategic choice analysis and decision tree analysis. Although decision analysis has a long history, particularly in management circles, and decision trees are a useful means of structuring such analysis, we use the term "litigation analysis" because it both refers specifically to the subject to which decision analysis is applied in this context and because it is slightly more broad than "BATNA-analysis" or "decision tree analysis," allowing that some techniques other than decision trees may be employed.

defendant negligent may depend on whether the judge rules that the plaintiff can discover the hospital's internal peer review reports related to the incident.

Decision trees are traditionally diagrammed in a fairly formal way to make them easier to chart and to read. *Decision nodes*, which identify an uncertainty that is completely within your control, are generally represented by a small square box. *Chance nodes*, which identify an uncertainty that is not within your control, are identified with a circle. In most legal disputes, the primary decision node represents a litigant's choice to litigate or settle. The branches following the choice to litigate will represent the various ultimate issues and influencing factors that could impact the litigation.

We can use Tammy's litigation against Dr. Sander to illustrate the process of creating a decision tree. Remember that Tammy's reservation value was $250,000—that was the least amount that she thought she should accept to settle the case. How did Tammy's attorney determine this reservation value? How could we use litigation analysis to calculate the expected value of her litigation alternative?

First, Tammy's lawyer must create the tree's structure by diagramming the basic issues that will have to be decided in court. Tammy's attorney tells her that she must overcome two hurdles: the possibility that the jury will find that Dr. Sander did not breach the standard of care (e.g., was not negligent) and the possibility that the jury will find that Dr. Sander's negligence did not cause Lyla's death. In addition, uncertainty exists about what amount of damages the jury might award. Tammy's lawyer believes the jury will choose between the maximum amount of $1,000,000, a "compromise" amount of $500,000, or a minimum amount representing medical costs of $200,000. Each of these three basic issues can be represented with a chance node. (See Figure 3.)

Figure 3

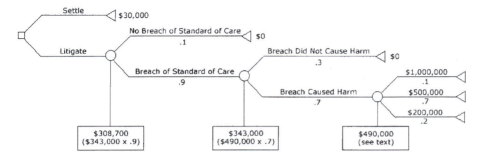

Next, Tammy's lawyer must attach probabilities to each of these chance nodes. Based on the best information he has available about the law, the facts, and the decision-makers, her attorney estimates a ninety

104   CHAPTER II   NEGOTIATION

percent chance of proving a breach of the standard of care and a seventy percent chance of then prevailing in convincing a jury that Dr. Sander's actions caused Lyla harm. He believes that there is only a ten percent chance that the jury would award $1,000,000 in damages, a similarly small chance of a small verdict of $200,000, and a seventy percent chance of a middle-of-the-road verdict of $500,000.

To calculate the expected value, one starts at the *right* of the tree and "rolls back" towards the decision node. Here the expected value of the jury's damages determination is $490,000: ($1,000,000 x .10 = $100,000) + ($500,000 x .70 = $350,000) + ($200,000 x .20 = $40,000) = $490,000. This is the expected value if Dr. Sander is found to have negligently caused Lyla harm, but he may not be. This $490,000 amount is multiplied by the probability of a causation determination (.70) to find that the expected value of the case upon the finding of negligence: $343,000. We continue to move towards the left, "rolling back" the tree, by multiplying this value of $343,000 by the probability that the jury *will* find Dr. Sander negligent (.90), for an expected value of litigation of $308,700.[11]

In addition, Tammy must adjust this expected value to account for her preferences regarding risk. A litigating party may be risk neutral, risk averse or risk preferring. Describing Tammy as risk neutral simply means that she is indifferent between accepting a fixed amount of money and taking a gamble that has the same expected value. For example, if Tammy is risk neutral she might be indifferent between accepting a cash payment of $308,700 and proceeding with litigation. But Tammy may be risk averse. She may be willing to pay a premium to avoid the risk inherent in gambling on litigation. For example, if Tammy is risk averse—she would rather have cash in hand than gamble—she might willingly accept *less* than $308,700 to reduce her uncertainty. Imagine that Tammy says she'd take $250,000 in cash rather than a chance at more, even though the expected value of the gamble is $308,700. In that case, we say that Tammy is willing to pay a $58,700 *risk premium*—$308,700 minus $250,000—to avoid the risk of losing in court. (If Tammy were risk *preferring*, she might demand *additional* compensation to give up the opportunity to gamble.) See D'Amato, Legal Uncertainty, 71 Calif.L.Rev. 1, 15 (1983).

This quick analysis shows how Tammy's lawyer can use litigation analysis to assist in valuing her litigation alternative. Her reservation value of $250,000 is tied to her best assessment of what will happen if she goes to court. By analyzing the structure of her case and the chances of succeeding at the various junctions that will determine its outcome, her lawyer can help her set a reservation value for her negotiations.

---

11. One can also perform sensitivity analysis to determine how sensitive the expected value is to changes in the probabilities associated with any given chance node. For example, instead of assuming a ninety percent chance that a judge will deny summary judgment, you might substitute a range of probabilities (from a 10 percent chance up to a ninety percent chance). You could then recalculate the tree to see the effects of changing that value. See Hoffer, Decision Analysis as a Mediator's Tool, 1 Harv. Neg.L.Rev. 113, 118–119 (1996).

We must note, however, that this discussion of litigation analysis is not meant to suggest that a lawyer can or should determine the value of her client's litigation alternative once and for all. The litigation game is fluid, not static. While negotiating with the other party, a lawyer may be simultaneously filing pre-trial motions, searching for new evidence, deposing the other side's witnesses, and researching novel legal theories in order to better her own case and worsen her opponent's. Events may take place that change the bargaining range because they change the expected outcome of the litigation—should the case go to trial. A new decision may come down from a higher court that will influence how a judge applies the law to the facts in dispute. A key witness may die or move away. One litigant may run out of money and be unable to continue the fight. Through various moves *away from the negotiating table*, a disputant or his lawyer may be able to change the game *at the table*.

NOTES AND QUESTIONS

1. There are various advantages to using a decision tree to model litigation. It can aid lawyer-client communication, making it easier for an attorney to explain the value of her client's case and its strengths and weaknesses. It can force attorneys or their clients to attain a more balanced perspective on a case than they might otherwise. It can promote earlier settlement by permitting negotiation to continue even in the face of uncertainty. Finally, it may help to persuade the other side to settle by making it easier to reach consensus on the value of litigation. The two sides might jointly create a decision tree, discovering along the way where their points of disagreement lie.

Obviously, however, one should not pretend that a decision tree gives a completely objective or reliable estimate of the expected value of litigation. Although litigation analysis may look scientific, it depends completely upon the probability assessments and damages estimates that a lawyer uses. As one text states, decision analysis is subject to the principle of "garbage in, garbage out." See Mnookin, Peppet and Tulumello, Beyond Winning: Negotiating To Create Value in Deals and Disputes 238 (2000).

Lax and Sebenius warn of the dangers of inflating your perception of your alternative:

> A negotiator's evaluation of alternatives is inherently subjective and, thus, depends on perceptions. Analysts and practitioners should, therefore, be sensitive to different possible perceptions of the same alternative. In an experiment at Harvard, the findings of which have been replicated in many contexts with students and executives, players were given detailed information about the history of an out-of-court negotiation over insurance claims arising from a personal injury case. They were not told whether the negotiators settled or if the case went into court. Each player was assigned to the role of either the insurance company or the [plaintiff]. After reading the case file, the players were privately asked to give their true probability estimates that the plain-

tiff would win the case and, given a win, the expected amount of the ultimate judgment. Systematically, those assigned the role of the plaintiff estimated the chances of winning and the expected amount of winning as much higher than those assigned the role of the insurance company defendant. Players who were not assigned a role prior to reading the case gave private estimates that generally fell between those of the advocates for each position. Similar results have been found in cases involving the worth of a company that is up for sale. Even given identical business information, balance sheets, income statements, and the like, those assigned to buy the company typically rate its true value as low, while those assigned to sell it give much higher best estimates. Neutral observers ranked the potential someplace in between.

These results, in combination with many other negotiation experiences, suggest that advocates tend to overestimate the attractiveness of their alternatives to negotiated agreement. If each side has an inflated expectation of its alternatives, no zone of possible agreement for negotiation may exist. Awareness of this common bias dictates a conscious attempt to be more realistic about one's own case, not to ''believe one's own line'' too much, and to be aware and seek to alter counterparts' estimates of their alternatives. * * *

Lax and Sebenius, The Power of Alternatives or the Limits of Negotiation, 1 Neg.J. 163, 169–170 (1985).

Despite the subjectivity of decision analysis, it can help litigants to think clearly about their disputes. Litigation analysis can help to reduce uncertainties, force clear thinking about a complex decision and initiate discussion about the strengths and weaknesses of one's case. By asking basic questions—Does the tree include all of the ultimate issues that may impact the outcome of the litigation? Are all the influencing factors represented? Do the probabilities seem reasonable?—a lawyer can test whether her decision tree is sound.

2. As the example of Tammy's litigation illustrates, a party's risk preferences can greatly influence the decision to settle. In general, do you think plaintiffs or defendants are more likely to exhibit risk aversion—to be willing to settle for a sure amount rather than gamble on the prospect of gaining a greater (or paying a lesser) amount? Why?

As we explore in Section C, below, psychological research has shown that people seem prone to take a sure gain over a gamble but to be risk preferring when trying to avoid a sure loss. This effect can have profound implications for dispute resolution. Professor Jeff Rachlinski, for example, tested the effect using the following hypotheticals. How would you behave in each of these two situations?

Version 1:

Imagine you are the plaintiff in a copyright infringement lawsuit. You are suing for the $400,000 that the defendant allegedly earned by violating the copyright. Trial is in two days and the defendant has offered to pay $200,000 as a final settlement. If you turn it down, you believe that you will face a trial where you have a 50% chance of winning a $400,000 award.

Do you accept the settlement?

Version 2:

Imagine you are the defendant in a copyright infringement lawsuit. You are being sued for the $400,000 that you allegedly earned by violating the copyright. Trial is in two days and the plaintiff has offered to accept $200,000 as a final settlement. If you turn it down, you believe that you will face a trial where you have a 50% chance of losing a $400,000 award.

Do you agree to pay the settlement?

Rachlinski, Gains, Losses, and the Psychology of Litigation, 70 S.Cal.L.Rev. 113, 127–128 (1996). See also Kahneman and Tversky, Choices, Values, and Frames, 39 Am. Psychologist 341, 342–344 (1984); Kahneman and Tversky, Prospect Theory: An Analysis of Decision Under Risk, 47 Econometrica 263, 268–269 (1979); Tversky and Kahneman, The Framing of Decisions and the Psychology of Choice, 211 Sci. 453 (1981).

These two hypotheticals are economically identical—in each, the expected value of proceeding to court is $200,000. Both the plaintiff and the defendant must choose between gambling on winning (or not losing) the $400,000 and walking away with a sure $200,000.

Yet when Rachlinski ran these hypotheticals with first-year Cornell Law School students, he found that 77% of the plaintiffs (Version 1) chose to settle while only 31% of the defendants (Version 2) settled. Psychological "framing effects" most likely account for the difference: plaintiffs frame their choice as between a sure gain and a gamble on a larger gain (and are risk averse and prone to take the sure gain), whereas defendants frame their choice as between a sure loss and a gamble on avoiding loss (and are risk seeking in hoping to avoid the sure loss). For further variations on this theme, see Korobkin and Guthrie, Psychological Barriers to Litigation Settlement: An Experimental Approach, 93 Mich.L.Rev. 107, 133 (1994).

Defendants' actual litigation behavior seems to follow the predictions of this theory. Rachlinsky notes that a study of litigation behavior found that defendants' final offer of settlement was consistently below the ultimate jury award. This is what we would expect given framing effects: risk-seeking defendants trying to avoid sure losses are likely to be reluctant to settle and therefore offer less than the expected value of litigation. See Rachlinski, Gains, Losses, and the Psychology of Litigation, 70 S.Cal.L.Rev. 113, 149–150 (1996). See also Gross and Syverud, Getting to No: A Study of Settlement Negotiations and the Selection of Cases for Trial, 90 Mich. L.Rev. 319 (1991).

3. A litigant should factor several additional considerations into her litigation analysis. Transaction costs such as attorney's fees, court costs and emotional strain will reduce the value of any award secured through

CHAPTER II NEGOTIATION

litigation. In addition, a litigant must consider the time value of money in comparing a settlement offer to the promise of a litigated victory. A dollar received today is worth more than a dollar received a year from now, because with prudent investment you can earn returns on the dollar over the course of the year. Thus, the expected value of litigation must be converted into a present value. To do so requires first determining the *discount rate*—the annual rate of interest you assume you could earn on the money were it received today. The present value is then calculated with the following formula: Present Value = Future Value / $(1+r)n$, where r = rate expressed as a decimal and n = number of periods. For example, if Tammy's case would take three years to litigate, her expected value is \$308,700 (not considering risk preferences), and her discount rate is ten percent, the present value of her expected return from her litigation alternative is roughly \$232,000.[12] If she invested \$232,000 today she would have \$308,000 in three years. This is a dramatic difference, and must be taken into account when comparing any settlement offer to the possibility of continuing with litigation.[13]

Because the time value of money can so change the present value of a decision to continue litigation, whether a damage award may include pre-judgment interest can be extremely important. Courts generally award pre-judgment interest in contract cases, and, in some jurisdictions, in non-contract cases involving wrongful death, personal injury, or property damage. Pre-judgment interest awards are usually based solely on pecuniary or compensatory damages, not punitive or other non-compensatory damages. Without the threat of a pre-judgment interest award, of course, a defendant has a great incentive not to settle: the interest-free use of the defendant's money during the litigation. If pre-judgment interest is available, however, and if the pre-judgment interest rate equals the actual interest rate in the marketplace, a plaintiff should not need to discount his or her expected value of settlement to account for the time value of money. This obviously can have a great effect on the settlement decision. But see Bernstein, Understanding the Limits of Court–Connected ADR: A Critique of Federal Court–Annexed Arbitration Programs, 141 U.Pa.L.Rev. 2169 n.231 (1993) (noting that courts often award pre-judgment interest at below market rates, benefiting defendants).

4. What would the decision tree in Tammy's litigation look like if you added the following issue to it? Assuming the probability estimates given are accurate, what is the expected value of Tammy's case when you take this additional issues into account?

Tammy's lawyer intends to file a discovery motion seeking access to the hospital's internal peer review board records regarding Tammy's case. This is a fairly controversial legal question in many states. On the one hand, the medical profession insists that internal peer review documents

---

12. \$308,700 / (1 + .10)3 = \$232,000.

13. It can sometimes be helpful to be able to calculate the *future* value of a present settlement offer. The formula for future value is simply: Future Value = Present Value x (1 + r)n.

should be confidential to permit doctors to critique and learn from each other without the threat of their communications surfacing in a later lawsuit. On the other hand, plaintiffs insist that society will most benefit if doctors feel pressure to change their ways from outside, not merely inside, their profession. Tammy's attorney believes that she is forty percent likely to win this motion (and sixty percent likely to lose). If the discovery motion is granted, however, Tammy's attorney believes that the likelihood of establishing that Dr. Sander's negligence caused Lyla harm will rise to ninety percent instead of seventy percent. If the motion is denied, the probability of establishing causation remains seventy percent, as shown in Figure 3.

5. For more in-depth discussion of decision trees and litigation analysis, see Victor, Litigation Risk Analysis and ADR, in ADR Practice Book 308 (1990); Aaron and Hoffer, Decision Analysis as a Method of Evaluating the Trial Alternative, in Mediating Legal Disputes 307 (1996); Hoffer, Decision Analysis as a Mediator's Tool, 1 Harv.Neg.L.Rev. 113 (1996); Victor, The Proper Use of Decision Analysis to Assist Litigation Strategy, 40 Bus.Law 617 (1984); Raiffa, The Art and Science of Negotiation 30 (1982).

B. STRATEGY

That negotiations can have value-creating opportunities or integrative potential in addition to distributive issues explains their underlying economic structure, but does not necessarily dictate the choice of strategy. Negotiators must constantly choose how to approach a given bargaining situation. All things being equal, most of us prefer more money (or whatever else is in dispute) rather than less; negotiators generally seek the best deal they can for themselves. The constant question, then, is whether trying to find integrative trades—expanding the pie—will lead you to a bigger slice, or whether bargaining hard from the outset will maximize your return in a given negotiation. Here we explore three common negotiation approaches: hard or competitive positional bargaining, "soft" or compromising positional bargaining, and problem-solving.

1. POSITIONAL BARGAINING

Roger Fisher, William Ury and Bruce Patton's negotiation text Getting to Yes labeled as "positional bargaining" the traditional haggling that most people associate with negotiation.

Roger Fisher, William Ury and Bruce Patton, Getting to Yes

3–4 (2d ed. 1991).

Whether a negotiation concerns a contract, a family quarrel, or a peace settlement among nations, people routinely engage in positional bargaining.

Each side takes a position, argues for it, and makes concessions to reach a compromise. The classic example of this negotiating minuet is the haggling that takes place between a customer and the proprietor of a secondhand store:

Customer	Shopkeeper
How much do you want for this brass dish?	
	That is a beautiful antique, isn't it? I guess I could let it go for $75.
Oh come on, it's dented. I'll give you $15.	
	Really! I might consider a serious offer, but $15 certainly isn't serious.
Well, I could go to $20, but I would never pay anything like $75. Quote me a realistic price.	
	You drive a hard bargain, young lady. $60 cash, right now.
$25.	
	It cost me a great deal more than that. Make me a *serious* offer.
$37.50. That's the highest I will go.	
	Have you noticed the engraving on that dish? Next year pieces like that will be worth twice what you pay today.

And so it goes, on and on. * * *

a. HARD POSITIONAL BARGAINING

We first explore "hard" or competitive positional bargaining. A negotiator employing this strategy stakes out a position and demands concessions. Usually the negotiator starts with an extreme position and concedes slowly. He may make threats to walk away from the negotiation or use commitment tactics to pressure the other side. The following excerpts explore the tactics and mindset associated with this approach.

Donald G. Gifford, A Context–Based Theory of Strategy Selection in Legal Negotiation

46 Ohio St.L.J. 41, 48–52 (1985).

* * * The basic premise underlying the competitive strategy is that all gains for one's own client are obtained at the expense of the other party.

The strategy aims to convince the opposing party that her settlement alternative is not as advantageous as she previously thought. Competitive tactics are designed to lessen the opponent's confidence in her case, thereby inducing her to settle for less than she originally asked. The competitive negotiator moves "psychologically against the other person," with behavior designed to unnerve the opponent. Competitive negotiators expect similar behavior from their opponents and therefore mistrust them. In undermining their opponents' confidence, competitive negotiators employ a strategy which often includes the following tactics:

1. a high initial demand;

2. limited disclosure of information regarding facts and one's own preferences;

3. few and small concessions;

4. threats and arguments; and

5. apparent commitment to positions during the negotiation process.

A negotiator who utilizes the competitive strategy begins with a high initial demand. Empirical research repeatedly demonstrates a significant positive relationship between a negotiator's original demand and his payoff. A high initial demand conceals the negotiator's minimum settlement point and allows the negotiator to grant concessions during the negotiation process and still achieve a favorable result. The negotiator's opening position may also include a false issue—a demand that the negotiator does not really care about, but one that can be traded for concessions from the opponent during the negotiation. Generally, the more that the negotiator insists upon a particular demand early in the negotiation, the larger the concession that ultimately will be obtained from the opponent in exchange for dropping that demand. In addition, the opponent may have evaluated the negotiator's case more favorably than the negotiator has; a high demand protects the negotiator from quickly agreeing to a less favorable settlement than that which he might later obtain. If the demand is high but credible, the opponent's response to the demand may also educate the negotiator about how the opponent evaluates her own case.

The competitive negotiator selectively and strategically shares information with his opponent. He does not disclose the least favorable terms to which his client would agree, that is, his minimum reservation point. * * * Conversely, the competitive negotiator selectively discloses information which strengthens his case and which undermines the opponent's case.

* * * The competitive negotiator makes concessions reluctantly, because concessions may weaken one's position through both "position loss" and "image loss." Position loss occurs because in most negotiations a norm exists against withdrawing a concession. Further, an early concession results in an opportunity loss for something that might have been extracted in exchange for the concession later in the negotiation process. Image loss occurs because after a concession, the opponent perceives that the negotiator is flexible; in the opponent's mind this may suggest that further

concessions can be obtained. * * * When possible, the competitive negotiator seeks to create the illusion in his opponent's eye that he is making a concession without diminishing his own satisfaction. This is done by either conceding on an issue the negotiator does not care about or appearing to make a concession without really making one.

The competitive negotiator obviously strives to force his opponent into making as many and as large concessions as possible while he makes few concessions, small in degree. To force concessions from his opponent, he employs both arguments and threats. In negotiations, arguments are communications intended to persuade the opponent to draw logical inferences from known data. For example, a plaintiff's attorney might describe a favorable eyewitness account of a collision and ask the defense counsel to infer the probability that her client will be found liable. * * * A threat, on the other hand, is a communication intended to inform the opponent that unless she agrees to a settlement acceptable to the negotiator, the negotiator or his client will act to the opponent's detriment. For example, a union negotiator might threaten that the union will strike if management refuses to make wage concessions.

* * * To the extent that the success of a negotiation strategy is measured by the payoff in a single negotiation involving the division of limited resources between two parties, studies of simulated negotiations suggest that the competitive strategy yields better results than other strategies for the negotiator. However, the competitive strategy suffers severe disadvantages. The likelihood of impasse is much greater for negotiators who employ the competitive strategy than for those who use other approaches. Competitive tactics engender tension and mistrust between the parties, which can give the appearance that the parties are farther apart than they really are. These negative attitudes may carry over into matters other than the current negotiation and may make continuing relationships difficult.

Gary Goodpaster, A Primer on Competitive Bargaining
J. of Disp.Res. 325, 346–348 (1996).

Generally, the competitive negotiator seeks to persuade the other party that she will not agree to or settle above or below a certain point. In devising a negotiating strategy, the competitor uses some general approaches and rules of thumb. These are:

Negotiation is an information game. The competitor treats negotiation as a game in which the party with the most accurate information wins. Thus, the competitor either seeks to gather as much information as possible while giving away as little as possible or gives and manipulates information in such a way that the other party is led indirectly to draw conclusions the competitor wishes it to draw. Realizing that the other party will decide what to do on the basis of what he or she thinks and believes, the competitor seeks to shape, manage, and manipulate the other party's perceptions of the situation and that party's available choices.

Take an opening position at the margin (high or low openers). The negotiator who opens with a high or low offer and makes few and small concessions generally has the most success in negotiation. As used here, "opens high" or "opens low" means at the extreme or far end of the potential bargaining range but sufficiently within the range to retain credibility. The competitive negotiator prepares an opening position by first estimating her best possible deal and then staking out an initial position considerably beyond that estimate while developing justifications for the latter position.

Treat concessions as a way to gain and disclose information. Concessions convey information about what a party wants and values, about the party's preferences and intentions, and about the party's perception of the other party. The skillful, competitive negotiator "reads" concessions to infer this information and plans her own concessions to give the other party only those impressions she wants it to have. Concessions are not only, and perhaps are not even principally, a way to give something to the other party to narrow differences, but are also a way to gain advantage. A skillful competitor crafts concessions to shape the perceptions and expectations of the other party.

Hang tough on concessions; do not make concessions one-for-one nor trade concessions equally. Concessions seem to beget concessions. In general, an expectation exists in bargaining that when one party makes a concession, then the other party will also make a concession in return. * * * Notwithstanding this expectation, it is not *always* necessary to give a concession in exchange for receiving one. * * *

* * *

Make small, infrequent, and declining concessions. As a corollary to the foregoing, the competitive negotiator makes it a practice to make small concessions and force the other party to work hard to gain any concessions. The aim is to send the message that there is not much to give: if there is to be a bargain, the other party will have to move much further than the competitor. The competitive negotiator also makes concessions in declining increments in order to suggest a convergence on his apparent bottom line. * * *

One effect of "hanging tough" and making small concessions is to shape or alter the other party's expectations or aspirations about what it can get out of the negotiation. Treating a negotiator's concessions as information about what can be achieved, the other party may alter its expectations in a way favorable to the negotiator.

Select an opening position by reference to the mid-point rule. Once two settlement offers are on the table, the natural settling point is the mid-point. This rule of thumb, while not always true, is true often enough that competitive negotiators can use it to good effect. Typically, the competitive negotiator will allow, or more likely, *get* the other party to make the first offer. This allows the competitor to set his or her offer at the most advantageous point, given the likelihood that once both offers are out, the

114 CHAPTER II Negotiation

negotiators will settle in the middle. Alternatively, a competitive negotiator simply starts with an extreme offer, hoping that the other party is either innocent or will overvalue the item being negotiated and will open with an offer more favorable to the competitor. In effect, the competitor's high opener draws the other party's opener in its direction. * * *

Link positions and concessions to convincing justifications or rationales. Experienced competitive negotiators know that they may not be able to persuade the other party to agree to settle at any particular point in the perceived bargaining range simply by hanging tough. * * * In bargaining situations, people want justifications for positions taken. Understanding this, in preparing for a negotiation, the competitor picks positions on the bargaining continuum that he can defend with some plausible justification. * * *

Thomas C. Schelling, An Essay on Bargaining

in Thomas C. Schelling, The Strategy of Conflict 22–28 (1960).

"Bargaining power," "bargaining strength," "bargaining skill" suggest that the advantage goes to the powerful, the strong, or the skillful. It does, of course, if those qualities are defined to mean only that negotiations are won by those who win. But, if the terms imply that it is an advantage to be more intelligent or more skillful in debate, or to have more financial resources, more physical strength, more military potency, or more ability to withstand losses, then the term does a disservice. These qualities are by no means universal advantages in bargaining situations; they often have a contrary value.

The sophisticated negotiator may find it difficult to seem as obstinate as a truly obstinate man. If a man knocks at your door and says that he will stab himself on the porch unless given $10, he is more likely to get the $10 if his eyes are bloodshot. The threat of mutual destruction cannot be used to deter an adversary who is too unintelligent to comprehend it or too weak to enforce his will on those he represents. * * *

Bargaining power has also been described as the power to fool and bluff, "the ability to set the best price for yourself and fool the other man into thinking this was your maximum offer." Fooling and bluffing are certainly involved; but there are two kinds of fooling. One is deceiving about the facts; a buyer may lie about his income or misrepresent the size of his family. The other is purely tactical. Suppose each knows everything about the other, and each knows what the other knows. What is there to fool about? The buyer may say that, though he'd really pay up to twenty and the seller knows it, he is firmly resolved as a tactical matter not to budge above sixteen. If the seller capitulates, was he fooled? Or was he convinced of the truth? Or did the buyer really not know what he would do next if the tactic failed? If the buyer really "feels" himself firmly resolved, and bases his resolve on the conviction that the seller will capitulate, and the seller does, the buyer may say afterwards that he was "not fooling."

Whatever has occurred, it is not adequately conveyed by the notion of bluffing and fooling.

How does one person make another believe something? The answer depends importantly on the factual question, "Is it true?" It is easier to prove the truth of something that is true than of something false. To prove the truth about our health we can call on a reputable doctor; to prove the truth about our costs or income we may let the person look at books that have been audited by a reputable firm or the Bureau of Internal Revenue. But to persuade him of something false we may have no such convincing evidence.

When one wishes to persuade someone that he would not pay more than $16,000 for a house that is really worth $20,000 to him, what can he do to take advantage of the usually superior credibility of the truth over a false assertion? Answer: make it true. How can a buyer make it true? If he likes the house because it is near his business, he might move his business, persuading the seller that the house is really now worth only $16,000 to him. This would be unprofitable; he is no better off than if he had paid the higher price.

But suppose the buyer could make an irrevocable and enforceable bet with some third party, duly recorded and certified, according to which he would pay for the house no more than $16,000, or forfeit $5,000. The seller has lost; the buyer need simply present the truth. Unless the seller is enraged and withholds the house in sheer spite, the situation has been rigged against him; the "objective" situation—the buyer's true incentive—has been voluntarily, conspicuously, and irreversibly changed. The seller can take it or leave it. This example demonstrates that if the buyer can accept an irrevocable *commitment* in a way that is unambiguously visible to the seller, he can squeeze the range of indeterminacy down to the point most favorable to him. It also suggests, by its artificiality, that the tactic is one that may or may not be available; whether the buyer can find an effective device for committing himself may depend on who he is, who the seller is, where they live, and a number of legal and institutional arrangements (including, in our artificial example, whether bets are legally enforceable).

If both men live in a culture where "cross my heart" is universally accepted as potent, all the buyer has to do is allege that he will pay no more than $16,000, using this invocation of penalty, and he wins—or at least he wins if the seller does not beat him to it by shouting "$19,000, cross my heart." If the buyer is an agent authorized by a board of directors to buy at $16,000 but not a cent more, and the directors cannot constitutionally meet again for several months and the buyer cannot exceed his authority, and if all this can be made known to the seller, then the buyer "wins"—if, again, the seller has not tied himself up with a commitment to $19,000. Or, if the buyer can assert that he will pay no more than $16,000 so firmly that he would suffer intolerable loss of personal prestige or bargaining reputation by paying more, and if the fact of his paying more would necessarily be known, and if the seller appreciates all this, then a loud declaration by

CHAPTER II NEGOTIATION

itself may provide the commitment. The device, of course, is a needless surrender of flexibility unless it can be made fully evident and understandable to the seller.

* * *

Some examples may suggest the relevance of the tactic, although an observer can seldom distinguish with confidence the consciously logical, the intuitive, or the inadvertent use of a visible tactic. First, it has not been uncommon for union officials to stir up excitement and determination on the part of the membership during or prior to a wage negotiation. If the union is going to insist on $2 and expects the management to counter with $1.60, an effort is made to persuade the membership not only that the management could pay $2 but even perhaps that the negotiators themselves are incompetent if they fail to obtain close to $2. The purpose—or, rather, a plausible purpose suggested by our analysis—is to make clear to the management that the negotiators could not accept less than $2 *even if they wished to* because they no longer control the members or because they would lose their own positions if they tried. In other words, the negotiators reduce the scope of their own authority and confront the management with the threat of a strike that the union itself cannot avert, even though it was the union's own action that eliminated its power to prevent the strike.

Something similar occurs when the United States Government negotiates with other governments on, say, the uses to which foreign assistance will be put, or tariff reduction. If the executive branch is free to negotiate the best arrangement it can, it may be unable to make any position stick and may end by conceding controversial points because its partners know, or believe obstinately, that the United States would rather concede than terminate the negotiations. But, if the executive branch negotiates under legislative authority, with its position constrained by law, and it is evident that Congress will not be reconvened to change the law within the necessary time period, then the executive branch has a firm position that is visible to its negotiating partners.

When national representatives go to international negotiations knowing that there is a wide range of potential agreement within which the outcome will depend on bargaining, they often seem to create a bargaining position by public statements, statements calculated to arouse a public opinion that permits no concessions to be made. If a binding public opinion can be cultivated and made evident to the other side, the initial position can thereby be made visibly "final."

These examples have certain characteristics in common. First, they clearly depend not only on incurring a commitment but on communicating it persuasively to the other party. Second, it is by no means easy to establish the commitment, nor is it entirely clear to either of the parties concerned just how strong the commitment is. Third, similar activity may be available to the parties on both sides. Fourth, the possibility of commitment, though perhaps available to both sides, is by no means equally available; the ability of a democratic government to get itself tied by public opinion may be different from the ability of a totalitarian government to incur such a commitment. Fifth, they all run the risk of establishing an immovable position that goes beyond the ability of the other to concede, and thereby provoke the likelihood of stalemate or breakdown.

NOTES AND QUESTIONS

1. Many negotiation analysts have described the various tactics that hard positional bargainers employ. See Churchman, Negotiation: Process, Tactics, Theory (1995) (describing fifty negotiation tactics); Genn, Hard Bargaining: Out of Court Settlement in Personal Injury Actions 134–139 (1987) (discussing hard bargaining in the litigation context); Reitz (ed.), Negotiation: Theory and Practice 49–67 (1985) (discussing aggressive and coercive tactics); Pruitt, Negotiation Behavior 72–76 (1981).

Roger Volkema lists eight common difficult tactics: an exaggerated first offer, speed-ups (setting false deadlines to impose time pressure), delays, drawing artificial bottom lines, exaggerating your BATNA, making false concessions to coax someone into reciprocating, inducing the other to invest time and effort—so that they'll then keep bargaining, and false authority limits. See Volkema, The Negotiation Toolkit 78–91 (1999). Mnookin, Peppet and Tulumello list ten: extreme claims followed by small, slow concessions, commitment tactics, take-it-or-leave-it offers, inviting unreciprocated offers, pushing until the other side "flinches," personal insults and feather ruffling, bluffing and lying, threats, belittling the other side's alternatives, and playing good cop, bad cop. See Mnookin, Peppet and Tulumello, Beyond Winning: Negotiating to Create Value in Deals and Disputes 24–25 (2000).

What "hard" positional tactics have you seen? Which do you most fear? Which have you used yourself? What are the advantages of a hard positional strategy? The disadvantages? In what contexts, about what subjects and with what people is this approach suitable? Does a positional strategy lead to fair agreements? To efficient, value-creating or integrative agreements? What different characteristics of a bargaining situation make it easier or more difficult to succeed in using this approach?

2. A hard positional bargainer often attempts to influence the other party's subjective understanding of the bargaining situation. Indeed, the positional strategy can seem like a game of illusions—each side starts with an extreme position and concedes slowly in an attempt to signal to the other that their reservation value is more extreme than it is in reality. The bluffs, threats and positioning characteristic of this approach can be purely arbitrary. I might say that I will take no less than $200,000 for my house, but we both know that I could be lying—I might willingly accept $150,000. See Lax and Sebenius, The Manager as Negotiator 119–121 (1986).

Some tactics, however, aim not at the other side's subjective *perceptions* of the bargaining situation but instead at the negotiation's actual structure. In other words, they attempt to alter the parties' actual reservation values. The Schelling excerpt on commitment tactics illustrates that sometimes limiting one's freedom of action can be of great benefit in negotiations. His example of a house purchase illustrates this counterintuitive notion. By committing to a third party, the house buyer constrains his freedom—because he commits to forfeiting a penalty if he pays more than $16,000—but simultaneously changes his own reservation value and thus the zone of possible agreement. Assuming his third-party commitment really is irrevocable, this tactic is not smoke and mirrors: he has altered the negotiation structure, not merely influenced the other side's perception of it.

When are such tactics commonly used? When are they appropriate or inappropriate?

b. SOFT POSITIONAL BARGAINING

Although positional bargaining is most often associated with extreme offers, threats, commitment tactics and other attempts to pressure one's opponent to submit, we must note that sometimes negotiators engage in a softer version of the same basic approach to negotiation. That is, they continue to trade offers and concessions—arguing between competing positions—but they do so in a more conciliatory way. Roger Fisher and his co-authors explain this in Getting to Yes:

> Many people recognize the high costs of hard positional bargaining, particularly on the parties and their relationship. They hope to avoid them by following a more gentle style of negotiation. Instead of seeing the other side as adversaries, they prefer to see them as friends. Rather than emphasizing a goal of victory, they emphasize the necessity of reaching agreement. In a soft negotiating game the standard moves are to make offers and concessions, to trust the other side, to be friendly, and to yield as necessary to avoid confrontation.
>
> * * *
>
> The soft negotiating game emphasizes the importance of building and maintaining a relationship. Within families and among friends much negotiation takes place in this way. The process tends to be efficient, at least to the extent of producing results quickly. As each party competes with the other in being more generous and more forthcoming, an agreement becomes highly likely. But it may not be a wise one. * * * [A]ny negotiation primarily concerned with the relationship runs the risk of producing a sloppy [e.g., economically inefficient] agreement.
>
> More seriously, pursuing a soft and friendly form of positional bargaining makes you vulnerable to someone who plays a hard game of positional bargaining. In positional bargaining, a hard game dominates a soft one. If the hard bargainer insists on concessions and makes threats while the soft bargainer yields in order to avoid confrontation and insists on agreement, the negotiating game is biased in favor of the hard player. The process will produce an agreement, although it may not be a wise one. It will certainly be more favorable to the hard

positional bargainer than to the soft one. If your response to sustained, hard positional bargaining is soft positional bargaining, you will probably lose your shirt.

Fisher, Ury and Patton, Getting to Yes 7–9 (2d ed. 1991).

A soft positional bargainer may start reasonably, concede generously and act pleasantly. He may avoid threats and try not to discuss his BATNA—which can sometimes seem threatening to the other side. He may make concessions to preserve his relationship with the other side.

We have all used this approach, and sometimes it has great advantages. If you are negotiating with a friend about where to go for dinner you may simply concede to her wishes rather than hold out for your first choice. Getting your way may not be worth it. The disadvantages, however, are obvious. You may get exploited. And, as with insisting on your position through hard positional bargaining, you may arrive at an inefficient agreement if you merely accept the other person's position rather than probing for integrative possibilities. Perhaps your friend wants Chinese and you want to go to your favorite Italian restaurant. Giving in and going for Chinese doesn't create the most possible value if another option could better meet both of your interests. Perhaps your friend really just wants to eat somewhere nearby because she is tired and doesn't feel like walking far. Maybe you want Italian because you prefer somewhere quiet where you can talk together, and your friend's proposed Chinese restaurant tends to be loud. A third option—the local hamburger joint—may meet these interests and create value. In terms of efficiency, giving in may be no better than holding out.

c. THE FIRST OFFER PROBLEM

A positional strategy—hard or soft—inevitably gives rise to a common negotiation dilemma: who should make the first offer or demand? Imagine responding to an advertisement in your local paper: "Used 27–inch Sony television set for sale. Two years old, good condition. Best offer." You call the owner and talk briefly about the set and its features. But then you hesitate. Should you make an offer? Or wait until the seller states an asking price? What are the advantages and disadvantages of each approach?

Making the first offer can confer several benefits. First, you may be able to anchor the bargaining around your first offer or demand. If you start low—"I'll give you $5 for the television"—your negotiation may center on that starting point and you may get a better price. Conversely, if the seller started high—"I want $150 for the TV, no less"—you might be inclined to revise your expectations upwards and make a counter-offer much closer to his starting point. "Research has shown that individuals often use a salient piece of information as an anchor on which to base their future judgments. Regardless of the level of the anchor, adjustments tend to be insufficient. Thus, different opening offers (anchors) will result in final outcomes which are biased in the direction of that offer." Weingart,

120 CHAPTER II NEGOTIATION

Thompson, Bazerman and Carroll, Tactical Behavior and Negotiation Outcomes, 1 Intl.J. of Conflict Mgt. 7, 9–10 (1990).

The disadvantage with making the first offer is obvious, however. If you offer too much or demand too little, you may exceed the other side's expectation of what is possible in your negotiation. For example, you might offer $50 for the television thinking that you were low-balling, but the other side's reservation value might be only $10. In trying to take advantage of the first offer, you instead give up more than you need to.

Allowing—or requiring—the other person to "go first" thus has advantages. They might similarly "over-offer" and exceed your expectations. And both sides know this. As a result, negotiations sometimes turn comical as each side tries to persuade the other to make the first move. Like two wrestlers circling in a ring, neither negotiator wants to jump first for fear that the other side will exploit their volunteerism.

Consider the following excerpts.

Harry Edwards and James J. White, The Lawyer as Negotiator
115–116 (1977).

Almost without exception it is desirable to cause the opposing party in a negotiation to make the first realistic offer. If one has made a serious miscalculation about his position, the opponent's first offer may save a considerable sum. Assume for example that a new and totally inexperienced law school graduate is seeking a job in a middle-sized city. From his very limited perspective he believes that the yearly wage for beginning lawyers in that town is $10,000. He is pleasantly surprised therefore when his prospective employer offers him $17,000 to begin. If the employee had made the first offer, it would have cost him $7,000 and perhaps more. Thus, causing the opponent to make the first realistic offer is most helpful in circumstances in which one regards his opponent's case as stronger than the opponent regards it.

A standard defense to an opponent's demand for a first offer is to give him a large demand. Thus, if convention calls for one party to make the first move, he may choose to make that move by giving an outrageous demand simply to get the negotiation underway. Such an exchange is commonplace in the negotiation of personal injury cases in which the plaintiff's lawyer will often start with the demand far in excess of anything he thinks the defense will grant him. In fact such a demand is not a first offer at all but simply a way of instituting negotiation without having to set the level at the outset.

In contexts other than personal injury such as commercial litigation and the purchase or sale of goods or land, the large demand rule is not widely used. One who makes an outrageous demand in such circumstances may find that he has killed the deal entirely by signaling to the other party that he is not truly interested. For that reason it is more important in those situations that one concentrate on getting the first offer from the opponent.

The challenging question is not why one wants the first offer, but how he procures that offer from his opponent. In some situations one can rely upon the customary practice to require the other side to make the first offer. For example it is customary practice in the employment field for the employer to commence with an offer. Usually the employee is not expected to come up with an initial request of a specific dollar figure. There are similar customs in other areas.

Of course the simplest method of procuring the first offer in contexts in which there is no convention is simply to ask the opponent to state his price. An experienced negotiator is likely to reply that he is willing to offer, "Whatever you think it is worth," but the inexperienced negotiator may simply respond with a realistic first offer.

David Lax & James Sebenius, The Manager as Negotiator

132–134 (1986).

One common school of thought on how to choose offers is nicely expressed by Henry Kissinger:

> If agreement is usually found between two starting positions, there is no point in making moderate offers. Good bargaining technique would suggest a point of departure far more extreme than what one is willing to accept. The more outrageous the initial proposition the better is the prospect that what one "really" wants will be considered a compromise.

But, beyond the risk of souring the atmosphere, such tactics may stimulate equally extreme counteroffers that may simply cancel the intended effects and increase the chances of impasse. If one invests an extreme offer with a great deal of credibility, eventual movement may damage the credibility of subsequent "firm" stands.

If this is so and Kissinger's advice need not always apply, is there anything to guide the choice of offers?

CHOOSING OPENING OFFERS

* * *

The choice of an effective opening offer and even the decision whether or not to make the first offer should also reflect a negotiator's perceptions about the counterpart's reservation value. When quite uncertain about the counterpart's reservation value, the negotiator may be better off letting the counterpart make the initial offer. Why? First, the negotiator hopes to gain information about the bargaining range from the offer. Second, the uncertainty inherently implies that there is a good chance a "moderate" opening offer would be too high or too low. An offer much worse than the counterpart's reservation value may provoke anger, sour the atmosphere, and raise questions of seriousness or good faith. For example, if [a] building owner's reservation value were much higher than [a buyer's] $320,000 offer, he might be offended by it and feel that the offering group is not really serious. Yet offering too high a price, say $550,000, runs the opposite risk: if the owner would have accepted $450,000, the buyers would have overpaid by $100,000. Thus, by refraining from making a first offer, a negotiator who is quite uncertain about the counterpart's reservation value avoids giving too much away and offering insultingly little.

But, the negotiator who defers when uncertain about the counterpart's reservation value bears another risk: his perceptions of the bargaining set may be manipulated by the opening offer. Thus, in this situation, many buyers make very low offers but try to make them seem soft or flexible. They hope to substantially reduce the counterpart's aspirations without being insulting, without unnecessarily giving up value, or risking committing to an unrealistic point.

By contrast, if the negotiator becomes fairly confident that the counterpart's reservation value lies in a small range, than he may clearly be best off making the opening offer. In this case, he does not expect to gain much information about the bargaining set from his counterpart's initial offer. Moreover, he is not likely to run the risks of either an insultingly low offer or an overly generous opening. For example, if the [buyer] attempting to buy the building were fairly confident, after studying the market and the actual competing potential buyers, that the owner's reservation value was between $425,000 and $475,000, the firm might offer something below this range. For example, the firm might offer $400,000, which it feels has a 90 percent chance of being below the owner's reservation value; or it might go lower still. Given the [buyer's] assessment, such an offer is likely to be outside the bargaining set, is unlikely to leave much profit for the owner, is close enough to entice him to bargain, and is chosen to guide the final agreement to a point just above the owner's reservation value.

Experimental results in distributive bargaining suggest that, within limits, the higher the opening offer, the better the outcome. But, what is acceptably high and what is insultingly extreme depends on the assumed norms. When making an offer to another member of the diamond industry in Switzerland, being 2 percent below the asking price might be insulting; when buying a used car in the United States, offers 20 to 40 percent below the asking price can be reasonable. Couching potentially extreme offers in "reasonable" trappings by appeal to "fair" principles and presenting them in a low-key manner may help mitigate the risk of adverse reaction. Finally, what is "high" depends on the degree of uncertainty about the counterpart's reservation value. Thus, a seller might choose an offer she thinks is 90 to 95 percent likely to be above the buyer's reservation value. The offer is likely to be much higher when she is more uncertain than when she is fairly confident.

ANCHORING

People often deal poorly with uncertainty. * * * When many people assess an uncertain quantity, they tend to jump to a point estimate of it and then adjust a bit around it to account for the uncertainty. By influencing a counterpart's point estimate of the quantity, a negotiator can locate where the small range of uncertainty will lie. One can thus "anchor" another's beliefs about the quantity in a way favorable to one's bargaining position.

For example, in one experiment, groups of college students were asked to name the percentage of the countries in the United Nations that are African. Before answering the question, a roulette wheel (modified to have the numbers one through one hundred) was spun in front of the students. For one typical group, the wheel stopped at 10 percent; for another group it landed at 65 percent. The first group was asked if the percentage of U.N. nations that are African was higher or lower than 10 percent (the number chosen by the spin of the wheel); the other group was asked whether the percentage was higher or lower than 65 percent. Then discussion was allowed to take place. In all other ways the groups were treated identically. Surprisingly, the first group's estimates were strikingly lower than those of the second: the mean of the first group's estimates was 24 percent while the mean of the second group's estimate was 45 percent! Thus, the clearly irrelevant piece of information—a randomly chosen starting point of 10 percent versus 65 percent—seemed strongly to anchor their perceptions about the proportion of U.N. member nations that are African.

A negotiator is typically uncertain about his counterpart's reservation value and aspirations. His own aspirations follow, in part, from these uncertain perceptions. And * * * social psychological experiments on "limits" (bottom lines or reservation values) suggest that [bargainers will often change their reservation value in the face of new information.]

When there is considerable uncertainty, a strong opening offer can sharply anchor perceptions of the bargaining set and aspirations. Prenegotiation tactics, initial discussions, and opening offers by the counterparts can favorably anchor a negotiator's perception of these values, cause him to reduce his own aspirations, and alter his reservation value. The building owner who demands $600,000, argues forcefully that this price is fair and reasonable, refuses for weeks to listen to other offers, and keeps returning discussions to his $600,000 price may strongly anchor toward $600,000 potential buyers' perceptions of what the owner will accept. Their original aspiration to pay much less will also likely be revised.

NOTES AND QUESTIONS

1. Do you agree with Edwards and White that making the first offer is a disadvantage best avoided? Or with Lax and Sebenius that it can confer benefits? Which makes you most comfortable? Does your answer depend on factors such as what issue is under negotiation or with whom you are negotiating?

2. Lax and Sebenius describe the anchoring effect that a first offer can have on subsequent negotiations. One study in the legal context found that subjects were nearly twice as likely to accept a settlement offer of $12,000 in a hypothetical product defect case if the offeror initially offered $2,000 (and then increased his offer to $12,000) than if the offeror initially offered $10,000 (and then increased his offer to $12,000). The researchers argue that the $2,000 initial offer anchors the plaintiff-offeree's expectations at a low figure, making the subsequent large increase seem like a major concession. See Korobkin and Guthrie, Opening Offers and Out of Court Settlement: A Little Moderation Might Not Go a Long Way, 10 Ohio St. J.Disp.Res. 1 (1994).

3. As we've seen, bargaining over a single issue—such as money—is difficult in part because every move you make sends signals to the other side about what your next move may be. If you make too generous an offer up front, for example, the other side will realize that you're willing to pay more than they expected and may try to take advantage of you. If you're too stingy, however, the other side may perceive you as overly zealous, not serious about settling, or personally offensive, and may stop negotiating with you. Thus, the very act of trying to settle may make settlement more difficult.

Professors Gertner and Miller have argued that using "settlement escrows" can help to overcome such strategic difficulties and to promote settlement. To create a settlement escrow one would simply appoint a mediator or agent to accept cash settlement offers from both parties to a lawsuit. If the offers did not "cross," the neutral would indicate that there was no settlement but would not disclose the amounts of the offers. If the offers crossed, the neutral would impose a settlement at the midpoint of the two offers. See Gertner and Miller, Settlement Escrows, 24 J. Leg.Stud. 87 (1995).

Not surprisingly, several Internet services now offer systems that operate much like these settlement escrows. The most common are online blind bidding mechanisms. When two disputing parties sign on to use one of these services, each is typically instructed to submit, in private, their offer or demand. The system's computer then compares these submissions and informs the parties either that their figures overlap—in which case the case is settled—or that the figures do not overlap—in which case the parties may have an opportunity to try again.

On www.clicknsettle.com, for example, the system settles a case in one of two ways. First, if a plaintiff's demand is lower than the defendant's offer, the case is settled for the plaintiff's demand. Second, if at any time the plaintiff's demand comes within 30 percent of the defendant's offer, the computer splits the difference between demand and offer and settles the case at that mid-point. The bidding process is blind; at no point does the computer reveal to you what your opponent has bid. Bids need not proceed in fixed rounds. Instead, a plaintiff could, for example, lower her demand several times unilaterally before getting a response from the defendant. On clicknsettle.com, offers must increase (and demands decrease) in no less than 5 percent increments.

Another site, www.cybersettle.com, is designed to aid settlement of insurance-related claims. The insurance carrier initiates the process by submitting claim information and three offers—one for each round of a blind three-round bidding process. The service then notifies the plaintiff's attorney, who may log on and make an online demand. If the insurance carrier's offer is greater than 85 percent of the plaintiff's demand, the case is automatically settled for the average of that amount (85 percent of the demand) and the offer. For example, if the carrier offered $90,000 and the plaintiff demanded $100,000, the case would settle because the offer is greater than $85,000 (85 percent of $100,000). The settlement amount would be $87,500 (the average of $90,000 and $85,000).

For a sample of such services, see www.clicknsettle.com; www.cybersettle.com; www.ussettle.com. Some sites assist users by offering free, secure, online communication services so that parties may negotiate directly. If parties fail to reach agreement, the site may refer them to a mediator. See www.squaretrade.com. For an overview of online systems, see Katsh and Rifkin, Online Dispute Resolution: Resolving Conflicts in Cyberspace (2001); Hang, Online Dispute Resolution Systems: The Future of Cyberspace Law, 41 Santa Clara L.Rev. 837 (2001).

4. This first offer problem is one of the reasons that negotiators often adopt a hard positional strategy and begin with *extreme* first offers. After all, starting with a reasonable position may just allow the other side to take advantage of you. Rather than fretting about how much to offer, however, or about whether to move first or not, Roger Fisher recommends changing the game completely—not engaging in a positional strategy (soft or hard) to begin with:

> There is little doubt that if both parties are playing the haggling game of positional bargaining, the best position to start with is often an extreme one. Rather than denying that statement, we question whether haggling is the best game to play.
>
> *Getting to YES* probably overstates the case against positional bargaining. The New York Stock Exchange demonstrates that thousands of transactions a day can successfully be concluded without discussing interests and with little concern for ongoing relationships. Yet most cases of what we all think of as negotiations involve more than one issue and also involve ongoing matters of implementation or future dealing. In such cases, I would suggest that taking an extreme position is rarely the best first move. Coming up with an extreme and unilaterally determined answer before understanding the other side's perception of the problem involves risks to one's credibility, to a cooperative problem-solving relationship, and to the efficient reaching of an agreement.

Fisher, Beyond *YES*, 1 Neg.J. 67, 67 (1985). In the next section we turn to an alternative to positional negotiation: a problem-solving strategy.

2. PROBLEM–SOLVING

Whereas negotiations typically focus on the parties' positions, offers and counteroffers, a problem-solving strategy centers more on the parties' underlying interests. The goal is to search for trades and creative agreements that can create value and to deal with distributive issues as amicably and efficiently as possible. This strategy does not *depend* upon there being integrative possibilities to create value, but it certainly is well suited to such negotiations. In this section we explore the basic components of a problem-solving approach.

a. THE BASICS OF A PROBLEM–SOLVING APPROACH

Roger Fisher, William Ury and Bruce Patton, Getting to Yes

40–50 (2d ed. 1991).

For a wise solution reconcile interests, not positions

* * * Since the parties' problem appears to be a conflict of positions, and since their goal is to agree on a position, they naturally tend to think and talk about positions—and in the process often reach an impasse.

Interests define the problem. The basic problem in a negotiation lies not in conflicting positions, but in the conflict between each side's needs, desires, concerns, and fears. The parties may say: "I am trying to get him to stop that real estate development next door."

Or "We disagree. He wants $100,000 for the house. I won't pay a penny more than $95,000."

But on a more basic level the problem is: "He needs the cash; I want peace and quiet."

Or "He needs at least $100,000 to settle with he ex-wife. I told my family that I wouldn't pay more than $95,000 for a house."

Such desires and concerns are *interests*. Interests motivate people; they are the silent movers behind the hubbub of positions. Your position is something you have decided upon. Your interests are what caused you to so decide.

The Egyptian–Israeli peace treaty blocked out at Camp David in 1978 demonstrates the usefulness of looking behind positions. Israel had occupied the Egyptian Sinai Peninsula since the Six Day War of 1967. When Egypt and Israel sat down together in 1978 to negotiate a peace, their positions were incompatible. Israel insisted on keeping some of the Sinai. Egypt, on the other hand, insisted that every inch of the Sinai be returned to Egyptian sovereignty. Time and again, people drew maps showing possible boundary lines that would divide the Sinai between Egypt and Israel. Compromising in this way was wholly unacceptable to Egypt. To go back to the situation as it was in 1967 was equally unacceptable to Israel.

Looking at their interests instead of their positions made it possible to develop a solution. Israel's interest lay in security; they did not want Egyptian tanks poised on their border ready to roll across at any time. Egypt's interest lay in sovereignty; the Sinai had been part of Egypt since the time of the Pharaohs. After centuries of domination by Greeks, Romans, Turks, French, and British, Egypt had only recently regained full sovereignty and was not about to cede territory to another foreign conqueror.

At Camp David, President Sadat of Egypt and Prime Minister Begin of Israel agreed to a plan that would return the Sinai to complete Egyptian sovereignty and, by demilitarizing large areas, would still assure Israeli security. The Egyptian flag would fly everywhere, but Egyptian tanks would be nowhere near Israel.

Reconciling interests rather than positions works for two reasons. First, for every interest there usually exist several possible positions that could satisfy it. All too often people simply adopt the most obvious position, as Israel did, for example, in announcing that they intended to keep part of the Sinai. When you do look behind opposed positions for the motivating interests, you can often find an alternative position which meets not only your interests but theirs as well. * * *

* * *

[Second, in] many negotiations * * * a close examination of the underlying interests will reveal the existence of many more interests that are shared or compatible than ones that are opposed.

* * *

Agreement is often made possible precisely because interests differ. You and a shoe-seller may both like money and shoes. Relatively, his interest in the fifty dollars exceeds his interest in the shoes. For you, the situation is reversed: you like the shoes better than the fifty dollars. Hence the deal. Shared interests and differing but complementary interests can both serve as the building blocks for a wise agreement.

How do you identify interests?

The benefit of looking behind positions for interests is clear. * * * How do you go about understanding the interests involved in a negotiation, remembering that figuring out *their* interests will be at least as important as figuring out *yours*?

Ask "Why?" One basic technique is to put yourself in their shoes. Examine each position they take, and ask yourself "Why?" * * *

Ask "Why not?" Think about their choice. One of the most useful ways to uncover interests is first to identify the basic decision that those on the other side probably see you asking them for, and then to ask yourself why they have not made that decision. What interests of theirs stand in the way? If you are trying to change their minds, the starting point is to figure out where their minds are now.

* * *

The most powerful interests are basic human needs. In searching for the basic interests behind a declared position, look particularly for those bedrock concerns which motivate all people. If you can take care of such basic needs, you increase the chance both of reaching agreement and, if an agreement is reached, of the other side's keeping to it. Basic human needs include:

— security

— economic well-being

— a sense of belonging

— recognition

— control over one's life

As fundamental as they are, basic human needs are easy to overlook. In many negotiations, we tend to think that the only interest involved is money. Yet even in a negotiation over a monetary figure, such as the amount of alimony to be specified in a separation agreement, much more can be involved. What does a wife really want in asking for $500 a week in alimony? Certainly she is interested in her economic well-being, but what else? Possibly she wants the money in order to feel psychologically secure. She may also want it for recognition: to feel that she is treated fairly and as an equal. Perhaps the husband can ill afford to pay $500 a week, and perhaps his wife does not need that much, yet she will likely accept less only if her needs for security and recognition are met in other ways.

Carrie J. Menkel–Meadow, When Winning Isn't Everything: The Lawyer as Problem–Solver

28 Hofstra L.Rev. 905, 915–918 (2000).

A good problem solver must take the problem, transaction, or matter presented by the client, analyze what the problem or situation requires, and then use creative abilities to solve, resolve, arrange, structure, or transform the situation so it is made better for the client, not worse. To do this, the lawyer must also take account of the other side, not as someone to be "bested" or beaten, but as someone with needs, interests, and goals as well. How can both or all parties (including the state and the defendant in a criminal case, the plaintiff-victim and the tortfeasor, the breaching contractors, buyer-sellers, the regulated and private industry, and the many responsible parties in a clean-up site in an environmental case) attempt to structure their negotiations so that they learn what they want to do and what they can do?

Here, the important observation of social psychologist George Homans is significant: people often have complementary interests. Individuals do not always value things exactly the same way—[I like] icing and my brother like[s] cake. By having many issues and many different preferences, individuals actually increase the possibility of reaching an agreement, whether it is settling a case or arranging a transaction. It may be useful if judges and litigators narrow the issues for trial, but it is detrimental to the settlement process to narrow issues. The more issues, the more likely trades or "log-rolls," as the legislators call them, will be possible. Therefore, seeing many issues and parties and all organizational needs and preferences is essential to good problem solving.

Before one starts to compete with the other side, it is useful to see if the pie for which one is fighting can be expanded, before one divides it, if one must. This is what negotiation theorists call "expanding the pie" or "value creation," before one gets to the nasty "value claiming" or pie-dividing stages. * * * So, one should always ask the journalist's basic questions of every matter: 1) What (What is at stake? What is the "res" of the dispute? Can it be changed, expanded or traded?); 2) When (Must one resolve this now? Are installments possible? Are there any tax consequences or contingency arrangements? What risk allocation and sharing is involved?); 3) Where (Where can something be moved or transferred? Can a change of forum or process be effected?); 4) Who (Who are all the relevant parties here? Can one add some people or entities with resources and the power to do things?); 5) How (What means may be used to solve the problem: money, land, or an apology?); and finally, 6) Why (Why are the parties here? What are the underlying reasons, motivations, or interests in this matter? Can one reconstruct the reasons for being here and look for new ways to resolve the issues?). Answering these questions often, not always, provides new insights and new resources for solving problems.

One still needs law and a lot of other knowledge to solve problems and structure transactions. As Gary Klein's work indicates, "pattern recognition" helps those with experience quickly analyze and diagnose a problem and select a single solution, which is abandoned if it does not work. Lawyers need life experiences and they need to be generalists who can recognize many different kinds of patterns. Specialization may be increasing because of a perception or belief that individuals can only recognize a limited number of "patterns" in their experiences. I want to suggest that good legal problem solving, however, also requires the cross-fertilization of solving problems across fields. Individuals develop creativity by translating from one realm to another * * * The cost sharing of clean-up sites in environmental law is related to market share settlement grids in mass torts. The "structured settlement" or annuity in tort can work in installment payments for other damages or employment settlements. * * * So, in this sense, problem solving is analytic, rigorous, intellectual, interdisciplinary, and certainly more than doctrinal learning. Lawyers must learn to think of themselves in terms of experts in problem solving who draw on a wide range of disciplines. Lawyers are intelligent; they work with words and concepts ("linguistic intelligence"). They must learn to be facile with more systems of thought, as well as with the experiences on the ground * * * of the people they serve.

Howard Raiffa, Post–Settlement Settlements

1 Neg.J. 9–12 (1985).

"It's all very well to talk about collegial, joint problem-solving negotiation processes, but my opponent has unreasonable aspirations and I'm not going to weaken my just claim by trying to be a nice guy. I'm going to bargain tough, for myself, by myself." No matter how much we might bemoan this state of affairs, we must recognize that a lot of disputes are settled by hard-nosed, positional bargaining. Settled, yes. But efficiently settled? Often not. Both sides are often so intent on justifying their individual claims that not much time is spent on creating gains to be shared. They quibble about sharing a small pie and often fail to realize that perhaps the pie can be jointly enlarged. Even where there is a modicum of civility and some cooperative behavior on the part of the negotiators, it is not easy to squeeze out joint gains.

Here's one suggestion for how such intransigent negotiators might be helped. Let them negotiate as they will. Let them arrive at a settlement, or let a judge or jury impose a settlement on them. Mr. Jones, one protagonist, might feel happy about the outcome—he got more than he expected—but Ms. Spencer, the other protagonist, is unhappy—she did not realize her just aspirations. But even in this case the negotiators might not have squeezed out the full potential gains. There may be another carefully crafted settlement that both Jones and Spencer might prefer to the settlement they actually achieved.

Now let's imagine that along comes an intervenor * * * and he asks Jones and Spencer after they have achieved their settlement if they would be willing to let him try to sweeten the contract for each. The intervenor carefully explains to Jones that he will have the security of the outcome level he has already achieved but that he (Jones) may have the opportunity to do still better. The intervenor proposes that after some analysis he will suggest an alternate settlement—a *post-settlement settlement*, if you will—that would replace the original settlement only on the condition that both parties agree to the change; and of course they would only do this if each prefers the new settlement proposal to the old one.

Is this pie in the sky? Can the intervenor deliver the goods? Not always, but then Spencer and Jones would not have lost anything in trying, except perhaps their time. But it is my contention that in really complex negotiations where a lot of issues are at stake, where uncertainties are involved, or where settlements could involve transactions and payments over time, jointly desirable post-settlement settlements more often than not could be achieved by an analytical intervenor. If successful, the intervenor would add a surplus value to each side, and he might be recompensed for his effort by getting a small proportional slice of this surplus (if there is such a surplus) from each of the protagonists. So everybody would be happy.

NOTES AND QUESTIONS

1. The search for integrative or value-creating agreements is central to the problem-solving strategy. Obviously this search requires seeking out information about the other side's preferences, priorities and interests. Problem-solving then requires creating possible agreements and testing for optimality. Fisher, Ury and Patton recommend "brainstorming" about possible options before choosing one agreement. This changes the typical positional pattern of proposing two opposed agreements and battling between them—instead, negotiators are urged to propose many possibilities before evaluating their merits. See Fisher, Ury and Patton, Getting to Yes (2d ed. 1991).

In the legal context, Mnookin, Peppet and Tulumello recommend separating negotiations over a legal dispute into "two tables"—one focused on estimating the expected value of the case (using decision analysis) and the other focused on discovering the parties' interests and coming up with joint gain solutions. See Mnookin, Peppet and Tulumello, Beyond Winning: Negotiating to Create Value in Deals and Disputes 226–227 (2000). Whereas lawyers may be more involved at the first "table," clients or principals may be more involved in the interest-based negotiations.

Raiffa's post-settlement settlement is another possible approach. Although he calls for a third-party intervenor, two parties can theoretically use the approach by simply reaching an initial agreement and then trying to improve upon it. Some suggest that parties can, and do, engage in such modification, and that it is essential in problem-solving negotiation. See Bazerman, Russ, and Yakura, Post–Settlement Settlements in Two–Party Negotiations, 3 Neg.J. 283–292 (1987).

2. Information sharing is at the heart of a problem-solving approach to negotiation. Without information about the other side's interests, preferences, priorities and resources, finding value-creating trades is unlikely. Not surprisingly, increased information exchange has been shown to lead to improved negotiation performance. See Thompson, Peterson and Brodt, Team Negotiation: An Examination of Integrative and Distributive Bargaining, 70 J. of Personality & Soc.Psychol. 66–78 (1996). And lack of information exchange is a constant problem. After conducting a meta-analysis of 32 negotiation experiments, Thompson and Hrebec conclude, "Remarkably few people provided or sought information about the other party's interests during negotiations (about 20% and 7%, respectively), even though they had ample opportunity and there were no obvious costs of information exchange." Thompson and Hrebec, Lose-Lose Agreements in Interdependent Decision–Making, 120 Psychol.Bull. 396–409 (1996).

Why don't parties seek out their counterparts' interests in negotiation? One answer is that sharing information in an attempt to collaborate may risk exploitation. This "negotiator's dilemma," which we explore in more detail below (p. 142), derives from the possibility that if I tell you my interests and needs in an attempt to facilitate value-creating trades, you may instead use that information to capture a greater amount of the surplus for yourself. The more you know about what I want, the easier it is to hold that information hostage and demand concessions from me on those issues I care about.

Another answer is what some researchers have called the "fixed pie bias." Negotiators tend to assume that they face a zero-sum situation, not a positive-sum or integrative opportunity:

The fixed-pie assumption * * * represents a fundamental bias in human judgment. That is, negotiators have a systematic intuitive bias that distorts their behavior: They assume that their interests directly conflict with the other party's interests. The fundamental assumption of a fixed-pie probably results from a competitive society that creates the belief in a win-lose situation. This win-lose orientation is manifested objectively in our society in athletic competition, admission to academic programs, industrial promotion systems, and so on. Individuals tend to generalize from these objective win-lose situations and apply their experience to situations that are not objectively fixed-pies. Faced with a mixed-motive situation requiring both cooperation and competition, it is the competitive aspect that becomes salient—resulting in a win-lose orientation and a distributive approach to bargaining. This in turn results in the development of a strategy for obtaining the largest share possible of the perceived fixed-pie. Such a focus inhibits the creativity and problem-solving necessary for the development of integrative solutions.

Bazerman, Negotiator Judgment: A Critical Look at the Rationality Assumption 27 Am.Behavioral Sci. 211 (1983).

In one study, for example, Thompson and Hastie found that sixty-eight percent of negotiators assumed that there would be no opportunities for mutual gains or value-creating. See Thompson and Hastie, Social Perception in Negotiation, 47 Org. Behavior & Human Dec.Processes 98–123 (1990). Fixed-pie assumptions can be self-fulfilling. Studies have shown that negotiators who assume there will be value-creating opportunities are more likely to use strategies to identify an opponent's preferences and interests. See Pinkley, Griffith, and Northcraft, Fixed Pie A La Mode: Information Availability, Information Processing, and the Negotiation of Suboptimal Agreements, 62 Org. Behavior & Human Dec.Processes 101– 112 (1995). Conversely, the fixed-pie assumption can lead negotiators to ignore information that would disprove their expectations. In one study, for example, Pinkley et al. found that twenty-five percent of experts and forty

B. STRATEGY **133**

percent of beginners failed to identify their negotiating counterpart's interests and preferences *even when told those preferences in advance*. See id.

What causes the fixed-pie bias? As Professor Max Bazerman notes above, researchers have suggested that perhaps we have a cultural norm of competition that people erroneously generalize to negotiation situations. See also Bottom and Paese, False Consensus, Stereotypic Cues, and the Perception of Integrative Potential in Negotiation, 27 J. Applied Soc.Psychol. 21 1919, 1920 (1997); Dieffenbach, Psychology, Society and the Development of the Adversarial Posture, 16 J. Legal Prof. 205 (1991). Do you agree? Is our culture so competitive that we assume that our interests are opposed to—rather than merely different from—others'?

3. Just as computers have become useful tools in resolving distributive issues by facilitating structured positional negotiations, some negotiation support systems (NSS) are designed to assist negotiators in analyzing a negotiation problem and finding joint gains. Some systems help bargainers prepare for a negotiation. Others structure the bargaining process in ways that promote finding efficient outcomes. For example, one system, called NEGOTIATION ASSISTANT, helps parties to disaggregate their preferences and priorities by answering a series of questions in preparation for a negotiation. This, in turn, facilitates finding trades and packages that create value. In addition, the system allows for "post-settlement settlements"—finding Pareto-superior settlements to whatever deal the parties reached. Early studies suggest that using such computerized tools can lead to more efficient negotiated outcomes. See Rangaswamy and Shell, Using Computers to Realize Joint Gains in Negotiations: Toward an "Electronic Bargaining Table," 43 Mgt. Sci. 1147 (1997). See also Yuan, Rose and Archer, A Web–Based Negotiation Support System, 8 Elec.Mkts. 13 (1998).

b. FAIRNESS AND NORMS

It is important to note that problem-solving is not limited to the integrative aspects of bargaining. Problem-solving skills are also helpful in resolving the distributive issues present in any negotiation. Consider the following excerpt from Roger Fisher, author of Getting to Yes:

> The guts of the negotiation problem, in my view, is not who gets the last dollar, but what is the best process for resolving that issue. It is certainly a mistake to assume that the only process available for resolving distributional questions is hard bargaining over positions. In my judgment it is also a mistake to assume that such hard bargaining is the best process for resolving differences efficiently and in the long-term interest of either side.
>
> Two men in a lifeboat quarreling over limited rations have a distributional problem. One approach to resolving that problem is to engage in hard bargaining. *A* can insist that he will sink the boat unless he gets 60 percent of the rations. *B* can insist that he will sink the boat unless he gets 80 percent of the rations. But *A*'s and *B*'s

shared problem is not just how to divide the rations; rather it is how to divide the rations without tipping over the boat and while getting the boat to safer waters. In my view, to treat the distributional issue as a shared problem is a better approach than to treat it as a contest of will in which a more deceptive, more stubborn, and less rational negotiator will tend to fare better. Treating the distributional issue as a problem to be solved ("How about dividing the rations in proportion to our respective weights?" or "How about a fixed portion of the rations for each hour that one of us rows?") is likely to be better for both than a contest over who is more willing to sink the boat.

* * * It is precisely in deciding such distributional issues that objective criteria can play their most useful role. * * *

* * *

Two negotiators can be compared with two judges, trying to decide a case. There won't be a decision unless they agree. It is perfectly possible for fellow negotiators, despite their self-interest, to behave like fellow judges, in that they advance reasoned arguments seriously, and are open to persuasion by better arguments. They need not advance standards simply as rationalizations for positions, but as providing a genuine basis for joint decision.

Fisher, Comment, 34 J. of Leg.Educ. 120, 121 (1984).

A central aspect of problem-solving is using norms or standards of fairness to resolve or diminish distributive conflicts. As the following excerpts demonstrate, research has shown that fairness is an important concern for most people. At the same time, many commentators have debated both the efficacy and availability of "objective criteria" in negotiation, and have questioned how useful norms are in resolving conflict.

Max H. Bazerman, Robert Gibbons, Leigh Thompson, and Kathleen L. Valley, Can Negotiators Outperform Game Theory?

in Debating Rationality: Nonrational Aspects of Organizational Decision Making 78 (1998).

* * * Substantial evidence exists that individuals place utility on fairness in ways that are inconsistent with the self-interest assumption. In a provocative set of experiments, Kahneman, Knetsch, and Thaler asked subjects to evaluate the fairness of the action in the following situation:

A hardware store has been selling snow shovels for $15. The morning after a large snowstorm, the store raises the price to $20. Please rate this action as:

Completely Fair—Acceptable—Unfair—Very Unfair

The two favorable and the two unfavorable categories were combined to indicate the proportion of respondents who judged the action acceptable or unfair. Despite the (short-run) economic rationality of raising the prices on the snow shovels, 82 percent of the respondents considered this action unfair. * * *

Fairness issues also arise in ultimatum games. [In an ultimatum game, one person—the offeror—is given a certain sum of money by the experimenter. The offeror must then make an offer to divide that sum of money with the offeree. If the offeree accepts the offer, then the money is in fact divided and both keep their sum. If the offeree rejects the offer, however, then the experimenter keeps the sum and neither subject receives anything.] A number of researchers have methodically studied how people respond to ultimatums. [G]ame theory predicts that player 1 will offer player 2 only slightly more than zero, and that player 2 will accept any offer greater than zero. Empirical observation suggests, however, that individuals incorporate fairness considerations into their choices. Player 1 demands less than 70 percent of the funds on average, while individuals in the role of player 2 sometimes reject profitable but unequal offers, and accept zero only 20 percent of the time it is offered. * * *

In recent work, Straub and Murnighan manipulated knowledge of the size of the pie in ultimatum games. When player 1 knew the size of the pie but player 2 did not, player 2s accepted lower offers and player 1s made lower offers. The latter evidence suggests that it is 1's evaluation of 2's requirement of fairness that drives 1's observed behavior when the size of the pie is common knowledge, rather than any absolute preference for fairness on the part of player 1. * * *

Fairness considerations may be so powerful that players will be willing to pay to punish their opponent if their opponent asks for too much. In two-stage, alternating-offer bargaining games, Ochs and Roth found that 81 percent of rejected offers were followed by disadvantageous counteroffers, where the party who rejected the initial offer demanded less than he or she had just been offered. Ochs and Roth argue that the players' utility for fairness may explain the results. * * * [P]arties realize that the other side may very well refuse offers perceived as unfair, despite the economic rationality of accepting them. * * *

Russell Korobkin, A Positive Theory of Legal Negotiation

88 Georgetown L.J. 1789, 1821–1829 (2000).

Many common negotiating tactics are best understood as attempts to establish a procedure that the other party will view as "fair" for agreeing on a deal point within the bargaining zone. In employing such tactics, the negotiator may have either of two motives. He might believe that the procedure is equitable to both parties, and the resulting deal point will thus create a mutually beneficial transaction in which neither side gets the better of the other. Alternatively, he might attempt to establish a procedure that will lead to an agreement that benefits him or his client substantially more than it benefits the other negotiator. Whether the negotiator's

CHAPTER II NEGOTIATION

motives are communitarian or individualistic, however, the procedures must have the appearance of equity in order to win acceptance.

1. The Reciprocity Norm: Exchanging Concessions

Perhaps the most common behavioral norm invoked in the negotiation process is reciprocity. When one person takes some action on behalf of another, it is assumed that the favor will be returned. The person who fails to reciprocate commits a social faux pas, which can lead to social ostracism and derision.

* * *

The reciprocity norm is a fundamental element of the negotiation process as well. When one party makes a concession, the other finds himself under a social obligation to do likewise. If Esau offers $150,000 for Jacob's catering business, and Jacob counters with $200,000, Esau might increase his offer to $160,000 for the primary purpose of obligating Jacob to make a reciprocal concession. Even if Jacob believes that his original $200,000 demand is below Esau's [reservation price,] meaning that Esau could pay that amount and still be made better off by completing the transaction, Jacob will find himself under immense pressure to lower his demand in the interest of fairness.

* * *

The failure of negotiators to reciprocate in some fashion when an opponent makes a concession will almost certainly increase the likelihood that bargaining will end in impasse. The reciprocity norm is so strong that most commentators strongly warn against negotiators making single, take-it-or-leave-it offers, often called ''Boulwarism'' after a famous negotiator known for this tactic. Boulwarism can be successful, but only if the offeror is able to justify her offer as consistent with another procedural or substantive fairness norm.

2. Procedural Equity: ''Splitting the Difference''

Absent situation-specific reasons to think that a particular substantive division of the bargaining zone is the most fair, negotiators often assume that an equal division, or ''parity,'' is consistent with fairness norms. Consequently, splitting the difference between the parties' [reservation prices] is often perceived as a fair procedure for reaching a deal point. * * *

Of course, while each party can estimate the other's [reservation price,] in most cases neither will know the other's [reservation price] precisely. Consequently, they may invoke the norm of strict procedural equality by agreeing to split the difference between the two initial offers, two later offers (after reciprocal concessions have been made), or what each party represents to be his [reservation price.] One problem with each of these shortcuts, however, is that a party who presents the more extreme offer or is more dishonest about his [reservation price] will succeed in capturing the majority of the cooperative surplus. * * *

B. Strategy

137

3. Focal Points

* * * Deal points within the bargaining zone can be called "focal points" if they have some special salience, or prominence, to the negotiating parties, compared to other possible deal points. Focal points can strike negotiators as neutral deal points, and thus, their selection often meets the parties' expectations of procedural fairness.

When negotiations are denominated in currency, round numbers are often natural focal points. Consider the following simple empirical demonstration. J. Keith Murnighan told students that a woman found a car she wished to buy with a sticker price of either \$10,650, \$2,650, or \$2,450, and asked what they thought the exact final sales price would be. The dominant responses were \$10,000, \$2,500, and \$2,000 respectively—all very round numbers. Since most car dealers bargain over the price of their wares, the reciprocity norm suggests that it is fair to expect they will offer some sort of discount off the sticker price in return for concessions made by the purchaser. What price would be a fair deal point resulting from reciprocal concessions? In the absence of a good reason to choose a different deal point, one that stands out from the others often seems about as neutral—and thus fair—a point as any.

* * *

C. SUBSTANTIVE FAIRNESS: SEEKING NEUTRAL DEAL POINTS

Singling out a deal point requires the parties to agree on what is fair. In many negotiations, agreement is achieved by the parties acting consistently with procedural norms of bargaining behavior such as reciprocity, splitting the difference, and selection of prominent focal points. The deal point that emerges from a procedurally fair process is accepted by the parties as itself fair, assuming it lies within the bargaining zone. In other negotiations, the parties instead negotiate over what specific deal point would be most substantively fair.

In the best-selling book, Getting to Yes, Fisher and his co-authors urge negotiators to "insist on using objective criteria," which might include such benchmarks as market price, historic price, historic profit level, or some conception of merit. In other words, the authors present a normative case for agreeing on a deal point via negotiations over the most substantively fair way to divide the cooperative surplus, which they can create by reaching an agreement. Calling such criteria "objective" is a misnomer because (1) any such criteria will benefit one party over the other as opposed to a different criteria and (2) none can be conclusively established by logical argument to be justifiable ways to divide the cooperative surplus. Nonetheless, they are critical concepts in legal negotiation because they facilitate the parties' agreement on a single deal point that both can perceive as fair.

1. Market Standards

Negotiating parties often justify the proposal of a specific deal point within a larger bargaining zone by reference to the market price of the good in question. * * * This price might be determined by averaging the sales prices of similar companies sold recently, by an independent appraiser's examination, or in some other generally accepted way.

* * *

2. Other Reference Transactions

A significant amount of research suggests that individuals make fairness judgments about a particular transaction based on other "reference transactions." When past transactions are used as reference points, proposed transactions are perceived as fair to the extent that they are consistent with the reference transactions. Fairness is based on the normalcy of the proposed transaction relative to its antecedents, not on the intrinsic justice of the referent. * * *

* * * Parties who have done business together in the past might contend that their past dealings are a natural reference point, and that a proposed transaction ought to take place on the past terms—possibly with an allowance for inflation—rather than current market prices. A seller might defend a proposed price on the ground that it provides him with a certain percentage profit, implicitly arguing the seller's cost is a fair reference point. A commercial buyer might ask a seller for terms embodied in an industry association's form contract on the grounds that trade custom is the appropriate reference point for the transaction.

* * *

3. Merits and Morals

When negotiating parties rely on procedural fairness norms to settle on a deal point, they implicitly agree that neither has a stronger claim to the cooperative surplus that their deal will create on the basis of merit or morality. But often times negotiators argue that fairness requires an unequal distribution of that surplus or, in other words, that to preserve equity in the relationship between the parties, one must be allocated the lion's share of the gains from trade.

Hoffman and Spitzer found that when one subject was given a unilateral right to receive $12—leaving the other subject with nothing—unless the subjects could agree on a method to divide $14 between them, the first subject bargained for a far larger share of the $14 stake when he "earned" the dominant role by beating the other subject in a simple game than when he won the role in a coin flip. Subjects, it seems, believe that unequal divisions are fair if one party is more deserving in some way external to the experiment, but not if one party merely has the good luck of being randomly assigned the role with more power.

Those results and others similar to them suggest that individuals often equate fairness with the "contribution principle": the allocation of the cooperative surplus proportional to contributions or "inputs" to the surplus. * * *

As an alternative to the contribution principle, either party might lay moral claim to the cooperative surplus by demonstrating relative poverty or need, such that an unequal division is necessary to ensure equal—or close to equal—outcomes. * * *

Leigh Thompson and Janice Nadler, Judgmental Biases In Conflict Resolution and How to Overcome Them

in Morton Deutsch and Peter T. Coleman (eds.), The Handbook of Conflict Resolution: Theory and Practice 213, 224–225 (2000).

Although people generally want what is fair, their assessments of fairness are often self-serving. Moreover, the fact that we have little or no self-awareness of this influence on our otherwise sound judgment heightens the intransigence of our views. Suppose you have worked for seven hours and have been paid $25. Another person has worked for ten hours doing the same work. How much do you think the other person should get paid? If you're like most people, you believe the other person should get paid more for doing more work—about $30, on average. This is hardly a self-serving response. Now, consider the reverse situation: the other person has worked for seven hours and been paid $25. You have worked for ten hours. What is a fair wage for you to be paid? Messick and Sentis found the average response to be about $35. The difference * * * illustrates the phenomenon of egocentric bias: people pay themselves substantially more than they are willing to pay others for doing the same task.

Consider another example. You are told about an accident in which a motorcyclist was injured after being hit by a car. After learning all the facts, you are asked to make a judgment of how much money you think is a fair settlement to compensate the motorcyclist for his injuries. Then, you are asked to play the role of either the injured motorcyclist or the driver of the car and to negotiate a settlement. Most of the time, people in this situation have no trouble coming to an agreement.

Now imagine doing the same thing, except that your role assignment comes first. That is, first you are asked to play the role of the motorcyclist or the driver, and then you learn all the facts, decide on a fair settlement, and finally negotiate. In this situation, the only thing that changes is that you learn the facts and make a fair settlement judgment through the eyes of one of the parties, instead of from the standpoint of a neutral observer. As it turns out, this difference is crucial. Instead of having no trouble coming to an agreement * * * people who know their roles from the beginning have a very difficult time coming to an agreement. The high impasse rate * * * is linked to self-serving judgments of fairness. The more biased the prenegotiation fair-settlement judgment, the more likely the later negotiation will result in impasse. * * *

In conflict situations, there are often as many proposed solutions as there are parties. Each party sincerely believes its own proposed outcome is fair for everyone. At the same time, each party's conception of fairness is

140 CHAPTER II NEGOTIATION

tainted by self-interest, so that each solution is most favorable to the party proposing it.

NOTES AND QUESTIONS

1. Experimental research, particularly on ultimatum games, shows that people are often willing to sacrifice in the name of fairness. In other words, most individuals would rather take a worse outcome than a slightly better agreement that they see as unfair. See e.g., Fehr and Gachter, Fairness and Retaliation: The Economics of Reciprocity, 14 J.Econ. Perspectives 159 (2000). For a discussion of ultimatum games and their use by game theorists, see Kramer, Shah and Woerner, Why Ultimatums Fail: Social Identity and Moralistic Aggression, in Coercive Bargaining in Negotiation as a Social Process 288–289 (1995).

This suggests that a skilled negotiator should consider whether others will likely see her proposals as fair, regardless of whether that negotiator actually cares about fairness as a social or moral good in itself. Fairness, in short, is effective. Are you willing to accept an "unfair" agreement just because it is better than your best alternative to negotiation? Or do you turn down such agreements if they seem unfair? What standard should you use to judge the fairness of a proposed agreement?

2. Thompson and Nadler point out that our judgments of fairness can be biased, and Korobkin notes that "objective criteria" are rarely truly objective. Given that the parties to a dispute will often disagree about what's fair and may seek to apply different (and self-serving) standards of fairness, are appeals to fairness helpful in negotiation?

In many transactions such standards or focal points may be obvious. If you are purchasing a used car, for example, the "blue book" will approximate the car's value. If you are buying a house, you might look at other recent sales in the neighborhood, the average price per square foot in your town, or what the house sold for most recently. Yet, what focal points, market standards, or reference transactions are likely to be available in most legal disputes? For example, what standards of fairness might you turn to in a medical malpractice litigation? In a product liability case? In a commercial contract litigation? For each of these examples, what types of information would you like to have to judge the fairness of the other side's proposed agreement? Is that information likely to be available?

3. Although appealing to fairness is a common problem-solving approach to resolving distributive issues, pursuing fair agreements can sometimes conflict with another central goal of problem-solving: seeking integrative or efficient solutions.[14] If you and I are negotiating over who should keep a

---

14. Social theorists, philosophers and economists have long debated whether Pareto efficiency is compatible with fundamental notions of fairness. See Sen, The Impossibility of a Paretian Liberal, 78 J.Pol.Econ. 152 (1970); Kaplow and Shavell, Any Non–Welfarist Method of Policy Assessment Violates the Pareto Principle, 109 J.Pol. Econ. (2001); Kaplow and Shavell, The Conflict Between Notions of Fairness and the Pareto Principle,

fossil that we found while hiking, several "fair" solutions might not be the most value-creating. We could split the fossil in two, each keeping an equal half. Although this might be fair, it is obviously inefficient. Neither gets what we really want. If we draw straws, our process might be fair but the outcome might be inefficient: I might get the fossil even if you value it more.

The basic point is that the choice of a division process to manage the distributive issues in a negotiation can make that division inefficient. For example, imagine that Sarah and Ned are divorcing and that they have six items to try to divide fairly (E.g., a car, their house, etc.). What should they do? One option is to flip a coin to see who goes first and then alternate. This may seem fair, but it may not be. If Sarah chooses first, she may come out ahead if Ned and Sarah value the items similarly. In addition, alternating may not produce an efficient allocation. If Ned thinks the six items are all equally valuable but Sarah finds two items valuable and six worthless, *both* would prefer to give Sarah her two valuable items (and Ned the other four items) than to alternate Sarah–Ned–Sarah–Ned–Sarah–Ned. The non-alternating solution gives Sarah one hundred percent of her total value (because she gets both of her valuable items) and Ned approximately sixty-seven percent of his total value (because he gets four items, which he values equally). In the pure alternating scheme, Sarah and Ned each receive only approximately fifty percent of their respective value. Thus, in some circumstances alternation can lead to an inefficient outcome—there is a division that would leave at least one party better off without leaving the other worse off. See Brams and Taylor, The Win–Win Solution: Guaranteeing Fair Shares to Everybody 26 (1999).

Another option is "divide and choose"—flip a coin to see who divides, and then that person creates two piles of items. The other person then gets to pick which pile he or she keeps and which pile the divider keeps. From an efficiency standpoint the problem is that the divider may not know the chooser's preferences. For example, imagine that Sarah and Ned were each given 100 points to distribute (in secret) among the six items to be divided. For example, if Sarah really wanted their Mercedes she could place fifty points on it in her list. (This would indicate that she thought the Mercedes was worth fifty percent of the total value of all the items, given that she put half of her points on that item.) Now imagine that Sarah tries to divide the items into two roughly equivalent piles. She places the Mercedes in one pile (because to her it is worth fifty points) and the other five items in the other pile (also worth fifty points). But Ned's perspective is quite different. He has allocated his points according to his preferences, and he doesn't much want the Mercedes. In his opinion, the piles are worth 10 points (for the car) versus 90 points. He'll obviously take the second pile, but this allocation may be inefficient. Imagine that two of the items Ned has received (a stereo and a painting) are worth nothing to Ned. Sarah, however, placed 10 points on each. If she got those items she would receive

1 Am.L. & Econ.Rev. 63 (1999); Chang, A Liberal Theory of Social Welfare: Fairness, Utility, and the Pareto Principle, 110 Yale L.J. 173 (2000).

142 CHAPTER II NEGOTIATION

70 points and Ned would still receive 90. The divide and choose method, although it can seem fair, may not have produced an optimal outcome. A third procedure is often referred to as "adjusted winner." In adjusted winner, each person again allocates 100 points to the items in question. Each person is then given those items on which he or she has placed more points. Thus, if Sarah put fifty points on the Mercedes but Ned allocated only 10 to it, Sarah would get the car. This initial distribution is efficient— each item goes to the person who most values it. When all of the items were distributed, Sarah and Ned could adjust the final distribution somewhat to make it more fair. For example, Sarah might have ended up with items equaling a total of 70 of her points, whereas Ned received a total of only 55 of his points. Sarah would then transfer items to Ned to even out the distribution. See id. at 69. See also Brams and Taylor, Fair Division: From Cake–Cutting to Dispute Resolution (1996); Brams and Taylor, A Procedure for Divorce Settlements, 13 Mediation Q. 191 (1996); Raiffa, Lectures on Negotiation Analysis (1996).

No approach is perfect. The point is that fairness, although helpful and important in deciding distributive issues, can create problems in terms of value creation or efficiency.

3. CHOOSING AN APPROACH

Imagine that you are preparing for a negotiation that you believe will involve both value-creating opportunities and, inevitably, distributive issues. You have a choice: bargain hard for distributive advantage, thereby perhaps sacrificing some undiscovered gains from trade if the negotiation fails to explore adequately the parties' interests and potential solutions, or attempt to set a more collaborative, problem-solving tone, thereby increasing your chances of enlarging the pie but perhaps simultaneously exposing yourself to an increased risk of exploitation. What should you do? Here we explore different perspectives on how to choose a negotiation strategy.

a. THE NEGOTIATOR'S DILEMMA

Unfortunately, the choice between strategies is not a simple one. On the one hand, the possibility of creating value may lead you to favor a problem-solving approach in which you share information and search for trades. On the other hand, adopting this collaborative stance may leave you vulnerable to exploitation. The very steps needed to expand the pie—in particular the sharing of information—may be disadvantageous when it comes time to carve the pie up. Consider the following description of this "negotiator's dilemma."

Robert H. Mnookin and Lee Ross, Barriers to Conflict Resolution: Introduction

in Arrow et al., eds., Barriers to Conflict Resolution 7–8 (1995).

Self-interested actors may fail to achieve efficient outcomes because their rational calculations induce them to adopt strategies and tactics that preclude such efficiency. Negotiators characteristically face a dilemma arising from the inherent tension between two different goals. The first goal consists of maximizing the joint value of the settlement—that is, the pool of benefits or size of the "pie" to be divided. The second goal consists of maximizing their own share of the benefit pool—that is, the size and attractiveness of their particular "slice" of the pie. Disputants * * * can affect the size of the pie and of their own slice in several ways; but often the strategies and tactics that maximize the size of the pie compromise their ability to achieve the largest possible slice. Conversely, negotiation ploys designed to increase the size of their own slice tend to stand in the way of maximizing, and may even shrink, the size of the pie.

* * *

The "negotiators' dilemma" that we have described is particularly clear with respect to the question of revealing versus concealing interests. Clearly, the parties have a strong incentive to ascertain each other's true interests. Accurate information about goals, priorities, preferences, resources, and opportunities is essential for the principals (or those negotiating on their behalf) to frame agreements that offer optimal "gain of trade"—that is, agreement tailored to take full advantage of asymmetries of interests. Such information may even allow the parties to create additional value, that is, to contribute complementary skills or resources that combine synergistically to offer the parties "win-win" opportunities that might not heretofore have been apparent.

At the same time, parties have a clear incentive to conceal their true interests and priorities—or even to mislead the other side about them. By feigning attachment to whatever resources they are ready to give up in trade, and feigning relative indifference to whatever resources they seek to gain (while concealing opportunities and plans for utilization of those resources), each party seeks to win the best possible terms of trade for itself. In other words, total frankness and "full disclosure"—or simply greater frankness and fuller disclosure than that practiced by the other side in a negotiation—leave one vulnerable in the distributive aspects of bargaining. Accordingly, the sharp bargainer is tempted, and may rationally deem it advantageous—to practice secrecy and deception.

Such tactics, however, can lead to unnecessary deadlocks and costly delays, or, more fundamentally, to failures to discover the most efficient trades or outcomes. A simple example illustrates the dilemma facing negotiators, and the barrier imposed by the strategic concealment or misrepresentation of information. Suppose Bob has ten apples and no oranges, while Lee has ten oranges and no apples. Suppose further that, unbeknownst to Lee, Bob loves oranges and hates apples, while Lee, unbeknownst to Bob, likes them both equally well. Bob, in service of his current resources and preferences, suggests to Lee that they might both be made better off through a trade.

Now, if Bob discloses to Lee that he loves oranges and doesn't eat apples, Lee might "strategically" but deceptively insist that he shares Bob's

CHAPTER II NEGOTIATION

preferences and, accordingly, propose that Bob give him nine apples (which he says have relatively little value to him) in exchange for one of his "very valuable" oranges. Bob might even agree, and thus sell his apples more cheaply than he could have sold them if he had concealed his taste for oranges and suggested a trade of five oranges for five apples (on the grounds that they "both might enjoy a little variety in their diet").

Note, however, that such an "even trade," while more equitable, would not really be efficient, because it fails to take full advantage of the differing tastes of the two parties. That is, a more efficient trade would be accomplished by an exchange of Bob's ten apples for Lee's ten oranges, perhaps with some "side payment" to sweeten the deal for Lee, or better still, with linkage to some other efficient trade—one in which it was Bob who, at little or no cost to himself, accommodated Lee's particular needs or tastes.

NOTES AND QUESTIONS

1. The "negotiator's dilemma" that Mnookin and Ross discuss was first articulated by Walton and McKersie in their early treatment of labor negotiations. See Walton and McKersie, A Behavioral Theory of Labor Negotiations (1965). See also Kelley, A Classroom Study of the Dilemmas in Interpersonal Negotiation, in Archibald (ed.), Strategic Interaction and Conflict (1966); Lax and Sebenius, The Manager as Negotiator (1986). For an in-depth discussion of the tension between creating and distributing value, see Mnookin, Peppet and Tulumello, Beyond Winning: Negotiating to Create Value in Deals and Disputes (2000).

2. Research suggests that negotiating parties often do *not* reach efficient agreements—they "leave value on the table" by settling on sub-optimal solutions to their conflicts. See Raiffa, The Art and Science of Negotiation 139 (1982); Bazerman, Magliozzi, and Neale, Integrative Bargaining in a Competitive Market, 34 Org. Behavior & Human Performance 294–313 (1985); Bazerman, Negotiator Judgment: A Critical Look at the Rationality Assumption, 27 Am.Behavioral Sci. 618–634 (1983). Why might this be? The negotiator's dilemma suggests one possible answer: strategic interaction prevents value-creation by inhibiting the exchange of information needed to find integrative trades. Because parties fear exploitation, they hold their cards close to their chest and therefore cannot exploit differences in resources and interests, relative valuations, forecasts, and time and risk preferences.

3. Despite the logic of the negotiator's dilemma, some studies show that it may not accurately portray bargaining. One study, for example, found that although "[i]nformation exchange appears to lead to a problem-solving atmosphere which allows negotiators to make tradeoffs," disclosing information did *not* affect the negotiators' distributive outcomes. "Although information sharing affected the integrativeness of the solution, the difference between the amount of information provided by each party did not impact the distribution of outcomes. * * * This suggests that negotiators should engage in information sharing without being overly concerned about

B. STRATEGY

145

being put at a disadvantage." Weingart, Thompson, Bazerman and Carroll, Tactical Behavior and Negotiation Outcomes, 1 Intl.J. of Conflict Mgt. 7, 27, 28 (1990). Have you found that this dilemma pervades your negotiations? What factors seem to exacerbate the tension, and what seems to ameliorate it? Are you personally more inclined towards seeking to create value through integrative trades or to try to claim more value in the distributive aspects of bargaining? In what situations, or with what sorts of people, do you tend towards—or should you tend towards—one sort of negotiation or the other?

b. SELF–INTEREST AND THE PRISONER'S DILEMMA ANALOGY

In 1984, a political scientist named Robert Axelrod published a seminal book titled *The Evolution of Cooperation*. In it he presented the results of computerized "tournaments" in which various human participants submitted computer programs designed to play repeated Prisoner's Dilemma games. Axelrod paired these programs off against each other in order to determine what program—or strategy—would most succeed in a repeat-play series of games.

Luce and Raiffa set out the classic definition of a Prisoner's Dilemma:

> Two suspects are taken into custody and separated. The district attorney is certain that they are guilty of a specific crime, but he does not have adequate evidence to convict them at a trial. He points out to each prisoner that each has two alternatives: to confess to the crime, or not to confess. If they both do not confess, then the district attorney states he will book them on some minor trumped-up charge such as petty larceny or illegal possession of a weapon, and they both will receive minor punishment. If they both confess they will be prosecuted, but he will recommend less than the most severe sentence; but if one confesses and the other does not, then the confessor will receive lenient treatment for turning state's evidence whereas the latter will get "the book" slapped at him. * * *

Luce and Raiffa, Games and Decisions 95 (1957).

In a Prisoner's Dilemma game, two players must simultaneously choose, without communicating, whether to "cooperate" or "defect." To simplify, imagine that if both players cooperate, each receives three points. If player A cooperates and B defects, B gets five points and A gets nothing. (Or, if B cooperates and A defects, A gets five points and B gets nothing.) If both defect, each gets one point. (See Figure 4.) The dilemma is that while mutual cooperation may be attractive, the temptation to defect—and the *fear* that the other player will succumb to that temptation—may lead to mutual defection and relatively low payoffs.

Economists assume that if two people are playing a prisoner's dilemma game only once, the optimal strategy for either player is to defect. Although mutual cooperation would be nice, each player will reason that the other is going to defect, and thus each will defect. Although this produces a collectively sub-optimal result, it is individually rational.

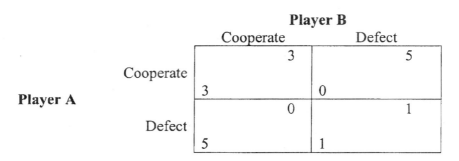

Figure 4

The analogy to negotiation is fairly obvious. In a given negotiation, we may both do better by cooperating—by adopting a problem-solving approach. But if you adopt such an approach and I "defect" or bargain hard, I may be able to exploit you and receive a bigger slice of the pie. Unfortunately, if we both defect and adopt a hard bargaining strategy we may each end up with a poor payoff. Our negotiation may stalemate, we may damage our relationship, and we may fail to find value-creating options. See Gilson and Mnookin, Disputing Through Agents: Cooperation and Conflict Between Lawyers in Litigation, 94 Colum.L.Rev. 509, 514–15 (1994).[15]

The game becomes more interesting, however, if played many times. David Lax and James Sebenius explain Axelrod's results:

> Axelrod's striking results have received widespread notice and scientific praise. * * * Axelrod asked a number of specialists from a broad sweep of related disciplines to submit computer programs to participate in a tournament of repeated plays of the Prisoner's Dilemma. Each program would be pitted against every other program for a large number of plays of the Prisoner's Dilemma; each program of "strategy" would be rated according to the total number of points obtained against the strategies of all its opponents. The strategies range from the simple—RANDOM which flipped a coin to decide whether to cooperate or defect and TIT–FOR–TAT which cooperated on the first play and in subsequent rounds merely repeated its opponent's immediately previous move—to many devilishly exploitative schemes, including some that calculated the rate at which the opponent defected and then defected just a little bit more frequently.

---

15. Negotiations over a legal dispute may be analogous to a repeat-play Prisoner's Dilemma in one of two ways. First, you might think of each communication or interaction between the parties as a choice point in which each can decide either to defect or to cooperate. Thus, over the course of a single piece of litigation the parties may interact many times, perhaps establishing a cooperative equilibrium over time. Second, you can treat a given litigation or negotiation as one "round" of the iterated Prisoner's Dilemma game, and assume that the potential benefits of repeat play arise only if the parties will negotiate together again in the future.

Axelrod's synthesis of his results is intriguing. First, the strategies that did well were "nice," they did not defect first. Second, they were "provocable" in that they punished a defection by defecting, at least on the next round. Third, they were "forgiving" in that after punishing a defection they gave the opponent the opportunity to resume cooperation. Thus, unlike other strategies that were less nice or forgiving, they did not become locked, after a defection, in a long series of mutual recriminations. Fourth, they were clear or "not too clever." Eliciting continued cooperation is sufficiently tricky that moves whose intentions were difficult to decipher tended to result in unproductive defections. Such strategies performed well because they were able to elicit cooperation and avoid gross exploitation. We call these strategies "conditionally open." The simplest of the submitted conditionally open strategies, TIT–FOR–TAT, actually won the tournament.

After disseminating these results, Axelrod ran a second tournament with a much larger number of participants. With TIT–FOR–TAT and other "nice" strategies as the contenders to beat, the second tournament brought forth a flood of even more clever, even more fiendish schemes. And, perhaps surprisingly, the best-performing strategies were conditionally open, and again, TIT–FOR–TAT won the tournament. The conclusions of these studies are of course only suggestive. The success of particular strategies depends on the population of submitted strategies. Yet, the studies imply that being open in each round to cooperation conditional on an opponent's openness elicits payoffs from cooperation sufficient to offset the costs of occasional defections.

Axelrod's results suggest the elements of a strategy for managing the tension between creating and claiming value. A negotiator can attempt to divide the process into a number of small steps and to view each step as a round in a repeated Prisoner's Dilemma. He can attempt to be conditionally open, warily seeking mutual cooperation, ready to punish or claim value when his counterpart does so, but ultimately forgiving transgressions. The attempt to create value is linked to an implicit threat to claim vigorously if the counterpart does, but also to the assurance that a repentant claimer will be allowed to return to good graces. Thus, both can avoid condemnation to endless mutual recriminations. Throughout the process, the negotiator may be better off if his moves are not mysterious.

Lax and Sebenius, The Manager as Negotiator: Bargaining for Cooperation and Competitive Gain 157–60 (1986). See also Axelrod, The Evolution of Cooperation (1984); Axelrod, The Complexity of Cooperation: Agent–Based Models of Competition and Collaboration (1997).

NOTES AND QUESTIONS

1. The Prisoner's Dilemma game has been used to analyze various litigation issues, including the problem of discovery abuse and the advantages of hiring a lawyer. See Setear, The Barrister and the Bomb: The dynamics of Cooperation, Nuclear Deterrence, and Discovery Abuse, 69 B.U.L.Rev. 569 (1989); Gilson and Mnookin, Disputing Through Agents: Cooperation and Conflict Between Lawyers in Litigation, 94 Colum.L.Rev. 509, 520–522 (1994). In the discovery context, for example, we might both be better off if we keep costs down by cooperating in exchanging information rather than waging a discovery battle with expensive depositions and document requests. At the same time, however, I may realize that by "defecting"—by holding back information or by imposing costs on you—I can gain advantage (if you do not reciprocate). Like a Prisoner's Dilemma, we may thus both "defect," allowing individually rational behavior to lead to a collectively irrational outcome.

Is the Prisoner's Dilemma a helpful metaphor for the negotiation process? In bargaining, unlike in a Prisoner's Dilemma game, the parties can communicate normally and are not confined to merely communicating by submitting a "cooperate" or "defect" bid. Their interaction may be face-to-face, whereas in a Prisoner's Dilemma game the interaction is usually handled through an intermediary. And in negotiation, the parties must bargain within a social and cultural context that may lead them to cooperate (or defect) more often than they would in a pure Prisoner's Dilemma. Such social influences can be extremely important. For example, in one experiment two sets of subjects played the same Prisoner's Dilemma game, with the same instructions, incentives, and opportunities to cooperate or defect. One group, however, was told that it was playing "The Community Game," while the other group was told that it was "The Wall Street Game." As you might expect, this social cue led to a higher rate of defection in the latter game than in the former. See Samuels and Ross, Reputations Versus Labels: The Power of Situational Effects in the Prisoner's Dilemma Game (unpublished manuscript, 1993).

Given such differences, how useful is the Prisoner's Dilemma in thinking about the choice between negotiation strategies?

2. Although Axelrod's analysis suggests that starting with an open, "nice" strategy can most often lead to a mutually-beneficial interaction, you may intuit that starting tough can reap benefits—if the other side is exploitable. Your approach, therefore, may be to try to claim value early in order to test the other side's mettle. If they give in, you walk away with the lion's share. If they don't, you can always switch to a more problem-solving approach.

Some fear that this strategy merely leads to mutual escalation and stalemate. Consider the following example: "In July, 1964, Undersecretary of State George Ball tried to dissuade Lyndon Johnson from sending U.S. ground forces to Vietnam en masse. Johnson intended to pressure the North Vietnamese to end the war on his terms, but Ball feared that escalation would become an autonomous force, impelling both sides to higher and higher levels of violence. 'Once on a tiger's back,' his memo argued, 'we cannot be sure of picking a place to dismount.' " O'Neill, Conflictual Moves in Bargaining: Warnings, Threats, Escalations, and Ultimatums, in Young (ed.), Negotiation Analysis 87 (1991).

Others, however, see this as a viable approach. Dean Pruitt, for example, argues that scholars have over-emphasized the risks of bargaining hard initially:

> While supported by certain lines of evidence, this indictment of contentious behavior seems overdrawn. Negotiations that reach reasonable agreements often go through an initial contentious stage followed by a later stage of joint problem solving. Furthermore, it can be argued that contending is often a necessary precursor to successful problem solving. Negotiators commonly start out with aspirations that greatly outstrip the integrative potential. In other words, their aspirations are so high that no degree of problem solving can yield a solution. Under such conditions, they are likely to engage in initial contentious behavior. During this stage, however, both parties often become more realistic about what aspirations can be sustained. If their actions have not produced too much antagonism, they can then enter a stage of joint problem solving that has prospects of yielding agreement because of their reduced aspirations.

Pruitt, Strategic Choice in Negotiation, 27 Am. Behavioral Sci. 167–194 (1983).

3. As Axelrod might predict, and as you might expect, research has shown that friends—who are by definition engaged in a long-term, repeat-play relationship—are more likely than strangers to manage conflict constructively. See Shah and Jehn, Do Friends Perform Better than Acquaintances? The Interaction of Friendship, Conflict and Task, Group Decision & Negot., 2, 149–165 (1993). Similarly, there is some evidence that small-town lawyers—who must interact repeatedly with each other and with those in their community—are less likely to engage in hostile or extremely competitive litigation. See Dieffenbach, Psychology, Society and the Development of the Adversarial Posture, 16 J.Leg.Prof. 205, 219–220 (1991) (discussing results of a study by Donald Landon).

More surprisingly, general studies of lawyer-negotiators lend some support to the notion that cooperation may be able to evolve and survive even in a largely adversarial environment, just as Axelrod showed in the Prisoner's Dilemma context:

> A study of American lawyer-negotiators reported by Professor Gerald R. Williams revealed that roughly 65 percent of a sample of attorneys from two major U.S. cities exhibited a consistently cooperative style of negotiation, whereas only 24 percent were truly competitive in their orientation. (11 percent defied categorization using these two labels). Roughly half of the sample was rated as "effective" negotiators by their peers. Most interesting, more than 75 percent of the "effective" group were cooperative types and only 12 percent were competitive. The remaining effective negotiators came from the pool of mixed strategy negotiators.
>
> In contrast to the stereotypes, this study suggests that a cooperative orientation is more common than a competitive orientation within

150 CHAPTER II Negotiation

at least one sample of professional negotiators in the United States. Moreover, it appears to be easier to gain a reputation for being effective (at least as rated by peers) by using a cooperative approach rather than using a competitive one.

The second study was conducted over a period of nine years by Neil Rackham and John Carlisle in England. Rackham and Carlisle observed the behavior of forty-nine professional labor and contract negotiators in real transactions. * * * The most effective of them displayed distinctly cooperative traits.

For example, the study examined the use of what the researchers called irritators at the negotiating table. Irritators are such things as self-serving descriptions of one's offer, gratuitous insults, and direct attacks on the other side's proposal—typical competitive tactics. The average negotiator used 10.8 irritators per hour of negotiating time; the more skilled negotiators used an average of only 2.3 irritators per hour.

In addition, skilled negotiators avoided what the researchers called defend/attack spirals, cycles of emotion-laden comments assigning blame or disclaiming fault. Only 1.9 percent of the skilled negotiators' comments at the table fell into this category, whereas the average negotiators triggered or gave momentum to defend/attack spirals with 6.3 percent of their comments. The profile of the effective negotiator that emerges from this study seems to reflect a distinct set of cooperative, as opposed to stereotypically competitive, traits.

Shell, Bargaining for Advantage: Negotiation Strategies for Reasonable People 12–14 (1999).

The Williams study has been repeated and expanded by Professor Andrea Schneider. She asked lawyers to rate the last attorney against whom they had negotiated. She found that lawyers thought that 54 percent of their "problem-solving" peers were "effective," whereas only 9 percent of their "adversarial" peers were effective. See Schneider, An Empirical Study of Negotiation Skills, 6 Dispute Resolution Magazine (Summer 2000).

These studies suggest that adversarial negotiators, although certainly prevalent, do not totally dominate the landscape in legal disputes and are not seen as being particularly effective. Other research, however, suggests that adversarial bargaining *is* most common. One study of civil litigation in New Jersey found that litigators thought that "positional" bargaining was used in 71 percent of the cases and problem-solving in approximately 16 percent. (Respondents indicated that both approaches were used together roughly 17 percent of the time.) See Heumann and Hyman, Negotiation Methods and Litigation Settlement Methods in New Jersey: "You Can't Always Get What You Want," 12 Ohio St.J.Disp.Resol. 253, 255 (1997).

What negotiation approach do you think is most common in legal disputes? On what do you base that assumption? How is legal negotiation commonly portrayed in films or television? In the press? Are such depictions accurate? At a more general level, do you believe that cooperation can evolve and flourish in a competitive world? Under what conditions?

4. Although Axelrod's work focused on repeat-play or iterated Prisoner's Dilemma games, some researchers have found that subjects cooperate even in one-shot games.

> How can cooperation in PD games be explained? In repeated games, the players have an ongoing relationship, so the decision to cooperate may reflect an attempt to influence the other player—by cultivating a reputation, by inducing reciprocity, and so forth. Cooperation can be explained as a social influence strategy that serves a player's long-run self-interest. The conditions under which a cooperative strategy optimizes a player's outcome have been explored analytically and empirically. In one-shot games, however, there is no ongoing relationship between players. Because social influence is impossible, cooperation is always suboptimal in terms of an individual's outcome. Nonetheless, subjects act as if social influence were possible: The rate of cooperation is as high as in repeated games. The explanation may be that subjects take the same approach to one-shot games as to repeated games: They follow rules of thumb learned through their experiences of interdependent decision making in everyday social contexts. That is, decision makers simplify dilemmas by introducing tacit assumptions about social relations—they respond to uncertainty by automatically drawing on mental representations of typical social contexts. In short, the explanation may be that you can take the decision maker out of a social context, but you can't take the social context out of the decision maker. * * *

> Ethical principles vary greatly across individuals and cultures, but a few that serve basic social functions are widely shared. One of these, reciprocity, has been called a "cement of society" because it leads to behaviors that hold together social organizations. Essentially, this norm obligates a person to match what another person has provided. It can be seen in interpersonal exchanges ranging from the explicit give-and-take of concessions in negotiation to the implicit turn taking of self-disclosure in conversation. A reciprocity norm benefits society by ensuring rewards for those who initiate exchanges of goods and services. It fosters trade, the formation of interpersonal interdependencies, and ultimately the establishment of stable social organizations. * * *

See Morris, Sim, & Girotto, Time of Decision, Ethical Obligation, and Causal Illusion: Temporal Cues and Social Heuristics in the Prisoner's Dilemma, in Kramer & Messick (eds.), Negotiation as a Social Process 210–213 (1995).

5. The tendency to defect in a one-shot Prisoner's Dilemma game may also be constrained by the possibility of distinguishing between "cooperators" and "defectors"—types of players. In experimental studies, subjects given only a short amount of time to interact with other subjects have been able to predict with both accuracy and confidence the likelihood that others will either cooperate or defect in a Prisoner's Dilemma game. If you can distinguish one type of player from another with even modest accuracy and modest effort, "the population settles at a stable mix of cooperators and defectors, one in which members of both groups have the same average payoff and are therefore equally likely to survive. There is a stable ecological niche, in other words, for both cooperators and defectors. This result stands in stark contrast to the traditional sociobiological prediction of universal defection in one-shot prisoner's dilemmas played by nonrelatives." Frank, Gilovich, and Regan, The Evolution of One–Shot Cooperation: An Experiment, 14 Ethology & Sociobiology 247–256 (1993).

Should this research influence your choice of strategies? Do you believe that you can accurately predict how a negotiating counterpart is going to behave? Although potentially accurate (and helpful), such predictions can be risky. Sometimes you may incorrectly assume that your counterpart is going to defect or be a hard bargainer. This may then become self-fulfilling, making it difficult or impossible in hindsight to determine who initiated the hard bargaining. As Morton Deutsch explains, "[s]elf-fulfilling prophecies are those wherein you engage in hostile behavior toward another because of a false assumption that the other has done or is preparing to do something harmful to you; your false assumption comes true when it leads you to engage in hostile behavior that then provokes the other to react in a hostile manner to you. The dynamics of an escalating, destructive conflict have the inherent quality of a *folie a deux* in which the self-fulfilling prophecies of each side mutually reinforce one another. As a result, both sides are right to think that the other is provocative, untrustworthy, and malevolent. Each side, however, tends to be blind to how it as well as the other have contributed to this malignant process." Deutsch, Cooperation and Competition, in Deutsch & Coleman, eds., The Handbook of Conflict Resolution: Theory and Practice (2000).

6. Research suggests that when people choose *not* to cooperate—choose to defect in a Prisoner's Dilemma game or perhaps, by analogy, to "bargain hard" rather than problem-solve—they are likely to rationalize that choice by denigrating their belief in their own self-efficacy. In other words, an individual may tell himself that there was "nothing he could have done to make a difference anyway" rather than believing that he walked away from a genuine chance to promote cooperation. See Kerr and Kaufman–Gilliland, "... and besides, I probably couldn't have made a difference anyway": Justification of Social Dilemma Defection via Perceived Self–Inefficacy, 33 J. of Experimental Soc.Psychol. 211–230 (1997). Have you ever found yourself explaining your behavior in this way? For example, if you've bargained hard—perhaps too hard—have you ever justified your actions by saying "there was nothing else I could do" or "they made me do it?" Is such reasoning justified?

7. The Prisoner's Dilemma may not be a perfect metaphor for negotiation because many disputes involve more than two parties . Multiparty disputes create the possibility of coalitions, in which two parties may join forces against a third. Such coalitions may shift, break apart, and re-form, and are notoriously difficult to model or predict. We do not focus on multiparty disputes here, but see Raiffa, The Art and Science of Negotiation (1982); Watkins and Rosegrant, Sources of Power in Coalition Building, 12 Neg.J. 47 (1996); Sebenius, Dealing with Blocking Coalitions and Related Barriers to Agreement: Lessons from Negotiations on the Oceans, the Ozone, and the Climate, in Barriers to Conflict Resolution 151 (Arrow et al., eds.,1995); Goodpaster, Coalitions and Representative Bargaining, 9 Ohio St.J. on Disp.Res. 243 (1994); Lax and Sebenius, Thinking Coalitionally: Party Arithmetic, Process Opportunism, and Strategic Sequencing, in Young, Negotiation Analysis 154 (1991); Touval, Multilateral Negotiation: An Analytic Approach, 5 Neg.J. 159 (1989).

8. What variables should influence your choice between strategies? Lax and Sebenius suggest a conditionally open strategy—start a negotiation willing to problem-solve but defend against exploitation if the other side bargains hard. When would this be good advice, and when might it be unwise? Consider how the following variables might influence your choice of approach:

- Is the negotiation a one-shot transaction, or will there be future dealings over time?

- Is it a single issue, primarily distributive negotiation, or are there multiple issues with integrative potential?

- Are the stakes high or low?

- How is the other side likely to act? Do they have a reputation for being a hard bargainer? Have you seen them negotiate in similar situations? What would *you* do if you were in their shoes?

- What are the negotiation norms in your community? Is problem-solving more common or is a hard, adversarial strategy the norm?

- What strategy does your client prefer?

- What strategy is more in line with your own personal style as a person or as an attorney? What strategy are you more skilled at?

c. WILL PROBLEM–SOLVING SACRIFICE MY CLIENT'S INTERESTS?

Many lawyers fear that adopting a problem-solving strategy will sacrifice their clients' interests in the name of cooperation. In a study of litigators in New Jersey, for example, Milton Heumann and Jonathan Hyman found that although litigators believed that problem-solving was used only 16 percent of the time, 61 percent thought that it should be used more. These lawyers, however, feared for their clients' interests. The following excerpt contains some of the lawyers' explanations of why positional hard bargaining seemed necessary, as well as the authors' explanation of the confusion that often exists between problem-solving, on the one hand, and "soft" positional bargaining in which one unilaterally over-discloses information, on the other.

Milton Heumann and Jonathan M. Hyman, Negotiation Methods and Litigation Settlement Methods in New Jersey: "You Can't Always Get What You Want"

12 Ohio St.J.Disp.Resol. 253, 262–265 (1997).

In their interviews, the litigators gave us vivid examples of how they act against their own preferences because they want to protect themselves against the positional excesses of the other side. Although they dislike it, they told us they must play a highly positional game of concealing their settlement positions. Candor about settlement positions is rarely the best policy. Lawyers learn that they must exaggerate demands and understate offers as part of the settlement ritual. Even when requested to divulge what they "really" want or what they "really" can offer, they learned that their "real" position only became the next starting point for another round of offers and demands. If they were honest about stating their positions and insisted on not budging once they had revealed what they would settle for, they came to be seen as inflexible and as an impediment to realistic settlement of the case.

* * *

We have set out several interview excerpts to illustrate the almost painful way attorneys learn that strategic bargaining is generally linked to some misrepresentation about true bargaining positions. We also include some excerpts from attorneys who found that the adversarial posture itself forced a sort of personal compromise with their own sense of truthful representation and required a slanting of issues with which they were not always comfortable.

[The practice of law] means never telling the truth; it means using tricks and scams. * * * The instinct [of a new attorney] to be honest is a disadvantage. I had to resort to lying.

* * *

[I learned to be an advocate, which means] learning to see with blinders. You learn to cloud weak things. * * *

* * *

[With experience] you become less naïve, learn the system. I try to be honest and straightforward, but I've learned that in certain circumstances you can't do that. [For example,] my firm [the insurance company he was representing] asked me to get a demand. I got a letter asking for $750,000, but I valued the case at $500,000 or less, the insurance company told me to go for a structured settlement of $400,000 or less but that they could go up to $500,000. I wrote a letter [to plaintiff's attorney] saying $100,000 up front, plus $100,000 structured. The plaintiff's attorney called me and said: "The offer is ridiculous. We won't consider it." I told him his 750 was high, and I asked him: "What do you really need?" His answer was "750, my client wants to net half a million and I need $250,000." I responded: "Let's avoid the game, cut through this nonsense, what do you really need." The attorney called me back and said: "Our rock bottom is half a million." I figured now we could settle, since I knew I had this amount. But when I called the insurance company, they now said they didn't want to pay it. Their feeling was that "if he says half a million, he'll take less." * * * [The attorney concluded by observing how] honesty can work against you. People expect you to play the game and if you don't . . .

* * *

As suggestive as these examples are, however, we do not think they confirm the working assumption that positional bargaining overwhelms problem-solving whenever the two meet. The lawyers in these excerpts are not describing a conflict between positional and problem-solving methods of negotiation. Instead, they are only describing a tension that inheres in the positional method of negotiating. The concealment or disclosure of settlement positions is a key issue—perhaps the key issue—of positional negotiation strategy, entirely independent of problem-solving strategies. Positional bargaining depends on each side eventually disclosing its settlement position, but it equally depends on each side initially concealing its true settlement positions and disclosing misleading settlement positions instead. Through misleading disclosures, each side tries to convince the other side that there is little left to give and that it would be better to settle for the proposed terms. But the concealment or disclosure of settlement positions forms only a minor sideshow for problem-solving negotiation. In contrast to advancing and defending settlement positions, the key to problem-solving methods of negotiation is maintaining focus on the underlying interests of the parties. At most, the stories we heard describe a conflict that arises within the four corners of the positional bargaining method. They do not describe the exploration of underlying interests or the crafting of mutually satisfactory agreements from those interests.

Robert Mnookin, Scott Peppet & Andrew Tulumello, Beyond Winning: Negotiating to Create Value in Deals and Disputes

321–322 (2000).

Will the client always be better off if a skilled lawyer adopts a problem-solving orientation rather than taking a more traditional adversarial approach? Our answer is straightforward: Usually, but not always.

The outcome of any negotiation depends on the behavior of the parties on both sides. Consider the following thought experiment. Imagine two lawyers—equally skilled—asked to represent the same client. One lawyer has a problem-solving orientation; the other is a hard bargainer. Each lawyer will represent this client in a series of negotiations where there is a random spread of lawyers and clients on the other side. In our view, clients do better, certainly in the long run, when represented by lawyers who have a problem-solving orientation. But common sense and anecdotal observation suggest that in *some* cases a competitive hard bargainer will achieve a better result for a client than a problem-solver—*if* the other side is represented by ineffective counsel so eager to settle the dispute or make a deal that he simply offers concession after concession. Adopting a problem-solving stance toward negotiations probably gives up some opportunities to fish for suckers who can be exploited with hard-bargaining tactics. But in large part, how you see this cost of problem-solving will depend on how likely you believe it is that those you negotiate against will be less skilled, intelligent, or sophisticated than you are. Assuming that more often than not those on the other side will be competent, then on average fishing for suckers may have a negative return.

Negotiators also fear that by adopting a collaborative posture their clients may be exploited. If I try to lead the way toward problem-solving, will my client be hurt? We think not. With an understanding of hard-bargaining tactics and how they work, an effective problem-solver can defend his client's interests. Will there be *any* cost of trying to lead with a problem-solving approach? Perhaps. But in most situations it's not so hard to change course quickly and take a defensive posture if necessary.

At the same time, if two problem-solving lawyers work together on opposite sides of the table, sometimes they will be able to create tremendous value for their clients and find outcomes that would simply be unimaginable using a traditional adversarial posture. Two companies in a dispute may realize that they can make millions doing a joint venture. * * * Even in contentious disputes, problem-solving lawyers may design creative processes to save their clients time and money. While there may be some downside risk to problem-solving, the upside benefit can be well worth it.

In short, if there is a sucker on the other side and future relationships don't matter very much, adopting a highly adversarial strategy * * * may sometimes lead to a higher pay-off. More often, it will lead to retaliation, and the net result may be no deal at all or simply much higher transaction costs.

NOTES AND QUESTIONS

1. Professor Robert Condlin suggests that lawyers have a "duty to compete" that may run counter to the problem-solving strategy:

> * * * While lawyers may not take action that is frivolous (i.e., primarily to harass or maliciously to injure) or prohibited by law, they must use any legally available move or procedure helpful to a client's bargaining position. Among other things, this means that all forms of leverage must be exploited, inflated demands made, and private information obtained and used whenever any of these actions would advance the client's stated objectives, even if such action would jeopardize a lawyer's long-term, working relationship with her bargaining counterpart.
>
> Lawyers also must show enthusiasm for the bargaining task. Once described as the obligation of zealous representation, and now ex-

pressed as the duty of diligence, this duty requires lawyers to act with "commitment and dedication to the interests of the client," and to "carry to a conclusion all matters undertaken" on the client's behalf. Lawyer bargainers, in other words, must develop and play out client-bargaining hands with energy and believability, and not undercut those efforts with a tone or attitude which indicates that their hearts are not in it, or that they do not believe what they say. Plausibility and sincerity are the most important attributes of effective bargaining maneuvers; the duty of competence requires the first, and the duty of diligence the second.

Condlin, Bargaining in the Dark: The Normative Incoherence of Lawyer Dispute Bargaining Role, 51 Md.L.Rev. 1, 71–72 (1992). Do you agree?

Although the Model Rules of Professional Conduct do not require "zealous advocacy" per se, Model Rule 1.3 does require "reasonable diligence" on behalf of a client. The earlier Canon 7 of the Model Code of Professional Responsibility stated that "a lawyer should represent a client zealously within the bounds of the law." And the even older Canon 15 of the ABA Canons of Professional Ethics stated that "[t]he lawyer owes 'entire devotion to the interest of the client, warm zeal in the maintenance and defense of his rights and the exertion of utmost learning and ability,' to the end that nothing be taken or be withheld from him, save by the rules of law, legally applied."

Does problem-solving square with these requirements? Given that problem-solving generally requires consideration of the other side's interests and concerns, and tailoring of agreements to dovetail your own client's needs with the other side's to create value, is a lawyer who pursues this approach letting down her client? When Mnookin, Peppet and Tulumello suggest that on *average* "fishing for suckers" will have a negative return, they implicitly admit that occasionally it may succeed in a given negotiation. Should a lawyer play the averages, or must she always seek to exploit the other side if that might be in her individual client's interests?

2. What should an attorney do if her client wants to adopt a hard bargaining strategy but she feels this is not necessarily in the client's best interest? Should she acquiesce? Try to persuade the client to change strategies? Withdraw from the representation? How clear must a lawyer be at the *start* of representation if she wants to take a problem-solving approach to the client's legal dispute? As a thought experiment, try writing down how you would explain to a new potential client that you preferred problem-solving to an adversarial strategy. What main points would you cover? How would you explain what "problem-solving" meant? What questions would your client likely have about your proposed approach?

C. PSYCHOLOGICAL AND SOCIAL ASPECTS OF BARGAINING

Choosing and executing a strategy may be complicated by a variety of psychological and social aspects of bargaining. In this Section we first

158 CHAPTER II NEGOTIATION

explore several psychological barriers to negotiating the resolution of legal disputes. We then turn to the problem of interpersonal style—what mix of interpersonal skills a negotiator should employ to be effective in dealing with her own client and the other side. Finally, we examine the role of race, gender, culture and stereotyping in the negotiation process.

1. PSYCHOLOGICAL BARRIERS TO CONFLICT RESOLUTION

Psychological aspects of bargaining were woven throughout Sections A and B. We have already seen, for example, that the fixed pie bias can diminish prospects for integrative bargaining, that negotiators are likely to have biased constructions of what should count as a fair outcome in a given dispute, and that anchoring effects can greatly increase the power of a first offer. Negotiation analysts, economists and legal scholars increasingly debate and explore the ways in which such psychological phenomena affect bargaining, litigation behavior and the legal system generally. See e.g., Sunstein, Behavioral Law and Economics (2000); Korobkin and Ulen, Law and Behavioral Science: Removing the Rationality Assumption from Law and Economics, 88 Cal.L.Rev. 1051 (2000); Jolls, Sunstein and Thaler, A Behavioral Approach to Law and Economics, 50 Stan.L.Rev. 1471 (1998); Mnookin, Why Negotiations Fail: An Exploration of Barriers to the Resolution of Conflict, 8 Ohio St.J. on Dis.Res. 235, 238–247 (1993).

a. COGNITION, PERCEPTION AND RECALL

The following excerpt reviews several additional psychological barriers to conflict resolution and offers remedial prescriptions to help lawyers overcome them. It is structured around several central questions that lawyers and clients must answer in a negotiation, including "How much is this case worth?", "How likely am I to win if this case goes to trial?", "How should I frame my offer?" and "How should I evaluate their offers?"

Richard Birke and Craig R. Fox, Psychological Principles in Negotiating Civil Settlements

4 Harv.Neg.L.Rev. 1, 7–12, 14–20, 42–47, 48–51 (1999).

Question 1: How much is the case worth?

* * *

1. *Psychology Relating to Preliminary Valuation: The Availability and Anchoring Heuristics*

Consider the following question: are there more male or female lawyers in America? To answer this question with complete accuracy would require demographic professional data. However, people render judgments on such matters all the time based on their own experience and intuition. In this case, for example, most people consult their memory and conclude that because it is easier to recall examples of male lawyers than female lawyers, the former are probably more common than the latter. They are using a mental short cut or heuristic to solve the problem. In this case, people automatically assume that when it is easier to recall examples of something, it tends to be more common. In the example of male and female attorneys, such reasoning provides the correct answer.

Now consider a different question: are there more murders or suicides each year in America? If you answered "murders," you might be surprised to learn that, in fact, suicides are much more common. In this second instance, the "availability heuristic"[27] fails because one's memories do not reflect a representative sampling of what exists in the world. Memories are often biased by vivid, extreme events that tend to receive extensive media coverage. Movies, television dramas, and news reports tend to make murder seem much more common than suicide.

There are many instances of such distortions. For example, people typically think that there is a higher percentage of African–American citizens in Los Angeles than African–American officers on the L.A. police force, that a higher proportion of top Hollywood actors than U.S. Congressmen are homosexual, and that it rains more in Seattle than it does in Northern Georgia. None of these apparent "facts" is true, but because it is easier to conjure images of African–American Los Angelinos than it is to conjure images of African–American L.A. police officers, openly gay actors than openly gay politicians, and rainy scenes of Seattle than rainy scenes of Georgia, most people automatically deem the former more common than the latter.

Media reporting facilitates availability distortions of legal matters as well. When people think of a tort case in contemporary society, they are likely to think of McDonald's coffee or Dow Corning breast implants. When thinking of a murder trial, O.J. Simpson may come to mind first. * * * Although people may be aware that these cases are atypical, their sensational portrayal by the media renders them readily available to memory. In fact, these cases are newsworthy precisely because they are not typical. However, when making predictions, people often fail to compensate for the gap between what is memorable and what is typical. If a lawyer knows that the upper end of jury awards in sexual harassment claims is 7.2 million dollars, she may realize that her case is worth less, but the fact that it is so easy to recall such notable cases * * * makes an extreme award seem possible.

This bias may be reinforced by a second psychological phenomenon: the tendency to anchor on a salient number and make insufficient adjustments in response to individuating details of the case at hand. For example, if a recent court award for a similar case comes to mind, people may be unduly influenced by this value in their assessment of the present case.

---

27. For a more detailed account of the psychology of the availability heuristic, see Amos Tversky & Daniel Kahneman, *Availability: A Heuristic for Judging Frequency and Probability*, 5 COGNITIVE PSYCHOL. 207 (1973). For an accessible introduction to different judgmental heuristics and associated biases, see Amos Tversky & Daniel Kahneman, *Judgment under Uncertainty, Heuristics and Biases*, 185 SCIENCE 1124 (1974).

160   CHAPTER II NEGOTIATION

Research shows that even when a focal number is not particularly relevant, it can exert a bias on judgment under uncertainty. * * *

People are especially susceptible to anchoring bias when they have little relevant experience or knowledge. However, expertise alone fails to provide protection from this tendency. In one study, several experienced real estate brokers were asked to provide information they used to appraise a piece of residential real estate and to estimate how accurately agents could appraise its value when given that information.[42] The brokers responded that the information should support an agent's estimate within five percent of the true value. Other groups of agents were given packets of information on a home that included a bogus listing price that was eleven percent above the true listing price or eleven percent below the true listing price. These two groups were asked to estimate the appraised value of the home. Although the agents explicitly denied that listing price affected their appraisals significantly, the manipulation of the bogus listing price led to a substantial difference in these values between the groups.

* * *

2. *Remediation*

To guard against bias when valuing a case, attorneys should research compiled statistics on outcomes of similar cases rather than relying exclusively on intuitive judgments which may be skewed by media reports of sensational cases. A thoughtful look at the class of comparable cases provides a reasonable starting point. Of course, the individuating circumstances of the present case are relevant considerations, but that judgment should be anchored on the average award in similar cases rather than on the outcomes of cases that happen to come to mind for idiosyncratic reasons. Psychological research in judgment under uncertainty suggests that people tend to undervalue base rates in their judgments of the case at hand. A modest investment of time researching comparable cases can help insulate against costly errors in valuation.

Question 2: How likely am I to win if this case goes to trial?

* * *

1. *Psychological Biases*

a. *Perspective Biases*

In general, people have great difficulty divorcing themselves from their idiosyncratic role sufficiently to take an objective view of disputes in which they are involved. In one study, researchers provided four groups of respondents with summary information pertaining to legal disputes.[57] In

---

42. *See* Gregory B. Northcraft & Margaret Neale, *Experts, Amateurs, and Real Estate: An Anchoring-and-Adjustment Perspective on Property Pricing Decisions*, 39 ORGANIZATIONAL BEHAV. & HUM. DECISION PROCESSES 84 (1987).

57. Lyle A. Brenner et al., *On the Evaluation of One–Sided Evidence*, 9 J. BEHAV.

the partisan conditions, respondents were given background information and either the plaintiff's or the defendant's arguments, but not both. In the neutral conditions, respondents were given either background information only or background information and both the plaintiff's and defendant's arguments. Participants in all conditions were asked to predict how many of twenty jurors would find for the plaintiff. Participants in the plaintiff condition predicted that a significantly higher proportion of jurors would find for the plaintiff than did participants in the defendant condition, despite the fact that both sides were aware that they were not provided with the other side's arguments. Participants in the neutral conditions (background only, or background and both sides' arguments) had a more balanced view than did participants in either of the partisan conditions.

Even when negotiators possess complete and shared information, they tend to assess the strength of their case in a self-interested (or "egocentric") manner. In one study, participants were randomly assigned to roles in a negotiation simulation involving a wage dispute between labor and management.[58] Both groups were given identical background information and asked to negotiate under the threat that a costly strike would occur if they failed to reach an agreement. Prior to negotiating, both groups were asked what they thought was a fair wage from the vantage point of a neutral third party. Despite the fact that both groups had been provided identical information, participants tended to be biased in a self-interested direction; that is, they tended to think a neutral third party would favor their side. Moreover, when members of a pair were farther apart in their predictions regarding the judgment of a third party, they tended to strike for longer periods of time. A similar pattern has been replicated with real money at stake in a simulated legal dispute negotiated under a regime of escalating legal fees.[59]

b. *Positive Illusions*

Egocentric biases are reinforced by so-called "positive illusions," which include unrealistic optimism, exaggerated perceptions of personal control, and inflated positive views of the self. For example, people tend to overestimate the probability that their predictions and answers to trivia questions are correct, at least for items of moderate to extreme difficulty. Overconfidence can inhibit negotiated settlements because if parties are overoptimistic about their ability to secure favorable litigated outcomes, they may set extreme reservation points. Indeed, one study found that overconfident negotiators were less concessionary and completed fewer deals than well-calibrated negotiators.[63] Also, in studies of final-offer arbitration, negoti-

---

DECISION MAKING 59 (1996).

58. Leigh Thompson & George Loewenstein, *Egocentric Interpretations of Fairness and Interpersonal Conflict*, 51 ORG. BEHAV. & HUM. DECISION PROC. 176 (1992).

59. *See* Linda Babcock et al., *Biased Judgments of Fairness in Bargaining*, 85 AM. ECON. REV. 1337 (1995); George Loewenstein

et al., *Self-Serving Assessments of Fairness and Pretrial Bargaining*, 22 J. LEGAL STUD. 135 (1993). * * *

63. *See* Margaret A. Neale & Max H. Bazerman, *The Effects of Framing and Negotiator Overconfidence on Bargaining Behaviors and Outcomes*, 28 ACAD. MGMT. J. 34 (1985).

ators on average overestimated the probability that their offers would be favored by the arbitrator. Presumably, these negotiators would have turned down settlement offers that, ex post, would have yielded more on average than did the arbitration.

Overconfidence stems, in part, from pervasive biases in the ways people pursue and evaluate evidence. Psychological studies have shown that people are more likely to seek information that confirms rather than discredits their hypotheses, and they tend to assimilate data in ways that are consistent with their prior views. In discovery, for example, attorneys are more likely to seek information that supports their viewpoint than they are to seek information that supports their opponents' cases. They work on "their side" of a case, and tend to construe the information that they find in a way that confirms their pre-existing beliefs about their odds of prevailing.

A second positive illusion is people's tendency to overestimate their ability to control outcomes that are determined by factors outside of their control. In one classic study by psychologist Ellen Langer, subjects bet more on a game of pure chance when they competed against a shy, awkward, poorly dressed individual than when they competed against a confident, outgoing, well-dressed person.[69] In a second study, subjects were offered one-dollar tickets to an office lottery. Each ticket consisted of two pictures of a famous football player, one of which was put into the box from which the winning ticket would be drawn. When participants were asked later at what price they would be willing to sell their ticket, those who had chosen the ticket for themselves demanded $6.87 on average, whereas those who had been assigned a ticket at random demanded only $1.96 on average. On the basis of these studies and other literature, Langer concludes:

> Whether it is seen as a need for competence, an instinct to master, a striving for superiority, or a striving for personal causation, most social scientists agree that there is a motivation to master one's environment, and a complete mastery would include the ability to "beat the odds," that is, to control chance events.[70]

When lawyers try to anticipate the outcome of a trial or a motion, there are many factors outside of their control. For example, appellate case law may change during the pendency of a case; or, the trial judge may recuse herself, become sick, or be elevated to a higher court. Witnesses may fail to appear or may be distracted by other events in their lives and be unable to prepare effectively or testify forcefully. Nevertheless, the lawyers may overestimate their ability to control a trial's outcome, and in turn, overvalue the claim.

A third variety of positive illusion is the tendency to hold overly positive views of one's own attributes and motives. For example, most people think that they are more intelligent and fair minded than average.

---

69. Ellen J. Langer, *The Illusion of Control*, 32 J. Personality & Soc. Psychol. 311 (1975).

70. *Id.* at 323 (internal citations omitted).

Ninety-four percent of university professors believe that they do a better job than their colleagues. More to the point, most negotiators believe themselves to be more flexible, more purposeful, more fair, more competent, more honest, and more cooperative than their counterparts.[74]

In a negotiation, this self-enhancing bias may lead an attorney to believe that she should hold out for a favorable settlement, because she is a more skilled attorney. Although skill among attorneys varies and it is rational to take skill into account when evaluating the worth of a case, lawyers at all skill levels are very likely to overestimate their abilities relative to those of their peers. This self-confidence may prove to be an effective bargaining tool to the extent that it sends a signal to her counterpart that the attorney is committed to seeing the case through to trial if necessary. However, if both sides overestimate their chances of prevailing in court, this bias will lead to excessive and costly discovery and litigation.

In sum, most people tend to make unrealistically optimistic forecasts regarding their own future outcomes. For example, an attorney may know that only twenty percent of appealed decisions in a particular practice area are overturned but nevertheless maintain that her odds of overturning an adverse ruling are higher—at least one in four, perhaps one in two. This perspective could eliminate the possibility of settlement in a case in which both sides agree on the value of a plaintiff's verdict and differ only in their assessment of the probability of a defense verdict. If the plaintiff feels that there is a forty percent chance that the verdict will be overturned and the defendant espouses the true base rate of twenty percent, the parties may not achieve a settlement that could have left them both better off than litigating through verdict.

2. *Remediation*

What can be done to circumvent these biases? Research suggests that egocentric biases may be very difficult to eliminate. It may be useful to actively anticipate arguments in favor of the opponent's case, but at least one study suggests that this tactic is not sufficient—perhaps because advocates easily generate counterarguments. However, this same study showed that egocentric bias was significantly mitigated when participants were asked to explicitly list weaknesses in their own case. Hence, to achieve a more balanced view of one's prospects, it is essential to make a concerted and sincere effort to play devil's advocate. Many experts recommend the use of test juries to perform this function.

As for optimistic overconfidence, experts suggest that this bias can be mitigated if lawyers take pains to adopt an outsider's perspective by seeking base rate statistics on cases that are similar in relevant respects to the present case, rather than relying solely on an insider's perspective that typically entails an analysis of plans and scenarios concerning the case at

---

74. *See* Roderick M. Kramer et al., *Self-Enhancement Biases and Negotiator Judgment: Effects of Self-Esteem and Mood*, 56 ORG. BEHAV. & HUM. DECISION PROCESSES 110 (1993).

hand. For example, a plaintiff's lawyer in a routine tort case might normally form an opinion of the probability of a jury verdict in his client's favor by assessing the credibility of each of his witnesses and the persuasive value of each piece of evidence he intends to offer. We suggest that this estimate would profit from a perusal of the local statistics about plaintiffs winning in similar cases. Of course, some further adjustment might be called for to account for cases that were too weak to withstand pretrial motions to dismiss.

Self-enhancing bias is arguably both a strength and a weakness. Many clients want to be represented by a counselor brimming with confidence—they may find this reassuring and also expect rosy prophesies to be self-fulfilling. On the other hand, if each attorney believes himself to be more honest, intelligent, and capable than the other, such tendencies can be counterproductive because they undermine incentives to settle. A little defensive humility is in order. Recognition of this pervasive tendency may allow attorneys to temper their expectations slightly and provide clients with more realistic assessments.

* * *

Question 8: How should I frame the offer?

* * *

Traditional economic analysis suggests that people should be sensitive to the impact of offers on final states of wealth, and that the particulars of how those offers are communicated should not matter.[173] Empirical studies of attorneys suggest that describing an offer in terms of gains versus losses can affect a lawyer's willingness to accept the offer. Certainly, lawyers choose words carefully, and this tendency extends to the crafting and communication of offers. However, for the most part, attorneys use this skill to avoid admitting or denying liability, or to avoid the accidental creation of exploitable weaknesses in their cases. Less thought goes into the question of how to frame an offer so that it is most likely to be accepted.

1. *The Psychology of Value and Framing*

Behavioral decision theorists have documented systematic violations of the standard economic assumption that people evaluate options in terms of their impact on one's final state of wealth. In particular, prospect theory assumes that people adapt to their present state of wealth and are sensitive to changes with respect to that endowment.[176]

173. *See, e.g.,* Amos Tversky, *Contrasting Rational and Psychological Principles of Choices, in* WISE CHOICES: DECISIONS, GAMES, AND NEGOTIATIONS 5 (Richard J. Zeckhauser, et al. eds. 1996).

176. Daniel Kahneman & Amos Tversky, *Prospect Theory: An Analysis of Decision under Risk*, 47 ECONOMETRICA 263 (1979); Amos Tversky & Daniel Kahneman, *Advances in Prospect Theory: Cumulative Representations of Uncertainty*, 5 J. RISK & UNCERTAINTY 297 (1992).

C. Psychological and Social Aspects of Bargaining

Second, people exhibit diminishing sensitivity to increasing gains and losses. For example, increasing an award from zero to $1000 is more pleasurable than increasing an award from $1000 to $2000; increasing an award from $2000 to $3000 is even less pleasurable, and so forth. Similarly, increasing a payment from zero to $1000 is more painful than increasing a payment from $1000 to $2000, and so on. One key implication of this pattern is that people's willingness to take risks differs for losses versus gains. For example, because $1000 is more than half as attractive as $2000, people typically prefer to receive $1,000 for sure than face a fifty-fifty chance of receiving $2,000 or nothing (i.e., they are "risk-averse" for medium probability gains). In contrast, because losing $1000 is more than half as painful as losing $2000, people typically prefer to risk a 50–50 chance of losing $2,000 or losing nothing to losing $1,000 for sure (i.e., they are "risk-seeking" for medium probability losses).

Third, prospect theory asserts that losses have more impact on choices than do equivalent gains. For example, most people do not think that a fifty percent chance of gaining $100 is sufficient to compensate a fifty percent chance of losing $100. In fact, people typically require a 50% chance of gaining as much as $200 or $300 to offset a 50% chance of losing $100.

Taken together, the way in which a problem is framed in terms of losses or gains can have a substantial impact on behavior in negotiations. First, loss aversion contributes to a bias in favor of the status quo because relative disadvantages of alternative outcomes loom larger than relative advantages. Hence, negotiators are often reluctant to make the tradeoffs necessary for them to achieve joint gains.[179] To illustrate, consider the case of two partners in a failing consulting firm. The joint office space and secretarial support costs are unduly burdensome, and each could operate productively out of their homes with minimal overhead costs. If they could divide their territory and agree not to compete, each could have a profitable career—but each would have to agree to give up half the firm's client base. Each partner may view the territory they retain as a gain that doesn't compensate adequately for the territory they must relinquish. Yet failure to make such a split consigns them to continuation in a losing venture.

Second, both loss aversion and the pattern of risk seeking for losses may lead to more aggressive bargaining when the task is viewed as minimizing losses rather than maximizing gains. Indeed, in laboratory studies, negotiators whose payoffs are framed in terms of gains (e.g., they were instructed to maximize revenues) tended to be more risk-averse than those whose payoffs are framed in terms of losses (e.g., they were instructed to minimize costs): the first group tended to be more concessionary but completed more transactions. Recently, Professor Rachlinski documented greater willingness to accept settlement offers in legal contexts when the offer is perceived as a gain compared to when it is perceived as a loss.

---

179. *See* William Samuelson & Richard Zeckhauser, *Status Quo Bias in Decision Making*, 1 J. Risk & Uncertainty 7 (1988). The authors also attribute status quo bias to * * * psychological commitments motivated by misperceptions of sunk costs, regret avoidance, or a drive for consistency.

CHAPTER II NEGOTIATION

Third, the attractiveness of potential agreements may be influenced by the way in which gains and losses are packaged and described. In particular, if a negotiator wants to present a proposal in its best possible light to a counterpart, he or she should attempt to integrate each aspect of the agreement on which the counterpart stands to lose (in order to exploit the fact that people experience diminishing sensitivity to each additional loss) and segregate each aspect of the agreement on which the counterpart stands to gain (in order to avoid the tendency of people to experience diminishing sensitivity to each additional gain). For instance, in the partnership dissolution example, it would be most effective to describe the territory forgone as a single unit (e.g., "everything west of highway 6 is mine") and the territory obtained in component parts (e.g., "and you will have the Heights neighborhood, the eastern section of downtown, everything north of there to the river, South Village, etc."), and least effective to describe the territory foregone in component parts (e.g. "I keep the west side of downtown, the riverfront, North Village, and everything between downtown and Ballard Square ...") and the territory obtained as a single unit (e.g., "everything east of highway 6 is yours").

2. *Remediation: Protecting Against Framing Effects*

Knowledge of the psychology of value can help a negotiator make offers appear more desirable to her counterpart, as described above. As for defending against inconsistency or manipulations by others, a negotiator should be aware that aspirations, past history, or previous offers may influence the frame of reference against which a negotiator perceives losses and gains; as a result, risk attitudes may be influenced by these transitory perceptions, which in turn influence how aggressively a negotiator bargains. Furthermore, negotiators must consciously overcome their natural reluctance to make concessions in order to exploit opportunities for trades that make both sides better off. Finally, in order to protect against mental accounting manipulations by others, a negotiator might develop a scoring system for each of the issues under consideration or translate everything into a unified dollar metric. By adding up points or dollars across all issues, the negotiator can focus on the value of the aggregate outcome to her client, rather than a piecemeal melange of incremental gains and losses that may have been creatively framed by her counterpart.

* * *

Question 9: How should I evaluate their offers?

* * *

When an attorney receives an offer from the other side, he is ethically obligated to transmit that offer to his client. He is not obligated to show the client a letter or play a voice-mail message or recite verbatim the offer with appropriate inflections. As the lawyer communicates the offer, the lawyer inevitably, if unwittingly, introduces a spin on the offer that may influence the client to consider it favorably or unfavorably. Usually the attorney's impression (and indeed, the client's) of the offer will be influenced to some degree by the identity of the offeror. In particular, if the attorney's dealings with the other side have been rancorous, the attorney may view any offer with a great deal of suspicion. Sometimes the relationship impedes impartial evaluation of an offer, causing a negotiator to reject an offer from an adversary that he should have accepted.

1. *Psychology of Reactive Devaluation*

Fixed-pie bias (i.e., the assumption that what is good for my counterpart must be bad for me) may contribute to *reactive devaluation*, which is a tendency to evaluate proposals less favorably after they have been offered by one's adversary.[186] In one classic study conducted during the days of Apartheid, researchers solicited students' evaluations of two university plans for divestment from South Africa. The first plan called for partial divestment, and the second increased investments in companies that had left South Africa. Both plans, which fell short of the students' demand for full divestment, were rated before and after the university announced that it would adopt the partial divestment plan. The results were dramatic: students rated the university plan less positively after it was announced by the university and the alternative plan more positively.

We hasten to note that the source of an offer may be diagnostic of its quality. It may be reasonable to view an offer more critically when the source is one's opponent, particularly if there is an unpleasant history between the parties. However, evidence from the aforementioned studies suggests that people tend to experience a knee-jerk overreaction to the source of the offer. If negotiators routinely undervalue concessions made by their counterparts, it will inhibit their ability to exploit tradeoffs that might result in more valuable agreements.

Consider an example of how reactive devaluation might manifest itself in a negotiation between lawyers. Imagine a simplified environmental cleanup action in which the parties are a governmental enforcement agency (represented by a single person) and a single responsible polluter. There may be two solutions to their problem. In one, the government effectuates the cleanup and sends a bill to the polluter. In the second, the polluter does the cleanup and the government inspects. Perhaps solution one meets more of the polluters' interests than solution two. One might suppose that the polluter would prefer this solution regardless of how it emerges as the agreed method. However, studies of reactive devaluation suggest that once the government tentatively agrees to that particular solution, the polluter may view the alternative solution more favorably. The apparent thought process is "if they held it back, it must be worse for them and therefore better for me than the one offered." The polluter may irrationally reorder her priorities and reject a deal simply because it was offered freely by an opponent.

---

186. *See* Lee Ross and Constance Stillinger, *Barriers to Conflict Resolution*, 7 Negotiation J. 389, 394–95 (1991) * * *

2. *Remediation*

Resisting the destructive effects of reactive devaluation will require negotiators to unlearn a pervasive assumption that most people carry with them. Negotiations are rarely fixed-sum and it is simply not true that what is good for one side is necessarily bad for the other. As mentioned above, both parties often have congruent interests or a mutual interest in exploiting tradeoffs on issues that they prioritize differently. To resist reactive devaluation, one must short-circuit a deeply ingrained habit. It is natural to react against freedom to choose, and when an opponent holds back one offer in favor of another, it's natural to yearn for the alternative option. However, it would be wise to critically examine this natural impulse and ask if this impulse is a rational response to a truly inferior offer or an emotional reaction against the other side's initiative.

Even if a lawyer can restrain herself from reactive devaluation, it may be very difficult to buffer this response in [her] counterpart. Certainly, it first may help to cultivate a cordial relationship with one's counterpart to the extent that this is possible, so that offers are regarded with less suspicion. Second, it may be helpful to ask a mutually trusted intermediary to convey a proposal. Some commentators have suggested that reactive devaluation can be overcome with the help of a mediator. Finally, if a party crafts a settlement package that would be mutually beneficial, it may be helpful to work with opposing counsel to make them feel as if the solution was jointly initiated or even that it was the opposing counsel's idea.

NOTES AND QUESTIONS

1. Some of the psychological phenomena described by Birke and Fox are heuristic in nature—they are mental shortcuts to simplify the process of making meaning out of our experiences. Such shortcuts can have great benefit—the availability heuristic described first, for example, obviously makes it much easier to make quick judgments without having to assess a situation completely. In conflict, however, as the old saying goes, sometimes a shortcut ends up being the longest way around. When coupled with the tendency to perceive a situation in a self-serving light, for example, simplifying one's perceptions may lead to intractable differences:

> [T]he need to simplify a conflict situation can lead to faulty perception about cause-and-effect relationships. People may falsely infer a relationship where none exists, or they may assume that a given action by one person results in an action by the other person. This effect, known as the "biased punctuation of conflict," occurs when people interpret interaction with their adversaries in other-derogating terms. Actor A perceives the history of conflict with another actor, B, as a sequence of B–A, B–A, B–A, in which the initial hostile or aggressive move was always made by B, obliging A to engage in defensive and legitimate retaliatory action. Actor B punctuates the same history of interaction as A–B, A–B, A–B, however, reversing the roles of aggressor and defender. Disagreement about how to punctuate

a sequence of events in a conflict relationship is at the root of many disputes. * * *

Thompson and Nadler, Judgmental Biases in Conflict Resolution and How to Overcome Them in The Handbook of Conflict Resolution: Theory and Practice 213, 214–219 (2000).

2. Birke and Fox discuss the importance of prospect theory and its implications for framing effects and risk aversion. As we saw in Section A, prospect theory can explain why plaintiffs are often risk averse and defendants risk-preferring. In most cases, if a defendant sees her choice as between a sure loss through settlement or a chance of avoiding loss through further litigation, the defendant may be prone to gamble to try to avoid the loss. Conversely, plaintiffs are often likely to take a sure gain through settlement rather than gamble on the possibility of greater gain through litigation.

Professor Chris Guthrie has also applied prospect theory to explain so-called frivolous litigation. Research has shown that "[w]hen choosing between low-probability gains and losses with equal expected values, . . . individuals make risk-seeking choices when selecting between gains and risk-averse choices when selecting between losses." Guthrie, Framing Frivolous Litigation: A Psychological Theory, 67 U.Chi.L.Rev. 163, 167 (2000). In other words, although normally a plaintiff may be risk-averse, when facing a low-probability of success, a plaintiff may be risk-preferring. For example, a plaintiff is more likely to choose to continue litigation and gamble on a five percent chance of a $1 million recovery than to accept a $50,000 settlement for that litigation, whereas a defendant will likely be risk-averse as between the same two choices and agree to settle. This may partly explain why plaintiffs pursue low-probability litigation so aggressively and why defendants may be willing to settle such claims.

3. Another psychological bias, called the "endowment effect," can also influence bargainers. The endowment effect is simple: people overvalue items they own as compared to items they don't. Individuals will demand more in compensation to give up something they already possess than they will offer as a payment to purchase the same item.

Many experiments have demonstrated this effect. In one classic study, experimenters gave some subjects a coffee mug and then offered them the choice to keep the mug or to sell it for an unspecified but predetermined price. These subjects had to write down the price at which they would sell their mug. Another group didn't receive mugs. Instead, they had to write down how much they were willing to spend to buy one. The researchers found that the median asking price for sellers was $7.12, whereas the median offer from buyers was $2.88. See Kahneman, Knetsch and Thaler, Experimental Tests of the Endowment Effect and the Coase Theorem, 98 J.Pol.Econ. 1325 (1990).

The endowment effect is related to loss aversion—those with a mug demand extra compensation to overcome what they perceive as a loss. Can you imagine ways in which the endowment effect may influence settlement negotiations in a legal dispute? When might a plaintiff, or a defendant, feel reluctant to give up something that they feel is already their entitlement or endowment?

For an argument that the behavior described as the endowment effect is not actually a cognitive error but instead can be explained in terms of self-interested "signaling," see Fremling and Posner, Market Signaling of Personal Characteristics 26–27 (U.Chi. Working Paper in L. & Econ.).

4. Birke and Fox briefly discuss the problem of overconfidence in negotiation-related judgments. Much research demonstrates that bargainers make self-serving and overconfident assessments, with obvious consequences:

> Conflicts and disputes are characterized by the presence of asymmetric information. In general, each side knows a great deal about the evidence and arguments that support its position and much less about those that support the position of the other side. The difficulty of making proper allowance for missing information * * * entails a bias that is likely to hinder successful negotiation. Each side will tend to overestimate its chances of success, as well as its ability to impose a solution on the other side and to prevent such an attempt by an opponent. Many years ago, we suggested that participants in a conflict are susceptible to a fallacy of initiative—a tendency to attribute less initiative and less imagination to the opponent than to oneself. The difficulty of adopting the opponent's view of the chessboard or of the battlefield may help explain why people often discover many new moves when they switch sides in a game. A related phenomenon has been observed in the response to mock trials that are sometimes conducted when a party to a dispute considers the possibility of litigation. Observers of mock trials have noted that the would-be litigators are often surprised and dismayed by the strength of the position put forth by their mock opponent. In the absence of such a vivid demonstration of their bias, disputants are likely to hold an overly optimistic assessment of their chances in court. More generally, a tendency to underestimate the strength of the opponent's position could make negotiators less likely to make concessions and thereby reduce the chances of a negotiated settlement. Neale and Bazerman (1983) illustrated this effect in the context of a final arbitration procedure, in which the parties submit final offers, one of which is selected by the arbitrator. Negotiators overestimated (by more than 15 percent, on the average) the chance that their offer would be chosen. In this situation, a more realistic appraisal would probably result in more conciliatory final offers.

Kahneman and Tversky, Conflict Resolution: A Cognitive Perspective, in Barriers to Conflict Resolution 47 (1995).

If you have ever been in the middle of a dispute—between two friends, two litigating parties, or two business partners, for example—you may have experienced such overconfidence effects first-hand. Both sides may seem supremely confident, so much so that to a third party their behavior and judgments seem almost comical. But when *you* are party to a dispute it is much more difficult to assess accurately your chances of success.

Reconsider the discussion of litigation analysis and decision trees in Section A. Is such analysis rendered worthless by the overconfidence bias? Or is litigation analysis a useful antidote to such psychological effects?

5. The phenomenon of reactive devaluation, covered at the end of the Birke and Fox excerpt, could theoretically have serious consequences for dispute resolution. If a party is likely to devalue an offer from the other side *merely because it comes from the other side*, finding solutions of any sort to a dispute may be jeopardized. Although the causes of this psychological effect are not entirely clear, the following excerpt summarizes two possibilities:

> One set of underlying processes involves changes in *perception, interpretation, or inference*, either about individual elements in a proposal or about the overall valence of that proposal. To the extent that the other side's initiative seems inconsistent with our understanding of their interests and/or past negotiation behavior, we are apt, perhaps even logically obliged, to scrutinize their offer rather carefully. That is, we are inclined to look for ambiguities, omissions, or "fine print" that might render the terms of that proposal more advantageous to the other side, and perhaps less advantageous to our side, than we had assumed them to be (or would have assumed them to be, had the question been asked) prior to their being offered. The results of such skeptical scrutiny—especially if the terms in question are unclear, complex, or imperfectly specified, and especially if trust vis-à-vis implementation of these terms is called for—are apt to be a revised assessment of what we stand to gain, both in absolute terms and relative to what we believe the other side stands to gain, from acceptance of the relevant proposal.

> This process of inference and deduction, as psychologists would be quick to note, could be even simpler and less cognitively demanding. Several theories of psychological consistency hold that any relevant object of judgment (including, presumably, a concession offer or a negotiation proposal) will be evaluated more negatively as a consequence of its linkage to a negative source (including, presumably, an enemy or adversary). In other words, no reinterpretation, in fact no consideration of content at all, need take place for devaluation to occur. One might simply reason that if "they" are offering a proposal it must be good for them; and if it is good for them (especially if "they" are adversaries who wish us harm) it must be bad for "us." Once again, although it is difficult to criticize such inferential leaps on purely normative grounds, the danger should be obvious. One can be led to conclude that any proposal offered by the "other side"—especially if that other side has long been perceived as an enemy—*must* be to our side's disadvantage, or else it would not have been offered. Such an inferential process, however, assumes a perfect opposition of interests,

or in other words, a true "zero-sum" game, when such is rarely the case in real-world negotiations between parties whose needs, goals, and opportunities are inevitably complex and varied.

The second type of underlying process or mechanism, suggested by demonstrations of the devaluation phenomenon in the Stanford divestment studies in which the source of the devalued proposal was not really an enemy of the recipient, is very different. This mechanism involves neither mindful nor mindless changes in interpretation, but rather changes in underlying *preferences*. Human beings, at least in some circumstances, may be inclined to reject or devalue whatever is freely available to them, and to covet and strive for whatever is denied them. Moreover, they may be inclined to do so even when no hostility is perceived on the part of the individual or institution determining what will or will not be made available. The familiar aphorism that "the grass is always greener on the other side of the fence" captures this source of human unhappiness and frustration very well, and it is easy to think of anecdotal examples in which children or adults, rather than "counting their blessings," seem to place inordinately high value on whatever commodity or opportunity is denied them.

* * *

The preceding discussion of the reactive devaluation phenomenon, and of the various processes that might underlie it, has some implication for those who seek to resolve disputes. Foremost, of course, is the likelihood that compromise proposals or concessions designed to demonstrate goodwill and prompt reciprocation will fail in their objectives. All too often, they will be dismissed as trivial and token, or received with coolness and expressions of distrust that serve to thwart the goal of negotiated agreement and to weaken rather than strengthen the hand of those who urge conciliation. Furthermore, such public dismissals or cool receptions are themselves apt to be misattributed—to be seen as the product of calculated strategy rather than genuine sentiment, or to be taken as evidence of a lack of good faith and seriousness in the pursuit of agreement. * * *

Two strategies for reducing reactive devaluation follow rather directly. Both are designed to discourage the recipients of a concession or compromise proposal from reinterpreting its terms or reordering their own preferences in ways that make the proposal seem less advantageous to them. The first strategy involves explicitly eliciting the potential recipients' values and preferences before making any concessionary proposal, and then explicitly linking the content of the subsequent proposal to those expressed values and preferences. * * *

A related strategy * * * would be for one side simply to offer the other a "menu" of unilateral concessions that it is willing to make as a gesture to initiate a cycle of future *reciprocal* concessions; and then to invite that other side to select the "pump-priming" concession of its choice.

Ross, Reactive Devaluation in Negotiation and Conflict Resolution, in Barriers to Conflict Resolution 34–40 (1995).

Do these ways to overcome reactive devaluation seem plausible? What of those suggested by Birke and Fox?

b. THE ROLE OF EMOTION

In addition to these cognitive and social psychological effects, the emotions play a critical role in disputes and in negotiation. The legal academy has become increasingly interested in the role of emotions in the law. See Bandes, The Passions of the Law (1999); Law, Psychology, and the Emotions, Symposium Issue, 74 Chi.–Kent L.Rev. 1423 (2000). The next two excerpts explore the role of attributions in creating and sustaining emotions in conflict and the steps a negotiator can take to deal with emotions in a dispute.

Keith G. Allred, Anger and Retaliation in Conflict: The Role of Attribution

in Morton Deutsch and Peter T. Coleman (eds.), The Handbook of Conflict Resolution: Theory and Practice 236, 243–244 (2000).

* * * Anger-driven conflict is often maladaptive in at least two respects. First, it is particularly destructive because, once angered at each other, parties in a conflict become less effective at solving the problems between them. One study found that negotiators who held each other responsible for harmful behavior in a previous interaction felt greater anger and less compassion toward each other than those who did not hold each other responsible for the same harmful behavior. Consequently, the angry negotiators had less positive regard for each other's interests in the negotiation. As a result, the negotiators who were angry with each other discovered fewer mutually beneficial solutions than the participants who were not angry with each other.

A second reason that angry, retaliatory conflicts are especially maladaptive is because they are frequently rooted in misperceptions that tend to escalate the conflict. Research on the actor-observer bias seems to suggest that a harmdoer attributes his or her behavior to external causes while the harmed party attributes the behavior to a disposition of the harmdoer. However, most actor-observer bias research has not examined situations in which the actor's behavior has a direct and negative impact on the observer. For example, many actor-observer bias studies investigate situations in which one person observes another in conversation or offering an opinion on a topic, rather than the situation [in which another's] behaviors have direct and negative impact * * *

A recent study investigated these situations in which the actor's behavior negatively affects the observer. * * * The results of the study indicated the presence of an *accuser bias*, the tendency for an observer negatively affected by an actor's behavior to attribute the behavior to causes under the control of the actor. For example, [if] Margaret is negatively affected by Robin's request that she come to work on Saturday, she is more likely to attribute the request to Robin's lack of organization than to her daughter's asthma attack. Consequently, Margaret is likely to feel greater anger and a stronger impulse to retaliate than she otherwise would. The accuser bias thus tends to make anger-driven conflict especially destructive because such conflicts are often rooted in exaggerated judgments of responsibility that lead to excessive anger and retaliation.

The destructive effects of the accuser bias are greatly exacerbated because the person who acts negatively falls victim to the opposite bias. The study documenting the accuser bias also revealed a *bias of the accused*, a tendency to attribute one's own harmful behavior to circumstances beyond one's control. In our example, Robin is likely to overattribute her need to have Margaret come in to her daughter's asthma attack, and underattribute it to her own lack of organization.

* * * The point of the research on the accuser bias and the bias of the accused is that, of the contributing causes of a harmful behavior, the accused tends to focus on those beyond her control, while the accuser focuses on those within the control of the accused. Consequently, the accuser holds the accused more responsible for the harmful behavior than the accused holds herself accountable.

* * *

In fact, research suggests that once these mutually derogating attributional patterns give rise to such dynamics they can become so entrenched that they define not only a unique and especially destructive type of conflict but an especially destructive type of relationship as well. * * * [D]ozens of studies investigating differences in attributional patterns among people in close relationships, mostly marital couples, have found similar results. In stressed or dissatisfied relationships, the parties consistently attributed each other's negative behavior to internal, controllable causes and attributed each other's positive behavior to external, uncontrollable causes. Consequently, people in stressed relationships felt negative emotions toward each other and had difficulty solving the problems that arose between them.

People in satisfied relationships, by contrast, tended to exhibit no such derogating pattern of attribution. In fact, people in some satisfied relationships exhibited a reversal of typical derogating attribution, attributing each other's negative behavior to external, uncontrollable causes and positive behavior to internal, controllable causes. * * *

Once established, both the stressed and satisfied marital patterns are self-fulfilling and self-perpetuating. That is, at some point the bias actually becomes an accurate perception. In a distressed relationship, the parties purposely behave negatively toward each other, although each sees his or her own negative behavior as the other person's just desserts for a prior negative act by that person. In a satisfied relationship, the parties intentionally act kindly toward each other. Nevertheless, * * * evidence suggests that attributional bias is the ultimate causal agent. In other words, the pattern is largely set in motion in the first place by the difference in attributional pattern. The research * * * thus suggests that once [two people] begin to exchange angry, retaliatory behavior—fueled by offsetting biases in judging how responsible each is for these behaviors—they face more than simply the destructiveness of a single angry conflict. They also run the risk of transforming their relationship into one characterized by chronic angry conflict.

Robert S. Adler, Benson Rosen, and Elliot M. Silverstein, Emotions in Negotiation: How to Manage Fear and Anger

14 Neg.J. 161, 167–177 (1998).

Anger in Negotiations

Two millennia ago, poet and satirist Horace wrote *Ira furor brevis est—* anger is a short madness. When we become truly furious, we may act in an utterly irrational way for a period of time. Although a temper tantrum may relieve pent-up feelings for a moment, we often find regret and negative recriminations following such displays. On this point, Queen Elizabeth I reportedly observed, "anger makes dull men witty, but it also keeps them poor."

Anger springs from many sources. On one hand, it may arise from the perception that someone has violated written or unwritten rules of behavior. In chimpanzee society, De Waal notes that members of a group exhibit what he terms *moralistic aggression*, that is, chimps perceived as stingy and unsharing are more likely to be attacked and refused favors than those that act in a more generous spirit. On a human level, someone who rudely breaks in line or recklessly cuts us off in traffic will likely ignite fires of indignation if we are the victims of these transgressions.

Anger also arises when one encounters snubs, rudeness, or anything that provokes a feeling of being unfairly diminished—we get angry because we feel vulnerable and exposed. In similar fashion, shame may trigger anger. If our egos are bruised in a manner that makes us feel small, we react defensively, and often in anger. The evolutionary basis for anger seems clear: anger motivates us to retaliate when we are attacked and to defend ourselves against those whom we believe are doing us harm. As with other emotions, what one feels at any given moment is both physical and situational. Fear may prompt a chimpanzee to flee from a more powerful lion, but anger will drive it to lash out at a weaker chimp who snatches a piece of food that it was about to eat.

In the negotiation context, a host of factors can contribute to anger and aggression. Citing a variety of studies, Barry and Oliver suggest the following examples where these negative emotions can arise in dyadic negotiations: where bargainers are accountable to angry constituents; where bargainers face time pressures; where they perceive the situation as win-lose with divergent goals between the parties; or, generally, where the parties are otherwise unconcerned with protecting a working relationship. In a study of anger in mergers and acquisitions, Daly found the following types of behavior likely to trigger anger: misrepresentation; making excessive demands; overstepping one's authority; showing personal animosity; questioning a representative's authority to negotiate; seeking to undermine a representative's authority by "going over his head"; and dwelling on unimportant details.

* * *

Dealing With Your Anger

The critical need for self-awareness. Virtually all researchers and commentators on emotions and negotiations insist that the first step necessary in controlling anger is self-awareness. If we cannot sense when our anger has been aroused, we will miss an opportunity to control it. Anger typically has physical manifestations, such as a rapid heartbeat, muscle tensing, increased sweating, or flushed face.

* * *

Determine situations that trigger inappropriate anger. In some cases, anger is an appropriate response to a provocative situation. At other times, we may instantly, and inappropriately, ignite in circumstances that most other bargainers would not find provocative. For example, some people react furiously to meetings that start a few minutes late. Others become livid at real or imagined slights to their dignity. Anger at these moments generally serves no useful purpose. Determining those things that trigger inappropriate anger may permit us to take steps to avoid them or to take preventative measures to control anger.

Decide whether to display anger. Recognizing how and why our anger arises does not mean that we should always avoid angry feelings or never display anger. But, if one can recognize the onset of anger, one can decide how best to deal with it. In some cases, we should reveal our feelings. For example, if a fellow negotiator has just falsely accused us of lying, we might want to demonstrate extreme displeasure in a way that persuades the other side that such charges are false and will not be tolerated. The trick is to do so in a manner that makes the point, but does not undermine the negotiation. This requires a careful assessment of the circumstances and of our opponent's reaction to our anger, and a measured approach to expressing our feelings.

* * *

Dealing With Your Opponent's Anger

Just as we need to develop a good instinct for determining when we become angry; we also need to be able to read our opponents' moods, particularly those involving frustration and anger. Here are some techniques that may be useful:

C. Psychological and Social Aspects of Bargaining 177

Defuse heated emotional buildups. Every good negotiator seeks to remain alert to the mood of a negotiation at all times. One should always seek to monitor opponents for anger. If one senses a rising temper on the other side, it may help to ask directly: "Mary, is something bothering you?" or "Tom, did my comment about the necessity of meeting deadlines disturb you?" or "Regina, you look angry. Are you?"

Assess the significance of angry displays. When an opponent erupts in anger, one should assess as carefully as possible the significance of the anger. Does it seem calculated? Can the person regain composure? In some cases, the other side may try to convey anger as a strategic maneuver to dislodge us from a firmly-held position. Dealing with such an approach calls for a different response than dealing with a truly lost temper. Trying to placate someone who is using anger strategically to gain concessions may well lead us to make overly generous offers.

Address an opponent's anger. In some cases, you may need to say something like, "Irv, I'm sure you're going to rethink the comments you've just made. I hope that you realize they were inappropriate. In the meantime, you've made me angry, so I need a break before we resume bargaining." It rarely hurts to acknowledge an opponent's anger even when one disagrees that it is justified. In some cases, an apology—even one felt to be undeserved—will help smooth the course of a negotiation. You should not apologize, however, in a way that leads an opponent to conclude that you have conceded a point that remains in dispute or that you are a weak negotiator. Thus, instead of offering a personal apology, you can—as easily and as effectively—simply apologize for the "bad situation."

* * *

Help an angry opponent save face. Perhaps the biggest deal breaker in negotiations is "face loss." Where parties feel they will lose face if they agree to an opponent's demands, they are likely to derail the negotiation even if it is not in their interest to do so. So critical is "face" to a negotiation that parties will hold to untenable positions that will cost them money or even provoke wars—Schoonmaker cites the example of two Latin American countries that fought a war because of angry feelings over a soccer match. Accordingly, one should always try to help an angry opponent save face especially if lost face is what triggered the outburst in the first place. * * *

NOTES AND QUESTIONS

1. Allred points out that the emotions are not wholly distinct from cognition and perception. If you think you've seen a coiled snake on the path, you're likely to jump in fear. But when you realize that it was merely a pile of old rope, your emotions calm, your heart rate may decrease, and you will experience the situation quite differently.

The actor-observer and accuser biases Allred discusses derive from what is known as the fundamental attribution error. We tend to assume that when others act in ways we dislike they do so because of their internal motivations, beliefs, or desires, whereas when *we* do something that others may dislike we attribute our own actions to circumstantial causes. You may, for example, assume that someone else is late because they're lazy; when you're late you know it's because your car broke down.

The angry emotions created by these misattributions can make negotiation much more difficult. The more anger and less compassion negotiators feel toward each other, the less willing they generally are to work together in the future. Similarly, high degrees of anger may make negotiators less likely to discover available joint gains. See Allred, Mallozzi, Matsui, and Raia, The Influence of Anger and Compassion on Negotiation Performance, 70 Org.Behav. & Human Dec. Proceses 175–187 (1997). However, anger does *not* seem to help negotiators claim more value for themselves. Id.

2. A dispute can become more emotional as the lawyers and clients involved negotiate about it. The other side's bargaining behavior may make you angry; their threats, bluffs, lying, delays, or other tactics may cause your blood to boil. Such behavior, and the emotion it engenders, may make you resist collaborating with the other side.

Adler, Rosen and Silverstein mention that "saving face" can be an important interest for many negotiators, and that loss of "face" can lead to angry reactions. Affronts to status are one way in which even seemingly innocent bargaining moves may generate an emotional reaction:

> [S]tudies indicate that bargainers whose social face has been affronted may resist making concessions, may fail to reach an agreement advantageous to them, and may engage in costly retaliation. These responses can be viewed as alternative ways of regaining self-esteem and social esteem.

> The affront to social face posed by an invalidation of a bargainer's position may be greatly reduced if the negotiator is able to assure the bargainer that he has not appeared personally weak and incapable. High-status bargainers whose position has been rejected and have no direct information concerning whether they have appeared effective as persons or not may try to assert that they are strong persons by resisting compromising.

Tjosvold and Huston, Social Face and Resistance to Compromise in Bargaining, 104 J. of Soc.Psychol. 57, 59 (1978).

3. Adler, Rosen and Silverstein suggest a fairly rational or cognitive approach to thinking through an emotional negotiation. First, they suggest thinking carefully about your own anger and whether displaying anger will be useful and appropriate. Second, they advise a negotiator to analyze an opponent's angry display and determine the best way to respond. Other commentators have likewise suggested that one should "think through" one's feelings in conflict situations rather than merely responding emotionally. See e.g., Stone, Patton and Heen, Difficult Conversations: How to Discuss What Matters Most 91–105 (1999). What are the advantages and disadvantages of such an approach? Will it work?

2. Interpersonal Style and Skill

These psychological barriers to dispute resolution affect the ways in which we think about and react to conflict. You may be unaware of their influence and yet subject to it. In addition to such psychological and emotional aspects of bargaining, however, we must consider the more social domain—the ways in which bargaining is an interpersonal event and is shaped by your interpersonal style and skills.

We each have different tendencies and our own style when faced with conflict. One's style differs from one's strategy:

> In settlement negotiation, it is not enough to say that one wants to negotiate "amicably" or "cooperatively." These words do not by themselves mean that someone wants to negotiate in a problem-solving manner. The words are as applicable to positional negotiation as they are to the problem-solving kind. For instance, one can negotiate positionally by using a pleasant, amicable outward "style" while still using a highly positional "strategy" of making and holding to settlement positions. Being cooperative might mean no more than making concessions to the bargaining positions taken by the other side. Not only is this an entirely positional kind of procedure, but it is also an ineffectual one. * * *

Heumann and Hyman, Negotiation Methods and Litigation Settlement Methods in New Jersey: "You Can't Always Get What You Want", 12 Ohio St.J. of Dis.Res. 253, 279–282 (1997).

In this Section we consider the different interpersonal skills needed to negotiate effectively.

Donald G. Gifford, Legal Negotiation: Theory and Applications

21 (1989).

It is important for the lawyer to distinguish style from strategy in a * * * negotiation for two reasons. First, many of the disadvantages of *competitive tactics*—the possibilities of deadlock and a premature breakdown of negotiation, and of generating ill-will and distrust with the other party—can be mitigated if the *style* of the negotiator is cooperative. Even when the substance being communicated to the other negotiator is very demanding and competitive, friendliness, courtesy and politeness help to preserve a positive working relationship.

Conversely, [a] lawyer needs to be able to identify *competitive tactics* even when the style of the negotiator is *cooperative*. Often, lawyers will be misled by the polite and friendly style of the other lawyer and assume that he is using *cooperative tactics, i.e.,* that his goals include a fair and just agreement and a positive, trusting working relationship between the parties. To the extent that the negotiator confuses cooperative style for cooperative substance, she may be inclined to reciprocate, and the resulting agreement will disadvantage her client.

Admittedly, the personal *style* of the negotiator often is intertwined with the negotiation strategy she is using in a specific negotiation or that she prefers to use. A negotiator who has an aggressive and forceful personal style frequently will succeed in causing the other negotiator to lose confidence in himself or his case, thereby inducing him to settle for less than he initially expected, a goal of the competitive strategy. In other instances, however, a negotiator who is courteous, personable and friendly may, through competitive strategic moves such as extreme opening demands and infrequent concessions, be even more successful in destroying the other party's confidence in his case and inducing unilateral concessions from him. Although a negotiator's personal style of interaction positively correlates with her preferred negotiating strategy, separating personal style from negotiation strategies and techniques yields new flexibility for the negotiator. It is possible for the negotiator with a *cooperative* personal *style* to adopt *competitive tactics* when it is advantageous, and naturally *competitive* individuals can adopt *cooperative tactics*.

Robert H. Mnookin, Scott R. Peppet and Andrew S. Tulumello, The Tension Between Empathy and Assertiveness

12 Neg.J. 217, 218–226 (1996).

* * * We propose that negotiation behavior can be conceptualized along two dimensions—*assertiveness* and *empathy*. By assertiveness, we mean the capacity to express and advocate for one's own interests. By empathy, we mean the capacity to demonstrate an accurate, non-judgmental understanding of another person's concerns and perspective.

Empathy and assertiveness are in "tension" because many negotiators implicitly assume that these two sets of skills represent polar opposites along a single continuum and that each is incompatible with the other. Some worry, for example, that to listen or empathize too much signals weakness or agreement; they perceive empathy to be incompatible with assertion. Others are concerned that if they advocate too strongly they will upset or anger their counterpart; they believe that assertion undermines empathy. Many negotiators fall somewhere in between. Not needing to dominate but preferring not to surrender control, they are unsure how much to assert. Or, open to understanding the other side but also wanting to secure the best possible outcome, they do not know how much to empathize. In short, many negotiators feel stuck. * * *

* * *

Our claim that empathy and assertiveness represent different dimensions [of negotiation behavior] can be illuminated by considering three common negotiation "styles." These are *competing*, *accommodating* and *avoiding*, each of which represents a different suboptimal combination of empathy and assertiveness. * * *

Competing

A competitive style consists of substantial assertion but little empathy. A competitor wants to experience "winning" and enjoys feeling purposeful and in control. Competitive negotiators exude eagerness, enthusiasm, and impatience. Because conflict does not make them feel uncomfortable, they enjoy being partisans. Competitive negotiators typically seek to control the agenda and frame the issues. They can stake out an ambitious position and stick to it, and they fight back in the face of bullying or intimidation.

The advantages of this style flow directly from this characterization. Competitors are not afraid to articulate and push for their point of view. With respect to distributive bargaining, they fight hard to get the biggest slice of any pie.

But this tendency also has disadvantages. Competitive negotiators risk provoking the other side and incur a high risk of escalation or stalemate. In addition, because competitive negotiators are often not good listeners, they have difficulty developing collaborative relationships that allow both sides to explore value-creating opportunities. They may also pay a high price in their relationships, as others, perceiving them as arrogant, untrustworthy, or controlling, avoid them. * * *

* * *

Accommodating

Accommodating consists of substantial empathy but little assertion. An accommodator prizes good relationships and wants to feel liked. Accommodators exude concern, compassion, and understanding. Concerned that conflict will disrupt relationships, they negotiate in "smoothing" ways to resolve difference quickly. Accommodators typically listen well and are quick to second-guess their own interests.

This style has straightforward advantages. Negotiators concerned with good relationships on balance probably do have better relationships, or at least fewer relationships marked by open conflict. Because they listen well, others may see them as trustworthy. Similarly, they are adept at creating a less stressful atmosphere for the negotiation.

One disadvantage of this tendency is that it can be exploited. Hard bargainers may extract concessions by implicitly or explicitly threatening to disrupt or terminate the relationship. Another disadvantage may be that accommodators pay insufficient attention to the substance of the dispute because they are unduly concerned about disturbing a relationship. Accommodators, therefore, can feel frustrated dealing with both substantive and interpersonal issues.

Avoiding

An avoiding style consists of low levels of empathy and assertiveness. Avoiders believe that conflict is unproductive, and they feel uncomfortable with explicit, especially emotional, disagreement. When faced with conflict, avoiders disengage. They tend not to seek control of the agenda or to frame the issues. Rather, they deflect efforts to focus on solutions, appearing detached, unenthusiastic, or uninterested.

At times, avoidance can have substantial advantages. Some disputes are successfully avoided. In other cases, avoiders may create a "chasing" dynamic in which the other side does all the work * * * Because they appear aloof, avoiders can have more persuasive impact when they do speak up. In addition, their reserve and cool-headedness makes it difficult for others to know their true interests and intentions.

The greatest disadvantage of this tendency is that avoiders miss opportunities to use conflict to solve problems. Avoiders often disengage without knowing whether obscured interests might make joint gains possible—they rarely have the experience of walking away from an apparent conflict feeling better off. Even when they do negotiate, avoiders leave value on the table because they refrain from asserting their own interests or flushing out the other side's. Avoiders fare poorly in the distributive aspects of bargaining.

* * *

* * * [W]e believe that a negotiator is most effective if she leads the way by successfully combining empathy and assertiveness. The normative task is to manage the tension between empathy and assertiveness by * * * helping design a process that permits the other side to do so as well. This often means agreeing to listen and empathize for a period on the condition that the other side agrees to try to do so later in the negotiation, and also discussing explicitly that a demonstrated understanding of the other's views should not be interpreted as agreement. In this way, a negotiation can sometimes evolve toward problem-solving even if it begins less productively.

Keith G. Allred, Distinguishing Best and Strategic Practices: A Framework for Managing the Dilemma Between Creating and Claiming Value

Neg. J. 387, 388–390 (2000).

This essay outlines a prescriptive framework for managing negotiation dilemmas * * * The prescriptive advice is based on drawing a distinction between "best practices" and "strategic practices." Best practices are defined as those that work well in terms of one or more dimensions of negotiation performance without diminishing one's performance on the other dimensions. For example, listening may be a practice that helps a negotiator create value and maintain the relationship with the other party without posing much risk to that negotiator's efforts to claim value. These are practices that pose no real dilemma. They tend to work well in most situations, regardless of what the other party does. The prescriptive advice is simply to use these practices in virtually all situations, even though there may be a tendency not to use them in certain situations. For instance, one may tend to listen less to an irritating and competitive other party, even though some situations could be handled more effectively by listening.

Strategic practices are defined as those that tend to work well in terms of one or more dimensions of negotiation performance, but that also tend to diminish one's performance on other dimensions. These are the practices, such as sharing information, that pose classic negotiation dilemmas. For example, full and truthful information sharing increases the chances of discovering an agreement that creates value and tends to enhance the relationship, but that information may also be exploited by the other party to gain a claiming-value advantage.

Accordingly, these practices work well in some situations and poorly in others. The key to generating prescriptive advice regarding strategic practices is to specify the conditions in which negotiators should use such practices more and those in which they should use them less. For example, a negotiator should probably share more information the more cooperative and trustworthy the other party is and the more significant and long-term the relationship is.

* * *

Asserting Facet

With respect to the asserting facet, the framework specifies three best practices and two strategic practices * * * The first best practice derives from prior work suggesting that working to develop and improve one's best alternative to a negotiated agreement (BATNA) is a practice that is effective in claiming-value terms without harming one in terms of creating value or maintaining the relationship. The second asserting best practice is based on research * * * indicating that effective professional negotiators * * * typically use a few of the most persuasive arguments available in support of the positions they advocate rather than diluting their persuasion efforts with a number of additional but weaker arguments. The third asserting best practice is derived logically. A minimally assertive practice of working to see that, where possible, one's own needs and interests are met would seem to present claiming-value advantages at little cost in terms of creating value or maintaining the relationship.

The first strategic asserting practice draws on research indicating that asserting practices such as taking extreme opening positions and being slow to make concessions can be used to gain a claiming-value advantage. A second strategic asserting practice that is similar is using one's power and authority to win a favorable outcome. While these practices can be effective in claiming-value terms, they can also compromise a negotiator's ability to create value and maintain the relationship. Accordingly, negotiators should be less willing to use them the more important, cooperative, trusting, and long-term the relationship with the other party is and the less important the interests the negotiator has at stake are.

Accommodating Facet

The framework identifies four best and one strategic practice with regard to accommodating * * * The accommodating best practices tend to involve accommodations in terms of the negotiation process rather than concessions on substantive issues. The first accommodating best practice draws on research on procedural and interactional justice suggesting that treating the other party with consideration and respect, even if one does not agree with the other party, will do a great deal to enhance the relationship without costing one anything in terms of substantive concessions. In fact, justice research suggests that such procedural and interactional accommodations will, in many ways, do more to prime the pump of trusting, cooperative interactions than will accommodation in the form of substantive concessions. Negotiators can provide the other party with a sense of procedural and interactional fairness through such actions as listening and seeking to understand and appreciate the other party's perspective.

The second accommodating best practice is drawn from research on attributional biases and anger in negotiation and conflict situations. This practice involves resisting the tendency to hold others more responsible for problems that arise than one holds oneself and resisting the tendency to retaliate angrily when one holds the other party responsible for problems.

The third and fourth best accommodating practices are based on * * * research on effective professional negotiators. That research indicated that effective negotiators do not use positive words such as "reasonable" and "generous" to describe their own proposals. The same research also indicated that effective negotiators do not immediately respond to the other party's proposal with a counterproposal.

Accommodation that takes the form of substantive concessions rather than process or interaction accommodations, logic would suggest, should be designated as strategic practices. While such substantive accommodations can help maintain the ongoing relationship, they clearly come at a claiming-value, and even a creating-value, cost. Negotiators should therefore be more willing to make such substantive concessions to the extent that the interests they have at stake are of limited importance and the relationship with the other party is important, cooperative, trusting, and ongoing.

Integrating Facet

Regarding the integrating facet, the framework specifies three best practices and two strategic practices * * * The first integrating best practice is based on research on logrolling that suggest that one should be willing to compromise on something of lesser importance in order to gain something of greater importance. The second integrating best practice is based on Pruitt's work suggesting that one should be firm in insisting that one's own interests and needs be fulfilled and flexible regarding the means by which those interests and needs are fulfilled. The third integrating best practice is based on Fisher, Ury, and Patton's work indicating that one should engage in collaborative consideration of how to fulfill both parties' underlying interests rather than engaging in positional bargaining.

The two strategic integrating practices involve the dilemmas of information exchange * * * Full, honest information exchange can facilitate the discovery of mutually satisfying solutions. However, information exchange can be exploited by the other party to gain a claiming-value advantage. Accordingly, two integrating practices regarding information exchange are strategic practices. First, one should be more willing to trust what the other party communicates the more cooperative and trustworthy the other party is and the more important and long-term the relationship is. Second, the more cooperative and trustworthy the other party is, and the longer and more important the relationship * * * the more willing negotiators should be to divulge their true interests, preferences, and alternatives to the other party.

Douglas Stone, Bruce Patton and Sheila Heen, Difficult Conversations

37–40, 167–168 (1999).

There's only one way to come to understand the other person's story, and that's by being curious. Instead of asking yourself, "How can they think that?!" ask yourself, "I wonder what information they have that I don't?" Instead of asking, "How can they be so irrational?" ask, "How might they see the world such that their view makes sense?" Certainty locks us out of their story; curiosity lets us in.

* * *

It can be awfully hard to stay curious about another person's story when you have your own story to tell, especially if you're thinking that only one story can really be right. After all, your story is so different from theirs, and makes so much sense to you. Part of the stress of staying curious can be relieved by adopting what we call the "And Stance."

We usually assume that we must either accept or reject the other person's story, and that if we accept theirs, we must abandon our own. [But who's] right between a person who likes to sleep with the window open and another who prefers the window closed?

The answer is that the question makes no sense. Don't choose between the stories; embrace both. That's the And Stance.

The suggestion to embrace both stories can sound like double-talk. It can be heard as "Pretend both of your stories are right." But in fact, it suggests something quite different. Don't pretend anything. Don't worry about accepting or rejecting the other person's story. First work to understand it. The mere act of understanding someone else's story doesn't require you to give up your own. The And Stance allows you to recognize that how you *each* see things matters, that how you each feel matters.

Regardless of what you end up doing, regardless of whether your story influences theirs or theirs yours, both stories matter.

The And Stance is based on the assumption that the world is complex, that you can feel hurt, angry, and wronged, *and* they can feel just as hurt, angry, and wronged. They can be doing their best, *and* you can think that it's not good enough. You may have done something stupid, *and* they will have contributed in important ways to the problem as well. You can feel furious with them, *and* you can also feel love and appreciation for them.

The And Stance gives you a place from which to assert the full strength of your views and feelings without having to diminish the views and feelings of someone else. Likewise, you don't need to give up anything to hear how someone else feels or sees things differently. Because you may have different information or different interpretations, both stories can make sense at the same time.

* * *

Scores of workshops and books on "active listening" teach you what you should *do* to be a good listener. Their advice is relatively similar—ask questions, paraphrase back what the other person has said, acknowledge their view, sit attentively and look them in the eye—all good advice. You emerge from these courses eager to try out your new skills, only to become discouraged when your friends or colleagues complain that you sound phony or mechanical. "Don't use that active listening stuff on me," they say.

The problem is this: you are taught what to say and how to sit, but the heart of good listening is authenticity. People "read" not only your words and posture, but what's going on inside of you. If your "stance" isn't genuine, the words won't matter. What will be communicated almost invariably is whether you are genuinely curious, whether you genuinely care about the other person. If your intentions are false, no amount of careful wording or good posture will help. If your intentions are good, even clumsy language won't hinder you.

Listening is only powerful and effective if it is authentic. Authenticity means that you are listening because you are curious and because you care, not just because you are supposed to. The issue, then, is this: Are you curious? Do you care?

NOTES AND QUESTIONS

1. Each of these excerpts stresses the importance of empathy and listening in negotiation. Empathy and listening have long been recognized as critically important skills in the resolution of conflict. The psychologist Carl Rogers used a simple rule to encourage his patients to demonstrate empathy for others: "Each person can speak up for himself only *after* he has first restated the ideas and feelings of the previous speaker accurately, and to that speaker's satisfaction." Rogers, On Becoming A Person 332 (1961). For an overview of current empathy-related research, see Duan and Hill,

The Current State of Empathy Research, 43 J. Counseling Psych. 261 (1996).

Empathy can help to overcome one of the causes of protracted conflict: mis-attributions about others' intentions and behavior. As we've seen, negotiators tend to assume that another's behavior was caused by that person's internal characteristics, and to under-attribute that behavior to external circumstances beyond the person's control. See Watson, The Actor and the Observer: How are Their Perceptions of Causality Divergent?, 92 Psychol.Bull. 682–700 (1982). This is particularly true in conflict situations. Are empathy and listening an effective antidote to these problems?

Listening and engaging in genuine dialogue has other obvious benefits. First, you may simply discover what the other person cares about—you may get to the heart of the matter. This may allow you to find a solution you would otherwise miss. Second, empathy may build respect and trust between the parties. Third, by demonstrating understanding of the other side's perspective and concerns you may defuse tensions and avoid polarization and escalation. Finally, your effective use of these interpersonal skills may build a context for collaboration or problem-solving. See Littlejohn and Domenici, Engaging Communication in Conflict 48–49 (2001).

2. For a discussion of the stages that children go through in developing empathy, see Hoffman, Empathy and Moral Development: Implications for Caring and Justice (2000) (exploring the reactive cry of the newborn on hearing other infants cry; "egocentric empathic distress," in which a small child seeks comfort upon seeing another person in distress; "quasi-egocentric distress," in which a toddler begins to try to help others but does so as *she* would like to be helped—patting, kissing, etc.—rather than in victim-appropriate ways; "sympathetic distress," in which a child understands that another's inner state differs from her own and offers more appropriate help; and "empathic distress," in which the suffering of others generates genuine empathy).

3. Stone, Patton and Heen suggest that empathy and listening will only be effective if they are genuine—if they reflect curiosity and concern on the part of the listener. Otherwise, they fear, the "listener" will simply be using tricks or techniques to try to accommodate the talker, and the talker will likely see through those techniques and spot the listener's disingenuousness. Do you agree? Can you "fake" listening? If not, how does one negotiate oneself into a stance of curiosity—particularly in a real conflict in which you disagree strongly with the other side?

4. Some claim that empathy may be dangerous to your negotiating position. One professional negotiator advises that you should "Put yourself in the shoes of your opponent, but do not remain there too long." He worries that empathy can lead a negotiator to sacrifice her own interests:

> The good negotiator feels the necessity to put himself or herself into the situation of the other side. This feeling is a natural byproduct of the negotiating process itself. Negotiation involves personal contact, communication, and interaction. The two parties are watching each

other like two boxing champions in the ring. They continually watch for signs that give insight into the other champion's mind. Very often, one negotiator openly invites the other to understand his or her situation. * * * You cannot reach an agreement without knowing as the Germans say, *wo die Schuh drückt*—where the shoe hurts.

* * *

Here lies the danger: Having put oneself in the shoes of the other fellow can lead to the road on which those shoes were marching—that is, seeking solutions which risk being beneficial to the other party alone. The right attitude in such a situation is to find answers that alleviate the burden of the other party while also providing satisfaction for yourself. Therefore, the more willing a negotiator is to assimilate, to feel the problems of the other side, the more that negotiator has to bear in mind the self-interested goals.

Nyerges, Ten Commandments for a Negotiator, 3 Neg.J. 21 (1987).

Do you agree with Nyerges? Are Mnookin, Peppet and Tulumello unrealistic when they counsel that empathy is a critical skill for lawyers in dispute resolution? One danger of demonstrating empathy for the other side's perspective is that your client may see you as disloyal—if you can understand their position it means you don't care enough about the client's. Does demonstrating empathy square with a lawyer's professional responsibilities to her client?

5. Not all assertions are created equal. Linguistic anthropologists have identified a variety of "powerless" speech patterns. These include:

Hedges: language that reduces the force of an assertion by allowing for exceptions or by avoiding commitments, such as "sort of," "a little," and "kind of"

Intensifiers: language that increases or emphasizes the force of an assertion, such as "very," "definitely," "very definitely," and "surely"

Hesitations: "meaningless" expressions, such as "oh, well," "let's see," "so, you see," "uh," "um," and "you know"

Questioning forms: use of rising question intonation at the end of what would otherwise normally be declarative sentences, such as "I weigh 125?" or "Definitely we could do that?"

Fairhurst and Sarr, The Art of Framing: Managing the Language of Leadership 175 (1996).

Research shows that use of these speech forms diminishes persuasive effect. "In one study, males and females heard the testimony of either a male or female witness who used either the powerful or powerless style to deliver the same substantive evidence. Regardless of whether the testimony was presented in transcript or through audiotape, and regardless of whether the witness or the rating audience was male or female, the powerful style resulted in greater perceived credibility of the witness." Id. at 176.

6. The therapeutic justice movement argues that as part of preparing for a negotiation, lawyers should identify with their clients' emotional concerns as well as typically legal and financial ones. See Kupfer Schneider, The Intersection of Therapeutic Jurisprudence, Preventative Law, and Alternative Dispute Resolution, 5 Psychol.Pub.Pol. & L. 1084, 1091 (1999). This requires that a lawyer demonstrate empathy for his client, listen carefully, and be willing to discuss or at least acknowledge the client's emotional state. Is this too much to ask of lawyers? Does it turn lawyers into therapists? How should a lawyer react to a very emotional or distraught client in a divorce case, for example, or in a corporate takeover situation? What is the lawyer's role in such moments?

3. GENDER, RACE, CULTURE AND STEREOTYPING

Many have tried to determine whether men and women bargain differently. Some studies suggest that women consider competitiveness less desirable than do men, see Lipman–Blumen, Connective Leadership: Female Leadership Styles in the 21st-Century Workplace, 35 Soc.Persp. 183, 200–201 (1992), and that they settle more frequently. See Kennard, Lawyers, Sex, and Marriage: Factors Empirically Correlated with the Decision to Settle, 2 Harv.Neg.L.Rev. 149, 149 (1997). Others suggest that women place a higher value on empathetic reasoning. See Jack and Jack, Moral Vision and Professional Decisions: The Changing Values of Women and Men Lawyers 56–58 (1989); Burton et al., Feminist Theory, Professional Ethics, and Gender–Related Distinctions in Attorney Negotiating Styles, 1991 J.Dis.Resol. 199, 200–203; Menkel–Meadow, Portia in a Different Voice: Speculations on a Women's Lawyering Process, 1 Berkeley Women's L.J. 39, 55 (1985). Some have found that women are more likely than men to be client-oriented in their practice. See Maiman et al., Gender and Specialization in the Practice of Divorce Law, 44 Me.L.Rev. 39, 51 (1992). And, perhaps most intriguingly, some have claimed that men tend to compete in conflict situations whereas women tend to compromise or cooperate. See Cahn, Styles of Lawyering, 43 Hastings L.J. 1039, 1045 (1992); Berryman–Fink and Brunner, The Effects of Sex of Source and Target on Interpersonal Conflict Management Styles, 53 S. Speech Comm.J. 38, 44 (1987); Komorita, Cooperative Choice in a Prisoner's Dilemma Game, 2 J. Personality & Soc.Psych. 741, 744 (1965); Rose, Bargaining and Gender, 18 Harv.J.L. & Pub.Pol. 547, 550 (1995).

Other scholars, however, have rejected both the empirical results and theoretical underpinnings of this pursuit. Many studies, for example, have failed to find significant gender-related differences in competition and cooperation in Prisoner's Dilemma games. See Craver and Barnes, Gender, Risk Taking, and Negotiation Performance, 5 Mich.J. Gender & L. 299, 318, 347 (1999) (citing studies and arguing that there is "no factual basis for assuming that women are weaker or less capable negotiators"); Burton, Farmer, Gee, Johnson and Williams, Gender–Related Distinctions in Attorney Negotiating Styles, 1991 J.Disp.Res. 199. And scholars have argued that seeking such differences is itself suspect:

We are hopefully past the days of the simplest gender stereotyping—men are competitive, women are cooperative; men talk and interrupt more, women use tentative language and seek to please the other; men threaten and assert; women seek to please and concede too much, although as the recent research * * * suggests, there may be some truth in some of the stereotypes, at least *under certain conditions*. If we have learned anything from the hundreds of studies conducted on gender and negotiation, it is that in negotiation gender (though a constant for the individual negotiator) is dynamic and interactive—that is, its significance and expression varies under different conditions and in different situations.

* * *

* * * The empirical results are all over the map. For every study which seems to suggest some gender difference (women are more cooperative; men are more competitive), there is another that finds no statistically significant difference in negotiation performance, whether measured by integrative and joint gain outcomes or by more competitive outcomes. Some of the studies have pointed to the situational or "moderating factor" complexity (such as one study which demonstrates that overly cooperative women may actually achieve poorer joint gain solutions because they "settle" too early, do not probe for more information, or fail to hold on to their own interests), but this is consistent with research that finds similar results for friends or others in close relationships who bargain with each other.

Menkel–Meadow, Teaching about Gender and Negotiation: Sex, Truths, and Videotape, Neg.J. 357, 358–359, 364 (2000). Deborah Rhode argues similarly:

The celebration of gender difference risks not only oversimplifying, but also overclaiming. Recent research raises substantial questions about how different women's voice in fact is. Psychological surveys generally find few attributes on which the sexes consistently vary. Even for these attributes, gender typically accounts for only about five percent of the variance. The similarities between men and women are far greater than the disparities, and small statistical distinctions do not support sweeping sex-based dichotomies. Most empirical studies of moral development or altruistic behavior do not find significant gender distinctions. Nor does related research on managerial behavior reveal the consistent sex-linked variations that relational feminism would suggest.

Rhode, Gender and Professional Roles, 63 Fordham L.Rev. 39, 42–43 (1994).

The following excerpts consider three quite different perspectives. The first examines gender and ethnic bargaining patterns. The second argues that *power*, not gender, accounts for any observable behavioral differences in negotiation. The last excerpt considers the effects of culture and stereotyping.

Christine Rack, Negotiated Justice: Gender and Ethnic Minority Bargaining Patterns in the Metro Court Study

20 Hamline J.Pub.L. & Pol. 211, 222–236 (1999).

2. Culture & Gender Negotiation Differences: Soft & Firm Bargaining

Gender and cultural theories, supported by self-report empirical findings, suggest that individuals socialized into collectivist and female social patterns would be more likely to have enhanced concern for the other party and would concede more readily.

In comparison to U.S. culture, Latin American cultural norms are described as "collectivist," oriented toward shared benefit outcomes. Persons from collectivist cultures theoretically hold a greater concern for the other party when he or she is an in-group member as opposed to an out-group member. In addition, Latin American cultures are theoretically more willing to view unequal power relations as legitimate. United States acculturation on the same scales is likely to encourage high self-concern, a willingness to challenge superiors, and a lack of in-group preference. Indeed, cross national studies using scenario techniques have consistently found that people from collectivist cultures are more apt than those from individualistic cultures to report themselves as conciliatory (compromising and obliging) in conflict situations if they do not avoid the conflict altogether.

Virtually all studies report significant gender effects, with women reporting that they are more likely to conciliate than men. In survey and scenario research, women within the United States and cross-nationally self-report a greater likelihood and/or preference for using collaborative strategies in conflict situations. However, the logical consequences of women's theoretical constructions as being more relational, particularistic, and giving are questionable. Research has found complications in outcomes, process, and perceptual distortions.

3. Bargaining Variables & Culture–Gender Differences

Cultural and gender differences are likely in all three variables that are known to affect negotiations: fairness rules, power differences, and the positivity or negativity of relationships.

a. Fairness or Distributional Norms

Shared fairness norms facilitate resolutions. Pruitt and Carnevale argue that shared fairness rules provide the basis for tacit bargaining leading to a rapid resolution. However, when disputants do not share a fairness rule, research and theoretical speculation suggest divergent probabilities; if they point in opposite directions, agreements reached by lengthy and complex bargaining might be truly balanced and integrative. Because fairness is at the heart of justice claims, however, divergent fairness rules might also narrow negotiations through positional rigidity.

Fairness rules, the "normative" expectations that structure exchange behavior and justice perceptions, are culturally learned and situationally evoked. Theory from Weber, Piaget and Ricoeur synthesized with anthropological research demonstrate four identifiable and inherent patterns of relational exchange called "structures," which could also be called distributional norms. These are normative expectations based on the primacy of need, authority, reciprocity, and modern market valuations.

The first, "communal sharing," is archetypally feminine and premodern. It is a need-based distributional norm similar to the exchange relationship found in the family, "primordial" collectivism, traditional and gift-based economies. Fiske's second exchange structure, "authority-ranking," is consistent with Latin American cultural generalizations suggesting a more ready acceptance of authority in hierarchical orders. It is a status-based distribution norm in which the unequal exchange favoring the superior is usually accepted as a legitimate inequality by the subordinate. It underlies the notion of judicial decisionmaking and public compliance based on status deference. Fiske's third exchange pattern, "equality matching," is a more masculine pattern of exchange, if only because men tend to have greater physical power and the willingness to use it. It is a reciprocity-based distribution norm involving strictly in-kind reciprocity. Finally, Fiske described the fourth model, "market pricing," as the market-based equity exchange model in modern capitalist society, wherein rewards are distributed according to input, and the input is valued in accordance with a market metric.

In addition to cultural learning, Fiske specifies that situational salience will determine which exchange norm or fairness rule will be applied. The question is whether the mediation situation suggested to nondominant parties that alternative norms should be applied.

b. Power Differences

Power differences between the parties have been closely studied in negotiation. As noted above, stronger parties tend to be advantaged in negotiations, an outcome achieved by higher claiming and undermatching concessions. The measure of greater power is the positive alternatives (court outcomes primarily) and the relative dependency of the weaker party on agreement. Corporate parties tend to have better court outcomes because the laws have been structured to affirm their rights according to rules they knew beforehand. In addition, previous experience can lead to greater power gained by developing strategic bargaining skills.

However, greater power, even when buttressed by weaker party dependence, does not immediately translate into dominance. Exchange researchers argue that normative constraints, including culturally-shaped justice norms and reciprocity, intervene between capacity and power use. Moreover, stronger parties are dependent on the other disputant for compliance with agreements they might make.

c. Positive & Negative Relationships

Trust and distrust, like the positive and negative relationships with which they are associated, tend both to be matched and to persist over time. Pruitt and Carnevale speculate that trusters tend to worry less about looking like suckers and would be more likely to make concessions and fill the gap produced by the other party's failure to concede at a deadline. Distrust is central to negative negotiating relationships, where bargainers tend to match contentious strategies (i.e., bargaining resistance and threats). In the absence of data, Pruitt and Carnevale theorized that past competition would result in less negativity if the competition was kept within normative boundaries rather than appearing as though the other party appeared to be trying to gain an unfair advantage, i.e., exploiting his or her bargaining partner.

d. Culture, Gender & Bargaining Variables

Theoretical and empirical arguments based on cultural and gender categorizations would suggest that Latinos and women might differ from dominant court players in all of the domains, fairness norms, power differences, and trust. Non-dominant groups may hold different fairness values, hold unequal power in negotiations with more dominant parties, and accept disadvantaged outcomes. Ridgeway explains that those who are traditionally perceived as less competent continue to be perceived that way persistently so that hierarchies are recreated through a process of self-fulfilling prophecy. Attempts to break free of others' expectations are often negatively misperceived and actively discouraged until less privileged actors retreat from trying.

Trust is particularly at issue for ethnic minorities because trust can be considered analogous to collectivist cultural patterns. But the trend of the predictions turns on the difference between outsiders and insiders. On the one hand, collectivist cultures might have distinct expressive motives in bargaining situations that appear as trusting but might be due to "face needs." Furthermore, collectivist identities would also, theoretically, be motivated to maintain the positive face of other parties, that is, to not subject them to shame. On the other hand, Hispanos have ample reason to distrust Anglos due to the historical memory of Anglo exploitation. Thus, past exploitation might establish Anglos as an outsider relation. The present bargaining situation is analyzed to more clearly indicate not only whether minorities did seem trusting toward Anglos, but also whether trust or distrust was warranted.

* * *

5. Summary

Cultural and gender theories suggest that minority and female disputants, who are more often socialized into collectivistic and relational patterns, will be soft bargainers. As a style, they will concede or conciliate more readily. But the empirical, historical, and theoretical specifics are contradictory, both for each group and in their relations with other parties.

* * *

Empirical research has failed to consistently support differences that are theorized for collectivistic culture groups. For example, although a collectivistic propensity for equality-based distribution norms was noted in scenario research, research has more consistently found a greater reported tendency for "lumping it" (i.e., conciliation and avoidance of overt conflict) among individuals socialized in nations considered collectivist.

Although women self-report that they would rather cooperate than compete, research has consistently shown status differences in which women seem to be more competitive when they held higher status positions and to be misperceived by others. Unlike cultural theories, gender theories based on relational psychology and particularistic moral reasoning have not been theorized to show an insider dynamic. Feminist theory, however, has focused on a fundamentally exploitative relationship between genders similar to the critical race theory applied to majority-minority ethnic relations. Predictions stemming from this theoretical orientation would suggest that men might more often exploit this relatively static "other-concern" or ethic of care.

Carol Watson, Gender Versus Power as a Predictor of Negotiation Behavior and Outcomes

10 Neg.J. 117, 119 (1994).[1]

Over the past ten to fifteen years, psychologists and sociologists have mounted a frontal assault on th[e] long-standing "different and inferior" assumption [about women] in many domains. Their work has shown the assumption to be frequently inaccurate. Recent literature reviews show, for example, that there are not clear gender differences in verbal ability, math ability, or spatial ability. Nor do there appear to be gender differences in more abstract characteristics or abilities such as moral reasoning or leadership. Nevertheless, the belief in significant, innate, gender differences refuses to die.

The probable reason for the durability of this belief is that, on a day-in, day-out basis, men and women *do* differ in countless ways that are apparent to each of us, researchers and members of the general public alike. One response to the dilemmas these differences have posed for women is advanced by the "cultural feminists" who have sought to fight society's inherent sexism by celebrating women as different from but superior to men. While such theories may be appealing because they highlight women's special qualities and help women feel good about themselves (rather than inferior or deficient), the "different-but-superior" argu-

---

1. This article is based on an earlier version. See Watson, Gender Differences in Negotiating Behavior and Outcomes: Fact or Artifact?, in Conflict and Gender 191 (1994).

ment does not hold up to the rigorous scrutiny of careful empirical investigation any better than does the more prevalent "different-and-inferior" argument.

An alternative perspective, offered in this article, is that gender differences do exist, but that those of significance relate to contextual rather than to innate personality factors. Contextual factors consist first and most obviously of the immediate situation and its particular demands. More broadly, however, the context of an individual's life includes all aspects in the environment of that individual's life—such as work, family, class, culture, etc.

Contextual factors have often been found to supplant personality factors in determining behavior * * * Nevertheless, researchers and the general public continue to make what psychologists have dubbed the "fundamental attribution error." This error consists of assuming that others behave the way they do because of internal personality characteristics rather than because of external situational demands.

Cooperative Women, Competitive Men?

* * * Early research suggested that women are "softer" negotiators than men, that they prefer an accommodating style, are generous, and are more concerned that all parties be treated fairly than they are about gaining positive substantive outcomes for themselves. These early studies also showed that men are "tough" negotiators who make many demands and few concessions, and that they are more concerned about winning positive substantive outcomes for themselves than about how the other party fares. Men were also found to be more flexible negotiators than women in that they seemed to use a tit-for-tat strategy more often, and were better at finding rational strategies that allowed them to maximize gains.

Although Rubin and Brown showed that these supposed gender differences in bargaining and negotiating were not consistently supported by research, there tends to be a continuing expectation that women will negotiate and bargain more cooperatively than men. Nevertheless, a few researchers have reached more negative conclusions. For instance, women have sometimes been found to lock into an unrelenting competitive stance when their partners refuse to cooperate, and this behavior has been construed by some as vindictive. * * *

The fact that negotiation researchers have often depicted women as cooperative might be construed to mean that the cultural feminist perspective (i.e., that women are different but superior) has predominated in the negotiation literature. This would be an incorrect assumption, however, because women's cooperativeness has generally been equated with weakness and ineffectiveness. * * * Thus, women have frequently been portrayed as "nicer" negotiators than men; and, since niceness does not help one to win, men have typically been credited with being more effective negotiators than women. * * *

* * *

* * * Interestingly, the literature on disputing shows differences in the behavior of high-and low-power negotiators that mirror the most commonly assumed gender differences in negotiator behavior and outcomes. That is, high-power negotiators tend to compete whereas low-power negotiators tend to cooperate. I am suggesting, then, that because women in American society are more likely to be found in low-power positions and occupations than men, we may have been misled into assuming that observed differences in the way men and women negotiate are due to gender when, in fact, they result from status and power differences.

* * *

Power generally leads to greater dominance, competitiveness, and success for both genders. On the one hand, this indicates that women are not softer or less effective negotiators * * * Given a reasonable degree of situational power, women are likely to be just as oriented toward beating their opponents as men are, and just as successful at doing so. Thus, there is no reason to mistrust women's negotiation abilities. * * *

On the other hand, this finding also implies that women are not nicer negotiators than men are. Women are not necessarily any more fair-minded or compassionate, despite what earlier research and some current feminist writers would have us believe. * * *

Jeffrey Z. Rubin and Frank E.A. Sander, Culture, Negotiation, and The Eye of The Beholder

7 Neg.J. 249 (1991).

To understand why culture should be so powerful in organizing stimulus, it is first necessary to understand the contributing role of labeling and stereotyping in our interpersonal perceptions. Social psychologists have observed that although we typically dismiss labeling (and the stereotyping to which it leads) as problematic, stereotyping has several apparent "benefits": First, it allows the perceiver to reduce a world of enormous cognitive complexity into terms of black v. white, good v. evil, friend v. enemy—thereby making it easier to code the things and people one sees. Second, armed with stereotypes, it becomes far easier to communicate in short-hand fashion with others, who we suspect share our views; "He's such a boy" conveys lots of (stereotypic) information very, very quickly, as does the time-worn phrase, "ugly American."

* * *

Robert Rosenthal and his colleagues have demonstrated the power of expectations and labels in an important series of experimental studies. In one of these experiments, teachers were told that some of the children in their elementary school classes had been identified as "intellectual bloomers," children who were likely to grow and develop substantially in the coming year. About other children (who had been privately matched with the "bloomers" in terms of measured aptitude) nothing was said. When an achievement test was administered at the end of the academic year, a shocking and important discovery was made: those children who had been labeled as intellectual bloomers scored significantly higher than those with whom they had been matched. In explanation, the researchers hypothesized that children who were expected to do very, very well were given more attention by their teachers; this increased attention, organized by a hypothesis that the child in question was a talented individual, created a self-fulfilling prophecy.

The label of culture may have an effect very similar to that of gender or intellectual aptitude; it is a "hook" that makes it easy for one negotiator (the perceiver) to organize what he or she sees emanating from that "different person" seated at the other side of the table. To understand how culture may function as a label, consider the following teaching exercise, used during a two-week session on negotiation conducted with a multinational, multicultural gathering. During one class session, the fifty or so participants were formed into rough national groups, and were asked to characterize their national negotiating style—as seen by others. That is, the task was *not* to describe true differences that may be attributable to culture or nationality, but to characterize the stereotypic perceptions that others typically carry around in their heads.

This exercise yielded a set of very powerful, albeit contradictory, stereotypic descriptions of different nationalities. To give a couple of examples, British participants characterized others' stereotypic characterizations of the British as "reserved, arrogant, old fashioned, eccentric, fair, and self-deprecating." A cluster of Arab participants from several Middle East nations characterized a "Levantine" negotiating style as "inclined to violence, aggressive, incohesive, indecisive, irrational, temperamental, emotional, impulsive, and romantic." The Irish self-characterization included such adjectives as "good social grease, people-oriented, fast-talking, good for a laugh, passionate but not serious, provincial, inefficient and undisciplined, unreliable and simple but shrewd." And a cluster of Central Americans listed other's stereotypes of them as negotiators as "idealistic, impractical, disorganized, unprepared, stubborn in arguments, and flowery in style."

Now imagine that you have begun to negotiate with someone from another culture, who at some point in the proceedings simply insists that he or she can go no further, and is prepared to conclude without agreement if necessary; in effect, says this individual, his BATNA has been reached, and he can do just as well by walking away from the table. How should you interpret such an assertion? If you share the general cluster of stereotypes described by the students, your interpretation will probably depend on the other person's culture or nationality. Thus, if the other negotiator is British, and (among other things) you regard the British as "fair," you may interpret this person's refusal to concede further as an honest statement of principle. The same behavior issuing from a Central American, however (someone you suspect of being "stubborn in arguments"), may lead you to suspect your counterpart of being stubborn and perhaps deceitful. Wouldn't you therefore be more likely to strike an agreement with a British than a Central American negotiator—despite the fact that each has behaved in the identical way?

If there is any truth to our surmise, you can see how powerful the effects of culture may prove to be, leading us (even before we have had a chance to gather information about our counterpart) to hold a set of expectations that guide and inform our judgments. Moreover, once our "hypotheses" about others are in place, it becomes very difficult to disprove them. We tend to gather interpersonal information in such a way that we pay attention only to the "facts" that support our preconceived ideas, ignoring or dismissing disconfirming data.

For example, if I believe that you are a defensive person, and then proceed to ask you why you are so defensive, I can be guaranteed of support for my hypothesis regardless of what you say * * *

What, then, are some implications of this brief essay for more effective negotiation across cultural/national boundaries? First, while cultural/national differences do exist, much of what passes for such differences may well be the result of expectations and perceptions which, when acted upon, help to bring about a form of self-fulfilling prophecy. Perhaps the best way to combat such expectations is to go out of one's way to acquire as much information as one can beforehand about the way people in other cultures view the kind of problem under consideration. Thus, if we are negotiating with a German about a health care contract, we should try to find out whatever we can about how Germans tend to view health care. Of course, in large countries, there may be regional variations that also need to be taken into account.

NOTES AND QUESTIONS

1. Do you believe that gender- and culture-based differences in negotiation behavior play a part in bargaining? Or do you agree with Watson, who suggests that power, not gender, is the actual driver of negotiation behavior? How would you test your views of whether such differences exist?

2. Like Rubin and Sander's excerpt on culture, many scholars now focus less on whether actual gender-based behavioral differences exist than on the different *perceptions* that negotiators have of each other because on gender, race or cultural difference. See Burrell et al., Gender–Based Perceptual Biases in Mediation, 15 Comm.Res. 447, 453 (1988). As Carol Rose puts it, "It is not as important that a gendered difference in tastes for cooperation actually exists, as that people simply think it exists." Rose, Bargaining and Gender, 18 Harv.J.L. & Pub.Pol. 547, 555 (1994). Are you persuaded by the argument that claims of gender- or culture-based difference are mostly stereotyping?

Consider the following five types of perceptual errors that may cause stereotyping. Do they seem likely to influence the negotiation process?

* * * Five major perceptual errors are typical: stereotyping, halo effects, selective perceptions, projections, and perpetual defenses. The first two—stereotyping and halo effects—are examples of perceptual distortion by *generalization*—small amounts of perceptual information are used to draw large conclusions about individuals. The last three—selective perception, projection, and perpetual defense—are examples of perceptual distortion by the *anticipation* of encountering another whom we believe to have certain attributes and qualities.

Stereotyping is a very common perceptual process. Stereotyping occurs when attributes are assigned to people solely on the basis of their membership in a particular social or demographic group. * * *

Halo effects in perception are similar to stereotypes. Rather than using a target individual's group membership as a basis for classification, halo effects occur when one attribute of an individual allows the perceiver to generalize about a wide variety of other attributes. A smiling person is judged to be more honest than a frowning or scowling person, even though there is no necessary relationship between a smile and honesty. * * *

Halo effects are likely to be as common as stereotypes in negotiation; we are likely to form rapid impressions of new opponents based on very limited initial information, such as their appearance or initial statements. We also maintain these judgments as we get to know people better, fitting each piece of "new" information into some consistent pattern. * * *

Selective perception occurs when the perceiver singles out certain information which supports or reinforces a prior belief, and filters out information which may not confirm that belief. Thus selective perception has the effect of perpetuating stereotypes or halo effects—quick judgments are formed about individuals on the basis of limited information, while any further evidence that might disconfirm the judgment is "filtered out" by attending only to the confirming information. An initial smile from the opponent, which leads the perceiver to believe that the opponent is honest, might also lead the perceiver to ignore statements by the opponent that he intends to be competitive and aggressive. The same smile, interpreted by the perceiver as a smirk, similarly leads the perceiver to ignore other information that the target wants to establish and honest and cooperative relationship. In both cases, the perceiver's own biases—predisposition to be cooperative or competitive—are likely to affect how the other's cues are selected and interpreted.

Projection occurs when an individual ascribes to others characteristics or feelings he possesses himself. * * * In negotiation, for example, it is extremely common for negotiators to claim that they want to be cooperative and to develop a positive relationship with the other negotiator, but that it is the opponent who is behaving uncooperatively and untrustingly. Such assertions often mask the negotiator's ability to admit to himself that he really wants to be deceptive and dishonest. * * *

Perpetual defense is the result of the same instinct for self-projection, and helps our perceptual apparatus defend us by "screening out," distorting, or ignoring information which is threatening or unacceptable to us. Information about ourselves or others which doesn't "fit" our self image, or the image of others, is likely to be denied, modified, distorted, or redefined to bring it into line with earlier judgments. * * *

It cannot be stated strongly enough that these perceptual distortions are frequently at the heart of breakdowns in communication between conflicting individuals. Perceptual biases tend to cast one's own position and behavior in more favorable terms, and to cast the other person ("the opponent") in more negative terms. These biases will affect the expectations that one has for his opponent, and lead to assumptions about the opponent: the position he is likely to take, his willingness to cooperate or make concessions, etc. Finally, these negative assumptions are likely to influence the party to assume a competitive, defensive stance in their initial negotiations. The tragic fallacy in this process is that if his assumptions are incorrect, there may be no way for the actor to discover it! By the time he is in a position to accurately judge the predisposition of his opponent, his own competitive mood and defensive posture have been interpreted by the opponent as offensive and antagonistic.

Lewicki and Litterer, Negotiation 166–169 (1985).

3. That others may stereotype you because of your gender may not be surprising, but research shows that gender may correlate with varied self-perceptions and self-confidence as well. In one study, researchers tested first-year law students for gender differences in their negotiation behavior and negotiated outcomes in a simulated negotiation. In addition, however, the students were asked to fill out questionnaires about their self-confidence and to assess their own negotiation abilities. Although ultimately the outcomes negotiated by men and women were very similar, women rated their abilities lower than men. See Farber and Rickenberg, Under–Confident Women and Over–Confident Men: Gender and Competence in a Simulated Negotiation, 11 Yale J.L. & Feminism 271, 291 (1999).

4. Regardless of whether gender, race and culture actually impact bargaining behavior, it is clear that some people may *treat* minorities and women differently in negotiations. For example, several studies by Ian Ayres of the Yale Law School have attempted to determine whether and why retail salespeople might discriminate in how they negotiate with minority and female car buyers. Ayres sent testers of different races and sexes to randomly selected car dealerships in the Chicago area to negotiate the purchase price of a given car model. The testers dressed similarly, arrived at their respective dealerships driving similar rented cars, and followed pre-arranged "scripts" so that all testers presented themselves to the dealerships in the same way.

The results were striking. Dealers offered white male testers lower initial and final offers than any other type of tester. Black male testers fared the worst, paying on average an extra $962 over white males on initial offers and an extra $1132 on final offers. See Ayres, Further Evidence of Discrimination in New Car Negotiations and Estimates of Its Cause, 94 Mich.L.Rev. 109, 116 (1995). Black females fared slightly better, paying approximately $470 more than white males on initial offers and $446 on final offers, and white females paid roughly $200 more than white males on both offers. In fact, "[t]he initial offer white male testers received was lower than the *final* offer 43.5 percent of nonwhite males received." Id. at 119. See also Ayres, Fair Driving: Gender and Race Discrimination in Retail Car Negotiations, 104 Harv.L.Rev. 817 (1991).

By comparing game theoretic models with the empirical data generated by his studies, Ayres tested several possible hypotheses regarding *why* car dealers might vary their offers depending on the race or gender of the potential buyer:

> [D]ifferent explanations of discrimination cause the dealer's choice of an initial offer, the size of concessions, and the speed of concessions, to vary. For example, sellers might offer a higher initial price to a black customer if they believe that black customers are averse to bargaining or if the sellers have a particular desire to disadvantage black customers. But game theory suggests that these two causes of discrimination will give rise to different concession rates: in particular, a desire to disadvantage blacks will cause sellers to hold out longer for a high price, implying a lower concession rate than a belief that black consumers are averse to bargaining. Our evidence of the dealers' initial offers and willingness to make concessions can thus be used to distinguish among competing causal theories

Ayres, Further Evidence of Discrimination in New Car Negotiations and Estimates of Its Cause, 94 Mich.L.Rev. 109, 120 (1995).

Ayres tested four reasons that sellers might offer higher prices to certain types of buyers: (1) sellers may have higher costs of bargaining with a disfavored group—if, for example, a male seller dislikes spending time with female buyers; (2) sellers may desire to disadvantage a disfavored group—the seller may feel a benefit from seeing that group pay higher prices; (3) sellers may believe that the disfavored group will pay more because it has higher costs of bargaining; or (4) sellers may believe that a disfavored group has a different (and higher) distribution of reservation prices than white males—that some black customers, for example, are "suckers" who are willing to pay more than most whites for a given car, perhaps because of a lack of information about the car's value. See id. at 124.

Of these possible explanations, Ayres argues that the second and fourth are the most robust. Sellers' offers and concession rates suggested a desire to disadvantage blacks and women. Indeed, "the seller's slow and small concessions to black males are consistent with the hypothesis that sellers enjoyed extracting dollars from black males *twice as much* as extracting dollars from white males." Id. at 132–133 (emphasis added). In addition, the data suggest that dealers believed that black males were willing to pay the most, and white males the least. Although the *average* black male is likely to be poorer than the average white male, dealers seemed to believe either that black males might pay more because they knew less about the car's value or because they knew less about the possibility of bargaining for a better price. See id. at 139–141.

D. PROFESSIONAL AND LEGAL FRAMEWORK FOR NEGOTIATION

1. CONSTRAINTS ON NEGOTIATION BEHAVIOR

In this section we consider various constraints on the negotiation behavior of a lawyer or her client. We begin with the constraints imposed by contract and tort law—constraints that apply equally to lawyers and clients. We then turn to the professional ethics codes that govern lawyers during bargaining and the possibility of post-settlement malpractice.

a. FRAUD, DURESS AND OTHER LIMITS ON BARGAINING

The bargaining behavior of lawyers and their clients is governed by tort, contract and agency law, as well as by specific statutes and regulations. The following excerpt considers various constraints, particularly in the context of unequal bargaining power.

Robert S. Adler & Elliot M. Silverstein, When David Meets Goliath: Dealing With Power Differentials in Negotiations

5 Harv.Neg.L.Rev. 1, 29–48 (2000).

* * * We now turn to an exploration of legal protections that apply in negotiation situations involving power imbalances.

Although the superior bargaining power of one party, standing alone, does not generally provide the basis for invalidating an agreement, the law does set limits within which bargainers must operate. These limits apply both with respect to the terms that can be negotiated and to the methods one can use to influence an opponent to agree to the terms. They are premised on the assumption that at some point in the bargaining process, power advantages can produce inequities so pronounced that the law must step in to protect the weak. In negotiations involving power imbalances, most abuses arise when the stronger party, either through threats or other overt displays of power, intimidates the other into entering an agreement so one-sided that it offends reasonable sensibilities. Of course, not all

D. Professional and Legal Framework for Negotiation

bargaining abuses result from overt power displays. Some arise from shifting the balance of power by exploiting trust or employing deceit.

Depending on the nature of the abuse, the law may take different approaches—regulating modestly where "arm's length" conditions exist or expansively where a "special relationship" requires protection for particularly vulnerable individuals. Where special relationships exist, special protections apply.

A. *Undue Influence*

When a relationship of trust and dependency between two or more parties exists, the law typically polices the relationship closely and imposes especially stringent duties on the dominant parties. * * *

Contract law imposes similar duties in the case of agreements involving undue influence in special relationships. Where one party—because of family position, business connection, legal authority or other circumstances—gains extraordinary trust from another party, the courts will scrutinize any agreements between them with great care to ensure fairness. Common examples of special relationships include guardian-ward, trustee-beneficiary, agent-principal, spouses, parent-child, attorney-client, physician-patient, and clergy-parishioner. To treat negotiations in these settings as arm's length interactions would invite "unfair persuasion" by the dominant parties either through threats, deception, or misplaced trust. Accordingly, the law imposes special obligations on those who play the dominant role in such relationships, requiring them to exercise good faith and to make full disclosure of all critical facts when negotiating agreements with dependent parties. In determining whether a dominant party in a special relationship exerted undue influence, the courts generally look to the fairness of the contract, the availability of independent advice, and the vulnerability of the dependent party. An agreement entered into as a result of undue influence is voidable by the victim.

B. *Protections in Arm's Length Transactions*

Under the "bargain theory" of contracts, parties negotiate at arm's length to exchange consideration. An arm's length transaction is one in which the parties stand in no special relationship with each other, owe each other no special duties, and each acts in his or her own interest. * * * This is not to suggest that parties are free to operate without rules, but it does mean that they are accorded substantial leeway in negotiating contracts. * * * Once one of the parties acts in a patently abusive manner, however, the law does provide protection, as, for example, with fraud, duress, and unconscionability.

1. *Fraud*

Negotiated agreements, to be binding, must be entered into by the parties in a knowing and voluntary manner. Lies undermine agreements by removing the "knowing" element from the bargain. That is, one induced by misrepresentations to purchase a relatively worthless item of personal

204 CHAPTER II NEGOTIATION

property typically buys the product "voluntarily"—in fact, eagerly—with enthusiasm generated by the false promise of the product's value. The catch is that because of the defrauder's lies, the victim has unfairly lost the opportunity to "know" the precise nature of what he or she has bought. * * *

* * *

Sadly, it appears that lying in negotiations occurs frequently—often to the great advantage of the liar—and dramatically shifts the power balance when it goes undetected. Unfortunately, those who fail to appreciate and take precautions against lies set themselves up to be victimized in their dealings.

Compounding the issue of lying in negotiations is drawing the distinction between what is permissible bluffing, or harmless puffing, and what is truly improper. Traditionally, the distinction, although difficult to draw with precision, is between a factual representation and mere generalized praise or opinion. Factual misrepresentations may constitute fraud, while generalized opinions usually do not. * * *

Lawyers have not always improved the moral climate of bargaining. Indeed, lawyers have adopted ethics rules that permit misrepresentations in certain negotiation settings based on the questionable premise that since the other side has no "right" to know this information, attorneys should not be held to speak honestly about it.

We acknowledge that the lines between proper and improper behavior are difficult to draw at times. We also recognize the general human proclivity to lie, including in negotiations. Nonetheless, we find ourselves persuaded by a careful analysis by Professor Richard Shell that, despite the casual approach that negotiators sometimes take towards the truth, the law actually had adopted a much stronger stance against misrepresentations than is generally recognized. Accordingly, we conclude that there is less room for playing with the truth than many negotiators believe possible.

2. *Duress*

Coercion, whether express or implied, takes many forms. One party, for example, might threaten to take its business elsewhere if its terms are not met. Another might threaten to file suit if its financial claims are not resolved. Still another might insist that it will no longer provide a discount or expedited delivery if a deal cannot be struck. These threats, designed to exert pressure on an opponent to secure his or her cooperation, generally fall into a category that the law would consider to be hard bargaining, but not illegal. At some point, however, coercion becomes objectionable. How does one distinguish between proper and improper behavior? * * *

* * *

Threatened action need not be illegal—even acts otherwise legal may constitute duress if directed towards an improper goal. For example, a threat to bring a lawsuit—normally a legitimate form of coercion—becomes abusive if "made with the corrupt intent to coerce a transaction grossly unfair to the victim and not related to the subject of such proceedings." Similarly, a threat to release embarrassing, but true, information about another person, although abhorrent, would not constitute duress (in the form of blackmail) unless accompanied by an improper demand for financial or other favors.

Should negotiators with a decided power advantage feel inhibited from pushing for as hard a bargain as they can in light of the law of duress? Generally, no. Judging from the language in the courts' opinions, hard bargainers should have little to fear from the doctrine of duress. * * * Trouble arises only when a party makes threats that lapse into the illegal, immoral and unconscionable. * * *

3. *Unconscionability*

The doctrine of unconscionability functions to protect bargainers of lesser power from overreaching by dominant parties. * * *

What is an unconscionable contract? * * * At a minimum, an unconscionable contract is one "such as no man in his senses and not under delusion would make on the one hand and no honest and fair man would accept on the other." Unconscionability seeks to prevent two evils: (1) oppression and (2) unfair surprise. * * * Substantive unconscionability includes the actual terms of the agreement; procedural unconscionability refers to the bargaining process between the parties.

Substantive unconscionability occurs where the terms of the contract are so onerous, unreasonable or unfair that someone with common sense hearing the terms could not help exclaiming at the inequality of the agreement. * * *

Procedural unconscionability * * * arises when contracts involve the element of unfair surprise. This typically takes the form of terms hidden in a mass of contract language, terms hidden in small print, or on the back of an agreement where one would not think to look, or the like. Procedural unconscionability also assumes another, less clearly delineated form, that of "oppressive" tactics. When the dominant party uses high-pressure tactics in circumstances that result in unfair control of the situation, the courts will intercede. * * * The abuse falls short of duress, but qualifies for judicial relief under the doctrine of unconscionability.

* * *

How concerned should a negotiator be—especially one with superior bargaining power—that pursuing an advantage in a contract will result in a court ruling that the agreement is unconscionable? Our best answer: some, but not much. For the most part, the courts have taken a cautious approach to finding unconscionability in negotiated agreements. The vast majority of successful unconscionability claims involve poor, often unsophisticated, consumers challenging oppressive adhesion contracts foisted on them by retail merchants or credit sellers. In fact, the courts have generally been unreceptive to unconscionability claims by middle class purchasers or

CHAPTER II NEGOTIATION

by merchants against other merchants. No doubt this reflects the general view that persons of greater sophistication suffer less contractual abuse and need less protection.

NOTES AND QUESTIONS

1. Adler and Silverstein suggest that the law of undue influence, fraud, duress, and unconscionability impose only minor constraints on a lawyer's negotiation behavior. Do you agree? If so, should these rules be strengthened to further limit how lawyers can bargain? What are the advantages and disadvantages of the status quo?

2. The law of contracts governs behavior toward third parties in negotiations. Most scholars agree that contract law generally imposes no duty of good faith in negotiations. One of the foremost legal scholars on contracts, Allen Farnsworth, argues that the duty of fair dealing does not attach until an agreement is signed:

> * * * Some scholarly writers have generalized from the cases decided on the grounds of misrepresentation and specific promise to argue that a general obligation of fair dealing may arise out of negotiations themselves, at least if the disappointed party has been led to believe that success is in prospect. Thus Summers wrote that if courts follow *Red Owl*, "it will no longer be possible for one party to scuttle contract negotiations with impunity when the other has been induced to rely to his detriment on the prospect that the negotiations will succeed." American courts, however, have been unreceptive to these arguments and have declined to find a general obligation that would preclude a party from breaking off negotiations, even when the success was in prospect. Their reluctance to do so is supported by the formulation of a general duty of good faith and fair dealing in both the Uniform Commercial Code and the Restatement (Second) of Contracts that, at least by negative implication, does not extend to negotiations.

> European courts have been more willing than American ones to accept scholarly proposals for precontractual liability based on a general obligation of fair dealing. But even in Europe it is difficult to find cases that actually impose precontractual liability where an American court would clearly not do so on other grounds. * * *

> It is perhaps not surprising that American courts have rarely been asked to hold that a general obligation of fair dealing arises out of the negotiations themselves when they have reached a point where one of the parties has relied on a successful outcome. Often the reason may be that, as suggested earlier, the disappointed parties to negotiations are unaware of the possibility of a generous measure of precontractual liability. But it may also be that they are not greatly dissatisfied with the common law's aleatory view of negotiations and recognize that the few claims that arise are fairly treated under the existing grounds of restitution, misrepresentation, and specific promise. As long as these grounds are not often invoked and have not been pushed to their

limits, there will be little pressure to add a general obligation of fair dealing.

There is ample justification for judicial reluctance to impose a general obligation of fair dealing on parties to precontractual negotiations. The common law's aleatory view of negotiations well suits a society that does not regard itself as having an interest in the outcome of the negotiations. The negotiation of an ordinary contract differs in this way from the negotiation of a collective bargaining agreement, in which society sees itself as having an interest in preventing labor strife. Although it is in society's interest to provide a regime under which the parties are free to negotiate ordinary contracts, the outcome of any particular negotiation is a matter of indifference.

There is no reason to believe that imposition of a general obligation of fair dealing would improve the regime under which such negotiations take place. The difficulty of determining a point in the negotiations at which the obligation of fair dealing arises would create uncertainty. An obligation of fair dealing might have an undesirable chilling effect, discouraging parties from entering into negotiations if chances of success were slight. The obligation might also have an undesirable accelerating effect, increasing pressure on parties to bring negotiations to a final if hasty conclusion. With no clear advantages to counter these disadvantages there is little reason to abandon the present aleatory view.

Farnsworth, Precontractual Liability and Preliminary Agreements: Fair Dealing and Failed Negotiations, 87 Colum.L.Rev. 217, 239–42 (1987).

Further, the Restatement (Second) of Contracts (1981) § 205, Comment C reflects the absence of a good faith requirement in negotiations:

c. *Good faith in negotiation.* This section, like Uniform Commercial Code § 1–203, does not deal with good faith in the formation of a contract. Bad faith in negotiation, although not within the scope of this Section, may be subject to sanctions. Particular forms of bad faith in bargaining are the subjects of rules as to capacity to contract, mutual assent and consideration and of rules as to invalidating causes such as fraud and duress. See, for example, §§ 90 and 208. Moreover, remedies for bad faith in the absence of agreement are found in the law of torts or restitution. For examples of a statutory duty to bargain in good faith, see, e.g., National Labor Relations Act § 8(d) and the federal Truth in Lending Act. In cases of negotiation for modification of an existing contractual relationship, the rule stated in this section may overlap with more specific rules requiring negotiation in good faith. See §§ 73, 89; Uniform Commercial Code § 2–209 and Comment.

3. Because contract law does not impose a duty of good faith on negotiators, lawyers still assume, often with good reason, that they are free during negotiations to change direction or walk away at any time. In some cases, however, this freedom may give rise to abuse of the bargaining process, and courts have begun to respond to such abuses. One case that

CHAPTER II NEGOTIATION

discusses some possible limits for negotiators is Hoffman v. Red Owl Stores, Inc., 26 Wis.2d 683, 133 N.W.2d 267 (1965), a staple of first year contracts classes. In Red Owl, the plaintiff operated a bakery and wanted to set up a grocery store. He contacted Red Owl Stores, which expressed interest in the venture. The Plaintiff stated that $18,000 was all the capital that he had available and the Red Owl negotiators repeatedly assured him that this amount would be sufficient for him to set up a business as a Red Owl Store. On the advice of Red Owl management, plaintiff bought the inventory and fixtures of a small grocery store to give him some experience; before the summer tourist season, he was told to sell his bakery business—that this was the only "hitch" in the entire plan. Time dragged on. At later meetings, the company raised the amount of capital required of plaintiff to $24,000, then to $26,000, and then to $34,000. Finally, the plaintiff had had enough and broke off negotiations. The Wisconsin Supreme Court held Red Owl liable to the franchisee even in the absence of a written agreement, applying the doctrine of promissory estoppel.

Contrast *Red Owl* with the case of Gray v. Eskimo Pie Corp., 244 F.Supp. 785 (D.Del.1965). There plaintiffs had conceived the idea of a circular ice cream product with a hole in the middle, which they referred to as an "ice cream donut." Realizing that mass production would be necessary for any real success, they looked around for a company which had the proper manufacturing equipment and national distribution network. They approached the Eskimo Pie corporation, which, after receiving samples of the product and full details on how it was made, indicated a definite interest in manufacturing and marketing it. For the next two years Eskimo Pie Corporation continued to express enthusiasm for the project, but it put plaintiffs off with an elaborate variety of excuses: its executives were out of the office or on "extended trips;" "preliminary engineering work" had to be done; and "major reorganization activities" were occurring within the company. Often the plaintiffs' urgent calls and telegrams were not returned. Meanwhile, Eskimo Pie had been doing a test run of its own "Eskimo Do-nuts," and eventually it launched this product nationwide. Plaintiffs were left "out in the cold"—without an agreement and ultimately without even any product. Plaintiffs sued.

The court concluded that the defendant was deliberately stalling for time while going forward with its own marketing and development plans. According to the court, "[t]hroughout its negotiations with plaintiffs, defendant failed to act with the degree and candor which honesty, fair dealing and a proper regard for business ethics required. Instead it followed a steadied course of seeming deception."[1] Nevertheless, the court concluded that on the facts the plaintiffs had failed to make a case for relief against the defendant. The plaintiffs had corresponded frequently with other large dairy companies during the time they were negotiating with Eskimo, and this made it reasonably clear that "plaintiffs had decided not to rely solely upon their contacts with defendant as a source of assistance but thereafter they persistently attempted to interest many other concerns in their

---

1. 244 F.Supp. at 794.

'SNONUTS.' "[2] The court also noted that no evidence was presented to show that plaintiffs would have benefited more by doing something other than what they did.

What does good faith mean in the context of these two cases? The Red Owl company appeared to be using the escalation game as a negotiating technique, as its negotiator encouraged Hoffman to increase his investment in successive increments. As Hoffman's sunk costs increased, so did the price of the franchise. To view it in the best light for Red Owl, its negotiator may not have fully appreciated the strategy he was following, or understood its impact, until late in the process. Is the unknowing use of escalation tactics a form of bad faith bargaining? Is the conscious use of such tactics bad faith per se? Perhaps the only mistake Red Owl made was in refusing to conclude a deal of some sort with Hoffman. Is an escalation strategy unethical if an agreement results, regardless of any inequities that might exist?

In contrast to Red Owl, the Eskimo Pie negotiators started out with an obvious intent to deceive plaintiffs and "steal" their idea. Why were they not held accountable for this "bad faith" behavior? The court seems to say that dishonest and deceptive behavior itself is not actionable, that you can benefit by this behavior if the other party either does not fully rely on the deception or cannot prove that it would have been better off absent the deceptive behavior. Does this serve as a realistic limit to bad faith negotiation? Is this consistent with legitimate expectations or custom in business negotiations?

4. Courts have imposed a good faith bargaining requirement in some statutory contexts, particularly in the labor arena. For example, in the late 1940's the National Labor Relations Act (NLRA) was passed requiring companies and labor unions to bargain in good faith. The General Electric Company's bargaining strategy, which came to be called Boulwarism after the General Electric vice president responsible for it, was ultimately found to violate this requirement. GE's approach to negotiations was simple. The company would collect all the available information about wage rates, economic conditions, market potential and other factors relevant to the negotiations. It would share this information with the union and listen to the union's comments. The management would then prepare a firm, fair and final offer for the labor union. Once submitted, GE refused to negotiate over or change its offer: it was a true take-it-or-leave-it approach. After extensive litigation, General Electric's approach was held to violate the NLRA. See N.L.R.B. v. General Electric Co., 418 F.2d 736 (2d Cir. 1969), cert. denied 397 U.S. 965 (1970).

Is this bad faith? Can a take-it-or-leave-it offer ever be an element of good faith bargaining, or must there always be concessions made on both sides? In the General Electric case, the court found that GE had engaged in a variety of additional actions that collectively amounted to bad faith, including developing a sophisticated campaign to sell its opening offer to

---

2. Id. at 795.

union employees, regardless of the employees' wishes or the offer's consequences. In the absence of such coercive measures, would a take-it-or-leave-it offer constitute bad faith?

b. A LAWYER'S PROFESSIONAL OBLIGATIONS IN SETTLEMENT NEGOTIATIONS

In addition to the substantive law of contract and tort, various professional codes govern attorneys' conduct in settlement negotiations. The most prominent standards are those in the ABA's Model Rules of Professional Conduct, promulgated in 1983. Adopted by roughly two-thirds of the states, the Model Rules replaced the ABA's earlier Model Code of Professional Responsibility, which was created in 1969. That, in turn, replaced the 1908 Canons of Professional Ethics.

Although the Model Rules are the dominant set of standards for lawyers, the Code still plays a significant role in many court and disciplinary body decisions. In addition, in 1997 the ABA commissioned a study to revise the Model Rules. That committee, named "Ethics 2000," has been circulating new versions of the Rules for consideration, and those revisions will undoubtedly play a more significant role over time. In addition, the American Law Institute recently issued its Restatement (Third) of the Law Governing Lawyers. Finally, a task force of the ABA's Section on litigation has recently circulated a draft set of Ethical Guidelines for Settlement Negotiations. Although the Guidelines do not have the binding force of the Model Rules, in some instances they more clearly articulate standards of behavior for negotiating lawyers.

In this section we consider some of the basic ethical dilemmas that lawyers face in negotiations. The first excerpt lays out several hypotheticals and reviews how they would be handled under the Model Rules. The second excerpt explores various disciplinary cases in which courts have questioned attorneys' negotiation behavior. The third excerpt challenges lawyers' tendencies to describe their lies with euphemisms. The final excerpt considers the ways in which lawyers attempt to justify their negotiation behavior and whether those justifications are persuasive.

Patrick Emery Longan, Ethics In Settlement Negotiations: Foreward
52 Mercer L.Rev. 807, 810–829 (2001).

II. LIMITS ON MISLEADING CONDUCT

[There are two initial] issues of truthfulness: misleading statements and the duty to disclose. Model Rule of Professional Conduct 4.1 covers these topics:

> In the course of representing a client a lawyer shall not knowingly: (a) make a false statement of material fact or law to a third person; or (b) fail to disclose a material fact to a third person when disclosure is

necessary to avoid assisting a criminal or fraudulent act by a client, unless disclosure is prohibited by Rule 1.6.

There are two issues lurking within and behind this rule. First, as to misrepresentation, comment two to Rule 4.1 contains a special qualification for statements in the context of settlement negotiations.[5] It exempts from the requirements of Rule. 4.1(a) certain statements that "[u]nder generally accepted conventions in negotiation" are not taken as statements of fact, such as the acceptability of a particular amount in settlement. In other words, there is room in negotiations for puffing and bluffing because those practices are what everyone involved expects. Second, the last phrase of Rule 4.1(b) appears to prohibit disclosure, even to prevent fraud, if Rule 1.6 would prohibit the disclosure. Rule 1.6 forbids disclosure of "information related to the representation of a client," absent client consent and with some very limited exceptions.[7] The exception, therefore, threatens to swallow the rule about disclosure.

Another relevant Model Rule is Rule 1.6(b), which permits a lawyer to withdraw from representation if the client "persists in a course of action involving the lawyer's services that the lawyer reasonably believes is criminal or fraudulent." For example, a client who lies to his or her lawyer and has the lawyer unwittingly repeat the lie to an opposing party may forbid the lawyer to reveal the falsity of the representation already made. The result might be fraud, perpetrated by the client through the lawyer. The attorney ethically may withdraw from the representation under these circumstances.

* * *

A.   The Limits of Representations

[We can consider] these and other issues in the context of three hypotheticals. The first concern[s] a case in which the plaintiff sought lost profits and the lawyer was trying to decide what he or she could say about the lost profits in negotiation in a variety of factual situations:

5. [Comment 2 states:] This Rule refers to statements of fact. Whether a particular statement should be regarded as one of fact can depend on the circumstances. Under generally accepted conventions in negotiation, certain types of statements ordinarily are not taken as statements of material fact. Estimates of price or value placed on the subject of a transaction and a party's intentions as to an acceptable settlement of a claim are in this category, and so is the existence of an undisclosed principal except where nondisclosure of the principal would constitute fraud.

7. Rule 1.6 states * * *:

(a) A lawyer shall not reveal information relating to the representation of a client unless the client consents after consulta-tion, except for disclosures that are impliedly authorized in order to carry out the representation, and except as stated in paragraph (b).

(b) A lawyer may reveal such information to the extent the lawyer reasonably believes necessary:

(1) to prevent the client from committing a criminal act that the lawyer believes is likely to result in imminent death or substantial bodily harm; or

(2) to establish a claim or defense on behalf of the lawyer in a controversy between the lawyer and the client * * *

CHAPTER II NEGOTIATION

You represent a plaintiff in a breach of contract action. You are seeking lost profits. What can you say in negotiations about the lost profits if:

(a) Your expert has come to no conclusion about their cause.

(b) Your expert has told you the breach did not cause the lost profits.

(c) Your expert has given you a range between $2,000,000 and $5,000,000 for the lost profits.

(d) Your expert says the maximum lost profit is $2,000,000.

(e) You do not have an expert; your client says the loss was $5,000,000.

It is common in negotiation for each side to emphasize the strength and persuasiveness of its evidence. On the other hand, each side in discovery has the opportunity to explore the other side's evidence. In this scenario, each side would be entitled to a report and a deposition of the other's testifying expert. Any statement about the expert would be a statement of fact. Because of the importance of expert testimony to this case, any statement of this sort would be material. The lawyer must be careful to tell only the truth to avoid violating Rule 4.1. Good lawyers, however, will test the assertions in discovery, consistent with the now-famous Russian proverb, "Trust, but verify."

Beyond the rules of ethics, however, it is proper to ask what the best strategy is for a lawyer in this negotiation. Here, any statement about the expert's conclusions probably will be the subject of discovery. If the statement is found to be false, the lawyer who made it will lose some credibility. That loss, which will likely survive the conclusion of this particular case and affect negotiations with the other lawyer in future cases, will cause these future negotiations to be more strained, more lengthy, and probably less fruitful. To the extent that the lawyer gains a reputation for untruthfulness as a result of statements about the expert, the lawyer may be impeding all his or her future negotiations. In other words, this hypothetical involves a happy situation in which it is both the right strategy and the smart strategy to tell the truth.

In a continuation of the same hypothetical, [we can consider] questions of representations about settlement authority and statements of fact that are literally true but, in context, potentially misleading:

In this breach of contract action, can you:

(a) tell opposing counsel that you will not settle for less than $3.5 million when you have authority to settle for $2 million?

(b) tell opposing counsel that five major buyers stopped buying from your client after the breach, knowing that they stopped buying for other reasons?

As discussed, comment 2 to Model Rule [4.1] defines statements about settlement authority not to be material. Technically, therefore, the lawyer should feel free to lie about his or her authority. Another strategy, however, and one that may be more effective in the long run, is simply to deflect any questions of authority with statements such as, "You know neither one of us can discuss our authority—let's talk about a fair settlement of this case." The reason a deflection may be more effective in the long run is the same reason exaggerations about the expert's conclusions may cause long term harm. You may be ethically permitted to lie about your authority, but if you do it, and the other lawyer catches you at it, he or she will not trust you again.

The misleading statement about the lost customers raises a persistent and subtle issue for lawyers about the use of language. The statement is literally true. These customers have left, and they did so at a time after the defendant's breach. The only reason the statement is made, however, is in the hope that the defendant will make the leap and conclude that the customers left *because* of the breach or, at least, that the plaintiff will attempt to prove that they did. The statement is, therefore, an intentionally misleading, sly use of language. It is reminiscent of former President Clinton's response to a question before the grand jury about his deposition testimony: "It depends on what the meaning of *is* is." The lawyer who engages in this type of deception is more clever, perhaps, than a straightforward liar, but the lawyer is no less worthy of condemnation. Once again, however, we can rely on the power of reputation to deter lawyers (at least those who care about their reputations) from engaging in these tactics. Word gets around.

B. *Disclosure of Factual Errors*

The second hypothetical concern[s] a duty to disclose facts when the other lawyer has made a settlement offer containing obvious mistakes:

> You represent the husband in a divorce action. You receive from opposing counsel a proposed property settlement with the following errors: (1) a transcription error that undervalues an asset; (2) an arithmetical error that undervalues an asset; (3) a valuation by purchase price of an asset when market value is much higher. All the errors work to your client's advantage. What, if anything, should you do about them?

To the extent that the first two errors are "scrivener's errors" (the other lawyer missed a typographical error or failed to add the numbers correctly), the lawyer has a duty to correct the mistakes.[15] The third problem may raise more difficult issues because the error may come from opposing counsel's conscious but erroneous judgment about what valuation is best for his or her client. Can the lawyer in the hypothetical take advantage of his or her adversary's error in judgment?

The question is a species of a fundamental, recurring question in an adversarial system. The lawyer owes a primary duty of loyalty to the client. In most respects, the lawyer is not expected to be his or her brother's keeper. One answer to the particular ethical question presented is to say

---

15. ABA Comm. on Ethics and Professional Responsibility, Informal Op. 86–1518 (1986).

that it is not the interesting or important question. The client is not perpetrating a fraud or a crime by taking advantage of a bad lawyer on the other side. There is no duty to disclose under Rule 4.1.

Abiding by the rules of ethics, however, is necessary but not always sufficient for good lawyering. Ethically, the lawyer need not correct every misstep of opposing counsel. But sometimes correcting the mistake would be the wise thing to do. For example, if the mistakes involved in the proposal were fundamental mistakes, ones that under the law of contract * * * would provide grounds later to void the transaction, then the lawyer may best serve his or her client by alerting opposing counsel to the mistakes now. If the parties to the transaction will have a continuing relationship, such as shared responsibility for minor children, the best strategy might be to correct the mistakes and buy some trust, which may be sorely needed later. Here, as in many situations, ethics tells you the options available, but the lawyer must still exercise good judgments among the options.

C. Disclosure of Legal Errors

The final hypothetical * * * highlight[s] the fact that Model Rule 4.1 forbids a lawyer from making a material misrepresentation about the law. The hypothetical does so in the context of an interaction with a young lawyer who is operating under a mistake about the state of the law:

> You represent the defendant in a personal injury case. In negotiation with plaintiff's counsel (a young, relatively inexperienced lawyer), it becomes clear to you that this lawyer believes his or her client's potential recovery is limited by a tort reform statute. You know that this statute has been found unconstitutional by the state supreme court. May you, and should you, correct opposing counsel's mistake about the law?

Most practicing lawyers would not think twice about taking advantage of this younger lawyer. Again, the client is not perpetrating fraud or a crime, and the client might be very happy to save some money because his or her adversary's lawyer is clueless. No rule of legal ethics requires the lawyer to be the opposing party's lawyer also. No rule requires that lawyers settle cases only on "fair" terms.

Again, however, the strictly ethical inquiry cannot end the discussion. For example, lawyers might find that taking advantage of the mistake in particular circumstances, such as a horrific injury to a young child, would be morally wrong although ethically permissible. The lawyer is free to counsel the client about nonlegal matters, such as the morality of leaving the injured child unable to obtain the life-long care the child needs. The lawyer is even free to seek to withdraw if assisting in a settlement under these circumstances would be repugnant to the lawyer.[19] Here, as in the

---

19. Model Rule of Professional Conduct 1.16(b) states in relevant part, "[A] lawyer may withdraw from representing a client if ... a client insists upon pursuing an objective that the lawyer considers repugnant or imprudent."

D. PROFESSIONAL AND LEGAL FRAMEWORK FOR NEGOTIATION

prior examples, the best lawyers consider all the circumstances and determine first whether the rules of ethics require a particular course of action and, if they do not, what under all the circumstances is the wisest choice.

* * *

IV. FAIRNESS IN SETTLEMENT NEGOTIATIONS

* * * Grouped under this heading are concerns about misusing the settlement process, overreaching with other lawyers' clients or an unrepresented party, making improper threats, and using confidential information that has been obtained improperly. The Model Rules deal with most of these issues, although sometimes only indirectly. Model Rule 4.4 forbids a lawyer from using means (not just in settlement, but generally) that "have no substantial purpose other than to embarrass, delay, or burden a third person." Rule 4.2 prohibits lawyers from contacting another lawyer's client without permission. Rule 4.3 contains protections for unrepresented persons and requires lawyers to correct any misunderstanding with these persons about their role. Rule 4.3 also forbids lawyers from stating or implying in this situation that they are disinterested. * * * The Model Rules do not contain a provision about improper threats although ABA Formal Opinions have been issued about threats of criminal prosecution and disciplinary action in civil matters.[37] * * *

* * *

A. Dealing With an Unrepresented Party

* * *

You represent the defendant in a product liability class action. The plaintiff is seeking class action certification but has not yet received it. You believe that you can settle the claims of many potential members of the class if you can negotiate with them directly. May you make settlement offers directly to them? May you emphasize to them that the cost of litigating their individual claims would be far greater than what they could hope to recover?

The issues are whether any contact is appropriate, and, if it is, what the lawyer can and cannot say.

The lawyer must first ensure that the court has not restricted direct contact. The Supreme Court of the United States has held that district courts can restrict communications with members of a putative class if the order is based upon a clear record and specific findings that the restrictions are necessary. If the court has not restricted communications, the defense lawyer faces another issue. If the class counsel represents the members of the putative class for purposes of Rule 4.2, then the defense lawyer may not

---

37. ABA Comm. on Ethics and Professional Responsibility, Formal Op. 363 (1992) (threats of criminal prosecution); ABA Comm. on Ethics and Professional Responsibility, Formal Op. 383 (1994) (threats of disciplinary action).

contact them directly. There is no consensus whether Rule 4.2 bars this sort of contact [in the class context]. * * *

If the contact is permitted, the lawyer must be wary of Model Rule 4.3's limits on what should be said and of Rule 4.1's prohibition on misleading statements of law or fact. * * *

B. Threats in Negotiations

The [following] hypothetical raises issues about documents that are sent to a lawyer improperly and the use the lawyer can or should make of them:

> Suppose the court certifies a class. During discovery, you receive an unsolicited letter from a former paralegal for the plaintiffs' law firm. The letter encloses a standard set of instructions for the plaintiffs' witnesses. The instructions arguably advise the witnesses to lie under oath about their exposure to the defendant's product. May you use the instructions in settlement negotiations? May you use the threat of a bar disciplinary proceeding or a criminal prosecution for obstruction of justice? In exchange for a favorable settlement, may you agree not to report the instructions the plaintiffs' lawyers had been giving?

* * *

* * * The documents have revealed conduct in violation of the Rules of Professional Conduct. May the lawyer threaten to report the misconduct in order to induce a settlement? The answer appears to be no. As discussed above, in Formal Opinion 94–383, the ABA concluded that the lawyer is "constrained" from using this sort of threat by the mandatory obligation to report the other lawyer's professional misconduct. * * *

The final issue is whether the lawyer can use the threat of a criminal referral in the settlement negotiations. The confidential witness instructions may be evidence of obstruction of justice. The Model Rules of Professional Conduct do not contain a prohibition on using a threat of criminal prosecution to settle a civil claim. However, the ABA has issued a formal opinion in which the lawyer's ability to use these threats is limited to situations in which the criminal and civil matters are related, the criminal charge is warranted on the facts and the law, the lawyer does not try to influence the criminal process, and the threat is not otherwise unlawful. In this situation, one issue would be whether the civil and criminal matters are "related" because the criminal activity arose in connection with the litigation and not the underlying facts of the case. The ABA Formal Opinion requires a relationship between the "facts or transaction" of the underlying civil claim and the criminal activity before a threat of criminal prosecution is permissible. A threat that concerns other activity, such as the way in which the lawyer conducts the litigation, would be improper. * * *

C. Good Faith in Negotiations

The next hypothetical raises a basic question about when and why the lawyer can engage in negotiations:

You choose not to use the plaintiffs' lawyer's instructions in an attempt to settle. In fact, your client has instructed you not to settle this case at all, ever, or even to negotiate. Your client believes any negotiation would be seen as a sign of weakness. You recognize, however, that a complete refusal to negotiate would irritate the magistrate judge assigned to the case. You also realize that you might be able to learn something about how the plaintiffs intend to prove damages if you engage them in negotiations. Your client would also be pleased if negotiations protracted the proceedings. What advice would you give your client about its current settlement posture?

Guideline 4.3.1 states that an attorney "may not employ the settlement process in bad faith." Model Rule 4.4 prohibits a lawyer from using means that only "embarrass, delay, or burden" a third person. What advice should the lawyer give when the client wants to use negotiation to curry favor with the judge, to conduct some informal discovery, and to delay the case?

Nathan M. Crystal, The Lawyer's Duty to Disclose Material Facts in Contract or Settlement Negotiations

87 Kentucky L.J. 1055, 1059–1074 (1998–99).

Any analysis of lawyers' disclosure obligations must begin with the fact that many court decisions have held that under some circumstances lawyers have an ethical duty to disclose information in connection with contract or settlement negotiations. * * *

* * *

Perhaps the most extreme example of nondisclosure occurs when a lawyer fails to reveal the death of a client. *Kentucky Bar Ass'n v. Geisler*[23] was a disciplinary action resulting from litigation arising out of an accident in which the plaintiff was struck by an automobile while he was walking on the street. The plaintiff died as a result of these injuries. Shortly after the plaintiff's death, his attorney contacted opposing counsel and negotiated a settlement. Defense counsel learned of the plaintiff's death when respondent returned the settlement documents signed by the plaintiff's son, who had been appointed as the administrator of his estate. Defense counsel did not attempt to rescind the settlement but instead sent the agreed order of dismissal to the court. However, defense counsel then filed a bar complaint against respondent. The Kentucky Supreme Court found respondent guilty of misconduct. The court reasoned that when the plaintiff died, any further communications by the lawyer without disclosure of the plaintiff's death were the equivalent of a misrepresentation of material fact in violation of Model Rule 4.1(a). * * *

Mississippi Bar v. Mathis[31] illustrates when a lawyer's nondisclosure is both the equivalent of a misrepresentation and a violation of disclosure

---

23. Kentucky Bar Ass'n v. Geisler, 938 S.W.2d 578 (Ky.1997).

31. Mississippi Bar v. Mathis, 620 So.2d 1213 (Miss.1993).

CHAPTER II NEGOTIATION

obligations under discovery rules. *Mathis* involved a claim by a beneficiary under accidental death insurance policies. The defendant insurance companies moved to have an autopsy performed to determine whether the insured's death was accidental. The attorney resisted the motion on various grounds. In connection with the motion by the insurance companies, the attorney never revealed that he and his client's son had secretly had an autopsy performed. * * * By failing to comply with discovery rules, Mathis violated DR 7–102(A)(3), which prohibits a lawyer, in his representation of a client, from concealing or knowingly failing to disclose that which he is required by law to reveal. The court also emphasized that Mathis's "failure to disclose is the equivalent of an affirmative misrepresentation." * * *

* * *

When a lawyer changes the terms of a settlement agreement or contract, the lawyer has an ethical obligation to disclose the changes to opposing counsel. In *In re Rothwell*,[44] attorney Rothwell represented a client in negotiations with his former employer. The employer had discharged Rothwell's client after he had moved from Ohio to South Carolina. To facilitate the move, the employer had loaned the employee funds to purchase a house. The company offered to buy back the house and to apply the proceeds to the employee's debt to the company. The company sent Rothwell a deed along with a letter asking Rothwell to have his client sign the deed. The letter stated, "We will expect your call if there are any questions." Rothwell modified the deed by inserting a paragraph discharging his client from all liability to the company. After his client signed the modified deed, Rothwell returned it with a letter to the company stating, "We are returning herewith your package to you duly executed. Once you have filed the deed of record, please forward on a clocked copy of same for our files. Thank you." Rothwell did not inform the company that the deed had been changed. In the disciplinary proceeding, Rothwell argued that he did not have a duty to disclose the change in the deed to the company and that his change was merely a counteroffer. The South Carolina Supreme Court rejected this argument, finding Rothwell in violation of several disciplinary rules * * * Rothwell received a public reprimand.

* * *

If a lawyer makes a representation that is true when made but later learns that the representation is now false, the lawyer has an ethical duty to inform the opposing party of this change. In *In re Williams*,[54] respondent represented a tenant in connection with a dispute with a landlord regarding the maintenance of his house. Williams wrote to the landlord to demand repairs and to inform the landlord that he would hold the rent in escrow until the repairs were made. In a subsequent letter, Williams informed the landlord that the tenant would contract for the repairs and would pay the cost from the rent held in escrow. A few days later, however, the tenant moved out of the house. The lawyer returned a rent check to the

44. *In re* Rothwell, 296 S.E.2d 870 (1982).

54. *In re* Williams, 840 P.2d 1280 (1992).

D. Professional and Legal Framework for Negotiation

tenant, but he did not inform the landlord that he had returned the check. The bar conceded that Williams had not engaged in misrepresentation because at the time he wrote to the landlord he intended to hold the rent in escrow. The court accepted this concession and treated the case as one involving nondisclosure rather than affirmative misrepresentation. Nonetheless, the court found Williams guilty of misrepresentation by failing to disclose that he was returning the rent check to the tenant.

* * *

Cases involving the death of a client, surreptitious changes in contracts, or failure to correct representations that are now known to be false are rather extreme situations. Courts, however, have disciplined lawyers for nondisclosure in much less egregious situations. *State ex rel. Nebraska State Bar Ass'n v. Addison*[60] dealt with nondisclosure of insurance coverage. The defendant attorney represented a pedestrian injured in a collision between two automobiles. As a result of his injuries, the client incurred hospital expenses of more than $100,000. The attorney engaged in negotiations with the business manager of the hospital, seeking a release of the hospital's lien in exchange for reduced payment of the client's bills. One driver had a liability policy with $100,000 coverage and a separate umbrella policy of $1 million; the other driver's coverage was limited to $50,000. During these negotiations, the attorney learned that the hospital's business manager was under the mistaken impression that there were only two insurance policies available to pay claims; the manager was unaware of the $1 million umbrella policy. Nonetheless, the attorney negotiated a release of the lien without disclosing the third policy. The Nebraska Supreme Court found that the attorney had violated DR 1–102(A)(4), which prohibits a lawyer from engaging "in conduct involving dishonesty, fraud, deceit, or misrepresentation."

* * *

Nondisclosure of significant mathematical errors has also been the basis for rescission of settlement agreements. For example, *Stare v. Tate*[101] was an action by an ex-wife to reform a property settlement agreement entered into by parties prior to their divorce and to enforce the agreement as reformed. The agreement was the result of extensive negotiations between parties who were both represented by counsel. The parties agreed that community property would be divided equally, but they disagreed about the value of a piece of real estate referred to as the "Holt property." The wife contended that the Holt property was worth $550,000, while the husband argued that the property had a value of no more than $450,000. The property was subject to a mortgage of approximately $300,000. The wife's attorney submitted a settlement offer based on a $550,000 valuation of the Holt property, but the attorney made a mathematical mistake of $100,000 in computing the equity in the property. The husband's lawyer

---

60. State *ex rel.* Nebraska State Bar Ass'n v. Addison, 412 N.W.2d 855 (Neb. 1987).

101. Stare v. Tate, 98 Cal. Rptr. 264 (Ct. App. 1971).

and his accountant spotted the error but did not reveal the mistake to the wife's attorney. They reasoned that the mistake was the equivalent of acceptance of the husband's valuation of the property. Acting on the husband's behalf, they presented a counteroffer that used the mistake by the wife's attorney. After some further negotiation, the parties reached agreement based largely on the terms of the husband's counteroffer. The mistake would probably never have come to light except that after the settlement agreement was signed, the husband sent a note to his wife gloating over the fact that she and her attorney had made a mistake. The California Court of Appeals held that the agreement should be reformed to reflect the wife's intent. * * *

Arthur Isak Applbaum, Ethics for Adversaries: The Morality of Roles in Public and Professional Life

104–108 (1999).

We are now positioned to answer the dangling question about lawyers. Are they liars? Both in the courtroom and out, lawyers—good lawyers—intentionally attempt to convince judges, jurors, litigants, and contracting parties of the truth of propositions that the lawyer believes to be false. The act of intentionally inducing a belief in others that one believes to be false ordinarily counts as deception, whatever else it may count as. When deception is accomplished by making an untrue statement, the deception is a lie. * * * [G]ood lawyers certainly are serial *deceivers*—indeed, deception in one of the core tasks and skills of legal practice. And, because sometimes lawyerly deception is accomplished by making untrue statements, sometimes lawyers—again, good lawyers—deceive by lying. But my stake in showing that many lawyerly deceptions are also lies is poetic, not moral. "Are lawyers deceivers?" doesn't have quite the same ring, but a yes answer does have approximately the same moral force. Since deception also is a presumptive moral wrong, the burden is on the practice of law to justify lawyerly deception as well as lying. The question of moral evaluation cannot be redescribed away.

Consider some examples of clear deception. Many lawyers spend much of their time in contract or settlement negotiations, and several common strategies for reaching agreement when the initial perceived zone of possible agreement is larger than a point involve inducing false beliefs about a number of matters: the alternatives of both parties to settlement, the proper assessment of probabilities when alternatives are uncertain, the proper valuation of those alternatives, the change in alternatives and their valuation over time, the proper assessment of probabilities when the outcome of a proposed agreement is uncertain, and the value of a proposed agreement to both parties. Some manipulation of belief in negotiation counts in the law as fraud, and some counts, both in the law and in positive legal ethics, as "puffing and bluffing." But no institutional redescription can do away with the prior description of "intentionally inducing a false belief," or can block counting intentionally inducing false belief as deception. Though the law and positive legal ethics may count certain representations as mere puffery or bluffery, legal rules and rules of professional practice cannot by themselves undo the prior description of deception. When puffing and bluffing is accomplished by making untrue statements, such as "My client will not accept anything less" when you have good reason to believe that this is not the case, or the disarming "That clause is standard boilerplate" when in fact it was specially drafted to cover a contingency that you have good reason to believe has a substantial chance of occurring, you are lying. That the law has some standard of what counts as a "material" misrepresentation of fact is of no consequence to the prelegal description. Because descriptions persist, the law does not determine what is or is not properly described as a lie.

* * *

The good lawyer claims that, in the practice of lawyering, convincing others to believe the truth of what the lawyer believes to be false no longer counts as deception. Rather, it counts as zealous advocacy. Now, it could be that rules of morality do not count certain untruthful behaviors as deceptions. Morality does not count fiction writing as deception, for instance. But the rules of the practice of *lawyering* cannot redescribe a lie as something else. * * *

The lawyer might concede that, for one side or another, most trials involve deception, but deny that it is the lawyer who is doing the deceiving. It is the client, not the lawyer, who deceives. The lawyer-in-role acts as an artificial person, personating or representing the will of the client, but the natural person who occupies the lawyer's role cannot be described as the author of deception. This, I argued earlier, is untrue. * * *

The lawyer is not lying only. She is also advancing legal rights of her client, fulfilling her professional obligations, taking her part in a system that, in equilibrium, seeks truth and justice—the list goes on. The lies lawyers tell and the deceptions they state may be justified. But that, to repeat the refrain, is an evaluative matter. We cannot evade the hard work of moral evaluation and justification by claiming for the action or actor a different description. Does "liar" misdescribe the lawyer?

Walter W. Steele, Jr., Deceptive Negotiating and High-Toned Morality

39 Vand.L.Rev. 1387, 1390–91 (1986).

* * * In a broad sense, justifications exist for this less than honest standard for negotiating. A lawyer's devotion to a client's interest is so compelling that some lawyers feel justified, if not compelled, to employ some deception when negotiating. This viewpoint assumes that clients have a right to a lawyer who engages in deception. Unfortunately, the Model Code of Professional Responsibility and its modern cousin, the Model Rules of Professional Conduct, do not adequately address whether or not clients have a right to a deceptive lawyer.

CHAPTER II NEGOTIATION

Another justification for less than honest and straight-forward negotiating is the belief that a convention exists among lawyers to mislead during negotiations. This viewpoint, when carried to its logical conclusion, means that lawyers expect to negotiate with one another much like the proverbial used car salesperson. What a curious postulate for a learned and "high toned" profession to adopt. One wonders how even the most experienced negotiator in a negotiation can tell the difference between an honest party upon whom he can rely, and a deceitful party, upon whom he should not rely.

A final justification for less than honest and straight-forward negotiating is that deceit is inherent to negotiation. Are misrepresentations essential to negotiations? Certainly non-lawyer negotiators engage in deception from time to time. Should we expect something else from lawyers? Consider the negotiating standards of two holy men, one a willing buyer and the other a willing seller. If their personal commitments to holiness prevented them from making the slightest misrepresentation or from engaging in any abuse of their bargaining positions, how would the ultimate outcome of the negotiations differ from the outcome achieved by two lawyer negotiators? If deceit is truly inherent to negotiation, the outcome achieved by the holy men could not be defined as the product of a negotiation. But if the results achieved by their methods are somehow better or fairer than the result achieved by lawyers, then perhaps the legal definition of negotiation should be changed.

None of these rationalizations of deceptive negotiating is fully satisfactory. As a consequence, each prevaricating negotiator relies upon one or some combination of them. Each negotiator feels more or less justified to deceive or abuse power when negotiating, depending upon how well the chosen rationalizations satisfy the moral imperative of that particular negotiator. The result might be thought of as a disco dance floor full of negotiators, some more adroit than others, some more at ease with the music than others, and each very definitely free to "do his own thing." Obviously, what is missing is a specific and reasonably thorough set of standards for negotiating.

NOTES AND QUESTIONS

1. Although the Model Rules provide some guidance for, and some constraint on, lawyers' behavior, these excerpts illustrate that lawyers still have considerable room to maneuver in ways that you might consider immoral even if they do not run contrary to the profession's ethical standards. Are the Rules sufficiently strict? Should the rules governing negotiation behavior set a minimum standard with which all lawyers must (and should be able to) comply—a floor—or an aspirational standard—a ceiling—at which all lawyers should aim even if they sometimes fail? Do you agree with the following assessment?:

[T]he reality of the situation supports the notion that the status quo ethical constraints in negotiation are adequate to protect societal and legal interests. Admittedly, the formal rules of ethical conduct do not directly speak to negotiation behavior, and when they do, they only address the most egregious conduct. However, there are a number of other external factors apart from the vacuum of a particular negotiation setting that act as a check on such unethical negotiation behavior. Among these are the professional forces surrounding a particular attorney's practice, the developing cooperative nature of negotiation itself and the market forces that affect a negotiator's decision. Taken together with formal rules of ethics, these factors insure that ethical standards are met during negotiation, while still honoring the ideals of the adversary system and the zealous advocacy of the client that are deeply imbedded within our existing legal system.

Rosenberger, Laissez-"Fair": An Argument for the Status Quo Ethical Constraints on Lawyers as Negotiators, 13 Ohio St.J. on Dis.Res. 611, 638 (1998).

2. As discussed in the Longan excerpt, Comment 2 to Model Rule 4.1 allows for certain types of misleading statements on the ground that all negotiators expect such behavior from their counterparts. Professor White has long championed that the profession's ethical standards should account for the realities of bargaining:

> A final complication in drafting rules about truthfulness arises out of the paradoxical nature of the negotiator's responsibility. On the one hand, the negotiator must be fair and truthful; on the other hand he must mislead his opponent. Like the poker player, a negotiator hopes that his opponent will overestimate the value of his hand. Like the poker player, in a variety of ways he must facilitate his opponent's inaccurate assessment. The critical difference between those who are successful negotiators and those who are not lies in this capacity both to mislead and not to be misled.

> Some experienced negotiators will deny the accuracy of this assertion, but they will be wrong. I submit that a careful examination of the behavior of even the most forthright, honest, and trustworthy negotiators will show them actively engaged in misleading their opponents about their true positions. That is true of both the plaintiff and the defendant in a lawsuit. It is true of both labor and management in a collective bargaining agreement. It is true as well of both the buyer and the seller in a wide variety of sales transactions. To conceal one's true position, to mislead an opponent about one's true settling point, is the essence of negotiation.

> Of course there are limits on acceptable deceptive behavior in negotiation, but there is the paradox. How can one be "fair" but also mislead? Can we ask the negotiator to mislead, but fairly, like the soldier who must kill, but humanely?

White, Machiavelli and the Bar: Ethical Limitations on Lying in Negotiation, Am.B.Found. Research J. 921, 927–38 (1980). Do you agree? Are the justifications and excuses for lying in negotiations more persuasive than the reasons for candor?

Some research has attempted to determine to what extent the Comment to Model Rule 4.1 actually reflects negotiation practice. Various empirical studies show that lawyers believe that both puffing and misrepresenting one's settlement range are ethical and appropriate. See Dahl, Ethics on the Table: Stretching the Truth in Negotiations, 8 Rev.Litig. 173, 183–93 (1989); Lewicki and Stark, Presentation, What's Ethically Appropriate in Negotiations: An Empirical Examination of Bargaining Tactics 18 (Behavioral Research and Bus. Ethics Conf., Nw.U., July 31–Aug. 4, 1994); Lempert, In Settlement Talks, Does Telling the Truth Have its Limits?, 2 Inside Litig. 1 (1988). Thus, even if an attorney knows her client will settle a personal injury case for $30,000, she can say that the client would like to settle in the $50,000 to $75,000 range.

What about lying about a client's reservation value? For instance, what if an attorney authorized to settle for $30,000 told opposing counsel that her client would settle for no less than $50,000? At first glance, lying about a client's reservation price may seem indistinguishable from misrepresenting a client's settlement range. However, to equate the two requires a broad interpretation of the exceptions to Model Rule 4.1. Lying about one's bottom line differs subtly but significantly from expressing one's desired settlement range. The former is an ultimatum, making an opposing negotiator think that unless she gives in to a demand, no settlement will be possible. It thus exerts leverage on the other side. In contrast, an intended settlement range is as subjective as a wish list, more like an opinion or a value estimate. Accordingly, most negotiators would not directly lie about a reservation value. Instead, they would find ways to artfully evade direct questions about settlement authority. See Dahl, Ethics on the Table: Stretching the Truth in Negotiations, 8 Rev.Litig. 173, 192–93 (1989).

For a survey of cases involving misrepresentation, see Perschbacher, Regulating Lawyers' Negotiations, 27 Ariz.L.Rev. 75 (1985); Shell, When Is It Legal To Lie in Negotiations?, 32 Sloan Mgt.Rev. 93 (Spring 1991).

3. Lawyers often argue that their role insulates them from moral criticism. As a participant in the adversary system, the argument runs, the lawyer is merely embodying the client's preferences and commands, and is not himself open to moral inquiry about the acceptability of his conduct. Particularly in the negotiation context where common practice may already seem to permit some behavior that would normally seem unethical, do the lawyer's role and the rules of the "game" insulate an attorney from moral scrutiny?

Arthur Applbaum critiques the reasoning of role morality, a prominent justification given by lawyers for conduct that would be considered unethical in other contexts. Applbaum summarizes the argument in favor of role morality:

[A]ctors occupying professional or public roles are not to make all-things-considered evaluations about the goodness or rightness of their actions, but rather, they are to act on restricted reasons for action, taking into account only a limited or partial set of values, interests, or fact. * * * Each adversary ought to do so (or more modestly, is permitted to do so) because, in the aggregate, the institution of multiple actors acting from restricted reasons properly takes into account the expansive set of reasons, values, interests, and facts.

Applbaum, Ethics for Adversaries: The Morality of Roles in Public and Professional Life 5–6 (1999). Applbaum is critical of the reasoning of role morality: "Good forms of social organization do not by themselves dictate the forms of moral reasoning particular actors within institutions ought to employ. The gap between what an institution may allow and what an actor within an institution may do is especially great when the action in question deceives, coerces, or violates persons in other ways." Further, Applbaum contends that role morality does not "justify circulating information one believes to be false," undercutting the rationale for allowing certain forms of misrepresentation in negotiation.

4. In addition to the moral questions raised by misrepresentation and nondisclosure, such behavior may cause inefficiencies. According to Howard Raiffa:

The art of compromise centers on the willingness to give up something in order to get something else in return. Successful artists get more than they give up. A common ploy is to exaggerate the importance of what one is giving up and to minimize the importance of what one gets in return. Such posturing is part of the game. In most cultures these self-serving negotiating stances are expected, as long as they are kept in decent bounds. Most people would not call this "lying," just as they would choose not to label as "lying" the exaggerations that are made in the adversarial confrontations of a courtroom. I call such exaggerations "strategic misrepresentations." The expression is not my own invention; it was used by game theorists and mathematical economists long before I adopted it.

* * *

* * * Bargainers are often advised that they should purposely add to the negotiation agenda issues that they do not really care about, in the hope that the other side will feel strongly about one of these superfluous issues—strong enough to be willing to make compensating concessions in return for dropping the offending issue. This questionable strategy can, of course, poison the atmosphere of the negotiations, with detriment to both parties.

Strategic misrepresentation can also cause inefficiencies. Consider a distributive bargaining problem in which there is a zone of agreement in actual, but not necessarily in revealed, reservation prices. An inefficiency can arise only if the parties fail to come to an agreement. By bargaining hard the parties may fail to come to an agreement, even though any point in the zone of agreement would yield a better outcome for both than the no-agreement state. Still, one cannot conclude from this observation that a negotiator should unilaterally and truthfully reveal his or her reservation price.

Contrast this situation with an integrative bargaining problem, in which it may be possible for the negotiators to enlarge the pie before cutting it. In order to squeeze out potential joint gains, the negotiators must do some joint problem solving. If both sides strategically misrepresent their value tradeoffs, then inefficient contracts will often result. In complicated negotiations where uncertainties loom large, there may be contracts that are far better for each negotiating party than the no-contract alternative, but it might take considerable skill at joint problem solving to discover those possibilities. Without the right atmosphere and without some reasonably truthful communication of values, such jointly acceptable contracts might never be discerned. It is my impression from observing many negotiation exercises that each negotiator is well advised to behave cooperatively and honestly (for example, by disclosing tradeoffs) in seeking joint gains, but to bargain more toughly when it comes to sharing the jointly created pie.

In general, I would advise negotiators to act openly and honestly on efficiency concerns; tradeoffs should be disclosed (if the adversary reciprocates), but reservation prices should be kept private. * * *

Raiffa, The Art and Science of Negotiation 142–144 (1982).

Even if deception creates market inefficiencies, many scholars contend that economic incentives adequately maintain ethical disclosure in negotiation. Robert Condlin argues that a negotiator with a reputation for cooperating will secure more favorable settlements over time and, consequently, have more clients and income over the long term. See Condlin, Bargaining in the Dark: The Normative Incoherence of Lawyer Dispute Bargaining Role, 51 Md.L.Rev. 1, 82 (1992). The market favors disclosure because the practical risks of not disclosing include injury to the negotiator's reputation. Thus, market forces may preserve ethical conduct because attorneys are concerned about the hidden costs of nondisclosure such as harms to reputation, to future clients, and to professional relationships. See Rosenberger, Laissez-"Fair": An Argument for the Status Quo Ethical Constraints on Lawyers as Negotiators, 13 Ohio St.J. on Dis.Res. 611 (1998). Using economic analysis, Geoffrey Peters advocates heightened disclosure requirements for negotiation. Peters says that in real-world negotiations, deception is almost always inefficient and that it rewards those who are skilled at lying. See Peters, The Use of Lies in Negotiation, 48 Ohio St.L.J. 1 (1987); but see Norton, Bargaining and the Ethic of Process, 64 N.Y.U.L.Rev. 493, 537–38 (contending that certain forms of misrepresentation are efficient and enable negotiators to arrive at accurate information); Wokutch and Carson, The Ethics and Profitability of Bluffing in Business, Westminster Inst.Rev. 77–83 (May 1981) (arguing that some degree of deception through bluffing is necessary to maintain economic profitability).

D. Professional and Legal Framework for Negotiation

Are economic incentives sufficient to deter lying and nondisclosure in negotiations? If so, why are the Model Rules, the law of fraud and other ethical codes necessary? Even if market forces encourage candor between lawyers in negotiations, clients may have competing incentives not to disclose. Constrained by client confidentiality, lawyers are pressured by clients to engage in hard-bargaining tactics at the same time that economic incentives encourage them to cooperate—a tension Robert Condlin refers to as the "bargainer's dilemma." How do lawyers deal with the bargainer's dilemma? See Condlin, Bargaining in the Dark: The Normative Incoherence of Lawyer Dispute Bargaining Role, 51 Md.L.Rev. 1, 84–85 (1992) (arguing that stylized, or slightly exaggerated, negotiation behavior is a common solution to the bargainer's dilemma).

5. One of the most common ethical dilemmas in negotiation involves corrective disclosure. Consider the following hypothetical:

> [A] mechanic testifies on the deposition that his customer (the father of a child who was killed in an auto accident after the mechanic worked on the car) did not request that the mechanic check the brakes but asked only for a "general checkup" of the car. Subsequently the mechanic comes to his lawyer and states that he "remembers" that the father of the dead child did tell him to check the brakes.

White, Machiavelli and the Bar: Ethical Limitations on Lying in Negotiation, Am.B.Found. Research J. 921, 936 (1980).

The problem of corrective disclosure is related to nondisclosure, becoming an issue when a representation that was originally true turns out to be false. In such a case, does the attorney have an obligation to provide the now-correct information? In a litigation context, an attorney has an ongoing obligation under Federal Rule of Civil Procedure 26(e) to inform the opposing side when material facts are no longer correct. However, the Model Rules do not explicitly cover negotiation ethics in situations where material facts turn out to be false. A draft proposal for a Model Rule that would have required corrective disclosure in negotiations was rejected. For some, the intentional omission resolves the issue in favor of nondisclosure. Further, White argues that the mechanic's attorney could withhold the information in good faith, reasoning that the faulty "memory" had been induced by a sense of guilt from being connected with the child's death. Scholars are split on the question of whether the mechanic's attorney would be required to disclose. Many cite cases of fraud in which attorneys or their clients were held liable for failing to correct a statement that was initially true. If disclosure is required, the mechanic example above may be a rare case where negotiation ethics are out of step with negotiation practice. White contends that most lawyers would not reveal a witness' recantation, and an empirical study supports his claim.[3]

3. See Dahl, Ethics on the Table: Stretching the Truth in Negotiations, 8 Rev.Litig. 173, 190 (1989).

228 CHAPTER II NEGOTIATION

6. Although misrepresentation and nondisclosure may be the most common ethical issues raised by negotiations, lawyers must consider others as well. In multiparty negotiations, for example, a given lawyer or law firm may represent more than one party, raising conflict of interest and loyalty concerns. Much has been written about the ethical quandaries raised by class action litigation. Concerns include that plaintiffs attorneys often cannot adequately represent all members of a class because of intra-class conflicts, that plaintiffs and defense attorneys may collude in settling for their own advantage and fees but to the detriment of class members, and that settlement classes are sometimes "feigned" or "friendly" actions created by the lawyers on both sides that do not truly meet the "case or controversy" requirement. See e.g., Coffee, Class Action Accountability: Reconciling Exit, Voice, and Loyalty in Representative Litigation, 100 Colum.L.Rev.370 (2000); Coffee, Class Wars: The Dilemma of the Mass Tort Class Action, 95 Colum.L.Rev. 1343 (1996); Hay and Rosenberg, "Sweetheart" and "Blackmail" Settlements in Class Actions: Reality and Remedy, 75 Notre Dame L.Rev. 1377 (2000); Koniak, Feasting While the Widow Weeps: Georgine v. Amchem Products, Inc., 80 Cornell L.Rev. 1045 (1995); Menkel–Meadow, Ethics and the Settlement of Mass Torts: When the Rules Meet the Road, 80 Cornell L.Rev. 1159 (1995).

In addition, multiparty cases sometimes raise ethical concerns about defense representation. When a given defense attorney represents more than one party under what is often known as a "joint defense agreement" or when multiple defendants agree to use separate representation but share costs, conflicts of interest can arise as the lawsuit progresses that may not have been obvious at the beginning of litigation. See Erichson, Informal Aggregation: Procedural and Ethical Implications of Coordination Among Counsel in Related Lawsuits, 50 Duke L.J. 381 (2000); Ashley and Wynne, Dealing with Conflicts in Joint Representation of Defendants in Mass Tort Litigation, 17 Rev.Lit. 469 (1998).

Finally, a particular type of settlement has gained some notoriety. In some cases involving multiple defendants, a plaintiff will settle with a given defendant prior to trial and agree with that settling defendant that any recovery at trial in excess of an amount fixed in the settlement agreement will lower the amount owed by the settling defendant. These agreements, known as Mary Carter agreements after the name of a prominent Florida case, Booth v. Mary Carter Paint Co.,[4] have been questioned for the incentives they provide the settling defendant to reveal confidences to the plaintiff so as to help the plaintiff win its lawsuit against the remaining litigants. In addition, because the settling defendant stays in the lawsuit (despite having "capped" its liability through the settlement device), some question whether such agreements may mislead judge and jury. Although the settling defendant purports to be in an adversarial posture vis-à-vis the plaintiff, their interests actually align. See Entman, Mary Carter Agreements: An Assessment of Attempted Solutions, 38 U.Fla.L.Rev. 521, 529 (1986). Although several states have banned Mary Carter Agreements,

---

4. 202 So.2d 8 (Fla.App.1967).

some commentators have justified them on economic grounds. See Bernstein and Klerman, An Economic Analysis of Mary Carter Agreements, 83 Geo.L.J. 2215 (1995). In addition, California courts have interpreted state statutes as allowing enforcement of "sliding scale recovery agreements"—the California equivalent of Mary Carter Agreements, only if in "good faith." That is, the amount of the settlement must be within the reasonable range of the settling tortfeasor's proportional share of the comparative liability for the plaintiff's injuries. See Tech–Bilt Inc. v. Woodward–Clyde & Assoc., 38 Cal.3d 488, 213 Cal.Rptr. 256, 698 P.2d 159 (1985).

(1) Alternatives

The shortcomings of the existing professional codes have called forth a variety of alternatives from scholars, practitioners and judges. Here we list and consider some of these approaches. As you read, compare the different proposals and consider which seems best suited to governing negotiating lawyers. Are these standards realistic? Operational? Sufficiently aspirational? Do they comport with your understanding of what negotiation requires? Will lawyers obey them? Can they be enforced?

Robert B. Gordon, Private Settlement as Alternative Adjudication: A Rationale for Negotiation Ethics

18 U. Mich.J.L.Ref. 503, 530 (1985).

Fairness to Other Participants

In conducting settlement negotiations,

(A) A lawyer shall at all times act in good faith and with the primary objective of resolving the dispute without court proceedings;

(B) A lawyer shall not

(1) Knowingly make any statement that contains a misrepresentation of material fact or law or that omits a fact necessary to make the statement considered as a whole not materially misleading;

(2) Knowingly fail to

(a) Disclose to opposing counsel such material facts or law as may be necessary to correct manifest misapprehensions thereof; or alternatively,

(b) Give reasonable indication to opposing counsel of the possible inaccuracy of a given material fact or law upon which opposing counsel appears to rely. Such indication may take the form of statements of unwillingness to discuss a particular matter raised by opposing counsel.

Walter Steele, Jr., Deceptive Negotiating and High-Toned Morality

39 Vand.L.Rev. 1387, 1402 (1986).

Obligation of Fairness and Candor in Negotiation

When serving as an advocate in court a lawyer must work to achieve the most favorable outcome for his client consistent with the law and the admissible evidence. However, when serving as a negotiator lawyers should strive for a result that is objectively fair. Principled negotiation between lawyers on behalf of clients should be a cooperative process, not an adversarial process. Consequently, whenever two or more lawyers are negotiating on behalf of clients, each lawyer owes the other an obligation of total candor and total cooperation to the extent required to insure that the result is fair.

James J. Alfini, Settlement Ethics and Lawyering in ADR Proceedings: A Proposal to Revise Rule 4.1

19 N.Ill.U.L.Rev. 255, 270–71 (1999).

Rule 4.1 Truthfulness in Statements to Others

In the course of representing a client a lawyer shall not knowingly:

   (a) make a false statement of ~~material~~ fact or law to a third person; or

   (b) assist the client in reaching a settlement agreement that is based on reliance upon a false statement of fact made by the lawyer's client; or

   (c) fail to disclose a material fact to a third person when disclosure is necessary to avoid assisting a criminal or fraudulent act by a client, unless disclosure is prohibited by Rule 1.6.

COMMENT:

Alternative Dispute Resolution

[2] A lawyer's duty of truthfulness applies beyond formal tribunals (see Rule 3.3) to less formal settings. The obligation to be truthful is particularly essential with the increased use by courts of dispute resolution alternatives such as mediation, arbitration, mini-trial, and summary jury trials to effect settlement. When representing a client in these less formal settings, the lawyer may often encounter situations where both the lawyer and his or her client participate freely in open and frank discussions unconstrained by rules of evidence or procedure. The lawyer should therefore inform the client of the lawyer's duty to be truthful and the lawyer's inability to assist the client in reaching a settlement agreement that is procured in whole or in part as a result of a false statement of material fact or law made by the client.

ABA Litigation Section, Ethical Guidelines for Civil Settlement Negotiations

(Draft 2001).

4.1.1. False Statements of Material Fact.

In the course of negotiating or concluding a settlement, a lawyer may not knowingly make a false statement of material fact (or law) to a third person.

4.1.2. Silence, Omission, and the Duty to Disclose Material Facts.

In the course of negotiating or concluding a settlement, a lawyer must disclose a material fact to a third person when doing so is necessary to avoid assisting a criminal or fraudulent act by a client, unless such disclosure is prohibited by the ethical duty of confidentiality.

4.1.3. Withdrawal in Situations Involving Misrepresentations of Material Fact.

If a lawyer discovers that a client will use the lawyer's services or work product to materially further a course of criminal or fraudulent conduct, the lawyer must withdraw from representing the client and may disaffirm any opinion, document or other affirmation. If a lawyer discovers that a client has used a lawyer's services in the past to perpetuate a fraud, now ceased, the lawyer may, but is not required to, withdraw, but disaffirming his/her prior opinion and work product is not permitted.

4.3.7. Exploiting Opponent's Mistake.

In the settlement context, a lawyer should not attempt knowingly to obtain benefit or advantage for himself or herself or his or her client as a result of an opponent's mistake which has been induced by the lawyer or which is obviously unintentional. Further, a lawyer may have an affirmative duty to disclose information in settlement negotiations if he or she knows that the other side is operating on the basis of a mistaken impression of material fact.

4.3.1. Bad Faith in the Settlement Process.

An attorney may not employ bad faith in the settlement process.

4.3.2. Duress and Extortionate Tactics in Negotiations.

A lawyer may not employ pressure tactics in negotiating a settlement that have no substantial purpose other than to embarrass or burden the opposing party.

Alvin B. Rubin, A Causerie On Lawyers' Ethics In Negotiation

35 LA.L.Rev. 577, 589–91 (1975).

The lawyer must act honestly and in good faith. * * * The lawyer may not accept a result that is unconscionably unfair to the other party.

Discussion Draft Of The Model Rules Of Professional Conduct

(Jan. 30, 1980).

Rule 4.2—Fairness to Other Participants

(a) In conducting negotiations a lawyer shall be fair in dealing with other participants.

Rule 4.3—Illegal, Fraudulent or Unconscionable Transactions

A lawyer shall not conclude an agreement, or assist a client in concluding an agreement, that the lawyer knows or reasonably should know is illegal, contains legally prohibited terms, would work fraud or would be held to be unconscionable as a matter of law.

Rex R. Perschbacher, Regulating Lawyers' Negotiations

27 Ariz.L.Rev. 75, 133–36 (1985).

5. *Duty to negotiate in good faith*

Commentators in legal ethics have regularly urged that lawyers owe a duty of fairness to their negotiation adversaries. Even these commentators, however, acknowledge the difficulty in establishing a set of legal rules that express and enforce the general duty of fairness. Fairness either includes or is related to the other restrictions on lawyer-negotiators discussed in this part of the article. But what the commentators have in mind is clearly something that goes beyond simply avoiding fraud, duress, and unconscionability. Judge Rubin suggests negotiating lawyers ought "to act honestly and in good faith."

Without an overhaul of the representational-adversary system, imposing a general good faith obligation on lawyer-negotiators is impossible. In part the problem is technical. Under agency law rules, lawyer-agents are privileged and do not incur liability to their client principals by refusing to perform illegal, unreasonable, or unethical acts. Thus, lawyers can respect their obligations to third parties outlined in this section without thereby violating duties and incurring liability to their clients. Currently, there is no general good faith obligation to third parties, and lawyers cannot act according to such a standard without incurring liability to their clients. If this were the only problem, the solution would be simple: add the general good faith obligation to the ethical rules and lawyers will be privileged to act in accord with it. But there are deeper problems.

There is a structural difficulty inherent in the adversary system. Other than rules of professional etiquette, the duties of negotiating lawyers depend upon the existence of a legally recognized relationship. We do not ordinarily talk in terms of a lawyer's duty of fairness to the client because the legally recognized lawyer-client relationship gives rise to the specific obligations of competence, communication, loyalty, and confidentiality. A duty to third parties is recognized only to the extent that the lawyer must not inflict intentional harm or, in those circumstances where the nominal adversary is dependent on the lawyer, to avoid creating an unreasonable risk of harm to the third party. Under current legal practice standards, expanding these limited third party duty rules is incomprehensible. If lawyers are required to respect their adversaries' rights throughout the course of representation, in the end the lawyer becomes representative of both parties and guarantor of the fairness of the transaction. The adversary system would have to be abandoned in negotiations. However desirable this may be as an ideal, it is unacceptable and unworkable in the profession today.

Although wholesale changes in negotiating lawyers' obligations to third parties are unlikely, incremental changes seem certain. One such change is an expansion of the duty to bargain in good faith. Currently, this obligation is restricted to labor negotiations and insurance, both highly regulated because of perceived special public interests. Most of the elements that comprise good faith bargaining in labor and insurance negotiations are either common to all negotiations, such as the proscription against misrepresentation, or are uniquely dependent on the substantive context, such as mandatory bargaining topics in labor law. Thus labeling them part of good faith bargaining does not carry any implications for a general fairness good faith principle in negotiations.

However, two ideals taken from both insurance and labor collective bargaining suggest possible directions for change. These are (1) limitations on negotiating only for purposes of delay, and (2) obstructing an adversary's access to information material to the negotiation. Even if these ideas do not constitute a duty of good faith bargaining in negotiations, they could eventually become the bases for possible damage claims against lawyers who fail to live up to their requirements. These two elements are similar to already recognized bases for relief under existing law. For example, negotiating solely for delay or to burden a third party resembles the tort of abuse of process. To recover for abuse of process, ordinarily an injured party must show use of legal process for a procedurally improper purpose and malice. Negotiation seldom involves the use of legal process, but by analogy sham negotiating can substitute for the procedurally improper use. Combined with malice such as using sham negotiations to coerce or extort money from a third party, misuse of apparent negotiations could become a part of the abuse of process tort or gain acceptance as a separate duty of good faith negotiation practice.

Obstructing access to information is more difficult to place with assurance. In labor law, access to information has developed in the form of the civil discovery rules. There must be an appropriate demand for the information; it must be relevant to the subjects under negotiation; and the adversary can provide it in several different forms. In good faith insurance settlement negotiations, the duty to provide information is actually part of the lawyer's duty of loyalty to the client—a duty to provide the client with information necessary to make informed choices concerning the subject of the representation. Obviously the duty of providing negotiation information is not one of full disclosure. Such an obligation would create an unresolvable conflict with the lawyer's duties of loyalty and confidentiality to the client. Instead it involves a duty of noninterference that should include familiar proscriptions on destruction or concealment of evidence, and that requires disclosure when the failure to do so would be deceptive or misleading to an adversary. This, then, takes into account the negligence-based duties toward third parties and requires some assessment of the opponent's position and the third party's need to rely on information held

CHAPTER II NEGOTIATION

exclusively by a lawyer for the adversary. Of course, this duty is unambiguous when the subject of negotiation is litigation (civil or criminal), and the information requested is subject to discovery or must be disclosed under existing constitutional, statutory, or regulatory standards.

NOTES AND QUESTIONS

1. How do you think the legal profession should govern lying, misrepresentation, puffing and bluffing, and nondisclosure in negotiations? Do you prefer the existing Model Rule 4.1, Gordon's approach, or Alfini's proposed rule? Are the ABA's proposed ethical guidelines helpful?

The debate surrounding truthfulness, good faith, and fairness standards in negotiation often centers around the proper role of rules themselves. Two divergent camps advocate alternative views on rulemaking. One side supports a minimalist code of ethics, while the other espouses a "high toned," or aspirational, ethic.

Minimalists contend that a certain amount of deception is inherent in negotiation. Further, enforcement of negotiation rules is more difficult because of the nonpublic setting of most negotiations. In light of the difficulty of achieving consensus on appropriate negotiation standards, most commentators assert that negotiation rules must reflect current negotiation practices. The Model Rules represent an ethical lowest common denominator, and individual negotiators may adopt higher ethical standards at their discretion. Finally, rules that set overly high standards will not be followed, casting all of the rules in doubt. For an example of the minimalist position, see White, Machiavelli and the Bar: Ethical Limitations on Lying in Negotiation, Am.B.Found. Research J. 921, 926 (1980); compare Steele, Deceptive Negotiating and High–Toned Morality, 39 Vand. L.Rev. 1387 (arguing that the intrinsic benefits of aspiring to higher ethical standards outweigh social costs).

In addition to Model Rule 4.1, most legal scholars formerly adopted a minimalist position toward disclosure in negotiations. However, in light of the American Bar Association's Ethics 2000 hearings on revisions to the Model Rules, there has been a recent resurgence in favor of aspirational standards. See e.g. Painter, Rules Lawyers Play By, 76 N.Y.U.L.Rev. 665 (2001) (arguing that aspirational rules could improve ethics norms, especially if combined with public reporting on lawyer compliance); Crystal, The Incompleteness of the Model Rules and the Development of Professional Standards, 52 Mercer L.Rev. 839 (2001) (discussing the recent trend in favor of aspirational standards in response to the limitations of the minimalist Model Rules); ABA Litigation Section, Ethical Guidelines for Civil Settlement Negotiations (Draft 2001) (proposing higher disclosure standards for negotiators).

2. One of the dangers of setting an aspirational standard in the professional ethics rules is that lawyers may then be more constrained in negotiations than non-lawyers. In other words, if the professional ethics codes are more strict than the law of fraud, a client may be disinclined to

D. Professional and Legal Framework for Negotiation 235

allow her lawyer to negotiate on her behalf. This argument, however, suggests that Model Rule 4.1 (or any replacement for it) might be unnecessary. Should we just do away with regulating negotiation behavior through professional ethics?

3. In addition to seeking to regulate misrepresentations and nondisclosure, many legal scholars have argued in favor of a fairness standard. Judge Alvin Rubin, for instance, argues in favor of a rule preventing negotiators from accepting "unconscionably unfair" results:

> The lawyer should not be free to negotiate an unconscionable result, however pleasing to his client, merely because it is possible, any more than he is free to do other reprobated acts. He is not to commit perjury to pay a bribe or give advice about how to commit embezzlement. The examples refer to advice concerning illegal conduct, but we do already, at least in some circumstances, accept the principle that some acts are proscribed though not criminal: the lawyer is forbidden to testify as a witness in his client's cause, or to assert a defense merely to harass his opponent; he is enjoined to point out to his client "those factors that may lead to a decision that is morally just." Whether a mode of conduct available to the lawyer is illegal or merely unconscionably unfair, the attorney must refuse to participate. This duty of fairness is owed to the profession and to society; it must supercede any duty owed to the client.

Rubin, A Causerie on Lawyer's Ethics in Negotiation, 35 La.L.Rev. 577, 591–92 (1975).

Arguments in favor of a fairness standard often appeal to the notion that lawyers owe duties to the public. The Model Rules, adopted almost a decade after Rubin's essay, give some support for such a duty. See Model Rules of Professional Conduct Preamble (rules should be "conceived in the public interest") and Rule 2.1 (in rendering advice, a lawyer may refer to "moral, economic, social and political factors").

Does Rubin's proposed rule make a negotiator his brother's (or counterpart's) keeper? Does it deprive the more skilled negotiator the benefits of her negotiating talent and experience? Using Rubin's criteria, what would an unconscionable settlement look like? Where would one draw the line between an unconscionably unfair and a merely unfair settlement?

Contract law allows a party to rescind a contract for an unconscionable agreement. Is in necessary to police unconscionable results before the deal is done? In a negotiation, a lawyer may not always have the ability to step back to assess power imbalances and value differentials. Is that a good enough reason not to impose a rule like Rubin's on the negotiator?

For a discussion of the early legislative history of the Model Rules and the reasons why a rule requiring fairness in negotiations was rejected, see Hazard, The Lawyer's Obligation to Be Trustworthy when Dealing with Opposing Parties, 33 S.C.L.Rev. 181 (1981).

(2) Dealing With Ethical Dilemmas

Robert H. Mnookin, Scott R. Peppet & Andrew S. Tulumello, Beyond Winning: Negotiating to Create Value in Deals and Disputes

286–93 (2000).

What If the Other Side Asks Me a Question I Don't Want to Answer?

Negotiating lawyers are sometimes caught off-guard when asked a question where a truthful answer would disadvantage their client. For example, if you were [negotiating a severance package on behalf of a client named Ed and Ed's employer] asked you "Does Ed have any other job offers?" what could you do to get out of the situation without violating the rules of professional conduct? [What if you feared that disclosing Ed's new job offer would lead to a smaller severance package from his existing employer?]

Attorneys approach such moments in various ways. Many refuse to answer such questions. Some might simply remain silent. Others may say "No comment," "I'm not at liberty to say," or "You'd have to ask my client." A lawyer might indicate that he cannot disclose information because to do so would violate client confidences. Given the exceedingly narrow scope of the Rule 1.6(b) exceptions, Rule 1.6(a)'s broad duty of confidentiality operates as a serious constraint on lawyers. The duty to keep client confidences is one of the central pillars of professional ethics. The attorney-client evidentiary privilege protects the attorney-client relationship from unauthorized revelation of information by an attorney. These walls around the relationship are meant to ensure that clients can talk openly and truthfully with their lawyers without fear that their secrets will become public knowledge.

The weakness of using Rule 1.6 as an excuse in a negotiation is that a client can always authorize a lawyer to disclose anything—and if the other side insists that you answer a question, they'll likely insist that you return to your client for permission to do so. The broader problem is that the other side may interpret your refusal to answer, whether you've invoked the rule explicitly or not, *as* an answer—in this case, that Ed *does* have other opportunities.

As a result, many attorneys try evasion in moments like this. They may try to change the subject. Or, rather than not answer, an attorney might answer a different question than the one asked—the politician's classic interview technique. Or a lawyer might respond by asking a question of his own, either to clarify or to change topics. In Ed's case, a lawyer might try to deflect the question by asking, "Who'd want to hire him?" Or "the job market is pretty tight right now, isn't it?" Of course, alert attorneys might expose such sleight of hand under persistent questioning.

A different sort of problem is posed if the lawyer on the other side asks you the limits of your settlement authority or "What is the least amount Ed is willing to accept as severance pay?" While the Model Rules suggest that an attorney has great leeway to misrepresent such information, it is often far better to refuse to answer and to explain why.

You can name the inherent problem with such difficult questions: they invite you to lie. "You know, I don't find questions like that all that helpful, and here's why. If I asked *you* that, although I think you're a decent person, I'd be setting you up to deceive me. It's just a tough question to answer, and it's tempting to bend the truth. I'd have very little confidence in your answer, and so I'm not sure that the question itself would serve me very well. My suggestion is that we table that question." By naming the strategic problem created by such a question, you can sometimes dissuade the other side from pursuing an answer to it. And you show that you understand the strategic landscape and their motivation for asking. This can take the power out of such inquiries.

The key is to prepare. Before you negotiate, make a list of the nightmare questions the other side might ask. Think of all the inquiries that would make you uncomfortable or tempt you to lie. Then prepare answers that could extricate you from those situations as gracefully as possible. Your answers may not be perfect, but you will be able to react more skillfully than if you simply deceive the other side.

What If I Think the Other Side is Lying or Being Misleading?

In negotiation, often the challenge is the other side's behavior, not yours. Some negotiators boast that they can see through the other side's lies and deception. Others fear that they cannot, and they seek advice on how to distinguish truth from falsehoods. Certainly there are sometimes cues when people lie, and it may be possible to become more skillful at identifying deceit. But research suggests that most people exaggerate their ability to detect lies. The stubborn fact is that people sometimes will lie to you, and often you won't know it. Even more often, you'll be unsure whether to trust the other side. What can you do if you fear that the other side is lying, being misleading, or not telling you material information?

SMOKE OUT DECEPTION

One technique is to smoke out unethical behavior. As we've seen, the Model Rules do not require attorneys to reveal much information voluntarily. As a result, asking direct questions and probing for information is indispensable to successful lawyering. Of course, if the other side doesn't want to answer your question, they may evade or refuse, just as you might if they asked you. And they might lie. But only by asking will you truly test their willingness to respond directly. You can't assume that they will otherwise provide you with material facts. As you probe, you can try to triangulate between the other side's statements to discover inconsistencies that demonstrate deception or an attempt to mislead.

VERIFY INFORMATION

Another way to deal with your doubts about the other side is to verify material information whenever possible. This is why due diligence is so

CHAPTER II NEGOTIATION

important in deal-making and discovery so important to litigation; each side must independently seek to verify material information about the other. Even if the seller says the house you're purchasing is in good condition, be sure to get an inspection anyway. Even if the other side insists that their company is doing well, have your accountant review their books.

Of course, verifying information is expensive. A strong, trusting relationship is valuable in part because it reduces this cost of doing business: you may not need to spend as much time and money on verification. Nevertheless, independently verifying critical information is often a central part of a lawyer's role.

CRAFT REPRESENTATIONS AND WARRANTIES TO HEDGE RISK

Deception works only if you rely on the other side's falsehood. If you doubt the other side, you can structure your negotiated agreement so that you do not rely upon their statements and so that you hedge the risk if it turns out that they have not told the truth.

Lawyers have a comparative advantage in negotiation because they can use their contracting and drafting skills to seek written representations about material facts. Rather than informally relying on the other side's verbal assurances, lawyers can build representations and warranties into agreements and condition settlement on the veracity of those representations. If the other side was exaggerating or lying, they may balk at making such a written representation. The request then serves to smoke out unethical behavior on the other side.

Warranties can also deter, or remedy, lies and nondisclosure. You should always be on the lookout for the lemons problem, for example. In any purchase and sale, the seller has an incentive to withhold information about the condition of the item in question. Seeking representations and warranties can reduce these risks and decrease the damage to you if they lie.

Contracting is thus the legal negotiator's most helpful tool in discovering and constraining misleading behavior on the other side. Don't just take them at their word—have them write their word down and warrant that it is true.

The danger, of course, is that if you find yourself not trusting the other side, you may be tempted to seek representations and warranties about *everything*. If the other side has demonstrated that they can't be trusted, what would in other cases be over-lawyering may be necessary. But you must calibrate your suspicions. Attorneys too easily get carried away and imagine that a written document provides complete protection. Representations and warranties are not a perfect cure. A breach of warranty must be detected and proved, and enforcement is both costly and imperfect.

GIVE THE OTHER SIDE A WAY TO SAVE FACE

When you've discovered or you suspect that the other side is lying or being misleading, you may want to end the negotiations. We certainly don't want to defend those who lie or mislead, nor to apologize for them. At the same time, before breaking off the negotiations or rubbing the other side's nose in their misdeeds, think carefully about what will best serve your client's overarching interests. If problem-solving is the approach you prefer, it may be more productive to deal with the other side's impropriety while giving them a way to save face.

Why? Because being caught lying is embarrassing. The other side may not want to continue negotiating with you if it is clear that you know they were trying to deceive. Moreover, if you acknowledge that you have found them out, *you* may no longer be able to negotiate with *them*: to preserve your reputation, you can't be known as a person who does business with liars. For example, imagine that you know your employee has falsified a few expense reports. You don't want to fire him, but you want him to change his behavior. However, you can't let him know that you know about the past transgressions, because then you would have to fire him: your company's policy would require it. In this situation, naming the ethical issue would make it harder to work together in the future, even if he was committed to no longer stealing from the company.

Often you can find creative ways to signal or hint to the other side that their unethical behavior won't work or has been found out, while leaving the message ambiguous enough to permit both sides to continue working together.

How Much Do I Have to Tell My Client?

It can be quite easy for a lawyer to manipulate his client to serve his own interests. For example, many lawyers admit to lowballing their clients in order to set achievable expectations. If the client doesn't expect much, then whatever settlement or deal the lawyer reaches will seem like a victory. Some lawyers may even lie to their clients to look good. For example, if the other side has made an oral offer of $50,000 to settle a client's claim, a lawyer might first tell the client that the other side offered $35,000, and then—days later—tell the client that after strenuous negotiations the other side increased the offer to $50,000.

Lawyers may also exaggerate in order to delay settlement and run up fees. An attorney might exaggerate negative comments made by the other side and try to excite his client into continuing litigation. Or he may twist his assessment of the value of the client's claim and argue that an existing settlement offer is insufficient. The lawyer, in short, may manipulate the client's perceptions for the lawyer's own ends.

Finally, lawyers sometimes withhold information for the opposite reason: to make ending a negotiation easier and quicker. This can be done in the name of serving the client's "real" interests. If a lawyer has spent a great deal of time counseling a stubborn and frustrating client, manipulating information may seem easier than continuing these difficult conversations. But his rationalization can also be merely a pretense for advancing the lawyer's interests at the client's expense.

Obviously, a lawyer should not lie to his clients. And saying the other side offered $35,000 when the offer was $50,000 is a lie that most lawyers would consider outrageous. But these situations are often less about lying per se than about shading the truth and not disclosing information. What do the Model Rules say about these issues? Model Rule 1.4 requires lawyers to keep clients "reasonably informed about the status of a matter and promptly comply with reasonable requests for information." Rule 1.4(b) requires lawyers to explain matters "to the extent necessary to permit the client to make informed decisions regarding the representation." And Comment 1 to Rule 1.4 says that when a *written* offer is obtained, the attorney "should promptly inform the client of its substance unless prior discussions with the client have left it clear that the proposal will be unacceptable."

Most commentators go further and urge attorneys to apply Rule 1.4 to a verbal offer as well. Although the Rule doesn't technically apply, the underlying purpose of Rule 1.4 is to keep a client "reasonably" informed about the progress of her legal matter. An attorney's failure to report back to a client should therefore be considered a violation of professional canons if the lawyer's actions leave the client so in the dark that the client cannot be said to be able to make an informed decision. This includes a failure to transmit a verbal settlement offer or an attempt to manipulate the client's impression of a settlement offer through lowballing or other tricks.

At the same time, it is important to note that the Model Rules leave an attorney a great deal of freedom and flexibility to decide for himself what amount of information-sharing should take place with his client. Even if an attorney must transmit both written and verbal settlement offers, there is information that the attorney may *not* be required to share. For example, the codes do not require an attorney to discuss what happened at the negotiation table, what was said, what strategy or tactics the attorney used, or how the other side reacted. If an attorney employs very aggressive hard-bargaining tactics, for example, and the other side reacts negatively and refuses to continue negotiating, is the attorney under a professional obligation to explain what tactics he used and what the consequences were? Or can the attorney merely advise the client that the other side has refused to continue discussions? The codes seem to suggest that if a client *asks* for such information, the lawyer must provide it. In the absence of a direct request, however, the lawyer might not have a duty to disclose such information to the client.

Nevertheless, attorneys should share such information with their clients, or at least negotiate explicitly with their clients about the kind of information that the client *wants*. Being interest-based and client-centered may require a shift in the lawyer's implicit stance toward the client. But at base, effective lawyering requires that a lawyer see her client as a person with valuable information from which the lawyer can learn, and as a person deserving the opportunity to make an informed choice about his legal affairs. The lawyer's job is to provide the client with the information he needs to make such choices.

Aren't I Supposed to Be a "Zealous Advocate"?

An attorney is supposed to champion the client's cause, and as a consequence, many lawyers claim that a duty of "zealous advocacy" requires them to do everything that isn't clearly forbidden. But this often places lawyers in an uncomfortable position. Because defending a client's interests is paramount, attorneys may fear that adopting any negotiating strategy other than extreme hard bargaining violates a basic duty to their client.

Under the Model Rules, this is nonsense. Rule 1.3 requires "reasonable diligence" on behalf of a client. Comment 1 to Model Rule 1.3 states that "a lawyer should act with commitment and dedication to the interests of the client and with zeal in advocacy upon the client's behalf. However, a lawyer is not bound to press for every advantage that might be realized for a client. A lawyer has professional discretion in determining the means by which a matter should be pursued." This comment suggests that attorneys retain significant flexibility in defining the bounds of zealous representation. The client's interests, conceived broadly, may be better served by a more constrained and reasoned approach to negotiation than by initiating a contest of wills or a war of attrition. So long as the client understands the risks and benefits of a problem-solving stance, there is no inherent contradiction between problem-solving and advocacy. Indeed, sometimes blindly going to war—even if the client insists upon it—may disserve the client's broader interests. As Elihu Root once said, "About half the practice of a decent lawyer consists in telling would-be clients that they are damned fools and should stop."

NOTES AND QUESTIONS

1. Many people believe that they can tell when others are lying. In fact, however, studies have found that most people have a very difficult time detecting others' lies. Analyzing nonverbal cues in the deceiver's behavior produces accurate results 45 to 60 percent of the time—roughly equivalent to tossing a coin. See Vrij, Edward, Roberts and Bull, Detecting Deceit Via Analysis of Verbal and Nonverbal Behavior, 24 J. Nonverbal Behavior 239 (2000); DePaulo, Stone and Lassiter, Deceiving and Detecting Deceit, in The Self and Social Life 323–370 (1985). (Some professionals, including law-enforcement officers and psychologists, have been shown to have better than average abilities in detecting lies. See Ekman, O'Sullivan and Frank, A Few Can Catch A Liar, 10 Am.Psychol. Survey 263 (1999).)

In general, most people assume that a liar's behavior will change during deception. See Anderson, DePaulo, Ansfield, Tickle and Green, Beliefs About Cues To Deception: Mindless Stereotypes or Untapped Wisdom?, 23 J. Nonverbal Behavior 67 (1999). We often assume that a deceptive person will become agitated or nervous, and therefore increase her bodily movements. People predict that a liar will avert her eyes, smile less frequently, and shift positions more frequently. People also associate lying with an increase in speech disturbances (such as "ahs" and "ums") and with changes in voice tone or pitch.

Although speech disturbances do generally occur more frequently during deception, liars generally *decrease* their bodily movements while lying. They tend to move deliberately and rigidly, and decrease the number of nonfunctional movements such as hand or leg movements. See Vrij and Mann, Telling and Detecting Lies in a High-stake Situation: The Case of a Convicted Murderer, 15 Applied Cognitive Psych. 187–203 (2001). Liars are often unaware of these changes, see Vrij, Edward and Bull, People's Insight Into Their Own Behavior and Speech Content While Lying, 92 British J. Psych. 373–389 (2001), and, interestingly, even people who have been told in advance that they are likely to decrease their bodily movements when lying—and who are thus trying to compensate for this tendency in order to avoid detection—often fail to incorporate this information and continue to display rigidity and decreased movement when lying. See Vrij, Semin and Bull, Insight Into Behavior Displayed During Deception, 22 Human Commun. Research 544, 545 (1996).

2. Should you lie in negotiations? The discussion in these various excerpts suggests many reasons not to lie, including economic, reputational, moral, and personal costs of lying. If detected, lying may hurt this negotiation, future negotiations, and your reputation generally.

Intriguingly, however, lying may do damage even if *undetected.* Research suggests that even if you are able to lie without detection, your undetected lie can *still* damage the long-term relationship with the other side. Why? Because an undetected liar often will, over time, begin to believe that his *counterpart*—the other person in relationship with him—is being dishonest. "For example, if a husband has an extramarital affair and does not tell his wife, then he may begin to see her as less honest as a result of his own infidelity. This *deceiver's distrust* could occur through one or a combination of three psychological processes: (a) a false consensus effect, in which the liar infers the level of dishonesty in others from his or her own salient behavior; (b) an ego-protective mechanism, in which the liar defends self-image by coming to believe that anyone would have acted the same way; and (c) a belief in a just world, in which the liar derogates the character of the victim of the deceit to maintain the belief that bad outcomes do not afflict good people." Sagarin, Rhoads and Cialdini, Deceiver's Distrust: Denigration as a Consequence of Undiscovered Deception, 24 Personality & Soc.Psychol.Bull. 1167, 1167 (1998).

3. Because of the gaps and conflicting ethical duties in the ethical codes, a negotiator will often face ethical dilemmas that cannot be resolved merely by consulting professional standards. In such a case, what should you do? Each person's moral code differs, and people may reasonably disagree about what constitutes ethical or unethical behavior. To aid in your personal deliberations, however, we reproduce a list of questions that has long circulated as folk wisdom for determining whether a given action is morally permissible. In reading it, think back to the various hypotheticals in the Longan excerpt and the disciplinary cases in the Crystal excerpt. Would the lawyers in those situations have acted as they did if they subjected their behavior to these various tests?

History

How do I guess that future historians are likely to judge conduct like this?

If, years hence, I myself look back at this conduct am I more likely to be proud or ashamed of it?

Will it be cited to my credit or will I have to defend it?

Philosophy

What are guiding principles of which my proposed action is an application?

Are those principles that I would commend to all?

Law

Is the proposed conduct legal?

Would the comparable conduct be legal within most countries?

Would the conduct be consistent with wise laws as they should be established and interpreted?

Religion

Is the proposed conduct consistent with the teachings of the world's religions?

Would the conduct be seen as an example of how a deeply religious person ought to behave?

Literature

How would I have to behave so that if a novelist or dramatist were basing his writing on this incident I might be the hero of that work?

Is the proposed conduct more like that of literary heroes or literary villains?

Family and Friends

Would I be pleased to learn that my father or mother had behaved as I propose to behave?

Would I be proud to learn that my child had behaved this way?

Would I want my child to use this bit of conduct as a guide for his future actions?

Publicity

If, through no doing of mine, a full account of my proposed conduct appeared on the front page of tomorrow's newspaper, is it more likely that I would be proud or embarrassed?

4. Roger Fisher has suggested that because the legal profession's ethical codes do not sufficiently constrain an attorney's behavior and therefore leave an attorney vulnerable to pressure to ''cheat'' from his or her client, lawyers should begin relations with their clients by laying out their *own* written code of negotiation practice. In a sample letter to a hypothetical client, Fisher suggests explaining the following to a potential client:

I would like to obtain your approval for my accepting this code as providing the general guidelines for any negotiations I may conduct on your behalf. I would also like you to know that I will follow these guidelines in any negotiations that you and I have with each other, for example over the question of fees. * * *

The reason I would like your approval of my following this code in my negotiations as your lawyer is to avoid any future misunderstanding. In addition, I would like to put to rest the canard that because I am a lawyer, I have a ''professional'' duty to you as my client to engage in sharp or deceptive practices on your behalf—practices that I would not use on my own behalf and ones that might damage my credibility or my reputation for integrity. Let me explain.

The Code of Professional Responsibility approved by the American Bar Association provides that a lawyer should advance a client's interest zealously. The Code * * * does little to clarify this standard, and the Bar Association has failed to adopt proposed changes that would more explicitly permit a lawyer to balance the duty to be a partisan on behalf of a client with the duty to adhere to ethical standards of candor and honesty.

The result is that, in the absence of client approval to do otherwise, it can be (and has been) argued that a lawyer should conceal information, bluff, and otherwise mislead people on behalf of a client even: (a) where the lawyer would be unwilling for ethical reasons to do so on his or her own behalf; and (b) where the lawyer's best judgment is that to do so is contrary to the public interest, contrary to wise negotiation practices, and damaging to the very reputation for integrity that may have caused the client to retain the lawyer.

* * *

I believe that it is not a sound practice to negotiate in a way that rewards deception, stubbornness, dirty tricks, and taking risks. I think it wiser * * * to deal with differences in a way that optimizes the chance of reaching a fair outcome efficiently and amicably; that rewards those who are better prepared, more skillful and efficient, and who have the better case as measured by objective standards of fairness; and that makes each successive negotiation likely to be even better. (This does not mean that a negotiator should disclose everything or make unjustified concessions.)

The attached code is intended to accomplish those goals.

Fisher, A Code of Negotiation Practices for Lawyers, 1 Neg.J. 105–110 (1995). Fisher's code then goes on to outline for lawyers their goals for a given negotiation, including to jointly consider the parties' interests, to seek efficient and creative options, to find a fair or legitimate solution, and to act honorably in ways that promote justice and honesty. Others have recommended that law firms fill the gap left by ethical codes. See e.g. Painter, Rules Lawyers Play By, 76 N.Y.U.L.Rev. 665, 732–740 (2001).

Will Fisher's approach work? How will most clients likely react to a lawyer who disseminates such a personal code? What are the advantages of having given a client such explicit guidance about your negotiation approach? The disadvantages?

c. MALPRACTICE

In addition to the constraints imposed by the substantive law and the professional ethics codes, a lawyer must concern herself with the possibility of a post-settlement malpractice action related to her behavior during the negotiation process. In the following excerpt Professor Epstein considers the viability of such actions.

Lynn A. Epstein, Post–Settlement Malpractice: Undoing the Done Deal

46 Cath.U.L.Rev. 453, 453–60 (1997).

Clients voice their approval to mediators and judges as a settlement agreement is reached. A release is signed, the file is closed, and from the lawyer's perspective, another case ends. The settled case joins an overwhelming majority of civil cases that are resolved in pretrial settlement. Buried within this figure, however, is a more troubling statistic: over twenty percent of civil cases will be resurrected in the form of malpractice actions initiated by dissatisfied clients. In those instances, and for various reasons substantiated by expert opinions, the client will charge that they could have received a better result in the settlement even though the client knowingly and willingly agreed to end the case.

In every state except Pennsylvania, a client is permitted to proceed with the theory that his attorney negligently negotiated an agreement despite the fact that the client consented to settlement. In *Muhammad v. Strassburger, McKenna, Messer, Shilobod & Gutnick*, 587 A.2d 1346 (Pa. 1991), the Pennsylvania Supreme Court determined that an attorney is immune from malpractice based on negligence where the client consented to settle. Court decisions after Muhammad, however, have uniformly rejected immunity for the attorney, permitting post-settlement malpractice actions to proceed in the same manner as the prototypical malpractice case.

* * *

I. Muhammad and its Successors

Conventional wisdom dictates that attorneys settle cases effectively, as an estimated ninety-five percent of civil cases are resolved by settlement. Yet, an emerging trend of post-settlement malpractice claims threatens the integrity of the settlement negotiation process. While malpractice actions

246 CHAPTER II NEGOTIATION

are on the rise, most attorneys reasonably believed they were insulated from liability because the client had consented to settlement, and because there was no affirmative wrongdoing by the attorney. Because so many factors influence a client's decision to settle, and because so many individuals, such as judges and mediators, are a part of the process, it would appear fundamentally unfair to hold the attorneys solely responsible for such malpractice claims. This is buttressed by a majority viewpoint which looks unfavorably upon malpractice claims that require the judiciary to infiltrate the negotiation process, a process traditionally viewed as immune from judicial scrutiny.

Balancing these competing interests, the Pennsylvania Supreme Court barred such malpractice actions to foster the negotiation and settlement process. In *Muhammad*, the Pennsylvania Supreme Court held that, absent fraud, an attorney is immune from suit by a former client dissatisfied with a settlement that the former client agreed to enter.

Pamela and Abdullah Muhammad sued the firm of Strassburger, McKenna, Messer, Shilobod and Gutnick for malpractice arising from the settlement of an underlying medical malpractice suit. In the underlying action, the Muhammads sued the physicians and hospital that performed a circumcision on their son who died as a consequence of general anesthesia used during the procedure. The Muhammads retained the Strassburger law firm. The physicians and hospital offered to settle the malpractice claim for $23,000, which was subsequently increased to $26,500 at the suggestion of the trial court. The Muhammads accepted the settlement offer. The Muhammads later grew dissatisfied with the amount received in settlement and instructed the Strassburger law firm to communicate this discontent to defense counsel. An evidentiary hearing ensued where the court upheld the settlement agreement, reasoning that the Muhammads agreed to the settlement amount and, thus, there existed a binding and enforceable contract.

Unable to reopen the medical malpractice proceeding, the Muhammads initiated a claim against the Strassburger law firm alleging legal malpractice, fraudulent misrepresentation, fraudulent concealment, nondisclosure, breach of contract, negligence, emotional distress, and breach of fiduciary duty. The court dismissed the fraud counts because the Muhammads had not pled fraud with specificity. Surprisingly, the court then barred the Muhammads from proceeding with their remaining negligence claim against the Strassburger firm, based on articulated public policy encouraging civil litigation settlement. In granting immunity, the court wrote:

> [W]e foreclose the ability of dissatisfied litigants to agree to a settlement and then file suit against their attorneys in the hope that they will recover additional monies. To permit otherwise results in unfairness to the attorneys who relied on their client's assent and unfairness to the litigants whose cases have not yet been tried. Additionally, it places an unnecessarily arduous burden on an overly taxed court system.

The court emphasized that this immunity extends to specific cases where a plaintiff agreed to settlement in the absence of fraud by the attorney. This is distinguished from the instance when a lawyer knowingly commits malpractice, conceals the wrongdoing, and convinces the client to settle in order to cover-up the malpractice. According to the court, in this instance, the attorney's conduct is fraudulent and actionable.

In a stinging dissent, Justice Larsen lamented that the majority established a "LAWYER'S HOLIDAY" by barring legal malpractice actions for negligence committed in the negotiation of civil case settlements. Contrasting the new declaration of immunity with the liability exposure of other professionals, Justice Larsen reasoned: "If a doctor is negligent in saving a human life, the doctor pays. If a priest is negligent in saving the spirit of a human, the priest pays. But if a lawyer is negligent in advising his client as to settlement, the client pays." *Muhammad* has suffered widespread criticism and is uniformly rejected in every reported opinion reviewing post-settlement legal malpractice litigation.

For example, in *Ziegelheim v. Apollo*, 607 A.2d 1298 (N.J.1992), the New Jersey Supreme Court rejected Muhammad, permitting a client to sue his attorney even though the client agreed to a settlement amount. Apollo represented Miriam Ziegelheim in a divorce action. The only issues litigated at the trial court level were payment of alimony, identification of marital property, and equitable distribution of that property. After reaching an agreement on these issues, both parties testified in open court "that they understood the agreement, that they thought it was fair, and that they entered into it voluntarily."

After consummation of the agreement, Mrs. Ziegelheim sued Apollo for legal malpractice, contending that he failed to discover information about her husband's assets which would have increased the amount she might have received in settlement. The trial court granted summary judgment for Apollo, holding that Mrs. Ziegelheim entered into the settlement agreement voluntarily with every indication that she clearly understood the terms of the agreement. The appellate division affirmed.

The New Jersey Supreme Court reversed, reasoning that the duty to provide reasonable knowledge, skill, and diligence provides the basis for a legal malpractice action even when the client consents to settlement of the underlying civil action. In addition to Zeigelheim's consent, the family court judge's proclamation that the settlement was "fair and equitable" did not preclude the legal malpractice action. The Supreme Court added:

> The fact that a party received a settlement that was "fair and equitable" does not mean necessarily that the party's attorney was competent or that the party would not have received a more favorable settlement had the party's incompetent attorney been competent. Thus, in this case, notwithstanding the family court's decision, Mrs. Ziegelheim still may proceed against Apollo in her negligence action.

The New Jersey Supreme Court tempered its decision by qualifying that it did not intend to "open the door" to legal malpractice suits by every former client who had previously agreed to civil suit settlement. The court cautioned that in order to state this genre of legal malpractice, a former

CHAPTER II NEGOTIATION

dissatisfied client must specify, with particularity, the alleged malpractice. Hence, a general plea by dissatisfied clients who later decide they should have obtained more money in settlement will not be successful. The court also reiterated that an attorney will not be held to an unrealistically infallible standard of securing the maximum outcome in settlement: an attorney's duty remains one of reasonable skill and knowledge.

While most courts are expeditious in determining that an attorney is not absolutely immune from legal malpractice actions when the client consents to settlement, they are also uniform in expressing a desire to foster protection over the negotiation process. In *Prande v. Bell*, 660 A.2d 1055 (Md. Ct. Spec. App. 1995), plaintiff Luisa Prande sued her former attorneys, John T. Bell and Elbert Shore (the Bell firm), alleging they negligently settled claims arising from her motor vehicle personal injury action. The Bell firm represented the plaintiff in two automobile accidents. In the first lawsuit, Prande accepted $7,500 to settle her personal injury suit in which she signed a release. According to the Bell firm, she verbally agreed to settle the second lawsuit for $3,000, but refused to sign the release.

Defendant Wishart then filed a motion to enforce the settlement. The plaintiff's attorney informed Ms. Prande that she should attend the hearing " 'in the event that you seek or wish to contest the matter of whether we had your authorization to accept a settlement.' " Prande failed to appear, and the court granted Wishart's motion, dismissing with prejudice the personal injury lawsuit. Prande then initiated a legal malpractice action against the Bell firm, claiming that it "negligently advised [her] to accept unreasonable and inadequate settlements of her claims." The lower court granted summary judgment for the Bell firm, ruling that the plaintiff merely wished "to relitigate the matters that have already been decided and resolved" by settlement, and concluding that permitting the legal malpractice action to proceed to trial would result in never-ending litigation.

The appellate court reversed, reasoning that when the client voluntarily accepts a settlement, she does not absolve her attorney from liability for negligence committed during settlement negotiation. Rejecting *Muhammad's* hard and fast rule, the court determined that the important public policy of encouraging settlements was outweighed by an attorney's responsibility to advise his client with the same skill, knowledge, and diligence in the negotiation of civil suit settlement as that which an attorney must employ in all other litigation tasks. The court also cautioned, however, that post-settlement malpractice actions involving an attorney's judgment and recommendation whether to settle is not malpractice simply because another attorney would not have recommended settlement. Thus, the court held that to recover, a plaintiff must allege specifically that the attorney's recommendation to settle is one that no reasonable attorney would have made.

Though *Prande* requires a higher standard for alleging malpractice, it focuses solely on the conduct of the attorney. Both *Prande* and *Apollo* ignore the client's role in negotiating civil case settlements, failing to examine the client's reasons for consenting to settlement. While ignoring these important factors, both cases establish guidelines for post-settlement legal malpractice which allow the cause to proceed only if the client alleges specific acts of negligence; typically such allegations are supported by expert testimony. Both courts seek to address the importance of safeguarding the negotiation process in an effort to encourage settlements and discourage clients from seeking redress based on bald assumptions that they should have received more money. * * *

* * *

In review, while other dissatisfied clients alleged they had been unable to comprehend or understand a settlement agreement, it is logical to infer that clients who claim to believe they are entitled to receive more money would have no difficulty "comprehending" the amount of money they did receive. Requiring an attorney to determine whether a client is competent to enter into a settlement agreement when there is no indication otherwise would be tantamount to imposing an unrealistic standard upon the attorney. To anticipate such an unrealistic defense, a properly diligent lawyer would be required to obtain an independent medical evaluation for a client before entering into a settlement agreement or, for that matter, prior to any agreement substantially affecting the course of ongoing litigation. Absent any prior patent evidence of incompetence, a lawyer should not be held to such an unwieldy standard.

NOTES AND QUESTIONS

1. In general, courts have found that a lawyer has both substantive and procedural duties to her client in the settlement process. The procedural duties include the duty to communicate serious settlement offers to the client, the duty to only make settlement offers to the other side with the client's permission, the duty to only accept a settlement offer with the client's consent, and the duty to inform a client of any conflict of interest. In addition, courts have held that an attorney may not use the negotiation process to cover up the lawyer's mistake. In other words, malpractice may be appropriate if a client is forced to accept a lower (or pay a greater) settlement amount because her attorney has encouraged settlement to cover up the attorney's negligence. On the substantive side, as Epstein explains, courts have sometimes found that a lawyer has failed to apply his or her substantive knowledge of the law to the client's case, thereby resulting in a sub-standard settlement agreement. Such malpractice actions are obviously significantly harder to establish. See Baker–Selesky, Negligence in Failing to Settle Lawsuits: Malpractice Actions and Their Defenses, 20 J. Leg. Prof. 191,196–197 (1995–1996).

As Epstein explains, courts have sometimes been reluctant to permit malpractice actions in the settlement context. Is this approach defensible, or is the *Muhammad* rule appropriate? What social policies does each approach promote?

2. Epstein criticizes the propensity for courts to use the likely result at trial as the standard for measuring whether malpractice has occurred. The jury in a malpractice action is asked to evaluate the settlement agreement about which the plaintiff has claimed malpractice. The jury's assessment of the settlement is said to be an objective standard for measuring a fair outcome. Epstein criticizes this ex post evaluation of the case's value, or "trial within a trial," because it ignores the negotiation process and subjective interests in the earlier negotiation. In the article, Epstein explains,

> Courts that apply the "trial within a trial" method to post-settlement malpractice claims typically ignore the fact that the client voluntarily agreed to settle the case, and instead focus on the result that would have occurred had the case gone to the jury. * * * By definition, however, every aspect of a negotiated settlement, particularly its conclusion, is a subjective evaluation premised on the client's needs and desires, coupled with the various influences that affect that client's ultimate decision to settle. * * *

> * * *

> * * * In post-settlement malpractice litigation analysis, courts tend to focus only on the result obtained (the settlement sum) to gauge the lawyer's liability exposure, ignoring the traditional factors preceding settlement. * * *

Epstein, Post–Settlement Malpractice: Undoing the Done Deal, 46 Cath. U.L.Rev. 453, 463–464 (1997).

If the jurors in a malpractice action are not allowed to consider the negotiation process and parties' interests in the prior settlement, how can they objectively weigh a fair outcome? If the prior settlement was an interest-based negotiation in which non-monetary tradeoffs occurred, how could the jury take that into account? For instance, a divorcing spouse may agree to a reduced monetary settlement for sole custody of the children, or for an apology, but in a subsequent malpractice action the jury may not be able to hear about the interest-based tradeoff. Thus, the "trial within a trial" may force a distributive lens on interest-based negotiations.

Epstein suggests that allowing the jury to consider the negotiation process and subjective interests of the parties would allow a jury to see that some settlements that appear one-sided are actually fair. However, there may be problems with this approach. As Epstein notes, courts are reluctant to weigh needs and interests that do not seem to comport with an objective malpractice standard. In addition, judges and legal scholars worry that opening up confidential negotiations to scrutiny will discourage settlement. Further, partisan perceptions and memories will likely cloud what actually happened in the negotiation.

3. To better protect a client's interests and prevent potential malpractice claims, Epstein suggests that attorneys consider the following four factors in settling a client's case:

D. PROFESSIONAL AND LEGAL FRAMEWORK FOR NEGOTIATION   **251**

* * * The *Prande* court, however, does provide minimum guidelines to which an attorney should adhere in advising a client regarding settlement. *Prande* provides that the lawyer should hold an appreciation of 1) the relevant facts; 2) the present and future potential strengths and weaknesses of his case; 3) the likely costs, both objectively (monetarily) and subjectively (psychological disruption of business and family life) associated with proceeding further in the litigation; and 4) the likely outcome if the case were to proceed further.

Epstein, Post–Settlement Malpractice: Undoing the Done Deal, 46 Cath. U.L.Rev. 453, 471 (1997).

In addition to being aware of the *Prande* factors, an attorney can have a client sign a "release and settlement agreement." Epstein suggests the following model release, which incorporates the *Prande* factors into a comprehensive statement of the case:

Pre–Settlement Statement of Client's Case

Before you, the client, decide to enter into a settlement agreement, you should understand your rights concerning this settlement. The purpose of this statement is to provide you with information concerning your case so that you may make an informed decision to settle your case. This statement is not part of the settlement agreement.

A.   Status of Your Case.

1.   The relevant facts of your case are _____.

2.   The following discovery has been conducted _____.

3.   The strengths of your case are _____.

4.   The weaknesses of your case are _____.

5.   The fees and costs of your case to date _____ until trial _____ through trial _____.

6.   The likely verdict of your case at trial is _____.

7.   This figure has been based on _____.

8.   You have offered/been offered _____ to settle your case.

9.   This settlement amount is/is not in the range of settlement figures for cases of your type. This range of settlement figures is based on

_____.

B.   Your Rights Concerning Settlement.

You, the client, have the sole decision whether to accept or reject this settlement. While your attorney may offer you advice as to whether to accept or settle your case, you are not obligated or required to follow your attorney's advice.

DO NOT SIGN THIS AGREEMENT if you do not understand any of the information provided to you in this statement.

Your attorney is required to answer any questions you may have concerning the settlement of your case. If you have any questions which your attorney cannot answer to your satisfaction, you have the right to seek the advice from another attorney of your choice or you may contact the bar association at _____. Signing this document does not waive your right to subsequently file a malpractice action against your attorney unless prohibited by state law. However, your attorney may use this document as a defense in a malpractice action if permitted by law.

Date: _____   Signature of Client _____

Date: _____   Signature of Attorney _____

Epstein, Post–Settlement Malpractice: Undoing the Done Deal, 46 Cath. U.L.Rev. 453, 472–474 (1997).

An attorney can use a signed post-settlement release in a subsequent malpractice action. The document sheds light on aspects of settlement that courts routinely ignore in their attempt to consider only "objective" factors in malpractice actions. Is this a reasonable precaution for attorneys to take? Should it be necessary? What implications does it have for the attorney-client relationship? How might it impact the ways attorneys negotiate on behalf of their clients?

4. A number of commentators have noted the difficulty of proving legal malpractice in negotiated settlements. For instance, Rex Perschbacher observes, "Because it is grounded in tort, a malpractice action requires proof of a duty to the plaintiff, a breach of that duty, causation, and damages. Proving this prima facie case is often burdensome for legal malpractice plaintiffs." Perschbacher, Regulating Lawyers' Negotiations, 27 Ariz.L.Rev. 75, 80–81 (1985).

In *Nicolet Instrument Corp. v. Lindquist & Vennum*, 34 F.3d 453, 455 (7th Cir.1994), Chief Judge Posner said that causation is the biggest obstacle to proving legal malpractice in negotiation:

Proof of causation is often difficult in legal malpractice cases involving representation in litigation—the vast majority of such cases—because it is so difficult, yet vital, to estimate what difference a lawyer's negligence made in the actual outcome of a trial or other adversary proceeding. (citation omitted). How many criminal defendants, required as they are to prove that their lawyer's ineffective assistance prejudiced them, succeed in overturning their convictions on this ground? Proof of causation is even more difficult in a negotiating situation, because while there is (at least we judges like to think there is) a correct outcome to most lawsuits, there is no "correct" outcome to a negotiation. Not only does much depend on the relative bargaining skills of the negotiators, on the likely consequences to each party if the negotiations fall through, and on luck, so that the element of the intangible and the unpredictable looms large; but there is no single "right" outcome in a bargaining situation even in principle. Every point within the range bounded by the lowest offer that one party will accept and the highest offer that the other party will make is a possible

D. Professional and Legal Framework for Negotiation

transaction or settlement point, and none of these points is "correct" or "incorrect."

5. While judgments of legal malpractice in settlement negotiations are rare, they are not unheard of. For example, in *Grayson v. Wofsey, Rosen, Kweskin and Kuriansky*, 231 Conn. 168, 646 A.2d 195 (1994), the Connecticut Supreme Court found a divorce attorney liable for legal malpractice, rejecting Pennsylvania's stringent malpractice standard established in *Muhammad v. Strassburger, McKenna, Messer, Shilobod & Gutnick*, 526 Pa. 541, 587 A.2d 1346 (1991). On the advice of her attorney, Elyn Grayson had agreed to settle a pending divorce suit against her husband. Later she filed a motion to open up the settlement agreement because an affidavit misrepresented the value of her former spouse's assets. The Connecticut Supreme Court affirmed a lower court judgment refusing to open up the settlement agreement.

Ms. Grayson also brought suit against her attorney for legal malpractice for negligently failing to conduct an adequate investigation of her husband's finances and improperly preparing for trial. This time, the Connecticut Supreme Court affirmed a $1.5 million jury verdict. Why would the court allow Ms. Grayson to sue her attorneys but not to open up the settlement agreement? Is the standard for proving legal malpractice easier than the standard for opening up a settlement agreement? The policy of encouraging settlement is undermined both by opening up settlement agreements and by low thresholds for legal malpractice. The *Grayson* court suggests that other policies such as attorney diligence outweigh the policy of encouraging settlement.

In rejecting the *Muhammad* rule, the court said:

> The defendants urge us to adopt a common law rule whereby an attorney may not be held liable for negligently advising a client to enter into a settlement agreement. They argue that, as a matter of public policy, an attorney should not be held accountable for improperly advising a client to settle a case unless that advice is the product of fraudulent or egregious misconduct by the attorney. The defendants contend that the adoption of such a rule is necessary in order to promote settlements, to protect the integrity of stipulated judgments, and to avoid the inevitable flood of litigation that they claim will otherwise result. They claim that such a rule is particularly appropriate if, as here, the court has reviewed and approved the settlement agreement.

> We have long recognized that the pretrial settlement of claims is to be encouraged because, in the vast number of cases, an amicable resolution of the dispute is in the best interests of all concerned. * * *

> We reject the invitation of the defendants, however, to adopt a rule that promotes the finality of settlements and judgments at the expense of a client who, in reasonable reliance on the advice of his or her attorney, agrees to a settlement only to discover that the attorney had failed to exercise the degree of skill and learning required of attorneys

CHAPTER II NEGOTIATION

in the circumstances. * * * Accordingly, like the majority of courts that have addressed this issue, we decline to adopt a rule that insulates attorneys from exposure to malpractice claims arising from their negligence in settled cases if the attorney's conduct has damaged the client.

Furthermore, we do not believe that a different result is required because a judge had approved the settlement of the plaintiff's marital dissolution action. Although in dissolution cases "[t]he presiding judge has the obligation to conduct a searching inquiry to make sure that the settlement agreement is substantively fair and has been knowingly negotiated" the court's inquiry does not serve as a substitute for the diligent investigation and preparation for which counsel is responsible. * * *

d. STABILITY OF SETTLEMENTS

As we have seen, a client's ability to sue her lawyer for settlement-related malpractice is connected to the courts' approach to post-settlement attempts to reopen a negotiated agreement. Often a client turns to malpractice only as a last resort. First, the client may try to revise the original settlement agreement to improve his or her deal. The courts' reluctance to entertain such claims is directly related to the tendency toward malpractice actions in this arena.

Like any contract, parties are free to modify a settlement agreement by mutual consent. If only one party seeks to change the agreement, however, courts are much more reluctant to acquiesce, because the courts favor and seek to promote the private settlement of disputes and resist undermining the stability of settlements. A party's ability to rescind a settlement agreement depends on whether the settlement is entered into as a private contract or as a consent decree. If parties privately agree to settle, the normal contract rules apply. Grounds for rescission include fraud, misrepresentation, mistake, duress or undue influence, incapacity of the parties, unconscionability, or impossibility. A private settlement ordinarily will not be reopened merely to examine the equities of the agreement, to reinvestigate the facts, or because one of the parties is now dissatisfied.[5]

Conversely, judicially approved settlements are easier to modify or rescind. As Larry Kramer notes, "[I]t is generally easier to obtain modification of a consent decree than a contract if circumstances change." For instance, Mnookin and Kornhauser say that in the case of divorce, "A court may at any time during the child's minority reopen and modify the initial decree in light of any subsequent change in circumstances. The parties entirely lack the power to deprive the court of this jurisdiction." However,

---

5. Although the grounds for rescinding agreements are limited, in some cases courts have allowed rescission to achieve just results and to serve public policy aims. For example, the Montana Supreme Court allowed an injured worker to rescind a settlement agreement with the state worker's compensation fund on grounds of unilateral mistake of law and mistake of fact because of confusion regarding a subrogation clause with the state fund. *Brown v. Richard A. Murphy, Inc.*, 261 Mont. 275, 862 P.2d 406 (1993).

Mnookin and Kornhauser observe that if no minor children are involved in the divorce, "In some American states a couple may make its agreement binding and final—i.e., not subject to later modification by a court."[6]

Larry Kramer, Consent Decrees and the Rights of Third Parties

87 Mich.L.Rev. 321, 324–31 (1988).

I. THE NATURE OF CONSENT DECREES

What exactly is a consent decree? Opinions have varied over the years, and there is still no consensus. One view is that a consent decree is merely a private contract between the parties. Another view treats a consent decree as a judgment of the court. The dominant modern view is that a consent decree is a hybrid, with elements of both contract and judgment. This view requires the court to decide whether a particular problem implicates the contract or judgment aspect of a consent decree; once the proper category is identified, the rules applicable to that category are applied.

But a consent decree is neither a contract nor a judgment—and it is both. This whole way of thinking about consent decrees is improper, for it leads courts to focus on outer appearance rather than underlying purpose. A consent decree is what it is: an agreement between the parties to end a lawsuit on mutually acceptable terms which the judge agrees to enforce as a judgment. What is critical is why the parties want judicial assistance and why the court agrees (or should agree) to provide it. If contract or judgment rules apply to consent decrees, it is because the nature of the parties' agreement or the reason for judicial assistance is such that the justification for a particular contract or judgment rule also makes sense for consent decrees. But the fact that consent decrees often resemble contracts or judgments does not mean that this will always by the case. There may be instances in which the appropriate rule for a consent decree is different from both contract and judgment rules.

In order to understand consent decrees properly, then, we need a fuller appreciation of the dynamics of the consent decree process: Why do parties want consent decrees? Why should courts agree to enforce them?

One party files a lawsuit against another. Rather than spend time and money and still risk losing at trial, the parties will usually negotiate a settlement. Negotiating a settlement is like negotiating any agreement against a background of uncertainty. If the plaintiff's minimum offer is less than the defendant's maximum offer, and if excessive second-guessing does not cause the bargaining process to falter, an agreement will be reached and the case will be voluntarily dismissed.

---

6. Mnookin & Kornhauser, Bargaining in the Shadow of the Law: The Case of Divorce, 88 Yale L.J. 950, 954–955 (1979).

In this, the typical settlement, there is no further judicial involvement. The agreement by which the plaintiff agrees to dismiss his lawsuit is an ordinary contract, and it can be enforced, modified or set aside as such.

Sometimes, however, the parties ask the court to enter their settlement as a decree. This has some rather important consequences. If either party fails to live up to the agreement, the other party can obtain contempt sanctions without having to file an independent lawsuit on the contract. This allows the party seeking enforcement to avoid some of the expense of a separate lawsuit. Perhaps more importantly, it enables the party seeking enforcement to avoid the court's docket queue and obtain sanctions more quickly than if a new lawsuit had to be filed. In addition, if the settlement is entered as a decree, the court may provide additional assistance (like appointing a monitor to oversee implementation) and will interpret the decree to help the parties resolve disputes before they reach the point of formal litigation.

It is easy, in light of these benefits, to see why a plaintiff might prefer a consent decree to a private contract. By speeding up the process and lowering the cost of enforcement, consent decrees enhance the plaintiff's ability to hold the defendant to his bargain. Indeed, the benefits of a consent decree are often indispensable to plaintiffs in public law or institutional reform litigation. The plaintiffs in these cases are frequently short on resources; they are typically represented by pro bono counsel or by counsel financed through government legal aid; often the class is unorganized and each member has only a small stake in the outcome. In addition, settlements providing for the installation of pollution control devices, the implementation of affirmative action, or the construction of new facilities to house prisoners or mental health patients can be extremely complicated. The parties often anticipate taking years to fulfill the agreement. Moreover, as the agreement grows more complex, it becomes increasingly likely that there will be disputes over its interpretation. Consequently, the availability of a consent decree may make a significant difference in the willingness of the plaintiff to settle.

The defendant's reasons for agreeing to a consent decree are somewhat different. Except in rare instances, the plaintiff's side of the bargain is simply to drop the lawsuit, and the defendant does not need a device to facilitate enforcement. Indeed, if anything, such devices are to the defendant's disadvantage. But the reduced expense of resolving disputes in the implementation phase is advantageous to the defendant as well as the plaintiff. Moreover, it is generally easier to obtain modification of a consent decree than a contract if circumstances change. Most importantly, if the plaintiff wants a consent decree badly enough, the defendant can obtain additional bargaining concessions in return.

But why should the court enter a consent decree? The answer, already suggested by the analysis above, is that making consent decrees available facilitates the settlement of difficult cases that might otherwise go to trial, furthering the strongly held policy favoring settlement over litigation. The reasons for this policy are well known. Settlement is more efficient for the parties, giving them more of what they hoped to gain at less cost. More importantly, settlement allows already overburdened judges to devote time to cases that are not settled voluntarily.

* * *

[A] consent decree is interpreted like a contract. According to the Supreme Court, this is because a consent decree is negotiated like a contract. But the terms of an ordinary judgment are often negotiated by the parties after liability has been determined through litigation, and the Court has never suggested that a litigated decree should be interpreted like a contract. Rather, the reason it makes sense to interpret a consent decree like a contract is that a consent decree represents only what the parties have agreed to do, and the court's participation in enforcing the decree is simply a means of encouraging the parties to make such agreements. The policy protecting justified party expectations that underlies contract law is thus fully applicable. With a litigated decree, by contrast, judicial participation is compelled by one party's invocation of right under substantive law. The court must therefore interpret the decree in light of what the substantive law requires to remedy a proven violation.

But contract law will not always be appropriate for consent decrees, and the court's participation may sometimes require the development of special procedures. For instance, in *Local 93, International Association of Firefighters v. City of Cleveland*, 478 U.S. 501 (1986), the Supreme Court held that a court cannot approve a consent decree unless it (1) determines that the consent decree "springs from and serves to resolve a dispute within the court's subject-matter jurisdiction"; (2) ensures that the consent decree comes "within the general scope of the case made by the pleadings"; and (3) satisfies itself that the consent decree "furthers the objectives of the law upon which the complaint was based." The exact reason for these requirements has puzzled some commentators, but they follow naturally from an understanding of consent decrees as a method of facilitating settlement by making judicial resources available, under certain circumstances, to help the parties enforce their agreement. The court is not "a recorder of contracts" from whom parties can freely purchase injunctions. The court only agrees to "record" and enforce a particular kind of contract: one that saves judicial resources by settling a lawsuit. The requirements for approval set forth in *Local 93* help insure that only such contracts are entered as consent decrees.

Moreover, the court is concerned with other interests in addition to facilitating settlement, and the pursuit or protection of these interests may impose limits on the consent decree device. Consider, for example, the question of modifying a consent decree over the objection of one of the parties. One might extend the argument for interpreting consent decrees according to principles of contract law to modification. But the Supreme Court held contract law inapplicable to consent decree modification in *United States v. Swift & Co.*, 286 U.S. 106 (1932). The Court explained that a consent decree is a "judicial act," an unsatisfying explanation made even more so by the fact that the Court articulated a test for modifying a

CHAPTER II NEGOTIATION

consent decree that is stricter than the test for modifying judgments entered after litigation. How, then, does one explain the rules governing consent decree modification?

An argument can be made that entering the parties' agreement as a judgment associates the court with a consent decree in a way that is not true of ordinary contracts. This, in turn, gives the court an institutional stake in the consent decree beyond protecting the parties' expectations, and justifies retaining additional power to modify the decree if, in the words of Justice Cardozo, the court is "satisfied that what it has been doing has been turned through changing circumstances into an instrument of wrong."

The hard question is deciding how broad this power should be. The *Swift* Court apparently thought that a narrow power would suffice. Courts today are often willing to modify consent decrees on a less stringent showing. I do not address this issue here. My point is simply to illustrate that beyond the question of whether a particular rule facilitates settlement lies the additional question of whether further adjustments are necessary because of the court's involvement in the enforcement process.

NOTES AND QUESTIONS

1. Formerly, consent decrees, sometimes referred to as "confession of judgments," were used primarily in antitrust cases. In recent years, the consent decree has been used in a wide range of cases. Consent decrees have been used to achieve broad institutional reforms such as school desegregation, environmental regulation and housing reform. See Note, The Modification of Consent Decrees in Institutional Reform Litigation, 99 Harv.L.Rev. 1020, 1020–21 (1986). In an effort to clear clogged dockets, courts have also increasingly filed consent decrees in lawsuits between private parties. Further, courts are often responsible for approving divorce settlements, a legal proceeding resembling a consent decree. See generally Mnookin and Kornhauser, Bargaining in the Shadow of the Law: The Case of Divorce 88 Yale L.J. 950, 954–55 (1979). Thus, judicially approved settlements are a common feature of the legal system.

2. Whether consent decrees in civil rights and institutional reform cases can bind similarly situated non-parties is an issue of much controversy. This is an important consideration for counsel in deciding whether to negotiate a consent decree, rather than going to trial. In Martin v. Wilks, 490 U.S. 755, 109 S.Ct. 2180, 104 L.Ed.2d 835 (1989), white firefighters were allowed to make a collateral attack on a consent decree entered in a suit brought by seven black firefighters that established goals for hiring blacks. The Court stated: "A judgment or decree among parties to a lawsuit resolves issues as among them, but it does not conclude the rights of strangers to those proceedings." Although there was no evidence that the settlement was collusive, any consent decree raises concerns that parties may sacrifice the interests of others in reaching a compromise settlement. See Laycock, Consent Decrees Without Consent: The Rights of Nonconsenting Third Parties, 1987 U.Chi.L. Forum 103. The Civil Rights Act of 1991, 42 U.S.C.A. § 2000e–2(n)(1), provides that "an employment practice that implements and is within the scope of a litigated or consent judgment or order that resolves a claim of employment discrimination under the Constitution or Federal civil rights laws may not be challenged" by a person who had actual notice of the proposed judgment sufficient to apprise him that it might adversely affect him or who was adequately represented by another person who had previously challenged the judgment.

3. Why should the consent decree be interpreted like a contract generally but like a judicial act when parties request modification? Courts encourage freely negotiated private settlements, yet they are more willing to actively administer agreements on which they put their seal of approval. Contract law encourages market activity through the freedom to contract. Similarly, courts encourage parties to craft their own negotiated settlements. In most cases, parties assume the risks of changing circumstances in private contracts. Thus, parties are normally responsible for evaluating exchanges and risks. A bad bargain or a foreseeable risk, therefore, will normally not allow for contract modification. However, when a court gets involved in the contracting process by accepting a consent decree, it often assumes the responsibility of ensuring that a bargain is at least nominally fair. For instance, a negotiated divorce settlement often must be judged to be fair or at least not unconscionable before a court will approve it. See Mnookin and Kornhauser, Bargaining in the Shadow of the Law: The Case of Divorce 88 Yale L.J. 950, 954 n. 15 (1979). If circumstances change to the detriment of one party, the court will be more likely to provide relief.

4. Andrew Kull argues that the availability of rescission as a remedy in settlement agreements has an important consequence in settlement negotiations. Rescission acts as a powerful deterrent against breach of the settlement agreement at the same time that it promotes opportunistic behavior:

> Let us assume (i) a breach by the defendant giving rise to a right of rescission on the part of the plaintiff, (ii) the absence of any broader relationship that would constrain the parties in their post-breach behavior, and (iii) mutual recognition that the cost of rescission to the defendant would exceed the harm to the plaintiff from the defendant's breach. Such circumstances, which are not particularly rare, make an opportunistic threat of rescission an implicit part of any settlement negotiations. Indeed, the practical consequences of a rescission alternative will predominantly be realized, not through the infrequent judicial decrees granting rescission and restitution, but in terms of enhanced settlement leverage for those plaintiffs for whom rescission is a credible option.

Kull, Restitution as a Remedy for Breach of Contract, 67 S.Cal.L.Rev. 1465, 1512–14 (1994).

e. JUDICIAL SANCTIONS

In addition to the threat of malpractice and the possibility of a settlement agreement unraveling after completion, parties and their attorneys must take into account the threat of judicial sanctions for improper litigation conduct. Judicial sanctions are available in a federal court under 28 U.S.C.A. § 1927, which permits sanctions for "multipl[ying] the proceedings in any case unreasonably and vexatiously." The discovery rules were amended in 1980 to provide for sanctions for failure to cooperate in discovery.[7] In 1983, Federal Rule of Civil Procedure Rule 11 was amended to provide broad new sanctions for a variety of litigation conduct. The risk of these sanctions constitutes a check on excessively adversarial behavior. This rule, amended again in 1993, sets forth the following requirements for representations made to a court:

Representations to Court. By presenting to the court (whether by signing, filing, submitting, or later advocating) a pleading, written motion, or other paper, an attorney or unrepresented party is certifying that to the best of the person's knowledge, information, and belief, formed after an inquiry reasonable under the circumstances,

(1) it is not being presented for any improper purpose, such as to harass or to cause unnecessary delay or needless increase in the cost of litigation;

(2) the claims, defenses, and other legal contentions therein are warranted by existing law or by a nonfrivolous[8] argument for the extension, modification, or reversal of existing law or the establishment of new law;

(3) the allegations and other factual contentions have evidentiary support or, if specifically so identified, are likely to have evidentiary support after a reasonable opportunity for further investigation or discovery; and

(4) the denials of factual contentions are warranted on the evidence or, if specifically so identified, are reasonably based on a lack of information or belief.

Several 1993 changes to Rule 11 softened the Rule's impact. First, the 1993 version of Rule 11 creates a "safe harbor" by requiring that a Rule 11 motion be served separately from other papers and that the served party be given twenty-one days to withdraw the challenged statement or submission. In other words, a lawyer or client can avoid sanctions by withdrawing any questionable representation to the court. Second, the 1993 amendments were intended to incent litigants to file Rule 11 motions quickly after an alleged violation, rather than waiting until after final judgment to raise Rule 11 issues. If a litigant delays in raising Rule 11 issues, they may be

---

7. Fed.R.Civ.Proc. 37(b)(2).

8. The 1983 version of Rule 11 required that such arguments be in "good faith," a standard that seemed overly subjective and was thus replaced in 1993 with the word "nonfrivolous."

D. Professional and Legal Framework for Negotiation — 261

found untimely.[9] Third, the 1993 amendments were clearly intended to make Rule 11 a tool to deter improper litigation conduct, not to compensate the alleged victim of that conduct.[10] Fourth, the amended rule permits factual assertions that are "likely to have evidentiary support after a reasonable opportunity for further investigation or discovery" or denials that are "reasonably based on a lack of information or belief." These "reasonable ignorance" provisions permit attorneys to pursue a case (or defend it) despite incomplete factual information about the issue at hand.

In the following case the court applies the 1993 version of Rule 11 to a litigant and his lawyer, ultimately holding that neither should be sanctioned under the Rule. What effects will this holding have on the negotiation behavior—and the lawyer-client relationships—of litigants?

Hadges & Kunstler v. Yonkers Racing Corp.

United States Court of Appeals, Second Circuit, 1995.
48 F.3d 1320.

■ Before Feinberg, Kearse and Altimari, Circuit Judges.

■ Feinberg, Circuit Judge:

[The Plaintiff George Hadges had filed various actions against defendant Yonkers Racing Corp. (YRC) for its alleged unfair refusal to permit him to pursue his career as a harness racehorse driver, trainer and owner. In 1989, the New York State Racing and Wagering Board had suspended Hadges's racing license for six months after determining that he had illegally passed wagering information to a member of the betting public at a race. Although the Racing Board then reissued his license, YRC denied him the right to work at the Yonkers racetrack. The district court granted summary judgment for YRC in 1990 (Hadges I). In 1992, Hadges began another suit against YRC in New York state court, but lost on all claims. He then appealed that decision. In 1993 he brought a § 1983 action in federal district court against the Meadowlands racetrack, alleging that the Meadowlands had barred him because of YRC's ban. He settled that suit. With a state court appeal pending regarding the New York state court suit, Hadges then brought a Rule 60(b) action in federal court in New York seeking to vacate Hadges I. He alleged that YRC had perpetrated fraud on the court by claiming that Hadges could continue to work at other tracks despite the YRC ban—which Hadges claimed was false. The district court ruled against Hadges and granted summary judgment for YRC. The district court also imposed sanctions under Rule 11 against Hadges and his lawyer Kunstler.]

B.   Facts underlying Rule 11 sanctions

In support of his claim for relief in the Rule 60(b) action, Hadges submitted a sworn statement that 1993 was his "fifth year . . . out of work,

9. See Ridder v. City of Springfield, 109 F.3d 288, 295 (6th Cir.1997).

10. See Advisory Committee Notes to the 1993 Amendments.

with the boycott by Yonkers still in effect." In addition, he stated that "there was a secret agreement among all of the racetracks, that barring a licensee from one, will result in his being barred from all." Plaintiff's memorandum of law, signed by Kunstler, also asserted that Hadges "has not worked for more than four years." Hadges claimed that he had applied to race at other tracks in New York State, but that these tracks refused to act upon the applications, thereby barring him from racing. He also asserted that upon the advice of a former attorney, Joseph A. Faraldo, he had written to the general managers of these tracks to apply for driving privileges in mid–1990 but received no reply. Hadges presented the court with an affidavit of Faraldo stating that Faraldo had so advised Hadges.

In response, YRC produced documents revealing that Hadges had in fact raced at Monticello Raceway five times in 1991 and seven times in 1993. The most recent race took place less than one month before Hadges submitted his affidavit stating that he had been banned from racing by all tracks in New York State for more than four years. YRC also submitted letters of current and former Racing Secretaries from race tracks in Saratoga, Batavia Downs, Fairmount Park, Vernon Downs and Buffalo who asserted that Hadges had not applied (or they had no recollection of his having applied) for racing privileges at their respective tracks in the relevant time period.

In a memorandum of law and notice of motion to dismiss the Rule 60(b) action, YRC requested that the court impose sanctions on Hadges and, if warranted, on his counsel for this misrepresentation and for failing to disclose the state court action to the district court. This method of requesting Rule 11 sanctions was, as set forth below, contrary to the procedural requirements of Rule 11 that took effect on December 1, 1993, five days before Hadges filed his complaint in the Rule 60(b) action and 15 days before YRC requested sanctions.

After YRC requested sanctions, Hadges submitted an affidavit dated December 28, 1993, admitting that he had raced in Monticello in 1991 and 1993, but explaining that he considered the races insignificant because he had earned less than $100 in the two years combined. That affidavit also described a so-called "scratching incident" that Hadges claimed had taken place at Yonkers Raceway on October 31, 1989. He stated that although his state racing license had been restored in 1989, New York State Racing Board judges "scratched" him from that race, in which he was to have ridden the horse "Me Gotta Bret." After this scratching incident, YRC informed him of its independent ban. Hadges argued to the district court that this sequence of events supported his theory that YRC was acting as a state agent in banning him and thus could be held liable in a § 1983 action. Hadges submitted to the court a "scratch sheet," purporting to document his version of the event.

YRC then submitted what the district court later described as "overwhelming proof" that the scratch sheet did not refer to an October 1989 race, but rather to a November 1987 race.

In its decision on the merits of the Rule 60(b) action, the district court found that Hadges had raced at Monticello in 1991 and 1993 but that he had made only a "minimal" amount of money. 845 F. Supp. at 1041. It also found that the legal basis for Hadges's Rule 60(b) action was not "so frivolous as to warrant Rule 11 sanctions." Id. However, the court was "quite concerned" that Hadges and Kunstler had attempted "to indicate that [Hadges] had not raced in four years when, in fact, he had privileges at Monticello in both 1991 and 1993." Id. The court stated that Hadges had "made matters worse by attempting to strengthen his claim of state involvement alleging that he was scratched from driving Me Gotta Bret on October 31, 1989 by the judges of the racing board." Id. The court further found that submission of the undated scratch sheet was a "flagrant misrepresentation ... suggesting the need for sanctions, certainly against the plaintiff and possibly against his counsel." Id. The judge invited Hadges and Kunstler to submit papers opposing the imposition of sanctions. The court did not refer to the nondisclosure of the state court action as a possible basis for sanctions.

Thereafter, Hadges submitted an affidavit admitting that he had made a misstatement about the scratching incident but expressing his objection to sanctions. He stated that this error was the result of a simple memory loss, and that the scratch sheet involved was bona fide proof of his having been scratched in 1987 rather than in 1989. He went on to describe yet another 1989 incident in which he had been scratched from racing the horse "Dazzling GT" at YRC. Hadges also submitted an affidavit of his then-assistant Erik Schulman, which also described the 1989 Dazzling GT scratching incident. Further, Hadges repeated that he had written to the General Managers (not the Racing Secretaries relied upon by YRC) of the various tracks to request driving privileges but had received no reply. He attached copies of the letters along with copies of postal receipts.

Kunstler also submitted a sworn response, which stated that he "had no idea" that the scratch sheet was from 1987 rather than 1989, and set forth the facts of the Dazzling GT incident. Kunstler maintained that the error regarding the date of the scratch sheet was unintentional but would not have affected the outcome of the case in any event. Regardless of its date, he argued, the scratch sheet was evidence that YRC was acting as an agent of the state Racing Board and could therefore be held liable in a § 1983 action. Thus, he maintained that submission of the document was not sanctionable. Kunstler's affidavit did not describe the efforts he had undertaken to verify his client's factual claims. YRC then submitted further affidavits stating that it had no records concerning the alleged Dazzling GT incident.

Thereafter, in the second ruling on appeal to us, the judge imposed a Rule 11 sanction of $2,000 on Hadges as an appropriate sanction for his misrepresentations. The judge also censured Kunstler under Rule 11 for failing to make adequate inquiry as to the truth of Hadges's affidavits and for failing to inform the court of the pending state court litigation. In the course of his opinion, the judge stated:

264   CHAPTER II NEGOTIATION

Mr. Kunstler is apparently one of those attorneys who believes that his sole obligation is to his client and that he has no obligations to the court or to the processes of justice. Unfortunately, he is not alone in this approach to the practice of law, which may be one reason why the legal profession is held in such low esteem by the public at this time.

Kunstler responded in a letter to the court, in which he argued that the court erred in sanctioning his client $2,000 and in censuring him. In particular, he objected to the court's characterization of him as an attorney "who believes that his sole obligation is to his client," and he objected to the court's charge that his approach to law practice was in part responsible for the low public esteem for the legal profession. Kunstler went on to state his opinion that the court's comment was "generated by an animus toward activist practitioners who, like myself, have, over the years, vigorously represented clients wholly disfavored by the establishment."

* * *

This appeal from the judgment for YRC in the Rule 60(b) action and from the two April 1994 rulings on sanctions followed.

II.   Discussion

* * *

B.   Rule 11 sanctions

As we have already noted, not only did the district court rule against Hadges regarding his claims of fraud on the court in Hadges I, but it went on to impose Rule 11 sanctions on both Hadges and Kunstler for their own misrepresentations and omissions. This determination was based on two principal grounds: (1) misstatement of the date of the alleged "scratching" incident and (2) misstatement regarding Hadges's lack of work in the years since the YRC ban. In addition, the court based Kunstler's censure on his failure to inform the court of the state court action. The court also found that Hadges's sanction was justified in part by the disqualification motion, referred to in note 2 above, which the court characterized as "bizarre." Hadges and Kunstler argue that the district court abused its discretion in imposing the Rule 11 sanctions.

As noted above, an amended version of Fed.R.Civ.P. 11 came into effect on December 1, 1993, five days before Hadges filed his complaint in the Rule 60(b) action in the district court.

* * *

1.   Hadges's sanction

Hadges argues that the district court abused its discretion in imposing sanctions on him. YRC argues that the sanctions were justified. We believe that Hadges is correct.

In imposing sanctions, the district court apparently did not take into account YRC's failure to comply with the revised procedural requirements of Rule 11. In this case, YRC did not submit the sanction request separately from all other requests, and there is no evidence in the record indicating that YRC served Hadges with the request for sanctions 21 days before presenting it to the court. Thus, YRC denied Hadges the "safe-harbor" period that the current version of the Rule specifically mandates. See advisory committee note to 1993 amendment * * *

If Hadges had received the benefit of the safe-harbor period, the record indicates that he would have "withdrawn or appropriately corrected" his misstatements, thus avoiding sanctions altogether. Hadges did in fact correct one of his misstatements by admitting in an affidavit, sworn to on December 28, 1993, just 12 days after YRC asked for sanctions, that he had raced at Monticello in 1991 and 1993. Thus, this misstatement is not sanctionable.

Hadges also explained and corrected his misstatement about the 1989 date of the first scratching incident and described another scratching incident in 1989 involving another horse (Dazzling GT). This correction was supported by his own affidavit sworn to on March 17, 1994, and the affidavit of Erik Schulman, sworn to on March 16, 1994. Both were filed with the district court on March 21, 1994, just one week after the court issued its order stating that it was considering imposition of sanctions. Apparently, YRC had not previously requested sanctions on the basis of the scratching incident. Although YRC subsequently questioned whether the Dazzling GT incident described by Hadges and Schulman had taken place, the district court did not rely on this as a basis for imposing sanctions. We note that Kunstler also filed an affidavit making similar retractions.

In addition to sanctioning Hadges for his factual misrepresentations, the district court ruled that sanctions were justified in part by the disqualification motion filed on Hadges's behalf. See note 2 above. In relying on the latter ground, the court imposed monetary sanctions on a represented party for making a legal contention that the court believed was not warranted by existing law or by a nonfrivolous argument for a change in existing law. Revised Rule 11 specifically prohibits imposition of monetary sanctions on the party on this basis. Fed.R.Civ.P. 11(b)(2) & 11(c)(2)(A).

Rule 11 also provides that a court may impose sanctions on its own initiative. Fed.R.Civ.P. 11(c)(1)(B). If a court wishes to exercise its discretion to impose sanctions sua sponte, it must "enter an order describing the specific conduct that appears to violate subdivision (b) and directing an attorney, law firm, or party to show cause why it has not violated subdivision (b) with respect thereto." Id. In this case, the court indicated that it was imposing sanctions in response to YRC's request and did not state that it was imposing sanctions on Hadges sua sponte. We doubt that sua sponte sanctions would have been justified here. The advisory committee note on the 1993 amendment specifically states that such sanctions "will ordinarily be [imposed] only in situations that are akin to a contempt of court." Hadges's conduct did not rise to that level.

266 CHAPTER II Negotiation

Thus, under all the circumstances, particularly the failure to afford Hadges the 21–day safe-harbor period provided by revised Rule 11, we believe that the sanction of Hadges should be reversed.

2. Kunstler's censure

Like Hadges, Kunstler did not receive the benefit of the safe-harbor period. The district court imposed sanctions on Kunstler for failing to adequately investigate the truth of Hadges's representations prior to submitting them to the court and for failing to disclose that Hadges had brought an action against YRC in New York state court. Kunstler argues that the court's censure of him was an abuse of discretion because the court was motivated by a personal or political animus against him and because his conduct was not sufficiently egregious to justify imposition of sanctions.

In our decisions concerning the former version of Rule 11 we have had occasion to address the reasonableness of an attorney's reliance on information provided by a client. In Kamen v. American Tel. & Tel. Co., 791 F.2d 1006 (2d Cir.1986), the plaintiff brought suit against her employer and supervisors under the Rehabilitation Act of 1973 and state law. Employers are not liable under the Rehabilitation Act unless they receive "federal financial assistance." 29 U.S.C. § 794. The employer sent letters to the plaintiff's attorney asserting that it did not receive federal financial assistance, but her attorney persisted in prosecuting the Rehabilitation Act suit. The district court agreed with the employer and dismissed the claims. Although plaintiff's attorney had submitted an affirmation stating that his client had advised him that the employer received federal grants, the district court imposed sanctions. We found that the district court abused its discretion because the attorney's reliance on his client's statements was reasonable. Kamen, 791 F.2d at 1007–12.

A few years later, we relied on Kamen in holding that "an attorney is entitled to rely on his or her client's statements as to factual claims when those statements are objectively reasonable." Calloway v. Marvel Entertainment Group, 854 F.2d 1452, 1470 (2d Cir.1988), rev'd in part on other grounds sub nom. Pavelic & LeFlore v. Marvel Entertainment Group, 493 U.S. 120, 107 L. Ed. 2d 438, 110 S. Ct. 456 (1989). This interpretation is in keeping with the advisory committee notes on former Rule 11, which indicates that the reasonableness of an inquiry depends upon the surrounding circumstances, including

> such factors as how much time for investigation was available to the signer; whether he had to rely on a client for information as to the facts underlying the pleading . . .; or whether he depended on forwarding counsel or another member of the bar.

Advisory committee note on 1983 amendment to Fed.R.Civ.P. 11.

In Calloway, at least one of the plaintiff's claims "was never supported by any evidence at any stage of the proceeding," and we affirmed the district court's imposition of sanctions. Calloway, 854 F.2d at 1470 & 1473.

D. Professional and Legal Framework for Negotiation

However, we went on to set forth a procedure for district courts to follow in analyzing whether an attorney has conducted a reasonable inquiry into the facts underlying a party's position.

> In considering sanctions regarding a factual claim, the initial focus of the district court should be on whether an objectively reasonable evidentiary basis for the claim was demonstrated in pretrial proceedings or at trial. Where such a basis was shown, no inquiry into the adequacy of the attorney's pre-filing investigation is necessary.

Id. at 1470.

The new version of Rule 11 makes it even clearer that an attorney is entitled to rely on the objectively reasonable representations of the client. No longer are attorneys required to certify that their representations are "well grounded in fact." Fed.R.Civ.P. 11 (1983) amended 1993. The current version of the Rule requires only that an attorney conduct "an inquiry reasonable under the circumstances" into whether "factual contentions have evidentiary support." Fed.R.Civ.P. 11(b) & (b)(3). Thus, the new version of Rule 11 is in keeping with the emphasis in Calloway on looking to the record before imposing sanctions.

In its first sanction decision in April 1994, the district court here stated:

> With respect to plaintiff's counsel, William M. Kunstler, the situation is not quite as clear. There is nothing to indicate that, on the serious factual misrepresentations made in plaintiff's papers, Mr. Kunstler had independent knowledge of their falsity. However, it is equally clear that he made no attempt to verify the truth of the plaintiff's representations prior to submitting them to the court.

Apparently, the district court did not focus, as Rule 11 now requires, on whether the pretrial proceedings provided "evidentiary support" for the factual misrepresentations with which the court was concerned.

It is clear that the record before the district court contained evidentiary support for Kunstler's incorrect statements. As to the scratching incident, the record included a sworn statement by Hadges describing an October 1989 incident in which he claimed to have been scratched from driving the horse "Me Gotta Bret." A scratch sheet, which did not reveal the year in which it was made out, was also part of the record. Kunstler later submitted an affidavit admitting the error and stating that he had no idea that the 1989 date was wrong. He further maintained that regardless of its date, the scratch sheet was relevant to show collaboration between the Racing Board and YRC in 1987, which would subject the latter to § 1983 liability. Moreover, it appears to be undisputed that most of the evidence YRC produced to persuade the court that the event had taken place in 1987 was within its possession, not Hadges's. See Kamen, 791 F.2d at 1012 (noting reasonableness of relying on client representations where "the relevant information [is] largely in the control of the defendants").

We also believe that the record contained evidentiary support for the claim that Hadges had not worked for four years. At the time the district court granted YRC summary judgment in Hadges's 60(b) action, it had before it Hadges's affidavit asserting that he had written to racetrack General Managers asking for driving privileges and had not received any replies. The record also contained attorney Faraldo's affidavit asserting that Hadges had followed his advice in writing these letters. Moreover, Kunstler represented Hadges in the Meadowlands suit in which Meadowlands admitted banning Hadges based upon the YRC ban. We believe that in light of his familiarity with the Meadowlands litigation and the sworn statements of his client and another attorney, Kunstler had sufficient evidence to support a belief that Hadges had not participated in harness horseracing in New York since the YRC ban. * * *

The district court also believed that censure of Kunstler was justified because "he had to be aware of the recent state court litigation, still on appeal, but made no mention of it in his initial papers." Kunstler concedes that he was aware of this litigation but maintains that he did not believe that it was necessary to bring the proceedings to the court's attention because the New York Supreme Court had not ruled on the merits of the state law blackballing claim. As noted above, we agree with the view that the state court opinion was not a decision on the merits of that issue. Even if it were, there would be no tactical advantage in not mentioning the state court ruling to the district court since YRC was a party to both actions (indeed, it was represented by the same law firm and the same attorney in both actions) and could be expected to inform the district court of the state court action if it were helpful.

Moreover, the portion of the court's opinion in the Rule 60(b) action that listed the possible bases for imposition of sanctions omitted any reference to Kunstler's nondisclosure of the state court action. Rule 11 specifically requires that those facing sanctions receive adequate notice and the opportunity to respond. See Fed.R.Civ.P. 11(c)(1)(A) & (B). Although YRC had requested sanctions on this ground, as discussed above, that request was procedurally improper. Thus, although Kunstler would have been wiser to alert the court to the state court proceedings, the nondisclosure was not a proper ground for sanctioning him.

YRC maintains that sanctions were justified because the motions to reargue and to disqualify the district court judge were frivolous. As noted above, the court referred to the disqualification motion as a reason for sanctioning Hadges. However, the court did not rely upon it as a ground for the censure of Kunstler, and we decline to do so here.

Finally, the remarks of the district court, which we have quoted in substantial part above, contribute to our conclusion that the sanction of Kunstler was unjustified. These remarks have the appearance of a personal attack against Kunstler, and perhaps more broadly, against activist attorneys who represent unpopular clients or causes. We find the court's criticism of Kunstler's law partner, Ronald L. Kuby, for his activities in another case, especially unwarranted. For all these reasons, we reverse the imposition of the sanction of censure on Kunstler.

III. Conclusion

We have considered all of the parties' remaining arguments and find that they are without merit.

We affirm the ruling of the district court denying Rule 60(b) relief. We reverse the Rule 11 sanction of Hadges and the censure of Kunstler.

NOTES AND QUESTIONS

1. How should the possibility of sanctions affect negotiations between parties? Should a party who believes his opponent's case is based on a frivolous claim or defense raise the possibility of sanctions as a means of getting a more favorable settlement? Would a party's willingness to talk settlement indicate that the opponent's case really isn't frivolous? Would an actual offer of settlement so indicate?

2. In applying the 1993 version of Rule 11, the *Hadges* court ultimately rejects sanctions against both the plaintiff and his lawyer on procedural grounds. In other words, both were saved by the safe harbor provision created in 1993 and by the diminished requirements regarding investigation of factual assertions. Is this justified? Given the extensive (and perhaps excessive) litigation waged by Mr. Hadges and the numerous seemingly unsupported assertions he made to the court, should the court have been able to use Rule 11 in this instance? Should the court have sanctioned him using 28 U.S.C.A. § 1927, which permits sanctions for "multipl[ying] the proceedings in any case unreasonably and vexatiously"?

What effects will the *Hadges* opinion have on lawyer-client relationships? What assumptions does the court make about how lawyers and clients should prepare for litigation or negotiation?

3. Rule 11 has been interpreted as imposing an objective standard for frivolousness. Does that mean that any party who loses a suit is a likely candidate for imposition of sanctions? Does this discourage parties from seeking redress when the present law seems to be against them or where the potential witnesses are biased in favor of their opponent?

4. Is there a way to factor in a value for the possibility of Rule 11 sanctions in determining the settlement value of a case? What considerations would go into determining the size of that discount? How should a lawyer factor the possibility of sanctions into a decision tree?

5. The federal rules were also amended in 1983 to encourage use of sanctions for violation of the discovery rules. One of the reasons was a feeling that lawyers would not seek, and judges would not award, sanctions. A federal district judge commented: "A lawyer who wants the option to abuse discovery when it is to his client's advantage will hesitate to seek sanctions when his client is the victim of such practices—especially if the sanctions are imposed on the attorney instead of, or in addition to, the client. As a result, a kind of gentlemen's agreement is reached, with the tacit approval of the bench, which is extremely convenient for the attorneys who avoid the just imposition of sanctions and extremely unfair to the litigants who pay more and wait longer for the vindication of their rights than they should." Renfrew, Discovery Sanctions: A Judicial Perspective, 67 Cal.L.Rev. 264, 272 (1979). Today, however, requests for such sanctions are commonplace. Have the beefed-up sanctions rules gone too far the other way, encouraging further disputes involving great personal acrimony over collateral matters like discovery?

f. FEE AND COST–SHIFTING AND OFFERS OF JUDGMENT

Parties must also consider the affects of an award of legal fees or other costs when deciding whether to press forward with litigation or seek settlement. The following excerpt explains the traditional "American Rule" regarding such awards, the ways in which offer of judgment rules work, and the incentives they create for bargaining parties.

Edward F. Sherman, From Loser Pays to Modified Offer-of-Judgment Rules: Reconciling Incentives to Settle With Access to Justice

76 Tex.L.Rev. 1863, 1863–77 (1998).

The "American rule" that parties will bear the cost of their own attorneys' fees in litigation, whether or not they win or lose, has a long pedigree going back to the earliest days of our republic. It stands in sharp contrast to the "English rule," long followed in Great Britain and most European nations, that the loser must pay the successful party's attorneys' fees. Historical explanations for the American departure from the English rule, such as the spirit of individualism in frontier societies, the conception of lawsuits as sporting contests, and hostility toward lawyers, are not very persuasive today. "Even if distrust of lawyers does survive," Professor John Dawson observed, "it provides no reason for denying indemnity to their clients." Indeed, the American rule cuts against a basic assumption of American remedies law—that a party with a valid claim should be made whole—because requiring a successful claimant to pay his own attorneys' fees considerably diminishes his remedy.

I. "Access to the Courts" Justification for the American Rule

Perhaps the strongest historical justification for the American rule is centered in the American faith in liberal access to the courts for righting wrongs. If a wronged party is deterred from filing and prosecuting a suit by the risk that he will have to pay the opposing party's attorneys' fees if the suit is unsuccessful, there is a concern that many wrongs could go unremedied in our society. That rationale is essentially pro-litigation, indeed pro-plaintiff, in the sense that it reflects a view that access to the courts by claimants should not be discouraged by the threat of substantial, potential penalties for losing. This view also reflects a certain wealth consciousness, particularly in this century when defendants in lawsuits have increasingly been corporations, business entities, institutions, and governmental bodies that are generally more able to bear the risk of penalties for losing than are plaintiffs. Thus, underlying the American rule is a concern that a well-heeled defendant is less likely to be deterred from defending a weak suit by the threat of having to pay its opponent's attorneys' fees than a plaintiff from prosecuting a possibly meritorious suit. Since plaintiffs are generally more risk averse than defendants, a "loser pays" rule impacts disproportionately on plaintiffs' access to the courts.

The pro-plaintiff nature of the American rule (or perhaps more properly pro-claimant, since a loser who is not required to pay the winner's attorneys' fees may be a counterclaimant or cross-claimant rather than a plaintiff) is particularly apparent in the way the rule has been applied in the twentieth century.

First, various common-law doctrines have accorded exceptions to the American rule, permitting recovery of attorneys' fees by a claimant (but not a defending party) against a losing party under certain circumstances—for example, under the theories of "common fund" and "private attorney general." The breach of the American rule in circumstances that only benefit plaintiffs gives added emphasis to the "access to the courts" rationale for the rule. One common-law doctrine that is an exception to the American rule does apply equally to claimants and their opponents—the "bad faith" doctrine that allows recovery of attorneys' fees when an opponent has acted "in bad faith, vexatiously, wantonly, or for oppressive reasons." The rationale is punitive, and fees may be awarded for bad faith either in filing and prosecuting a case or in defending it. This doctrine provides one of the few vehicles for shifting attorneys' fees to a victorious defendant, but "bad faith" is a more demanding standard than the "prevailing party" standard that usually governs fee shifting of plaintiffs' attorneys' fees.

Second, a large number of statutes have been passed since the 1930s to allow recovery of attorneys' fees by a prevailing party despite the American rule. Most of these statutes apply only to prevailing plaintiffs. The justification for such fee shifting has been based on providing an incentive for parties to vindicate their rights under the particular statute (for example, the Civil Rights Act) and to make them whole by not diminishing their damage award through a requirement that they pay their own attorneys. Thus the "access to the courts" concern underlies the departure from the American rule in most attorney's fee shifting statutes, serving as an exception that actually reinforces the pro-plaintiff rationale of the American rule.

II. Attack on the American Rule Gives Way to Modified Offer of Judgment Proposals

Although the American rule remains a bedrock of American jurisprudence, it has increasingly come under attack in recent years. In the early 1980s, Florida passed a "loser pays" rule that shifted legal fees to the losing party in medical malpractice suits as part of "malpractice reforms" sought by doctors and insurance companies. "The rule was not at all what the doctors expected," however, and they "quickly came to the support of its repeal when many fee awards proved uncollectable—except for those against losing doctors." The "tort reform" and "competitiveness" movements of the 1980s and 1990s, particularly supported by business interests, mounted a new attack on the American rule, calling for state legislatures and Congress to replace it with the English "loser pays" rule. Little headway was made, however, until the Republican "Contract with America" burst upon the political scene with the GOP sweep of the congressional elections in 1994.

One of the major planks of the Contract with America was the "loser pays" rule. Early in its first hundred days, the 104th Congress introduced the Common Sense Legal Reforms Act of 1995 which required the application of the "loser pays" rule in actions arising under state law but brought in federal courts under diversity jurisdiction. The proposed rule was modified by provisions that attorneys' fees recovered by the winning party could not exceed those of the losing party, and that the court could limit awards under special circumstances. Along the way, however, resistance to the "loser pays" rule arose, and its advocates shifted to an offer of judgment procedure as an acceptable substitute. A bill was introduced to replace the "loser pays" provision in the Common Sense Legal Reforms Act with a provision that allowed any party to make an offer of judgment to an opposing party. If this offer of judgment were refused, and the ultimate judgment were not more favorable than the original offer, the offeree would have to pay the offeror's costs, including its attorneys' fees up to an amount equal to the offeree's attorneys' fees.

The House of Representatives passed this bill on March 7, 1995, prompting the American Bar Association to convene a task force to study and report back quickly on the desirability of this expanded offer of judgment practice. The task force report presented an alternative proposal * * * that would expand the offer of judgment to allow plaintiffs to invoke it and to allow shifting of attorneys' fees. However, it also included safeguards to ensure that access to the courts and the parties' right to trial by jury would not be chilled. That report was narrowly adopted by the ABA House of Delegates in the spring of 1995, after it debated whether the alternative proposal would adequately guarantee access to the courts. Meanwhile the bill that had been passed by the House stalled in the Senate, and the congressional session ended without action being taken. A similar bill was introduced in 1997 in the 105th Congress, the ABA again opposed it, and it did not become law.

This legislative history highlights the nexus between "loser pays" and expanded offer of judgment rules. Both accomplish the shifting of attorneys' fees—under the "loser pays" rule automatically to the winner, while under the offer of judgment rule to an offeree who refused his opponent's offer to settle and did not do better at trial. Both deter parties' willingness to prosecute a suit by threatening to shift the successful party's attorneys' fees. The offer of judgment rule, however, requires an additional step—a party must first make an offer of judgment to settle for a certain sum as a prerequisite to being allowed to invoke the fee shifting provisions. Offer of judgment thus has an added settlement potential because, in order to invoke it, a party must be prepared to settle if his offer is accepted. Because fee shifting will only occur if the offeree does not do better in the final judgment than in the offer, the offeror has an incentive to make an offer that will be better than what he expects the judgment might be. The offer of judgment rule is thus less directly punitive than the "loser pays" rule, and the manner in which it creates incentives is more complex. It is also more susceptible to fine-tuning, although the drafting job to create the desired incentive structure and to factor for competing policies is enormously complicated.

III. Incentives Under Fee Shifting Structures

The incentives created by fee shifting have been the subject of considerable analysis but limited empirical research. The most traditional form of fee shifting is the shifting of court costs to the losing party upon the completion of a trial or appeal. "Loser pays" and offer of judgment rules are an extenuation of that concept. But while the justification for fee shifting of court costs is based on fairness and making the winning party whole, fee shifting of attorneys' fees is viewed today as a significant means of inducing settlement. Incentives for settlement have thus become the principal focus for analysis of these rules.

A. "Loser Pays" Rule

There has been much debate in the law and economics literature over the effect of fee shifting rules on settlement. Richard A. Posner and Steven Shavell have concluded that fee shifting of the English "loser pays" type would decrease the likelihood of settlement. They viewed parties as pursuing litigation because they are overly optimistic about their chances at trial, which causes them to discount the amount of attorneys' fees they will have to pay, and thus makes settlement less attractive. This position has been challenged by John J. Donohue III, who argued that Posner and Shavell failed to consider the Coase theorem and instead presented a model showing that the settlement rate would be identical under the American and British rules. John C. Hause also argued that fee shifting rules raise the stakes, creating an incentive to spend more at trial and, by increasing the projected costs, a heightened expectation of benefits from settlement. Keith N. Hylton differentiated between a "filing effect" and a "settlement effect." He concluded that "defendants who can credibly commit to large litigation expenses are less likely to be sued under the British than under the American rule," while "the incentive to litigate rather than to settle a dispute is greater under the British than under the American rule." Perhaps the most that can be said with confidence is that the variables and details affecting incentives are sufficiently complex that, as Donohue remarked, "until a better empirical foundation has been established, the existing theoretical arsenal is still too weak to resolve many of the ultimate questions of interest."

* * *

There is, however, reason to believe that the "loser pays" rule can have a disproportionate impact depending on the wealth of a litigant. "Loser pays" has the effect of a blunderbuss rather than a rifle because it shifts all of the winning party's attorneys' fees to the loser no matter their relationship to the amount of damages in issue. The prospect of having to pay the winner's attorneys' fees, plus one's own lawyer, presents a formidable risk to any litigant. It falls equally on plaintiffs and defendants. An individual or small business with limited means, whether a plaintiff or defendant, is likely to be more severely affected by the risk than a well-heeled opponent, especially one who is a repeat player (such as an insurance company) capable of spreading risk over a large number of cases. The rule could encourage a well-heeled party to raise the stakes by hiring more expensive counsel in anticipation of shifting its cost to its opponent (although this assumes that increased attorneys' fees will necessarily improve chances of winning, and it is not at all clear that a rational prosperous litigant would always make that assumption). Much more likely is that a poorly financed litigant would accept an unfavorable settlement because of the relative degree of risk imposed by potential fee shifting. "The rule would deter some litigation," Judge Schwarzer concludes, "but it would do so more on the basis of a litigant's risk averseness than the merits of the litigant's case." Based on this disparate impact, the Economist in 1995 called for the abolition of the English rule on the grounds that it makes no economic sense and denies judicial access to most citizens.

* * *

B. Offer of Judgment

The offer of judgment device was included in Rule 68 when the Federal Rules of Civil Procedure were adopted in 1938. It was new to federal procedure, being borrowed from the practice of a few states. Today twenty-nine states and the District of Columbia have rules similar in language and effect to Rule 68.

Rule 68 provides that any party defending a claim may make a settlement offer to the plaintiff. If the plaintiff rejects the offer and does not receive a more favorable judgment at trial, he must pay the defendant's court costs and fees incurred after the date of the offer. The final judgment must result from an actual trial and not by way of settlement or voluntary dismissal.

An offer of judgment must meet a few simple criteria. It must be served on the adverse party more than ten days before the trial begins and must be for a definite sum, including "costs then accrued." The requirement for a definite sum aims at fostering settlement; an "ambiguous" offer does not give the plaintiff sufficient information to "make reasonable decisions regarding the conduct of litigation." Ambiguous offers, however, are open to clarification, including oral clarification, and clarifications are generally not treated as attempted revocations.

The Rule 68 offer of judgment procedure has been subjected to a great deal of analysis relating to its legal administrative feasibility and economic justification. It is a paradigm for lawyers and academics to try their hand at modeling, structuring, and drafting in hopes of achieving myriad goals. Let us consider some of the features of its incentive structure.

1. Limitations Reducing Its Usefulness.—Two factors have particularly limited parties' resort to Rule 68: only defendants may use it, and only court costs, and not attorneys' fees, are shifted. The Judicial Conference of the United States proposed in 1983 and 1984 to amend the rule because it "has rarely been invoked and has been considered largely ineffective as a means of achieving its goals." The amendments would have made the Rule available to both parties, allowed an offer to be made up to thirty days before trial, and required that the offer remain open for thirty days. A party who refused an offer and did not obtain a more favorable judgment would have to pay the costs and expenses (including reasonable attorneys' fees) incurred by the offeror after making the offer. The rigor of the fee shifting would be lessened by allowing a reduction to the extent that the fees shifted were found by the court to be excessive or unjustified, and by prohibiting fee shifting if the offer was found to have been made in bad faith. These proposals were never adopted by the Rules Advisory Committee.

Although proposals for changes in Rule 68 have primarily focused on expanding it to apply to offers by plaintiffs and recovery of attorneys' fees, a number of proposals have also tinkered with the basic terms of what triggers cost shifting. One of the more interesting proposals came from the local rule experimentation fostered by the Civil Justice Reform Act of 1990 (CJRA). For example, the CJRA-generated plan adopted in 1993 by the United States District Court for the Eastern District of Texas provides that "a party may make a written offer of judgment" and "if the offer of judgment is not accepted and the final judgment in the case is of more benefit to the party who made the offer by 10%, then the party who rejected the offer must pay the litigation costs incurred after the offer was rejected." "Litigation costs" is defined to include "those costs which are directly related to preparing the case for trial and actual trial expenses, including but not limited to reasonable attorneys' fees, deposition costs and fees for expert witnesses." If the plaintiff recovers either more than the offer or nothing at trial, or if the defendant's offer is not realistic or in good faith, the cost shifting sanctions do not apply. Chief Judge Robert M. Parker reported that in the rule's first two years, hundreds of parties made offers of judgment, generally resulting in settlement at a subsequently negotiated figure. No sanctions had to be granted under the rule for failure of the offeree to have obtained a judgment less than 10% better than the offer. There is a question, however, as to whether such a local federal rule is inconsistent with Rule 68, and similar modification of Rule 68 has not been followed in other local rules.

2. Extension of Rule 68 to Attorney Fee Shifting Statutes.—Although Rule 68's limitation of shifting court costs has provided little incentive for parties to make an offer because the potential recovery is so small, that defect also diminishes the concern that the Rule will have the effect of denying access to the courts. A 1985 Supreme Court interpretation of Rule 68, however, directly impacts a plaintiff's willingness to go to a full trial in a case in which a prevailing plaintiff may be entitled to attorneys' fees. In *Marek v. Chesny*,[79] the Court held that when a statute awards attorneys' fees to a prevailing party "as part of" costs (as does the Civil Rights Attorney's Fees Award Act of 1976 which was applicable in *Marek*), a prevailing plaintiff who does not obtain a judgment more favorable than the defendant's offer loses the right to recover his attorneys' fees. The Court read the word "costs" which the offeree is required to pay under Rule 68, as "intended to refer to all costs properly awardable under the relevant substantive statute or other authority." Thus whenever a statute awards attorneys' fees to a prevailing party "as part of costs," or with similar language, a plaintiff offeree who obtains a favorable judgment on liability that is less favorable than the offer loses his right to attorneys' fees as prevailing party. The dissent expressed doubt that the rule was intended to condition fee shifting on whether particular statutes passed over the years referred to attorneys' fees as "part of costs," often without an appreciation of the impact of such language on the application of Rule 68.

Marek has been viewed by the plaintiffs' bar, and particularly the pro-bono and civil-rights bar, as a backdoor way to deny prevailing plaintiffs their attorneys' fees, and thus, as a hindrance to access to the courts. It did create the potential for strategic use of a Rule 68 offer by defendants. A defendant can put the plaintiff's recovery of his attorneys' fees in jeopardy by making a lump sum offer and specifying that this sum is intended to include costs. The dilemma of the plaintiff's lawyer in such a situation can be intense: Any statutory attorneys' fees it might recover can be a negotiable item on the table, and his client, who has no liability for those statutory fee amounts if not awarded, has discretion to accept or reject the settlement offer.

The Court intensified this dilemma in *Evans v. Jeff D.*[89] That case involved a section 1983 class action suit which the defendant would only settle if the plaintiff's lawyer waived his statutory fees. The plaintiff's reluctant agreement to the settlement was conditioned on the court's specific approval of the waiver along with the settlement, both of which the district court provided. On appeal, the Ninth Circuit reversed, holding such agreements unfair per se, barring unusual circumstances, because of inherent conflicts that the negotiation tactic generates between the plaintiff and his lawyer. The Supreme Court reversed, holding that a settlement offer may link the merits with a waiver of statutory attorneys' fees, confirming "the possibility of a tradeoff between merits relief and attorney's fees."

Evans enables defendants in pro-bono and civil-rights cases to offer a settlement in which the plaintiffs waive attorneys' fees for which they have no personal liability. This poses a classic conflict between the interests of

79. 473 U.S. 1 (1985).   **89.** 475 U.S. 717 (1986).

settlement and access to courts. It is true that by jettisoning their attorneys' right to recover attorneys' fees, plaintiffs may more often be able to achieve an attractive settlement. Yet the practice may make many lawyers, including even public interest groups, unwilling to take cases in reliance on statutory sources for adequate fees. Especially in civil-rights cases, in which clients often are unable to pay for legal services, lawyers may rely on statutory attorneys' fees. Several bar associations responded to the decision in *Evans* by adopting ethics opinions insisting that a defense lawyer violates the code of ethics by making a settlement contingent on the plaintiff's lawyer waiving or limiting his rights to a statutory fee. Congressional attempts to overrule *Marek v. Chesny*, however, have failed.

3. Applicability to a Defendant's Verdict.—Rule 68 provides that cost shifting will take place "if the judgment finally obtained by the offeree is not more favorable than the offer." This language seems to apply only when the offeree obtains a verdict less favorable than the offer; it makes no reference to the situation when the verdict is in favor of the defendant. In *Delta Air Lines, Inc. v. August*,[96] the Supreme Court held that "the plain language of Rule 68 confines its effect to . . . [cases] in which the plaintiff has obtained a judgment" which is for less than the offer of judgment.[97] There is irony in this interpretation of Rule 68: a plaintiff who suffers a defendant's judgment at trial might end up better off under the attorney's fee shifting provision than if there had been a plaintiff's verdict that was less favorable than the offer that the plaintiff turned down. The virtue of this literal interpretation of the rule, however, is to prevent defendants from making token, rather than serious, offers for small amounts (say $1) in order to invoke cost shifting in every case in which there is a defendant's verdict. For this reason, proposals to change Rule 68 generally have chosen to leave the Delta interpretation intact.

4. The Offer Process.—Under Rule 68, offers last only a short period of time, but can be renewed. The offeree has ten days to accept an offer. Acceptance is carried out by serving notice on the offeror, must be unconditional, and cannot purport to accept only part of the offer tendered. While Rule 68 does not expressly provide that the offer is irrevocable during the ten-day period, this seems to be the best interpretation and has been adopted by at least one federal court. However, in "exceptional" circumstances, such as fraud on the part of the plaintiff, the court may approve revocation of an offer. An offer that is unaccepted at the end of ten days is "deemed withdrawn." An unaccepted offer is not admissible for anything other than establishing costs, should the offeree obtain a judgment that is less favorable than the offer.

Rule 68 does not preclude the possibility of multiple offers. Once an offer is deemed withdrawn, the offeror is free to make another as long as it is made at least ten days before the beginning of trial. According to the Advisory Committee Note to the 1946 Amendment of the rule, if the offeror makes several successive offers, the offer which is "equal to or greater than

---

96. 450 U.S. 346 (1981).

97. *Id.* at 351.

278 CHAPTER II NEGOTIATION

the judgment ultimately obtained" sets the date for determining the defendant's cost savings.

5. When a Judgment is "Less Favorable" Than the Offer.—To determine whether an offer is more favorable than the judgment, Rule 68 requires a comparison of the offer (including pre-offer costs) with the "judgment finally obtained." It has been said that the Supreme Court favors a comparison that would include pre-offer costs on both sides of the comparison, adding these costs to the jury award and to the offer of judgment. But that approach has also been criticized as contrary to the language of the rule that only speaks of comparing the "judgment finally obtained," arguably meaning that pre-offer costs should not be added to the judgment for purposes of comparison. In a 1986 civil rights case, the Seventh Circuit held that pre-offer costs and attorneys' fees should be added to the jury award for comparison with the offer of judgment.

When comparing the offer to the judgment, courts are divided as to how to quantify any nonmonetary relief which was obtained. Some courts have declined to attempt to put any value on nonmonetary relief. Other courts, however, try to take nonmonetary relief into account and have found it sufficient to offset a substantial difference between a monetary offer and a judgment that includes nonmonetary relief.

NOTES AND QUESTIONS

1. Various commentators have examined the effect of fee-shifting procedures on settlement behavior. See e.g., Donohue, The Effects of Fee Shifting on the Settlement Rate, 54 Law & Contemp.Probs. 195 (1991). One observer concludes that Rule 68's primary effect "is not to encourage settlement but to benefit defendants and harm plaintiffs by shifting downward the relevant settlement range." Miller, An Economic Analysis of Rule 68, 15 J.Leg.Stud. 93 (1986). The argument is as follows: A defendant will make a lower settlement offer under Rule 68 than he would otherwise, knowing the effect that the added impact of cost-shifting will have on the plaintiff's decision. The plaintiff, for his part, will accept something less than he otherwise would, knowing the increased cost of not surpassing the offer at trial. Thus, the entire settlement range is shifted downward. The effect is even more pronounced if the plaintiff is risk-averse (as many are) and the defendant is risk-neutral. See Chung, Settlement of Litigation Under Rule 68: An Economic Analysis, 25 J.Leg.Stud. 261 (1996).

2. In a recent article Bruce Merenstein has argued that the only legitimate benefit of Rule 68 is the discouragement of vexatious or frivolous litigation, a benefit that can be captured using the more discretionary standards found in Federal Rule of Civil Procedure 11. Merenstein contends that Rule 11, which permits a court to sanction attorneys, law firms, or parties that submit papers to the court for an improper purpose—such as to harass or cause unnecessary delay—could be extended to "provide that all offers of settlement and refusals of such offers must not be presented for any improper purpose, as well as be 'warranted by existing law or by a nonfrivolous argument for the extension, modification, or reversal of existing law or the establishment of new law' and be supported by evidence obtained after a reasonable pre-offer (or pre-refusal) inquiry." Merenstein, More Proposals to Amend Rule 68: Time to Sink the Ship Once and For All, 184 F.R.D. 145 (1999). This would eliminate the gambling quality of Rule 68 while still punishing the most egregious problems of litigation abuse.

Is cost-shifting—and fee-shifting—a wise approach to managing the problem of excessively adversarial or bad faith litigation behavior? Do you favor a strict rule-bound approach, such as Rule 68, or a more discretionary approach, such as that permitted to judges under Rule 11?

g. CONFIDENTIALITY

Lawyers and litigants must also consider the possibility that information exchanged during settlement discussions could adversely affect future litigation. The following excerpt considers the rules that govern the confidentiality of settlement-related information. Given the "minefield" the excerpt describes, will lawyers and clients be significantly constrained as they negotiate for fear that their statements may later be used against them?

Jane Michaels, Rule 408: A Litigation Mine Field

19 Litig. 34, 34–38, 71 (Fall 1992).

Suppose that you have three settlement negotiations to conduct. In each, a client will send you on a mission requiring detailed, but slightly different, knowledge of Rule [of evidence] 408. Before beginning the negotiations, your first step is to review the Rule carefully, along with the policies supporting it. Rule 408 reads as follows:

> Evidence of (1) furnishing or offering or promising to furnish, or (2) accepting or offering or promising to accept, a valuable consideration in compromising or attempting to compromise a claim which was disputed as to either validity or amount, is not admissible to prove liability for or invalidity of the claim or its amount. Evidence of conduct or statements made in compromise negotiations is likewise not admissible. This rule does not require the exclusion of any evidence otherwise discoverable merely because it is presented in the course of compromise negotiations. This rule also does not require exclusion when the evidence is offered for another purpose, such as proving bias or prejudice of a witness, negativing a contention of undue delay, or proving an effort to obstruct a criminal investigation or prosecution.

After reading, and re-reading, Rule 408, you manage to distill its language into a useful checklist. The first two sentences of the Rule exclude two kinds of evidence. They provide that the Rule may be used to exclude: (a) offers of compromise; and (b) conduct and statements made in compromise negotiations, if four requirements are met:

(1) there is an actual dispute;

(2) the dispute is over validity or amount of the claim;

(3) efforts are made to compromise the dispute; and

(4) the evidence is offered to prove the validity or amount of the claim.

The third and fourth sentences of Rule 408 have been labeled by some as exceptions to the general exclusionary rule. More properly considered, however, these sentences merely clarify the limits of the Rule's application. The third sentence confirms that Rule 408 is not a discovery privilege. The fourth states that settlement evidence is not automatically excluded if offered to prove something other than the validity or amount of the claim, and so it actually reiterates one of the four requirements of the general rule.

Knowing the policies behind a rule can help guide its application. Two reasons are commonly advanced for the exclusion of compromise evidence: (a) a desire to encourage the extrajudicial resolution of disputes; and (b) lack of relevance.

* * *

Your first mission begins Monday morning. You have a meeting with a potential client, Austek, Inc., which has invented a revolutionary computer chip. Megabite Corp., a manufacturer of personal computers, had entered into an oral agreement with Austek in which Megabite purchased the right to use the computer chip in exchange for Megabite's promise to pay Austek 10 percent of the gross receipts from the sales of computers containing the Austek chip. Megabite has refused to remit the 10 percent royalty. Austek asserts it is owed $5 million in royalties, but does not have underlying documentation to support the amount. The president of Austek has come to you for help.

Was There a Dispute?

In reviewing what has already happened, you learn that, two weeks ago, Megabite called your client and said that it was sending a check for $150,000, which would satisfy the entire amount owed.

The $150,000 is an offer of compromise that will be excluded by Rule 408, right?

Wrong. The offer will not be excluded under Rule 408 because there was not an actual dispute when the offer was made. The language of Rule 408 does not mention a dispute requirement, but the courts have read one in. The reasoning is simple: In order to compromise a dispute, there must be a dispute to compromise. * * *

Not surprisingly, the actual dispute requirement has been litigated frequently. Having to look for, or define, the precise moment when a difference becomes a "dispute" has produced scattered results. Facts matter a lot, and formulas are not helpful. The Federal Circuit has held, for example, that an acknowledged "probability" of an eventual court battle is not sufficient to invoke Rule 408 protection if the claim has not yet been contested. *Deere & Co. v. International Harvester Co.*, 710 F.2d 1551, 1556 (Fed.Cir.1983).

* * *

Since there has been no explicit assertion of conflicting rights in your case, you decide that there is probably no dispute, even under the more liberal *Alpex [Computer v. Nintendo Co., Ltd.*, 770 F. Supp. 161 (S.D.N.Y. 1991),] standard. Thus, you conclude Megabite's $150,000 offer will be admissible if there later is litigation.

On Tuesday morning, you set up a conference call to discuss a settlement between your client and Megabite. Before the meeting, Megabite's attorney—doing a little study of his own—looks at the second sentence of Rule 408, which states that "Evidence of conduct or statements made in compromise negotiations is likewise not admissible." He thinks everything he is about to say will never be heard in court. That turns out to be a mistake.

During the negotiations, Megabite offers $200,000 for a release of all claims. You refuse this offer on Austek's behalf and threaten to enjoin Megabite from using the Austek chip. Megabite knows that your client does not have the money to engage in protracted litigation. In pure mockery, Megabite's lawyer admits that it owes the $5 million, but simply refuses to pay. He tells you that unless Austek accepts the $200,000 offer, Megabite will tie the case up so long that it will get all the benefits it wants out of Austek's computer chip. Your client is concerned because the chip will be obsolete in three years.

Megabite's admission of liability is protected by the second sentence of Rule 408 because it was made in compromise negotiations, right?

Wrong. Megabite has stepped on a Rule 408 mine. You happily inform your client that Megabite's statements are admissible because Megabite has admitted that there is no dispute over the "validity or amount" of the claim. Megabite's admission of liability for the full $5 million bars exclusion under Rule 408, and the admission itself can be introduced at trial. *See Cassino v. Reichhold Chemicals, Inc.*, 817 F.2d 1338 (9th Cir.1987).

You jot down some notes to support this exception, just in case you have to argue it at trial. You find support in a careful reading of the Rule itself. The second sentence of Rule 408 says that "statements made in compromise negotiations" are "likewise not admissible." The word "likewise" refers back to the restrictions on offers of compromise contained in the first sentence of Rule 408. Thus, statements made in compromise negotiations are excluded on the same basis as the offers themselves. The first sentence states that an offer to compromise a claim that was "disputed as to either validity or amount" is not admissible. The word "likewise" then makes a dispute "as to either validity or amount" a condition precedent to exclusion of statements made in negotiations as well.

* * *

282 CHAPTER II NEGOTIATION

Megabite has unconditionally admitted liability and the amount due, but refuses to settle. You realize that Megabite is strong-arming your client with a threat of litigation attrition. Megabite hopes to chisel down the amount required to settle. In effect, Megabite is trying to force a buy-out of Austek's rights in the chip.

Having Megabite's admission of full liability safely in your pocket as admissible evidence, you should now have some leverage. But, still undaunted, Megabite refuses to settle. There will be a trial. Suppose for a moment you can go ahead in time to that proceeding.

Megabite lists Mr. Third as a potential trial witness. Mr. Third had once been in the same position as your client, Austek. Mr. Third had sold Megabite the right to install his microprocessors in the same computers as the Austek chips, in exchange for 5 percent of the gross revenues of all computers sold with his microprocessors. Like your client, Mr. Third had not received any royalty payments. Six months ago, Mr. Third told you that Megabite sold 10,000 computers containing both his microprocessors and your client's chips. In fact, Mr. Third offered to testify on behalf of your client.

You learn, however, that at trial Mr. Third intends to testify that Megabite sold only 200 computers containing Austek's chips. This undermines your entire damages theory. Your heart races; your mind grapples for a solution.

During pretrial investigations, you have also discovered that Mr. Third settled his claim with Megabite two months ago. You immediately approach the judge and seek permission to use evidence of the settlement to impeach the credibility of Mr. Third.

Megabite's counsel confidently recites the general rule that evidence of making or accepting a settlement offer is excluded by Rule 408. Opposing counsel correctly states that settlements with third parties are also excluded under Rule 408.

Bias or Prejudice

But you hold the trump card. The fourth sentence of Rule 408 states that settlement evidence is not excluded when offered to prove something other than the validity or amount of the claim. The evidence is admissible to prove bias or prejudice of a witness. Having settled his own dispute with a party, a third-party witness might be swayed toward, or occasionally against, the litigant. The paradigm example is a Mary Carter agreement. Such a settlement agreement may give the witness a financial stake in the outcome of the trial. *See Brocklesby v. United States*, 767 F.2d 1288, 1293 (9th Cir.1985). In extreme cases, you may be able to show that a very generous settlement is fundamentally payment for testimony, rather than a resolution of liability.

You have correctly understood the exception, but you have not won the argument yet. A conflict exists between the right to cross-examine a witness for bias and the policy of encouraging settlement. Rule 408 makes an explicit exception for proof of "bias or prejudice" and seems to set that as a policy superior to encouraging settlements. Nonetheless, trial courts strike a balance between these competing policies. Regardless of the purpose for which the evidence is offered, there is a danger that the jury may view the evidence as an implied admission, creating a possibility that future settlement may be deterred. *See Weir v. Federal Ins. Co.*, 811 F.2d 1387, 1395 (10th Cir.1987). Sometimes the evidence may not come in, even to show bias.

Opposing counsel also reminds the court that Rule 408 is a rule of exclusion, not admissibility. Although Rule 408 may not bar settlement evidence if offered to show bias, the evidence must still satisfy all the other rules of evidence. That includes Rule 403, which permits a court to refuse evidence that is unduly confusing or prejudicial. The trial judge must weigh the need for the settlement evidence against the potential of discouraging compromise negotiations and the chance of unfair prejudice. Rule 403 may require exclusion in many instances.

Limited Admissibility

You retort that Mr. Third had previously agreed to testify for Megabite. After listening to arguments from both attorneys, the judge determines that the chance of jury confusion is outweighed by your interest in revealing Mr. Third's bias. He allows you to present evidence of the settlement with Mr. Third.

Even though you seem to have won, the judge warns you that the settlement with Mr. Third will not be admissible to impeach a Megabite representative. The bias exception takes on a different character if the witness to be impeached is a party, because such a witness has an obvious interest in the outcome of the trial. For such a witness, the additional proof of bias offered by settlement evidence is probably minimal; it will more likely be seen as an admission of liability. As a result, settlement evidence offered to impeach Megabite will be excluded under a combination of Rules 408 and 403.

* * *

* * * A prior inconsistent statement made during a settlement discussion may not be used for impeachment. Although the Rule does not expressly prohibit the use of settlement evidence for other methods of impeachment, admitting prior inconsistent statements for such a purpose would eviscerate Rule 408.

After this excursion through the lawbooks, you return to the Austek/Megabite litigation. Through discovery, you have obtained an intraoffice report in which Megabite's sales manager admits that Megabite owes your client "$4 million or $5 million." Will this smoking gun document be admissible? Megabite claims that it must be excluded under Rule 408, because the report was specifically prepared for use in compromise negotiations after the lawsuit was filed. If the report was actually prepared for settlement purposes, the policies of Rule 408 will require its exclusion. *See Ramada Development Co. v. Rauch*, 644 F.2d 1097 (5th Cir.1981).

The intent of the party making the report is an important question. Were it otherwise, the Rule would be open to abuse. An unscrupulous party seeking to keep a damaging report out of evidence could do so by merely saying that the report was produced for settlement purposes. Courts, however, do not accept this argument absent objective, good-faith evidence of settlement intent. For example, in *Blue Circle Atlantic, Inc. v. Falcon Material, Inc.*, 760 F.Supp. 516 (D.Md.1991), the court ruled that Rule 408 does not apply to intraoffice memoranda unless communicated to the other side in an attempt to settle.

After hearing more about the context of the sales manager's preparation of the report, the court excludes it from evidence. However, effective impeachment of Mr. Third, combined with Megabite's pre-suit admissions of liability, convince the jury that your client deserves full recovery. In the final analysis, Megabite was blown away in the Rule 408 mine field.

Come back now to the present and embark upon your second settlement mission of the week. Wednesday afternoon brings a reunion with an old friend who seeks your assistance. The friend, Ms. Reliable, was unexpectedly discharged from her job. She asks you if she has a suit. After reviewing the facts, you determine that she has a strong chance of proving wrongful discharge or sex discrimination. You file the claim.

As you will soon learn, counsel for the defendant employer is more familiar with the intricacies of Rule 408 than Megabite's lawyer. Defendant's counsel telephones to suggest a settlement conference Thursday over breakfast. Since conduct and statements made during compromise negotiations are inadmissible under Rule 408, you agree.

During the compromise negotiation, the employer admits that most of the employees it has let go recently were women. Is this statement admissible?

No. In its greatest departure from the common law, the second sentence of Rule 408 provides that statements of fact made in compromise negotiations are inadmissible. * * *

The common law rule had two main problems. First, the admissibility of factual statements hindered the negotiation process because parties could not speak freely. Second, often fights occurred over which comments fell within a prefatory "without prejudice" statement.

Rule 408 solves these problems by excluding all conduct and statements made in compromise negotiations. Thus, parties can speak freely about the facts of the disputed matter without fear of the subsequent admissibility of those conversations.

Your client's former employer has come to this settlement meeting with an objective. The company wants to generate evidence that will limit backpay damages if the matter goes to trial. Specifically, it wants to demonstrate that Ms. Reliable has rejected a reasonable offer of reinstatement.

Opposing counsel knows that the definition of the word "compromise" provides an implicit exception to Rule 408's evidentiary ban. A compromise is an agreement reached by mutual concession. Each side agrees to relinquish something to which it believes itself entitled. If an offer does not require Ms. Reliable to release her legal claim against the employer, then it seeks no compromise within the meaning of Rule 408, and there is no exclusion. In other words, offers not requiring a release are not excluded by Rule 408. * * * Presenting Ms. Reliable with an offer that does not require a release would be easy. But the company wants to have it both ways: It wants to create evidence of the reinstatement offer to cut off backpay damages, but not have to pay additional salary should Ms. Reliable accept the offer.

* * *

By now, as a Rule 408 veteran, you see exactly what is happening. The employer plans to circumvent the Rule 408 exclusion by resorting to ambiguity. If the terms of the offer are ambiguous, Ms. Reliable will be uncertain as to whether acceptance requires her to waive her legal claim. The former employer wants to make the terms of the offer vague, but just clear enough to convince a judge that Ms. Reliable was not being asked to release her claim, so that the offer will not be excluded under Rule 408.

Fortunately, you have just read a case holding that offers presented during compromise negotiations are inadmissible, unless the offering party can prove that the offer did not require a release of claims. *See Pierce v. F.R. Tripler & Co.*, 955 F.2d 820 (2d Cir. 1992). The burden of clarifying ambiguity should fall on your adversary. You inform opposing counsel of the *Pierce* case.

Your opponent is not easily deterred, however. Later in the negotiations, she says "We are making a reinstatement offer without prejudice." This time, opposing counsel has skillfully used the language of Rule 408, creating admissible evidence that could limit the damages awarded to your client. Because the offer was made "without prejudice," its acceptance would not have required Ms. Reliable to waive her claim against the employer. Falling outside the purview of Rule 408, the offer is admissible. Of course, to set up this evidence, opposing counsel had to take the risk that Ms. Reliable might accept. Disregarding your sound advice, however, Ms. Reliable rejects the offer.

At trial, Ms. Reliable wins on the liability issue, but the offer of reinstatement "without prejudice" is admitted. Opposing counsel's careful use of Rule 408's compromise requirement has limited the damages awarded to your client.

Name Theft

Your third and final mission comes from an old and dear client: A–One Airlines. A–One has come to you because a small air cargo company is operating under the name "A–One Cargo." Your client is a first-class operation that scorns any association with a slipshod outfit like A–One Cargo. The airline owns the right to use the name "A–One," and it wants you to get the cargo company to change its name—quickly.

Your client wants to avoid an ugly battle in the courts and would prefer to settle. You call counsel for the cargo company and set up a meeting. You suggest that all parties sign a written agreement in advance, stating their intent to meet in a compromise negotiation under Rule 408.

During negotiations, the cargo company says it will change its name if your client pays $20,000, plus the expenses of a new logo design and reprinting the company stationery. Your client likes the idea but is reluctant to pay any money. After all, there might be another A–One operation out there. Your client fears that the terms of the settlement might be revealed if a future plaintiff makes a discovery request.

You consult the third sentence of Rule 408, which states: "This rule does not require the exclusion of any evidence otherwise discoverable merely because it is presented in the course of compromise negotiations." From reading the Rule and interpretive case law, you conclude that, while the intent of Rule 408 is to foster settlement negotiations, there is only one means used to effectuate that policy: exclusion from evidence at trial. Rule 408 does not create a broad discovery privilege. *NAACP Defense and Education Fund, Inc. v. United States of Justice*, 612 F. Supp. 1143, 1146 (D.D.C.1985).

Doing more research, you determine that your client does have some protection. Third parties will not be able to compel discovery of settlement material if their sole aim is to expose your client's prior negotiations with others. A–One Airlines is not required to disclose settlement material unless, as required by Rule 26(b)(1), there is a showing that the material sought through discovery will be relevant to the issues in another case or will lead to the discovery of evidence admissible there. *See Morse/Diesel, Inc. v. Trinity Indus., Inc.*, No. Civ. 5781 (SWK), 1992 WL 76896 (S.D.N.Y. April 10, 1992).

* * *

Discovery of Settlements

Assessing the risks, you advise your client that future litigants might be able to compel discovery of the A–One Cargo settlement, but that it cannot be used against A–One Airlines in a later suit to prove the validity or amount of the claim. You must, however, warn your client of certain risks. For example, factual admissions made during compromise negotiations are more likely to be discoverable in another suit, because they are more likely to lead to admissible evidence. In addition, the settlement could be subject to discovery if the evidence will be used to demonstrate bias. With these concerns reviewed and carefully examined, your client signs the settlement papers, satisfied that the risks have been well identified.

At the end of your various settlement discussions, you take a moment to reflect. Although intended to encourage settlement negotiations and to assure that negotiators can speak freely during settlement discussions without creating admissible evidence, Rule 408 contains numerous exceptions. They make it a mine field—but one that can be negotiated successfully.

NOTES AND QUESTIONS

1. The Michaels article begins by referring to the policy of encouraging settlement. In judicial opinions concerning settlement practice, the policy of encouraging settlement is an overriding concern. In close cases regarding post-settlement issues such as malpractice, confidentiality, and collateral attack, the policy of encouraging settlement often tips the scales in favor of one side. Thus, parties in post-settlement disputes are well advised to discuss the ways in which their legal position favors, or at least does not discourage, settlement.

2. Whether to discourage similar suits, prevent future liability, or preserve a positive public image, parties often seek to protect the terms of private settlements. In such a case, the public's right to know may outweigh the policy of encouraging settlement. Carrie Menkel–Meadow has discussed the policy questions raised by confidential settlement. While parties may prefer private settlement terms, many groups claim a right to know stemming from the First Amendment and the common law. Public interest groups and the media attempt to disclose public harms. Public officials encourage open discussion of issues pertaining to the public interest. Plaintiff's lawyers want to share information with others and to prevent some plaintiffs from trading large settlements for promises of secrecy. In response to the controversy, many state legislatures have adopted "sunshine laws" precluding confidential settlements in cases involving public issues. See Menkel–Meadow, Public Access to Private Settlements: Conflicting Legal Policies, 11:6 Alt. to the High Cost of Litig. 85 (Jun. 1993). For further discussion, including an analysis of the legal procedures available to parties seeking to protect settlement terms, see Dore, Secrecy by Consent: The Use and Limits of Confidentiality in the Pursuit of Settlement, 74 Notre Dame L.Rev. 283 (1999).

3. As Michaels' article makes clear, Federal Rule of Evidence 408 leaves many statements made in settlement negotiations subject to discovery. However, parties can mutually agree through private contract to maintain the confidentiality of settlement negotiations. The degree of deference a court will afford such a contract depends on the circumstances. Contracts that violate public policy are routinely disregarded. Courts may also view private contracting as infringing on the court's power to consider evidence or as conflicting with Rule 408. As Wayne Brazil notes, "Confidentiality contracts that threaten none of these more compelling public policies, however, may be enforceable * * * " See generally Brazil, Protecting the

Confidentiality of Settlement Negotiations, 39 Hastings L.J. 955, 1026–28 (1988).

4. The Advisory Committee that drafted Rule 408 made no recommendation about whether parties should be able to use lies in settlement negotiations to impeach their opponents at trial. Some legal scholars have suggested that allowing parties to impeach their counterparts with inconsistent statements made during negotiations would not undercut the policy rationale behind Rule 408, and it would promote ethical negotiation behavior. See Rambo, Impeaching Lying Parties with their Statements during Negotiation: Demysticizing the Public Policy Rationale Behind Evidence Rule 408 and the Mediation–Privilege Statutes, 75 Wash.L.Rev. 1037 (2000); Hjelmeset, Impeachment of Party by Prior Inconsistent Statement in Compromise Negotiations: Admissibility Under Federal Rule of Evidence 408, 43 Clev.St.L.Rev. 75 (1995).

The exclusion provided in Rule 408 must be read in conjunction with the standards for discovery in the Federal Rules. Rule 26(b) allows discovery "regarding any matter, not privileged, which is relevant to the subject matter involved in the pending action." Furthermore, that rule states that "[I]t is not ground for objection that the information sought will be inadmissible at the trial if the information sought appears reasonably calculated to lead to the discovery of admissible evidence." This broad scope of discovery could be seen to come into conflict with the Rule 408 exclusion for offers in compromise. Consider the following case:

Young v. State Farm Mutual Automobile Insurance Company

U.S. District Court, S.D. West Virginia 1996.
169 F.R.D. 72

■ FEINBERG, UNITED STATES MAGISTRATE JUDGE.

This is a civil action in which Plaintiffs, a partnership of attorneys, seek to recover legal fees in connection with the representation of Defendant Michael Pritchard, who was seriously injured in an automobile accident at the conclusion of a high speed chase involving Fayetteville, West Virginia police officers and a Fayette County Deputy Sheriff.

Defendants State Farm Mutual Insurance Company and State Farm Fire and Casualty Company (collectively referred to as "State Farm") insured the automobile in which Pritchard was riding when he was injured. Plaintiff Ralph Young served as local counsel in the trial of Pritchard's case against the driver of the automobile. *Michael Pritchard, Jr. v. Town of Fayetteville,* No. 5:89–1457 (S.D.W.Va. Aug. 30, 1993). Defendant Sutherland was Pritchard's lead attorney at the trial. The jury awarded Pritchard more than $15 million in damages payable by the driver, Smith.

Subsequently, Smith, Pritchard, and the owner of the automobile sued State Farm for unlawful trade practices and bad faith in connection with the Pritchard case, *Smith v. State Farm Mut. Auto. Ins. Co.*, No. 94–C–54–S (Cir.Ct. McDowell Co., W.Va.), removed to United States District Court, No. 1:95–0100 (S.D.W.Va. Mar. 13, 1996). Plaintiffs notified the *Smith v. State Farm* litigants of their claim to attorneys' fees. State Farm then settled with Smith, Pritchard and the owner, and the unlawful trade practices/bad faith case was dismissed. The *Smith v. State Farm* parties agreed that their settlement agreement would be confidential.

It is clear to the Court that all parties to the *Pritchard v. City of Fayetteville* case recognized that the insurance policy limits on the automobile driven by Smith were totally inadequate to compensate the damages suffered by Mr. Pritchard. The trial of *Pritchard v. City of Fayetteville* was conducted for the purpose of establishing the amount of damages, not the issue of liability, which was conceded. It is also clear that State Farm was the only available source of money to satisfy the verdict in favor of Pritchard, if recovery could be had against State Farm on the bad faith/unlawful trade practices claim. The underlying action and the insurance action were two separate cases, involving some different attorneys, but they were related.

In this civil action, Plaintiffs claim that they are owed a share of the settlement paid by State Farm to Pritchard on behalf of Smith. Plaintiffs sue Defendants Sutherland and Pritchard for breach of contract of an oral contingency fee agreement (Count I), and for *quantum meruit* (Count II); they sue all Defendants for enforcement of attorney's lien (Count III). Defendants Sutherland and Pritchard admit that Plaintiff Ralph Young is entitled to receive a reasonable attorney's fee according to the legal doctrine of *quantum meruit* but deny any liability based on a contingency. State Farm has moved to dismiss pursuant to Fed.R.Civ.Proc. 12(b)(6), asserting lack of privity of contract with Plaintiffs, and lack of services rendered by Plaintiffs to State Farm.

Now pending before the Court are Plaintiffs' Motions to Compel and the Motion for Protective Order filed by Defendants Sutherland and Pritchard. Plaintiffs seek disclosure by Defendants Sutherland and Pritchard of [certain matters, including the] amount and terms of the settlement between Mr. Pritchard and State Farm, the amount of all attorneys' fees received by Mr. Sutherland,* * * or by any other person, from the above settlement proceeds; whether funds were escrowed; [and] any portion of the file maintained by Sutherland in connection with the bad faith action. * * *

Plaintiffs request the following information from State Farm: "the amount and terms of the settlement in question, the escrow-related information, if any, and information concerning the identity of the person or persons at State Farm who made a decision not to honor plaintiffs' attorneys' fee lien."

State Farm resists disclosure based upon relevancy and the confidentiality provision of the settlement agreement. No privilege is asserted. * * *

The issues posed by the Complaint in this case are:

1. Did Plaintiffs have an agreement with Defendants Sutherland and Pritchard concerning the amount of Plaintiffs' attorneys' fees for services rendered?

2. If so, what were the terms of that agreement?

3. If attorneys' fees are payable to Plaintiffs, how much is payable, and who is liable for the payment?

The issues raised by the pending Motions are:

1. Should the settlement agreement between Sutherland/Pritchard and State Farm be disclosed to Plaintiffs, despite the agreement's provision to maintain its confidentiality?

2. Should the Court compel Defendants Pritchard, Sutherland and State Farm to answer the additional discovery requested by Plaintiffs concerning the settlement?

These discovery issues are of first impression in the Fourth Circuit and the District Courts within that Circuit.

* * *

When the requested discovery concerns a confidential settlement agreement, the majority of courts considering the issue have required the requesting party to meet a heightened standard, in deference to Federal Rule of Evidence 408, and the public policy to encourage settlements and to uphold confidentiality provisions. In Bottaro v. Hatton Associates, *96 F.R.D. 158, 159 (E.D.N.Y.1982)*, the court noted that *Rule 26(b)* itself provides that "[i]t is not ground for objection that the information sought will be inadmissible at the trial if the information sought appears reasonably calculated to lead to the discovery of admissible evidence." The Bottaro court held as follows:

> Given the strong public policy of favoring settlements and the congressional intent to further that policy by insulating the bargaining table from unnecessary intrusions [*Fed.R.Evid. 408*], we think the better rule is to require some particularized showing of a likelihood that admissible evidence will be generated by the dissemination of the terms of a settlement agreement. The Bottaro court found that the showing had not been made, and refused disclosure.

In Morse/Diesel, Inc. v. Fidelity and Deposit Co. of Maryland, *122 F.R.D. 447, 451 (S.D.N.Y.1988)*, the court used the heightened standard analysis, found that the required showing had been made, and ordered disclosure of the settlement materials. A similar result was reached in Fidelity Federal Savings and Loan Ass'n v. Felicetti, *148 F.R.D. 532, 534 (E.D.Pa.1993)*. The Felicetti court characterized the heightened standard as "switch[ing] the burden of proof from the party in opposition to the discovery to the party seeking the information." In Lesal Interiors, Inc. v. Resolution Trust Corp.,

D. PROFESSIONAL AND LEGAL FRAMEWORK FOR NEGOTIATION

153 F.R.D. 552, 562 (D.N.J.1994), the court applied the heightened standard, and refused disclosure.

In Vardon Golf Co. v. BBMG Golf Ltd., *156 F.R.D. 641, 650–51 (N.D.Ill.1994)*, the court concluded that the Bottaro standard overstated the nature of the proponent's burden. Rather than require a "particularized showing," the court noted that *Rule 26(b)* considers what is "reasonably calculated to lead to the discovery of admissible evidence."

> "[W]e hold that where information sought in discovery would not be admissible due to an exclusionary rule in the Federal Rules of Evidence, the proponent of discovery may obtain discovery (1) by showing that the evidence is admissible for another purpose other than that barred by the Federal Rules of Evidence or (2) by articulating a plausible chain of inferences showing how discovery of the item sought would lead to other admissible evidence. The proponent may do this by simply articulating what kind of information it reasonably expects to find in the documents sought and how this will lead to other admissible evidence. The proponent need not show that the information expected is in fact in the items sought, but need only articulate why it is reasonable to believe that information of that nature would be revealed were discovery permitted."

Despite the lessened standard, the court refused disclosure in Vardon Golf.

At least one court has rejected the Bottaro heightened standard, has applied the normal relevancy standard of *Rule 26(b)*, and has placed the burden on the party opposing discovery to establish some good cause or sound reason for withholding the material. Bennett v. La Pere, *112 F.R.D. 136, 140 (D.R.I.1986)*. In Bennett, the court found that the requested documents were relevant and not privileged and that no sound reason had been shown to withhold them from disclosure. Moreover, the Bennett court opined that disclosure would enable the parties to appraise the case realistically, to consider settlement, and to avoid protracted litigation. "So long as the policy of the Rules is the promotion of the 'just, speedy, and inexpensive' resolution of cases, then fair settlements must always be encouraged. Fairness cannot be achieved when one said is needlessly blindfolded." Id. *at 141*.

The case which is closest in its facts to the instant action is McCullough v. Nichols, *No. 9404CV0093, 1995 WL 679265, *2 (Mass.Dist.Ct. Aug. 3, 1995)*, in which the plaintiff-attorneys sued their former clients for breach of contract and, alternatively, in *quantum meruit,* for failure to honor a written fee agreement and to pay attorneys' fees. Defendants counterclaimed, alleging failure of adequate representation. The court held as follows:

> [I]t is my view that when private parties to a civil action enter into an agreement providing for the non-disclosure of settlement terms, the privilege from disclosing those terms that is thereby created must yield to a request for discovery by a third party attorney in an independent action for recovery of counsel fees against one of the settling parties for

services performed in connection with the subject matter of the case that was settled in circumstances in which the terms and conditions of the prior settlement are central to the third party cause of action.

The threshold question is whether the requested discovery, including the disclosure of the confidential settlement agreement, is relevant to this litigation. Any discussion of relevancy in the context of discovery must begin with *Fed.R.Civ.Proc. 26(b)*, which provides that "[p]arties may obtain discovery regarding any matter, not privileged, which is relevant to the subject matter involved in the pending action. . . ." *Federal Rule of Evidence 401* defines "relevant evidence" as "evidence having any tendency to make the existence of any fact that is of consequence to the determination of the action more probable or less probable than it would be without the evidence." "All relevant evidence is admissible." *Fed.R.Evid. 402*. Courts have construed *Rule 26(b)* to permit very broad discovery, encompassing "any matter that bears on, or that reasonably could lead to other matter that could bear on, any issue that is or may be in the case." Oppenheimer Fund, Inc. v. Sanders, *437 U.S. 340, 351, 98 S.Ct. 2380, 2389, 57 L.Ed.2d 253 (1978).*

Review of the pleadings in the instant case reveals that Plaintiffs allege that there was an oral contingency fee contract between Plaintiff Young and Defendant Pritchard's attorneys, with the fee to be determined upon the successful outcome of both the underlying action and the insurance action. Defendants Pritchard and Sutherland admit that there was an implicit agreement to compensate Plaintiff Young for his services, and that the amount of the fee was not agreed. They deny the existence of a contingency fee agreement, and contend that Plaintiff Young can recover a fee based only on *quantum meruit.*

* * *

It is evident, and the Court so finds, that the requested discovery material is relevant to the issues in this case. Contrary to Defendants' position, a District Court's determination of an attorney's fee is not a simple mathematical calculation of "percentage multiplied by verdict," or "number of hours multiplied by hourly rate." A District Court's responsibility in a dispute over attorneys' fees requires review of each attorney's performance and role in the cases which are relevant to the dispute, in light of the Johnson factors. In determining whether the fee is fixed or contingent (factor 6), Plaintiffs should be able to examine Defendant Sutherland's file and to question him concerning his understanding as to whether Plaintiff Young's fee was fixed or contingent. The results obtained (factor 8) cannot be determined without knowing what State Farm paid to settle with Pritchard, Sutherland, and Smith. A large verdict has little value unless the judgment is actually paid in whole or in part.

Having determined that the requested discovery material is relevant, the next question is whether it is privileged. As noted above, Defendants Sutherland and Pritchard have waived the attorney-client and work product privileges as to discovery [requested of them]. State Farm does not assert any privilege. Therefore, the Court concludes that the requested discovery material is relevant and not privileged.

The next inquiry is whether the requested discovery material is admissible. * * * If the confidential settlement agreement or related discovery material were offered into evidence at the trial of this case, it would not be offered to prove State Farm's liability for bad faith or unfair trade practices, nor to prove the invalidity of the claim that State Farm engaged in bad faith or unfair trade practices, nor to prove the amount of the claim against State Farm. Presumably the settlement agreement and the related discovery materials would be offered into evidence for other purposes, that is, to prove the nature of the agreement with Plaintiff Young, and the results obtained in the subject cases. While it is the decision of the presiding District Judge to determine whether evidence is admissible, this Magistrate Judge considers it probable that the confidential settlement agreement and the related discovery materials would be admissible for the purposes stated. At a minimum, the Court finds that the confidential settlement agreement and the related discovery materials constitute information which is reasonably calculated to lead to the discovery of admissible evidence. *Fed.R.Civ.Proc. 26(b)*.

Having determined that the discovery requests are relevant and not privileged, and that the discovery material is probably admissible (or likely to lead to admissible evidence), the Court notes that applicable cases support disclosure. Bottaro, *96 F.R.D. at 160;* Morse/Diesel, Inc., *122 F.R.D. at 451;* Vardon Golf Co., *156 F.R.D. at 650–51;* McCullough, supra, *1995 WL 679265, at *2.* The weight of authority and *Rule 26(b)* itself impose upon the requesting party a greater burden to establish the relevancy, and to gain discovery, of otherwise inadmissible non-privileged confidential settlement documents. But if the requesting party shows that the "information appears reasonably calculated to lead to the discovery of admissible evidence," then it is probably discoverable. It is appropriate to protect confidential settlement agreements, but not if such protection prevents necessary discovery.

The settlement agreement contains specific terms bearing on the disposition of files and the relationships among attorneys and represented parties which directly affect this litigation. Moreover, the hand-written note attached to document #63 suggests that Plaintiff Young and Pritchard's first attorney discussed Young's receiving a contingent fee based on the outcome of both the underlying action and the insurance action if verdicts were rendered. If the confidentiality provision were enforced against Plaintiffs, then Plaintiffs would probably be blocked in their efforts to obtain documentary and testamentary evidence concerning any agreement concerning their fees.

For the reasons stated and after careful consideration of the terms of the settlement agreement, the facts of the underlying and insurance actions, and all the cited cases, the Court holds that the confidential settlement agreement signed by Defendants Sutherland, Pritchard and State Farm, and the other discovery materials that it protects by its

294 CHAPTER II Negotiation

confidentiality provision, are discoverable because Plaintiffs have demonstrated their relevance and probable admissibility (or likelihood of leading to admissible evidence). The Court concludes that the requested discovery, including the settlement agreement, is likely to lead to the discovery of admissible evidence relevant to the issues posed by this case, i.e., the existence, terms, and proper enforcement of any agreement between Plaintiffs, on the one hand, and Defendants Sutherland and Pritchard, on the other hand.

For these reasons, it is hereby **ORDERED** that Plaintiffs' Motions to Compel with respect to Defendants Pritchard and Sutherland * * * are granted in part * * *

It is further **ORDERED** that Plaintiffs' Motions to Compel with respect to State Farm * * * are granted as follows, but any disclosure shall be subject to a protective order:

1. Amount and terms of the settlement: granted;

2. Escrow-related information: granted; and

3. Identity of person who decided not to honor the attorney's lien: granted.

It is further **ORDERED** that no disclosure shall be made unless and until all parties execute an agreed protective order.

NOTES AND QUESTIONS

1. Are Rule 408 and Rule 26(b) in conflict? Were they properly reconciled in this case? How should courts respond to discovery requests pertaining to previous settlement agreements?

2. The plaintiffs in *Young* claim that the settlement agreement was relevant to their claim for attorneys' fees which were contingent upon success in both the underlying claim and the bad faith action. What is the link between the agreement and their claim for fees? Was it critical that the agreement contained "specific terms bearing on the disposition of files and relationships among attorneys and represented parties?" Would that be admissible to prove that plaintiff Young had a contingent fee contract, or would it just lead to admissible evidence?

3. How does the court deal with the conflict in the case law concerning the standard to apply under the interface between Rule 408 and Rule 26(b), i.e., *Bottaro* requires "some particularized showing of a likelihood that admissible evidence will be generated by the dissemination of the terms of a settlement agreement," while *Bennett* rejected such a heightened standard and simply applied the "relevancy" standard of Rule 26(b)? The court states that Rule 26(b) imposes "upon the requesting party a greater burden to establish the relevancy, and to gain discovery, of otherwise inadmissible non-privileged confidential settlement documents." Did it find that plaintiffs discharged that burden, or did its finding that the information was reasonably calculated to lead to the discovery of admissible evidence result in its applying a lesser standard?

4. In *Bottaro*, non-settling defendants sought to discover the nature of the plaintiff's settlement agreement with a settling defendant. How could discovery of the terms of the settlement reasonably lead to admissible evidence? Defendants argued that it might lead to admissible evidence on the question of damages. However, the court found that there was no particularized showing of a likelihood of leading to admissible evidence and refused to compel disclosure of the settlement agreement. Could the fact that the settling defendant paid the plaintiff a large sum lead to admissible evidence concerning damages? Might it not indicate that plaintiff had a stronger case than the defendants thought (or if the settlement was small, that he had a weaker case). The court in *Bennett* required disclosure to a non-settling defendant Hospital of a settlement agreement between the plaintiff and defendant Physicians, stating "the damages which the plaintiffs can collect from the Hospital if they successfully prosecute what remains of the case will depend to some extent on the terms, amount, and value of the Physicians' settlement."

5. In *Botarro*, would the details of the settlement agreement be relevant to determining whether, and in what amount, remaining defendants would be entitled to contribution against a settling defendant? The *Bottaro* decision, however, stated that "while it is true that a settling defendant's liability for contribution depends on whether he paid his share of any damage award, this determination cannot be made until a final judgment has been rendered." It further stated that "even then, the settlement would not be evidence relevant to any issue in this case other than a ministerial apportionment of damages, a mathematical computation which the Court rather than the jury will perform." Must a defendant wait until a final judgment to discover the settlement amount for purposes for determining contribution? Would the interests of settlement be better served by allowing discovery of that information earlier so that all claims might be resolved at one time? What if the state procedure provides for comparing the negligence of settling defendants with that of the remaining defendants in the primary suit (see Tex. Civ.Prac. & Rem.Code § 33.003 et seq.)?

6. Rule 408 clearly prohibits introduction of the fact or amount of a settlement for the purpose of proving liability or the amount of damages due. But it may be introduced for "another purpose, such as proving bias or prejudice or interest of a witness or a party." Could the defendants in *Bottaro* have succeeded on a theory that they wanted to use the settlement information to impeach the settling defendant if he testified? When there is a "Mary Carter agreement" between plaintiff and a settling defendant (an agreement by which the settling defendant retains a financial interest in the plaintiff's recovery against non-settling defendants), evidence of the agreement may be introduced for the purpose of impeaching the settling defendant. See General Motors Corp. v. Simmons, 558 S.W.2d 855, 858 (Tex.1977). Should the same be true when there is no "Mary Carter

296 CHAPTER II Negotiation

agreement," but the defendant desires to show that the settling defendant was "paid off" in return for testimony favorable to the plaintiff?

7. The discovery rules also offer the possibility of protection of confidentiality through a court protective order, as in incorporating a mediation agreement of confidentiality or in sealing a mediation record. Rule 26(c) provides that a court may "for good cause shown ... make any order which justice requires to protect a party or person from annoyance, embarrassment, oppression, or undue burden or expense." Rule 26(c)(7) specifically provides for a protective order that "a trade secret or other confidential research, development, or commercial information not be disclosed or be disclosed only in a designated way."

2. JUDICIAL PROMOTION OF SETTLEMENT

A lawyer's efforts to use litigation procedures to help assure a more successful negotiation can be made more effective if a judge assumes responsibility for managing the litigation with a goal of resolving the dispute voluntarily, fairly, and efficiently. Judicial administrators at both the federal and state levels currently emphasize the judge's role in promoting settlement.[11]

Federal Rule of Civil Procedure 16, adopted in 1938, provides the primary tool for judicial supervision of litigation through the pretrial conference. It was amended in 1983 to provide for two types of pretrial conferences—"scheduling and planning" and "final." Among the subjects to be discussed at pretrial conference are "establishing early and continuing control so that the case will not be protracted because of lack of management," "discouraging wasteful pretrial activities," "improving the quality of the trial through more thorough preparation," and "facilitating settlement."

Rule 16(c)(9) now expressly provides that "settlement and the use of special procedures to assist in resolving the dispute when authorized by statute or local rule" may be considered and acted upon during pretrial conferences. Explicit reference to settlement was added to Rule 16 in 1983; as the Advisory Committee then acknowledged, it had "become commonplace to discuss settlement at pretrial conferences." In 1993 the treatment of settlement promotion was expanded, and the Advisory Committee explained this expansion as follows:

> Even if a case cannot immediately be settled, the judge and attorneys can explore possible use of alternative procedures such as mini-trials, summary jury trials, mediation, neutral evaluation, and non-binding arbitration that can lead to consensual resolution of the dispute without a full trial on the merits.

---

11. See Miller, The August 1983 Amendments to the Federal Rules of Civil Procedure: Promoting Effective Case Management and Lawyer Responsibility 11–34 (Fed.Judicial Center 1984).

But these devices can be employed only when authorized by statute or local rule. This reflects in part the decentralization accomplished by the Civil Justice Reform Act, 28 U.S.C.A. § 471 et seq., which allowed each district to authorize, or not, the use of alternative dispute resolution. A sizable number of districts decided to adopt such ADR methods, but some specifically rejected them.

a. THE PROPER ROLE OF THE JUDGE

Judicial encouragement of settlement has long been practiced in federal and many state courts; until the advent of the ADR movement, this was primarily accomplished through a settlement conference with the judge who used a combination of jaw-boning and veiled threats to move the parties towards settlement.[12] The courts have uniformly held that such settlement procedures must not have the effect of coercing the parties into settling.

In a typical case, *Kothe v. Smith*,[13] the Second Circuit reversed sanctions against the defendant after he refused to settle before trial (on the judge's recommendation of a $20,000 to $30,000 settlement figure), but settled for $20,000 after one day of trial. The Second Circuit concluded that an "attorney should not be condemned for changing his evaluation of the case after listening to [the opponent's] testimony during the first day of trial."[14] The process used in *Kothe* was a judicial settlement conference, authorized by Federal Rule of Civil Procedure 16, which the appellate court viewed as "designed to encourage pretrial settlement discussions," but not to "impose settlement negotiations on unwilling litigants." "Pressure tactics to coerce settlement," it said, "simply are not permissible."[15]

An ABA-sponsored study of lawyers in four federal districts concluded that "85 percent of the responding attorneys from the entire four-district sample agree that involvement by federal judges in settlement discussions is likely to improve significantly the prospects of achieving settlement."[16] The data, summarized in the following selection, provide interesting insight into the relationships of lawyers and judges in the negotiation area.

Wayne D. Brazil, Settling Civil Disputes

44–46 (1985).

Why do lawyers say that judicial involvement can significantly improve prospects for achieving settlement? Our data do not provide a definitive answer, but they offer clues and suggest hypotheses. Even though a large percentage of cases ultimately settle, the process through which the parties eventually reach agreement often is difficult to launch, then can be awk-

---

12. See E. Donald Elliott, Managerial Judging and the Evolution of Procedure, 53 U.Chi.L.Rev. 306 (1986); Paul Reidinger, Then It's Settled, A.B.A.J., July 1989, at 92.

13. 771 F.2d 667 (2d Cir.1985).

14. Id. at 670.

15. Id. at 669.

16. Wayne D. Brazil, Settling Civil Suits 39 (1985).

ward, expensive, time-consuming, and stressful. The route to resolution can be tortuously indirect and travel over it can be obstructed by emotion, posturing, and interpersonal friction. Counsel and clients can be distracted by irrelevancies and resources can be consumed by feints or maneuvers designed primarily to save face with opponents or to retain credibility with the people paying the bills. Parties and lawyers can be slow to feel confidence in the wisdom or fairness of proposals developed through such an awkward, adversarial process, a process in which people assume that their opponents are not disclosing significant information and are offering only self-serving assessments of the implications of evidence and the relative strengths of competing positions.

Since at least some of these problems burden private settlement negotiations in many cases, lawyers well might feel that federal judges can make significant contributions to the settlement process by reducing frictions and removing obstacles that otherwise would impede it. As we will demonstrate, the pattern of lawyer responses to our questions suggests an important unifying hypothesis; judicial involvement is likely to improve prospects for achieving settlement because judges are professional decision makers.

Litigators, by contrast, are professional advocates. The skills that are central to the litigator's professional self-image and role revolve around marshalling evidence and arguments for one side, selecting and packaging information to make it as persuasive as possible. Lawyers are trained to uncover evidence, then to arrange its display to others; the others have ultimate responsibility to decide what the evidence means. Thus the litigator's job is to present persuasively, not to judge dispassionately.

Judges, on the other hand, are paid to make decisions, and to do so rationally and impartially. Good judges know that their central responsibility is to resolve disputes fairly, to terminate conflicts by making neutral decisions. Judges also know that the data on which they must make decisions will be presented to them by advocating litigators seeking persuasive advantages. To achieve their objective of making rational decisions in this environment, good judges become skillful at cutting through verbal and emotional camouflage to identify pivotal issues, at ferreting out key evidence, assessing credibility and analyzing strengths and weaknesses of arguments. The pursuit of fair solutions teaches judges to probe, to ask about matters not presented. The responsibility to make decisions puts a premium on efficiency. The responsibility to decide rationally sharpens the judge's analytical edge.

A judge who enters the settlement dynamic with these instincts and skills is in a position to make unique and valuable contributions. The presence of a judicial officer can create an expectation of decision making and can help overcome lawyers' and litigants' natural resistance to realistically assessing their positions. The judge can initiate settlement discussions earlier than counsel otherwise would and can relieve lawyers of the onus of being the first to suggest discussion of settlement. Some lawyers are reluctant to initiate settlement talks because they are afraid that raising the issue of settlement will be perceived by their opponents as a sign of weakness. That fear might help explain why so many of our respondents think settlement conferences should be mandatory in most actions in federal court and that judges should take steps to encourage settlement even when no one has asked them to do so.

Our data indicate, however, that lawyers believe that initiating dialogue about settlement is by no means the principal contribution judges can make to the process. What judges have to contribute to settlement that lawyers value most is skill in judging. Lawyers value penetrating, analytical exposition and thoughtful, objective, knowledgeable assessment. They want the judges' opinions. They want the judges' suggestions. They want the perspective of the experienced neutral. Data we discuss in a subsequent section shows that a judge's opinion that a settlement offer is reasonable is likely to have a great effect on a recalcitrant client, especially if that client is not often involved in litigation.

There also are many ways judges can contribute to the quality of the settlement dialogue itself: they can defuse emotions, set a constructive and analytical tone, help parties focus on the pertinent matters, and ask questions that expose underdeveloped areas. Judges can help keep litigants talking when they otherwise might retreat into noncommunication. In these and other ways, a judicial officer can improve the civility, efficiency, and efficacy of the negotiation process.

Thus, we infer that when lawyers say judicial involvement is likely to improve significantly prospects for achieving settlement, they mean that the right kind of judicial activism can initiate the process earlier, expedite it, and lead to earlier agreement by improving litigant and lawyer confidence in the fairness or wisdom of specific settlement proposals.

NOTES AND QUESTIONS

1. The survey data showed that a majority of litigators (90% in one judicial district) preferred that judges in settlement conferences "actively offer suggestions and observations" for the settlement of the case. Opinions were sharply divided, however, as to whether the "settlement judge" should be the same judge who would ultimately try the case. What reasons might litigators have for wanting a different judge at trial than at the settlement conference?

2. Two sitting judges, speaking to an audience of other judges, used the following language to describe the judge's role in settlement negotiations:

> One of the fundamental principles of judicial administration is that, in most cases, the absolute result of a trial is not as high a quality of justice as is the freely negotiated, give-a-little, take-a-little settlement. * * * Therefore, it is essential as part of your procedures to provide some techniques that will maximize the possibility of freely negotiated settlements in cases for which you are responsible. * * *

There's no point in talking about settlement at a time when the parties are not well enough informed to rationally discuss the elements in the case, and so that they can tell you enough about it so you can make an intelligent contribution to an evaluation of the case. * * *

If you get to that point, then you are faced with the question as to what your role should be. I always say, "Do you want me to participate in your discussions, or do you want to go off and have them by yourselves?" This is because * * * the use of judge time in settlement negotiations is valuable only if desired. * * *

We are catalysts in settlement. Our role is not that of a traditional judge. Our role at that stage is that of a mediator.

Panel Discussion, Comments by Judge Hubert L. Will, The Role of the Judge in the Settlement Process (Fed. Judicial Center 1983).

I thought it might be well for us to examine our own experiences as practicing lawyers, and think a little bit about why cases settle, because I think that helps us best to analyze the judge's role in the settlement process. * * *

[T]here appear to be two primary factors that lead to settlement. One is anxiety, and the other is the necessity for doing something. Now, none of us like anxiety. * * * It's not a desirable human emotion. * * * [A]nd lawyers, sharing with their clients the desire to eliminate anxiety, want to get rid of it. We eliminate anxiety, of course, by replacing uncertainty with certainty.

But that alone of itself won't settle anything because we are capable of tolerating anxiety for long periods. So, the second thing that seems to me to be an important component of the settlement process is the need to do something by a certain time. All settlement procedures are more efficient if there is a more or less inexorable trial date.

Panel Discussion, Comments by Judge Alvin B. Rubin, The Role of the Judge in the Settlement Process (Fed. Judicial Center 1983).

3. A Colorado state district court issued an administrative order that parties in civil cases who settle after the case has been scheduled for trial shall be assessed a fine of no less than $550 for failure to resolve the case in a timely manner. Do you see any problems, either in terms of policy or due process, with this rule? See Raymond Lloyd Co. v. District Court for the Twentieth Judicial District, 732 P.2d 612 (Colo.1987).

Agent Orange Settlement Conference

In 1967 the United States military forces faced serious obstacles in their efforts to support the Government of South Vietnam. The war, which had begun (for the U.S.) in the early 1960's and had been escalating rapidly since 1965, included an estimated 500,000 American military personnel and showed few signs of completion. A major problem was the infiltration of

North Vietnamese guerillas throughout South Vietnam under cover of heavy forestation and undergrowth. An obvious solution, recognizable immediately to the military mind, was to create and apply a chemical that would eliminate the foliage, thereby exposing the enemy to rifle fire. Several American chemical firms prepared the defoliant, named Agent Orange, and the U.S. military used it to spray enormous forested areas in rural South Vietnam. The results were not only disappointing in terms of military strategy, but disastrous (at least allegedly) for the health of those required to live and work in an Agent Orange environment.

In 1978, three years after the last Americans left Vietnam, many veterans and their families filed individual and class action lawsuits in federal court against the chemical companies responsible for manufacturing and distributing Agent Orange. The plaintiffs complained of multiple diseases caused by exposure to the defoliant. By the conclusion of the district court case in 1985, it involved a plaintiff class of over 2.4 million veterans and family members, seven defendant corporations, the U.S. Government as a potential indemnitor, a docket sheet containing 375 pages and roughly 6,000 entries, and one entire room full of filed documents.

The lawyers settled this complex case on Monday, May 7, 1984, the date set for trial to begin, after intense nonstop settlement discussions led by Judge Jack B. Weinstein throughout the weekend. In the following selection, Professor Schuck describes the final three months:

Peter H. Schuck, The Role of Judges in Settling Complex Cases: The Agent Orange Example

53 U.Chi.L.Rev. 337, 344–348 (1986).

In February 1984, Weinstein requested and obtained permission to retain, at the defendants' expense, an unnamed consultant to develop a settlement strategy and plan. That consultant was later revealed to be Ken Feinberg, a lawyer whom Weinstein knew and trusted. Feinberg was not only knowledgeable about toxic tort litigation, but also had a reputation as an effective mover, shaker, and conciliator. By mid-March, he had prepared a settlement plan. It stated no dollar amount but contained three sections: an analysis of the elements for determining the aggregate settlement amount, especially the various sources of uncertainty and the likely number and nature of claims; a discussion of alternative criteria for allocating any liability among the chemical companies; and a discussion of alternative criteria for distributing any settlement fund to claimants. This document, which the judge made available to the lawyers, occasioned considerable disagreement but succeeded in setting the terms for the negotiations that followed.

On April 10, less than three weeks before trial, Weinstein appointed three special masters for settlement. Feinberg and David I. Shapiro, a prominent class action expert and skillful negotiator, would work with the lawyers. Leonard Garment, a Washington political insider, would explore

CHAPTER II Negotiation

what resources the government might contribute to a settlement. Feinberg and Shapiro immediately identified three major obstacles to settlement: the parties were more than *a quarter of a billion dollars* apart; each side was deeply divided internally over whether and on what terms to settle (and in defendants' case, how to allocate liability); and the government was manifestly unwilling to contribute toward a settlement fund or even to participate in settlement negotiations.

The judge and special masters decided to convene an around-the-clock negotiating marathon at the courthouse during the weekend before the trial. The lawyers were ordered to appear on Saturday morning, May 5, with their "toothbrushes and full negotiating authority." On that morning, while preliminary jury selection work was proceeding in another room, Weinstein met with the lawyers and gave them a "pep talk" about settlement. Then the special masters undertook a grueling two-day course of shuttle diplomacy, holding separate meetings with each side interspersed with private conferences with Judge Weinstein. On several occasions, the judge met privately with each side.

Several features of the discussion were particularly salient in generating the settlement agreement. First, the court did not permit the two sides to meet face-to-face until the very end, after the terms of the deal had been defined. This strategy preserved the court's control over the negotiations and prevented them from fragmenting. In particular, it stymied the plaintiffs' lawyers in their last-ditch effort to improve on the deal by settling with five of the defendants and isolating Monsanto and Diamond Shamrock, the two companies they thought most vulnerable to liability and punitive damages.

Second, the masters attempted to break log-jams in the negotiations by helping the lawyers to predict the consequences of the various approaches under consideration, and by proposing alternative solutions. For example, when the chemical companies' lawyers expressed the fear that a settlement would be rendered worthless if a large number of veterans decided to opt out of the class and sue on their own, Shapiro devised a "walk-away" provision that would minimize those concerns. The tax implications of a settlement were also questions that the masters helped to clarify.

Third, when especially difficult issues arose that threatened to derail the settlement, the parties agreed to be bound by the judge's decision. The most important example of the judge acting as arbitrator involved perhaps the most difficult question facing the defendants—how to allocate liability among themselves. Another example involved the question of one of the defendants' "ability to pay" its share.

Fourth, the judge and his special masters, while being careful not to be duplicitous, did emphasize different things to each side. In their discussions with plaintiffs' lawyers, they stressed the weakness of the evidence on causation, the novelty of many questions of law in the case, the consequent risk of reversal on appeal of a favorable verdict, the prospect that they might lose everything if they rejected settlement, and the enormous costs of continued litigation. To the defendants' lawyers, they stressed the pre-

D. Professional and Legal Framework for Negotiation

sumed pro-plaintiff sympathies of Brooklyn juries, the reputational damage that protracted litigation and unfavorable publicity would cause their clients, and the high costs of the trial and of the inevitable appeals.

Fifth, a common theme in all discussions was the pervasive *uncertainty* that surrounded the law, the facts, the duration and ultimate outcome of the litigation, and the damages likely to be awarded. By almost all accounts, it was this uncertainty that proved to be the decisive inducement to settlement. On one count, however, Judge Weinstein left little doubt in the lawyers' minds: the court, having crafted and taken responsibility for the settlement, was in a position to make it stick.

Sixth, the imminence and ineluctability of trial "concentrated the minds" of the lawyers as nothing else could have done. This deadline imparted to their deliberations an urgency and a seriousness that swept aside objections that might have undermined negotiations in less compelling circumstances. The lawyers' growing physical and mental exhaustion during that weekend of feverish intensity abetted the conciliatory effect. As one plaintiff's lawyer later complained in his challenge to the validity of the settlement, "the Judge wore us all down with that tactic."

Seventh, the judge and special masters displayed a degree of skill, sophistication, imagination, and artistry in fashioning the settlement that almost all the participants viewed as highly unusual. But even this would not have availed had Judge Weinstein not inspired an extraordinary measure of respect, even awe, in the lawyers, and had the special masters not been viewed as enjoying the authority to speak and make commitments for him.

Eighth, the settlement was negotiated without any agreement (or even any serious discussion) of how the settlement fund would be distributed among the claimants, and without reliable information as to the number of claims that would be filed. The first, of course, was of great interest to the plaintiffs and a matter of indifference to the defendants. The second, however, was significant to both sides. It is not at all certain that settlement could have been reached had the parties been required to resolve these issues in advance. The problem was not simply that preparation of a distribution plan required an immense amount of analysis. A protracted process of political compromise and education was also needed to gain support for the plan, a process whose results even now remain doubtful and perhaps legally vulnerable.

Ninth, the lawyers on the PMC [Plaintiffs' Management Committee] at the time of the settlement possessed very different personalities, ideologies, and incentives than those of the group of lawyers that had launched the case and carried it through its first five years. These differences likely affected the lawyers' disposition to settle. The veterans' passionate desire for vindication at trial, quite apart from their wish for compensation, had strongly driven their chosen lawyer, Victor Yannacone, during the earlier stages of the litigation. Yet the PMC's deliberations concerning the settlement were strongly influenced by lawyers who had only the most attenuated relationship to the veterans. And under the terms of an internal fee-

304   CHAPTER II NEGOTIATION

sharing agreement, these lawyers would be secured financially by even a "low" settlement.

Finally, the court was prepared to allocate substantial resources to the quest for a settlement. Judge Weinstein devoted a great deal of his own time to thinking through and implementing a settlement strategy. His three special masters for settlement commanded high compensation and worked long hours. Their billings to the court totaled hundreds of thousands of dollars, even excluding the massive amount of work they later invested in connection with the distribution plan.

According to virtually all of the lawyers who participated in the negotiation of the Agent Orange settlement, Judge Weinstein's distinctive intervention was essential to the settlement. It is possible, of course, that the lawyers are wrong, and that a pretrial settlement would have been reached even without Weinstein's intervention—or, at the very least, that a settlement would have been reached after some witnesses had testified and "blood" had been drawn. But the court's settlement activity was regarded as crucial by those in the best position to know.

NOTES AND QUESTIONS

1. The Agent Orange settlement cannot be used as a guide for lawyers in the typical lawsuit since the case was anything but typical. Several lessons, however, emerge: 1) the settlement process in a complex litigation often needs a manager—if a lawyer does not serve in that role (in addition to his role as advocate), the judge or a master may; 2) creativeness and flexibility are frequently indispensible to settlement; 3) a judge has many available and appropriate resources which can improve the climate for settlement; 4) the judge can easily assume the role of a "mediator with muscle," giving rise to charges of possible overreaching and coercion; and 5) a trial deadline is perhaps the single most effective tool promoting settlement.

2. One ambitious form of structured negotiation and settlement is the Asbestos Claims Facility, created in 1984 by representatives of insurance companies and manufacturers of asbestos products in an attempt to resolve the tens of thousands of asbestos cases pending (and still to be filed) in state and federal courts around the country. The Facility, governed by a Board of Directors with equal representation from manufacturers and insurers, provided adjusters who made offers of compensation to asbestos victims who submitted claims to it. If the claimant rejected the offer, he could pursue relief in court. The Facility also provided ADR procedures for claims by producers against insurers. See description in Richard L. Marcus & Edward F. Sherman, Complex Litigation 835–36 (1985). The Facility had a modest success in resolving claims, but some asbestos manufacturers and insurers and many plaintiffs chose to stay out. Why would claimants spurn such a non-binding settlement process?

b.   FORM OF PARTICIPATION REQUIRED

Lawyers recognize that judicial involvement can improve the chances for settlement, and they welcome "the right kind of judicial activism," as

D. PROFESSIONAL AND LEGAL FRAMEWORK FOR NEGOTIATION

Judge Brazil's article notes. A central issue is, of course, what form of participation by parties and their lawyers is helpful to achieving the goal of a fair settlement efficiently arrived at. To what degree can a court require such participation in judicial settlement conferences without distorting the existing balance of interaction of the parties? These same questions are equally important for other mandated forms of ADR, such as mediation and evaluative and "trial run" processes.

Edward F. Sherman, Court–Mandated Alternative Dispute Resolution: What Form of Participation Should Be Required?

46 SMU L.Rev. 2079, 2089–92, 2094–96 (1993).

Over the past several years some judges in ordering parties to participate in ADR proceedings have included a provision that they must participate in good faith. A number of states have also adopted, by statute or rule, a good faith participation requirement for mediation or ADR.[17] A good faith participation requirement is obviously premised on the belief that since ADR is non-binding, it will be a futile exercise unless the parties engage in it with willingness to present their best arguments and to listen to those of the other side with an open mind.

1. Inadequacy of Case Precedents for Policy Guidance

There is remarkably little case law that examines policy issues as to the propriety of a requirement of good faith participation in ADR. A good faith standard first appeared in a 1983 amendment to Rule 16, the pretrial conference rule on which the authority for federal courts' annexation of ADR processes has been based. Rule 16(f) provides for sanctions, upon motion or a judge's own initiative, for a party's or its attorney's failing to obey a scheduling or pretrial order, being "substantially unprepared to participate in the conference," or failing "to participate in good faith." There have been few reported cases on the application of the Rule 16 good faith participation requirement. It is usually failure to appear[18] or lack of preparation[19] rather than the quality of participation, that has resulted in sanctions. That is not surprising since a settlement conference with a judge

---

17. *See, e.g.,* Me.Rev.Stat.Ann. tit. 19 § 214 (West Supp.1992) (requiring a good faith effort to mediate in mandatory domestic mediation); Minn.Stat.Ann. § 583.27 (West 1988 & Supp.1992) (requiring good faith mediation in farm mortgage mediations with authority in mediator to determine that a party is "not participating in good faith").

18. *See* Barsoumian v. Szozda, 108 F.R.D. 426 (S.D.N.Y.1985) (sanction of $300 attorney fees and $200 court costs imposed on plaintiff's attorney for failure to appear at pre-trial conference); In re McDowell, 33 B.R. 323 (Bankr.N.D.Ohio 1983) (default judgment entered against defendant for failure of his lawyer to appear at pre-trial conference).

19. *See* Flaherty v. Dayton Elec. Mfg. Co., 109 F.R.D. 617, 618–19 (D.Mass.1986) (sanction of payment of opposing counsel's fees and costs of preparation for pre-trial conference entered against plaintiff's attorney who was "substantially unprepared" in not knowing her client's injuries, medical expenses, lost earnings, or whether worker's compensation payments had been received).

CHAPTER II NEGOTIATION

is usually informal, leaving both the judge and attorneys considerable leeway in how they will participate.[20] Only recently has there been an emphasis on attendance and participation by the parties themselves, raising a host of new issues about participation. Thus Rule 16 precedents offer little guidance as to the scope of the good faith participation requirement in ADR.

* * *

2. *Inadequacy of the Collective Bargaining Analogy*

A possible source for policy guidance in applying the "good faith participation" requirement is collective bargaining. Under the labor laws, unions and management that are required to engage in collective bargaining must bargain in good faith.[21] Is that an apt analogy for ADR? Both ADR and collective bargaining would undoubtedly benefit from the parties' good faith participation. But there are differences in ADR which suggest that such participation is not as critical to the process as in collective bargaining and that the content of "good faith participation" is more difficult to determine.

First, the necessity for demanding good faith participation is less in ADR than in collective bargaining. The failure of an ADR proceeding simply means that the parties are relegated to their basic constitutional right to a trial. Failure of collective bargaining, on the other hand, can have severe social consequences—labor unrest, non-cooperation, and strikes. The fact that there is no reasonable fall-back process after unsuccessful collective bargaining underlines the importance of forcing the parties to meet a certain level of participation.

Second, the labor laws impose positive duties on management and labor to participate in collective bargaining that do not exist in the procedural context of ADR. Negotiation in good faith is viewed as critical to labor's rights to share in the determination of contract provisions. The good faith participation duty in collective bargaining refers to "a *bilateral* procedure whereby the employer and the bargaining representative *jointly* attempt to set wages and working conditions for the employees."[22] In effect, the conduct of the collective bargaining process itself is a playing out of the substantive rights guaranteed in the labor laws.

There is no similar substantive entitlement of parties in an ADR proceeding. A party has no right to force another party to accept its participation in shaping a settlement agreement. The authority for ADR in court rules and orders is only procedural, with express limitations on enlarging or modifying substantive rights. If the ADR is not successful, it

---

20. *See* R. Lawrence Dessem, Pretrial Litigation: Law, Policy and Practice 477–83 (1991).

21. 29 U.S.C. §§ 158(a)(5), (b)(3); (d) (1988).

22. Charles Morris, The Developing Labor Law 574 (2d ed. 1983) (referring to General Elec. Co., 150 NLRB 192 (1964)), *enforced,* 418 F.2d 736 (2d Cir.1969), *cert. denied,* 397 U.S. 965 (1970) (emphasis in original).

D. Professional and Legal Framework for Negotiation

will be followed by a trial where the parties' substantive rights can be vindicated.

* * *

3. *Incompatibility with Values and Objectives of Litigation*

If the ADR and collective-bargaining precedents provide little policy analysis, they do at least demonstrate that too expansive a "good faith participation" requirement may not be compatible with the four principles underlying the values and objectives of court-mandated ADR [which were set out earlier in the article]. Although in a nonbinding ADR proceeding, a broad participation requirement may not be *coercive* in the *Kothe* sense in which a judge attempts to impose his settlement figure on the parties, the higher the level of participation required, the greater the coercion by forcing a party to present its case in a manner not of its choosing. This shades into an invasion of *litigant autonomy* by interfering with the party's choice as to how to present its case. A legitimate claim of litigant autonomy can be made as to those matters of case presentation as to which the parties have superior expertise and can best perform in the interests of accuracy and efficiency. Under the principle of providing the *equivalent of a day in court,* the good faith participation requirement could result in a freer exchange of information and views, but, by requiring the parties to participate as they might not have chosen to do in a trial, it does not necessarily enhance their feeling of having had a fair proceeding. For the equivalent of a day in court, no greater degree of participation should be required than is needed for fairness under the ADR process (which places a high value on litigant autonomy and lack of coercion). This shades into the fourth principle—*calculated to achieve its process purposes*—which insists that the parties not be required to perform unnecessary or futile acts that are not reasonably likely to result in settlement. Imposing collective-bargaining kinds of good faith requirements on the parties seems as likely to result in satellite litigation over sanctions as to improve the possibility of settlement.

Exchange of Position Papers and Objective Information

If a "good faith participation" requirement is undesirable in ADR, there are forms of participation that would enhance the likelihood of success that rely on objective conduct and therefore are more easily enforced by courts. For any form of ADR to succeed, there must be some indication of the parties' positions on the relevant issues and some exchange of basic factual information. Requiring the parties to provide each other and the third-party neutral with position papers and other relevant information lays a basis for meaningful consideration of the case without mandating specific forms of presentation or interaction with the other party. It encourages further oral participation and interaction without having to specify its form, since once having submitted a position paper, parties and counsel are less likely to refuse to discuss their positions at the ADR proceeding.

308 CHAPTER II NEGOTIATION

A reasonable order would be that the parties provide a position paper in advance of the ADR proceeding which would include a plain and concise statement of: (1) the legal and factual issues in dispute, (2) the party's position on those issues, (3) the relief sought (including a particularized itemization of all elements of damage claimed), and (4) any offers and counter-offers previously made.[23] This is a shortened list of the kinds of items that are routinely required by federal courts in proposed pretrial orders under the authority of the Rule 16 pretrial conference rule.

The order might also require the parties to provide to the other side in advance, or to bring to the ADR proceeding, certain documents, such as current medical reports or specific business records. It would thus also serve as a discovery or subpoena order. Such an order may not be necessary if discovery has already been conducted in the normal course of the litigation (although updating of documents, such as medical records, is still often necessary). Courts should be aware of the interplay between on-going discovery in the case and any production provisions contained in an ADR order. The two should be coordinated so as not to conflict. When ADR is ordered early in the litigation before discovery, some form of abbreviated discovery may be necessary if the ADR proceeding is to be meaningful.[24] On the other hand, there is a growing tendency for courts to stay ordinary discovery if a scheduled ADR proceeding could make full discovery unnecessary.[25] Courts should take care to insure that ADR not be used strategically as a vehicle to delay or frustrate normal discovery. If a stay of discovery is granted, the court should require the ADR proceeding to take place within a reasonably short time period.

MINIMAL MEANINGFUL PARTICIPATION

Although exchange of position papers and objective information often provides an alternative to mandating a specific level of participation in ADR, there can still be a need for a minimal level of oral participation by the parties if the process is to have a genuine hope of success. It is not easy to fashion a term to describe what that minimal level should be because the necessary degree of participation varies with the type of ADR process involved. For want of a better term, I have adopted the language used by some courts that require the parties to participate "in a meaningful

---

23. Fed.R.Civ.P. 16(a), (b), & (c). These items are culled from a larger list required by Local Rule 235-7 of the U.S. District Court for the Northern District of California.

24. Abbreviated discovery may be accomplished by court order or agreement of the parties. Consider the following description of discovery in "fast track settlement" in automobile product liability cases:

In a fast track settlement, the plaintiff and defendant agree shortly after the defendant has answered the lawsuit to forego formal discovery and court action for a specified period to pursue settlement. It usually in-

volves the plaintiff voluntarily producing the vehicles to the defendant for inspection and voluntarily producing documents and other information requested by the defendant, which it needs for its settlement evaluation.

W. Douglas Matthews & Timothy F. Lee, *Identifying and Developing a Crashworthiness Case*, 26 Texas Trial Lawyers Forum No. 4, 17, at 21 (1992).

25. *See* Wagshal v. Foster, 1993 WL 86499 (D.D.C.1993) (discovery stayed pending parties' resort to mandatory ADR procedure with "case evaluator").

manner."[26] Although hardly a model of certainty and precision, a "minimal meaningful participation" standard avoids the subjectivity of "good faith participation" by suggesting that the degree of participation required to be "meaningful" is related to the goal of the ADR procedure. Since the methodology and objectives of ADR processes vary a good deal, the "minimal meaningful participation" standard allows flexibility of participation depending on the particular process involved in each case.

NOTES AND QUESTIONS

1. What "minimal meaningful participation" should be required of a party in a settlement conference? What more is required than simply attending?

2. Should "good faith participation" ever be required for a settlement conference?

3. Consider the following settlement conference rule from the U.S. District Court for the Central District of California:

Rule 23. Mandatory Settlement Procedures

23.1. Policy. It is the policy of the Court to encourage disposition of civil litigation by settlement when such is in the best interest of the parties. The Court favors any reasonable means to accomplish this goal. Nothing in this rule shall be construed to the contrary. The parties are urged first to discuss and to attempt to reach settlement among themselves without resort to these procedures.

23.2. Proceeding Mandatory. Unless exempted by this rule or otherwise ordered by the Court, the parties in each civil case shall participate in one of the settlement procedures authorized by this rule.

* * *

23.2.2. *Excuses.* A judge either on application of a party or sua sponte may excuse counsel in any case from compliance with this rule.

23.3. Time for Proceedings. No later than forty-five (45) days before the final Local Rule 9 pretrial conference, the parties shall participate in one of the approved settlement procedures set forth in this rule and selected by the parties. Except in the case of Settlement Procedure No. 1, a Notice of Settlement Procedure Selection, signed by counsel for both sides, shall be filed not later than fourteen (14) days before the date scheduled for the settlement procedure. The notice shall state the settlement procedure selected, the name of the settlement officer and the date, time and place of the settlement procedure.

23.4. Court-Ordered Proceedings. If the parties do not file a timely Notice of Settlement Procedure Selection (and the Court has not consented

---

26. *See, e.g.,* W.D.Tex.R. CV–87(f)(2) (providing for "appropriate sanctions" against a party who "fails to participate in the [court-annexed] arbitration process in a meaningful manner").

310 CHAPTER II NEGOTIATION

to engage in Settlement Procedure No. 1), the Court may order the parties to participate in any of the settlement procedures approved by this rule.

23.5. Approved Settlement Procedures.

23.5.1. Settlement Procedure No. 1. With the consent of all parties and the concurrence of the Court, the parties shall appear before the judge assigned to the case for such settlement proceedings as the judge may conduct.

23.5.2. Settlement Procedure No. 2. With the consent of the Court, the parties shall appear before a judge of the Court, other than the judge assigned to the case, or a magistrate judge for settlement proceedings.

23.5.3. Settlement Procedure No. 3. The parties shall appear before an attorney for settlement proceedings. If the parties agree on this procedure but are unable to agree upon an attorney to conduct it, an attorney shall be appointed by the Court.

23.5.4. Settlement Procedure No. 4. The parties shall appear before a retired judicial officer or other private or non-profit dispute resolution body for mediation-type settlement proceedings.

23.6. Requirements for Settlement Procedures. Regardless of the settlement procedure selected, the parties shall:

23.6.1. Submit in writing to the settlement officer, in camera (but not file), a letter (not to exceed five (5) pages) setting forth the party's statement of the case and the party's settlement position, including the last offer or demand made by that party and a separate statement of the offer or demand the party is prepared to make at the settlement conference. This confidential settlement letter shall be delivered to the settlement officer, at least five (5) days before the date of the conference. Such confidential settlement letters shall be returned to the submitting party at the conclusion of the settlement proceedings.

23.6.2. Each party shall appear at the settlement proceeding in person or by a representative with full authority to settle the case, except that parties residing outside the District may have such an authorized representative available by telephone during the entire proceeding.

23.6.3. Each party shall be represented at the settlement proceeding by the attorney who is expected to try the case, unless excused by the settlement officer.

23.6.4. Each party shall have made a thorough analysis of the case prior to the settlement proceeding and shall be fully prepared to discuss all economic and non-economic factors relevant to a full and final settlement of the case.

23.7. Optional Requirements for Settlement Procedures. Without limitation, the settlement officer may require any of the following procedures in any settlement proceeding:

(a) An opening statement by each counsel.

(b) With the agreement of the parties, a "summary" or "mini-trial", tried either to the settlement officer or to a jury.

(c) Presentation of the testimony, summary of testimony or report of expert witnesses.

(d) A closing argument by each counsel.

(e) Any combination of the foregoing.

23.8. Report of Settlement. If a settlement is reached it shall (i) be reported immediately to the judge's courtroom deputy clerk, and (ii) timely memorialized.

23.9. Confidentiality of Proceedings. All settlement proceedings shall be confidential and no statement made therein shall be admissible in any proceeding in the case, unless the parties otherwise agree. No part of a settlement proceeding shall be reported, or otherwise recorded, without the consent of the parties, except for any memorialization of a settlement.

c. OBLIGATION TO ATTEND

Edward F. Sherman, Court–Mandated Alternative Dispute Resolution: What Form of Participation Should Be Required?

46 SMU L.Rev. 2079, 2103–08 (1993).

Court orders that the parties participate in ADR proceedings often provide that they must attend with "full authority to settle the case" and, in the case of a corporate party or governmental body, that a representative attend who has authority to settle. Such orders raise questions, first, as to what persons are included when parties are ordered to attend, and, second, as to what kind of settlement authority the parties and/or attorneys must have.

1. Mandatory Client Attendance

The conviction that it is essential for the parties to attend settlement proceedings has been relatively late in coming. The original pretrial conference rule (Rule 16), promulgated in 1937, authorized federal courts only to "direct the attorneys for the parties to appear before it for a conference." In 1983 it was amended to include, in addition to the attorneys, "any unrepresented parties."[27] Increasingly, however, courts have come to the conclusion that attendance of the parties themselves, whether represented by counsel or not, increases the possibility of success of both settlement

---

27. Fed.R.Civ.P. 16(a), as amended, 1983. The Manual for Complex Litigation 365 (2d ed. 1985) provides in its Sample Order Setting Initial Conference: "Each party represented by counsel shall appear through its attorney who will have primary responsibility for its interests in this litigation. Parties not represented by counsel are expected to appear in person or through a responsible officer."

312   CHAPTER II   NEGOTIATION

conferences and newly emerging ADR proceedings. A 1993 amendment to the rule allows courts to require that "a party or its representative be present or reasonably available by telephone in order to consider possible settlement of the dispute." (Rule 16(c)(16)).

Professor Riskin has made an examination of the advantages and disadvantages of client attendance that offers useful guidance for courts. Advantages include giving the client a chance to tell his story in his own words, learning about the strengths and weaknesses of both sides, permitting him to act on new information, allowing cooperation and momentum to build in the offer process, clearing up miscommunications about facts and interests between lawyers and clients, and providing the information to spot opportunities for problem-solving solutions. Disadvantages include the risk that the client may give away valuable information that could leave him vulnerable to exploitation or weaken his case, that exposure to the other side's behavior will anger or harden some clients, or that direct communication will cause a flare-up and loss of objectivity.[28]

On balance, required attendance of individual parties at ADR proceedings is consistent with the four principles of court-mandated ADR.[29] Client participation reduces coercion by providing full information to the person who must ultimately decide whether to settle and enhances litigant autonomy by allowing the client to participate in the presentation of his own case. It strengthens the feeling of the parties that they have had their day in court. Its compatibility with the ability of the ADR process to achieve its objectives varies with the process. It is certainly consistent with the objectives of "facilitative" ADR* by including the client as an active participant in searching for solutions. It may not be as important in "evaluative" or "trial run" ADR,[†] as the attorney usually plays the key role in summarizing and presenting the case, but the client can often add a

---

28. Riskin, The Represented Client in a Settlement Conference: The Lessons of G. Heileman Brewing Co. v. Joseph Oat Corp., 69 Wash.U.L.Rev. 1059, 1099–1102 (1991).

29. *Id.* at 1107 n. 167. Riskin concludes that client attendance is more likely to be useful in an ADR process that has such features as "participatory lawyer-client relationships, problem-solving negotiation, and judicial interventions emphasizing facilitation rather than pressure." *Id.* at 1106. He recommends that the "judicial host" in a settlement conference should "1. routinely require attendance of represented clients, and representatives of organizational clients with full settlement authority, in the absence of a suitable, and suitably presented objection, and 2. take appropriate measures to ensure that the client's presence is worthwhile to the client." *Id.* at 1106–07.

* [In "facilitative" ADR, the neutral views her role only as facilitating communica-

tion, and avoids giving an evaluation of the strengths of the parties' cases, opinions as to outcome in a court, or recommendations for terms of settlement. Judicial settlement conferences and mediation are often "facilitative" depending on the approach of the judge or mediator.—Eds.]

† [In "evaluative" ADR, the neutral may provide an evaluation of the strengths of the cases, opinions as to outcome, and recommendations for settlement. Examples are early neutral evaluation (ENE) and settlement conferences and mediations in which an "evaluative" approach is taken. In "trial run" ADR, the parties are provided with an opportunity to present their cases in shortened form to a neutral or neutrals who render a non-binding decision. Examples are court-annexed arbitration, mini-trial, and summary jury trial.—Eds.]

critical aspect to both the case presentation and the negotiation that is expected to follow.

An exception to this analysis is when a named party has no real interest in the case. This frequently arises in personal-injury or property-damage cases filed against a fully insured defendant. Under standard insurance policy provisions, the insurance company has sole authority over the defense of cases, including whether to settle or go to trial. The insurance company representative, therefore, is the crucial person on the defense side for settlement negotiations. The insured defendant may have some interest in the case since its conduct is in question, but determination of that issue may have no monetary consequences to it. Most insured defendants are content to leave settlement matters to the insurance company, with no interest in devoting time and emotional capital to participating in settlement negotiations. An appropriate court order, therefore, would not require an insured defendant to attend when it has no realistic exposure over policy limits and when its consent to settle is not required. It is quite different, however, if there is any realistic possibility of recovery against the defendant above policy limits. The paradigm example arises when a plaintiff offers to settle within policy limits in a state that provides for recovery against an insurance company for bad faith failure to settle. [Then] the defendant has a significant interest to preserve in the settlement negotiations, and, in fact, its desire to escape exposure by having the insurance company settle within policy limits may provide an interesting dynamic in the settlement proceedings.

Difficult questions also arise when the client is not an individual but a corporation. A broad range of issues in this context was explored by a Seventh Circuit en banc decision, *G. Heileman Brewing Co., Inc. v. Joseph Oat Corp.*

* * *

2. Scope of Settlement Authority

Courts also routinely include in ADR orders a requirement that the parties and counsel come to the proceeding with settlement authority.[30] This is based on the frequent experience that a settlement is less likely to be achieved if persons not in attendance must approve the settlement agreed upon. Coming without full settlement authority has also been seen as an illegitimate tactic used by parties, particularly insurance companies, to allow the negotiator to claim inability to bargain outside of a prescribed range and to allow absent officials to disavow agreements made by their negotiating representative as outside their authority.[31]

---

30. *See, e.g., In re Air Crash Disaster at Stapleton International Airport,* 720 F.Supp. 1433, 1441 (D.Colo.1988) (settlement conference order that "Representatives of all parties, with full settlement authority, shall attend the settlement conference and participate fully in all negotiations. The court ex-

pressly notes that the presence of counsel of record does not fulfill the requirement of the presence of an individual with settlement authority.").

31. *See* Chester L. Karrass, Give and Take 96–97 (1974).

CHAPTER II NEGOTIATION

Lockhart v. Patel provides an extreme example of an insurance company's noncompliance with such an order. After a non-binding summary jury trial that awarded the plaintiff $200,000 for a lost eye in a medical malpractice case, the plaintiff agreed to settle for $175,000, but the attorney for the doctor's insurer told the judge he was only authorized to offer $125,000 and not to negotiate any further. The judge then called a settlement conference, directing the defense attorney to bring the home-office representative of the insurance company who had issued these instructions and a representative with equal authority. He said: "Tell them not to send some flunky who has no authority to negotiate. I want someone who can enter into a settlement in this range without having to call anyone else."[32]

The defense attorney brought an adjuster from the local office who advised the court that her instructions from the home office were to reiterate the previous offer "and not to bother to call them back if it were not accepted." The judge then made findings that the insurer "had deliberately refused to obey the order of the court," striking the pleadings of the defendant, declaring him in default, and ordering a show cause hearing why the insurer should not be punished for criminal contempt. Later that day, the insurer settled for $175,000. At the contempt hearing, the judge accepted the assurances of the insurer that "it had all been a misunderstanding" and permitted it to purge itself with a letter of apology from its Chief Executive Officer.

Lockhart is an appropriate fact situation for sanctions. Defendant's refusal to send a representative with any settlement authority at all, other than to reiterate the previous offer, insured that the conference would be a futile proceeding. Requiring settlement authority does not coerce a party into settling for any specific amount, and litigant autonomy cannot justify ignoring a requirement directed at avoiding wasteful negotiation tactics.

The hard cases arise when the representative's settlement authority is more ambiguous than in *Lockhart*. Assume that an insurance company sends a representative with authority to settle only up to $10,000, on the basis that it has thoroughly reviewed the case and is convinced that there is no liability at all and, that, in any event, the reasonable damages are much smaller than that amount. Surely the company should not be required to give its representative authority to settle at a higher amount when it has concluded that there is no justification for doing so. But the key inquiry is what the representative's instructions are. If he is sent without authority to consider any settlement above $10,000, this is essentially a "no authority" case as in *Lockhart*. A court should be entitled to require that the representative at least be open to hearing the arguments of the other side with the possibility of settling at any amount found to be persuasive, even though the representative understands that the company has evaluated the case as not worth more than $10,000. If his authority and instructions are

---

32. 115 F.R.D. 44, 45 (E.D.Ky.1987).

so limited that he is deaf to any persuasion, then he is not the proper representative with adequate authority that the court has ordered.

A further question, however, is whether the representative must himself possess full authority to settle. Would it be sufficient to have a representative at the regional office with broader settlement authority be available by phone? What is troubling with this approach is that the person with the ultimate authority cannot be subjected to the discussion that takes place in the settlement conference, thus undermining the effectiveness of the process. On the other hand, requiring the representative to be the person with ultimate settlement authority can impose enormous burdens on that official's time or force her to delegate the authority further down the line than she finds it prudent to do.

G. Heileman Brewing Co., Inc. v. Joseph Oat Corp. wrestled with these issues. * * *

G. Heileman Brewing Co. v. Joseph Oat Corp.

United States Court of Appeal, Seventh Circuit.
871 F.2d 648.

■ Before BAUER, CHIEF JUDGE, CUMMINGS, WOOD, JR., CUDAHY, POSNER, COFFEY, FLAUM, EASTERBROOK, RIPPLE, MANION and KANNE, CIRCUIT JUDGES.

■ KANNE, CIRCUIT JUDGE.

May a federal district court order litigants—even those represented by counsel—to appear before it in person at a pretrial conference for the purpose of discussing the posture and settlement of the litigants' case? After reviewing the Federal Rules of Civil Procedure and federal district courts' inherent authority to manage and control the litigation before them, we answer this question in the affirmative and conclude that a district court may sanction a litigant for failing to comply with such an order.

I. Background

A federal magistrate ordered Joseph Oat Corporation to send a "corporate representative with authority to settle" to a pretrial conference to discuss disputed factual and legal issues and the possibility of settlement. Although counsel for Oat Corporation appeared, accompanied by another attorney who was authorized to speak on behalf of the principals of the corporation, no principal or corporate representative personally attended the conference. The court determined that the failure of Oat Corporation to send a principal of the corporation to the pretrial conference violated its order. Consequently, the district court imposed a sanction of $5,860.01 upon Oat Corporation pursuant to Federal Rule of Civil Procedure 16(f). This amount represented the costs and attorneys' fees of the opposing parties attending the conference.

II. The Appeal

Oat Corporation appeals, claiming that the district court did not have the authority to order litigants represented by counsel to appear at the pretrial settlement conference. Specifically, Oat Corporation contends that, by negative implication, the language of Rule 16(a)(5) prohibits a district court from directing represented litigants to attend pretrial conferences. That is, because Rule 16 expressly refers to "attorneys for the parties and any unrepresented parties" in introductory paragraph (a), a district court may not go beyond that language to devise procedures which direct the pretrial appearance of parties represented by counsel. Consequently, Oat Corporation concludes that the court lacked the authority to order the pretrial attendance of its corporate representatives and, even if the court possessed such authority, the court abused its discretion to exercise that power in this case. Finally, Oat Corporation argues that the court abused its discretion to enter sanctions.

A. Authority to Order Attendance

First, we must address Oat Corporation's contention that a federal district court lacks the authority to order litigants who are represented by counsel to appear at a pretrial conference. Our analysis requires us to review the Federal Rules of Civil Procedure and district courts' inherent authority to manage the progress of litigation.

Rule 16 addresses the use of pretrial conferences to formulate and narrow issues for trial as well as to discuss means for dispensing with the need for costly and unnecessary litigation. As we stated in Link v. Wabash R.R., 291 F.2d 542, 547 (7th Cir.1961), aff'd, 370 U.S. 626, 82 S.Ct. 1386, 8 L.Ed.2d 734 (1962):

> Pre-trial procedure has become an integrated part of the judicial process on the trial level. Courts must be free to use it and to control and enforce its operation. Otherwise, the orderly administration of justice will be removed from control of the trial court and placed in the hands of counsel. We do not believe such a course is within the contemplation of the law.

The pretrial settlement of litigation has been advocated and used as a means to alleviate overcrowded dockets, and courts have practiced numerous and varied types of pretrial settlement techniques for many years. Since 1983, Rule 16 has expressly provided that settlement of a case is one of several subjects which should be pursued and discussed vigorously during pretrial conferences.

The language of Rule 16 does not give any direction to the district court upon the issue of a court's authority to order litigants who are represented by counsel to appear for pretrial proceedings. Instead, Rule 16 merely refers to the participation of trial advocates—attorneys of record and pro se litigants. However, the Federal Rules of Civil Procedure do not completely describe and limit the power of the federal courts. HMG

Property Investors, Inc. v. Parque Indus. Rio Canas, Inc., 847 F.2d 908, 915 (1st Cir.1988).

The concept that district courts exercise procedural authority outside the explicit language of the rules of civil procedure is not frequently documented, but valid nevertheless. The Supreme Court has acknowledged that the provisions of the Federal Rules of Civil Procedure are not intended to be the exclusive authority for actions to be taken by district courts. Link v. Wabash R.R., 370 U.S. 626, 82 S.Ct. 1386, 8 L.Ed.2d 734 (1962).

In *Link,* the Supreme Court noted that a district court's ability to take action in a procedural context may be grounded in " 'inherent power,' governed not by rule or statute but by the control necessarily vested in courts to manage their own affairs so as to achieve the orderly and expeditious disposition of cases." 370 U.S. at 630–31, 82 S.Ct. at 1389 (footnotes omitted). This authority likewise forms the basis for continued development of procedural techniques designed to make the operation of the court more efficient, to preserve the integrity of the judicial process, and to control courts' dockets. Because the rules form and shape certain aspects of a court's inherent powers, yet allow the continued exercise of that power where discretion should be available, the mere absence of language in the federal rules specifically authorizing or describing a particular judicial procedure should not, and does not, give rise to a negative implication of prohibition.

Obviously, the district court, in devising means to control cases before it, may not exercise its inherent authority in a manner inconsistent with rule or statute. As we stated in Strandell v. Jackson County, 838 F.2d 884, 886 (7th Cir.1988), such power should "be exercised in a manner that is in harmony with the Federal Rules of Civil Procedure." This means that "where the rules directly mandate a specific procedure to the exclusion of others, inherent authority is proscribed."

In this case, we are required to determine whether a court's power to order the pretrial appearance of litigants who are represented by counsel is inconsistent with, or in derogation of, Rule 16. We must remember that Rule 1 states, with unmistakable clarity, that the Federal Rules of Civil Procedure "shall be construed to secure the just, speedy, and inexpensive determination of every action." This language explicitly indicates that the federal rules are to be liberally construed. There is no place in the federal civil procedural system for the proposition that rules having the force of statute, though in derogation of the common law, are to be strictly construed.

"[The] spirit, intent, and purpose [of Rule 16] is ... broadly remedial, allowing courts to actively manage the preparation of cases for trial." In re Baker, 744 F.2d 1438, 1440 (10th Cir.1984) (en banc), cert. denied, 471 U.S. 1014, 105 S.Ct. 2016, 85 L.Ed.2d 299 (1985). Rule 16 is not designed as a device to restrict or limit the authority of the district judge in the conduct of pretrial conferences. As the Tenth Circuit Court of Appeals sitting en banc stated in Baker, "the spirit and purpose of the amendments to Rule 16 always have been within the inherent power of the courts to manage

318 CHAPTER II NEGOTIATION

their affairs as an independent constitutional branch of government." Id. at 1441.

We agree with this interpretation of Rule 16. The wording of the rule and the accompanying commentary make plain that the entire thrust of the amendment to Rule 16 was to urge judges to make wider use of their powers and to manage actively their dockets from an early stage. We therefore conclude that our interpretation of Rule 16 to allow district courts to order represented parties to appear at pretrial settlement conferences merely represents another application of a district judge's inherent authority to preserve the efficiency, and more importantly the integrity, of the judicial process.

To summarize, we simply hold that the action taken by the district court in this case constituted the proper use of inherent authority to aid in accomplishing the purpose and intent of Rule 16. We reaffirm the notion that the inherent power of a district judge—derived from the very nature and existence of his judicial office—is the broad field over which the Federal Rules of Civil Procedure are applied. Inherent authority remains the means by which district judges deal with circumstances not proscribed or specifically addressed by rule or statute, but which must be addressed to promote the just, speedy, and inexpensive determination of every action.

B. Exercise of Authority to Order Attendance

Having determined that the district court possessed the power and authority to order the represented litigants to appear at the pretrial settlement conference, we now must examine whether the court abused its discretion to issue such an order.

At the outset, it is important to note that a district court cannot coerce settlement. Kothe v. Smith, 771 F.2d 667, 669 (2d Cir.1985).[33] In this case, considerable concern has been generated because the court ordered "corporate representatives with authority to settle" to attend the conference. In our view, "authority to settle," when used in the context of this case, means that the "corporate representative" attending the pretrial conference was required to hold a position within the corporate entity allowing him to speak definitively and to commit the corporation to a particular position in the litigation. We do not view "authority to settle" as a requirement that corporate representatives must come to court willing to settle on someone else's terms, but only that they come to court in order to consider the possibility of settlement.

As Chief Judge Crabb set forth in her decision which we now review:

33. Likewise, a court cannot compel parties to stipulate to facts. J.F. Edwards Constr. Co. v. Anderson Safeway Guard Rail Corp., 542 F.2d 1318 (7th Cir.1976) (per curiam). Nor can a court compel litigants to participate in a nonbinding summary jury trial. Strandell, 838 F.2d at 887. In the same vein, a court cannot force a party to engage in discovery. Identiseal Corp. v. Positive Identification Sys., Inc., 560 F.2d 298 (7th Cir.1977).

There is no indication ... that the magistrate's order contemplated requiring Joseph Oat ... to agree to any particular form of settlement or even to agree to settlement at all. The only requirement imposed by the magistrate was that the representative [of Oat Corporation] be present with full authority to settle, should terms for settlement be proposed that were acceptable to [Oat Corporation].

If this case represented a situation where Oat Corporation had sent a corporate representative and was sanctioned because that person refused to make an offer to pay money—that is, refused to submit to settlement coercion—we would be faced with a decidedly different issue—a situation we would not countenance.

The Advisory Committee Notes to Rule 16 state that "[a]lthough it is not the purpose of Rule 16(b)(7) to impose settlement negotiations on unwilling litigants, it is believed that providing a neutral forum for discussing [settlement] might foster it." These Notes clearly draw a distinction between being required to attend a settlement conference and being required to participate in settlement negotiations. Thus, under the scheme of pretrial settlement conferences, the corporate representative remains free, on behalf of the corporate entity, to propose terms of settlement independently—but he may be required to state those terms in a pretrial conference before a judge or magistrate.

As an alternative position, Oat Corporation argues that the court abused its discretion to order corporate representatives of the litigants to attend the pretrial settlement conference. Oat Corporation determined that because its business was a "going concern":

It would be unreasonable for the magistrate to require the president of that corporation to leave his business [in Camden, New Jersey] to travel to Madison, Wisconsin, to participate in a settlement conference. The expense and burden on the part of Joseph Oat to comply with this order was clearly unreasonable. Consequently, Oat Corporation believes that the district court abused its authority.

We recognize, as did the district court, that circumstances could arise in which requiring a corporate representative (or any litigant) to appear at a pretrial settlement conference would be so onerous, so clearly unproductive, or so expensive in relation to the size, value, and complexity of the case that it might be an abuse of discretion. Moreover, "[b]ecause inherent powers are shielded from direct democratic controls, they must be exercised with restraint and discretion." However, the facts and circumstances of this case clearly support the court's actions to require the corporate representatives of the litigants to attend the pretrial conference personally.

This litigation involved a claim for $4 million—a claim which turned upon the resolution of complex factual and legal issues. The litigants expected the trial to last from one to three months and all parties stood to incur substantial legal fees and trial expenses. This trial also would have preempted a large segment of judicial time—not an insignificant factor. Thus, because the stakes were high, we do not believe that the burden of requiring a corporate representative to attend a pretrial settlement conference was out of proportion to the benefits to be gained, not only by the litigants but also by the court.

Additionally, the corporation did send an attorney, Mr. Fitzpatrick, from Philadelphia, Pennsylvania to Madison, Wisconsin to "speak for" the principals of the corporation. It is difficult to see how the expenses involved in sending Mr. Fitzpatrick from Philadelphia to Madison would have greatly exceeded the expenses involved in sending a corporate representative from Camden to Madison. Consequently, we do not think the expenses and distance to be traveled are unreasonable in this case.

Furthermore, no objection to the magistrate's order was made prior to the date the pretrial conference resumed. Oat Corporation contacted the magistrate's office concerning the order's requirements and was advised of the requirements now at issue. However, Oat Corporation never objected to its terms, either when it was issued or when Oat Corporation sought clarification. Consequently, Oat Corporation was left with only one course of action: it had to comply fully with the letter and intent of the order and argue about its reasonableness later.

We thus conclude that the court did not abuse its authority and discretion to order a representative of the Oat Corporation to appear for the pretrial settlement conference on December 19.

C. Sanctions

Finally, we must determine whether the court abused its discretion by sanctioning Oat Corporation for failing to comply with the order to appear at the pretrial settlement conference. Oat Corporation argues that the instructions directing the appearance of corporate representatives were unclear and ambiguous. Consequently, it concludes that the sanctions were improper.

Absent an abuse of discretion, we may not disturb a district court's imposition of sanctions for failure of a party to comply with a pretrial order. The issue on review is not whether we would have imposed these costs upon Oat Corporation, but whether the district court abused its discretion in doing so.

Oat Corporation contends that the presence of Mr. Fitzpatrick, as an attorney authorized to speak on behalf of the principals of Oat Corporation, satisfied the requirement that its "corporate representative" attend the December 19 settlement conference. Oat Corporation argues that nothing in either the November 19, 1984 order or the December 14, 1984 order would lead a reasonable person to conclude that a representative or principal from the Joseph Oat Corporation was required to attend the conference personally—in effect arguing that sanctions cannot be imposed because the order failed to require a particular person to attend the conference.

We believe that Oat Corporation was well aware of what the court expected. While the November order may have been somewhat ambiguous,

D. Professional and Legal Framework for Negotiation

any ambiguity was eliminated by the magistrate's remarks from the bench on December 14, the written order of December 18, and the direction obtained by counsel from the magistrate's clerk.

III. Conclusion

We hold that Rule 16 does not limit, but rather is enhanced by, the inherent authority of federal courts to order litigants represented by counsel to attend pretrial conferences for the purpose of discussing settlement. Oat Corporation violated the district court's order requiring it to have a corporate representative attend the pretrial settlement conference on December 19, 1984. Under these circumstances, the district court did not abuse its discretion by imposing sanctions for Oat Corporation's failure to comply with the pretrial order.

■ Posner, Circuit Judge, dissenting.

Rule 16(a) of the Federal Rules of Civil Procedure authorizes a district court to "direct the attorneys for the parties and any *unrepresented* parties to appear before it for a [pretrial] conference." The word I have italicized could be thought to carry the negative implication that no represented party may be directed to appear—that was the panel's conclusion—but I hesitate to so conclude in a case that can be decided on a narrower ground.

The main purpose of the pretrial conference is to get ready for trial. For that purpose, only the attorneys need be present, unless a party is acting as his own attorney. The only possible reason for wanting a represented party to be present is to enable the judge or magistrate to explore settlement with the principals rather than with just their agents. Some district judges and magistrates distrust the willingness or ability of attorneys to convey to their clients adequate information bearing on the desirability and terms of settling a case in lieu of pressing forward to trial. The distrust is warranted in some cases, I am sure; but warranted or not, it is what lies behind the concern that the panel opinion had stripped the district courts of a valuable settlement tool—and this at a time of heavy, and growing, federal judicial caseloads. The concern may well be exaggerated, however. The panel opinion may have had little practical significance; it is the rare attorney who will invite a district judge's displeasure by defying a request to produce the client for a pretrial conference.

The question of the district court's power to summon a represented party to a settlement conference is a difficult one. On the one hand, nothing in Rule 16 or in any other rule or statute confers such a power, and there are obvious dangers in too broad an interpretation of the federal courts' inherent power to regulate their procedure. One danger is that it encourages judicial high-handedness ("power corrupts"); several years ago one of the district judges in this circuit ordered Acting Secretary of Labor Brock to appear before him for settlement discussions on the very day Brock was scheduled to appear before the Senate for his confirmation hearing. The broader concern illustrated by the Brock episode is that in their zeal to settle cases judges may ignore the value of other people's time. One reason people hire lawyers is to economize on their own investment of

322 CHAPTER II NEGOTIATION

time in resolving disputes. It is pertinent to note in this connection that Oat is a defendant in this case; it didn't want its executives' time occupied with this litigation.

On the other hand, die Not bricht Eisen ["necessity breaks iron"]. Attorneys often are imperfect agents of their clients, and the workload of our district courts is so heavy that we should hesitate to deprive them of a potentially useful tool for effecting settlement, even if there is some difficulty in finding a legal basis for the tool. Although few attorneys will defy a district court's request to produce the client, those few cases may be the very ones where the client's presence would be most conducive to settlement. If I am right that Rule 16(a) empowers a district court to summon unrepresented parties to a pretrial conference only because their presence may be necessary to get ready for trial, we need not infer that the draftsmen meant to forbid the summoning of represented parties for purposes of exploring settlement. The draftsmen may have been unaware that district courts were asserting a power to command the presence of a represented party to explore settlement. We should hesitate to infer inadvertent prohibitions.

The narrowly "legal" considerations bearing on the question whether district courts have the power asserted by the magistrate in this case are sufficiently equivocal to authorize—indeed compel—us to consider the practical consequences for settlement before deciding what the answer should be. Unfortunately we have insufficient information about those consequences to be able to give a confident answer, but fortunately we need not answer the question in this case—so clear is it that the magistrate abused his discretion, which is to say, acted unreasonably, in demanding that Oat Corporation send an executive having "full settlement authority" to the pretrial conference. This demand, which is different from a demand that a party who has not closed the door to settlement send an executive to discuss possible terms, would be defensible only if litigants had a duty to bargain in good faith over settlement before resorting to trial, and neither Rule 16 nor any other rule, statute, or doctrine imposes such a duty on federal litigants. There is no federal judicial power to coerce settlement. Oat had made clear that it was not prepared to settle the case on any terms that required it to pay money. That was its prerogative, which once exercised made the magistrate's continued insistence on Oat's sending an executive to Madison arbitrary, unreasonable, willful, and indeed petulant. This is apart from the fact that since no one officer of Oat may have had authority to settle the case, compliance with the demand might have required Oat to ship its entire board of directors to Madison. Ultimately Oat did make a money settlement, but there is no indication that it would have settled sooner if only it had complied with the magistrate's demand for the dispatch of an executive possessing "full settlement authority."

* * *

■ COFFEY, CIRCUIT JUDGE, with whom EASTERBROOK, RIPPLE and MANION, CIRCUIT JUDGES, join, dissenting.

D. PROFESSIONAL AND LEGAL FRAMEWORK FOR NEGOTIATION 323

* * * Unlike the majority, I am convinced that Rule 16 does not authorize a trial judge to require a represented party litigant to attend a pretrial conference together with his or her attorney because the rule mandates in clear and unambiguous terms that only an unrepresented party litigant and attorneys may be ordered to appear.

[The opinion goes on to reject "inherent authority" to compel the presence of represented parties.]

■ EASTERBROOK, CIRCUIT JUDGE, with whom POSNER, COFFEY, and MANION, CIRCUIT JUDGES, join, dissenting.

Our case has three logically separate issues. First, whether a district court may demand the attendance of someone other than the party's counsel of record. Second, whether the court may insist that this additional person be an employee rather than an agent selected for the occasion. Third, whether the court may insist that the representative have "full settlement authority"—meaning the authority to agree to pay cash in settlement (maybe authority without cap, although that was not clear). Even if one resolves the first issue as the majority does, it does not follow that district courts have the second or third powers, or that their exercise here was prudent.

The proposition that a magistrate may require a firm to send an employee rather than a representative is puzzling. Corporate "employees" are simply agents of the firm. Corporations choose their agents and decide what powers to give them. Which agents have which powers is a matter of internal corporate affairs. Joseph Oat Corp. sent to the conference not only its counsel of record but also John Fitzpatrick, who had authority to speak for Oat. Now Mr. Fitzpatrick is an attorney, which raised the magistrate's hackles, but why should this count against him? Because Fitzpatrick is a part-time rather than a full-time agent of the corporation? Why can't the corporation make its own decision about how much of the agent's time to hire? Is Oat being held in contempt because it is too small to have a cadre of legal employees—because its general counsel practices with a law firm rather than being "in house"?

At all events, the use of outside attorneys as negotiators is common. Many a firm sends its labor lawyer to the bargaining table when a collective bargaining agreement is about to expire, there to dicker with the union (or with labor's lawyer). Each side has a statutory right to choose its representatives. 29 U.S.C. § 158(b)(1)(B). Many a firm sends its corporate counsel to the bargaining table when a merger is under discussion. Oat did the same thing to explore settlement of litigation. A lawyer is no less suited to this task than to negotiating the terms of collective bargaining or merger agreements. Firms prefer to send skilled negotiators to negotiating sessions (lawyers are especially useful when the value of a claim depends on the resolution of legal questions) while reserving the time of executives for business. Oat understandably wanted its management team to conduct its construction business.

As for the third subject, whether the representative must have "settlement authority": the magistrate's only reason for ordering a corporate representative to come was to facilitate settlement then and there. As I understand Magistrate Groh's opinion, and Judge Crabb's, the directive was to send a person with "full settlement authority". Fitzpatrick was deemed inadequate only because he was under instructions not to pay money. E.g.: "While Mr. Fitzpatrick claimed authority to speak for Oat, he stated that he had no authority to make a [monetary] offer. *Thus,* no representative of Oat or National having authority to settle the case was present at the conference as the order directed" (magistrate's opinion, emphasis added). On learning that Fitzpatrick did not command Oat's treasury, the magistrate ejected him from the conference and never listened to what he had to say on Oat's behalf, never learned whether Fitzpatrick might be receptive to others' proposals. (We know that Oat ultimately did settle the case for money, after it took part in and "prevailed" at a summary jury trial—participation and payment each demonstrating Oat's willingness to consider settlement.) The magistrate's approach implies that if the Chairman and CEO of Oat had arrived with instructions from the Board to settle the case without paying cash, and to negotiate and bring back for the Board's consideration any financial proposals, Oat still would have been in contempt.

Both magistrate and judge demanded the presence not of a "corporate representative" in the sense of a full-time employee but of a representative with "full authority to settle". Most corporations reserve power to agree (as opposed to power to discuss) to senior managers or to their boards of directors—the difference depending on the amounts involved. Heileman wanted $4 million, a sum within the province of the board rather than a single executive even for firms much larger than Oat. Fitzpatrick came with power to discuss and recommend; he could settle the case on terms other than cash; he lacked only power to sign a check. The magistrate's order therefore must have required either (a) changing the allocation of responsibility within the corporation, or (b) sending a quorum of Oat's Board.

Magistrate Groh exercised a power unknown even in labor law, where there is a duty to bargain in good faith. 29 U.S.C. § 158(d). Labor and management commonly negotiate through persons with the authority to discuss but not agree. The negotiators report back to management and the union, each of which reserves power to reject or approve the position of its agent. We know from Fed.R.Civ.P. 16—and especially from the Advisory Committee's comment to Rule 16(c) that the Rule's "reference to 'authority' is not intended to insist upon the ability to settle the litigation"—that the parties cannot be compelled to negotiate "in good faith". A defendant convinced it did no wrong may insist on total vindication. Rule 68, which requires a party who turns down a settlement proposal to bear costs only if that party does worse at trial, implies the same thing. Yet if parties are not obliged to negotiate in good faith, on what ground can they be obliged to come with authority to settle on the spot—an authority agents need not carry even when the law requires negotiation? The order we affirm today compels persons who have committed no wrong, who pass every requirement of Rules 11 and 68, who want only the opportunity to receive a decision on the merits, to come to court with open checkbooks on pain of being held in contempt.

Settling litigation is valuable, and courts should promote it. Is settlement of litigation more valuable than settlement of labor disputes, so that courts may do what the NLRB may not? The statutory framework—bona fide negotiations required in labor law but not in litigation—suggests the opposite. Does the desirability of settlement imply that rules of state law allocating authority within a corporation must yield? We have held in other cases that settlements must be negotiated within the framework of existing rules; the desire to get a case over and done with does not justify modifying generally applicable norms.

* * *

■ RIPPLE, CIRCUIT JUDGE, with whom COFFEY, CIRCUIT JUDGE, joins, dissenting.

I join the dissenting opinions of Judge Coffey and Judge Manion. I write separately only to emphasize that the most enduring—and dangerous—impact of the majority's opinion will not be its effect on the conduct of the pretrial conference, but on the relationship between the Judiciary and the Congress in establishing practice and procedure for the federal courts. Recognizing that the line between substance and procedure is at best an indistinct and vague one, the two branches of government have established a long tradition of shared responsibility for this aspect of governance. That tradition is embodied principally—although not exclusively—in the Rules Enabling Act. 28 U.S.C. § 2072. That Act was designed to foster a uniform system of procedure throughout the federal system, supplemented but not altered, by local rules to take care of local problems. Experimentation at the local level in areas where policy choices have not been made at the national level is permitted. Moreover, there is no question that the judicial officer retains a substantial degree of inherent authority to deal with individual situations—as long as that authority is exercised in conformity with the policies embodied in the national rules. However, the Rules Enabling Act hardly contemplates the broad, amorphous, definition of the "inherent power of a district judge" articulated by the majority.

NOTES AND QUESTIONS

1. The majority opinion in Heileman conceded that circumstances could arise in which requiring a corporate representative to appear "would be so onerous, so clearly unproductive, or so expensive in relation to the size, value, and complexity of the case that it might be an abuse of discretion." However, it found no such situation here, where the claim was sizable ($4 million) and turned on complex factual and legal issues, where the trial was expected to be lengthy (one to three months), and where the corporation had sent an attorney from Philadelphia to speak for the principals, whose expenses would not have exceeded sending a corporate representative from

Camden. Would any of these facts, if changed, have made the attendance order impermissible?

2. Judge Posner, dissenting, expressed the concern "that in their zeal to settle cases judges may ignore the value of other people's time." Surely there are circumstances when an attorney can adequately represent a party and when requiring a non-attorney representative is unnecessarily wasteful. How does the majority opinion deal with this point? Do the efficiency and proportionality considerations identified by the majority provide appropriate guidance for case-by-case determinations?

3. Judge Easterbrook, also dissenting, argued that many firms send their lawyer to negotiate in collective bargaining or merger talks, and that a lawyer is no less suited to negotiating in a settlement conference. It is important to have in attendance the person who will make the ultimate decision to settle so that she can hear, see, and participate in the proceedings, in short, so that she can be affected by the discussion and interaction with the other side and the judge? Would an appropriate test be that if a lawyer is the sole representative she should be essentially the alter ego of the corporate decisionmaker, with the same knowledge, interests, and settlement authority?

4. Can a court require an insurer to attend a settlement conference? In In re Novak, 932 F.2d 1397 (11th Cir.1991), the district court in a malpractice action directed the defendant's lawyer to find out who at the defendant's insurer had "full settlement authority" after the lawyer stated in a pretrial conference that he would have to check with the insurer before increasing defendant's settlement offer. On being told that the person with such authority was Novak, the judge ordered him to appear for a settlement conference and fined him when he did not. The appellate court agreed with *Heileman* that there is inherent power to require a party to send a person with full settlement authority to a pretrial conference, but held that there is no similar authority to require a nonparty insurer to attend. It added, however, that the court could threaten sanctions against the insured party as a way to coerce cooperation from the party's insurer. Id. at 1406–08.

5. The 1993 amendments to Rule 16(b) provide that "[i]f appropriate, the court may require that a party or its representative be present or reasonably available by telephone in order to consider possible settlement of the dispute." The note also mentioned that this might include "a representative from an insurance company." Citing *Heileman,* the note states that the telephone provision "is not intended to limit the reasonable exercise of the court's inherent powers."

CHAPTER III

MEDIATION

A. THE SOURCES OF CONTEMPORARY MEDIATION

When parties are unable to resolve their dispute through discussion and negotiation, a logical next step is to seek the assistance of a third party to facilitate communication and the search for a solution. "Mediation" is the broad term used to describe the intervention of third parties in the dispute resolution process. The term "conciliation" is sometimes used to describe the same process of involving third parties, usually in the context of labor relations when neutral intervention is used to break a stalemate, domestic relations, or international commercial matters. Although distinctions between mediation and conciliation are sometimes made, today the two terms are essentially synonyms.

Mediation probably predates the formal creation and enforcement of law, for humans in the social state seem to have a natural instinct to seek the guidance of others in settling differences between individuals. Indeed, formal legal structures may have developed out of informal attempts by family members, neighbors, and friends to mediate between disputing individuals. The Classical Chinese viewed the use of mediation as superior to recourse to law for settlement of disputes. F.S.C. Northrop has described the view of the Confucian Chinese that "litigation" was a "second best" solution to disputes:

> The "first best" and socially proper way to settle disputes, used by the "superior man," was by the method of mediation, following the ethics of the "middle way." This consisted in bringing the disputants to something they both approved as a settlement of the dispute, by means of an intermediary. This middle man served largely as a messenger. Proper behavior prescribed that he refuse even to arbitrate the differences at the request of the disputants. "Good" dispute settling consisted in conveying the respective claims of the disputants back and forth between them until the disputants themselves arrived at a solution which was approved by both.[1]

In many societies, mediation through a third party has been a favored alternative to formal legal processes. The mediator may be chosen because of special qualities, for example, the "prestige-mediators" among the Singapore Chinese, the "big man" among the Ifugao tribe, or the Iranian bazaar mediators.[2] On the other hand, the mediator may simply be a friend or a disinterested person. The "Book of Discipline" of the Society of Friends stated that when differences arise between persons, their friends shall "forthwith speak to and tenderly advise, the persons between whom the difference is, to make a speedy end thereof; and if that friend or those friends do not comply with their advice, that then they take to them one or two friends more, and again exhort them to end their difference."[3]

---

1. Northrop, The Mediational Approval Theory of Law in American Legal Realism, 44 Va.L.Rev. 347, 349 (1958). See also Luban, Some Greek Trials: Order and Justice in Homer, Hesiod, Aeschylus and Plato, 54 Tenn. L.Rev. 280 (1987), describing Greek approaches to the conflicting objectives of "justice" and "reconciliation."

2. P.H. Gulliver, Disputes and Negotiations: A Cross–Cultural Perspective 214 (1979).

3. Rules of Discipline of the Yearly Meeting 3 (New Bedford 1809). The Rules go on to provide, if mediation is not successful, for "arbitration" by a group composed of persons selected by each party and third persons selected by the parties' arbitrators. Id. at 7.

A. The Sources of Contemporary Mediation

Mediation has often existed alongside formal legal structures, offering a community-based, consensual alternative to legal remedies. In African societies, tribal "moots" were an informal mediation process which continued after the imposition of colonial law:

> A court system, established by the British, was primarily adjudicative, while a tribal "moot" performed an integrative, conciliatory function. Whereas the court was characterized by social distance between judge and litigants, rules of procedure which narrowed the issues under discussion, and a resolution which ascribed guilt or innocence to a defendant, the moot emphasized the bonds between the convenor and the disputants, it encouraged the widening of discussion so that all tensions and viewpoints psychologically—if not legally—relevant to the issue were expressed, and it resolved disputes by consensus about future conduct, rather than by assessing blame retrospectively.[4]

The Development of Contemporary Mediation: One Process or Many?

Mediation as we find it today in the United States is the product of a variety of historical influences and sources. The term "mediation" describes at best a loosely-knit set of values, objectives, and techniques derived from a variety of sources over the past fifty years. At the risk of oversimplification, some of the principal developments include the following:

1. Labor Mediation

Labor disputes were the first significant area in which mediation was routinely used in this country. Attempts at mediating labor disputes were made in the 19th century both in England and the United States. Government-sponsored mediation dates from 1913 when the Department of Labor appointed "commissioners of conciliation"[5] to be made available to the parties in labor disputes.[6] Resort to mediation increased in the 1930's, with the passage of national collective bargaining legislation, as a means of dealing with impasses between a union and management in the collective bargaining process. Mediation thus served as a form of "social intervention" through outside neutrals to assist labor and management to find a

---

4. Danzig, Toward the Creation of a Complementary, Decentralized System of Criminal Justice, 26 Stan.L.Rev. 1, 42–3 (1973). See also Galanter, Justice in Many Rooms: Courts, Private Ordering, and Indigenous Law, 19 J. of Legal Pluralism & Unofficial Law 1 (1981); Nader, Styles of Court Procedure: To Make the Balance, in L. Nader (ed.), Law in Culture and Society (1969).

5. The term "conciliation," often used in the labor context, describes the process for "bringing of disputing parties together, under circumstances and in an atmosphere most conducive to the discussion of the problem in an objective way for the purpose of seeking a solution to the issue or issues involved." Walter A. Maggiolo, Techniques of Mediation in Labor Disputes 10 (1971). The two terms are often used interchangeably.

6. They were reconstituted in 1947 as the Federal Mediation and Conciliation Service, which continues to function today in providing arbitrators and mediators for labor disputes. See 29 U.S.C. § 171.

socially-desirable solution. Thus labor mediators were often more activist and directive in their mediating style, sometimes using cajoling, warnings, reality testing, and appeals to higher interests to achieve an agreement.[7]

A unique feature of collective bargaining mediation is that the participants are chosen from the complex organizational structures of labor and management. The mediator is therefore dealing with experienced and well-prepared adversaries and generally starts at a higher level of understanding and structuring of positions than in community and family dispute mediation. The challenge here is not only to facilitate communication and understanding between the participants but also to recognize the large constituencies behind them that will have to be persuaded of the merits of any agreement. Labor mediation thus requires the mediator to be sensitive not only to the agreement that can be achieved between the company and union but also to the need for approval by the union bureaucracy and rank-and-file, on the one hand, and the different management teams on the other. The issues are at times amorphous, the agenda generally flexible and open-ended, and the role of the mediator expansive and active.

In contrast to collective bargaining mediation, mediation of employee grievances is generally performed by a single or a small number of representatives on each side. Arbitration is still the principal process for resolving employee grievances under union-management contracts, particularly in the public sector, but "grievance mediation" is increasingly being used as an alternative. It is said to offer "substantial promise of resolving grievances more quickly, inexpensively, and informally than arbitration," to be more satisfactory to employees because of its "cathartic value," and to improve "the parties' problem-solving ability and their relationship in a way that arbitration cannot."[8]

In grievance mediation, the issues are limited to those that have arisen in the individual case. Even here, however, the resolution of grievances in the labor context may have important precedential effect on the institutional parties that may far outweigh the interest of the individual. Thus, there is a potential policy overlay in even the simplest individual grievance dispute. This may affect the mediator's role, causing him to be more activist than his counterpart in other forms of mediation.

2.   FAMILY LAW MEDIATION

Family law was an early arena for application of mediation. Even in the 19th century, mediation was sometimes provided by churches, schools, and community groups in situations of family break-up. In the 1930's, American divorce courts began to recommend mediation to the parties, and in 1939, California created the Conciliation Court, with parties allowed to go through conciliation, usually in an uncontested divorce, as an alternative

---

7.   See Deborah M. Kolb, The Mediators (1983).

8.   Goldberg, The Mediation of Grievances Under a Collective Bargaining Contract: An Alternative to Arbitration, 77 Nw. L.Rev. 270, 314 (1982).

to the normal adversary divorce process.[9] The rapid spread of no-fault divorce in the last several decades has further spurred the movement towards replacing an adversary divorce trial with a mediated settlement. In the last decade, California mandated conciliation for issues of child custody or visitation as a prerequisite to a divorce trial,[10] and judges in some other states have imposed this requirement through court rule.

The demand for divorce mediation led to a specialized group of family mediators around the country with training and experience in that process. Family mediators have been in the forefront of the movement to require training and other requirements for mediators and to devise rules of professional conduct for mediators. Many family law mediators are mental health, psychology, or counseling professionals, but lawyers have increasingly become involved as mediators.[11]

Some family-law mediators bring a "therapeutic" dimension to mediation, encouraging the parties to recognize and confront the underlying emotional issues and, where appropriate, to work on their relationship.[12] Although there is no agreement among family mediators as to whether a "therapeutic" dimension is appropriate,[13] family mediation generally devotes considerable attention to non-legal emotional and relationship issues. The complexity of issues that must be resolved concerning child custody, property division, and future relationships, plus the confusion and distraction caused by family miscommunication, are often cited as warranting a more activist mediator role. In addition, face-to-face mediation is not always viewed as desirable in divorce mediation, and "shuttle mediation," with only a limited face-to-face meeting between the parties, has attracted support in certain divorce situations. Recently a development referred to as the "collaborative divorce" movement has integrated mediation techniques into a process particularly used in family law cases that stresses the integral collaborative role of the parties in structuring a workable agreement.[14]

---

9. California now requires conciliation where child custody is in issue. West's Ann. Cal.Civ.Code § 4607. See also Ohio Rev.Code § 4117.14; West's A.I.C. 20–7.5–1–12; 20–7.5–1–13.

10. West's Ann.Cal.Civ.Code § 4607.

11. One model of divorce mediation is to use two mediators, one with training in psychology or a related field and one with training in law. It is sometimes urged that they be of different sexes. This "luxury" model of divorce mediation, however, cannot be afforded in many divorce situations. The "stripped-down" model of mediation has to rely on volunteer mediators from a community dispute resolution center, religious organization, or social service agency, or, at times, simply on a local family lawyer. Sometimes, community mediation services refuse to me-

diate divorces when child custody or division of property is at issue, in recognition that specialized training and legal knowledge is needed.

12. Silbey & Merry, Mediator Settlement Strategies, 8 Law & Policy 7 (1986).

13. Compare Roberts, Systems or Selves? Some Ethical Issues in Family Mediation, 10 Mediation Q. 3 (1992) with Haynes, Mediation and Therapy: An Alternative View, 10 Mediation Q. 21 (1992).

14. See Herman, Collaborative Divorce: A short Overview, 4 Divorce Litig. 68 (April 2001) (the parties sign an agreement that there will be no contested hearings or motions and no formal discovery, they will make full disclosure of all relevant financial information, and their attorneys will refrain from sending "attack" letters or acting in any

332 CHAPTER III MEDIATION

3. COMMUNITY MEDIATION

Community mediation was the next significant development in American ADR. Neighborhood Justice Centers sprang up in the 1960's under the impetus of federal government grants under the poverty and other Great Society programs.[15] At the same time, there was increased interest at the local level in establishing alternatives to courts, and community mediation centers were established with sponsorship from local governments, churches, charities, and community organizations. Specialized forms of mediation were developed by particular institutions and government agencies to attempt to resolve misunderstandings in such areas as community-police relations, race relations, hospital and health care services, environmental protection, and divorce and family-law problems.

A central theme of the community mediation movement was that mediation was a way to empower disputants to build stronger community ties and resolve their disputes without having to rely on the power establishment of courts, police, and government agencies and to frame the issues and devise solutions of their own making.[16] Community mediation services also shared a common methodological approach to dispute resolution. Although the exact form of mediation varied from center to center, a standard methodology gradually became accepted, spread by mediator trainers and training handbooks. This "classical mediation" model taught that since it is desirable for people to resolve their own disputes, the mediator should use a "non-directive" style that encourages the parties to communicate but eschews influencing them by such "directive" conduct as expressing opinions, using stratagems to bring them around to certain positions, or giving evaluations of their cases. Since voluntariness is important, mediation should be initiated by the parties who should not be coerced into engaging in it. Since parties are more likely to abide by agreements that they have worked out between themselves, the mediator should only be a facilitator for discussion and problem solving and should not attempt to influence the parties in favor of or against particular solutions. And since the legal system is distrusted, both because of its coercive procedures and the inflexibility of the law, mediation should encourage parties to resolve disputes without concern for how the legal system would resolve them if the case went to trial.

This social empowerment theme of the community mediation movement moderated in the 1970's as store-front community justice centers gave way to more staid "dispute resolution centers" operated by largely

manner detrimental to the future relationship of the parties); Practicing Therapeutic Jurisprudence: Law as a Helping Profession (eds., Dennis P. Stolle, David B. Wexler, & Bruce J. Winick) (2000). This movement is related to the "collaborative law" techniques advocated for business and other kinds of disputes. See section 5, n. 23, below.

15. See Shonholtz, Neighborhood Justice Systems: Work, Structure, and Guiding Principles, 5 Mediation Q. 3 (1984).

16. Id.

middle-class volunteers. But notions of "empowerment," "party ownership of the conflict," and "the value of voluntary resolution of conflict within a community framework" still retain an important influence in mediation across the country.

4. SETTLEMENT PROMOTION

Concern in the late 1970's and 1980's over a "litigation boom" led to a movement to promote settlement to relieve court congestion. The related "case management movement" within the courts[17] urged judges and court personnel to undertake active management of court cases in the interests of getting an early resolution, including the use of ADR.[18] Emphasis was placed on promoting settlement as early in the litigation process as possible in order to conserve court resources and reduce the parties' litigation costs. This objective was especially attractive to business interests and traditional defendants in law suits, and defense-oriented organizations and lobbies urged both the voluntary use of ADR before suit and its mandatory use in the courts. An organization with many of the Fortune 500 corporations as its members, the Center for Public Resources, was formed to encourage corporations to use ADR in place of litigation and devised and promoted various ADR processes like the mini-trial.[19] The "settlement promotion" dimension was also aided by research and academic scholarship in such areas as "game theory" which shifted the traditional mediation orientation from social-science and psychology to applied economics and statistical analysis as scholars experimented with incentive models that could lead to settlements.[20]

The "settlement promotion" movement initially focused on ADR processes other than mediation. New or hybrid forms of ADR emerged—such as the mini-trial, summary jury trial, court-annexed arbitration, and mediation-arbitration hybrids. However, mediation proved more popular than had been anticipated, and it has become the principal ADR process invoked by institutions and courts. Nevertheless, there has been an impact on the nature and style of mediation, and a more directive and evaluative kind of mediation has emerged.

17. See Sherman, A Process Model and Agenda for Civil Justice Reforms in the States, 46 Stanford L.Rev. 1553, 1562 (1994).

18. Court ADR programs range from voluntary programs like "Settlement Week," when court rooms are used for mediations and any party can put the case on the mediation docket, to "court-annexed ADR" as an integral part of the litigation process (see Chapter IV). The Federal Alternative Dispute Resolution Act of 1998 provides that each district court "by local rule, require that litigants in all civil cases consider the use of an alternative dispute resolution process at an appropriate stage in the litigation."

19. See Center for Public Resources, CPR Model Minitrial Procedure (1989). CPR changed its name in 1994 to CPR Institute for Dispute Resolution. It asks its members to sign a pledge: "In the event of a business dispute between our company and another which has made or shall make a similar statement, we are prepared to explore with that other party resolution of the dispute through negotiation or ADR techniques before pursuing full-scale litigation."

20. See, e.g., R. Axelrod, The Evolution of Cooperation (1984); Brown, The Superpower Dilemma: Can Game Theory Improve the U.S.–Soviet Negotiating Relationship?, 2 Negotiation J. 371 (1986).

334 CHAPTER III MEDIATION

5. COOPERATIVE PROBLEM-SOLVING

During the 1980's, a new approach to corporate and institutional management, as well as the art of negotiation, incorporated emerging techniques of cooperative problem-solving. In the corporate world, the Japanese had devised new management methods that involved all employees in collaborative processes to recommend policies and monitor quality, and these concepts were quickly assimilated into American management practices.[21] In the field of dispute resolution, Professors Roger Fisher and William Ury published an important little book, *Getting to Yes*, that provided a popularized synthesis of cooperative problem-solving techniques.[22] They rejected the traditional competitive approach to negotiation for what they called "principled negotiation" that involved an attempt to discover mutual interests and solutions for mutual gain. Although "interest-based" negotiation was not new to mediation, the "win-win" approach advocated by the authors captivated both mediation professionals and millions of readers. By the mid–1980's, it began to be applied to public policy disputes, with an elaborate scheme for involving all "stake-holders" in collaborative problem-solving.[23] (See further discussion in section 7, below) A recent variation of cooperative problem-solving is the "collaborative law" movement that involves the parties agreeing to a team approach requiring foreswearing litigation, full disclosure of relevant information, and special settlement counsel with training in the method.[24]

The "problem-solving" dimension was always a part of the traditional mediation model. But for some mediators it has taken on a central role, arguably overshadowing other aspects of the mediation process. One critique of this development comes from advocates of a "transformational" effect in mediation who urge that mediation offers an opportunity to transform the parties by "engendering moral growth."[25] This approach views the emphasis on problem-solving as too heavy-handed and robbing

---

21. See, e.g., the Total Quality Management (TQM) program, discussed in Goldberg, The Quest for TQM, 79 A.B.A. Journal 52 (Nov. 1993).

22. Roger Fisher & William Ury, Getting to Yes: Negotiating Agreement Without Giving In (1981, 2d ed. 1991, with B. Patton). See also Roger Fisher, Elizabeth Kopelman & Andrea Kupfer Schneider, Beyond Machiavelli: Tools for Coping With Conflict (1994). Roger Fisher & Scott Brown, Getting Together: Building a Relationship That Gets to Yes (1988); William Ury, Getting Past No: Negotiating With Difficult People (1991).

23. See Lawrence Susskind & Jeffrey Cruikshank, Breaking the Impasse: Consensual Approaches to Resolving Public Disputes (1987).

24. See Arnold, Collaborative Dispute Resolution: An Idea Whose Time Has Come, in 16 American L. Inst. & A.B.A., Course of Study Materials, 379 (2000); Jackson, Collaborative Innovation (Journal of the American Institute of Collaborative Professionals), 1 The Collaborative Quarterly 1 (October 1999); Rack, Settle or Withdraw: Collaborative Lawyering Provides Incentive to Avoid Costly Litigation, Disp. Resol. Mag. 8 (Summer 1998).

25. Robert A. Baruch Bush & Joseph P. Folger, The Promise of Mediation: Responding to Conflict Through Empowerment and Recognition 2 (1994); Baruch Bush, Defining Quality in Dispute Resolution: Taxonomies and the Anti–Taxonomies of Quality Arguments, 66 Denv.U.L.Rev. 335 (1989).

the parties of the moral autonomy to confront each other and devise their own forms of resolution of their conflict.

6. EVALUATIVE MEDIATION

A dramatic influx of lawyers into the ranks of trained mediators occurred in the late 1980's and 1990's as court annexation of ADR created a need (or at least an opportunity) for mediators and other third-party neutrals who had a background in the legal issues involved in law suits. Some lawyers did not easily take to the traditional non-directive style of mediation, relying instead on their legal knowledge and experience to "reality test" with the parties about the strength of their cases and to predict court outcomes. One organization, JAMS (Judicial Arbitration and Mediation Service), primarily provided former judges as ADR neutrals in the conviction that the parties often wanted some sort of evaluation of their cases by a person who could speak with experience and authority about how a court might resolve the dispute. Thus a new form of "evaluative" mediation has emerged, although most mediators use an evaluative approach in tandem with other techniques. The degree of evaluation used by attorney mediators trained in a more "evaluative" model often varies according to the kind of case and the expressed desires of the parties.

7. PUBLIC POLICY DISPUTE RESOLUTION

Concern over the high cost, delay, and inflexibility sometimes associated with resolving public policy disputes through litigation and formal governmental agency administrative determinations lead over the past couple of decades to the development of new techniques for dealing with such disputes. "Public policy disputes" is a broad term used to refer to disputes involving government agencies and bodies, and at times private institutions or corporations, concerning such matters of public interest and regulation as the environment, economy, labor and employment, education, and public health and welfare. As a result of the work of mediator specialists in these kinds of disputes, public policy dispute resolution has become a distinct subset of mediation. However, procedures can involve a mix of processes including mediation, collaborative problem-solving, consensus building, non-binding arbitration, and mini trial. Negotiated rulemaking ("neg-reg") is a specialized collaborative process by which governmental agencies involve interested groups in administrative rule making.[26]

Since public policy disputes often involve many parties and groups interested in the outcome ("stake-holders"), as well as divided jurisdiction and responsibilities among various governmental and private entities, special techniques for identifying stake holders, encouraging coalitions, and

---

26. See Haygood, Negotiated Rule Making: Challenges for Mediators and Participants, 20 Mediation Q. 77 (Summer 1988).

CHAPTER III MEDIATION

structuring the dialogue and problem-solving process have been developed.[27] This field was promoted in the late 1980's and early 1990's by grants from the National Institute for Dispute Resolution (NIDR, a non-profit organization created by foundations to provide funding for the creative development of ADR) to establish Public Policy Dispute Resolution Centers in some twenty states.[28] The movement was also fueled by legislation and administrative rules at both the national and state level to require agencies to adopt dispute resolution procedures for a variety of their functions, including regulation, enforcement, rule-making, and internal personnel matters.[29]

8. Systems Design

As corporations, institutions, and governmental entities increasingly turned to ADR when disputes and law suits arose, it became apparent that procedures could be established to invoke ADR processes at certain stages of disputes.[30] Systems design is the science of determining what processes should be invoked and at what stages of institutional operations. Actual disputes in such areas as personnel, business relations, and general business operations might be headed off by identifying in advance situations likely to result in conflict and providing mechanisms for dealing with them. The purpose of systems design is to institutionalize procedures for conflict avoidance, control, and finally resolution. Brown and Root, a large construction company with international operations, was one of the first to set up procedures for resort to ADR in many of its operations. It was followed by similar systems designs by manufacturing companies, service industries, hospitals and health care, insurance companies, and government agencies. Typically a systems design calls for a graduated resort to ADR processes, going from informal to more formal (for example, informal consultation, mediation, fact-finding, non-binding arbitration, and, in some cases, binding arbitration).

---

27. See Susskind & Ozawa, Mediated Negotiation in the Public Sector, in Negotiation Theory and Practice 401 (J. William Breslin & Jeffrey Z. Rubin, ed. 1991); Potapchuk, New Approaches to Citizen Participation: Building Consent, National Civic Rev. 158 (Spring 1991); Denise Madigan, Gerald McMahon, Lawrence Susskind & Stephanie Rolley, New Approaches to Resolving Local Public Disputes (1990); Susan Carpenter & W.J.D. Kennedy, Managing Public Disputes (1988); Lawrence Susskind & Jeffrey Cruikshank, Breaking the Impasse (1987).

28. See Adler, State Offices of Mediation: Thoughts on the Evolution of a National Network, 81 Ky. L. J. 1013 (1992–93).

29. See Administrative Dispute Resolution Act of 1990, 5 U.S.C. § 571 et seq.

(1994); Negotiated Rulemaking Act, Pub. Law 101–648 (1990); Suskind, Babbitt & Segall, When ADR Becomes the Law: A Review of Federal Practice, 9 Negotiation J. 59 (1993).

30. See Ury, Brett, & Goldberg, Dispute Systems Design: An Introduction, 5 Negotiation J. 357 (1989) ("It is now time to adopt a broader perspective, asking how [dispute resolution] procedures can be most effectively used to form an integrated system for dealing not with just a single dispute, but with the stream of disputes that arise in nearly all relationships, organizations, and communities."); Murray, Dispute Systems Design, Power, and Prevention, 6 Negotiation J. 105 (1990).

B. THE MEDIATION PROCESS

9. CYBERMEDIATION

The Internet provided an essentially cost-free means of instant communication which has lead to online dispute resolution, generally mediation or arbitration, either non-binding or binding.[31] The growth of internet businesses also gave rise to a host of new disputes over purchases, quality of goods, and technical failures as to which cybermediation offers an inexpensive and speedy form of dispute resolution. The forms of cybermediation offered by various web sites differ considerably. One form, especially directed to disputes where there is insurance, involves blind-bidding by claimants and insurance adjustors. Both sides enter their numbers, and if they are within 30%, or $5,000, of each other, there will be an automatic settlement at the median amount.[32] In another form, especially directed to low-value consumer disputes, the claimant fills out a questionnaire and the web site contacts the other party. If that party will not settle, a human mediator conducts communication with either or both parties on a secure messaging web site.[33] Yet another form provides a "virtual courthouse" in which a claimant types in a description of the dispute, omitting personal identifying information, the other party is notified and is given a chance to submit a response. Visitors at the site can register to be jurors, are given access to information as to other cases, can ask questions, and then post their comments and judgments. Judgments are non-binding.[34]

These processes have been criticized as either being a corruption of the mediation process by not having the parties meet face-to-face, or a corruption of the arbitration process by either being too mechanical or obtaining advisory opinions from persons whose reliability cannot be judged. On the other hand, it is said that "the Web sites can be helpful if you have a particular dispute but don't want to spend a lot of time and money to resolve it."[35] Whether there should be rules and guidelines for cybermediation is a continuing topic of debate.

B. THE MEDIATION PROCESS

Mediation is a process by which the parties, assisted by a neutral third person, "attempt to systematically isolate points of agreement and disagreement, explore alternative solutions, and consider compromises for the purpose of reaching a consensual settlement of the issues relating to their conflict."[1] Underlying this process is the philosophy that any agreement

---

31. See Frangos, Turning to the Internet to Settle a Dispute, Wall Street J. (June 24, 2001).

32. See Colter, Dispute–Resolution Service Says There is a Market for Settlement Information, Wall Street J. (Nov. 8, 1999) (describing CyberSettle.com); id. (describing ClickNsettle.com).

33. See Miller, Legal sites help untangle Web disputes, USA Tech Report, July 10,

2000, and Frangos, id. (describing SquareTrade.com).

34. See Miller, id. (describing iCourthouse.com).

35. See Frangos, id.

1. Chang, "Nonadversarial Representation: Rule 2.2 and Divorce Mediation," in A

should be voluntarily arrived at by the parties. It is believed that the parties will be more satisfied, and thus more likely to abide by the agreement, if it is of their own creation, and there is evidence to support this premise.[2]

Mediation is "fundamentally a process of assisted negotiation."[3] Thus negotiation strategy is central to what goes on in mediation, and the principles of negotiation theory and practice studied in the last chapter have a direct bearing on the conduct of a mediation. The major difference between negotiation and mediation is the presence of the mediator, and her neutrality is critical to the success of the process. Neutrality does not mean that the mediator is a passive observer, but she must always be conscious of avoiding the appearance of partiality.

A mediator is essentially a facilitator of communication between the parties, assisting them to engage in a dialogue directed toward mutual resolution of their dispute. The mediator's role can vary with the circumstances and the kind of mediation that the mediator and the parties have agreed upon. The roles may include being a facilitator of communication, arranger of processes to inform and enlighten the disputants, impresario of a structured dialogue, encourager of problem-solving, generator of possible solutions, or shuttle-diplomat using control of the information flow to focus on areas of agreement without the risks of much face-to-face confrontation by the parties.

Voluntariness is at the heart of the mediation process. The strength of mediation is that it permits the parties to achieve their own resolution of a dispute without being bound to a formal, and possibly inflexible, legal solution.[4] Research supports the conclusion that disputing parties will be more satisfied, and thus more likely to abide by an agreement, if it is of their own creation. For example, a study of small claims disputes in Maine found a higher compliance rate with settlements that resulted from mediation than from a court-ordered judgment.[5] This conclusion is not surprising if the result is a mutually-acceptable solution to the dispute and the parties

---

Study of Barriers to the Use of Alternative Methods of Dispute Resolution, Vermont Law School Dispute Resolution Project 112 (1984).

2. See McEwen & Maiman, Mediation in Small Claims Court: Achieving Compliance Through Consent, 18 Law & Society Rev. 11, 40–47 (1984) (finding a higher percentage of parties comply with a mediated settlement than with a court-ordered judgment).

3. Marcel, Why We Teach Law Students to Mediate, Journal of Dispute Resolution 77 (1987).

4. Fuller, Mediation—Its Forms and Functions, 44 Southern California Law Review 305, 308, 325–26 (1971); Stulberg and Montgomery, Design Requirements for Medi-

ator Development Programs, 15 Hofstra Law Review 499, 504 (1987).

5. See McEwen and Maiman, Mediation in Small Claims Court: Achieving Compliance Through Consent, 18 Law & Society Review 11 (1984). See also Vidmar, An Assessment of Mediation in a Small Claims Court, 41 Journal of Social Issues 127 (1985); McEwen and Maiman, The Relative Significance of Disputing Forum and Dispute Characteristics for Outcome and Compliance, 20 Law & Society Review 439 (1986); Vidmar, Assessing the Effects of Case Characteristics and Settlement Forum on Dispute Outcomes and Compliance, 21 Law & Society Review 155 (1987).

feel a sense of obligation to comply with its terms. The trick is to bring disputing parties to a state of mind in which this result is achievable.

Advocates of mediation view it as an "empowering" process by which the parties are given, by the very nature of the process, the power to confront each other on both a moral and personal level.[6] This is a heady concept, and one might well be skeptical of the ability of the process to break through the existing pattern of relationships between the parties to move them to view the dispute from a different perspective. But mediation advocates believe that the very act of participating in a mediation, accompanied by the mediator's demand for a commitment to participate in good faith and the mediator's assistance in identifying shared values, can alter the existing dynamic between the parties. By forcing the parties to hear each other's justifications and to confront each other's feelings, mediation seeks to empower the less powerful party to invoke shared community standards to support his position. The ultimate objective is to bring the parties to a mutual acceptance of standards of fairness and broad equity that might not be possible in a formal legal proceeding.

Despite the philosophical preference that mediation be undertaken voluntarily by the parties, participation must sometimes be encouraged, indeed, even pressured or coerced. Parties may be required to mediate by a judge or government official, as when mediation is made a prerequisite for being allowed to go to trial, for prosecuting a criminal complaint, or for receiving some government benefit such as staying in a low-income housing project, avoiding expulsion from school, or obtaining enforcement of zoning, land use, or other regulations.[7] Experience suggests that such coerced participation may still be beneficial in bringing the parties into a process where cooperation can ultimately arise.[8] It should be remembered that coerced participation is not coerced agreement; no party to mediation can be forced to enter an agreement.

A key aspect of the mediation process is to make the parties confront the realities of their firmly-held perceptions and positions. Mediators may reality-test with parties at various stages in the mediation. Coming to an awareness of error in one's perceptions or of weakness in one's positions may result from open sessions in which the opposing parties present their arguments and points of view or from private sessions with one party (a "caucus") in which the party can discuss frankly and in confidence its doubts, ultimate interests, and bottom lines.[9] Reality-testing seeks to get

---

6. See C. Moore, *The Mediation Process: Practical Strategies for Resolving Conflict* (1986).

7. See N. Rogers and R. Salem, *A Student's Guide to Resolving Conflicts Without Litigation* 10 (New York: Matthew Bender & Co., 1984); J. Murray, A. Rau, and E. Sherman, *Processes of Dispute Resolution: The Role of Lawyers* 279–81 (New York: Foundation Press, Inc., 1989).

8. See Pearson and Thoennes, *Divorce Mediation: An Overview of Research Results,*

19 Columbia Journal of Law & Social Problems 451 (1985); Wall & Schiller, *Judicial Involvement in Pre–Trial Settlement: A Judge is Not a Bump on a Log,* 6 American Journal of Trial Advocacy 27 (1982).

9. See Moore, *The Caucus: Private Meetings That Promote Settlement,* 16 Mediation Quarterly 87 (1987).

340 CHAPTER III MEDIATION

parties with an exaggerated view of the wrong done them, or of the strength of their position, to come to a more realistic understanding of the dispute.

Mediation is a flexible process, and thus it is impossible to describe specific "procedures" for its conduct. In addition, there are many forms of mediation, and some are more formal, or follow more set patterns, than others. The "classical" form of mediation that has been taught and used for decades in such areas as family law and community dispute resolution centers is still central to the approach taken by most mediators. Many of the steps and techniques involved—such as having the parties begin by each stating the problem, allowing for ventilation of feelings and emotions, and encouraging joint problem-solving—are applicable to all forms of mediation.

1. FORMAT OF THE "CLASSICAL" MEDIATION

There are many different formats for the conduct of a mediation, and mediations trainers and training manuals often use their own terminology, order, and emphasis in outlining how a mediation ought to be conducted. But there is general agreement as to the key stages of mediation and what they ought to contain. Mediation in the "classical" non-directive style that is still the dominant kind of mediation in this country might contain the following stages:

Introductory Remarks by the Mediator[s]
Statement of the Problem by the Parties
Information Gathering
Problem Identification
Problem Solving: Generating Options and Bargaining
Writing of Agreement[10]

a. INTRODUCTORY REMARKS BY MEDIATOR(S)

The purpose of this stage is to:

(1) Explain the process to the parties (e.g., that the mediator is not a judge and is there to help them communicate and try to reach a solution, that the mediator may use a caucus to talk with them privately and confidentially at some time, that all communications in the mediation are confidential, and that if they reach an agreement the mediator will assist them to put it in writing which, when signed, is legally enforceable as a contract).

(2) State the ground rules (e.g., that they should not interrupt when the other is talking, that they can write down on the pad in front of them any points they want to make later, and that they should avoid name-calling),

---

10. This description is taken from John S. Murray, Alan S. Rau, & Edward F. Sherman, Dispute Resolution: Materials for Continuing Legal Education III–7–9 (National Institute for Dispute Resolution 1991).

(3) Insure that the parties have no problem with the mediator (i.e., any prior relationship or conflict of interest), and

(4) Establish realistic expectations of the process and the parties' commitment to engaging in it.

The mediator's introductory remarks are often short, taking up no more than five or ten minutes. However, some mediators use this phase to go beyond a perfunctory setting out of the guidelines and taking care of housekeeping rules to prepare the parties emotionally for the mediation, gather certain information, and discuss the parties' expectations. Consider the following:

Jay Folberg & Alison Taylor, Mediaton: A Comprehensive Guide to Resolving Conflicts Without Litigation

39–43 (1994).

Beyond introductions and reviewing guidelines, this stage is used to gather relevant information about the participants' perceptions of the conflict, their goals and expectations, and the conflict situation. Essential information should be gathered during this stage:

- The participants' motivation to use mediation

- The immediate background and precipitating events of the conflict

- The interactional and communication styles of the participants

- The present emotional state of the participants

- Arrangements for legal processes and the involvement of other participants

- The presenting problem as opposed to the hidden agenda

- Immediate safety and security concerns for each participant and their dependents.

The sequence shown in Table 4 helps elicit this information and serves as a guide to the mediator for facilitating the introductory session. Not all the steps presented here will be followed in every case. The order of the steps in all stages must remain flexible to fit the dynamics of each case. Each case is different and the mediation process must not be rigid. The process must be adapted as needed. It should be noted that guidelines, employment agreements, and worksheets are optional tools that may or may not be needed in mediation settings. These, as well as the confirmation of case data (step 3), are contingent on the content and context of mediation.

342 CHAPTER III MEDIATION

Table 4. The Eight Steps of Stage 1.

Step	Data Obtained
1. Brief introductions and seating	Nonverbal impressions
2. Preparatory statement by mediator (repeated if one participant is late)	Present emotional state of participants; legal processes
3. Confirm case date	Immediate background and precipitating events; involvement of attorneys, advocates; safety concerns
4. Handover discussion to participant	Interactional and communication styles; emotional stages
5. Discuss expectations	The presenting problem vs. hidden agendas or conflicts
6. Review guidelines	Interactional styles; emotional states
7. Review and sign employment agreement	Participants' motivation
8. Discuss worksheets	Immediate security concerns

In our *introductions* (step 1), we prefer to avoid small talk. We allow the participants to determine where they sit in individual chairs or couches arranged in a semicircle or other conversation area; at the apex, near a small table or desk, is the mediator's chair. The seating chosen by the participants can be a helpful nonverbal clue about their relationships and attitudes. The positioning of the mediator's chair and the distance between the mediator and each participant can be used to indicate the mediator's neutral stance. Three aspects must be considered in all physical settings for mediation: comfort, communication, and control (Neighborhood Justice Center of Atlanta, 1982). Additional parties, such as spouses, friends, lawyers, advocates, interpreters, and related professionals, may have to attend mediation sessions for convenience in decision making or because of legal requirements. These participants must be dealt with immediately— before the actual session begins, if possible. Mediators should develop policies concerning additional persons in the sessions.

The second step begins with a *preparatory statement* that outlines the roles of both mediator and participants and rewards the participants for having made the risky decision of coming to the session. If one participant arrives later than the other, we summarize all that has been said to the other participant, no matter how redundant it may be for those who arrived earlier. For those who were on time, this summary recapitulates material that may have been missed because of anxiety; it also confirms, by behavior, the scrupulous neutrality the mediator must maintain. It shows that what is said to one participant will be said to all.

The next step is to *confirm case* data—whatever the mediator knows about the participants and their situation—in the presence of all. This review serves the same purpose as the repetition for latecomers: It confirms by action that the mediator is not keeping secrets. The information should be the same as that gathered on the contact sheet and will then become part of the case file.

The next step is the *handover* to the participant—a definitive signal from the mediator, usually verbal, that indicates the need for the person to become an active part of the communication. For example: "It must be hard to open up after all the problems, but please try to tell us your perspective." We often find it best to encourage the more passive participant or the one who is more upset. The more passive is thereby urged to become a true participant; the more upset is allowed a legitimate way to vent feelings of anger, anxiety, hopelessness, and vindictiveness. The handover shows the mediator's willingness to openly confront the major emotional tendencies and displays a truthful picture of the interactions. It is important not only to encourage such involvement but also to reward it verbally, since to express deep personal feelings is risky and threatening to the participants. Such phrases as "Thanks for sharing some important points of concern for you" will provide the reward. We believe this openness reduces any tendencies toward passive-aggressive behavior, which can undermine later negotiations.

Another technique that may be helpful in certain cases is to have a protocol. The complainant (the one who has brought the issues to mediation, the one who is seeking resolution, or simply the one who first contacted you) goes first in all dealings as a general policy, followed by the respondent. The terms *complainant* and *respondent* stem from the adversarial legal perspective and are more appropriate in some settings than others. However, the terminology does help remind the mediator that participants have often entered mediation from such adversarial positions. It also reminds mediators that the concerns of the person who has brought the case to mediation should be addressed by the end of the mediation process.

The *discussion of expectations or positions* tends to expose hidden agendas or "icebergs"—conflicts that are only barely acknowledged by the participants. By using open questions and silence, the mediator can facilitate discussion while maintaining control and providing recognition and encouragement by means of interpretations and summary. The participants should be doing most of the talking and will often become incensed at each other's perceptions. At this point the emotional level of the session often begins to rise. The mediator can let each participant "tell their side of things" while the other participant and the mediator listen in silence, or each participant can explain the situation to the mediator, who can ask pertinent questions. Allowing uninterrupted story-telling is best when

344 CHAPTER III MEDIATION

participants are openly angry, verbally abusive, or even explosive. Interrupting is best when both participants are controlled. Both styles allow participants to hear the other's views of the issues.

The next step, *reviewing the mediation guidelines,* helps calm the tension—partly because it is a break in the sequence, partly because it once again reminds the participants that they will not be *allowed* to get out of control despite their strong emotions. It sets up explicit expectations. Participants can take an emotional time-out from their initial anxiety while the mediator is busy explaining the structure. Some mediators use separate mediation guidelines; others incorporate guidelines into the employment contract. Either method is acceptable provided the mediator reviews the guidelines with the participants to verify that they are understood and acceptable. We find it important at this time to emphasize the natural inclination of the participants to become discouraged or disinterested in continuing the mediation at critical points in the process. During the review of the guidelines, we legitimize this natural tendency to defend against pain but point out that such defenses have negative consequences and are avoidable. Here are some examples of specially contracted consequences: Serious lateness is given a financial penalty; withdrawal from mediation requires a written statement; noncompliance with a guideline will result in an *impasse* and termination of the session by the mediator.

The guidelines or the employment contract should address the question of whether the participants will be allowed to talk separately with the mediator. Separate sessions are a common practice in environmental, labor, commercial, and crisis mediation but are less frequent in family mediation. Separate caucusing may be an effective mediation technique, but it does raise significant ethical considerations. Participants are encouraged by some mediators to talk to them separately if they are feeling discouraged or want to end mediation. This gives the mediator a chance to discuss concerns privately, get a better understanding of the underlying conflicts, and encourage without embarrassment. It must be established in the guidelines, however, that an acknowledgment of the separate conversation and its general contents will be conveyed to the other participant in the next mediation session.

Other issues that fall in the category of setting guidelines should be discussed at this step: (1) disclosure of information within mediation (discovery), (2) confidentiality, (3) fees and payment, (4) length of sessions, (5) how the mediator will function should the participants be unable to make a decision later in the process, (6) provision for legal input and processing, (7) review and revision, and (8) termination.

The next step, *signing the employment agreement,* is an overt method of gaining cognitive, if not emotional, commitment to mediation on the part of the participants; it is also a legal necessity for the mediator. If the mediator has been skillful up to this point, the participants will have enough information about the process (and emotional relief) to feel good about mediation. Many, nonetheless, express their doubts and fears at this time ("I'll sign it, but I'm not sure it will work for us"), and the mediator should acknowledge expressed ambivalence and the reversibility of this commitment should mediation not work.

NOTES AND QUESTIONS

1. The mediator's introductory remarks may include reference to an agreement to mediate if one is signed in advance. The most important aspects of such an agreement might be confidentiality (see III, section D, infra) and mediation fees.

2. One sample agreement contains the following provision (James C. Malamed, Sample Agreement to Mediate, *www.mediater.com/articlesmelamed6.cfm* (May 4, 2001)):

Full Disclosure: Each party agrees to fully and honestly disclose all relevant information and writings as requested by the mediator and all information requested by any other party of the mediation if the mediator determines that the disclosure is relevant to the mediation discussions.

Do you see any problems with this rule?

b. STATEMENT OF THE PROBLEM BY THE PARTIES

The mediation begins by asking the parties to state the problem as they see it. If one of the parties has brought the matter to mediation, that party will usually be asked to go first. This stage is designed to allow the parties to frame the issues and also provides the mediator with information as to the basic facts and some insight into the emotional and relational matters involved. There is no need to have a comprehensive statement of the facts and problems at this point; such information may come out in other stages of the mediation. When the attorneys are the principal participants in a mediation (as, for example, in some Settlement Week mediations), they may make the statement of the problem. They are obviously more likely to place the factual discussion into the context of legal rights and duties, and for this reason, mediators often ask the parties, in addition, to make a statement of their own.

Beginning the mediation by asking the parties to state the problem as they see it is designed to allow them to frame the issues and set the agenda. Consider the following analysis of a mediation over a complaint that Spruce's barking dog is interfering with his neighbor Smith's ability to study, from Shaw, Divorce Mediation: Some Keys to the Process, 9 Mediation Q. 27 (1985):

Suppose the mediator, having heard this statement of the problem by Smith and Spruce, said, "Let's talk about the issue of the howling dog." Consider the course of the discussion that is likely to ensue: "My dog does not howl." "Your dog has barked endlessly day and night for weeks." "None of the other neighbors have complained." "If you don't shoot that dog, I will." "Why don't you find some other place to live if you don't like it."

Characterizing the issue as "the howling dog" presents two major problems. The first is that the mediator has adopted the issue as framed by one of the parties. The issue so framed assumes a judgment that the dog howls. This leads clearly and inevitably to an offensive-defensive debate between Smith and Spruce.

A mediator who simply accepts the statement of the problem in the terms used by one or the other of the parties is locked into that person's perceptions of the dispute, perceptions that are a large part of the reason the parties have reached a stalemate and sought outside help. A principal opportunity afforded by mediation is the mediator's ability to perceive the dispute in a different way from the parties and thereby to help them discuss and resolve the dispute effectively.

The second major problem with framing the issue as "the howling dog" (or indeed even as "the dog") is a more subtle one. Even if the characterization of the dog as howling is eliminated, the discussion that ensues will focus on the dog's behavior. How often has the dog barked in the past? During what hours? How loud? Have other neighbors been bothered?

Mediation is not a search for the truth. While the truth or falsity of the facts the parties bring may be relevant to a court proceeding, they are not what the issues are all about in mediation.

What if Smith is right that the dog is loud, noisy, beyond Spruce's control, and disturbing to the neighborhood? Perhaps the solution is indeed for Spruce to get rid of the dog. If it is established that the dog's barking is in fact not constant and that none of the other neighbors have complained, then Spruce's position that Smith should "put up or shut up" becomes more persuasive.

Consider the difference in the discussion that would ensue with respect to both the matters in dispute and the possible range of solutions if the mediator characterized the issues as "Smith's study time" and "Spruce's protection." The process would unfold very differently. Is Smith's need for quiet time greatest at night? Would Spruce be willing to take her dog to obedience school in exchange for Smith's studying in the library several nights a week for a defined period?

Is Shaw correct in stating that "[m]ediation is not a search for the truth"? What obligation does a mediator have towards insuring that the truth, at least as to the facts, is presented?

Ventilation: The term "ventilation" refers to a party's expression of strong feelings, anger, or emotions, often directed at the opposing party. In some mediations, parties will ventilate at their first opportunity to talk when asked to give their statement of the problem. In other mediations, ventilation will take place at a number of the early stages of the mediation, or at a later stage, or not at all. Lawyers are often uncomfortable with such displays, but ventilation can be an important component of mediation so long as it serves to make each side aware of the depth of concerns of the other. It can be used constructively to lead to a rehabilitation of the relationship of the parties or to expressions of apology or understanding of the feelings of the other. Ventilation is spontaneous and can take place at almost any time. The good mediator must carefully monitor the situation to assure that ventilation is not so abusive as to undermine the possibility of agreement or so lengthy and unrelated to the critical issues as to detract from constructive problem-solving.

c. INFORMATION GATHERING

This is the time for the parties to talk about the dispute, preferably between themselves, with the mediator unobtrusively guiding the discussion. It should allow a full exchange between the parties of the facts as they see them, the history of the dispute, and their opinions and emotions. It should also permit responding to accusations and clearing up of misunderstandings. Mediators should use open-ended questions and summarize in neutral language useful points that have been made.

The "information gathering" stage can be enhanced by a skillful mediator who allows the parties to reveal the information they feel important, but who also assists them with appropriate questions and probing. Consider the techniques suggested by Ernie Odom, The Mediation Hearing: A Primer, in Joseph E. Palenski & Harold M. Launer, Mediation: Context and Challenges 12 (1986):

1. Mediators ask questions that cannot be answered by a simple "yes" or "no." Many times mediators sense that there is more to the case than the disputants are willing to tell. In such instances, mediators may want to elicit additional facts by encouraging the parties to speak at greater length. If a party is responding rather than contributing to the discussion, it will be difficult to evoke more than the information already given. Also, it may seem to the disputants that the mediators, not the parties, are controlling the discussion. This may give the disputants the feeling that the mediators are resolving the dispute, not the disputants themselves.

The mediators use questions requiring a descriptive answer: "Why do you say that?" "What do you mean by that?" "What happened?" "How do you feel about this?" The basic idea is to call on the disputant to explain how or why, to describe something.

2. Mediators preface Key Words with "what about" or "how about." This is another technique mediators use to encourage a reluctant disputant to contribute additional information. By using these opening phrases, they try to move the discussion in a particular direction. Once the disputant starts talking, the mediators can key in on specific areas deemed important.

For example, in a dispute between neighbors, a mediator may lead with, "What about your relationship with your other neighbors?" This question requires the disputant to consider information not yet discussed. Once the party is encouraged to reflect on new factors, pertinent information may come to light that may never have surfaced if the conversation had been more tightly controlled.

3. Mediators repeat back Key Words. A third technique found effective in drawing out information is to repeat certain key phrases the party used in his or her previous answer. The purpose of this technique is to keep the dialogue going and gather as much information as possible by leading the disputant from one thought to the next.

4. Mediators summarize back. The advantage of repeating key words has been discussed. Sometimes mediators may feel an even greater elaboration may be necessary. They may find it helpful to summarize their understanding of the point the person is trying to make. In some instances, this is necessary to clarify the positions.

For example, a mediator may say, "Am I to understand you feel that ...?" Great care must be taken to assure that the summarization comes out sounding as impartial as possible; the mediator runs the serious risk of further confusing the issue by either misconstruing the person's thoughts or phrasing remarks in such a way that the opposing party is led to believe the mediator is taking sides or offering unfair advantage to the other party.

Caucus: A "caucus" is a private meeting between the mediator and one of the parties, its counsel, or both. The caucus allows the mediator to work individually with parties "to improve their attitudes and perceptions of the other, design procedures to test the accuracy of perceptions, or plan activities that will change negative attitudes." Moore, *The Caucus: Private Meetings That Promote Settlement*, 16 Mediation Q. 87, 89 (1987). A caucus can permit the mediator to talk frankly with one party, even discussing weak points in that party's case. Doing this in the presence of the other party, on the other hand, might give the impression that the mediator favors the other party's side. A caucus may also allow the mediator to test the willingness of the party to accept certain positions or solutions. A caucus may be initiated by any party or the mediator, although it is usually by the mediator. The mediator will have to decide what mix of open sessions with the parties present or of caucuses with only one party will be most useful.

Care must be taken in the way the mediator introduces the caucus. Generally the parties are told in the opening remarks that a caucus with either or both of them may be held and that its purpose is to clarify certain matters and not to make a private deal without the other. One commentator suggests: "Once the mediator initiates the caucus, he or she should take (1) steps to join psychologically with the party and build rapport, trust, and confidence in the mediator and the process, and (2) actions to assist the party in overcoming the specific barriers to settlement.... Statements such as 'I can see why it has been so tough to negotiate' or 'Looks like it's been pretty hard on you in the session' may indicate to the parties an interest in and empathy for how they are feeling." Moore, supra, at 93.

What is said in a caucus is held in confidence, but the mediator may set the ground rules by informing the party at the beginning of the caucus that, for example, anything that is said will not be kept from the other party or that he will convey certain kinds of information about the caucus to the other party.

B. The Mediation Process

d. PROBLEM IDENTIFICATION

This stage seeks to identify the problem (or a set of problems), to discover the interests of each party, and to find common goals. Problem identification may be a separate stage or may simply take place as part of the information gathering. It may not be useful to pursue all issues. The mediator should seek to focus on issues that the parties indicate a sustained commitment to pursuing. Problem identification may also need to include identification of the needs of the parties and the risks arising from a failure to settle the dispute.

Susan S. Silbey & Sally E. Merry,[11] Mediator Settlement Strategies

8 Law & Policy 7, 12–19 (1986).

In general, mediators regulate the account that is being developed by interpretation and reinterpretation of disputants' statements, determinations of relevance and irrelevance of statements, and styles of discourse. Mediators usually begin by asking questions that will elicit discussion and explanation of what has occurred to bring the parties to mediation. They are looking for a starting narrative and will ask disputants to expand upon simple statements such as "he struck me" to the circumstances and history of the blow. They will then broaden the discussion to encompass other events and circumstances, seeking areas of agreement, shared values, and shared experiences that could be emphasized and built upon for a settlement. "Tell me about how things were before all this started" is a common way of beginning this search. Although there is no single set of questions that can guarantee discovering commonalities, the broadening and searching process is indicated by such statements as: "Did you ever like each other?"; "Do you belong to the same church?"; "Do the children play together?"; "Had anything like this ever happened before the new neighbors moved in?"; and "Was there a time when you were friends or had good relations in the past?"

Selecting Issues

Through this process mediators uncover a broad range of problems to discuss and acknowledge. From this range of issues, mediators select the ones most likely to be settled. In one case, for example, in which lovers quarreled about the damage the man caused to the woman's apartment in a fit of jealousy, the mediators explored at some length the history of the relationship, their interest in continuing to see each other and the prospects for a future together. Unable to achieve consensus on these issues,

11. The authors are, respectively, professors of sociology and anthropology at Wellesley College. They spent three years studying a court-related mediation program which handled primarily criminal cases arising out of neighborhood, marital, family, and interpersonal disputes, and a community-based mediation program located in a social service agency which received both interpersonal and small claims case referrals.

the mediators returned to and focused upon the particular damages and losses sustained in the quarrel.

Mediators also establish an appropriate discourse by eliminating issues or people from the discussion. For example, some parties arrive with an extensive apparatus of legalistic "evidence" of past offenses such as logs of harassing phone calls, pictures of offensively parked cars, and bills and receipts from transactions. When this evidence points to fundamental conflicts or irresolvable issues of fact, the mediators define this legalistic, evidentiary mode of discourse as irrelevant and shift the discussion to feelings, morality, and an examination of how future relations should be ordered. Most of the discussion then deals with moral justifications of behavior, of character, and of being reasonable. There is very little explicit discussion of norms. Parties and mediators clearly assume that they share the same "paradigm of argument", and therefore leave norms unstated and implicit.

On the other hand, mediators will seek to narrow disputes, not by defining and eschewing legalistic discourse as irrelevant, but by turning directly to the law and legal charges as means of eliminating other unmanageable issues. They will frequently say that they cannot deal with all the issues presented at this time, but are here to deal with a specific criminal complaint. Thus the legal mode of discourse, which previously may have been irrelevant, is pulled back into the discussion as a means of eliminating other troublesome issues, some of which the mediators may have dredged up themselves.

In addition to eliminating issues, mediators will attempt to eliminate parties from the dispute. Parties will be told that the agreement deals only with the person who signed the original complaint and the person accused, so that the interests and concerns of others present at the session or involved in the dispute are eliminated.

Concretizing Issues

Once the dispute has been broadened and issues amenable for settlement or more appropriate for discussion have been selected, the next step is to concretize the issues. Mediators will often push for agreements by asking directly, "What is it you are looking for in an agreement?", thereby casting aside all issues but those that constitute a "bottom line." Mediators reshape general complaints and demands into specific behavioral requests. They will make concrete demands for respect between neighbors, more care between spouses, and better service by business people, focusing on a few specific points rather than general attitudinal orientations. For example, a man furious at the loud music next door might be urged to accept a promise that the music will be turned down at 10:00 p.m. every weekday night and 12:00 p.m. on the weekends. Parents quarreling with children about their friends, their social life, and their lack of respect may end up agreeing to have the child phone in nightly at 11:00 p.m. At first glance, this may seem to be a major redefinition of the family problem; however, it is possible to regard this agreement as a behavioral acknowledgement of parental authority and self-control on the part of the child, which was a substantial part of the original disagreement.

Insofar as possible, issues of insult and injury are transformed into property demands. The conversion of interpersonal injuries into property exchanges is the essence of tort law and has a long history in small-scale societies; the same approach is pursued here. For example, a man who was continually harassed by a neighbor's teenage son, which included a barrage of chocolate donuts at his door, reluctantly accepted the price of a gallon of paint to repaint the door as a settlement. Similarly, mediators will rephrase demands and accounts in order to eliminate emotionally loaded language which might connote moral blame or liability.

Postponing Issues

Finally, when problems seem too difficult to resolve in one session, or simply unresolvable, mediators postpone them. They suggest a future mediation session or a limited time to a present agreement; although only 6 per cent of the cases in the court-affiliated program and 13 per cent of the cases in the community program were postponed, 44 per cent of the agreements in the family program called for a second session. Typically, such agreements read, "X agrees not to drink for three weeks and to pay his wife $80 a week until the next mediation session, scheduled in three weeks." Or, they might read, "X agrees to talk to Mrs. Jones about the placement of the fence while Y agrees to talk to his tenant about his working hours. They will return to mediation in two weeks to discuss the results of their inquiries."

Sometimes, issues which are not easily resolved are sent to counseling, thus suggesting that they belong in a therapeutic arena and not in a process designed to settle "disputes" of legitimate differences. Alcoholics, spouse-abusers, parents who cannot control their children, and husbands and wives who continually fight are routinely sent to counseling. The family mediation program increased the use of social services for almost half the families.

* * *

From [our observations of mediation sessions in a two-year study of mediation programs] we constructed two ideal types of mediation styles: the bargaining and the therapeutic.

These mediation styles are modal/ideal types constructed by synthesizing and typifying the characteristics of over forty mediators. They do not categorize mediators, but describe instead regular patterns of dealing with problems. A single mediator usually uses both styles to some extent, and a single mediation session has some elements of each style. Any particular mediator may adopt one or another strategy, depending upon the particular problem or case, and strategies may change within the duration of any mediation session. Neither the relationship of the parties, nor the type of case (small claims, spouse abuse, neighborhood dispute), nor the sex of the mediator seems to determine which style eventually predominates. Media-

CHAPTER III MEDIATION

tion strategies develop through interaction with the parties who come to mediation with sets of expectations, wants and skills with which they endeavor to impose their view of things upon the situation. Thus the degree to which a mediation session is a bargaining or therapeutic event is constructed by implicit negotiation between the parties. Nevertheless, where the parties are known to have longstanding relations, or the issues are emotional ones, mediators often begin with the therapeutic approach. Mediators who are known to adopt one style more than the other may be assigned to cases on this basis. Moreover, mediator strategies seem to become more pronounced and stylized toward one or the other mode with increased experience.

In the bargaining mode, mediators claim authority as professionals with expertise in process, law, and the court system, which is described as costly, slow and inaccessible. The purpose of mediation is to reach settlement. The bargaining style tends toward more structured process, and toward more overt control of the proceedings. In the bargaining style, mediators use more private caucuses with disputants, direct discussion more, and encourage less direct disputant communication than in the therapeutic style. Moreover, in the bargaining style the mediators tend to write agreements without the parties present, summarizing and synthesizing what they have heard from the parties. The job of the mediator is to look for bottom lines, to narrow the issues, to promote exchanges, and to sidestep intractable differences of interest. Typically disputants will be asked directly "What do you want?", ignoring emotional demands and concentrating on demands that can be traded off. Following this bargaining mode, mediators seem to assume that conflict is caused by differences of interest and that the parties can reach settlement by exchanging benefits. When parties resist, the role of the mediator is to become an "agent of reality" and to point to the inadequacy of the alternatives, the difficulty of the present situation and the benefits of a settlement of any kind.

By contrast, the therapeutic style of mediation is a form of communication in which the parties are encouraged to engage in a full expression of their feelings and attitudes. Here, mediators claim authority based on expertise in managing personal relationships and describe the purpose of mediation as an effort to help people reach mutual understanding through collective agreements. Like the bargaining style, the therapeutic mode also takes a negative view of the legal system; but, instead of emphasizing institutional values and inadequacies, the therapeutic style emphasizes emotional concerns, faulting the legal system for worsening personal relationships. In this mode, agreement writing becomes a collective activity, with mediators generally maximizing direct contact between the parties wherever it may lead. Following the therapeutic style, mediators will typically ask, "How did this situation start?", or, "What was your relationship beforehand?" They rely more heavily upon expanding the discussion, exploring past relations, and going into issues not raised by the immediate situation, complaint or charge. There is less discussion of legal norms than within the bargaining mode, and statements about alternatives tend to focus upon appropriateness of process rather than particular outcomes. In addition, the therapeutic mode tends to emphasize the mutuality, reciprocity, and self-enforcement of the agreement in contrast to court or program monitoring. * * *

The communication approach assumes that misunderstandings or failures of communication, rather than fundamental differences of interest, are the source of conflict, and that with sufficient "sharing" of feelings and history the empathy required for consensus and harmony will be achieved. It assumes that the expression of conflict will help resolve it and that the recognition of shared norms and underlying shared interests will lead to the maintenance of good relationships. Questions typical of the therapeutic approach are generally open, yet probing: "Tell me how you feel about that," or "Are there other things you want to talk about?" It is assumed that parties do not always know what they want and that the job of mediation is to help them define their real wants by exploring their lives and values. Mediators who are more typically therapeutic are often stymied in a way that mediators who are typically bargaining are not, when direct conflicts of interest emerge. Moreover, because of the length of sessions in the therapeutic mode (often four hours or more) there is a sense of wearing the parties down. The mandate for the mediator is clear: to facilitate conversation, not to bargain. Bargaining mediation takes a pragmatic view that parties should settle because they must and because they need to live together, while therapeutic mediation emphasizes the value of handling conflict through rational discourse.

Two cases can serve as examples of mediation style. The first is a case in which the dominant mediator style was bargaining; the second is a case in which the mediator style was essentially therapeutic.

The first case concerns a dispute between a married couple and their teenage daughter over her defiance, overuse of the family's telephone, unwillingness to help with chores, and her spending patterns. The parents filed an application for a complaint against their daughter in juvenile court. In the mediation session, the two mediators begin by asking the family (mother, father, daughter) to describe the situation. After a half-hour discussion, the mediators meet privately, decide that the phone is the major issue and begin to talk about what an agreement might look like. In a private caucus with the child, they ask her to discuss further what is bothering her and whether she thinks it is getting worse. They soon begin asking for suggestions: "What would be a reasonable arrangement for the phone?"; "Is your sister old enough to clean up after herself, and would she be willing to help?"; "If we were going to work out some rules for everyone in the house, what could we work out that might work?" After forty minutes of exploring specific options, the mediators again hold a private discussion, then invite the mother in by herself.

In the private session with the mother, they ask her who does the chores, how the children are punished for failure to do them, and if there is a curfew. They ask the mother what she sees as the problem with the phone, chores, and friends and what she would like to see changed in the family. The mediators then summarize the three major issues: the phone,

CHAPTER III MEDIATION

going out, and how the members of the family deal with one another. They ask the mother to be specific about the chores her daughter is expected to do and when she is to do them. Together, they hammer out a list of rules for chores, phone use, and curfews.

One hour later, the father is called in for a brief (20–minute) session with the mother and the mediators. The mediators again stress that they are working out an arrangement in which the daughter knows what she has to do. In a final private discussion with the daughter, the mediators ask her if she had any other thoughts or concerns. They present the specific proposals and ask if she agrees to them. Their proposals include a promise that her father will talk to her calmly instead of yelling at her. These provisions are incorporated into a formal written document which parents and daughter sign, with the mediators serving as witnesses. The session lasts three hours and fifteen minutes, and the family members seem satisfied.

In this session, the mediators structured the discussion around specific issues through questions which narrowed rather than expanded the dispute. The extensive use of caucusing enabled them to control the exchange of information and to develop and transfer acceptable arrangements. They took an active role in working out the details, rather than encouraging the parties to talk directly to one another or to formulate arrangements entirely on their own. They typically asked clarifying or informational questions or ones which invited the parties to narrow the problem. As this example shows, the extensive use of private sessions with individual parties maximizes the control of the mediators. The parents, searching for guidance and help, did not seem unhappy with this level of intervention by the mediators.

A therapeutic mediation session is a contrast in many ways. One example also concerns a family conflict, but the style of the mediator (there was only one in the session) was quite different. Instead of closing down the emotional issues, the mediator constantly sought to open them up and to expand the frame of the discussion.

The dispute concerns debts which a young man, in his late 20s, had acquired during his marriage. The couple are now living separately and in the process of filing for a divorce. He wants his ex-wife to help him bear the burden of these consumer debts, while she claims that he spent money irresponsibly and she is not liable. He sued her for $750 in small claims court, and the mediation program invited the couple to try mediation. The couple has a hearing in probate court about their divorce in two months, where they expect to settle financial issues and the contested custody of their 10–year–old child. This couple married interracially but found the racial barriers increasingly difficult to handle. The man drank and was violent to his wife, which persuaded her to leave him. He blames the stress of the interracial marriage and her lack of support for his behavior. She wants the divorce and he is resisting it strongly.

The mediator begins this session by allowing the parties to inspect the bills and argue over the amount of the debt and the degree of liability of each. After 35 minutes of mutual accusations about money and past poor behavior, the mediator caucuses with the woman and asks her about the bills and how much she is willing to pay. He then inquires what, besides the bills, she would like to see in an agreement. She replies that she would like the agreement to be final so that he would not come back and go over the incidents between them over and over again. At this point, the mediator asks her to tell him about the incidents and anything else that is bothering her, promising not to convey this to her husband. She responds that, if it is helpful, she will give her version of the incidents, but she is not sure that it is relevant. One hour and ten minutes later, she has thoroughly reviewed the reasons for the breakup of the marriage, her feelings about the divorce, and the nature of the divorce settlement.

In the next caucus, with the man, the mediator spends one hour hearing the husband's version of the conflict and his feelings about the divorce. The mediator then brings them back together and asks the man what he would like from the woman. They renew discussion of the unpaid bills and again try to decide who is responsible for each bill; this is the point at which they began two-and-one-quarter hours earlier. They cannot agree upon responsibility, but finally settle on a plan in which the wife would make a regular, monthly small contribution for one year, at which time the agreement would be renegotiated. Although unwilling to acknowledge responsibility for the bills, the wife is willing to agree to this payment schedule because she expects that the upcoming divorce decision will eventually change this agreement, as well as their relationship. The final discussion of a payment schedule lasts forty-five minutes, and the entire mediation session takes three-and-one-half hours. The woman leaves feeling angry that she has made a concession she does not like, while the man is pleased. Both say they want another session, although they do not come again, nor does the woman make all the payments she promised.

In this session, the mediator began with a narrow financial problem, expanded it into far broader and more emotional areas, even when the parties resisted slightly, then returned at the end to the narrower problem of negotiating the money. Behind his strategy was the theory that the expression of feelings is a necessary precondition to reaching a resolution. As a result, he pursued a strategy we have labeled therapeutic. He constantly invited them to expand the arena of discussion and to move into other facets of their conflict. It is impossible to say if a mediator could have produced the same or a better settlement through focused bargaining, but it is clear that this approach differs a great deal from the bargaining approach. This mediation was unusual for a therapeutic session in its use of private sessions for the bulk of the mediation process, but not unusual in the scope of issues considered and the role of the mediator in probing into feelings.

Comments from mediators about the techniques they use to settle cases further illustrate the differences between the two mediation styles. As these statements suggest, mediator strategies grow out of assumptions about the nature of conflict, conflict resolution, and their own particular

CHAPTER III MEDIATION

capacities and skills. When asked how they settle cases, for example, several mediators expressed a view of their work which leads them to adopt a bargaining mode:

(a) I get people talking, then focus on some issues to get to agreement points. You can't just keep talking.

(b) I take a ball of broad issues and expand it by breaking it down into concrete ones. I see what issues really matter to them and I work on those.

(c) As a mediator, your job is to convince one or the other party to give up something; to negotiate together. The essence of the process is negotiation. You don't accept blame from others of each other, and you also don't accept their version of the facts. I am firm with a loud-mouth. In small claims cases, I say that when a person won't settle, I will give it back to the judge and the judge will give him only 30 days to pay.

Here, mediators express a view which leads them to adopt the more therapeutic approach:

(a) My strategy is to try to get the recalcitrant person to see the other's view. If the other person doesn't do it, I do it in caucus myself. It usually works to point out how the other person sees things—that usually produces an agreement.

(b) I look for people's concerns, the reasons why this issue is important to each of them, and try to create an environment where they feel safe enough to articulate that concern. I do this by being open and non-judgmental and by listening to their feelings.

(c) I try just to get people talking, to get them to explain their side fully so that the other side really understands them. The problem is that people don't understand each other's thinking. I try to help them look for solutions.

NOTES AND QUESTIONS

1. Are any of the techniques described by Silbey and Merry for nudging parties toward settlement inconsistent with the consensual nature of mediation?

2. Is the mediator who adopts a therapeutic approach more likely to impose her values on the bargaining process? Should there be a distinction between imposing her values and seeking to serve valid mediation objectives such as a consensual agreement? Is the notion of mending the relationship and achieving reconciliation, if possible, a proper objective? Is the bargaining approach likely to overlook an opportunity for the mediator to move the parties toward reconciliation?

3. Do any of the following three examples of mediator pressure described in David E. Matz, Mediator Pressure and Party Autonomy: Are They Consistent With Each Other?, 10 Negotiation J. 359, 359–363 (1994), violate the party's autonomy? How do they differ in terms of mediator directiveness?

B. The Mediation Process   **357**

Example 1

A party seeking to dissolve a partnership has spoken for fifteen minutes (in private caucus) about the ways in which his partner has betrayed the business. You as the mediator have been largely silent, taking notes. In passing, the party mentions that his partner had developed all of that part of their business that takes place in the Southeastern part of the United States. You see in this comment the potential for a useful step in dividing up the partnership assets; so, in your first substantive move in fifteen minutes, you ask for more detail about the partner's relationship with the Southeast. The party stops describing his partner's betrayal, shifts focus to comply with your request, and answers your question.

Example 2

Same case as just described. Same moment in the case. Except that the party has been describing his partner's betrayal for twenty minutes, and for the last five minutes has been repeating earlier accusations. You have listened actively, summarized for him twice, and asked him several questions seeking clarification. Now he has begun his third repetition of the betrayal charges. His reference about the partner's link to the Southeast was made ten minutes ago, and you now ask him for more details about it. The party ignores your question and continues to redescribe the betrayal. You make the judgment that not only is his redundancy of no use but, without stronger intervention, the party will continue to wallow in the agony of his past, effectively preventing any movement toward a resolution.

So you say: "I believe I understand how you see the painful parts of your past relationship with your partner. (And here you summarize again.) Is there anything new from that history that you wish me to hear? You have told me the same facts now several times, and it is not a good use of our time to go over them again. I am interested, however, in your partner's relationship to the Southeast. I asked about that before. Is there a reason you'd rather not talk about it?" The party responds by saying that of course he wants to describe his partner's work in the Southeast. And he proceeds to do so.

Example 3

Same scene as variation two. But instead of telling you about the work in the Southeast, the party responds by saying, "No, there is no reason not to discuss my partner's work in the Southeast. Let me tell you how he has betrayed me in the Southeast too." And he proceeds to start such a description.

There are, of course, a number of steps you could take at this point, but you are now sufficiently concerned about whether this party is willing or able to discuss settlement at all that you choose to say: "I am perplexed and troubled. You told me you came to mediation seeking a settlement, but I think you are having a difficult time letting go of the past. Until you let go, however, I think there is no way to explore settlement. There are a number of topics we can discuss that may move us toward settlement. One

358 CHAPTER III MEDIATION

of them is your partner's work in the Southeast. If you have some others, perhaps we should turn to those. If you are ready to discuss any one of them now, fine. If not, then I think we should end the mediation." The party responds, "Oh fine, if you insist. I'll tell you about the Southeast." And he does.

4. Professor Harold I. Abramson, Business Mediation Representation: Representing Clients in a Problem–Solving Process (2002), sees an appropriate role for a mediator in turning the parties from an adversary to a problem-solving approach:

> If your client or the other side slips backward into an adversarial approach, the mediator can coax the regressing person back into a problem-solving mode. The mediator can do this by posing carefully crafted questions. If the other side starts the mediation with an opening offer strategy of an extreme proposal, for example, the mediator can ask whether all proposals could be deferred until after the parties gather more information, including sharing information about each other's interests. If the other party insists on ten million dollars in damages, the mediator may search behind the party's position by asking for a reasoned explanation for the level of damages. If the other side approaches the problem as a narrow legal dispute, the mediator may ask whether other issues should be addressed in the mediation. If the other party treats the dispute as distributive—one gains at the expense of the other, the mediator may ask integrative-oriented questions about the party's interests and opportunities to increase value and expand the pie. These reactive moves by the mediator can temper your need to react. Instead, you can defer to the mediator's moves to prod the adversarial person into a problem-solving mode.

e. PROBLEM SOLVING: GENERATING OPTIONS AND BARGAINING

This stage seeks to have the parties explore all possible options for resolving the dispute. It too may not take place as a separate stage but as part of a free-flowing exchange of information, positions, feelings, and problem identification. Ideally concrete suggestions should come from the parties, although the mediator may have to use various techniques for encouraging creative option-generating. It may also be necessary for the mediator to assist the parties in identifying ways to marshal resources in order to achieve a feasible solution. Option-generating will often be followed by negotiating and bargaining as the parties work out their demands and concessions.

Christopher W. Moore, The Mediation Process
204–206, 212–216 (1986).

I will discuss two overall strategies and then proceed to explore specific procedural moves mediators and negotiators use to develop settlement options.

The Building–Block Approach to Settlement. The *building-block approach* requires disputants to divide an issue into subissues or component parts. Fisher (1964) refers to this procedure as *fractionation.* Ideally, these smaller components are more manageable units for problem solving. Each of these subissues is sequentially resolved and combined with the settlements of previous issues. When combined in a building-block approach, these agreements allow the parties to develop an elaborate and complete settlement. Procedurally the parties move from the settlement of specific subissues toward a total package which settles the dispute. The parties may agree to accept as final agreements on each subissue, or may delay final settlement until agreement can be reached on all the issues in dispute.

Problems or issues are divided into smaller components because (1) disputants may see and understand smaller issues more easily than those that are complex and many-faceted, (2) dividing issues into components prevents moves to join or link unrelated subjects that block agreement, and (3) dividing issues into components may depoliticize or isolate issues that prevent settlement.

There are two ways to divide issues into smaller components. First, the mediator may suggest that the definition of what is being discussed be narrowed. Second, the mediator or a negotiator may ask parties to look at an issue and ask them to divide it into component subissues. Obtaining the involvement of the parties in subissue definition can create greater commitment to the process.

Negotiation over how privacy could be maintained for single-family homeowners if condominiums were built close to their residences illustrates fractionation and the building-block approach. The mediators and the parties divided the problem of privacy into several subissues: visual privacy, auditory privacy, and congestion. To accomplish visual privacy, the parties generated solutions that (1) reduced building height so that second-floor dwellers could not see into the backyards or windows of the single-family homes, (2) provided for berms and fences to shield single-family homes from views of the condominiums, (3) graduated building heights so that condominiums close to single-family homes were one story in height and those further away were gradually increased to two or three stories, and (4) shielded lights in the condominium parking lot to prevent the light from entering single-family home windows. Similar solutions were generated to handle auditory and congestion problems. By dividing the problem or issue into smaller pieces and solving the component parts, the parties were ultimately able to forge a comprehensive settlement.

Agreement in Principle Approach to Settlement. The second major strategy for defining issues and progressing toward a settlement is the *agreement in principle* or *formula* approach. This procedure requires negotiators to create or identify a bargaining formula or set of general principles that will guide the shape of the final settlement. This approach is the polar opposite of the building-block approach in that it requires negotiators to reach a general level of agreement and then initiate steps to define the specifics. This approach is often appropriate when underlying values of the disputants are similar or when superordinate goals can be identified.

The agreement in principle or formula approach to settlement is often not as familiar to disputants as the building-block approach. The mediator may have to be more directive in educating the parties about the procedure. The mediator may either directly reframe the issue to be resolved in broader terms and then encourage the parties to generate general principles of agreement, or may explain the philosophy behind the strategic approach and turn the implementation over to the negotiators.

An example of the agreement in principle approach occurred in the Metropolitan Water Roundtable negotiations in Denver, Colorado, among water suppliers, environmentalists, ranchers, and recreation interests. The parties were initially stalled over whether additional water was needed in the Denver area and over a proposal to construct a dam at a particular site.

After an intensive educational process, all the parties agreed that the water was needed and that a dam was needed somewhere on the eastern side of the Rocky Mountains. After agreeing on these two principles, the parties began to investigate how the water needs could be met using a variety of sources—conservation, groundwater, transmountain exchanges— and the location and size of a new dam. By reaching a series of agreements in principle on several different levels, the parties were able to progress toward agreement. * * *

Parties in mediation have used numerous processes to generate settlement options. These procedures have several characteristics in common. First, they attempt to generate several options so that the parties can move from a bipolar view of solutions to a multipolar approach. Second, they attempt to separate the stage of generating options from the later evaluative or assessment stage. This separation ensures that the search process will be more comprehensive and complete and not inhibited by premature judgments. Third, they focus the effort of the negotiators on the issue or problem and not on the other party. The dispute is depersonalized so that the parties aim their attacks not at the people in the negotiations but at the issues that divide them. I will now discuss six common procedures mediators or negotiators can initiate to generate settlement options.

Brainstorming. Brainstorming is a procedure in which a group of people generate a variety of ideas or options for consideration. The mediator or a negotiator begins the process by framing an issue into a problem. A *problem* is a restatement of an issue into a "how-to" format. "How can enough resources be found to send a wife to school so that she can be self-supporting?" "How can an outstanding bill be paid by a company with limited assets?" "How can a popular recreation area be maintained while still allowing companies to explore for minerals?"

The parties are then instructed to speak one at a time and suggest as rapidly as possible a list of alternative solutions that might meet the needs of the parties. The mediator should instruct them to avoid stating purely self-serving options and should caution them against making verbal or nonverbal judgments of practicality or acceptability during the session. The mediator should inform them that assessment and evaluation of the options will be initiated after they have generated a substantial number of solutions, and he or she should encourage them to build and modify each other's ideas as long as the results incline them toward an option that might meet more of their interests. The mediator should record alternatives on a pad or wall chart, taking care to record accurately and keep the session going. When the parties have generated a number of options or have exhausted their resources, they may shift to an assessment procedure.

Brainstorming can be conducted (1) as a whole group activity, (2) individuals or teams, (3) within subgroups of a team, or (4) in subgroups composed of delegates or representatives of each of the parties. Brainstorming as individuals, teams, or team subgroups may be used when disputants do not trust other parties and are uncomfortable disclosing options publicly, but want to enlarge their settlement alternatives. The mediator may randomly assign subgroups with members from opposing parties when he or she or a negotiator wants to maximize participation and increase personal contact between disputants by using small groups. Brainstorming in a subgroup with specifically assigned membership may be used to group or more evenly distribute moderates from opposing negotiating teams. Moderate team members are more likely to come up with integrative solutions that will meet the needs of all parties than subgroups composed of hard-line negotiators.

Utilizing Nominal Group Process. Building on the basic small group process concept that individuals invent and groups evaluate, the nominal group process seeks to maximize individual creativity to help a group solve a problem. In this process, the issue is stated in problem format to the participants. Individuals list independently within a specific time limit all possible alternatives that might resolve the group's differences. They then form small subgroups of about five members each. All ideas are shared and recorded within the small group, with each member offering one suggestion at a time. These ideas are then elaborated on, discussed, and assessed for merit.

Discussion Groups or Subgroups. People in conflict are often hindered from generating options because groups are too large in size to be manageable for problem solving, high-level interaction, or candor. This may be especially true for multi-party community disputes. Small, informal discussion groups are often helpful for alternative generation. In disputes with multiple parties, the entire group may delegate subissues or problems to small working groups or committees, charging them to propose an integrative solution that can be referred back to the main group for final decision.

Developing Hypothetical Plausible Scenarios. Parties may occasionally be encouraged to develop possible settlement options by engaging in hypothetical scenario development. The mediator describes the issue as a problem and then charges individuals or small groups to develop hypothetical scenarios, in narrative form, about how the problem can be overcome.

362 CHAPTER III MEDIATION

Scenarios should describe procedural, substantive, and psychological outcomes and processes used to incline the parties from their present stance to the preferred result. This approach, when used in small groups of disputants from all parties, often produces greater commitment to cooperative solutions. Once the scenarios are developed, the groups may present each until the negotiators have heard all the possibilities. The parties then assess whole scenarios and individual components for relevant alternative solutions to their dispute.

Single Text Negotiating Document. Hypothetical plausible scenarios can often be developed into a single text negotiating document. Either a party or the mediator may initiate this procedure. The first step is to identify the interests of all parties. The initiator should then develop a text or proposal that might satisfy the majority of the interests and resolve the dispute. This document becomes a draft settlement text that is circulated between the parties for comments and revision. Each party should have an opportunity to modify the text to better meet his or her needs. Gradual revision often results in a single text that is acceptable to all disputants.

President Carter used this procedure in 1978 to negotiate the Camp David accords between Israel and Egypt. A similar procedure was used in the Law of the Seas negotiations. The one-text approach is helpful for two-party disputes and almost a necessity for a multiparty dispute.

Using Outside Resources. Parties are often frustrated by a myopic view of the conflict when generating viable alternatives. This condition may result from proximity to or lack of objectivity toward issues in dispute. Disputants may also be limited by their own experiences or possess inadequate data. The use of outside resources, initiated by either the parties or the mediator, may be of great assistance to the negotiations. Often the mediator can enhance the acceptability of a move to obtain outside help because of his or her perceived neutrality.

Outside resources can take the form of specific information or experts in the topic under discussion. For example, in child custody disputes, mediators may want the couple to read *Mom's House, Dad's House* (Ricci, 1980) or *Joint Custody and Co–Parenting* (Galper, 1980) so that they may obtain ideas outside of mediation on how to establish a new parenting relationship. For companies trying to negotiate the structure of a new employee-management grievance procedure, representatives may want to consult books on organizational dispute resolution (Bazerman and Lewicki, 1983; Blake and Mouton, 1984).

Outside resource persons may be substantive or procedural experts on the issue. Lawyers, assessors, or accountants; other parties who have had similar conflicts and have resolved them, such as government officials, managers, or parents; or individuals from other disciplines or backgrounds may have data to contribute.

Bargaining: The Effect of Legal Rules

The very essence of mediation is that the parties are free to reach their own resolution of the dispute. Much like negotiation, mediation is a form of private ordering by which the parties may choose a settlement quite different from the rights and obligations set out in the law. This raises questions, however, as to what role legal rules should play in the mediation process.

Even though mediation is a form of private ordering, it is still conducted against the backdrop of the legal system. The parties are aware that if the mediation fails, the dispute may be resolved in a trial through formal application of legal rules. Thus the bargaining that takes place in mediation is performed "in the shadow of the law," as Professors Mnookin and Kornhauser described in the context of divorce:

> Divorcing parents do not bargain over the division of family wealth and custodial prerogatives in a vacuum; they bargain in the shadow of the law. The legal rules governing alimony, child support, marital property, and custody give each parent certain claims based on what each would get if the case went to trial. In other words, the outcome that the law will impose if no agreement is reached gives each parent certain bargaining chips—an endowment of sorts.

Robert H. Mnookin & Lewis Kornhauser, *Bargaining in the Shadow of the Law: The Case for Divorce,* 88 Yale L.J. 950, 968 (1979).

Mnookin and Kornhauser assert that law provides a framework for parties to invoke a process of private ordering:

> We see the primary function of contemporary divorce law not as imposing order from above, but rather as providing a framework within which divorcing couples can themselves determine their postdissolution rights and responsibilities. This process by which parties to a marriage are empowered to create their own legally enforceable commitments is a form of "private ordering." Id. at 950.

If mediating parties bargain in the shadow of the law, where do they get their information about the law? In the case of divorce, where most parties have legal representation, the information usually comes from their lawyers. But what little research has been done on the interaction between clients and attorneys incident to giving legal advice is not heartening. Consider the following account from a study based on interviews with parties and lawyers in divorce cases from Erlanger, Chambliss, & Melli, Participation and Flexibility in Informal Processes: Cautions from the Divorce Context, 21 Law & Soc'y Rev. 585, 598–600 (1987):

> The hypothesis that endowments will structure the bargaining process because parties will bargain with judicial review in mind is also problematic. First, it assumes parties have access to legal information, or at least to information about their judge's expectations regarding child support and property division. The parties we interviewed received most of their legal information from their attorneys. Thus, to the extent that formal endowments exist, they are subject to attorneys' interpretations, which potentially alters the entitlements created by the law. At the very least, then, we would argue that the shadow of the

law is being cast by the lawyers, who declare their expectations of judicial behavior. * * *

Perhaps more fundamentally, the existence of consistent formal criteria for decision making is itself debatable. Several of the lawyers we interviewed report that they have difficulty discerning court standards and that they cannot predict the outcomes of court processes. Some lawyers also indicate they feel uncomfortable trying to advise clients about what is fair or what to aim for in a given divorce case. One lawyer remarks: "So much of it is judgmental.... [Clients] ask questions like 'Is it fair?' and I just want to say—forgive my language—'Well, shit, I don't know, I'm just guessing like you'".

Even the lawyers in our sample who do think there are set standards and who do say they can predict outcomes differ in their opinion of the content of those court standards; obviously, they cannot all be correct. Some lawyers attempt to "divide hardship," that is, to make each parent absorb equal deficiencies of income. Others measure the adequacy of support by looking at the custodial parent's budget, trying to make sure the custodian can make ends meet, or by looking at the supporting parent's ability to pay. Still others focus on a flat amount of support per child. Many lawyers also stress that their settlement strategy in any given case depends heavily on who is representing the other spouse. Thus, it is doubtful that parties receive consistent legal information and advice.

Over 90% of divorce cases, according to most estimates, are settled through stipulation, and it is the rare case that is completely litigated. This fact opens the possibility that the shadow of the law, which presumably constrains negotiating parties, is instead cast by them. In other words, in litigation, judges may be following the patterns they see in informal settlements rather than the other way around; thus, instead of "bargaining in the shadow of the law," one should refer to "litigating in the shadow of informal settlement." Even one who accepts the logic of this argument might still defend the endowments assumption. One could say that what matters is not some abstract analysis about who sets the patterns but rather the participants' *perceptions* of that process. Parties who feel constrained will act as if they are, whether or not they in fact are.

To our respondents, however, legal constraints are decidedly less important than the other pressures we have discussed; many parties even disregarded the advice of their attorneys. For instance, in some cases in which the client was impatient to settle, the lawyer's dissatisfaction with the terms was ignored:

> My lawyer ... wanted to wait until fall to make sure, to try to get a better handle on if [my husband's] business was successful. He thought my name should remain on it as part-owner.... I really wanted to get out of it, and didn't want to just mess around. I mean [he may have been] right—[but] I didn't care who was right at that point, and I still don't. It was more important to get out of the marriage.

While lawyers are often accused of stirring up trouble in divorce cases, it is clear that in some cases, they are unable to do so even when they

B. THE MEDIATION PROCESS

think it is necessary to protect their client's interests. Against custody threats and other tactics, a lawyer's reassurances and support may be insufficient to keep clients from folding, as one lawyer explains:

> Her husband was using the threat of a custody issue to keep his payments down and she was insisting that I follow that approach. In other words, I take it very easy on him and as I recall, even from the beginning, no support [was] ordered.... She wanted me to forget about the father's responsibility to the children as far as money goes.... She was such a basket case.... He had just frightened her to death.

Thus, even if the "shadow of the law" is a factor in informal settlement decisions, it is not the only factor, and its impact should not be overestimated.

Despite widespread acceptance of the "bargaining in the shadow of the law" thesis, there are strong roots in the mediation tradition that emphasize its ex-legal nature. Consider the following:

Lenard Marlow, The Rule of Law in Divorce Mediation

9 Mediation Q. 5, 10–13 (1985).

[The author is a fellow of the American Academy of Matrimonial Lawyers and Director of legal services of Divorce Mediation Professionals in New York.]

Divorce mediation rejects the idea that legal rules should be used as weapons to improve one party's position at the expense of the other. Similarly, it rejects the idea that these legal rules and principles embody any necessary wisdom or logic. In fact, it views them as being arbitrary principles, having little to do with the realities of a couple's life and not superior to the judgments that the couple could make on their own. What relevance do these rules and principles have in mediation then, and why is it necessary to know them?

Whether laws are fair or unfair, parties believe them to be significant and this shapes their expectations. This is just a fact. If the law says that when title to a couple's home is in the husband's name alone, and that the wife will not have an interest in it, then the husband does not expect to have to give her any portion of it—this is so whether the wife feels this to be fair or unfair. This is a reality with which a mediator must deal. However, unlike a lawyer in an adversarial setting, he is not bound by it. He does not believe that these rules embody any necessary logic, let alone guarantee any necessary justice. They may be limiting factors, but they are not absolutes. In fact, from his standpoint, the problem is that the expectations created by these rules and principles will produce an agreement between the parties that is not fair. In this instance, therefore, the law is an obstacle to a fair agreement. The mediator's job is to effect a fairer agreement than the law would provide, despite the expectations that the husband (in this case) has based on the law.

366 CHAPTER III MEDIATION

In other instances, the mediator will treat the law not as an obstacle to overcome but will use it as a protective shield. For instance, a lack of agreement between the parties is occasioned by the fact that they disagree as to whether it is fair that the wife should have an interest in her husband's business. As arbitrary as the law may be in its determination (at one time it may have said no, at another time it may have said yes), the mediator can, nevertheless, invoke it as a means of resolving the disagreement when all else fails. When the husband refuses to concede that his wife should have any interest in his business, the mediator intervenes and says, "But that is the law." In this instance, he invokes the law not for the purpose of resolving the disagreement but to end it. The law is a reality, and although it may go against the husband's intentions, he cannot deny it.

The mediator is trying to effect change, in this case, a change from a lack of agreement to an agreement. Moreover, the mediator does not view these legal rules and principles as embodying either wisdom or justice, and does not believe that they represent a necessary yardstick by which to judge the agreement that has been concluded. Rather, these legal rules and principles are simply realities that can either limit or aid the mediation process.

How does this view of the law affect the way a mediator would treat legal rules and principles? To begin with, if a mediator suggested to a couple that they seek legal counsel, it would be so that they could each determine what their rights and obligations were and to thereby assure that their agreement accurately mirrored those rights and obligations. It would be difficult to find out exactly what their rights were (that is, the parties could not find out, save by going to court, what a court would decide in their particular case). Nor would the parties' agreement necessarily be better if it exactly resembled the one that the law would give them— assuming they could find out what such an agreement would be without going to court.

If the mediator suggested that the couple consult with attorneys, it would be for very different reasons. The first reason would be to avoid concluding an agreement that one or the other of the parties would later feel was unfair. Perhaps it would be extremely unfair in a particular instance for one of the parties to share in the other's pension (for instance, if the husband does not have a pension but his parents are extremely wealthy and he will be well provided for in his old age and the wife, on the other hand, will need every penny of her own pension to support herself when she retires.) Before the husband waives his interests in her pension, however, it would be better that he knows that legally he has an interest in it. The disposition that the law would make in this case would not necessarily be fairer. (Since the court could not take cognizance of the husband's future inheritance, or therefore consider it, it might be far less fair.) It is that the mediator does not want to jeopardize the efficacy of the agreement as one that both of the parties can live with. This might occur if the husband concluded an agreement without being aware that he could

B. The Mediation Process   **367**

legally make claims on his wife's pension and later might feel that he had been taken advantage of.

Another instance in which the mediator might recommend that the parties consult with an attorney would be as a strategy to break an impasse, for example if the couple disagreed as to whether it was fair that the wife should share in her husband's pension. It is not the purpose of mediation to have endless philosophical debates as to what is ultimately fair or unfair; there will be as many opinions on that issue as there are people who are asked. If the couple does not start out with a common view of what is fair or unfair, and if the mediator is unable to produce a common view, then there must be a way to break the impasse. In this case, referring the couple for legal counsel (to find out what the law says) may serve to do that, since the couple will feel obligated to accept what the law says. Since this is the only reason why the mediator is referring the couple for legal counsel, it is not necessary (as would be the case if legal rules and principles were viewed as rights) that they consult with separate attorneys. The only question at issue is whether the law in the particular jurisdiction would give the wife an interest in her husband's pension. In fact, one lawyer is preferable, since the mediator wants an answer, not a range of legal opinions.

Since legal rules and principles are therefore simply a means to an end and are used by a mediator as an intervention of strategy to achieve a desired result, the mediator does not consider himself slavishly bound to them. Rather, he is free to deal with them in a far less constricted manner. Suppose, for example, that there is a dispute between a husband and a wife as to how long she will have the right to live in their marital residence with their children. The husband asks the mediator (who happens to be a lawyer), "How long do I have to let her live in the home?" What he is of course asking is how long the law will allow her to live there. The husband is now attempting to use the law as a strategy, not because he feels that the legal answer makes sense or is right, but simply because he believes that the law will support his opinion. The mediator, of course, does not believe that there are or should be legal answers to personal questions. More important, the mediator's job is to impress this fact on the husband. Instead of answering the question, therefore, the mediator asks the husband, "Tell me, how are your children taking your separation? If they were required to leave their home and be uprooted from their community at this time, do you think that this would make it more difficult for them? And what about your son who is in the tenth grade? Do you think it would be a good idea to disrupt the continuity of his high school experience by being required to relocate to a new school district before he graduates?" In short, what the mediator is doing is forcing the husband to deal with the resolution of this issue on the basis of the same kinds of practical considerations that the couple used during their marriage (for instance they bought their home because they felt it would be a good place to raise their children and because they wanted them to have the benefit of the good schools in the area), rather than on the basis of what would be the result if they

CHAPTER III MEDIATION

applied arbitrary legal rules and principles that have little to do with their lives.

NOTES AND QUESTIONS

1. Do you agree with Marlow's observations that there is no need to have the parties to a divorce mediation consult with separate attorneys, "as would be the case if legal rules and principles were viewed as rights?" Surely legal rules and principles *are* rights, even if the parties choose not to follow them exactly in their mediation agreement. Are you satisfied with his conclusion that "one lawyer is preferable, since the mediator wants an answer, not a range of legal opinions?" Are the parties' interests adequately represented by sending them to the same lawyer so the mediator can get "an answer?"

2. What happens in a mediation when the values of the parties—deriving from either community or personal standards—are in conflict with the law? Is it the duty of the mediator to point out the conflict?

3. Should a mediator be expected to inform herself of the applicable law? Is it realistic to expect that of a non-lawyer mediator? Should a mediator also be expected to inform the parties of the law? Or should that be their own responsibility? Parties engaged in a negotiation surely understand that although they bargain against the backdrop of the law, they choose, by entering a negotiated agreement, to make their own arrangement and to forego the legal procedures available to them, such as discovery from the opponent and examination of witnesses. Is the same true of parties to a mediation? Unlike negotiation where there is no one comparable to a mediator to preside, parties to a mediation have reasonable expectations that the mediator will insure that fair procedures are followed. Are they also entitled to expect the mediator to insure that they are adequately apprised of their legal rights? Should they at least be warned that they may be giving up certain legal rights? When the mediation is conducted under institutional auspices, as in a court-mandated Conciliation Court, shouldn't they expect a process that gives them more protection than the rough-and-tumble of a negotiation? Would the same be true of a mediation to which they were coerced to attend by a court's or prosecutor's letter?

4. May not a mediator simply seek to change the parties' frame of reference regarding absolute compliance with rules of law, rather than rejecting them? Consider the following comments in Stulberg & Montgomery, Design Requirements for Mediator Development Programs, 15 Hofstra L.Rev. 499, 504 (1987):

> What distinguishes the mediator's frame of reference from that of other intervenors is that a mediator cajoles parties to agree to settlement terms that are legally permissible even if not legally required. For instance, a mediator might prod a landlord to consider letting a tenant remain in his apartment and accept a schedule of periodic payments for rent in arrears even though the application of the pertinent legal rules in that jurisdiction would incontrovertibly result

in a favorable judgment for the landlord. Similarly, a mediator might try to persuade a tenant to consider paying for a necessary improvement to the apartment, even though it is arguably an expense that the landlord should absorb, if the tenant's so acting might induce the landlord to renew the lease for a stated term. * * * What gives mediated negotiations their flexibility is that the mediator is not simply a compliance officer who blindly demands obedience to one set of rules.

5. Concerning the relative benefits and risks of an "alegal" mediation process, consider the following comments from Riskin, Mediation and Lawyers, 43 Ohio St.L.J. 29, 34–5 (1982):

[I]n mediation—as distinguished from adjudication and, usually, arbitration—the ultimate authority resides with the disputants. The conflict is seen as unique and therefore less subject to solution by application of some general principle. The case is neither to be governed by a precedent nor to set one. Thus, all sorts of facts, needs, and interests that would be excluded from consideration in an adversary, rule-oriented proceeding could become relevant in a mediation. Indeed, whatever a party deems relevant is relevant. In a divorce mediation, for instance, a spouse's continuing need for emotional support could become important, as could the other party's willingness and ability to give it. In most mediations, the emphasis is not on determining rights or interests, or who is right and who is wrong, or who wins and who loses because of which rule; these would control the typical adjudicatory proceeding. The focus, instead, is upon establishing a degree of harmony through a resolution that will work for these disputants.

A danger inheres in this alegal character: individuals who are not aware of their legal position are not encouraged by the process to develop a rights-consciousness or to establish legal rights. Thus, the risk of dominance by the stronger or more knowledgeable party is great. Accordingly, for society to maximize the benefits of mediation while controlling its dangers, it must carefully adjust the role of lawyers in the mediation process.

Though mediation agreements typically neither set nor follow legal precedent, they often have important legal consequences. Frequently, the mere making of an agreement defers legal action by one of the disputants or the government. The agreement itself may establish or avoid legally enforceable rights. To reduce the danger that less powerful persons unwittingly will give up legal rights that would be important to them, they must be afforded a way of knowing about the nature of the adversary process and the result it would likely produce. But the very presentation of the rules that would probably govern a decision if the matter were litigated may impel parties toward adopting the predicted results, rather than regarding the law as simply one factor—to be blended with a variety of economic, personal, and social considerations—in reaching a decision. At the same time, if such information is

370 CHAPTER III MEDIATION

not readily available to them, they are not necessarily free from influence by the law; they may be basing their decisions to mediate and their judgments during mediation upon inaccurate assumptions about what result would follow from adversary processing.

f. WRITING OF AGREEMENT

If an agreement is reached, the mediator will assist in setting it down in writing, insuring that each party understands fully what the terms are and making the terms as concrete as possible. The mediator, or more likely the center or institution with which she is connected, may serve as the conduit for transfer of funds or other compliance with an agreement. Mediation centers also often maintain a copy of agreements for future reference if needed.

The Significance of Consent in Compliance with Mediation Agreements

A recurring theme in mediation literature is that mediation works because the parties have consented to participate and because any agreement must be mutually acceptable. "By definition," Professors Folberg and Taylor have written, "a consensual agreement, whether reached through mediation or direct negotiation, reflects the participants' own preferences and will be more acceptable in the long run than one imposed by a court. In the process of mediation, participants formulate their own agreement and make an emotional investment in its success. They are more likely to support its terms than those of an agreement negotiated or imposed by others."[12]

Like many processes, mediation does not always live up to its advance billing, and the touted element of consent is a prime example. If mediation were strictly limited to situations in which the parties' participation is entirely consensual, many of its contemporary uses would be foreclosed. As appreciation of the utility of mediation has grown, so too have mediation devices in which the parties are encouraged or pressured in a variety of ways into participation.

The most obvious form of coerced participation is in a dispute that has been the subject of a criminal complaint. Professor Nancy Rogers and mediator Richard Salem provide the following example:

> Mediation workers in New York City interview complainants in minor assault, cohabitant violence, criminal trespass and related cases at the Municipal Court in Manhattan. If the intake worker deems the case appropriate for mediation, the respondent will be "served" by the complainant or by mail, with a form, headed "Criminal Court of the City of New York," listing the allegations and requesting the party to

---

12. Jay Folberg & Alison Taylor, Mediation: A Comprehensive Guide to Resolving Conflicts Without Litigation 10 (1984).

appear at the mediation center "at which time an inquiry will be made of the said allegation." If the respondent fails to appear, the form warns, "a criminal action against you may be commenced without your having an opportunity to be heard."[13]

Similar kinds of pressure arise when government agencies require parties to go through mediation as a prerequisite, for example, to being allowed to continue to rent an apartment in a low-income housing project, to receive welfare or other assistance, to avoid expulsion of a child from school, or to obtain enforcement of zoning, land use, or other governmental regulations. Pressure may also arise in the private sector, for instance, when an employer requires an employee to mediate with a disputing co-employee or with an outsider, like a merchant, over an ongoing dispute.

Mediation mandated by law is the ultimate form of coercion. This includes requirements in some states for mediation in cases involving child custody or visitation,[14] labor disputes,[15] and employment discrimination.[16]

Even where participation in mediation is not coerced, parties often agree to participate in it because of pressure. Pressure that a party may not be able to resist can come from a judge or prosecutor who "encourages" mediation, a counsellor or member of the clergy, members of the family or friends, or even the opposing party. Thus in some mediations, at least one party is a reluctant participant. This does not mean, of course, that a resulting mediation is not voluntary, but it signifies that the degree of cooperativeness may vary considerably from party to party and that the mediator must be aware of this possibility. It should also be remembered that coerced participation is not coerced agreement; no party to mediation can be forced to enter an agreement.

The consensual nature of mediation is often claimed to promote compliance by the parties with the result. If the parties have been free to formulate their own agreement, the conventional wisdom goes, they are more willing to abide by it. But parties come away from mediation with varying attitudes, just as do parties from litigation. It is human nature to relive the mediation, rehashing what one would have liked to have said or liked to have presented. Parties to a mediation sometimes feel surprised or unfairly treated as do litigants. Like the audience at an auction, mediating parties are sometimes capable of being swept up in the flow of the proceeding, resulting in later regrets. An objective of a mediator, of course, is to prevent the mediation from having this effect and to insure that any settlement is acceptable to both sides. But the success of mediation in terms of individual satisfaction and compliance is still a matter of some dispute.

---

13. Nancy H. Rogers & Richard A. Salem, A Student's Guide to Mediation and the Law 19–20 (1987).

14. See West's Ann.Cal.Civ.Code § 4607; Me.Rev.Stat.Ann. title 19, § 752(4).

15. See Ohio Rev.Code § 4117.14; West's A.I.C. 20–7.5–1–12, 20–7.5–1–13.

16. See 42 U.S.C.A. § 2000e–4(g).

Craig A. McEwen & Richard M. Maiman, Mediation in Small Claims Court: Achieving Compliance Through Consent

18 Law & Soc'y Rev. 11, 40–47 (1984).

[The authors, professors of sociology/anthropology at Bowdoin College and of political science at University of Southern Maine, studied small claims disputes in Maine in the late 1970's, concluding that mediation is more likely to produce greater compliance by the parties than litigation.]

For consensual agreements the key to closure is litigant satisfaction. Even where satisfaction is contextually dependent in the sense that an outcome is satisfactory because it is "least undesirable," feelings of satisfaction are likely to respond to a range of considerations that will have little or no influence when solutions are imposed. These include values and norms embedded in non-legal institutions, tastes for risk, and the idiosyncratic ways in which time, money, and aggravation can be relatively weighted. While settlements are no doubt shaped by the parties' shared expectations of what going to court means, the fact that so many variables may come into play creates substantial pressure to break the mold of traditional adjudicative outcomes. Thus, it is not surprising that mediation and negotiation produced six of the seven outcomes we observed in which the defendant was obliged to do something other than pay money to the plaintiff, and twelve of the fourteen in which the plaintiff undertook some obligation to the defendant.

Facilitating the free consideration of multiple variables is the fact that consensual settlements do not have to be explicitly justified. The legitimacy of a judge's decision depends on an explicit, reasoned connection between the result and a general rule, but an individual or group can explain a decision to settle on vague and general grounds—"it's fair" or "it's the best I could expect".[1] When rationales do not have to be well articulated, decisions can more easily reflect idiosyncratic value preferences, feelings that are not easily identified, and inconsistencies that are hard to reconcile. By contrast, when a judge articulates a reason for a decision, he or she provides a clear target for dissatisfaction and criticism. This may happen even where it is possible to advance reasons that the disadvantaged party would accept, since the judge may not know which of the possible justifications for his or her decision are acceptable. The failure to articulate reasons provides no escape so long as the parties expect a decision accompanied by reasons.[2]

---

[1] For this reason, groups in conflict may find it more difficult to achieve consent than individuals in conflict. The representatives of a group must articulate reasons for accepting or rejecting a proposed outcome in order to convince the group to endorse a position. This process requires articulation of criteria by which an outcome can be judged and thus moves the decision process closer to adjudication.

[2] When a jury renders a verdict and in certain forms of arbitration, such as baseball salary arbitration, there is no expectation that the verdict will be accompanied by supporting reasons.

The consensual settlement process has an important interpersonal component as well, although this aspect of the process may vary substantially depending on the type and extent of participation allowed the parties to the dispute. In particular, interaction in mediation or negotiation often has a strong normative character. Bargainers use norms as levers to persuade other parties to accept particular settlements (e.g., "Don't you think it's fair that you pay me something for using my property?"). Bargainers also remind one another of the practical consequences of their decisions (e.g., "You can save time and aggravation."). Mediators similarly highlight relevant norms, mutual obligations, and the practical implications of choices, but they do it from the vantage point of a formally disinterested third party. They also provide a third party's view of the relative merits of the conflicting cases. This allows each party to make what may be a more realistic prediction of the likely results of adjudication and so may help induce a settlement. Conversely, by highlighting the merits of opponents' positions, mediators may lead both parties to exaggerate their risks of loss in adjudication. Where a pair of predictions is unrealistic in this way, the chance of settlement is high.

* * *

[O]ne might well ask why any small claims defendants meet their obligations at all. The power of the small claims court to enforce compliance is extremely limited. Self-interest seems to invite defiance, and defiance does occur, although considerably more often in adjudicated than in mediated or negotiated cases. But complete defiance, even in adjudication, is the exception rather than the rule. This suggests that losing litigants extend legitimacy to judicial judgments and/or that they exaggerate the likelihood of punishment should they fail to comply. When a judgment confirms a consensual settlement, these pressures toward compliance may be reinforced and are complemented by others we have identified.

Consent, unlike command, brings with it an assumption of responsibility for the settlement and for its implementation. This sense of responsibility, along with general normative pressures to live up to commitments, can weigh heavily on disputants, even those who may regret having given consent in the heat of negotiation or mediation. The more explicit these pressures, the more effective they are. Our data suggest that the personal and immediate commitments generated by consensual processes bind people more strongly to compliance than the relatively distant, impersonal obligations imposed by authorities. * * *

Our data on small claims mediation and adjudication provide strong evidence that consent is a powerful adjunct to command in securing compliance with behavioral standards. Consent enlists a sense of personal obligation and honor in support of compliance, and consensual processes are more open than command to the establishment of reciprocal obligations and of detailed plans for carrying out the terms of an agreement. Consent may also be more likely than command to leave both parties—not just the winner—with the feeling that the outcome was fair or just. These characteristics of consent mean that consensual solutions are more likely to be

CHAPTER III MEDIATION

complied with than those imposed by adjudication, at least when they are ratified by a court or backed up by the threat of adjudication.

NOTES AND QUESTIONS

1. Following the McEwen and Maiman study of Maine small claims disputes, Professor Neil Vidmar conducted a study of small claims disputes in Ontario. Vidmar, The Small Claims Court: A Reconceptualization of Disputes and an Empirical Investigation, 18 Law & Soc'y Rev. 515 (1984); Vidmar, An Assessment of Mediation in a Small Claims Court, 41 J. Social Issues 127 (1985). He concluded that a case characteristic, namely whether the defendant admits partial liability, is more important than effects produced by the type of procedural forum. McEwen and Maiman, looking at his data, disagreed. McEwen & Maiman, The Relative Significance of Disputing Forum and Dispute Characteristics for Outcome and Compliance, 20 Law & Soc'y Rev. 439 (1986). Regarding their conclusion that there is greater compliance with consensual, than with authoritative, decisions, Vidmar commented [Vidmar, Assessing the Effects of Case Characteristics and Settlement Forum on Dispute Outcomes and Compliance, 21 Law & Soc'y Rev. 155, 162–63 (1987)]:

> In systematic observations of 204 mediated hearings I and the members of my research team uncovered the fact that defendants owing money were given subtle and not-so-subtle hints about the need for compliance and the possible sanctions if compliance was not forthcoming. This occurred even when specific payment arrangements were not made by the referee. Interestingly, these kinds of pressures were more likely to be exerted in Partial Liability cases than in No Liability cases. In contrast, observations of 73 trials yielded not a single instance of discussions of payment; judges dealt only with liability and damage assessment. Thus while I cannot rule out the possibility that defendants owing money derived a sense of obligation through consensual processes, there is evidence suggesting that in mediation obligations were emphasized in an authoritative, coercive way while in adjudication payment obligations were completely ignored. * * *

> McEwen and Maiman and I agree, I think, that both forum type and case characteristics play their part in contributing to dispute outcomes and compliance, so the real issue for future research should be how and when these factors combine with one another. The methodological message of my reply to the reanalysis by McEwen and Maiman is that just because a procedure is labeled as mediation or adjudication that does not necessarily make it so. We must examine the process of resolution and do so on a case-by-case basis.

2. Other studies have also found that there is greater compliance with mediation awards than with adjudicated judgments. Pearson & Thoennes, Divorce Mediation: An Overview of Research Results, 19 Colum.J.L. & Soc.Probs. 451 (1985). However, a recent study of four small claims courts in Massachusetts found that "defendants in mediated cases were only marginally more likely to comply with the specified monetary award or agreement than were defendants in the adjudication group." Wissler, Mediation and Adjudication in the Small Claims Court: The Effects of Process and Case Characteristics, 29 Law & Soc'y Rev. 323, 349 (1995). It also found that "compliance was not significantly related to the defendants' assessments of the fairness of or satisfaction with the process or the outcome. This is consistent with Vidmar's (1985) finding of no relationship between compliance and outcome satisfaction but at variance with McEwen and Maiman's (1984) finding that judgments of outcome fairness affected compliance.... These data suggest that compliance may be affected more by the nature of the outcome (and by the ability to pay) than by characteristics of the dispute resolution process."

3. If McEwen and Maiman's study correctly indicates that mediation is better able than adjudication to create a sense of obligation to make payments, what theory would account for that? Is it that the consensual nature or the interpersonal contact of mediation create a greater sense of personal obligation? But isn't this largely dependent on the individual parties' perceptions of the process and the result? Is it that mediation just leaves the participants with a better feeling than litigation? If so, how do we explain that, even as found by McEwen and Maiman, the satisfaction level is only slightly higher? Is deterrence a key ingredient in parties' willingness to make payments under each system? What will happen to a party who violates a court order to make payments as opposed to one who violates a mediation agreement?

4. The merits of involuntary mediation continue to be debated. McEwen & Milburn, Explaining a Paradox of Mediation, 9 Negotiation J. 23, 34 (1993), note that "mediation appears to be particularly powerful and effective in resolving conflicts when parties are most reluctant to enter the process voluntarily." They explain this as the product of processes of "dispute selection" and "dispute elaboration" which cause the parties to make and rebuff claims in order to gain leverage, resulting in a "metadispute" which focuses narrowly on their differences rather than the solution. They see "communities," however, as providing social pressures to enter mediation: "Larger 'communities' of interested parties often push disputants to undertake mediation. The pressure they apply includes legal mandates to use mediation as a condition for proceeding further in the legal process [and] the risk of diminished community reputation among kin and neighbors."

C. THE ROLE OF THE MEDIATOR

One of the strengths of mediation is said to be that it permits the parties to achieve their own resolution of a dispute without being bound to

376 CHAPTER III MEDIATION

a formal, and possibly inflexible, legal solution. Professor Lon Fuller noted this quality of mediation (Fuller, Mediation—Its Forms and Functions, 44 S. Cal. L. Rev. 305, 308, 325–26 (1971)):

> [M]ediation is commonly directed, not toward achieving conformity to norms, but toward the creation of the relevant norms themselves. This is true, for example, in the very common case where the mediator assists the parties in working out the terms of a contract defining their rights and duties toward one another. In such a case there is no pre-existing structure that can guide mediation; it is the mediational process that produces the structure.

> * * *

> This quality of mediation becomes most visible when the proper function of the mediator turns out to be, not that of inducing the parties to accept formal rules for the governance of their future relations, but that of helping them to free themselves from the encumbrance of rules and of accepting, instead, a relationship of mutual respect, trust and understanding that will enable them to meet shared contingencies without the aid of formal prescriptions laid down in advance. Such a mediational effort might well come into play in any of the various forms of mediation between husband and wife associated with "family counseling" and "marriage therapy." In the task of reestablishing the marriage as a going concern the mediator might find it essential to break up formalized conceptions of "duty" and to substitute a more fluid sense of mutual trust and shared responsibility. In effect, instead of working toward achieving a rule-oriented relationship he might devote his efforts, to some degree at least, in exactly the opposite direction.

A corollary of the thesis that mediation agreements must be voluntarily arrived at is that a mediator may not impose his or her perceptions, values, or judgments on the parties. Virtually all mediators, no matter their style or philosophical orientation, would agree with this proposition. However, there is a considerable difference of opinion among mediators as to how it is to be implemented. The traditional nondirective model of mediation demands that a mediator take great care in not revealing her views or in suggesting solutions during the mediation. On the other hand, even the nondirective mediator is hardly passive. "Mediators work towards settlement of cases by controlling interaction and communication in the mediation session." Silbey & Merry, Mediator Settlement Strategies, 8 Law & Policy 7 (1986). They may, for example, assert control over what issues will be discussed, whether to broaden or narrow the focus, the degree to which ventilation of emotions will take place, the point at which to move from identification of issues to solutions, and reality testing with the parties as to their perceptions and values or the strength of their cases. See Matz, Mediator Pressure and Party Autonomy: Are They Consistent with Each Other?, 10 Negotiation J. 359 (1992).

1. MEDIATOR ADVANTAGES

Richard A. Posner, Mediation

American Bar Association Section of Dispute Resolution, 11th Annual Frank E.A. Sander Program: The 21st Century Lawyer: Problem Solver or Case Processor? (July 8, 2000).

An attenuated version of the Alphonse and Gaston problem arises when parties employ the standard step-wise method of negotiation, in which each starts with his "dream" position and gradually backs off from it until convergence occurs. The problem here is that each party will be reluctant to depart more than one or two steps from his opening position, because it signals weakness. The other party will figure: "since my opponent started at X, but quickly moved to X–1 and then X–2, I'll be stubborn and see how much farther down he's prepared to come." But with both parties thinking this way, convergence is unlikely.

Both the convergence of the parties' estimates, and, if there is convergence, negotiation to a mutually agreeable settlement point within an overlapping settlement range, are less likely if the parties' minds are fogged by emotion, and specifically the kinds of emotion typically aroused by serious struggles. Anger begets righteousness, and a sense of righteousness is likely to increase confidence that the judiciary, as the repository of justice, will rule in one's favor. Anger may also make it difficult to perceive the merits of the opposing party's position. On both counts anger is likely to increase mutual optimism about the outcome of the litigation and thus reduce the probability of a settlement. The litigants are more likely to be angry than their lawyers, but, especially in a protracted dispute, the lawyers tend to identify with their clients and feel the client's anger or indignation as their own.

Reference to the lawyers brings into view still another reason why settlement negotiations may fail. I do not think it is unduly cynical to observe that lawyers often are not the perfect agents of their clients. They have their own pecuniary and other interests which may tug them in the direction opposite to where the client would want to go if he knew the score. Litigation can be extremely lucrative for lawyers, making them reluctant to truncate it by settling the case. The danger of these "agency costs," as economists refer to the conflict of interest between principal and agent, is enhanced by the emotionality of litigation, which may as I suggested earlier fog the lawyers' thinking, and by the fact that trial lawyers bring a different perspective to a dispute from the disputants, one that emphasizes the importance of winning as distinct from negotiating a satisfactory compromise.[1] But this point also identifies a potential disad-

---

1. For a helpful discussion of principal-agent problems in negotiation, see Jeffrey Z. Rubin and Frank E. A. Sander, "When Should We Use Agents? Direct vs. Representative Negotiation," in *Negotiation Theory*

378 CHAPTER III MEDIATION

vantage of a judge or ex-judge as mediator. Judges are accustomed to making dichotomous decisions, rather than to seeking common ground between the litigants. Their strength—a superior ability to predict the "no contract" alternative (that is, what will happen if the dispute is not resolved)—may be offset by a habit of making rather than facilitating decisions resolving conflicts.

The agency-costs problem can be especially serious when settlement negotiations occur while a case is awaiting decision on appeal. A lawyer who lost in the trial court will not redeem his loss by settling the case on appeal; on the contrary, a settlement will extinguish his chance for vindication through a reversal of the lower-court judgment by the appellate court. This consequence of settlement may make him very reluctant to recommend a settlement to the client. We need not assume that any such reluctance would be a sign of bad faith; the lawyer may be quite unaware of the concern with vindication that is driving his reluctance to settle on terms acceptable to his opponent.

A mediator, I need hardly remind *this* group, is a neutral third party who, unlike an arbitrator (a private judge), has no decisional power. He might seem impotent, therefore, to bring about a settlement. Yet actually a mediator can help make a negotiation a success in a variety of ways—by, in Howard Raiffa's words, (1) bringing parties together; (2) establishing a constructive ambience for negotiation; (3) collecting and judiciously communicating selected confidential information; (4) helping the parties to clarify their values and to derive responsible reservation prices; (5) deflating unreasonable claims and loosening commitments; (6) seeking joint gains; (7) keeping negotiations going; and (8) articulating the rationale for agreement.[2] I am particularly interested in points (3) through (6), which pertain to the informational, strategic, emotional, and agency-cost issues that retard settlement. Mediation bears on all these issues:

Since the mediator can meet with the parties separately and his discussions with them are confidential, they are likely to be more candid with him than they would be with each other, enabling him to form a more accurate impression of the actual strengths and weaknesses of their respective positions than they are and to communicate *this* impression to them in a credible fashion. He can thus help them to converge to a common estimate of the likely outcome of the case if it is litigated to judgment. It helps if he has relevant expertise that the parties and their lawyers lack; one reason I was asked to mediate the Microsoft case [Judge Posner served as mediator in 1999 in the antitrust suit, United States v. Microsoft Corp., which did not result in a settlement of the case at that time—Eds.] was that, as a judge, I could be assumed to have greater insight into likely judicial reactions to the case than the parties or their lawyers.

Since the mediator can make proposals for settlement, neither party need know whether a proposal made to it is emanating from the opposing

---

and Practice (J. William Breslin and Jeffrey Z. Rubin eds. 1991), at 81.

2. Howard Raiffa, *The Art and Science of Negotiation* 108—109 (1982).

party or from the mediator. Hence neither party need be identified as the one that made the first proposal to settle, thus signaling weakness. The parties will therefore have a greater incentive to make a proposal to the mediator for (covert) transmission to the other party than they would have to make a proposal directly to the other party. The case will not settle, however, if either or both parties consider that, all things considered, the cost of litigation is lower than the cost of settlement.

The parties may make their "dream" offers to the mediator, in an effort to signal strength to him, just as they would do in an unmediated negotiation. But he need not, unless the party insists, convey that offer to the other side. He can short-circuit the step-wise method of negotiation by paring down each side's opening proposal before presenting it to the other side. That way neither side is induced to signal strength by refusing to recede from an extreme initial negotiating position.

As Brown and Ayres point out in an important article on the economics of mediation, the mediator is both a conduit of information between the opposing sides and an impediment to transparent communication between them.[3] When a mediator formulates a proposal to one party, that party will infer that the proposal reflects information conveyed to the mediator by the other party; but because the information will be fuzzied up by the mediator, that other party will be giving up less in the way of strategically valuable information (should mediation fail and the case go to trial) than if he had to communicate with his opponent face to face. In the Microsoft mediation, I told each party that I would not report anything it told me to the other side without the party's express permission, but it was implicit that in formulating proposals to each side I would be using information furnished me by the other side, and some of that information could be inferred from the proposal.

The mediator is not the object of the parties' anger. His presence is a soothing one and encourages each party to make a realistic assessment of its chances if the litigation continues. And when he is negotiating with each party separately, and thus masking the anger of each from the other, they can negotiate a settlement without ever having to be in the same room with each other.

Finally, the mediator can reduce the problem of agency costs by dealing directly with the parties. In a case that I did mediate successfully, I asked lawyers for both sides to bring their principals (the presidents of the corporations that were the parties in the case) to the settlement conference. I explained to each that he should view settlement in strictly business terms. For the plaintiff, it was an opportunity to "sell" an asset (the plaintiff's claim) for a higher net price than a later sale was likely to produce. For the defendant, it was an opportunity to "buy" a form of

---

3. Jennifer Gerarda Brown and Ian Ayres, "Economic Rationales for Mediation," 80 *Virginia Law Review* 323 (1994).

insurance against an uncertain future liability, namely the risk of an adverse judgment.

Some evidence in support of an analysis tying mediation to the economic model of settlement (as I have tried to do) comes from an empirical study by Douglas Henderson. He found that, just as the economic model of settlement predicts,[4] mediation is less likely to succeed in bringing about a settlement the larger the stakes in the case.[5] Because the costs of litigation do not increase in proportion to the stakes (a $10 million case does not cost ten times as much to litigate as a $1 million case), they are a greater incentive to settlement the smaller the stakes are. This by the way is one reason why relatively few cases settle at the appeals stage; most of the costs of litigation have already been incurred. Another reason is that the fact that the case didn't settle before judgment in the trial court indicates that it may never have been a very good candidate for settlement. A third reason, as I noted earlier, is that the lawyer for the losing side may be reluctant for reasons of reputation to give up the chance of vindication by reversal.

Henderson also found that the longer the mediation continued, the more likely it was to be successful.[6] This makes sense in light of my analysis too. The greater the benefits of settlement relative to litigation, the more time and effort (and legal fees) the parties will invest in a settlement procedure, such as mediation, and the greater investment is likely to produce a greater "return," which in this context means a greater likelihood of settlement.

2. Mediator Control of the Process

John M. Haynes, Mediation and Therapy: An Alternative View

10 Mediation Q. 21, 22–30 (1992).

[The author responds to Marian Roberts' article, Systems or Selves: Some Ethical Issues in Family Mediation, 10 Mediation Q. 3 (1992), which argued that "the integrity of the mediation process is threatened" by "the importation into mediation practice of family systems theory via the system approach of most family therapists." Under this approach, she wrote, "the family is understood as a system of mutually interacting and interdependent parts that can be understood only as constituents of the whole," and the "site of pathology" is not the individual but the family. "[B]elievers in systems therapy adopt a mode of intervention that places the therapist as knowing expert in a position of exceptional power in relation to the family."]

4. Richard A. Posner, *Economic Analysis of Law* 610 (5th ed. 1998).

5. Douglas A. Henderson, "Mediation Success: An Empirical Analysis," 11 *Ohio State Journal on Dispute Resolution* 105, 144 (1995).

6. Id. at 143.

Professional power is derived from two sources: asserted power by the intervenor and attributed power that is unilaterally assigned to the professional by the client.

In therapy the claim to power is clear and the therapist makes no apology for having this power. The therapist claims power over both the process and the content. This situation is not unique to family systems therapists. Psychoanalysis, for example, is guided by the analyst who determines what to comment on or what to ignore. The response of the therapist to the client defines the content and the process of the session. If the client raises issue A, which the analyst believes to be unimportant or a cover for another more relevant issue, the therapist ignores issue A and directs the client to talk about other things until issue B or some other acceptable (to the analyst) issue is raised by the client.

The same is true of the attorney-client interview. Counsel focuses on the legal content of the dialogue while ignoring the irrelevant nonlegal items. Inherent in any professional-lay dialogue is the responsibility of the professional to direct the dialogue in a way through which the professional can be useful to the client. "Useful" in this sense is defined as the ability of the professional to use his or her special training and expertise to help the client. In every professional-lay dialogue the professional exercises power to direct the dialogue in a way that enables her to be professional and use her professional knowledge and skills. This situation is equally true for mediation.

The therapist or the attorney thus decides what things will be handled and how they will be handled. In addition, the assumptive contract between the therapist-attorney and client is that the professional will ultimately direct the client to the answer either by sharing a legal interpretation, offering insightful comments, making behavioral prescriptions, or using family system therapy strategies.

The power relationship in mediation is less clear, and thus may be more dangerous to the client. For we actually assert power in controlling the process but deny power in relation to the content. The assumed contract in mediation is that the mediator will assist the clients to resolve specific problems *on their own terms*. In divorce, these problems include the amount and duration of child and maintenance support, the appropriate division of assets, and future parenting roles.

The professional-client relationship is inherently imbalanced because the client requests an interaction with the professional *because* the professional has more knowledge (often one of the determinants of power). As Roberts has so clearly demonstrated, the mediator's management of the negotiations, problem solving, decision making, and context knowledge is the key to successful mediation.

The mediator can divest himself or herself of some of this attributed power by defining the areas in which he or she is willing and able to exercise power. I have stated elsewhere that the mediator must control the process and the family must control the outcome. Laying this out clearly at the beginning of the mediation as part of the contract with the client sets the stage for power divestiture. The mediator should make it clear that he or she is neutral as to the outcome—the product of the content over which the family as a unit must have total control.

A safeguard against the mediator's misuse of power is that any agreement must be acceptable to both parties if it is to be formalized. Thus, the balance of power rests relatively equally between the clients in the content-outcome area because each side can veto an agreement. An agreement cannot be thrust on one party against its will. The mediator *can* influence the direction of the agreement sufficiently to make one client regret it in the future, but it is doubtful that a mediator can thrust a totally unwanted agreement on a client since if he or she attempts to do so, the alternative arena (the court) will become more attractive to the pressured client.

The mediator has power whether or not she wants it. She can limit her power by limiting her use of it. It is not family systems theory per se that creates the problem of asserted power; instead, it is the relationship of the professional to the client. In raising this question, Roberts has provided mediation with a major service by helping us to understand the dangers of power and by alerting us to the need to control that power and limit it to the content.

However, the mediator does exercise power when managing the process because true process neutrality can often benefit one side at the expense of the other. Families choose mediation because they want someone to regulate a dispute and provide an environment in which a self-determined solution can be found. The mediator cannot proclaim process neutrality. He or she cannot stand aside while one party verbally abuses the other, cannot permit secrecy, and must intervene to assure that all parties understand the issues and the data that determine the issues. He or she cannot allow one party to unilaterally define the problem: the problem definition *must* be mutual. Thus, if party A defines the issue in a way that benefits him, the mediator should not accept that definition of the problem but rather work with the parties to create a new problem definition that is mutual and the solution of which benefits both parties. The mediator's neutrality is confined to the content of the agreement. He or she is not neutral on the process; indeed, he or she continually exercises power to control the process to assure a mutual problem definition, a neutral environment, and a joint decision that is mutually acceptable.

* * *

[T]here are times when the mediator discusses concepts of fairness with the family. At other times he or she moves them, as part of process control, within his or her predetermined standards of fairness, without explaining the way they achieve this standard of fairness. For example, I frequently use the strategy of "joining the liar." If I believe the husband is withholding information, for example, I eschew the strategy of challenging him on the issue. Rather, I will say something like, "OK, you say those items were sold ten years ago and the proceeds shared by the family at that time. What evidence can we produce to convince Mary that this is so?''

As we explore how the husband might produce the evidence, the mediator "colludes" with the "liar" and the lack of evidence becomes clearer and clearer, often causing a change in the position or behavior of the "liar." Of course, if he can produce the necessary documentation, the issue will also be resolved in that fashion.

While doing this I tend to side with the husband, while gently undermining his position. Since this is a process issue I do not have to be informative. Instead, I have to be in control. I have not explained my strategy to the client and he has not given his informed consent to be undermined. Few mediators would argue with this strategy in dealing with disclosure. But most *would* disagree if a similar strategy was used when the couple are deciding how to divide a certain asset once it is disclosed.

There are times when the mediator uses the Milan therapist's reframing techniques that engage the clients' participation. Reframing is designed to change the parties' perception of a situation or event. The mediator summarizes. The summary takes the key content of what party A says and condenses it to demonstrate that the mediator has heard party A and, at the same time, to provide party B with the content of party A's statement. The mediator "launders" the original statement to remove all emotional flack and focuses on the meaningful negotiations content of the remark. In addition, the mediator may reorder the priority or importance of A's content, or deliberately ignore certain content parts of A's statement. In doing so, the mediator informs the parties of what he or she thinks is important and unimportant and suggests the best direction for the parties to take in the subsequent negotiations.

The similarity to reframing is close. However, it is not the summary that provides a potential problem, but instead it is what the mediator does with the client's response to the summary that can cause problems. If party A accepts the mediator's summary, the mediation proceeds on the basis of the new statement. If party A argues with the mediator's summary, the mediator immediately accepts A's position and resummarizes to conform with A's position. Likewise, if party B argues with the mediator's summary of party A's statement, the mediator puts it back to party A to be sure that any argument is between A and B, not between the mediator and A or B.

Roberts argues that reframing techniques "elevate reinterpretation over action for change." Hopefully, I have demonstrated that reframing in the form of summarizing can indeed be the basis of action for change. She also argues that the professional must operate out of a set of moral standards. But the task of the mediator is to help the participants develop and articulate their own unique set of moral precepts.

She raises a number of important points with which I agree and that I find useful in clarifying the appropriate mediation role, including not conducting therapy under the guise of mediation, safeguarding against the

Guidelines for Some Mediator Behaviors

The core of mediation is reconnecting people to their own inner wisdom or common sense. The trauma of the events leading up to divorce and divorce itself often robs people of their clarity and ability to focus on legitimate self-interest. The role of the mediator—insofar as any therapy takes place in mediation—is to put people back in touch with their own decision-making process and the common sense that has taken them through life so far.

Let's look at some of the ways the mediator conducts the session so as to encourage this outcome. The more the mediator conducts a session using questions, the more he or she encourages and facilitates the parties' decision making. In answering these questions, the parties move toward solutions. Each time a client answers a question, he or she owns the answer. The same idea, when flatly asserted by the mediator, is in danger of being equally flatly rejected or incorporated into the clients' thinking if they think the statement is an imperative. In mediation, questions are the preferred form of dialogue.

When asking questions, the mediator does not give advice. Statements are reserved for process discussions, leaving content discussions to be conducted in the question form. Thus, it can be said that a major issue for a mediator is to *avoid the imperative.* In order to avoid the imperative the mediator must accept the couple's right to make the decisions—even if the decisions are not those the mediator would choose for them.

During discussions on content the mediator avoids giving commands to the couple to do or not to do something that affects the outcome. However, imperatives during the process discussions are appropriate. Thus a command not to interrupt the other while he is speaking is acceptable because the imperative controls the process and assures a balance. On the other hand, the command to sell the house is unacceptable because it invades the couple's right to make decisions.

In content discussions the mediator helps the clients explore the consequences of a given action. This is done through questions, not through imperatives. The client examines each idea and the consequences through the mediator's questions. Some are looked at carefully, others discarded almost immediately. The choice concerning the extent of the examination lies with the client, as does the ultimate selection.

When the client makes a decision, the outcome makes a difference to what happens to that person (and possibly to other members of the family) in the future. Knowing the difference between the effects of deciding one way versus the effects of deciding another is the key to long-term satisfaction with the decision.

The language of the mediator is important. Appropriate behavior (language is our prime behavior) during process discussions can be inappropriate during content discussions. The range of appropriateness is wide, making determination of whether a statement is an imperative less clear as the mediator moves across the range. That is, it would probably be clear that (1) "You should sell the house" is an imperative, and therefore inappropriate. But are the following imperatives? (2) "Have you considered selling the house?" (3) "You may want to consider selling the house." (4) "Do you want to consider selling the house as one of your options?" If these are not imperatives, what is the distinction between them?

Statement 1 is a clear command to act. Question 2 allows the party to consider or not consider the act. However, question 2 could also be an embedded suggestion if the client hears it as a suggestion to act; in that situation it becomes an imperative. Statement 3 is an offering to the client that places the right of selection on the client. As in 2, this may be received by the client as a suggestion/imperative. Statement 4, on the other hand, places the offer in the context of a range of options explicitly making the right of selection the clients'.

We might say that the differences between the statements is also between *telling* someone to sell the house (1, 2, and 3) and *getting* them to sell the house. The former, *telling*, requires only a simple imperative, directly or indirectly, from the mediator. The latter, *getting*, requires a continuing dialogue and justification to convince the couple to follow the mediator's advice and sell the house.

The act of getting someone to act on your imperative requires that you first state the imperative "sell the house." Thus, if the mediator avoids using imperatives either by *telling* parties or by *suggesting* they do something, she will not have to move to the next stage of *getting* them to act. The mediator can control her behavior by not attempting to get the client to act on her advice. She can be aware that when she is selling the client a particular idea she is *getting* them to do what she feels is best.

Imperatives are made because the person issuing the imperative believes that his or her command is correct, factually or morally. Thus, "Sell the house" is stated when the mediator believes that this act is in the clients' self-interest and is therefore morally correct. In this situation the mediator makes a moral judgment about the best course of action. In doing so he or she also makes a moral judgment about the clients as they determine which course to take. Moral judgments, which are usually associated with the verbs *should, could,* and *ought,* are therefore imperatives.

Moral judgments are also linked to the mediator's sense of duty. Hopefully, the mediator is always clear as to what his or her sense of duty is. This clarity is useful in helping the mediator to avoid deciding what the client's sense of duty is. For example, increasingly women are deciding that the children and they themselves will be better off if the father becomes the residential parent. The mediator's sense of duty might well be that mothers have a duty to be present for their children. If the mediator conveys this sense of duty to the mother, then the mediator makes it difficult for the mother to assert her definition of duty which might be that mothers who are starting out in a career should relinquish the primary parenting role to a father who can provide more time and nurturing to them. When the mediator's sense of duty or moral value clashes with the client's, the client's moral duty must prevail.

Thus, one of Roberts' central points carries an additional important warning. The danger of using therapy in mediation is that therapy often leads to advocacy because the shift to therapy permits a more frequent use of the professional's moral judgment.

Imperatives can also be avoided if the mediator provides options rather than single commands. The statement "You may sell the house or not sell the house—the choice is yours," provides the couple with options that, hopefully, will cause them to explore options rather than follow a single command. The options can be further enhanced by the mediator explaining the consequences of each action:

- If you sell the house you will have to either buy another or rent a place.
- If you rent, will the income from your proceeds from the sale cover the rental costs?
- If you later decide to reenter the housing market, will your investment of the proceeds have kept pace with the change in the value of housing?

In looking at the other side of the coin, the mediator may ask,

- If you keep the house, what percentage of your assets are tied up in housing?
- Are there other things you could do with this asset?
- Can you afford to maintain this size house?
- What is the emotional cost of selling?
- Could you rent part of the house to help pay the costs?
- Would you be better off in smaller quarters?

One question standing alone could be an embedded suggestion; received by the client, it could be interpreted as pressure. When all of the questions are asked together, they lessen the impact of each embedded suggestion because the group of questions expands the available options. The clients are not asked to accept a single solution but to consider a range of possibilities.

Maintaining Process Control Through Strategic Techniques

Client control of content is essential. Therefore, questions that lead to option development are the best modes of mediator behavior. Process control calls for different approaches. It is in the area of process control that mediators can usefully use strategies drawn from other forms of practice.

One useful systems strategy is that of paradox. Paradox is frequently used in therapy to put the client into a bind, thus forcing him or her to make a choice. The choice the therapist looks for is one that requires change in client perceptions or behavior.

The mediator can also use paradox to move couples from fighting about their *linked* marital past into negotiating about their *independent* futures. When normal strategies to bring a couple away from their ongoing fight and back to the task before them fail, the mediator might say, "You are right. It would be crazy to give up this constant fighting. You both seem to enjoy it and perhaps you should just stay in this stage for a while and come back to mediation in six months when you are ready to negotiate." Invariably, this kind of statement brings a firm denial from the couple. They do [not] want to stay in the unsatisfying state of constant marital fights; they just don't know how to let go of them. The paradox of giving them permission to stay in the past makes them recognize that if they accept this permission they are doomed to spend more of their future lives stuck in unproductive stasis. In order not to accept the permission, they must recognize where they are, how unsatisfying their present state is, and then focus on the future.

Neither the mediator nor the therapist explains what he or she is doing. The impact of the paradox is the same in both arenas and it appears to be equally effective for mediators and therapists. The issue, therefore, is when is a paradox ethical? It *is* appropriate when used as a means of process control. But it is useful in management of content negotiations? Since the goal of a paradoxical intervention is to force the client to make choices, provided the paradox does not dictate which choice the client should make, the intervention would appear to be valid in content discussions. But, if the mediator's paradox omits options and instead offers a forced choice, then it is wrong.

NOTES AND QUESTIONS

1. Does the style of mediation advocated by Haynes cross over into an impermissible form of therapy? Does he adequately justify the mediator's use of power? Are there any points at which you think his approach is too directive?

2. Are strategies used in therapy—such as paradox—appropriate in mediation? Does their effectiveness indicate that mediators should have training in psychology? Are similar skills and devices used by lawyers in negotiating? Does that make them appropriate for a mediator? Can a mediator be too manipulative? Is it appropriate that "neither the mediator nor the therapist explains what he or she is doing"?

3. Do you agree with Roberts that reframing techniques "elevate reinterpretation over action for change"? Is the basis of action for change that Haynes sees as arising from reframing too intrusive on party autonomy?

James C. Freund, The Neutral Negotiator: Why and How Mediation Can Work to Resolve Dollar Disputes

18–48 (Prentice Hall Law & Business, 1994).

[The author, a retired partner of Skadden, Arps, Slate, Meagher & Flom LLP, has remained active in the mediation field. His article on

388 CHAPTER III MEDIATION

mediating dollar disputes was awarded the 1994 First Prize for Professional Articles by the CPR Institute for Dispute Resolution. Mr. Freund has prepared the following excerpt of that article for this casebook. The italicized material in brackets represents his brief summaries of certain lengthier material appearing in the original article.]

This article is about mediating one-shot money disputes where there is no continuing relationship between the parties and the alternative is acrimonious litigation. It's difficult ground for many reasons–ambivalence over whether to settle, an atmosphere of distrust, the fear of conveying weakness, the special problems litigators face. The biggest hurdle is to find a settlement number that both sides can buy into, since it will invariably be at odds with any litigated outcome. As a result, the parties are often trapped between the rock of expensive, inefficient litigation and the hard place of unavailing negotiations.

The introduction of a neutral mediator into the situation can help alleviate many of these problems. For this to happen, in my view, the mediator has to play an activist, judgmental role—not merely function as a facilitator. The mediator has to serve as an "agent of reality" to guide the parties on how the various issues are likely to play out in litigation; discourage "digging in" and prod the parties to move in constructive directions; and help them bridge the final gap, often by proposing the terms of a possible compromise. For these and other reasons, I believe the prime skill called for in a mediator is his or her negotiating ability. A mediation is definitely a negotiation, in which a prime negotiator is the mediator himself.

In serving as a mediator, I have developed my own method for resolving these cases, which I've dubbed The 12 Step Negotiation Program for Dollar Disputes. I'll show you how it's designed to work in a hypothetical situation, based on an actual case (with names and facts changed to preserve anonymity).

The Put Case

Parent Corporation owns 80% of Company's shares; the other 20% is owned by Executive, the Company CEO. Their stockholders' agreement provides that, at certain times, Executive can "put" all his Company shares to Parent (i.e., at Executive's option, he can require Parent to purchase his 20% interest) at a formula price. The price is calculated by multiplying Company's net income for the most recent twelve months by an industry-wide price-earnings multiple (determined at the time of the put) derived from external sources, and dividing the result by five (to reflect Executive's 20% interest). At the time the contract was signed, the external sources for obtaining industry-wide multiples (including the best known and most widely consulted source) all produced multiples in the low teens.

In 1992, Executive gives notice he is putting his shares to Parent, accompanying the notice with his calculation of the formula price. The net income figure he uses, based on the unaudited books of Company prepared under his direction, is $2 million. And now, lo and behold, the price-earnings multiple emanating from that best known outside source is 30! He multiplies the \$2 million by 30, and, after dividing the result by five, arrives at a \$12 million price for his shares.

Parent disagrees sharply with Executive's calculation. In the first place, Parent believes that Company's net income should be substantially reduced by a variety of audit adjustments (such as an increased reserve for accounts receivable) and also to account for various inter-company items between Company and Parent (such as the need for Company to reimburse Parent for services performed for Company's benefit by certain Parent employees). The aggregate effect of such adjustments, in Parent's view, reduces Company's net income from Executive's \$2 million figure to \$1 million.

In addition, Parent disagrees with Executive on what the proper price-earnings multiple should be. Parent argues that the multiple produced by using Executive's best known outside source is aberrationally high due to unforeseen developments (big losses reported by several component companies, which greatly skew the overall results). Parent points instead to a less widely used alternative source, which has eliminated the effect of such skewing and produces a more normalized multiple of *15*. Multiplying \$1 million by 15 and dividing by five, Parent takes the position that, instead of the \$12 million Executive seeks, the correct price for the put shares is \$3 million.

The parties try to reach a compromise price, but direct negotiations fail-at which point there's a race to the courthouse in order to obtain the most hospitable jurisdiction. The resulting lawsuit and counterclaim transcend mere money, alleging fraud, dereliction of duty, and much else. * * *

[The parties decide to see if mediation can help to resolve the dispute and select me as the mediator. What follows is a summary of the 12 steps.]

1. Setting the Ground Rules and Lineup

[The crucial ground rules involve such matters as confidentiality, the non-binding nature of the process, and the role of the mediator.]

Just a word on the lineup. I can't overemphasize the importance of having at least one business—person present on each side who has authority to make the deal. * * * In the Put Case, I'm pleased to find that, in addition to counsel, Executive is present in person, and both the chief executive officer and chief financial officer of Parent are appearing on its behalf. Still, the opening moments are far from auspicious. When we all come together for the first time in my conference room, I notice some extended hands that don't get shaken. There's a palpable tension in the air. Let's hope this proves to be more artifice than reality.

2. Presenting those "Winning" Positions

Undoubtedly, some mediators try to downplay the differences between the parties right from the start—moving briskly into the search for common ground, along the lines of a Getting *to* Yes-style negotiation. That's not my style, and I think the contrast derives from a different approach I take to negotiation. * * *

[In brief, Getting to Yes disciples aim at intrinsic fairness, which I find an elusive goal. I preach the gospel of mutual satisfaction, resulting from a strenuous process with plenty of give and take, so both sides are reassured they ended up with the best deal possible. In this spirit, I want to give each side—and particularly the litigators involved—the chance to vent here, in lieu of a trial. And who knows—they may actually influence the executive on the other side, while the mediator is sure to pick up useful information.]

So, in advance of the Put Case mediation, I ask the parties to furnish me with separate written statements (''not too lengthy'') setting forth their views on the principal issues and referencing the key documents involved in the controversy (such as the ''put'' agreement itself).

Now the Put Case proceedings begin, with all the participants together in one room. I consider this lineup necessary for steps two through four of a one-shot dollar dispute mediation. (After that, as you'll see, I like to separate the parties and generally don't bring them back together again unless and until agreement is reached.) Following my brief discussion of the ground-rules and other preliminary remarks designed to demystify the process, I allow each side to make a short (generally under 30 minutes) oral statement of its views on the important issues in dispute. *[The arguments I hear in the Put Case are about what I expect; I listen in vain for signs of a conciliatory nature. But I do notice certain things, mainly from their choice of issues and degree of emphasis, that I'll use later on.]*

3. Probing for Weakness and Enlightenment

With everyone still together in one room, I now direct questions to both sides concerning the facts of the matter, the legal and accounting principles involved, the positions each has taken on the issues, and certain points raised which have thus far gone unanswered. * * * The questioning and the interplay bring out certain nuances of the issues which can prove helpful to me later on. *[I learn, for example, that it now looks like the Company may receive close to 100% of what it's owed on one large doubtful account.]* * * *

I try to ask my questions in as neutral a vein as possible, and certainly never in a disparaging tone. A mediator's most precious commodity is the presumption of neutrality with which he or she starts out. If the mediator loses that, he can no longer be effective. * * *

4. Rehashing the Prior Settlement Negotiations

If you share my views of negotiating as a process and the mediator as a neutral negotiator who joins the proceedings along the way, you'll agree that the history of the negotiations which preceded the mediation is of real significance. So, for my fourth step, I ask the parties while they're still together in the same room-to describe the course the negotiations have taken, both before and after filing of the lawsuit, including the important detail of how they happened to arrive at the mediation table. * * *

In the Put Case, I'm actually surprised to learn that in their initial negotiations the parties progressed from the $3 million-$12 million range of their extreme positions—the same ones to which they reverted for the mediation—to a more reasonable *$5* million-*$9.5* million range. At that point, however, both sides appear to have become exhausted by the effort, since (according to their report) each stiffened noticeably, and the race to the courthouse ensued.

And this, in my view, is about all that can be accomplished in a one-shot dollar dispute with everybody at the same table. So, at this juncture, I break the parties apart and put them in separate rooms for the remainder of the mediation—not just to lower the tension level but to encourage candor through private discourse.

5. *Evaluating the Merits*

In the fifth step, the mediator meets separately with each of the parties for the first time. * * * The technique I favor for resolving a one-shot dollar dispute through mediation gets away from traditional positional bargaining. I would not typically coax Side A to improve its offer, convey A's improved offer to Side B, urge B to improve its offer, convey that to A, and so on. Rather, I try to have each side work with me to approach a resolution level at which each feels comfortable and the dispute can be settled-without either side knowing, until the end, just where its adversary stands. To bring the parties to this level of comfort, I need to discuss with each of them the merits of the issues underlying the dispute.

The concomitant of my approach is that, at this point, it would be premature for the mediator to deal with the numbers involved in the dispute, and even worse to suggest the dollar level of an ultimate compromise. * * *

In attempting to assess where the parties stand on the merits, I'm sure many mediators would initiate this process by asking each side in private for its "real" feelings about the issues—to get at the differences between public and private positions. I prefer another method, which I use in the Put Case. I tell each side how I feel about the various issues. *[This keeps the parties from "digging in" to what will undoubtedly be intermediate positions, while allowing me to have a moderating influence on the attitudes they ultimately express.]* * * *

So, I tell Executive and his lawyer how I come out on each issue, but in very general terms, without attempting to put any dollar values on my evaluation at this time. * * * My presentation is in the nature of, "Well, issue #1 could go either way; #2 should come out your way as a matter of equity, but Parent's technical argument can't be ignored; #3 is strong for you, but not conclusive; #4 is hands down for Parent"—and so on. For each judgment, I give the basis of my reasoning. I phrase some of my judgments in terms of how I think the issue would play out in court, and others in terms of what I see as an appropriate resolution of that issue based on other factors.

CHAPTER III MEDIATION

Take, for instance, the issue involving reimbursement of Parent for services performed for the Company's benefit by certain Parent employees. I give great weight (in Executive's favor) to the fact that although these services were performed over several years, Parent never saw fit to charge Company for them, or even to raise the issue of reimbursement, until this controversy began. * * *

The big issue, of course, is the appropriate price-earnings multiple. * * * The result obtained through Executive's approach appears to represent a quantum leap from what the parties originally envisaged when they contracted (although Executive does make some arguments to the contrary, which are unconvincing). By contrast, Parent's approach provides a more equitable (if somewhat conservative) outcome; yet it clearly constitutes a less straightforward reading of the pertinent provision of the agreement. Difficult questions of contractual interpretation abound—most notably, is the language of the contract provision clear as a matter of law, or sufficiently ambiguous that the court will look beyond the words to try to derive the real intentions of the parties? And, if so, what were those intentions? *[Bottom line, although a court could go either way, for settlement purposes the merits appear to favor Executive, because of the hurdles Parent would have to overcome at trial.]* * * *

So, after I finish my survey of the issues, I say to Executive and his lawyer, "Now, I'm not asking you to agree with all my evaluations—in fact, I assume you probably have a number of reservations—but what I want to know is whether there are any particular issues on which you feel I'm way off base?" Those are the ones I want to focus on, and I'm content with what might be termed "tacit non-disagreement" on the unspecified residue.

Executive and his lawyer do disagree with me on several key issues, and let me know about it, but they don't feel obliged to run down the entire list. *[Often, in these cases, the issues a party feels most strongly about are not the largest dollar issues, but those where a seemingly sacred principle lurks beneath the money involved. It's hard to influence his posture on such issues of principle, although he may be willing to swap, for my acquiescence on a principled—but—smallish issue, a larger dollar issue that doesn't move him so deeply.*

In one case, where Executive's argument on an issue of principle for him makes excellent sense, I let him know he has altered my view. It's important for the parties and their lawyers to feel that they can have a positive impact on the proceedings; moreover, it gives more credibility to the mediator's tough stance on a different issue down the road.]

I then proceed to the other conference room and go through a similar exercise with Parent's team. My views on the merits are roughly similar to those I conveyed to Executive, although not always expressed in the same words or with the same degree of emphasis. The response I receive is comparable to what I heard from Executive. Here too, I find myself changing my views on one "hot button" issue in response to the persuasive comments of Parent's officers. * * *

C. The Role of the Mediator 393

6. Determining a Realistic Expectation

This is a good moment to send the parties out to lunch. The time has come, I tell them, for me to go off by myself and do some homework. *[Basically, the mediator now has to work out a strategy to bring these seemingly irreconcilable parties together.]*

At the core of the mediator's strategy is his formulation of a realistic expectation as to where the settlement can be effected. This is not something he shares with the parties—at least, not yet—but is rather for his own guidance. What figure is most likely to resolve this dollar dispute? What number can the mediator envision each side ultimately accepting? It won't be the best price that either party might achieve if his adversary caves in, but rather a hardheaded look at what's feasible to achieve-what price both parties would shake on rather than return to court. * * *

[To accomplish this, I go down two roads simultaneously, the first of which is attempting to attach dollar values to my views on the various issues.] For example, there's a dispute about the appropriate accrual for vacation pay in the Company income statement. Executive has no accrual at all in his computation; at the other extreme, Parent accrues into the 1992 income statement not only amounts from the current year but also amounts relating to prior years (since these were never previously accrued). Based on generally accepted accounting principles, the merits lay more with Parent here; but for purposes of settlement, a good outcome is obtainable through accruing the larger component for the current year and forgetting about the lesser amount from prior years (the inclusion of which would have the effect of unduly penalizing Executive for past omissions).

On the other hand, take a different accounting issue with no such logical dividing point, and which, if decided in Parent's favor, would reduce Executive's net income computation by $100,000. If I believe the issue could go either way, I'm inclined to use a $50,000 income reduction figure. If the merits clearly favor Executive, my reduction might be $25,000, or, if Executive's case is truly compelling, even $10,000.

The second road I go down simultaneously consists of asking myself what I think is the most feasible dollar amount at which settlement of this dispute can occur. To a large extent, this is a matter of feel, utilizing my negotiating experience in other deals and disputes and then trying to apply good judgment to the determination. *[This involves an assessment of such matters as each party's expectation, leverage factors, the need for funds, and their anxiety to settle.*

I end up with two numbers, which are hopefully in the same ballpark. They may well be closer to the position taken by one side, requiring the other party to move a greater distance—always a tough problem. This calls for an assessment of why the other party is being unrealistic, in order to know how to proceed.]

I manage, through a combination of the merits and assessing feasibility, to work out a realistic expectation for settling this case at $6.8 million. My analysis, oversimplified, is that the merits on the various accounting and intercompany adjustments tend to favor Parent, but this is partly balanced by Executive's better case on the price-earnings multiple. The net effect of the non-dollar factors points somewhat in Parent's direction. In particular, and even though Executive has been careful not to concede that it has any effect on the outcome, I sense that Executive feels some pressure to reach a settlement in 1992. *[This is for tax reasons.]*

The number I've selected ($6.8 million) is closer, in absolute dollar terms, to the highest number Company offered in the aborted negotiations ($5 million) than it is to the lowest number Executive indicated he was prepared to take ($9.5 million). *[But since equivalent dollar concessions always represent a greater percentage shift for the buyer than the seller, I'll use this disparity to counter Executive's cries of anguish.*

The mediator has to think like a negotiator and give himself some room to maneuver, since nothing will be accepted without a struggle.] In the Put Case, having determined that $6.8 million is the optimum place to expect a settlement, I decide to aim Executive at the $6.5 million level and point Parent toward the vicinity of $7 million.

In planning to deal with Executive, I turn my primary attention to the price-earnings multiple; for him, this is clearly the key item—he feels he outsmarted Parent on this point in the contract and doesn't want to have the fruits of his victory snatched away. You'll recall that, in Executive's computation, he used a multiple of 30, while Parent countered with 15. The mid-point of these two numbers is 22.5. So, in order for Executive to feel he has won a clear victory here, I reckon he has to end up with a multiple of at least 25. Now I work backwards to derive the net earnings. At the $6.8 million level of my realistic expectation for Executive's 20% of Company's shares, this translates to a total Company value of $34 million. Using the 25 multiple, earnings have to be around $1,360,000—considerably less than halfway between Parent's $1 million and Executive's $2 million initial computations. Then I have to make minor modifications to both earnings and multiple to arrive at my starting point, which for Executive is $6.5 million.

In reflecting on how to deal with Parent (and especially its sharp-eyed CFO), I realize that the key lies in the income statement adjustments, many of which seem to rise to the level of sacred principles in his mind. Because of this, I feel the need to end up with earnings no greater than $1.3 million. At the $6.8 million realistic expectations this results in a multiple of around 26¼. But how would I explain such an odd number? Then it hits me—a quite logical (and serendipitous) computation, indeed. Since I'm letting Parent know that in my view he definitely has the worst of the argument on the multiple, I tell him that the multiple I'm using represents the midpoint between Executive's initial position (30) and the midpoint of their two positions (22½)—which just happens to work out to 26¼.

[As you can see, there's no question in my mind that, for the dollar dispute mediator, a pocket calculator is a more important tool than the rules of evidence!]

7. Reporting Dollar Findings

In the seventh step, I share my dollar analysis of the dispute with each side separately. I go first to Executive and take him through the issues, now attaching dollars and numbers to the views on the merits I expressed at our last meeting. [*I end up at around $6.5 million. Later I perform a similar exercise for Parent arriving at a $7 million result. I invite them to point out any places where they take strong issue with my calculations.*

Where, as here, the resulting gap between their thinking and mine isn't too wide, I let it lie for now. If the difference were quite large, I would have to press the issue—although this is good ground for the mediator, whose neutral stance gives his judgment on the merits added stature.]

8. Generating a Settlement Range

For the first time in the whole process, this is now the right moment for me to quiz the parties separately on where they might be willing to settle the dollar dispute. My hope is that, having postponed "popping the question" until this eighth step—and after extensive discussions of the issues, and exposure to my views on the merits translated into dollars— what I'll hear from them now will be a lot closer to my realistic expectation than if I had posed the same question at an earlier point in the proceedings.

I make it clear to each participant that I'll hold his answer in confidence and not reveal it to the other side. * * *

I think the best a mediator can hope to get from each party at this point is a number lying somewhere between the "valuation" number which the mediator presented to that party in Step 7 and a number based on that party's differing view of the merits. This is precisely Executive's reaction to my query, to wit: "Well, even though my calculations suggest that I should be getting at least $7.5 million for my stock, in the interests of settling this today, I would take $7.1 million." A good ways from the $6.5 million I suggested he consider, but less distant from the $6.8 at which I'm aiming.

No matter what number a party provides in reply to my question—or what unyielding language (verbal and body) accompanies it—I figure there's some more give there. Let's face it, the parties are going to negotiate with the mediator—which is just what I would be doing if I were sitting in their seats. * * *

[*If a party's number is reasonable, I don't negotiate it at this point. (If it's excessive, I have to confront the situation more directly.) Fortunately, Parent's $6.6 million figure (viewed against the $7 million I'd aimed them at and my $6.8 million silent target) is encouraging. I now have a settlement range (which only I am privy to) of $7.1 million to $6.6 million. Still, the final mile is often the toughest, and the outcome remains in doubt.*]

9. Setting Things Up for the Finale

The ninth step is somewhat more free-form than its predecessors, and can be handled through various means. The way I see it, in most cases the parties will be reluctant to make any immediate move from their "real" settlement numbers to an actual resolution. While the movement at the end of a dollar dispute negotiation may not be large in terms of absolute amounts, these final steps are often the most difficult to take psychologically. For this, the parties need some breathing room. * * * So, I envision a break in the mediation occurring at this point.

[The interval I'm thinking of is a brief one, such as overnight. If this isn't possible, and the interruption would be lengthy—raising the spectre of the parties reverting to extreme positions—then I would probably press ahead while everyone is still together.]

Before meeting with each of the parties for Step 9, the mediator has to reassess the realistic expectation he formulated back in Step 6, on the basis of developments that have occurred since that time. Perhaps one side is showing such resistance—in terms of either the merits or its willingness to advance a realistic settlement number—that the mediator realizes he won't be able to achieve his expectation. It may be time to aim at a different, more feasible, goal with a new strategy to point the parties in that direction.

This, however, is not what has occurred in the Put Case. It turns out that I estimated pretty well; and depending on how the endgame plays out, my $6.8 million expectation (or something slightly higher) should produce a deal—if the parties can just get there.

Now I go back to each of the parties separately. I tell each that progress has occurred, although not enough to do a deal. (Each side knows, of course, how far it has moved, but I don't reveal what the other side has done—citing the pledge of confidentiality that I gave each of them.) What I want to convey is that movement will be needed from both sides if something constructive is to happen here.

[With each side, I return briefly to the merits of various (but differing) issues—particularly those where the other side is refusing to budge and my view on the merits is in accord with such refusal. I'm looking for signs of flexibility, softening the parties up for what lies ahead, and searching for insights usable in the endgame.]

I try to strike a balance here between, on the one hand, keeping the parties upbeat about the prospects for an ultimate resolution of their dispute through the mediation, and on the other hand, alerting them that there's a real possibility of failure if they're not a little more flexible.

10. *Looking for Signs of Movement*

When the mediation resumes the next day, I begin by asking each side in separate caucus what constructive movement they've come up with overnight. The replies don't surprise me. Instead of some new proposal that helps to bridge the gap, each party has a newly minted additional justification for a harder-nosed position than the "more generous" figure he proffered privately twelve hours earlier.

A mediator has to be prepared for this. The constructive mood of yesterday's mediation doesn't easily survive the cold shock of a night off! What's more, each side wants me to convey this fresh justification to the other side—just to show they mean business and to send a clear message as to who ought to be thinking about a move at this juncture.

This isn't a very encouraging development, but frankly, it doesn't worry me too much. Even though things seem to be going in the wrong direction, I see this as a final gesture of defiance—a last salute to the ambivalence about settling that most litigants feel before the endgame begins in earnest. And it has the added virtue of laying the groundwork for a creative compromise. I'm not even disturbed when, having communicated Executive's message to Parent, the latter responds with its own argument on a different issue pointing in the opposite direction, which I dutifully communicate to Executive. * * *

11.   *Proffering a Creative Compromise*

Now, with things at a standstill, it's time for the mediator to offer up a creative compromise in Step 11. This is what I worked on overnight—a new twist that gets away from the rigidity of the inexorable numbers in a one-shot dollar dispute. In general terms (not necessarily applicable to the Put Case), it can serve to enlarge the pie in some way, or make something contingent on a future event, or use the transfer or pricing of goods and services creatively—all in the interests of adding a new element to the equation. The imaginative solution shouldn't be too complex; it ought to flow from the situation without introducing an entirely foreign element; and above all, it can't be premised on the good faith of one or the other party down the road. (So, for instance, anything based on a future computation of earnings is definitely off limits in the Put Case.)

First, I ask each of the parties separately if they have any thoughts as to a creative compromise. If either does, then I would explore it with the proponent. But if they don't (which is the case here), then I ask them if they would like me to present a possible creative compromise. Each of them is curious, and since (by definition) it's something new that's not on the table, neither feels threatened by it. So they give me the green light to proceed. * * *

Here, I try my solution out on Executive first, because I see him as someone who's more inclined to roll the dice than Parent. "Look," I tell him, "Parent says the best-known source for deriving the price-earnings multiple produces an aberrational result at the present time. You've been arguing that this isn't really the case. So, here's a way for each of you to put a little of your money where your mouth is. You complete the stock purchase with a fixed payment of $6.2 million, plus an escrowed contingency payment of up to $1 million, payable a year from now, based on the multiple taken from the best-known source at that time—when any aberrational items should, by all rights, have been expunged. If the multiple is actually higher than the current level of 30, you get the whole $1 million. If it's under the current level of 15 that Parent considers normalized, you get nothing. And for each of the 15 points (whole multiples of earnings) between these two extremes that the anniversary multiple exceeds, you get $66,666."

Executive, after a skeptical initial reaction, becomes intrigued with the possibilities and starts negotiating with me about the relative size of the fixed and contingent payments, the date of determination for the contingency, the levels I've picked for the outside numbers, and so on.

[I end up ceding a little of the room I've left myself in return for Executive's agreement to the compromise. I assure him I'll only tell Parent that Executive is "considering any proposal," at least until Parent tells me it's willing to go along. Then I go through the same exercise with Parent.]

Parent ultimately balks at it—the CEO claiming that his conservative board of directors would be unhappy with the uncertain "crapshoot" element it embodies. This may, in fact, be the case; but the rejection might also reflect Parent's concern that a big chunk of that "aberration" is— likely to stick around for another year!

Still, the creative proposal has served an important role, in at least three respects. One, as my attempt at a solution, it lays the groundwork for me to make a more mundane proposal later on if the impasse persists. Two, it keeps things rolling at a crucial point when the parties appear to be backsliding. And three, it sets them up for the final—not particularly creative—dollar compromise.

12. *Splitting the Difference*

Now, having reported back to Executive that Parent isn't willing to make the contingent deal, I do what any smart negotiator should do at this point I shut up. Sure, I know what the next step has to be, but I want it to come from the parties, if possible, rather than be initiated by me.

If I were really a positive thinker, I might hope that Executive or Parent would, at this juncture, suggest a reasonable compromise on which they're willing to settle. My actual aspirations are more modest. What I'm hoping for is that both sides—or at least one—will ask me to suggest a fixed dollar compromise number to resolve the dispute.

My silence works; Executive makes the request. I reply that I'm willing to proffer a settlement number, but only if Parent also wishes me to; and I ask Executive whether he has any objection to my telling Parent that Executive has requested this. My reason for proceeding in this fashion is that, although neither of them will be agreeing in advance to accept the number I put forth, the pressure on each to do so will be heavy indeed following a joint request.

Executive approves my approach to Parent on that basis. Parent is more wary, but also accedes. *[If neither side were to ask me to do this and all movement toward a final solution had halted, then I would probably put the question to each of them as to whether they wanted me to suggest a compromise.]*

I consider it important to explain to the parties how I arrived at the number—and I always like to do this before I trot out the number itself. The reason here is obvious; once the mediator proclaims the number, no one listens to anything else. Besides, this placement has the advantage of underlining that the number is the product of my reasoning—not something I just backed into and am now trying to justify.

My number is $6,825,000. I go through the calculations (previously discussed under Step 7) that get me there, which include slightly different components for each side, although ending up at the same place.

This is also the time to trot out any arguments I've saved (or even ones I may have used previously) as to why it's in a party's best interests to settle rather than fight. * * *

When I encounter initial resistance, I resort to pointing out the relative insignificance of this final move. For Parent, the $225,000 increase called for is only about 3% of the deal. Come on, I say; if you're willing to do the deal at $6.6 million, what's the problem with $6.825 million? (Well, they say, we have to draw the line somewhere—which is the usual, though rarely a devastating, rejoinder.) And I encourage the parties to think about the perils of having to second-guess themselves. Listen, I say to Executive, if you don't make the deal, and then the jury buys most of Parent's arguments and comes in at $4 million, aren't you going to feel terrible that you didn't grab the $6.8 million plus?

Of course, no one wants to be the first to agree to the compromise. So in communicating my number to Executive, I make it clear that, if he's agreeable to it, I won't apprise Parent of that fact. I'll simply tell Parent that I've proposed the same number to Executive, who is reflecting on it.

After much apparent soul-searching, Executive agrees to accept the compromise. Now, I go off to try to sell it to Parent. (I likewise tell Parent's officers that, if they're willing to agree to the number, I won't reveal this to Executive unless and until Executive has signified his willingness to settle at that figure.) The Parent officers back and fill for a while, but finally agree to accept the number; and the deal is made. * * *

[*I consider this to be a realistic example of how mediation can work in a one-shot dollar dispute, overcoming the bad feelings engendered by litigation and bridging a major gap in the hard line positions of the parties.*]

NOTES AND QUESTIONS

1. Freund's approach is quite different from Haynes', but they both exert great control over the process. Is the difference in approach simply that one is a lawyer trying to make a deal and the other is a psychologist addressing relationships? Can either one of them really be called facilitative?

2. Note the importance of timing in Freund's steps. When were breaks of critical importance?

CHAPTER III MEDIATION

3. Despite a highly activist style, how did Freund avoid having the parties feel that he was either partisan or pushing his own solutions?

4. Consider the following from Peter Contuzzi, Should Parties Tell Mediators Their Bottom Line?, 6 Dispute Resolution Mag. 30, 31–32 (Spring 2000):

> If we want negotiators to be candid with the mediator during the separate meetings, we mediators must do more than explain confidential information protections or appeal to the more rigorous ethical obligations some argue should apply in mediations. We must show them how being honest with the mediator serves their self-interest, and offer techniques that not only lessen the risks of candor, but perhaps even reward it. . . .

> Timing is obviously of paramount importance here, and effective mediators normally will not ask this type of question (as well as discourage "What do you think it's worth?" type questions *from* the negotiators) until the last phase of the negotiation. . . . Are there mediation process techniques, to be employed at the end of a money negotiation that will otherwise conclude in a stalemate, which can allow a negotiating party to find out simply and without risk if its bottom line would be acceptable to the other side, and which also encourage candid responses?

> In a separate meeting, I can of course ask a party to disclose its bottom line to me and then ask the other party whether that number would be acceptable *if* it could be obtained. This garden variety "What if" technique offers at least some protection since the hypothetical language used does not constitute a formal settlement proposal.

> That can be a pretty thin veil, though, and some negotiators will speculate that the hypothetical number has already been approved by the other party. Alternatively, I can ask each party to tell me its bottom line and then advise them, for example, whether the numbers are the same or (without disclosing the actual numbers) whether they overlap, are near each other or far apart.

> While they have the virtue of simplicity, these common techniques lack both sufficient incentives for candor and protections against manipulation. They may also leave unclear what will happen next if they do not produce an agreement. For example, the parties may be wary of winding up with an unwanted value opinion or a settlement proposal from the mediator that they suspect may be nothing more than a splitting of the difference between their confidential bottom line numbers. Given these risks and uncertainties, how candid can they afford to be?

> To address these shortcomings, I have experimented for several years with a technique in money negotiations I call the Safety Deposit Box. Mine is a deadline-oriented process, and if the parties are not

close to agreement as we approach the end of the allotted time, I sometimes convene a joint meeting to tell them that there is a final technique that is often effective at this point. I ask them to think of me as a Safety Deposit Box and explain that numbers go into the box but not out—they remain locked in the box. My explanation continues with words similar to the following:

"I will separate you one last time in a few minutes and ask you to put your final bottom line number into the Safety Deposit Box. Please give careful thought to your number, because it will be used by me in several ways.

"These numbers will not be disclosed unless, as happens occasionally, they are the same. If they are the same, I will bring you together to sign a settlement agreement. A few times in the past, these numbers have overlapped, i.e., the plaintiff's final number was lower than the defendant's. That is the one and only situation in which the midpoint between your final numbers will arbitrarily become the settlement amount.

"If there is a gap of any significance between your final numbers, I will inform each party that a gap exists, without disclosing either number or the size of the gap. You may then choose among three options: 1) to keep your number confidential; 2) to disclose your number to the other side; or 3) to condition your disclosure on the other party's agreeing to disclose its number to you.

"If this step does not lead to an agreement, the mediation will conclude with a brief joint meeting during which you will have an opportunity to decide if you wish to move on to the optional last stage of the process—a joint request for a final settlement proposal from the mediator. If you jointly request a settlement proposal from me, I will use the final numbers you put in the Safety Deposit Box in the following way:

"Sometimes, I believe the final number of one party is significantly more fair than the other. Then I adopt that same number as my own number in my proposal. In fact, my preference is to do this in order to provide an extra incentive for you to be as candid as possible when putting your number in the Safety Deposit Box. I obviously do not indicate if my number is an adopted one, although if you have already chosen to disclose your final number, the other side will know that.

"Sometimes, however, I develop my own number. It is my strong policy *not* to propose the midpoint between your two numbers. My proposed number will always be closer to whichever of your numbers I consider more fair.

"You will have some time to consider the proposal and then respond confidentially to me with a simple "yes" or "no." If you say "yes," you are entitled to bear the other party's response, but your "yes" is not communicated by me to the other party unless it also said "yes." If you say "no," you are not entitled to hear the other party's response. The case either settles for the proposed terms or else nobody's position changes.

"Before I separate you again and ask you to spend a few minutes discussing what your final bottom line number will be for the Safety Deposit Box, are there any questions?"

In short order, I obtain their bottom lines. If their numbers are close, a little shuttling normally produces a mutually acceptable number. If their numbers are not close, I convene a final joint meeting and offer them the option of a final settlement proposal from the mediator (normally faxed to them the following day so I have some time to reflect). I explain that I will do my best to provide them with a proposal that reflects my opinion of the case's settlement value and meets my standard of fairness: reasonable to my mind as well as comfortable to my conscience. I also advise them that in the past, there have been some cases in which I declined a request for a proposal because I could not develop one that met my standard of fairness. I make a proposal only if both parties jointly request it, and I wait outside the room while they decide.

Thus, each party knows exactly how its Safety Deposit Box number will be used during these final steps. Each maintains complete control over disclosure of its number and each has veto power over the making of a settlement proposal by the mediator. If they jointly decide to request a proposal, it will not be a mindless one "splitting the difference." I am required to either adopt or at least be nearer to one party's number. My stated preference for the adoption alternative provides an incentive for honesty, but the ambiguity created by the other option (combined with my not saying which alternative applies) provides cover for a party which would like a proposal but does not want its final number revealed under any circumstances.

. . . When I use this technique, it is only when we are near our deadline and the parties remain substantially apart (normally after a full day of negotiating), so the overlap scenario is by far the rarest. However, in a significant minority of cases, the numbers placed in the Safety Deposit Box have either been the same or close enough so that sonic follow-up shuttling quickly produced agreement.

The most common result is for there to be a significant gap between the final numbers. The option most frequently chosen by the parties has been keeping their numbers confidential, but many have selected conditional disclosure. Unilateral disclosure has occurred in only a few cases. More often than not, the parties jointly request a final settlement proposal, and a majority of these cases then settle. Even in the cases that do not settle, the parties often express procedural satisfaction with the control they maintain and with the clearly defined "end game."

3. PROVIDING INFORMATION

One of hallmarks of classical facilitative mediation is that the mediator only facilitates discussion and does not provide advice or recommendations for resolving the dispute. But just as facilitative mediators use methods for directing and moving the parties, mediators may serve as the source for certain kinds of information or for insuring that such information is made available. The need is much greater when the parties are not represented by attorneys, but even when they are, the mediator is not a potted plant when it comes to insuring that necessary information is elicited. Since a high proportion of mediators are attorneys, how they deal with legal information is of particular interest.

Sandra E. Purnell, The Attorney as Mediator–Inherent Conflict of Interest?

32 U.C.L.A. L. Rev. 986, 1008–(1985).

In disputes with important legal dimensions, a legally trained mediator can contribute to effective decision making by providing the parties with fair, accurate, and impartial legal information. In a divorce case, for example, the attorney-mediator may explain the state's marital property system to the parties. When the parties' conflict concerns an environmental issue, the attorney-mediator may explain the relevant cases and statutes on environmental pollution, zoning, or nuisance. Generally, the mediator can make both parties aware of the legal rules applicable to their situation and of the broad parameters within which a court might resolve their dispute. Additionally, the attorney-mediator might explain the policies or nonlegal concerns that might influence a court's decision.

Of course, court decisions cannot be predicted with mathematical accuracy. Thus, the attorney-mediator cannot tell the parties exactly how their case will be resolved if they do not reach an agreement through mediation. She can merely explain the legal principles that a court might consider in reaching a resolution. These are the same principles that would function as bargaining chips if the parties, through their attorneys, engaged in settlement negotiations. The mediator's role is to put the legal principles or "chips" into the hands of the parties themselves. The parties may choose to use their chips to extract the most favorable settlement they can, or they may view the legal principles as a general framework within which to fashion a solution that expresses as fully as possible their own social, economic, political, and ethical views. Whatever their approach, the legal principles are available equally to both parties to use as they see lit.

The essential question is whether providing impartial legal information is equivalent to giving legal advice to a client—and thus constitutes practicing law. Under the definition developed above, legal advice consists of applying law to the specific facts of the client's case provided to the attorney in confidence, As a corollary, when the factual basis of the attorney's opinion is not confidential, when the legal information given is general rather than tailored to the specific facts of the client's situation, or when the legal dimension of the attorney's work is a minor element in her overall responsibilities, the attorney is not engaged in the practice of law. Legal advice is inherently partial: the attorney's goal is not to educate her client about the law but to marshal her knowledge to his service by formulating the best possible legal position she can given the facts of his particular situation. When practicing law, the attorney is not a technician but an advocate. Cases analyzing the "practice of law" have held that attorneys giving business, accounting, and labor relations advice were not practicing law, even when their judgments were dictated by legal considerations. Patent attorneys, for example, often act as legal consultants to their employers. When these attorneys provide general legal and business information, courts have found them not to be engaged in the practice of law; but when legal principles are applied to confidential details of the client's situation, especially when litigation is in view, patent attorneys have been held to be practicing law.

Based on this definition and these analogous cases, the mediator may be viewed as a dispenser of general legal information who is not engaged in the practice of law. First, the legal information a mediator gives is presented in an objective, impartial form. It is not adapted to the parties' specific situation or marshaled to support a particular solution. Second, the mediator obtains information from both parties and, while she may meet with them separately, she makes no promise to protect confidential information as between the parties. Since the parties meeting with the mediator are the primary antagonists and disclose all relevant information to each other as well as to the attorney-mediator, they cannot be giving confidential information to their attorney for the purpose of representation. Third, any legal information the attorney-mediator provides is given to both parties equally. In several mediation models the mediator is required to provide legal information only in the presence of both parties. The lack of confidentiality and the presence of both antagonists underscore the attorney-mediator's role as a technical advisor rather than an advocate. Finally, as the preceding survey of mediator conduct indicates, providing legal information is a relatively small part of the mediator's contribution to conflict resolution. She must also facilitate communication between the parties, and suggest alternative ways to achieve the parties' goals.

No bright line can be drawn between giving advice and providing impartial information. The parties may sometimes interpret legal information as legal advice. Where the law clearly favors one party, for example, the other may feel that the mediator's statement of the legal principle is sufficiently prejudicial to amount to advocating the opponent's position. Even when the attorney-mediator presents only objective summaries of legal principles, she necessarily selects aspects of the law she considers relevant and frames them in a meaningful way—a process involving editorial choices that may reflect her own values and her sense of how the principles should be applied to the particular dispute. Furthermore, a lawyer's training is directed toward advocacy. An attorney is trained to approach facts and law as materials from which she can construct convincing arguments. It may be unreasonable to expect the attorney-mediator to be objective without specific training in the somewhat alien skill of objectivity. The law should recognize, however, that an important distinction exists between legal information and legal advice and acknowledge that the

C. THE ROLE OF THE MEDIATOR   **405**

mediator who actually does provide impartial legal information to both parties is not, on that basis, "acting as a lawyer."

4. DEALING WITH POWER IMBALANCES

Power imbalances, or at least potential power imbalances, arise in every mediation. They can arise out of personality features: one party may be more forceful, articulate, smarter, tougher, have been dominant in the prior relationship between the parties, or be more willing to take the risk of going to court. They can arise out of strategic considerations: one party may have superior information, better access to legal advice, or a better ability to find favorable witnesses or evidence. They can arise out of the inherent strength of one's case: one party may have a more sympathetic position or a stronger legal position.

One of the most challenging tasks for a mediator is how to deal with power imbalances. Not all power imbalances are real. The sources of the parties' power may be different and, because the comparative strengths are difficult to assess, one party may not fully appreciate that it has countervailing powers of its own. Mediators often deal with such situations by trying to enhance the perception of equal power. Techniques include encouraging each party to list its bases of power and then identifying the costs and benefits to each from exercising that power. See Gary Bellows & Bea Moulton, Assessment: Framing the Choices, in The Lawyering Process 998–1017 (1978).

Another method is to shift the focus from power relationships to interests by calling attention to the process of how the parties' needs can be satisfied. See Christopher W. Moore, The Mediation Process 280 (1987). The openness of the mediation process is seen as enabling the mediator to remind the parties that they have agreed to certain process values such as respect for the other party and a commitment not to intimidate. Davis & Salem, Dealing with Power Imbalances in the Mediation of Interpersonal Disputes, 6 Mediation Q. 17, 21 (1984).

Situations in which there is unequal power may arise from one or both parties having a misperception of their strengths or weaknesses or from a genuine "asymmetrical relationship" in which one party is actually in a weaker position and both parties are aware of it. Consider the following discussion by Moore of mediator tactics in such situations (Moore, supra note 2, 281–82 (1987)):

> Mediators work with both weaker and stronger parties to minimize the negative effects of unequal power. When a mediator encounters a situation in which the balance of power is unequal, the weaker party bluffs about his or her power, and the stronger party accepts the bluff, the mediator should usually meet with the bluffing party to educate him or her about the potential costs of being found out or called on to carry out the bluff. The other party's discovery of the deception can lead to a deterioration in relationships and may lead to retaliation if the victim of the bluff is the stronger party.

If the intervenor is successful in convincing the party that the costs of bluffing are too high, the mediator and the party should jointly search for a way to retreat from the bluff or minimize the importance of power dynamics in the context of the negotiations. Retreating from a bluff or minimizing the effects of bluff can often be achieved by ceasing to make threatening statements or false promises and obscuring the explicitness of statements describing the consequences of disagreement.

In power situations in which parties appear to have an asymmetrical relationship and the bases of power are different, the mediator may attempt to obscure the strength of influence of both parties. Mediators can pursue this strategy to create doubt about the actual power of the parties by questioning the accuracy of data, the credibility of experts, the capability of mobilizing coercive power, or the degree of support from authority figures. These techniques will prevent the parties from ascertaining the balance of power. If a party cannot determine absolutely that he or she has more power than another, he or she usually does not feel free to manipulate or exploit an opponent without restraint.

By far the most difficult problem mediators face regarding power relationships is the instance in which the discrepancy between the strength of means of influence is extremely great. The mediator, because of his or her commitment to neutrality and impartiality, is ethically barred from direct advocacy for the weaker party, yet is also ethically obligated to assist the parties in reaching an acceptable agreement. * * *

[T]he mediator should initiate moves to assist the weaker party in mobilizing the power he or she possesses. The mediator should not, however, directly act as an organizer to mobilize or develop new power for the weaker disputant unless the mediator has gained the stronger party's approval. To act as a secret advocate puts the mediator's impartiality and effectiveness as a process intervenor at risk.

Empowering moves may include assisting the weaker party in obtaining, organizing, and analyzing data and identifying and mobilizing his or her means of influence; assisting and educating the party in planning an effective negotiation strategy; aiding the party to develop financial resources so that the party can continue to participate in negotiations; referring a party to a lawyer or other resource person; and encouraging the party to make realistic concessions.

5. ISSUES OF FAIRNESS OF SETTLEMENT AND DISCRIMINATORY IMPACTS ON WOMEN AND MINORITY PARTICIPANTS

Related to the question of power imbalances is that of the mediator's role in assuring fairness. There is general agreement that a mediator should insure fairness in process, but whether she should also take steps to insure that the final agreement is fair is a more controversial issue. A continuing debate in mediation literature is that of mediator neutrality versus accountability.[7] The classical position is that the mediator should avoid taking responsibility for the fairness of the settlement.[8] If the parties, acting with consent after an open discussion that is fair in process terms, decide on a solution, it is said that the mediator should not impose her view of what the result should have been. This view gains support from the reality that there is no easily-agreed upon objective standard as to what is fair in the particular case. This resolution, however, continues to be troubling to some:

> One student, however, in observing a divorce mediation, saw that the mediator very clearly assessed whether a certain financial settlement would be fair and adequate for the wife, and that when he found it would not be, encouraged the wife to refuse it and pressured the husband to make a more generous offer. Troubled by the role conflicts inherent in adopting this kind of judgmental posture as mediator, the student grasped much more powerfully the conflict between the neutrality and accountability arguments in mediation theory. He also saw that the orthodox theory may simply not apply when mediators face the practical test of sitting passively by and watching a disadvantaged party willingly accept a grossly unfair settlement.[9]

Although it is often said that mediators are not to take responsibility for the fairness of a settlement, clearly the concern with power imbalances reflects the mediator's obligation to insure that the process is fair. But some studies have indicated that certain groups which have been historically disadvantaged in our society are also disadvantaged in the mediation process. Consider the following feminist critique:

Trina Grillo, The Mediation Alternative: Process Dangers for Women

100 Yale L.J. 1545 (1991).

The western concept of law is based on a patriarchal paradigm characterized by hierarchy, linear reasoning, the resolution of disputes through the application of abstract principles, and the ideal of the reasonable person. Its fundamental aspiration is objectivity, and to that end it separates public from private, form from substance, and process from policy. This objectivist paradigm is problematic in many circumstances, but never more so than in connection with a marital dissolution in which the custody

---

7. Compare Susskind, Environmental Mediation and the Accountability Problem, 6 Vt.L.Rev. 1 (1981) with McCrory, Environmental Mediation—Another Piece of the Puzzle, 6 Vt.L.Rev. 49 (1981).

8. Stulberg, The Theory and Practice of Mediation: A Reply to Professor Susskind, 6 Vt.L.Rev. 85, 86–87 (1981).

9. Bush, Using Process Observation to Teach Alternative Dispute Resolution: Alternative to Simulation, 37 J.Legal Educ. 46, 52 (1987).

of children is at issue, where the essential question for the court is what is to happen next in the family. The family court system, aspiring to the ideal of objectivity and operating as an adversary system, can be relied on neither to produce just results nor to treat those subject to it respectfully and humanely.

There is little doubt that divorce procedure needs to be reformed, but reformed how? Presumably, any alternative should be at least as just, and at least as humane, as the current system, particularly for those who are least powerful in society. Mediation has been put forward, with much fanfare, as such an alternative. The impetus of the mediation movement has been so strong that in some states couples disputing custody are required by statute or local rule to undergo a mandatory mediation process if they are unable to reach an agreement on their own. Mediation has been embraced for a number of reasons. First, it rejects an objectivist approach to conflict resolution, and promises to consider disputes in terms of relationships and responsibility. Second, the mediation process is, at least in theory, cooperative and voluntary, not coercive. The mediator does not make a decision; rather, each party speaks for himself. Together they reach an agreement that meets the parties' mutual needs. In this manner, the process is said to enable the parties to exercise self-determination and eliminate the hierarchy of dominance that characterizes the judge/litigant and lawyer/client relationships. Third, since in mediation there are no rules of evidence or legalistic notions of relevancy, decisions supposedly may be informed by context rather than by abstract principle. Finally, in theory at least, emotions are recognized and incorporated into the mediation process. This conception of mediation has led some commentators to characterize it as a feminist alternative to the patriarchally inspired adversary system.

* * * I conclude that mandatory mediation provides neither a more just nor a more humane alternative to the adversarial system of adjudication of custody, and, therefore, does not fulfill its promises. In particular, quite apart from whether an acceptable result is reached, mandatory mediation can be destructive to many women and some men because it requires them to speak in a setting they have not chosen and often imposes a rigid orthodoxy as to how they should speak, make decisions, and be. This orthodoxy is imposed through subtle and not-so-subtle messages about appropriate conduct and about what may be said in mediation. It is an orthodoxy that often excludes the possibility of the parties' speaking with their authentic voices.

Moreover, people vary greatly in the extent to which their sense of self is "relational"—that is, defined in terms of connection to others. If two parties are forced to engage with one another, and one has a more relational sense of self than the other, that party may feel compelled to maintain her connection with the other, even to her own detriment. For this reason, the party with the more relational sense of self will be at a disadvantage in a mediated negotiation. Several prominent researchers have suggested that, as a general rule, women have a more relational sense of self than do men, although there is little agreement on what the origin of this difference might be. Thus, rather than being a feminist alternative to the adversary system, mediation has the potential actively to harm women.

Some of the dangers of mandatory mediation apply to voluntary mediation as well. Voluntary mediation should not be abandoned, but should be recognized as a powerful process which should be used carefully and thoughtfully. Entering into such a process with one who has known you intimately and who now seems to threaten your whole life and being has great creative, but also enormous destructive, power. Nonetheless, it should be recognized that when two people themselves decide to mediate and then physically appear at the mediation sessions, that decision and their continued presence serve as a rough indication that it is not too painful or too dangerous for one or both of them to go on.

* * *

Principles and Fault in Mediation

The introduction of mediation into family court processes was another part of the effort to make the adversary system fit the realities of divorce more closely. Mediators stepped into the increasingly uncertain legal world of dissolution with a new process which minimized the role of principles and fault. Mediation appeared to provide the opportunity to bring the lessons of context and subjective experience to dissolution proceedings. In mediation, the parties' legal rights would not be central. Instead of relying solely on abstract principles and rules, parties and mediators could attend to the reality of complex relationships. Precedent, legal rules and a legalized formulation of the facts might be seen as irrelevant to the mediation process and an unnecessary constraint on the mediator. Individuals could be seen in relation to one another, and morality treated as "a question of responsibilities to particular people in particular contexts."

The informal law of the mediation setting requires that discussion of principles, blame, and rights, as these terms are used in the adversarial context, be deemphasized or avoided. Mediators use informal sanctions to encourage the parties to replace the rhetoric of fault, principles, and values with the rhetoric of compromise and relationship. For example, mediators typically suggest that the parties "eschew[ ] the language of individual rights in favor of the language of interdependent relationships." They orient the parties toward reasonableness and compromise, rather than moral vindication. The conflict may be styled as a personal quarrel, in which there is no right and wrong, but simply two different, and equally true or untrue, views of the world.

Are All Agreements Equal?

The reason for the lack of focus on values and principles in many models of mediation is, in part, simply practical. If the essence of mediation entails trading off interests and compromising, each person's interests are important, but which person violated societal values and why he did so, is not. To the extent that principles and faultfinding based on those principles enter into the discussion, reaching an agreement might be delayed or disrupted. Deemphasizing principles also might appear to be the sensible approach in a society that is increasingly pluralistic in terms of cultures, religions, and varieties of family structures. Where there are conflicting moral codes, as there often are when couples divorce, making the only standard for agreement be that it is accepted by both parties means that it will not be necessary for a third party to decide which moral code is superior.

Sometimes, however, all agreements are not equal. It may be important, from both a societal and an individual standpoint, to have an agreement that reflects cultural notions of justice and not merely one to which there has been mutual assent. Many see the courts as a place where they can obtain vindication and a ruling by a higher authority. It is also important in some situations for society to send a clear message as to how children are to be treated, what the obligations of ex-spouses are to each other and to their children, and what sort of behavior will not be tolerated. Because the mediation movement tends to regard negotiated settlements as morally superior to adjudication, these functions of adjudication may easily be overlooked. * * *

Formal Equality

Context is also destroyed by a commitment to formal equality, that is, to the notion that members of mediating couples are, to the extent possible, to be treated exactly alike, without regard for general social patterns and with limited attention to even the history of the particular couples. Thus, it becomes close to irrelevant in determining custody that the mother may have been home doing virtually all the caretaking of the children for years; she is to move into the labor market as quickly as possible. It is assumed that the father is equally competent to care for the children. In fact, it frequently is said that one cannot assume that a father will not be as competent a caretaker as the mother just because he has not shown any interest previously:

> Many women have told me, "He never did anything with the children. If he is given even part-time responsibility for them, he'll ignore them, he won't know what to do."
>
> Research has shown, however, that little correlation exists between men's involvement with the children before and after divorce.... When they gain independent responsibility for the children, many men who were relatively uninvolved during the marriage become loving and responsive parents after divorce. [R. Adler, Sharing the Children 33 (1988)]

In mediation, insistence on this sort of formal equality results in a dismissal of the legitimate concerns of the parent who is, or considers herself to be, the more responsible parent. Such concerns are often minimized by characterizing them as evidence of some pathology on the part of the parent holding them. The insistence of a mother that a young child not be permitted to stay overnight with an alcoholic father who smokes in bed might be characterized as the mother needing to stay in control. Or the mediator might suggest that it is not legitimate for one party to assume that the other party will renege on her obligations, simply because she has done so in the past. In the example above, once [the wife] was in mediation, she was treated exactly equally with [the husband] even though their past parental performance had been dramatically different. The point is not that mothers never inappropriately desire to stay in control, or that people who have not fulfilled their obligations once will continue to fail to do so, but rather that by defining the process as one in which both parties are situated equally, deep, heartfelt, and often accurate concerns either are not permitted to be expressed or are discounted.

Equating fairness in mediation with formal equality results in, at most, a crabbed and distorted fairness on a microlevel; it considers only the mediation context itself. There is no room in such an approach for a discussion of the fairness of institutionalized societal inequality. For example, women do not have the earning power that men have, and therefore are not in an economically equal position in the world. All too often mediators stress the need for women to become economically independent without taking into account the very real dollar differences between the male and female experience in the labor market. While gaining independence might appear to be desirable, most jobs available for women, especially those who have been out of the labor market, are low paying, repetitious, and demeaning. Studies show that women in such dead-end jobs do not experience the glories of independence, but rather show increased depression. * * *

Mandatory Mediation and the Promise of Self–Determination

Mediation permits persons to speak for themselves and make their own decisions. This self-determination can be empowering. Patterns of domination characteristic of adversary adjudication are challenged in two ways: no outside decisionmaker is present, and the client need not be the passive recipient of a lawyer's advice and decisionmaking. Instead, he can explore alternatives, create options, and make decisions. In private, voluntary mediation, I have found that many say that they have chosen mediation so that they, and not a lawyer, will be in charge of their own destinies. In this very immediate way, mediation can challenge the hierarchical, professionalized way that family law is usually practiced.

This dynamic is fundamentally altered when mediation is imposed rather than sought or offered. When mandatory mediation is part of the court system, the notion that parties are actually making their own decisions is purely illusory. First, the parties have not chosen or timed the process according to their ability to handle it. Second, they are not allowed to decide themselves how much their lawyers should participate, but instead are deprived of whatever protection their lawyers have to offer. Finally, they are not permitted to choose the mediator, and they often cannot leave without endangering their legal position even if they believe the mediator is biased against them. * * *

Mediation literature has addressed the problem of unequal bargaining power between the parties by suggesting that the mediator use a variety of techniques to "balance the power." These techniques entail empowering or supporting the less powerful party or disempowering the more powerful party. For example, a mediator might provoke a conflict, forbid the discussion of certain issues, or advise a party who seems to be at an economic disadvantage to see a financial counselor. These suggestions share the premise that the mediator can recognize power disparities when they occur and intervene to lessen their impact. But, as I have attempted to show, benign intervention may not always be possible. When a mediator analyzes and attempts to correct a power imbalance, she can no longer claim to be simply a facilitator of the couple's process; rather, she is taking an active role in affecting the outcome of that process. But the mediator, due to her own internal processes, may not in fact have a sufficiently clear vision of the interaction between the divorcing spouses to make a considered decision about if and how the power needs to be balanced. The existence of partiality, countertransference, and projection on the part of mediators explains why mediators' attempts to redress imbalances cannot necessarily be relied upon to meet the problem of unequal bargaining power.

NOTES AND QUESTIONS

1. Power imbalances are a recurring spectre in divorce mediation where there may be a long history of dominance of one spouse by another, often a wife by a husband. One spouse may also be in a superior economic position, again often a husband who has greater earning power and social mobility. There may also be imbalances of knowledge, experience, sophistication with business and property matters, and negotiating ability, that can be gender-specific. A prominent feminist critique of mediation in family law disputes is that it reinforces the gender-advantage of the husband and removes the protection of the legal process. See Woods, Mediation: A Backlash to Women's Progress on Family Law Issues, 19 Clearinghouse Rev. 431, 435 (1985):

> Mediation can be effective if and only if (1) the issue is capable of resolution through modification of perceptions, attitudes and/or behavior; (2) relative parity of power exists between the parties; (3) there is no need for punishment, deterrence or redress; and (4) the parties are capable of entering into and carrying out an agreement. These criteria are not met in divorce or family law mediation.

* * *

> Mediation trivializes family law issues by relegating them to a lesser forum. It diminishes the public perception of the relative importance of laws addressing women's and children's rights in the family by placing these rights outside society's key institutional system of dispute resolution—the legal system—while continuing to allow corporate and other "important" matters to have unfettered access to that system. Loss of one's children and protection of one's physical safety

should be considered too important to entrust to any other but the legal system.

Professor Grillo sounds similar themes, but is her critique even more basic to the nature of mediation? Does her critique extend beyond family-law cases?

2. In a spirited response to Professor Grillo, Professor Rosenberg argued:

(1) Many of Professor Grillo's statements and stories do not represent what actually happens at a typical mediation session. Instead, they effectively capture and magnify only the worst possible abuses of the process. Because many potential users of mediation and many policymakers are either unfamiliar or only marginally familiar with mediation, it is dangerous to allow these misrepresentations and distortions to go unchallenged; (2) To the extent that mandatory mediation presents some real problems, society may be better served by attempting to correct those problems than by abandoning mandatory mediation in areas where it has already proved to be very helpful. Although Professor Grillo does not adequately explore that possibility, many states that have mandatory mediation have already enacted legislation that addresses her concerns; and (3) Professor Grillo's article suggests that mediation may be dangerous for women. While anything can be dangerous to anyone at some time, mandatory mediation is generally helpful both to women and to men, and an overwhelming number of the women and men who have been through mandatory mediation approve of it strongly.

Rosenberg, In Defense of Mediation, 33 Ariz.L.Rev. 467, 467–8 (1991).

3. As we have seen, there are techniques for dealing with power imbalances. These may have to be applied in the divorce context with an awareness of gender relationships in our society. See Folger & Bernard, Divorce Mediation: When Mediators Challenge the Divorcing Parties, 10 Mediation Q. 5, 20 (1985) (studies indicate that female mediators intervene more often than males on behalf of either spouse). It is also argued that divorce mediations should not take place without the presence of attorneys to provide support and information. Can these techniques ever be adequate to justify mediation in which there is a seriously-dominated wife?

4. The California compulsory mediation approach to child custody and visitation issues is much debated. There is concern that the parents will be less likely to mediate in good faith, see Schepard, Philbrick & Rabino, Ground Rules for Custody Mediation and Modification, 48 Albany L.Rev. 616 (1984), or that they will refuse to cooperate, leaving custody decisions to be decided by the courts, see Evarts & Goodwin, The Mediation and Adjudication of Divorce and Custody from Contrasting Premises to Complementary Processes, 19 Idaho L.Rev. 277 (1984). However, the Denver Custody Mediation Project study, in which mediation services were offered but not required, indicates that while only about 50% of parents chose to mediate when given the choice, one of them was usually eager to mediate. Pearson et al., The Decision to Mediate: Profiles of Individuals

Who Accept and Reject the Opportunity to Mediate Contested Child Custody and Visitation Issues, 6 J. of Divorce 17 (1982). This suggests that compulsory mediation may only be compulsory for one of the parties in most cases. The same study reports that 80% of those exposed to the mediation process reached agreement, and that 90% of parties who mediated were satisfied with the process (compared with a 50% satisfaction rate with the courts). Pearson & Thoennes, Mediating and Litigating Custody Disputes: A Longitudinal Evaluation, 17 Fam.L.Q. 497, 504, 514 (1984). Does the high agreement and satisfaction rates for mediation demonstrate the success of the process or simply reflect that those who chose to use it were a self-selected group more predisposed to satisfactory settlements?

5. Many of the themes in the feminist critique have been raised in reference to mediation involving minorities or poor people. A groundbreaking study published in 1985 concluded that informal mechanisms like mediation injure the poor and disempowered. Delgado, Dunn, Brown, Lee, & Hubbert, Fairness and Formality: Minimizing the Risk of Prejudice in Alternative Dispute Resolution, 1985 Wis.L.Rev. 1359, 1360–61, 1375–91. It also opined that mediation may allow recognition of racial and ethnic prejudice to the disadvantage of minorities. Id. at 1387–91. See also Delgado, ADR and the Dispossessed: Recent Books About the Deformalization Movement, 13 L. & Soc. Inquiry 145, 151–54 (1988) (higher risk of prejudice in ADR proceedings); Hermann, The Dangers of ADR: A Three-Tiered System of Justice, 3 J.Contemp.Legal Issues 117 (1990).

6. MEDIATOR APPROACHES AND ORIENTATIONS

As a wide spectrum of people have become trained as mediators over the past several decades and mediation has expanded beyond its traditional family, labor, and community boundaries, there has been great experimentation with different mediator styles, approaches, and orientations. As we have seen, even the traditional "non-directive" or "facilitative" approach is really a diversity of approaches depending on the circumstances. However, distinctive approaches and orientations have emerged and had labels put on them.

The "facilitative versus evaluative" dichotomy was perhaps the first to be recognized and debated by mediators. As lawyers and former judges came to dominate the ranks of mediators, the classical "facilitative," or non-directive, model of mediation was challenged by a more directive "evaluative" orientation. Lawyers and former judges may be selected, or may consider themselves to have been selected, because of their knowledge of the law and their familiarity with the litigation system. They therefore may be more inclined to evaluate and not merely to facilitate.

In the classical non-directive form of mediation, a mediator strives to be only a facilitator and not to interject her views, values, or solutions into the process or the agreement. Under this model, the mediator should not desire, nor have the authority, to impose a particular settlement. It is recognized that the mediator has an influence on the mediation by her role in helping to define the problem and in encouraging the parties to consider options for its solution, but it is not her role to provide evaluation of the strength of the parties' cases or estimates of the probable outcome in a court.

Despite the classical model, some mediation processes always embraced greater mediator activism in the belief that to be a good facilitator, the mediator must use a variety of techniques to encourage and shape a settlement. This can be seen in the "muscle mediation" often practiced in collective bargaining mediation. The influx of attorneys as mediators has given rise to a different form of mediator directiveness—"evaluative mediation" in which the mediator may actually give her opinion of the merits of the parties' cases or suggest solutions or settlement terms.

The differences in approach between the two models reflect differences in philosophical outlook. However, much of mediation today is something of a hybrid, with the mediator using the techniques that seem to be called for in the particular context. As has been seen, even under the classical nondirective model, the mediator may take a more active role in order to facilitate an agreement. She may use a variety of devices such as focusing the parties on the issues that will achieve a resolution, clearing up the facts and any misconceptions, encouraging understanding of the other party's position, and avoiding unfairness in the mediation process. And, as we have seen, a nondirective mediator may use a variety of techniques and strategies to raise doubts in the parties' minds as to the strength of their positions and cases.

Consider the following proposal for classifying mediator orientations according to facilitative and evaluative approaches as a means of getting both parties and the mediator to determine in advance the type of mediation that is desired:

Leonard L. Riskin, Mediator Orientations, Strategies and Techniques

12 Alternatives 111, 111–112 (1994).

The classification system starts with two principal questions: 1. Does the mediator tend to define problems **narrowly** or **broadly**? 2. Does the mediator think she should **evaluate**—make assessments or predictions or proposals for agreements—or **facilitate** the parties' negotiation without evaluating?

The answers reflect the mediator's beliefs about the nature and scope of mediation and her assumptions about the parties' expectations.

Problem Definition

Mediators with a **narrow** focus assume that the parties have come to them for help in solving a technical problem. The parties have defined this problem in advance through the **positions** they have asserted in negotiations or pleadings. Often it involves a question such as, "Who pays how much to whom?" or "Who can use such-and-such property?" As framed, these questions rest on "win-lose" (or "distributive") assumptions. In other words, the participants must divide a limited resource; whatever one gains, the other must lose.

The likely court outcome—along with uncertainty, delay and expense—drives much of the mediation process. Parties, seeking a compromise, will bargain adversarially, emphasizing positions over interests.

A mediator who starts with a **broad** orientation, on the other hand, assumes that the parties can benefit if the mediation goes beyond the narrow issues that normally define legal disputes. Important interests often lie beneath the positions that the participants assert. Accordingly, the mediator should help the participants understand and fulfill those interests—at least if they wish to do so.

The Mediator's Role

The **evaluative** mediator assumes that the participants want and need the mediator to provide some direction as to the appropriate grounds for settlement—based on law, industry practice or technology. She also assumes that the mediator is qualified to give such direction by virtue of her experience, training and objectivity.

The **facilitative** mediator assumes the parties are intelligent, able to work with their counterparts, and capable of understanding their situations better than either their lawyers or the mediator. So the parties may develop better solutions than any that the mediator might create. For these reasons, the facilitative mediator assumes that his principal mission is to enhance and clarify communications between the parties in order to help them decide what to do.

The facilitative mediator believes it is inappropriate for the mediator to give his opinion, for at least two reasons. First, such opinions might impair the appearance of impartiality and thereby interfere with the mediator's ability to function. Second, the mediator might not know enough—about the details of the case or the relevant law, practices or technology—to give an informed opinion.

Each of the two principal questions—Does the mediator tend toward a narrow or broad focus? and Does the mediator favor an evaluative or facilitative role?—yield responses that fall along a continuum. Thus, a mediator's orientation will be more or less broad and more or less evaluative.

Strategies and Techniques Of Each Orientation

Each **orientation** derives from assumptions or beliefs about the mediator's role and about the appropriate focus of a mediation. A mediator employs **strategies**—plans—to conduct the mediation. And he uses **techniques**—particular moves or behaviors—to effectuate those strategies. Here are selected strategies and techniques that typify each mediation orientation.

C. The Role of the Mediator   417

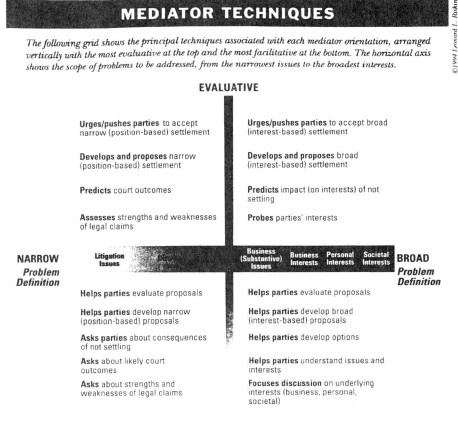

Evaluative–Narrow

The principal strategy of the evaluative-narrow mediator is to help the parties understand the strengths and weaknesses of their positions and the likely outcome at trial. To accomplish this, the evaluative-narrow mediator typically will first carefully study relevant documents, such as pleadings, depositions, reports and mediation briefs. Then, in the mediation, she employs evaluative techniques, such as the following, which are listed from most to least evaluative:

Like the evaluative-narrow, the facilitative-narrow mediator plans to help the participants become "realistic" about their litigation situations. But he employs different techniques. He does not use his own assessments, predictions or proposals. Nor does he apply pressure. Moreover, he probably will not request or study relevant documents, such as pleadings, depositions, reports, or mediation briefs. Instead, because he believes that the burden of decision should rest with the parties, the facilitative-narrow mediator might ask questions—generally in private caucuses—to help the participants understand both sides' legal positions and the consequences of non-settlement. Also in private caucuses, he helps each side assess proposals in light of the alternatives.

Here are examples of the types of questions the facilitative-narrow mediator might ask:

- What are the strengths and weakness of your case? Of the other side's case?
- What are the best, worst, and most likely outcomes of litigation? How did you make these assessments? Have you thought about [other issues]?
- How long will it take to get to trial? How long will the trial last?
- What will be the associated costs—in money, emotions, or reputation?

Evaluative–Broad

The evaluative-broad mediator also helps the parties understand their circumstances and options. However, she has a different notion of what this requires. So she emphasizes the parties' interests over their positions and proposes solutions designed to accommodate these interests. In addition, because the evaluative-broad mediator constructs the agreement, she emphasizes her own understanding of the circumstances at least as much as the parties'.

Like the evaluative-narrow mediator, the evaluative-broad mediator is likely to request and study relevant documents, such as pleadings, depositions, and mediation briefs. In addition, she tries to uncover the parties' underlying interests by such methods as:

- Explaining that the goal of mediation can include addressing underlying interests.
- Encouraging the real parties, or knowledgeable representatives (with settlement authority) of corporations or other organizations to attend and participate in the mediation. For instance, the mediator might invite such individuals to make remarks after the lawyers present their opening statements, and she might include them in most settlement discussions.
- Asking about the participants' situations, plans, needs and interests.
- Speculating about underlying interests and asking for confirmation.

Facilitative–Broad

The facilitative-broad mediator seeks to help the parties define, understand and resolve the problems they wish to address. She encourages them to consider underlying interests rather than positions and helps them generate and assess proposals designed to accommodate those interests. Specifically, she might:

- Encourage the parties to discuss underlying interests in joint sessions. To bring out such interests, she might use techniques such as those employed by the evaluative-broad mediator.

C. The Role of the Mediator **419**

- Encourage and help the parties to develop their own proposals (jointly or alone) that would respond to underlying interests of both sides.

The facilitative-broad mediator does **not** provide assessments, predictions or proposals. However, to help the participants better understand their legal situations, she will likely allow the parties to present and discuss their legal arguments. In addition, she might ask questions such as those listed for the facilitative-narrow mediator and focus discussion on underlying interests.

In a broad mediation, however, legal argument generally occupies a lesser position than it does in a narrow one. And because he emphasizes the participants' role in defining the problems and in developing and evaluating proposals, the facilitative-broad mediator does not need to fully understand the legal posture of the case. Accordingly, he is less likely to request or study litigation documents, technical reports or mediation briefs.

However, the facilitative-broad mediator must be able to quickly grasp the legal and substantive issues and to respond to the dynamics of the situation. He needs to help the parties realistically evaluate proposals to determine whether they address the parties' underlying interests.

NOTES AND QUESTIONS

1. What kinds of cases would you think most suitable for each of the four orientations described by Professor Riskin?

2. One of the ways to distinguish mediators' philosophical view of the role of the mediator is in the use of the caucus. Extensive use of caucuses may reflect a more activist and directive model of mediation. Such a model may use open sessions primarily to describe the process to the parties and to allow them to state their positions, but leave the hard bargaining, particularly regarding dollar-settlement figures, to caucuses. The mediator then becomes something of a shuttle-diplomat, taking offers back and forth between the parties and reality-testing with them in private. Mediators who advocate this model maintain that parties' intemperate statements that, for example, this is their "last offer," or that the other's side's offer is "absurd" or "an insult," or that they "would just as soon go to trial," are less harmful if restricted to a caucus. The mediator is then able to choose what information, and what degree of intensity, to convey to the other party as she perceives it useful in the interests of effecting a settlement.

In contrast, the classical model of mediation favors a broader use of open sessions, using a caucus only when the parties seem to be at an impasse, when their positions are so extreme that private reality-testing is necessary, or when it is necessary to deal privately with highly personal matters that a party would not want to divulge in front of the opposing party. The advantage of open sessions is that the parties can hear the arguments of the other party and his attorney and begin to reassess their case from a less one-sided point of view. Open sessions also remove the risk that the mediator who keeps the parties apart in caucuses will come to be

420   CHAPTER III MEDIATION

perceived as unduly manipulative or will be distrusted as the conveyor of information and offers.

3. Consider the following comments on the consequences of the Riskin grid in Joseph B. Stulberg, *Facilitative Versus Evaluative Mediator Orientations: Piercing the "Grid" Lock*, 24 Florida State U. L. Rev. 985, 991–995 (1997):

A. There Is No Criterion for Critiquing Mediator Performance (Whether Facilitative or Evaluative) Other than the Single Dimension of the Efficiency with Which Parties Reach (or Fail to Reach) the Stated Goal of the Mediator's Orientation

Consider the evaluative mediator. She is portrayed as someone who provides guidance to parties as to appropriate settlement terms in light of the legal, industry, or technology considerations with which the mediator is reasonably conversant. In such circumstances, what counts as "good" or "bad" mediating? Presumably, the assessment turns completely on whether the mediator was successful in getting the parties to accept her assessment of the outcome and the settlement terms offered. However, that is simply to define good and bad in terms of efficiency in reaching a settlement, Whether the mediator listened to the parties or their counsel, captured their concerns, or crafted an agreement compatible with their values is irrelevant. The only test of success is whether the mediator convinced the parties to accept an outcome. To paraphrase H.L.A. Hart's wonderful example, mediating is simply the case of "the gunman writ large"; that is, if the mediator is articulate, adept with figures, or in any other manner dangerously persuasive, then, on the Riskin grid, such, conduct is not subject to criticism if the parties reach agreement. We may observe that the mediator could have achieved the same results even if she had been less blustery, more subtle, less belligerent, or less authoritative, but such observations are simply comments about style. Nothing in principle is improper about the mediator bullying someone into an agreement as long as there is some operative notion that the parties "voluntarily" agreed to the outcome (for example, they had counsel, were not compelled under duress to accept the terms, etc.). There is no sense in which we can say of the mediator's performance, "You should not do that," where "should" appeals to some value other than whether (and how quickly) the parties accepted (the mediator's) proposed settlement terms.

Similar comments hold true for evaluating the performance of the facilitative mediator. The primary mission of the facilitative mediator, according to Riskin, "is to clarify and to enhance communication between the parties in order to help them decide what to do." If the mediator asked questions in carefully crafted and open-ended language, crystallized issues in neutral terms, thoughtfully designed a discussion agenda that enabled parties to reorient and enrich their understanding of one another, effectively but indirectly probed for possible options, or thoughtfully prompted parties to think about the consequences of not settling, and all of those efforts still failed to lead the parties to an enhanced understanding of their situation or improved communication (let alone a resolution), we cannot, according to the grid, say of that individual that she mediated well but was not successful. All we can say is that she was not effective in having the parties achieve the stated goal.

The general structure of this criticism, then, is that by letting a thousand flowers bloom in the name of mediation, the grid embraces whatever values a particular orientation espouses. Since all orientations are "mediation," no commanding, independent analytical framework for evaluating mediator performance emerges. By necessity, we are constrained to evaluating the conduct from the frame of reference of the quadrant within which one finds oneself. That evaluation reduces everything to a matter of efficiency, not propriety. Riskin, on pain of contradiction, must be wedded to this analytical consequence. For if he were to begin to offer some goals and values (for example, that mediation is consensual and participatory) as being distinctive of the mediation process, thus indicating standards against winch one can evaluate mediator conduct, then the gate is opened to ask why those values, but not others, were included. Since the grid, has no way in principle of foreclosing any values from being acceptable, it relinquishes all claims to establishing a noninstrumental foundation on which to critique mediator conduct.

B. The Marketplace Vision of the Delivery of Mediation Services Cannot Do What Its Advocates Propose

Some argue that the intervener should adopt the orientation that the parties desire. [FN36] If parties or their counsel want an evaluation, the mediator should provide it. If they want facilitation, the mediator should act accordingly. The mediator who can service the broadest client base is that individual who adapts her orientation to market demands.

However, this analysis collapses in an instructive way. Consider the situation in which Party A or her lawyer indicates that she prefers a mediator with an evaluative-narrow orientation, and Party B or her lawyer indicates that she prefers a mediator whose orientation is facilitative-broad. ii one assumes that the parties are ordered to appear in mediation, how should the mediator proceed? The obvious answer is that the mediator must choose which orientation to adopt. That choice might be influenced by the mediator's convictions about the values of conversations and settlement discussions or her probabilistic assessments of which style will appeal to the largest segment of the financially paying mediation clients; the reasons, at this level, are irrelevant. The compelling insight is that the mediator must choose which orientation to adopt, not the parties. Thus, the market-demand analysis simply folds.

C. Some Orientations May Incorporate Practices That Systematically Favor the Participation of One Party over Another

Assume that the grid accurately describes acceptable mediation practices. Do the orientations share a consistency of values in their process guidelines? I do not believe they do.

For example, recent communication literature suggests that conversational patterns among males and females are importantly different. Some patterns appear to be characteristic of males—for exam pie, argumentative comments designed to assert a certain dominance in the conversational relationship—whereas other styles that emphasize relational connections appear more congruent with female orientations. Acknowledging that much of the analytical and empirical work in this area is quite tentative, I do believe that it is sufficiently rich to at least ask the following question: In a conference conducted pursuant to the evaluative-narrow orientation, would the structure of the conversation, with the advocates presenting the ease, submitting facts, and proffering argumentative conclusions to the third-party intervener, operate to favor one gender over another? If any plausibility attaches to the claim that such an argumentative flavor might favor males over females, then certainly the mediator must revisit her claim that she is conducting a conversation that is without bias, for the game is skewed from the outset. From this admittedly guarded perspective, the facilitative approach then appears to at least leave open the possibility of a more equitable conversational climate. In that important sense, the structure of the conversation can either support or undermine a viable notion of power balance and equality as being valued features of the problem-solving process....

D. The Scope of Usefulness of the Mediation Process Is Unnecessarily Constrained

The image of mediation portrayed in the grid is governed by a conception of mediation as being an alternative to some other identifiable decision making procedure, To play upon the well-worn phrase, the mediation captured by the grid is being conducted in the "shadow of a trial." If the parties do not resolve their differences in mediation, then some other dispute resolution forum—most likely an adjudicatory one (trial, arbitration, or administrative hearing)—will take place.

Mediation, however, has far more extensive uses than that—and when one envisions its applications, some mediator orientations are immediately deemed irrelevant. An evaluative-narrow orientation for a peer mediator in a high school converts the peer into a school guidance counselor. When the Department of Justice dispatches a team of mediators to service racial conflicts or the Federal Mediation and Conciliation Service assigns a mediator to help management and union bargaining teams resolve a private-sector collective-bargaining impasse, the last thing parties will embrace is someone who has come to tell them how to live their lives. In short, parties operating in important contexts in which mediation is used have no tolerance for the evaluative orientation. The response, "Well, for certain types of disputes, certain orientations would not be effective or well-suited," is not sufficient. The mismatch in orientation stems from the fact that dissimilar values and goals make the intervention something different. That insight leads to the more fundamental flaw generated by the grid's analysis, namely that the proffered distinction between evaluative and facilitative is not persuasive.

C. The Role of the Mediator

Robert A. Baruch Bush & Joseph P. Folger, The Promise of Mediation: Responding to Conflict Through Empowerment and Recognition

pp. 5–12 (1994).

One of the cases recently mediated at a court-annexed community mediation program in Queens, New York, illustrates in a general way what transformative mediation looks like. The case, a dispute involving an assault charge, shows in concrete terms what gets accomplished in mediation when at least some transformative opportunities for empowerment and recognition are realized.

The Sensitive Bully

Regis, a large, stern-looking middle-aged black man, had filed an assault charge against Charles, a young black man of medium height and slight build. Regis came to the mediation with his thirteen-year-old son, Jerome; Charles came alone. After the mediator provided an opening statement about the purpose and ground rules of mediation, he asked Regis to explain why he was there. In a loud, agitated voice and rambling style, Regis said he was fed up with what had been dished out to his son. He said that this guy (pointing across the table to Charles) chased and attacked Jerome and Jerome's friends several times over the past few months. The last time he attacked Jerome, Regis said he had enough. He went after this guy and "pinned him to the street." He said he didn't want to punch him out, just let him know that this would not happen again. As Regis said this, he pulled a silver badge out of his shirt pocket, raised his voice, and said threateningly that he was a correctional officer at Rykers Island Penitentiary and that he "wanted this guy locked up."

The mediator intervened at this point and asked Regis how well he knew Charles. Regis said he did not know him at all. All he knew was that this guy didn't live in the neighborhood. He thought he walked through the area on his way to work and that was when he would harass Jerome and his friends. The mediator then asked whether he knew why Charles might have come after his son. Regis said that Jerome was a minor so any reason would be out of the question. If Charles had an issue with Regis's son, he should have brought it to Regis, not attack a thirteen-year-old. The mediator raised a few other questions to clarify what happened since the altercations, then asked whether Regis wanted to say anything else. Regis said he wanted this guy locked up so he would leave his son alone.

The mediator then asked Regis's son to describe how he saw the dispute. Jerome seemed somewhat withdrawn and reluctant to speak. He said that his "father told everything there was to say." He was asked whether he wanted to add anything to his father's statements. He said no.

Then the mediator turned to Charles and asked him to describe how he saw things. Answering with an undefensive, lump-in-the-throat tone, he started by saying, "Maybe I made a mistake, maybe it wasn't right. I'm not even sure it was always him [looking at Jerome]. But he was always in the group. That I do know." He said that all he wanted to do was to be able to walk through the area as he always had to catch the bus on his way to work or to visit his girlfriend, Claudia. The mediator asked whether Claudia lived in the neighborhood. He said she did. He said that nearly every time he walked through the block or approached his friend's house, Jerome and his friends were there "saying words" to him. He used this expression several times, without being more specific. He said he tried to ignore the kids but finally went up to them and said, "Look, I don't know you—I don't even know your names. Why are you bugging me? I'm not starting with any of you. I just want to walk through the neighborhood." Charles then said Regis attacked him and warned him to leave his son alone. Still speaking somewhat pensively, Charles said he did not want to have anything to do with this guy's family and that he would be willing to walk a different way to get to the bus stop or Claudia's.

At this point Regis interrupted Charles. He started to say that Charles could continue to walk through the neighborhood. He didn't have to walk a different way. The mediator interrupted Regis and asked him to write down what he wanted to say and save it until after Charles finished.

Charles repeated that he didn't need to walk close to Jerome's house anymore but he was worried that if "something else came up, something I didn't have anything to do with, I don't want to be blamed for it." The mediator asked for several clarifications about whether any other factors contributed to the incidents with Jerome and his father. Charles indicated that there was nothing else between them—he did not know Jerome or his father at all. Finally, the mediator asked whether Charles wanted to say anything else at this point. He asked specifically whether Charles wanted to say more about the "words" from Jerome and his friends that had bothered him so much. Charles said no. It was obviously a sensitive subject.

After offering a brief summary of both men's accounts, the mediator turned back to Regis and asked him what he had wanted to say while Charles was speaking. Regis looked toward his son and said, somewhat sternly, "I know kids can be cruel. I told Jerome and his friends not to be cruel, not to throw rocks when we all live in glass houses. I told him that little things like that can lead to larger things like this." He then changed the focus of his comments, turned directly toward the mediator, and said, "You know, he [pointing across the table to Charles] has a bad limp. And I told Jerome not to be cruel."

During the silence that followed Regis's revealing comments, the mediator noticed that Charles had an elevated heel on one of the boots he was wearing; clearly, this condition was the subject of the "words" he had referred to. The mediator asked Charles if he knew that Regis had talked to Jerome and his friends about not being cruel. Charles said he didn't know what Regis had said to them. But he was clearly affected by what Regis had just said.

The mediator then focused on what both parties wanted to see happen. Both men offered their sense of what might prevent future problems. There was a discussion of ways in which Charles could get to Claudia's house and catch the bus without walking near Jerome's block. This was followed by a discussion of ways to deal with Jerome's friends and their attitudes and actions toward Charles. Various options were raised and considered. When the parties had focused on certain steps as the ones they felt would resolve the situation, the mediator asked them to help draw up what they wanted to include in a final settlement. In the end, the agreement included (1) a statement that Charles would not attack Jerome and his friends, (2) a statement that Jerome would not name-call and would ask his friends not to name-call, (3) a description of the route Charles would walk through the neighborhood when he caught the bus and visited Claudia, and (4) a commitment that the parties would exchange addresses so that if any issues came up or if Charles was thought to be involved in any incidents with Jerome or his friends, the two men could contact each other directly to discuss the matter.

* * *

The terms the parties agreed to in this case alleviated a serious and potentially volatile dispute between two relative strangers. The agreement addressed Regis's concerns about protecting his son's safety, and it met Charles's need to walk, unharassed, through the neighborhood. In this sense, the case is a classic instance of successful mediation: it produced a settlement that reflected workable solutions to a problem that had escalated severely.

But in another sense, the agreement reached was a very minor part of what this mediation accomplished. In fact, when the parties agreed on a settlement at the end of the session, it was almost an anticlimax. And the subsequent agreement-writing endeavor seemed somewhat contrived. It was as if these men were being asked to demonstrate that the subtle exchange that had just occurred between them could fit into a settlement framework. It felt as if the terms they were being encouraged to articulate—where Charles would and would not walk, what Jerome would not say to Charles and what he would say to his friends—did not greatly matter, because something had taken place that made any specific agreement unnecessary. It seemed clear that Charles would not attack Jerome, even if he walked through Jerome's neighborhood and was taunted about the limp the way he had been in the past. Given this sense, drafting an agreement about Charles's route through the neighborhood appeared almost superfluous, as if fulfilling some preordained ritual of agreement writing rather than documenting what the parties had actually accomplished.

What happened during the session was much more powerful than the terms of the agreement the parties ultimately signed. These two men came to see each other differently, by recognizing that they were alike—that they both wanted and deserved each other's acknowledgment as fellow human beings. In stating that he may have made a mistake in attacking the abusive teens, Charles acknowledged the father's outrage at the threat to his son's well-being. Even Charles's undefensive demeanor suggested that he was in touch with the father's concern about his son. In stating that Jerome and his friends were cruel, Regis acknowledged the emotional pain

CHAPTER III MEDIATION

someone with a severe limp could feel at such ridicule. When Regis revealed that he had told his son "we all live in glass houses," Regis acknowledged that he, too, may have wounds that could easily be opened by careless words or teenage pranks. He acknowledged that he shared, with Charles, in the vulnerabilities of being human.

It was this exchange of acknowledgments that made it very unlikely that Charles would attack, even if insults were hurled in the future. Being in earshot of such ridicule simply didn't matter half as much now that Charles knew, firsthand, that someone understood the pain such insults could inflict. He had something to draw from—a source of strength—that would mute the hurt, even if Regis could not change his son or his son could not change his friends. The connection Charles made with another human being, in this mediation, would help buffer him from thoughtless cruelties.

Both men also found, through their interactions with each other during the mediation session, capacities within themselves to address a problem in ways they may never have learned in the streets of Queens, or in the court in which the original assault charge was filed. They had examined their own feelings, considered the consequences of moving toward or against each other, and relied on their own (sometimes intuitive) insights about human strengths and frailties in deciding what to say to each other and in making commitments to each other. They both knew, at some level, that during the hour and a half session *they* had made choices—about revealing parts of themselves, about acknowledging concerns for each other—that had powerful, reparative effects. They were aware, at some level, that they themselves had made decisions and commitments that redirected an escalation that easily might have ended up in Queens' homicide files. As a result of this experience of their own power to redirect events, they left the session with a greater awareness of their own potential resources—resources they could draw from when confronted with other escalating circumstances. * * *

What the Sensitive Bully case (and others like it) suggests is that an approach to practice is possible that realizes the transformative potential of the mediation process. But taking this approach means turning off a road that the mediation movement has been following for some time. It means seeing that a crossroads lies ahead and that staying on mediation's current course may mean missing a promising route. Our goal is to offer a clear road map of the choices, a map that describes where mediation is and where it might (or might not) head.

The crossroads we see facing the mediation movement is reflected in the difference between two approaches to mediation that are described and contrasted in this book. Each has roots reaching back to the beginnings of the mediation movement; each is connected to a different dimension that has always been seen as one of the potentials of the mediation process. The first approach, a *problem-solving approach*, emphasizes mediation's capacity for finding solutions and generating mutually acceptable settlements. Mediators make moves that influence and direct parties—toward settlements in general, and even toward specific terms of settlement. As the mediation movement has developed, the problem-solving potential of mediation has been emphasized more and more, so that this kind of directive, settlement-oriented mediation has become the dominant form of practice today.

The second approach, a *transformative approach* to mediation, emphasizes mediation's capacity for fostering empowerment and recognition, as illustrated in the most general way by the Sensitive Bully dispute. Transformative mediators concentrate on empowering parties to define issues and decide settlement terms for themselves and on helping parties to better understand one another's perspectives. The effect of this approach is to avoid the directiveness associated with problem-solving mediation. Equally important, transformative mediation helps parties recognize and exploit the opportunities for moral growth inherently presented by conflict. It aims at changing the parties themselves for the better, as human beings. In the course of doing so, it often results in parties finding genuine solutions to their real problems. However, as the movement has grown and developed, the transformative potential of mediation has received less and less emphasis in practice.

NOTES AND QUESTIONS

1. Baruch Bush and Folger maintain that mediation can engender "moral growth" through "empowerment" and "recognition." They define empowerment as "the restoration to individuals of a sense of their own value and strength and their own capacity to handle life's problems" and recognition as "the evocation in individuals of acknowledgment and empathy for the situation and problems of others." How were these values fostered in the case of the sensitive bully?

2. Consider the following example given by Baruch Bush and Folger (supra, at 126–7) of engendering "recognition" in a mediation over a criminal complaint filed by C, a black woman, and W3, a black neighbor, against R, a white man who had discharged a firearm at W3's dog:

[Caucus with R] R said that last year the dog had bitten his daughter through the garden fence. R told W3 that if it happened again "the dog would die." He then related the current incident about the dog. R was returning from dinner at a local restaurant with his family. He raced an older daughter home while carrying a smaller child. When he ran past W3's fence, the dog jumped up, startled him and caused him to drop the baby, which he caught in time. He was very angry, swore at the dog, called it "a black son of a bitch," pointing out that the dog happens to be black all over. Then there was "the discharging of firearms," but at the dog (presumably in the direction of, or to frighten, the dog), not at human beings. R said he was jumpy these days because he had been shot "in three places" in another part of town a year before. The mediators then explored with R the conditions of the dog's confinement and whether it was necessary for him to pass by the yard in which the dog was kept. These issues were not clarified very well. R said he would not fire the gun again. He then explained how the gun (which he spoke about obliquely as if its existence were still in question) had been dismantled, partly buried and partly thrown out with the garbage. He was very sorry about it. His wife does not want any guns in the house ever again.

Comment: R is saying in effect, as he indicated earlier, that he is sorry for what happened, that he felt scared and threatened, and that he did not want to hurt anyone. He is asking to be seen, not as a violent or bad person, but as someone who made a mistake and wants to do the right thing. R's statements here both offer recognition *to* C and ask for recognition *from* C, in indirect fashion. The mediators largely ignore this entire dimension of what R is saying, continuing to focus on the mechanics of separating R and the dog. They miss entirely the possibility presented here for encouraging greater recognition among the parties after the caucus with R.

Alternative: The mediators could emphasize the possible grounds for developing recognition that were implicit in R's comments. One approach would be to say, "You seem to be saying that you are really sorry about what happened, that you felt somewhat worried or threatened yourself in the situation and maybe got carried away, but that you certainly didn't and don't want anyone hurt. Is that close to what you're saying? If so, then let me say that I don't know if C and W3 really understand that so clearly. Would you be willing to say that to them again, in so many words, or maybe let me try to convey that to them? If it's put to them in the right way, I think they might understand, and it might help work things out. There doesn't seem to be much to lose by trying it. Is this something you would be comfortable with?" Even this much serves to help R express recognition for C's situation, as in the earlier move in connection with the apology. Beyond this, it opens up the possibility of working with C and W3, translating these comments of R to evoke recognition of R from them.

3. How does the transformative approach endorsed by Baruch Bush and Folger differ from the kind of "control of the process" methods described by Silby & Merry and Haynes? Is it less manipulative? Is it less intrusive? Is it a more moral position?

4. Why do Baruch Bush and Folger find the problem-solving approach inadequate? Is the transformative approach any less directive?

5. Is the transformative approach suitable for most mediations? Can mediation expect to change parties' attitudes? Should it?

6. Consider the following comments in a review of the Bush & Folger book by Carrie Menkel–Meadow, The Many Ways of Mediation: The Transformation of Traditions, Ideologies, Paradigms, and Practices, 11 Negotiation J. 217, 235–38 (1995):

Bush and Folger want to rachet up our expectations and practice of transformative mediation, as long as we "transform" in their image.

In what has to be one of the most astonishing statements ever made about human beings (at least most psychologists would probably think so), Bush and Folger promote transformative mediation because, they suggest, people are easier to change than situations. In a critique of more conventional mediation, Bush and Folger suggest that too much mediation is focused on "problem solving" or as they label it, the "Satisfaction Story." The goal, they write, is "for satisfying the genuine human needs of the parties to individual disputes," through more directive and manipulative action by mediators to reach agreements and settlements between the parties to concrete problems. * * *

Bush and Folger argue that mediation is uniquely adapted to engage individuals in moral growth and change, and that human growth is, after all, more important than material wealth. They posit that solving problems will not change the world so only by changing people (to focus more on their moral potential than their appetites) will we achieve a "better world."

Bush and Folger's book, though an interesting effort, exposes the difficulties of articulating what "transformative mediation" should be. What goals should any process serve? From what to what are we seeking to transform people? Who are the "we's" that preside over this transformation? Though I support the basic precepts of building party competence (empowerment) and mutual understanding across difference (recognition and empathy), Bush and Folger's descriptions of these processes reveal that their model is no less manipulative or content-based than the problem-solving model they critique. Their claim for "process neutrality" seems potentially more dangerous for the almost New Age-human potential movement-religious fervor which seems to inspire it. If conflict is the matériel of mediation, why should process always trump outcome? Why is individual growth process privileged over other processes? In mediation, isn't relationship process as important as individual process? And also, can't relationships of people *to* their conflict be changed in mediation, without necessarily changing the relationship between the people (e.g., in divorce mediation)?

* * *

At the same time that Bush and Folger are vague about standards for measuring their own model of mediation, they are remarkably judgmental and conclusionary about what they say about other models of mediation. They argue that problem-solving mediation inevitably leads to over-directive practices by mediators, but the empirical support for this claim is very weak and supported by mostly anecdotal observations and selected stories. How does this jibe with the stories told by Community Boards critics that, in fact, too much time is spent on expressing feelings (empowerment and recognition) and not enough on settling cases or solving community and group problems? That Bush and Folger should critique mediators for globalizing and narrowly diagnosing problems seems highly ironic, given their own globalizing and conclusionary statements about mediation practice with little empirical rigor. They suggest, somewhat naively, that problem-solving mediators have an "interest" in conflict resolution and mediation and then seem to ignore the fact that their own transformative mediators will also have agendas and interests that may not be the parties' own.

Why have Bush and Folger shifted the focus entirely away from the group or community to the individual? In conflict resolution, isn't the relationship often the key unit of analysis, standing between the individual and group process? [T]he authors provide a useful catalogue of how empowerment and recognition can be articulated. They assert, however, that empowerment "is independent of any particular outcome of the mediation". How anyone could feel empowered if they did not get at least some of what they needed or expected from a mediation seems a bit much to ask. Similarly, if recognition is the achievement of understanding of the other, one wonders whether there are never limits on mediation: Should we have tried to understand Hitler?

In their attempt to distinguish transformative mediation from directive problem solving, the authors exhort mediators not to frame issues and prematurely diagnose problems. But at the same time, they encourage mediators to facilitate perspective taking by "reframing, reinterpreting and translating ... to make the parties more intelligible to each other". Thus, seemingly without realizing it, the authors have created a model which simply relocates the directiveness of mediators; instead of solving the problem, they will orchestrate the communication.

* * *

I propose a reconciliation here by suggesting that "transformative mediation" is possible (and indeed desirable)—but only if we define our terms more clearly, state our goals more modestly and inclusively, and remain sensitive to the social and political situations and institutions in which we do our work. Mediation does, after all, occur in a material world, with parties who seek particular ends and mediators who must make a living, as well as live out their theoretical and political fantasies. Transformative mediation can occur anywhere, but is it less likely in particular settings, just as some medical delivery systems may limit the provision of medical care?

In short, transformative mediation, like all processes, must be contextualized. No process can do all things, or any one thing for all people. * * * For me, mediation is transformative because it is educational. At its best, we learn about other people, other ways to conceptualize problems, ways to turn crises into opportunities, creative new ways to resolve complex issues and interact with each other. And we learn about ourselves and, perhaps, new ways to negotiate our next problem. But mediation has not solved racial and class inequalities in the world (neither has anything else so far), nor the violence in Bosnia, nor the food shortage in Somalia, nor the drug trafficking in Colombia and on the streets of our inner cities. Mediation cannot transform all people—neither can intensive therapy. So we must consider what we can realistically do.

Does the Bush & Folger "transformative" approach really shift the focus away from the community to the individual? Are there genuine differences between the use to which they and Menkel–Meadow would put a transformative perspective?

D. THE ROLE OF THE PARTY'S ATTORNEY

The role of attorneys in mediation is to advise the client about the availability of ADR, to provide pre-mediation advice necessary for participation in the mediation, to participate in the process in good faith to the extent that it calls for attorney participation, and to protect the party's legal interests in connection with any agreement reached.

1. DUTY TO ADVISE CLIENTS ABOUT ADR

Lawyers today clearly fail to meet their professional obligations if they do not advise their clients as to the availability of ADR procedures. A number of states, through court rule or standards of professional responsibility, require attorneys to discuss the availability of ADR with their clients and consider its use.[1] The advice should take place at the earliest appropriate stage and all stages thereafter at which ADR might be a reasonable alternative to litigation. That would include the time of drafting a contract about which there could be some dispute in the future, when any dispute arises, when litigation is being considered, and throughout the litigation process.

a. ADVICE IN ADVANCE PLANNING SITUATIONS

A lawyer should advise a client of the availability of ADR mechanisms when drafting contracts that might contain such clauses.[2] A lawyer who advises commercial clients, corporations and other business entities, or clients with on-going business or institutional operations, should inform them of the growing range of "systems designs" available for institutionalizing ADR into everyday operations. This involves training of personnel to be aware of ADR options in dealing with disputes from the lowest level upwards and utilizing ADR at various phases of the development of a dispute.[3]

---

1. See Schmitz, Giving Meaning to the Second Generation of ADR Education, 1999 J. Disp. Resol. 29; Rogers & McEwen, Employing the Law to Increase the Use of Mediation and to Encourage Direct and Early Negotiations, 133 Ohio St. J. on Disp. Resol. 831 (1998); Moberly, Ethical Standards for Court–Appointed Mediators and Florida's Mandatory Mediation Experiment, 21 Fla.St. U.L.Rev. 701, 723–26 (1994).

2. See Freund & Millhauser, ADR—A Conversation, Nat.Law J. (Feb. 27, 1989) (containing model contractual clauses).

3. See Millhauser, The Next Step in Alternative Dispute Resolution: Building an Effective Dispute Handling System Within

CHAPTER III MEDIATION

b. ADVISING A CLIENT CONTEMPLATING LITIGATION

The availability of ADR should be discussed with the client at the earliest stage of contemplated litigation. There is, however, no certain time for invoking ADR. It may be useful early on, but it may also be beneficially invoked at various stages of litigation right up to trial itself.

An attorney, acting in the interests of her client, can and should seek to influence the decision as to the type of ADR selected. Obviously, if an express form of ADR has already been mandated by contract—as when there is a clause requiring binding arbitration or mini-trial—that form must be followed, although, even then, both parties could choose to supersede it or modify it with voluntary resort first to another process (such as mediation). Where there is no advance selection of processes, an attorney may be able to petition the court to mandate a particular ADR process. In such cases the attorney should be prepared to provide valid, neutral reasons that the preferred process is most likely to result in settlement.

Attorneys may also be able to influence the opposing attorney's willingness to select a particular process. An open and fair approach that seeks the best process that is likely to result in settlement is most likely to succeed with an opponent. It should be remembered that a process will only be beneficial if the opponent also finds it fair and is willing, for example, to participate in good faith in a mediation or to accept an advisory opinion or case evaluation in a reality-testing process. To overcome an opponent's mind set about ADR can be a genuine test of an attorney's negotiation skills.

Part of the role of advising and influencing the selection of an ADR process is to consider what parties or representatives of parties are crucial to a settlement and therefore should be involved in a mediation or ADR proceeding. If the client is a corporation or business entity, the attorney should study the organization structure, as it operates both in theory and in practice, to determine whom she should bring to the mediation.[4] Likewise, she should encourage the opponent to bring those persons most likely to be able to accomplish a settlement.[5]

An essential part of advising the client concerning the availability of ADR is the consideration of the cost-benefits of ADR versus litigation. An attorney may want to itemize the likely expenses of the litigation route to give the client a full picture of the risks of not settling. The relatively small costs of ADR—quite minimal if a court-annexed method is used, still small if mediation is used, and more expensive but still cheap by comparison if a

the Corporation, Corporate Counsel's Q. (Oct. 1989); Millhauser, "Integrating ADR Into Law Firm Practice," in Containing Legal Costs—ADR Strategies for Corporations, Law Firms, and Government (CPR Legal Program 1988).

4. See discussion of "Obligation to Attend" in relation to settlement conferences, Chap. II, section E, 3, supra, which is also relevant to mediation.

5. See discussion of "Scope of Settlement Authority" in relation to settlement conferences, Chap. II, section E,3, supra, which is also relevant to mediation.

formal reality-testing method like mini-trial is used—should be brought home to the client. Attorneys sometimes fail to appreciate that the preparation that goes into ADR is often not wasted even if ADR does not succeed since it involves a comprehensive review of the evidence and legal issues and a realistic case evaluation. Where relevant, the attorney should also discuss possible relational benefits from ADR. If the parties have a relationship that could be preserved, as among parties to a business contract, the possibility of mending that relationship should be discussed. Finally, the flexibility of ADR in fashioning a settlement that could address each side's interests should be mentioned to the client.

c. CONSIDERATIONS FAVORING USE OF MEDIATION

Considerable study has been devoted to analyzing the factors that favor the use of particular ADR devices, which has been referred to as "fitting the forum to the fuss."[6] It is said that when disputed issues of law are central to a dispute, an "evaluative" or "trial run" process may be more useful. When on-going relationships are involved, mediation is particularly suitable both to probe the real issues in dispute and to seek a resolution that might preserve the relationship. When there are questions of credibility of the parties, mediation can sometimes go to the heart of the problem and assist the parties to work through and possibly resolve their different perceptions of the truth. Finally, if there are strong equities on one side, mediation provides a process for allowing that side to confront the other side with fairness issues and to promote an equitable solution.

2. PRE-MEDIATION ADVICE AND PREPARATION

Attorneys should carefully prepare the party for mediation, as they would for a deposition or trial appearance. It is critical that the party understand in advance the nature of the process, what will go on, what is expected of him, and the strategic concerns of his lawyer. Such preparation, however, should not rob the mediation process of spontaneity. A mediation cannot be written as a scenario in advance with the party and attorney simply stating memorized lines. In many forms of mediation, the process depends for its chance of success upon spontaneity and give-and-take among the parties and attorneys. One objective of the process is to come to a better understanding of one's own position and the strengths and weaknesses of both sides through frank and open interchange.

Pre-mediation advice to the party should include full information as to important legal aspects of the case. That does not mean that the party will necessarily address them in the mediation. The party and attorney may decide that the attorney will play the primary role as to such legal discussions. But the party should be aware of the issues and how they relate to his case and to the strategic concerns affecting his case.

---

6. See Sander & Goldberg, Fitting the Forum to the Fuss: A User–Friendly Guide to Selecting an ADR Procedure, 10 Negotiation J. 49 (1994), a selection of which is in Chap. IV, B, 2, supra.

The party should also be instructed as to what is protected in the mediation by confidentiality and what is not.[7] If there are matters that the attorney feels must not be disclosed, she should so inform the party. However, a conscious decision in advance of a mediation that certain matters will not be disclosed should normally be eschewed. Participation in good faith in a mediation requires a degree of mutual trust and openness. Certainly giving misleading answers to questions by a mediator or other party in order to preserve confidentiality should be avoided. If there are areas in which the attorney feels confidentiality must be maintained, the party or attorney should normally be straightforward in stating, if asked, that they will not go into such matters.

The attorney should discuss options and possible solutions with the party before the mediation. The party should be aware of possible fall-back positions and concessions. Again, however, this does not mean that a perfect scenario can or should be sketched out for the mediation. Options and solutions may arise which the attorney and party had not thought of. To the extent the attorney is able to do so, she should prepare the party to be receptive to the notion that their purpose in the mediation is not necessarily to "win," but rather to resolve the dispute in a satisfactory way, and that satisfaction may involve a variety of objectives including mending relationships and bringing closure to the hurt feelings and disruption of lives caused by on-going litigation.

The attorney should run through the mediation process, explaining the aspirations for the parties jointly resolving the dispute, the role of the mediator, the lack of the attorney's control of the process, the ground rules including such matters as not interrupting, the respective roles of the attorney and party as they have agreed upon it, and procedural devices such as the caucus. She should also discuss the obligation to participate in good faith and its importance to taking full advantage of the opportunity which the mediation offers in getting the dispute settled.

Advising the client about how to act in the mediation is of great importance. Most clients will not have participated in a mediation and, because it is an informal proceeding may be misled into believing that there is no need for rehearsing their role. In fact, a client may be more at risk in a mediation than in a trial because the rules of evidence do not apply and the attorney is less able to object to leading questions, irrelevant tangents, or overbearing or seductive conduct by the opposing party or its attorney. Consider the following advice for prepping the client:

John W. Cooley, Mediation Advocacy

91–95.
1996 (National Institute for Trial Advocacy).

The client should face the mediator when, speaking

It is important for you to advise your client to face the mediator when speaking. If your client talks across the table to the opposing party and

---

7. See discussion of confidentiality at section E.

opposing counsel, it is quite possible that either or both of them will interpret what your client is saying as accusatory or demeaning. This may arouse anger in one of them and perhaps cause an outburst and an interruption of your client's story. The opponent's outburst, in turn, may cause your client to react emotionally and perhaps say something in front of the mediator that is embarrassing or even harmful to your case.

Apart from avoiding these unpleasant happenings, having your client face the mediator when speaking has other benefits. Your client's eye contact with the mediator will help to make his message more persuasive to the mediator. Persuading the mediator is important because, even though mediators are duty-bound to remain neutral and impartial regarding the parties and the subject matter of the dispute, they are human beings whose perceptions and actions can have a great impact on the quality of the ultimate settlement. They are constantly vigilant for clues to finding the true heart of the conflict, the relative credibility and/or memory acuity of the parties, and their essential needs and interests. By maintaining eye contact with the mediator, your client can begin to build trust and rapport with the mediator and convey forthrightness of purpose, desire, and motivation to achieve a joint goal. This kind of bonding with the mediator has the effect of building a type of teamwork atmosphere that can spill over into caucuses and, through the mediator's shuttle pollination, positively reinforce the problem-solving efforts of both sides. Making sure your client faces the mediator also carries with it the added benefit of having the opposing party and counsel actually listen to what your client is saying without feeling threatened. Equally as important, it gives *you* the opportunity to observe the body language of the opposing party and counsel while your client is speaking. An opponent's frown or a smirk made while your client is giving a factual presentation may communicate the opponent's denial or assent to your client's version of the events giving rise to the dispute.

The client should speak to be understood

When preparing a client for mediation, allow him to rehearse the factual presentation in your presence. Listen very carefully while your client gives this practice presentation. Is it organized? Does it begin at the beginning and touch on all necessary points? Is it a fair, honest statement of what occurred? Does the client use terminology that can be understood by both the mediator and the opponents? This last question is a very important one. Clients with industrial, medical, or technical expertise may use words or expressions that are common to their everyday experience, but that are like a foreign language to others present at the mediation session. In the rehearsal session with your client, listen for such words, and when you hear one, stop your client and have him define it in simple terms. Impress on your client the importance of using words that everyone understands at the mediation conference. Point out to him that big words not only can communicate arrogance and insensitivity, but also can be boring, distracting, and misleading and in the worst case scenario, can precipitate very unpleasant results. When Benjamin Franklin was quite young, he once said to his mother, "I have ingested an acephalous mollus-cous." Fearful that the young Benjamin had swallowed something poison-ous, his mother forced him to take a large dose of castor oil. The next day, the effects of the medicine having subsided, Ben confided to his mother that he "had eaten nothing but an oyster." While recuperating from the resultant vigorous spanking, young Ben vowed never again to use big words when little words would do.

The client should state only facts

In the presentation rehearsal and at the mediation conference itself, your client should state only facts. He should be careful not to confuse facts with exaggeration and hyperbole. If your client finds it necessary to offer speculation or hearsay regarding a part of his story, he should label it as such when speaking to ensure that no one will be misled. Making these distinctions between fact and conjecture can have a very positive influence on listeners. It communicates that the speaker is making a determined effort to be fair and objective in his recollection of events. It also conveys an openness to have his recollection refreshed by the opponent, thereby imparting to the listeners an attitude of flexibility and an inclination to cooperativeness.

Conversely, a speaker's overstatement, embellishment, or stretching of the truth usually inspires listeners to be apprehensive and cautious about accepting all of the speaker's message. If the speaker misrepresents an important fact—even innocently—a listener may lose complete confidence in the speaker's ability to be truthful, may refuse to communicate with the speaker, or may become vindictive.

The client should never argue

Retraining from arguing is a cardinal rule everyone should observe at the mediation. "Arguing" carries at least two connotations. The first type of "arguing" makes a point persuasively with the purpose of convincing a listener to the speaker's point of view. That type of arguing is certainly well within the scope of permissible mediation behavior. What is taboo is "arguing" of the second type—making an argument, anger-based, that is combative and offensive and does nothing but distract listeners from the task at and. Most such arguments consist of isolated or periodic episodes of seemingly endless blustering and pointless discourse, resulting in a total waste of everyone's time. Admittedly, arguments of the first type and arguments of the second sometimes produce very similar effects. Consider the story of a young lawyer who had been talking for about four hours in court to twelve jurors, who, when he had finished, felt like lynching him. After the young lawyer took his seat at counsel table, his opponent, a crusty old professional, rose slowly to his feet. After glancing quickly toward the jury, then down at his watch, he looked pleasantly at the judge and said, "Your Honor, I will follow the example of my friend who has just finished and submit the case without argument."

The client should display no reaction to settlement offers

Because no one really knows what the true settlement value of a case is before the settlement agreement is actually reached, you should counsel your client not to display any reaction to any settlement offer—either verbally or nonverbally. If your client is the plaintiff, and the defendant's offer is much higher than anticipated, your client's reaction of shock and elation or statements of "sounds great!" or "hot dog!" may preclude you from later convincing your opponent that your client wants (or needs) more to settle the case. If your opponent makes what she thinks is a reasonable offer to settle, and your client scoffs at it and verbally berates the opposing party, your client's reaction might anger the other side sufficiently to cause them to withdraw from the mediation. If your client is a defendant, impulsive reactions could do similar damage to the potential for successful negotiations. It should be emphasized that verbal reactions are not the only type of prohibited reactions to settlement offers. As pointed out in subsection 4.4.1, facial expressions can communicate what people are thinking. In the proper context, they can be a strong asset. In the wrong context, they can be a devastating liability. Counsel your client to display no body reactions—even facial reactions—to settlement offers.

The client should behave as if before a jury

Advise your client that, although he will not be under oath during a mediation session, he should speak narratively and answer questions as if under oath. Your client should make every effort to give the appearance to the mediator and opposing party and counsel alike that he is trustworthy and honest. The best advice to your client is "be yourself—don't try to be the person you think the mediator, or anyone else, wants or expects you to be." Tell your client to tell his story to the mediator "straightforwardly and sincerely," and if appropriate, "empathically." If your client tries to pretend to be someone he is not, the masquerade will undoubtedly fail, and it will probably adversely affect the success of the negotiations. No one easily tolerates a phony. That statement is as true with respect to mediations as it is with trials, and its truth was aptly demonstrated in an incident that occurred in a Kansas court some years back. A tall, awkward, somewhat timid fellow was called to testify as a witness for the defendant in a civil case. Defense counsel said to him, "Now sir, take the stand and tell your story like a preacher." "No sir!" roared the judge. "I want you to tell the truth!"

The client should neither answer nor ask difficult questions

At times during the course of the mediation, the opposing counsel or the mediator may direct difficult questions to your client. Difficult questions might be defined as those that require some knowledge of the law to answer, seek information beyond the specific expertise of a client, or require a client to make or imply an admission against interest without having available the necessary information to give a full explanation. During the premediation preparation, advise your client that when such questions are posed during the mediation session, your client should defer to you for an answer. You should also have an understanding with your client before you go to the mediation session that when someone asks your client a question during the course of the mediation, your client will pause slightly before answering to permit you to interject, if you think it necessary, to answer the question or to provide a reason why it cannot be answered at that particular time.

By the same token, you should caution your client not to ask the other side or the mediator difficult questions during the course of the mediation. Actually, better advice would be for your client not to ask the mediator or the other side any questions without first clearing the questions with you privately. After you screen the question, you may decide that it is appropriate to ask, and you may determine that your client is the appropriate one to ask it. Or, you may conclude that it would be better if you asked the question. Inappropriate questions posed by a client can sometimes have the effect of undermining a negotiating strategy, exposing a negotiation tactic, revealing the client's gullibility, threatening the other side, disclosing clues to your bottom line, or demonstrating the client's lack of knowledge, skill, ability, or competence. As to the last effect, consider this historical example. Mozart was once asked by a lad how to write a symphony. "You're a very young man," Mozart replied and then asked, "Why not begin with ballads?" "But you composed symphonies when you were ten years old," the youth urged. "Yes," said Mozart, "but I didn't ask 'how'."

3. Representing the Client in Mediation

The role played by an attorney in representing her client in mediation may vary depending on the type of case, the nature of the client, and the style of the mediator. The following are examples of the differing kinds of participation that an attorney may perform:

a. DEGREE OF PARTICIPATION

(1) Attorney as Non–Participant

The classical model of mediation once envisioned the parties mediating without attorneys being present. This model was particularly favored by family-law mediators who often viewed attorneys as hindrances to resolving the dispute out of court. Today that attitude has changed a good deal (in part because attorneys have become more sensitive to how mediation works), but there may still be valid reasons in a particular case for the attorney not to directly participate in a mediation.

In such a situation, the attorney must protect the party's interests by insuring that the party has adequate legal advice both in advance in order properly to participate in the mediation and after the mediation in connection with any settlement. The attorney's legal advice, however, may be counterproductive if it prevents the party from engaging in the mediation in good faith and unduly restricts the options available. The attorney must walk a thin line between adequately advising the party about legal aspects and so preconditioning the party that creative and useful approaches to settlement are impossible.

In family mediations where attorneys may not play a central role in the mediation discussions or, may not even be present at all stages, they still provide a critical source of information and advice as to legal matters as well as strategy. Consider Judy K. Dougherty & Josefina M. Rendon, Models, Styles and the Process of Family Mediation, Alternative Resolutions 22, 25 (June 2001):

> During the actual mediation, the lawyer may help with evaluations, clarification of issues, legal questions, development of options, consideration of the range of possible judicial rulings for particular issues and development of tradeoffs. The attorney is in direct contact with the client during this stage. Often, in mediations where the attorneys are not present, memos of each session are prepared by the mediator so that the particular legal questions are clear and so the attorneys can point out problem areas before a final agreement is solidified and owned' by the parties.

(2) Attorney as Silent Advisor

There are also mediation models in which attorneys sit through the mediation with their client but do not take an active role. Some dispute resolution centers encourage attorneys not to sit at the table with the parties, but rather on the periphery where they can still intervene or give advice if necessary. Arguably under these circumstances the attorney has a better chance to judge how and when to provide legal advice without risking undermining the creativity of the process. Normally attorneys should resist the temptation to interject themselves into the mediation, and such intervention should only take place if necessary to protect the client's rights and interests (the "I'm not a potted plant" situation).

(3) Attorney as Co–Participant

If the attorney attends the mediation, she may sit at the table with her client and be a co-participant in the discussion. They may both participate in all phases of the negotiation, or they may decide among themselves on more specialized roles. Obviously the attorney is more likely to address the legal issues while the party may focus more on the factual and emotional issues. The attorney will be in a position to consult privately with the party at the table, although this can detract from the spontaneity of the discussion and generate defensiveness on the other side. Considerable advance thought should be given to how the respective roles will be conducted.

(4) Attorney as Dominant or Sole Participant

Finally, there are mediation models in which the attorney is the dominant or sole participant. The attorney may either not be accompanied by the client at all (as in some court-ordered settlement conferences) or may come with the client who, however, does not take an active role in the mediation (as in some settlement-week mediations). Such mediations are necessarily more focused on legal issues and the application of law to fact.

In such mediations, however, the attorneys should give consideration to how the human side of their client and the client's position can best be conveyed, including having the client speak to certain matters.

Consider the following account of the role of attorneys in divorce mediation in Maine:

Craig McEwen & Nancy Rogers, Bring the Lawyers Into Divorce Mediation

Disp.Resol.Mag. 8–10 (1994).

Since 1984, Maine has mandated mediation in contested divorce cases involving minor children. Mediation is not confined to questions of custody and visitation, but may include financial matters as well. Maine lawyers have counseled thousands of clients going through this mandatory process. The results of interviews with 88 Maine divorce lawyers lead us to believe that mandatory mediation can be fair if it includes all divorce-related issues, and if lawyers are encouraged to participate with their clients. The interviews also reveal that the assumptions leading mediation proponents and critics to ignore our approach are in fact myths.

The *first myth* that critics and advocates of mandatory mediation share is that lawyers disappear when mediation begins. For advocates the disappearance of lawyers is often a goal because presumably it diminishes adversary conduct, empowers parties, and reduces costs. For critics it is a central problem because lawyers are seen as guardians of client rights, and their absence disadvantages weaker parties especially.

In Maine, however, divorce lawyers do not vanish when mediation starts. Indeed, 95 percent of those attorneys interviewed reported that they always or usually attend mediation sessions with their clients. Not only do lawyers attend, but they participate actively, though selectively, on behalf of their clients. Their presence and participation are premised on concerns about fairness because they recognize, as one lawyer said, that "mediation is like a crucible and bad decisions can be made." That is, even the best and most balanced mediation can create a momentum toward settlement that may lead parties to disregard their interests. But lawyers are also concerned about unfairness resulting from pressures from the other party and from the mediator. One lawyer reflected a common view among those interviewed: "I'm there to protect [my client] if I think things are not being run fairly and to watch out for his or her interests, but primarily it's up to him or her, the mediator, and the other spouse." Lawyers also recognize that some clients may need support in articulating their interests and concerns if fair results are to be achieved. As one lawyer said, "It depends on the client, but I'll tell them, 'If you want to talk, feel free to talk. The mediator would rather have you talk, but if you prefer me to talk, that's fine.'"

Thus, unlike the common picture of a lawyerless process, Maine divorce mediation involves lawyers actively, and they participate with an eye toward fairness.

A *second myth* about divorce mediation is that lawyer participation would spoil the mediation process for parties by permitting attorneys to take over the process. Further, it is supposed, lawyers will argue the law and pursue aggressive adversarial tactics in mediation, ruining efforts at settlement. This view is shared by many advocates of mediation and has produced statutes or court rules in five states prohibiting lawyer participation in custody mediation altogether or limiting the attorney role to observer. Opponents of mandatory mediation, on the other hand, assume that lawyers, by providing the vigorous advocacy necessary to assert and protect client rights, would thwart a mediation process that "steamrolls" the parties.

The view of lawyers as habitual spoilers proves erroneous in Maine. That state reports settlement rates of about 50 percent in its fairly short, single-session mediations, a figure comparable to those in many other divorce mediation programs where lawyers do not participate. Settlements even with lawyers present seem to happen because the mediator's demeanor and the mediation setting encourage lawyers to behave in accord with the professional norm of the "reasonable lawyer," who discourages unrealistic client expectations, refrains from identifying with the client emotionally, resists inflating demands, understands the likely legal outcome, and engages straightforwardly in the settlement process. In fact, lawyers sometimes report that the usual structure of mediation sessions discourages antagonistic conduct by lawyers: "It's easy to be Tarzan over the telephone, it really is. It's real hard to pull that garbage when the client [is right there]."

Even with their lawyers present, clients participate because that is the expectation of the mediator. Thus, one lawyer's description of her relationship to her client in mediation was typical of Maine lawyers: "I want to sit back and listen, and I'm not going to interrupt unless I feel that you've misstated something or you're misinformed on an area or need some counseling."

This client involvement allows parties to voice their feelings and to identify and deal with intensely important emotional issues that may block settlement. Said one lawyer: "I'm much more inclined to let the client talk in the mediation room.... [I]t's one of the few times [the parties] have the opportunity to be face-to-face, and they need to get some stuff off their chest, and it can be done in that setting safely and usefully." The chance for parties to talk is prized and encouraged by most lawyers. "This is the only opportunity I have," said another lawyer, "to have [the other spouse] sitting there listening to my client's point of view. He's probably never done it before in his life. Now he's got someone who's describing what her life is going to be like, going through her budget."

Parties in Maine engage actively in most mediation sessions, express their feelings, and participate in settlement discussions. Their chances of achieving a fair result are increased both by the support of legal counsel and by their opportunity to take a leading role in crafting a divorce settlement for themselves.

Most attorneys agree that representing a client in a mediation is quite different from a trial and that the kind of adversary tactics that may be used before a jury may not serve the interests of persuading the other side to settle. However, although the style may be less adversary, a great deal of strategy is at work. Consider the following thoughts from attorneys about tactics at various phases of a mediation.

b. ATTORNEY'S OPENING STATEMENT

David M. Stern, Mediation: An Old Dog with Some New Tricks

24 Litigation 31, 35 (Summer 1998).

Trial lawyers are familiar with opening statements and their importance. Knowing how to give one is invaluable. There is, however, a crucial difference between an opening statement in a mediation and one at trial. At trial, the neutrals—judge and jury—are your primary audience. At a mediation, your audience is primarily the client on the other side of the table. By force of habit, you will be inclined to address the mediator. Stifle the urge. Your true audience consists of the hostile sea of faces on the other side of the table, and more so the unfamiliar client faces than your more familiar fellow lawyer. You need not ignore the mediator, but you must remember that he is merely a facilitator, not a decision-maker. Winning him over is good, often helpful. It *is* important that he understand your position so that he can forcefully convey it to your adversary in private session. But remember, your opponent is infinitely more important than the mediator. The mediator can persuade, but the opponent can write—or accept—a check. As such, it is to your opponent that you must address your case. He is your most important audience, the person who can now hear—without benefit of the filtering his own lawyer will provide—just why his case is in trouble and why it is in his interest to settle, Mediation is unique in this respect. At trial, a client may absorb this fact a? he watches the judge or jury turn against him. At mediation, the client is effectively the judge and jury, and it is incumbent upon you to make him feel the heat.

There is disagreement among commentators about how tough an opening statement can or should be. Some commentators feel that an excessively aggressive opening can destroy the goodwill that the simple act of agreeing to mediate has created, making negotiation more difficult and agreement less possible. This author respectfully dissents. While it is never appropriate, in any setting, to be vicious, mean or disrespectful to anyone, particularly someone you wish to persuade, that does not mean that you cannot be tough and aggressive in presenting your case. It is unlikely that your opponent has gotten a raw, uncensored view of how strong your case is, and how passionate your client is about fighting. This is your opportunity to convey that fact to the other side. Do so with logic and reason. Make it clear that you are a tough advocate, and a very articulate one at that. Assemble the facts and the law in the best possible way so that, at the end of your presentation, the key decisionmaker on the other side feels, somewhere in the pit of his stomach, that you might just beat him in court.

If you feel a need to be more moderate, let your client do it. After a 10– or 15–minute opening, when you sit down and thank those who have listened to you, your client can "spontaneously" say something like:

> As you can tell, we feel very strongly about the case. But, I want to make it clear. art behalf of my company, that we are here not to perpetuate this litigation, but to settle it. If we must fight, we will, and we do believe we will succeed. However, we also think, and I know that my esteemed colleague (opponent) Ms. X believes, that reaching a negotiated settlement is best for all concerned.

If this sounds like the old game of "good cop, bad cop," it is.

Eric Galton, Mediation of Medical Negligence Claims

28 Capital University Law Rev. 321 (2000).

[A] lawyer for a party is traditionally given an opportunity to make an opening presentation at mediation. The opening presentation by counsel is not and should not be a jury argument. An ill-conceived or intemperate opening presentation by a lawyer may doom a mediation.

Consider a story an excellent plaintiff's lawyer told me. The lawyer's best friend was a physician who had been sued. The physician confided in his friend that a mistake had been made and that the matter was scheduled for mediation. The physician not only consented to settlement, but very much believed the family was entitled to compensation. His best friend advised the physician that mediation was an excellent way to resolve the dispute.

At the mediation, the family's attorney made a hostile, threatening opening presentation and concluded by suggesting the physician had "murdered" the deceased. The physician, who would have otherwise settled the dispute, was so offended that he declared the mediation to be over and left. Unfortunately, the case was tried and resulted in a verdict adverse to the physician.

A defense lawyer, in a case I mediated, made a similar mistake, which we were fortunately able after runny hours to overcome. The defense lawyer, during his opening presentation, accused a mother of such terrible prenatal care that it was like "putting a bullet to your unborn child's head." While the mother's prenatal care was in fact far from perfect, the mother reacted so poorly to the defense lawyer's remark that she almost refused to continue with the mediation.

My point is that the lawyer's role at mediation, especially during the opening presentation, is very different than the lawyer's role at trial. An attack on a physician's competency usually dooms the mediation to failure. Personal attacks on the motivations or behavior of the claimants have a similar effect.

Compare and contrast such approaches with a remarkable and effective approach by a plaintiff's lawyer in the failure to diagnose a cancer case. The plaintiff's lawyer advised the physician that the physician deservedly enjoyed a reputation of the highest competency. The lawyer went on to tell the physician about his best childhood friend who went on to enjoy a stellar career as a Golden Glove second baseman in the major leagues. The lawyer described a play in the deciding sixth game of the World Series in which his friend inexplicably let a ball go through his legs and allowed the winning run. The lawyer described his friend's grief and sadness over the misplay and advised the physician that this was how be saw this case; i.e., an otherwise stellar physician made a human mistake, just as his best friend had done. The physician, who had not consented to settle the dispute prior to the mediation, agreed to settle during the first private caucus and attributed his willingness to do so to the respectful tone and grace of the plaintiff's lawyer during his opening presentation.

The role of the lawyer at mediation is to be aware and empathetic of the feelings of all participants involved in the dispute. When mistakes are made in medical procedures, all participants experience grief and pain. Losing a loved one is extremely painful. A physician whose human error results in the death or injury of a patient carries a great burden as well.

c. USE OF THE CAUCUS

The caucus is one of the most critical elements of many mediations, and an attorney needs to have given careful thought to how she will conduct herself and advise her client to act in the caucus. In considering the following, you may want to recall how the caucus is used from the mediator's point of view (see III, B, 1, c):

John W. Cooley, Mediation Advocacy

116–123 (National Institute for Trial Advocacy 1996).

How to use the mediator and the caucusing
process for the best results

The caucus is an important instrument that the mediator uses to achieve settlements. The main virtue of the caucus is that it eliminates one of the principal barriers to dispute settlement—direct confrontation between the parties. By following the guidelines suggested below, you can, from behind the scenes, use the mediator's negotiating prowess and the nonconfrontational benefits of the caucusing process to orchestrate optimal settlement results for your client. But make sure that you alert your client to what you are doing so that he does not inadvertently spoil the symphony. Once when Leopold Stokowski was conducting the Philadelphia Orchestra in the Leonore Overture no.3, a famous offstage trumpet call twice failed to sound on cue. When the performance concluded, Stokowski rushed into the wings, ready to give the delinquent trumpet player a tongue-lashing. To his surprise, he found the tuxedoed musician struggling in the arms of a burly security officer. "I tell you, you can't blow that darn thing in here," the officer was saying, "there's a concert going on!" The moral of this story is, first and foremost, let your client know what is going on at all times during the course of the mediation.

- **Take charge of the initial caucus.**

From the beginning of the very first caucus, let the mediator know that the mediator and you are on the same team. You both have the goal of settling the case. Be collaborative. The mediator is your teammate and messenger. Whether representing a plaintiff or defendant, you should begin by giving an honest summary of the strong points of your case and its weak points together with the strong and weak points of the other side's case. If you do this, the mediator will be impressed with your preparedness and reasonableness. If you do not do this, the mediator will ask questions that will elicit precisely the same information but over a longer period of time. By acknowledging your weaknesses and the other side's strengths you deprive the mediator of an opportunity to use them to adjust your first offer or demand. Also, immediately after you give your summary of strengths and weaknesses, go right into making your first proposal for settling the case. You need not hem and haw about it. You have given the matter a lot of thought in your preparation.

- **Make a reasonable first offer or demand through the mediator.**

If the first settlement offer or demand is a dollar figure, explain to the mediator in detail how you arrived at the figure. The first offer or demand should be highly favorable to your client and reasonable in the sense that it should not offend or insult the other side. A $500 response to a $50,000 demand would most likely insult the ordinary plaintiff. It may even cause the mediation to terminate. If the mediator has any questions, answer them directly and succinctly.

- **Do not disclose your bottom line to the mediator up front.**

If you are an advocate for the plaintiff, do not tell the mediator in the initial caucuses the minimum amount you would accept to settle the case. First of all, the defendant, despite his prior statements to the contrary, may be willing to pay much more than you think to resolve the matter. If, as plaintiff's advocate, you tell the mediator up front your minimum acceptable figure, the mediator will not feel compelled to settle the case at a figure much more than that and will feel satisfied if the case settles at or near your figure. Second, you should not reveal your minimum acceptable figure up front because it may change during the mediation session. The defendant may reveal information that greatly increases the value of your case or that significantly undermines his position. Or, you may discover

CHAPTER III MEDIATION

information which causes you to value your case at a lower level. If you committed to a minimum acceptable figure at the beginning of the mediation, you may feel psychologically inhibited from moving off it, thus sacrificing an opportunity to settle at a slightly lower amount. If you are an advocate for the defendant, do not disclose to the mediator the maximum amount you are willing to spend on the case and then expect the mediator to "play" within that constraint during a series of caucuses. First of all, by doing that you surrender to the mediator most, if not all, of your control over the ongoing negotiation and mediation processes. Second, it places the mediator in an awkward ethical position vis-à-vis the opposing side. As the process progresses, the mediator cannot be totally honest with the opposing side if asked by that side whether there is any flexibility in the offers. In effect, the opposing side will be negotiating directly with the mediator without even knowing it. A mediator in that position will have a great deal of difficulty remaining neutral. If the opposing side will accept in full settlement half of the maximum amount the mediator knows is available for settlement, does the mediator have a duty to disclose that more money is available? If asked? If not asked? Does the mediator in such situation have a duty to withdraw? These are difficult ethical dilemmas. The better practice is not to put mediators in these ethical predicaments.

- **Listen carefully to the mediator and watch for clues about the other side's strategy or bottom line.**

When the mediator reports back with the other side's response to your proposal, the mediator will have gained much information about the other side's strategy, tactics, and maybe even its bottom line. The mediator will be primarily engaged in communicating the substance of the other side's response to you. However, the mediator's tone of voice, word selection, or body language may provide useful clues about what the other side is really thinking. As to word selection, the mediator may use the following phrases, which may in fact have the meanings shown:

Mediator	**Possible Meaning**
"... *finally* they've made some movement."	"They should and could have made more movement."
"The defendant says he *personally* cannot pay a penny more."	"Defendant may get someone else to contribute to the settlement."
"The defendant says there's no way plaintiff can be reinstated to his job *at this time*."	"Reinstatement may be possible later when the company reorganizes."
"Plaintiff wants as much as he can get, *no matter how long it takes*."	"Plaintiff would accept payment of the settlement in installments."
"The plaintiff *cannot forgive* the defendant for humiliating her by those sexual remarks."	"Plaintiff needs an apology before she can settle the case."

D. The Role of the Party's Attorney

Through body language the mediator might unconsciously provide clues to the other side's true interests or concerns. Also, if you simply ask them, some mediators will freely share their perceptions of the emotional state of participants on the opposing side during caucuses.

- **Orchestrate your mediator-carried messages to effectuate your changing strategy and tactics.**

Before going into the caucusing phase of a mediation session, you should consider in advance and discuss with your client the possible caucusing scenarios and what your caucusing tactics might be for various scenarios. Assume that you represent a plaintiff in a personal injury case and that you have decided to adopt a competitive strategy in the mediation. Assume further that your premediation demand was $50,000 and the insurance company's offer was $5,000. In keeping with your competitive strategy, you have determined that you will make very manor monetary concessions in the first three caucuses. You have determined the reasonable settlement range to be somewhere between $20,000 and $25,000.

During the mediation, after the first caucus, assume that you authorize the mediator to communicate a reduction of your premediation demand by only $2,500 to $47,500 "because of the strength of your case on the liability issue." The insurance company, acknowledging to the mediator in caucus that the plaintiff will probably be able to establish liability and that the insurance company's first offer was intentionally nominal, responds by doubling its first offer and authorizing the mediator to communicate a $10,000 offer.

Maintaining your competitive strategy, you move to $45,000 after the second caucus, and the insurance company responds competitively by increasing its offer only to $12,000. In the third caucus, you remain competitive, reducing your demand only to $40,000 and using the competitive tactic of threatening a walkout by having the mediator communicate to the insurance company counsel, "If the insurance company does not get more realistic in its offer, the plaintiff is going to walk out of the mediation."

The insurance company counsel responds by moving to $17,000 but tells the mediator to communicate to you, "She's nearing the limit of her authority." Hearing that, you interpret it to mean that the insurance company is approaching the lower end of the settlement range estimated by the insurance company. It appears that your estimated settlement range and the estimated settlement range of the insurance company overlap. You have two choices now: (1) continue your competitive strategy and reduce your demand by a small increment or (2) become more cooperative by reducing your demand by a significant increment (using the accommodating tactic of creating movement), but still not within your estimated settlement range. If you follow strategy 1, the insurance company may terminate the mediation. If you follow strategy 2, you may get the insurance company to make an offer within your estimated reasonable settlement range.

You decide to go with the more cooperative strategy 2 and reduce your demand from $40,000 to $30,000 with instructions to the mediator to convey to the insurance company, "The plaintiff is approaching its movement limit." You also use the compromising tactic of reciprocity by asking the mediator to communicate, "The $10,000 reduction represents plaintiffs good faith interest in settling the case, and plaintiff expects a reciprocal expression of good faith by the defendant." The insurance company counsel moves to $22,000 and conveys to the plaintiff through the mediator that counsel has reached the limit of its authority.

At this point, you decide to use the compromising tactic of splitting the difference and instruct the mediator to suggest that solution—$26,000—to the other side. The insurance company counsel asks for a recess, calls the supervising adjuster on the case, and tells the mediator to convey to the plaintiff its final offer—$23,500. After discussing the pros and cons with your client, you accept the insurance company's offer, which in fact falls within your estimated reasonable settlement range.

The important point to remember is that the mediator is your negotiation conduit. Convey through the mediator to the other side those statements that effectuate your chosen tactics and that you would ordinarily say to opposing counsel personally if negotiating face-to-face.

- **Refrain from using the mediator to communicate extra-mediation threats.**

Do not expect the mediator to be willing to communicate extramediation threats to the other side. Extramediation threats are those that relate to topics or people not directly related to the dispute or to the commonly understood consequences flowing from the nature of the dispute, its processing, and its resolution. Parties make such extramediation, irrelevant threats for the specific purpose of gaining an unfair advantage in the mediation. For example, to encourage a defendant to accept the plaintiffs settlement proposal, a mediator could not ethically communicate a threat by the plaintiff to expose defendant's alleged illicit conduct (marital cheating, alcoholism, tax evasion) to his wife, his employer, or the government, respectively. Communicating these types of threats would place the mediator squarely in the role of a blackmailer or an accessory to blackmail.

Mediators, of course, routinely communicate to one side or the other threats directly related to the dispute or the process. These types of threats merely reflect the existing power, authority, or opportunities available to one party vis-à-vis the other in the particular dispute and would ordinarily be legitimate tactics in conventional dispute negotiation. Sometimes the threats are present in the minds of the mediation participants but are not verbalized. Threats that are related to the dispute include the following: to contract with alternate suppliers (in a business dispute mediation); to strike (in a labor mediation); and to withdraw financing (in a construction case). Threats related to the process might include threats to conclude the session, to walk out of the mediation, and to proceed to trial.

D. The Role of the Party's Attorney 449

- **Hold back some information favorable to you or unfavorable to the opposing side until the final caucuses.**

The timing of the release of information can be a very powerful settlement tool for you in mediation, just as one move in chess or the calculated playing of one bridge hand can change the whole complexion of victory and loss. It is not necessary to show the mediator every relevant document in the initial joint session. In many situations it is most effective to show some documents in the initial joint session and mention others. Then in the sequential caucuses have the mediator read the critical documents with you, answer the mediator's questions, and suggest that the mediator have the other side respond to or explain passages in the documents in a subsequent caucus. These critical documents contain either information favorable to you or unfavorable to your opponents. The other side, after being presented with the documents you have supplied to the mediator, may indeed respond with other documents that the mediator will bring back to you for explanation. Be prepared for that, and either show the mediator those documents up front or know in advance precisely what you are going to say in response to them. If the other side has no adequate response to your documents, you may have provided the mediator with exactly what he needs to elicit a major concession from the other side regarding settlement.

- **Take the time necessary to caucus with your client privately.**

In caucus when the mediator brings you the other side's response to your settlement proposal, and after you have assured yourself that you fully understand it, consider telling the mediator that you need a few minutes to caucus with your client. Caucusing with your client not only will assist you in determining your client's needs and interests at *that particular time* in the mediation, but also may assist you in better evaluating the proposal and in formulating a reasoned response to it.

- **When you state a proposal or make a movement off a demand or offer, provide the mediator with several supporting reasons why you did it and why the new proposal should be acceptable to the other side.**

When you provide the mediator with a settlement proposal in response to one from the other side, it is very important to state several supporting reasons why you are modifying your former proposal and why the newly formulated proposal should be satisfactory to the other side. This will assist the mediator in explaining to the other side that your new proposal is principled—that is, that your movement is rationally based and that you are not simply "caving in" to the other side's more meritorious demands.

- **Know what aspects of your case are confidential and advise the mediator at the end of each caucus concerning what information should not be disclosed to the other side.**

Normally, at the end of each caucus the mediator will ask you if any of the information discussed in the caucus is confidential. The mediator does this so that she knows what information you do not want communicated to

CHAPTER III MEDIATION

the other side with your counterproposal for settlement. If the mediator fails to ask about confidential information, make sure that you remember to tell her the specific information you want to keep confidential. If, as the mediation proceeds, you believe that certain confidential information may give you increased leverage at a particular stage, you can authorize the mediator to disclose it to the other side at that time.

- **Do not tell the mediator that you want to make or accept a settlement proposal that you have no authority to make or accept.**

When you communicate a firm settlement proposal to the mediator with instructions to convey it to the other side, make sure that you have authority from the client to make the proposal. If the proposal is unauthorized, you may destroy the chance to settle the case, cause the other side to become antagonistic and adversarial, or worse yet, cause the other side to hold your client to the agreement or suffer adverse consequences. This situation sometimes arises when the advocate is present at the mediation with a corporate representative who believes that a proposal will be authorized by the company but later finds out that the company will not back it up. Likewise, when you agree to accept a proposal conveyed by the mediator to you from the other side, make sure that you have the authority to accept it. If you are not sure that you have the authority to make or accept a settlement proposal, simply tell the mediator to relate to the other side that the your offer or acceptance of the proposal is contingent on your client's approval.

- **Refrain from talking about your fees or the mediator's fees as elements of the settlement.**

In the caucuses do not include the mediator in your discussions about how your fees and the mediation expenses need to be factored into the settlement equation. These may be appropriate topics for discussion between you and your client, but they are irrelevant to the mediator. Discussing the mediator's fees in his presence is embarrassing to the mediator and actually puts the mediator in the position of possibly having or appearing to have a monetary stake in the continuing caucusing with the other side. This may impact, either actually or impliedly, on the mediator's duties of neutrality and impartiality to the parties.

NOTES AND QUESTIONS

Consider the comments of attorney-mediator Jeffrey Krivas, A Winning Formula for Mediation, www:mediate.com/articles.krivas6.cfm (May 4. 2001), concerning collaboration with the mediator in the caucus: "Generally the mediator will use this time to talk to you about the strengths and weaknesses of your case. While you probably know them by now, oftentimes the mediator can give you a snapshot of your opponent's position in an impartial way that actually allows you to become more objective and therefore more effective as an advocate. Rather than sit back and simply answer questions from the mediator, work together with the mediator by asking what he thinks is the best approach to achieve your goals. Ask the mediator what has worked in other cases where parties were looking to get lots of money from the other side. Get specific examples of techniques the mediator has used. Decide together what might be the most effective technique in your case, realizing that you need to be flexible in the approach. You can't always put a nice neat bow around every case and seal it shut. You need to allow the mediator some ability to size up the other side and determine whether the competitive strategy you discussed would work or whether you should revisit that decision."

d. IMPASSE

Elizabeth Allen & Donald D. Mohr, Your Role in a Client's Mediation

California Bar Journal (Sept. 1999).

If it appears to you that negotiations have come to a stalemate, buy some time. Don't burn your bridges by declaring an impasse. Rather, agree to adjourn the mediation "for now." It's best to schedule a time to reconvene, in the event that someone comes up with a new idea. A week down the road, everyone will have had a chance to think about the offers. Sometimes the passage of time alone changes the circumstances, sheds new light on a proposal, or results in someone coming up with a different possibility. Don't give up just because you reach the end of one session. Many mediations take two or more sessions to complete, which is why it's usually better to schedule two half-days than one full one in the first place.

Jeffrey Krivas, A Winning Formula for Mediation

www.mediate.com/articles.krivas6.cfm (May 4, 2001).

Don't ever be afraid of an impasse in the negotiations. A good mediator will not let the parties simply walk away without trying to come up with some alternatives. At this point, you might suggest that the mediator make a proposal to settle the case. The proposal would be presented confidentially to each side and only the mediator would know whether it has been accepted by all parties. That way, you don't get punished for making a big move at the end. The other side will only know you made the move If the case settles, which is your goal in the first place. This will also result in the other side moving upward toward your goal because the mediator's proposal is usually a type of compromise that leaves both sides equally unhappy.

Formulas like this are educational models to consider. In the final analysis, you should feel free to utilize the style and approach that has succeeded for you in the past, knowing that you now have some additional tools and insight to draw from in the future. "Tit for Tat" allows you the flexibility to compete in order to avoid being vulnerable, yet cooperate in order to achieve a mutually beneficial and lasting outcome.

CHAPTER III MEDIATION

4. POST-MEDIATION REPRESENTATION

The role of the attorney is usually not over with the termination of a mediation. If a settlement is not reached, the dispute will go on. That could mean now deciding to file a suit, going forward with an already-existing suit, or attempting to resolve the dispute in other ways. It should be kept in mind that a failure to get a settlement does not always mean the mediation was wasted. Sometimes the mediation will provide the basis for a later settlement or a partial settlement if there were aspects of the mediation on which some agreement can be based. Sometimes lack of success demonstrates only that mediation was not the proper form of ADR or that mediation at that particular time could not work, and further use of ADR should still be explored. An attorney should use an unsuccessful mediation as a learning experience on which further attempts to resolve the dispute can be built.

If a settlement is reached, the attorney will have to insure that it is actually carried out. This can involve such technical matters as insuring that the settlement agreement is properly filed or converted into a judgment, as required by local law, to make it legally enforceable.[8] Often there are practical matters of compliance that must be carried out—handing over of property, removal of goods, cancellation of debts, drawing up of new contracts to comply with agreement terms, or future action or conduct of the parties. The mediator rarely plays a role in such compliance matters, and the full responsibility therefore falls on the attorneys. Settlement under private ordering lacks the formal assistance of the courts, except when a settlement agreement is converted into a judgment.

5. ATTORNEY AS MEDIATOR

The second context in which the lawyer may confront mediation is as a mediator himself. If he acts as a formal mediator in a dispute not involving present or past clients, there are few professional problems. He is required to clearly differentiate his role as a lawyer from that of a mediator.[9] As a mediator, for example, he is not to give legal advice. But so long as the roles are kept separate, a lawyer may act as a mediator, and many do in such areas as divorce and family law, commercial matters, and community disputes.

A more difficult question arises when a lawyer seeks to mediate, either formally or informally, in a dispute involving one of his clients. The 1969

---

8. Concerning the legal effect of a settlement agreement, see, e.g., D.R. by M.R. v. East Brunswick Board of Education, 838 F.Supp. 184 (D.N.J.1993) (mediation settlement agreement is a binding enforceable contract); Snyder–Falkinham v. Stockburger, 249 Va. 376, 457 S.E.2d 36 (1995) (client's later attempt to withdraw from mediation

settlement agreement is not good cause for setting it aside).

9. See Comment, The Attorney As Mediator—Inherent Conflict of Interest?, 32 UCLA L.Rev. 986 (1985); Pirie, The Lawyer As Mediator: Professional Responsibility Problems or Profession Problems?, 63 Canadian Bar Rev. 378 (1985).

American Bar Association Code of Professional Responsibility specifically addressed the issue of the lawyer as mediator in a case involving a client:

A lawyer is often asked to serve as an impartial arbitrator or mediator in matters which involve present or former clients. He may serve in either capacity if he first discloses such present or former relationships. After a lawyer has undertaken to act as an impartial arbitrator or mediator, he should not thereafter represent in the dispute any of the parties involved.[10]

The Model Rules of Professional Conduct, Rule 2.2, provides specific guidelines for lawyer mediation, allowing him to act as an intermediary between clients if:

(1) the lawyer explains the advantages and risks associated with common representation and obtains each client's consent to the common representation;

(2) the lawyer reasonably believes that the matter can be resolved on terms compatible with the clients' best interests, that each client will be able to make adequately informed decisions in the matter and that there is little risk of material prejudice to interests of any of the clients if the contemplated resolution is unsuccessful; and

(3) the lawyer reasonably believes that the common representation can be undertaken impartially and without improper effect on other responsibilities the lawyer has to any of the clients.[11]

The comment goes on to warn:

In considering whether to act as intermediary between clients, a lawyer should be mindful that if the intermediation fails the result can be additional cost, embarrassment and recrimination. In some situations the risk of failure is so great the intermediation is plainly impossible. For example, a lawyer cannot undertake common representation of clients between whom litigation is imminent or who contemplate contentious negotiations. More generally, if the relationship between the parties has already assumed definite antagonism, the possibility that the clients' interests can be adjusted by intermediation ordinarily is not very good.

The desire that a lawyer act as mediator seems to arise most often in family-law cases, sometimes because the parties want to avoid the cost of hiring an outside mediator. A 1981 opinion of the New York City Bar Association Committee on Professional and Judicial Ethics stated that the Code "does not impose a per se bar to lawyers participating in divorce mediation activities."[12] But it warned that "[t]he lawyer may not participate in the divorce mediation process where it appears that the issues

---

10. Code of Professional Responsibility, 1969, EC 5–20.

11. See Standards of Practice for Lawyer Mediators in Family Disputes (Adopted by the House of Delegates of the ABA, 1984).

12. N.Y. City Bar Assoc. Comm. on Professional and Judicial Ethics, Op. No. 80–23 (1981), 7 Fam.L.Rep. 3097.

CHAPTER III MEDIATION

between the parties are of such complexity or difficulty that the parties cannot prudently reach a resolution without the advice of separate and independent legal counsel."[13] Consider the following discussion of possible models for lawyers who serve as mediators in divorce cases:

Leonard L. Riskin, Mediation and Lawyers
43 Ohio St.L.J. 29, 37–41 (1982).

A lawyer may function explicitly as a divorce mediator, * * * by representing one of the spouses, leaving the other unrepresented; both of the spouses; or neither of the spouses.

Each of these models has strengths and weaknesses.

[*Representing One of the Spouses*]

Parties who have independent counsel can benefit from an adversarial look at their position. A prediction of the likely results of adversary processing is necessary for an informed, fully voluntary decision about a mediated solution. Sometimes lawyers also aid the mediation process by urging their clients to accept a reasonable compromise. There is a concomitant likelihood, however, that a lawyer's advice will work to undermine a mediation. Of course, this occasionally will be in the client's best interest. But some lawyers may tend to deliver advice in a way that exaggerates the importance of the adversary perspective and the accuracy of their predictions. When this occurs, the client may be drawn away inappropriately from a mediated resolution. But the risk of inappropriate disruption by outside lawyers also is directly related to the level of the parties' commitment to nonadversarial processing. A person who truly wanted to resolve his problem in a nonadversarial, personal fashion—if he is satisfied with the results of mediation—would not be inclined to give high value to the possible advantages proffered by the adversary lawyer.

[*Representing Both of the Spouses*]

One way to lessen the likelihood of a lawyer's undermining a mediation is to employ an impartial attorney to advise both parties, but this raises a number of worries. There are, as examples, mild possibilities of charges of aiding in the unauthorized practice of law (a violation of DR 3–101(A)) or practicing law in association with or otherwise sharing fees with a layman (a violation of DR 3–102(A)). The most substantial concern, however, is the enormous difficulty of giving impartial or neutral legal advice if the parties have conflicting interests. This raises the spectre of breaching the requirement of Canon 5 that a lawyer exercise independent professional judgment on behalf of a client. A recent opinion imposed, *inter alia,* the conditions that "the issues not be of such complexity that the parties cannot prudently reach resolution of the controversy without the advice of separate and independent legal counsel," and that the lawyer advise the parties of the limitations and risks of his role and of the advantages of independent legal

13. Id. at 3099.

counsel, obtain their informed consent, give legal advice only in the presence of both, and refrain from representing either in a subsequent proceeding concerning divorce. If one lawyer advises the couple, each partner is deprived of the benefit of an adversarial look at his or her situation. * * *

When a lawyer functions explicitly as a mediator while representing both of the parties, or just one of the parties while leaving the other unrepresented, the principal professional responsibility concern is again the Canon 5 requirement that a lawyer exercise independent professional judgment on behalf of a client. Bar associations have traditionally prohibited dual representation in matrimonial cases, but have recently shown some signs of liberalization. The Ohio state bar ethics committee recently permitted a lawyer to draft a separation agreement for a couple so long as he was representing one of the parties and the other was protected by giving a knowing consent. The Arizona committee also has permitted dual representation, as has a California appellate court in limited circumstances, including full disclosure of risks.

The *Model Code of Professional Responsibility,* EC 5–20, permits a lawyer to mediate in a matter that involves "present or former clients ... if he first discloses such ... relationships ... and [does not] thereafter represent in the dispute any of the parties involved." The Wisconsin bar ethics committee has ruled that a lawyer who educated the parties about their legal rights and responsibilities, mediated disputes during the negotiations, drafted documents, and appeared in court would find himself beyond the protection of EC 5–20, even though each party would receive independent legal review of the agreement and the lawyer would not represent either party subsequently. And, of course, there are significant risks of a malpractice action.

The principal danger of dual representation is that one of the parties will take unfair advantage of the other, knowingly or not. With this in mind, Rule 2.2 of the proposed final draft of the American Bar Association *Model Rules of Professional Conduct* would apply where a lawyer represents both parties.

This model offers significant potential advantages to clients who wish to save time and money and avoid an adversarial confrontation. Yet when assets or interests that the parties consider significant are involved, they will usually want the benefit of a partisan look at their case.

[Representing Neither of the Spouses]

The most recent development—the lawyer serving as divorce mediator but not representing either party—has earned the qualified approval of the Boston and Oregon bar ethics committees. The Oregon opinion imposed the conditions that the attorney

1. ... must clearly inform the parties he represents neither of them and they both must consent to this arrangement;

2. ... may give legal advice only to both parties in the presence of each other;

3. ... may draft the proposed agreement but he must advise, and encourage, the parties to seek independent legal counsel before execution of the agreement; and

4. ... must not represent either or both of the parties in the subsequent legal proceedings.

This model seems to offer the best possibilities for the appropriate use of law and lawyers in mediation of some matters that normally pass through the adversary process. The attorney-mediator can attempt to provide impartial legal information while making clear the risks to the clients in his doing so. The outside consultations with lawyers can defend against the possibility of bias (deliberate or not) in the lawyer-mediator's work and reduce the chances that one party will inappropriately exercise power over the other.

Another advantage is that information about what a court would do can be integrated into the mediation process in a way that suits the needs of the parties. Because he is an expert on law, the lawyer-mediator can help the parties free themselves, when appropriate, from the influence of legal norms so that they can reach for a solution that is appropriate to them. In addition, the experienced lawyer who functions as a mediator can offer a variety of business arrangements to accomplish the objectives of the parties. These options can become part and parcel of the decision process, and the law-trained mediator who is present at all the sessions and thoroughly familiar with the various needs of the parties can propose alternatives finely tuned to such needs. Moreover, the lawyer-mediator can, better than the lay mediator, identify a myriad of legal issues that must be addressed in the final agreement, and press the disputants to reach decisions. He can incorporate the results in a draft final agreement, which—because of the lawyer-mediator's skill in identifying issues and preparing documents— would be less vulnerable to upending by the outside lawyers than would one drafted by a nonlawyer.

Lance J. Rogers, Lawyer–Mediators Wanting Ethical Guidance Must Look Beyond Attorney Ethics Standards

66 U.S. Law Week 2307 (November 25, 1997).

As the debate continues over whether the public is ill-served by the adversary system, more and more lawyers are expanding–and even replacing–traditional law practice with services that focus on cooperative dispute resolution. But, such lawyers seeking guidance on ethical issues will obtain little help from attorney professional responsibility rules, which are geared for adversarial litigation and generally do not apply to the mediation scenario.

A lawyer mediating disputes between non-clients must instead seek guidance from a patchwork of local ethics rules and ethics committee opinions, state statutes, and dispute resolution organization codes. Even though mediation of one form or another is used in a majority of states, there are few licensing requirements for mediators and no comprehensive set of ethical standards.

Lawyer as "Intermediary." Most states' rules of legal ethics are patterned after the American Bar Association's Model Rules of Professional Conduct. However, the Model Rules only envision a role for lawyers as "intermediaries" seeking to help two or more clients resolve a potential controversy. Model Rule 2.2.

Although some courts and commentators use the terms "mediation" and "intermediation" interchangeably, the Model Rules on intermediation do not apply to a lawyer who functions as an impartial mediator or arbitrator between non-clients.

The lawyer-intermediary maintains an attorney-client relationship with each party throughout the mediation process. That relationship makes the attorney responsible not only for fashioning an acceptable resolution but also for seeing that the interests of each client are fully represented. Thus, the lawyer-intermediary relationship triggers a codified set of duties and responsibilities that are more rigorous and regulated than the mediator's general duty to be impartial.

States Offer Guidance. A few states have expressly recognized that lawyers may mediate disputes between non-clients and have spelled out some standards for ethical behavior. Typically, those guidelines require impartiality, emphasize the parties' right to withdraw, and further require the lawyer-mediator to encourage the parties to secure independent legal advice before signing a legal agreement.

Regardless of the nature of the mediation dispute, most jurisdictions forbid lawyer-mediators from later representing one of the mediation parties in a suit involving substantially similar issues.

Lawyer-mediators seeking ethical guidance should also look to state statutes and local rules that govern the conduct of all persons holding themselves out as mediators. Generally, these local rules require some minimal level of competence, training, and impartiality by the mediators. Moreover, the rules tend to emphasize confidentiality, limit the scope and nature of advertising, and prohibit mediation if there is a conflict of interest.

Finally there are several general codes of ethics that lawyers should consult:

> * The American Bar Association's *Standards of Practice for Lawyer–Mediators in Family Disputes*. Developed by the ABA Family Law Section in 1984, the standards provide that a lawyer-mediator has a duty to be impartial, to maintain confidences, and to ensure that the mediation participants make informed decisions. The mediator also is obliged to suspend or terminate mediation whenever continuation of the process would harm one or more of the participants and has a continuing duty to advise each of the mediation participants to obtain legal review prior to reaching any agreement.

458 CHAPTER III MEDIATION

* AAA Code of Ethics for Arbitration in Commercial Disputes. The American Arbitration Association's Code of Ethics sets out six primary canons of conduct that describe the arbitrator's duty to act with fairness, impartiality, and diligence and to maintain confidences.

* Ethical Standards of Professional Responsibility of the Society of Professions in Dispute Resolution (SPIDR). These standards, adopted by *SPIDR* in 1989, provide that the "neutral" must be competent, honest, unbiased, and diligent. Moreover, the neutral must alert the parties to situations where unrepresented interests should be taken into consideration.

* Center for Dispute Resolution (CDR) Code of Conduct. This code emphasizes the mediator's obligation to educate the parties about the process, to remain sensitive to the parties' needs, to avoid playing an adversarial role, to maintain confidentiality, and to reach a settlement that is seen as fair and equitable by all parties. The code prohibits mediators from offering legal advice and stresses that the mediator's role "should not be confused with that of an attorney who is an advocate for a client."

* Association of Family and Conciliation Courts (AFCC) Model Standards of Practice for Family and Divorce Mediation. These standards, completed in 1984, set out 13 guidelines dealing with impartiality, initiation of the mediation process, costs and fees, confidentiality, disclosure, advertising, and training and education. The standards suggest that a mediator's actual or perceived neutrality may be compromised by profession, or even social, relationships with one of the participants before or after the mediation is completed. The standards further provide that whenever the mediation may affect a participant's legal rights, the mediator shall advise the parties to seek independent legal advice before formalizing any agreement or settlement.

* Model Standards of Conduct for Mediators. These guidelines were prepared from 1992 to 1994 by a joint committee composed of two representatives from the ABA, two delegates from the AAA, and two from SPIDR. The Model Standards have been approved by the Councils of the ABA Section of Litigation and Section of Dispute Resolution.

Not surprisingly perhaps, these last standards are quite similar to those already established by the AAA and SPIDR. The standards divide the mediator's responsibilities into nine major guidelines that spell out the duty to remain impartial, avoid apparent conflicts of interest, maintain, confidences, act diligently and competently, and be truthful when advertising and discussing fees. The standards caution that mediators should refrain from providing professional advice and should instead advise the parties to seek outside professional advice when appropriate. * * *

Unauthorized Practice of Law. A lawyer-mediator naturally brings legal training and experience to the mediation and, indeed, may have been chosen precisely because of this expertise. While that expertise alone will not trigger the full panoply of legal ethical duties, offering legal advice to the parties may be viewed as engaging in the practice of law and therefore could bring the state's professional conduct rules into play.

Several ethics committees have suggested that lawyers may participate in divorce mediation services provided that the lawyer's services do not require legal judgment but rather call for the sort of mediation services that non-lawyers typically perform.

Other ethics committees, however, have concluded that lawyers performing mediation services are engaged in the practice of law, and therefore that the lawyers may not join non-lawyers in such a service with running afoul of Model Rule 5.4(b) or Model Code DR 3–103(A), which bar lawyers from engaging in the practice law with non-lawyers.

Duty of Impartiality. Another concern for attorneys involves the debate over the lawyer-mediator's role as an impartial go-between. Some have argued that mediators who seek a "fair" result are paternalistic and violate their pre-eminent duty to be impartial and neutral. Stuhlberg, *The Theory and Practice of Mediation: A Reply to Professor Susskind,* 6 Vt. L.Rev. 85, 86–87 (1981). Others have insisted that mediators have a duty to ensure that both parties have an equal opportunity to participate, even if this involves "empowering" one of the parties to assure that they have equal footing. Susskind, *Environmental Mediation and the Accountability Problem,* 6 Vt.L.Rev. 1, 14–15 (1981): Kelly, *Power Imbalance in Divorce and Interpersonal Mediation,* 13 Med.Q. 85 (1995). Yet a third view suggests that regardless of what label mediators give to their role, they still must struggle with their own subtle biases and preconceived notions when establishing the boundaries of what is "fair" or "neutral." See Cobb and Rifkin, *Practice and Paradox: Deconstructing Neutrality in Mediation,* 16 L. & Soc. Inquiry (1991).

For the lawyer-mediator, the tension between being neutral and being fair is even more problematic because the lawyer brings specialized knowledge and experience to the relationship and it is unlikely that he or she can conduct the mediation without drawing from that knowledge. Indeed, the clients no doubt view the lawyer-mediator's background as one of the advantages of having a lawyer mediate the dispute, and fully expect the lawyer to refer to that expertise when mediating their dispute.

NOTES AND QUESTIONS

1. A Commission on Ethics and Standards in ADR sponsored by Georgetown University and CPR Institute for Dispute Resolution issued a Proposed Model Rule of Professional Conduct for the Lawyer as Third Party Neutral in 1999. The Preamble cited the need for guidance for lawyers who "now commonly serve as third party neutrals, either as facilitators to settle disputes or plan transactions, as in mediation, or as third party decision makers, as in arbitration": "When lawyers serve as ADR neutrals they do not have partisan 'clients,' as contemplated in much of the Model Rules, but rather serve all of the parties. Lawyer neutrals do not 'represent' parties, but have a duty to be fair to all participants in the process and to execute different obligations and responsibilities with respect to the parties

CHAPTER III MEDIATION

and to the process." The proposed rule, running almost twenty pages double-spaced, establishes standards as to diligence and competence, confidentiality, impartiality, conflicts of interest, fees, and fairness and integrity of the process. Other proposed rules that may affect the ethical standards for attorney-mediators are the American Bar Association's Ethics 2000 Commission and the American Law Institute's Restatement of the Law Governing Lawyers.

2. For a reasoned argument that there is a difference between giving "legal advice," which an attorney-mediator may not do, and giving "legal information," which he should be able to do in order to be an effective mediator, see Weckstein, In Praise of Party Empowerment–And of Mediator Activism, 33 Willamette L. Rev. 501 (1997).

3. Suppose a lawyer regularly represents a businesswoman in all of her affairs. The lawyer has also handled some of her personal affairs with her husband, such as a will and retirement plan. Can the lawyer agree to mediate between the husband and wife in a divorce that involves child custody?

The answer to this question requires careful working through of the provisions of the applicable rules. First, the *Standards of Practice for Lawyer Mediators in Family Disputes* is not directly applicable because they are premised on the lawyer-mediator not having previously represented one of the parties (see § III(A)). Therefore, one must look to the *Model Rules of Professional Conduct.* [see Appendix D].

Rule 2.2 requires the lawyer-mediator to "explain the *advantages and risks* associated with common representation." The primary risk is that once a lawyer represents multiple clients, such clients are deemed to waive the attorney-client privilege as to the other commonly-represented clients. Thus the lawyer here, if bound by Rule 2.2, must inform both husband and wife of the consequences of waiver of the attorney-client privilege. This could be a disadvantage for the wife if, for example, the lawyer has been told confidences about her assets or business affairs that she wants to keep confidential from the husband. Even if the parties had worked out all of the details of the divorce and had simply brought the agreement to the lawyer to draft up in legal form, he would still seem to be acting in a joint-representational capacity and thus to be bound by Rule 2.2. Rule 2.2(a)(2) also focuses on the compatibility of the lawyer serving as mediator with "the clients' best interests," a troubling question for the wife in this hypo.

4. Suppose a real estate lawyer who normally represents landlords in drafting leases agrees to mediate disputes between a landlord and tenants. Should the lawyer disclose to the tenants who agree to submit to mediation that he normally represents landlords? Does the tenant have a right to see a record of prior mediations?

5. In Poly Software International, Inc. v. Su, 880 F.Supp. 1487 (D.Utah 1995), a copyright infringement suit, defendants moved to disqualify plaintiff's attorney for having served as a mediator in an earlier dispute involving some of the same parties and events. The court adopted a "substantially factually related matter" test to hold that the mediator, who had heard frank discussions relating to these matters during the mediation, could not then represent a party in a different, but related action. In Fields–D'Arpino v. Restaurant Associates, Inc., 39 F.Supp.2d 412 (S.D.N.Y. 1999), a law firm was disqualified from representing their corporate client in an employment discrimination case because a member of the firm had served as a "neutral, third party" in a meeting with the client and the employee plaintiff. The plaintiff was aware that the mediator's firm was her employer's outside counsel. N.Y. Code of Professional Responsibility EC 5–20 states: "A lawyer who has undertaken to act as an impartial arbitrator or mediator should not thereafter represent in the dispute any of the parties involved." The court rejected the argument that only the lawyer who acted as mediator should be disqualified. It noted that the firm "has not even attempted to implement screening procedures that would prevent its attorney-mediator from sharing confidential information disclosed by the plaintiff during the mediation with other attorneys in the firm."

E. CONFIDENTIALITY IN MEDIATION

In the usual case, what was said in mediation will be of no further legal relevance after the mediation is over. But there are occasions on which someone will attempt to discover what was said in a mediation or to use it as testimony in a future proceeding. This is more likely to occur when no agreement was reached in the mediation and the dispute later goes to trial (or to some other form of resolution, such as arbitration). Even when an agreement was reached in the mediation, there may be a future attempt to discover what was said or to use it in testimony. This can occur when there is a disagreement between the parties as to what the mediated agreement was or when one party seeks to enforce the agreement and the other claims that it was obtained improperly. A later proceeding for which mediation testimony is sought may be based directly on the dispute that was the basis of the mediation (for example, a suit between partners who had tried to mediate their differences) or on a matter separate from that dispute (for example, a suit by a creditor, against one of the partners, as to which something said in the mediation is relevant).

Many proponents of mediation claim that confidentiality is critical to the success of the process. They maintain that parties will not speak freely if confidentiality is not guaranteed and that the ability to get to the heart of the dispute will be jeopardized. They also argue that the independence of the mediator would be undermined if she could be required to testify about the mediation at some future time. Consider the following discussion of the need for confidentiality:

Lawrence R. Freedman & Michael L. Prigoff, Confidentiality in Mediation: The Need for Protection

2 Ohio St.J. Dispute Res. 37, 39 (1986).

Effective mediation requires candor. A mediator, not having coercive power, helps parties reach agreements by identifying issues, exploring possible bases for agreement, encouraging parties to accommodate each others' interests, and uncovering the underlying causes of conflict. Mediators must be able to draw out baseline positions and interests which would be impossible if the parties were constantly looking over their shoulders. Mediation often reveals deep-seated feelings on sensitive issues. Compromise negotiations often require the admission of facts which disputants would never otherwise concede. Confidentiality insures that parties will voluntarily enter the process and further enables them to participate effectively and successfully.

Fairness to the disputants requires confidentiality. The safeguards present in legal proceedings, qualified counsel and specific rules of evidence and procedure, for example, are absent in mediation. In mediation, unlike the traditional justice system, parties often make communications without the expectation that they will later be bound by them. Subsequent use of information generated at these proceedings could therefore be unfairly prejudicial, particularly if one party is more sophisticated than the other. Mediation thus could be used as a discovery device against legally naive persons if the mediation communications were not inadmissible in subsequent judicial actions. This is particularly important where a mediation program is affiliated with an entity of the legal system, such as a prosecutor's office.

The mediator must remain neutral in fact and in perception. The potential of the mediator to be an adversary in a subsequent legal proceeding would curtail the disputants' freedom to confide during the mediation. Court testimony by a mediator, no matter how carefully presented, will inevitably be characterized so as to favor one side or the other. This would destroy a mediator's efficacy as an impartial broker.

Privacy is an incentive for many to choose mediation. Whether it be protection of trade secrets or simply a disinclination to "air one's dirty laundry" in the neighborhood, the option presented by the mediator to settle disputes quietly and informally is often a primary motivator for parties choosing this process.

Mediators, and mediation programs, need protection against distraction and harassment. Fledgling community programs need all of their limited resources for the "business at hand." Frequent subpoenas can encumber staff time, and dissuade volunteers from participating as mediators. Proper evaluation of programs requires adequate record keeping. Many programs, uncertain as to whether records would be protected absent statutory protection, routinely destroy them as a confidentiality device.

In opposition to a broad claim for mediation confidentiality is our tradition that all relevant evidence should be available in judicial proceedings. The right to "every man's evidence" is a basic procedural principle only outweighed in the case of certain limited privileges.

Professor Eric D. Green points out that there are a number of considerations bearing on the degree of confidentiality that should be accorded.[1] These include *what* should be confidential (i.e., the fact of settlement, its terms, statements by parties, documents and evidence disclosed by parties, statements by or notes of the mediator, or the mediator's impressions, opinions, or recommendations); *who* should be able to enforce confidentiality (i.e., parties, non-party participants such as witnesses, the mediator, interested non-participants, or the courts and public agencies); and *against whom* confidentiality can be enforced (parties, the mediator, non-party participants, private third parties, or public third parties). It is apparent that the justification for confidentiality may be more or less compelling, depending on the combination of these factors (Green provides five charts for this purpose).

Green sees the paradigm case for confidentiality as one in which (a) one party to a mediation, (b) to advance its own interests, tries to (c) introduce either the (d) statements of another party or the impressions, notes, or opinions of the mediator (e) in subsequent litigation over the same event (f) between the same parties (g) when the interests of third parties and the public are not involved. Do you agree that these factors make the strongest case for confidentiality? What factors would weaken the case?

Our inquiry in this section will be focused on the scope of the present legal protections for confidentiality in mediation, and whether they are adequate. Those protections will be discussed under the categories of (1) Evidentiary Exclusion for Compromise Discussions, (2) Discovery Limitations, (3) Mediation Privileges, and (4) Contractual Agreements of Confidentiality.

1. EVIDENTIARY EXCLUSION FOR COMPROMISE DISCUSSIONS

Federal Rule of Evidence 408 (and a large number of state rules based on it) expands the common law privilege by excluding from evidence both offers to compromise and "evidence of conduct or statements made in compromise negotiations," if introduced "to prove liability for or invalidity of the claim or its amount."

The elements necessary for Rule 408 exclusion have been discussed in Chapter II (see II, D, 2, e). An issue that arises in the context of a negotiated settlement is whether the terms of a settlement between the defendants and other parties can be discovered by persons not parties to that settlement. That issue can also arise out of a mediated settlement. Can a mediation be analogized to a settlement negotiation to satisfy the Rule 408 requirement that an offer be made "to compromise a claim which was disputed?" The policy behind the rule, to promote "the out-of-court settle-

---

1. Green. A Heretical View of a Mediation Privilege, 2 Ohio St.J. Dispute Res. 1, 32 (1986).

CHAPTER III MEDIATION

ment of disputes,''[2] should apply to any form of settlement discussion, whether it be an informal negotiation between counsel or parties, a structured settlement conference, or a mediation. There has been little occasion for courts to rule on the application of Rule 408 to mediation. But unless a mediation is so limited as to exclude any discussion of settlement of a dispute, it would seem to apply. The judge in one case, in which evidence arising in an EEOC conciliation was sought to be introduced in a later trial, stated that "it probably is inadmissible under Fed.R.Evid. 408."[3]

Colorado settled any uncertainty as to whether the rule protecting settlement discussions applies to mediation by passing a statute that "[m]ediation processes shall be regarded as settlement negotiations." It provides that "no admission, representation, or statement made in mediation not otherwise discoverable or obtainable shall be admissible as evidence or subject to process requiring the disclosure of any matter discussed during mediation proceedings."[4]

Rule 408 applies to unsuccessful as well as successful compromise discussions and thus should accord protection regardless of the outcome of a mediation. It also specifically provides that it "does not require the exclusion of any evidence otherwise discoverable merely because it is presented in the course of compromise negotiations." This is intended to prevent a participant from immunizing otherwise available evidence simply by presenting it during mediation. "If, for example, evidence of child abuse already existed, it does not become inadmissible because it is additionally blurted out during custody mediation."[5]

Rule 408 has a number of limitations that severely restrict the scope of its protections regarding mediations. First, it only applies to subsequent litigation and is inapplicable, for example, in subsequent administrative or legislative hearings. It also provides no protection against public disclosure of information revealed in mediation. Second, it only protects parties to a subsequent litigation, and thus mediation participants who are not parties to the litigation (including the mediator) cannot invoke its protections. Third, although it protects not only offers to compromise but also "evidence of conduct or statements made in compromise negotiations," some narrow court interpretations have found that not everything said in a negotiation has a sufficient relationship to discussions of settlement to come under the rule.[6]

Rule 408 is limited to the situation in which a party in a subsequent litigation seeks to introduce mediation evidence to prove liability or the amount of damages. Further, it does not apply if the evidence is introduced

2. J. Weinstein, 2 Weinstein's Evidence 408–3 (1986).

3. U.S. Equal Employment Opportunity Comm'n v. Air Line Pilots Ass'n Intern., 489 F.Supp. 1003, 1008 n. 4 (D.Minn.1980), rev'd on other grounds, 661 F.2d 90 (8th Cir.1981).

4. Colo.Rev.Stats. § 13–22–307 (Supp. 1985).

5. J. Folberg & A. Taylor, Mediation: A Comprehensive Guide to Resolving Conflicts Without Litigation 271 (1984).

6. See Thomas v. Resort Health Related Facility, 539 F.Supp. 630 (E.D.N.Y.1982) (defendant's offer of unconditional reinstatement made to cut off plaintiff employee's right to back pay found to be unrelated to discussions for settling the whole law suit).

for another purpose such as bias, negating undue delay, and obstruction (which, although specifically cited, are only examples of other purposes).[7]

Finally, Rule 408 has to be read in light of the broad discovery permitted by the federal discovery rules which allow discovery "regarding any matter, not privileged, which is relevant to the subject matter involved in the pending action."(Rule 26(b)). That rule further states that "[i]t is not ground for objection that the information sought will be inadmissible at the trial if the information sought appears reasonably calculated to lead to the discovery of admissible evidence." Even the broad scope of discovery under the rules, however, contains limitations which may provide some confidentiality protection for mediations. First, discovery may not be made as to any privileged matter. Mediations may fall in this category if a privilege has been accorded in the particular jurisdiction (as will be discussed in the next subsection). Second, information sought to be discovered must be relevant and must at least be reasonably calculated to lead to admissible evidence.

The provision in Rule 26(c) that a court may "for good cause shown . . . make any order which justice requires to protect a party or person from annoyance, embarrassment, oppression, or undue burden or expense" provide a further protection for mediation confidentiality. Rule 26(c)(7) specifically refers to grounds for a protective order that "a trade secret or other confidential research, development, or commercial information not be disclosed or be disclose only in a designated way." Information disclosed in a mediation would be appropriate for protection under Rule 26(c) if "good cause" is shown by demonstrating a particular need for protection. See Cipollone v. Liggett Group, Inc., 785 F.2d 1108, 1121 (3d Cir.1986). Such protection might be provided even if a formal mediation privilege (as will be discussed in the next section) were not available. Professor Moore comments that "[t]here is no true privilege against discovery of trade secrets or other 'confidential' business information, but the courts nevertheless will exercise their discretion to avoid unnecessary disclosure of such information." 4 Moore's Federal Practice (2d ed.) 2519–2520. In Adler v. Adams, No. 675–73C (W.D.Wash., May 3, 1979), a court used a balancing test in granting a motion to quash a subpoena to a mediator in an environmental case. It used an analogy to Hickman v. Taylor, 329 U.S. 495, 508, 67 S.Ct. 385, 91 L.Ed. 451 (1947), deeming the mediator's communications to be protected "work product".

NOTES AND QUESTIONS

1. What if suit is brought to enforce a mediation agreement and the plaintiff seeks to introduce testimony as to what was said in order to prove

---

7. See Belton v. Fibreboard Corp., 724 F.2d 500, 505 (5th Cir.1984) (fact of settlement by co-defendants was admissible to explain why they were not in court); Central Soya Co., Inc. v. Epstein Fisheries, Inc., 676 F.2d 939, 944 (7th Cir.1982) (evidence of settlement was admissible to show partial forgiveness of debt in guaranty case); Breuer Electric Manufacturing Co. v. Toronado Systems of America, Inc., 687 F.2d 182, 185 (7th Cir.1982) (evidence of settlement negotiations was admissible in hearing to set aside default to show defendant's awareness of claim).

CHAPTER III MEDIATION

what the agreement was? Is this a purpose *other* than proving liability for the claim or its amount, so that the testimony would not be protected under Rule 408? Is this a situation in which confidentiality would undermine the effectiveness of mediation by making it more difficult to enforce the agreement?

2. What if testimony as to what was said or agreed upon in the mediation is introduced only for the purpose of impeaching a party or witness? Is it outside the protection of Rule 408? See Brocklesby v. United States, 767 F.2d 1288, 1293 (9th Cir.1985) (indemnity agreement could be introduced to attack credibility of witnesses); John McShain, Inc. v. Cessna Aircraft Co., 563 F.2d 632, 635 (3d Cir.1977) (release could be introduced to show consultant was released in return for testimony); Reichenbach v. Smith, 528 F.2d 1072, 1075 (5th Cir.1976) ("Rule 408 codified a trend in case law that permits cross-examination concerning a settlement for the purpose of impeachment").

3. Consider the following hypothetical suggested by Professor Green in reference to the applicability of Rule 408 (and in relation to the other bases for confidentiality discussed in subsections 2 through 4 that follow this subsection):

> Jane and Frank Smith have decided to divorce. They have been married twelve years and have two children, Mary, 7 and Peter, 5.
>
> The Smiths engage Patrick Brave, an experienced divorce mediator, to help them work out a separation agreement covering custody and property issues. During mediation, Jane admits to Patrick during a private session that she does not really want custody of the children, but is only using the custody issue as a device to get a better property settlement. In addition, Jane tells Patrick that the children might be better off with Frank because she doesn't seem to be able to control herself with the children very well; she has lost her temper with them on a number of occasions and found herself hitting them in the face. She gave Mary a black eye last week.
>
> Later, at a joint session, Jane admits that she is using the custody issue as leverage for a larger property settlement. Upon hearing this, Frank gets mad and breaks off the mediation.
>
> Frank's lawyer schedules Patrick's deposition. At Patrick's deposition, the lawyer asks Patrick to repeat what Jane has told him about her interest in custody of the children and about her feelings with regard to the best interest of the children. Frank's lawyer also asks Patrick if he has any information or opinions about what would be in the best interest of the children. At trial, Patrick is called as a witness by Frank's lawyer and asked the same questions.
>
> Jane obtains custody of Mary and Peter. Six months later, at the request of Mary's second grade teacher, the Department of Social Services conducts an investigation into Jane's treatment of the children. The DSS social worker asks Patrick what he knows about Jane's care and treatment of the children.

2. MEDIATION PRIVILEGE

Some jurisdictions recognize a mediation privilege. Such a privilege may be created by court or by statute. At common law, a sizable number of privileges were recognized, reaching such status situations as attorney-client, clergyman-penitent, physician-patient, and husband-wife. The modern trend is to narrow the number of privileges. The Federal Rules of Evidence provide that privilege will be governed by "the principles of the common law in the light of reason and experience,"[8] and the federal courts have severely cut back on the range of privileges. The Supreme Court, in rejecting a constitutionally-based reporter's privilege, has indicated that claims of privilege should be carefully scrutinized in light of their denial of the right to evidence and that courts should ordinarily defer to the legislative branch for the creation of privileges.[9]

a. JUDICIALLY CREATED PRIVILEGE

Professor Wigmore provided the classic statement of conditions which should be met in creating a privilege, which has been followed by many courts:

(1) The communications must originate in a confidence that they will not be disclosed;

(2) This element of confidentiality must be essential to the full and satisfactory maintenance of the relationship between the parties;

(3) The relationship must be one which in the opinion of the community ought to be sedulously fostered; and

(4) The injury that would inure to the relationship by the disclosure of the communications must be greater than the benefit thereby gained for the correct disposal of the litigation.[10]

The first condition would normally be satisfied in the mediation setting. Mediators usually tell parties that the mediation is confidential, thus creating an expectation that it will be held in confidence. The expectation, however, must be reasonable in terms of the courts' willingness to recognize it. Thus the means by which mediators inform clients of confidentiality could be important. A written statement, signed by the mediator and parties, would be best, but sometimes, as in initial telephone conversations, this is not possible. In such situations, the expectation of confidence may be insufficient and, if it is to be protected, a statutory privilege would be needed.

The second condition—that confidentiality be essential to the full and satisfactory maintenance of the relationship—is not easily proven. How does one, for example, demonstrate that confidentiality is essential to the relationship between physician-client or husband-wife? Professor Green

---

8. Federal Rules of Evidence, Rule 501.

9. Branzburg v. Hayes, 408 U.S. 665, 92 S.Ct. 2646, 33 L.Ed.2d 626 (1972).

10. Wigmore on Evidence § 2285 (McNaughton ed. 1961).

CHAPTER III MEDIATION

points out that mediation has flourished in many states without a privilege and argues that on occasions when confidentiality is essential, a limited, rather than absolute privilege, is sufficient.[11] Consider the following comments by Gary Kirkpatrick in favor of a privilege:[12]

[S]uppose I came to you as a mediator for assistance with my spouse and had embarrassing things to tell. I will want you to understand me and my situation, since I can expect that you will be able to help me only if you have an opportunity to know all of the relevant data. Otherwise, you are making guesses about the situation, and creating alternatives that cannot help because they apply to other circumstances. If you, as the mediator, pledge confidentiality, I will be more likely to feel comfortable and speak more openly than if I am unsure about your discretion. People * * * must feel secure that their secrets will not be passed along to friends, family, the press, and foes. The revelation of secrets in court is only one of many fears. * * *

It [may be] contended that the belief that mediators would become personae non grata is also insufficiently substantiated. Would marriages cease, lawyers be without work, doctors without patients if the principals were required to testify? Probably not. The mediator-client relationship probably would not cease either, although this relationship is more fragile than those between attorneys and clients, husbands and wives, doctors and patients, all of which are more established and recognized. But the validity of the contention that mediators would be spurned if their testimony was admissible is not necessary for the privilege to be desirable. Rather, it is sufficient that the confidentiality privilege would help the mediator-client relationship. This could perhaps be best established through polling potential clients to determine if they would continue using mediators if they could be subpoenaed, and by research that would make experimental determinations of the effect of subpoenability. * * *

It [may be said] that the privilege could prevent finding the guilty party. This is a broad attack against any privilege, and on the face of it is undeniable. However, several considerations bring this legitimate concern into focus. First, forcing the mediator to testify does not mean that the truth will come out. The mediator can lie; this means that the innocent will sometimes lose their case. Also, if the clients are aware that the mediator can be subpoenaed, they have a motive for lying to the mediator. The mediator may then unwillingly (or otherwise) transmit the lies uttered during the mediation. Once again, the innocent may suffer. The mediator's testimony may not be excluded as hearsay evidence, especially if the trial is without jury. The mediator could testify about what he remembers without having to testify to the truth of what he heard and could affirm or deny previous testimony of the clients.

---

11. Green, A Heretical View of the Mediation Privilege, 2 Ohio St.J. on Dispute Res. 1, 32 (1986).

12. Kirkpatrick, Should Mediators Have a Confidentiality Privilege?, 9 Mediation Q. 85, 94–6 (1985).

The mediator usually views the problem as a conflict to be solved, not as a situation in which someone is to be blamed and punished. Therefore, the mediator may not make a good witness in the adversarial setting, which is designed to discover who or what is right, because his orientation will probably lead him away from making that judgment.

The contention that secrecy and privilege serve the guilty must be considered along with the belief that the unabridged access to private lives leaves the innocent subject to the unjust examination of life's details. The rights associated with privacy are, of course, subject to abuse by criminals and sociopaths, who use the shield of privacy to rob, murder, and abuse others. For example, the need to obtain a search warrant may delay police officers looking for a drug dealer while the accomplice meanwhile destroys evidence. Or an abusive spouse may relentlessly pursue the victim after very brief stays in jail. But the criminal justice system hopes to secure the rights of those who may be unjustly accused by their enemies or by the misinformed and assumes innocence until guilt is proven. Similarly, privileged relationships may be misused but they can nonetheless be justified.

Thus, while acknowledging that privileged communication does have its drawbacks, there are benefits as well. It seems that the benefits could prevail in some circumstances because the need for privacy is legitimate and basic and must be respected because of the practical benefits that accrue from recognizing the confidentiality privilege.

Wigmore's last two conditions—that the relationship be one that the community strongly believes should be fostered and that the injury from disclosure outweigh the benefit to be gained—are also subject to debate. Green argues that "there is a substantial and respectable body of opinion that holds that mediation and other informal methods of dispute resolution ought not be encouraged,"[13] and that "given the unwillingness of courts to strike the balance between injury to the relationship and benefit to the justice system in favor of executive privilege and reporter's privilege, it is doubtful that courts will conclude that the balancing of interests" will come out in favor of a mediation privilege.[14]

Several courts have wrestled with the issue of a common-law privilege and, under certain circumstances, have found it appropriate. Consider the following cases:

Sheldone v. Pennsylvania Turnpike Commission

U.S. District Court, W.D. Pa., 2000.
104 F.Supp.2d 511.

■ CAIAZZA, UNITED STATES MAGISTRATE JUDGE

[Plaintiffs, members of International Brotherhood of Teamsters, Local 30, who are employed by the Commission, filed suit alleging that the

---

13. Green, supra note 4, at 33.   **14.** Id. at 34.

470 CHAPTER III MEDIATION

Defendant violated the Fair Labor Standards Act, 29 U.S.C. § 201, *et seq.* ("the FLSA"), by "imposing a fluctuating hours method of compensation." Plaintiffs' counsel noticed the deposition of an authorized agent of the Commission pursuant to Rule 30(b)(6), seeking to conduct an examination regarding "[t]he mediation [of] the grievance filed by Roger Haas and Michael Pandolfo heard on May 21, 1999, before Mediator Michael W. Krchnar, Jr."] The Defendant's motion seeks to preclude the discovery "through any method ..., including [the] Plaintiffs' noticed deposition," of "[a]ll mediation communications and mediation documents." As the basis for its request, the Commission urged the Court to recognize a federal "mediation privilege" precluding discovery of such communications and documents.]

The Plaintiffs explain that the Mediation constituted the "third step of a grievance procedure under" a "Memorandum of Understanding" between the Commission and Local 30 * * *. Their opposition brief alleges Mr. Haas testified at his deposition that one of the Commission's attorneys stated that it "settled out of court" another lawsuit brought by many of the same Plaintiffs here because the Commission "found out it was illegal to pay [them] ... straight time for overtime." The Plaintiffs argue that this purported admission is "extremely significant to [their] claims of retaliation" and to the Commission's affirmative defense that it acted with a good faith belief it was not violating the law. They also assert the purported admission is highly relevant to their claim that the fluctuating hours method of compensation actually results in "less compensation for overtime hours than under the 'straight time' method" allegedly referenced during the Mediation.

In asking this Court to recognize a federal mediation privilege, the Defendant correctly identifies *Federal Rule of Evidence 501* as authority for the creation of evidentiary privileges under the federal common law. *Rule 501* provides:

> [T]he privilege of a witness, person, government, State, or political subdivision ... shall be governed by the principles of the common law as they may be interpreted by the courts of the United States in the light of reason and experience.

Id.[1]

The parties agree that the four factors annunciated by the Supreme Court in Jaffee v. Redmond, *518 U.S. 1, 116 S.Ct. 1923, 135 L.Ed.2d 337 (1996)* provide the standards for determining whether a potential federal evidentiary privilege should be recognized, and this Court joins the other federal courts that have focused on these same standards. *See, e.g., In re*

---

1. The second clause in *Rule 501*, which directs that privileges relevant to "element[s] of ... claim[s] or defense[s] as to which State law supplies the rule of decision" are determined by state law, is inapplicable here because the Plaintiffs' claims are asserted under a federal statute.

Air Crash Near Cali, Colombia on Dec. 20, 1995, 959 F.Supp. 1529, 1533–34 (S.D.Fla.1997) (*Jaffee* factors provide "a useful framework" for analyzing claim of privilege); *Folb v. Motion Picture Indus. Pension & Health Plans,* 16 F.Supp.2d 1164, 1171 (C.D.Cal.1998) (same); *cf. generally Pearson,* 211 F.3d at 66–67 (*quoting* and *citing* general principles annunciated in *Jaffee*).

The four relevant factors are:

(1) whether the asserted privilege is "rooted in the imperative need for confidence and trust";

(2) whether the privilege would serve public ends;

(3) whether the evidentiary detriment caused by an exercise of the privilege is modest; and

(4) whether denial of the federal privilege would frustrate a parallel privilege adopted by the states. *See Jaffee,* 518 U.S. at 9–13, 116 S.Ct. 1923.

Each of these factors weigh in favor of recognizing the mediation privilege in this case.

1. *The Mediation Privilege is Rooted in the Imperative Need for Confidence and Trust.*

Mediation "is the process in which an independent, impartial, trained, neutral third party, or mediator, facilitates the resolution of a dispute by assisting in reaching a voluntary agreement."

Both federal and state courts have recognized that confidentiality is essential to the mediation process. The federal circuit court in *Lake Utopia Paper Ltd. v. Connelly Containers, Inc.,* 608 F.2d 928 (2d Cir.1979) succinctly articulated why confidentiality is necessary:

> If participants cannot rely on the confidential treatment of everything that transpires during [mediation] sessions *then counsel of necessity will feel constrained to conduct themselves in a cautious, tight-lipped, non-committal manner more suitable to poker players in a high-stakes game than to adversaries attempting to arrive at a just resolution of a civil dispute. This atmosphere* if allowed to exist *would surely destroy the effectiveness of a program which has led to settlements ...,* *thereby expediting cases at a time when ... judicial resources ... are sorely taxed. Id.* at 930 (emphasis added).

The need for confidence and trust in the mediation process is further evidenced by federal statute, the local rules of federal district courts in Pennsylvania and other states, and state statutes from across the country. The Alternative Dispute Resolution Act of 1998, which requires each federal district court to "provide litigants in all civil cases with at least one alternative dispute resolution process, including ... mediation," expressly directs the courts to adopt local rules "provid[ing] for the confidentiality of the alternative dispute resolution processes and to prohibit disclosure of confidential dispute resolution communications." *See* 28 U.S.C. § 652(d).

CHAPTER III MEDIATION

As directed by Congress, the District Courts of Pennsylvania have adopted provisions addressing the confidentiality of mediation communications and documents. This District's Local Rule, for example, provides:

All counsel and parties shall treat as confidential all written and oral communications made in connection with or during any conference and no such communications may be disclosed to anyone not involved in the litigation. *Nor may any such communication be used for any purpose (including impeachment) in the civil action or in any other proceedings.* Except for a written settlement agreement or any written stipulations executed by the parties or their counsel, *no party or counsel shall be bound by anything done or said at any [mediation] conference[ ].*

See W. Dist. Local R. 16.3.5(E)[2] (emphasis added); *see also* M. Dist. Local R. 16.8.6(c) (mediation "proceeding shall not be used by any adverse party for any reason in the litigation at issue"); E. Dist. Local R. 53.2.1(5)(e) ("nothing communicated during the mediation process[,] including any oral or written statement made by a[n] ... attorney or other participant ... [,] shall be placed in evidence, made known to the trial court or jury, *or construed for any purpose as an admission*").

Finally, as noted by another district court that adopted the federal mediation privilege, forty-nine states and the District of Columbia have adopted "a mediation privilege of one type or another." *See Folb,* 16 F.Supp.2d at 1179 (*citing* Pamela A. Kentra, *Hear No Evil, See No Evil, Speak No Evil: the Intolerable Conflict for Attorney–Mediators Between the Duty to Maintain Mediation Confidentiality and the Duty to Report Fellow Attorney Misconduct,* B.Y.U. L.Rev. 715 (1997)). Based on the foregoing, it is beyond doubt that the mediation privilege is rooted in the imperative need for confidence and trust.

2. *The Mediation Privilege Would Serve the Public Ends of Encouraging Settlement and Reducing Court Dockets.*

As noted above, mediation is intended to facilitate and promote the voluntary conciliation, compromise and resolution of civil actions. Absent the mediation privilege, parties and their counsel would be reluctant to lay their cards on the table so that a neutral assessment of the relative strengths and weaknesses of their opposing positions could be made. Assuming they would even agree to participate in the mediation process absent confidentiality,[3] participants would necessarily "feel constrained to

---

2. To be sure, this District's Local Rule does not govern the instant motion because the Rule addresses "court-annexed mediation," *i.e.,* mediation ordered by the Court. *See* W. Dist. Local R. 16.3.1, 16.3.3(B). Nevertheless, the District Court's adoption of the confidentiality provisions in Rule 16.3 reveals its recognition of "the imperative need for confidence and trust" in the mediation process. *See* discussion *supra* at 513.

3. "Parties who fear that the results of an unsuccessful mediation attempt will come back to haunt them in a court of law will have little incentive to cooperate and compromise...." *See Willis,* 1998 WL 812110 at *2.

conduct themselves in a cautious, tight-lipped, non-committal manner more suitable to poker players in a high-stakes game than to adversaries attempting to arrive at a just resolution of a civil dispute." *Lake Utopia,* 608 F.2d at 930. The effectiveness of mediation would be destroyed, thereby threatening the well established public needs of encouraging settlement and reducing court dockets.

3. *The Evidentiary Detriment Caused by Exercise of the Mediation Privilege is Modest.*

In *Jaffee,* the Supreme Court explained why the psychotherapist-patient privilege it recognized for the first time caused only a modest evidentiary detriment:

> If the privilege were rejected, *confidential conversations between psychotherapists and their patients would surely be chilled,* particularly when it is obvious that the circumstances that give rise to the need for treatment will probably result in litigation. *Without a privilege, much of the desirable evidence to which litigants such as petitioner seek access—for example, admissions against interest by a party—is unlikely to come into being.* This unspoken "evidence" will therefore serve no greater truth-seeking function than if it had been spoken and privileged. *Id.,* 518 U.S. at 11–12, 116 S.Ct. 1923 (emphasis added).

This analysis presents the most compelling basis for adopting and applying the mediation privilege in this case. If the Commission had not participated in the Mediation, the admission against interest purportedly made by one of its attorneys would not likely have come into being. This Court sees no reasoned basis for allowing the Plaintiffs to enjoy the benefit of an alleged admission arising through the mediation process when it seems doubtful that such an admission would have otherwise come into existence.

The Court notes, though, that the rationale underlying the mediation privilege does not justify precluding the Plaintiffs' discovery of the alleged admission or the facts underlying it independent and outside the scope of the mediation process. *See* Fed.R.Evid. 408 ("This rule does not require the exclusion of any evidence otherwise discoverable merely because it is presented in the course of compromise negotiations."); *see also* Pamela A. Kentra, *Hear No Evil,* B.Y.U. L.Rev. at 735 (noting that certain states' mediation privilege statutes contain an "otherwise discoverable information" exception); *see also, e.g.,* 42 Pa. Cons.Stat. § 5949(b)(4) ("Any document which otherwise exists, or existed independent of the mediation and is not otherwise covered by this section, is not subject to this privilege."). In any event, a discussion of the Plaintiffs' potential attempts to discover information outside the scope of the Mediation would be premature, as the Defendants have only requested protection of "[a]ll mediation communications and mediation documents...." In sum, the Supreme Court's analysis in *Jaffee* confirms that the evidentiary detriment caused by an exercise of the mediation privilege is modest.

474   CHAPTER III   MEDIATION

4. *Denial of the Federal Mediation Privilege Would Frustrate a Parallel Privilege Adopted by the States.*

As noted above, nearly all of the states have adopted a mediation privilege. *See* Appendix in *Hear No Evil*, B.Y.U. L.Rev. at 757–75, which contains a chart summarizing mediation privilege statutes for the many states. The states' "promise[s] of confidentiality" regarding mediation "would have little value if the [participants] were aware that the privilege would not be honored in . . . federal court." *See Jaffee*, 518 U.S. at 13, 116 S.Ct. 1923. Thus, a "[d]enial of the federal privilege . . . would frustrate the purposes of the state legislation that was enacted to foster" confidentiality in the mediation process. Based on the foregoing analysis, this Court concludes that all of the factors in *Jaffee* counsel in favor of recognizing a federal mediation privilege here. Like the psychotherapy-patient privilege adopted in that case, the mediation privilege creates a "public good transcending the normally predominant principle of utilizing all rational means for ascertaining truth." *See Jaffee*, 518 U.S. at 9.

Nothing in the Plaintiffs' opposition brief demonstrates the contrary. First, for reasons articulated above, their suggestion that "[n]o private interest is furthered" by adopting the privilege is entirely without merit. Under the first prong in *Jaffee,* Plaintiffs' counsel apparently attempts to distinguish the Mediation from the "normal mediation process," stating that Local 30 "had no recourse" once mediation did not result in a settlement. Aside from the obvious fact that the *Plaintiffs* have enjoyed the recourse of filing a federal lawsuit, Counsel provides no legal authority for the proposition that Local 30's potential rights are in any way relevant to the privilege issue.

Nor can the Plaintiffs support their suggestion that the Mediation was "essentially meaningless" because the Commission was not bound by any findings of the mediator. By definition, mediation is a non-binding dispute resolution technique through which "a neutral third party" . . . *facilitates the resolution of a dispute* by assisting parties *in reaching a voluntary agreement.* The very nature of this process mandates a need for confidence and trust so that the parties can honestly and openly discuss the strengths and weaknesses of their positions in an attempt to reach a voluntarily settlement. The Plaintiffs' "private interest" arguments are of no avail.

So too are their arguments regarding "public interest." Under this prong, the Plaintiffs merely reiterate their claim that the mediation process here was meaningless and they state that the privilege "would only give the [Commission] a license to lie and encourage disingenuity." *See id.* The Plaintiffs' sentiments notwithstanding, Congress, the legislatures of nearly every state, and this and other District Courts have recognized the valuable role that mediation plays in our judicial system. Additionally, this Court fails to see how an adoption of the mediation privilege creates a license for litigants to lie or to be disingenuous. To the contrary, the privilege fosters mediation participants' candor and honesty regarding the validity of their positions by alleviating their "fear[s that] an unsuccessful mediation attempt will come back to haunt them in a court of law."

E. CONFIDENTIALITY IN MEDIATION **475**

Regarding the third prong in *Jaffee,* the Plaintiffs suggest that the Commission's purported admission "would have been spoken with or without a privilege because" the Defendant agreed to participate in the Mediation. This argument turn's the reasoning in *Jaffee* on its head. The *Jaffee* Court concluded that, if the privilege at issue there "*were rejected,* confidential conversations ... would surely be chilled," thereby making it unlikely for "admissions against interest by a party" like the purported one here "to come into being." This is the appropriate analysis, and it demonstrates precisely why the Plaintiffs should not be afforded the benefit of the purported admission.

Regarding the fourth prong in *Jaffee,* the Plaintiffs' arguments simply cannot explain away the nearly unanimous voices of state legislatures from across the country adopting mediation privileges. The only other argument the Plaintiffs present in opposing an application of the mediation privilege is their contention that the Commission "waived the privilege by putting" mediation communications and documents "at issue" in this case. A review of the record, however, reveals the contrary. The mediation issue arose only after Mr. Haas and an agent of Local 30 referenced it in their depositions. The Plaintiffs have not and cannot support their assertion that discussions in depositions of the Mediation by them or agents of Local 30 somehow effectuated a waiver of the privilege on behalf of the Commission.[4]

Having concluded that the federal mediation privilege will be adopted and applied in this case the Court must, to the extent possible, define the contours of the privilege. Because this District's Local Rule 16.3 addresses standards regarding the appropriate scope of confidentiality in the mediation process (albeit, within the context of court-annexed mediation), the Court concludes that the Rule is an appropriate starting point for defining the privilege. Accordingly, the mediation privilege recognized herein shall comport with the following standards:

- The privilege protects from disclosure "all written and oral communications made in connection with or during" a mediation conducted before a "neutral" mediator.

- No such written or oral communication may be "used for any purpose (including impeachment) in the civil action or in any other proceedings."

- "Except for a written settlement agreement or any written stipulations executed by the parties or their counsel, no party or counsel shall be bound by anything done or said" during the mediation process.

In addition, this Court has already concluded that the most compelling reason for recognizing the mediation privilege is the Plaintiffs' lack of

---

4. Nor have the Plaintiffs demonstrated that Defense counsel's following up on Mr. Haas' references to the Mediation in his deposition, without immediately asserting the mediation privilege, renders the instant motion untimely or otherwise inappropriate. Finally, this magistrate judge fails to see how the Defendant's assertion of the affirmative defense that it acted on a good faith belief that its conduct was lawful constitutes a waiver of the mediation privilege. *Cf. generally United States v. Liebman,* 742 F.2d 807, 811 n. 4 (3d Cir.1984) (refusing to find waiver of privilege "on a speculative basis").

entitlement to any admission of the Defendant that, but for the mediation process, would not have come into being. If the Plaintiff is able to elicit any admissions (or facts underlying them) outside the scope of the mediation process, however, the rationale for the privilege would no longer apply. Accordingly, this Court concludes and therefore holds that the mediation privilege does not protect from disclosure "any evidence otherwise" and independently "discoverable merely because it [wa]s presented in the course of" the Mediation. Accordingly, the Plaintiffs remain free to conduct discovery independent of, and unrelated to, the mediation process.

Finally, the Court notes that the elements listed above are by no means intended to be an exhaustive recitation of the standards governing the mediation privilege. Numerous court and legislatures have recognized exceptions and/or limitations to the privilege not implicated in this case. These issues must be saved for another day.

NOTES AND QUESTIONS

1. In finding little evidentiary detriment caused by exercise of the privilege, the court in *Sheldone* states that "it seems doubtful that such an admission would have otherwise come into existence" because the attorney would not have made the admission against interest. Can't the same be said of all mediations or negotiations—that admissions wouldn't be made if the individual hadn't thought it was confidential? That would seem to justify a blanket privilege for all mediations, and courts have not been willing to do that. Or should we look to the particular circumstances of each mediation to determine if the speaker had a reasonable expectation of confidentiality? The trouble with that approach is that judicially created privileges would vary from case to case. Would it be appropriate to consider under this prong of *Jaffee* how important the admission is for the plaintiffs to make out their case, independent of whether it would have been made outside of the mediation?

2. The mediation in *Sheldone* was the third step of a grievance procedure between the Commission and the union. Arguably the mediation was mandated, unlike many mediations which are voluntary. Does that make mediation confidentiality more or less compelling?

3. In N.L.R.B. v. Joseph Macaluso, Inc., 618 F.2d 51 (9th Cir.1980), the court created a privilege for a mediation between a union and a company conducted by the Federal Mediation and Conciliation Service (FMCS) relating to stalled collective bargaining negotiations. Thereafter, the National Labor Relations Board (NLRB) found the company had engaged in unfair labor practices by failing to execute a formal contract and pay back-compensation after having reached an agreement with the union at the mediation. The company claimed no agreement was reached and, on appeal to an administrative law judge, sought to subpoena the mediator to testify on this question. The court held the testimony was privileged, concluding that "the public interest in maintaining the perceived and actual impartiality of federal mediators does outweigh the benefits derivable from [the mediator's] testimony." It relied heavily on the intent of Congress in creating the FMCS of encouraging mediation in the interests of resolving labor disputes and the existence of an FMCS regulation that provided that no employee of the FMCS could be required, in response to a subpoena, to disclose information acquired in the performance of his duty. Do you think the court in *Macaluso* would have reached the conclusion that "the complete exclusion of mediator testimony is necessary to the preservation of an effective system of labor mediation" without the provisions in the FMCS statute and regulations suggesting limitations on the subpoena power and the desirability that mediators not be required to testify? Is the privilege recognized in *Macaluso* limited to the labor mediation situation or to the FMCS? See *Drukker Communications, Inc. v. N.L.R.B.*, 700 F.2d 727, 731–34 (D.C.Cir.1983) (NLRB testimony accorded qualified privilege). Is the need for privilege really any greater in labor relations than other mediation situations?

4. The court in *Macaluso* concluded that the public interest in confidentiality outweighs "the interest in obtaining every person's evidence." Should the balancing of the potential injury from disclosure against the harm resulting from denial of the testimony be made on the basis of the facts in the particular case or on the general policies of availability of evidence versus mediation confidentiality? In *Macaluso*, unlike *Sheldone*, the testimony was not simply an admission that might not have been made outside of the mediation, but related to a "fact" as to whether an agreement had been reached in the mediation, and the only alternative sources for the mediator's testimony was the conflicting testimony of the parties. Shouldn't the uniqueness of his testimony cut against finding a privilege? If one party is lying about what happened in the mediation, why isn't it critical to the success of mediation *as a process* that the mediator be able to set the record straight?

Fenton v. Howard

Arizona Supreme Court, 1978.
118 Ariz. 119, 575 P.2d 318.

■ HAYS, JUSTICE

Guillermo Martinez, real party in interest, sustained severe facial scarring as a result of an automobile accident involving Bruce Parsil, the other real party in interest. As a result of the facial scarring, Martinez claimed his marriage began to deteriorate. About a year later, he filed for dissolution of his marriage. He and his wife participated in counseling through the Court of Conciliation. Later Martinez brought an action against Parsil for personal injuries. Some of the damages alleged in the personal injury action were for emotional stress resulting from the scarring of Martinez's face. Martinez subpoenaed Don Crawford, the assistant director of the Court of Conciliation of Pima County, for the purpose of taking his deposition. The subpoena required Crawford to bring to the

478 CHAPTER III MEDIATION

deposition "any and all documents, records, reports, and/or notes concerning counseling services rendered to the above-named Plaintiff."

Pima County Superior Court Judge Norman S. Fenton indicated in a minute entry that at the request of Crawford, the court on its own motion quashed the subpoena. Martinez moved to set aside the order quashing the subpoena. Citing A.R.S. § 25–381.16,[1] Judge Fenton refused to set aside the order on the basis that the confidential nature of the counseling at the Conciliation Court was the very heart of the Conciliation Court's effectiveness in rendering proper service to the persons it served. Although Martinez and his wife had signed forms authorizing Crawford to release information relevant to Martinez's emotional problems, the court stated that the "form" authorization was inadequate to cover the unique situation where more than communications by the plaintiff was involved, and the "form" did not cover the confidentiality of such things as the counselor's notes and observations. Martinez then brought a Special Action in the Court of Appeals alleging that the lower court had abused its discretion. * * * The Court of Appeals granted the relief requested by Martinez and ordered Judge Fenton to vacate the order quashing the subpoena.

* * *

[W]e believe that the subpoena as presently written is overbroad. A.R.S. § 25–381.16 gives a privilege to the *communications of the parties* to persons acting for the Conciliation Court and to reports of outside resource agencies. This does not mean that other matters coming to the attention of the Conciliation Court during the counseling of the parties must be freely and easily disclosed. Every court has inherent power to do those things which are necessary for the efficient exercise of its jurisdiction. See State v. Superior Court, 39 Ariz. 242, 5 P.2d 192 (1931). The jurisdiction of the Conciliation Court is set forth in A.R.S. § 25–381.08 which provides:

> "Whenever any controversy exists between spouses which may, unless a reconciliation is achieved, result in the legal separation, dissolution or annulment of the marriage or in the disruption of the household, and there is any minor child of the spouses or either of them whose welfare might be affected thereby, the conciliation court shall have jurisdiction over the controversy, and over the parties thereto and all persons having any relation to the controversy, as further provided in this article. Added Laws 1962, Ch. 119, § 1. As amended Laws 1973, Ch. 139, § 3."

The Conciliation Court's jurisdiction is further defined by A.R.S. § 25–381.01 which states:

> "The purposes of this article are to promote the public welfare by preserving, promoting and protecting family life and the institution of matrimony, to protect the rights of children, and to provide means for

---

1. [ed.] "Hearings or conferences ... shall be held in private.... All communications, verbal or written, from the parties to the judge, commissioner or counselor in a proceeding under this article shall be deemed confidential communications, and shall not be disclosed without the consent of the party making such communication."

the reconciliation of spouses and the amicable settlement of domestic and family controversies. Added Laws 1962, Ch. 119, § 1.''

Under these statutes and State v. Superior Court, supra, the Conciliation Court may refuse to disclose matters not made privileged by A.R.S. § 25–381.16, if disclosure will hamper the Conciliation Court in carrying out its purposes.

However, the court's right to protect its ability to function effectively by prohibiting disclosure must be balanced by the need of a litigant for the information sought. When, as in this case, a person claims that information in the custody of the Conciliation Court will be necessary, or very helpful, to him in another proceeding, an in-camera hearing must be held to determine the need for disclosure and the harm to the Conciliation Court if the desired disclosure is allowed. The judge should order disclosure of that material shown to be appropriate by a just balancing of the needs of the individual for the information and the need of the Conciliation Court for confidentiality.

■ CAMERON, C.J., STRUCKMEYER, V.C.J., and GORDON, J., concur.

■ HOLOHAN, JUSTICE, specially concurring.

* * *

I part company with the majority on the resolution of this case as one involving the ''inherent powers'' of the judiciary. The majority leave the impression that the Conciliation Court system may be disrupted by requiring one of the conciliation counselors to testify at a deposition, and of course a judge has inherent power to prevent this. There is no suggestion or inference in the statute that the counselors of the Conciliation Court are entitled to any special treatment or have a personal privilege protecting their so-called work product.

The only privilege of confidentiality belongs to the parties appearing in the Conciliation Court. A.R.S. § 25–381.16(D). If there is a waiver of that privilege I find nothing implied in the statute which gives the counselors or director any basis to object to giving testimony on the matters conducted by them.

The form of consent to disclosure submitted by the parties to conciliation was inadequate to cover the situation. The consent form was the usual release of information form used in personal injury litigation. It authorized release of information to the signer's attorney. Since the deposition would involve disclosure to others not covered by the form, the waiver was not broad enough to waive the statutory privilege created by A.R.S. § 25–318.16(D). The Judge of the Conciliation Court was, therefore, justified in quashing the subpoena.

NOTES AND QUESTIONS

1. McCormick observes, regarding evidentiary privileges, that ''the right to object does not attach to the opposing party as such, but to the person vested with the outside interest or relationship fostered by the particular privilege." Charles T. McCormick, Handbook of the Law of Evidence 152 (1954). Whose interest is protected by the privilege in *Fenton*? If the purpose of the privilege is to encourage the *parties* to speak freely during mediation, what is the need for it when, as in *Fenton,* the plaintiff and his wife both signed forms authorizing the mediator to release the information? Does the privilege then run to the *mediator*? If so, what purpose is served by such a privilege? Is it to protect the mediator's interest in preserving his neutrality? How valid is that interest? It has been said that a mediator's neutrality is not compromised by testimony under subpoena and with consent of both parties and that "what's really at stake is careerism and professional self-interest." 2 BNA ADR Rptr. No. 8 (1988) (reporting on speech by Professor Eric Green). Do you agree? Is there more justification for protecting mediator neutrality in the case of an institutional mediator (as in *Macaluso* where the mediator was under the FMCS)?

2. Is the privilege in *Fenton* limited to court testimony, or would it apply to any attempt outside of court to obtain testimony from the mediator, as in an administrative proceeding? Could it be used to prevent the mediator voluntarily from disclosing what went on in the mediation, as to the press? Note that although "communication privileges often cover licensed professionals who are under an ethical duty not to disclose such information without a waiver from the client," most mediators are not licensed or certified and therefore are subject to discipline only from their employer if there is one. Tort or contract remedies may be available to a wronged party for violation of confidentiality, and one federal statute creates criminal penalties for mediator disclosure of information obtained in confidence (see 42 U.S.C.A. § 2000g–2).

3. The Arizona confidentiality statute, as noted in the concurring opinion in *Fenton,* provides a privilege only to the parties since it allows disclosure only with their consent. How did the court in *Fenton* reach the position that the mediator may assert a privilege? Is this a common-law or statutory privilege?

4. A confidentiality privilege may arise from state constitutional provisions. In Garstang v. Superior Court of Los Angeles County, 39 Cal.App.4th 526, 46 Cal.Rptr.2d 84 (2d Dist.1995), the plaintiff in a slander suit sought to compel an ombudsperson to answer deposition questions as to what was said in a session. The session was held between the plaintiff and her co-workers at Cal Tech concerning allegations that plaintiff had obtained a promotion through sexual favors. Plaintiff sought to elicit testimony that admissions were made in the session by co-workers that she had been treated unfairly. The court of appeals found that the California mediator confidentiality statute did not apply because, even if an ombudsman could be considered a mediator (which it did not decide), the parties had not executed the required confidentiality statement. However, the court found a qualified privilege for private institutions not to disclose communications

E. CONFIDENTIALITY IN MEDIATION **481**

made before an ombudsman in an attempt to mediate an employee dispute, based on the California constitutional right of privacy.

b. STATUTORY MEDIATION PRIVILEGE

A number of states have extended a statutory privilege to mediation. They range from short, broadly-stated provisions to long, narrowly-drawn statutes. The passage of a statute rarely resolves all issues as to mediation confidentiality. Often there are difficult problems of interpretation and application. There may be situations which the drafters did not foresee. Grants of confidentiality sometimes have not taken into account hard cases in which the policy favoring confidentiality is less compelling and the need for disclosure is greater. The variety of statutory approaches indicates that there is not yet a totally satisfactory solution to confidentiality questions. Consider the following survey of state statutory approaches to mediation confidentially.

Ellen E. Deason, Enforcing Mediated Settlement Agreements: Contract Law Collides With Confidentiality
35 U.C.Davis L.Rev. 33 (2001)

General mediation statutes protect confidentiality by relying on privileges, evidentiary exclusions, testimonial incapacity, or some combination of these or other legal mechanisms to prevent testimony regarding mediation communications in legal proceedings. The evidentiary limitations in many mediation statutes are broad enough to prevent a party from supporting a claim that an agreement was reached by introducing evidence about what transpired during the mediation. The scope of statutory coverage does vary, however, thus affecting the extent of protection. For example, many statutes protect "mediation communications," but this term is variously defined to include statements, documents, actions and/or agreements reached as a result of mediation.

Moreover, a statute's protection for mediation depends not only on what is encompassed by its definitions, but just as importantly on its exceptions. These exceptions to confidentiality also vary greatly in content and scope, and hence create significant differences among the states in the manner and extent to which they permit proof of mediated agreements. Evidentiary statutes can, however, be grouped according to five major approaches legislatures have taken to confidentiality when the parties dispute the existence of a mediated settlement. These are considered below, moving from the most to the least protective of confidentiality.

a. "Complete Confidentiality"

First, there are statutes written in absolute terms that make no exception to their confidentiality protections for the purpose of enforcing a mediated settlement agreement. They can be read to make an agreement that comes out of mediation as confidential as the mediation process. Some of these statutes protect mediation communications and documents with comprehensive evidentiary exclusions that do not contemplate exceptions.[32]

---

32. *See, e.g.,* ARK. CODE ANN. § 16–7–206 (Michie 1999); ME. R. EVID. § 408; MASS. GEN. LAWS ANN. ch. 233, § 23C (West, Lexis 2000); MO. ANN. STAT. § 435.014 (West 1992); NEV.

CHAPTER III MEDIATION

Others establish privileges, provide for waivers by the parties and/or the mediator, and enumerate some exceptions to confidentiality, but fail to make any type of exception for evidence to establish a settlement.[33] Under the terms of these statutes, this evidence is admissible only if the relevant mediation participants consent to waive their privilege. It is hard to know whether a jurisdiction with an evidentiary exclusions or a privilege of this type really intends to preclude mediation disclosures completely whenever an agreement is challenged or has instead overlooked the issue.

Many states have probably overlooked the issue. Texas, for example, makes confidential, among other things, "any record made at an alternative dispute resolution procedure."[34] The statute makes no exception when the record is a written agreement that resulted from mediation. Thus, if taken literally, the statute means that any mediated agreement between the parties, whether written or oral, must remain confidential. But if all settlements resulting from mediation were completely confidential, there would be no avenue available to enforce them, creating tension with the purpose of the Texas Act to use ADR to help bring litigation to a close. As Dean Edward Sherman has observed, given the stated purpose of the Act to encourage the use of ADR, "it would be anomalous to believe that the Act really intended to prevent the agreement from being disclosed."[35]

b. Narrow Exception for Memorialized Settlements

Second, there is a group of statutes that anticipate the possible need for evidence that the parties reached an agreement, but are structured to place evidence of confidential mediation communications and documents off limits. These statutes typically establish a mechanism to exclude evidence of the mediation (such as a privilege) but create an exception for documented settlements. Usually they mandate that the agreement must be written and signed by the parties,[36] although California also requires language that

---

REV. STAT. § 48.109 (Michie 1996); R.I. GEN. LAWS § 9–19–44 (1997).

33. *See, e.g.,* ARIZ. REV. STAT. ANN. § 12–2238 (West 1994); KAN. STAT. ANN. § 60–452a (Supp. 1999); MINN. STAT. ANN. § 595.02 subd 1a (West 2000); N.J. STAT. ANN. § 2A:23A–9 (West 2000); OKLA. STAT. ANN. tit. 12, § 1805 (West 1993); S.D. CODIFIED LAWS § 19–13–32 (Michie Supp. 2000); TEX. CIV. PRAC. & REM. CODE ANN. §§ 154.053(c), 154.073 (Vernon Supp. 2000); UTAH CODE ANN. § 78–31b–8 (LEXIS Supp. 2000) (court-annexed ADR).

34. TEX. CIV. PRAC. & REM. CODE ANN. § 154.073(b).

35. Edward F. Sherman, *Confidentiality in ADR Proceedings: Policy Issues Arising From the Texas Experience*, 38 S. TEX. L. REV. 541, 545 (1997). *See also* Eric R. Galton & Kimberlee K. Kovach, *Texas ADR: A Future*

So Bright We Gotta Wear Shades, 31 ST. MARY'S L.J. 949, 969 (2000).

36. *See, e.g.,* COLO. REV. STAT. § 13–22–302(2.5) (West 1997) (court-annexed ADR) ("mediation communication" covered by privilege defined to exclude written, executed settlement agreements); CONN. GEN. STAT. § 52–235d(b)(2) (Supp. 2000) FLA. STAT. ANN. § 44.102(3) (West Supp. 2001) (court-ordered mediation) (exception to privilege limited to executed settlement agreements); MONT. CODE ANN. § 26–1–813 (3) (1999) (exception to confidentiality for signed, written agreement); N.C. GEN. STAT. § 7A–38.1 (*l*) (1999) (court mediation program) (creating exception to evidentiary exclusion of mediation statements and conduct for proceedings to enforce a settlement, but specifying that only written, signed settlements shall be enforceable); OHIO REV. CODE ANN. § 2317.023 (Anderson 1998) (mediation provisions do not affect admissi-

E. Confidentiality in Mediation   **483**

the parties intend the agreement to be enforceable.[37] Some permit an alternative record of the agreement so long as the parties' assent is made plain. These alternatives to a writing foster flexibility at the mediation table and can include tape recording or other means that allow the parties to retrieve the specifics of the agreement.[38] But the key for admissibility of the mediated settlement is usually some form of memorialization.

By combining a privilege for mediation with an exception for memorialized settlements, these statutes protect the details of mediation from disclosure (unless the parties consent to that disclosure) whether or not the parties entered into a written agreement. When there is no documented settlement, there is no exception to the privilege that would allow a party to prove the existence of an agreement. When there is a documented settlement it can be introduced but, absent other exceptions or consent, the privilege prevents a party from invading the confidentiality of the mediation to argue that there was no agreement in spite of the document.

The Uniform Mediation Act, recently approved by NCCUSL, would fall within this group of statutes. It would establish a mediation privilege subject to an exception for a "record" of an agreement "signed by all parties to the agreement."[39] The drafters' remark that this exception is notable for what it does not include—that is, oral agreements.[40] Thus, a mediated settlement agreement would need to be memorialized as a prerequisite to enforcement because the privilege would prevent a party from relying on mediation communications to demonstrate an agreement. I argue below that this is the most appropriate balance between confidentiality and settlement enforcement when the existence of an agreement is in dispute.

---

bility of written, signed settlement agreement); 42 PA. CONS. STAT. ANN. § 5949(b)(1), (c) (West 2000) (written and signed settlement admissible to enforce agreement unless agreement specifies it is unenforceable or not intended to be binding); VA. CODE § 8.01–576.10 (Michie, LEXIS 2000) (court ADR program) (written settlement agreement not confidential unless the parties agree otherwise in writing); WASH. REV. CODE ANN. § 5.60.070(1)(e) (West 1995) (exception to mediation privilege for written agreement signed by the parties resulting from a mediation proceeding); WIS. STAT. ANN. § 904.085(4)(a) (West, LEXIS 1999) (inadmissibility provisions inapplicable to any written agreement, stipulation or settlement made during or pursuant to mediation).

37. *See, e.g.,* CAL. EVID. CODE § 1123 (written and signed settlement agreement reached pursuant to mediation is admissible if it states it is admissible or enforceable).

38. *See, e.g.,* CAL. EVID. CODE §§ 1118, 1124 (oral agreement admissible if recorded by court reporter or sound recording and reduced to writing and signed within 72 hours); FLA. R. CIV. PRO. 1.730 (agreement may be electronically or stenographically recorded by stipulation of the parties); N.C. SUPER. CT. MEDIATED SETTLEMENT CONF. R. 4(C) (same); *see also* Carr v. Runyan, 89 F.3d 327, 330 (7th Cir.1996) (recognizing agreement that mediator dictated and all parties affirmed on tape); Regents of Univ. Cal. v. Sumner, 42 Cal.App.4th 1209, 50 Cal.Rptr.2d 200 (1st Dist.1996) (recognizing tape recorded agreement); Plum Creek Timber Co. v. Hillman, 95 Wash.App. 1061, 1999 WL 350830 (1999) (enforcing tape recorded agreement stipulated to in writing).

39. UNIF. MEDIATION ACT § 7(a)(1) (2001). A "record" is defined as "information that is inscribed on a tangible medium or that is stored in an electronic or other medium and is retrievable in perceivable form." *Id.* § 3(9).

40. UNIF. MEDIATION ACT § 7(a)(1), Reporter's Working Notes (Proposed Official Draft, 2001).

CHAPTER III MEDIATION

c. Case-by-case Approach

Third, rather than making an across-the-board judgment that only written and signed documents are admissible to establish a mediated settlement, some legislatures leave this to a case-by-case determinations by the courts. In its mediation statute, Louisiana authorizes a judge to admit testimony on mediation communications in order to interpret or enforce a settlement agreement, but only if the judge first decides that the evidence is necessary to prevent fraud or manifest injustice.[41] Ohio and Wisconsin also grant similar discretion to their courts but do not limit the context to settlement enforcement. In these states the provision is intended to cover circumstances not anticipated or not resolved by the legislature: courts may make exceptions to mediation confidentiality in situations not covered by their confidentiality statutes.[42] This case-by-case approach opens the door for a court to pierce the confidentiality of mediation even when contract formalities have not been observed. But the standard for disclosures is high: as construed by the Ohio Supreme Court, the statutory requirement of "manifest injustice" requires a "clear or openly unjust act."[43]

This case-by-case approach gives the courts flexibility, but limits mediation disclosures in order to keep them rare. The disadvantage is that the court's judgment on confidentiality cannot be determined in advance, at the time of the mediation, when the parties to the mediation need the assurance. Moreover, because a court, rather than a bright-line rule, is the gatekeeper for confidentiality, the very possibility of an exception may stimulate unnecessary litigation .

d. Broad Exception for Settlement Enforcement

Fourth, a few legislatures have decided that when the enforceability of a mediated settlement is at issue, confidentiality must give way to the extent necessary to determine if an agreement was reached. Presumably this represents a policy determination to elevate enforceability of settlements over the risks potential disclosures pose for the mediation process. These jurisdictions make a full exception to their mediation confidentiality protections, without regard to whether the disputed agreement is written or oral.

For example, mediation communications and documents are admissible in Iowa under an exception to the parties' mediation privilege that applies whenever the information is relevant to determining the existence of an agreement that resulted from mediation or to enforcing such an agree-

---

41. *See* La. Rev. Stat. Ann. § 9:4112(B)(1)(c) (West Supp. 2000).

42. *See, e.g.,* Ohio Rev. Code Ann. § 2317.023(C)(4) (Anderson 1998); Wis. Stat. Ann. § 904.085(4)(e) (West 2000) (exception to prevent manifest injustice limited to proceedings distinct from the dispute that was mediated). The "manifest injustice" language originated in the Administrative Dispute Res-

olution Act of 1990, 5 U.S.C. § 574(a)(4)(A), (b)(5)(A) (1994 & Supp. IV 1998).

43. *See* Schneider v. Kreiner, 83 Ohio St.3d 203, 699 N.E.2d 83, 86 (Ohio 1998) (refusing to create a confidentiality exception to protect a party from potential criminal charges for failing to comply with mediated agreement).

E. Confidentiality in Mediation

ment.[44] Wyoming, which also has a mediation privilege, makes an exception any time one of the parties seeks judicial enforcement of a mediated settlement agreement.[45] Oregon's statute similarly provides an exception to confidentiality in a proceeding to enforce an agreement, but only to the extent "necessary to prosecute or defend the matter."[46] The confidentiality provision in the federal Administrative Dispute Resolution Act makes an exception to mediation confidentiality that permits parties to disclose communications relevant to determining the existence or meaning of a mediated agreement or to the enforcement of such an agreement.[47]

Although these statutes create broad exceptions, there are also signs of compromise to protect confidentiality to some degree. Iowa is more protective of the mediator's privilege than the parties' privilege, requiring the consent of all parties before the mediator can testify about mediation communications relevant to a claimed settlement.[48] This consent requirement lessens the likelihood that a mediator will be required to testify, thus limiting the potential damage to the mediation process. The Administrative Dispute Resolution Act also differentiates between party and mediator testimony. While permitting disclosures to enforce a settlement as an exception to the parties' confidentiality obligations, it does not contain a parallel exception to the provisions that govern mediator confidentiality.[49] Finally, Oregon attempts to mitigate the threat its broad exception poses to confidentiality by permitting courts to seal the records of enforcement proceedings to prevent further disclosure of mediation communications.[50] In spite of these safeguards, however, this approach to settlement enforcement, like a case-by-case analysis, casts doubt on the promise of confidentiality for mediation through the possibility that one party will allege an oral agreement.

e. No Statutory Coverage

Finally, many mediations take place without any statutory protection for confidentiality other than the inadequate evidentiary exclusion of Federal Rule of Evidence 408 and its widely-adopted state equivalents, which do not apply to discovery or administrative/ proceedings and which exclude statements made in mediations from evidence only in limited circumstances.[51] Approximately half the states lack a comprehensive media-

---

44. Iowa Code § 679C.2(7) (West Supp. 2000).

45. Wyo. Stat. Ann. § 1–43–103(c)(v) (LEXIS 1999). *See also* General Order Governing the Appellate Conference Program ¶ 8 (5th Cir. Mar. 27, 2000) (exception to privilege in a proceeding to enforce a settlement agreement).

46. Or. Rev. Stat. § 36.222(4) (1999).

47. 5 U.S.C. § 574(b)(6). At least one federal district court local mediation rule

makes a similar exception. In the District of Idaho, parties cannot use mediation communications in any pending or future proceeding, except in a separate legal action brought to enforce a mediated settlement. D. Idaho R., Order 130(r).

48. Iowa Code § 679C.3(6).

49. 5 U.S.C. § 574(a), (b).

50. Or. Rev. Stat. § 36.222(4).

51. Indiana has interpreted its version of the rule to strengthen the protection for

486 CHAPTER III MEDIATION

tion statute and thus cannot be included in any of the four categories described above. Instead, state statutes that establish particular mediation programs may include separate confidentiality provisions, creating a patchwork of protections made up of one or more of these approaches. This leaves mediations that fall outside the scope of these statutes without confidentiality protection, and in many states the holes in statutory coverage may allow a substantial number of mediations to slip through.[52] By default, agreements from mediations without confidentiality protection are subject to the jurisdiction's normal contract rules for proving settlements unless they are covered by a special writing requirement.

Three Statutory Approaches

Colo.Rev.Stat. § 13–22–307 (Supp.1995)

Confidentiality

(1) **Dispute resolution meetings** may be closed at the discretion of the mediator.

(2) Any party or the mediator or mediation organization in a mediation service proceeding or a dispute resolution proceeding shall not voluntarily disclose or through discovery or compulsory process be required to disclose any information concerning any mediation communication or any communication provided in confidence to the mediator or a mediation organization, unless and to the extent that:

(a) All parties to the dispute resolution proceeding and the mediator consent in writing; or

(b) The mediation communication reveals the intent to commit a felony, inflict bodily harm, or threaten the safety of a child under the age of eighteen years; or

(c) The mediation communication is required by statute to be made public; or

---

mediation communications. In Maine, the Rule 408 protections are stronger for court-sponsored domestic relations mediation: conduct or statements by a party are not admissible for any purpose. ME. R. EVID. 408(b). *See also* MO. ANN. STAT. § 435.014 (West 1992); NEV. REV. STAT. § 49.109(3) (Michie 1996); S.D. CODIFIED LAWS § 19–13–32 (Michie Supp. 2000) (all labeling mediation as a settlement negotiation, but conferring protection more consistent with an evidentiary exclusion than with Rule 408).

52. In Illinois, for example, mediations have statutory protection for confidentiality only if they concern human rights issues. 775 ILL. COMP. STAT. § 5/7B–102(E) (West 1996). The primary source of confidentiality is state court rules that protect confidentiality only for court-annexed mediation programs. As a further problem, even when specialized statutes do provide for confidentiality, they may define their protection too narrowly, leaving crucial communications or documents open for disclosure and creating variation in confidentiality protection within a single state.

(d) Disclosure of the mediation communication is necessary and relevant to an action alleging willful or wanton misconduct of the mediator or mediation organization.

(3) Any mediation communication that is disclosed in violation of this section shall not be admitted into evidence in any judicial or administrative proceeding.

(4) Nothing in this section shall prevent the discovery or admissibility of any evidence that is otherwise discoverable, merely because the evidence was presented in the course of a mediation service proceeding or dispute resolution proceeding.

(5) Nothing in this section shall prevent the gathering of information for research or educational purposes, or for the purpose of evaluating or monitoring the performance of a mediator, mediation organization, mediation service, or dispute resolution program, so long as the parties or the specific circumstances of the parties' controversy are not identified or identifiable.

Mass.Ann.Laws ch. 233, § 23C

All memoranda, and work product prepared by a mediator and a mediator's case files, shall be confidential and not subject to disclosure in any judicial or administrative proceeding involving any of the parties to any mediation. And any communication made in the course of and relating to the subject matter of any mediation and which is made in the presence of such mediator by any participant, mediator or other person shall be a confidential communication and not subject to disclosure in any such judicial or administrative proceeding; provided, however, that the provisions of this section shall not apply to the mediation of labor disputes.

For the purposes of this section a mediator shall mean a person not a party to a dispute who enters into a written agreement with the parties to assist them in resolving their disputes and has completed at least thirty hours of training in mediation and who either has four years of professional experience as a mediator or is accountable to a dispute resolution organization which has been in existence for at least three years or one who has been appointed to mediate by a judicial or governmental body.

Texas Civil Practice and Remedies Code

Title 7, chapter 154.

AN ACT relating to alternative dispute resolution procedures.

Sec. 154.002. POLICY. It is the policy of this state to encourage the peaceable resolution of disputes, with special consideration given to disputes involving the parent-child relationship, including the mediation of issues involving conservatorship, possession, and the support of children,

CHAPTER III MEDIATION

and the early settlement of pending litigation through voluntary settlement procedures.

* * *

Sec. 154.023. MEDIATION. (a) Mediation is a forum in which an impartial person, the mediator, facilitates communication between parties to promote reconciliation, settlement, or understanding among them. (b) A mediator may not impose his own judgment on the issues for that of the parties.

* * *

Sec. 154.073. CONFIDENTIALITY OF COMMUNICATIONS IN DISPUTE RESOLUTION PROCEDURES. (a) Except as provided by Subsections (c) and (d), a communication relating to the subject matter of any civil or criminal dispute made by a participant in an alternative dispute resolution procedure, whether before or after the institution of formal judicial proceedings, is confidential, is not subject to disclosure, and may not be used as evidence against the participant in any judicial or administrative proceeding.

(b) Any record made at an alternative dispute resolution procedure is confidential, and the participants or the third party facilitating the procedure may not be required to testify in any proceedings relating to or arising out of the matter in dispute or be subject to process requiring disclosure of confidential information or data relating to or arising out of the matter in dispute.

(c) An oral communication or written material used in or made a part of an alternative dispute resolution procedure is admissible or discoverable if it is admissible or discoverable independent of the procedure.

(d) If this section conflicts with other legal requirements for disclosure of communications or materials, the issue of confidentiality may be presented to the court having jurisdiction of the proceedings to determine, *in camera,* whether the facts, circumstances, and the context of the communications or materials sought to be disclosed warrant a protective order of the court or whether the communications or materials are subject to disclosure.

NOTES AND QUESTIONS

1. How would you describe the difference in approach in the Colorado, Massachusetts, and Texas statutes?

2. Consider the following criticisms of the Massachusetts statute in Green, A Heretical View of a Mediation Privilege, 2 Ohio St.J.Dispute Res. 1, at 29–30 (1986):

"The primary problem with the Massachusetts statute, as with all statutes of this sort that I have seen, is that it is both over-inclusive and under-inclusive. The act is over-inclusive because, unlike the attorney-client privilege, the husband-wife privilege, and the evidentiary exclusionary rule, it contains no exception for bad faith, illegal conduct, fraud, or any other abuse of the mediation process, nor any exception when other important values are at stake. Exceptions to prevent such results arguably could be inferred by a court, but there is not a textual hook in the statute on which to peg such judicial legislation. Moreover, if exceptions are to be inferred on an ad hoc basis, what is the advantage of a statute that appears absolute but which, in fact, is subject to case-by-case determination? Would it not be better simply to leave matters to courts to apply a public policy approach to mediation results and fruits?

The statute is under-inclusive in that it applies only to judicial or administrative proceedings involving former parties to the mediation. By implication, an attempt to discover or use mediation results or fruits in other circumstances is not privileged, even though protection may be appropriate. The statute is under-inclusive for the further reason that it applies only to mediation conducted by a 'mediator' as the term is defined in the second paragraph of the statute. To qualify, a mediator must have certain training and experience and must act pursuant to a written agreement with the parties. Again, the negative implication is that mediation conducted by anyone else or without a written agreement is to be totally discoverable and admissible. Many mediators, such as internal ombudsmen in corporations, educational institutions, and governmental agencies constantly conduct mediation without any opportunity to enter into a written agreement with the parties. Confidentiality is probably more important and appropriate for such mediation than other mediation covered by the statute, yet the existence of the statute invites judicial interpretation that is not covered, and hence not confidential.''

3. What kinds of mediation information are protected by the Texas statute under the term "communication relating to the subject matter of any civil or criminal dispute made by a participant in an alternative dispute resolution procedure, whether before or after the institution of formal judicial proceedings"? Would the specific details of a settlement be a "communication"? Who may invoke the statute's protections?

4. Even an ADR statute with a broad confidentiality provision may fail to provide protection for all mediations. For example, a 1999 Texas Attorney General Opinion concluded that a victim-offender mediation conducted by the Texas Department of Criminal Justice is not a mediation under the ADR Act and therefore not entitled to the Act's confidentiality protections. *Op. Tex. Att'y Gen., Open Records Decision No. 659 (1999)*. The Texas legislature had amended the Code of Criminal Procedure to provide that "before accepting a plea of guilty or a plea of nolo contendere and on the request of a victim of the offense, the court may assist the victim and the defendant in participating in a victim-offender mediation program." To participate, the offender had to admit guilt or otherwise accept responsibility for the crime, and a judge could impose mediation as a condition of probation. In this case, a prosecutor sought to obtain videotapes of a victim-

CHAPTER III MEDIATION

offender mediation in the belief that they might provide evidence of other serious offenses by the offender. The Opinion found this was not a mediation within the meaning of the ADR Act "[b]ecause the objective of the department's victim-offender mediation is to provide a means for the victims and offenders to therapeutically and emotionally cope with the aftermath of the commission of a crime rather than resolving any civil or criminal dispute." It noted that the stated purpose of the ADR Act is to "encourage the peaceable resolution of disputes" and "the early settlement of pending litigation through voluntary settlement procedures." Victim-offender mediation, the Opinion found, "does not involve the resolution of a criminal dispute because, before mediation commences, the offender has been adjudicated of the crime [and] the offender has admitted guilt and has accepted responsibility for the crime."

Mediators have criticized the Opinion as lacking an understanding of the mediation process. They argue that mediation does not distinguish between therapeutic effects and resolving elements of a crime or cause of action. Mediation instead takes a holistic approach to a dispute, recognizing that emotional and personal issues may be as critical to ultimate resolution as are the elements of the crime or cause of action. Although an offender may have admitted guilt or responsibility, various aspects of a "dispute" may still need to be resolved in a mediation. It is true that the victim/offender program, as the Opinion pointed out, "is a personal process between victim and offender and is totally separate from and can have no bearing on an offender's particular judicial/appellate proceedings." Nevertheless, mediators argue, the emotional closure sought by the victim may constitute a part of the dispute that is still unresolved even after the offender accepts responsibility. The confidentiality that encourages that closure is as necessary for victim-offender mediations as in mediations where responsibility has not yet been decided.

5.   Consider the following arguments for four exceptions to confidentiality in Sherman, A Process Model and Agenda for Civil Justice Reforms in the States, 46 Stanford L.Rev. 1553, 1580–82 (1994):

> *Information to the court regarding compliance with its order.* A court that has ordered the parties to participate in ADR has a valid interest in obtaining certain information about the proceeding to determine if the parties complied with its order. This need may arise when one party seeks sanctions against another for not complying with requirements specified in the order (such as exchanging information or position papers, having adequate authority to settle, or participating in good faith). This situation presents a need for an exception to confidentiality to permit the court to obtain information relevant to determining compliance with its order.
>
> *Information relating to the meaning or enforcement of an agreement resulting from ADR.* In a suit to enforce an agreement resulting from an ADR proceeding, one party may seek to introduce communications made in the proceeding that relate to the meaning or enforceability of the agreement. If, for example, there is a dispute over the

meaning of a key provision and recourse to testimony from the parties or a third-party neutral could resolve it, a court may avoid inaccuracy and unfairness by allowing the testimony. Likewise, a party is entitled to raise fraud, coercion, illegality, mutual mistake, and other contract defenses in a suit to enforce, modify, or void an agreement. Exclusion of such evidence—for example, that a husband in a divorce mediation, upon being asked about his assets, failed to reveal that he has $500,000 in a Swiss bank account—jeopardizes the integrity of the ADR process.

The fear driving the insistence on an absolute rule of confidentiality, however, is that parties attempting to avoid a settlement agreement will always be able to find some ambiguity in the terms of an ADR settlement or to claim some contract defense, and there will be nothing left of ADR confidentiality. This concern might be alleviated by excepting from confidentiality only extreme situations involving genuine uncertainty as to critical clauses in the agreement or raising aggravated defenses like fraud, and then only for the limited purpose of determining the precise issue in controversy. But the "floodgates" concern remains a powerful one, and accommodating the need for accuracy and integrity of the process, on one hand, with the need for confidentiality to make the process work, on the other, presents a difficult challenge.

Information relevant to third-party malpractice. If a third-party neutral is charged with malpractice (such as intentional disclosure of a party's confidences made in a caucus), the confidentiality rule would effectively prevent proof of wrongdoing. This might be a happy solution for neutrals, but it is inconsistent with the fact that most states have chosen not to immunize them for wrongful acts in the performance of their ADR duties. This situation involves only a small number of cases, and an exception to confidentiality for communications relating to neutral malpractice seems appropriate.

Public access to information relevant to the public interest. A number of states have rules or statutes guaranteeing public access to certain kinds of proceedings or information deemed within the public interest. "Open meetings and records" acts, for example, are intended to ensure that decision-making in government is open to public scrutiny. While such statutes only affect ADR when a government agency is a party, ADR is increasingly being used in administrative and public policy law contexts. A clash between open meetings laws and ADR confidentiality may arise when a mediation order in a suit to which the government is a party requires the parties to send a representative with settlement authority. If the mediation is considered a "meeting" under the particular open meetings act (usually defined as any deliberation of a government body at which formal action is taken), then it must be open to the public.

An ADR confidentiality rule, and courts issuing orders to participate in ADR, should try to make them compatible with open meetings act requirements. For example, a court may have to recognize that a government agency's representative at a confidential mediation is not able to possess full authority to settle. He may be limited to agreeing to preliminary understandings with the other party, leaving the ultimate agreement to settle for a deliberative session of the governing board of the agency, which must be open to the public.

In recent years, a host of new rules and statutes have made settlement agreements matters of public record. These rules strive to protect public health and safety and promote greater integrity in attorneys and clients. ADR, on the other hand, promotes resolution without publicity, making it especially attractive to defendants facing claims of flagrant product defects, professional malpractice, or environmental pollution. By making discovery and the terms of a settlement open to the public, state open-litigation rules conflict with ADR confidentiality. Some compromise solutions may be possible, such as according confidentiality only to communications made in the actual ADR proceeding, but not to discovery nor to all the terms of an agreement. Before adopting ADR confidentiality, states or courts should carefully consider trying to harmonize it with policies or rules that favor open litigation.

6. Does a state mediator's confidentiality privilege apply in a federal court? Under the doctrine of Erie Railroad Co. v. Tompkins, 304 U.S. 64, 58 S.Ct. 817, 82 L.Ed. 1188 (1938), a federal court in a diversity case is required to apply the substantive law of the state in which it sits. Matters of privilege have generally been found to be substantive under *Erie*. The Federal Rules of Evidence provides that matters of privilege are governed "by the principles of the common law as they may be interpreted by the courts of the United States in the light of reason and experience," but, in diversity cases, "shall be determined in accordance with State law." Rule 501. In Smith v. Smith, 154 F.R.D. 661 (N.D.Tex.1994), a securities fraud and RICO case (and therefore within "federal question" jurisdiction), a federal magistrate judge quashed a subpoena served on a mediator appointed by a state court in a related state-court suit. Defendants sought to obtain the mediator's testimony to refute the plaintiff's claim that defendants had made misrepresentations in the mediation that resulted in a settlement agreement. The district judge found that federal law would govern whether there was a mediator privilege and declined to determine whether one existed in this case, noting the Supreme Court's reluctance to confer new privileges. However, it upheld the quashing of the subpoena on the ground that the magistrate relied on comity and the expectations of the parties who agreed that the Texas ADR Act's mediator privilege provision would apply. See also Deason, Predictable Mediation Confidentiality in the U.S. Federal System, Ohio S.J.Dis.Resol. (2001).

c. CARVING OUT EXCEPTIONS FROM MEDIATION CONFIDENTIALITY

The movement to create statutory mediation confidentiality statutes has given rise to a debate over how broad confidentiality protection should be. Although some earlier statutes, like Texas, were stated in absolute

E.   CONFIDENTIALITY IN MEDIATION   **493**

terms, drafters have increasingly been crafting carefully-worded exceptions in recognition of special situations in which confidentiality may result in unfairness. The drafting of the Uniform Mediation Act provided a forum for this debate, and the act went through a number of emanations of exceptions, often eliciting much disagreement and heat. Courts have also gotten into the act when confronted with vagueness in statutory confidentiality provisions or with troubling situations if the full scope of confidentiality were to be accorded. Courts increasingly have to reconcile ADR confidentiality provisions with evidentiary privilege rules (which are sometimes parallel and sometimes somewhat different) and the interplay of contract law and evidentiary rules like the parole evidence rule.

(1) Exception for Evidence of the Mediated Agreement

When a broad statute, like Texas', makes confidential "any record made at an alternate dispute resolution procedure,"[1] can that mean that if an agreement is put in writing and signed by the parties at the mediation, it is confidential? How can a mediation achieve its purpose if the very agreement that results is confidential and therefor cannot be introduced for any purpose, including presentation to a court for enforcement? "It would be anomaolous to believe that the [Texas] Act really intended to prevent the agreement from being disclosed."[2] More difficult situations, however, arise when the parties later disagree as to what a particular provision of the agreement meant[3] or when the only agreement was oral. In those situations, testimony by the parties or the mediator may become critical to whether the agreement can be enforced or can be modified by parole evidence. Just how this issue is dealt with in a mediation confidentiality statute may be critical to whether such evidence can be admitted into evidence.

Vernon v. Acton

Supreme Court of Indiana, 2000.
732 N.E.2d 805.

■ DICKSON, JUSTICE

The plaintiff-appellants, Kirk and Martha Vernon, are appealing from a judgment granting motions to enforce an oral pre-trial mediation settlement agreement and to impose attorney fees filed by the defendant-appellee, Adam Acton. Denying the existence of any agreement, the plaintiffs raised multiple issues on appeal. The Court of Appeals affirmed. *Vernon v. Acton*, 693 N.E.2d 1345 (Ind.Ct.App.1998). We granted transfer and requested additional briefing regarding issues related to the Indiana Rules for Alternative Dispute Resolution (A.D.R.Rules). We now reverse the

---

1. Tex. Civ. Prac. & Rem. Code Ann. § 154.073(b).

2. Sherman, Confidentiality in ADR Proceedings: Policy Issues Arising from the Texas Experience, 38 So. Tex. L. Rev. 541, 545 (1997).

3. See III, F, on enforceability of agreements.

trial court, concluding that the mediator's testimony regarding the alleged oral settlement agreement was confidential and privileged and that it was not admissible pursuant to the A.D.R. Rules incorporated in the parties' written agreement to mediate.

This case arises from an automobile collision involving vehicles driven by plaintiff Kirk Vernon and defendant Adam Acton. Prior to filing a complaint for damages, the plaintiffs and the defendant engaged in a voluntary pre-suit mediation pursuant to a written agreement establishing the terms and conditions of the mediation process. The defendant contends that the session produced an oral agreement to settle the plaintiffs' claims for $29,500.00. A few days after the mediation session, the defendant's insurance company issued a check and a release form to the plaintiffs. The plaintiffs returned both unsigned and promptly filed a complaint against the defendant alleging negligence and seeking damages for physical injuries and loss of consortium. In his answer, the defendant asserted various affirmative defenses and a counterclaim seeking damages for breach of the settlement agreement and attorney fees. Both parties timely filed demands for jury trial. Two months later, the defendant filed a "Motion to Enforce Settlement Agreement," along with a "Motion for Attorney's Fees."

The trial court heard evidence on the defendant's pre-trial motions and made the following determinations: that the plaintiff had accepted the defendant's settlement offer; that there was an oral agreement that the plaintiffs would execute a release of all claims in exchange for $29,500.00; that the defendant did not breach the confidentiality provisions of the Agreement to Mediate or the A.D.R. Rules by disclosing statements made during the mediation process; and that the defendant was entitled to $8,000.00 in attorney fees from the plaintiffs because the lawsuit was a frivolous, unreasonable, and groundless action in light of the settlement agreement.

The plaintiffs contend that, during the hearing on the defendant's pre-trial motions to enforce settlement agreement and for attorney fees, the trial court erroneously admitted evidence regarding the alleged settlement in contravention of the parties' mediation agreement, *A.D.R. Rule 2.12*, and *Indiana Evidence Rule 408*. The defendant asserts that only the statements made during the mediation process *before* settlement were confidential. He argues that neither the parties' agreement, the A.D.R. Rules, nor the Evidence Rules prohibit evidence of an oral settlement agreement reached in mediation.

At the trial court evidentiary hearing, David Young, a claims representative for Farmers Insurance, the defendant's insurance company, testified regarding events that occurred on October 23, 1995, at the Indianapolis offices of National Alternative Dispute Resolution Services, Inc. Young; the mediator, Paul S. Petticrew; the plaintiffs; their attorney, Kirk A. Knoll; and his investigator, Clifford Somers, attended the mediation, held pursuant to a signed Agreement to Mediate. The mediation session lasted about three and one-third hours on a single day. Over the plaintiffs' objection, the trial court permitted Young to testify that, at the conclusion of the mediation session and while at the mediator's offices, "We agreed to settle the claim at $29,500." Young stated that he delivered the settlement check and release to Somers a few days after the mediation session. Over repeated objections by plaintiffs' counsel, the mediator, Petticrew, testified that the parties reached agreement in separate rooms, after which he brought them together for the purpose of summarizing the terms of the agreement. Petticrew stated that "[t]he parties had reached an agreement of $29,500 in full and final satisfaction of the claims" and that "the parties agreed that the adjustor was to deliver a check for $29,500 along with a release to the claimants' attorney's office." Record at 305–06. At no time did Petticrew prepare or submit a written version of the agreement to the parties to be signed. However, five months later, on March 18, 1996, in response to a request from Young, Petticrew issued a written report on the mediation, stating in part: "After three and one third hours of negotiation through the pre-litigation mediation process, the parties reached an agreement for a full and final settlement of claimants' claims for twenty-nine thousand five hundred dollars ($29,500.00)."

In response to the trial court overruling the plaintiffs' objections and admitting evidence of the existence of an alleged oral settlement agreement, plaintiff Kirk Vernon testified that, when he left the meeting with the mediator, he did not believe that he had entered into a binding agreement. Sowers, the investigator for the plaintiffs' attorney, testified that, at the time of leaving the mediator's office, an offer had been extended but the plaintiffs had unresolved questions regarding whether they had to pay back their medical insurance carrier. To establish their contention that there was no meeting of the minds, the plaintiffs also attempted to present testimony during the hearing regarding statements and events during the portion of the mediation session that preceded the mediator's summary, but the trial court sustained the defendant's objections to this testimony. The plaintiffs contend that the trial court's decision had the effect of allowing the parties to testify as to the legal conclusion that an agreement had been reached but excluded evidence of the facts relevant to whether the alleged agreement existed.

The trial court ruled that it could hear evidence that an agreement was reached, but that *A.D.R. Rule 2.12* prevented it from receiving evidence of "what went on during the mediation process." Record at 228. The Court of Appeals upheld the trial court's judgment, based upon *Indiana Evidence Rules 402* and *408* and its view that the confidentiality provisions in the parties' written agreement to mediate could not supersede the Rules of Evidence. *Vernon*, 693 N.E.2d at 1348–50.

This mediation was entered into pursuant to a written Agreement to Mediate. The agreement required confidentiality in conformity with state law and Supreme Court Rules. Both parties claim that by their Agreement to Mediate they intended to be governed by the A.D.R. Rules. They dispute the scope, but not the applicability, of the A.D.R. mediation confidentiality rule. Each party presented arguments both to the trial court and to the

CHAPTER III MEDIATION

Court of Appeals based on the A.D.R. Rules. The trial court's decision was grounded solely upon the A.D.R. Rules. We note that the A.D.R. Rules would not have otherwise applied to this pre-suit mediation,[1] *see Anderson v. Yorktown Classroom Teachers Ass'n*, 677 N.E.2d 540, 542 (Ind.Ct.App. 1997). However, because each of the parties intended to be governed by the A.D.R. mediation confidentiality rule, and to guide the bench and bar, we will analyze the mediation in this case as governed by the A.D.R. Rules.

At the time of the mediation in this case, the Indiana A.D.R. Rules provided in pertinent part:

RULE 2.12 CONFIDENTIALITY

Mediation shall be regarded as settlement negotiations. Evidence of (1) furnishing or offering or promising to furnish, or (2) accepting or offering or promising to accept, a valuable consideration in compromising or attempting to compromise a claim which was disputed as to either validity or amount, is not admissible to prove liability for or invalidity of the claim or its amount. *Evidence of conduct or statements made in the course of mediation is likewise not admissible.* This rule does not require the exclusion of any evidence otherwise discoverable merely because it is presented in the course of the mediation process. This rule also does not require exclusion when the evidence is offered for another purpose, such as proving bias or prejudice of a witness, or negating a contention of undue delay. Mediation meetings shall be closed to all persons other than the parties of record, their legal representatives, and other invited persons. *Mediators shall not be subject to process requiring the disclosure of any matter discussed during the mediation, but rather, such matter shall be considered confidential and privileged in nature. The confidentiality requirement may not be waived by the parties, and an objection to the obtaining of testimony or physical evidence from mediation may be made by any party or by the mediators.*

This rule provides for confidentiality in mediation to the extent provided for in other settlement negotiations. This remained so when we revised and renumbered the rule as *A.D.R. Rule 2.11* in December of 1996 (effective March 1, 1997), modifying it to read: "Mediation shall be regarded as settlement negotiations as governed by *Ind. Evidence Rule 408*," the language of which we specifically set forth in this A.D.R. Rule. Likewise,

---

1. The A.D.R. Rules apply only to "all civil and domestic relations litigation filed" in Indiana trial courts, subject to certain exceptions not relevant to this case. *A.D.R. 1.4.* By their terms, they do not apply to a mediation not instituted pursuant to judicial action in a pending case. Although not in effect at the time of the mediation in the present case, this Court has since expressly recommended the Pre–Suit Mediation Guidelines developed by the Indiana State Bar As-

sociation. A.D.R. Guideline 8 (adopted Dec. 4, 1998, effective Jan. 1, 1999). The Pre–Suit Guideline suggests that the parties should, by private agreement, protect the confidentiality of the pre-suit mediation process in accordance with the A.D.R. Rules. A.D.R. Guideline 8.4 & Form B(5). Strongly favoring the amicable resolution of disputes without resort to litigation, this Court encourages the use of mediation and other amicable settlement techniques and procedures.

E. CONFIDENTIALITY IN MEDIATION 497

this evidence rule has, from the time of its adoption in 1994, provided: "Compromise negotiations encompass alternative dispute resolution." *Ind. Evid. R. 408.* Although the mediation confidentiality rule declares that "[e]vidence of conduct or statements made in the course of mediation is likewise not admissible," the rule also provides:

> This rule does not require exclusion of any evidence otherwise discoverable merely because it is presented in the course of the mediation process. This rule does not require exclusion when the evidence is offered for another purpose, such as proving bias or prejudice of a witness, or negating a contention of undue delay. *A.D.R. 2.12 (1995). Evidence Rule 408* contains a parallel provision.

We note that, in general, settlement agreements need not be in writing to be enforceable. *Ind. Farmers Mut. Ins. Co. v. Walters,* 221 Ind. 642, 646, 50 N.E.2d 868, 869 (1943); *Klebes v. Forest Lake Corp.,* 607 N.E.2d 978, 982 (Ind.Ct.App.1993). However, when a settlement agreement is reached in mediation, the mediation rules required that "it shall be reduced to writing and signed." *A.D.R. 2.7(E)(2).*[2] In *Silkey v. Investors Diversified Serv., Inc.,* 690 N.E.2d 329 (Ind.Ct.App.1997), the Court of Appeals confronted the issue of "what effect, if any, should be given to the oral agreement reached by the parties at the conclusion of a mediation." *Id.* at 331–32. Unlike the present case, the parties in *Silkey* agreed that an agreement was reached, and the claim presented was whether the agreement was enforceable even though it was not signed. Noting that the terms of the agreement were not in dispute, the Court of Appeals held that the trial court acted properly in ordering the parties to reduce their agreement to writing and to file it with the court. *Id.* at 334. The *Silkey* court did not address the admissibility of evidence to establish the existence and terms of an alleged oral mediation settlement agreement.

Because of the nature of the mediation process and its significant and increasing role, considerable attention has been given to whether claims of oral mediation settlement agreements should be enforceable. We note that the March 2000 discussion draft of a proposed Uniform Mediation Act under consideration by the National Conference of Commissioners on Uniform State Laws provides that "a record of an agreement between two or more disputants" shall not be protected by privilege or prohibition against disclosure, Section 8(a)(1), and the Reporter's Notes provide the following thoughtful explanation:

> This exception is noteworthy only for what is not included: oral agreements. The disadvantage of exempting oral settlements is that

---

2. At the time of the mediation, *A.D.R. 2.7(E)(2)* stated: "If an agreement is reached, it shall be reduced to writing and signed. The agreement shall then be filed with the court. If the agreement is complete on all issues, it shall be accompanied by a joint stipulation of disposition." Amendments to this subsection adopted December 23, 1996, effective March 1, 1997, added the phrase "and signed by the parties and their counsel" to the end of the first sentence and the phrase "In domestic relations matters" to the beginning of the second sentence. Similarly, A.D.R. Guideline 8.8 states: "If an agreement to settlement is reached, it should be reduced to writing promptly and a copy provided to all parties."

nearly everything said during a mediation session could bear on either whether the disputants came to an agreement or the content of the agreement. In other words, an exception for oral agreements has the potential to swallow the rule. As a result, mediation participants might be less candid, not knowing whether a controversy later would erupt over an oral agreement. Unfortunately, excluding evidence of oral settlements reached during a mediation session would operate to the disadvantage of a less legally-sophisticated disputant who is accustomed to the enforcement of oral settlements reached in negotiations. Such a person might also mistakenly assume the admissibility of evidence of oral settlements reached in mediation as well. However, because the majority of courts and statutes limit the confidentiality exception to signed written agreements, one would expect that mediators and others will soon incorporate knowledge of a writing requirement into their practices. *See Ryan v. Garcia,* 27 Cal.App.4th 1006, 33 Cal.Rptr.2d 158 (1994) (privilege statute precluded evidence of oral agreement); *Hudson v. Hudson,* 600 So.2d 7 (Fla.App.1992) (privilege statute precluded evidence of oral settlement); *Cohen v. Cohen,* 609 So.2d 783 [785] (Fla.App.1992) (same); Ohio Rev.Code § 2317.02–03 (Baldwin 1998). Nat'l Conf. of Comm'rs on Unif. State Laws, Uniform Mediation Act, Draft Report, Section 8, Reporter's Note 2, Subsection 8(a)(1), Record of an Agreement (Mar. 2000) <http://www.law.upenn.edu/ bll/ulc/ulc_frame.htm>.

We agree with this approach. Notwithstanding the importance of ensuring the enforceability of agreements that result from mediation, other goals are also important, including: facilitating agreements that result from mutual assent, achieving complete resolution of disputes, and producing clear understandings that the parties are less likely to dispute or challenge. These objectives are fostered by disfavoring oral agreements, about which the parties are more likely to have misunderstandings and disagreements. Requiring written agreements, signed by the parties, is more likely to maintain mediation as a viable avenue for clear and enduring dispute resolution rather than one leading to further uncertainty and conflict. Once the full assent of the parties is memorialized in a signed written agreement, the important goal of enforceability is achieved. We decline to find that the enforcement of oral mediation agreements is a sufficient ground to satisfy the "offered for another purpose" exception to the confidentiality rule and Evidence Rule 408.

We therefore hold that the mediation confidentiality provisions of our A.D.R. Rules extend to and include oral settlement agreements undertaken or reached in mediation. Until reduced to writing and signed by the parties, mediation settlement agreements must be considered as compromise settlement negotiations under the applicable A.D.R. Rules and Evidence Rule 408.

Having previously granted transfer, thereby vacating the opinion of the Court of Appeals, we now reverse the judgment of the trial court and remand this cause for a jury trial.

E. CONFIDENTIALITY IN MEDIATION **499**

■ SHEPARD, C.J., SULLIVAN, BOEHM, and RUCKER, JJ., concur.

NOTES AND QUESTIONS

1. *Vernon* demonstrates the interrelationship between confidentiality provisions of ADR statutes (in Indiana, however, provided for by court rule) and the enforceability of settlement agreements. The court notes that settlement agreements need not be in writing to be enforceable. Although the Indiana ADR rule said that an agreement reached in mediation "shall be reduced to writing and signed" (later amended to add "by the parties and their counsel"), this was not read as prohibiting the enforcement of an oral mediated agreement. However, the ADR rule's confidentiality provisions both tracked Federal Rule of Evidence 408 and protected mediators from being subject to process requiring disclosure. On what basis did the court conclude that this oral mediation agreement could not be enforced?

2. *Vernon* was distinguished in Reno v. Haler, 734 N.E.2d 1095 (Ind.App. 2000), where the parties signed the mediator's handwritten notes of an agreement. The wife later refused to sign the typewritten agreement, claiming that she remembered the agreement as providing for sole and not joint custody as stated in the agreement. The court found that Indiana A.D.R. Rule 2.7(A)(3) required the mediator to ensure that the parties understood the consequences of decisions regarding children and that there was no evidence he had failed in this duty. Parties do not have an absolute right to repudiate an agreement (Gabriel v. Gabriel, 654 N.E.2d 894, 898 (Ind. App.1995)), and, absent evidence of "some unfairness, unreasonableness, manifest inequity in the terms of the agreement, or that the execution of the agreement was procured through fraud, misrepresentation, coercion, duress, or lack of full disclosure," the agreement would be upheld. See III, F, 2, for further discussion of enforcement of repudiated agreements.

3. Oral mediation agreements are disfavored for the reasons given in *Vernon* and the quote from the proposed Uniform Mediation Act, but it is not always the confidentiality rules that prevent their enforcement. In Thermos Co. v. Starbucks Corp. 48 U.S.P.Q.2d 1310 (N.D.Ill.1998), the parties in a mediation reached an oral agreement on all the issues concerning an alleged patent infringement but one (whether there was a method to "design around" that would avoid infringing the patent). The court found that oral settlement agreements reached in mediation are enforceable (Carr v. Runyan, 89 F.3d 327, 329–33 (7th Cir.1996)), and "the fact that a settlement agreement calls for the parties to reach another agreement in the future—in other words, an 'agreement to agree'—will not prevent the settlement from being enforced." (S and T Mfg. Co., Inc. v. County of Hillsborough, 815 F.2d 676, 678–9 (Fed.Cir.1987)). However, it found that although the parties reached "an agreement in principle" to all of the terms of a settlement, "their minds never met as to how the remaining 'design around' issue would be resolved." It drew an analogy to U.S. v. Orr

Constr. Co., 560 F.2d 765 (7th Cir.1977), which held that although a contract can call for the parties to reach another agreement in the future, there was inadequate meeting of the minds as to the content of "proper legal releases" called for in the agreement.

4. In Wilmington Hospitality, L.L.C. v. New Castle County, 2001 WL 291948, the parties engaged in a mediation over several days, but a draft agreement was never signed. One party sought to enforce the terms of an agreement that it said could be gleaned from four letters exchanged between the parties. The court refused to admit evidence of the letters, rejecting the argument that the ADR confidentiality statute only applied to communications made at the mediation conference. The letters were made, it found, "in connection with" the mediation and were therefore covered by the statute. Under this reasoning, why wouldn't a signed agreement also be confidential and therefore inadmissible?

(2) Exception for Testimony Relevant to Sanctions Sought for Improper Participation in Mediation

Foxgate Homeowners' Association, Inc. v. Bramalea California, Inc.

Supreme Court Of California, 2001.
25 P.3d 1117.

■ BAXTER, JUSTICE

The questions we address here are independent of the issues in the underlying lawsuit. Instead, we face the intersection between court-ordered mediation, the confidentiality of which is mandated by law (Evid. Code, §§ 703.5, 1115–1128), and the power of a court to control proceedings before it and other persons "in any manner connected with a judicial proceeding before it" (Code Civ. Proc., § 128, subd. (a)(5)), by imposing sanctions on a party or the party's attorney for statements or conduct during mediation. (See Code Civ. Proc., §§ 128.5, 1209; Bus. & Prof. Code, § 6103.)

The Court of Appeal held that, notwithstanding section 1119, which governs confidentiality of communications during mediation and section 1121, which limits the content of mediators' reports, the mediator may report to the court a party's failure to comply with an order of the mediator and to participate in good faith in the mediation process. In doing so, the mediator may reveal information necessary to place sanctionable conduct in context, including communications made during mediation. The court concluded, however, that in this case the report included more information than necessary. It therefore reversed a trial court order imposing sanctions on defendants and defendants' attorney. We granted review to consider whether sections 1119 and 1121 are subject to any exceptions.

We conclude that there are no exceptions to the confidentiality of mediation communications or to the statutory limits on the content of

E. Confidentiality in Mediation

mediator's reports. Neither a mediator nor a party may reveal communications made during mediation. The judicially created exception fashioned by the Court of Appeal is inconsistent with the language and the legislative intent underlying sections 1119 and 1121. We also conclude that, while a party may do so, a mediator may not report to the court about the conduct of participants in a mediation session. We nonetheless affirm the judgment of the Court of Appeal, as that judgment sets aside the order imposing sanctions.

The underlying litigation is a construction defects action in which the defendants are the developers Bramalea, Ltd. (now Bramalea, Inc.), a Canadian corporation, and its subsidiary Bramalea California, Inc., a California corporation (collectively Bramalea), and various subcontractors. The plaintiff is a homeowners association made up of the owners of a 65–unit Culver City condominium complex developed and constructed by defendants. In a comprehensive January 22, 1997 case management order (CMO), made pursuant to Code of Civil Procedure section 638 et seq.,[1] the superior court appointed Judge Peter Smith, a retired judge, as a special master to act as both mediator and special master for ruling on discovery motions. Judge Smith was given the power to preside over mediation conferences and to make orders governing attendance of the parties and their representatives at those sessions. The CMO specifically provided that Judge Smith was to "set such ... meetings as [he] deems appropriate to discuss the status of the action, the nature and extent of defects and deficiencies claimed by Plaintiffs, and to schedule future meetings, including a premediation meeting of all experts to discuss repair methodology and the mediation...." Defendants were ordered to serve experts' reports on all parties prior to the first scheduled mediation session. The order confirmed that privileges applicable to mediation and settlement communications applied. The parties were ordered to make their best efforts to cooperate in the mediation process.

Bramalea, Ltd. was (and continues to be) represented by Ivan K. Stevenson who also acted as cocounsel for Bramalea California, Inc. The record reflects that, on the morning of September 16, 1997, the first day of a five-day round of mediation sessions of which the parties had been notified and to which the court's notice said they should bring their experts and claims representatives, plaintiff's attorney and nine experts appeared

---

1. Code of Civil Procedure section 638 now provides in part: [¶] "A referee may be appointed upon the agreement of the parties filed with the clerk, or judge, or entered in the minutes or in the docket, or upon the motion of a party to a written contract or lease that provides that any controversy arising therefrom shall be heard by a referee if the court finds a reference agreement exists between the parties:

"(a) To hear and determine any or all of the issues in an action or proceed-

ing, whether of fact or of law, and to report a statement of decision thereon;

"(b) To ascertain a fact necessary to enable the court to determine an action or proceeding."

Code of Civil Procedure section 639, subdivision (a)(5) permits the court, without agreement of the parties, "to appoint a referee to hear and determine any and all discovery motions and disputes relevant to discovery in the action and to report findings and make a recommendation thereon."

for the session. Stevenson was late and brought no defense experts. Subsequent mediation sessions were cancelled after that morning session because the mediator concluded they could not proceed without defense experts.

Plaintiff filed its first motion under Code of Civil Procedure section 128.5, for the imposition of sanctions of $24,744.55 on Bramalea and Stevenson (Bramalea/Stevenson) for their failure to cooperate in mediation. The sanctions sought reflected the cost to plaintiff of counsel's preparation for the sessions, the charges of plaintiff's nine experts for preparation and appearance at the mediation session, and the payment to the mediator, which was no longer refundable. Plaintiff's memorandum of points and authorities and declaration of counsel in support of the motion for sanctions recited a series of actions by Bramalea and Stevenson that, plaintiff asserted, reflected a pattern of tactics pursued in bad faith and solely intended to cause unnecessary delay. The actions described included objections to the schedule and attempts to postpone the mediation sessions, and culminated with Stevenson's appearance without experts at the mediation session at which architectural and plumbing issues were to be discussed. The motion recited that when asked by plaintiff's counsel if he would have expert consultants present for the future mediation sessions, Stevenson replied that "I can't answer that." When asked why he had arrived without expert consultants, Stevenson replied: "This is your mediation, you can handle it any way you want. I'm here, you can talk to me." In an ensuing conversation Stevenson said that regardless of settlement between plaintiff and the subcontractors, who had not appeared in the case, Bramalea would not allow the subcontractors to get out of the case and, in a cross-complaint, sought indemnity from them.

On September 18, two days after the aborted mediation session, Judge Smith filed the report that is the object of this dispute with the superior court. [The report recited various "obstructive bad faith tactics" of Mr. Stevenson in "trying to derail the mediations." "It became apparent," it said, "that Mr. Stevenson's real agenda was to delay the mediation process so he can file a Motion for Summary Judgment" and noted that "it has been the experience of the mediator, in past mediations, that this tactic can be used to cut the amount of plaintiff's claims." The superior court denied the plaintiff's motion for sanctions without prejudice "as Bramlea was then in a Canadian bankruptcy proceeding." Plaintiff later filed a second motion for sanctions which was granted.]

On appeal, Bramalea/Stevenson contended, inter alia, that the superior court violated the confidentiality of mediation when the judge considered the report of the mediator in assessing the events and communications that occurred during the September 1997 mediation in imposing sanctions on them.

The Court of Appeal reversed the sanctions order and remanded the matter to the superior court because that court had not complied with the requirement of Code of Civil Procedure section 128.5, subdivision (c), that the court enter an order that "recite[s] in detail the conduct or circumstances justifying the order.'' Because the issue was one of great importance whose determination was necessary to a final resolution of the matter, and to give guidance to the superior court as to the matters it could properly consider on remand, the Court of Appeal addressed and rejected appellant's claim that the mediator was barred by section 1121, which prohibits most reports regarding mediation and consideration by the court of such reports, from reporting conduct during mediation to the court.

The Court of Appeal concluded that the rule precluding judicial construction of an unambiguous statute (Code. Civ. Proc., § 1858; *Hughes v. Board of Architectural Examiners* (1998) 17 Cal.4th 763, 775) should not apply here. It invoked instead the rule that permits judicial construction of an apparently unambiguous statute where giving literal meaning to the words of the statute would lead to an absurd result or fail to carry out the manifest purpose of the Legislature. (*Times Mirror Co. v. Superior Court* (1991) 53 Cal.3d 1325, 1334, fn. 7.) With regard to the latter, the court acknowledged that the purpose of the confidentiality mandated by section 1119, which makes evidence of anything said during mediation inadmissible and undiscoverable, is to promote mediation as an alternative to judicial proceedings and that confidentiality is essential to mediation. The Court of Appeal reasoned, however, that it should balance against that policy recognition that, unless the parties and their lawyers participate in good faith in mediation, there is little to protect. It concluded that the Legislature did not intend statutory mandated confidentiality to create an immunity from sanctions that would shield parties who disobey valid orders governing the parties' participation. The Court of Appeal also expressed doubt that section 1121 was intended to preclude a report to the trial court if the parties engaged in improper conduct by attacking or threatening to attack an opposing party. In sum, section 1121 was not intended to shield sanctionable conduct.

Relying on the statement of purpose offered by the California Law Revision Commission at the time the section was proposed, the Court of Appeal concluded that section 1121 served to preserve mediator neutrality and prevent coercion of the parties. * * *

The Court of Appeal acknowledged that it was creating a nonstatutory exception to the confidentiality requirements. The court described the exception as narrow, permitting a mediator or party to report to the court only information that is reasonably necessary to describe sanctionable conduct and place that conduct in context. The report in this case was not so limited. It included extraneous information, recommendations, conclusions, and characterized the conduct and statements reported, all matters for argument by the parties, not a report by a neutral. The Court of Appeal cautioned: ''The report should be no more than a strictly neutral account of the conduct and statements being reported along with such other information as required to place those matters in context.'' The Court of Appeal directed the trial court to disregard any portions of the report or the declarations submitted by the parties that did not conform to this limitation.

Bramalea/Stevenson claim that any exception that permits reporting to the court and sanctioning a party on the basis of a mediator's report of conduct or statements allegedly undertaken in bad faith during mediation violates the statutes that guaranty confidentiality of mediation. And, notwithstanding the limited scope of the exception the Court of Appeal believed it had created, numerous amici curiae with an interest in alternative dispute resolution urge the court to enforce the statutory rule of absolute confidentiality.

Discussion

At the time Judge Smith submitted his September 18, 1997 report to the superior court, former section 1152.6 (Stats. 1995, ch. 576, § 8) provided: "A mediator may not file, and a court may not consider, any declaration or finding of any kind by the mediator, other than a required statement of agreement or nonagreement, unless all parties in the mediation expressly agree otherwise in writing prior to commencement of the mediation. However, this section shall not apply to mediation under Chapter 11 (commencing with Section 3160) of Part 2 of Division 8 of the Family Code."

The report was not authorized by former section 1152.6, but, as noted above, no party objected, either before or at the hearing on plaintiff's first motion for sanctions, to the superior court's consideration of the report.

When the motion for sanctions at issue here was heard, former section 1152.6 had been repealed and replaced by section 1121 (Stats. 1997, ch. 772, § 3), which retains and enlarges the substance of former section 1152.6. Section 1121 provides: "Neither a mediator nor anyone else may submit to a court or other adjudicative body, and a court or other adjudicative body may not consider, any report, assessment, evaluation, recommendation, or finding of any kind by the mediator concerning a mediation conducted by the mediator, other than a report that is mandated by court rule or other law and that states only whether an agreement was reached, unless all parties to the mediation expressly agree otherwise in writing, or orally in accordance with Section 1118."

Section 1119, subdivision (c), enacted at the same time (Stats. 1997, ch. 772, § 3) provides: "All communications, negotiations, or settlement discussions by and between participants in the course of a mediation or a mediation consultation shall remain confidential." Sections 1119 and 1121 became effective on January 1, 1998. (Cal. Const., art. IV, § 8, subd. (c).)

The language of sections 1119 and 1121 is clear and unambiguous, but the Court of Appeal reasoned that the Legislature did not intend these sections to create "an immunity from sanctions, shielding parties to court-ordered mediation who disobey valid orders governing their participation in the mediation process, thereby intentionally thwarting the process to pursue other litigation tactics." The court therefore crafted the exception in dispute here. As stated and as applied, the exception created by the Court of Appeal permits reporting to the court not only that a party or attorney has disobeyed a court order governing the mediation process, but

E. Confidentiality in Mediation **505**

also that the mediator or reporting party believes that a party has done so intentionally with the apparent purpose of derailing the court-ordered mediation and the reasons for that belief.

Appellants contend that the legislative policies codified in sections 1119 and 1121 are absolute except to the extent that a statutory exception exists. The only such exception they acknowledge is the authority of a mediator to report criminal conduct. They argue that the report of the mediator, which plaintiff submitted to the court with its motion for sanctions and which the court considered, was a form of testimony by a person made incompetent to testify by section 703.5,[2] and violated the principle that mediators are to assist parties in reaching their own agreement, but ordinarily may not express an opinion on the merits of the case. In permitting consideration of any part of the report, the Court of Appeal has created a vague and inconsistent exception to the mandate of confidentiality, one that the Legislature did not authorize.

* * *

We do not agree with the Court of Appeal that there is any need for judicial construction of sections 1119 and 1121 or that a judicially crafted exception to the confidentiality of mediation they mandate is necessary either to carry out the purpose for which they were enacted or to avoid an absurd result. The statutes are clear. Section 1119 prohibits any person, mediator and participants alike, from revealing any written or oral communication made during mediation. Section 1121 also prohibits the mediator, but not a party, from advising the court about *conduct* during mediation that might warrant sanctions. It also prohibits the court from considering a report that includes information not expressly permitted to be included in a mediator's report. The submission to the court, and the court's consideration of, the report of Judge Smith violated sections 1119 and 1121.

Because the language of sections 1119 and 1121 is clear and unambiguous, judicial construction of the statutes is not permitted unless they cannot be applied according to their terms or doing so would lead to absurd results, thereby violating the presumed intent of the Legislature. (*Diamond Multimedia Systems, Inc. v. Superior Court* (1999) 19 Cal.4th 1036, 1047; *California School Employees Assn. v. Governing Board* (1994) 8 Cal.4th 333, 340.) Moreover, a judicially crafted exception to the confidentiality mandated by sections 1119 and 1121 is not necessary either to carry out the legislative intent or to avoid an absurd result.

---

2. Section 703.5: "No person presiding at any judicial or quasi-judicial proceeding, and no arbitrator or mediator, shall be competent to testify in any subsequent civil proceeding, as to any statement, conduct, decision, or ruling, occurring at or in conjunction with the prior proceeding, except as to a statement, or conduct that could (a) give rise to civil or criminal contempt, (b) constitute a crime, (c) be the subject of investigation by the State Bar or Commission on Judicial Performance, or (d) give rise to disqualification proceedings under paragraph (1) or (6) of subdivision (a) of Section 170.1 of the Code of Civil Procedure. However, this section does not apply to a mediator with regard to any mediation under Chapter 11 (commencing with Section 3160) of Part 2 of Division 8 of the Family Code."

The legislative intent underlying the mediation confidentiality provisions of the Evidence Code is clear. The parties and all amici curiae recognize the purpose of confidentiality is to promote "a candid and informal exchange regarding events in the past.... This frank exchange is achieved only if the participants know that what is said in the mediation will not be used to their detriment through later court proceedings and other adjudicatory process." (Nat. Conf. of Comrs. on U. State Laws, U. Mediation Act (May 2001) § 2, Reporter's working notes, [¶] 1; see also Note, *Protecting Confidentiality in Mediation* (1984) 98 Harv. L.Rev. 441, 445. ["Mediation demands ... that the parties feel free to be frank not only with the mediator but also with each other.... Agreement may be impossible if the mediator cannot overcome the parties' wariness about confiding in each other during these sessions."].)

As all parties and amici curiae recognize, confidentiality is essential to effective mediation, a form of alternative dispute resolution encouraged and, in some cases required by, the Legislature. Implementing alternatives to judicial dispute resolution has been a strong legislative policy since at least 1986. * * *

To carry out the purpose of encouraging mediation by ensuring confidentiality, the statutory scheme, which includes sections 703.5, 1119, and 1121, unqualifiedly bars disclosure of communications made during mediation absent an express statutory exception.

Heretofore the only California case upholding admission, over objection, of statements made during mediation in which no statutory exception to confidentiality applied, was *Rinaker v. Superior Court* (1998) 62 Cal. App.4th 155 (*Rinaker*), a case that is clearly distinguishable. There, a juvenile court judge conducting a jurisdictional hearing in a delinquency matter (Welf. & Inst. Code, § 602) ordered disclosure by a volunteer who had mediated a civil harassment action between the victim and juveniles who had engaged in a rock throwing incident. The minors who were the subject of the hearing claimed that the victim's statements at the mediation session differed from his testimony at the delinquency hearing. The Court of Appeal held that, although a delinquency proceeding is a civil action within the meaning of Evidence Code section 1119 and the confidentiality provisions were applicable, that statutory right must yield to the minor's due process rights to put on a defense and confront, cross-examine, and impeach the victim witness with his prior inconsistent statements. (*Pennsylvania v. Ritchie* (1987) 480 U.S. 39, 51–52; *Davis v. Alaska* (1974) 415 U.S. 308, 315–319.) To maintain confidentiality to the extent possible, however, the Court of Appeal stated that the juvenile court judge should first have held an in camera hearing to weigh the minors' claim of need to question the mediator against the statutory privilege to determine if the mediator's testimony was sufficiently probative to be necessary. (*Rinaker, supra,* 62 Cal.4th at pp. 169–170.)

Although criticized (see Reuben, *Strictly in Confidence,* Cal. Law. (Sept. 2000) p. 31), *Rinaker* is consistent with our past recognition and that of the United States Supreme Court that due process entitles juveniles to some of the basic constitutional rights accorded adults, including the right to confrontation and cross-examination. In this matter, however, plaintiffs have no comparable supervening due-process-based right to use evidence of statements and events at the mediation session.

In the only other reported case arising in California in which a mediator's testimony about events during mediation was compelled and admitted, a federal magistrate judge, Wayne Brazil, an expert in mediation law, ruled that the testimony of a mediator could be compelled notwithstanding sections 703.5 and 1119, which were held to be applicable (Fed. Rules Evid., rule 501, 28 U.S.C.), because the evidence was necessary to establish whether a defaulting party had been competent to enter into a settlement that another party sought to enforce. (*Olam v. Congress Mortgage Company* (N.D.Cal.1999) 68 F.Supp.2d 1110.) There plaintiff had waived confidentiality and defendant had agreed to a limited waiver of confidentiality, and the agreement in question fell within the exception of section 1123 for settlement agreements resulting from mediation if the agreement provided that it was enforceable. Nonetheless, the magistrate judge was not satisfied that the waivers were an adequate basis on which to compel the mediator's testimony, as the mediator had not waived the mediation privilege. After considering *Rinaker*, in which the magistrate judge noted the mediator had not invoked section 703.5, the magistrate judge concluded that a similar weighing process should be used to determine if the parties' interest in compelling the testimony of the magistrate outweighed the state's interest in maintaining confidentiality of the mediation. After doing so, the magistrate judge concluded that the testimony was the most reliable and probative evidence on the issue, and there was no likely alternative source, the testimony was crucial if the court was to be able to resolve the dispute and was essential to doing justice in the case before him. (*Olam,* at p. 1139.)

That case, too, is distinguishable as Bramalea/Stevenson have not waived confidentiality.

The mediator and the Court of Appeal here were troubled by what they perceived to be a failure of Bramalea to participate in good faith in the mediation process. Nonetheless, the Legislature has weighed and balanced the policy that promotes effective mediation by requiring confidentiality against a policy that might better encourage good faith participation in the process. Whether a mediator in addition to participants should be allowed to report conduct during mediation that the mediator believes is taken in bad faith and therefore might be sanctionable under Code of Civil Procedure section 128.5, subdivision (a), is a policy question to be resolved by the Legislature. Although a party may report obstructive conduct to the court, none of the confidentiality statutes currently makes an exception for reporting bad faith conduct or for imposition of sanctions under that section when doing so would require disclosure of communications or a mediator's assessment of a party's conduct although the Legislature presumably is aware that Code of Civil Procedure section 128.5 permits

508 CHAPTER III MEDIATION

imposition of sanctions when similar conduct occurs during trial proceedings.

Therefore, we do not agree with the Court of Appeal that the court may fashion an exception for bad faith in mediation because failure to authorize reporting of such conduct during mediation may lead to "an absurd result" or fail to carry out the legislative policy of encouraging mediation. The Legislature has decided that the policy of encouraging mediation by ensuring confidentiality is promoted by avoiding the threat that frank expression of viewpoints by the parties during mediation may subject a participant to a motion for imposition of sanctions by another party or the mediator who might assert that those views constitute a bad faith failure to participate in mediation. Therefore, even were the court free to ignore the plain language of the confidentiality statutes, there is no justification for doing so here.

Plaintiff's motion for sanctions and the trial court's consideration of the motion and attached documents violated both sections 1119 and 1121. The motion had attached both the report of Judge Smith and a declaration by plaintiff's counsel reciting statements made during the mediation session. Section 1121 prohibits the submission by anyone to a court and consideration by the court of "any report, assessment, evaluation, recommendation, or finding of any kind by the mediator concerning a mediation conducted by the mediator." Plaintiff violated this section as did the court. Plaintiff also violated subdivision (c) of section 1119 in counsel's declaration and by submitting the report. Both documents included communications in the course of the mediation.[3] The court violated subdivision (a) of section 1119 when it admitted in evidence at the sanctions hearing "anything said . . . in the course of . . . mediation."

The remedy for violation of the confidentiality of mediation is that stated in section 1128: "Any reference to a mediation during any subsequent trial is an irregularity in the proceedings of the trial for purposes of Section 657 of the Code of Civil Procedure. Any reference to a mediation during any other subsequent noncriminal proceeding is grounds for vacating or modifying the decision in that proceeding, in whole or in part, and granting a new or further hearing on all or part of the issues, if the reference materially affected the substantial rights of the party requesting relief."

Inasmuch as the superior court's sole basis for imposing sanctions on Bramalea/Stevenson was allegations in and the material offered in support of the motion for sanctions, it is clear that reference to the mediation materially affected their rights and that the Court of Appeal did not err in setting aside the order imposing sanctions. If, on remand, plaintiff elects to pursue the motion, the trial court may consider only plaintiff's assertion

---

3. To the extent that the declaration of counsel stated that the mediator had ordered the parties to be present with their experts, there was no violation. As noted earlier, neither section 1119 nor section 1121 prohibits a party from revealing or reporting to the court about noncommunicative conduct, including violation of the orders of a mediator or the court during mediation.

and evidence offered in support of the assertion that Bramalea engaged in conduct that warrants sanctions. No evidence of communications made during the mediation may be admitted or considered.

The judgment of the Court of Appeal is affirmed.

■ Concurring: GEORGE, C.J., KENNARD, J., WERDEGAR, J., CHIN, J., BROWN, J.

NOTES AND QUESTIONS

1. An initial question in the *Foxgate* case might be whether Mr. Stevenson should have been sanctioned if the mediator's report had been allowed to be considered by the trial judge. Was his objective of delaying a mediation to prepare a motion for summary judgment a valid tactic? Should parties have to go through a mediation if a summary judgment might dispose of the case? Was the mediator right that such motions are generally delaying tactics aimed at getting a lower settlement? Did the fact that Mr. Stevenson's client was on the verge of bankruptcy make his recalcitrance a valid tactic?

2. Assuming that Mr. Stevenson's tactics were a violation of the participation requirement for a court-ordered mediation (see Chap. IV, A, 6, supra), how can such conduct be deterred if sanctions are thwarted by preventing the parties or the mediator from testifying about what an attorney like Mr. Stevenson did in the mediation? In distinguishing the *Rinaker* and *Olam* cases, did the California Supreme Court leave open any effective avenues for enforcing sanctions? Are there any circumstances that could overcome the *Foxgate* holding disallowing testimony about mediation behavior?

3. The *Foxgate* court rejected the approach taken by the federal magistrate judge in *Olam v. Congress Mortgage Co., 68 F.Supp.2d 1110 (N.D.Cal. 1999).* There, after a party claimed a mediated agreement had resulted from undue influence and lack of capacity due to her emotional state, both parties sought to require the mediator to testify, waiving their own privileges, but the mediator asserted a privilege not to testify. In determining what California law requires, the magistrate applied a balancing of the values, rights, and interests involved. To do this, he heard the testimony in closed court under seal. He found a strong interest in "doing justice" that favored overriding confidentiality because the mediator's testimony would "greatly improve the court's ability to determine reliably what the pertinent facts were" and was the only source of "disinterested neutral evidence." He also distinguished between what is often called "facilitative" mediation used to "explore underlying interests and feelings and to build settlement bridges" and "an adjudicative/evaluative model with a clear focus on evidence and law." He felt that less harm would be done in allowing evidence of what was said under the latter model. He found that the kind of testimony sought in this case was likely to be reliable and to avoid compromising confidential communications:

510 CHAPTER III MEDIATION

[T]he parties and I assumed that the testimony from the mediator that would be most consequential would focus not primarily on what Ms. Olam said during the mediation, but on how she acted and the mediator's perceptions of her physical, emotional, and mental condition. The purpose would not be to nail down and dissect her specific words, but to assess at a more general and impressionistic level her condition and capacities. That purpose might be achieved with relatively little disclosure of the content of her confidential communications. Id. at 50–51.

Should the California Supreme Court in *Foxgate* have taken a more policy-oriented approach, and if so, would the policies stated in *Olam* favor denying confidentiality?

4. The *Foxgate* decision has been criticized as making too literal a reading of the confidentiality statute and passing the responsibility off to the legislature to create an express exception, rather than weighing the policies itself. Do you agree?

5. Can an attorney be sanctioned for disclosing mediation documents in an unsealed motion to the court for sanctions against the opposing attorney? In Lawson v. Brown's Day Care Center, Inc., 776 A.2d 390 (Vt.2001), the defense attorney did that to support his claim that the opposing attorney had (1) violated state law when, during the mediation, he proposed settlement terms under which defendants would have to refrain from making or authorizing "any claims, complaints or allegations, civil or criminal, against any parties or other persons" arising out of the lawsuit, and (2) violated the state disciplinary rule prohibiting lawyers from engaging in "illegal conduct involving moral turpitude" by making a negotiating demand that the plaintiff's attorney forgo any criminal or disciplinary complaint against him. After reading the cover and title pages, the judge returned the disclosure unread and, after a hearing, imposed a $2,000 sanction on the defense attorney for violating mediation confidentiality. The appellate court noted that the lower court had not made a finding that the filing was made for an improper purpose or in bad faith, as opposed to disclosing unethical conduct, and remanded for such a determination if sanctions were to be imposed. See also Toon v. Wackenhut Corrections Corp., 250 F.3d 950 (5th Cir.2001)(sanctions against counsel were appropriate where he acted in bad faith in intentionally filing a motion to enforce a settlement agreement unsealed, exposing the terms to the public in disregard of the confidentiality provision of the agreement).

d. CONTRACTUAL AGREEMENTS OF CONFIDENTIALITY

A contractual agreement by which the parties and mediator agree not to disclose information arising in the mediation can, if properly executed, provide protection of confidentiality. Many mediation programs routinely require such an agreement at the beginning of the mediation. The ABA Standards of Practice for Lawyer Mediators in Family Disputes, sec. II.A., provide:

At the outset of the mediation, the participants should agree in writing not to require the mediator to disclose to any third party any statements made in the course of mediation. The mediator shall inform the participants that the mediator will not voluntarily disclose to any third party any of the information obtained through the mediation process, unless such disclosure is required by law, without the prior consent of the participants. The mediator shall inform the participants of the limitations of confidentiality such as statutory or judicially mandated reporting.

Like any contract, such an agreement must satisfy the requirements for a valid contract, and thus must be written with sufficient clarity and specificity to constitute a proper manifestation of mutual consent. "[A]greements not to disclose have been ruled valid against disclosure outside litigation. Thus, for example, a professional [psychiatrist] has been held liable for promising confidentiality and then writing an article about conversations with the client [Doe v. Roe, 93 Misc.2d 201, 400 N.Y.S.2d 668, 674–75 (N.Y.Sup.Ct.1977)]." Nancy H. Rogers & Richard A. Salem, A Student's Guide to Mediation and the Law 98 (1987).

Simrin v. Simrin

California District Court of Appeals, 1965.
233 Cal.App.2d 90, 43 Cal.Rptr. 376.

■ STONE, JUSTICE.

Appellant, the mother of four minor children, seeks their custody by modification of the final decree of divorce which awarded custody to the father. The interlocutory decree and custody order was entered March 29, 1962, and became final April 14, 1963. This motion to modify the custody provisions of the decree was filed three months later. Appellant also moved for attorney fees and costs.

Respondent husband countered with an improperly noticed motion to modify the child custody provisions of the final decree by reducing from each weekend to one weekend a month, the mother's right to have the children visit with her.

The trial court denied appellant's motion for change of custody, denied her attorney fees, and granted the husband's motion to reduce the mother's visitation rights to one weekend a month.

Since the welfare of the children was the paramount issue and only one year and four months had elapsed between the original custody order and the mother's motion to modify it, the court allowed evidence to be introduced concerning the conduct of the mother and father prior to the divorce as well as during the interval between the final decree and the hearing on the motion to modify.

The evidence leaves no doubt as to the wisdom of the trial court in awarding custody of the children to the father in the first place, and the case narrows to whether the mother proved rehabilitation during the interval between the original custody award and the hearing on the motion.

In these circumstances we are guided by Sanchez v. Sanchez, 55 Cal.2d 118, at page 121, 10 Cal.Rptr. 261, at page 535, 358 P.2d 533, at page 263:

> "The rule is, of course, that 'In a divorce proceeding involving the custody of a minor, primary consideration must be given to the welfare of the child. The court is given a wide discretion in such matters, and its determination will not be disturbed upon appeal in the absence of a manifest showing of abuse. "Every presumption supports the reasonableness of the decree." ' "

Following the rule of Sanchez, we find no abuse of discretion in the order denying the wife's petition for modification, and limiting the mother's right to have the children visit with her to one weekend each month.

From the printed page, without the advantage of observing the witnesses and the children, the trial judge's decision is within the bounds of his discretion. The most favorable testimony adduced by the mother was that of her psychiatrist. But his testimony left room for doubt that sufficient time had elapsed for a determination of whether appellant had become rehabilitated. Clearly, there is no room for conjecture when the welfare of children is involved, and in accordance with the well settled principles enunciated in the Sanchez case, the trial court resolved conjecture in the best interests of the children; "every presumption supports the reasonableness of the decree."

We turn from the sufficiency of the evidence to alleged errors in the trial.

* * *

A more intricate question arises from the court's ruling that a rabbi who acted as a marriage counselor for the parties need not reveal conversations with them. The wife called as a witness a rabbi, who declined to testify, not on the ground of privilege, but that he undertook marriage counseling with the husband and wife only after an express agreement that their communications to him would be confidential and that neither would call him as a witness in the event of a divorce action. He imposed the condition so they would feel free to communicate with him. After lengthy voir dire examination of the rabbi, the husband, and the wife, the court ruled that the rabbi need not relate the confidential communications.

The husband asserted the communications were privileged under Code of Civil Procedure section 1881, subdivision (3); the wife, on the other hand, waived any privilege that might exist. The question of waiver of joint husband-and-wife privilege was argued, but we think the question academic for under the statute there is no privilege here in the first place. Section 1881, subdivision (3), is limited to confessions in the course of discipline enjoined by the church. It would wrench the language of the statute to hold that it applies to communications made to a religious or spiritual advisor acting as a marriage counselor. We think this result regrettable for reasons of public policy expressed below in our discussion of the agreement, but the wording of the statute leaves us no choice.

E. Confidentiality in Mediation

As to the agreement, appellant argues that to hold her to her bargain with the rabbi and with her husband is to sanction a contract to suppress evidence contrary to public policy. However, public policy also strongly favors procedures designed to preserve marriages, and counseling has become a promising means to that end. The two policies are here in conflict and we resolve the conflict by holding the parties to their agreement. If a husband or wife must speak guardedly for fear of making an admission that might be used in court, the purpose of counseling is frustrated. One should not be permitted, under cover of suppression of evidence, to repudiate an agreement so deeply affecting the marriage relationship. For the unwary spouse who speaks freely, repudiation would prove a trap; for the wily, a vehicle for making self-serving declarations.

It is true, as appellant points out and as respondent concedes, there is no California case in point. But two analogies are close aboard. Since appellant stresses the trial or evidentiary aspects of the agreement, we note, first, the analogy to statements that are made in offer of compromise and to avoid or settle litigation, which are not admissible in evidence. Likewise, statements made to a counselor in an effort to save a marriage, as here, should not be admissible since they, too, are made for the purpose of settling a dispute, to save a marriage and to prevent litigation. The other analogy is to proceedings in the conciliation court. Of them Mr. Witkin says in his work, California Evidence, section 477(b), page 533:

"Proceedings of Conciliation Court. The superior court sitting as a conciliation court conducts its proceedings in private . . ., and communications from parties to the judge, commissioner or counselor are deemed made 'in official confidence' under C.C.P.1881(5), supra, § 438. (C.C.P. 1747.)"

We do not equate a confidential communication made to a churchman acting as a marriage counselor, with a communication made in a judicial proceeding. The analogy holds nonetheless, since the purpose of making such communications confidential in each instance is to encourage the husband and wife to speak freely and to preserve the marriage.

NOTES AND QUESTIONS

1. The court in *Simrin* notes that a contract to suppress evidence is contrary to public policy. Wigmore said that "no pledge of privacy * * * can avail against demand for the truth in a court of justice." 8 John H. Wigmore, Evidence in Trials at Common Law § 2286, at 528 (1964). Here the court found that the testimony of the psychiatrist introduced by the mother "left room for doubt that sufficient time had elapsed" to determine that she had become rehabilitated. Thus the rabbi's testimony appears to have been of critical importance. Why then did the need for confidentiality override the mother's need for the evidence? Did the court engage in a balancing of the two policies, or simply rule that confidentiality agreements must be enforced? Would there have been any protection of confidentiality without the agreement?

514 CHAPTER III MEDIATION

2. In *Simrin* the rabbi acted as a marriage counselor rather than a formal mediator. Does the court's reliance on the policy favoring confidentiality in California Conciliation Court proceedings suggest that similar confidentiality agreements would be upheld in all forms of mediation?

3. Despite the protection that California courts have accorded to mediation confidentiality, due process concerns may undermine that protection. In McLaughlin v. Superior Court for San Mateo County, 140 Cal.App.3d 473, 189 Cal.Rptr. 479 (1983), it was held that both parties are entitled to call as a witness or cross-examine a Conciliation Court counselor who renders a report to the judge. The notion is that the parties must be able to examine the counselor to insure that her recommendation has a basis in the facts and law and is not influenced by bias. What does this do to mediation confidentiality? Jay Folberg & Alison Taylor, Mediation 280 (1984), observe that "allowing the mediator to make a recommendation and testify creates an untenable Hobson's choice for divorcing parents: either refrain from being candid in mediation discussions or reveal relevant confidences knowing that they can be used later against your individual interests. This challenge has been countered with the argument that parties to a court-compelled mediation are unlikely to reveal confidences that would threaten their desired custody resolution, whether or not those confidences would be revealed in court."

4. If a contractual agreement does not contain any exceptions, would it be upheld when a statute imposes a duty to report certain information or events, for example, reports of felonies, child neglect or abuse, or gunshot wounds? Even if there is no such express statute, should a court weigh the policy favoring such disclosure against that favoring confidentiality under the agreement?

F. ENFORCEABILITY OF MEDIATION AGREEMENTS

Mediation agreements, like contracts and court judgments, are not always complied with. When that happens the question arises as to what remedies are available to invoke the coercive power of the courts to enforce the agreement.

Enforceability of mediation agreements may be critical to obtaining an agreement. The parties may want to know that the agreement is final and effective. This is especially true in such areas as labor, commercial, and public-law dispute mediation. There the usual expectation is that any agreement reached will be a legally enforceable contract, and it is usually drawn up by lawyers.

Some advocates of community dispute mediation do not view legal enforceability as central to its objectives. Particularly where the parties have an ongoing relationship, as in a family or church, it is said that the nature of the relationship is critical and that failure of compliance calls for

F. ENFORCEABILITY OF MEDIATION AGREEMENTS

a return to mediation or renegotiation rather than court action.[1] Since empirical evidence suggests that mediated agreements have a higher compliance rate than court judgments,[2] it is argued that judicial enforcement does not enhance the mediation process. It is further argued that focusing on legal enforceability during mediation can undermine the process of trust and reconciliation and may require the parties to consult legal counsel, undercutting the desire to avoid legalism.

Whatever the attractiveness of such arguments in certain contexts such as church mediations, the desire for closure of the dispute is generally viewed as requiring an expectation of enforcement. Most mediation centers retain the agreement in their files and offer their services in helping to assure compliance. Centers often hold in escrow sums of money to be paid by one party until the other party complies with its part of the agreement. Sometimes they oversee and assist in exchanges of property and other tangible forms of compliance. If the center's assistance fails to accomplish compliance, the only recourse may be to seek enforcement by a court. Mediation centers are not comfortable with that turn of events; court proceedings may threaten mediation confidentiality and signal failure of the process. But increasingly parties are told both in advance of mediation and upon signing an agreement that it is legally enforceable, and mediators find such expectations necessary for closure.

To be legally enforceable, settlement agreements must of course satisfy the requisites of contract law. The general policy favoring enforcement of settlement agreements, and specific policies underlying certain causes of action, may enhance enforceability.[3] "The power of a trial court to enter a judgment enforcing a settlement agreement has its basis in the policy favoring the settlement of disputes and the avoidance of costly and time-consuming litigation."[4] An agreement to settle a federal suit need not be in writing to be enforceable.[5] However, in some states, settlement agreements must be in writing.[6] In some states, also, an attorney who signs a settle-

---

1. See Note, The Dilemma of Regulating Mediation, 22 Hous.L.Rev. 841, 864–65 (1985).

2. See Note, Enforceability of Mediated Agreements, 1 Ohio St.J. of Dispute Res. 385, 385 n. 5 (1986).

3. See Fulgence v. J. Ray McDermott & Co., 662 F.2d 1207, 1209 (5th Cir.1981) (Title VII includes a congressionally mandated policy of encouraging settlement); Strange v. Gulf & South American Steamship Co., 495 F.2d 1235, 1237 (5th Cir.1974) (agreement challenged on grounds of mutual mistake).

4. Kukla v. National Distillers Products Co., 483 F.2d 619, 621 (6th Cir.1973).

5. Bergstrom v. Sears, Roebuck and Co., 532 F.Supp. 923, 932 (D.Minn.1982).

6. N.Y.Civ.Prac.R. 2104.7 (McKinney 1976 & Supp.1987); Moore v. Gunning, 328 So.2d 462 (Fla.App.1976) (applying West's F.S.A.R.Civ.P. 1.030). Cf. Vernon's Ann.Tex. R.Civ.Proc. 11 ("Unless otherwise provided in these rules, no agreement between attorneys or parties touching any suit pending will be enforced unless it be in writing, signed and filed with the papers as part of the record, or unless it be made in open court and entered of record.")

516 CHAPTER III MEDIATION

ment agreement must have actual, rather than apparent, authority in order to bind the client unless the client ratifies it or accepts partial satisfaction.[7] Of course, the entry of a settlement agreement as a judgment of the court gives it the effect of a judgment, with the attendant rights to judicial enforcement remedies.

A mediation agreement that is intended by the parties to be a contract is enforceable under the rules of contract law. Some contracts, however, are not enforceable for public policy reasons. This may include contracts that interfere with highly personal matters relating to family life and social mores. Mediation agreements sometimes involve this sort of agreement, and the parties should be aware that they are not legally enforceable. There is also sometimes a question as to whether the parties actually intended an agreement to be legally enforceable. A Minnesota statute provides that the effect of a mediated settlement agreement is to be "determined under principles of law applicable to contract"; however, under the statute such an agreement is *not* binding unless it contains "a provision stating that it is binding," as well as provisions stating that the parties were advised in writing that (a) the mediator has no duty to protect their interests or provide them with information about their legal rights; (b) signing a mediated settlement agreement may adversely affect their legal rights; and (c) they should consult an attorney before signing a mediated settlement agreement if they are uncertain of their rights.[8]

Assuming that the nature of a mediation agreement would admit of judicial enforcement, enforceability is determined by reference to contract law. There must be a manifestation of mutual assent and consideration. Consideration is rarely a problem since a mediation agreement will generally involve a bargained-for exchange, whether of tangible goods, promises, forbearance, or the creation, modification or destruction of a legal relation.[9] The most likely defenses to the manifestation of mutual consent are duress, mistake, or fraud or misrepresentation.

The question of duress may arise when a party comes to a mediation under pressure, as when a prosecutor or court orders him to mediate or suffer certain consequences. Under certain Neighborhood Justice Center programs, for example, a party may receive a letter from an intake official informing him of the complaint and the time and place of the hearing and containing the notation that "failure to appear may result in this complaint being referred to an appropriate criminal or civil law enforcement agency for possible charges in accordance with the law."[10] "If a party's manifestation of assent is induced by an improper threat by the other party that leaves the victim no reasonable alternative, the contract is voidable by the victim."[11] A threat is improper if it threatens criminal prosecution, but not

---

7. See citations in Nancy H. Rogers & Richard A. Salem, A Student's Guide to Mediation and the Law 157 (1987).

8. Minn.Stat.Ann. § 572.35 (West 1986).

9. Restatement of Contracts, § 75 (1932).

10. Note, The Dilemma of Regulating Mediation, supra note 1, at 845 n. 34.

11. Restatement, Second, Contracts § 175.

F. Enforceability of Mediation Agreements

if it threatens the use of the civil process unless made in bad faith.[12] It might be argued that the threat in the letter quoted above was not to coerce an agreement but merely to encourage the recipient to talk about the dispute in mediation. If it were made clear at the outset of the mediation that any agreement would be entirely voluntary, duress would seem difficult to establish in that case.

A defense based on mistake may arise more often as to a mediation agreement than other forms of contract. The process seeks to assure the parties that by settling the dispute themselves without intermediaries, they can rely on the actual facts of which they have the best knowledge. But since the proceeding is not adversary, there is greater likelihood of a mistake as to an essential element of the agreement which, if it satisfies the legal criteria for mistake, will prevent enforceability.[13]

Fraud or misrepresentation may also occur in a mediation. To establish the defense of misrepresentation, there must be an assertion or omission that is not in accord with the facts, that is either fraudulent or material, and that is justifiably relied on by the recipient in manifesting his assent.[14] It is possible that one party may misrepresent a material fact and that the best efforts of the mediator will not succeed in bringing out the true state of the facts. In such a case, the defense of misrepresentation would prevent enforcement.

Unconscionability provides another possible defense to the enforcement of a mediation agreement. At times, the mediation process fails to prevent serious power imbalances, and an agreement is markedly unfair to one party. Sometimes the extent of the unfairness may not be fully appreciated until a later time. Under the unconscionability clause of the Uniform Commercial Code[15] and those jurisdictions that recognize unconscionability as a defense,[16] a court may refuse to enforce the contract or any provision thereof.

Enforcement remedies create special problems in the context of mediation agreements. When, as in community dispute mediation, the mediator is often not a lawyer, the agreement may be written in layman terms or inartful legal jargon. That may be perfectly satisfactory to enable a court to enforce it if the terms are clear and unambiguous. But if the terms are vague, ambiguous, or contradictory, problems arise. For specific performance, a higher degree of specificity is generally required, and the terms must be certain in all particulars essential to enforcement.[17] Inartful drafting is not necessarily fatal to the enforcement of contracts. Courts have held that even though the draftmanship leaves something to be

12. Restatement, Second, Contracts § 179.

13. Restatement, Second, Contracts § 152.

14. A. Farnsworth, Contracts 232 (1982); Restatement, Contracts §§ 162–64.

15. Uniform Commercial Code § 2–302.

16. See Restatement, Contracts § 208.

17. Manss–Owens Co. v. H.S. Owens & Son, 129 Va. 183, 105 S.E. 543, 547 (1921).

518 CHAPTER III MEDIATION

desired and could have been more clearly stated, the contract should be specifically enforced if its intent can be determined.[18]

Courts should give consideration to the nature of the mediation process in striving to determine the intent of an agreement. They should be apprised of the fact that the parties voluntarily engaged in a process involving mutual discussion in an attempt to resolve the dispute and achieve reconciliation. In such a process, drafting requirements should be liberal if the intent can be divined. Furthermore, it might be argued "that the harm suffered from denial of the specific performance order would be more than just that of the parties involved, but would also include the harm to the program of public knowledge that settlements are not enforced on their terms."[19] There are, however, occasions when mediation contracts simply lack the specificity necessary for specific enforcement.

In addition, specific performance will not be enforced if "the character and magnitude of performance would impose on the court burdens in enforcement or supervision disproportionate to the advantages gained from enforcement and the harm suffered from denial."[20] An agreement, for example, that calls for a party "to stay away" from the other might fail under that standard.

Damages, in lieu of specific performance, seems an inappropriate remedy for mediation, at least in agreements dealing with relationships and other intangibles. The goal of mediation is to allow the parties to structure their own resolution of the dispute, and damages would seem contrary to that objective. In such cases, the inadequacy of damages, as required for specific performance, should generally be easily demonstrated: damages fail to carry out the parties' resolution and could be difficult to prove for breach of an agreement that seeks to define interpersonal relations and nontangible benefits. It has been suggested that "if a damage award is made, it should be made on the original dispute, and not on the agreement reached in settlement of the original dispute."[21] On the other hand, in such areas as labor, commercial, public law, and even certain family law (as with property settlements) disputes, damages may provide an adequate substitute for the loss of compliance with the mediation agreement.

1. WRITTEN AGREEMENTS: COMPLETENESS, AMBIGUITY, AND PAROL EVIDENCE

Hardman v. Dault

Texas Court of Appeals–San Antonio, 1999.
2 S.W.3d 378.

■ PAUL W. GREEN, JUSTICE.

Hardman owned 19 acres of land securing his real estate lien note payable to Dault. Hardman defaulted on the note and, pursuant to the

---

18. Wilkinson v. Vaughn, 419 S.W.2d 1, 6 (Mo.1967).

19. Freedman, Are Mediation Agreements Enforceable? 9 (ABA Spec.Comm. on Alt. Means of Dis.Res.).

20. Restatement, Second, Contracts § 366.

21. Freedman, supra, at 7.

terms of a deed of trust, Dault initiated non-judicial foreclosure proceedings against the property. Hardman filed suit to stop the foreclosure, and Dault filed a counterclaim to enforce the note and seek foreclosure of the vendor's lien. The trial court ordered the dispute to mediation, which was conducted on December 16, 1996. The mediation was successful.

Pursuant to the mediated settlement, the parties signed a memorandum setting out the terms of the settlement as follows:

The parties below agree to enter a Take Nothing Judgment in this matter based upon the following conditions, and in full & final settlement of all claims stated herein:

1. Dault agrees to dismiss the foreclosure action against Hardman, with prejudice;

2. Hardman agrees to pay to Dault an amount of $50,000, over ten years, at a compound rate of 8.5%, with the first payment due on or before April 1, 1998, and an acceleration clause conditioned on 3 missed payments (not consecutively), secured by the subject property of this suit;

3. Hardman agrees to dismiss this lawsuit with prejudice;

4. All parties pay their own costs, expenses, and attorneys fees;

5. Final documents to be signed by 1–1–97.

Dault tendered "final documents" to Hardman on December 30, 1996, but Hardman refused to sign them. Dault then amended his counterclaim to seek enforce of the settlement agreement; his motion for summary judgment on the settlement agreement was granted.

* * *

Enforceability of Settlement Agreement

Hardman claims the mediated settlement was only tentative and the parties did not intend their memorandum agreement to be binding. Specifically, Hardman points to the January 1, 1997 deadline imposed in the agreement for signing "final documents" as evidence the settlement was not intended to be final.

A mediated settlement agreement is enforceable in the same manner as any other contract. Tex. Civ. Prac. & Rem. Code Ann. § 154.071(a) (Vernon 1997); *Martin v. Black*, 909 S.W.2d 192, 195 (Tex.App.—Houston [14th Dist.] 1995, writ denied). An agreement is enforceable if it is "complete within itself in every material detail, and [ ] contains all of the essential elements of the agreement." *Padilla v. LaFrance*, 907 S.W.2d 454, 460 (Tex.1995). The intent of the parties to be bound is an essential element of an enforceable contract, *see Foreca, S.A. v. GRD Development Co., Inc.*, 758 S.W.2d 744, 746 (Tex.1988), and is often a question of fact. *Id.* But where

CHAPTER III MEDIATION

that intent is clear and unambiguous on the face of the agreement, it may be determined as a matter of law. *Cf. Padilla,* 907 S.W.2d at 461–62.

The settlement memorandum in this case sets out the essential terms of the agreement. No material or essential detail was left out. All that remained were the "final documents" necessary to carry out the agreement. Hardman claims the parties contemplated that signing final documents by January 1, 1997 was a condition precedent to the formation of an enforceable agreement. Since the documents were not signed by the deadline, Hardman says there was no contract. The issue, then, is whether the contemplated documentation was a condition precedent to the formation of a contract or simply a memorial of an already enforceable contract.

In *Foreca, S.A. v. GRD Development Co., Inc.,* the supreme court addressed the same issue. In that case, two offer letters contained language specifically making them subject to "satisfactory legal documentation." *See* 758 S.W.2d at 744–45. The court held the "subject to" language raised a fact issue concerning whether the parties intended the letters to be binding. *See id.,* 758 S.W.2d at 746. Similarly, in *Martin v. Black,* a settlement memorandum prepared pursuant to a mediated settlement contained language that "the parties' understandings are subject to securing documentation satisfactory to the parties." *See* 909 S.W.2d at 196. Following *Foreca,* the Houston court held that the "subject to" language left a fact issue on the question of the parties' intent to be bound by the settlement memorandum.

There is no "subject to" language in the settlement memorandum in this case, however. The "final documents" provision neither suggests nor infers that the parties intended that the agreement was to be subject to any subsequent action by the parties, or that the signing of documents was to be a condition precedent to the formation of an enforceable contract. Thus, since the settlement agreement contains all essential terms, and there being no fact issue concerning whether the parties intended the settlement agreement to be binding, the partial summary judgment enforcing the written settlement agreement is affirmed.

NOTES AND QUESTIONS

1. The court's finding in *Hardman* that the language in the agreement—"Final documents to be signed by 1–1–97"—did not detract from the finality of the agreement was an attempt to apply the intent of the parties. Would the parties have also understood, in *Foreca,* that saying that the letters of understanding were "subject to" "satisfactory legal documentation" evidenced an intent that the agreement not be final? Why wouldn't the parties have understood "satisfactory legal documentation" as an objective criterion easily verifiable by lawyers and not as failing to reach agreement on an essential element?

2. What items are so material to an agreement that failure to include them makes it unenforceable? In Coulter v. Carewell Corp. of Oklahoma, 21 P.3d 1078 (Okla.Cir.App.Div. 2, 2001), a wrongful death case, the parties signed a mediation agreement that said: "We intend the above agreement to be a legally binding and enforceable settlement contract and acknowledge that we entered into the same without coercion and duress." Counsel for the defendant was to draft the settlement agreement and send it to the plaintiff for her signature. She refused, objecting to a broad release clause, and then moved in court to enforce the settlement without the release, apparently on the theory that the agreement was complete without it and that she had not agreed to it. The appellate court noted that a release need not be negotiated during mediation, but still enforced the agreement containing the release on the ground that it "contained an implied promise to execute the release." Under what circumstances might failure to agree on the terms of a release make an agreement unenforceable? The court in *Coulter* said that the plaintiff had not argued that "the release materially altered the financial terms agreed upon in the mediation agreement." What if she had so argued? What if the plaintiff had disavowed the whole agreement (rather that trying to enforce it without the release)? What if the agreement had not specifically stated that the parties intended it to be legally binding?

Cain v. Saunders

Court of Civil Appeals of Alabama 2001.
2001 WL 499167.

■ THOMPSON, JUDGE

J.M Cain, Jr., sued Charles L. Saunders, Jr. The action was related to Saunders's agreement to guarantee certain debts of Cain. Saunders moved for a summary judgment. [Cain and Saunders mediated Cain's breach-of-contract claim and his claim alleging failure to act in a commercially reasonable manner, and reached an agreement; the parties executed a written settlement agreement.] Saunders filed a motion seeking to have the settlement agreement enforced. The trial court conducted a hearing on Saunders's motion and heard more evidence. On June 15, 2000, the trial court entered a judgment "in accordance with" the terms of the settlement agreement. Cain appealed.

The relevant portion of the parties' settlement agreement provides: "3. Mr. Saunders will transfer ownership of the 2 [MONY] policies (death benefit of $19,022 and $12,300) to Mr. Cain. Saunders waives and releases any claim to all policies identified in the August 14, 1991, document."

During the June 14, 2000, hearing on his motion to enforce the parties' settlement agreement, Saunders objected to Cain's testimony regarding Cain's understanding of the cash values of the life-insurance policies; Saunders argued that the parties' settlement agreement was not ambiguous and that, therefore, parol evidence was not admissible. Saunders also objected to Cain's testimony regarding the positions the parties took during the course of their mediation; he argued that that testimony was barred by Rule 11, Alabama Civil Court Mediation Rules, which provides that information used in a mediation is confidential. The trial court granted Saunders continuing objections to all of that testimony. The trial court stated

CHAPTER III MEDIATION

that it would consider the testimony only if it determined that the parties' settlement agreement was ambiguous.

At the June 14, 2000, hearing, Cain testified that he thought the two life-insurance policies referenced in paragraph 3 of the parties' settlement agreement had a total cash value of approximately $20,000. In fact, the combined cash value of those two policies was less than $10,000. Saunders testified that he also thought the life-insurance policies' cash values were higher. Cain testified that he would not have entered into the settlement agreement had he known the actual cash values of the two life-insurance policies.

In its judgment, the trial court determined that paragraph 3 of the parties' settlement agreement was not ambiguous and that, therefore, the agreement was due to be enforced. The trial court entered a judgment incorporating the terms of the parties' settlement agreement.

In his brief on appeal, Cain argues that the parties' settlement agreement should be set aside on the grounds of mutual mistake and because there was no "meeting of the minds." However, before the trial court, Cain did not seek to rescind or set aside the settlement agreement. He did not file any motion seeking such relief in the trial court, and he did not file any document in opposition to Saunders's motion to enforce the settlement agreement. At the June 14, 2000, hearing, Saunders objected to Cain's attempts to introduce parol evidence regarding the parties' beliefs regarding the cash values of the life-insurance policies. The trial court granted Saunders a continuing objection to that testimony. Thus, it cannot be said that the issue whether the settlement agreement should be rescinded or set aside was tried by the implied consent of the parties. *See* Rule 15(b), Ala.R.Civ.P. We interpret Cain's argument on appeal as addressing whether the trial court properly concluded that the settlement agreement was unambiguous and was due to be enforced.

A settlement agreement is as binding on the parties as any other contract, and it will be enforced by the courts. *Coaker v. Washington County Bd. of Educ.*, 646 So.2d 38 (Ala.Civ.App.1993). A settlement agreement may be reopened only for fraud, accident, or mistake. *Nero v. Chastang*, 358 So.2d 740 (Ala.Civ.App.1978). Where the terms of a written settlement agreement are clear and unambiguous, the terms of that agreement may not be varied by the introduction of parol evidence regarding a mutual mistake of fact. *State Farm Mut. Auto. Ins. Co. v. Brackett*, 527 So.2d 1249 (Ala.1988). *See also Marriot Int'l, Inc. v. deCelle*, 722 So.2d 760 (Ala.1998); *Clark v. Albertville Nursing Home, Inc.*, 545 So.2d 9 (Ala.1989).

> "[I]n the absence of fraud, a release supported by a valuable consideration, unambiguous in meaning, will be given effect according to the intention of the parties from what appears within the four corners of the instrument itself, and parol evidence may not be introduced to establish the existence of a mutual mistake of fact when the release was signed as a basis for a rescission of that release."

Cleghorn v. Scribner, 597 So.2d 693, 696 (Ala.1992).

F. Enforceability of Mediation Agreements

Cain has made no allegation of fraud against Saunders.

Whether an agreement is ambiguous is a question of law to be determined by the court. *Austin v. Cox,* 523 So.2d 376 (Ala.1988). An agreement is ambiguous if it is susceptible to more than one meaning. *Bain v. Gartrell,* 666 So.2d 523 (Ala.Civ.App.1995). However, an agreement is not rendered ambiguous simply because the parties assign different meanings to it. *Wayne J. Griffin Elec., Inc. v. Dunn Constr. Co.,* 622 So.2d 314 (Ala.1993). Parol evidence regarding the terms of an agreement is admissible only where an ambiguity exists. *F.W. Woolworth Co. v. Grimmer,* 601 So.2d 1043 (Ala.Civ.App.1992). In his brief on appeal, Cain makes no argument that paragraph 3 of the settlement agreement was ambiguous, nor does he argue that because the agreement was ambiguous, parol evidence was admissible to establish the alleged mutual mistake of the parties.

We agree with the trial court that paragraph 3 of the parties' settlement agreement is unambiguous. That provision clearly identifies the consideration, i.e., the life-insurance policies, that Saunders would provide to Cain. Because the parties' settlement agreement was not ambiguous, parol evidence was not admissible to alter the terms of that agreement. *Cleghorn v. Scribner,* supra; *F.W. Woolworth Co. v. Grimmer,* supra.

We conclude that the trial court correctly determined that the parties' settlement agreement was unambiguous and that, therefore, it was due to be enforced without regard to parol evidence regarding the parties' intentions or understandings in entering into the settlement. We recognize that the result reached in applying the parol-evidence rule might not always seem equitable where a mutual mistake inures to the benefit of one of the settling parties at the expense of the other. However, in this case, both parties were represented by counsel and each had ample opportunity to draft the settlement agreement in a manner to fully protect his rights.

Affirmed.

■ PITTMAN, J., concurs.

■ CRAWLEY, J., concurs in the result.

■ YATES, PRESIDING JUDGE, dissenting.

The trial judge refused to allow parol evidence because he found the language in the settlement agreement to be unambiguous. When a party alleges mutual mistake, the task of the trial court should not be to interpret the language of the contract, but to determine whether the contract was valid. In order for a contract to be valid, there must be a meeting of the minds, which cannot exist if there is a mutual mistake. The fact that the settlement agreement is couched in unambiguous terms, or that the parties knew what words were used and were aware of their ordinary meaning, or that the parties were negligent in failing to discover the mistake before signing the instrument, should not preclude the admission of parol evidence. Where a mutual mistake of fact is alleged, or where fraud is alleged, parol evidence should be admissible to show the true intent and understanding of the parties.

> "It is practically the universal rule that in suits to reform written instruments on the ground of fraud or mutual mistake, parol evidence is admissible to establish the fact of fraud or of a mistake and in what it consisted, and to show how the writing should be corrected in order to conform to the agreement or intention which the parties actually made or had. The nature of the action is such that it is outside the field of operation of the parol evidence rule, since the court does not receive parol testimony to vary the contract of the parties but to show what their contract really was. If the rule were otherwise and parol evidence was not admissible in an action for reformation, a rule adopted by the courts as a protection against fraud and false swearing—that is, the parol evidence rule—would become the instrument of the very fraud it was designed to prevent, and the reformation or correction of a written instrument would rarely, if ever, be accomplished. Evidence of fraud or mistake is seldom found in the instrument itself, and unless the parol evidence may be admitted for the purpose of procuring its reformation, the aggrieved party would have as little hope of redress in a court of equity as in a court of law. Moreover, a general merger clause in a written contract, to the effect that it expresses the entire agreement and that no asserted extrinsic representations are binding, will not, of itself, bar parol evidence for the purpose of reforming the instrument on the ground of mistake ."

66 Am.Jur.2d *Reformation of Instruments* § 118 (1973).

I find persuasive *Beck v. Reynolds*, 903 P.2d 317 (Okla.1995). In *Beck*, a patient had released his medical-malpractice claims against his physician after settling with the physician's insurer for the limits of the physician's liability policies. Both parties understood that the settlement was for $201,000—which they understood to be the combined policy limits of the physician's two insurance policies. The patient filed a "motion to compel settlement," requesting a judgment against the insurer for $900,000 after learning that the actual limit of one of the policies was $1,000,000. The Oklahoma Supreme Court held that no mutual consent had existed to support the settlement between the patient and the physician's insurer, because, given the mutual mistaken of fact, there had been no meeting of the minds. Therefore, I dissent.

■ MURDOCK, JUDGE, dissenting.

* * *

As indicated by the plurality, Cain did not seek from the trial court a formal order of rescission of the settlement agreement. He presumably saw no need to do so. The settlement agreement was still executory, and Cain had repudiated it based on the mutual mistake of fact.

Thus, it was Saunders who invoked the aid of the court and sought an order relating to the agreement, namely, one to require Cain to perform. It was as a *defense to Saunders's motion* that Cain presented the issue of the parties' mutual mistake.

The trial court's order states that the court ordered the agreement "specifically enforced" based on its find[ing] that "the settlement agreement is not ambiguous." Moreover, because of its finding that the agreement was not ambiguous, the trial court thought it was foreclosed from considering parol evidence to show the parties' mutual mistake of fact and, concomitantly, the court did not reach the latter issue.

Two issues are raised by the parties. The first is whether the trial court erred in enforcing the parties' settlement agreement in light of the parties' mutual mistake of fact—and similarly erred in refusing to consider parol evidence to show the mutual mistake—because the court had found the agreement to be unambiguous. The second issue is whether the Alabama Civil Court Mediation Rules prevented introduction of parol evidence from the parties' mediation process in order to show that the settlement agreement achieved in that process was a result of a mutual mistake of fact and therefore should not have been enforced.

I. *Mutual Mistake of Fact as Shown by Parol Evidence*

Saunders argues that the provision of the contract calling for the transfer of the two life-insurance policies is unambiguous. Consequently, according to Saunders, the trial court refused to consider parol evidence to determine the provision's "true meaning."

I agree that the provision is unambiguous. Its meaning is clear: two assets, namely, two particular insurance policies, are to be transferred from Saunders to Cain under this provision. The issue presented by Cain, however, is not whether this provision is ambiguous. The issue presented by Cain is whether there was a mutual mistake of fact as to the underlying value of the assets to be transferred.

It is a well-established rule of contract law that a mutual mistake of fact concerning a basic assumption on which a contract is made can, alone, make that contract unenforceable. The existence of such a mutual mistake is not dependent on the presence of fraud or ambiguity. Instead, a mutual mistake is recognized as a separate and independent ground for relief from the terms of a contract. * * *

Fundamentally, however, it is important to note that, in order to serve as a basis for relief from a contract, a mistake must be as to an *existing* fact. In *Boles v. Blackstock*, 484 So.2d 1077 (Ala.1986), our Supreme Court recognized the distinction between a mutual mistake as to an existing fact and a mutual mistake as to some future condition or occurrence. Quoting from § 151 of the *Restatement (Second) of Contracts*, the Court noted that a "mistake" such as will prevent the enforcement of a contract is "a belief that is not in accord with the facts" and that the "erroneous belief must relate to the facts as they exist *at the time of the making of the contract*." 484 So.2d at 1082 (emphasis in original).

526 CHAPTER III MEDIATION

In the present case, the trial court specifically entered a judgment to enforce the terms of the parties' executory settlement agreement based on its finding that the agreement was "not ambiguous." As a result of this finding, the trial court declined to consider parol evidence. Saunders is correct to the extent that he asserts that parol evidence is not admissible to "vary the terms" of an unambiguous agreement. However, because Alabama law also recognizes that a party may obtain relief from a contract based on a mutual mistake of fact, the trial court erred in refusing to consider parol evidence for *that* purpose.

II. The Admissibility of Parol Evidence from the Parties' Mediation

Saunders also argues that the Alabama Civil Court Mediation Rules do not allow the introduction of the parol evidence upon which Cain relied at trial. Saunders cites the provisions of Rule 11 of those Rules, which, in relevant part, provides as follows:

> "Each party shall maintain the confidentiality of the information received during the mediation and shall not in any arbitral, judicial, or other proceeding rely on or introduce as evidence:
>
>> "(a) Views expressed or suggestions made by another party with respect to a possible settlement of the dispute;
>>
>> "(b) Admissions made by another party in the course of the mediation proceedings...."

> "The court shall neither inquire into, nor receive information about, the positions of the parties taken in mediation proceedings; the facts elicited or presented in mediation proceedings; or the cause or responsibility for termination or failure of the mediation process."

When an agreement is reached in mediation, however, and that very agreement is challenged in a subsequent court action as having been a result of fraud or mutual mistake occurring in the course of the mediation, the Alabama Civil Court Mediation Rules were not intended to prevent the injured party from proving such fraud or mistake. The use of the mediation process does not immunize the resulting contract from scrutiny under otherwise-applicable substantive law pertaining to the enforceability of contracts.

A careful examination of the language of Rule 11 supports this interpretation, particularly as it applies to the present case. Saunders relies primarily upon the concluding paragraph of Rule 11; however, it is that concluding paragraph that underscores the fact that Rule 11 contemplates that the views and admissions exchanged in the course of attempting to negotiate a mediated settlement will not be disclosed when that negotiation is *unsuccessful*. Specifically, the concluding clause of Rule 11 contemplates that there has been a "termination or failure of the mediation process." Thus, the parties are protected in any statements they make to one another in the course of attempting to settle their dispute if the mediation fails and they are forced to resort to a court action to resolve their underlying claims.

In this regard, Rule 11 of the Alabama Civil Court Mediation Rules is comparable to Rule 408 of the Alabama Rules of Evidence. Rule 408 provides that evidence of offers or acceptances of particular consideration in return for the proposed compromise of a claim "is not admissible to prove liability for or invalidity of the claim or its amount" and that "[e]vidence of conduct or statements made in compromise negotiations is likewise not admissible." Ala.R.Evid., Rule 408. However, "[t]his rule does not require the exclusion of any evidence otherwise discoverable merely because it is presented in the course of compromise negotiations." *Id.*

In other words, Rule 408 does not preclude admission, in a subsequent judicial proceeding, of a compromise offer or a related statement proffered for some purpose other than the one specifically precluded (proof of validity or invalidity of the underlying claim). If the settlement agreement, itself, is being sued upon or asserted as a defense to a claim, Rule 408 does not apply. *See* 1 Charles W. Gamble, *McElroy's Alabama Evidence* § 188.01(6)(e) (5th ed.1996). Thus, Rule 408 does not prevent the use of representations made during the settlement discussions to establish that a resulting settlement was the product of fraud or a mutual mistake that occurred in those discussions.

Similarly, Rule 11 of the Alabama Civil Court Mediation Rules does not prevent a trial court from admitting evidence of fraud or mistake occurring in the course of mediated settlement negotiations where, as here, the issue before the court is the impact of the alleged fraud or mistake on the resulting settlement agreement.

NOTES AND QUESTIONS

1. It is a familiar doctrine that parol evidence is not admissable concerning an unambiguous contract. In *Cain*, was the provision in the agreement that the defendant would transfer ownership of two policies to the plaintiff ambiguous? Both the majority and the dissent found that it was not, and the majority notes that a provision is not ambiguous just because the parties assign different meanings to it. Why do the dissents maintain that parol evidence is nevertheless admissible? Can a claim of mutual mistake be adequately presented without resort to parol evidence? Does admitting parol evidence in such a case undermine the finality of a mediated agreement?

2. The defendant argued that even if contract law would permit parol evidence in this situation, the Alabama rule governing mediation confidentiality would not. How does the appellate court get around the seemingly broad guarantee of confidentiality in the Alabama court rule and Alabama's equivalent of Federal Rule of Evidence 408 (see discussion of Rule 408 in Chapter II, D, 2, e, and in III, E, 1).

2. ENFORCING MEDIATED SETTLEMENT AGREEMENT REPUDIATED BEFORE ENTRY OF JUDGMENT

Many state mediation/ADR statutes and rules state that an agreement resulting from mediation or ADR "is enforceable in the same manner as

528   CHAPTER III MEDIATION

any other written contract."[22] Does this mean that a mediated agreement must be sued on like any other contract as a separate cause of action in which proof of a valid contract must be made, or that it can be treated as a consent judgment in a pending case as to which judgment can be entered without further evidence? In many jurisdictions the parties to a mediated agreement in a pending suit can come before the court and have the agreement entered as a consent judgment. But what if one of the parties repudiates the agreement before a consent judgment is entered?

The Texas courts have wrestled with this issue in a variety of situations, and the Texas cases are instructive as to how other jurisdictions that have not addressed this issue might rule. A majority of Texas courts have held that if one of the parties withdraws consent before the court renders its judgment, a consent judgment cannot be entered. Therefore, even after the parties enter mediation, negotiate extensively, and agree to terms embodied in a written ADR agreement, one party may unilaterally render the agreement unenforceable by withdrawing consent before the agreement is entered as a court judgment.

A minority view among Texas courts holds that agreements reached pursuant to the ADR Act can be enforced even after a party has repudiated the agreement. In Matter of Marriage of Ames, 860 S.W.2d 590 (Tex.App.— Amarillo 1993, no writ), the parties ordered to mediation by the court reached a community property settlement agreement. The agreement was signed by the parties and their attorneys. Two weeks later, one party to the settlement withdrew consent. He asserted that he was permitted to do so under the provisions of the Texas Family Code which allows an agreement to be revised or repudiated before rendition of a divorce or annulment. Texas Family Code Section 3.631(a). However, the Family Code also states that the agreement may not be revised or repudiated if it is binding under some other rule of law. This express exception meant, in the *Ames* court's view, that the Texas ADR Act controlled over the Family Code. The court concluded that the ADR statute specifically provided for enforcement of ADR agreements notwithstanding repudiation by one of the parties: "We interpret this statute to mean, inter alia, that a party who has reached a settlement agreement disposing of a dispute through alternative dispute resolution procedures may not unilaterally repudiate the agreement." The court noted that the express policy of the ADR Act is the early settlement of pending litigation through voluntary settlement procedures. If parties were free to repudiate their agreements, the court reasoned, disputes would not be finally resolved, and traditional litigation would recur.

Most Texas courts have not followed *Ames*, even in situations where unfairness arises from the repudiation of the agreement. Cary v. Cary, 894 S.W.2d 111 (Tex.App.—Houston [1st Dist.] 1995, no writ), like *Ames*, involved a divorce proceeding that was referred to mediation. The parties executed a written agreement, but before the court could enter the agreement as its judgment, the wife repudiated the agreement. The husband

---

22. Tex. Civ. Prac. & Rem. Code § 154.071(a).

F. ENFORCEABILITY OF MEDIATION AGREEMENTS

then moved to render a final decree of divorce based on the agreement reached. After a hearing, the trial court rendered its decree based on parties' agreement over the objection of the wife. The Houston Court of Appeals overturned the judgment of the trial court, expressly rejecting *Ames*: "We disagree with the Amarillo court and adhere to the concept that consent of the parties is required up to the moment of rendition of the consent judgment, no matter how the agreement was reached." The *Cary* court found that nothing in the Texas ADR Act gives heightened dignity to an agreement reached through mediation. Thus, when a party has repudiated an agreement prior to its entry as a judgment, it is only enforceable through a separate cause of action in contract.

In order to enforce a settlement entered as a consent judgment, a party must affirmatively request the court to take action. In Pickell v. Guaranty Nat. Life Ins. Co., 917 S.W.2d 439 (Tex.App.—Houston [14th Dist.] 1996), a suit by an insurance agent against his company, the Court of Appeals affirmed a default judgment entered against an agent who, believing his case settled after mediation, failed to appear in court. The parties had reached an agreement whereby the insurance company was to pay the agent $10,000 and his lawyer $3,800. The mediator sent the trial court a letter stating that the case was settled and enclosing a copy of the settlement, but the case was not removed from the trial docket. After a hearing at which the insurance company presented evidence of its damages, the court entered a default judgment of $267,681 for the insurance company.

The judgment was affirmed on appeal. *Pickell* rejected the agent's claim that since the parties executed a settlement agreement, the trial court had no option but to enter judgment in accordance with the agreement. In the court's view, the fact that a settlement agreement was executed at mediation did not relieve the party of his obligation to appear at trial. Nor did the settlement agreement preclude a default judgment when a party failed to appear. The court noted that the agent did not move the court to continue or change the dates set for the pretrial conference and trial because of the settlement and did not file amended pleadings raising a defense or asking for affirmative relief based on the mediated settlement agreement. Nor did the agent file a motion for summary judgment based on the agreement. According to the *Pickell* court, "[t]he court cannot take action on the mediated settlement agreement without an affirmative request to do so." The court acknowledged that the result in the case was harsh. However, where the party seeking to enforce the settlement did not file amended pleadings or a summary judgment motion, the settlement agreement was not effective.

When a party to a settlement agreement repudiates the agreement before the court enters it as a judgment, the agreement can only be enforced as a cause of action in contract. In Martin v. Black, 909 S.W.2d 192 (Tex.App.—Houston [14th Dist.] 1995), the court was called on to enforce a mediated settlement agreement which had been repudiated by one of the parties. The parties had voluntarily agreed to mediate, resulting in an agreement outlined in two handwritten documents or "term sheets"

530 CHAPTER III MEDIATION

signed by the parties and their counsel and advisors. The agreements called for the parties to draft a number of documents, including the final settlement agreement and final judgment. The agreements provided also that the parties' understandings were subject to securing documentation satisfactory to the parties. Subsequently, one party repudiated the agreement. The trial court held that the term sheets were clear and unambiguous. Therefore, as a matter of law they constituted binding and enforceable settlement agreements. It then entered a final judgment on the settlement agreements, and denied a motion for a new trial from the party who repudiated the agreement.

The Court of Appeals reversed, noting that the Texas ADR statute only provides that a written settlement agreement is enforceable in the same manner as any other written contract. The statute does not order courts to follow a special procedure applicable only to mediated settlement agreements. Because a mediated settlement agreement is enforceable under contract law, the same procedures used to enforce and enter judgment on other contracts apply to mediated settlement agreements. Under the rules of civil procedure, the applicable vehicles for obtaining judgment on a dispute over whether a contract exists are: (1) a motion for summary judgment if no fact issue exists, or (2) a non-jury or jury trial if a fact issue does exist. Where one of the parties contests its intent to be bound by a mediated settlement agreement, the court may enter a judgment only under one of these procedures. The *Martin* court went on to find that an issue of fact existed as to the intent of one of the parties to be bound by the agreement and reversed the lower court's judgment and remanded the case for trial.

In Cadle Co. v. Castle, 913 S.W.2d 627 (Tex.App.—Dallas 1995, writ denied), one party repudiated the agreement before the court entered it as a judgment. The party seeking enforcement of the agreement filed a "Motion to Enforce Settlement Agreement." The court conducted a hearing on the motion. Without hearing evidence, the trial judge concluded that the terms of the written settlement agreement should be "incorporated" into a final judgment.

On appeal, the party seeking to enforce the agreement took inspiration from *Ames*. It argued that § 154.071 of the ADR Act creates a summary procedure whereby the trial court can enter judgment based on the agreement without a trial, evidentiary hearing, or underlying petition or counterclaim asserting breach of contract. The party argued further that the broad public policy behind the ADR statute, i.e., early settlement of pending litigation, required such a reading . The Dallas Court of Appeals disagreed. It held that the act merely states that ADR agreements are to be enforced like any other contract and allows the trial court, in its own discretion, to incorporate settlement terms into the final judgment. The ADR Act did not establish a summary procedure bypassing the need to seek enforcement of a repudiated settlement agreement in contract: "We do not believe the legislature intended section 154.071(b) to be used to enter a judgment on the merits of a cause of action without a party having the right to be confronted by appropriate pleadings, have an opportunity to conduct discovery and assert defenses, or a chance to have the dispute determined by a judge or jury." The court then found that the party seeking to enforce the agreement had failed to present proper pleadings and proof to support an action for breach of contract and that the entry of the settlement agreement as a judgment was invalid.

The Texas Supreme Court dealt with the issue in an oblique fashion in Mantas v. Fifth Court of Appeals, 925 S.W.2d 656 (Tex.1996). *Mantas* arose from a suit in which one party obtained a judgment in a commercial dispute. The judgment debtor appealed, whereupon the appellate court ordered the parties to mediate, and the parties reached and signed a settlement agreement. Pursuant to the agreement, the judgment debtor gave the other party a $160,000 check in full satisfaction of the judgment. The other party signed a release of judgment, a joint motion to dismiss the appeal, and an agreed order dismissing the appeal. Later the same day, before any documents were filed with the appellate court, the party to whom the check was paid withdrew his consent from the settlement agreement. The check was never returned. The party who paid the check then asked the appellate court to enforce the settlement agreement or alternatively to order the other party to return the check. Relying on *Cadle*, the court held that enforcement of a disputed settlement agreement, even if reached at court-ordered mediation, must be determined in a cause of action for breach of contract under normal rules of pleading and evidence. It refused to order the return of the $160,000 check prior to the resolution of a suit to enforce the settlement agreement or to abate the appeal pending resolution of a suit in contract to enforce the settlement agreement.

The Texas Supreme Court declined to grant mandamus relief to compel the appellate court to enforce the settlement agreement. A written settlement agreement can not be enforced as a consent judgment when one party withdraws its consent before the court renders judgment on the agreement. Instead, the party seeking to enforce the agreement must pursue a separate breach of contract claim subject to normal rules of pleading and proof. In the *Mantas* court's view, the payment of the $160,000 check did not alter procedural requirements or authorize the court summarily to enforce the settlement agreement. Similarly, it held that the appellate court was correct not to order repayment of the check, since this was a matter which had to be settled through an enforcement suit in contract. However, the Supreme Court concluded that the appellate court was in error in refusing to abate the appeal pending resolution of a suit in contract to enforce the settlement agreement. Thus, it granted conditional mandamus relief in the form of a temporary abatement of the appeal pending resolution of the enforcement suit.

One Texas court, *Alvarez v. Reiser, 958 S.W.2d 232 (Tex.App.–Eastland 1997), writ denied,* reached the same result as *Ames*, but did not base its decision on the policy underlying the ADR Act, but on a provision of the Texas Family Code. *Alvarez*, like *Ames*, involved the enforcement of a

532 CHAPTER III MEDIATION

mediated divorce settlement where one party, the wife, repudiated the agreement before a judgment was entered on the agreement. The appellate court found that the trial court was required to enter judgment on the mediated settlement agreement because the agreement included a provision highlighting the irrevocability of the settlement in accordance with the Texas Family Code. The court stated, "mediated settlement agreements complying with [the Family Code] are binding, and a party to such an agreement is entitled to a judgment. Unilateral withdrawal of consent does not negate the enforceability of the agreement and a separate suit for enforcement is not necessary." *See also Pollard v. Merkel, 1999 WL 72209 (Tex. App.–Dallas 1999, n.w.h.)(not designated for publication)* (refusing to enter a judgment based on a mediated agreement in a divorce proceeding where one party has repudiated the agreement).

G. REGULATING PROFESSIONAL CONDUCT IN MEDIATION AND ALTERNATIVE DISPUTE RESOLUTION

Mediators have always been aware that the performance of their functions requires compliance with strict professional standards. The difficulty is in determining the source of those standards. Until recently, mediators from different professions looked to the professional standards of their own profession. But as the mediator profession became more eclectic and as mediation became court-annexed, there have been increasing demands for uniform professional standards. This development has been accompanied by a movement for credentialing of ADR professionals by some authoritative body.

1. STANDARDS OF PROFESSIONAL CONDUCT

Edward F. Sherman, Introduction to Symposium on Standards of Professional Conduct in Alternative Dispute Resolution

1995 J. of Dispute Resolution 95.

Mediators and ADR neutrals increasingly view themselves as a part of a distinct profession.[1] Many are already associated with another profession—lawyers, psychologists, therapists, social workers—and are subject to the standards of those professions. However, there is a growing consensus

---

1. The concept of professionalism, writes Burton J. Bledstein, has evolved out of an attempt "to define a totally coherent system of necessary knowledge within a precise territory, to control the intrinsic relationships of their subject by making it a scholarly as well as an applied science, to root social existence in the inner needs and possibilities of documentable wordly processes." Bledstein, The Culture of Professionalism 88 (1976). A concomitant feature is a sense of responsibility to the clients of the profession and an obligation to comply with the professional standards of conduct and ethics.

G. Regulating Professional Conduct 533

that ADR raises distinctive issues of professional conduct that cannot be fully comprehended by the codes of the individual professions.

ADR is unique in being interdisciplinary and interprofessional. ADR neutrals perform in a distinctive role and not as members of their own profession. The ADR process demands adherence to policies like voluntariness, respect for party autonomy, and confidentiality, which, in turn, make special ethical demands on ADR neutrals. Thus there are compelling reasons to contemplate an interdisciplinary code of conduct that addresses the professional duties and obligations of ADR neutrals.

Standards of conduct for ADR has been a much discussed and debated topic over the past decade, both as to source and content.[2] The two principal sources of standards have been the professions and the government.

The standards of conduct of individual professional groups are still the primary source of regulation in most states. Codes of professional conduct tailored to mediation and ADR have been issued by various professional organizations.[3] In addition, consortia of professional groups and umbrella organizations that include a number of individual professions have promulgated standards. Most recently, three prestigious organizations—the American Arbitration Association, the American Bar Association, and the Society of Professionals in Dispute Resolution (SPIDR)—formed a Joint Committee on Standards of Conduct. In 1994 it issued a draft of proposed standards of conduct for mediators which would affect the members of those organizations.[4] Such groups, however, lack enforcement power, and have to rely upon the individual professions to undertake enforcement sanctions against one of their members.

A long-awaited study of qualifications by SPIDR issued in 1989 concluded that no single entity, but rather a variety of professional organizations, should establish qualifications; that the greater the degree of choice the parties have over the ADR process, the less mandatory should be the qualification requirements; and that the qualification criteria should be based on performance, rather than on paper credentials.[5]

The second source of standards for conduct of ADR professionals comes from various forms of government regulation. Particularly as courts have begun to "annex" ADR processes as an integral part of litigation procedures, there has been increasing concern with providing regulation of ADR neutrals through legislation or court rule. Some states have assigned

---

2. *See* M. Shaw, Selection, Training, and Qualification of Neutrals (National Symposium on Court Connected Dispute Resolution Research Working Paper for the State Justice Institute, Oct. 15–16, 1993).

3. *See, e.g.,* Ethical Standards of Professional Responsibility (SPIDR) (1987), see Appendix; Professional Standards of Practice for Mediators (Mediation Council of Illinois, 1985); Code of Professional Conduct for Me-

diators (Colorado Center for Dispute Resolution, 1982).

4. *See* Joint Committee on Standards of Conduct, Standards of Conduct for Mediators, see Appendix E.

5. Report of the Commission on Qualifications of the Society of Professionals in Dispute Resolution (SPIDR) (1989).

CHAPTER III MEDIATION

responsibility for establishing training and qualification standards, credentialing, and supervising of ADR professionals to a governmental or quasi-governmental body. In Florida, for example, the Florida Supreme Court adopted procedural rules for mediation and arbitration,[6] as well as standards for qualifications and professional conduct.[7] The Office of the State Courts Administrator was established in the Supreme Court building to administer and monitor the regulations governing ADR practice. A Mediator Qualifications Board composed of three regional divisions has power to investigate complaints, hold hearings, and impose sanctions for violations of the standards.[8]

If there is no agreement as to the source of the professional standards in ADR, there is also no consensus as to content. However, there is a good deal of agreement as to what standards should be addressed. For example, a Texas Task Force on Professional Standards[9] concluded, after surveying ADR practitioners, that an interdisciplinary code should address:

1. *Neutrality of ADR neutrals* (including the duty to make full disclosure in advance as to qualifications, prior experience, and compensation to insure against conflicts of interest, and to refrain from imposing the neutral's views on the parties or using coercion or undue influence in attempting to obtain a resolution of the dispute).

2. *Professional responsibilities* (including preserving the integrity of the ADR process, maintaining skills and training, and only taking cases within one's competency level).

3. *Advance notice to clients* of relevant matters (including the ADR process, techniques to be used, and enforceability of any agreement).

4. *Avoidance of impropriety* (including use of information obtained in the process and relationships with referral sources).

5. *Duty and scope of confidentiality.*

6. *Avoidance of professional misconduct* (including such matters as limitations on advertising).

7. *Fair and equitable fee structure* (fully disclosed to clients in advance).

This is a fairly representative list of the kinds of matters that ADR codes seek to address. There is less agreement, however, as to the exact standards that should apply within these areas. Furthermore, once one moves from standards of conduct to requirements as to qualifications, training, and credentialing, there is even less agreement in the ADR community.

---

6. *See* In re Amendment to Florida Rules of Civil Procedure, 563 So.2d 85 (Fla. 1990).

7. Florida Rules of Civil Procedure, Professional Conduct, and Rules of Discipline for Certified and Court–Appointed Mediators, Rules 10.010–10.290 (May 28, 1992).

8. *Id.* at Rules 10.190–10.290.

9. Report of the Task Force on the Quality of Alternative Dispute Resolution Practice in the State of Texas (1993).

G. REGULATING PROFESSIONAL CONDUCT

535

NOTES AND QUESTIONS

1. The search for, discussion of, and debate over ethical standards governing mediation continues apace in many different quarters. Somewhat different issues arise as to the nature of the mediation participants–mediators, attorney-mediators, or counsel. The Uniform Mediation Act, a project of the National Conference of Commissioners on Uniform State Laws, has occupied the attention over the last several years of a large number of mediation experts. Although ethics is not its central focus, professional and ethical considerations abound. State commissions continue to draft ethics codes. See Krohnke, Decisions Standards Raise Policy Issues as Minnesota Drafts an ADR Code of Ethics, 15 Alternatives 3 (January 1997). And a body of useful academic writing on ethics issues continues to grow. See Kovach, New Wine Requires New Wineskins: Transforming Lawyer Ethics for Effective Representation in a Non–Adversarial Approach to Problem Solving: Mediation, 28 Fordham Urban. L. J. 935 (2001); Alfini, Settlement Ethics and Lawyering in ADR Proceedings: A Proposal to Revise Rule 4.1, 19 No. Ill. U. L. Rev. 255 (199); Nolan–Haley, Informed Consent in Mediation: A Guiding Principle for Truly Educated Decision-making, 74 Notre Dame L. Rev. 775 (1999); Menkel–Meadow, Ethics in Alternative Dispute Resolution: New Issues, No Answers from the Adversary Conception of Lawyers' Responsibilities, 38 S.Tex. L. Rev. 407 (1997); Feerick, Toward Uniform Standards of Conduct for Mediators, 38 S. Tex. L. Rev. 455 (1997); Henikoff & Moffitt, Remodeling the Model Standards of Conduct for Mediators, 2 Harv. Negotiation L. Rev. 87 (1997); Symposium, Focus on Ethics in Representation in Mediation, 4 Disp. Res. Mag. (Winter 1997).

2. Examine the Standards of Conduct for Mediators approved by the American Arbitration Association, Society of Professionals in Dispute Resolution, and the American Bar Association Section on Dispute Resolution, in Appendix E. How are the seven matters listed in the extract above that the Texas Task Force recommended for an interdisciplinary code dealt with? Are there points on which the Code is insufficiently specific?

3. A recurring ethical problem for mediators is raised by the following hypothetical posed by Professor Edward Sherman at the 1995 annual meeting of the American Association of Law Schools: In a suit for wrongful death by a grandson of the deceased, the mediator happens to look at the applicable wrongful death statute over lunch and learns that a grandson is not covered by the statute, and therefore plaintiff has no cause of action. The defendant has already offered $25,000, but the plaintiff's last offer was $200,000. Neither party appears to be aware that the statute provides no cause of action. What should the mediator do under these circumstances?

Consider the comments of various members of the panel and audience:

PROFESSOR LELA LOVE, Cardozo School of Law, Yeshiva University. This problem is troubling because important values are at stake, each value pulling the mediator in a different direction. I will describe the competing values, point out several alternative courses of action, and then describe what I would do.

Informed consent is an important value, incorporated into the Joint Committee Standards of Conduct [Standard I; Comments (second comment): "A mediator ... should help ... the parties make informed decisions."] The comment suggests that this should be done by making "the parties aware of the importance of consulting other professionals." Mediators want the parties to base their understandings and decisions on as much information as possible, to be "playing with a full deck." In this problem, it appears that both parties are lacking a critical piece of information that would radically change their litigation option. The mediator naturally wants the parties to have the information.

A second important value is mediator impartiality. This value is recognized by the Standards as "central" to the mediation process [Standard II. Impartiality: A Mediator Shall Conduct the Mediation in an Impartial Manner.]. Here the information known to the mediator is very advantageous to one of the parties but is devastating to the other party. If the mediator provides the information, she will color the parties' perceptions of her impartiality, jeopardizing her ability to mediate effectively. The mediator does not want this result.

Third, the mediator's role should not be mixed with that of another profession. The Standards call on the mediator to "refrain from providing professional advice" [Standard VI, (fourth comment): "Mixing the role of a mediator and the role of a professional advising a client is problematic, and mediators must strive to distinguish between the roles. A mediator should therefore refrain from providing professional advice."] The mediator's job is to facilitate negotiation, not to give legal advice. In this problem, the mediator has discovered statutory language which appears to negate the grandson's cause of action. If the mediator delivers the information, without doing careful legal research, he may miss some potential exception, or plausible argument for an exception, that a zealous advocate would find. In this hypothetical, giving this highly charged information is closely related to giving professional advice and can be dangerous where the mediator does not fully take on the responsibility of the professional advocate. Here, the mediator does not want to step into the role of a lawyer and be responsible for providing information about the parties' legal rights, which can easily be construed as an opinion.

Finally, the value of party self-determination argues against directive moves by the mediator. The line between information and advice is not a bright one. While the mediator has happened upon information that will influence the parties, she is also aware there is other (unknown) information that might also influence the parties. Providing this particular information is going to be directive, which the mediator does not want to be. So what should the mediator do? I will describe a few possibilities.

The mediator can do nothing with the information, withhold it from the parties and simply continue to mediate. Doing nothing maintains a clear separation between the role of mediator and attorney. In addition, the mediator's impartiality is not compromised in the eyes of the parties. However, doing nothing here neglects the value of informed consent. The mediator has information that will affect the parties but, instead of imparting it, allows the parties to "fly blind" into an agreement they might not accept if they had the mediator's information. If the parties come to an agreement and then discover this piece of information the next day, at least one of them will have a very unhappy surprise. The durability of the agreement will be affected if a party feels the agreement is unfair. While the parties were enabled to arrive at an outcome based on self-determination, it is not as good an outcome as it would be if it sat on the bedrock of adequate information. So this choice is not satisfactory.

The mediator can provide the information, either throwing out the relevant statutory provision in a joint session or in private caucuses. Either way, providing the information is directive. There is a world of information; the mediator stumbled across one piece of information; providing it outright is bound to suggest that the mediator endorses the information and that it should influence the parties. I can imagine the defendant saying, "I withdraw my offer of $25,000," or becoming absolutely inflexible. And I can imagine the grandson storming out of the mediation, feeling that his bargaining position has been undermined and that the mediator took sides. So this choice does not seem satisfactory.

The mediator can urge the parties to get legal advice. This course of action is safe and does not conflict with other values, except perhaps an interest in making mediation efficient in terms of cost and speed. This course of action also is in keeping with the Standards. During any mediation, the mediator will consistently be urging the parties to obtain and share information and advice about their situation from a variety of sources, including professionals. In many cases, urging the parties to get appropriate professional advice will resolve the dilemma raised by this problem.

However, in some circumstances the parties do not want or cannot afford to get legal advice, and then the mediator still has the problem of a failure of informed consent. Or it may be that the parties' lawyers have not considered the information the mediator has! In these cases, in addition to the general urging to get legal advice, I believe the mediator should raise specific issues and questions that the parties have not addressed, urging the parties to get more information and legal advice, and/or urging the lawyers to do their homework with respect to the particular issue the mediator raises as well as other issues the mediator may not see. This urging, however, must be done in a non-directive way. I believe the mediator, in a caucus with each party, should explore whether the party has considered the risk of

538 CHAPTER III MEDIATION

litigation and has weighed any potential weaknesses of positions that are being asserted. The mediator should feel that the party understands the importance of adequate information and understands that there are questions regarding the application of a statutory provision to his or her case. If the mediator does this, he has done his job. He should not cross the line into giving legal advice as to what is or is not a cause of action or into giving legal information which can easily be construed as advice. Asking questions comports with the mediator's role, but giving or suggesting answers does not.

* * *

PROFESSOR DONALD WECHSTEIN, University of San Diego School of Law. One, I fully agree that self-determination is the key. Two, I don't see how you can have informed self-determination if you have uninformed determiners. So if there is key information that the parties are lacking, they are not engaging in informed self-determination. Consequently, there has to be some way in which they can become informed. I agree with what was just said that the mediator should be the source of that information only as a last resort. In addition to suggesting they consult counsel, you might want to suggest that they consult written materials, or in fact in some cases, in information-based mediation, which, incidentally at least in California, the AAA uses almost exclusively because that's what the parties want. You can provide in advance key information on things like spousal support schedules and things of that nature. But if push comes to shove, if a party is making a stupid self-determination because the party is not informed, I think the mediator either has to withdraw or get the information out in some way.

* * *

DEAN JAY FOLBERG, University of San Francisco School of Law. I'm curious about the hypothetical which I think is a good one. In the Northern District of California where the court has both an early neutral evaluation and a mediation program, this issue has come up because the judges are in disagreement about whether the early neutral evaluators or the mediators, all of whom were very experienced federal litigators, should, in cases in which the parties are represented by attorneys, inform the attorneys or the parties, when there is a mistaken notion of law of which the neutral is aware. And the court is divided on that, and looking at your hypothetical let's try to make it a little more realistic. In a wrongful death case involving a claim of $200,000 there surely will be attorneys on each side. And I'm assuming that the monetary defendant will be an insurance company. That raises the question, is this notion of informed consent changed in its application when we realize that the supposed uninformed party is an insurance company represented by sophisticated counsel? That doesn't mean that they won't make mistakes, so it's not totally unrealistic that they might not be aware of a new statute, though it's unlikely. I think all of us with our humanistic values may say, well I do believe in informed consent if this grandson didn't know, sure, we'd have to do something. However, is informed consent applicable in the same way given an insurance company and representation by sophisticated counsel and our own sense of justice? And secondly, given that there are attorneys, does that change the notion of what the role of a mediator might be, assuming a lawyer-mediator who does know that one of the attorneys is wrong?

* * *

PROFESSOR FRANK EVANS, South Texas College of Law. I've never heard someone say it's inappropriate to ask questions. Here's this case, why do you think you can get around [it]? * * * I'm talking about lawyer cases where lawyers are there, you're not worried about dealing directly with a client. * * * I think if you've got a lawyer, what I'd do is take him out so I don't embarrass him in front of his client, the one that's going to be affected by it negatively, and say, "have you read this case? You ought to look at it because here you are claiming this and this is what it may do to you." But it seems, that's just the way I do it, there may be a better way, but I don't see that violates any premise of confidentiality, it doesn't put anybody at a disadvantage and all you've done is bring something home to them. It's where you deal pro bono and this kind of question has been with the dispute resolution centers forever. Here you're sitting, you're supposed to be concerned about balance of power, but you're not supposed to get into the act. And suppose you've got somebody with their fence six inches over or two feet over on somebody else's property, the statute of limitations is about to run and you're sitting there helping them get an agreement that will avoid that statute of limitations impact, and you don't tell anybody. That's the tough one. I don't know the answer to what to do there.

2. LIABILITY OR IMMUNITY OF MEDIATORS & ADR NEUTRALS

Wagshal v. Foster

United States Court of Appeals, D.C. Circuit, 1994.
28 F.3d 1249.

■ Before: SILBERMAN, WILLIAMS and RANDOLPH, CIRCUIT JUDGES.

■ STEPHEN F. WILLIAMS, CIRCUIT JUDGE:

This case presents the issue of whether a court-appointed mediator or neutral case evaluator, performing tasks within the scope of his official duties, is entitled to absolute immunity from damages in a suit brought by a disappointed litigant. The district court found such immunity and we agree.

* * *

540   CHAPTER III   MEDIATION

In June 1990, appellant Jerome S. Wagshal filed suit in D.C. Superior Court against Charles E. Sheetz, the manager of real property owned by Wagshal. In October 1991 the assigned judge, Judge Richard A. Levie, referred the case to alternative dispute resolution pursuant to Superior Court Civil Rule 16[1] and the Superior Court's alternative dispute resolution ("ADR") program. While the program does not bind the parties (except when they agree to binding arbitration), participation is mandatory. See Superior Court Rules of Civil Procedure 16(j).

Judge Levie chose "neutral case evaluation" from among the available ADR options, and appointed Mark W. Foster as case evaluator.[2] Pursuant to the order of appointment, the parties signed a "statement of understanding" providing (among other things) that the proceedings would be confidential and privileged, and that the evaluator would serve as a "neutral party". Moreover, the parties were not allowed to subpoena the evaluator or any documents submitted in the course of evaluation, and "[i]n no event [could the] mediator or evaluator voluntarily testify on behalf of a party." Wagshal signed in January 1992 (under protest, he alleges).

After Foster held his first session with the parties, Wagshal questioned his neutrality. Foster then asked that Wagshal either waive his objection or pursue it; if Wagshal made no response waiving the objection, Foster would treat it as a definite objection. Receiving no response by the deadline set, and later receiving a communication that he regarded as equivocal, Foster wrote to Judge Levie in February 1992, with copies to counsel, recusing himself. The letter also reported to the judge on his efforts in the case and recommended continuation of ADR proceedings. In particular, Foster said that the case was one "that can and should be settled if the parties are willing to act reasonably", and urged the court to order Wagshal, "as a precondition to any further proceedings in his case, to engage in a good faith attempt at mediation." He also urged Judge Levie to "consider who should bear the defendant's costs in participating" in the mediation to date.

Judge Levie then conducted a telephone conference call hearing in which he excused Foster. Wagshal's counsel voiced the claim that underlies this suit—that he thought Foster's withdrawal letter "indicates that he had certain feelings about the case. Now, I'm not familiar with the mediation process but as I understood, the mediator is not supposed to say, give his opinion as to where the merits are." On that subject, Judge Levie said, "I don't know what his opinions are and I'm not going to ask him because

---

1. Superior Court Rule 16(b) provides in part: "At [the initial scheduling and settlement] conference the judge will ... explore the possibilities for early resolution through settlement or alternative dispute resolution techniques...."

2. We use the terms "case evaluator" and "mediator" interchangeably in this opin-

ion. Each acts as a neutral third party assisting the parties to a dispute in exploring the possibility of settlement, the principal difference being that implicit in the name: the case evaluator focuses on helping the parties assess their cases, while the mediator acts more directly to explore settlement possibilities.

that's part of the confidentiality of the process." Neither Wagshal nor his counsel made any objection or motion for Judge Levie's own recusal.

Judge Levie soon after appointed another case evaluator, and Wagshal and the other parties settled the *Sheetz* case in June 1992. In September 1992, however, Wagshal sued Foster and sixteen others (whom he identified as members of Foster's law firm) in federal district court, claiming that Foster's behavior as mediator had violated his rights to due process and to a jury trial under the Fifth and Seventh Amendments, and seeking injunctive relief and damages under 42 U.S.C. § 1983. Besides the federal claims, he threw in a variety of local law theories such as defamation, invasion of privacy, and intentional infliction of emotional distress. His theory is that Foster's conduct as case evaluator forced him to settle the case against his will, resulting in a far lower recovery than if he had pursued the claim.

The district court granted the defendants' motion to dismiss with prejudice, holding that Foster, like judges, was shielded by absolute immunity. We affirm.

* * *

We may quickly dispatch Wagshal's claim to injunctive relief. While such a claim is not barred by judicial immunity, Wagshal lacks standing to seek such an injunction on behalf of others, and has alleged no likelihood whatever that he himself will again suffer the alleged injury.

Foster's first line of defense against the damages claim was the assertion of quasi-judicial immunity. The immunity will block the suit if it extends to case evaluators and mediators, so long as Foster's alleged actions were taken within the scope of his duties as a case evaluator.

Courts have extended absolute immunity to a wide range of persons playing a role in the judicial process. These have included prosecutors, law clerks, probation officers, a court-appointed committee monitoring the unauthorized practice of law, a psychiatrist who interviewed a criminal defendant to assist a trial judge, persons performing binding arbitration and a psychologist performing dispute resolution services in connection with a lawsuit over custody and visitation rights. On the other hand, the Supreme Court has rejected absolute immunity for judges acting in an administrative capacity, court reporters charged with creating a verbatim transcript of trial proceedings, and prosecutors in relation to legal advice they may give state police. The official claiming the immunity "bears the burden of showing that such immunity is justified for the function in question."

We have distilled the Supreme Court's approach to quasi-judicial immunity into a consideration of three main factors: (1) whether the functions of the official in question are comparable to those of a judge; (2) whether the nature of the controversy is intense enough that future harassment or intimidation by litigants is a realistic prospect; and (3) whether the system contains safeguards which are adequate to justify dispensing with private damage suits to control unconstitutional conduct.

542   CHAPTER III MEDIATION

In certain respects it seems plain that a case evaluator in the Superior Court's system performs judicial functions. Foster's assigned tasks included identifying factual and legal issues, scheduling discovery and motions with the parties, and coordinating settlement efforts. These obviously involve substantial discretion, a key feature of the tasks sheltered by judicial immunity and the one whose absence was fatal to the court reporter's assertion of immunity in *Antoine v. Byers & Anderson, Inc.*, 113 S.Ct. 2167, 2170–71 (1993). Further, viewed as mental activities, the tasks appear precisely the same as those judges perform going about the business of adjudication and case management.

Wagshal protests, however, that mediation is altogether different from authoritative adjudication, citing observations to that effect in radically dissimilar contexts. See, *e.g., General Comm. of Adjustment v. Missouri–Kan.–Tex. R.*, 320 U.S. 323, 337, 64 S.Ct. 146, 152–53, 88 L.Ed. 76 (1943) ("The concept of mediation is the antithesis of justiciability."). However true his point may be as an abstract matter, the general process of encouraging settlement is a natural, almost inevitable, concomitant of adjudication. Rule 16 of the Federal Rules of Civil Procedure, for example, institutionalizes the relation, designating as subjects for pre-trial conferences a series of issues that appear to encompass all the tasks of a case evaluator in the Superior Court system: "formulation and simplification of the issues", "the possibility of obtaining admissions of fact and documents", "the control and scheduling of discovery", and a catch-all, "such other matters as facilitate the just, speedy, and inexpensive disposition of the action." Fed.R.Civ.P. 16(c). Wagshal points to nothing in Foster's role that a Superior Court judge might not have performed under Superior Court Rule 16(c), which substantially tracks the federal model. Although practice appears to vary widely, and some variations raise very serious issues, see, e.g., *G. Heileman Brewing Co. v. Joseph Oat Corp.*, 871 F.2d 648 (7th Cir.1989) (en banc), it is quite apparent that intensive involvement in settlement is now by no means uncommon among federal district judges.

Wagshal does not assert that a case evaluator is performing a purely administrative task, such as the personnel decisions—demotion and discharge of a probation officer—at issue in *Forrester v. White*. Because the sort of pre-trial tasks performed by a case evaluator are so integrally related to adjudication proper, we do not think that their somewhat managerial character renders them administrative for these purposes.

Conduct of pre-trial case evaluation and mediation also seems likely to inspire efforts by disappointed litigants to recoup their losses, or at any rate harass the mediator, in a second forum. Although a mediator or case evaluator makes no final adjudication, he must often be the bearer of unpleasant news—that a claim or defense may be far weaker than the party supposed. Especially as the losing party will be blocked by judicial immunity from suing the judge, there may be great temptation to sue the messenger whose words foreshadowed the final loss.

The third of the Supreme Court's criteria, the existence of adequate safeguards to control unconstitutional conduct where absolute immunity is

G. REGULATING PROFESSIONAL CONDUCT **543**

granted, is also present. Here, Wagshal was free to seek relief from any misconduct by Foster by applying to Judge Levie. Alternatively, if he thought Foster's communications might prejudice Judge Levie, he could have sought Levie's recusal under Superior Court R.Civ.P. 63–I, Bias or Prejudice of a Judge. The avenues of relief institutionalized in the ADR program and its judicial context provide adequate safeguards.

Wagshal claims that even if mediators may be generally entitled to absolute immunity, Foster may not invoke the immunity because his action was not taken in a judicial capacity, and because he acted in complete absence of jurisdiction.

Wagshal's argument that the acts for which he has sued Foster are not judicial (apart from the claim against mediators generally) rests simply on his claim that Foster's letter to Judge Levie, stating that he felt he "must recuse" himself and giving his thoughts on possible further mediation efforts and allocation of costs, breached Foster's obligations of neutrality and confidentiality. We assume such a breach for purposes of analysis. But "if judicial immunity means anything, it means that a judge 'will not be deprived of immunity because the action he took was in error . . . or was in excess of his authority.' " Mireles v. Waco, 502 U.S. 9, 112 S.Ct. 286, 116 L.Ed.2d 9 (1991) (quoting Stump v. Sparkman, 435 U.S. 349, at 356, 98 S.Ct. at 1104–05). Accordingly "we look to the particular act's relation to a general function normally performed by a judge". Applying the same principle to case evaluators, we have no doubt that Foster's announcing his recusal, reporting in a general way on the past course of mediation, and making suggestions for future mediation were the sort of things that case evaluators would properly do.

* * *

We hold that absolute quasi-judicial immunity extends to mediators and case evaluators in the Superior Court's ADR process, and that Foster's actions were taken within the scope of his official duties. The judgment of the district court is

Affirmed.

NOTES AND QUESTIONS

1. Do you agree that court-appointed mediators should enjoy immunity because they function like court officers? Isn't this contrary to the emphasis on mediator independence?

2. There is considerable disagreement between jurisdictions as to the liability of mediators for acts done in the performance of their duties. There is no general rule of immunity although some courts and some statutes have granted some form of immunity, although often qualified.

3. Consider the Texas ADR statute which was amended in 1993 to accord qualified immunity to certain ADR neutrals. V.T.C.A., Civ.Prac. & Rem. Code § 154.055. It applies not only to court-appointed procedures, but to any ADR procedure "whether before or after the institution of formal judicial proceedings." It thus applies to mediators in proceedings conducted by Dispute Resolution Centers, or on agreement of the parties to a dispute, even though no suit has been filed. However, it only applies to "volunteer" third parties, that is persons who do not receive compensation for their services other than a small stipend intended to be reimbursement for expenses incurred.

The scope of the Texas immunity only reaches negligence. It accords immunity from civil liability for any act or omission within the course and scope of a neutral's duties, but not for an act with wanton and willful disregard of the rights, safety, or property of another. Neutrals are thus immunized from suit for negligence in the performance of their duties or for professional malpractice, so long as their conduct did not rise to the level of gross negligence. This would include the broad range of acts for which a third party could be sued, such as divulging confidential information to the other party, failing to warn either party of their rights or interests, incorrectly stating any fact or law, or favoritism displayed towards one party. However, intentional acts, like accepting a bribe from one party or purposely divulging confidential information to assist one side might fall under the wanton and willful disregard exception.

4. Court employees acting as conciliators have also been accorded quasi-judicial immunity. Meyers v. Contra Costa County Department of Social Services, 812 F.2d 1154 (9th Cir.1987). However, the National Standards of Court–Connected Mediation Programs, issued by the Center for Dispute Settlement in 1992, question denial of "recourse to litigants injured by incompetent service" where the mediator has received a fee.

CHAPTER IV

COURT–ANNEXED ADR PROCESSES

When the term "alternative dispute resolution" came into general usage several decades ago, it referred to processes like mediation and arbitration that were truly alternative to the court system. Since that time, ADR processes that once operated independently of the court system are now often invoked as an integral part of litigation. Although it has been urged that the word "alternative" should now be dropped, the original name (and its acronym ADR) seems too widely used to make the change stick. The term "court-annexed" is also something of a misnomer because ADR can be integrated into the litigation process in a variety of ways not necessarily comprehended by the word "annexed." Again, however, the term is used today to describe a wide variety of relationships between the ADR process and an on-going litigation. This relationship ranges from a formal order incorporating ADR into the litigation schedule to more informal court action that merely acquiesces in, recognizes, or validates resort to an ADR process before the trial of the case will go forward.

This chapter will consider the types of ADR processes that have most commonly been annexed by courts and will then turn to the principal issues that are peculiar to the court annexation of ADR.

A. A RANGE OF PROCESSES

Over the last two decades of intense court experimentation with ADR, a range of favored processes with somewhat differing techniques, objectives, and rationales has emerged. These processes have in common the nonbinding intervention of third-party neutrals to assist the parties in achieving settlement. The processes differ, however, as to a number of features which may affect a decision to select them for different kinds of disputes. One of the most significant features is the *procedural formality* of the process. The chart below places the most prominent of the court-annexed processes (which will be considered in detail in the next section) on a continuum based on the degree of formality.

Mediation	Judicial Settlement Conference	Early Neutral Evaluation (ENE)	Court– Annexed Arbitration	Mini– Trial	Summary Jury Trial

On the left are processes that are the least formal procedurally, mediation, for example, being a relatively unstructured dialogue between

546 CHAPTER IV COURT-ANNEXED ADR PROCESSES

the parties sitting around a table, and judicial settlement conference being an informal discussion with the judge. As we move along the continuum towards the right, the processes involve greater procedural formality with more clearly differentiated roles for the participants and a prescribed format governing the presentation of cases. At the right end are the most formal processes, for example, mini-trial which uses a trial format, and summary jury trial which very much resembles a court trial.

This chart only compares the six processes as to *procedural formality*, but additional characteristics that might influence the choice of a process could also be charted. One might, for example, compare the processes as to *degree of intrusiveness of the neutral*. The six processes would be in roughly the same order along the continuum as in the chart above. On the left would be processes like mediation where the role of the neutral is primarily "facilitative"[1] and "non-directive."[2] Of course, as we have seen, there are today considerable differences in mediator styles. The classical form of mediation is primarily facilitative (and therefore belongs on left-end of the chart), but some mediators take a more directive role (which would move their mediations towards the center). As we move along the continuum towards the right, the neutral takes on a more "directive" or "evaluative" role, as in ENE or court-annexed arbitration. At the far right, the neutral's role becomes almost "adjudicative,"[3] as in the summary jury trial.

Another characteristic on which the six processes could be charted is the *time when the process is invoked*. On this chart, however, the six processes would not be in the same order as in the chart above. On the left would be processes, like ENE, that are intended to be invoked early in the litigation, with resultant cost savings if the case can be settled. In the middle would be a process like court-annexed arbitration that normally takes place after some discovery. On the right are processes that normally take place after extensive discovery and preparation, like mini-trial and summary jury trial. Mediation and judicial settlement conference, on the other hand, can not really be placed at any one point on the continuum because they may be invoked at various stages of the litigation.

1. The term "facilitative" is frequently used to describe the approach to mediation by which a mediator attempts to promote communication between the parties, including an understanding of each other's views of the dispute and of their respective interests. It is often contrasted with an "evaluative" approach in which a mediator goes beyond facilitating communication to provide evaluations of the respective cases of the parties and estimates of how the dispute might be resolved in the courts.

2. The term "non-directive" is frequently used to describe the approach to mediation by which a mediator avoids attempting to influence the parties by such "directive" conduct as expressing opinions, openly challenging positions and values, manipulating the parties to bring them around to certain positions, or proposing specific solutions to resolve the dispute.

3. The term "adjudicative" describes a process in which a neutral or neutrals renders a decision on the merits as opposed to allowing decision-making to come from the parties. In nonbinding ADR processes of the type we are considering, any such decision is not final, but the rendering of a nonbinding decision still has elements of adjudication not found in processes in which the neutral has no such authority.

A.   A RANGE OF PROCESSES   **547**

With this brief introduction to the various continua of characteristics that differentiate the six court-annexed ADR processes, we will consider each process individually.

1.   MEDIATION

Over the last two decades mediation has become "court-annexed" in many jurisdictions. Statutes and court rules now often either encourage or require the parties to a law suit to mediate as an integral part of the litigation process. Since mediation has been considered extensively in the last chapter, we will only mention here some of the distinctive features and problems that arise in the context of court-annexation. First, court-annexed mediation is often not voluntary, the parties being ordered by the court to participate. This poses questions as to the degree of participation required and the availability of sanctions for non-compliance. Second, the method for selection of mediators takes on particular importance when the mediation is ordered by the court rather than the parties agreeing on a mediator outside of court. Third, court-ordered mediators increasingly expect to be paid for their services, requiring rules for how they will be compensated. Finally, since court-ordered mediation takes place under the auspices of the court, the court must assure itself that the process is fair and efficient. This gives rise to difficult questions as to qualifications of mediators, professional standards of conduct, and degree of court monitoring.

Duty to Participate in Mediation and Sanction Power of the Court

The duty to participate in settlement conferences and court's sanction powers in this regard have been discussed in some detail in Chapter II. Many of the policies and issues are similar to mediation. There is general agreement that parties can be required to participate in a court-ordered mediation. See Decker v. Lindsay, 824 S.W.2d 247, 250–51 (Tex.App.—Houston [1st Dist.] 1992) (holding that a court "can compel [the parties] to sit down with each other" in a mediation and "to come together in court-ordered ADR procedures"); Kurtz v. Kurtz, 538 So.2d 892, 894–95 (Fla. IV–56 App.1989) (rejecting due process and illegal delegation challenges to mandatory mediation where visitation rights are involved).

Likewise parties can be required to come to a court-ordered mediation with settlement authority. The Fifth Circuit, in *In re Stone 986 F.2d 898 (5th Cir.1993)* (per curiam), recommended a "practical approach" to settlement-authority requirements imposed on governmental bodies, such as allowing the official with ultimate authority to be fully prepared and available by telephone at the time of the conference. This practical approach, however, would not be appropriate in every circumstance. In *In re United States*, 149 F.3d 332 (5th Cir.1998) (per curiam), the Fifth Circuit held a district court could, without abusing its discretion, order the government to send a person with full settlement authority to a mediation. In explaining the Fifth Circuit's holding, Judge Dennis stated "[t]his case is substantially different from *Stone* in that (a) it is an exceptional case rather than routine litigation; (b) it involves specifically ordered mediation

548   CHAPTER IV   COURT–ANNEXED ADR PROCESSES

... and [(c)] the government agreed to mediation." In Nueces County v. De Pena, 953 S.W.2d 835 (Tex.App.–Corpus Christi 1997), the appellate court found that the county executive did not have to attend under an order requiring the attendance of the person with settlement authority. The reason was that he could only settle with the concurrence of the commissioner's court. Therefore should all the members of a commissioner's court be required to attend? Is there any alternative to this unmanageable situation?

Court orders to mediate sometimes require that the parties "participate in good faith." Is it possible to have a "good faith participation" standard that does not improperly interfere with the parties' right not to yield or settle? Compare Sherman, Court–Mandated Alternative Dispute Resolution: What Form of Participation Should be Required?, 46 S.M.U.L.Rev. 2079, 2089–94 (1993) with Kovach, New Wine Requires New Wineskins: Transforming Lawyer Ethics for Effective Representation in a Non–Adversarial Approach to Problem Solving: Mediation, 28 Fordham Urban. L. J. 935, 961–64 (2001).

In Texas Parks and Wildlife Department v. Davis, 988 S.W.2d 370 (Tex. App.–Austin 1999, n.w.h.), the appellate court reversed the trial court's imposition of sanctions for failure to negotiate in good faith in a court-ordered mediation. The court emphasized that the defendant had filed an objection to the mediation but had attended it and made an offer during the course of the mediation. It concluded that "it cannot be said that [the defendant] did not participate in the mediation." Obviously a party need not make an offer in order to satisfy the "good faith participation" requirement. In contrast, a decision by another appellate court in the same state, Texas Department of Transportation v. Pirtle, 977 S.W.2d 657 (Tex. App.–Fort Worth 1998, writ ref'd), upheld the assessment of costs, including attorney's and mediator's fees, against a party for a bad faith failure to participate in a court-ordered mediation. It found that he had not filed an objection to the mediation order but then had "pretty much told [the court] from the beginning they weren't going to mediate" or settle a disputed liability case. Note that in Texas, as in a number of other states that authorize court-ordered mediation, parties may object to the order to mediate, but the court has the ultimate authority to order it or not. What might be persuasive reasons to object to a mediation order? That the parties had already discussed settlement and couldn't agree? That matters of principle are at stake that should not be compromised? That the parties have insufficient information because too little discovery has taken place?

2.   JUDICIAL SETTLEMENT CONFERENCE

Although the traditional model of an American judge is of a passive umpire who "views the case from a peak of Olympian ignorance,"[4] judges

---

4. Frankel, The Search for Truth: An Umpireal View, 123 U.Pa.L.Rev. 1031, 1042 (1975).

have often taken an active hand in encouraging settlement. This was often done in the past without express authority in state or federal court rules. The degree of activism would vary with the judge, ranging from detached encouragement of settlement in the abstract to personal jawboning and none-too-subtle telegraphing of the judge's views on the facts and the law.

Federal Rule of Civil Procedure 16 was amended in 1983 to list settlement as one of the proper subjects for discussion at pretrial conferences.[5] In 1993, this was expanded to include "settlement and the use of special procedures to assist in resolving the dispute when authorized by statute or local rule."[6] Promotion of settlement has also been viewed as a function of inherent judicial power. In addition, some state rules and statutes explicitly authorize judges to discuss settlement with the parties. On the other hand, judges in both state and federal courts have sometimes been disqualified for bias for becoming too personally involved in promoting settlement. It is this concern that has increasingly lead to calls for assigning a "settlement" judge or magistrate, who will not try the case, to conduct settlement conferences.

A judicial settlement conference is usually an informal discussion around a table with the judge. It was placed on the left end of the *procedural formality* continuum chart because of its informal setting and relative lack of format. It would also go on the left end of an *intrusiveness of the neutral* continuum because most judges perform only a facilitative role, taking great care to preserve their neutrality and not to reveal their opinions. However, the role of the judge varies with the individual, and with a more activist judge, the judicial settlement conference might have to be moved to the right on the chart.

3. EARLY NEUTRAL EVALUATION (ENE)

The Early Neutral Evaluation (ENE) program, now used in a number of federal and state courts, was first created by the U.S. District Court for the Northern District of California.[7] Under it, a neutral—usually a respected lawyer with expertise in the subject matter of the case—meets with the parties and their lawyers for two hours not long after the filing of the case and gives them a frank assessment of their cases. "Typically, one of the clients begins a narrative presentation of the case, without being led by the lawyer. After both sides have presented, the evaluator asks questions. The evaluator tries to help the parties to identify common ground, and to convert this to stipulations or informal agreements. The effort during the process is to isolate the areas of disagreement most central to the case."[8]

After the discussion, the evaluator leaves the room and writes her evaluation of the value of the case and two or three key analytical points. If the evaluation indicates liability, the evaluator ascribes a range of damages.

---

5. Fed.R.Civ.P. 16(c)(7) (1983).

6. Fed.R.Civ.P. 16(c)(9) (1993).

7. See Brazil, Kahn, Newman & Gold, Early Neutral Evaluation: An Experimental

Effort to Expedite Dispute Resolution, 69 Judicature 279 (1986).

8. Lawyers Get Tips on Using Early Neutral Evaluation, 4 ADR Rep. 124, at 124–25 (April 12, 1990).

550 CHAPTER IV COURT-ANNEXED ADR PROCESSES

Before giving the parties the evaluation, she asks if they wish to discuss settlement before they see it. Some 25% of cases settle at this point. If they opt not to discuss settlement, the evaluator explains the evaluation. She then "outlines a case development plan, identifying key areas of disagreement and suggesting ways to posture the case and to conduct discovery as efficiently as possible. The evaluator is required to do case planning. The parties are required to listen, but not to agree. They may decide to come back for a follow-up settlement conference."[9]

ENE provides a fairly pristine form of "evaluative" ADR. Although the outside attorney may facilitate discussion, her principal role is to hear each side's case and give them an objective assessment. Unlike mediation, both the presentations and the evaluation tend to be couched in terms of the legal issues.

ENE serves as both an early planning and settlement device. It provides an early pretrial conference that adds the feature of a neutral third-party to the mix. Building on this concept, a 1993 ABA proposal for civil justice reforms in the states would require a "meet and confer" conference between the parties and their attorneys within 20 days after the filing of responses to the complaint to consider a comprehensive trial plan, including the possibility of settlement, suitability of the case for ADR, simplification of the issues, and formulation of a discovery plan.[10] The conferences would be conducted by volunteer attorneys, called "court facilitators," who would have training in both case management and ADR and would, if desired by the parties, make a non-binding evaluation.[11] This proposal indicates how malleable the various ADR devices are and how the concept of ENE can be intermixed with other pretrial management objectives.

Reliance on volunteers, on the other hand, could indicate a lack of long-term commitment to the process. Attorneys have often volunteered to provide ADR services when programs are new, but as time passes the number of volunteers can dwindle. Commitment to pay ADR professionals is the best way to assure that an ADR program will last long-term. Concern has also been expressed with the message that staffing ADR with volunteers conveys. In a society in which the cost of services is often viewed as an indication of their value, parties may not treat volunteer evaluations with sufficient seriousness. Of course, the cost need not necessarily be borne by the courts. In many court-annexed mediation programs, mediators' fees are borne by the parties as costs.

4. COURT-ANNEXED ARBITRATION

In 1952, Pennsylvania adopted a court-supervised system of mandatory, non-binding arbitration for certain cases. The experiment was based on

---

9. Id.

10. American Bar Association Ad Hoc Committee on Civil Justice Improvements, Discussion Drafts: Civil Justice Improvement Proposals (Dec. 13–14, 1993), discussed in Sherman, A Process Model and Agenda for Civil Justice Reforms in the States, 46 Stan. L.Rev. 1553, 1556, 1566, 1572–73 (1994).

11. Id. at 1572–3.

the premise that parties were more likely to settle if they were given an opportunity to present their cases in an abbreviated form to three neutral attorneys who would render a non-binding judgment. This would provide an opportunity to "reality test" by comparing the presentation of their case with that of their opponent and to see how neutrals who were familiar with the law would assess the cases.

About half the states now have court-annexed arbitration programs,[12] and the federal courts began to experiment with programs in the 1970's. Under the encouragement of Attorney General Griffin Bell, three federal districts were designated for pilot programs. Two of the districts (E.D.Pa. and N.D.Cal.) still operate their programs, while the third (D.Conn.) disbanded its program in 1982 in preference for a mediation program.[13] In 1985 the Administrative Office of the U.S. Courts obtained funding from Congress for mandatory programs in eight new pilot districts, and voluntary programs in eight additional districts were added in 1989 as a result of the Judicial Improvements and Access to Justice Act of 1988. Over a quarter of the 94 federal district courts provided for court-annexed arbitration in their "cost and delay reduction" plans submitted pursuant to the Civil Justice Reform Act of 1990,[14] and court-annexed arbitration remains one of the principal mandatory ADR mechanisms used by courts today.[15]

Consider the following description of the court-annexed arbitration program in Pittsburgh:

Jane W. Adler, Deborah R. Hensler, & Charles Nelson, Simple Justice: How Litigants Fare In The Pittsburgh Court Arbitration Program

9–14, 87–94 (1983).

At the beginning of each court day, the parties whose cases have been scheduled for hearing assemble in the arbitration center, a room that once served as a courtroom but that has since been remodeled to produce a large waiting room surrounded by six smaller hearing rooms. Panels of three arbitrators each assemble in each of these hearing rooms. Arbitration cases are called and assigned numbers in the daily queue of cases awaiting hearing. The panels then begin hearing the first set of cases. As soon as a panel completes hearing and deliberating on a case, a new case is sent in to that hearing room, in the order of the assigned numbers. Because the length of time required for hearings varies, this system results in a more or less random assignment of arbitrators to cases. * * *

---

12. McIver & Keilitz, Court–Annexed Arbitration: An Introduction, 14 Just.Syts.J. 123 (1991).

13. Meierhoefer, Court–Annexed Arbitration in Ten District Courts 14 (Federal Judicial Center 1990).

14. 28 U.S.C.A. § 473(a)(6).

15. Elizabeth Plapinger & Donna Stienstra, Source Book on Federal District Court ADR and Settlement Procedures (Federal Judicial Center 1996).

The parties themselves play no role in choosing the arbitrators, nor do they have a formal opportunity to object to their assignment. This "rough and ready" procedure for random assignment contrasts sharply with the more elaborate and often time-consuming procedures for randomly assigning arbitrators that many jurisdictions use to guard against arbitrator bias.

The Pennsylvania Supreme Court rules require that arbitrators be "active" members of the bar and that the chairman of each panel have a minimum of three years of experience in practice. * * *

Some counties use a computer to randomize arbitrator assignment, but in Pittsburgh the arbitration director uses a manual, less standardized procedure to choose panel members. Wherever possible he seeks a balance between plaintiff and defense attorneys. The chairman is seen as the linchpin; and if there is a solid, experienced person in this spot, the other two members may be an attorney only a few months out of law school and an unknown quantity summoned for the first time.

* * *

Arbitrators are not expected to do any advance preparation for hearings. Their task is simply to listen to both sides present their case and then to make an on-the-spot decision on the dispute. Hearings generally last 30–45 minutes. After each hearing, the arbitrators deliberate briefly and record their decision. Each panel sits for several hours, hearing cases in order, until all of the scheduled cases have been heard. Arbitrators are paid $100 a day, and they generally hear four or five cases during the time they sit. * * *

The arbitrators' decision is transmitted by mail that day to the parties. Any party wishing to appeal the award must request a trial de novo within 30 days and accompany the appeal with a payment reimbursing the court for the cost of arbitrating his suit.

* * *

In place of the trial paradigm, most litigants used a very simple standard for evaluating arbitration: They wanted an opportunity to have their case heard and decided by an impartial third party. When this requirement was met, they reported that the arbitration process had been "fair." When asked why they had come to this conclusion, they were unlikely to offer elaborate rationales. "They heard us both out, listened the same to both sides," or "We got an equal chance to tell our stories," were typical responses.

Hypothetical questions from the interviewers, implying that suits elsewhere are frequently resolved by attorneys and adjudicators without the appearance of the parties, seemed puzzling to many respondents, who assumed that the only fair way to decide their case was the process that they had experienced. A few attorneys made comparative comments about arbitration, noting that some of their clients' cases would have received shorter shrift and rougher justice in other jurisdictions. But individual litigants themselves made no reference to such alternatives, taking it for granted that they had a right to appear in person, to be heard fully, and to be treated even-handedly. Where this right had been recognized, essentially nothing more was demanded. Even the identity and qualifications of the arbitrators were unimportant, so long as neutrality was assured.

More than 80 percent of the individual litigants whom we interviewed found their hearings "fair" according to this simple standard.

* * *

Our interview data suggest that arbitration's informal procedures may lead some litigants to infer that they were treated unfairly. A "rough and ready" procedure for assigning arbitrators to cases, administered in a flexible fashion so as to accommodate parties and attorneys' schedules, may in some circumstances lead litigants to believe that their case has been matched with arbitrators who are predisposed in favor of one of the disputants. The use of volunteer attorneys as adjudicators may give rise to speculations about the influence of personal motivations on the decision-making process that might not occur to the litigant if the adjudicator were a black-robed judge. Allowing the arbitrators broad discretion in determining the pace of the hearing may lead litigants to wonder whether they have been granted a proper opportunity to present their cases.

* * *

Our interviews suggest further that the average citizen's notion of "fairness" does not incorporate the judicial robes, formal procedures, or the various components of due process that are the hallmark of trial. But his notion of fairness is not simply cheap, quick dispute resolution. Rather, the average individual seems to believe that a "fair" dispute resolution procedure is one that provides an opportunity for a hearing of the facts of the case before a neutral third-party adjudicator. Our data suggest that ability to appeal the arbitration award contributes to individuals' perceptions that the process is fair. We find no evidence in our interview data that the typical individual litigant envisions a model of "first-class" justice against which the arbitration process is judged and found wanting. Rather, individual litigants appear to believe that it is appropriate to tailor dispute resolution procedures to the nature of the disputes and, perhaps, that it is acceptable to invest smaller amounts of resources on resolving simple disputes than might be required to dispose of more complicated cases.

Attorneys who make frequent use of the arbitration program clearly assess acceptability on different grounds. They are more likely to measure the arbitration process against trial court procedures and arbitrators against judges, and they sometimes find the program wanting on both grounds. Institutional litigants, however, compare the court arbitration program to other mechanisms for disposing of civil claims with which they are familiar: for insurance companies, inter-company arbitration; for banks, institutional collection procedures. But the predictability of outcomes is probably the institutional litigants' most important criterion for assessing the arbitration program. An institutional litigant judging that an award is outside the expected range is likely to appeal. The availability of a quick

554 CHAPTER IV COURT-ANNEXED ADR PROCESSES

and inexpensive appeal process may therefore be an essential aspect of arbitration's acceptability to these litigants.

NOTES AND QUESTIONS

1. What sorts of cases should be channeled into court-administered arbitration? The existing programs are generally limited to claims for money damages, and the principal criterion has been the amount of money claimed. The federal district court programs based on local rules sweep more broadly than the Pennsylvania plan, and often divert cases involving under $100,000 into compulsory arbitration (the Northern District of California proposed a raise to $150,000 in 1988).

In deciding which cases are suitable for court-supervised arbitration, should the amount of damages claimed be the deciding factor? Under the federal court programs, there are also subject-matter limitations: In some programs only actions based on a negotiable instrument or contract or for personal injury or property damage are sent to compulsory arbitration (*e.g.,* Rule 300–9(c) (W.D.Tex.)); others include all civil actions but explicitly exclude social security and prisoners' civil rights cases (e.g., Local Civil Rule 8 § 3(A) (E.D.Pa.); Local Arbitration Rule § 3(A) (E.D.N.Y.)). In addition, courts are sometimes given discretion to exempt cases that are otherwise arbitrable where a party has shown good cause for relief by demonstrating "the existence of significant and complex questions of law or fact" in the action (*e.g.,* Rule 300–9(d)(3) (W.D.Tex.)). The Department of Justice recommended that district court arbitration rules exempt any case "in which the objectives of arbitration would not appear to be realized, because the case involves complex or novel legal issues, or because legal issues predominate over factual issues * * *." 28 C.F.R. § 50.20(b)(5) (statement of policy).

2. How should the arbitrators be chosen? The usual procedure is random selection, as in Pennsylvania. Would a better system be to specially select arbitrators for balance (e.g., as between plaintiff's and defendant's lawyers), type of legal specialty, or age and experience? Would you want arbitrators who specialize in that area of the law or those who are non-specialists and who might bring a broader perspective to the evaluation? Should the attorneys have a role in the selection? It is common in federal programs to allow each side to strike one name from a list of five arbitrators furnished by the court. Rule 300–9(e)(1) (W.D.Tex.). Consider Hensler, What We Know and Don't Know About Court–Administered Arbitration, 69 Judicature 270, 278 (1986): "If the attorneys have some say in the selection, they may be more inclined to accept the award, but providing for attorney participation may require a cumbersome and time-consuming process. If the court is in charge of assigning the arbitrators, the process may be expedited but litigant and attorney satisfaction may decrease." Should there be a requirement that arbitrators have practiced a certain number of years?

3. Court-annexed arbitration is generally expected to take place early in the litigation, without an opportunity for full discovery. It is viewed as a quick and inexpensive alternative to litigation: Judge Harry Edwards has referred to it as a "poor man's mini-trial." Edwards, Alternate Dispute Resolution: Panacea or Anathema?, 99 Harv.L.Rev. 668, 673 (1986). Can a case be properly arbitrated without full discovery? Note that parties are encouraged to "decide what discovery is crucial to the hearing and conduct that discovery in advance of arbitration." Handbook of Alternative Dispute Resolution 50 (State Bar of Texas 1987). Is this feasible?

4. Should arbitrators have subpoena and other supervisory powers? In some state programs, they are selected immediately before the arbitration and thus have no opportunity to exercise such powers. In federal programs, they are usually assigned in advance and thus could enter orders governing such matters as a continuance and discovery. Under the Mandatory Arbitration Program of the D.C. Superior Court, arbitrators have the authority to issue subpoenas, rule on evidence, decide discovery disputes, compel the production of documents, enter judgment by default or consent, and stay execution of such judgments if the parties agree to schedule payments. Do you see any problem with these powers?

5. The rules of evidence in court-annexed arbitration are relaxed. See Rule CV–87(f)(4)a (W.D.Tex.): "In receiving evidence, the arbitrators shall be guided by the Federal Rules of Evidence, but they shall not thereby be precluded from receiving evidence which they consider to be relevant and trustworthy and which is not privileged." Are there any constraints on what the arbitrators will hear under this rule? Can an arbitration provide a realistic trial run if lax rules of evidence permit material to be received that would not be admissible at trial?

6. Court-annexed arbitrators need not necessarily be lawyers, and some programs have used such experts as architects, engineers, accountants, and doctors. There may also be mixed panels of lawyers and other experts. Would a decision from such experts really tell much about how a jury would decide the case?

7. Court-annexed arbitration rules often impose sanctions against a party who rejects the arbitral award and seeks a *de novo* trial in order "to serve as a brake or deterrent on the taking of frivolous and wholly unjustified appeals." Application of Smith, 381 Pa. 223, 233, 112 A.2d 625, 630, appeal dismissed, 350 U.S. 858 (1955). Sometimes the penalty is small. Rule CV 87(h)(3) (U.S.Dist.Ct., W.D.Tex.) requires the party seeking a trial to deposit with the court an amount equal to the fees of the arbitrators ($100 each for three arbitrators), which is forfeited if the final judgment is not more favorable than the arbitration award. In Pennsylvania, any party who wishes a trial must reimburse the state for all fees paid to the arbitrators. See also West's Ann.Cal.Civ.Pro.Code § 1141.21 (party who does not obtain more favorable result than in arbitration must pay arbitrators' fees to county and the other party's court costs and expert witness fees). Some programs impose stiffer sanctions but make them dependent on the outcome of the appeal. In one Michigan program a party who rejects a unanimous valuation of the panel must compensate his opponent for the costs at trial—including attorney's fees—if he does not improve his position by at least 10% over the figure proposed by the arbitrators. Shuart, Smith & Planet, Settling Cases in Detroit: An Examination of Wayne County's "Mediation" Program, 8 Just.Sys.J. 307 (1983).

Do these sanctions for requesting a trial abridge the right to jury trial?

8. Are multiple arbitrators necessary for effective arbitration, or is one enough? Consider Hensler, supra note 2 above, at 277: "If only one arbitrator is required to hear each case, it will be easier to administer the program and easier to meet the demand for volunteer arbitrators. But attorneys may be more inclined to question the decision of a single arbitrator, leading to a higher rate of appeal. If three or five arbitrators are required, the task of administering the program will be greater, and the per case costs for arbitrator fees may be more, but practitioners may be more inclined to accept the arbitration outcome."

9. In a diversity case, a federal court is required to apply the state arbitration requirements. See Woods v. Holy Cross Hospital, 591 F.2d 1164 (5th Cir.1979) (upholding dismissal of suit where there was no prior hearing before a malpractice review panel as required by a state law requiring that the chairman of the three-member review panel be a state judge and that the findings be admissible in evidence at trial). However, a federal court is not required to apply a state statute that would "impinge upon the broad procedural powers of the federal district courts to control and further techniques for settlement." Seck v. Hamrang, 657 F.Supp. 1074 (S.D.N.Y.1987). See generally Alexander, State Medical Malpractice Screening Panels in Federal Diversity Actions, 21 Ariz.L.Rev. 959 (1979).

10. Mandatory court-annexed arbitration has been challenged on various constitutional grounds, including the right to a jury trial, equal protection, and due process. None has succeeded, primarily because there is a right to trial de novo, and courts have concluded that the benefits of settlement promotion outweigh the burden of participation. See Davis v. Gaona, 260 Ga. 450, 396 S.E.2d 218 (1990); Firelock, Inc. v. District Court of 20th Judicial Dist., 776 P.2d 1090 (Colo.1989); Kimbrough v. Holiday Inn, 478 F.Supp. 566 (E.D.Pa.1979).

11. What if a party refuses to come to court-annexed arbitration, or attends but refuses to participate? New England Merchants National Bank v. Hughes, 556 F.Supp. 712 (E.D.Pa.1983), denied a right to trial *de novo* to a defendant who offered no excuse for failing to appear, thus resulting in a final judgment for the plaintiff in the amount of $31,000 that the arbitrators had awarded. The court found no deprivation of the constitutional right to jury trial, observing that under those circumstances "the goals of the arbitration program and the authority of this Court would be seriously undermined" if the defendant were allowed to demand a trial. Compare Lyons v. Wickhorst, 42 Cal.3d 911, 231 Cal.Rptr. 738, 727 P.2d 1019 (1986) (finding no power under state statutes to dismiss action with prejudice for not participating, but with disagreement among the justices as to whether such sanction might be constitutional).

12. Court orders referring cases to ADR use a variety of terms to describe what is expected of the parties, such as to "participate in good faith," to attend with "meaningful participation;" to "fully cooperate and participate," or simply to "attend and participate." Consider two cases that have found a party's participation in court-annexed arbitration to be inadequate:

In Gilling v. Eastern Airlines, Inc., 680 F.Supp. 169 (D.N.J.1988), a suit by a passenger against an airline, the parties were ordered to participate in a court-annexed arbitration. The defense counsel presented only summaries of her position and read a few passages from deposition testimony and answers to interrogatories. When asked by the arbitrator at the end of the proceeding whether she wanted any damage award that he might make to be broken down into compensatory and punitive damages, she said "Do what you want, or, we don't care what you do, we won't pay it anyway." The arbitrator found that she merely "went through the motions," rendering the proceeding "a sham." In awarding sanctions, the court deferred to the arbitrator's judgment in weighing "the earnestness of the defendants' presentation against the gravity of the plaintiffs' allegations and the defendants' potentially sizeable exposure to liability" and to "his overall assessment of the meaningfulness of their participation."

In the second decision, McHale v. Alcon Surgical, Inc., 1992 WL 99658 (E.D.Pa.1992), plaintiffs' request that a scheduled court-annexed arbitration be continued because it interfered with a planned Mexican vacation was denied. Plaintiffs' lawyer came to the arbitration without them and spent about 15 minutes presenting their case. The three arbitrators ruled in defendant's favor, and defendant moved to strike plaintiffs' request for a trial de novo on the ground of failure to comply with the local rule calling for participation "in a meaningful manner." The court granted the motion, finding that the proceeding "was, at best, less than a shadow of the arbitration trial Congress ordained" (this was one of the ten congressional pilot court-annexed arbitration projects). To be "meaningful," the court said, "arbitration must at least resemble the rudiments of a traditional civil trial. In a trial involving bodily injury to the plaintiff, this would include the plaintiff's live direct testimony and cross-examination, medical records and other evidence documenting the reality and extent of plaintiff's injury, and evidence of the defendant's breach of some legal duty to the plaintiff. Plaintiffs adduced nothing that began to approach even one of these rudiments." The district court decision was reversed, without opinion, in 993 F.2d 224 (3d Cir.1993).

Do you agree with the district court opinions in *Gilling* and *McHale* ? Does the degree of participation demanded by the court go too far in restricting party autonomy?

13. Early studies indicated that the trial rate of cases diverted to court-annexed arbitration was substantially lower than the rate at which comparable cases would have gone to trial in the absence of the program. See Levine, Court–Annexed Arbitration, 16 J.Law Reform 537, 542–43 (1983). However, more recent studies have not proven a statistically significant reduction in trial rates in most of the state programs. Keilitz, Court–

Annexed Arbitration, in Nat'l Symposium on Court–Connected Dispute Resolution Research 43 (Nat'l Center for State Cts. and State Jus.Instit. 1994). Average appeal rates from arbitrators' judgments in state programs are 40 to 60%. Id. at 42–43. However, the settlement rates of all cases are high, and it is difficult to determine to what degree the added effort involved in court-annexed arbitration results in more settlements.

Evaluations of federal programs show similar results. In the ten mandatory federal district court programs, a majority of arbitration hearings did not settle the case and ended with a demand for trial de novo. However, the parties felt the arbitration award was a good starting point for settlement negotiations and that the hearing was not a waste of time. 84% of the attorneys approved of the process, and 80% of the litigants felt it was fair. When no demand for a de novo trial was made, 68% of the attorneys reported cost savings; on the other hand, when there was a demand for trial de novo, 60% found no cost savings. Voluntary Arbitration in Eight Federal District Courts: An Evaluation 6 (Federal Judicial Center 1994).

A review in 1993 of ten years of arbitration programs around the country also found the evidence mixed on whether they reduced case processing time and court costs. See Hensler, Does ADR Really Save Money? The Jury's Still Out, Nat.L.J., at C2 (April 11, 1994). See also Bernstein, Understanding the Limits of Court–Connected ADR: A Critique of Federal Court–Annexed Arbitration Programs, 141 U.Pa.L.Rev. 2169 (1993) (public court-annexed arbitration cannot capture most of the benefits available from private consensual programs and may decrease access to justice for poorer and more risk-adverse litigants by adding an additional layer of costly procedure).

14. If there is a lack of proof that court-annexed arbitration saves money, there is more encouraging evidence as to the satisfaction rate of litigants and attorneys. An 1989 study interviewed litigants whose tort cases were resolved by trial, court-annexed arbitration, and judicial settlement conference. Those with trials and arbitrations felt they were fairer than those with settlement conferences and also expressed higher satisfaction rates. E. Allen Lind, et al., The Perception of Justice: Tort Litigants' Views of Trial, Court–Annexed Arbitration, and Judicial Settlement Conferences 44–74 (Rand Institute for Civil Justice 1989). "Although the monetary outcome of the case appears to have had a modest impact on outcome satisfaction, the outcome had little or no effect on the perceived fairness of the procedures or satisfaction with the system." Id. at 52. * * * The study found that the litigants wanted "a dignified, careful, and unbiased hearing," "to exercise some control over the handling of their cases," and "procedures with which they could feel comfortable, but [not necessarily] less formal procedures." It concluded that "the findings do not reveal much interest on the part of litigants in very informal, high-participative, simplified procedures" while "[a]lternative procedures less formal than trial can be quite acceptable, as can be seen in the litigants' generally favorable reactions to court-annexed arbitration." The 1993 study of ten years of programs also found that court-annexed arbitration enjoyed a high satisfaction rate. Keilitz, supra note 16 above.

15. Concerns over the mandatory nature of many federal court-annexed arbitration programs surfaced in 1993 when the House of Representatives passed a bill to require all districts to adopt arbitration programs. H.R. 1102 (103d Cong., 2d Sess.). The bill was opposed by several federal judges and others in testimony before a Senate Subcommittee on the ground that mandatory programs were "an 'alien intrusion' on due process rights and an easy out for judges wishing to 'coerce settlement' rather than try cases." "Court Arbitration Bill Faces Tough Fight in Senate," 5 World Arbit. & Med.Rep. 127 (June 1994). Ultimately, the pilot programs were renewed for three more years, but districts were not required to adopt programs.

5. THE MINI-TRIAL

Words sometimes catch the public imagination and take on a life of their own, and so it is with the "mini-trial." This term was attached by a New York Times story to a formal settlement device created in 1977 in connection with a corporate patent infringement dispute. It is not strictly speaking a trial at all, but a process that combines elements of adjudication with other processes such as negotiation and mediation. It refers to a proceeding, usually presided over by a neutral advisor, in which each side presents its case in shortened form to the representatives of the parties who have settlement authority, often the Chief Executive Officers, as a prelude to settlement negotiations between them. The term is sometimes used inaccurately to refer to any form of shortened or summarized trial (rather than using the more specific titles, such as "summary jury trial" or "court-annexed arbitration").

The mini-trial was created for corporate disputes and was intended to be conducted privately as an alternative to the court system. Although mini-trials are used most often in this context, the process is amenable to noncorporate disputes and to court annexation. Its distinctive features of presenting the evidence to the parties' decision makers and having a "neutral advisor" preside but also be available to give her personal evaluations if asked can work well in a variety of contexts. The Texas ADR Act specifically lists the mini-trial as one of the ADR processes that can be ordered by a court, and mini trials have been ordered in both state and federal courts, usually on the request of the parties. Because a mini-trial is usually invoked in an on-going litigation, and even when conducted privately outside the court system there may be a stay of court proceedings to allow it to take place, the process has been included in this section on court-annexed ADR processes.

Ronald L. Olson, An Alternative for Large Case Dispute Resolution

6 Litigation 22 (Winter 1980).

[The author served as one of the counsel in the 1977 *TRW* case for which the mini-trial was devised.]

In the case for which the mini-trial was developed, the plaintiff, Telecredit, Inc., of Los Angeles, held several patents on computerized charge-authorization and credit-verification devices. The defendant, TRW, Inc., was a manufacturer of those devices. In response to Telecredit's contention that its patents were infringed by TRW's devices, TRW alleged that Telecredit's patents were invalid and unenforceable. Telecredit sought not only substantial damages for past infringement, but also an injunction restraining future infringement. The injunction would have destroyed one of TRW's major product lines.

When the mini-trial concept was developed, the parties had already obtained expert opinions to support their positions and had slugged their way through extensive, tedious, and costly discovery. While the case was somewhat simplified by earlier discovery, TRW's exposure was not materially lessened, and the parties were as far apart on the merits as they were when suit was filed. The parties had spent hundreds of thousands of dollars on discovery, and more remained before the case would be brought even to the threshold of a lengthy trial.

The procedure eventually developed called for a six-week schedule of expedited but limited discovery, the exchange of position papers and exhibits, and a two-day mini-trial. At the mini-trial each side could present through two, top-management representatives its "best case" on the issues of infringement, validity, and enforceability. Management on each side could then independently assess the theories, strengths, and weaknesses of the respective positions. Opposing management could next meet without counsel and try to resolve the dispute from the new perspectives obtained at the mini-trial.

There was also a mutually selected "neutral advisor" for the mini-trial. The advisor—in this case a lawyer and former Court of Claims judge with widely recognized expertise in patent law—was there strictly to *moderate* the proceedings; he was not authorized to impose, or even to "jaw-bone," to reach a compromise of the dispute. Rather, in the event management did not resolve the dispute in their initial discussions after the mini-trial, the advisor was to submit a written and nonbinding opinion discussing the relative strengths and weaknesses of the parties' positions and predicting the likely outcome of courtroom trial. Thereafter, management was to meet again to try to resolve the dispute with the added spur of the advisor's opinion. We believed that the party against whom the advisor opined would be willing to make significant concessions. More generally, we thought that the conclusions of the advisor would cause the parties to be more realistic in their evaluations and demands as they discussed disposition of the case immediately after the mini-trial. On a practical level the advisor's opinion, although nonbinding, would be coercive because the persons involved would have to explain to auditors and corporate superiors why they ignored the advisor.

The procedure included these other significant aspects:

- The parties postponed all pending discovery in the case, except discovery viewed as absolutely necessary to prepare for the mini-trial, with no waiver of the right to take further discovery if the case was not settled. Partial depositions, for example, could be taken without prejudicing the right to take a full deposition of the same person at a later time.

- By mutual agreement, any discovery disputes that arose during the six weeks of expedited, limited discovery could be submitted to the advisor for his "advice."

- The parties would initially share the fees and expenses of the advisor—with assessment against the eventual losing party in the event that a settlement could not be reached and a trial was conducted.

- The parties stipulated about basic source material to be submitted to the advisor before the mini-trial.

- The parties exchanged in advance and submitted to the advisor all exhibits to be used at the mini-trial and short briefs in the form of "introductory statements."

- The advisor could submit written questions to the parties' technical experts before the mini-trial.

- The rules of evidence would not apply during the mini-trial.

- There would be unlimited scope for the material offered during each party's presentation at the mini-trial. The advisor could ask clarifying questions, but was explicitly told he could not preside like a judge or arbitrator or limit the parties' presentations.

- There was insulation of the mini-trial procedure and its results from the court. Resort to the court on any aspect of the mini-trial was forbidden. The written submissions prepared specifically for the mini-trial and the oral statements made during the mini-trial were inadmissible at trial for any purpose, including impeachment. However, evidence that was otherwise admissible was not rendered inadmissible by use at the mini-trial.

- The advisor was disqualified as a trial witness, consultant, or expert for either party, and his advisory opinion could not be used for any purpose in any dispute between the parties.

The presentations were made primarily by attorneys, with significant participation by the parties' experts, each a noted computer authority. Telecredit also presented a former employee of one of its licensees, and TRW used one of its scientists to present a technical aspect of its case.

The mini-trial's question and answer sessions were particularly useful in defining and narrowing each side's contentions. Where difficulties arose, the advisor aided the discussion with his questions. Occasionally, the advisor's comments indicated where he felt serious problems existed for each side. This participation by a neutral observer was particularly helpful in bringing home to the participants the strengths and weaknesses of their cases.

CHAPTER IV   COURT-ANNEXED ADR PROCESSES

Immediately after the mini-trial ended, top management for each side met privately without lawyers. Within one-half hour, they reached in principle an agreement that became the basis for resolving the dispute. Although the details took several weeks to tie up, the drain on both corporations' treasuries was plugged, and a case that had threatened to occupy the time and energy of a federal court for months was terminated without an additional day of court time.

NOTES AND QUESTIONS

1. The mini-trial is peculiarly the result of concerns by corporate officers that business litigation has become too costly and cumbersome. A principal philosophical thrust is, as indicated by Olson, that it "returns the dispute to the businessmen." But why isn't traditional negotiation sufficient? Why the need for a formalized procedure? The answer in part may be that when business deals go sour, the persons involved are too close to the dispute to be able to settle it among themselves. Traditionally they have turned to lawyers, partly to bail them out and partly to shift the blame if litigation turns out badly. Lawyers, in turn, have relied on the adversary litigation process, because it is what they know and what they can do. Whether or not the corporate manager who oversees the litigation was personally responsible for the matter that is in litigation, he is unlikely to advance his career through continued association with that unhappy episode. Throughout the litigation the lawyers are likely to have to combat this tendency in order to force the client to take some responsibility for the conduct of the case. By shifting the responsibility for the outcome back to the client, advocates of the mini-trial argue, it can perform an important function. The process also directly involves the decision-makers who have settlement authority in the settlement process. The decision-makers may, for the first time, hear the weak points in their case when there is a summarized presentation of the evidence.

2. The mini-trial attempts to reduce the influence of both the lawyers and the business personnel who were involved in the arrangements that gave rise to the dispute, by presenting the case to the Chief Executive Officers or their delegees. It worked in the *TRW* case where substantial stakes were involved, litigation had proven costly, positions had hardened, and there was room for compromise. Is it less likely to be effective if a company's integrity is on the line, major public policy issues dominate, the monetary stakes are not substantial, there are unresolved legal issues, or the credibility of contradictory witnesses from each company is central?

3. What is lost when a case that might have taken weeks or months to try is squeezed into a two-day mini-trial? Although witnesses may be presented in a mini-trial, lengthy examination and cross-examination is not possible. The virtues and vices of summarization of evidence is also considered in connection with summary jury trial (IV, A, 6).

4. Is a contract clause requiring the parties to submit any dispute to a mini-trial legally enforceable? This may depend on the specificity of the language and the context of the dispute. The usual remedy for breach of contract is damages, but how could a dollar figure be placed on a failure to engage in a mini-trial? Is a mini-trial clause therefore specifically enforceable because damages are inadequate? Would administering such specific enforcement cause the same kinds of difficulties that has led courts to refuse specific enforcement of contracts for personal services? Professor Green argues that "it may be possible to specifically enforce a mini-trial clause by setting forth the procedures to be followed at the mini-trial in detail," making the court's job of supervising performance easier.

5. One of the attractions of the mini-trial is its confidentiality. It is a form of settlement negotiation and therefore enjoys the protections of Federal Rule of Evidence 408. Those protections should apply to all parts of a mini-trial, including the information-exchange, neutral advisor's opinion or comments, negotiations, and any settlement. But since Rule 408 only prohibits admissibility, rather than discovery, further privilege is necessary.

A contract clause that statements, documents, results, or other information arising in a mini-trial will not be admissible in a later trial or proceeding is standard. But while a court may be willing to specifically enforce a non-disclosure clause against the parties, can third-parties be prevented from using discovery devices to obtain the information? Green suggests incorporating the mini-trial agreement in a court order, thus entitling it to the protection of Rule 26(c)(7) for "trade secret or other confidential research, development, or commercial information." But he notes that courts have allowed subsequent litigators access even to previously sealed court records, and that the government may have special powers to discover evidence, as under anti-trust statutes.

6. The reputation or prestige of the neutral advisor is often considered to be critical to the success of the mini-trial. The CPR (Center for Public Resources) Institute for Dispute Resolution, which pioneered the use of the mini-trial, maintains a list of well-known and respected lawyers and businesspersons who have agreed to serve as neutral advisors.

7. Detailed mini-trial procedures have been drawn up by various organizations. See, *e.g.,* Eric Green, The CPR Legal Program Mini–Trial Handbook, in Corporate Dispute Management (1985), which sets out procedures for a six week schedule, with two weeks for discovery and a 2½ day hearing. Plaintiff's case-in-chief is presented on the first afternoon; defendant's rebuttal and plaintiff's response on the second morning; defendant's case-in-chief on the second afternoon; and plaintiff's rebuttal and defendant's response on the third morning. Negotiations without the advisor are held on the third afternoon. Some mini-trials have provided for shortened depositions, *e.g.,* half a day for an expert witness. Although unusual, a mini-trial without a neutral advisor is also possible.

8. One creative use of the mini-trial is as a trial within a trial. In a product liability case where the defendant manufacturer believed it could demonstrate through cross-examination of the plaintiff that his fall had not been caused by a defective ladder, the parties were $10,000 apart on the eve of trial. The defendant made the following proposition, as described by Jeffrey B. Gold, A New Approach in ADR: A Mini–Trial at Trial, 24 The Brief 77, 78 (Summer 1995):

> We offered to keep our $65,000 offer (the "low" figure) on the bargaining table if the plaintiff-husband would take the stand and testify. After the plaintiff-husband testified, the plaintiffs would have an hour to decide whether to accept the "low" figure. If they declined to do so, the defendants would then have an hour to agree to pay the "high" figure of $75,000. In the unlikely event that the plaintiffs refused to accept the "low" figure and the defendant refused to pay the "high" figure, the plaintiffs would present the remainder of their case, the defendants would present their case, and (barring a last-minute settlement) the case would go to the jury as if the parties had never attempted this ADR/negotiation technique during the trial.
>
> The mini-trial at trial would be completely invisible to the jury, and no one but the parties and the court would know that the parties had introduced a dispute resolution technique into the trial. Naturally, we insisted that any stipulation with respect to the high/low offers would be made on the record and be subject to specific performance.

* * *

> If, after the husband's testifying, the plaintiffs felt that the husband had held his own, they could decline the lower offer, recognizing that if the defendants found the husband's testimony unworthy of belief, the case could still go to a jury, which might rule against them. If the plaintiffs felt that the husband was "beat up," they would gladly accept the $65,000; if not, the defendants would in all likelihood be unwilling to try the case to conclusion over $10,000 once the plaintiffs had testified and withstood counsel's best cross-examination. There is great incentive for both the plaintiffs and defendants to view their case closely after entering into a stipulation of this type, because otherwise they still face the jury system model, "to the victor belongs the spoils." Although our proposal was well received, it never was implemented because it stimulated further discussion that resulted in settlement.

6. SUMMARY JURY TRIAL

The summary jury trial is a shortened trial, usually lasting less than a day, in which the lawyers summarize their cases before a jury empanelled under usual procedures. A judge or magistrate presides. The jury verdict is advisory and non-binding—although the jurors are not usually told this explicitly. It was developed by Judge Thomas Lambros, of the U.S. District Court for the Northern District of Ohio, and is now in use in a number of federal and state courts.

Judge Lambros conceived of the device in 1980 while trying two personal injury suits that he believed should have settled: "The reason that they didn't was that counsel and their clients felt that they could obtain a better resolution from a jury than from their pretrial settlement negotiations. It occurred to me that if only the parties could gaze into a crystal ball and be able to predict, with a reasonable amount of certainty, what a jury *would* do in their respective cases, the parties and counsel would be more willing to reach a settlement rather than going through the expense and aggravation of a full jury trial."[16]

Thomas D. Lambros, Summary Jury Trial—An Alternative Method of Resolving Disputes

69 Judicature 286, 286–290 (1986).

* * *

The day of the summary jury trial begins with the arrival of prospective jurors at the jury commissioner's office. If another judge is commencing a jury trial on the same day, the jurors who are called for that proceeding but not actually empanelled may be used in the summary jury trial. To expedite selection of the summary jury, the jury commissioner provides the prospective jurors with a questionnaire. * * *

While the potential jurors are completing their questionnaires, the presiding judicial officer meets with counsel. This meeting gives the court and the parties an opportunity to review the case in an environment that is very similar to that existing just prior to a regular civil jury trial. The same factors that often cause settlement of cases immediately prior to a regular trial will often produce a settlement prior to the summary jury trial proceeding.

In order for the meeting to be of benefit, it is important for counsel to have their cases in a state of complete trial readiness. Each party should be required to file a trial memorandum, proposed voir dire questions, and proposed jury instructions. If an extensive presentation is anticipated, the court may also require the parties to submit exhibit lists and lists of witnesses whose testimony will be summarized during the proceeding. During this meeting, counsel are required to present all procedural and evidentiary questions which foreseeably will arise during the course of the summary jury trial. Resolution of these questions during this meeting minimizes the need for objections during the actual summary jury trial and thus contributes to the flowing character of the proceeding.

* * *

Summary jury trial format

The format of a summary jury trial is very similar to that of a traditional civil jury trial. A judge or magistrate presides over the court, which is formally brought to order. Attendance of the parties with complete settlement authority is required.

It is best if the judge who will try the case conducts the summary jury trial because, through presiding over the summary jury trial, the judge will

---

16. Lambros, The Summary Jury Trial, 103 F.R.D. 461, 463 (1984).

obtain a thorough understanding of the issues presented by the case and the strengths and weaknesses of each parties' position. The judge's participation in the summary jury trial will also facilitate an open and frank discussion of the evidence during post-summary jury trial settlement negotiations. Because the jury remains the ultimate trier of fact, the outcome of a subsequent trial probably will not be affected by the participation of the judge who presided over the summary jury trial. Indeed, the quality of the actual jury trial may be improved because the judge will have become intimately acquainted with the legal issues posed by the case.

As an alternative, the judge may decide to assign a summary jury trial to a magistrate, thereby freeing the judge to conduct traditional trials. This procedure can also be very effective, but it is important that the judge and the magistrate communicate in detail about the case prior to the time that the magistrate assumes responsibility for the proceeding. The magistrate should have a thorough understanding of the issues posed by the case and the parties' settlement positions. If a magistrate conducts the summary jury trial, it is recommended that he or she participate with the judge in the post-summary jury trial settlement negotiations.

The judge opens the summary jury trial with a few introductory remarks in which he or she introduces the trial participants and explains briefly what the case is about. The judge then explains the summary jury trial procedure to the jury. The judge normally states that the lawyers have reviewed all of the relevant materials and interviewed all of the witnesses and now have been asked to condense all of the evidence and present it to the jury in a narrative form. They are also told that the attorneys will be permitted to summarize both the evidence and legal arguments in support of their respective positions.

The prospective jurors are advised that at the conclusion of the case they will be instructed on the applicable law and the use of the verdict form. They are further advised they are expected to consider the case just as seriously as they would if the case was presented to them in the conventional manner and that their verdict must be a true verdict based on the evidence. They are further told that the proceeding will be completed in a single day and that their verdict will aid and assist the parties in resolving their dispute. Nothing more is said about the non-binding nature of the summary jury trial; nothing more need be said. Although the jurors are not misled to believe that the proceeding is equivalent to a binding jury trial, the non-binding character of the proceeding is not emphasized. By adopting this balance the judge may candidly explain the procedure without minimizing the jurors' responsibilities.

Following the judge's introduction of the case to the prospective jurors, the judge conducts a brief voir dire generally posing questions to the jury collectively. This process is expedited through the use of the completed juror profile forms. The judge may make additional inquiries of the jury based on voir dire questions proposed by the attorneys. Counsel are normally permitted to exercise challenges for cause as well as peremptory challenges, although the number of challenges should be limited, and counsel should be encouraged to accept the jurors as they find them, since prolonged voir dire will defeat the goal of conducting the summary jury trial efficiently.

Jury selection is followed by the presentations of counsel. Although the goal of expedited presentation is always kept in mind, the length and format of the proceeding may be adjusted to accommodate the particular needs of the case. Counsel are usually given one hour each for the presentations. This period is usually broken down so that plaintiff devotes approximately 45 minutes to its case in chief, followed by defendant being given a similar period for its main presentation. A 15 minute period may then be given to the parties for their respective rebuttal and surrebuttal. The total time of the proceeding may be extended if the case involves particularly complex issues or more than two parties. It is recommended that each side give the jury a three-to-five minute overview of its case before the formal presentations. This will give the jury a "fix" on the whole case, obviating the need to wait a full hour before learning about the defense.

Fair presentations

As with all other aspects of the summary jury trial process, form should not be allowed to overcome substance. The judge must be especially sensitive to a commonsense notion of fairness. This concept must necessarily extend beyond technical questions of whether the summary by counsel of the evidence is accurate, to such questions as whether the jury is being given a fairly accurate sense of the weight of the evidence. For example, if plaintiff can support a crucial fact in its case only through the rather questionable testimony of one witness, while defendant can present five independent witnesses to confirm the opposite, counsel for plaintiff should not be able to speak of that fact as proof beyond refutation.

Lawyers should also be reminded by the court of Disciplinary Rule 7–106 regarding trial conduct, in particular that portion of the disciplinary rule that forbids a lawyer from asserting personal knowledge of the facts in issue or personal opinions as to the justness of a cause or the credibility of a witness. It is true that the effectiveness of the trial attorney as an advocate will have a marked effect upon the results of the summary jury proceeding; this is no less true, however, at the time of trial and is a factor that each party should be weighing in evaluating the settlement value of the case.

In making their presentations to the jury, counsel are limited to representations based on evidence that would be admissible at trial. Although counsel are permitted to mingle representations of fact with legal arguments, considerations of responsibility and restraint must be observed. Counsel may only make factual representations supportable by reference to discovery materials. These materials include depositions, stipulations, signed statements of witnesses, and answers to interrogatories or requests for admissions. Additionally, an attorney may make representations based on the assurance that he or she has personally spoken with a witness and is repeating what that witness stated. Discovery materials may be read aloud but not at undue length. Counsel may submit these materials in full to the jury for their consideration during deliberations. Each juror is provided a note pad and is permitted to take notes.

Physical evidence, including documents, may be exhibited during a presentation and submitted for the jury's examination during deliberations. These exhibits may be marked for identification, but are returned to the appropriate party at the end of the proceeding.

By virtue of the nature of the summary jury trial, objections during the proceeding are not encouraged. However, in the event counsel overstep the bounds of propriety as to a material aspect of the case, an objection will be received and, if well taken, will be sustained and the jury instructed appropriately.

Jury deliberations

At the conclusion of the summary jury trial presentations, the jury is given an abbreviated charge dealing primarily with the applicable substantive law and, to a lesser extent, with such boilerplate concepts as burden of proof and credibility. The jury is normally given a verdict form containing specific interrogatories, a general inquiry as to liability, and an inquiry as to the plaintiff's damages. The jurors are encouraged to return a unanimous verdict and are given ample time to reach such a consensus. However, if, after diligent efforts, they are unable to return a unanimous verdict, each juror should be given a verdict form and should be instructed to return a separate verdict. These separate views will be of value to the lawyers in exploring settlement.

Once the jury has been excused to deliberate, the court may engage the parties in settlement negotiations. These negotiations have a special sense of urgency in that they are conducted in the shadow of an imminent verdict. The negotiations are informed by the perspectives gained through observation of the summary jury trial.

When the jurors complete their deliberations, the court receives their unanimous verdict or individual verdicts. At this time, the judge, the attorneys, the parties, and the jurors engage in a dialogue unique to summary jury trial. The judge may ask the jurors a broad variety of questions ranging from the general reason for the decision to their perceptions of each party's presentation. Counsel may also inquire of the jurors both as to their perspectives on the merits of the case and their responses to the style of the attorneys' presentations. This dialogue affords an opportunity to gain an in-depth understanding of the strengths and weaknesses of the parties' respective positions. The dialogue may serve as a springboard for meaningful settlement negotiations.

NOTES AND QUESTIONS

1. Should an attorney be allowed to refer to facts or testimony not contained in formal discovery such as a deposition? Note that Judge

Lambros would permit "a professional representation that counsel has spoken with the witness and is repeating that which the witness stated." What problems do you see with this?

2. Is there any check on a counsel's misstating what he has been told in private by a potential witness? Indeed, is there any check on a counsel's misstating or embellishing his summary of the deposition or other discovery? The primary check is the ability of the opposing counsel to set the record straight in her own presentation. Objections are possible, though not encouraged. Perhaps most importantly, an important consideration to keep in mind about the summary jury trial is that it is not a trial, but a settlement procedure. This feature serves in part to answer the objection that, without strict rules of evidence in an informal proceeding that discourages objections, attorneys may be tempted to over-state or misstate their case. Since the jury's opinion is advisory only, it may be of little use to get a favorable advisory opinion from the jury but have the other side turn it down because of its perception that the case was not fairly presented. As in a negotiation, there is an incentive for both sides to appear straightforward and forthcoming in order to lay the basis for an agreed-upon settlement.

3. Advocates of summary jury trials claim that they effect a high settlement rate. See Cook, A Quest for Justice: Effective and Efficient Alternative Dispute Resolution Processes, 1983 Detroit College L.Rev. 1129, 1133 (use by federal judges in Michigan, Pennsylvania, Oklahoma, Massachusetts, and Ohio resulted in a 94% settlement rate after the summary trial). Federal judges continue to report a higher settlement rate of cases after summary jury trial than in other cases. Summary Jury Trials Gain Favor, Nat.L.J. 1 (June 10, 1985).

4. Critics, however, have asked whether the cases that settle after summary jury trials would not have settled anyway. Applying an economic model to an admittedly "crude" set of statistics, Judge Richard A. Posner of the U.S. Court of Appeals for the Seventh Circuit, concluded that summary jury trials did not result in a decrease in the number of trials nor an increase in judicial efficiency. Posner, The Summary Jury Trial and Other Methods of Alternate Dispute Resolution: Some Cautionary Observations, 53 U.Chi.L.Rev. 366, 377–85 (1986). He also found the technique "lavish" because a judge must devote a full day to settling one case.

5. Critics have also questioned summary jury trial verdicts as an accurate indication of what a jury in a full trial would do. Judge Posner argued: "The jury's principal function is to determine the credibility of witnesses, yet there are no witnesses in the summary jury trial. The credibility assessed is that of the lawyers. A jury may react quite differently when confronted with the actual witnesses." Posner, supra at 374. Furthermore, he feared that lawyers may hold back some of their best evidence or arguments in an effort to surprise the opponent at the real trial. A number of lawyer critics have claimed that summary jury trial results are distorted, citing examples of cases in which the verdict at a full trial, after failure to settle, was quite different from that of the summary jury trial. Summary

570 CHAPTER IV COURT-ANNEXED ADR PROCESSES

Jury Trials Assailed as Inaccurate and Ineffective, 4 BNA Civil Trial Manual 96, 97–8 (Mar. 23, 1988).

6. Judge Lambros contemplated that a decision to use a summary jury trial will be made at the final pre-trial conference, presumably after discovery is complete. Some judges, however, have also used summary jury trials early in the litigation. There would obviously be more significant savings of time and trial preparation costs if settlement could be achieved early on. One of the objections to the summary jury trial, as seen by the criticisms of Judge Posner (note 4), is that it really doesn't offer much of a savings in trial preparation or lawyer and judge time. An even more fundamental question is whether something important isn't lost by foregoing full discovery. Can "expedited" discovery—the taking of only critical depositions and documents—provide enough basis for a fair appraisal of a case? The answer might differ according to the type of case. Where the plaintiff must prove difficult matters of intent—as in a civil rights or securities fraud case—or must rely on extensive documentation—as in a product liability case—he may be disadvantaged by having to present his case in a summary jury trial on the basis of limited discovery. On the other hand, overdiscovery is a needless litigation cost, and all parties involved may grant a certain indulgence to a plaintiff in a summary jury trial, knowing that he may have a still stronger case with fuller discovery. If a fair settlement is thereby obtained at an early stage, all parties may benefit.

7. Consistent with the emphasis on confidentiality in settlement negotiations, the summary jury trial is closed to the public. This was challenged by a number of newspapers that had been excluded from a summary jury trial involving the design of a nuclear power plant; the papers brought suit claiming that they had been denied their First Amendment right of access to the "trial." The newspapers argued that trials are public events, but the judge rejected the analogy (117 F.R.D. at 601). The district court in addition issued a gag order restraining communications between the jurors and the press and public, and sealing the transcript and the list of jurors; the court continued these orders in effect after the parties had reached a settlement. The Sixth Circuit affirmed, holding that the newspapers' claim of a public "right to know" had no validity with respect to summary jury trials: "At every turn the summary jury trial is designed to facilitate pretrial settlement of the litigation, much like a settlement conference," and "[s]ettlement techniques have historically been closed to the press and public." In addition, where a party has a legitimate interest in confidentiality, public access would be detrimental to the effectiveness of the summary jury trial in facilitating settlement [and thus] would have significant adverse effects on the utility of the procedure as a settlement device. Therefore, allowing access would undermine the substantial governmental interest in promoting settlements. Cincinnati Gas & Electric Co. v. General Elec. Co., 117 F.R.D. 597 (S.D.Ohio 1987), aff'd 854 F.2d 900 (6th Cir. 1988).

Is it proper for a court to use its facilities for secret dispute resolution in this manner? Would it affect your answer to know that the plaintiff in *Cincinnati Gas* alleged that due to poor design the nuclear reactor was unable to withstand the pressures generated and therefore was unable to contain radioactive steam. After the secret summary jury trial, the case was settled for an amount reportedly exceeding $75 million. Should the press and residents of the area where the reactor is located have been given access to the evidence summarized during the summary jury trial?

8. If the summary jury trial is actually a private settlement device, does the court have authority to summon jurors to participate in it? In Hume v. M & C Management, 129 F.R.D. 506 (N.D.Ohio 1990), another judge in Judge Lambros' district, Judge Battisti, ruled that 28 U.S.C.A. § 1866(g), which empowers courts to summon jurors under threat of fine or imprisonment, does not authorize summoning them for summary jury trials. He further found that the basic jury statute, 28 U.S.C.A. § 1861, was not intended to apply to summary jury trials and expressed concern that summary jury trials could adversely affect the jury system by depleting the supply of jurors for real trials and demoralizing citizens assigned to participate in trials that are not real.

Following his order in *Hume,* Judge Battisti suspended all criminal and civil jury trials pending before him on the ground that the fact that some potential jurors might have served in summary jury trials "may impermissibly alter the jury selection process." United States v. Exum, 748 F.Supp. 512 (N.D.Ohio 1990). However, after the passage of the Civil Justice Reform Act of 1990, which provided that federal district courts should consider the use of ADR devices including the summary jury trial, see 28 U.S.C.A. § 473(a)(6), he vacated those orders. The Act seems to resolve any doubts about the power of judges to use ordinary court processes to summon summary jury trial jurors.

9. An interesting hybrid is a "summary jury with ceilings and floors." It is a variation of "high-low arbitration" in which the parties agree in advance to a high and low figure. If the figure awarded by the arbitrator falls below the agreed-upon low, it will be increased to the amount of the low. If if it is above the agreed-upon high, it will be reduced to the amount of the high. This gives the parties greater advance certainty by avoiding the risks of unduly high or low awards. See Schneider, Summary Jury Trials and Ceilings and Floors, 17 Litigation 3 (Summer 1991), for an account of a successful use of this approach in a summary jury trial. The judge concluded: "With a 'ceiling' and a 'floor' and with a vastly more economical proceeding, the parties benefit significantly from having traded away all the tried-and-true but enormously expensive trappings of the typical jury trial."

10. The Tort Claimants Committee in the Dow Corning bankruptcy proposed a summary jury trial process to provide data to aid the court in estimating the value of nondisease breast implant claims. See In re Dow Corning Corp., 211 B.R. 545 (Bkrtcy.E.D.Mich.1997). The process, which

CHAPTER IV   COURT-ANNEXED ADR PROCESSES

was not adopted, called for six different summary jury trials designed to produce 384 jury verdicts within a 60–day period.

Judicial Power to Require Participation in Summary Jury Trial

Strandell v. Jackson County

United States Court of Appeals, Seventh Circuit, 1987.
838 F.2d 884.

■ Before WOOD and RIPPLE, CIRCUIT JUDGES, and GORDON, SENIOR DISTRICT JUDGE.

■ RIPPLE, CIRCUIT JUDGE.

Mr. Tobin represents the parents of Michael Strandell in a civil rights action against Jackson County, Illinois. The case involves the arrest, strip search, imprisonment, and suicidal death of Michael Strandell. In anticipation of a pretrial conference on September 3, 1986, the plaintiffs filed a written report concerning settlement prospects. The plaintiffs reported that they were requesting $500,000, but that the defendants refused to discuss the issue. At the pretrial conference, the district court suggested that the parties consent to a summary jury trial. * * *

Mr. Tobin informed the district court that the plaintiffs would not consent to a summary jury trial, and filed a motion to advance the case for trial. The district court ordered that discovery be closed on January 15, 1987, and set the case for trial.

During discovery, the plaintiffs had obtained statements from 21 witnesses. The plaintiffs learned the identity of many of these witnesses from information provided by the defendants. After discovery closed, the defendants filed a motion to compel production of the witnesses' statements. The plaintiffs responded that these statements constituted privileged work-product; they argued that the defendants could have obtained the information contained in them through ordinary discovery. The district court denied the motion to compel production; it concluded that the defendants had failed to establish "substantial need" and "undue hardship," as required by Rule 26(b)(3) of the Federal Rules of Civil Procedure.

On March 23, 1987, the district court again discussed settlement prospects with counsel. The court expressed its view that a trial could not be accommodated easily on its crowded docket and again suggested that the parties consent to a summary jury trial. On March 26, 1987, Mr. Tobin advised the district court that he would not be willing to submit his client's case to a summary jury trial, but that he was ready to proceed to trial immediately. He claimed that a summary jury trial would require disclosure of the privileged statements. The district court rejected this argument, and ordered the parties to participate in a summary jury trial.

On March 31, 1987, the parties and counsel appeared, as ordered, for selection of a jury for the summary jury trial. Mr. Tobin again objected to the district court's order compelling the summary jury trial. The district

A. A RANGE OF PROCESSES 573

court denied this motion. Mr. Tobin then respectfully declined to proceed with the selection of the jury. The district court informed Mr. Tobin that it did not have time available to try this case, nor would it have time for a trial "in the foreseeable months ahead." The court then held Mr. Tobin in criminal contempt for refusing to proceed with the summary jury trial. ** * * The district court filed a memorandum opinion setting forth its reasons for ordering a summary jury trial. The district court noted that trial in this case was expected to last five to six weeks, and that the parties were "poles apart in terms of settlement." It further noted that summary jury trials had been used with great success in such situations.

* * *

We begin by noting that we are presented with a narrow question: Whether a trial judge may *require* a litigant to participate in a summary jury trial to promote settlement of the case. We are *not* asked to determine the manner in which summary jury trials may be used with the consent of the parties. Nor are we asked to express a view on the effectiveness of this technique in settlement negotiations.

In turning to the narrow question before us—the legality of *compelled* participation in a summary jury trial—we must also acknowledge, at the very onset, that a district court no doubt has substantial inherent power to control and to manage its docket. That power must, of course, be exercised in a manner that is in harmony with the Federal Rules of Civil Procedure. * * *

In this case, the district court quite properly acknowledged, at least as a theoretical matter, this limitation on its power to devise a new method to encourage settlement. Consequently, the court turned to Rule 16 of the Federal Rules of Civil Procedure in search of authority for the use of a mandatory summary jury trial. In the district court's view, two subsections of Rule 16(c) authorized such a procedure. As amended in 1983, those subsections read:

The participants at any conference under this rule may consider and take action with respect to.

(7) the possibility of settlement or the use of extrajudicial procedures to resolve the dispute;

(11) such other matters as may aid in the deposition of the action.

Fed.R.Civ.P. 16(c)(7), (11).

Here, we must respectfully disagree with the district court. We do not believe that these provisions can be read as authorizing a *mandatory* summary jury trial. In our view, while the pretrial conference of Rule 16 was intended to foster settlement through the use of extrajudicial procedures, it was not intended to require that an unwilling litigant be sidetracked from the normal course of litigation. The drafters of Rule 16 certainly intended to provide, in the pretrial conference, "a neutral forum" for discussing the matter of settlement. Fed.R.Civ.P. 16 advisory committee's note. However, it is also clear that they did not foresee that the

574   CHAPTER IV · COURT-ANNEXED ADR PROCESSES

conference would be used "to impose settlement negotiations on unwilling litigants.... " *Id.; see also* 6 C. Wright, A. Miller & M. Kane, *Federal Practice and Procedure* § 1525 (Supp.1987) ("As the Advisory Committee Note indicates, this new subdivision does not force unwilling parties into settlement negotiations."). While the drafters intended that the trial judge "*explor[e]* the use of procedures other than litigation to resolve the dispute,"—including "*urging* the litigants to employ adjudicatory techniques outside the courthouse,"—they clearly did not intend to *require* the parties to take part in such activities. Fed.R.Civ.P. 16 advisory committee's note (emphasis supplied). As the Second Circuit, commenting on the 1983 version of Rule 16, wrote: "Rule 16 ... was not designed as a means for clubbing the parties—or one of them—into an involuntary compromise." *Kothe v. Smith,* 771 F.2d 667, 669 (2d Cir.1985).

* * *

Our decision is consistent with two decisions issued by this court prior to the 1983 amendments to Rule 16. In *J.F. Edwards Constr. Co. v. Anderson Safeway Guard Rail Corp.,* 542 F.2d 1318 (7th Cir.1976), the court ruled that a district court could not use Rule 16 to compel parties to stipulate facts to which they could not voluntarily agree. One year later, in *Identiseal Corp. v. Positive Identification Sys.,* 560 F.2d 298 (7th Cir.1977), this court reiterated that Rule 16 was noncoercive when it determined that district courts lacked the power to order that a party undertake further discovery. The court said:

The limit of the court's power was to compel plaintiff to consider the possibility of conducting discovery, and there is no evidence in the record that plaintiff's attorney rejected the district court's preferred method of litigating the action without giving it serious consideration. Although *J.F. Edwards* and *Identiseal* antedate the amendments to Rule 16, nothing in the amended rule or in the Advisory Committee Notes suggests that the amendments were intended to make the rule coercive.

The use of a mandatory summary jury trial as a pretrial settlement device would also affect seriously the well-established rules concerning discovery and work-product privilege. *See* Fed.R.Civ.P. 26(b)(3); *see also Hickman v. Taylor,* 329 U.S. 495, 67 S.Ct. 385, 91 L.Ed. 451 (1947). These rules reflect a carefully-crafted balance between the needs for pretrial disclosure and party confidentiality. Yet, a compelled summary jury trial could easily upset that balance by requiring disclosure of information obtainable, if at all, through the mandated discovery process. We do not believe it is reasonable to assume that the Supreme Court and the Congress would undertake, in such an oblique fashion, such a radical alteration of the considered judgments contained in Rule 26 and in the case law. If such radical surgery is to be performed, we can expect that the national rule-making process outlined in the Rules Enabling Act will undertake it in quite an explicit fashion.[1]

---

1. Legislation has been offered in Congress that would allow district courts to convene mandatory summary jury trials. *See* H.R. 473, 100th Cong., 1st Sess., 133 Cong.

A. A RANGE OF PROCESSES **575**

The district court, in explaining its decision to compel the use of the summary jury trial, noted that the Southern District of Illinois faces crushing caseloads. The court suggested that handling that caseload, including compliance with the Speedy Trial Act, required resort to such devices as compulsory summary jury trials. We certainly cannot take issue with the district court's conclusion that its caseload places great stress on its capacity to fulfill its responsibilities. However, a crowded docket does not permit the court to avoid the adjudication of cases properly within its congressionally-mandated jurisdiction. As this court said in *Taylor v. Oxford*, 575 F.2d 152 (7th Cir.1978): "Innovative experiments may be admirable, and considering the heavy case loads in the district courts, understandable, but experiments must stay within the limitations of the statute."

Judgment of contempt vacated.

Arabian American Oil Co. v. Scarfone

United States District Court, Middle District of Florida, 1988.
119 F.R.D. 448.

■ KOVACHEVICH, DISTRICT JUDGE.

This cause is before the Court on Defendants', Robert Work and Jerry Konidaris, motions to excuse participation in summary trial. Mr. Work's motion was filed March 22, 1988, alleging that there is no possibility of settlement in the case, that even if settlement were possible the settlement must occur between Plaintiff and Defendant Scarfone, and that he desires to avoid the expenditure of time and money that participation in the summary trial would require.

* * *

Konidaris joins the motion of Defendant Work, adding the factor that he is an individual with limited financial resources who lives and works in Greece and that it would be "absolutely meaningless and highly expensive for KONIDARIS to have to attend a Summary Jury Trial through himself or through his counsel."

* * *

Rule 16(a)(1) and (5) and (c)(11) has been cited as a basis for the utilization of summary trial procedures. That rule gives the court the power to direct parties to appear before it for various purposes, including expediting the disposition of the action; facilitating the settlement of the case; and taking action in regard to matters which may aid in the disposition of the action. Rule 16 calls these procedures conferences, but what is in a name. The obvious purpose and aim of Rule 16 is to allow courts the discretion and processes necessary for intelligent and effective case man-

Rec.H. 157 (daily ed. Jan. 7, 1987) ("Alternative Dispute Resolution Promotion Act of 1987"); S. 2038, 99th Cong., 2d Sess., 132 Cong.Rec.S. 848 (daily ed. Feb. 3, 1986) ("Alternative Dispute Resolution Promotion Act of 1986").

agement and disposition. Whatever name the judge may give to these proceedings their purposes are the same and are sanctioned by Rule 16.

Statistically, the Middle District of Florida has the worst record in the nation for protracted trials; an accumulation of lengthy, untried causes, literally awaiting decades for trial disposition are delayed because of their extraordinary projected trial time. This Court has effectively utilized summary trials since 1985; without it, opportunity for resolution is delayed, and, justice is denied. The parties herein have had ample notice of this procedure; in fact, the January 1988 summary trial setting would have been held, but for courtroom space limitations. Defendants, for the first time, now raise objections on the eve of the April 12 and 13 summary trial; this constitutes a two-day investment on a *real* trial projected by the parties to consume 210 courtroom hours, or, seven courtroom weeks. Litigants are entitled to their day in court, but not, to somebody else's day.

Under Article Three of the U.S. Constitution, definite work is assigned to, or expected of, the trial court; that is our duty. The inherent jurisdiction of the trial court to determine, set, and use management policies should not be abrogated; it is in the best position to identify, separate, process, and complete *all* of the cases for which it is held responsible, accountable, and exists to perform. Without the authority to perform the task, the ultimate mission of the courts of the United States—to promptly administer justice in all matters properly before the court—is adversely affected.

The summary trial represents one alternative dispute resolution process which courts are employing in an effort to secure to civil litigants just, speedy, and inexpensive determination of their claims (Rule 1, Fed.R.Civ. P.) of which litigants may be otherwise deprived because of the overwhelming and overburdening caseloads which befall many district courts. The summary trial does not abolish any substantive rights of the parties; they are still entitled to a binding trial, if the summary proceedings do not lead to ultimate settlement of the cause of action.

Even if the summary procedures do not culminate in settlement of the case, the value of the summary trial in crystalizing the issues and the proof is immeasurable to the later binding trial, to which all parties come more fully prepared and rehearsed in their roles and the trial procedure. All attorneys and parties must be treated equally. Many attorneys come to trial prepared; *others do not.* After the jury is sworn in an involved case, it is an embarrassing professional exercise before the court and jury to see lawyers floundering in their presentations due to inadequate preparation, whether it be the facts from witnesses, or the law in proposed jury instructions and verdict interrogatories. The reality is that too many will *not* get ready until the day of a trial; a summary trial *forces* that day and that preparation!

This Court finds the summary trial to be a legitimate device to be used to implement the policy of this Court to provide litigants with the most expeditious and just case resolution. The Court does not find the *Strandell* case from the Seventh Circuit persuasive or binding precedent to this Court.

A. A RANGE OF PROCESSES   577

* * * Any contention that individual defendants should be excused from participation based on reasons, such as inability to appear for financial reasons, should be addressed by the magistrate before whom the summary trial is scheduled.

NOTES AND QUESTIONS

1. The Sixth Circuit followed *Strandell* in In re NLO, Inc., 5 F.3d 154 (6th Cir.1993), holding that courts may not compel participation in a summary jury trial (id. at 158):

> "Requiring participation in a pre-trial conference, even if settlement is explored, is permitted under Rule 16(a), and justifiably so, for it may facilitate settlement at very little expense to the parties and the court. A jury trial, even one of a summary nature, however, requires at minimum the time consuming process of assembling a panel and (one would hope) thorough preparation for argument by counsel, no matter how brief the actual proceeding. Compelling an unwilling litigant to undergo this process improperly interposes the tribunal into the normal adversarial course of litigation."

Would counsel's preparation for a summary jury trial necessarily be wasted if the case goes to a full trial? Other lower courts have taken the same position as *Arabian American Oil*. See Twitty v. Minnesota Mining and Manufacturing Co., 16 Pa. D. & C. 4th 458 (C.P. of Philadelphia County 1993)("conducting a summary jury trial using jurors ... does not constitute an obstruction of justice, the misuse of a jury, or the deprivation of [plaintiff's] right to a jury trial"); McKay v. Ashland Oil, Inc., 120 F.R.D. 43, 46 (E.D.Ky.1988).

2. The Civil Justice Reform Act of 1990 authorized each district court "to refer appropriate cases to ADR programs that have been designated for use in a district court or that the court may make available, including mediation, mini-trial, and the *summary jury trial*." 28 U.S.C.A. § 473(a)(6). Did this overrule *Strandell* by authorizing mandatory referral to summary jury trials, or did it only refer to voluntary referral? The statutory language and legislative history are unclear. The *NLO* opinion concluded that § 473(a) only referred to voluntary referral, pointing out that § 473(b) spoke of *required* participation and did not mention summary jury trials. NLO, supra at 158, footnote 1. However, that portion of § (b) dealt with very different procedures—methods to reduce discovery costs—and that could explain why summary jury trials were not mentioned in that context. The Senate Report states that "§ (a)(6) eliminates any doubt that might exist in some courts" "as to whether the summary jury trial is an authorized procedure permissible in the Federal courts." Judicial Improvement Act of 1990, Senate Rpt. No. 101–416, 8 U.S.Code Congressional & Administrative News 6802, 6846 (101st Cong., 2d Sess.1990). However, the case cited as being overruled (Hume v. M & C Management, 129 F.R.D. 506 (N.D.Ohio 1990)), refused to order a summary jury trial solely for lack of authority to use the normal jury summons procedure and did not address whether

CHAPTER IV COURT-ANNEXED ADR PROCESSES

otherwise there was authority for mandatory summary jury trials. Curiously, the Report does not mention *Strandell* at all. This strengthens the *NLO* position that *Strandell* was not overruled by § 473(a)(6), especially since the Report specifically referred to two other relevant cases—noting that *Hume* would be overruled by § (a) and, in connection with § (b), approving the majority *Heileman* view that courts may require the presence of representatives with settlement authority.

3. Does the judge in *Arabian American Oil* answer the *Strandell* objection that a compelled summary jury trial affects discovery and work-product privileges? Is an attorney entitled not to disclose his best case until trial? If so, why shouldn't the federal court practice of requiring parties to identify their witnesses and to indicate the substance of their expected testimony also be considered an invasion of the work-product privilege?

4. Consider the following argument that plaintiff's being forced to reveal work product in *Strandell* was not sufficient prejudice to warrant refusal to participate in the summary jury trial: "The plaintiff's attorney was not required to put on any specific evidence in the summary jury trial. Given due regard for litigant autonomy, he would certainly have been entitled, for example, to hold back the work-product evidence for sole use at trial. Of course, that could mean that he would not do as well with the summary jury as he hoped he would do at trial. But that is a strategic choice he had to make—either hold back his work-product and possibly weaken his case in the summary jury trial, or risk all on the trial. Since the summary jury trial is nonbinding, all he risked was an adverse summary jury trial verdict that might conceivably weaken his bargaining position for settlement before trial." Sherman, Court–Mandated Alternative Dispute Resolution: What Form of Participation Should Be Required?, 46 S.M.U.L.Rev. 2079, 2101–02 (1993).

5. Can *Strandell* be reconciled with *Heileman Brewing* (supra Chap. II), a later decision by the same circuit court, which upheld mandatory participation in a settlement conference? Is a distinguishing characteristic that participation at a settlement conference is less demanding than at a summary jury trial, and less likely to force a party to reveal strategy and information it wants to keep confidential until trial?

6. Is inability to participate in a summary jury trial for financial reasons a valid justification? Note that *American Arabian Oil* left this issue to the magistrate. What criteria should he use?

7. Was *Strandell* a less appropriate case for a summary jury trial than *American Arabian Oil?* Judge Lambros emphasizes that effective pretrial conferencing involves care in selecting cases for a summary jury trial. Would a proper pretrial conference have weeded the *Strandell* case out as inappropriate for summary jury trial? If one of the parties is unwilling to talk settlement and opposes a summary jury trial, what is the value of holding one?

B. ADMINISTERING COURT-ANNEXED ADR

Elizabeth Plapinger & Donna Stienstra, ADR and Settlement in the Federal District Courts: A Sourcebook for Judges and Lawyers

Alternative Dispute Resolution: The Litigators Handbook, eds. Nancy F. Atlas, Stephen K. Huber, & E. Wendy Trachte–Huber, 399, 406–15 (ABA Section of Litigation 2000)

Court–Based ADR Programs: How Many, What Kind, and How Old?

Mediation has emerged as the primary ADR process in the federal district courts. In marked contrast to five years ago when only a few courts had court-based programs for mediation, over half of the ninety-four districts now offer—and, in several instances, require—mediation. Most mediation offered in the federal courts is administered wholly by the courts; only a few districts provide mediation through referral to bar groups or private ADR provider organizations.

Arbitration is the second most frequently authorized ADR program, but falls well short of mediation in the number of courts that have implemented it. In addition to eighteen statutorily authorized courts, two others (Northern District of Alabama and Eastern District of Washington) offer arbitration as the second step of a combined mediation/arbitration procedure. Several others authorize use of arbitration but have not established court-annexed programs.[1] The infrequent adoption of arbitration may be in part the result of uncertainty over whether courts other than those authorized by statute may establish arbitration programs.[2]

Use of early neutral evaluation (ENE) has increased from two courts five years ago, but still is used in only fourteen courts. Limited ENE adoption under the CJP.A may reflect uncertainty about the nature of this relatively new form of ADR or about its relation to mediation. Recently, one of the first two courts to use ENE—the District of Columbia—

---

[1]. 28 U.S.C. §§ 651–58 authorizes ten courts to require participation in arbitration, hence the designation "mandatory," and ten to offer arbitration, which the parties may use at their option, hence the designation "voluntary" (two courts designated as voluntary arbitration courts have not implemented programs). Mandatory arbitration involves an "automatic" referral process; that is, cases meeting the eligibility requirements, such as case type and dollar amount, are automatically referred to ADR. The statutory arbitration programs are funded by congressional appropriations.

[2]. Although the Civil Justice Reform Act of 1990 recommends that courts consider authorizing referral of appropriate cases to ADR (28 U.S.C. § 473(a)(6)), the statute does not include arbitration among the ADR methods it lists, leading some to conclude that arbitration remains limited to those courts authorized by 28 U.S.C. §§ 651–58. *See, e.g.,* Memorandum from William R. Burchill, Jr., general counsel, Administrative Office of the U.S. courts (AO), to Abel J. Mattos, court Administration Division, AO (July 5, 1991) (the CJRA does not appear to authorize arbitration in other courts) (on file with the Research Division of the Federal Judicial center).

580   CHAPTER IV   COURT-ANNEXED ADR PROCESSES

disbanded its program, finding it unnecessary in light of the court's substantial mediation program.

Settlement week and case valuation, the last two forms of court-wide ADR programs, are found in even fewer courts, with three offering a settlement week program and two offering case valuation. Both case valuation programs are in Michigan, where the federal court programs are based on a state program.

Just over half the courts report authorization or use of the summary jury trial. With little information about past practices, we do not know whether this represents a change, but our guess is that, as with other forms of ADR, the number of courts authorizing summary jury trial has grown substantially over the past five years. The level of usage reported by most courts is, however, very low—generally around one or two cases a year.

Also noteworthy is the number of courts that now offer a variety of ADR options. During the past several years, most of the ten courts authorized to establish mandatory arbitration programs in the 1980s have added mediation to their offerings. It is not uncommon today to find at least two ADR procedures available in many federal courts, and at least six courts now offer a full array of options, including arbitration, mediation, early neutral evaluation, and summary jury trial.

The range and number of federal district court ADR programs is particularly noteworthy in light of their recency: most have been implemented since 1990. Although there are some long-standing programs, in particular several arbitration and mediation programs that date from the 1970s, and despite the 1983 authorization provided by amendments to Federal Rule of Civil Procedure 16, use of "extra-judicial procedures to resolve the dispute" did not fully emerge until the 1990s.[3]

A complete picture of each court's approach to settlement attests to the continuing viability of judicial settlement efforts and the expanding role of magistrate judges in settlement. Most courts, even those with substantial ADR programs, provide judicial settlement assistance. Particularly noteworthy are the many courts—at least a third—that have designated magistrate judges as the court's primary settlement officers. While in-depth study of judicially hosted settlement procedures was beyond the scope of this project, our work demonstrates continuing experimentation in the courts to determine the best mix of judicial and nonjudicial settlement programs.

How Many Cases in ADR?

Of great interest to many is the number of cases going into these ADR programs. For several reasons, these numbers should be used cautiously. First, the courts were asked for the number of cases *referred* to ADR, not how many cases actually participated in or were resolved by ADR. Second,

---

3. In 1993, further amendment of Rule 16 altered the language to "use of special procedures to assist in resolving the dispute."

because ADR caseloads are not reported nationally, and in many courts the procedures for recording ADR information are rudimentary, the courts themselves frequently offered their ADR figures as only approximations. Third, large numbers should not be equated with a successful program and smaller numbers with a less successful one. A mediation program that targets complex cases, for example, may be a great success in the court's and litigants' eyes if it resolves two dozen cases a year, whereas a voluntary arbitration program that is available for all civil cases but attracts only a few each year may be a great disappointment.

It seems safe, nonetheless, to say that courts with automatic referral by case type, as in the mandatory arbitration programs and a few mediation programs, have fairly substantial ADR caseloads—for example, 1,235 arbitration cases in New Jersey, 292 mediation cases in the Middle District of North Carolina. The voluntary arbitration courts with opt-out instead of opt-in procedures also have significant caseloads—for example, 266 cases in the Western District of Pennsylvania.[4] Mandatory referral is not, however, essential for moving large numbers of cases into mediation, as we can see from the 414 cases in the Northern District of Oklahoma and the 580 cases in the Northern District of Texas. Early neutral evaluation also draws a good number of cases in several districts, as shown by the 89 cases in the Northern District of Ohio.

It is almost impossible at this time to draw any conclusions about the effectiveness of ADR from these ADR caseload figures. The tables show the substantial variation across courts, but close examination of referral processes, local attitudes toward ADR, the nature of the caseload, and other variables is needed before this variation can be explained. Fortunately, several courts are planning evaluations of their ADR programs, and two national studies required by the CJRA will also contribute to our understanding.[5]

Referring Cases to ADR: The Shift from Referral by Case Type to the Judge as ADR Catalyst and Educator

During the past several years, there has been substantial attention in the federal courts to the issue of *how* cases are referred to ADR, a debate centered largely on the pros and cons of mandatory versus voluntary referral to arbitration. With the emergence of mediation as the primary ADR process, however, and the abandonment of several mandatory arbitration programs,[6] the principal referral mechanisms used today are notably different from those used a few years ago.

---

4. In opt-out procedures, cases eligible for arbitration are automatically referred but then may opt-out of the process with no questions asked. In opt-in programs, cases enter the arbitration process only at the initiative of the parties.

5. The study of the ten pilot and ten comparison districts, being conducted by the

Rand Corporation, and the study of the five demonstration districts, being conducted by the Federal Judicial Center, will be reported to Congress by the Judicial Conference of the united States in December 1996.

6. Two mandatory arbitration courts (Western District of Michigan and Western District of Missouri) have decided to make

CHAPTER IV COURT-ANNEXED ADR PROCESSES

Few of the mediation programs refer cases mandatorily and automatically by case type. Most leave to the judge or parties the identification of cases suitable for ADR.

Whether the referral is made sua sponte or at the request of one or more parties (both of which are authorized in most programs), the judge has become the focal point for identifying cases appropriate for ADR and for educating attorneys and parties about it. Rather than remaining in the background, as in the mandatory arbitration programs, the newer forms of ADR expect the judge to be very much at the center of ADR use.

Even within the arbitration programs, the picture is much more nuanced than the terminology suggests. In the so-called mandatory programs, for example, the referral is only presumptively mandatory. Courts with these programs provide mechanisms for seeking removal from arbitration, and some courts readily grant such removal. Variation is also found in the voluntary programs, with several courts adhering to the textbook model of participation only if the parties voluntarily come forward, but with several others automatically referring cases on the basis of objective criteria and then permitting unquestioned opt-out by the parties.[7]

Nonetheless, a significant change has taken place with the advent of mediation, which places greater emphasis on judicial involvement in the ADR referral than arbitration has.

ADR Obligations of Attorneys and Litigants

Along with the increased ADR responsibility that rests with the judge, a similar responsibility now falls on attorneys and parties. Courts expect attorneys to be knowledgeable about ADR in general and about the court's ADR programs in particular. Many courts' local rules now require attorneys to discuss ADR with their clients and opponents, to address in their case management plan the appropriateness of ADR for the case, and to be prepared to discuss ADR with the judge at the initial Rule 16 scheduling conference.

These rules indicate the extent to which the courts now expect attorneys to work with the judge to determine whether ADR should be used in a case and, if so, what kind of ADR should be used. The attorneys' and judge's responsibilities merge at the initial case management conference, which in many courts has become the critical event—or the first of several—in determining how and when ADR will be used in the case.

In the ADR event itself—that is, the mediation session, the ENE conference, or the summary jury trial—clients are generally required to attend.[8] Most courts have not, however, defined the level or kind of participation required by parties and their counsel.

---

arbitration one of several ADR options offered by the court, and one (Eastern District of North Carolina) has ended its program.

7. Participation rates in three of the four voluntary courts with opt-out procedures are similar to participation rates in courts with presumptively mandatory referral. *See* David Rauma & Carol Krafka, Voluntary Arbitration in Eight Federal District Courts: An Evaluation (Federal Judicial Center 1994).

8. In many courts, cases involving unrepresented parties are not referred to ADR.

Timing of the ADR Session and Integration into Case Management

With the emphasis on case-by-case screening for ADR and the importance of the Rule 16 conference has come a shift in the timing of ADR—or perhaps a recognition that ADR can be used earlier in the case has prompted the emphasis on the Rule 16 conference. In any event, whereas in the past many considered ADR appropriate only for trial-ready cases, now ADR is more often integrated into a court or judge's overall case management practices and is considered much earlier in the case.

This is and has been particularly true of ENE, which was designed to provide an early evaluation of a case's merits and was not originally intended as a settlement device. Even for settlement-oriented procedures such as mediation the process is now likely to occur earlier in the case. It occurs very early in some courts, such as the Western District of Missouri, where the first mediation session is held within thirty days of filing of the answer, and the Eastern District of Pennsylvania, where the conference is held as soon as possible after the first appearance of the defendant. Across all courts, it is not uncommon today for discovery planning to be linked to the mediation process and for the mediation session to take place before discovery has been completed.

The Central Role of Attorney–Neutrals and Court Rosters

Although some courts provide mediation or early neutral evaluation through judges or magistrate judges, most of the courts' ADR programs rely on nonjudicial neutrals, [M]ost of the mediators, arbitrators, and other neutrals used by the courts are attorneys, with other professionals occasionally authorized to serve in that role.

Not only are attorneys the mainstay of most ADR programs, but in nearly every district the court has created its own roster rather than relying on an already-established list of neutrals or turning to private-sector ADR providers for these services.[9] For example, of the forty-three mediation programs that use non-judge neutrals, only three rely on an outside organization, such as a bar association or state mediation program, to provide the ADR services. In contrast, one court (Western District of Missouri) has brought one of its ADR processes fully in-house by hiring an experienced litigator to serve as the court's neutral in cases referred to mediation.

Most courts set eligibility criteria for inclusion on the roster, and a significant number of courts include on the roster any person certified as an ADR neutral by a bar association or state court system. This is true for training as well, with some courts accepting as sufficient the training neutrals have received from other court systems or organizations. On the other hand, some courts completely control the training of their neutrals,

---

9. The bright line between court rosters and private ADR providers is becoming less clear as increasing numbers of lawyers participating in court ADR programs also provide ADR services in the private sector, either in law firms or as part of ADR provider organizations.

CHAPTER IV COURT-ANNEXED ADR PROCESSES

either by conducting the training themselves or by screening and hiring trainers.

The emergence of court-managed rosters has brought with it a number of new questions for the courts. One of the most obvious is the question of training. Given the great range of approaches courts take to training—including requiring none—can litigants have confidence in the courts' ADR processes? Should minimum national training standards be established? A less obvious but also important question is whether neutrals have judicial immunity. Few of the courts' rules speak to this question (perhaps in a belief that the question is more appropriate for case law).[10] Only slightly more address the question of conflicts of interest between the neutral attorney's role as mediator and his or her role as counsel. When and under what circumstances, for example, is an attorney-neutral barred from serving as counsel in future disputes?[11]

As these issues become more urgent, a few individual federal courts (and some state court systems) are developing ethical guidelines or standards of practice for the neutrals on their rosters.[12] Several professional organizations of lawyers and ADR neutrals are also engaged in efforts to define ethical standards for ADR practice.[13] These issues are prompting commentators to ask an even more fundamental question: Are rosters of attorneys the optimum method for providing ADR services or should judges, court staff, or private sector ADR providers deliver these services instead?

Fees for ADR: Parties Generally Must Pay

In a significant shift from past practice, most courts now require parties to pay a fee to the neutral (except in the arbitration programs,

---

10. A number of courts cite a recent District of Columbia Circuit decision on this question. See Wagshal v. Foster, 28 F.3d 1249 (D.C.Cir.1994) (granting mediators and neutral evaluators in the District of Columbia Superior Court absolute quasi-judicial immunity when performing their official duties).

11. In a recent decision in the District of Utah, an attorney who had mediated between two parties was disqualified, along with his firm, from representing one of the parties in subsequent litigation involving both. See Poly Software Int'l, Inc. v. Yu Su, 880 F. Supp. 1487 (D.Utah 1995). See also Cho v. Superior Ct. of La.; Cho Hung Bank, Real Party in Interest (95 C.D.O.S. 8237, Oct. 19, 1995) (entire law firm disqualified when retired judge who had conducted mediation-like meetings involving two parties joined law firm representing one of the parties).

12. See District of Utah Manual on Alternative Dispute Resolution for Court-Appointed Arbitrators and Mediators. Section IV

contains the Code of Ethics for Court-Appointed Arbitrators and Mediators; Section V contains Information Regarding Court-Appointed Arbitrator and Mediator Liability Issues. The Northern District of Oklahoma is also developing a code of ethics for its neutrals. See also Florida Rules for Certified and Court-Appointed Mediators (adopted by the Florida Supreme Court, May 1992) and Ethical Guidelines for Mediators (adopted by the Alternative Dispute Resolution Section of the State Bar of Texas in 1994).

13. The CPR Institute for Dispute Resolution, in conjunction with the Georgetown University Law Center, is developing ethical guidelines and standards of practice for attorneys in ADR. See also the proposed Joint Standards of Conduct for Mediators drafted by the American Bar Association Section of Dispute Resolution, the American Arbitration Association, and the Society for Professionals in Dispute Resolution.

where arbitrator fees are paid from congressional appropriations). In the first mediation programs, the neutrals generally provided their services pro bono. Today, of the forty-one courts offering attorney-based mediation, only nine provide that service pro bono (and one, as already mentioned, provides mediation through a staff mediator). Three others generally offer mediation without fees, although in some circumstances the parties may be required to pay the mediator. The remaining courts—that is, two-thirds of the courts with mediation programs—require that parties pay a fee.

The courts generally use one of four different approaches to determine the fee: market rate, court-set rate, pro bono, or court-set fee after a specified number of pro bono hours. A market-rate fee, found in ten courts, is the most common; a number of these courts, however, reserve the right to review the reasonableness of the fee. Eight courts specify a set fee, which may be either an amount per hour (for example, $150 per hour) or an amount per session (for example, $250 per session). Five courts authorize both a market-rate and court-set fee, reserving to the judge the discretion to determine which type of fee arrangement is best for each case. In four courts the neutral must serve pro bono for a specified number of hours, ranging from one to six, before the parties must pay either a court-set or market-rate fee.

In recognition that some parties cannot afford to pay a fee, a number of courts—e.g., nine of the forty-three attorney-based mediation programs—include special provisions in their rules regarding low-income or indigent parties, generally waiving the fee altogether. To provide this service, some courts require those selected from the court's roster to serve pro bono for a specified number of hours or cases.

Interestingly, there appears to be little relationship between whether fees are assessed and whether the referral to ADR is mandatory or made only with party consent. While some voluntary programs assess a fee and some do not, most of the courts that require participation in ADR also require payment of a fee.

Increasing Formalism and Institutionalization of ADR

With the Civil Justice Reform Act and its encouragement of district-wide examination, ADR has taken on a programmatic character, rather than relying on the initiatives of individual judges as in earlier ADR efforts.[14] Evidence for the growing institutionalization of ADR within the courts can be seen in the formal rules and procedures adopted by the courts, which usually apply to the court as a whole and replace the individual judge-based procedures of the past. While generally leaving to the judge's discretion whether ADR should be used in an individual case, the rules spell out the procedures to be followed once a case has been referred. Additionally, a number of courts have developed ADR brochures

---

14. As is true with most of the patterns discussed here, arbitration stands apart. As statutory programs funded from appropria-tions, these programs have been program-matic and court-wide from their inception.

that are given to parties at filing to alert them to the court's ADR options. A body of judicial decisions about various components of these ADR programs is also emerging.[15]

Further evidence of ADR's institutionalization is the emergence of specialized staff. Nearly a dozen courts have appointed an ADR administrator or director whose full-time responsibility is to manage and monitor the court's ADR programs. The administrator's duties are often broad and include recruitment and training of the court's neutrals, assistance in identifying cases appropriate for ADR, and ongoing evaluation of program quality. While some courts have created these positions because they have special funding as experimental courts under the CJRA, others support such positions from their general budget. Even when courts have not been able to or have not wanted to fund a full-time, high-level position, many have assigned part-time ADR responsibilities to a member of the clerk's office staff.

There are a number of administrative steps, procedures, and issues that must be worked out when ADR is annexed to the judicial system. They are sometimes resolved by statutes, occasionally by case law, but more frequently by court rules, orders, or practice.

1. REFERRAL OF CASES TO ADR

The referral process is critical to the success of court-annexed ADR. It will decide what cases are referred to ADR, which process will be used, and what neutrals will be appointed.

Whether or not courts adopt mandatory ADR, voluntary requests for ADR by the parties are always more desirable. An increasing number of states impose an obligation on counsel to discuss ADR with their clients and consider its use.[1] Requiring the parties to consider ADR as early as

---

15. *See, e.g., supra* notes 10 & 11. *See also* Cincinnati Gas & Elec. Co. v. General Elec. Co., 854 F. 2d 900 (6th Cir.1988) (summary jury trial maybe ordered closed to the public); GTE Directories Serv. Corp. v. Pacific Bell Directory, 135 F.R.D. 187 (N.D.Cal. 1991) (disclosure of privileged documents for use in an ENE session does not, by itself, waive privilege, as long as the party states its intention to retain the privilege); Kimbrough v. Holiday Inn, 478 F. Supp. 566 (E.D.Pa. 1979) (upholding mandatory arbitration program in one of the ten pilot courts and rejecting Seventh Amendment challenge); Hume v. M & C Management, 129 F.R.D. 506 (N.D.Ohio 1990) (federal courts have no authority to summon citizens to serve as jurors

in summary jury trials). *And see* Strandell v. Jackson County, 838 F.2d 884(7th Cir.1987), and *In re* NLO, Inc., 5 F.3d 154(6th Cir.1993) (judge cannot order parties to participate in a summary jury trial); *cf.* McKay v. Ashland Oil Co., 120 F.R.D. 43 (E.D.Ky.1988), and Arabian Am. Oil Co. v. Scarfone, 119 F.R.D. 448 (M.D.Fla.1988).

1. See, e.g., The Texas Lawyer's Creed—A Mandate for Professionals, § II(11) (1989) ("I will advise my client regarding the availability of mediation, arbitration, and other alternative methods of resolving and settling disputes."); see also Moberly, Ethical Standards for Court–Appointed Mediators and Florida's Mandatory Mediation Experiment, 21 Fla.St.U.L.Rev. 701, 723–26 (1994)

B. Administering Court-Annexed ADR   **587**

possible can save time and money by improving chances for an early, mutually-acceptable resolution. If there is a requirement for an early conference to consider case management, scheduling, and discovery (as in federal courts), ADR should be on the checklist. Discovery schedules and deadlines should be made with an eye towards when and how ADR might be used. For example, if a "facilitative" ADR process like mediation is to be used early in the litigation, the discovery order might provide for "expedited discovery" limited to a small number of depositions of critical persons and production of key documents that are needed for an informed mediation.

Statutes and rules vary as to the role of the parties in the referral process. Some courts automatically refer certain categories of cases to ADR, or to a particular ADR process, without direct involvement of the parties in the process. Some rules require the court to confer with the parties before referring a case to ADR.[2] Some rules give the parties a short period of time to object to any such referral, but with ultimate power in the court to overrule objections.[3] Some courts have administrative personnel screen cases, applying either general criteria, or sometimes detailed criteria, as to when and what kind of ADR is useful.[4] Such screening, however, is costly, and many courts do not have the trained personnel to conduct it effectively.

One model for involving the parties in the ADR referral decision is a rule proposed by an ABA study. The parties would be required to consider the use of ADR at a "meet and confer" conference held shortly after the case is filed. If they agree upon an ADR method or provider, the court must respect their choice unless it believes it unsuitable to the case. If the parties do not agree, the court will appoint a neutral from a list prepared by a standing panel on ADR neutrals that reviews applications from neutrals and annually prepares a list of those qualified.[5]

2. Selecting the Process

The range of basic ADR processes that have already been discussed in this chapter, plus an ever expanding number of new and hybrid processes,

(discussing a movement by professional groups and law firms to require attorneys to advise clients of ADR options).

2. See, e.g., V.T.C.A., Civ.Prac. & Rem. Code § 154.021 ("the court shall confer with the parties in the determination of the most appropriate alternative dispute resolution procedure"). In actuality, Texas courts often make the referral without consultation, and only confer if there is an objection. Alan S. Rau & Edward F. Sherman, Rau & Sherman's Texas ADR and Arbitration Statutes 10–11 (1994).

3. See, e.g., V.T.C.A., Civ.Prac. & Rem. Code § 154.022.

4. In Washington, D.C., the Multi–Door Dispute Resolution Division of the Superior

Courts uses a computer program that applies a large number of variables to assess the appropriateness of various types of ADR for a particular case. Gray, Multi–Door Courthouse, in National Symposium on Court–Connected Dispute Resolution Research: A Report on Current Research Findings—Implications for Courts and Future Research Needs 109 (Susan Keilitz ed., 1994).

5. American Bar Association Ad Hoc Committee on Civil Justice Improvements, Discussion Drafts: Civil Justice Improvement Proposals 13–14 (Dec. 13–14, 1993), discussed in Sherman, A Process Model and Agenda for Civil Justice Reforms in the States, 46 Stan. L.Rev. 1553, 1572–1573 (1994).

is one of the strengths of the ADR movement. There has been constant experimentation and innovation as courts pick and choose among a wealth of alternative processes. That variety of processes, however, presents a challenge to a court both as to choosing a manageable number that will work and in devising procedures for selecting the right process for each case. One might think that courts should be authorized to use all the processes, but each process requires its own administrative structure and trained neutrals. Courts may have to make some hard choices in determining which processes they have the resources to implement and which are most likely to work. Of the 94 federal district court plans submitted under the 1990 Civil Justice Reform Act (CJRA), about two-thirds authorize judicial settlement conferences, half authorize mediation, half authorize summary jury trial, a quarter authorize court-annexed arbitration, and a fifth authorize summary jury trial.[6]

A good deal of attention has been given in recent years to applying the right ADR process to each dispute. The continuum chart on *procedural formality* at the beginning of this chapter—as well as possible other charts on *intrusiveness of the neutral* and *timing*—reflect some of the factors that go into selecting the right process. Consider the following discussion of this issue:

Frank E.A. Sander & Stephen B. Goldberg, Fitting the Forum to the Fuss: A User–Friendly Guide to Selecting an ADR Procedure

10 Negotiation J. 49, 51-2, 54-60 (1994).

Mary Stone has worked for the past two years as an accounting manager at the Smith Corporation, a manufacturer of menswear. She is one of only two women in the Accounting Department.

Stone is an attractive single woman of 32. The fact that she is somewhat overweight has made her the object of various jokes around the office, some of them of an explicit sexual nature. Sometimes she will find a crude cartoon on her desk when she arrives in the morning (e.g., a recent one depicted a couple in bed, with the caption "Fat girls are best."); at other times she hears whispered comments about her as she passes by. Although this objectionable behavior has been going on for about four months, it has really got to Stone recently. Last week, she discussed the situation with the director of the Department of Human Resources, who urged her to see the sexual harassment counselor, Jane Willard. Willard promised to send around to the accounting department a reminder about the company's policies on sexual harassment.

Stone has now come to see you, an attorney who specializes in sexual harassment cases. Mindful of the recent emphasis on various ways of

---

6. E. Plapinger & D. Steinstra, Source Book on Federal District Court ADR and Settlement Procedures (Federal Judicial Center and CPR, 1995).

resolving disputes outside the courts, you wonder whether this case might be suitable for alternative dispute resolution (ADR).

* * *

3. CLIENT GOALS

How do you, as Stone's attorney, prepare for your initial interview with your client? Is she eager to remain at the company (perhaps because alternative employment opportunities are scarce) and hence wants to resolve this situation with the least disruption and fuss? Or is she so angry that she is determined to have some outside neutral pronounce her "right," and thus vindicate her position?

Answers to questions like these are critical in determining what dispute resolution procedure is appropriate in this case. The fact that Stone has decided to come to an attorney indicates that she is dissatisfied with the present posture of the dispute. But should she file a lawsuit or seek some other way of resolving the problem? If she has an emotional need for vindication, she will have to resort to some form of adjudication, either in court or—if the company is willing—through private means, such as arbitration or private judging. Private adjudication, in addition to assuring confidentiality, is often faster and cheaper than a court decision. In arbitration and private judging, there is also an opportunity to participate in the selection of the adjudicator and thus to obtain particular expertise. In addition, arbitration almost guarantees finality, since a reviewing court will hardly ever overturn an arbitrator's decision. If Stone wants public vindication, however, or a binding precedent, only court will do.

A form of third-party vindication is available through the minitrial, the summary jury trial, and early neutral evaluation, since in each of these processes a neutral third party evaluates the contentions of the parties. Because these processes are both abbreviated and nonbinding, however, they will not always satisfy a client's desire for vindication.

If Stone wants the opinion of a neutral concerning the merits of her claim less for vindication than as a means of convincing the company that she has a strong claim, and is entitled to a reasonable settlement, then any of the nonbinding evaluative procedures (minitrial, summary jury trial, neutral evaluation) has promise. Choosing among these options will depend on such factors as the client's other goals and the extent to which each procedure is likely to overcome the barriers to settlement, factors that are discussed later in this article.

What if there were other employees with similar complaints of sexual harassment? In that case Stone might again want some formal declaration concerning the illegality of the conduct in question, which then could be used as a precedent in other cases. The company, viewing the problem from its vantage point, might have a similar preference for some type of reasoned adjudication (probably via a court decision, but possibly through arbitration or private judging).

CHAPTER IV COURT-ANNEXED ADR PROCESSES

But suppose instead that Stone is eager to keep her job and simply wants the annoying conduct to stop. Perhaps a transfer will accomplish that goal. If the company is willing to meet her halfway, it may be desirable to involve a mediator who can help facilitate this kind of solution in a quiet, confidential manner.

Of course, client goals may change as time passes, conditions change, and feelings wax or wane. Stone may start out bent on vengeance via public vindication and damages. But, as she considers giving up a job she finds satisfying, except for the harassment, her priority may shift from vindication and damages to retaining her job, if she can be assured that the employer has taken steps to protect her from harassment, and perhaps also to protect potential future victims.

These, then, are some of the considerations that lawyers and clients must examine with regard to processes that might meet client objectives. The value of various procedures in meeting specific client objectives is set forth in Table 1.

Table 1

Extent to Which Dispute Resolution Procedures Satisfy Client Objectives
Procedures

| Objectives | Nonbinding | | | | Binding | |
	Mediation	Minitrial	Summary Jury Trial	Early Neutral Evaluation	Arbitration, Private Judging	Court
Minimize Costs	3	2	2	3	1	0
Speed	3	2	2	3	1	0
Privacy a	3	3	2	2	3	0
Maintain/Improve Relationship b	3	2	2	1	1	0
Vindication c	0	1	1	1	2	3
Neutral Opinion d	0	3	3	3	3	3
Precedent e	0	0	0	0	2	3
Maximizing/ Minimizing Recovery	0	1	1	1	2	3

0 = Unlikely to satisfy objective   2 = Satisfies objective substantially
1 = Satisfies objective somewhat   3 = Satisfies objective very substantially

a. We believe that a summary jury trial and a neutral evaluation offer less privacy than the other ADR processes, in which the neutral is selected by the parties. In the summary jury trial, a judge or magistrate, as well as a jury, is present; in neutral evaluation, the neutral will typically be a court-appointed attorney. If, however, the neutral evaluator is selected by the parties, neutral evaluation will offer as much privacy as the other ADR processes. Conversely, if a mediator, minitrial neutral, or arbitrator were imposed by the court, that procedure would receive a lower privacy rating.
b. We have given early neutral evaluation a lower rating than the summary jury trial or the minitrial for the capacity to maintain relationships. While all three procedures are relatively brief and thus do little harm to the relationship, the summary jury trial and the minitrial typically involve negotiations between the principals; and such negotiations sometimes have the potential of mending a frayed relationship. If a particular early neutral evaluation were to involve negotiations between the principals, it would receive the same rating as the summary jury trial or the minitrial.
c. Since a need for vindication may be satisfied by an apology, mediation that results in an apology can satisfy the need for vindication. However, in our experience, apologies rarely occur in mediation (see Goldberg, Sander, and Rogers, 1992: 137–139).

d. We have assigned the same ranking to all the procedures that provide any kind of neutral evaluation. But if one were to take account of the basis for making the evaluation, the procedures that provide for a full presentation of the evidence and arguments (namely, court and arbitration) would receive a higher score. A neutral evaluation which follows a full presentation of evidence and argument is likely to be given greater weight by the parties than is a neutral opinion based upon a more truncated presentation.

e. Although mediation normally seeks to provide a solution to the specific dispute, the parties could also agree on a new rule for future cases and thus obviate the need for a formal precedent.

An important point to note is that the values assigned to each procedure in Table 1 (as well as in Table 2, which follows) are not based on empirical research but rather upon our own experience, combined with the views of other dispute resolution professionals. Moreover, the numerical values assigned to each procedure are not intended to be taken literally, but rather as a shorthand expression of the extent to which each procedure satisfies a particular objective.

If, for example, the client's goals are to maintain the relationship and receive a neutral opinion while also maximizing privacy, adding the numerical scores would lead to the following result: mediation 6; minitrial 8; summary jury trial 7; early neutral evaluation 6; arbitration 7; and court 3. One could not, however, conclude from these scores that the minitrial is the preferred procedure. Our analysis of the capacity of each procedure to meet various goals is not that precise. The most that one could conclude at this point in the analysis would be that some ADR procedure is preferable to court.

The next step in the analysis is to list the client's goals in order of priority. If the client is primarily interested in a prompt and inexpensive resolution of the dispute that also maintains or improves the parties' relationship—which is typical of most clients in most business disputes—mediation is the preferred procedure. Mediation is the only procedure to receive maximum scores on each of these dimensions—cost, speed, and maintain or improve the relationship—as well as on assuring privacy, another interest which is present in many business disputes. It is only when the client's primary interests consist of establishing a precedent, being vindicated, or maximizing (or minimizing) recovery that procedures other than mediation are more likely to be satisfactory.

It should be clear from this discussion that our evaluation is based on assumptions concerning how ADR procedures are typically structured. If the procedures are structured differently, by court order or party design, the extent to which they will satisfy client goals will also differ. For example, mediation will generally cost the parties less and be faster than a summary jury trial or the minitrial, which require preparing to present evidence and arguments in a structured setting, but that is not always the case. Some parties will provide for a comparatively simple minitrial, with a minimum of preparation, while others will participate in a lengthy, somewhat formal mediation that will be expensive and time-consuming. Similarly, we have assumed that mediation is a process distinct from neutral evaluation, and have set the point values in Table 1 accordingly. But some mediators also perform evaluative functions, and some neutral evaluators attempt to mediate. Hence, Table 1 should be understood only as a general guide, subject to modification if the procedures involved differ from the norms on which the table was based.

A related point is that the processes listed in Tables 1 and 2 are discussed more or less in isolation. Often however, it is possible to blend or link different processes (e.g., mediation and evaluation) to develop a hybrid process. Indeed, Tables 1 and 2 can be used as a guide for designing a process that promises to achieve the client's objectives and, where settlement is sought, that is likely to overcome the envisioned impediments.

One final point concerning client goals: Some contend that ADR should be avoided altogether when one party will be sure to win if the matter is litigated. We disagree. First, the likely loser may be persuaded, through the use of one of the evaluative ADR procedures, to concede, thus sparing both parties the costs of litigation. An agreed-upon outcome is also more likely to be fully complied with than a court order. Alternatively, the likely loser may offer, in ADR, a settlement that is better in non-monetary terms than what could be achieved in litigation; such a settlement preserves, and often enhances, the parties' relationship. Thus, the prospect of a victory in litigation is not reason enough for avoiding ADR.

Impediments to Settlement and Ways of Overcoming Them

In some circumstances, a settlement is not in the client's interest. For example, the client may want a binding precedent or may want to impress other potential litigants with its firmness and the consequent costs of asserting claims against it. Alternatively, the client may be in a situation in which there are no relational concerns; the only issue is whether it must pay out money; there is no pre-judgment interest; and the cost of contesting the claim is less than the interest earned on the money. In these and a small number of other situations, settlement will not be in the client's interest.

Still, a satisfactory settlement typically is in the client's interest. It is the inability to obtain such a settlement, in fact, that impels the client to seek the advice of counsel in the first place. The lawyer must consider not only what the client wants but also why the parties have been unable to settle their dispute, and then must find a dispute resolution procedure that is likely to overcome the impediments to settlement. Note, however, that, even though it may initially appear that the parties seek a settlement, sometimes an examination of the impediments to settlement reveals that at least one party wants something that settlement cannot provide (e.g., public vindication or a ruling that establishes an enforceable precedent).

[The authors discuss various impediments to settlement, along with the likelihood that various ADR processes will overcome them: Poor Communication; The Need to Express Emotions;

Different View of Facts; Different Views of Legal Outcome if Settlement Is Not Reached; Issues of Principle; Constituency Pressure; Linkage to Other Disputes; Multiple Parties with Diverse Interests; Different Lawyer/Client Interests; The Jackpot Syndrome.]

A Rule of Presumptive Mediation

Mediation will most often be the preferred procedure for overcoming the impediments to settlement. It has the greatest likelihood of overcoming all impediments except different views of facts and law, and the jackpot syndrome. Furthermore, a skilled mediator can often obtain a settlement without the necessity of resolving disputed questions of fact or law. Thus, there is much to be said for a rule of "presumptive mediation"—that mediation, if it is a procedure that satisfies the parties' goals, should, absent compelling indications to the contrary, be the first procedure used.

Under this approach, the mediator would first attempt to resolve the dispute by using customary mediation techniques. In doing so, the mediator would gain a clearer sense of the parties' goals and the obstacles to settlement than could be obtained by counsel prior to mediation. If mediation were not successful, the mediator could then make an informed recommendation for a different procedure. For example, if the parties were so far apart in their views of the facts or law that meaningful settlement negotiations could not take place, the mediator might recommend a referral to one of the evaluative procedures to move the parties closer to a common view of the facts and law. Once that had been accomplished, mediated settlement negotiations would recommence.

One of the strengths of this approach is that the mediator's process recommendation might be more readily accepted by both parties than would the suggestion of either of their attorneys, since attorney suggestions are sometimes suspected of being based on tactical considerations. Thus, the approach of "presumptive mediation" seems promising, particularly when the parties are having difficulty in agreeing upon an ADR procedure.

The presumption in favor of mediation would be overcome when the goals of one or both parties could not be satisfied in mediation, or mediation was clearly incapable of overcoming a major impediment to settlement. The most common situation in which this could occur would be when either party has a strong interest in receiving a neutral opinion, obtaining a precedent, or being vindicated, and is unwilling to consider any procedure that forecloses the possibility of accomplishing that objective.

---

4. SELECTING THE NEUTRAL(S)

There is also great diversity in the way neutrals are selected under court-annexed ADR programs. In a number of programs the neutral is selected by the judge just like other judicial surrogates like special masters or guardians ad litem. On the opposite end of the spectrum is a random or rotation method of selection. This approach avoids charges of cronyism and patronage in court appointments. It also provides an opportunity for more qualified neutrals to get appointments, and this, in turn, fosters a larger active ADR profession. Some judges, however, feel that they have the duty to select the neutral whom they consider best qualified for the particular case and that random or rotation methods have no place in the appointive process. A random-selection method also adds another level of administra-

594 CHAPTER IV COURT-ANNEXED ADR PROCESSES

tive work to the selection process and possible delay before a case can go forward with ADR. A middle position is for a court to give the parties a reasonable period of time (say ten days) to select the neutral, subject to final court approval. If the parties cannot agree on a choice, the court would make the selection either on its own or from a previously-approved list.[7]

5. WHO PAYS FOR COURT-ANNEXED ADR?

Should the services of neutrals be provided by courts or paid for by the parties? In California, which mandates mediation in certain family law cases, mediators are employees of the court and provided without charge. In contrast, most court-annexed ADR programs rely on appointment of private mediators and other neutrals. Federal district court CJRA plans generally provide that the fees of ADR neutrals are to be charged to the parties as court costs.

Under many court-annexed programs, the court sets "a reasonable fee" for the services of the neutral, which is taxed against the parties "as other costs of suit." How is a "reasonable fee" determined? An analogy can be found in cases where the prevailing party is entitled to recover reasonable attorney's fees. Courts look to such factors as the usual prevailing fee for similar services in the community, the hours spent, and whether there were any special risks, difficulties, or benefits in performing the services which would warrant a higher fee.[8] Setting a reasonable fee for third party neutrals may actually be easier since such factors as risk in performing legal services for a contingent fee, difficulties and weaknesses in the case, and benefit to the client would not be relevant. The key factors would seem to be the hourly fee charged, the prevailing fee for similar services, whether that fee was reasonable under the circumstances, and the number of hours spent.

There is a further question as to whether the parties must accept a court-appointed mediator or third-party neutral and his fee schedule, or whether they should be allowed to make their own selection, including one from a community-based low-fee or non-fee service. It has been urged that in appointing an ADR neutral, a court should consider the parties' preferences concerning fees.[9] Some courts require, as a condition for being on a

---

7. See, e.g., Rules and Legislation Committee, Texas State Bar Association, Proposed New Order of Referral to Mediation, Alternative Resolutions 11 (State Bar of Texas, Winter 1992); ABA Ad Hoc Committee, supra note 5, at 18.

8. Among the factors that may be considered in setting a reasonable attorneys' fee in federal courts are 1) time and labor required, 2) novelty and difficulty of the questions, 3) skill requisite to perform the legal service properly, 4) preclusion of employment by the attorney due to acceptance of the case,

5) customary fee, 6) whether the fee is fixed or contingent, 7) time limitations imposed by the client or circumstances, 8) amount involved and results obtained, 9) experience, reputation, and ability of the attorneys, 10) undesirability of the case, 11) nature and length of the professional relationship with client, and 12) awards in similar cases. Johnson v. Georgia Highway Express, Inc., 488 F.2d 714 (5th Cir.1974).

9. The model "Pretrial Settlement Facilitation Procedures" drafted by the American Bar Association Ad Hoc Committee on

court-appointed ADR neutral roster, willingness to accept *pro bono* appointments.[10]

6. APPELLATE ADR

Appellate courts have generally been behind trial courts in developing ADR programs. However, in recent years several viable models for appellate ADR have been developed, and a number of federal and state appellate court programs have emerged. All twelve federal circuits have settlement conference offices or plan to open one in the near future, and about twenty-five state appeals courts have active programs.[11]

The U.S. Court of Appeals for the Second Circuit pioneered the concept of appellate mediation in 1974. Its Civil Appeals Management Plan (CAMP) began with one staff attorney who selected those cases that seemed most suitable for settlement. Today it has three conference attorneys, each conducting at least three mediation conferences per day. Cases selected go to a mandatory pre-argument conference, usually within 20 days of docketing. In 1994, 45% of mediated cases settled or were dismissed.[12]

Appellate cases seem particularly well suited to ADR since there are few imponderables; the facts, the record, and the judgment are all known, and the range of possible outcomes is narrowed. But parties and lawyers who have gone through a trial (or other court proceeding) are sometimes so emotionally committed to their position, and so angry about the tactics of the other side, that settlement is difficult. For this reason, mandatory ADR helps each side to save face and provides a structure for reaching agreement.

A good example of an appellate ADR program is that adopted by the U.S. Court of Appeals for the D.C. Circuit in 1987 for mandatory mediation of cases on a random basis. Relying on experience from five circuit courts of appeals and a number of state appellate courts, the program cited the following four critical factors: (a) the primary goal must be achieving settlements, rather than refining cases, (b) the mediators should be special-

---

Civil Justice Improvements provides: "The ADR neutral and the parties will determine the fees for the ADR. If the neutral and parties cannot agree as to the fees, the court may appoint another neutral or determine that the fees sought by the originally appointed neutral are reasonable and that the ADR should proceed with the neutral. The fees will be assessed as costs, to be shared equally by the parties, unless the court, in its discretion, determines that some other allocation is warranted. The court may on its own motion, or the motion of a party, review the reasonableness of the fees." Reaching Common Ground: A Summit on Civil Justice Systems Improvements § 14 at p. 16 (ABA Ad Hoc Committee on Civil Justice Improvements, Dec. 1993). The Commentary also states: "Since public

and not-for-profit neutrals and providers are eligible for the approved list of ADR neutrals, the court should consider appointing an ADR neutral who will serve *pro bono* if the payment of the neutral's fees would cause hardship to the parties." *Id.* at 21.

10. See Application Form, Travis County, Texas List of ADR Providers, II, C: "If called upon by the Court to do so, I hereby agree to accept up to two mediation referrals, at least one non-settlement week, per year on a *pro bono* basis."

11. Dick, The Surprising Success of Appellate Mediation, 13 Alternatives to the High Cost of Litigation 41, 48 (1995).

12. *Id.* at 48.

ly trained in mediation techniques, (c) attorneys and parties must attend at least the first conference, and (d) the conference must be scheduled soon after an appeal is filed.[13]

Under the D.C. Circuit procedures, the mediator schedules the initial meeting within 45 days of assignment. Counsel prepare, within 15 days, position papers of not more than 10 pages, outlining their views on key facts and legal issues. These papers are not given to opposing counsel unless the mediator requests it. The mediator may also require production of key documents.

The initial meeting must be attended by counsel or other person with authority to settle the case. Parties are encouraged, but not required, to attend. All proceedings and statements made are privileged and are not subject to disclosure. If the mediator makes any suggestion as to the advisability of a change in a party's position, counsel are required to transmit these suggestions to their client. They must advise their clients that the mediator is an experienced attorney selected by the court to act as an impartial volunteer to help reach agreement and avoid further expense and uncertainty.

Any agreement reached will be reduced to writing. If no agreement is reached, the mediator notifies the Circuit Executive and the case is returned to the clerk's office for normal processing. If more time is needed, a joint stipulation can be submitted to hold the appeal in abeyance to allow the parties to continue settlement negotiations.

The federal appellate ADR programs differ on a number of points, including whether they use staff attorneys or outside volunteers, whether they focus on settlement or also deal with case management, and what style of mediation is used. Under the Sixth Circuit program, the emphasis is on settlement rather than case management. Virtually all civil appeals are mediated by five conference attorneys (three of them working part-time). A more "rights-based" or "evaluative" style is favored. "When it is appropriate, and when we can confidently do so," says the senior staff counsel, "we will offer our assessment of the legal merits of an appeal." The D.C. Circuit, however, follows a more "interest-based" or "facilitative" philosophy. Under the Ninth Circuit's program, case management and docket control is provided if mediation is not successful. About half of the civil docket goes to mediation conducted by six staff attorneys who screen incoming appeals based on a docketing statement filed by each party. In contrast, the Seventh Circuit's program selects cases on a random basis.[14]

A key issue in appellate ADR is whether clients should attend, and there is disagreement on this point between the programs. Some courts do not allow clients to participate without prior permission from the mediator. Other courts either invite or "strongly encourage" client attendance.[15]

---

13. "Appellate Mediation," 1 BNA ADR Rep. 75 (June 11, 1987).

14. Dick, supra note 11, at 28–29, 50.

15. Id. at 50.

Snow White and the Wicked Queen submit the fairness question to binding arbitration.

Drawing by Lorenz; © 1991
The New Yorker Magazine, Inc.

CHAPTER V

ARBITRATION

A. THE PROCESS OF PRIVATE ADJUDICATION

1. INTRODUCTION

William M. Landes & Richard A. Posner, Adjudication as a Private Good

8 J. Legal Stud. 235, 235–40 (1979).

Adjudication is normally regarded as a governmental function and judges as public officials. Even economists who assign a highly limited role

598 CHAPTER V ARBITRATION

to government consider the provision of judicial services as indisputably apt function of government; this was, for example, Adam Smith's view. Few economists (and few lawyers) realize that the provision of judicial services precedes the formation of the state; that many formally public courts long had important characteristics of private institutions (for example, until 1825 English judges were paid out of litigants' fees as well as general tax revenues); and that even today much adjudication is private (commercial arbitration being an important example).

* * *

1. *Introduction.* A court system (public or private) produces two types of service. One is dispute resolution—determining whether a rule has been violated. The other is rule formulation—creating rules of law as a by-product of the dispute-settlement process. When a court resolves a dispute, its resolution, especially if embodied in a written opinion, provides information regarding the likely outcome of similar disputes in the future. This is the system of precedent, which is so important in the Anglo–American legal system.

* * *

The two judicial services are in principle severable and in practice often are severed. Jury verdicts resolve disputes but do not create precedents. Legislatures create rules of law but do not resolve disputes. In the Anglo–American legal system rule formation is a function shared by legislatures and (especially appellate) courts; elsewhere judicial law making tends to be less important.

2. *Dispute Resolution.* Imagine a purely private market in judicial services. People would offer their services as judges, and disputants would select the judge whom they mutually found most acceptable. The most popular judges would charge the highest fees, and competition among judges would yield the optimum amount and quality of judicial services at minimum social cost. This competitive process would produce judges who were not only competent but also impartial—would thus fulfill the ideals of procedural justice—because a judge who was not regarded as impartial could not get disputes submitted to him for resolution: one party would always refuse.

A voluntary system of dispute resolution does not presuppose that the dispute has arisen from a consensual relationship (landlord-tenant, employer-employee, seller-buyer, etc.) in which the method of dispute resolution is agreed on before the dispute arose. All that is necessary is that when a dispute does arise the parties to it choose a judge to resolve it. Even if they are complete strangers, as in the typical accident case, the parties can still choose a judge to determine liability.

Although dispute resolution could thus be provided (for criminal as well as civil cases) in a market that would operate free from any obvious elements of monopoly, externality, or other sources of "market failure," it may not be efficient to banish public intervention entirely. Public intervention may be required (1) to ensure compliance with the (private) judge's decision and (2) to compel submission of the dispute to adjudication in the first place. The first of these public functions is straightforward, and no more compromises the private nature of the adjudication system described above than the law of trespass compromises the private property rights system. The second function, compelling submission of the dispute to judge, is more complex. If A accuses B of breach of contract, the next step in a system of private adjudication is for the parties to select a judge. But suppose B, knowing that any impartial judge would convict him, drags his feet in agreeing to select a judge who will hear the case, rejecting name after name submitted by A for his consideration. Although a sanction for this kind of foot-dragging (a sanction analogous to the remedies that the National Labor Relations Board provides for refusals to bargain collectively in good faith) is conceivable, there may be serious difficulty in determining when the bargaining over the choice of the judge is in bad faith—it is not bad faith, for example, to reject a series of unreasonable suggestions by the other side.

Two ways of overcoming the submission problem come immediately to mind. The first is for the parties to agree on the judge (or on the method of selecting him) before the dispute arises, as is done in contracts with arbitration clauses. This solution is available, however, only where the dispute arises from a preexisting voluntary relationship between the parties; the typical tort or crime does not. * * *

Another type of private solution to the problem of enforcement and the selection of a private judge is available when both parties to the dispute are members of the same (private) group or association. The group can expel any member who unreasonably refuses to submit to an impartial adjudication (perhaps by a judge selected by the group) or to abide by the judge's decision. To the extent that membership in the group confers a value over and above alternative opportunities, members will have incentives to bargain in good faith over the selection of the judge and to abide by his decision. In these circumstances dispute resolution can operate effectively without public intervention.

* * *

3. *Rule Production.* Private production of rules or precedents involves two problems. First, because of the difficulty of establishing property rights in a precedent, private judges may have little incentive to produce precedents. They will strive for a fair result between the parties in order to preserve a reputation for impartiality, but why should they make any effort to explain the result in a way that would provide guidance for future parties? To do so would be to confer an external, an uncompensated, benefit not only on future parties but also on competing judges. If anything, judges might deliberately avoid explaining their results because the demand for their services would be reduced by rules that, by clarifying the meaning of the law, reduced the incidence of disputes. Yet, despite all this, private judges just might produce precedents. We said earlier that competitive private judges would strive for a reputation for competence and

600   CHAPTER V ARBITRATION

impartiality. One method of obtaining such a reputation is to give reasons for a decision that convince the disputants and the public that the judge is competent and impartial. Competition could lead private judges to issue formal or informal "opinions" declaring their interpretation of the law, and these opinions—though intended simply as advertising—would function as precedents, as under a public judicial system. * * *

The second problem with a free market in precedent production is that of inconsistent precedents which could destroy the value of a precedent system in guiding behavior. If there are many judges, there is likely to be a bewildering profusion of precedents and no obvious method of harmonizing them. An individual contemplating some activity will have difficulty discovering its legal consequences because they will depend on who decides any dispute arising out of the activity.

* * *

[A] system of voluntary adjudication is strongly biased against the creation of precise rules of any sort. Any rule that clearly indicates how a judge is likely to decide a case will assure that no disputes subject to the rule are submitted to that judge since one party will know that it will lose. Judges will tend to promulgate vague standards which give each party to a dispute a fighting chance.

2.   ARBITRATION AND DISPUTE RESOLUTION

The traditional model of arbitration is precisely that of the "private tribunal"—private individuals, chosen voluntarily by the parties to a dispute in preference to the "official" courts, and given power to hear and "judge" their "case." The materials that follow explore the ramifications of this model, which is still the prevalent one. "Arbitration," however, cannot be so easily pigeon-holed, and in recent years the term has come to serve for a broad spectrum of dispute resolution processes. We will see later in this section how other models of arbitration have altered our conventional view of the process. Arbitration, for example, is sometimes imposed by law as a *mandatory,* non-consensual form of dispute resolution (See Section E.1 infra), and it has also been used to resolve kinds of disputes different from the traditional sort of "cases" which might otherwise have found their way into the judicial system.

There are many reasons why parties may choose arbitration as a more "efficient" means of dispute settlement than adjudication. To begin with, it seems likely that a dispute processed through arbitration will be disposed of more quickly than if the parties had made their way through the court system to a final judgment. In the commercial arbitration cases administered by the American Arbitration Association in 1999, an average of 114 days elapsed between the date the case was assigned to an arbitrator and the date the file was closed (by award or otherwise); the median processing time was 101 days. Arbitration tends to be a speedier process in part because it allows the parties to bypass long queues at the courthouse door and to schedule hearings at their own convenience. In addition, as we will see, arbitration procedure is relatively "informal"; pre-trial procedures, pleading, motion practice, and discovery are substantially streamlined or in many cases completely eliminated. And the arbitrator's decision is likely to be final: There is no delay imposed by any appeal process, and court review is highly restricted. It is not surprising, therefore, that surveys of practicing attorneys indicate that arbitration is overwhelmingly considered a speedier means of dispute resolution than either jury trial or bench trial; see Stipanowich, Rethinking American Arbitration, 63 Ind.L.J. 425, 460 (1988). Any savings in time and in related pre-and post-trial work are also likely to be reflected in savings in expense—for example, in lawyers' fees—although there can be no assurance that this will always be the case.

There may be other benefits as well. Taking a dispute out of the courtroom and into the relative informality of arbitration may reduce the enmity and heightened contentiousness which so often accompany litigation, and which work against a future cooperative relationship. The privacy of the process may also contribute to a lessening of hostility and confrontation. An arbitration hearing (unlike a trial) is not open to the public, and unless the result later becomes the subject of a court proceeding it is not a matter of public record.

Finally, the parties themselves are able to choose their "judges." They are free, therefore, to avail themselves of decision-makers with expert knowledge of the subject matter in dispute. The arbitrator may have a similar background to the parties, or be engaged in the same business; he is likely, then, to be familiar with the presuppositions and understandings of the trade. The usefulness of such expertise is particularly apparent when a contract dispute hinges on interpretation of the agreement—which in turn may depend on the content of trade custom and usage—or when the dispute is over whether goods sold meet the necessary technical standards. In such cases arbitration avoids the task (which may in some cases be insuperable) of educating judge or jury as to the content of these industry norms. In short, "the evidence from arbitration is that a single qualified lay judge is superior to six or twelve randomly selected laymen—on reflection, a not implausible suggestion."[1]

Lon Fuller, Collective Bargaining and the Arbitrator

1963 Wisc.L.Rev. 3, 11–12, 17.

Labor relations have today become a highly complicated and technical field. This field involves complex procedures that vary from industry to industry, from plant to plant, from department to department. It has developed its own vocabulary. Though the terms of this vocabulary often seem simple and familiar, their true meaning can be understood only when they are seen as parts of a larger system of practice, just as the umpire's

---

1. Landes & Posner, Adjudication as a (1979).
Private Good, 8 J.Legal Stud. 235, 252

CHAPTER V ARBITRATION

"You're out!" can only be fully understood by one who knows the objectives, the rules and the practices of baseball. I might add that many questions of industrial relations are on a level at least equal to that of the infield fly rule. They are not suitable material for light dinner conversation.

In the nature of things few judges can have had any very extensive experience in the field of industrial relations. Arbitrators, on the other hand, are compelled to acquire a knowledge of industrial processes, modes of compensation, complex incentive plans, job classification, shift arrangements, and procedures for layoff and recall.

Naturally not all arbitrators stand on a parity with respect to this knowledge. But there are open to the arbitrator, even the novice, quick methods of education not available to courts. An arbitrator will frequently interrupt the examination of witnesses with a request that the parties educate him to the point where he can understand the testimony being received. This education can proceed informally, with frequent interruptions by the arbitrator, and by informed persons on either side, when a point needs clarification. Sometimes there will be arguments across the table, occasionally even within each of the separate camps. The end result will usually be a clarification that will enable everyone to proceed more intelligently with the case. There is in this informal procedure no infringement whatever of arbitrational due process. On the contrary, the party's chance to have his case understood by the arbitrator is seriously impaired if his representative has to talk into a vacuum, if he addresses his words to uncomprehending ears.

The education that an arbitrator can thus get, say, in a half an hour, might take days if it had to proceed by qualifying experts and subjecting them to direct and cross examination. The courts have themselves recognized the serious obstacle presented by traditional methods of proof in dealing with cases involving a complex technical background.

* * *

Courts have in fact had difficulty with complicated commercial litigation. The problems here are not unlike those encountered in dealing with labor agreements. There are really few outstanding commercial judges in the history of the common law. The greatest of these, Lord Mansfield, used to sit with special juries selected from among experienced merchants and traders. To further his education in commercial practice he used to arrange dinners with his jurors. In Greek mythology it is reported that Minos prepared himself for a posthumous career as judge of shades by first exposing himself to every possible experience of life. It is not only in labor relations that the impracticability of such a program manifests itself.

NOTES AND QUESTIONS

1. Consider the possible use of arbitration in the following circumstances, and weigh its advantages and disadvantages from the perspective of dispute settlement:

A. The Process of Private Adjudication 603

In 1986, the Hunt brothers of Dallas filed two lawsuits in federal court seeking a total of $13.8 billion against some of the country's biggest banks. The banks were accused of fraud, breach of contract, and banking and antitrust law violations after they refused to restructure about $1.5 billion in debts owed by certain Hunt companies, including Placid Oil Company. In December 1986 the Hunts hired a Houston attorney, Stephen Susman, to take charge of the two lawsuits. Placid Oil was then involved in Chapter 11 bankruptcy proceedings. In a court filing seeking the bankruptcy judge's approval to represent Placid, Susman proposed to charge $600 per hour for his time:

> If the Susman firm is terminated by the Hunts for any reason other than malpractice—or the Hunts drop their lawsuits—the firm can pocket the entire retainer [of $1 million]. A malpractice or fee dispute would be arbitrated by the dean of the University of Texas School of Law, Mr. Susman's alma mater. A decision by the dean is final, the fee agreement says.

The Wall Street Journal, December 30, 1986, p. 4.

2. Later in this chapter we will consider in some detail the conduct of an arbitration proceeding, see Section D, infra. An arbitration, like a trial, entails the adversary presentation of evidence and argument before a neutral third party; as we will see, however, the rules of procedure and of evidence that constrain behavior at "trial" will be noticeably lacking. One federal court has observed that "[t]he present day penchant for arbitration may obscure for many parties who do not have the benefit of hindsight that the arbitration system is an inferior system of justice, structured without due process, rules of evidence, accountability of judgment and rules of law." Stroh Container Company v. Delphi Industries, Inc., 783 F.2d 743, 751 n. 12 (8th Cir.1986). As we proceed through this chapter, you should continue to ask if it is appropriate to consider arbitration as an "inferior system of justice." In what sense may this be true? Is the process merely another, somewhat streamlined, form of "trial"? Is there a danger that the pervasive influence of the judicial model may make it difficult for us to assess arbitration on its own terms? And in any event, isn't it clear that "whether to accept rougher justice in exchange for cost savings" is always "a question for contracting parties themselves"? Nagel v. ADM Investor Services, Inc., (65 F. Supp.2d 740, 745 N.D. Ill. 1999).

3. Lawyers are quick to perceive the advantages that inhere in the expeditious, "businesslike," expert settlement of a controversy provided by arbitration. These are largely advantages of "efficiency." However, whether arbitration ultimately turns out to be a blessing or a curse may in fact depend upon the tactical position of the particular client. Rapid resolution of a dispute may in theory benefit everyone; nevertheless the party against whom a claim is being asserted will probably find that there are offsetting advantages in delaying the ultimate reckoning. The larger of the disputants may also prefer to exploit the fact that its smaller opponent does not have the financial resources for an extended struggle. In addition, a party for whom the stakes and risk of loss are high may for that reason become less

604 CHAPTER V ARBITRATION

interested in "informality"—and more reluctant to chance a decision without having taken every possible advantage of the full panoply of legal procedures, including the ability to play out his hand to the bitter end. Similarly, a party who is aware that his case is a weak one may not always find a knowledgeable arbiter to be desirable; he may prefer instead to take his chances with a decision maker who is somewhat less expert and considerably more malleable. The General Counsel of Refac Technology Development Corporation has in fact written this about his company's patent litigation strategy:

> [I]f patent validity or infringement is questionable, why take a chance with an arbitration expert who will know exactly how weak the patent is and how dubious infringement is? It makes sense to take one's chance with a judge inexperienced in the technical and legal aspects involved. If the infringer is much bigger than the patentee or an entire industry has copied the patent, a jury trial would be much more beneficial than arbitration because of the sympathy and deep-pocket doctrine that can be played to the hilt.

Sperber, Overlooked Negotiating Tools, 20 Les Nouvelles 81 (June 1985).

4. The newly-appointed curator of drawings at the Getty Museum in Los Angeles came to believe that some of the Museum's expensive and highly-publicized acquisitions were in fact forgeries. "Some of the drawings were so patently bogus that they began to annoy me to look at them," he said. He was, however, instructed by the Museum director not to inform the Getty's trustees about the drawings' dubious authenticity. Over a number of years the relationship between the Museum and the curator worsened: The curator complained that the drawings department was being denied an adequate budget and gallery space—and in his opinion, the Museum "was punishing him and subverting his credibility in order to cast doubt on his forgery claims." He eventually sued the Museum for defamation, and the parties reached a settlement: The curator was to receive a large monetary payment and agreed to resign; the Getty promised to publish an exhaustive catalogue he had written of the Museum's drawings collection, part of which was devoted to the forgery allegations. The catalogue, however, was never published—and the curator was convinced that the Getty's intention was in fact to bury it in order to minimize embarrassment to the Museum. He later filed another suit, in which his allegations of fraud centered on the Getty's failure to publish his catalogue; the case was sent to arbitration.

In the course of the proceedings, the Getty's lawyers filed a motion with the arbitrator to keep the curator from discussing with the press anything discovered during the case: "The Getty argued that arbitration is an inherently confidential proceeding and so [the curator] should not be permitted to say anything to the media, especially about the forgeries." The motion, however, was denied—the arbitrator noting that after all, "Erin Brockovich was an arbitration." Peter Landesman, "A Crisis of Fakes," New York Times Magazine, March 18, 2001, at pp. 37, 38–40.

As we will see, arbitration has been used in a number of diverse contexts, to resolve many different types of disputes. However, it has flourished most in situations where parties to a contract have or aspire to have a continuing future relationship in which they will regularly deal with each other. The paradigm is the relationship between management and union in the administration of a collective bargaining agreement, or, perhaps, the relationship between a buyer and a seller of fabric in the textile industry. In both cases there is a history and a likelihood of continued mutual dependence by which both parties may profit; there also exist non-legal sanctions allowing either party to withdraw from (or seek to adjust) the relationship, or at least to withhold vital future cooperation. All this makes it easier to settle in advance on arbitration as a less disruptive method than litigation for resolving any future disputes. It also tends to induce the parties to comply with arbitration decisions once they are handed down (as does the feeling, in a long-term relation, that "awards are likely to be equalized over the long run and that erroneous awards can be dealt with through negotiation"[2]). In both cases there is an understandable reluctance to assert officially-defined legal "rights," or to rely on formal, technical arguments or on accusations of misconduct or impropriety—all of which may seem inappropriate in the context of a "family row" and which may hurt the prospects of future collaboration. And in both cases the parties may be more willing in advance to entrust to arbitrators the task of working out the details of their arrangement in accordance with the common values, the "shared norms," of the trade or of the "shop."

William M. Landes & Richard A. Posner, Adjudication as a Private Good

8 J.Legal Stud. 235, 245–47 (1979).

[I]f one party to a dispute expects that an impartial arbitrator would rule against him, he has an incentive to drag his feet in agreeing to the appointment of an arbitrator. Consistently with this point, writers on arbitration agree that the problem of selection makes arbitration a virtually unusable method of dispute resolution where there is no preexisting contractual or other relationship between the disputants. This suggests a clue to the superior ability of primitive compared to advanced societies to function without public institutions of adjudication. Primitive communities tend to be quite small and their members bound together by a variety of mutually advantageous relationships and interactions. Expulsion, outlawry, ostracism, and other forms of boycott or collective refusal to deal are highly effective sanctions in these circumstances. Another way of putting this point is that reputation, a factor recognized in the literature as deterring people from breaking contracts even in the absence of effective legal sanctions, is a more effective deterrent in a small community, where news

2. Getman, Labor Arbitration and Dispute Resolution, 88 Yale L.J. 916, 922–23 (1979).

CHAPTER V ARBITRATION

travels rapidly throughout the entire circle of an individual's business and social acquaintances, than in large, modern, impersonal societies.

Yet even in modern society, certain trade, religious, and other associations correspond, to a degree, to the close-knit, primitive community. For example, securities or commodities exchanges whose members derive substantial benefits from membership can use the threat of expulsion as an effective sanction to induce members to submit to arbitration. So can a religious association in which excommunication is regarded by members as a substantial cost[30]; so can a university. Exchanges, religious associations, and (private) universities are in fact important examples of modern "communities" in which private adjudication (whether called arbitration or something else) is extensively utilized in preference to public adjudication.

In The Matter of the Arbitration Between Mikel and Scharf

Supreme Court, Special Term, Kings County New York, 1980.
105 Misc.2d 548, 432 N.Y.S.2d 602, aff'd, 85 A.D.2d 604, 444 N.Y.S.2d 690 (1981).

■ ARTHUR S. HIRSCH, J.

This is a motion to confirm an arbitration award rendered by a rabbinical court.

[Respondents are the shareholders of a corporation that operates a nursing home. In 1973, the corporation agreed to lease premises from a partnership. Negotiations on behalf of the partnership were conducted primarily by Barad, one of the partners, and the agreed monthly rental was $25,208.

[In 1977 respondents contacted Barad and told him that because of business reverses, they would have to vacate the premises unless there were a substantial reduction in rent. After negotiations, an oral agreement was reached to reduce the monthly rental by $8000, and a writing to this effect was signed by respondents on behalf of the corporation and by Barad on behalf of the landlord.]

During the negotiations, respondents had met with other partners besides Barad, but at no time had they come in contact with petitioner or with his father, who acted as his son's surrogate in the arbitration proceedings and from whom petitioner had received the 6% interest in the partnership. * * *

In November, 1977, respondents received notice from the Union of Orthodox Rabbis to appear before a rabbinical court for a *"Din Torah"* or arbitration of a claim brought against them by petitioner. Respondents testified they refused to appear at first on grounds that they had no

---

30. The threat of excommunication was, for example, the ultimate sanction for refusal to submit to, or obey the decision of, the medieval English ecclesiastical courts, which had an immense jurisdiction covering matrimonial disputes, perjury, and a variety of other matters as well as strictly religious disputes.

knowledge of petitioner, but did appear after receiving written notice that refusal would result in the court's invoking a "sirov."

The first meeting of the rabbinical court, presided over by the requisite three rabbis, took place on Sunday, May 14, 1978. The respondents appeared with their attorney, who was present as their legal representative and to testify as witness to all meetings between [landlord] and [tenant], at which the attorney was present.

Respondents are persistent in their claim that theirs was a special appearance before the rabbinical tribunal to establish that there was never a business nor contractual relationship between the claimant and themselves, and therefore, a *Din Torah,* or arbitration, would be improper and invalid. Their participation thereafter was to obtain a determination on this limited issue, i.e., whether a *Din Torah* should be convened and not for a determination as to the merits of the claim.

The respondents were required by the court to sign a Hebrew Document entitled a "Mediation Note" which, in effect, is an agreement to voluntarily arbitrate "the dispute existing" between the parties. Respondent Asher Scharf, who has a complete understanding of the Hebrew language, contends that much discussion ensued until it was unequivocally established that the "dispute" referred to in the "Mediation Note" was the question of the propriety of having a *Din Torah* and that he overcame his conceded reluctance to sign the document when he was assured by the court of the limited scope of the dispute. Respondents were summoned and attended two additional meetings. At the insistence of the rabbinical court, respondents' attorney did not attend any meeting after the first. On December 31, 1978, a written judgment of the rabbinical court was rendered, in which respondents were directed, among other things, to pay to petitioner a lump sum of $9,000 and to make monthly payments of 6% of $23,000, representing petitioner's share of the rental due and owing to the [landlord].

Petitioner has moved for an order confirming the award, with respondents opposing and moving to vacate the award on numerous grounds.

Rabbinical Court–Din Torah

As earlier indicated, the customary arbitration proceeding was not utilized by the parties. An accepted, but more unusual forum was selected, that of arbitration by a tribunal of rabbis conducting a *Din Torah.*

The beginnings of Jewish arbitral institutions are traceable to the middle of the second century. Throughout the centuries, thereafter, in every country in which Jews have been domiciled, Jewish judicial authority has existed, via the institute of arbitration conducted by special rabbinical courts. Orthodox Jews, prompted by their religious, national feelings, accepted Jewish judicial authority, by resorting to the arbitration procedure of their own free will. This method of arbitration has the imprimatur of our own judicial system, as a useful means of relieving the burdens of the inundated courts dealing with civil matters. Through Talmudic sages, it is

608 CHAPTER V ARBITRATION

learned that special rules or procedures have been provided under which the rabbinical courts function as a *Din Torah* (literally translated as torah judgment), with Judaic or torah law as its basis. * * *

In addition to the procedural rules established by Judaic Law, there are state, civil, procedural rules for arbitration (CPLR, Article 75) to which the rabbinical court, as an arbitration forum, must also adhere.

* * *

Respondents [challenge] the rabbinical court's award, claiming first, the arbitration agreement was entered involuntarily, under duress and is consequently void, [and] second, charging the arbitrators with misconduct * * *.

Involuntary Agreement–Duress

Both parties are members of the orthodox Jewish community. Respondent's denial of the existence of any disputable issue between themselves and petitioner convinced them to refuse to appear for a *Din Torah* and they would not have done so had they not received the threat of a "sirov." Rabbis testifying for respondents stated that a sirov, literally translated as contempt of court, is a prohibitionary decree that subjects the recipient to shame, scorn, ridicule and ostracism by his coreligionists, fellow members of his community. Ostensibly, he is ostracized and scorned. Other Jews refuse to eat or speak with him. He is discredited and dishonored. The respondents maintain that the draconian measures of a sirov are sufficiently threatening so as to compel their compliance with the demand to appear. They claim they would have become outcasts among their friends and coreligionists. However, from other testimony, it appears that the sirov, while most assuredly ominous in its potential power, is honored in its breach. The court cannot, of course, know the actual state of mind of respondents and it may be that their fear of a sirov decree was real. However, it seems more plausible that if respondents believed the consequences so fearful, they would not, at this point, be willing to defy the rabbinical court by refusing to accept the arbitrator's determination. Undoubtedly, pressure was brought to bear to have them participate in the *Din Torah,* but pressure is not duress. Their decision to acquiesce to the rabbinical court's urgings was made without the coercion that would be necessary for the agreement to be void.

Misconduct

CPLR 7511 (subd [b], par. 1, cl [i]) allows for the vacation of an award if the rights of a party are prejudiced by corruption, fraud or misconduct. Courts have used the term misconduct to denote actions of fundamental unfairness, whether intentional or unintentional.

Respondents charge misconduct by the rabbinical tribunal in their refusal to permit respondents to have legal representation and, further, to hear testimony or accept material documents offered by respondents' attorney, as witness to the lease negotiations. This, they contend, violated their due process rights. Respondents appeared at the first meeting with their attorney, Abraham Bernstein. From the beginning, it became apparent the tribunal would not tolerate the presence of an attorney at a *Din Torah*. Petitioner's father strenuously objected, claiming he had no attorney to represent petitioner. At first, attorney Bernstein was not permitted to speak, but later was allowed to make a short statement in which he attempted to establish the fact that a lease was executed between the corporation tenant and the landlord partnership without personal involvement of the parties and when he offered to submit the lease and other documents for the perusal of the court, the papers were returned to him. Thereafter, he interjected himself wherever possible to explain respondents' position regarding the lack of legal connection between the parties. For the most part, the court refused to acknowledge him, quelling his attempts to speak or take part in the proceedings. He was not permitted to ask questions of petitioner or his father, who at all times acted as representative and voice of petitioner.

* * *

Biblical law requires that parties appear before a magistrate in person and not by proxy (*Deuteronomy* 19:17). For many years, this supported a Jewish judicial prejudice against proxies, including attorneys and even interpreters, it being determined essential that argument be heard directly from the mouths of litigants or witnesses. There was a tradition, however, that the high priest, when sued in court, could appoint an attorney to represent him (*Talmud Yerushalmi,* Sanhedrin 2:1, 19d). It may be this tradition that precipitated the admittance of defense attorneys into rabbinical courts. Where the parties were present to give testimony, thus permitting Judges to perceive their demeanor and evaluate their credibility, legal counsel was no longer considered to be anathema. The rabbinical court in the instant matter obviously did not abide by this accepted legal concept.

The tribunal's proclivity for conducting their court under outdated concepts resulted in inadvertent violations. Respondents were denied due process. The right of counsel, which is a constitutional right, is further enunciated in Article 75 of the CPLR, and is an unwaivable right. Consequently, respondent's participation without counsel, after receiving the court's warning to appear alone, did not have a negative effect on their inherent right to legal representation, the deprivation of which is sufficient to vitiate the award.

Respondent Asher Scharf's unrebutted testimony indicated that at a session he attended, one of the three rabbi arbitrators called him out to talk with him privately. The rabbi argued for a cash settlement, to be paid by respondent on the grounds that petitioner was a poor student. Scharf testified the rabbi asked, ''Well, what does a few thousand dollars mean to you?''

Under Judaic law (*Deuteronomy* 1:17), a Judge must judge impartially in favoring the rich or the poor. In an interpretation of this portion of the Torah, the foremost authority, Rashi, in *Commentary Rashi,* states that the version should be understood as follows: A judge "should not say: 'This is a poor man and his fellow (opponent) is rich and he will consequently obtain some support in a respectable fashion.' "

To ensure fairness, it is axiomatic and imperative that an arbitrator's impartiality be above suspicion. The rabbinical court was obviously prejudiced against respondents because of their affluence and considered the financial status of the parties above the issues. Such conduct, forbidden by the Torah, the law under which the rabbinical court has jurisdiction, constitutes another instance in which the tribunal deviated from its own *Din Torah* precepts.

The procedural format of the sessions was haphazard; no prescribed order was followed. A rabbinical court normally operates in a set manner, with presentation of claims, counterclaims, testimony of witnesses and cross-examinations conducted in a fairly orderly manner. This is not to say that any formal hearings are required. However, it appears that no semblance of administrative court proceeding, formal or informal, was followed by this rabbinical court. Witnesses were not called, real evidence was not accepted and no recognizable and required *Din Torah* procedure was followed. Under these highly unusual and chaotic conditions, a fair award could not be given.

* * *

Despite the established and well-grounded precedent that courts rarely set aside an arbitration award, in this instance the court finds it obligatory to vacate the award of the rabbinical court for the reasons enunciated above. A new arbitration proceeding will not be scheduled, as the court is convinced that no legal dispute exists between these particular parties.

NOTES AND QUESTIONS

1. Closely-knit Jewish communities throughout the Western world developed—out of necessity—a long-standing proscription against submitting intragroup disputes to hostile or uncomprehending secular courts. See Congregation B'nai Sholom v. Martin, 382 Mich. 659, 173 N.W.2d 504 (1969). At the same time such communities developed their own systems of dispute resolution. With assimilation into the wider society, the role of these autonomous tribunals has naturally declined; even today, however, a practice of rabbinical "arbitration" still persists in Jewish communities. The majority of cases heard in this country by Jewish courts seem to concern divorce matters. See, e.g., Avitzur v. Avitzur, 58 N.Y.2d 108, 459 N.Y.S.2d 572, 446 N.E.2d 136 (1983). For the modern history of Jewish tribunals, see Note, Rabbinical Courts: Modern Day Solomons, 6 Col.J.Law & Soc.Prob. 48 (1970); Israel Goldstein, Jewish Justice and Conciliation (1981); James Yaffe, So Sue Me! The Story of a Community Court (1972).

2. In a business or employment dispute, it is usually understood by the parties that a Jewish rabbinical tribunal "may seek to compromise the parties' claims, and is not bound to decide strictly in accordance with the

A. The Process of Private Adjudication

governing rules of Jewish law, but may more carefully weigh the equities of the situation." See Kingsbridge Center of Israel v. Turk, 98 A.D.2d 664, 469 N.Y.S.2d 732, 734 (1983). Is that what the tribunal attempted to do in the principal case?

3. Professor Marc Galanter has written that "[j]ust as health is not found primarily in hospitals or knowledge in schools, so justice is not primarily to be found in official justice-dispensing institutions. People experience justice (and injustice) not only (or usually) in forums sponsored by the state but at the primary institutional locations of their activity—home, neighborhood, workplace, business deal and so on * * *." This social ordering, found in a variety of institutional settings (such as universities, sports leagues, housing developments, and hospitals) he refers to as "indigenous law." He notes that although

> indigenous law may have the virtues of being familiar, understandable and independent of professionals, it is not always the expression of harmonious egalitarianism. It often reflects narrow and parochial concerns; it is often based on relations of domination; its coerciveness may be harsh and indiscriminate; protections that are available in public forums may be absent.

Galanter, Justice in Many Rooms: Courts, Private Ordering, and Indigenous Law, 19 J. Pluralism & Unofficial L. 1, 17–18, 25 (1981).

4. For further discussion of court review of "arbitration" awards, see Section C.4.a, infra.

3. Arbitration and the Application of "Rules"

The Landes and Posner excerpt at the beginning of this chapter introduces another recurrent theme in these materials. Many writers suggest that arbitration, as a voluntary and private process, may not proceed by formulating, applying, and communicating general principles of decision, or "rules." A number of related points form an essential backdrop for this discussion.

First of all—particularly outside the field of labor arbitration—arbitrators (unlike judges) commonly do not write reasoned opinions attempting to explain and justify their decisions. In fact the American Arbitration Association, which administers much commercial arbitration, actively discourages arbitrators from doing so. In addition, we do not in any event expect that an arbitrator will decide a case the way a judge does. We do not expect that he will necessarily "follow the law"—or indeed apply or develop any body of general rules as a guide to his decision. An arbitrator, it is said, "may do justice as he sees it, applying his own sense of law and equity to the facts as he finds them to be and making an award reflecting the spirit rather than the letter of the agreement."[1] Furthermore, a decision by any particular arbitrator will not necessarily control the result of later cases involving

---

1. In the Matter of the Arbitration between Silverman and Benmor Coats, Inc., 61 N.Y.2d 299, 308, 473 N.Y.S.2d 774, 779, 461 N.E.2d 1261, 1266 (1984).

other parties—or, indeed, have any precedential value at all for later arbitrators. And finally, an arbitrator's decision is not subject to later review and correction by a court to insure that general rules of law have been complied with. The highly restricted role courts play in passing on the decisions of arbitrators, and the implications of a system in which elaborate reasoned awards are rare, are discussed in some detail in Section C.4 infra.

What are some of the implications of a system of private justice in which cases are "decided," but without the use or communication of consistent rules of decision? When cases are diverted into a private forum, operating without a formal system of precedent, any judicial function of shaping future activity may be neglected. In addition, it may be more difficult for private parties to predict the future results of cases heard in these private tribunals. Information disseminated by courts in the form of precedents is used every day by private actors in routine decisions concerning which claims they should assert, and under what circumstances they should settle those claims. With no certainty as to the rule a particular arbitrator would apply—and with no consistent application of rules across the entire community of "competing" arbitrators, purporting independently to decide particular cases without reference to each other or to generally accepted rules—any firm basis on which to build future conduct is undermined:

> You cannot say today that a check need not contain an unconditional promise or order to pay to be negotiable and tomorrow that it must. You cannot say today that F.O.B. means free on board and tomorrow that it means only that the seller must get the goods as far as his shipping room. And so on. Mankind needs an irreducible minimum of certainty in order to operate efficiently. That irreducible minimum would seem to be better handled by the courts than by arbitration even though in the particular case the result would have been better decided in arbitration.[2]

However, unless the parties to an arbitration are "repeat players"—with a stake in the rules applied that extends beyond the result in the particular case—creating and promulgating "rules" of decision could from their point of view serve only to confer a benefit on *other* people, at the cost of increasing the duration and the expense of their own proceedings.

Of course, much of the above discussion has to be qualified. Any dichotomy between an ad hoc, particularistic system of private arbitration and a rule-and precedent-bound judiciary can easily be overstated. All first-year law students know that such a characterization can grotesquely exaggerate the predictability of court decisions and the meaningfulness of rules of decision in predicting or explaining the results of litigation. And even in the absence of a formal system of precedent, criteria of decision can be agreed on, developed, and communicated in other ways: by private

---

2. Mentschikoff, The Significance of Arbitration—A Preliminary Inquiry, 17 Law & Contemporary Problems 698, 709 (1952).

associations, through past practice and the evolution of trade custom, and particularly through the pre-existing contractual relations of the parties. Lawyers who are experienced in arbitration tend to feel that they are able to predict the results of arbitration with some certainty, at least in part because these sources supply rules of decision likely to be consistently applied. It is, of course, a separate question whether the rules so applied will be consonant with officially-declared public values, or whether the arbitration process may implicate important public policy concerns which should be reserved to the official court system. This is a subject which is explored further in later sections.

In addition, the arbitration of disputes arising under collective bargaining agreements has come to evolve certain unique characteristics, distinguishing it from other forms of private dispute resolution. It does appear to be the general practice for *labor* arbitrators to write explanations and justifications—sometimes elaborate ones—for their decisions; these decisions are often publicly reported, cited to later arbitrators, and relied on in later cases. "An extensive survey of labor arbitration disclosed that 77 percent of the 238 responding arbitrators believed that precedents, even under *other* contracts, should be given 'some weight.' "[3]As we will see, there has developed a "common-law" of labor arbitration. In addition, the growth of labor arbitration over the last 50 years to a central place in the settlement of labor disputes has been accompanied by the development of the profession of "labor arbitrator." In the commercial area it may be unusual for an arbitrator to decide more than one or two cases a year, but for many labor arbitrators arbitration constitutes a primary source of their livelihood. One may suspect that Landes and Posner's point concerning the advertising value of reasoned opinions may have particular relevance here.

4. "RIGHTS" ARBITRATION AND "INTEREST" ARBITRATION

"Interest" arbitration is distinguished from the more familiar grievance or "rights" arbitration by the fact that in the former situation the designated neutral is employed to determine the actual contract terms which will bind the parties during the life of their new agreement, while in the latter situation the arbitrator is only empowered to decide disputes concerning the interpretation and application of the terms of an already existing contract. The grievance arbiter is generally precluded from adding to or modifying the terms of the contract in dispute.[4]

The distinction between "rights" and "interest" arbitration is a familiar one. You will often see reference to it, particularly in relation to the arbitration of labor-management disputes. The paradigm of a "rights" arbitration is a hearing on the grievance of an employee alleging that he has been discharged "without just cause." The paradigm of an "interest" arbitration is a hearing held at the expiration of a collective bargaining

---

3. Frank Elkouri & Edna A. Elkouri, How Arbitration Works (4th ed. 1985) 418.

4. Craver, The Judicial Enforcement of Public Sector Interest Arbitration, 21 B.C.L.Rev. 557, 558 n. 8 (1980).

614 CHAPTER V ARBITRATION

agreement, after negotiations over a union's demand for higher wage rates in a "new" contract have failed. While "interest" arbitration remains an unusual and infrequent device in comparison to other forms of arbitration, it is quite commonly resorted to in resolving disputes over the terms of employment of public employees. Public employees, such as police or school teachers, are usually forbidden to engage in strikes; economic pressure, and the usual tests of economic strength used in the private sector to determine contract terms after a bargaining impasse, are therefore limited in the public interest. "Interest" arbitration to determine the terms of a new contract when bargaining fails provides a common alternative mechanism. In many cases, in fact, state statutes impose this as a *mandatory* means of settlement. See Section E.1 infra. Such legislation in effect gives to public employee unions the "right" to resort to the arbitration mechanism to determine the future terms of employment.

Now compare the following three cases. Are these examples of "rights" or of "interest" arbitration? What precisely are the differences, if any, between them?

(a) A law firm entered into a lease of space in an office building. The term of the lease was ten years. At the firm's request, a clause was added to the lease by which it would have the option to renew the lease for an additional ten years; it provided that "rental for the renewal term shall be in such amount as shall be agreed upon by the parties based on the comparative rental values of similar properties as of the date of the renewal and on comparative business conditions of the two periods." The lease contained a general arbitration clause providing that "all disputes relating to" the lease shall be settled by arbitration. The parties fail to agree on a rental for the renewal term.

(b) A coal supply agreement provided that for a period of ten years a coal company would tender and a power company would purchase specified quantities of coal. There was a base price per ton, and a provision for the calculation of adjustments in base price upon changes in certain labor costs and in "governmental impositions." The agreement also provided:

> Any gross proven inequity that may result in unusual economic conditions not contemplated by the parties at the time of the execution of this Agreement may be corrected by mutual consent. Each party shall in the case of a claim of gross inequity furnish the other with whatever documentary evidence may be necessary to assist in effecting a settlement.

Another clause called for "any unresolved controversy between the parties arising under this Agreement" to be submitted to arbitration. Four years later, after a rapid escalation in the price of coal, the open market price of coal of the same quality was more than three times the current adjusted base price under the agreement. The coal company requested an adjustment in the contract price which the power company adamantly rejected.[5]

---

5. See Georgia Power Co. v. Cimarron Coal Corp., 526 F.2d 101 (6th Cir.1975).

A. The Process of Private Adjudication

(c) An agreement between a newspaper and its employees was to last for three years, with a provision that "this contract shall remain in effect until all terms and conditions of employment for a succeeding contract term are resolved either through negotiation or through arbitration." After a bargaining deadlock, the union moved for arbitration. The employer presented to the arbitrator a number of items which it wanted included in the agreement for the new term, including the right to make layoffs on account of automation or the introduction of new processes. The Union also presented a number of issues to the arbitrator, including "wages; mailers brought up to mechanical department [wage] scale; proof room brought up to composing room scale; pension; sick leave; vacations; increased mileage; grievance procedure; jurisdiction of jobs—need for job descriptions; holidays; jury and witness duty; overtime after thirty hours during holiday weeks; night differential; life insurance; option under Blue Cross for eyeglasses; option under Dental Plan for payment for dentures; paid uniforms for pressmen; addition of grandparent and guardian to funeral leave."

As these examples illustrate, it may sometimes be difficult satisfactorily to distinguish an "interest" dispute from one concerning "rights." Moreover, from a broader perspective, even in what are assumed to be "rights" disputes (such as employee grievances) the process of interpretation must necessarily involve considerable flexibility. In complex and long-term relationships there will inevitably be some uncertainty concerning matters inadvertently (or purposely) left open when the contract was entered into, or where past solutions are no longer neatly adapted to changed needs. When the parties participate in this procedure, they are in a very real sense taking part in a process which "involves not only the settlement of the particular dispute but also interstitial rule-making"[6]—a process aimed at creating, refining, and elaborating for the future the rules which will govern their relationship.

The supposed distinction between "rights" and "interest" arbitration may then be—as are most distinctions in the law—a mere question of degree or emphasis. However, this is not to say that it is without analytic utility or practical importance. Parties to a contract who are considering arbitration as a device to handle future disputes must ask themselves a number of questions. The distinction between "rights" and "interest" arbitration forces them to ask some important ones. To what extent is arbitration suitable for establishing the basic structure, the essential parameters of the relationship? What important differences are there between doing this, and asking the arbitrator merely to spell out the implications of a bargain they have hammered out for themselves? Are there reasons to

---

6. See Feller, A General Theory of the Collective Bargaining Agreement, 61 Cal-if.L.Rev. 663, 744–45 (1973).

CHAPTER V ARBITRATION

hesitate before confiding this task to arbitrators as a substitute for their own bargaining? A few of the relevant considerations are suggested in the paragraphs that follow.

Assume that the parties know from the outset—either because of a mandatory statutory procedure, or a contractual agreement—that they will later be able to turn to arbitration to determine their future rights. How might this affect the dynamics of the bargaining process? Is it likely that one or the other of them may assume more extreme positions at the bargaining stage, trusting that an arbitrator will later seek out a middle ground? Is there a danger that the parties may use the possibility of arbitration as a crutch, and resort to it too readily rather than face the hard issues themselves? Is it likely that negotiators will resort to the arbitration mechanism to insulate themselves from the dissatisfaction of their own constituencies—union members, or taxpayers—who might personally hold them accountable for inevitable concessions made in negotiation?

If the contract confides to arbitrators the ultimate responsibility for determining the essential rights of the parties in the future, what standards are the arbitrators to use? The possible value choices are far more diverse, the possible criteria of decision far more nebulous, than in cases where an arbitrator acts more "judicially" in deciding whether particular goods are defective or whether certain employee conduct merited discharge.

In Twin City Rapid Transit Co., 7 Lab.Arb. 845 (1947), a collective bargaining agreement between a privately-owned company and an employee union provided that "if at the end of any contract year the parties are unable to agree upon the terms of a renewal contract, the matter shall be submitted to arbitration." In his decision, the arbitrator wrote:

Arbitration of contract terms * * * calls for a determination, upon considerations of policy, fairness, and expediency, of what the contract rights ought to be. In submitting this case to arbitration, the parties have merely extended their negotiations—they have left it to this board to determine what they should, by negotiation, have agreed upon. We take it that the fundamental inquiry, as to each issue, is: what should the parties themselves, as reasonable men, have voluntarily agreed to?

In answering that question, we think that prime consideration should be given to agreements voluntarily reached in comparable properties in the general area. For example, wages and conditions in Milwaukee, the city of comparable size nearest geographically to Minneapolis and St. Paul, whose transit company is neither bankrupt, municipally owned, nor municipally supported, might reasonably have had greater weight in the negotiations between the parties than Cleveland or Detroit, both municipally owned and farther distant, or Omaha and Council Bluffs, more distant in miles and smaller in population. Smaller and larger cities, however, and cities in other geographical areas should have secondary consideration, for they disclose trends and, by indicating what other negotiators, under different circumstances, have found reasonable, furnish a guide to what these parties, in view of the differing circumstances, might have found reasonable. * * * To repeat, our endeavor will be to decide the issues as, upon the evidence, we think reasonable negotiators, regardless of their social or economic theories might have decided them in the give and take process of bargaining. We agree with the company that the interests of stockholders and public must be considered, and consideration of their interests will enter into our considerations as to what the parties should reasonably have agreed on.

NOTES AND QUESTIONS

1. Does the inquiry in *Twin City Rapid Transit* ("what should the parties themselves, as reasonable men, have voluntarily agreed to?") seem meaningful to you in light of your understanding of the negotiation process? Should the arbitrator try to reconstruct the murky totality of the bargaining process, including the various dimensions of bargaining power, when the parties' own negotiations have failed? Can he do so? Or is he necessarily reduced to acting as a "legislator" and mandating what he thinks the "fair" result would be? Presented with all the outstanding bargaining issues with which the arbitrator was faced in case (c) above, how does he go about distinguishing between issues as to which the parties have reached a serious impasse and "throwaway" issues placed on the table for bargaining advantage? Is it feasible to impose criteria in advance on the arbitrator, by statute or contract? Or to structure the process so as to limit the scope of his discretion?

2. Of course, *courts* daily adjudicate grievances and disputes concerning "rights." Do they *also* handle types of disputes which might be characterized as "interest" disputes? In contracts cases, as you remember, the traditional wisdom is that courts "interpret" agreements, but they will not "make a contract for the parties" or enforce arrangements where the parties have merely "agreed to agree." The received learning has it that

> "[b]efore the power of law can be invoked to enforce a promise, it must be sufficiently certain and specific so that what was promised can be ascertained. Otherwise, a court, in intervening, would be imposing its own conception of what the parties should or might have undertaken, rather than confining itself to the implementation of a bargain to which they have mutually committed themselves. * * * [A] mere agreement to agree, in which a material term is left for future negotiations, is unenforceable."

Joseph Martin, Jr. Delicatessen, Inc. v. Schumacher, 52 N.Y.2d 105, 436 N.Y.S.2d 247, 417 N.E.2d 541 (1981).

Is that distinction in contract law the equivalent of the "rights"/"interest" dichotomy?

An economist would say that when courts insist on a certain level of clarity and completeness in the terms of a contract, they are attempting to insure that the deal is "allocatively efficient"—roughly, that it serves to

618 CHAPTER V ARBITRATION

reallocate resources to higher-valued uses—and that they do so by assuring that the deal has been bargained out by the parties themselves, in terms of their own assessments of their own interests. They may also be trying to prevent parties from taking a "free ride" on the public court system by shifting onto the courts the burden of determining contract terms. Do any of the same objections apply to "interest" arbitration?

The reluctance of courts to help in fashioning bargains left incomplete by the parties may be changing. Compare Sun Printing & Publishing Ass'n v. Remington Paper & Power Co., 235 N.Y. 338, 139 N.E. 470 (1923)—a wooden mainstay of the Contracts curriculum—with David Nassif Associates v. United States, 557 F.2d 249 (Ct.Cl.1977), 644 F.2d 4 (Ct.Cl.1981). See also Uniform Commercial Code §§ 2–204(3), 2–305. Or is it fair to say that courts, like arbitrators, have been doing much the same thing all along, under the guise of "interpretation"—but without admitting it?

3. Recall Lon Fuller's suggestion that the adjudicative process may not be well-suited to resolve what he calls "polycentric" or "many-centered" disputes, in which the resolution of any one issue may have "complex repercussions" for other aspects of the dispute. See Chapter I, supra p. 24. Are any of the "interest" disputes we are looking at here "polycentric"? Do Fuller's objections apply to arbitration as well as to the judicial process? How might an "interest" arbitrator proceed so as to minimize the problems that Fuller raises?

4. The arbitrator in an "interest" arbitration may be asked to determine the wages to be paid to employees in a "new" or renewal contract. How relevant in such a determination is the employer's claim of financial hardship or inability to pay? Is the answer in any way dependent on whether the arbitrator suspects the employer's "hardship" is due to managerial inefficiency, or to general conditions in a declining industry?

In one case an arbitrator, granting a union's requested wage increase, rejected the employer's claim by writing that

> The *price of labor* must be viewed like any other commodity which needs to be purchased. If a new truck is needed, the City does not plead poverty and ask to buy the truck for 25% of its established price. It can shop various dealers and makes of truck to get the best possible buy. But in the end the City either pays the asked price or gets along without a new truck.

In re City of Quincy, Illinois and International Association of Machinists, 81 Lab.Arb. 352, 356 (1982).

Compare In re School Board of the City of Detroit and Detroit Federation of Teachers, 93 Lab. Arb. 648 (1989). In this case the arbitrator accepted the union's argument that in terms of comparison with other school districts the salary position of Detroit schoolteachers "is too far down in the ranks, * * * is deteriorating and eroded by inadequate increases and the cost of living"; "the Union's contention that [a] 7% [increase] is necessary to preserve the *status quo ante* is a sound one." Nevertheless the arbitrator ordered a wage increase of only 5%:

The deficit incurred by the district, coupled with its continued precarious financial position, * * * all make it clear that these are perilous times for the state of education in Detroit. * * * We must be certain that any award involving salaries does not detract from or interfere with the district's educational program. * * * [T]he fact is that Detroit is very much at the margin and the voters might rebuke the District if an excessive wage increase was perceived to capture all available funds, without any consideration of educational enhancement.

5. In the case of a public employer, can the arbitrator weigh the claims of employees against other claims to public funds? Should the arbitrator take into account the employer's ability to pass on any increase in wages to others—to taxpayers or to the customers of a public utility? This may of course entail the exercise of some delicate judgment on matters of social and economic policy. In addition, the arbitrator is a creature of contract, hired and paid by employer and union: Is it appropriate for him in the course of making his decision to weigh the interests of those who are *not* parties to the agreement? See In re Nodak Rural Elect. Coop. and Int'l Bro. of Elect. Workers, 78 Lab.Arb. 1119 (1982) (rural North Dakota electrical cooperative; "This arbitrator grew up on an Iowa farm in the 1930's so he understands the meaning of a depressed farm economy and is sympathetic to the farmer's current conditions. * * * It is not likely that it would be wise for either the company or the union to ignore the condition of the farm economy. After all, the farmers and Nodak employees are dependent on each other. The farmers must be able to pay their bills in order for Nodak employees to retain their jobs and get paid.").

6. Can an existing "interest" arbitration clause be invoked in order to obtain inclusion of a similar clause in a *new* contract? Courts that have answered "no" have reasoned in this way:

The contract arbitration system could be self-perpetuating; a party, having once agreed to the provision, may find itself locked into that procedure for as long as the bargaining relationship endures. Exertion of economic force to rid oneself of the clause is foreclosed, for the continued inclusion of the term is for resolution by an outsider. Parties may justly fear that the tendency of arbitrators would be to continue including the clause * * *.

[T]he perpetuation of [interest] arbitration clauses in successive contracts may well serve to increase industrial unrest. Under [interest] arbitration, an outsider imposes contract terms, perhaps * * * unguided by any agreed-upon standards. In these circumstances, a disappointed party can readily believe that the arbitrator lacked appreciation of its needs or failed to apply appropriate standards, for example, "fair wages." * * * The result is that a party's dissatisfaction with an award may be aggravated by doubts about its legitimacy. The likelihood that one party will feel aggrieved by a contract arbitration award increases as parties move from contract to contract. The factors which determine the parties' relative strength for strikes and lockouts often changes with the passage of time. * * * Courts cannot bind the parties in

620 CHAPTER V ARBITRATION

perpetuity to forego use of economic weapons in support of bargaining positions.

NLRB v. Columbus Printing Pressmen & Assistants' Union No. 252, 543 F.2d 1161, 1169–70 (5th Cir.1976).

The *Columbus Printing* court also held that in negotiating the terms of a collective bargaining agreement, a union may not insist on the inclusion of an "interest" arbitration clause; to bargain to an "impasse" on this issue would constitute an "unfair labor practice."

B. SOME FREQUENT USES OF ARBITRATION

1. COMMERCIAL ARBITRATION

William C. Jones, Three Centuries of Commercial Arbitration in New York: A Brief Survey

1956 Wash.U.L.Q. 193, 209–10, 218–19.

[I]t is commonplace among those who write about arbitration that it has been in use for centuries.

* * *

[E]nough material on arbitration has been uncovered to show fairly conclusively that arbitration was in constant and widespread use throughout the colonial period in New York. * * * Seemingly, arbitration was used primarily in situations where the decision would not be entirely for one side or the other, but where there was, rather, considerable area for negotiation. The settlement of an account resulting from a long course of dealing between two merchants is an example. Land boundaries and the distribution of the proceeds from a privateering expedition are others. Evidently, from the way in which individuals felt it worthwhile to advertise in the newspapers their willingness to arbitrate, there was some social pressure to arbitrate a dispute before taking it to court, and even to submit it to arbitration after the suit was begun. This tends to substantiate a feeling that one function of arbitration was to supply a final stage in the negotiation process between two disputants and that a willingness to negotiate was highly esteemed in the community.

* * *

[T]he existence of the practice of extensive arbitration over so long a period of time in the mercantile community tends to show that, as used by merchants, arbitration is not really a substitute for court adjudication as something that is cheaper or faster or whatever,[112] but is rather a means of dispute settling quite as ancient—for all practical purposes anyway—as

---

112. Though, interestingly enough, arbitration was presented as such an alternative in the eighteenth century in almost the same language as is used today.

court adjudication, and that it has, traditionally, fulfilled quite a different function. The primary function of arbitration is to provide the merchants fora where mercantile disputes will be settled by merchants. This, in turn, suggests that merchants wish to form, and have for a long time succeeded in forming, a separate, and, to some extent, self-governing community, independent of the larger unit. For law this means that courts may perform, in the commercial field at least, a different function from that which we usually assign to them. In many cases, they may not be the primary fora for adjudication. If this is true, when they are called upon to decide a commercial case in one of these areas, it will be either after another adjudicatory agency has acted or because the other system cannot, or will not, cope with the case. In some areas, courts may almost never get a case. * * * Insofar as this area, in which arbitration is and—most importantly—has always been the primary dispute-settling agency, is an important one (and an area which includes stockbrokers, produce brokers, coffee merchants, etc., seems to be such an area), it cannot really be said that one has studied commercial law, in the sense of the rules that actually guide the settlement of disputes involving commercial matters, if he has studied only the reports of appellate courts and legislation. We cannot even understand the significance of the "law" contained in the reports and statutes until we have studied arbitration decisions. * * *

Having gone so far with hypothesis, one may be forgiven for going a little farther and suggesting that the existence of a sufficient sense of community identity or separateness on the part of merchants to cause them to have a separate adjudicatory system tends to show that there is a mercantile community which is, to a considerable degree, self-governing. This community has existed in this form for centuries. Its existence suggests that there may be others—religious and educational communities come to mind.

Soia Mentschikoff, Commercial Arbitration

61 Col.L.Rev. 846, 848–54 (1961).

The first thing to be noted is that although commonly thought of as a single type phenomenon, both the structure and the process of commercial arbitration are determined by the different institutional contexts in which it arises. There are three major institutional settings in which commercial arbitration appears as a mechanism for the settlement of disputes.

The simplest is when two persons in a contract delineating a business relationship agree to settle any disputes that may arise under the contract by resort to arbitration before named arbitrators or persons to be named at the time of the dispute. In this, which can be called individuated arbitration, the making of all arrangements, including the procedures for arbitration, rests entirely with the parties concerned. Although we do not know, we believe that the chief moving factors here are: (1) a desire for privacy as, for example, in certain crude oil situations where such arrangements exist; (2) the availability of expert deciders; (3) the avoidance of possible legal difficulties with the nature of the transaction itself; and (4) the random acceptance by many businessmen of the idea that arbitration is faster and less expensive than court action.

A second type of arbitration arises within the context of a particular trade association or exchange. The group establishes its own arbitration machinery for the settlement of disputes among its members, either on a voluntary or compulsory basis, and sometimes makes it available to non-members doing business in the particular trade. A particular association may also have specialist committees, which are investigatory in character, with the arbitration machinery handling only the private disputes involving nonspecialist categories of cases. * * *

The third setting for commercial arbitration is found in administrative groups, such as the American Arbitration Association, the International Chamber of Commerce, and various local chambers of commerce, which provide rules, facilities, and arbitrators for any persons desiring to settle disputes by arbitration. Many trade associations with insufficient business to warrant separate organizations make special arrangements with one of these groups to process disputes that arise among their members.

* * *

Factors Determining the Need for Arbitration

At this point it is useful to distinguish between those factors that can be said to produce a need for arbitration machinery in commercial groups and those factors that merely make it desirable. The reasons commonly given for arbitration—speed, lower expense, more expert decision, greater privacy—are appealing to all businessmen, and yet not all utilize arbitration. It seems reasonably clear, therefore, that for some trades these factors are of greater importance than for others, and that for some trades there must be countervailing values in not resorting to arbitration. We postulated three factors as being theoretically important in determining whether or not a particular trade needed institutionalized use of arbitration, and incorporated questions relating to these factors in our trade association questionnaire.

The first factor was the nature of the economic function being performed in relation to the movement of the goods by the members of the association. We postulated that persons primarily buying for resale, that is merchants in the original sense of the term, were much more likely to be interested in speed of adjudication, and that since price allowance would be a central remedy for defects in quality or, indeed, for nondelivery, the speed and low cost characteristics of arbitration would be particularly attractive to them, thus leading to the creation of institutionalized machinery. The trade associations in which such merchants constitute all or part of the membership reported as follows: 48 percent use institutionalized machinery, 34 percent make individual arrangements for arbitration, and only 18 percent never arbitrate. These figures are to be contrasted with the reports from those trade associations that stated that their memberships did not include any merchants. In those groups 23 percent reported the existence of institutionalized arbitration, 44 percent reported individual arrangements, and 33 percent reported no arbitration whatever.

The second major factor that we thought would be important in determining the need for arbitration was the participation of the members of the association in foreign trade. Apart from the enhanced possibility of delay inherent in transnational law suits, when the parties to a transaction are governed by different substantive rules of law, resort to the formal legal system poses uncertainty and relative unpredictability of result for at least one of the parties. This uncertainty and unpredictability is increased by the fact that the very rules governing the choice of the applicable law are themselves relatively uncertain and are not uniform among the nations of the world. Faced with such an uncertain formal legal situation, any affected trade group is apt to develop its own set of substantive rules or standards of behavior as the controlling rules for its members. Obviously, when a trade group develops its own rules of law, it requires as deciders of its disputes persons who are acquainted with the standards it has developed. Since this knowledgeability does not reside in the judges of any formal legal system, the drive toward institutionalized private machinery is reinforced.

* * *

The third factor that we thought would bear on the need for arbitration machinery relates to the kind of goods dealt with by the members of the association. One of the major areas of dispute among businessmen centers on the quality of the goods involved. If, therefore, the goods are such as not to be readily susceptible of quality determination by third persons, arbitration or, indeed, inspection, is an unlikely method of settling disputes. If goods are divided into raws, softs, and hards, the differences in their suitability for third party adjudication becomes relatively clear. On the whole, raws are a fungible commodity, one bushel of #1 wheat being very much like another bushel of #1 wheat. On the other hand, hards, which consist of items like refrigerators and automobiles, are not viewed by their producers as essentially fungible, however they may appear to the layman. We did not believe that Ford would like to have General Motors sitting on disputes involving the quality of Ford cars, or vice versa. Moreover, quality differentials in raws can normally be reflected by price differentials, but defects in hard goods frequently affect their usefulness and therefore price differential compensation is not feasible. Thus, the normal sales remedy for raws has come to be price allowance, whereas the normal sales remedy for hard goods has come to be repair or replacement. Raws, involving fungibility and ease of finding an appropriate remedy, are therefore highly susceptible to third party adjudication, whereas hard goods tend to move away from such adjudication. Soft goods, which are an intermediate category and range from textiles to small hardware, we thought would constitute a neutral category.

In our survey of exchanges dealing in grain and livestock, 100 percent of those responding reported the use of institutionalized arbitration. There are, of course, other reasons for such a unanimous response by the exchanges, but the nature of the goods involved is a very important one. The trade association survey showed that of all the reporting associations, dealings in raws, 46 percent had machinery, 29 percent made individual arrangements, and only 25 percent never arbitrated. On the other hand, only 4 percent of those reporting hards as their basic goods had machinery, 46 percent made individual arrangements, and 50 per cent never arbitrated. * * *

To the extent that the factors leading to institutionalized machinery reinforce each other, as, for example, in the case of an association reporting that its members have an import relationship to foreign trade, deal in raws, and consist of merchants, the existence of arbitration machinery rises to approximately 100 percent. When the contrary report is made, that is, that the membership consists of manufacturers of hard goods engaged only in domestic business, the percentage drops off to about 8 percent.

We can thus say that the presence of institutionalized arbitration is a strong index of the existence of a generally self-contained trade association having its own self-regulation machinery and that the forces leading to institutionalized arbitration also, therefore, tend to lead to the creation of self-contained, self-governing trade groups.

Note: The American Arbitration Association

The AAA is a private non-profit organization founded in 1926 "to foster the study of arbitration, to perfect its techniques and procedures under arbitration law, and to advance generally the science of arbitration." It works actively to publicize and promote arbitration. Of far greater importance, however, is its central role in the administration of much of the arbitration that takes place in this country. The parties to a contract will frequently stipulate that disputes which later arise are to be arbitrated under the auspices of the AAA. This means, for one thing, that the proceedings will automatically be governed by AAA rules. In a commercial case, the AAA's "Commercial Arbitration Rules" will resolve questions concerning the method of choosing arbitrators, their powers, time limits for various steps in the proceedings, and the conduct of the hearing. There are also alternative sets of rules available for adoption in particular trades. In the construction industry for example, use of the AAA's Construction Industry Arbitration Rules (recommended by such trade groups as the American Institute of Architects and the American Society of Civil Engineers) has become standard. The AAA also administers a large number of labor arbitrations under its Voluntary Labor Arbitration Rules, and uninsured motorist accident arbitrations under its Accident Claims Arbitration Rules. In all these cases, using contracts that incorporate pre-existing bodies of rules saves the parties the burden, costs, and delay of having to negotiate and spell out an entire code for the conduct of the arbitration.

Over 194,000 arbitration cases were filed with the AAA in 2000. Of these, 17,791 were commercial cases; 4,677 were construction cases; 13,680 were labor cases, and 2,049 were individual employment cases. (By far the largest part of the AAA's arbitration caseload was made up of uninsured-

B. SOME FREQUENT USES OF ARBITRATION

motorist and no-fault insurance cases).[1] The Association maintains a panel of 6000 arbitrators willing to serve in commercial cases (and another panel of more than 3000 arbitrators for construction cases); the parties select their arbitrators from a number of names suggested by AAA administrators, who furnish information concerning the background and experience of the candidates. The AAA itself will appoint the arbitrator to hear the case if the parties cannot agree on a name. In addition, during the course of the proceeding the AAA staff will furnish a variety of administrative services, concerning, for example, notice to the parties, pre-hearing conferences, and the scheduling, location, and conduct of the hearing—all intended to insure that the process runs smoothly and that the chances of a successful later challenge to the award are minimized. Selection of arbitrators and arbitration procedure are discussed in some detail at Section D.1.a, infra.

While the AAA remains the dominant arbitral institution in the United States, it has in recent years been subject to increasing competition for business from a number of more entrepreneurial for-profit rivals, including Judicial Arbitration & Mediation Services, Inc., (JAMS) and National Arbitration Forum (NAF). See Pollock, "Arbitrator Finds Role Dwindling as Rivals Grow," Wall St. J., April 28, 1993 at B1.

NOTES AND QUESTIONS

A survey of textile disputes arbitrated through the AAA found that much textile arbitration was handled by a relatively small group of lawyers: Only five lawyers were counsel to 43 of the 182 parties who submitted to arbitration in one of the years studied. "When asked to compare the predictability of an arbitrator's decision to that of a judge or the verdict of a jury, each of the five lawyers replied without hesitation that the decision of an arbitrator was by far the 'most predictable,' that a judge's decision was 'predictable at some but not all times,' and a jury's decision was 'virtually one of pure chance.' "Bonn, The Predictability of Nonlegalistic Adjudication, 6 Law & Soc'y Rev. 563 (1972). However, the author attributed this predictability largely to the fact that sellers would carefully "screen" or "preselect" cases they took to arbitration. Sellers would pursue arbitration primarily against "buyers who are marginal firms or who have weak or specious claims"; where a buyer had "a strong case, say one based on a legitimate quality claim," and was a good future business prospect, sellers would choose instead to settle the dispute informally.

In another survey of textile arbitration cases the same author found that out of 78 cases, "business relations were resumed" following the arbitration in only 14. Bonn, Arbitration: An Alternative System for Handling Contract Related Disputes, 17 Admin.Sci.Q. 254, 262 (1972). Is this clearly an indication that arbitration may be as "lethal to continuing relations" as litigation? Cf. Galanter, Reading the Landscape of Disputes:

---

[1] American Arbitration Association, *Dispute Resolution Times*, April–June 2001, at pp. 1, 19.

626 CHAPTER V ARBITRATION

What We Know and Don't Know (And Think We Know) About Our Allegedly Contentious and Litigious Society, 31 U.C.L.A.L.Rev. 4, 25 n. 117 (1983). See also Baruch Bush, Dispute Resolution Alternatives and the Goals of Civil Justice: Jurisdictional Principles for Process Choice, 1984 Wisc.L.Rev. 893, 992–93. Bush suggests that the "informality" of arbitration may well contribute to reducing hostility between the parties—especially in comparison with litigation—in that it limits the amount and intensity of "direct party confrontation" in the form of evidentiary and procedural contentions. He argues, however, that this function is far more likely to be accomplished by a process like mediation that is aimed directly at facilitating mutual understanding and sympathy.

2. INTERNATIONAL COMMERCIAL ARBITRATION

Many of the same factors inducing parties to choose arbitration as a dispute settlement technique in domestic commercial transactions are likely to be present when the transaction expands across national boundaries. Indeed, as Professor Mentschikoff points out, the involvement of more than one body of law and more than one court system is likely to provide even further impetus to nonjudicial dispute resolution. The time, expense, and procedural complexities of litigating in another country's courts are likely to be considerable. There may not even be any effective protection against parallel litigation proceeding simultaneously in the courts of the United States and of a foreign country. There is likely to be far greater uncertainty with respect to the rules of decision that will govern the dispute in a foreign tribunal, and thus as to the outcome; the rules of "conflict of laws" will not always give a bankable answer even to the question of *which* nation's law will apply to the transaction. In addition, the "foreign" party to the litigation will not only feel disadvantaged by his relative unfamiliarity with the "rules of the game," but may also doubt how fairly and even-handedly he will be treated in comparison to his "local" opponent.

Another troubling cause of unpredictability in international litigation stems from uncertainty as to when and to what extent a judgment obtained in one country will be enforceable in another. A favorable decision against a French supplier in a New York court, for example, may be of little value if the courts of France will not recognize the New York judgment. However, "[c]ompared with ordinary court decisions, arbitration is far ahead as far as enforcement in other countries is concerned."[2] In many countries, enforcement of a foreign arbitral award is simpler and more assured than is enforcement of a foreign judgment—a difference in outcome perhaps explained by the common tendency to regard an arbitral award as "the outcome of contractual relationships, rather than of the exercise of state powers."[3] This favorable treatment of foreign arbitral awards has been

---

2. Sanders, International Commercial Arbitration—How to Improve its Functioning?, [1980] Arbitration 9.

3. Gardner, Economic and Political Implications of International Commercial Arbitration, in Martin Domke (ed.), International Trade Arbitration 20–21 (1958).

reinforced by international treaty. See the United Nations Convention on the Recognition and Enforcement of Foreign Arbitral Awards, infra Appendix G.

It is therefore not surprising that in international commercial contracts, arbitration clauses "not only predominate but are nowadays almost universal" and are "virtually taken for granted."[4] The Supreme Court has on a number of occasions recognized the unique value of international arbitration in promoting "the orderliness and predictability essential to any international business transaction," and has drawn from it a strong policy favoring international commercial arbitration. See Scherk v. Alberto–Culver Co., 417 U.S. 506, 516 (1974); Mitsubishi v. Soler, infra p. 766. It has been suggested that international arbitrators have been moving towards a "common law of international arbitration"—that they have been developing a "customary law of international contracts"[5] that stresses general norms of conduct suited to international business practices independent of the rules of particular bodies of national law. This is particularly marked in arbitration decisions dealing with such thorny recurring problems in international trade as the effect on contracts of "impossibility" (*force majeure*) or currency fluctuations.

Parties to international transactions often prefer to proceed with arbitration outside of any institutional framework, and to administer the arbitration themselves on an "ad hoc" basis. However, dispensing with the administrative support of organizations like the AAA is not likely to be successful in cases where the level of cooperation and trust between the parties is low and one of them may be dragging his feet in resolving the problem. In addition, where a recognized institution has supervised the arbitration, the institution's reputation may lend credibility to the award should a national court ever come to review the arbitration. There exist a large number of other organizations besides the AAA which compete in the administration of international commercial arbitrations; by far the most important of these is the International Chamber of Commerce (ICC), based in Paris.

It is inevitable that international arbitration will often turn out to be considerably more protracted and expensive than its domestic counterpart. The ICC in particular is often criticized on this account. In ICC proceedings the administrative charges paid to the ICC for its services, and the fees paid to the arbitrators themselves, are calculated on the basis of the amount in dispute between the parties. In a $10 million case these may range from a bare—and unlikely—minimum of $62,550 to a maximum, if three arbitrators are used, of $441,800. The most articulate apologists for ICC arbitration respond to criticisms of excessive expense with a plea that:

4. Kerr, International Arbitration v. Litigation, [1980] J. Business Law 164, 165, 171.

5. W. Laurence Craig, William Park, & Jan Paulsson, International Chamber of Commerce Arbitration 638 (3rd ed. 2000). See also Rene David, Arbitration in International Trade §§ 16 ("Search for an autonomous commercial law"), 17 (1985).

628   CHAPTER V   ARBITRATION

the cost must be evaluated in relation to the alternatives. Certainly, ICC arbitration seems cheaper than abandoning one's rights altogether. Litigation, even in one's own home courts, is not necessarily a less expensive alternative, given the possibility of one or more appeals. More importantly, it simply is not always reasonable to expect that one's home forum will be acceptable to a foreign contracting party. ICC arbitration is too often compared—unrealistically and unfairly—with a perfect world in which there are no administrative difficulties, no judicial prejudice against foreign parties, no language problems, no uncooperative parties, and where the just always prevail at no cost to themselves.[6]

NOTES AND QUESTIONS

1. In many countries the government assumes a far more active role in economic transactions—particularly those involving capital investment and the exploitation and development of national resources—than it does in the United States. The foreign state or one of its instrumentalities will often be a party to such contracts, which are likely to have political and economic implications and symbolic importance far greater than in the case of domestic transactions. This can be a factor which complicates the question of dispute resolution. A foreign state will understandably be reluctant to submit to the jurisdiction of the courts of another sovereign (as, of course, the foreign investor will be reluctant to submit to the courts of the host country.) However, developing countries in particular have long been sensitive to the implications of submitting to *any* forum where the location or the decision-maker is foreign, and such reluctance has been extended to foreign arbitrations as well.

This unwillingness to submit to foreign arbitration is probably most marked in Latin American countries, where historical memory of one-sided international "arbitrations" dominated by European or North American partners is still vivid. A Brazilian writer has recently argued that:

> Functioning as an active element to denationalize (or internationalize) the contract, arbitration by removing a dispute from resolution by local courts applying local law, takes it to a plane where the rules are made by the great international commercial interests, a process from which Third World countries normally are excluded.

Quoted in Nattier, International Commercial Arbitration in Latin America: Enforcement of Arbitral Agreements and Awards, 21 Tex.Int'l L.J. 397, 407 (1986). See also Echeverria & Siqueiros, Arbitration in Latin American Countries, in Sanders (ed.), Arbitration in Settlement of International Commercial Disputes 81, 82 (1989) (the failure of arbitration to take root in Latin America "may only be explained as a consequence of the traditional view that international arbitration was a surrogate for diplomatic interven-

---

6. W. Laurence Craig et al., supra n.5 at 29–30, 744 ("Calculating ICC Administra- tive Expenses and Fees of Arbitrators Accord- ing to the ICC Schedule").

tion by the great powers"). For many years the "Calvo doctrine," incorporated in several Latin American constitutions or statutes, made impossible the litigation or arbitration abroad of state contracts and required foreign investors to consent to the dispute resolution processes of local courts.

In many Latin American countries, in fact, the validity even of agreements between *private* parties to submit disputes to foreign arbitral tribunals has been uncertain. This traditional attitude, however, has gradually been changing. In recent years a number of such countries have enacted modern arbitration laws providing for the enforcement of arbitration agreements and awards, and have become parties to international arbitration treaties such as the New York Convention (see Appendix G), the similar Inter–American Convention on International Commercial Arbitration, (see Appendix H), and the Convention on the Settlement of Investment Disputes (the ICSID Convention; see note (2) infra). Brazil's new arbitration law, adopted in 1996, for the first time made pre-dispute arbitration clauses specifically enforceable—although doubts have persisted as to the constitutionality of this legislation. See Wald et al., Some Controversial Aspects of the New Brazilian Arbitration Law, 31 U. Miami Inter–Amer. L. Rev. 223 (2000)(enactment of the new law "signifies a true cultural revolution whose significance is only now being recognized by the judiciary"; "[u]nder the pressures of huge caseloads," Brazilian courts are abandoning their traditional hostility to arbitration and recognizing its increasing importance); Barral & Prazeres, Trends of Arbitration in Brazil, Mealey's Int'l Arb. Rep., Aug. 2000, at p. 22. See also Trevino, The New Mexican Legislation on Commercial Arbitration, 11 J.In'tl Arb. 5 (1994); Siqueiros, Mexican Arbitration—The New Statute, 30 Tex.Int'l L.J. 227 (1995).

2. In December 1985, Walt Disney Productions and the French Government signed a letter of intent for the construction of a new Disneyland, to be located near Paris. France and Spain had both competed vigorously for this project, which French officials estimated would involve long-term American investment of as much as $6.7 billion and the creation of more than 30,000 jobs. The French Government had made commitments to build rail and highway networks linking the site to Paris and to develop an infrastructure, including roads and telephone trunk lines, for the area.

The contract negotiations, however, proved extremely difficult. Political opposition to the project—French Communists denounced it as "the encroachment of an alien civilization next to the city of enlightenment"—figured in the parliamentary elections held throughout France in March 1986. Another major snag was Disney's demand that any disputes which might later arise out of the French Government's undertakings be resolved by arbitration through the International Center for the Settlement of Investment Disputes (ICSID).

ICSID was established by treaty in 1966 to provide a neutral forum for the resolution of disputes between states and foreign investors, and to reduce the fear of political risks that might discourage the flow of private foreign capital to developing countries. ICSID functions under the auspices of the World Bank and is a "public" body, administered by representatives of the various participating governments. Only 57 cases have as yet been referred to the Center; most of these have involved disputes arising out of mining, construction, or joint venture agreements with developing states in sub-Saharan Africa and Latin America. See generally Ibrahim Shihata & Antonio Parra, The Experience of the International Centre for Settlement of Investment Disputes, 14 ICSID Rev.-Foreign Investment L.J. 299 (1999).

Fear was expressed in France that acceding to Disney's demand would create a "precedent" by which all new foreign investments might have to go to arbitration. And one French official was said to have commented that "Disney's request for ICSID was shocking and a bit dumb. France is not a banana republic." International Herald Tribune, March 15, 1986, pp. 1, 15; see also Washington Post, August 21, 1986, p. C8; "The Real Estate Coup at Euro Disneyland," Fortune, April 28, 1986, p. 172.

The agreement between Disney and the French Government was finally signed in March 1987. It did contain a provision for dispute settlement by arbitration—but through the ICC, to take place in France.

3. In concluding commercial contracts with foreign businesses, negotiators from the People's Republic of China invariably try to obtain an agreement that any future disputes will be arbitrated in China by the China International Economic and Trade Arbitration Commission ("CIETAC"). CIETAC today has a caseload that makes it one of the world's busiest arbitration centers. Under CIETAC rules, each party to a dispute selects one arbitrator from the Commission's list of arbitrators; the third and presiding member of the panel is chosen by CIETAC itself and is in most cases an employee of the Commission. Most of the arbitrators on CIETAC's list are Chinese nationals, although more than a fourth of the names on the list are now from foreign countries. Some insight into the nature of an arbitration conducted by CIETAC can be gleaned from this account by a leading official of the organization:

> A foreign buyer ordered 500 cases of goods from a Chinese seller. According to the contract, the goods were to be shipped from a Chinese port to Hong Kong and then transshipped from Hong Kong to the port of destination. Upon arrival at the port of destination, part of the goods were found damaged. The buyer claimed against the seller for compensation of the losses incurred * * * on the grounds that the packing was defective. The seller argued that the packing was not defective because it was the normal packing he used for exporting the goods and no extra or special requirements for packing were specified in the contract. * * * The buyer then applied to [CIETAC] for arbitration. With the consent of both parties, the arbitration tribunal decided the case according to principles of conciliation. It was the opinion of the arbitration tribunal that although no extra or special requirements for packing were specified in the contract, the seller knew that the goods were to be transshipped at Hong Kong, which was different from shipment directly from a Chinese port to the port of destination. The packing should be suitable for that specific transportation. However, the nails and the wood used for the packing were not appropriate for

the purpose. The arbitration tribunal proposed an appropriate compensation to the buyer for his losses. The seller accepted the arbitration tribunal's proposal but pointed out that the amount claimed by the buyer was too large and asked for a reduction. The arbitration tribunal consulted the buyer and eventually the buyer agreed to reduce his claim by seventy percent. Both parties came to a compromise agreement from which the arbitration tribunal delivered a Conciliatory Statement and closed the case.

Tang, Arbitration—A Method Used by China to Settle Foreign Trade and Economic Disputes, 4 Pace L.Rev. 519, 533–34 (1984). For more recent developments, see also Harpole, How China Organizes Arbitral Tribunals, Disp. Res. J., Jan. 1997 at p. 72; Blay, Party Autonomy in Chinese International Arbitration, 8 Am. Rev. Int'l Arb. 331 (1997); Peerenboom, The Evolving Regulatory Framework for Enforcement of Arbitral Awards in the People's Republic of China, 1 Asian–Pac. L. & Policy J. 12 (2000).

CIETAC acts under the supervision of the China Chamber of International Commerce, which is nominally a non-governmental organization whose mission is to promote foreign investment and trade by promoting links between foreign companies and the Chinese government. Its arbitrators may understandably be reluctant to finally adjudicate the merits of a dispute between a Western trading company and a domestic state unit, since such a decision might well affect the future business relations between the parties. Cf. Chew, A Procedural and Substantive Analysis of the Fairness of Chinese and Soviet Foreign Trade Arbitrations, 21 Tex.Int'l L.J. 291, 330–34 (1986). In addition, a general aversion to formal third-party adjudication and a predilection for conciliation and compromise have long marked Chinese legal culture. See, e.g., Schwartz, On Attitudes Toward Law in China, in Katz (ed.), Government Under Law and the Individual 27–39 (1957). In any event, as this excerpt illustrates, CIETAC will proceed to "decide" a dispute only in those cases where its efforts to induce a voluntary agreement through conciliation have failed. To what extent does this model correspond to the American understanding of the arbitration process? See also the discussion of "Med–Arb" at Section E.3 infra.

4. Fujitsu (Japan's largest computer company) developed and marketed IBM-compatible operating system software, which IBM claimed was in violation of its copyrights. The companies agreed to submit the dispute to two arbitrators (a law professor and a retired computer executive) under AAA auspices. The arbitrators were determined from the outset "to avoid becoming engulfed in an extensive adjudicatory fact-finding process with respect to hundreds of programs previously released by [Fujitsu]." "While this might determine in particular instances whether IBM's intellectual property rights had been violated, it would not directly address and resolve the parties' dispute with respect to [Fujitsu's] ongoing use of IBM programming material in its software development process."

Through their mediation efforts, the parties came instead to agree on the concept of a "coerced license" that was to be administered by these arbitrators into the future. The arbitrators' award allowed the Japanese company to examine IBM programs in a "secured facility" for a period of five to ten years and, "subject to strict and elaborate safeguards," to use such information in its software development; this would provide Fujitsu with a "reasonable opportunity to independently develop and maintain IBM–compatible operating system software." Fujitsu was to "fully and adequately compensate" IBM for such access in amounts to be determined by the arbitrators. In effect the arbitrators' award and subsequent decisions "will constitute the applicable intellectual property law until the end of the Contract Period, notwithstanding copyright decisions of U.S. or Japanese courts * * *." One of the arbitrators later commented that their decisions "will be considerably more detailed than existing copyright law, because there haven't been all that many cases and they haven't got into as many areas as we've gotten into." Wall.St.J., July 1, 1988, p. 4. See also Johnston, The IBM–Fujitsu Arbitration Revisited—A Case Study in Effective ADR, 7 Computer Law. 13 (May 1990).

5. Athletes participating in the Olympic Games are required to sign entry forms in which they agree to settle all Games-related disputes through arbitration before the Court of Arbitration for Sport. The CAS was created in 1984 by the International Olympic Committee, but is now more or less independent, and operates under the general supervision of the International Council of Arbitration for Sport. (The ICAS is composed of twenty "high-level jurists," four of whom are appointed respectively by the IOC, by the Association of National Olympic Committees, and by the International Federations that govern individual sports such as swimming and gymnastics—with the remaining members chosen by those already appointed). The ICAS in turn selects a panel of 150 arbitrators who are supposed to have "legal training and who possess recognized competence with regard to sport": "From the professor of Sports Law, to the lawyer who once won an Olympic wrestling medal, the paths of 'specialization' are diverse." See Kaufmann–Kohler, "Art and Arbitration: What Lessons Can be Drawn from the Resolution of Sports Disputes," 11 Studies in Art Law 123, 128 (1999).

The CAS makes arbitrators available on-site at each Olympics, with a commitment to render awards within 24 hours after the demand for arbitration. (Under its rules, however, the "seat" of every arbitration panel is deemed to be in Lausanne, Switzerland, and the arbitration is to be governed by Swiss law). CAS jurisdiction is by no means limited to the Olympics: It is a permanent body that may decide any "matters of principle relating to sport or matters of pecuniary or other interests brought into play in the practice or the development of sport"; its case load of around 20 arbitrations per year has included disputes involving such matters as substance abuse, eligibility for competition, and the interpretation of endorsement contracts or contracts between athletes and agents or managers. Perhaps the most highly-publicized award, however, was made at the 2000 Sydney games: A 16–year old Romanian gymnast was stripped of her gold medal by the IOC after testing positive for a banned substance—apparently she had been given two over-the-counter cold pills by the team's doctor. It was conceded that neither her intent, nor the effect of the drug, had been to enhance her performance. The CAS arbitration panel, made up of arbitrators from Australia, Switzerland, and the United States, nevertheless upheld the IOC's decision: "A strict liability test must be applied," it said in a brief opinion, "the consequence being automatic disqualification as a matter of law and in fairness to all other athletes."

6. As we have seen, the practice in domestic commercial arbitration is to dispense with reasoned opinions. In contrast, parties in international cases *do* usually expect arbitrators to provide a written opinion that sets out the reasons for their award. The ICC requires its arbitrators to give reasoned awards; under the ICSID treaty, an award may be "annulled" by an ad hoc appellate committee if "the award has failed to state the reasons on which it is based." This expectation of a reasoned opinion in international arbitration reflects in part the pervasive influence of Continental legal systems, where unreasoned awards are often considered contrary to public policy and thus unenforceable. See Rene David, Arbitration in International Trade 319–328 (1985); W. Laurence Craig, William Park & Jan Paulsson, International Chamber of Commerce Arbitration § 19.04 (3rd ed. 2000).

3. LABOR ARBITRATION

A collective bargaining agreement between an employer and the union that represents the firm's employees is likely to be a complex document. It will deal with a large number of subjects, among many other things setting wages and other terms of employment, imposing limits on the employer's right to discharge or discipline employees, and providing for seniority for purposes of layoffs, promotion, and job assignments. It will constitute, in short, an overall framework for employer-employee relations.

Most agreements also spell out a process by which the inevitable questions of interpretation and application arising during the life of the contract will be settled. There are typically a number of steps in this process: At the beginning, for example, there may be informal attempts to adjust a grievance on the shop floor by consultations between the employee's immediate supervisor and the union shop steward; if the dispute is not settled at this stage it will move to successively higher levels. The agreement is likely to make it clear that at all stages work is not to be interrupted because of the dispute but is to continue pending a final settlement, and is likely also to impose strict time limits to insure that a grievance is heard and processed speedily. The final stage in the grievance process, to handle those "cases that are not winnowed out by the process of day-to-day negotiation,"[7] is likely to be binding arbitration. The Department of Labor estimates that more than 96% of all collective bargaining agreements—covering a total of almost 6 ½ million workers—provide for arbitration of grievance disputes.[8]

---

7. Getman, Labor Arbitration and Dispute Resolution, 88 Yale L.J. 916, 919 (1979).

8. U.S. Dept. of Labor, Characteristics of Major Collective Bargaining Agreements 112 (1981).

CHAPTER V ARBITRATION

Section 301 of the Labor Management Relations Act of 1947 (the Taft–Hartley Act) granted jurisdiction to federal district courts to hear suits for violation of collective bargaining agreements "in an industry affecting commerce." In Textile Workers Union v. Lincoln Mills, 353 U.S. 448 (1957), the Supreme Court held that § 301 was "more than jurisdictional," and that it "authorizes federal courts to fashion a body of federal law for the enforcement of these collective bargaining agreements." "Plainly the agreement to arbitrate grievance disputes is the *quid pro quo* for an agreement not to strike." Federal policy therefore was that promises to arbitrate grievances under collective bargaining agreements should be specifically enforced, and that "industrial peace can be best obtained only in that way."

Federal courts have for the past thirty years engaged in "fashioning" a federal common law dealing with the enforcement of arbitration agreements—to such an extent that it is not an exaggeration to say that the field of "labor law" is now to a large degree the law of labor arbitration. In 1960, in what is still the Supreme Court's most significant pronouncement on the subject, Justice Douglas undertook an evaluation of the purpose and function of labor arbitration and of the central place it occupies in our system of workplace bargaining. Some extracts from his discussion follow.

United Steelworkers of America v. Warrior & Gulf Navigation Co.

Supreme Court of the United States, 1960.
363 U.S. 574, 80 S.Ct. 1347, 4 L.Ed.2d 1409.

■ Opinion of the Court by MR. JUSTICE DOUGLAS.

* * *

The present federal policy is to promote industrial stabilization through the collective bargaining agreement. A major factor in achieving industrial peace is the inclusion of a provision for arbitration of grievances in the collective bargaining agreement.

Thus the run of arbitration cases * * * becomes irrelevant to our problem. There the choice is between the adjudication of cases or controversies in courts with established procedures or even special statutory safeguards on the one hand and the settlement of them in the more informal arbitration tribunal on the other. In the commercial case, arbitration is the substitute for litigation. Here arbitration is the substitute for industrial strife. Since arbitration of labor disputes has quite different functions from arbitration under an ordinary commercial agreement, the hostility evinced by courts toward arbitration of commercial agreements has no place here. For arbitration of labor disputes under collective bargaining agreements is part and parcel of the collective bargaining process itself.

* * *

A collective bargaining agreement is an effort to erect a system of industrial self-government. When most parties enter into [a] contractual relationship they do so voluntarily, in the sense that there is no real compulsion to deal with one another, as opposed to dealing with other parties. This is not true of the labor agreement. The choice is generally not between entering or refusing to enter into a relationship, for that in all probability preexists the negotiations. Rather it is between having that relationship governed by an agreed-upon rule of law or leaving each and every matter subject to a temporary resolution dependent solely upon the relative strength, at any given moment, of the contending forces. The mature labor agreement may attempt to regulate all aspects of the complicated relationship, from the most crucial to the most minute over an extended period of time. Because of the compulsion to reach agreement and the breadth of the matters covered, as well as the need for a fairly concise and readable instrument, the product of negotiations (the written document) is, in the words of the late Dean Shulman, "a compilation of diverse provisions: some provide objective criteria almost automatically applicable; some provide more or less specific standards which require reason and judgment in their application; and some do little more than leave problems to future consideration with an expression of hope and good faith." Gaps may be left to be filled in by reference to the practices of the particular industry and of the various shops covered by the agreement. Many of the specific practices which underlie the agreement may be unknown, except in hazy form, even to the negotiators. Courts and arbitration in the context of most commercial contracts are resorted to because there has been a breakdown in the working relationship of the parties; such resort is the unwanted exception. But the grievance machinery under a collective bargaining agreement is at the very heart of the system of industrial self-government. Arbitration is the means of solving the unforeseeable by molding a system of private law for all the problems which may arise and to provide for their solution in a way which will generally accord with the variant needs and desires of the parties. The processing of disputes through the grievance machinery is actually a vehicle by which meaning and content are given to the collective bargaining agreement.

Apart from matters that the parties specifically exclude, all of the questions on which the parties disagree must therefore come within the scope of the grievance and arbitration provisions of the collective agreement. The grievance procedure is, in other words, a part of the continuous collective bargaining process. It, rather than a strike, is the terminal point of a disagreement.

* * *

The labor arbitrator's source of law is not confined to the express provisions of the contract, as the industrial common law—the practices of the industry and the shop—is equally a part of the collective bargaining agreement although not expressed in it. The labor arbitrator is usually chosen because of the parties' confidence in his knowledge of the common law of the shop and their trust in his personal judgment to bring to bear

636 CHAPTER V ARBITRATION

considerations which are not expressed in the contract as criteria for judgment. The parties expect that his judgment of a particular grievance will reflect not only what the contract says but, insofar as the collective bargaining agreement permits, such factors as the effect upon productivity of a particular result, its consequence to the morale of the shop, his judgment whether tensions will be heightened or diminished. For the parties' objective in using the arbitration process is primarily to further their common goal of uninterrupted production under the agreement, to make the agreement serve their specialized needs. The ablest judge cannot be expected to bring the same experience and competence to bear upon the determination of a grievance, because he cannot be similarly informed.

Arbitration of labor disputes serves, then, to give "meaning and content" over time to the vague or ambiguous terms of the collective bargaining agreement. In addition, the very existence of this dispute resolution mechanism itself may affect the dynamic of the parties' relationship. Through the processing of a grievance dispute, for example, useful information may be communicated about the needs and attitudes of one party to the agreement, and about potential trouble spots in the relationship. Another function of labor arbitration was highlighted by Justice Douglas in a formulation which has now attained something of the status of a cliché: In a companion case to *Warrior & Gulf,* Justice Douglas noted that "[t]he processing of even frivolous claims may have therapeutic values of which those who are not a part of the plant environment may be quite unaware."[9]

Just what does it mean to claim that labor arbitration can have a "therapeutic" function? It has been suggested that the ability to participate in the selection of a neutral decisionmaker, and to present one's own story to him in an informal, "non-threatening" atmosphere, may be "empowering" for each of the parties to the dispute.[10] It is important also to bear in mind here that any particular grievance under a collective bargaining agreement is likely to be that of the individual *employee,* who may have been dismissed or whose job classification may have been changed. However, the parties to the bargaining agreement are the employer and the *union;* the union, as the exclusive representative of all the employees in the bargaining unit, is in exclusive control of the administration of the contract and controls access to the grievance procedure at every stage. In these circumstances, pursuing even a hopeless claim to arbitration has at least the virtue of giving the employee the assurance that his case has been heard and that he has been taken seriously. Grievance arbitration may thus serve as a "safety valve for troublesome complaints"[11] the employee's

---

9. United Steelworkers of America v. American Mfg. Co., 363 U.S. 564, 568 (1960).

10. See, e.g., Abrams, Abrams & Nolan, Arbitral Therapy, 46 Rutgers L.Rev. 1751, 1765, 1767, 1769 (1994).

11. Cox, Current Problems in the Law of Grievance Arbitration, 30 Rocky Mt.L.Rev. 247, 261 (1958).

presence at the hearing watching management witnesses subjected to "searching and often embarrassing cross-examination" may result in "a kind of catharsis that helps to make even eventual defeat acceptable" to the grievant.[12]

Carrying a case through the arbitration process may have other advantages for the union. It is often more politic for union representatives to "pass the buck" to the arbitrator, who they know will reject the grievance, than to be obliged *themselves* to convince their constituent that he is wrong and that the claim should be dropped. In addition, a union that is found to have "arbitrarily" refused to pursue an employee's grievance to arbitration, or to have "process[ed] it in a perfunctory fashion," may well be open to a suit by the employee for "unfair representation."[13] Nevertheless, the fact remains that the overwhelming proportion of employee grievances are screened or settled without resort to arbitration, just as the overwhelming proportion of lawsuits are settled before trial. It has been estimated that a grievance rate of 10 to 20 per 100 employees per year is "typical" in this country.[14] If any substantial proportion of those cases were to go to arbitration the entire grievance system would collapse.

Awards handed down by labor arbitrators generally reveal considerable sensitivity to those considerations mentioned by Justice Douglas in his paean to labor arbitration in *Warrior & Gulf*—the need to reduce tensions and to foster a good working relationship within the plant setting, the need to pay attention to the "common law of the shop" and to the "customs and practices which the parties have come to consider as settled patterns of conduct."[15] Some selections from recent arbitral awards give a good flavor of how labor arbitrators purport, at least, to see their role in the process. Would you expect to find opinions like these written by "judges"?

(a) The employee had worked for the employer for eight years and had never been disciplined. He was discharged for being disrespectful to the Company President ("If you don't like the way I'm doing the work, do it yourself") in the presence of a number of the company's other employees. The arbitrator held that the employer did not have "proper cause" to discharge the employee and that he should be reinstated, although without recovering back pay or accruing seniority or vacation benefits for the seven months he was off work:

> Since discharge is in essence "capital punishment" in the work place, it is necessary to examine with extreme care all of the evidence before determining whether it is appropriate or not. This would include the facts and circumstances leading to the discharge, the grievant's length of service, the degree of aggravation involved in the offense, whether

---

12. Aaron, The Role of the Arbitrator in Ensuring a Fair Hearing, 35 Proc.Nat'l Acad.Arb. 30, 32 (1983).

13. Vaca v. Sipes, 386 U.S. 171 (1967); see also Bowen v. U.S. Postal Service, 459 U.S. 212 (1983).

14. See Feller, A General Theory of the Collective Bargaining Agreement, 61 Cal. L.Rev. 663, 755 (1973).

15. See In re Standard Bag Corp. and Paper Bag, Novelty, Mounting, Finishing and Display Workers Union, 45 Lab.Arb. 1149 (1965).

the conduct was intended or rather an accidental outburst, the grievant's past record and finally whether the events are likely to recur were the grievant to be reinstated. * * *

Management's main argument was that it would be difficult for [the President] to run his operation with employees knowing that they could talk back to the President of the Company and get away with it. However, with this employee having been off work for over seven months without pay, I doubt that any employee will seriously think that he "got away with" very much. Upholding the discharge would be the most severe form of industrial penalty, but giving the grievant his job back without the seven months of back pay is still a very significant penalty. In salary alone that amounts to approximately $6,000.00 of gross earnings. (The grievant did not collect unemployment compensation and has not worked.) * * *

On the day he returns to work, but as a condition precedent to returning to work, the grievant will apologize to [the President] either privately or in front of the employees of Stylemaster. (The presence or lack thereof of other employees to be at the discretion of the Company.)

In re Stylemaster, Inc. and Production Workers Union of Chicago, 79 Lab.Arb. 76 (1982).

(b) A collective bargaining agreement provided that the employer, a grocery chain, would remain closed on January 1 "contingent upon similar limitations being contractually required of other organized food stores and/or being generally observed by major unorganized food competitors in the cities in which the Employer operated." The arbitrator found that the employer violated this agreement by opening on January 1. He then turned to the question of the proper remedy to be granted the Union. The arbitrator denied the Union's request for punitive damages, since he was "of the view that they are bad medicine when administered to a participant in an ongoing, union-management relationship." Although the employer's violation was "clear and unmistakable," "it is always hard to say that a beleaguered competitor, as Kroger undoubtedly considered itself, acted subjectively in bad faith. Moreover, it seems to me that a healing process is what is most needed in the relations between this Company and the Union, and I question whether punitive damages will contribute to that end." Nor, he held, was there any basis for awarding damages to the employees: "I do not mean that it would be impossible to attach a dollar value to a January 1 with family and friends, perhaps in front of the TV set watching a bowl game * * * but I do not find that such a showing was made here."

However, to prevent "unjust enrichment," the arbitrator did award to the union "restitution of any profits that may be attributable to the Company's operations on January 1." In re The Kroger Company and United Food and Commercial Workers, 85 Lab.Arb. 1198 (1985).

(c) The employee had worked for the employer for twenty-two years as a messenger; her job was to pick up and deliver advertising proofs and

B. Some Frequent Uses of Arbitration 639

materials to customers. She was discharged for failing to report to work at the scheduled time: This was apparently "the fourth occurrence of this behavior in the past six months," and four months previously, she had been suspended for three days without pay in a similar incident. The arbitrator held that the discharge should be set aside, and that the employee should be returned to her former position without loss of seniority:

> When [the grievant] was testifying at the Arbitration Hearing my personal observation of her demeanor and appearance indicated that she was emotionally distraught beyond the customary nervous reaction of a witness. I * * * believe that [the grievant] deserved compassionate understanding. * * *

> If Grievant performed with reasonable competency essentially the same messenger duties for about twenty-two years and only during the past year * * * did she demonstrate incompetence there must be some reason. It could be possible that Grievant suddenly developed a contemptuous disregard for her supervisor's instructions, It is more likely that some other explanation accounts for her recent erratic work performance. * * *

> It was not until the Arbitration Hearing that the [employer's] supervisor learned that [the grievant] lived with her mother who was suffering with Alzheimer's disease and Grievant had to assist her. Grievant, at 43 years of age, is within the age span of 40 to 54 years that physicians believe that the climacteric usually occurs. This aging process, commonly called the change of life, in women sometimes produces sudden emotional changes that usually are temporary but which disrupt normal activities. Such a condition could interfere with a woman's required work activities and responsibilities. * * *

> The evidence proves that [the grievant's] work performance during the last year had declined to an unacceptable level. The time she has been suspended from work shall be considered a disciplinary penalty to impress upon her, and other employees, the necessity of conforming to proper standards of conduct. Perhaps this lengthy period [grievant] has been off duty provided an opportunity to regain her health and emotional stability.

> It probably would be beneficial to both bargaining unit employees and Management if specific rules for reporting off and obtaining sick leave or vacation days would be set forth in writing and distributed to all employees in this department. In the past there seems to have been considerable laxity in enforcement of reporting off and attendance requirements and also some ambiguity as to what attendance standards employees were expected to observe.

In re Pittsburgh Post–Gazette and Pittsburgh Typographical Union, 113 Lab. Arb. 957 (1999).

640 CHAPTER V ARBITRATION

Note: Compromise Decisions

POSNER: The arbitration literature says—something that is very difficult to find out independently—that arbitrators are not supposed to compromise. Arbitrators are supposed to decide a dispute as if they were judges.

LEFF: The literature says that for the same reason that signs in subways say, "Don't Smoke," because there is a very strong tendency to smoke and therefore you have to say it over and over again. That reflects the fact that arbitrators compromise a great deal * * *.[16]

Observers often note that arbitrators have a propensity to tailor their decisions so as to make them acceptable to both parties. Such a criticism is heard most vociferously perhaps with respect to labor arbitrators, although it is by no means confined to the labor area. It is often supposed that this is done to insure the future "acceptability" of the arbitrator *himself*. Labor arbitrators are paid, often quite handsomely, for their work; what would be more natural than for this to create an incentive to try to assure themselves of repeat business? This incentive may often result in compromise decisions, "splitting the difference" so as not to appear unduly to favor either of the two parties whose future goodwill must be retained. A similar dynamic might be reflected in a *course* of decisions by the same arbitrator which over time, taken together, appears to show a rough balance between awards favorable to labor and those favorable to management.

As might be expected, this tendency to engage in compromise decisions appears particularly marked in "interest" arbitrations. In such cases the arbitrator is likely to be aware that the stakes riding on his decision are high, that the impact of his decision may be great and felt in all sorts of ways that he cannot be sure of in advance, and that intense dissatisfaction with a "mistaken" award may adversely affect the working relationship of the parties for some time to come. Do you expect that judges are often impelled to take such considerations into account in deciding cases?

Compare the following two excerpts, whose authors appear to take sharply differing views of the propriety of this behavior and of its function within the context of labor-management relations:

A proportion of arbitration awards, no one knows how large a proportion, is decided not on the basis of the evidence or of the contract or other proper considerations, but in a way calculated to encourage the arbitrator's being hired for other arbitration cases. It makes no difference whether or not a large majority of cases is decided in this way. A system of adjudication in which the judge depends for his livelihood, or for a substantial part of his livelihood or even for substantial supplements to his regular income, on pleasing those who hire him to judge is per se a thoroughly undesirable system. In no proper system of justice should a judge be submitted to such pressures. On the contrary, a judge should be carefully insulated from any pressure of this type.

---

16. Discussion by Seminar Participants, 8 J.Legal Stud. 323, 345 (1979).

B.   Some Frequent Uses of Arbitration **641**

Paul R. Hays, Labor Arbitration: A Dissenting View 112–13 (1966).

Compare Getman, Labor Arbitration and Dispute Resolution, 88 Yale L.J. 916, 928–930 (1979):

> In none of the literature is it suggested that an arbitrator's desire to promote acceptability might affect the process in a way that is basically desirable. However, if, as I contend, economic efficiency is promoted by arbitration partly because through it the parties conclude their negotiations, then it is likely that the desire to maintain acceptability plays a useful role in helping to achieve the resolution that the parties would have achieved had they had the opportunity to negotiate with respect to the issues in dispute. Such a resolution would by definition further the goal of efficiency.

> The negotiating process reflects both the relative economic strength and the differing priorities of the parties. * * * Economic strength is necessarily a factor in arbitration because it shapes the language of the collective-bargaining agreement, which is always the starting point, and sometimes the sole basis, for the arbitrator's decision. The parties' priorities are more difficult to ascertain. The arbitrator must pay careful attention to the clues that the parties give concerning how strongly they feel about a particular case. My judgment is that the need to maintain acceptability makes arbitrators more attentive to such clues than judges and more likely than judges would be to utilize them in their decision. Arbitrators whose decisions over time accurately reflect the priorities of the parties are likely to maintain and enhance their acceptability more than arbitrators who take either a more narrowly judicial role or a personally activist role. Thus, the process of selection will tend to produce arbitrators and a body of arbitral precedent that facilitate and extend the process of negotiation. * * *

> The careful selection process also motivates arbitrators to try to please both sides, if possible, with their decision. Thus, the split award and the decision in which it is difficult to tell which side has won are frequent in labor relations. Although the parties constantly insist it is contrary to their wishes, this system of giving a little bit to each side permits the process to achieve the results of successful negotiation.

NOTES AND QUESTIONS

1. As Getman suggests, it is almost inevitable that in the course of a hearing an arbitrator will receive some intimation from the parties or their attorneys as to what an "acceptable" settlement will look like, and that he will be influenced by such hints or suggestions. In an extreme case this may even take the form of what is called a "rigged award." The union representative and the management may actually *agree* between themselves as to

642 CHAPTER V ARBITRATION

how a case should be resolved; this understanding is conveyed to the arbitrator, who incorporates it in the final award as "his" decision without openly revealing that it is in fact the result of the parties' compromise. The hearing itself then becomes a mere charade. The practice of the "rigged award" has been often and scathingly condemned as "the crassest infringement of adjudicative integrity," "the most severe criticism which could be made of arbitration," "vicious" and "a shocking distortion of the administration of justice." See Fuller, Collective Bargaining and the Arbitrator, 1963 Wisc.L.Rev. 3, 20 (1963); Eaton, Labor Arbitration in the San Francisco Bay Area, 48 Lab.Arb. 1381, 1389 (1967); Paul R. Hays, Labor Arbitration: A Dissenting View 113, 65 (1966).

Why might the parties want the arbitrator to proceed in this way, when they could simply "settle" the case and withdraw it from the purview of the arbitrator? And just *why* is the arbitrator not entitled to do this? What is wrong with the "rigged award"? Might there be a difference if this practice is used in "interest" arbitration rather than with respect to a "rights" dispute? Finally, if the arbitrator is unwilling merely to rubber-stamp the parties' understanding, how should he proceed? What as a practical matter is he able to do?

2. Some writers have suggested that the "procedures for arbitration that have been developed in the context of labor relations make the technique particularly adaptable to prison problems." To resolve disputes arising out of grievances by prison inmates, "third-party neutrals who have particular expertise in corrections may be chosen by both prisoners and the officials. Furthermore, the parties could stipulate in advance the rules to be followed and the issues to be settled." Goldfarb & Singer, Redressing Prisoners' Grievances, 39 Geo.Wash.L.Rev. 175, 316 (1970); see also Keating, Arbitration of Inmate Grievances, 30 Arb.J. 177 (1975). Do you agree?

4. ARBITRATION OF CONSUMER DISPUTES

The Bank of America, the nation's second-largest bank, has 11.5 million checking and savings accounts in California and has issued a total of 7 million credit cards nationwide. In the summer of 1992 the Bank announced that all its contracts with depositors and credit-card holders would henceforth contain arbitration clauses. Under the Bank's new contract, any individual disputes would be decided by arbitration under the commercial rules of the AAA; any complaints brought as class actions would be "referred" to a neutral under California's "rent-a-judge" statute (See p. 900 infra.) Notice of the arbitration clause was sent to the bank's customers as "stuffers" in their monthly statements; cardholders, for example, were told that if they continued to use their cards after receiving the notice, the arbitration provision would apply to all past and future transactions.

During the 1980's a number of California banks, including the Bank of America, had already begun to experiment with using arbitration in other product lines, particularly mid-range commercial loans. This was in reac-

B. Some Frequent Uses of Arbitration 643

tion to a series of pro-borrower "lender liability" cases which seemed to broaden the scope of the duties owed to a borrower by a bank:

> [The banks] concluded that both their exposure and their transaction costs could be reduced by the adoption of arbitration provisions. First, they believed that their exposure would be both more predictable and better contained with arbitration. In their view, arbitrators generally had a better grasp of underlying contractual issues than juries and were less likely to consider factors outside those presented in the case at issue; for example, the fact that the bank is a large institution able to spread out any losses relative to the individual, who may be forced into extreme hardship. Firms also believed that arbitrators were less likely to award punitive damages. Furthermore, firms anticipated that the fact that disputes would be heard before an arbitrator would, in turn, affect plaintiffs' and plaintiffs' attorneys' calculus in deciding whether to bring suit in the first place; as possible verdicts declined, plaintiffs would be less likely to bring suit.[17]

In the first few years of the program, fewer than 20 disputes between the Bank and its customers went as far as arbitration. And in 1998, the Bank's arbitration mechanism was held on narrow grounds to be unenforceable: The California Court of Appeals held that under the original terms of its customer agreements, the Bank had no right to unilaterally impose this modification on its credit-card holders. (See p. 707 infra). However, the Bank's introduction of arbitration clauses in its customer contracts was closely watched, and its example apparently encouraged other companies to follow its lead. Shortly after the Bank's announcement California's second-largest bank, Wells Fargo, also modified its deposit and credit-card contracts to include a mandatory "Comprehensive Dispute Resolution Program." The Program would apply only to claims of more than $25,000 (the limit for claims that can be brought in municipal court in California), and to both individual and class action suits. Under the Program, if any dispute could not be settled by good-faith negotiation or mediation, the dispute would then be submitted to a "rent-a-judge" process under the auspices of Judicial Arbitration and Mediation Services, Inc. (JAMS), or, if both parties prefer, to a JAMS arbitration. In addition, First USA, the nation's second-largest issuer of credit cards and a unit of Chicago-based Bank One, has also begun to require its customers to arbitrate any disputes under the auspices of the "National Arbitration Forum."

Indeed, the possibilities for the use of arbitration in consumer contracts seem endless. Securities brokers invariably insist that individual investors who wish to open a margin or an option account agree to arbitration, and a substantial and increasing number of brokerage firms require arbitration even for investors wishing to open a cash account. Such

---

17. Erik Moller, Elizabeth Rolph, & Patricia Ebener, Private Dispute Resolution in the Banking Industry 12–13 (RAND 1993).

644   CHAPTER V   ARBITRATION

a requirement is "never or almost never waived or negotiated."[18] After a customer orders a Gateway computer over the phone, the computer will eventually arrive in a box containing all the necessary equipment—along with a copy of Gateway's "Standard Terms and Conditions," which includes the obligation to arbitrate any disputes. The nation's second largest home-warranty company, Home Buyers Warranty Corp., now requires homeowners to agree to arbitration of any warranty claims.[19] Arbitration clauses can be found in many contracts of insurance.[20] And in 1994, the makers of Honey Nut Cheerios conducted a "sweepstakes" in which individuals with winning "game cards" would be entitled to certain prizes. (The odds were 1 in 10,000 that winners would receive a Sega Genesis Home Entertainment System with a Sega Cartridge—"you will receive either Dr. Robotnik's Mean Bean Machine or Toe Jam & Earl in Panic on Funkatron.") The back of the cereal box contained dense and lengthy rules by which "[a]s a condition of entering this contest," the participant agreed that "any and all disputes, claims and causes of action arising out of or connected with this contest, or any prizes awarded shall be resolved individually, without resort to any form of class action, and exclusively by arbitration under the rules of the American Arbitration Association in Minneapolis, Minnesota."[21]

Note: Medical Malpractice: Disputes Between Doctors and Patients

A dramatic increase in the number and size of medical malpractice claims and awards first entered the public consciousness during the 1970's, under the banner of the "malpractice crisis." The threatened effects of this "crisis" on the health and insurance industries spawned a large variety of legislative responses. These have ranged from tinkering with the formal legal standard of negligence or the statute of limitations in malpractice cases, to more dramatic reforms such as abolishing the collateral source rule or imposing ceilings on recoverable damages or on attorney's contingent fees. Among these legislative "reforms" there inevitably appeared changes in the *process* by which malpractice claims could be asserted, and attempts to divert such claims entirely from the time-honored system of tort litigation.

(a) Some states have imposed preliminary hurdles on malpractice litigation by *requiring* that claims first be submitted to a "medical review"

---

18. U.S. General Accounting Office, Securities Arbitration: How Investors Fare 28–30 (1992).

19. The arbitration is to be administered by Construction Arbitration Services of Dallas, which will "appoint arbitrators from its panel of persons knowledgeable in residential construction," CAS Rules for the Arbitration of Home Warranty Disputes, R.3. If CAS is for any reason unable to conduct the arbitration, then the AAA will instead administer the arbitration under its own rules. See

Home Buyers Warranty Corp., Home Buyers Warranty Booklet, at p. 6. See also Blumenthal, "Shaky Support: Some Home Buyers Find Their Warranties Can Be Nearly Useless," Wall St.J., Nov. 30, 1994 at p. 1.

20. See, e.g., 2 Alan Widiss, Uninsured and Underinsured Motorist Insurance § 26.4 (2d ed. 1992).

21. "Honey Nut Cheerios/Sega Sweepstakes Official Rules"; see also Wall St.J., June 30, 1994, p. 1.

B. Some Frequent Uses of Arbitration

645

or "professional liability review" panel. (These may sometimes be called "arbitration boards.") Under some statutes, this required panel must consist of three physicians.[22] Another common pattern is for the panel to consist of a physician, an attorney, and a member of the "general public"[23]; still other states simply provide for a "tripartite board" (with one member named by each party and a chairman selected by the other two members or by the court) without specifying the profession or background of the arbitrators. Under the various statutes the fees and expenses of the arbitrators may be shared equally by the parties, may be assessed by the arbitrators as an element of costs, or may in some cases come directly from state funds.

If either party is dissatisfied with the arbitration award, he has the right to demand a trial de novo to be held in the regular state courts. In consequence it is often said that the review panels serve not so much to "decide" disputes, as to provide "an expert opinion" based on evidence submitted to them—that they act "in the nature of a pretrial settlement conference," or that, by giving the parties a preliminary, disinterested evaluation of the merits of a claim, they serve an "advisory" function and help to "promote an early disposition of many cases by a voluntary settlement."[24] You have already been introduced to dispute resolution processes that can serve similar functions in Chapter IV. In a number of states, however, decisions of review panels are given somewhat greater clout by being made admissible in any later trial of the malpractice claim.[25]

(b) There has been some experimentation also with the use of *voluntary* agreements to arbitrate malpractice claims between a patient and a medical defendant. As in the case of traditional arbitration, such agreements can be entered into either prior to treatment or as the submission of an existing dispute; where such an agreement is made, the arbitrator's decision will be binding on both parties.

In a number of states, statutes expressly authorize the arbitration of medical malpractice disputes:[26] These statutes are intended not only to encourage agreements to arbitrate but also to regulate the process; they

22. See, e.g., Neb.Rev.St. § 44–2841 (each party selects one physician and the two thus chosen select a third; panel also includes attorney who acts in "advisory capacity" and has no vote).

23. See, e.g., Md.Code, Courts & Jud.Proceed. §§ 3–2A–03, 3–2A–04 (state "Health Claims Arbitration Office" circulates lists of arbitrators in each category to the parties, who may strike unacceptable names); Del.Code Tit. 18, §§ 6804, 6805 (each panel consists of two "health care providers," one attorney, and two "lay persons" chosen from a "list of 100 objective and judicious persons of appropriate education and experience" maintained by the Commissioner of Insurance).

24. Prendergast v. Nelson, 199 Neb. 97, 256 N.W.2d 657, 666–67 (1977).

25. E.g., La.S.A.–Rev. Stat. 40:1299.47(H) (report of the "expert opinion" of the panel is "admissible," but not "conclusive").

26. E.g., Alaska Stat. ch. 55 § 09.55.535; S.H.A.Ill.Comp.Stat. ch. 710 § 15/1; La.S.A.–Rev.Stat. § 9:4232; Ohio Rev. Code Tit. 27, § 2711.22; West's Ann.Cal.Code Civ.Proc. § 1295; see Pietrelli v. Peacock, 13 Cal.App.4th 943, 16 Cal.Rptr.2d 688, 689 (1993) ("The purpose of § 1295 was to encourage and facilitate arbitration of medical malpractice disputes"); cf. N.Y.–McKinney's C.P.L.R. 7550 et seq. (limited to HMO's).

646 CHAPTER V ARBITRATION

commonly provide, for example, that notice that an agreement contains an arbitration clause must be printed in conspicuous "bold red type," and that an agreement to arbitrate "may not be made a prerequisite to receipt of care or treatment" by a doctor or hospital.[27] In other jurisdictions, voluntary arbitration agreements between patients and health care providers may also be enforceable under the state's general arbitration statute.

It appears that agreements for binding arbitration are not as yet widespread in the medical setting—although recent surveys do suggest "a dynamic innovation environment," since "organizations that are well positioned to stimulate use of agreements are aware of them, and alert to information that may demonstrate they have value." One California study reveals that while only 9% of physicians and hospitals in the state use arbitration agreements, 60% of the physicians using such agreements have adopted them since 1990—"suggesting that a reasonably persistent diffusion process is underway in the physician community."[28] About a third of the responding physicians and hospitals that did *not* use arbitration agreements attributed their reluctance to the fear that such agreements "set the wrong tone" for the patient,[29] creating "an uncomfortable situation."[30] Other possible reasons for the current lack of physician enthusiasm also might be suggested: For example, the supposed propensity of arbitrators to indulge in compromise decisions might not be attractive to physicians who in malpractice cases "possess a strong interest in vindicating their conduct."[31] And even where claims are subject to an arbitration agreement, defense attorneys will commonly fail to move to dismiss lawsuits filed by patients: Some defense attorneys in fact prefer to keep a case in court despite the existence of an arbitration agreement—apparently "for fear that a physician arbitrator would easily recognize that in that particular case, a deviation in the standard had occurred."[32]

In sharp contrast to the limited use by individual physicians and hospitals, the same California survey revealed that 71% of the state's HMO's do use binding arbitration agreements with their subscribers. Such arbitration agreements are usually designed by HMO's to apply to contract disputes only—and not to claims alleging medical malpractice. However, an important exception to this finding is the nation's largest HMO, Kaiser Permanente—which *does* require all of its subscribers in California and in three other states to agree to arbitrate any medical malpractice claims, as well as any other disputes arising out of their health care plans. (Over 6

---

27. West's Ann.Cal.Code Civ.Proc. § 1295(b); Alaska Stat. ch. 55, § 09.55.535(a).

28. Rolph et al., Arbitration Agreements in Health Care: Myths and Reality, 60 Law & Contemp. Probs. 153, 171–72, 180 (1997).

29. Id. at 175.

30. See U.S. General Accounting Office, Medical Malpractice: Few Claims Resolved

Through Michigan's Voluntary Arbitration Program 6 (1990).

31. Metzloff, Alternative Dispute Resolution Strategies in Medical Malpractice, 9 Alaska L.Rev. 429, 440 (1992).

32. Whitelaw, Health Care Arbitration in Michigan: An Effective Method of Alternative Dispute Resolution, 72 Mich. Bar J. 1158, 1162 (1993).

million Kaiser subscribers are subject to mandatory arbitration agreements).

Kaiser's arbitration program was originally designed to be self-administered—with "administrative functions performed by outside counsel retained to defend Kaiser in an adversarial capacity."[33] Kaiser claimed that plaintiffs in its arbitrations tended to win about half of the time—although arbitration was also thought to "reduce the likelihood of excessive awards."[34] However, in 1997 the California Supreme Court refused to compel arbitration against the estate of a deceased plan participant—finding that Kaiser had engaged in fraud both "in the inducement "and "in the application" of the arbitration agreement: An independent statistical analysis of Kaiser arbitrations found that in only 1% of all Kaiser cases was a neutral arbitrator appointed within the 60–day period mandated by the plan; on average it took 863 days to reach a hearing in a Kaiser arbitration. For the court, a fraud claim could be premised on Kaiser's conduct in setting up a self-administered arbitration system "in which delay for its own benefit and convenience was an inherent part"—and yet nevertheless "persist[ing] in its contractual promises of expeditiousness."[35] As a result of such criticisms, Kaiser has since re-designed its arbitration mechanism to provide for independent administration. It has appointed the Law Offices of Sharon Lybeck Hartmann—"a boutique firm specializing in monitoring consent decrees and injunctions and in alternative dispute resolution, primarily in the field of civil rights"—to serve as the "Office of the Independent Administrator," and to write rules of procedure for Kaiser arbitrations, to create a panel of qualified neutrals, and to monitor the progress of the arbitrations "to assure that each case moves as expeditiously as possible." The OIA began administering arbitrations in March 1999; its first annual report can be found at www.slhartmann.com/oia.

Nevertheless a recent report by the California Research Bureau—the research arm of the California Legislature—has been highly critical of both the fairness and efficiency of patient-insurer arbitration. This 2000 report covered 50 health plans, although most of its data came from Kaiser. The Bureau noted that 12% of all Kaiser arbitrations under the OIA were dismissed on summary judgment (by contrast, the summary judgment rate in civil litigation was only 0.6%): This was attributed in part to the fact

---

33. Engalla v. Permanente Medical Group, Inc., 15 Cal.4th 951, 64 Cal. Rptr.2d 843, 849, 938 P.2d 903 (1997).

34. U.S. General Accounting Office, Medical Malpractice: Alternatives to Litigation 8–9 (1992); see also "Med–Mal Arbitration in California: Murky Results," Legal Times, Sept. 13, 1993 at 10. Cf. Zuckerman et al., Information on Malpractice: A Review of Empirical Research on Major Policy Issues, 49 Law & Contemp.Probs. 85, 103–06 (1986) (summarizing results of empirical studies of medical malpractice arbitration; "a major problem in assessing the attributes of arbitration is that so few cases have been arbitrated," and "controlled comparisons with conventional litigation are difficult to conduct").

35. Engalla v. Permanente Medical Group, Inc., supra n.33 at 853, 858 (held, "there is evidence to support the [plaintiff's] claims that Kaiser fraudulently induced [plaintiff] to enter the arbitration agreement in that it misrepresented the speed of its arbitration program, a misrepresentation on which [plaintiff's] employer relied by selecting Kaiser's health plan for its employees").

648 CHAPTER V ARBITRATION

that it is "easier to file an arbitration claim" than to institute litigation (so that arbitrators see more plaintiffs who probably would never make it to court), and in part to the fact that many Kaiser arbitrations are conducted *pro se* (so that the claimant "may be unable to present evidence correctly or even understand what evidence needs to be presented."). Large malpractice awards are apparently less common in arbitration than in comparable jury trials: Excluding summary judgment, patients were successful in only 35% of the cases arbitrated; 45% of the awards were under $100,000, and only 6% were more than $1 million. The report pointed out that during the selection process, the health plan is likely to have far more information than the claimant with respect to the track record of potential arbitrators, and is therefore "in a good position to make informed decisions": Thirty percent of the Kaiser arbitration claims were decided by eight repeat arbitrators, most of whom were likely to rule in favor of the defense. (None of the arbitrators in cases awarding more than $1 million had a second reported case). As a consequence—"[b]ecause the potential earnings, relative to the costs of preparing a case, are too limited"—lawyers are seldom willing to take such arbitration cases on a contingency basis.[36]

NOTES AND QUESTIONS

1. In this section you have been introduced to a use of arbitration quite different from the models presented in the labor and commercial areas. You can see that the term "arbitration" is commonly applied to describe any number of different processes, developing along different lines and responding to different needs. Indeed, the long-standing acceptability and respectability of "arbitration" make it a useful term to be co-opted by innovators in the dispute resolution field.

Some of the attributes traditionally claimed for arbitration may be present here as well. In consumer arbitration, an arbitrator is typically asked to apply fairly straightforward rules of decision to limited and tractable fact questions; in addition, the stakes are likely to be small and the procedure extremely informal. In such circumstances there are likely to be advantages, at least to the plaintiff, of reduced delay and costs—similar to the advantages often claimed for small claims courts. Studies indicate also that arbitration, at least where it is voluntary in inception and binding in result, may bring similar benefits to medical malpractice claimants in the form of increased speed and reduced expense. See, e.g., Note, Medical Malpractice Arbitration: A Patient's Perspective, 61 Wash.U.L.Q. 123, 153–155 (1983).

However, there are also some significant differences. The usefulness of arbitration may be diluted where the parties do not (as they may in labor and commercial disputes) "have an interest in the pie of continued collaboration." See Henry M. Hart & Albert M. Sacks, The Legal Process 315

---

36. Nieto & Hosel, Arbitration in California Managed Health Care Systems 2, 19 (CRB 2000).

B. Some Frequent Uses of Arbitration 649

(1994). Especially where the parties' autonomy in the choice of the process or in the selection of arbitrators is reduced, the decision-makers are no longer "their" arbitrators, spelling out the meaning of "their" agreement in terms of their probable preferences or past practice. It then becomes more appropriate to view arbitration not as part of the world of "private ordering" but simply as a form of economic regulation. Particularly in the field of medical malpractice such regulation is often responsive to a not-very-well-hidden agenda, as the following excerpt indicates:

> The push for the arbitration of malpractice claims * * * must not be seen as linked to the general interest in alternative dispute resolution mechanisms exhibited over the past two decades. This examination of alternative mechanisms has had as its primary goal the identification of fora and procedures suitable for the resolution of meritorious claims that, for essentially economic reasons, had been excluded from the litigation system. In direct contrast, malpractice claims have always been guaranteed judicial resolution because of the contingency fee system. * * *

> There are two primary goals set forth by those propounding the arbitration of malpractice claims: first, to chill attorney interest in what are labelled *vel non* as frivolous or unmeritorious claims; and second, to reduce the size of damage awards in meritorious claims. Neither goal is related to providing a resolution for otherwise unresolvable claims. Both are intimately linked, however, to the widely held belief that the judiciary is unwilling or unable to exercise effective control over juries in civil trials. * * *

> Arbitration and pretrial review of medical malpractice claims serve different legislative goals. At the most general level, both are designed to freeze or slow the acceleration of the size of malpractice insurance premiums. The effect of pretrial review, however, is to chill plaintiff interest in pursuing marginal claims, both practically and psychologically, and to encourage settlement by forcing additional plaintiff expenditure without providing for concomitant recovery. Arbitration, on the other hand, is viewed primarily as a constitutionally safe method of avoiding jury determinations of liability and quantum of damages.

Terry, The Technical and Conceptual Flaws of Medical Malpractice Arbitration, 30 St. Louis U.L.J. 571, 572–73, 586 (1986).

2. A Florida statute provides that either party to a medical malpractice suit may request a "medical arbitration panel" to determine damages. An agreement by both parties to participate in arbitration binds both to the panel's decision. In such a case the plaintiff's noneconomic damages will be capped at $250,000 per incident and "calculated on a percentage basis with respect to capacity to enjoy life" (so, for example, a finding that the plaintiff had suffered a "50% reduction in his capacity to enjoy life" would warrant an award of not more than $125,000 in noneconomic damages). No punitive damages may be awarded, but the plaintiff is entitled to attorneys' fees of up to 15% of the award. If the defendant offers to arbitrate but *the plaintiff refuses,* the plaintiff may proceed to trial, although his noneconom-

650 CHAPTER V ARBITRATION

ic damages at trial will be limited to $350,000 per incident. If, however, it is the *defendant who refuses arbitration*, the plaintiff may proceed to trial without any limitation on damages at all—and in addition is entitled to recover attorneys' fees up to 25% of the award.

What incentives are this statute intended to create? See West's Fla. Stat.Ann. §§ 766.207, 766.209, 766.211, 766.212; University of Miami v. Echarte, 618 So.2d 189 (Fla.1993).

3. One common provision in statutes regulating medical malpractice arbitration is a "cooling off period." The Ohio statute, for example, allows a patient to "withdraw" his consent to arbitrate by written notice within 60 days "after the termination of the physician-patient relationship" (in the case of a hospital, within 60 days after the patient's discharge). Ohio Rev.Code Tit. 27 § 2711.23(B).

What is the point of a statutory "cooling off" period? Is it that a patient may *retroactively* withdraw his consent to arbitrate disputes over treatment already received? The Louisiana statute, however, is explicit that while an arbitration agreement is "voidable" within 30 days after "the date of execution," it is nevertheless "binding" as to acts of malpractice committed "prior to the revocation date." La.S.A.–Rev.Stat. § 9:4233.

4. Another area where there has been recent experimentation with use of the arbitration process has been in disputes between consumers and automobile manufacturers. General Motors and some other manufacturers, for example (including Honda, Nissan, and Volkswagen) have agreed to submit disputes over new-car warranties to the "Auto Line" program administered by the Better Business Bureau. In this program, the consumer's complaint is heard by volunteer arbitrators—"lawyers, professors, accountants, company executives, housewives, trade association personnel"—who have gone through a short training program but who have no necessary background in either the law or in automobile mechanics; they are told to "make common sense adjudications based on their own sense of fairness." General Motors Corp. v. Abrams, 897 F.2d 34, 37 (2d Cir.1990). "In the vast majority of cases both parties represent themselves, and do not find it necessary to involve an attorney." The arbitrators will hear any claims under an automobile warranty, although they will not consider claims for consequential damages such as for personal injury or lost wages. The program is funded by the manufacturer, operates at no cost to the consumer, and is designed to resolve any complaint within 40 days after filing. The manufacturer generally agrees in advance to be bound by the award. The consumer, however, is free either to reject any unfavorable award and pursue a warranty claim in court, or indeed, to bypass the arbitration process entirely. See generally the BBB's web site at http://www.dr.bbb.org/autoline.cfm.

5. As part of the expansion of consumer protection legislation over the last two decades, most states have enacted so-called "lemon laws" aimed at insuring that automobile manufacturers conform the vehicle to any express warranty. These statutes grant additional rights to the consumer by requiring the manufacturer to refund the purchase price or provide the consumer a new replacement vehicle if it cannot correct any defect after a "reasonable number of attempts."

State "lemon laws" also commonly provide that where the manufacturer has set up or participates in a qualified "third party dispute resolution process" to hear warranty claims, then the consumer must first assert any "lemon law" claims through such a process. See Tanner Consumer Protection Act, Cal. Civ. Code § 1793.22 (c), (d). A number of states such as California have "certified" the BBB's AutoLine program as meeting the minimum standards of the state lemon law. A recent survey by California's Department of Consumer Affairs indicated that an "AutoLine" arbitration decision was in the consumer's favor 58% of the time, but that consumers reported they were "satisfied with the arbitration process" in 64% of the cases, and that they "would recommend the arbitration process to others" in 66% of the cases. Apparently a post-arbitration lawsuit was filed by the consumer in only 8% of the cases. 1999 Annual Consumer Satisfaction Survey, "Arbitration Certification Program," available at *http://www.dca.ca.gov/acp/survey_99.htm*. Cf. Harrison v. Nissan Motor Corp., 111 F.3d 343 (3d Cir. 1997)(Pennsylvania "lemon law"; held, BBB AutoLine mechanism is not "arbitration" within the Federal Arbitration Act, so circuit court had no appellate jurisdiction under FAA to review a district court's refusal to dismiss the consumer's complaint for failure to "first resort" to the AutoLine program).

In New York, by contrast, consumers have the option of selecting arbitration under AAA auspices as an alternative to any process that the manufacturer sets up or sponsors. A consumer is free to initiate an AAA arbitration under the state "lemon law" even if she has already resorted to the manufacturer's own non-binding process and been denied relief. Most notably, AAA arbitration is made *mandatory* for the manufacturer at the consumer's option. If the consumer elects AAA arbitration and pays a filing fee she will, however, be bound by the result in the same way as the manufacturer. See N.Y.Gen.Bus.Law § 198–a(k), (m).

6. Disputes between attorneys and clients over legal fees constitute the major share of all attorney-client conflict—it has even been said that such disputes constitute "the principal source of public dissatisfaction with the judicial system." Anderson v. Elliott, 555 A.2d 1042, 1049 (Me.1989). Litigation over fees is a highly unsatisfactory method of dispute resolution for the attorney; a suit over unpaid fees virtually guarantees a counterclaim for malpractice, so that "fee suits can be ugly affairs." Charles Wolfram, Modern Legal Ethics § 9.61 at 554 (1986). And litigation may be equally unattractive for the client. In addition to the cost, it may be difficult even to find a local lawyer willing to handle a fee case against another attorney; there is also the risk that in such litigation confidential information that had earlier been revealed to the attorney may become part of the public record. See Model Rules of Professional Conduct, Rule 1.6(b)(2), in Appendix D, infra.

As a consequence, a number of states have made binding arbitration of fee disputes mandatory for the attorney at the request of a client. See, e.g.,

652   CHAPTER V ARBITRATION

Anderson v. Elliott, supra; In re LiVolsi, 85 N.J. 576, 428 A.2d 1268 (1981). In most other states, state or local bar associations offer programs by which attorney and client can voluntarily enter into binding arbitration after a fee dispute has arisen. These arbitration programs are usually administered by the bar association, and attorneys serve as the arbitrators (although in larger cases, where a panel of three arbitrators is used, it is common for one lay person to sit on the panel along with the attorneys.) See generally Alan Rau, Resolving Disputes Over Attorneys' Fees: The Role of ADR, 46 S.M.U.L.Rev. 2005 (1993).

In addition, lawyers are increasingly experimenting with *pre-dispute* arbitration agreements, entered into with the client at the time the attorney is retained. Such agreements frequently purport to cover not only fee disputes but also later claims of malpractice. See, e.g., McGuire, Cornwell & Blakey v. Grider, 765 F.Supp. 1048 (D.Colo.1991) (agreement bound client to submit to arbitration "any fee disputes * * * and claims by you regarding [the firm's] handling of your matter," although it expressly permitted the firm to "[collect] amounts due to it in other ways, including litigation").

Might such pre-dispute agreements raise ethical problems for the attorney? Is any guidance to be found in Rule 1.8 of the Model Rules of Professional Conduct? In some ethics opinions Rule 1.8 has been thought to make such agreements impermissible unless the client has actually been "counseled by another attorney" before signing: See, e.g., Md. State Bar Comm. on Ethics Dock. 90–12 (1989) ("If the client refuses to seek independent counsel, then the lawyer is prohibited from entering into such a written agreement"). See also D.C. Bar Legal Ethics Comm., Op. 211 (1990)("the lawyer entering into a retainer agreement with a client for arbitration of all disputes, including malpractice, could not adequately explain the tactical considerations of arbitration versus litigation to the lay client—considerations such as lack of formal discovery, lack of a jury trial, and the closed nature of arbitration proceedings"); cf. Op. 218 (1991)(agreement calling for mandatory arbitration of *fee* disputes before the bar association's Attorney–Client Arbitration Board is ethically permissible given that the Board's procedures and rules are "relatively simple to understand" and that counseling is provided by the Board staff). An Ohio opinion concludes that since "it is impractical to expect most clients to 'hire a lawyer to hire a lawyer,'" the practice of requiring clients to prospectively agree to arbitrate legal malpractice disputes should be generally "discouraged"—and that such arbitration should in all cases "be a voluntary decision made by a client after opportunity to consider the facts and circumstances of the dispute." Ohio Bd. Comm. Griev. & Discip. Op. 96–9 (1996),

Other opinions indicate that a lawyer may contractually require arbitration of malpractice claims only if he "fully discloses, in writing and in terms that can be understood by the client, the advantages and disadvantages of arbitration" and "gives the client a reasonable opportunity to seek the advice of independent counsel," State Bar of Ariz. Op. 94–05 (1994); see also Pa. Bar Ass'n Comm. on Legal Ethics & Prof. Resp., Formal Op. 97–140 (1997)(it is not necessary to require that the client actually consult independent counsel "because such would mean that a client would have to consult a lawyer to retain a lawyer, and such could go on indefinitely"). In still other states, by contrast, pre-dispute arbitration clauses for malpractice claims are freely permitted on the ground that they do not limit the attorney's liability at all—but "merely select the forum in which liability will be determined," Calif. State Bar, Ethics Op. 1989–116 (1989); see also Maine Bd. of Bar Overseers Prof. Ethics Comm'n Op. 170 (1999)(the suggestion that someone is necessarily prejudiced by having to proceed to arbitration reflects a "jaundiced view of arbitration"). Is this rationale convincing?

7. Do you expect that resolution of consumer and malpractice claims that is "private"—that is, that uses non-"official" decision makers, does not establish precedent or communicate its decisions in reasoned opinions, and is otherwise withdrawn from public scrutiny—is likely to have the deterrent or accident-reduction effects of tort litigation?

8. Arbitration clauses found in consumer transactions are increasingly being challenged on the ground that they are not enforceable as contracts—because, for example, they are "unconscionable" contracts of adhesion. See the discussion at pp. 699–711 infra; see also p. 781 infra (Magnuson–Moss Act and "public policy").

C. ARBITRATION AND THE COURTS

1. INTRODUCTION

The traditional attitude of judges towards arbitration has been one of considerable hostility, "explained," if at all, by ritual invocation of the phrase that agreements to submit disputes to arbitration "oust the jurisdiction of the courts." Perhaps this rhetorical flourish masked some concern over the diversion from the court system of cases implicating public values, or fear that private tribunals might ignore or undermine the enforcement of "legal" rules. Somewhat more cynically, one might also suppose that it originated in considerations of competition for business, at a time when judge's salaries still depended on fees paid by litigants.

At common law, if the parties did voluntarily submit a dispute to arbitration *and* the arbitrator proceeded to render an award, the award would be considered binding. Barring some exceptional defense such as arbitrator misconduct, the award could be enforced in a separate court action brought by the successful plaintiff. However, purely *executory* agreements to arbitrate had little force. A party could refuse to honor such an agreement and could revoke it at any time; a court would not specifically enforce an agreement to arbitrate existing or future disputes. While damages could in theory be awarded for breach of this contract, how could they possibly be calculated?[1] So a potential "defendant" could deprive the arbitration agreement of any effect simply by giving notice of his objection and refusing to participate in the process. A potential "plaintiff" could, after revocation, simply bring his own lawsuit, and the court would hear the case without regard to the agreement to arbitrate. A readable summary of the situation at common law can be found in Judge Frank's opinion in Kulukundis Shipping Co. S/A v. Amtorg Trading Corp., 126 F.2d 978 (2d Cir.1942).

Beginning with New York in 1920, most states have now passed statutes completely reversing the common law position on arbitration. The Uniform Arbitration Act, on which many modern state statutes have been modeled, was adopted by the National Conference of the Commissioners on Uniform State Laws in 1955.[2] The Federal Arbitration Act (FAA) was enacted in 1925. All of these statutes are quite similar in their broad outlines, although there is considerable variation in detail. The Federal Act, because of its overwhelming importance, is set out in Appendix F, infra. Read the text of the Act carefully: It is deceptively simple for a statute which has grown to assume such pervasive importance. What does the Act do to change the common law attitude towards arbitration? How does it assure the enforceability of agreements to arbitrate?

The situation is further complicated by the fact that even in states with "modern" statutes modeled on the New York or Uniform Act, the statute is usually not interpreted to be exclusive. As a consequence, "common law arbitration" still survives. Thus, even where the arbitration statute has not been complied with—for example, where there has been no written agreement to arbitrate or where the subject matter of the dispute has been specifically excluded from the coverage of the statute—the arbitrator's decision will have the same binding force it would have at common law, as long as consent to arbitrate has not been revoked and the parties have proceeded without objection to an award. See, e.g., L.H. Lacy Co. v. City of Lubbock, 559 S.W.2d 348 (Tex.1977) (arbitration statute did not apply to construction contracts); see generally Sturges and Reckson, Common–Law and Statutory Arbitration: Problems Arising From Their Coexistence, 46 Minn.L.Rev. 819 (1962).

Nor have state arbitration statutes frozen the independent *development* of the common law. On the contrary, in a number of places they seem to have aided in its growth. Increasingly, decisions can be found where courts will rely on the "pro-arbitration" policy of the state statute to enforce an arbitration agreement *outside* the statute's substantive scope,

---

1. See Munson v. Straits of Dover S.S. Co., 102 Fed. 926 (2d Cir.1900) (plaintiff sought damages, in the form of lawyer's fees and costs incurred in defending a lawsuit, for breach of agreement to arbitrate; held, plaintiff entitled to nominal damages only; judicial process is "theoretically at least, the safest and best devised by the wisdom and experience of mankind.").

2. A revised version of the Uniform Arbitration Act was approved by the NCCUSL at its Annual Meeting in August, 2000. The Revised Uniform Arbitration Act is available at http://www.law.upenn.edu/bll/ulc/ulc_frame.htm.

and *despite* one party's prior attempt to "revoke." See Olshan Demolishing Co. v. Angleton Independent School District, 684 S.W.2d 179 (Tex.App.— Houston [14th Dist.] 1984) (agreement to arbitrate lacked statutory notice; "[e]ncouraging arbitration will reduce some of the backlog in our trial courts"); Kodak Mining Co. v. Carrs Fork Corp., 669 S.W.2d 917 (Ky.1984) (statute then in force applied only to submission of existing disputes to arbitration).

2. THE FEDERAL ARBITRATION ACT AND STATE LAW

a. PREEMPTION OF STATE LAW

The FAA was enacted before *Erie v. Tompkins* (in 1938) called for a fundamental rethinking of the relationships between state and federal courts. Over the last 50 years, problems of federalism in the enforcement of arbitration agreements have surfaced on a number of occasions. Only recently have some fundamental issues been more or less settled.

Bernhardt v. Polygraphic Co. of America, Inc., 350 U.S. 198 (1956), was a diversity case in federal court. The contract provided that any future disputes would be settled by arbitration; the transaction was assumed *not* to "involve" interstate commerce. At that time, Vermont law made an agreement to arbitrate revocable at any time before an award was actually handed down. In such circumstances, could the federal court enforce the arbitration agreement? The Supreme Court said "no": In the absence of a "transaction involving commerce," *state* law on arbitration was to be applied in federal courts in diversity cases. Arbitration was therefore "substantive" for *Erie* purposes: "The change from a court of law to an arbitration panel may make a radical difference in ultimate result." Furthermore, the Court said, the "procedures" for enforcing arbitration agreements in section 3 of the Federal Act were limited by section 2; applying the FAA, therefore, even in a federal court, is dependent on the existence of "a transaction involving commerce."

It later became settled that the FAA had been enacted as an exercise of Congress' commerce and admiralty powers. The Act thus laid down substantive rules of decision, binding on federal courts even in diversity cases as long as interstate or foreign commerce or maritime matters were involved. In this respect, though, the FAA remains something of an anomaly among federal statutes: Although enacted under Congress' commerce power, of itself it confers no federal question *jurisdiction.* Therefore, an action to enforce an arbitration agreement under the Act does not "arise under" federal law but requires an *independent* source of federal jurisdiction, such as diversity or some other federal statute.

This line of cases raised still further questions: In cases that *do* involve foreign or interstate commerce, does the body of law fashioned by federal courts bind *state* courts as well? For example, would a Vermont court, in such a case, still be free to hold an arbitration agreement revocable, or is Vermont law to that effect preempted by the FAA?

Southland Corporation v. Keating

Supreme Court of the United States, 1984.
465 U.S. 1, 104 S.Ct. 852, 79 L.Ed.2d 1.

■ CHIEF JUSTICE BURGER delivered the opinion of the Court.

This case presents the questions (a) whether the California Franchise Investment Law, which invalidates certain arbitration agreements covered by the Federal Arbitration Act, violates the Supremacy Clause and (b) whether arbitration under the federal Act is impaired when a class-action structure is imposed on the process by the state courts.

Appellant Southland Corp. is the owner and franchisor of 7–Eleven convenience stores. Southland's standard franchise agreement provides each franchisee with a license to use certain registered trademarks, a lease or sublease of a convenience store owned or leased by Southland, inventory financing, and assistance in advertising and merchandising. The franchisees operate the stores, supply bookkeeping data, and pay Southland a fixed percentage of gross profits. The franchise agreement also contains the following provision requiring arbitration:

> "Any controversy or claim arising out of or relating to this Agreement or the breach hereof shall be settled by arbitration in accordance with the Rules of the American Arbitration Association ... and judgment upon any award rendered by the arbitrator may be entered in any court having jurisdiction thereof."

Appellees are 7–Eleven franchisees. Between September 1975 and January 1977, several appellees filed individual actions against Southland in California Superior Court alleging, among other things, fraud, oral misrepresentation, breach of contract, breach of fiduciary duty, and violation of the disclosure requirements of the California Franchise Investment Law, Cal.Corp.Code § 31000 et seq. Southland's answer, in all but one of the individual actions, included the affirmative defense of failure to arbitrate.

In May 1977, appellee Keating filed a class action against Southland on behalf of a class that assertedly includes approximately 800 California franchisees. Keating's principal claims were substantially the same as those asserted by the other franchisees. After the various actions were consolidated, Southland petitioned to compel arbitration of the claims in all cases, and appellees moved for class certification.

The Superior Court granted Southland's motion to compel arbitration of all claims except those claims based on the Franchise Investment Law. The court did not pass on appellees' request for class certification. Southland appealed from the order insofar as it excluded from arbitration the claims based on the California statute. Appellees filed a petition for a writ of mandamus or prohibition in the California Court of Appeal arguing that the arbitration should proceed as a class action.

The California Court of Appeal reversed the trial court's refusal to compel arbitration of appellees' claims under the Franchise Investment

Law. That court interpreted the arbitration clause to require arbitration of all claims asserted under the Franchise Investment Law, and construed the Franchise Investment Law not to invalidate such agreements to arbitrate. Alternatively, the court concluded that if the Franchise Investment Law rendered arbitration agreements involving commerce unenforceable, it would conflict with § 2 of the Federal Arbitration Act and therefore be invalid under the Supremacy Clause. The Court of Appeal also determined that there was no "insurmountable obstacle" to conducting an arbitration on a classwide basis, and issued a writ of mandate directing the trial court to conduct class-certification proceedings.

The California Supreme Court, by a vote of 4–2, reversed the ruling that claims asserted under the Franchise Investment Law are arbitrable. The California Supreme Court interpreted the Franchise Investment Law to require judicial consideration of claims brought under that statute and concluded that the California statute did not contravene the federal Act.

* * *

The California Franchise Investment Law provides:

"Any condition, stipulation or provision purporting to bind any person acquiring any franchise to waive compliance with any provision of this law or any rule or order hereunder is void." Cal.Corp.Code Ann. § 31512.

The California Supreme Court interpreted this statute to require judicial consideration of claims brought under the state statute and accordingly refused to enforce the parties' contract to arbitrate such claims. So interpreted the California Franchise Investment Law directly conflicts with § 2 of the Federal Arbitration Act and violates the Supremacy Clause.

In enacting § 2 of the federal Act, Congress declared a national policy favoring arbitration and withdrew the power of the states to require a judicial forum for the resolution of claims which the contracting parties agreed to resolve by arbitration. * * *

We discern only two limitations on the enforceability of arbitration provisions governed by the Federal Arbitration Act: they must be part of a written maritime contract or a contract "evidencing a transaction involving commerce" and such clauses may be revoked upon "grounds as exist at law or in equity for the revocation of any contract." We see nothing in the Act indicating that the broad principle of enforceability is subject to any additional limitations under state law.

The Federal Arbitration Act rests on the authority of Congress to enact substantive rules under the Commerce Clause. In Prima Paint Corp. v. Flood & Conklin Mfg. Co., 388 U.S. 395 (1967) [infra p. 690], the Court examined the legislative history of the Act and concluded that the statute "is based upon ... the incontestable federal foundations of 'control over interstate commerce and over admiralty.'" The contract in *Prima Paint,* as here, contained an arbitration clause. One party in that case alleged that the other had committed fraud in the inducement of the contract, although not of the arbitration clause in particular, and sought to have the claim of fraud adjudicated in federal court. The Court held that, notwithstanding a contrary state rule, consideration of a claim of fraud in the inducement of a contract "is for the arbitrators and not for the courts." The Court relied for this holding on Congress' broad power to fashion substantive rules under the Commerce Clause.

At least since 1824 Congress' authority under the Commerce Clause has been held plenary. Gibbons v. Ogden, 9 Wheat 1, 196 (1824). In the words of Chief Justice Marshall, the authority of Congress is "the power to regulate; that is, to prescribe the rule by which commerce is to be governed." The statements of the Court in *Prima Paint* that the Arbitration Act was an exercise of the Commerce Clause power clearly implied that the substantive rules of the Act were to apply in state as well as federal courts.

* * *

Although the legislative history is not without ambiguities, there are strong indications that Congress had in mind something more than making arbitration agreements enforceable only in the federal courts. The House Report plainly suggests the more comprehensive objectives:

"The purpose of this bill is to make valid and enforceable agreements for arbitration contained *in contracts involving interstate commerce* or within the jurisdiction or admiralty, *or* which may be the subject of litigation in the Federal courts." HR Rep No. 96, 68th Cong, 1st Sess, 1 (1924). (emphasis added).

This broader purpose can also be inferred from the reality that Congress would be less likely to address a problem whose impact was confined to federal courts than a problem of large significance in the field of commerce. The Arbitration Act sought to "overcome the rule of equity, that equity will not specifically enforce an[y] arbitration agreement." The House Report accompanying the bill stated:

The need for the law arises from . . . . the jealousy of the English courts for their own jurisdiction. . . . This jealousy survived for so lon[g] a period that the principle became firmly embedded in the English common law and was adopted with it by the American courts. The courts have felt that the precedent was too strongly fixed to be overturned without legislative enactment. . . .

Surely this makes clear that the House Report contemplated a broad reach of the Act, unencumbered by state-law constraints.

* * *

Justice O'Connor argues that Congress viewed the Arbitration Act "as a procedural statute, applicable only in federal courts." If it is correct that Congress sought only to create a procedural remedy in the federal courts, there can be no explanation for the express limitation in the Arbitration Act to contracts "involving commerce." For example, when Congress has authorized this Court to prescribe the rules of procedure in the federal

C. ARBITRATION AND THE COURTS

659

Courts of Appeals, District Courts, and bankruptcy courts, it has not limited the power of the Court to prescribe rules applicable only to causes of action involving commerce. We would expect that if Congress, in enacting the Arbitration Act, was creating what it thought to be a procedural rule applicable only in federal courts, it would not so limit the Act to transactions involving commerce. On the other hand, Congress would need to call on the Commerce Clause if it intended the Act to apply in state courts. Yet at the same time, its reach would be limited to transactions involving interstate commerce. We therefore view the "involving commerce" requirement in § 2, not as an inexplicable limitation on the power of the federal courts, but as a necessary qualification on a statute intended to apply in state and federal courts.

Under the interpretation of the Arbitration Act urged by Justice O'Connor, claims brought under the California Franchise Investment Law are not arbitrable when they are raised in state court. Yet it is clear beyond question that if this suit had been brought as a diversity action in a federal district court, the arbitration clause would have been enforceable. The interpretation given to the Arbitration Act by the California Supreme Court would therefore encourage and reward forum shopping. We are unwilling to attribute to Congress the intent, in drawing on the comprehensive powers of the Commerce Clause, to create a right to enforce an arbitration contract and yet make the right dependent for its enforcement on the particular forum in which it is asserted. And since the overwhelming proportion of all civil litigation in this country is in the state courts, we cannot believe Congress intended to limit the Arbitration Act to disputes subject only to *federal*-court jurisdiction.[9] Such an interpretation would frustrate congressional intent to place "[a]n arbitration agreement ... upon the same footing as other contracts, where it belongs." HR Rep No. 96, 68th Cong, 1st Sess, 1 (1924).

In creating a substantive rule applicable in state as well as federal courts,[10] Congress intended to foreclose state legislative attempts to undercut the enforceability of arbitration agreements.[11] We hold that 31512 of the California Franchise Investment Law violates the Supremacy Clause.

---

9. While the Federal Arbitration Act creates federal substantive law requiring the parties to honor arbitration agreements, it does not create any independent federal question jurisdiction under 28 USC § 1331 or otherwise. This seems implicit in the provisions in § 3 for a stay by a "court in which such suit is pending" and in § 4 that enforcement may be ordered by "any United States district court which, save for such agreement, would have jurisdiction under title 28, in a civil action or in admiralty of the subject matter of a suit arising out of the controversy between the parties."

10. The contention is made that the Court's interpretation of § 2 of the Act ren-

ders §§ 3 and 4 "largely superfluous." This misreads our holding and the Act. In holding that the Arbitration Act preempts a state law that withdraws the power to enforce arbitration agreements, we do not hold that §§ 3 and 4 of the Arbitration Act apply to proceedings in state courts. Section 4, for example, provides that the Federal Rules of Civil Procedure apply in proceedings to compel arbitration. The Federal Rules do not apply in such state-court proceedings

11. * * * Justice Stevens dissents in part on the ground that § 2 of the Arbitration Act permits a party to nullify an agreement to arbitrate on "such grounds as exist at law or in equity for the revocation of any

660 CHAPTER V ARBITRATION

The judgment of the California Supreme Court denying enforcement of the arbitration agreement is reversed; as to the question whether the Federal Arbitration Act precludes a class-action arbitration and any other issues not raised in the California courts, no decision by this Court would be appropriate at this time. As to the latter issues, the case is remanded for further proceedings not inconsistent with this opinion.

■ JUSTICE STEVENS, concurring in part and dissenting in part.

The Court holds that an arbitration clause that is enforceable in an action in a federal court is equally enforceable if the action is brought in a state court. I agree with that conclusion. Although Justice O'Connor's review of the legislative history of the Federal Arbitration Act demonstrates that the 1925 Congress that enacted the statute viewed the statute as essentially procedural in nature, I am persuaded that the intervening developments in the law compel the conclusion that the Court has reached. I am nevertheless troubled by one aspect of the case that seems to trouble none of my colleagues.

For me it is not "clear beyond question that if this suit had been brought as a diversity action in a federal district court, the arbitration clause would have been enforceable." The general rule prescribed by § 2 of the Federal Arbitration Act is that arbitration clauses in contracts involving interstate transactions are enforceable as a matter of federal law. That general rule, however, is subject to an exception based on "such grounds as exist at law or in equity for the revocation of any contract." I believe that exception leaves room for the implementation of certain substantive state policies that would be undermined by enforcing certain categories of arbitration clauses.

The exercise of state authority in a field traditionally occupied by state law will not be deemed preempted by a federal statute unless that was the clear and manifest purpose of Congress. Moreover, even where a federal statute does displace state authority, it "rarely occupies a legal field completely, totally excluding all participation by the legal systems of the states.... Federal legislation, on the whole, has been conceived and drafted on an ad hoc basis to accomplish limited objectives. It builds upon legal relationships established by the states, altering or supplanting them only so far as necessary for the special purpose." P. Bator, P. Mishkin, D. Shapiro,

contract." We agree, of course, that a party may assert general contract defenses such as fraud to avoid enforcement of an arbitration agreement. We conclude, however, that the defense to arbitration found in the California Franchise Investment Law is not a ground that exists at law or in equity "for the revocation of *any* contract" but merely a ground that exists for the revocation of arbitration provisions in contracts subject to the California Franchise Investment Law. Moreover, under this dissenting view, "a state policy of providing special protection for franchisees

... can be recognized without impairing the basic purposes of the federal statute." If we accepted this analysis, states could wholly eviscerate Congressional intent to place arbitration agreements "upon the same footing as other contracts" simply by passing statutes such as the Franchise Investment Law. We have rejected this analysis because it is in conflict with the Arbitration Act and would permit states to override the declared policy requiring enforcement of arbitration agreements.

& H. Wechsler, Hart and Wechsler's The Federal Courts and the Federal System 470–471 (2d ed. 1973).

The limited objective of the Federal Arbitration Act was to abrogate the general common-law rule against specific enforcement of arbitration agreements, and a state statute which merely codified the general common-law rule—either directly by employing the prior doctrine of revocability or indirectly by declaring all such agreements void—would be pre-empted by the Act. However, beyond this conclusion, which seems compelled by the language of § 2 and case law concerning the Act, it is by no means clear that Congress intended entirely to displace state authority in this field. Indeed, while it is an understatement to say that "the legislative history of the ... Act ... reveals little awareness on the part of Congress that state law might be affected," it must surely be true that given the lack of a "clear mandate from Congress as to the extent to which state statutes and decisions are to be superseded, we must be cautious in construing the act lest we excessively encroach on the powers which Congressional policy, if not the Constitution, would reserve to the states."

The textual basis in the Act for avoiding such encroachment is the clause of § 2 which provides that arbitration agreements are subject to revocation on such grounds as exist at law or in equity for the revocation of any contract. The Act, however, does not define what grounds for revocation may be permissible, and hence it would appear that the judiciary must fashion the limitations as a matter of federal common law. In doing so, we must first recognize that as the " 'saving clause' in § 2 indicates, the purpose of Congress in 1925 was to make arbitration agreements as enforceable as other contracts, but not more so." The existence of a federal statute enunciating a substantive federal policy does not necessarily require the inexorable application of a uniform federal rule of decision notwithstanding the differing conditions which may exist in the several States and regardless of the decisions of the States to exert police powers as they deem best for the welfare of their citizens. Indeed the lower courts generally look to state law regarding questions of formation of the arbitration agreement under § 2, which is entirely appropriate so long as the state rule does not conflict with the policy of § 2.

A contract which is deemed void is surely revocable at law or in equity, and the California Legislature has declared all conditions purporting to waive compliance with the protections of the Franchise Investment Laws, including but not limited to arbitration provisions, void as a matter of public policy. Given the importance to the State of franchise relationships, the relative disparity in the bargaining positions between the franchisor and the franchisee, and the remedial purposes of the California Act, I believe this declaration of state policy is entitled to respect.

* * *

[A] state policy of providing special protection for franchisees, such as that expressed in California's Franchise Investment Law, can be recognized without impairing the basic purposes of the federal statute. Like the majority of the California Supreme Court, I am not persuaded that Congress intended the pre-emptive effect of this statute to be "so unyielding as to require enforcement of an agreement to arbitrate a dispute over the application of a regulatory statute which a state legislature, in conformity with analogous federal policy, has decided should be left to judicial enforcement."

Thus * * * I respectfully dissent from [the Court's] conclusion concerning the enforceability of the arbitration agreement. On that issue, I would affirm the judgment of the California Supreme Court.

■ JUSTICE O'CONNOR, with whom JUSTICE REHNQUIST joins, dissenting.

The majority opinion decides three issues. First, it holds that § 2 creates federal substantive rights that must be enforced by the state courts. Second, though the issue is not raised in this case, the Court states that § 2 substantive rights may not be the basis for invoking federal-court jurisdiction under 28 U.S.C. § 1331. Third, the Court reads § 2 to require state courts to enforce § 2 rights using procedures that mimic those specified for federal courts by FAA §§ 3 and 4. The first of these conclusions is unquestionably wrong as a matter of statutory construction; the second appears to be an attempt to limit the damage done by the first; the third is unnecessary and unwise.

One rarely finds a legislative history as unambiguous as the FAA's. That history establishes conclusively that the 1925 Congress viewed the FAA as a procedural statute, applicable only in federal courts, derived, Congress believed, largely from the federal power to control the jurisdiction of the federal courts.

In 1925 Congress emphatically believed arbitration to be a matter of "procedure." At hearings on the Act congressional Subcommittees were told: "The theory on which you do this is that you have the right to tell the Federal courts how to proceed."

* * *

Since *Bernhardt*, a right to arbitration has been characterized as "substantive," and that holding is not challenged here. But Congress in 1925 did not characterize the FAA as this Court did in 1956. Congress believed that the FAA established nothing more than a rule of procedure, a rule therefore applicable only in the federal courts.

* * *

Yet another indication that Congress did not intend the FAA to govern state-court proceedings is found in the powers Congress relied on in passing the Act. The FAA might have been grounded on Congress' powers to regulate interstate and maritime affairs, since the Act extends only to contracts in those areas. There are, indeed, references in the legislative history to the corresponding federal powers. More numerous, however, are the references to Congress' pre-Erie power to prescribe "general law" applicable in all federal courts. At the congressional hearings, for example: "Congress rests solely upon its power to prescribe the jurisdiction and duties of the Federal courts." * * * Plainly, a power derived from Congress' Art III control over federal-court jurisdiction would not by any flight of fancy permit Congress to control proceedings in state courts.

* * *

Section 2, like the rest of the FAA, should have no application whatsoever in state courts. Assuming, to the contrary, that § 2 *does* create a federal right that the state courts must enforce, state courts should nonetheless be allowed, at least in the first instance, to fashion their own procedures for enforcing the right. Unfortunately, the Court seems to direct that the arbitration clause at issue here must be *specifically* enforced; apparently no other means of enforcement is permissible.[20]

It is settled that a state court must honor federally created rights and that it may not unreasonably undermine them by invoking contrary local procedure. " '[T]he assertion of federal rights, when plainly and reasonably made, is not to be defeated under the name of local practice.' " Brown v. Western Ry. Co. of Alabama, 338 U.S. 294, 299 (1949). But absent specific direction from Congress the state courts have always been permitted to apply their own reasonable procedures when enforcing federal rights. Before we undertake to read a set of complex and mandatory procedures into § 2's brief and general language, we should at a minimum allow state courts and legislatures a chance to develop their own methods for enforcing the new federal rights. Some might choose to award compensatory or punitive damages for the violation of an arbitration agreement; some might award litigation costs to the party who remained willing to arbitrate; some might affirm the "validity and enforceability" of arbitration agreements in other ways. Any of these approaches would vindicate § 2 rights in a manner fully consonant with the language and background of that provision.

The unelaborated terms of § 2 certainly invite flexible enforcement. At common law many jurisdictions were hostile to arbitration agreements. That hostility was reflected in two different doctrines: "revocability," which allowed parties to repudiate arbitration agreements at any time before the arbitrator's award was made, and "invalidity" or "unenforceability," equivalent rules that flatly denied any remedy for the failure to honor an arbitration agreement. In contrast, common-law jurisdictions that enforced arbitration agreements did so in at least three different ways—through actions for damages, actions for specific enforcement, or by enforcing sanctions imposed by trade and commercial associations on members who violated arbitration agreements. In 1925 a forum allowing any one of

---

20. If my understanding of the Court's opinion is correct, the Court has made § 3 of the FAA binding on the state courts. But * * * § 3 by its own terms governs only *federal-court* proceedings. Moreover, if § 2, standing alone, creates a federal right to specific enforcement of arbitration agreements §§ 3 and 4 are, of course, largely superfluous.

And if § 2 implicitly incorporates §§ 3 and 4 procedures for making arbitration agreements enforceable before arbitration begins, why not also § 9 procedures concerning venue, personal jurisdiction, and notice for enforcing an arbitrator's award after arbitration ends? One set of procedures is of little use without the other.

664   CHAPTER V ARBITRATION

these remedies would have been thought to recognize the "validity" and "enforceability" of arbitration clauses.

This Court has previously rejected the view that state courts can adequately protect federal rights only if "such courts in enforcing the Federal right are to be treated as Federal courts and subjected pro hac vice to [federal] limitations...." Minneapolis & St. Louis R. Co. v. Bombolis, 241 U.S. 211 (1916). As explained by Professor Hart:

> "The general rule, bottomed deeply in belief in the importance of state control of state judicial procedure, is that federal law takes the state courts as it finds them.... Some differences in remedy and procedure are inescapable if the different governments are to retain a measure of independence in deciding how justice should be administered. If the differences become so conspicuous as to affect advance calculations of outcome, and so to induce an undesirable shopping between forums, the remedy does not lie in the sacrifice of the independence of either government. It lies rather in provision by the federal government, confident of the justice of its own procedure, of a federal forum equally accessible to both litigants."

In summary, even were I to accept the majority's reading of § 2, I would disagree with the Court's disposition of this case. After articulating the nature and scope of the federal right it discerns in § 2, the Court should remand to the state court, which has acted, heretofore, under a misapprehension of federal law. The state court should determine, at least in the first instance, what procedures it will follow to vindicate the newly articulated federal rights.

The Court rejects the idea of requiring the FAA to be applied only in federal courts partly out of concern with the problem of forum shopping. The concern is unfounded. Because the FAA makes the federal courts equally accessible to both parties to a dispute, no forum shopping would be possible even if we gave the FAA a construction faithful to the congressional intent. In controversies involving incomplete diversity of citizenship there is simply no access to federal court and therefore no possibility of forum shopping. In controversies *with* complete diversity of citizenship the FAA grants federal-court access equally to both parties; no party can gain any advantage by forum shopping. Even when the party resisting arbitration initiates an action in state court, the opposing party can invoke FAA § 4 and promptly secure a federal court order to compel arbitration. See, e.g., Moses H. Cone Memorial Hospital v. Mercury Construction Corp., 460 U.S. 1 (1983).

Ironically, the FAA was passed specifically to rectify forum-shopping problems created by this Court's decision in Swift v. Tyson, 16 Pet. 1, 10 L.Ed. 865 (1842). By 1925 several major commercial States had passed state arbitration laws, but the federal courts refused to enforce those laws in diversity cases. The drafters of the FAA might have anticipated *Bernhardt* by legislation and required federal diversity courts to adopt the arbitration law of the State in which they sat. But they deliberately chose a different approach. As was pointed out at congressional hearings, an additional goal of the Act was to make arbitration agreements enforceable even in federal courts located in States that had no arbitration law. The drafters' plan for maintaining reasonable harmony between state and federal practices was not to bludgeon States into compliance, but rather to adopt a uniform federal law, patterned after New York's path-breaking state statute, and simultaneously to press for passage of coordinated state legislation. The key language of the Uniform Act for Commercial Arbitration was, accordingly, identical to that in § 2 of the FAA.

In summary, forum-shopping concerns in connection with the FAA are a distraction that do not withstand scrutiny. The Court ignores the drafters' carefully devised plan for dealing with those problems.

Today's decision adds yet another chapter to the FAA's already colorful history. In 1842 this Court's ruling in Swift v. Tyson set up a major obstacle to the enforcement of state arbitration laws in federal diversity courts. In 1925 Congress sought to rectify the problem by enacting the FAA; the intent was to create uniform law binding only in the federal courts. In Erie R. Co. v. Tompkins, 304 U.S. 64 (1938), and then in Bernhardt v. Polygraphic Co., 350 U.S. 198 (1956), this Court significantly curtailed federal power. In 1967 our decision in *Prima Paint* upheld the application of the FAA in a *federal-court* proceeding as a valid exercise of Congress' Commerce Clause and admiralty powers. Today the Court discovers a federal right in FAA § 2 that the state courts must enforce. Apparently confident that state courts are not competent to devise their own procedures for protecting the newly discovered federal right, the Court summarily prescribes a specific procedure, found nowhere in § 2 or its common-law origins, that the state courts are to follow.

Today's decision is unfaithful to congressional intent, unnecessary, and, in light of the FAA's antecedents and the intervening contraction of federal power, inexplicable. Although arbitration is a worthy alternative to litigation, today's exercise in judicial revisionism goes too far. I respectfully dissent.

NOTES AND QUESTIONS

1. The California Labor Code regulates in an elaborate way the payment of employee wages. (For example, § 201.5 requires that discharged employees in the motion picture business must be given their earned and unpaid wages within "24 hours after discharge excluding Saturdays, Sundays, and holidays."). Section 229 provides:

> Actions to enforce the provisions of this article for the collection of due and unpaid wages claimed by an individual may be maintained without regard to the existence of any private agreement to arbitrate.

In 1973 the Supreme Court sustained a challenge to this statute, commenting sympathetically that it "was due, apparently, to the legislature's desire to protect the worker from the exploitative employer who would demand that a prospective employee sign away in advance his right to resort to the

666 CHAPTER V ARBITRATION

judicial system for redress of an employment grievance. * * * It may be, too, that the legislature felt that arbitration was a less than adequate protection against awarding the wage earner something short of what was due compensation." Merrill Lynch, Pierce, Fenner & Smith, Inc. v. Ware, 414 U.S. 117, 131 (1973). More recently, however, the California statute has been struck down as in conflict with the FAA. Perry v. Thomas, 482 U.S. 483 (1987).

2. Now that § 2 of the FAA makes arbitration agreements enforceable in state courts, does the enforcement mechanism provided by the *rest* of the Act accompany it? To what extent are state courts required to supply remedies equivalent to those in § 3 (stay of court proceedings) and § 4 (order to compel arbitration)? Compare footnote 10 of the majority opinion in *Southland* with footnote 20 of Justice O'Connor's dissent. What about Justice O'Connor's suggestion that specific performance of arbitration agreements is not necessary to vindicate the federal right because damages might be an acceptable alternative?

Section 4 provides for a jury determination of contested issues concerning the "making of the arbitration agreement." But a state might prefer that these issues be decided by a *court,* see Rosenthal v. Great Western Fin. Securities Corp., 14 Cal.4th 394, 58 Cal.Rptr.2d 875, 926 P.2d 1061 (Cal. 1996).

> To have a court rather than a jury pass on the existence of an arbitration agreement hardly appears to undermine or frustrate the arbitration process; moreover, a bench trial of the issue should not be expected to "frequently and predictably" lead to different outcomes. State rules denying a jury trial are certainly consistent both with the summary nature of the proceeding, and with the traditional treatment of these specific performance actions as equitable—and they can only result in making arbitration a speedier and more efficient process. It is not particularly clear in any event what role the choice of a jury in § 4 was intended to play in the overall statutory scheme: For some reason it is only "the party alleged to be in default"—presumably the party who has "failed, neglected, or refused" to proceed with arbitration— who under § 4 is entitled to ask for a jury trial; the party "aggrieved" by such "failure, neglect, or refusal" has no equivalent right. After such an analysis it might be concluded that state law ought to govern on such matters, even where the parties themselves have not expressly chosen to adopt such law.

Alan Rau, "Does State Arbitration Law Matter At All? Part II: A Continuing Role for State Law," in ADR & The Law 208, 211 (15th ed. 1999).

3. The same question can be raised in relation to other FAA provisions. Might § 12 (time limits for seeking to vacate or modify an award) apply to the states? See Jeereddi A. Prasad, M.D., Inc. v. Investors Associates, Inc., 82 F. Supp.2d 365 (D.N.J.2000)(state law permitted challenges to arbitration awards to be raised in opposition to a motion to confirm the award, even after 90 days; held, this contravenes federal policy favoring quick resolution of arbitrations and the enforcement of arbitration awards; "in the absence of contractual intent to the contrary, the FAA trumps the New York rule"). What about § 16 (appealability of trial-court orders dealing with arbitration)? See Bush v. Paragon Property, Inc., 165 Or.App. 700, 997 P.2d 882 (Or.App.2000)("Congress is without power under Article I to require a state to modify its normal judicial procedures, at least when those procedures do not absolutely defeat the congressional purpose").

4. Virginia law requires automobile manufacturers to submit their standard franchise agreements to the Department of Motor Vehicles for approval. Saturn Corporation, a subsidiary of General Motors, includes binding arbitration clauses in all franchise agreements with its dealers. The Department refused to approve the Saturn agreement unless it contained "an opt out provision" for dealers; its position was that while arbitration clauses were permissible, they could not be made "nonnegotiable." Saturn's challenge to the Department's action was successful: State law that "singles out" arbitration clauses, or treats them "more harshly than other contracts," is preempted by the FAA; since Virginia "has no general contract law restricting nonnegotiable provisions in standardized contracts, Virginia may not bar automobile manufacturers from making arbitration provisions a nonnegotiable term of doing business. * * * If a dealer does not wish to agree to nonnegotiable arbitration provisions, the dealer need not do business with Saturn." Saturn Distribution Corp. v. Williams, 905 F.2d 719 (4th Cir.1990).

5. Under Florida law, every arbitration agreement between a securities dealer and a customer must give the customer "the option" of arbitrating before the AAA "or other independent nonindustry arbitration forum" as well as before an "industry forum" such as a stock exchange. On what grounds could it be argued that such state law conflicts with the FAA? See Securities Industry Ass'n v. Lewis, 751 F.Supp. 205 (S.D.Fla.1990).

6. Under the Michigan Franchise Investment Act, any "provision requiring *that arbitration or litigation* be conducted outside this state" is "void and unenforceable if contained in any document relating to a franchise." Is this part of the statute preempted by the FAA? See Flint Warm Air Supply Co., Inc. v. York Int'l Corp., 115 F. Supp.2d 820 (E.D.Mich.2000); see also OPE Int'l L.P. v. Chet Morrison Contractors, Inc., 258 F.3d 443 (5th Cir.2001).

7. Individual investors opened an account with a discount brokerage firm registered in Delaware; the account agreement contained an arbitration clause. The firm advised the investors to buy certain stock that declined dramatically in value. The investors complained to the Division of Securities of the Delaware Department of Justice, and the state later instituted proceedings against the firm, alleging "fraudulent and unethical practices" in violation of state law in connection with the sale of stock. The state sought to impose fines and to revoke the firm's registration, and it also sought rescission of the stock transactions between the firm and the individual investors. The brokerage firm then brought suit to enjoin the state from pursuing this rescission action on behalf of the investors, alleging that the state could not properly pursue rescission since the firm

CHAPTER V ARBITRATION

"had a contractual right to arbitrate [the investors'] claims." The rescission remedy "circumvents [the firm's] rights under the FAA and thus violates the Supremacy Clause." What result? See Olde Discount Corp. v. Tupman, 1 F.3d 202 (3d Cir.1993).

8. The FAA applies to any "maritime transaction" or "contract evidencing a transaction involving commerce." (§ 2). For many years it remained unclear just how broadly this language should be read as a Congressional exercise of control over "commerce." The FAA is the only federal statute that uses the word "involving" to describe a relation to interstate commerce, and different courts adopted different standards as to when transactions were considered to "involve" commerce for purposes of the Act. See, e.g., Metro Industrial Painting Corp. v. Terminal Construction Co., Inc., 287 F.2d 382, 388 (2d Cir.1961) (Lumbard, C.J., concurring) (FAA should apply only when the parties "contemplated substantial interstate activity," for only then would the Act advance their expectations at the time of contracting).

However, the Supreme Court has recently made it clear that § 2 is to be given the broadest possible scope. The phrase "involving" commerce is the "functional equivalent" of "affecting" commerce, the Court held, and both terms "signal an intent to exercise Congress's commerce power to the full." If a transaction "in fact" involves commerce, it is within the FAA even if the parties had never contemplated any connection to interstate commerce. The FAA therefore applied to a contract in which homeowners obtained a lifetime "Termite Protection Plan" from the local office of a Terminix franchisee. It followed that state courts were obligated to enforce the arbitration clause in such a contract—even though under a state statute invalidating pre-dispute arbitration agreements, the clause would be unenforceable. Allied–Bruce Terminix Cos., Inc. v. Dobson, 513 U.S. 265 (1995).

The Supreme Court of Alabama has since held that a contract between a religious order (which owned and operated a monastery in the state) and a local construction company for repairs to the monastery, did not come within the FAA. There was no evidence that tools, equipment, or workers had moved across state lines (although the contractor was in turn to pay a percentage of the project cost to a plaster specialist resident in Texas.) The Alabama court found that the Supreme Court's decision in *Terminix* had been limited by the Court's opinion just three months later in United States v. Lopez, 514 U.S. 549 (1995)—in which the Court upheld a challenge to the constitutionality of the Gun–Free School Zones Act of 1990 (which made it a federal offense for any individual to possess a firearm in a "school zone"). According to the Alabama court, after *Lopez* Congress' Commerce power could extend only to matters that "substantially affect interstate commerce." Sisters of the Visitation v. Cochran Plastering Co., Inc., 775 So.2d 759 (Ala.2000); see also Southern United Fire Ins. Co. v. Knight, 736 So.2d 582 (Ala.1999) (insurance policy issued in Alabama between Alabama resident and Alabama insurer to cover the former's pick-up truck for personal use does not come within FAA; the insurer "does not ... allege that Knight has traveled outside the State or that he ever will").

Is *Sisters of the Visitation* a case of simple misunderstanding? Wasn't the real problem in *Lopez* that neither the statute, nor the underlying regulated behavior, had anything to do with "commerce" or any sort of economic enterprise *in the first place*—whether "interstate" or not? As emphasized by Justice Kennedy's concurring opinion, "here neither the actors nor their conduct have a commercial character, and neither the purpose nor the design of the statute have an evident commercial nexus." 514 U.S. at 580. See also United States v. Morrison, 529 U.S. 598 (2000)(Congress has no authority to enact Violence Against Women Act providing a federal civil remedy for the victims of gender-motivated violence; "gender-motivated crimes of violence are not, in any sense of the phrase, economic activity"). By contrast, isn't it clear that Congress' power to regulate economic activity extends to activity "that might, through repetition elsewhere," or "when viewed in the aggregate," come to substantially affect commerce—even though the effect may be de minimis in an individual case? See Wickard v. Filburn, 317 U.S. 111 (1942)(upholding the application of the Agricultural Adjustment Act to the growing of wheat for home consumption).

Perhaps, however, there is more going on in the Supreme Court of Alabama than a simple misreading of constitutional precedent: The *Sisters of the Visitation* opinion stressed that an expansive application of the FAA "would tend to defeat the doctrine of federalism, making that doctrine a hollow shell," and would "stifle" the efforts of the states to develop "creative" solutions "other than those that catch the fancy of Congress." (The court noted that even though Alabama law makes pre-dispute arbitration clauses unenforceable, the state still does have a "robust alternative dispute resolution program"—apparently consisting of non-binding judicial mediation!) *Sisters of the Visitation*, 775 So. 2d at 764. Cf. Stephen J. Ware, Money, Politics and Judicial Decisions: A Case Study of Arbitration in Alabama, 15 J. of Law and Politics 645 (1999), which concludes that there is a "strong correlation" in the state "between a justice's source of campaign funds and how that justice votes in arbitration cases": "Justices whose campaigns are funded by plaintiffs' lawyers are all Democrats and oppose arbitration, while justices whose campaigns are funded by business are nearly all Republicans and favor arbitration."

9. The question whether the FAA applies to individual employment agreements also remained unsettled for many years. See the proviso to § 1 of the Act. A consensus gradually emerged in the lower courts, under which the § 1 exclusion should be narrowly limited to workers—like seamen and railroad employees—who are actually engaged "in the transportation industries or in the actual movement of goods in interstate commerce." E.g., Hampton v. ITT Corp., 829 F.Supp. 202 (S.D.Tex.1993) ("plaintiffs' employment in the loan servicing industry does not place them within [this] narrow category"). On this interpretation, except for workers literally engaged in interstate transportation, the FAA would apply to employment contracts to the same extent as to any other contract. The Supreme Court, narrowly divided 5–4, finally ratified this general understanding in Circuit City Stores, Inc. v. Adams, 532 U.S. 105 (2001). Justice Kennedy for the Court asserted that "the text of the FAA forecloses the construction" that all employment contracts are excluded from the scope of the Act: The "application of the maxim *ejusdem generis*" provides an "insurmountable textual obstacle" to that reading; in addition, "the plain meaning of the words 'engaged in commerce' [in § 1] is narrower than the more open-ended formulations 'affecting commerce' and 'involving commerce.' " And the Court should not, he added, "chip away at *Southland [v. Keating]* by indirection."

There has been little pressure to apply the Federal Arbitration Act to collective bargaining agreements, given the well-developed body of law enforcing arbitration clauses under § 301 of the Labor Management Relations Act—although, as the Supreme Court has noted, even in such cases "the federal courts have often looked to the [FAA] for guidance," United Paperworkers Int'l Union v. Misco, Inc., 484 U.S. 29, 40 n. 9 (1987). Cf. Coca–Cola Bottling Co. of New York v. Soft Drink & Brewery Workers, 242 F.3d 52 (2d Cir. 2001)("Given the difference in eras [between the respective dates of the two statutes] and the intervening revolution in labor policy, adherence to the FAA in Section 301 cases may led to anomalous or even bizarre results").

10. An insured was injured in an automobile accident and made a claim under the uninsured motorist provision of his policy. The policy contained an arbitration clause, which provided that if the damages awarded by the arbitrators exceeded the statutory minimum coverage for uninsured motorists ($25,000), then either party might demand a trial de novo. The arbitrators awarded the insured $45,000. The court held that the insurer had no right to a new trial; the trial de novo provision was unenforceable since it "would result in complete frustration of the very essence of the public policy favoring arbitration" and would operate "to defeat goals designed to promote judicial economy and respect for the judicial system." Schmidt v. Midwest Family Mutual Ins. Co., 426 N.W.2d 870 (Minn.1988).

What precisely is the nature of the "public policy" argument here? Are you convinced?

b. PREEMPTION AND CHOICE OF LAW: THE PROBLEM OF MULTI-PARTY DISPUTES

Many disputes that may be amenable to settlement by arbitration are considerably more complex than the simple two-party disputes we have been considering throughout this chapter. In a number of common fact patterns, several related players have an interest in resolving a controversy that has arisen out of a single transaction. For example:

(i) The Owner of a new building will have entered into separate contracts with the General Contractor (who is responsible for construction) and with an Architect (who acts as the Owner's representative in designing and overseeing the project). Owner may make a claim against Contractor for alleged defects in construction; Contractor may answer that any defects are attributable to Architect's failings in specifying materials or in inspecting the work. Should Contractor's defense be upheld, Owner may wish to assert a claim against Architect for negligence. Another common scenario is a claim by Contractor against Owner: Contractor may claim that he was unable to comply with the plans and specifications for the project because they called for the use of materials that were unobtainable; this, he asserts, caused him delay and economic loss. Should Contractor's claim be upheld, Owner's position will be that he is entitled to indemnification from Architect for anything he owes to Contractor.[1]

(ii) An owner of a ship suitable for transporting cargo will typically concern himself only with building, financing, and maintaining the vessel, and will enter into a long-term lease of the ship to a Charterer. Charterer may himself be only a middleman speculating on increases in shipping rates; he may then "subcharter" the vessel to someone actually interested in carrying cargo for particular voyages. During the course of one such voyage, the ship may suffer structural damage. Shipowner will seek compensation from Charterer; Charterer in turn will claim that the Subcharterer is responsible for the damage and will seek indemnity from him.[2]

(iii) The Egyptian Government purchased wheat from four American suppliers; it then chartered a vessel from a Shipper to carry the cargo from Texas to Egypt. During loading, it was discovered that the wheat contained insects; Shipper had to delay loading to fumigate the cargo, and claimed damages for the delay from the Government. The Government naturally took the position that it could not be held liable: "The flour must have been contaminated either before loading, in which case the Suppliers would be liable, or after loading, in which case [the Shipper] would be liable."[3]

In these cases, the party "in the middle"—for example, the Owner in case (i)—has an obvious interest in a single proceeding to resolve the interrelated disputes. If the Owner must first assert a claim against Contractor, and only later seek to hold Architect responsible, he is faced with more than just the duplication of time and expense inherent in separate proceedings. There is in addition the real possibility of inconsistent results in the two forums. In a first proceeding, the Owner may be unable to overcome the Contractor's defense based on deficiencies in the project specifications. In a *later* proceeding, however, it may be found that the defect was caused by poor workmanship rather than by the Architect's

---

1. See, e.g., Consolidated Pacific Engineering, Inc. v. Greater Anchorage Area Borough, 563 P.2d 252 (Alaska 1977); Litton Bionetics, Inc. v. Glen Construction Co., Inc., 292 Md. 34, 437 A.2d 208 (1981).

2. See Miller, Consolidated Arbitrations in New York Maritime Disputes, 14 Int'l Bus.Lawyer 58 (1986).

3. In the Matter of the Arbitration Between the Egyptian Co. for Maritime Transport and Hamlet Shipping Co., Inc., 1982 A.M.C. 874 (S.D.N.Y.1981).

CHAPTER V ARBITRATION

negligence in preparing the plans—leaving the Owner "holding the bag" alone. In such a case the Owner would much prefer to be able to sit back and let the Contractor and Architect fight out between themselves the cause of the construction defects.

Suppose, now, that the agreement between Owner and Contractor contains a clause providing for the arbitration of all disputes; however, the agreement between Owner and Architect contains no arbitration clause. In such a case there will in all probability be no way to insure that all the claims are heard at the same time in a single proceeding. Certainly a party who has never agreed to arbitrate a dispute cannot be coerced into the process. By contrast, one powerful advantage of litigation is that a court with jurisdiction over all the interested parties can bring them all into the action. In a lawsuit against Contractor, Owner would be able to join a claim "in the alternative" against Architect (see Fed.R.Civ.P. 20(a)); if he is a defendant, Owner can "implead" Architect as a "third-party defendant." (See Fed.R.Civ.P. 14(a)). And if there are pending separate "actions involving a common question of law or fact," a court "may order a joint hearing or trial of any or all of the matters in issue in the actions" or may "order all the actions consolidated." (Fed.R.Civ.P. 42(a)).

What if *both* contracts (between Owner and Contractor, and between Owner and Architect) contain provisions for the arbitration of future disputes? In such a case the Owner might wish to have the various arbitration proceedings "consolidated"—that is, heard jointly before a common arbitration panel.

The long-standing policy of the AAA is that it will not consolidate separate arbitration proceedings unless all the parties consent or unless all the agreements explicitly provide for consolidation. The AAA has little incentive to force consolidation upon unwilling parties—and may, in fact, fear that doing so will impair the enforceability of the resulting award. So parties in the Owner's position will often attempt to seek a court order for the consolidation of the separate arbitrations. Once a court order has been issued, the AAA is off the hook and is then willing to administer the consolidated arbitrations.

The willingness of courts to order consolidated arbitration varies greatly. Some courts will do so even over the objections of one of the parties—at least when the arbitration agreement does not expressly forbid this. Such a power is asserted "as an incident of the jurisdiction statutorily conferred on a court generally to enforce arbitration agreements";[4] it will be stressed that "the same considerations of adjudicative economy that argue in favor of consolidating closely related court cases argue for consolidating closely related arbitrations."[5]

---

4. Litton Bionetics, Inc., 437 A.2d at 217.

5. Connecticut General Life Ins. Co. v. Sun Life Assurance Co. of Canada, 210 F.3d 771 (7th Cir.2000)("practical considerations [are] relevant to disambiguating a contract, because parties to a contract generally aim at obtaining sensible results in a sensible way")(Posner, J.).

C. Arbitration and the Courts

However, the general trend seems to be hostile to ordering consolidation of related arbitrations without the express consent of the parties to all the agreements. Many courts find the absence of "privity" between the Architect and the Contractor a barrier to ordering consolidated arbitration: To do so, it is suggested, would be to "rewrite" the contracts which these parties entered into. "A court is not permitted to interfere with private arbitration agreements in order to impose its own view of speed and economy."[6] And even if a court would generally be willing to order that the Owner–Contractor and the Owner–Architect arbitrations be heard together, further questions are still likely to arise. If it seems impossible to dovetail the provisions of two arbitration agreements that differ in important respects—for example, if one agreement calls for arbitration in Texas and the other in California, or if the agreements call for administration by different institutions—it may be expected that a court will refuse to consolidate the arbitrations.[7]

If the Owner—who may expect to be "in the middle" in most controversies—does not have the assurance that he will be able to settle all related disputes at the same time through consolidated arbitration, he might in some cases simply prefer to avoid arbitration completely. Some Owner–Contractor agreements in fact contain an "escape clause," freeing the Owner from any obligation to submit disputes with the Contractor to arbitration if the Owner, "in order to fully protect its interests, desires in good faith to bring in or make a party to any [dispute] * * * the Architect, or any other third party who has not agreed to participate in and be bound by the same arbitration proceeding."[8]

Assume, however, that the Owner has not been able to negotiate for the inclusion of such an "escape clause." The Owner is a party to an arbitration agreement with the Contractor, but not with the Architect. When the Contractor demands arbitration, the Owner may argue that for the sake of "efficiency," a court should refuse to compel arbitration so that the entire dispute can be resolved in one judicial proceeding.

This was the fact pattern presented to the Supreme Court in Moses H. Cone Memorial Hospital v. Mercury Construction Corp., 460 U.S. 1 (1983). Owner had filed a state court action against Contractor—seeking a declaratory judgment that their dispute was not arbitrable—and also against Architect, claiming indemnity for any liability to Contractor. Contractor

---

6. American Centennial Ins. Co. v. National Casualty Co., 951 F.2d 107 (6th Cir. 1991); see also Baesler v. Continental Grain Co., 900 F.2d 1193 (8th Cir.1990) (no power to consolidate "absent a provision in an arbitration agreement authorizing consolidation"); Government of the United Kingdom v. Boeing Co., 998 F.2d 68 (2d Cir.1993); Pueblo of Laguna v. Cillessen & Son, Inc., 101 N.M. 341, 682 P.2d 197 (1984).

7. See Hyundai America, Inc. v. Meissner & Wurst GmbH & Co., 26 F.Supp.2d

1217 (N.D.Cal.1998)(consolidation of related arbitrations—one to take place in San Francisco under California law, and the other to take place in Eugene, Oregon under Oregon law—"would run contrary to the principal goal of the FAA which is to enforce agreements into which the parties have entered.").

8. See Garden Grove Community Church v. Pittsburgh–Des Moines Steel Co., 140 Cal.App.3d 251, 191 Cal.Rptr. 15 (1983).

CHAPTER V ARBITRATION

then brought an action in *federal* court against Owner, under § 4 of the FAA, to compel arbitration. Owner, having taken the care in his own action to join a defendant who was not subject to an arbitration agreement, was then in a position to argue that Contractor's action should be stayed, so that the entire dispute could be disposed of in the parallel *state* action. Otherwise, he asserted, there would have to be "piecemeal litigation." The Supreme Court held that it was an abuse of discretion for the district court to grant a stay of the federal action, which at the time was "running well ahead of the state suit." To the Court, Owner's argument was misconceived: If the dispute between Owner and Contractor were in fact arbitrable, then "piecemeal litigation" was inevitable no matter *which* court, state or federal, decided the question of arbitrability. For "the relevant federal law *requires* piecemeal resolution when necessary to give effect to an arbitration agreement."

By contrast, however, some states have been more receptive to such arguments by the Owner. See, e.g., Prestressed Concrete, Inc. v. Adolfson & Peterson, Inc., 308 Minn. 20, 240 N.W.2d 551 (1976) ("Where arbitration would increase rather than decrease delay, complexity, and costs, it should not receive favored treatment"); County of Jefferson v. Barton–Douglas Contractors, Inc., 282 N.W.2d 155 (Iowa 1979) ("prospect of multiple proceedings carrying a potential for inconsistent findings provides a basis for overriding the freedom to contract for arbitration"). In California, a statute expressly permits a court to order consolidation of separate arbitrations when "[t]he disputes arise from the same transactions or series of related transactions" and "[t]here is common issue or issues of law or fact creating the possibility of conflicting rulings by more than one arbitrator or panel of arbitrators." At the same time, however, the statute provides that a court may *stay arbitration,* or *refuse enforcement* of an arbitration agreement, if one of the parties is also a party to pending *litigation* with a third party "arising out of the same transaction," and if there is a "possibility of conflicting rulings on a common issue of law or fact." West's Ann.Cal.Code Civ.Proc. § 1281.2(c); § 1281.3. Following *Southland v. Keating,* would such a refusal or stay of arbitration pursuant to the California statute violate federal law?

Volt Information Sciences, Inc. v. Board of Trustees of the Leland Stanford Junior University

Supreme Court of the United States, 1989.
489 U.S. 468, 109 S.Ct. 1248, 103 L.Ed.2d 488.

■ CHIEF JUSTICE REHNQUIST delivered the opinion of the Court.

Unlike its federal counterpart, the California Arbitration Act, Cal.Civ. Proc.Code Ann. § 1280 et seq., contains a provision allowing a court to stay arbitration pending resolution of related litigation. We hold that application of the California statute is not pre-empted by the Federal Arbitration Act, in a case where the parties have agreed that their arbitration agreement will be governed by the law of California.

C. ARBITRATION AND THE COURTS

675

Appellant Volt Information Sciences, Inc. (Volt), and appellee Board of Trustees of Leland Stanford Junior University (Stanford) entered into a construction contract under which Volt was to install a system of electrical conduits on the Stanford campus. The contract contained an agreement to arbitrate all disputes between the parties "arising out of or relating to this contract or the breach thereof."[1] The contract also contained a choice-of-law clause providing that "[t]he Contract shall be governed by the law of the place where the Project is located." During the course of the project, a dispute developed regarding compensation for extra work, and Volt made a formal demand for arbitration. Stanford responded by filing an action against Volt in California Superior Court, alleging fraud and breach of contract; in the same action, Stanford also sought indemnity from two other companies involved in the construction project, with whom it did not have arbitration agreements. Volt petitioned the Superior Court to compel arbitration of the dispute.[2] Stanford in turn moved to stay arbitration pursuant to Cal.Civ.Proc.Code Ann. § 1281.2(c), which permits a court to stay arbitration pending resolution of related litigation between a party to the arbitration agreement and third parties not bound by it, where "there is a possibility of conflicting rulings on a common issue of law or fact."[3] The Superior Court denied Volt's motion to compel arbitration and stayed the arbitration proceedings pending the outcome of the litigation on the authority of § 1281.2(c).

The California Court of Appeal affirmed. The court acknowledged that the parties' contract involved interstate commerce, that the FAA governs contracts in interstate commerce, and that the FAA contains no provision permitting a court to stay arbitration pending resolution of related litigation involving third parties not bound by the arbitration agreement.

---

1. The arbitration clause read in full as follows: "All claims, disputes and other matters in question between the parties to this contract, arising out of or relating to this contract or the breach thereof, shall be decided by arbitration in accordance with the Construction Industry Arbitration Rules of the American Arbitration Association then prevailing unless the parties mutually agreed [sic] otherwise.... This agreement to arbitrate ... shall be specifically enforceable under the prevailing arbitration law."

2. Volt's motion to compel was apparently brought pursuant to § 4 of the FAA, and the parallel provision of the California Arbitration Act, Cal.Civ.Proc.Code Ann. § 1281.2; the motion cited both Acts as authority, but did not specify the particular sections upon which reliance was placed. Volt also asked the court to stay the Superior Court litigation until the arbitration was completed, presumably pursuant to § 3 of the FAA, and the parallel provision of the Cali-

fornia Arbitration Act, Cal.Civ.Proc.Code Ann. § 1281.2(c)(3).

3. Section 1281.2(c) provides, in pertinent part, that when a court determines that "[a] party to the arbitration agreement is also a party to a pending court action or special proceeding with a third party, arising out of the same transaction or series of related transactions and there is a possibility of conflicting rulings on a common issue of law or fact[,] ... the court (1) may refuse to enforce the arbitration agreement and may order intervention or joinder of all parties in a single action or special proceeding; (2) may order intervention or joinder as to all or only certain issues; (3) may order arbitration among the parties who have agreed to arbitration and stay the pending court action or special proceeding pending the outcome of the arbitration proceeding; or (4) may stay arbitration pending the outcome of the court action or special proceeding."

676 CHAPTER V ARBITRATION

However, the court held that by specifying that their contract would be governed by " 'the law of the place where the project is located,' "the parties had incorporated the California rules of arbitration, including § 1281.2(c), into their arbitration agreement. Finally, the court rejected Volt's contention that, even if the parties had agreed to arbitrate under the California rules, application of § 1281.2(c) here was nonetheless pre-empted by the FAA because the contract involved interstate commerce.

The court reasoned that the purpose of the FAA was " 'not [to] mandate the arbitration of all claims, but merely the enforcement . . . of privately negotiated arbitration agreements.' "While the FAA therefore pre-empts application of state laws which render arbitration agreements unenforceable, "[i]t does not follow, however, that the federal law has preclusive effect in a case where the parties have chosen in their [arbitration] agreement to abide by state rules." To the contrary, because "[t]he thrust of the federal law is that arbitration is strictly a matter of contract," the parties to an arbitration agreement should be "at liberty to choose the terms under which they will arbitrate." Where, as here, the parties have chosen in their agreement to abide by the state rules of arbitration, application of the FAA to prevent enforcement of those rules would actually be "inimical to the policies underlying state and federal arbitration law," because it would "force the parties to arbitrate in a manner contrary to their agreement." The California Supreme Court denied Volt's petition for discretionary review. * * * We now hold that we have appellate jurisdiction and affirm.

Appellant devotes the bulk of its argument to convincing us that the Court of Appeal erred in interpreting the choice-of-law clause to mean that the parties had incorporated the California rules of arbitration into their arbitration agreement. Appellant acknowledges, as it must, that the interpretation of private contracts is ordinarily a question of state law, which this Court does not sit to review. But appellant nonetheless maintains that we should set aside the Court of Appeal's interpretation of this particular contractual provision for two principal reasons.

Appellant first suggests that the Court of Appeal's construction of the choice-of-law clause was in effect a finding that appellant had "waived" its "federally guaranteed right to compel arbitration of the parties' dispute," a waiver whose validity must be judged by reference to federal rather than state law. This argument fundamentally misconceives the nature of the rights created by the FAA. The Act was designed "to overrule the judiciary's longstanding refusal to enforce agreements to arbitrate," and place such agreements " 'upon the same footing as other contracts,' " Scherk v. Alberto–Culver Co., 417 U.S. 506, 511, 94 S.Ct. 2449, 2453, 41 L.Ed.2d 270 (1974) (quoting H.R.Rep. No. 96, 68th Cong., 1st Sess., 1, 2 (1924)). Section 2 of the Act therefore declares that a written agreement to arbitrate in any contract involving interstate commerce or a maritime transaction "shall be valid, irrevocable, and enforceable, save upon such grounds as exist at law or in equity for the revocation of any contract," and § 4 allows a party to such an arbitration agreement to "petition any United States district court

... for an order directing that such arbitration proceed in the manner provided for in such agreement."

But § 4 of the FAA does not confer a right to compel arbitration of any dispute at any time; it confers only the right to obtain an order directing that "arbitration proceed *in the manner provided for in [the parties'] agreement.*" Here the Court of Appeal found that, by incorporating the California rules of arbitration into their agreement, the parties had agreed that arbitration would not proceed in situations which fell within the scope of Calif.Code Civ.Proc.Ann. § 1281.2(c). This was not a finding that appellant had "waived" an FAA-guaranteed right to compel arbitration of this dispute, but a finding that it had no such right in the first place, because the parties' agreement did not require arbitration to proceed in this situation. Accordingly, appellant's contention that the contract interpretation issue presented here involves the "waiver" of a federal right is without merit.

Second, appellant argues that we should set aside the Court of Appeal's construction of the choice-of-law clause because it violates the settled federal rule that questions of arbitrability in contracts subject to the FAA must be resolved with a healthy regard for the federal policy favoring arbitration. Brief for Appellant, citing Moses H. Cone Memorial Hospital v. Mercury Construction Corp., 460 U.S. 1, 24–25 (1983) (§ 2 of the FAA "create[s] a body of federal substantive law of arbitrability, applicable to any arbitration agreement within the coverage of the Act," which requires that "questions of arbitrability ... be addressed with a healthy regard for the federal policy favoring arbitration," and that "any doubts concerning the scope of arbitrable issues ... be resolved in favor of arbitration"); Mitsubishi Motors Corp. v. Soler Chrysler–Plymouth, Inc., 473 U.S. 614, 626 (1985) (in construing an arbitration agreement within the coverage of the FAA, "as with any other contract, the parties' intentions control, but those intentions are generously construed as to issues of arbitrability"). These cases of course establish that, in applying general state-law principles of contract interpretation to the interpretation of an arbitration agreement within the scope of the Act, due regard must be given to the federal policy favoring arbitration, and ambiguities as to the scope of the arbitration clause itself resolved in favor of arbitration.

But we do not think the Court of Appeal offended the *Moses H. Cone* principle by interpreting the choice-of-law provision to mean that the parties intended the California rules of arbitration, including the § 1281.2(c) stay provision, to apply to their arbitration agreement. There is no federal policy favoring arbitration under a certain set of procedural rules; the federal policy is simply to ensure the enforceability, according to their terms, of private agreements to arbitrate. Interpreting a choice-of-law clause to make applicable state rules governing the conduct of arbitration—rules which are manifestly designed to encourage resort to the arbitral process—simply does not offend the rule of liberal construction set forth in

678 CHAPTER V ARBITRATION

Moses H. Cone, nor does it offend any other policy embodied in the FAA.[5]

The question remains whether, assuming the choice-of-law clause meant what the Court of Appeal found it to mean, application of Cal.Civ. Proc.Code Ann. § 1281.2(c) is nonetheless pre-empted by the FAA to the extent it is used to stay arbitration under this contract involving interstate commerce. It is undisputed that this contract falls within the coverage of the FAA, since it involves interstate commerce, and that the FAA contains no provision authorizing a stay of arbitration in this situation. Appellee contends, however, that §§ 3 and 4 of the FAA, which are the specific sections claimed to conflict with the California statute at issue here, are not applicable in this state-court proceeding and thus cannot pre-empt application of the California statute. While the argument is not without some merit,[6] we need not resolve it to decide this case, for we conclude that even if §§ 3 and 4 of the FAA are fully applicable in state-court proceedings, they do not prevent application of Cal.Civ.Proc.Code Ann. § 1281.2(c) to stay arbitration where, as here, the parties have agreed to arbitrate in accordance with California law.

The FAA contains no express pre-emptive provision, nor does it reflect a congressional intent to occupy the entire field of arbitration. But even when Congress has not completely displaced state regulation in an area, state law may nonetheless be pre-empted to the extent that it actually conflicts with federal law—that is, to the extent that it "stands as an obstacle to the accomplishment and execution of the full purposes and objectives of Congress." The question before us, therefore, is whether application of Cal.Civ.Proc.Code Ann. § 1281.2(c) to stay arbitration under this contract in interstate commerce, in accordance with the terms of the arbitration agreement itself, would undermine the goals and policies of the FAA. We conclude that it would not.

The FAA was designed "to overrule the judiciary's long-standing refusal to enforce agreements to arbitrate," and to place such agreements " 'upon the same footing as other contracts.' "While Congress was no doubt aware that the Act would encourage the expeditious resolution of disputes, its passage "was motivated, first and foremost, by a congressional desire to

---

5. Unlike the dissent, we think the California arbitration rules which the parties have incorporated into their contract generally foster the federal policy favoring arbitration. As indicated, the FAA itself contains no provision designed to deal with the special practical problems that arise in multiparty contractual disputes when some or all of the contracts at issue include agreements to arbitrate. California has taken the lead in fashioning a legislative response to this problem, by giving courts authority to consolidate or stay arbitration proceedings in these situations in order to minimize the potential for contradictory judgments. See Calif.Civ.Proc.Code Ann. § 1281.2(c).

6. While we have held that the FAA's "substantive" provisions—§§ 1 and 2—are applicable in state as well as federal court, see Southland Corp. v. Keating, we have never held that §§ 3 and 4, which by their terms appear to apply only to proceedings in federal court, are nonetheless applicable in state court. See Southland Corp. v. Keating, supra, n. 10 (expressly reserving the question whether "§§ 3 and 4 of the Arbitration Act apply to proceedings in state courts"); see also id. (O'CONNOR, J., dissenting) (§§ 3 and 4 of the FAA apply only in federal court).

C. ARBITRATION AND THE COURTS

enforce agreements into which parties had entered." Accordingly, we have recognized that the FAA does not require parties to arbitrate when they have not agreed to do so, nor does it prevent parties who do agree to arbitrate from excluding certain claims from the scope of their arbitration agreement. It simply requires courts to enforce privately negotiated agreements to arbitrate, like other contracts, in accordance with their terms.

In recognition of Congress' principal purpose of ensuring that private arbitration agreements are enforced according to their terms, we have held that the FAA pre-empts state laws which "require a judicial forum for the resolution of claims which the contracting parties agreed to resolve by arbitration." *Southland Corp. v. Keating; Perry v. Thomas.* But it does not follow that the FAA prevents the enforcement of agreements to arbitrate under different rules than those set forth in the Act itself. Indeed, such a result would be quite inimical to the FAA's primary purpose of ensuring that private agreements to arbitrate are enforced according to their terms. Arbitration under the Act is a matter of consent, not coercion, and parties are generally free to structure their arbitration agreements as they see fit. Just as they may limit by contract the issues which they will arbitrate, so too may they specify by contract the rules under which that arbitration will be conducted. Where, as here, the parties have agreed to abide by state rules of arbitration, enforcing those rules according to the terms of the agreement is fully consistent with the goals of the FAA, even if the result is that arbitration is stayed where the Act would otherwise permit it to go forward. By permitting the courts to "rigorously enforce" such agreements according to their terms, we give effect to the contractual rights and expectations of the parties, without doing violence to the policies behind by the FAA.

The judgment of the Court of Appeals is

Affirmed.

■ JUSTICE O'CONNOR took no part in the consideration or decision of this case.

■ JUSTICE BRENNAN, with whom JUSTICE MARSHALL joins, dissenting. * * *

The Federal Arbitration Act requires courts to enforce arbitration agreements in contracts involving interstate commerce. The California courts nonetheless rejected Volt's petition to compel arbitration in reliance on a provision of state law that, in the circumstances presented, permitted a court to stay arbitration pending the conclusion of related litigation. Volt, not surprisingly, suggested that the Supremacy Clause compelled a different result. The California Court of Appeal found, however, that the parties had agreed that their contract would be governed solely by the law of the State of California, to the exclusion of federal law. In reaching this conclusion the court relied on no extrinsic evidence of the parties' intent, but solely on the language of the form contract that the "law of the place where the project is located" would govern.

This Court now declines to review that holding, which denies effect to an important federal statute, apparently because it finds no question of

680   CHAPTER V ARBITRATION

federal law involved. I can accept neither the state court's unusual interpretation of the parties' contract, nor this Court's unwillingness to review it. * * *

Arbitration is, of course, "a matter of contract and a party cannot be required to submit to arbitration any dispute which he has not agreed so to submit." Steelworkers v. Warrior & Gulf Nav. Co., 363 U.S. 574, 582 (1960). I agree with the Court that "the FAA does not require parties to arbitrate when they have not agreed to do so." Since the FAA merely requires enforcement of what the parties have agreed to, moreover, they are free if they wish to write an agreement to arbitrate outside the coverage of the FAA. Such an agreement would permit a state rule, otherwise pre-empted by the FAA, to govern their arbitration. The substantive question in this case is whether or not they have done so. And that question, we have made clear in the past, is a matter of federal law.

Not only does the FAA require the enforcement of arbitration agreements, but we have held that it also establishes substantive federal law that must be consulted in determining whether (or to what extent) a given contract provides for arbitration. We have stated this most clearly in Moses H. Cone Memorial Hospital v. Mercury Construction Corp., 460 U.S. 1, 24–25:

> "Section 2 [of the FAA] is a congressional declaration of a liberal federal policy favoring arbitration agreements, notwithstanding any state substantive or procedural policies to the contrary. The effect of the section is to create a body of federal substantive law of arbitrability, applicable to any arbitration agreement within the coverage of the Act. * * * The Arbitration Act establishes that, as a matter of federal law, any doubts concerning the scope of arbitrable issues should be resolved in favor of arbitration, whether the problem at hand is the construction of the contract language itself or an allegation of waiver, delay, or a like defense to arbitrability." * * *

The Court recognizes the relevance of the *Moses H. Cone* principle but finds it unoffended by the Court of Appeal's decision, which, the Court suggests, merely determines what set of procedural rules will apply. I agree fully with the Court that "the federal policy is simply to ensure the enforceability, according to their terms, of private agreements to arbitrate," but I disagree emphatically with its conclusion that that policy is not frustrated here. Applying the California procedural rule, which stays arbitration while litigation of the same issue goes forward, means simply that the parties' dispute will be litigated rather than arbitrated. Thus, interpreting the parties' agreement to say that the California procedural rules apply rather than the FAA, where the parties arguably had no such intent, implicates the *Moses H. Cone* principle no less than would an interpretation of the parties' contract that erroneously denied the existence of an agreement to arbitrate.[8]

---

8. Whether or not "the California arbitration rules ... generally foster the federal

policy favoring arbitration" is not the relevant question. Section 2 of the FAA requires

While appearing to recognize that the state court's interpretation of the contract does raise a question of federal law, the Court nonetheless refuses to determine whether the state court misconstrued that agreement. There is no warrant for failing to do so. The FAA requires that a court determining a question of arbitrability not stop with the application of state-law rules for construing the parties' intentions, but that it also take account of the command of federal law that "those intentions [be] generously construed as to issues of arbitrability." Thus, the decision below is based on both state and federal law, which are thoroughly intertwined. In such circumstances the state-court judgment cannot be said to rest on an "adequate and independent state ground" so as to bar review by this Court. With a proper application of federal law in this case, the state court's judgment might have been different, and our review is therefore not barred. * * *

Construed with deference to the opinion of the California Court of Appeal, yet "with a healthy regard for the federal policy favoring arbitration," it is clear that the choice-of-law clause cannot bear the interpretation the California court assigned to it.

Construction of a contractual provision is, of course, a matter of discerning the parties' intent. It is important to recall, in the first place, that in this case there is no extrinsic evidence of their intent. We must therefore rely on the contract itself. But the provision of the contract at issue here was not one that these parties drafted themselves. Rather, they incorporated portions of a standard form contract commonly used in the construction industry. That makes it most unlikely that their intent was in any way at variance with the purposes for which choice-of-law clauses are commonly written and the manner in which they are generally interpreted.

It seems to me beyond dispute that the normal purpose of such choice-of-law clauses is to determine that the law of one State rather than that of another State will be applicable; they simply do not speak to any interaction between state and federal law. A cursory glance at standard conflicts texts confirms this observation: they contain no reference at all to the relation between federal and state law in their discussions of contractual choice-of-law clauses. See, e.g., R. Weintraub, Commentary on the Conflict of Laws s 7.3C (2d ed. 1980); E. Scoles & P. Hay, Conflict of Laws 632–652 (1982); R. Leflar, L. McDougal, & R. Felix, American Conflicts Law § 147 (4th ed. 1986). The same is true of standard codifications. See Uniform Commercial Code § 1–105(1) (1978); Restatement (Second) of Conflict of Laws § 187 (1971). Indeed the Restatement of Conflicts notes expressly that it does not deal with "the ever-present problem of determining the

courts to enforce agreements to arbitrate, and in *Moses H. Cone* we held that doubts as to whether the parties had so agreed were to be resolved in favor of arbitration. Whether California's arbitration rules are more likely than federal law to foster arbitration, i.e., to induce parties to agree to arbitrate disputes, is another matter entirely. On that question it is up to Congress, not this Court, to "fashio[n] a legislative response," and in the meantime we are not free to substitute our notions of good policy for federal law as currently written.

CHAPTER V ARBITRATION

respective spheres of authority of the law and courts of the nation and of the member States." Id., § 2, Comment c. * * * Choice-of-law clauses simply have never been used for the purpose of dealing with the relationship between state and federal law. There is no basis whatever for believing that the parties in this case intended their choice-of-law clause to do so.

Moreover, the literal language of the contract—"the law of the place"—gives no indication of any intention to apply only state law and exclude other law that would normally be applicable to something taking place at that location. By settled principles of federal supremacy, the law of any place in the United States includes federal law. * * * In the absence of any evidence to the contrary it must be assumed that this is what the parties meant by "the law of the place where the Project is located." * * *

Most commercial contracts written in this country contain choice-of-law clauses, similar to the one in the Stanford–Volt contract, specifying which State's law is to govern the interpretation of the contract. See Scoles & Hay, Conflict of Laws, at 632–633 ("Party autonomy means that the parties are free to select the law governing their contract, subject to certain limitations. They will usually do so by means of an express choice-of-law clause in their written contract"). Were every state court to construe such clauses as an expression of the parties' intent to exclude the application of federal law, as has the California Court of Appeal in this case, the result would be to render the Federal Arbitration Act a virtual nullity as to presently existing contracts. I cannot believe that the parties to contracts intend such consequences to flow from their insertion of a standard choice-of-law clause. Even less can I agree that we are powerless to review decisions of state courts that effectively nullify a vital piece of federal legislation. I respectfully dissent.

NOTES AND QUESTIONS

1. The *Volt* case raised many more questions than it answered. Even after *Volt,* the extent to which rules of state law that restrict arbitration can continue to be applicable in contracts otherwise falling within the FAA remained "murky." See Ian Macneil, Richard Speidel, & Thomas Stipanowich, Federal Arbitration Law § 10.9.2.2 (1994). This question will often recur throughout this chapter; see e.g., pp. 688–690 infra (state requirements of conspicuous notice for arbitration clauses); pp. 824–834 infra (state law prohibiting arbitrators from awarding punitive damages).

2. In what sense is it accurate to say—as the Court does in *Volt*—that the California "rules" involved in that case "are manifestly designed to encourage resort to the arbitral process"?

3. Under Rule 81(a)(3) of the Federal Rules of Civil Procedure, the federal rules apply "in proceedings under" the FAA "to the extent that matters of procedure are not provided for" in that statute. When a federal court is asked to compel arbitration, does this Rule give it the same power to order consolidation of related arbitrations involving a "common question of law or fact" as it would have to consolidate "actions" under Rule 42(a)? Or

C. ARBITRATION AND THE COURTS 683

does the Rule simply mean that a court can consolidate two *judicial* proceedings to compel *two separate* arbitrations, or to enforce two separate awards, where there are common issues going to arbitrability or enforcement? See Robinson v. Warner, 370 F.Supp. 828 (D.R.I.1974) (relying on Rule 81 to order consolidation of arbitration proceedings); cf. Government of the United Kingdom v. Boeing Co., 998 F.2d 68 (2d Cir.1993) (§ 4 of the FAA precludes use of the Federal Rules to consolidate arbitrations "absent the parties' consent.")

4. The result of the Supreme Court's decision in *Moses H. Cone* was that arbitrability would be decided in federal court, even though a state court proceeding raising the same question was pending. What might be the advantages to the plaintiff of a federal court determination of arbitrability? Note that under § 6 of the FAA, the plaintiff's request for an order compelling arbitration would be treated as a motion; the Act envisages "an expeditious and summary hearing, with only restricted inquiry into factual issues." The federal district court could therefore have resolved the matter "in very short order." 460 U.S. at 22 & n. 26. Are the summary procedures envisaged by the Act available in state as well as federal courts?

5. Even if an overall dispute must be settled in "piecemeal" fashion, in separate proceedings, it should at least be possible for any lawsuit (say, between the Owner and the Architect) to be stayed until the conclusion of the arbitration between the Owner and the Contractor. See Hikers Industries, Inc. v. William Stuart Industries (Far East) Ltd., 640 F.Supp. 175 (S.D.N.Y.1986). In *Hikers* the exclusive licensee of a trademark brought suit against both his licensor and a retailer to whom the licensor had sold goods allegedly in violation of the license. The licensee had an arbitration agreement only with the licensor; however, the court held that "sound judicial administration" dictated that the suit be stayed as to the *retailer* also. The court noted that since the licensee's claims against the retailer were "derivative" of his claims against the licensor, the arbitrator's decision would be "helpful" and would "provide the court with insight into the issues of law and fact." (Note that a stay would also prevent the licensee from taking advantage of federal discovery in order to aid it in arbitration with the licensor.) The stay was to be lifted, however, if the licensor-licensee arbitration was not completed within six months.

Does this procedure tend to avoid duplication of effort and inconsistent results? In the suit against the retailer, what would be the effect of an arbitrator's decision that the licensor's sales were not in violation of the license agreement?

Where two *arbitration* proceedings are pending which cannot for some reason be consolidated, may a court order that one proceeding be stayed until the other is concluded?

6. St. Margaret's Hospital entered into a number of written contracts concerning additions and renovations to the building—there was a contract with Triangle to perform electrical work, and a contract with McBro to act as construction manager. Each contract contained identical arbitration clauses. Triangle later brought suit in tort (for negligence and interference with contract) against McBro, alleging that McBro had harassed and hampered its work. McBro's motions for a stay pending arbitration, and for an order compelling arbitration, were granted: Although there was no written agreement between the parties, Triangle was "equitably estopped" from asserting this argument, since its claims were "intimately founded in and intertwined with the underlying contract obligations." "The close relationship of the three entities here involved," and "the close relationship of the alleged wrongs to McBro's contractual duties to perform as construction manager, give one pause." McBro Planning & Development Co. v. Triangle Electrical Construction Co., Inc., 741 F.2d 342 (11th Cir.1984). In the course of its opinion the court naturally had no occasion to discuss whether there should be consolidation of any related arbitration proceedings involving the three parties.

7. "If the parties haven't expressly provided for consolidation in their agreements, then for a court to order consolidation would violate the principle that arbitration is consensual." True or false? See Dominique Hascher, Consolidation of Arbitration by American Courts: Fostering or Hampering International Commercial Arbitration, 1 J. Int'l Arb. 127, 134 (1984)(true; "if it had been the parties' intention to submit their disputes to a multiparty arbitration setting, they would have so provided in their contracts"); to the same effect is "A Critique of the Uniform Arbitration Act (2000)," World Arb. & Med. Rep., April 2001 at pp. 94, 100–101. But cf. Alan Rau & Edward Sherman, Tradition and Innovation in International Arbitration Procedure, 30 Tex. Int'l L.J. 89, 113–115 (1995)(false; "as in most cases of contractual silence we are left with the need for some sort of default rule"; the problem of multiparty disputes is best approached "as one more inquiry into the choice of an appropriate presumption").

8. The new Revised Uniform Arbitration Act follows California's statute in reversing the usual default rule and in creating a new background rule in favor of consolidation. Under § 10 of the Act, a court may order consolidation of separate arbitration proceedings where:

> (2) the claims subject to the agreements to arbitrate arise in substantial part from the same transaction or series of related transactions;
>
> (3) the existence of a common issue of law or fact creates the possibility of conflicting decisions in the separate arbitration proceedings; and
>
> (4) prejudice resulting from a failure to consolidate is not outweighed by the risk of undue delay or prejudice to the rights of or hardship to parties opposing consolidation.

Section 10 (c) also adds—through an unnecessary excess of caution—that a court may nevertheless not order consolidation "of the claims of a party to an agreement to arbitrate which prohibits consolidation."

3. THE AGREEMENT TO ARBITRATE

a. ARBITRATION CLAUSES AND CONTRACT FORMATION

Under the modern federal and state statutes we have just been introduced to, the first requisite, of course, is an *enforceable agreement* providing for arbitration between the parties to the dispute. Where an arbitration clause calls for arbitration of any *future* dispute that may arise out of a contractual relationship, the clause may well be a small, little-noticed part of a much more complex document. Parties are likely to plan primarily for their performance, and only desultorily for what may happen should trouble arise from non-performance. And where firms exchange forms printed in advance, without separately agreeing (or even paying particularly careful attention) to everything that these forms contain, the challenge to the legal system to make some sense out of the transaction is at its most intense. The stage is then set for what lawyers and law students are trained to call "the battle of the forms."

Whether an arbitration clause has become part of a valid and enforceable contract is at least in the first instance a question of ordinary contract law. You may recall in fact the rather tortured attempt of the Uniform Commercial Code to provide some solution to the "battle of the forms" problem. UCC § 2–207 provides that

(1) A definite and seasonable expression of acceptance or a written confirmation which is sent within a reasonable time operates as an acceptance even though it states terms additional to or different from those offered or agreed upon, unless acceptance is expressly made conditional on assent to the additional or different terms.

(2) The additional terms are to be construed as proposals for addition to the contract. Between merchants such terms become part of the contract unless:

(a) the offer expressly limits acceptance to the terms of the offer;

(b) they materially alter it; or

(c) notification of objection to them has already been given or is given within a reasonable time after notice of them is received.

Assume that an exchange of forms creates a contract under UCC 2–207(1) but that only the *second* form contains a clause providing for the arbitration of future disputes. Does this clause become part of the contract?

The New York Court of Appeals considered this question in In the Matter of the Arbitration Between Marlene Industries Corp. v. Carnac Textiles, Inc., 45 N.Y.2d 327, 408 N.Y.S.2d 410, 380 N.E.2d 239 (1978). This case involved conflicting forms sent in confirmation of an *oral order* placed by the buyer; the seller's "acknowledgment" form, sent last, alone provided for arbitration but was not made "expressly conditional" on the buyer's assent to that or any other term. The Court of Appeals held that:

the inclusion of an arbitration agreement materially alters a contract for the sale of goods, and thus, pursuant to section 2–207(2)(b) it will not become a part of such a contract unless both parties explicitly agree to it.

It has long been the rule in this State that the parties to a commercial transaction "will not be held to have chosen arbitration as the forum for the resolution of their disputes in the absence of an express,

686 CHAPTER V ARBITRATION

unequivocal agreement to that effect; absent such an explicit commitment neither party may be compelled to arbitrate." The reason for this requirement, quite simply, is that by agreeing to arbitrate a party waives in large part many of his normal rights under the procedural and substantive law of the State, and it would be unfair to infer such a significant waiver on the basis of anything less than a clear indication of intent.

Since an arbitration agreement in the context of a commercial transaction "must be clear and direct, and must not depend upon implication, inveiglement or subtlety ... [its] existence ... should not depend solely upon the conflicting fine print of commercial forms which cross one another but never meet." Thus, at least under this so-called "New York Rule", it is clear that an arbitration clause is a material addition which can become part of a contract only if it is expressly assented to by both parties. Applying these principles to this case, we conclude that the contract between Marlene and Carnac does not contain an arbitration clause; hence, the motion to permanently stay arbitration should have been granted.

In New York, therefore, an arbitration clause has been said to be a "per se material alteration" of any agreement.[1] Cf. Jack Greenberg, Inc. v. Velleman Corp., 1985 U.S. Dist. Lexis 17132, *5 n. 1 (E.D.Pa.1985) (clause provided for arbitration under AAA rules "as supplemented or modified by the Meat Importers Council of America, Inc.'s Arbitration Rules"; held, "[e]ven assuming that it was not a per se material alteration, I would conclude that the clause here was material in that it would deprive Greenberg of its right to come into court to enforce the contract, without first bringing its claim before the Meat Importers Council of America").

NOTES AND QUESTIONS

1. The UCC does not define the term "materially alter." However Comment 4 to UCC § 2–207, in giving some examples, refers to clauses that would "result in surprise or hardship if incorporated without express awareness by the other party." The idea seems to be that a clause which is sufficiently important and unusual that a party would expect to have his attention specifically directed to it, should not come into the contract by way of a form that is by hypothesis commonly unread. Examples in Comment 5 of clauses which by contrast "involve no element of unreasonable surprise" are couched in terms of what is "within the range of trade practice" or "customary trade tolerances."

In many industries, of course, arbitration is a routinely-invoked, standard method of dispute resolution. Courts have even been willing to take "judicial notice" of the "common practice" of arbitration in the textile business. See Helen Whiting, Inc. v. Trojan Textile Corp., 307 N.Y. 360,

---

1. Supak & Sons Mfg. Co., Inc. v. Pervel Industries, Inc., 593 F.2d 135, 136 (4th Cir.1979).

367, 121 N.E.2d 367, 370 (1954). Given the widespread acceptance of arbitration in these industries, could it be argued that an arbitration clause would not, in light of the policies behind UCC § 2–207, be a "material alteration"? See Schulze and Burch Biscuit Co. v. Tree Top, Inc., 831 F.2d 709 (7th Cir.1987) (given the prior course of dealing between the parties, the buyer "had ample notice" that the seller's confirmation might include an arbitration clause; the clause was therefore not a material alteration to the contract). Cf. Chelsea Square Textiles, Inc. v. Bombay Dyeing & Manufacturing Co., Ltd., 189 F.3d 289 (2d Cir. 1999), which held that an importer was obligated to arbitrate with a textile manufacturer even though the arbitration clause was "nearly illegible" and was "printed on very thin, tissue-style paper, which resulted in some of the text being obscured by typing on the reverse side": "We believe that a textile buyer is generally on notice that an agreement to purchase textiles is not only likely, but almost certain, to contain a provision mandating arbitration in the event of disputes."

2. Might the practice of dispute resolution through arbitration be so widespread in a given trade, or so well-established in the prior dealings of the parties, that under ordinary contract principles arbitration might be an implied term of the bargain *from the very beginning* ? If so, then the arbitration term would not even be an "addition" to or an "alteration" of the contract *at all*. See UCC §§ 1–201(3), 1–205(3). In Schubtex, Inc. v. Allen Snyder, Inc., 49 N.Y.2d 1, 424 N.Y.S.2d 133, 399 N.E.2d 1154 (1979), a seller had confirmed a buyer's oral order by sending a form with an arbitration clause, and the buyer (as he had done several times in the past) retained the form without objection. The Court of Appeals conceded that "a determination that [the] oral agreement included a provision for arbitration could in a proper case be implied from a course of past conduct or the custom and practice in the industry," but concluded that such evidence was lacking in that case. Three judges, including the author of the *Marlene* opinion, concurred in the result but "strongly disagree[d]" with such a suggestion:

> It is true, of course, that evidence of a trade usage or of a prior course of dealings may normally be utilized to supplement the express terms of a contract for the sale of goods. General rules of contract law, however, are not always applicable to arbitration clauses because of overriding policy considerations. * * * "[T]he threshold for clarity of agreement to arbitrate is greater than with respect to other contractual terms." * * * Where there exists good reason to require an explicit agreement, * * * it would seem most imprudent to allow a presumption of intent to supplant the need for such an agreement.

3. Sometimes the writings exchanged by the parties will *not* create a contract under UCC § 2–207(1): A second form, for example, may simply provide that it is not an "Expression of Acceptance" at all, and that any acceptance is "expressly conditioned" on the other party's assent to its terms. E.g., Commerce & Industry Ins. Co. v. Bayer Corp., 433 Mass. 388, 742 N.E.2d 567 (Mass. 2001)(only the first form contained an arbitration clause; held, arbitration agreement is not enforceable because "a contract never came into being"). Nevertheless, the parties may recognize the existence of a contract by their conduct—for example, by shipping, accepting, and paying for the goods before any dispute arises. In such a case, § 2-207(3) provides that the terms of the contract consist of "those terms on which the writings of the parties agree, together with any supplementary terms incorporated under any other provisions of this Act." May an agreement to arbitrate be brought into the contract in such circumstances as a "supplementary term" implied from custom and usage?

Recall that the FAA provides for the enforceability of "*a written provision*" in a contract to submit future disputes to arbitration. Section 6 of the Revised Uniform Arbitration Act makes enforceable "*an agreement contained in a record*" to arbitrate future disputes. (A "record" is defined as "information that is inscribed on a tangible medium or that is stored in an electronic or other medium and is retrievable in perceivable form."). Do either or both of these statutes require the arbitration clause to be an *express* part of a valid written agreement—preventing an arbitration provision from being incorporated into a contract solely on the basis of custom, trade usage, or past dealing? See C. Itoh & Co. (America) Inc. v. Jordan Intern. Co., 552 F.2d 1228 (7th Cir.1977).

4. The United Nations Convention on Contracts for the International Sale of Goods, ratified by the United States in 1986, applies to all contracts for the sale of goods between parties "whose places of business are in different [Contracting] states." With respect to the formation of contracts, the Convention provides that a second printed form (e.g., a seller's "acknowledgement") that contains any additions to or modifications or the original offer may be treated as an acceptance, unless the additions or modifications "materially alter" the offer. If they *do* "materially alter" it, then the second form is presumed to be a counter-offer rather than an acceptance—with the result that no contract is formed at all. And additional or different terms "relating to the settlement of disputes" are *always* deemed to be "material" alterations, thereby preventing the formation of any contract by correspondence. Art. 19(3).

5. A number of state statutes have traditionally imposed special requirements on the formation of arbitration agreements—presumably to guard against "surprise" and to insure that consent to arbitration has been knowing and informed. The Missouri arbitration statute, for example, requires a statement in ten point capital letters adjacent to or above the signature line, reading "THIS CONTRACT CONTAINS A BINDING ARBITRATION PROVISION WHICH MAY BE ENFORCED BY THE PARTIES." V.A.M.S. § 435.460. Another model singles out certain types of arbitration agreements and conditions their validity on the parties' having first received independent legal advice. The Texas statute requires that any agreement for arbitration in a contract where an individual acquires real or personal property, services, or money or credit, for an amount of $50,000 or less, must be signed by the attorneys of both parties. The same requirement applies to agreements to arbitrate any personal injury claim. Tex.Civ. Prac. & Rem.Code § 171.001.

All such statutes are now presumably dead letters in light of the Supreme Court's recent decision in Doctor's Associates, Inc. v. Casarotto, 517 U.S. 681 (1996). In *Casarotto,* the Court was faced with a Montana statute requiring notice that a contract is subject to arbitration to be "typed in underlined capital letters on the first page of the contract": The Court struck down the state statute on the predictable ground that by enacting the FAA, "Congress precluded States from singling out arbitration provisions for suspect status, requiring instead that such provisions be placed upon the same footing as other contracts."

6. An arbitration agreement might also run afoul of disclosure requirements applied generally to wide classes of contracts. New York, for example, imposes precise legibility requirements (not less than "eight points in depth or five and one-half points in depth for upper case") for printed contracts in all "consumer transactions." An arbitration clause in a customer's agreement with a stockbroker was invalidated for failure to meet this requirement in Hacker v. Smith Barney, Harris Upham & Co., Inc., 131 Misc.2d 757, 501 N.Y.S.2d 977 (Special Term 1986), aff'd, 136 Misc.2d 169, 519 N.Y.S.2d 92 (Sup.Ct.1987).

The court in *Hacker v. Smith Barney* perfunctorily dismissed a preemption argument based on *Southland v. Keating.* But *Hacker* is rather easily distinguishable from *Southland* and *Casarotto,* isn't it?

7. What about the "New York Rule" on contract formation exemplified by the *Marlene* case, supra? Is it likely that the FAA has any preemptive effect on this rule? The Tenth Circuit, rejecting this argument, noted that UCC § 2–207 is "a general principle of state law controlling issues of contract formation." "Presumptions against including terms, such as the New York rule, are routinely applied to any term considered significant to the contracting parties," such as disclaimers of warranty; "§ 2–207 does nothing under its general, or its specific New York application, to restrict enforcement of agreements to arbitrate to which the parties have expressly assented." Avedon Engineering, Inc. v. Seatex, 126 F.3d 1279 (10th Cir. 1997). The Second Circuit, on the other hand, has pointed out that the *general* New York law of contracts (unlike the rule in *Marlene*) requires that "nonarbitration agreements be proven only by a mere preponderance of the evidence"; it therefore followed that *Marlene*'s "discriminatory treatment of arbitration agreements * * * is preempted." Progressive Casualty Ins. Co. v. C.A. Reaseguradora Nacional De Venezuela, 991 F.2d 42 (2d Cir.1993).

8. A Texas statute (now repealed) made all arbitration agreements unenforceable unless a notice of arbitration was "typed in underlined capital letters, or rubber-stamped prominently, on the first page of the contract." In one case, a contract provided that arbitration was to take place "pursuant to the laws of the State of Texas," but omitted the required statutory notice. The court held that on the authority of the *Volt* case, this choice-of-law provision allowed the notice requirement to escape federal preemption:

690   CHAPTER V   ARBITRATION

"[T]he Texas Act prevails over the FAA and the arbitration agreement is unenforceable because it does not conform to the Texas Act." American Physicians Service Group, Inc. v. Port Lavaca Clinic Associates, 843 S.W.2d 675 (Tex.App.—Corpus Christi 1992); *accord,* Al's Formal Wear of Houston v. Sun, 869 S.W.2d 442, 443–44 n. 3 (Tex.App.—Houston 1993). Can this possibly be right? Does the "party autonomy" rationale of *Volt* have any relevance here?

9. The owner of containerized cargo equipment leased the equipment to two shipping companies, which in turn insured the equipment. The contract of insurance between the shipping companies and the insurer contained an arbitration clause. After the equipment was damaged, the owner brought suit against the insurer. (The two shipping companies had gone out of business.) Does the insurer have the right to stay the proceedings and compel arbitration? See Interpool Ltd. v. Through Transport Mutual Ins. Ass'n Ltd., 635 F.Supp. 1503 (S.D.Fla.1985).

An employee's agreement with his employer, a brokerage firm, provided that any future disputes arising out of his employment or termination of employment would be subject to arbitration. The employee later brought suit against the firm for wrongful termination; at the same time, his wife also filed suit alleging loss of consortium as a result of the firm's actions toward her husband. On the firm's motion to stay all the proceedings and compel arbitration, what result? See Prudential Ins. Co. of Amer. v. Shammas, 865 F.Supp. 429 (W.D.Mich.1993) (motion granted); cf. Merrill Lynch, Pierce, Fenner & Smith, Inc. v. Longoria, 783 S.W.2d 229 (Tex. App.—Corpus Christi 1989) (motion properly denied as to wife).

b.   THE "SEPARABILITY" OF THE ARBITRATION CLAUSE

Prima Paint Corp. v. Flood & Conklin Mfg. Co.

Supreme Court of the United States, 1967.
388 U.S. 395, 87 S.Ct. 1801, 18 L.Ed.2d 1270.

■ MR. JUSTICE FORTAS delivered the opinion of the Court.

This case presents the question whether the federal court or an arbitrator is to resolve a claim of "fraud in the inducement," under a contract governed by the United States Arbitration Act of 1925, where there is no evidence that the contracting parties intended to withhold that issue from arbitration.

The question arises from the following set of facts. On October 7, 1964, respondent, Flood & Conklin Manufacturing Company, a New Jersey corporation, entered into what was styled a "Consulting Agreement," with petitioner, Prima Paint Corporation, a Maryland corporation. This agreement followed by less than three weeks the execution of a contract pursuant to which Prima Paint purchased F & C's paint business. The consulting agreement provided that for a six-year period F & C was to furnish advice and consultation "in connection with the formulae, manufacturing operations, sales and servicing of Prima Trade Sales account." These services were to be performed personally by F & C's chairman, Jerome K. Jelin, "except in the event of his death or disability." F & C bound itself for the duration of the contractual period to make no "Trade Sales" of paint or paint products in its existing sales territory or to current customers. To the consulting agreement were appended lists of F & C customers, whose patronage was to be taken over by Prima Paint. In return for these lists, the covenant not to compete, and the services of Mr. Jelin, Prima Paint agreed to pay F & C certain percentages of its receipts from the listed customers and from all others, such payments not to exceed $25,000 over the life of the agreement. The agreement took into account the possibility that Prima Paint might encounter financial difficulties, including bankruptcy, but no corresponding reference was made to possible financial problems which might be encountered by F & C. The agreement states that it "embodies the entire understanding of the parties on the subject matter." Finally, the parties agreed to a broad arbitration clause, which read in part:

"Any controversy or claim arising out of or relating to this Agreement, or the breach thereof, shall be settled by arbitration in the City of New York, in accordance with the rules then obtaining of the American Arbitration Association...."

The first payment by Prima Paint to F & C under the consulting agreement was due on September 1, 1965. None was made on that date. Seventeen days later, Prima Paint did pay the appropriate amount, but into escrow. It notified attorneys for F & C that in various enumerated respects their client had broken both the consulting agreement and the earlier purchase agreement. Prima Paint's principal contention, so far as presently relevant, was that F & C had fraudulently represented that it was solvent and able to perform its contractual obligations, whereas it was in fact insolvent and intended to file a petition under Chapter XI of the Bankruptcy Act shortly after execution of the consulting agreement. Prima Paint noted that such a petition was filed by F & C on October 14, 1964, one week after the contract had been signed. F & C's response, on October 25, was to serve a "notice of intention to arbitrate." On November 12, three days before expiration of its time to answer this "notice," Prima Paint filed suit in the United States District Court for the Southern District of New York, seeking rescission of the consulting agreement on the basis of the alleged fraudulent inducement. The complaint asserted that the federal court had diversity jurisdiction.

Contemporaneously with the filing of its complaint, Prima Paint petitioned the District Court for an order enjoining F & C from proceeding with the arbitration. F & C cross-moved to stay the court action pending arbitration. F & C contended that the issue presented—whether there was fraud in the inducement of the consulting agreement—was a question for the arbitrators and not for the District Court. * * *

The District Court granted F & C's motion to stay the action pending arbitration, holding that a charge of fraud in the inducement of a contract

692 CHAPTER V ARBITRATION

containing an arbitration clause as broad as this one was a question for the arbitrators and not for the court. * * * The Court of Appeals for the Second Circuit dismissed Prima Paint's appeal.

* * *

[The Court first determined that "[t]here could not be a clearer case of a contract evidencing a transaction in interstate commerce."]

Having determined that the contract in question is within the coverage of the Arbitration Act, we turn to the central issue in this case: whether a claim of fraud in the inducement of the entire contract is to be resolved by the federal court, or whether the matter is to be referred to the arbitrators. The courts of appeals have differed in their approach to this question. The view of the Court of Appeals for the Second Circuit, as expressed in this case and in others, is that—except where the parties otherwise intend—arbitration clauses as a matter of federal law are "separable" from the contract in which they are embedded, and that where no claim is made that fraud was directed to the arbitration clause itself, a broad arbitration clause will be held to encompass arbitration of the claim that the contract itself was induced by fraud.[9] The Court of Appeals for the First Circuit, on the other hand, has taken the view that the question of "severability" is one of state law, and that where a State regards such a clause as inseparable a claim of fraud in inducement must be decided by the court.

With respect to cases brought in federal court involving maritime contracts or those evidencing transactions in "commerce," we think that Congress has provided an explicit answer. That answer is to be found in § 4 of the Act, which provides a remedy to a party seeking to compel compliance with an arbitration agreement. Under § 4, with respect to a matter within the jurisdiction of the federal courts save for the existence of an arbitration clause, the federal court is instructed to order arbitration to proceed once it is satisfied that "the making of the agreement for arbitration or the failure to comply [with the arbitration agreement] is not in issue." Accordingly, if the claim is fraud in the inducement of the arbitration clause itself—an issue which goes to the "making" of the agreement to arbitrate—the federal court may proceed to adjudicate it. But the statutory language does not permit the federal court to consider claims of fraud in the inducement of the contract generally. Section 4 does not expressly relate to situations like the present in which a stay is sought of a federal action in order that arbitration may proceed. But it is inconceivable that Congress intended the rule to differ depending upon which party to the arbitration agreement first invokes the assistance of a federal court. We hold, therefore, that in passing upon a § 3 application for a stay while the parties arbitrate, a federal court may consider only issues relating to the

---

9. The Court of Appeals has been careful to honor evidence that the parties intended to withhold such issues from the arbitrators and to reserve them for judicial resolution. We note that categories of contracts otherwise within the Arbitration Act but in which one of the parties characteristically has little bargaining power are expressly excluded from the reach of the Act. See § 1.

making and performance of the agreement to arbitrate. In so concluding, we not only honor the plain meaning of the statute but also the unmistakably clear congressional purpose that the arbitration procedure, when selected by the parties to a contract, be speedy and not subject to delay and obstruction in the courts.

* * *

In the present case no claim has been advanced by Prima Paint that F & C fraudulently induced it to enter into the agreement to arbitrate "[a]ny controversy or claim arising out of or relating to this Agreement, or the breach thereof." This contractual language is easily broad enough to encompass Prima Paint's claim that both execution and acceleration of the consulting agreement itself were procured by fraud. Indeed, no claim is made that Prima Paint ever intended that "legal" issues relating to the contract be excluded from arbitration, or that it was not entirely free so to contract. Federal courts are bound to apply rules enacted by Congress with respect to matters—here, a contract involving commerce—over which it has legislative power. The question which Prima Paint requested the District Court to adjudicate preliminarily to allowing arbitration to proceed is one not intended by Congress to delay the granting of a § 3 stay. Accordingly, the decision below dismissing Prima Paint's appeal is

Affirmed.

■ MR. JUSTICE BLACK, with whom MR. JUSTICE DOUGLAS and MR. JUSTICE STEWART join, dissenting.

The Court here holds that the United States Arbitration Act, as a matter of federal substantive law, compels a party to a contract containing a written arbitration provision to carry out his "arbitration agreement" even though a court might, after a fair trial, hold the entire contract—including the arbitration agreement—void because of fraud in the inducement. The Court holds, what is to me fantastic, that the legal issue of a contract's voidness because of fraud is to be decided by persons designated to arbitrate factual controversies arising out of a valid contract between the parties. And the arbitrators who the Court holds are to adjudicate the legal validity of the contract need not even be lawyers, and in all probability will be nonlawyers, wholly unqualified to decide legal issues, and even if qualified to apply the law, not bound to do so. I am by no means sure that thus forcing a person to forgo his opportunity to try his legal issues in the courts where, unlike the situation in arbitration, he may have a jury trial and right to appeal, is not a denial of due process of law. I am satisfied, however, that Congress did not impose any such procedures in the Arbitration Act. And I am fully satisfied that a reasonable and fair reading of that Act's language and history shows that both Congress and the framers of the Act were at great pains to emphasize that nonlawyers designated to adjust and arbitrate factual controversies arising out of valid contracts would not trespass upon the courts' prerogative to decide the legal question of whether any legal contract exists upon which to base an arbitration.

* * *

694 CHAPTER V ARBITRATION

Let us look briefly at the language of the Arbitration Act itself as Congress passed it. Section 2, the key provision of the Act, provides that "[a] written provision in ... a contract ... involving commerce to settle by arbitration a controversy thereafter arising out of such contract ... shall be valid, irrevocable, and enforceable, *save upon such grounds as exist at law or in equity for the revocation of any contract.*" (Emphasis added.) Section 3 provides that "[i]f any suit ... be brought ... *upon any issue referable to arbitration* under an agreement in writing for such arbitration, the court ... *upon being satisfied that the issue involved in such suit ... is referable to arbitration under such an agreement,* shall ... stay the trial of the action until such arbitration has been had ..." (Emphasis added.) The language of these sections could not, I think, raise doubts about their meaning except to someone anxious to find doubts. They simply mean this: an arbitration agreement is to be enforced by a federal court unless the court, not the arbitrator, finds grounds "at law or in equity for the revocation of any contract." Fraud, of course, is one of the most common grounds for revoking a contract. If the contract was procured by fraud, then, unless the defrauded party elects to affirm it, there is absolutely no contract, nothing to be arbitrated. Sections 2 and 3 of the Act assume the existence of a valid contract. They merely provide for enforcement where such a valid contract exists. These provisions were plainly designed to protect a person against whom arbitration is sought to be enforced from having to submit his legal issues as to validity of the contract to the arbitrator. * * *

Finally, it is clear to me from the bill's sponsors' understanding of the function of arbitration that they never intended that the issue of fraud in the inducement be resolved by arbitration. They recognized two special values of arbitration: (1) the expertise of an arbitrator to decide factual questions in regard to the day-to-day performance of contractual obligations,[13] and (2) the speed with which arbitration, as contrasted to litigation, could resolve disputes over performance of contracts and thus mitigate the damages and allow the parties to continue performance under the contracts. Arbitration serves neither of these functions where a contract is sought to be rescinded on the ground of fraud. On the one hand, courts have far more expertise in resolving legal issues which go to the validity of a contract than do arbitrators.[15] On the other hand, where a party seeks to rescind a contract and his allegation of fraud in the

---

13. "Not all questions arising out of contracts ought to be arbitrated. It is a remedy peculiarly suited to the disposition of the ordinary disputes between merchants as to questions of fact—quantity, quality, time of delivery, compliance with terms of payment, excuses for non-performance, and the like. It has a place also in the determination of the simpler questions of law—the questions of law which arise out of these daily relations between merchants as to the passage of title, the existence of warranties, or the questions of law which are complementary to the questions of fact which we have just mentioned." Cohen & Dayton, The New Federal Arbitration Law, 12 Va.L.Rev. 265, 281 (1926).

15. "It [arbitration] is not a proper remedy for ... questions with which the arbitrators have no particular experience and which are better left to the determination of skilled judges with a background of legal experience and established systems of law." Cohen & Dayton, supra, at 281.

inducement is true, an arbitrator's speedy remedy of this wrong should never result in resumption of performance under the contract. And if the contract were not procured by fraud, the court, under the summary trial procedures provided by the Act, may determine with little delay that arbitration must proceed. The only advantage of submitting the issue of fraud to arbitration is for the arbitrators. Their compensation corresponds to the volume of arbitration they perform. If they determine that a contract is void because of fraud, there is nothing further for them to arbitrate. I think it raises serious questions of due process to submit to an arbitrator an issue which will determine his compensation.

* * *

The avowed purpose of the Act was to place arbitration agreements "upon the same footing as other contracts." The separability rule which the Court applies to an arbitration clause does not result in equality between it and other clauses in the contract. I had always thought that a person who attacks a contract on the ground of fraud and seeks to rescind it has to seek rescission of the whole, not tidbits, and is not given the option of denying the existence of some clauses and affirming the existence of others. Here F & C agreed both to perform consulting services for Prima and not to compete with Prima. Would any court hold that those two agreements were separable, even though Prima in agreeing to pay F & C not to compete did not directly rely on F & C's representations of being solvent? The simple fact is that Prima would not have agreed to the covenant not to compete or to the arbitration clause but for F & C's fraudulent promise that it would be financially able to perform consulting services.

* * *

Prima here challenged in the courts the validity of its alleged contract with F & C as a whole, not in fragments. If there has never been any valid contract, then there is not now and never has been anything to arbitrate. If Prima's allegations are true, the sum total of what the Court does here is to force Prima to arbitrate a contract which is void and unenforceable before arbitrators who are given the power to make final legal determinations of their own jurisdiction, not even subject to effective review by the highest court in the land. That is not what Congress said Prima must do. It seems to be what the Court thinks would promote the policy of arbitration. I am completely unable to agree to this new version of the Arbitration Act * * *.

NOTES AND QUESTIONS

1. There is a good review of authority in Ericksen, Arbuthnot, McCarthy, Kearney & Walsh, Inc. v. 100 Oak Street, 35 Cal.3d 312, 197 Cal.Rptr. 581, 673 P.2d 251 (1983). A law firm, complaining that the air conditioning in its offices was defective, brought suit against its landlord for breach of contract, of the covenant of quiet enjoyment, and of the warranty of habitability. The lease provided for arbitration "in the event of any dispute

* * * with respect to the provisions of this Lease exclusive of those provisions relating to payment of rent." The lessor filed a motion to compel arbitration; the lessee responded that "[g]rounds exist for revocation of the agreement to arbitrate the alleged controversy in that [lessee] was falsely and fraudulently induced to enter into the lease agreement." The Supreme Court of California noted that "[t]he high courts of our sister states with cognate arbitration acts have followed the rule in *Prima Paint* with near unanimity" and held that the lessor's motion should have been granted:

> [T]he issue of fraud which is asserted here "seems inextricably enmeshed in the other factual issues of the case." Indeed, the claim of substantive breach—that the air conditioning did not perform properly—is totally embraced within the claim of fraud—that the lessor knew, at the time of the lease, that the air conditioning would not perform. Thus, if the trial court were to proceed to determine the fraud claim it would almost certainly have to decide the claim of substantive breach as well, and the original expectations of the parties—that such questions would be determined through arbitration—would be totally defeated. However the fraud claim were determined, there would be virtually nothing left for the arbitrator to decide.

Two dissenting judges found the majority's result "Incredible!" and commented that "[t]his is resupination: logic and procedure turned upside down."

2. The court in *Ericksen* apparently assumed that the contract between the parties did not fall within the FAA. When dealing with a contract that *is* within the scope of the Federal Act, would a state court be free in any event to ignore the rule of separability established by *Prima Paint?* Cf. Rhodes v. Consumers' Buyline, Inc., 868 F.Supp. 368 (D.Mass.1993) ("the parties intended" that New York arbitration law govern the arbitration clause, and "under New York law, the arbitration clause of a void and unenforceable contract is itself void and unenforceable").

3. The question of "separability" is posed also by challenges on a number of other contract-law grounds to the validity of the overall agreement. For example:

    i. "Illegality"; see *Nuclear Electric Ins. Ltd. v. Central Power & Light Co.,* 926 F.Supp. 428 (S.D.N.Y.1996)(Texas Insurance Code rendered "unenforceable" any contract of insurance entered into by an unauthorized insurer; held, since "the claim of unenforceability does not specifically relate to the arbitration provision" but to "the entire policy," any claim that the policy is rendered unenforceable under Texas law "must be submitted to the arbitrator"); Wolitarsky v. Blue Cross of California, 53 Cal.App.4th 338, 61 Cal.Rptr.2d 629 (Cal.App.1997)(policyholders argued that insurance dispute could not be arbitrated because the policy discriminated against women, in violation of the state Civil Rights Act, by imposing an additional deductible for maternity care; held, when "the alleged illegality goes to only a portion of the contract (that does not include the arbitration agreement), the entire controversy, including the issue of illegality, remains arbitrable").

ii. "Unconscionability"; see Bondy's Ford, Inc. v. Sterling Truck Corp., 147 F.Supp.2d 1283 (M.D.Ala.2001)("To the extent that Bondy's Ford claims that other provisions of the dealer's agreement, such as the waiver of punitive damages, render the contract void because they are unconscionable, the validity or invalidity of these provisions may be argued to the arbitral tribunal, and do not clearly implicate the arbitration clause itself").

iii. Failure of a "meeting of the minds," Bratt Enterprises, Inc. v. Noble International, Ltd., 99 F.Supp.2d 874 (S.D.Ohio 2000)("Plaintiff does not claim that there was any 'mutual mistake' in the negotiation of the arbitration clause itself").

iv. Duress and "coercion through bribery," Republic of the Philippines v. Westinghouse Electric Corp., 714 F.Supp. 1362 (D.N.J.1989) ("if plaintiffs could demonstrate that the coercion or duress were directed specifically to the arbitration clause, this would satisfy *Prima Paint* and it would be appropriate to have a hearing on the issue").

v. Frustration of purpose, Unionmutual Stock Life Ins. Co. of Amer. v. Beneficial Life Ins. Co., 774 F.2d 524 (1st Cir.1985) (defendant "never argued * * * that the arbitration clause itself was invalid because of either mutual mistake or frustration of purpose").

vi. "Agreement to Agree," Republic of Nicaragua v. Standard Fruit Co., 937 F.2d 469 (9th Cir.1991) (in determining whether "Memorandum of Intent" was a "binding contract for the purchase and sale of bananas, or merely an 'agreement to agree' at some later date," the district court "improperly looked to the validity of the contract as a whole" and "ignored strong evidence in the record that both parties intended to be bound by the arbitration clause"; court should instead have "considered only the validity and scope of the arbitration clause itself").

vii. Lack of "Consideration," see Cline v. H.E. Butt Grocery Co., 79 F. Supp.2d 730 (S.D.Tex.1999)(employee claimed that the employer's unilateral right to amend or terminate its occupational injury plan made its promises "illusory," but that "is an attack on the [plan] as a whole, and not the arbitration provision itself," and is therefore "properly referable to an arbitrator"); Matter of Exercycle Corp. v. Maratta, 9 N.Y.2d 329, 214 N.Y.S.2d 353, 174 N.E.2d 463 (N.Y. 1961)(although employment agreement contained an arbitration clause, the employer opposed arbitration, arguing that since the employee had the right to quit at any time, the employment contract was "lacking in mutuality" and therefore unenforceable; held, "the question whether the contract lacked mutuality of obligation" "is to be determined by the arbitrators, not the court").

4. Compare Stevens/Leinweber/Sullens, Inc. v. Holm Development & Management, Inc., 165 Ariz. 25, 795 P.2d 1308 (1990). In this case a General Contractor entered into a standard-form construction contract with the Owner, providing that future disputes would be submitted to arbitration in accordance with the Construction Industry Arbitration Rules of the AAA. The contract also contained a non-standard clause drafted by the Owner, giving the Owner "the unilateral option of selecting either arbitration or litigation as the means of dispute resolution"; the Owner in fact had the right to reconsider its choice of dispute resolution "at any time, prior to a final judgment in the ongoing proceeding." The court noted that Arizona's arbitration statute contained language very similar to § 4 of the FAA and that it therefore "embod[ied] the concept of separability endorsed by the United States Supreme Court in *Prima Paint*." "Because under the separability doctrine the arbitration provision is an independent and separate agreement, [the Owner] cannot 'borrow' consideration from the principal contract to support the arbitration provision. As a result, we conclude that the arbitration provision, which clearly lacks mutuality, is void for lack of consideration. * * * [Owner's] contention that the arbitration provision should be considered in isolation from the principal contract only when it is necessary to preserve the parties' agreement to arbitrate is without merit."

Note that the *overall* construction contract in *Holm* was not challenged on the ground of lack of "mutuality" or "consideration." See 1 A. Corbin, Contracts §§ 125 ("One Consideration Exchanged for Several Promises"), 164 (1963). This is truly "separability" with a vengeance, isn't it?

5. In some cases, by contrast, courts rebel at carrying the notion of "separability" to its logical extreme. Are the following cases consistent with *Prima Paint* ?

i. Several local government authorities opened securities accounts with a brokerage firm, and later brought suit alleging that they had lost over $8 million as a result of the firm's unlawful conduct. The firm moved to stay the proceedings based on arbitration clauses in the customer agreements; the plaintiffs countered that the agreements were invalid because the individual purporting to sign on their behalf was not authorized to do so. The court held that this threshold issue whether the plaintiffs were bound by the customer agreements should be decided by the district court and not by the arbitrator: "A contrary rule would lead to untenable results. Party A could forge party B's name to a contract and compel party B to arbitrate the question of the genuineness of its signature." Three Valleys Municipal Water Dist. v. E.F. Hutton & Co., Inc., 925 F.2d 1136 (9th Cir.1991).

ii. A brokerage firm's customers (who could not read English) alleged that an employee of the firm had misrepresented to them that they were merely opening a money market account rather than a securities trading account. The court held that the customers were entitled to a trial on this issue, and that it was error to compel arbitration of the customers' claims before doing so: "Where misrepresentation of the character or essential terms of a proposed contract occurs, assent to the contract is impossible. In such a case there is no contract at all." Cancanon v. Smith Barney, Harris, Upham & Co., 805 F.2d 998 (11th Cir.1986). See also Strotz v. Dean Witter Reynolds, Inc., 223 Cal.App.3d 208, 272 Cal.Rptr. 680 (1990) (customer of brokerage firm alleged that she had not been told that the document entitled "Option Client Information" was actually a contract, the terms of which were set forth on the back of the form; "if a party is unaware he is signing any contract, obviously he also is unaware he is agreeing to arbitration").

6. The Supreme Court in Scherk v. Alberto–Culver Co., 417 U.S. 506 (1974), characterized an agreement to arbitrate as "in effect, a specialized kind of forum-selection clause that posits not only the situs of suit but also the procedure to be used in resolving the dispute." Consider Marra v. Papandreou, 216 F.3d 1119 (D.C.Cir.2000). Here the plaintiff was an investor in a consortium that had won a license from the government of Greece to operate a casino near Athens. The license agreement contained no arbitration clause—it did, however, provide that any dispute concerning the license would be settled "by the Greek courts." After local political opposition to the casino developed, the Greek government revoked the license, citing legal defects. The plaintiff filed suit in the United States for breach of contract; it argued that—because the Greek government purported to have revoked the license "from the time it came into effect"—the government should be estopped from seeking refuge in the forum selection clause, which was a provision of a "nonexistent" license. The court nevertheless held that the forum selection clause was enforceable and that the plaintiff was required to file suit in Greece: The clause was properly understood as

> severable from the contract in which it is contained. Therefore while the Greek government's denial of its contractual obligations to Marra relieves her of her duty to perform her side of the contract's terms (for instance, she is no longer obligated to pay the annual license fee), that action does not work a repudiation of the forum-selection clause unless it is specifically directed at the clause itself. Were this not the case ... the value of a forum-selection clause would be significantly diminished, since it will often be the case that a plaintiff can plausibly allege that the defendant's nonperformance constitutes a "repudiation" of its contractual obligations precluding it from recourse to the clause.

c. CONTRACTS OF ADHESION AND UNCONSCIONABILITY

Broemmer v. Abortion Services of Phoenix, Ltd.

Supreme Court of Arizona, En Banc, 1992.
173 Ariz. 148, 840 P.2d 1013.

■ MOELLER, VICE CHIEF JUSTICE. * * *

In December 1986, plaintiff, an Iowa resident, was 21 years old, unmarried, and 16 or 17 weeks pregnant. She was a high school graduate earning less than $100.00 a week and had no medical benefits. The father-to-be insisted that plaintiff have an abortion, but her parents advised against it. Plaintiff's uncontested affidavit describes the time as one of considerable confusion and emotional and physical turmoil for her.

Plaintiff's mother contacted Abortion Services of Phoenix and made an appointment for her daughter for December 29, 1986. During their visit to the clinic that day, plaintiff and her mother expected, but did not receive, information and counselling on alternatives to abortion and the nature of the operation. When plaintiff and her mother arrived at the clinic, plaintiff was escorted into an adjoining room and asked to complete three forms, one of which is the agreement to arbitrate at issue in this case. The agreement to arbitrate included language that "any dispute aris[ing] between the Parties as a result of the fees and/or services" would be settled by binding arbitration and that "any arbitrators appointed by the AAA shall be licensed medical doctors who specialize in obstetrics/gynecology." The two other documents plaintiff completed at the same time were a 2–page consent-to-operate form and a questionnaire asking for a detailed medical history. Plaintiff completed all three forms in less than 5 minutes and returned them to the front desk. Clinic staff made no attempt to explain the agreement to plaintiff before or after she signed, and did not provide plaintiff with copies of the forms.

After plaintiff returned the forms to the front desk, she was taken into an examination room where pre-operation procedures were performed. She was then instructed to return at 7:00 a.m. the next morning for the termination procedure. Plaintiff returned the following day and Doctor Otto performed the abortion. As a result of the procedure, plaintiff suffered a punctured uterus that required medical treatment.

Plaintiff filed a malpractice complaint in June 1988, approximately 1 1/2 years after the medical procedure. By the time litigation commenced, plaintiff could recall completing and signing the medical history and consent-to-operate forms, but could not recall signing the agreement to arbitrate. Defendants moved to dismiss, contending that the trial court lacked subject matter jurisdiction because arbitration was required. In opposition, plaintiff submitted affidavits that remain uncontroverted. The trial court considered the affidavits, apparently treated the motion to dismiss as one for summary judgment, and granted summary judgment to the defendants. Plaintiff's motion to vacate, quash or set aside the order, or to stay the claim pending arbitration, was denied.

On appeal, the court of appeals held that although the contract was one of adhesion, it was nevertheless enforceable because it did not fall outside plaintiff's reasonable expectations and was not unconscionable. * * * We granted plaintiff's petition for review. * * *

Some of the parties and amici have urged us to announce a "bright-line" rule of broad applicability concerning the enforceability of arbitration agreements. Arbitration proceedings are statutorily authorized in Arizona, A.R.S. §§ 12–1501 to–1518, and arbitration plays an important role in dispute resolution, as do other salutary methods of alternative dispute resolution. Important principles of contract law and of freedom of contract are intertwined with questions relating to agreements to utilize alternative methods of dispute resolution. We conclude it would be unwise to accept the invitation to attempt to establish some "bright-line" rule of broad

C. ARBITRATION AND THE COURTS

applicability in this case. We will instead resolve the one issue which is dispositive: Under the undisputed facts in this case, is the agreement to arbitrate enforceable against plaintiff? We hold that it is not.

I. The Contract Is One of Adhesion

* * * [T]he enforceability of the agreement to arbitrate is determined by principles of general contract law. The court of appeals concluded, and we agree, that, under those principles, the contract in this case was one of adhesion.

An adhesion contract is typically a standardized form "offered to consumers of goods and services on essentially a 'take it or leave it' basis without affording the consumer a realistic opportunity to bargain and under such conditions that the consumer cannot obtain the desired product or services except by acquiescing in the form contract." Wheeler v. St. Joseph Hosp., 63 Cal.App.3d 345, 356, 133 Cal.Rptr. 775, 783 (1976). The *Wheeler* court further stated that "[t]he distinctive feature of a contract of adhesion is that the weaker party has no realistic choice as to its terms." Likewise, in Contractual Problems in the Enforcement of Agreements to Arbitrate Medical Malpractice, 58 Va.L.Rev. 947, 988 (1972), Professor Stanley Henderson recognized "the essence of an adhesion contract is that bargaining position and leverage enable one party 'to select and control risks assumed under the contract.' " (quoting Friedrich Kessler, Contracts of Adhesion—Some Thoughts About Freedom of Contract, 43 Colum.L.Rev. 629 (1943)).

The printed form agreement signed by plaintiff in this case possesses all the characteristics of a contract of adhesion. The form is a standardized contract offered to plaintiff on a "take it or leave it" basis. In addition to removing from the courts any potential dispute concerning fees or services, the drafter inserted additional terms potentially advantageous to itself requiring that any arbitrator appointed by the American Arbitration Association be a licensed medical doctor specializing in obstetrics/gynecology. The contract was not negotiated but was, instead, prepared by defendant and presented to plaintiff as a condition of treatment. Staff at the clinic neither explained its terms to plaintiff nor indicated that she was free to refuse to sign the form; they merely represented to plaintiff that she had to complete the three forms. The conditions under which the clinic offered plaintiff the services were on a "take it or leave it" basis, and the terms of service were not negotiable. Applying general contract law to the undisputed facts, the court of appeals correctly held that the contract was one of adhesion.

II. Reasonable Expectations

Our conclusion that the contract was one of adhesion is not, of itself, determinative of its enforceability. "[A] contract of adhesion is fully enforceable according to its terms unless certain other factors are present which, under established legal rules—legislative or judicial—operate to render it otherwise." Graham v. Scissor–Tail, Inc., 28 Cal.3d 807, 171

Cal.Rptr. 604, 611, 623 P.2d 165, 172 (1981) To determine whether this contract of adhesion is enforceable, we look to two factors: the reasonable expectations of the adhering party and whether the contract is unconscionable. As the court stated in *Graham:*

> Generally speaking, there are two judicially imposed limitations on the enforcement of adhesion contracts or provisions thereof. The first is that such a contract or provision which does not fall within the reasonable expectations of the weaker or "adhering" party will not be enforced against him. The second—a principle of equity applicable to all contracts generally—is that a contract or provision, even if consistent with the reasonable expectations of the parties, will be denied enforcement if, considered in its context, it is unduly oppressive or "unconscionable."

* * *

The comment to [Restatement (Second) of Contracts § 211] states in part: "Although customers typically adhere to standardized agreements and are bound by them without even appearing to know the standard terms in detail, they are not bound to unknown terms which are beyond the range of reasonable expectation." The Restatement focuses our attention on whether it was beyond plaintiff's reasonable expectations to expect to arbitrate her medical malpractice claims, which includes waiving her right to a jury trial, as part of the filling out of the three forms under the facts and circumstances of this case. Clearly, there was no conspicuous or explicit waiver of the fundamental right to a jury trial or any evidence that such rights were knowingly, voluntarily and intelligently waived. The only evidence presented compels a finding that waiver of such fundamental rights was beyond the reasonable expectations of plaintiff. Moreover, as Professor Henderson writes, "[i]n attempting to effectuate reasonable expectations consistent with a standardized medical contract, a court will find less reason to regard the bargaining process as suspect if there are no terms unreasonably favorable to the stronger party." In this case failure to explain to plaintiff that the agreement required all potential disputes, including malpractice disputes, to be heard only by an arbitrator who was a licensed obstetrician/gynecologist requires us to view the "bargaining" process with suspicion. It would be unreasonable to enforce such a critical term against plaintiff when it is not a negotiated term and defendant failed to explain it to her or call her attention to it.

Plaintiff was under a great deal of emotional stress, had only a high school education, was not experienced in commercial matters, and is still not sure "what arbitration is." Given the circumstances under which the agreement was signed and the nature of the terms included therein, [we are compelled] to conclude that the contract fell outside plaintiff's reasonable expectations and is, therefore, unenforceable. Because of this holding, it is unnecessary for us to determine whether the contract is also unconscionable.

C. Arbitration and the Courts

III. A Comment on The Dissent

In view of the concern expressed by the dissent, we restate our firm conviction that arbitration and other methods of alternative dispute resolution play important and desirable roles in our system of dispute resolution. We encourage their use. When agreements to arbitrate are freely and fairly entered, they will be welcomed and enforced. They will not, however, be exempted from the usual rules of contract law * * *. * * *

The dissent is concerned that our decision today sends a "mixed message." It is, however, our intent to send a clear message. That message is: Contracts of adhesion will not be enforced unless they are conscionable and within the reasonable expectations of the parties. This is a well-established principle of contract law; today we merely apply it to the undisputed facts of the case before us.

Those portions of the opinion of the court of appeals inconsistent with this opinion are vacated. The judgment of the trial court is reversed and this case is remanded for further proceedings consistent with this opinion. * * *

■ Martone, Justice, dissenting.

The court's conclusion that the agreement to arbitrate was outside the plaintiff's reasonable expectations is without basis in law or fact. I fear today's decision reflects a preference for litigation over alternative dispute resolution that I had thought was behind us. I would affirm the court of appeals.

We begin with the undisputed facts that the court ignores. At the top [of the agreement to arbitrate] it states in bold capital letters "PLEASE READ THIS CONTRACT CAREFULLY AS IT EFFECTS [sic] YOUR LEGAL RIGHTS." Directly under that in all capital letters are the words "AGREEMENT TO ARBITRATE." The recitals indicate that "the Parties deem it to be in their respective best interest to settle any such dispute as expeditiously and economically as possible." The parties agreed that disputes over services provided would be settled by arbitration in accordance with the rules of the American Arbitration Association. They further agreed that the arbitrators appointed by the American Arbitration Association would be licensed medical doctors who specialize in obstetrics/gynecology. Plaintiff, an adult, signed the document. * * *

The court seizes upon the doctrine of reasonable expectations to revoke this contract. But there is nothing in this record that would warrant a finding that an agreement to arbitrate a malpractice claim was not within the reasonable expectations of the parties. On this record, the exact opposite is likely to be true. For all we know, both sides in this case might wish to avoid litigation like the plague and seek the more harmonious waters of alternative dispute resolution. Nor is there anything in this record that would suggest that arbitration is bad. Where is the harm? In the end, today's decision reflects a preference in favor of litigation that is not shared by the courts of other states and the courts of the United States. * * *

CHAPTER V ARBITRATION

NOTES AND QUESTIONS

1. Is it critical to the court's decision in *Broemmer* that under the contract the arbitrators were required to be "medical doctors who specialize in obstetrics/gynecology"?

Cf. Graham v. Scissor–Tail, Inc., 28 Cal.3d 807, 171 Cal.Rptr. 604, 623 P.2d 165 (1981), relied on by the court in *Broemmer. Graham* involved a contract for a series of concerts entered into between a promoter and Leon Russell, a recording artist and leader of a musical group. The contract was on a standard form prepared by Russell's union, the American Federation of Musicians, and provided that any disputes would be submitted to the International Executive Board of the Federation for final determination. After a dispute arose over the amount due to Russell out of the proceeds of the concerts, the Board issued an award in favor of Russell on the basis of a recommendation by a "referee"—a former executive officer of the union— named by the union president. The California Supreme Court refused to confirm this award. The court first found the agreement to be a "contract of adhesion"—"a standardized contract, which, imposed and drafted by the party of superior bargaining strength, relegates to the subscribing party only the opportunity to adhere to the contract or reject it." "All concert artists and groups of any significance or prominence" are members of the A.F. of M., and the promoter "was required by the realities of his business" to sign A.F. of M. form contracts with any concert artist with whom he wished to deal. Given that adhesion contracts are widely used and are "an inevitable fact of life for all citizens," that fact alone could not render the contract invalid. However, the court went on to find the agreement "unconscionable and unenforceable" because "it designates an arbitrator who, by reason of its status and identity, is presumptively biased in favor of one party":

> [W]hen as here the contract designating [the] arbitrator is the product of circumstances suggestive of adhesion, the possibility of overreaching by the dominant party looms large; contracts concluded in such circumstances, then, must be scrutinized with particular care to insure that the party of lesser bargaining power, in agreeing thereto, is not left in a position depriving him of any realistic and fair opportunity to prevail in a dispute under its terms. * * * [W]e * * * must insist— most especially in circumstances smacking of adhesion—that certain "minimum levels of integrity" be achieved if the arrangement in question is to pass judicial muster.

Further discussion of the selection of arbitrators and of arbitrator impartiality appears in Section D.1 infra.

2. Absent such elements of potential bias on the part of the arbitrators that the court found in *Graham,* under what circumstances is an arbitration clause in an adhesion contract likely to be found unenforceable?

Many state courts are inclined to strike down such clauses as "unconscionable" when they suspect that one party was not aware of the clause or that adequate efforts were not made to bring it to his attention. One such

C. Arbitration and the Courts

case is Wheeler v. St. Joseph Hospital, 63 Cal.App.3d 345, 133 Cal.Rptr. 775 (1976), also relied on in *Broemmer*. Wheeler was admitted to the hospital one evening "for an angiogram and catheterization studies in connection with a coronary insufficiency." On admission he signed a form entitled "CONDITIONS OF ADMISSION" which included a paragraph entitled "ARBITRATION OPTION." There was a blank space which the patient could initial to indicate his refusal of arbitration, but Wheeler did not do so. After the tests were performed, Wheeler suffered a brainstem infarction rendering him a total quadriplegic. The court held that he was not required to submit his malpractice claim to arbitration. According to his wife he had signed the admission form without reading it, and neither of them was aware that it contained an arbitration clause; "it was hurriedly signed under the stressful atmosphere of a hospital admitting room without any procedures calculated to alert the patient to the existence of the 'ARBITRATION OPTION.' Nor was the patient given a copy of the agreement to permit him to study its terms under less anxious circumstances":

> Although an express waiver of jury trial is not required, by agreeing to arbitration, the patient does forfeit a valuable right. The law ought not to decree a forfeiture of such a valuable right where the patient has not been made aware of the existence of an arbitration provision or its implications. Absent notification and at least some explanation, the patient cannot be said to have exercised a "real choice" in selecting arbitration over litigation. We conclude that in order to be binding, an arbitration clause incorporated in a hospital's "CONDITIONS OF ADMISSION" form should be called to the patient's attention and he should be given a reasonable explanation of its meaning and effect, including an explanation of any options available to the patient. These procedural requirements will not impose an unreasonable burden on the hospital. The hospital's admission clerk need only direct the patient's attention to the arbitration provision, request him to read it, and give him a simple explanation of its purpose and effect, including the available options. Compliance will not require the presence of the hospital's house counsel in the admission office.

4. A patient was admitted to the hospital for surgery. The hospital's "standard procedure" was to have the admitting clerk explain to patients that they were signing an arbitration agreement "to settle all grievances that they have against the hospital outside of court before an arbitration panel." The trial court found the arbitration agreement binding and dismissed the patient's malpractice action; *held*, reversed. The patient's waiver of his right to a jury trial was not "knowing," since there was insufficient evidence that he had read the agreement or was even aware that it contained an arbitration clause: "Surely, in a criminal proceeding, the prosecution could not withstand a *Miranda* challenge merely by presenting a police officer's testimony that it was his 'usual practice' to inform suspects of their rights before attempting to obtain confessions." Nor was the waiver "intelligent," since the agreement did not disclose the composition of the arbitration panel. Under Michigan law, one member of the panel was required to be a doctor or hospital administrator. The court found a

CHAPTER V ARBITRATION

"substantial likelihood that a health care provider's decisions will be swayed by *unconscious subliminal bias,* impossible to detect"; it therefore held that the patient must be fully informed in advance not only of the composition of the arbitration panel but also that doctors and hospital administrators on such panels may have "an incentive to minimize the number and size of malpractice awards, because their malpractice insurance rates are directly affected by those awards." Finally, the waiver was not "voluntary," in part because on signing the agreement upon admission to the hospital, the patient was in "considerable pain." Moore v. Fragatos, 116 Mich.App. 179, 321 N.W.2d 781 (1982).

5. If the patients in any of the preceding cases had had the opportunity to consult you in advance of treatment, would you have advised them that it was in their best interests to sign the arbitration agreement? Is it likely that the "disclosures" required in cases like *Wheeler and Moore* will have the same effect?

6. Investors entered into a margin account agreement with a stock brokerage firm. The firm later sold securities worth $3 million that were held in the account as collateral for the repayment of loans it had made to the investors. The investors brought suit claiming that this sale violated the agreement; the firm moved to compel arbitration in accordance with an arbitration clause. The investors asserted that they had been "fraudulently induced" to enter into the arbitration agreement by the firm's "failure to disclose the effect of the arbitration clause." The court held that the investors were not entitled to a jury trial of this issue:

> We know of no case holding that parties dealing at arm's length have a duty to explain to each other the terms of a written contract. We decline to impose such an obligation where the language of the contract clearly and explicitly provides for arbitration of disputes arising out of the contractual relationship. This is not a criminal case; the [plaintiffs'] argument that there was no "showing of intelligent and knowing waiver of the substantive rights at issue" is simply beside the point. * * * We see no unfairness in expecting parties to read contracts before they sign them.

Cohen v. Wedbush, Noble, Cooke, Inc., 841 F.2d 282 (9th Cir.1988). Is this consistent with the cases in the preceding notes? Cf. In re Rangel, 45 S.W.3d 783 (Tex.App.-Waco 2001), where the court enforced Orkin's "Limited Lifetime Subterranean Termite Agreement" containing an arbitration clause: The homeowner "was 75 years old, had never attended school, was functionally illiterate, and was hard of hearing." Nevertheless "at no time" did he "ask any questions regarding, or request any explanations of," the contract; the arbitration provision "was never hidden" from him, and he had "the opportunity to read and reject the terms of the contract within three business days."

7. In addition to one party's lack of awareness of the arbitration clause, what other defects might there be in an arbitration agreement which could give rise to an argument of unconscionability? See Henderson, Contractual

Problems in the Enforcement of Agreements to Arbitrate Medical Malpractice, 58 Va.L.Rev. 947, 994 (1972):

Assuming the conventional expectations test is applied widely to medical arbitration clauses, it is essential to underscore the point that the primary reason for application of such a test is that the disadvantaged bargaining party is harmed or unfairly overreached. The factor of harm or prejudice measures the range of reasonable expectation induced by a standardized contract. * * * So unless it can be said that a medical arbitration term operates in a coercive or oppressive manner, it is difficult to see that the courts will regard it as exceeding the expectations of the average patient who accepts it.

One possible illustration of an arbitration clause that "operates in a coercive or oppressive manner" might be Patterson v. ITT Consumer Financial Corp., 14 Cal.App.4th 1659, 18 Cal.Rptr.2d 563 (1993). Plaintiffs, "individuals of modest means, some self-employed or temporarily jobless," borrowed "relatively small amounts of money." The loan agreements provided that any disputes "shall be resolved by binding arbitration by the National Arbitration Forum, Minneapolis, Minnesota." The court found this arbitration provision "unconscionable and thus unenforceable." The NAF's rules were unclear as to just where the arbitration would be held, but "the provision on its face suggests that Minnesota would be the locus for the arbitration"—and "[w]hile arbitration per se may be within the reasonable expectation of most consumers, it is much more difficult to believe that arbitration in Minnesota would be within the reasonable expectation of California consumers." In addition, in order to obtain a participatory hearing the consumer was required to prepay a substantial hearing fee; a rule explaining the NAF's process for waiver of the fee was "incomprehensible."

8. The Bank of America's arbitration program for all its depositors and credit-card holders (see pp. 642–643 supra) was quickly challenged in court. The plaintiffs argued that "the Bank's unprecedented ADR provision does not fall within the reasonable expectations of the Bank's consumer account-holders," and that "the Bank's unilateral imposition of ADR deprives consumers without their consent of rights that are constitutionally guaranteed." (Plaintiffs' Trial Brief, pp. 23, 25). Outside of court, the plaintiffs' attorney put the matter somewhat more dramatically: "[A]rbitration, like sex, must be based on consent, not on coercion." 1 ABA Disp.Res.Mag., p. 5 (Summer 1994).

The plaintiffs were successful in having the Bank's arbitration clause held unenforceable in Badie v. Bank of America, 67 Cal.App.4th 779, 79 Cal.Rptr.2d 273 (Cal.App.1998). The credit-card agreements had provided that the Bank "may change any term, condition, service or feature of your Account at any time"—such change-of-terms provisions had in fact been standard industry practice since bank credit cards first became available in the 1960's. Nevertheless the court held that it was a violation of the covenant of good faith and fair dealing for the Bank to "attempt to 'recapture' a foregone opportunity by adding an entirely new term, which

CHAPTER V ARBITRATION

has no bearing on any subject * * * addressed in the original contract and which was not within the reasonable contemplation of the parties when the contract was entered into''; the absence of any such limitation "would open the door to a claim that the agreements are illusory." There was nothing that would have alerted a customer to the possibility that the Bank might one day in the future invoke this provision to add clauses that were not "integral to the Bank/creditor relationship". Nor was the customer's failure to close an account after receiving the "bill stuffers" sufficient to constitute a waiver of his right to a jury trial—because the Bank's notice was not "direct, clear and unambiguous" and was not "designed to achieve knowing consent" to arbitration. Federal policy favoring arbitration, added the court, "does not even come into play unless it is first determined that the Bank's customers agreed to use some form of ADR to resolve disputes regarding their deposit and credit card accounts"—a determination that in turn "requires analysis of the account agreements in light of ordinary state law principles" governing contracts.

9. The following year, Delaware enacted a statute that permitted a bank to amend any revolving credit plan "in any respect, whether or not the amendment * * * was originally contemplated or addressed by the parties or is integral to the relationship between the parties." Such amendment "may change terms by the addition of new terms" "of any kind whatsoever," expressly including "arbitration or other alternative dispute resolution mechanisms," and notice of any such amendment may be sent by the bank "in the same envelope with a periodic statement." 5 Del. Code § 952 (1999).

The Delaware statute was applied to bind credit card customers of First USA Bank to an arbitration clause in Marsh v. First USA Bank, N.A., 103 F. Supp.2d 909 (N.D.Tex.2000): It was enough for the Bank to show that notice of the arbitration clause was designed to be routinely included in monthly credit-card statements, and that there were in place "multi-level quality assurance controls" to "detect errors." To the same effect is Herrington v. Union Planters Bank, N.A., 113 F.Supp.2d 1026 (S.D.Miss. 2000) ("plaintiffs' apparent failure to read the revisions to their accounts is irrelevant to the issue of whether they agreed to arbitrate or are subject to those changes").

10. The use of arbitration clauses by Gateway in the direct sales of its computers (see p. 644 supra) has also been the subject of a flurry of recent litigation. The clause was enforced by the Seventh Circuit in Hill v. Gateway 2000, Inc., 105 F.3d 1147 (7th Cir.1997). Under Gateway's standard terms, the "form in the box" would govern unless the customer returned the computer within 30 days. Therefore, the court held, the contract had not been formed when the telephone order was placed, nor when the goods were delivered—but only *after* the customer had retained the computer beyond that time limit. "By keeping the computer beyond 30 days, the Hills accepted Gateway's offer, including the arbitration clause." Judge Easterbrook pointed out that "cash now-terms later" transactions were quite common in our economy, for example, in air travel and insurance transactions; "cashiers cannot be expected to read legal documents to customers before ringing up sales." And of course, "a contract need not be read to be effective; people who accept take the risk that the unread terms may in retrospect prove unwelcome."

Hylton, Agreements to Waive or to Arbitrate Legal Claims: An Economic Analysis, 8 Sup. Ct. Econ. Rev. 209, 252 (2000), argues that "rational apathy" may justify enforcement of arbitration clauses in "shrink wrap" and other cases where consumers purchase goods before reading or understanding the contract terms. If consumers are likely to misperceive the probability that an injury will arise, one explanation is that "it is costly to discover information about the probability of loss, and the expected rewards for discovering such information are too low to justify the research costs. The expected rewards may be too low because either the probability or the severity of harm, even after the [possibility of filing a lawsuit] is removed, is extremely low." Rational apathy may exist because consumers "rationally discount the deterrence benefits connected to their right to sue. In other words, they do not expect a significant change in the firm's conduct if the parties agree to resolve their disputes in the arbitration regime."

At least one court has declined to follow *Hill*, and has insisted that the proper analysis should instead be under § 2–207 of the UCC. The court in Klocek v. Gateway, Inc., 104 F.Supp.2d 1332 (D.Kan.2000) denied Gateway's motion to dismiss a consumer's breach of warranty suit. For purposes of the motion, it assumed that an offer to purchase the computer had been made by the consumer, and that Gateway had accepted the offer, "either by completing the sales transaction in person or by agreeing to ship and/or shipping the computer to plaintiff". "Because the plaintiff was not a 'merchant,' " Gateway's "additional" arbitration term could become part of the agreement under § 2–207(2) only if the plaintiff had "expressly agreed" to it—and merely retaining the computer was insufficient to show such express agreement.

11. The terms of Gateway's standard arbitration clause were found to be "substantively unconscionable" in Brower v. Gateway 2000, Inc., 246 A.D.2d 246, 676 N.Y.S.2d 569 (1998). The clause, as originally drafted, provided for arbitration to take place in Chicago under ICC rules. The court held that the "possible inconvenience of the chosen site" did not "alone" rise to the level of unconscionability. However, "the excessive cost factor that is necessarily entailed in arbitrating before the ICC is unreasonable and surely serves to deter the individual consumer from invoking the process." (For the smallest of cases ICC rules required an advance payment of $4000—greater than the cost of most Gateway products—of which the $2000 registration fee was nonrefundable even if the consumer prevailed at the arbitration.). Nevertheless, the court did not strike down the arbitration clause in its entirety—instead, it remanded the case to the trial court "so that the parties have the opportunity to seek appropriate substitution of an arbitrator" pursuant to § 5 of the FAA. More recently, the standard Gateway arbitration clause has been amended so that it now requires an arbitration administered by the "National Arbitration Forum"; the arbitration is to be held "at any reasonable location near [the customer's] residence."

12. Are general state contract-law principles of unconscionability applicable to a contract within the coverage of the FAA? The Supreme Court suggested in *Perry v. Thomas* that under § 2 of the FAA "state law, whether of legislative or judicial origin, is applicable *if* that law arose to govern issues concerning the validity, revocability, and enforceability of contracts generally." However, a "state-law principle that takes its meaning precisely from the fact that a contract to arbitrate is at issue does not comport with this requirement of § 2. * * * Nor may a court rely on the uniqueness of an agreement to arbitrate as a basis for a state-law holding that enforcement would be unconscionable, for this would enable the court to effect what we hold today the state legislature cannot." 482 U.S. 483, 492–93 n. 9. Lower courts seem to have had considerable difficulty in applying this principle. See, e.g., Meyers v. Univest Home Loan, Inc., 1993 WL 307747 (N.D.Cal.1993) ("Notwithstanding *Perry,* the court reads the controlling precedent to require that the instant dispute be resolved under principles of federal law only").

13. "When introduced as a method to control soil erosion, kudzu was hailed as an asset to agriculture, but it has become a creeping monster. Arbitration was innocuous when limited to negotiated commercial contracts, but it developed sinister characteristics when it became ubiquitous." In re Knepp, 229 B.R. 821 (Bankr.N.D.Ala.1999).

The *Knepp* court held that an arbitration clause in a contract for the sale of a used car was "void under the doctrine of unconscionability": The buyer lacked "meaningful choice," since "in today's market it is virtually impossible" to purchase an automobile without the sales contract containing an arbitration clause." The court noted that since "automobiles are a necessity in our society," consumers can ill afford to forsake this necessity even at the price of their constitutional rights." Under such reasoning, what *other* clauses in a standard sales, employment, or insurance contract could one justify invalidating?

14. Contracts of adhesion drafted by franchisors, brokerage firms, or insurers often give rise to a large number of claims presenting common questions. The repercussions of the defendant's actions may be widespread, but the monetary harm to individual claimants may be so insignificant that the expense even of arbitration proceedings would not be warranted. And a victory in arbitration for one particularly determined claimant would not necessarily lead to any recovery for any others, or alter the defendant's behavior.

Presumably, a defendant's motion to compel arbitration may no longer be denied simply on the ground that a class action would be a more suitable means of resolving the problem. See Dunham, The Arbitration Clause as Class Action Shield, 16 Franchise L.J. 141 (1997)("strict enforcement of an arbitration clause should enable the franchisor to dramatically reduce its aggregate exposure"); Johnson v. West Suburban Bank, 225 F.3d 366 (3d

Cir. 2000)(consumer borrowers can be forced to arbitrate their claims under the Truth in Lending Act even if doing so prevents them from bringing class actions; while the statute "clearly contemplates" class actions, it does not "create a right to bring them"); cf. Caudle v. AAA, 230 F.3d 920 (7th Cir.2000)(Easterbrook, J.) ("A procedural device aggregating multiple persons' claims in litigation does not entitle anyone to *be* in litigation; a contract promising to arbitrate the dispute removes the person from those eligible to represent a class of litigants").

But are class actions and arbitration agreements necessarily and inherently incompatible? Would it be feasible or desirable to expand the notion of "consolidation" to permit these similar cases to be heard together in a "class arbitration"? Cf. McCarthy v. Providential Corp., 1994 WL 387852 (N.D.Cal.)("Consolidation and class actions are both methods of adjudicating numerous individual actions involving common questions of law or fact"; the rationale of the consolidation cases "leads to the conclusion that the court cannot compel arbitration on a class basis where the agreement did not specifically provide for it"); cf. Blue Cross of California v. Superior Court of Los Angeles County, 67 Cal.App.4th 42, 78 Cal.Rptr.2d 779 (Cal.App.1998)(judicial consolidation of arbitrations is authorized by the California Code of Civil Procedure, see p. 674 supra, and "the interests of justice that would be served by ordering classwide arbitration are likely to be even more substantial in some cases than the interests that are thought to justify consolidation"). For a comprehensive discussion of this problem, see Sternlight, As Mandatory Binding Arbitration Meets the Class Action, Will the Class Action Survive?, 42 Wm. & Mary L. Rev. 1 (2000)(suggesting that the dispute over the permissibility of classwide arbitration may be simply a "decoy," which has "distracted observers from the companies' true goal: total evisceration of consumer and employment class actions").

15. Can an arbitration clause be enforceable if it purports to supersede class actions *that have already been filed*, where the consumer is a member of the putative class? The 2001 amendments to Fleet Bank (R.I.)'s credit card agreement so provide (arbitration "will not apply to Claims asserted in lawsuits filed by you against us ... before the Effective Date of this Arbitration Provision," but it will apply "to all other Claims, even if the facts and circumstances giving rise to the Claims existed before the [Effective Date] and even if some third party has initiated a class action against us, purporting to assert a Claim against us on your behalf prior to [the Effective Date]"; consequently the credit-card holder "may not participate in a class action or class-wide arbitration" unless he is a member of a class "which has already been certified on the effective date of this arbitration provision"). Cf. Jess Bravin, "Banks Seek to Halt Suits By Cardholders," Wall St. J., May 2, 2001.

d. "ARBITRABILITY"

Even if a valid agreement to arbitrate exists, that does not end the matter. The question may still arise whether the particular dispute falls within the ambit of the agreement—that is, whether the parties have

712   CHAPTER V   ARBITRATION

agreed to submit *this* matter in controversy to decision by arbitration. In the United States this is often referred to as an inquiry into whether the dispute is "arbitrable"—in effect, an inquiry into the "subject matter jurisdiction" of the arbitrator to hear the case.

AT & T Technologies, Inc. v. Communications Workers of America

Supreme Court of the United States, 1986.
475 U.S. 643, 106 S.Ct. 1415, 89 L.Ed.2d 648.

■ JUSTICE WHITE delivered the opinion of the Court.

The issue presented in this case is whether a court asked to order arbitration of a grievance filed under a collective-bargaining agreement must first determine that the parties intended to arbitrate the dispute, or whether that determination is properly left to the arbitrator.

I

AT & T Technologies, Inc. (AT & T or the Company) and the Communications Workers of America (the Union) are parties to a collective-bargaining agreement which covers telephone equipment installation workers. Article 8 of this agreement establishes that "differences arising with respect to the interpretation of this contract or the performance of any obligation hereunder" must be referred to a mutually agreeable arbitrator upon the written demand of either party. This Article expressly does not cover disputes "excluded from arbitration by other provisions of this contract."[1] Article 9 provides that, "subject to the limitations contained in the provisions of this contract, but otherwise not subject to the provisions of the arbitration clause," AT & T is free to exercise certain management functions, including the hiring and placement of employees and the termination of employment.[2] "When lack of work necessitates Layoff," Article 20 prescribes the order in which employees are to be laid off.[3]

1. Article 8 provides, in pertinent part, as follows:

If the National and the Company fail to settle by negotiation any differences arising with respect to the interpretation of this contract or the performance of any obligation hereunder, such differences shall (provided that such dispute is not excluded from arbitration by other provisions of this contract, and provided that the grievance procedures as to such dispute have been exhausted) be referred upon written demand of either party to an impartial arbitrator mutually agreeable to both parties.

2. Article 9 states:

The Union recognizes the right of the Company (subject to the limitations contained in the provisions of this contract, but otherwise not subject to the provisions of the arbitration clause) to exercise the functions of managing the business which involve, among other things, the hiring and placement of Employees, the termination of employment, the assignment of work, the determination of methods and equipment to be used, and the control of the conduct of work.

3. Article 20 provides, in pertinent part, "[w]hen lack of work necessitates Layoff, Employees shall be Laid–Off in accordance with Term of Employment and by Layoff groups as set forth in the following

On September 17, 1981, the Union filed a grievance challenging AT & T's decision to lay off 79 installers from its Chicago base location. The Union claimed that, because there was no lack of work at the Chicago location, the planned layoffs would violate Article 20 of the agreement. Eight days later, however, AT & T laid off all 79 workers, and soon thereafter, the Company transferred approximately the same number of installers from base locations in Indiana and Wisconsin to the Chicago base. AT & T refused to submit the grievance to arbitration on the ground that under Article 9, the Company's decision to lay off workers when it determines that a lack of work exists in a facility is not arbitrable.

The Union then sought to compel arbitration by filing suit in federal court pursuant to § 301(a) of the Labor Management Relations Act, 29 U.S.C. § 185(a). Ruling on cross-motions for summary judgment, the District Court reviewed the provisions of Articles 8, 9, and 20 and set forth the parties' arguments as follows:

> "Plaintiffs interpret Article 20 to require that there be an actual lack of work prior to employee layoffs and argue that there was no such lack of work in this case. Under plaintiffs' interpretation, Article 20 would allow the union to take to arbitration the threshold issue of whether the layoffs were justified by a lack of work. Defendant interprets Article 20 as merely providing a sequence for any layoffs which management, in its exclusive judgment, determines are necessary. Under defendant's interpretation, Article 20 would not allow for an arbitrator to decide whether the layoffs were warranted by a lack of work but only whether the company followed the proper order in laying off the employees."

Finding that "the union's interpretation of Article 20 was at least 'arguable,'" the court held that it was "for the arbitrator, not the court to decide whether the union's interpretation has merit," and accordingly, ordered the Company to arbitrate.

The Court of Appeals for the Seventh Circuit affirmed. The Court of Appeals understood the District Court to have ordered arbitration of the threshold issue of arbitrability. The court acknowledged the "general rule" that the issue of arbitrability is for the courts to decide unless the parties stipulate otherwise, but noted that this Court's decisions in *Steelworkers v. Warrior & Gulf Navigation Co.*, 363 U.S. 574 (1960), and *Steelworkers v. American Mfg. Co.*, 363 U.S. 564 (1960), caution courts to avoid becoming entangled in the merits of a labor dispute under the guise of deciding arbitrability. From this observation, the court announced an "exception" to the general rule, under which "a court should compel arbitration of the arbitrability issue where the collective bargaining agreement contains a standard arbitration clause, the parties have not clearly excluded the arbitrability issue from arbitration, and deciding the issue would entangle

[subparagraphs stating the order of layoff]." Article 1.11 defines the term "Layoff" to mean "a termination of employment arising out of a reduction in the force due to lack of work."

the court in interpretation of substantive provisions of the collective bargaining agreement and thereby involve consideration of the merits of the dispute."

All of these factors were present in this case. Article 8 was a "standard arbitration clause," and there was "no clear, unambiguous exclusion from arbitration of terminations predicated by a lack of work determination." Moreover, although there were "colorable arguments" on both sides of the exclusion issue, if the court were to decide this question it would have to interpret not only Article 8, but Articles 9 and 20 as well, both of which are "substantive provisions of the Agreement." The court thus "decline[d] the invitation to decide arbitrability," and ordered AT & T "to arbitrate the arbitrability issue."

* * *

We granted certiorari and now vacate the Seventh Circuit's decision and remand for a determination of whether the Company is required to arbitrate the Union's grievance.

II

The principles necessary to decide this case are not new. They were set out by this Court over 25 years ago in a series of cases known as the *Steelworkers Trilogy: Steelworkers v. American Mfg. Co.; Steelworkers v. Warrior & Gulf Navigation Co.*; and *Steelworkers v. Enterprise Wheel & Car Corp.,* 363 U.S. 593 (1960). These precepts have served the industrial relations community well, and have led to continued reliance on arbitration, rather than strikes or lockouts, as the preferred method of resolving disputes arising during the term of a collective-bargaining agreement. We see no reason either to question their continuing validity, or to eviscerate their meaning by creating an exception to their general applicability.

The first principle gleaned from the *Trilogy* is that "arbitration is a matter of contract and a party cannot be required to submit to arbitration any dispute which he has not agreed so to submit." This axiom recognizes the fact that arbitrators derive their authority to resolve disputes only because the parties have agreed in advance to submit such grievances to arbitration.

The second rule, which follows inexorably from the first, is that the question of arbitrability—whether a collective-bargaining agreement creates a duty for the parties to arbitrate the particular grievance—is undeniably an issue for judicial determination. Unless the parties clearly and unmistakably provide otherwise, the question of whether the parties agreed to arbitrate is to be decided by the court, not the arbitrator.

The Court expressly reaffirmed this principle in *John Wiley & Sons, Inc. v. Livingston,* 376 U.S. 543 (1964). The "threshold question" there was whether the court or an arbitrator should decide if arbitration provisions in a collective-bargaining contract survived a corporate merger so as to bind the surviving corporation. The Court answered that there was "no doubt" that this question was for the courts. " 'Under our decisions, whether or not the company was bound to arbitrate, as well as what issues it must arbitrate, is a matter to be determined by the Court on the basis of the contract entered into by the parties.' ... The duty to arbitrate being of contractual origin, a compulsory submission to arbitration cannot precede judicial determination that the collective bargaining agreement does in fact create such a duty."

The third principle derived from our prior cases is that, in deciding whether the parties have agreed to submit a particular grievance to arbitration, a court is not to rule on the potential merits of the underlying claims. Whether "arguable" or not, indeed even if it appears to the court to be frivolous, the union's claim that the employer has violated the collective-bargaining agreement is to be decided, not by the court asked to order arbitration, but as the parties have agreed, by the arbitrator. "The courts, therefore, have no business weighing the merits of the grievance, considering whether there is equity in a particular claim, or determining whether there is particular language in the written instrument which will support the claim. The agreement is to submit all grievances to arbitration, not merely those which the court will deem meritorious."

Finally, it has been established that where the contract contains an arbitration clause, there is a presumption of arbitrability in the sense that "[a]n order to arbitrate the particular grievance should not be denied unless it may be said with positive assurance that the arbitration clause is not susceptible of an interpretation that covers the asserted dispute. Doubts should be resolved in favor of coverage." *Warrior & Gulf,* 363 U.S. at 582–583. Such a presumption is particularly applicable where the clause is as broad as the one employed in this case, which provides for arbitration of "any differences arising with respect to the interpretation of this contract or the performance of any obligation hereunder.... " In such cases, "[i]n the absence of any express provision excluding a particular grievance from arbitration, we think only the most forceful evidence of a purpose to exclude the claim from arbitration can prevail." *Warrior & Gulf,* 363 U.S., at 584–585.

This presumption of arbitrability for labor disputes recognizes the greater institutional competence of arbitrators in interpreting collective bargaining agreements, "furthers the national labor policy of peaceful resolution of labor disputes and thus best accords with the parties' presumed objectives in pursuing collective bargaining." The willingness of parties to enter into agreements that provide for arbitration of specified disputes would be "drastically reduced," however, if a labor arbitrator had the "power to determine his own jurisdiction...." Cox, Reflections Upon Labor Arbitration, 72 Harv.L.Rev. 1482, 1509 (1959). Were this the applicable rule, an arbitrator would not be constrained to resolve only those disputes that the parties have agreed in advance to settle by arbitration, but instead, would be empowered "to impose obligations outside the contract limited only by his understanding and conscience." This result undercuts the longstanding federal policy of promoting industrial harmony through the use of collective-bargaining agreements, and is antithetical to the function of a collective-bargaining agreement as setting out the rights and duties of the parties.

With these principles in mind, it is evident that the Seventh Circuit erred in ordering the parties to arbitrate the arbitrability question. It is the court's duty to interpret the agreement and to determine whether the parties intended to arbitrate grievances concerning layoffs predicated on a "lack of work" determination by the Company. If the court determines that the agreement so provides, then it is for the arbitrator to determine the relative merits of the parties' substantive interpretations of the agreement. It was for the court, not the arbitrator, to decide in the first instance whether the dispute was to be resolved through arbitration.

The Union does not contest the application of these principles to the present case. Instead, it urges the Court to examine the specific provisions of the agreement for itself and to affirm the Court of Appeals on the ground that the parties had agreed to arbitrate the dispute over the layoffs at issue here. But it is usually not our function in the first instance to construe collective-bargaining contracts and arbitration clauses, or to consider any other evidence that might unmistakably demonstrate that a particular grievance was not to be subject to arbitration. The issue in the case is whether, because of express exclusion or other forceful evidence, the dispute over the interpretation of Article 20 of the contract, the layoff provision, is not subject to the arbitration clause. That issue should have been decided by the District Court and reviewed by the Court of Appeals; it should not have been referred to the arbitrator.

The judgment of the Court of Appeals is vacated, and the case is remanded for proceedings in conformity with this opinion.

■ JUSTICE BRENNAN, with whom THE CHIEF JUSTICE and JUSTICE MARSHALL join, concurring.

I join the Court's opinion and write separately only to supplement what has been said in order to avoid any misunderstanding on remand and in future cases.

The Seventh Circuit's erroneous conclusion that the arbitrator should decide whether this dispute is arbitrable resulted from that court's confusion respecting the "arbitrability" determination that we have held must be judicially made. Despite recognizing that Article 8 of the collective-bargaining agreement "is a standard arbitration clause, providing for arbitration of 'any differences arising with respect to the interpretation of this contract or the performance of any obligation hereunder,' "and that "there is no clear, unambiguous exclusion [of this dispute] from arbitration," the Court of Appeals thought that "there [were] colorable arguments both for and against exclusion." The "colorable arguments" referred to by the Court of Appeals were the parties' claims concerning the meaning of Articles 9 and 20 of the collective-bargaining agreement: the Court of Appeals thought that if the Union's interpretation of Article 20 was correct and management could not order lay-offs for reasons other than lack of work, the dispute was arbitrable; but if AT & T's interpretation of Article

20 was correct and management was free to order lay-offs for other reasons, the dispute was not arbitrable under Article 9. Because these were the very issues that would be presented to the arbitrator if the dispute was held to be arbitrable, the court reasoned that "determining arbitrability would enmesh a court in the merits of th[e] dispute," and concluded that the arbitrability issue should be submitted to the arbitrator.

The Court of Appeals was mistaken insofar as it thought that determining arbitrability required resolution of the parties' dispute with respect to the meaning of Articles 9 and 20 of the collective-bargaining agreement. This is clear from our opinion in *Steelworkers v. Warrior & Gulf Navigation Co.* In *Warrior & Gulf,* the Union challenged management's contracting out of labor that had previously been performed by Company employees. The parties failed to resolve the dispute through grievance procedures, and the Union requested arbitration; the Company refused, and the Union sued to compel arbitration under § 301 of the Labor Management Relations Act, 29 U.S.C. § 185. The collective-bargaining agreement contained a standard arbitration clause similar to Article 8 of the AT & T/CSA contract, i.e., providing for arbitration of all differences with respect to the meaning or application of the contract. We held that, in light of the congressional policy making arbitration the favored method of dispute resolution, such a provision requires arbitration "unless it may be said with positive assurance that the arbitration clause is not susceptible of an interpretation that covers the asserted dispute. Doubts should be resolved in favor of coverage."

The Company in *Warrior & Gulf* relied for its argument that the dispute was not arbitrable on a "Management Functions" clause which, like Article 9 of the AT & T/CWA agreement, excluded "matters which are strictly a function of management" from the arbitration provision. We recognized that such a clause "might be thought to refer to any practice of management in which, under particular circumstances prescribed by the agreement, it is permitted to indulge." However, we also recognized that to read the clause this way would make arbitrability in every case depend upon whether management could take the action challenged by the Union; the arbitrability of every dispute would turn upon a resolution of the merits, and "the arbitration clause would be swallowed up by the exception." Therefore, we held that, where a collective-bargaining agreement contains a standard arbitration clause and the "exception" found in the Management Functions clause is general, "judicial inquiry ... should be limited to the search for an explicit provision which brings the grievance under the cover of the [Management Functions] clause...." "In the absence of any express provision excluding a particular grievance from arbitration, ... only the most forceful evidence of a purpose to exclude the claim from arbitration can prevail...."

The Seventh Circuit misunderstood these rules of contract construction and did precisely what we disapproved of in *Warrior & Gulf*—it read Article 9, a general Management Functions clause, to make arbitrability depend upon the merits of the parties' dispute. As *Warrior & Gulf* makes

718 CHAPTER V ARBITRATION

clear, the judicial inquiry required to determine arbitrability is much simpler. The parties' dispute concerns whether Article 20 of the collective-bargaining agreement limits management's authority to order lay-offs for reasons other than lack of work. The question for the court is "strictly confined" to whether the parties agreed to submit disputes over the meaning of Article 20 to arbitration. Because the collective-bargaining agreement contains a standard arbitration clause, the answer must be affirmative unless the contract contains explicit language stating that disputes respecting Article 20 are not subject to arbitration, or unless the party opposing arbitration—here AT & T—adduces "the most forceful evidence" to this effect from the bargaining history. Under *Warrior & Gulf,* determining arbitrability does not require the court even to consider which party is correct with respect to the meaning of Article 20.

NOTES AND QUESTIONS

1. The presumption of arbitrability established by the *Steelworkers* "Trilogy" rested in large part on the unique value that arbitration was thought to have, as a "substitute for industrial strife," in the context of the administration of a collective bargaining agreement. See the excerpts from Justice Douglas' opinion in the *Warrior and Gulf* case, supra p. 634. Is there any reason to apply a similar presumption in other areas? See Schneider Moving & Storage Co. v. Robbins, 466 U.S. 364, 104 S.Ct. 1844, 80 L.Ed.2d 366 (1984) (*Steelworkers* presumption of arbitrability "is not a proper rule of construction" in a case brought against employers by the trustees of certain multi-employer trust funds).

In cases within the coverage of the FAA, the statute's "liberal federal policy favoring arbitration agreements" has led to a similar presumption that "any doubts concerning the scope of arbitrable issues should be resolved in favor of arbitration." Moses H. Cone Memorial Hospital v. Mercury Construction Corp., 460 U.S. 1, 24–25, 103 S.Ct. 927, 941, 74 L.Ed.2d 765 (1983); see also Mitsubishi Motors Corp. v. Soler Chrysler–Plymouth, infra p. 766. Courts applying the FAA will tend even in commercial arbitration cases to cite routinely and to rely indiscriminately on the labor precedents. See, e.g., In the Matter of the Arbitration Between the Singer Co. and Tappan Co., 403 F.Supp. 322, 330 (D.N.J.1975), aff'd, 544 F.2d 513 (3d Cir.1976) (if the policy of judicial noninterference in labor cases is grounded on the belief that "a labor arbitrator is better able to decide complex labor issues than a judge, then it can likewise be said here that the accounting complexities which led to disagreement between well known and highly regarded accounting firms should likewise be best left for arbitration").

2. The *Steelworkers* "Trilogy" is also thought to stand for the principle that questions of "arbitrability" are not affected by the fact that the claim asserted may clearly be without any substantive merit. "Issues do not lose their quality of arbitrability because they can be correctly decided only one way." New Bedford Defense Prods. Div. v. Local No. 1113, 258 F.2d 522,

526 (1st Cir.1958). Is the same proposition true, as a general matter, of the "subject matter jurisdiction" of a court?

In an influential article relied on by Justice Douglas in the "Trilogy," Professor Cox argued that a dispute can rarely be confidently labeled as "frivolous" until "its industrial context," "the parties' way of life and general industrial practice," have all been brought to light: "Since the true nature of a grievance often cannot be determined until there is a full hearing upon the facts, the reasonable course is to send all doubtful cases to arbitration * * *." Cox, Reflections Upon Labor Arbitration, 72 Harv. L.Rev. 1482, 1515, 1517 (1959). Recall also the frequently-made claim that in collective bargaining cases the airing even of claims that *are* clearly "frivolous" might have a "therapeutic" or "cathartic" value. Is this likely to be true of disputes outside of the collective bargaining area?

3. A collective bargaining agreement provided that any layoffs would be in order of seniority, provided that "aptitude and ability [were] equal." One year after the agreement had expired, the employer laid off a number of senior employees, and the Union brought a grievance. The Supreme Court (in a 5–4 decision) held that this dispute did not "arise under" the expired agreement and was therefore not arbitrable. The grievances "would be arbitrable only if they involve rights which accrued or vested under the Agreement, or rights which carried over after expiration of the Agreement * * * as continuing obligations under the contract," and this was not the case: Since aptitude and ability "do not remain constant, but change over time," they "cannot be said to vest or accrue." The Court rejected the Union's argument that this was an issue of contract interpretation that should be submitted in the first instance to the arbitrator: The presumption of arbitrability cannot be applied "wholesale in the context of an expired bargaining agreement, for to do so would make limitless the contractual obligation to arbitrate. * * * [W]e must determine whether the parties agreed to arbitrate this dispute, and we cannot avoid that duty because it requires us to interpret a provision of a bargaining agreement." A footnote in the opinion conceded that the Court's determination that the dispute was not arbitrable "does, of necessity, determine that * * * the employees lacked any vested contractual right to a particular order of layoff." Litton Financial Printing Div. v. NLRB, 501 U.S. 190, 111 S.Ct. 2215, 115 L.Ed.2d 177 (1991).

Is *Litton* consistent with *AT & T?* See also Independent Lift Truck Builders Union v. Hyster Co., 2 F.3d 233 (7th Cir.1993) (after *Litton,* "the rule that courts must decide arbitrators' jurisdiction takes precedence over the rule that courts are not to decide the merits of the underlying dispute").

4. Any "presumption" in favor of arbitration remains, at least in theory, only a rule of construction. The ultimate goal is to effectuate the parties' intent, and the presumption can be overcome by language or other evidence indicating an intent to *exclude* certain items or claims from the arbitrator's consideration. See, e.g., Instructional Television Corp. v. National Broadcasting Co., 45 A.D.2d 1004, 357 N.Y.S.2d 915 (1974) (clause provided that "[a]ny unresolved questions of fact, as distinguished from questions of law, shall at the behest of either party be submitted to arbitration").

Conversely, it is at least conceivable that the parties could go so far as to entrust to the arbitrator *alone* the authority to determine the scope of his own jurisdiction. After all, is not a dispute about "arbitrability" a dispute (in the language of the arbitration clause involved in *Warrior & Gulf*) "as to the meaning and application of [one of] the provisions of [the] Agreement"? However, is it likely that the parties will have wanted to do this? Are arbitrators likely to be entirely objective in deciding whether or not they have the authority to hear the merits of a case? "Once they have bitten into the enticing fruit of controversy, they are not apt to stay the satisfying of their appetite after one bite." Trafalgar Shipping Co. v. International Milling Co., 401 F.2d 568, 573–74 (2d Cir.1968) (Lumbard, C.J., dissenting). The Supreme Court has warned that lower courts "should not assume" that contracting parties have empowered the arbitrator to decide questions of arbitrability, in the absence of "clear and unmistakable evidence that they did so." First Options of Chicago v. Kaplan, 514 U.S. 938, 944 (1995).

5. The AAA recommends the following standard arbitration clause for use in all commercial contracts:

> Any controversy or claim arising out of or relating to this contract, or the breach thereof, shall be settled by arbitration in accordance with the Commercial Arbitration Rules of the American Arbitration Association, and judgment upon the award rendered by the Arbitrator(s) may be entered in any Court having jurisdiction thereof.

One of the advantages of arbitration is that this grant of jurisdiction can be limited or tailored to meet the particular needs and circumstances of the parties. However, more detailed clauses are likely to invite litigation over arbitrability, and may invite courts to speculate as to just what the parties were aiming at. And the departure from hallowed formulas may leave the door open to idiosyncratic judicial rulings.

For example, in Beckham v. William Bayley Co., 655 F.Supp. 288 (N.D.Tex.1987) the parties had provided for arbitration of "any disagreement * * * as to the intent of this contract." The plaintiff, a general contractor, complained that the casements and doors delivered by the defendant were warped and otherwise defective. The court held that this complaint concerning the defendant's *performance* under the contract was not covered by the arbitration clause. The court did not suggest *why* the parties might have wanted to distinguish between disputes over "intent" and disputes over "performance." (Aren't issues of the quality of "performance" precisely the kind of factual questions for which arbitration may be most suited?) See also United Offshore Co. v. Southern Deepwater Pipeline Co., 899 F.2d 405 (5th Cir.1990) (clause provided for arbitration of "any controversy or claim * * * arising out of the interpretation of the provisions of the agreement"; held, arbitrator was "powerless to decide matters on which the agreement was silent; '[i]t is clear that the parties intended

C. ARBITRATION AND THE COURTS 721

that only the contract be interpreted by the arbitrator and not general principles of justice or industry custom or course of dealing between the parties' '").

6. The "separability" principle of *Prima Paint* is also nominally a rule of construction. See fn. 9 of the Supreme Courts opinion, p. 692 supra. A court will frequently compel arbitration only after indulging in mock deference to the parties' presumed "intention" to entrust to the arbitrator the question whether the overall agreement had been induced by fraud. See, e.g., Weinrott v. Carp, 32 N.Y.2d 190, 344 N.Y.S.2d 848, 298 N.E.2d 42 (1973) (proceeding to confirm arbitration award; "technical argument about separability or nonseparability has often obscured the main goal of the court's inquiry which is to discern the parties' intent"). It need hardly be pointed out that this is usually little more than a fiction: It will be rare indeed that parties resisting arbitration will be able to present sufficient evidence to satisfy "their heavy burden of proving an intent not to arbitrate" the issue of fraudulent inducement. See Stateside Machinery Co., Ltd. v. Alperin, 591 F.2d 234 (3d Cir.1979).

Nevertheless, judicial reliance on rules of construction may occasionally entail some curious consequences in terms of party planning and drafting. In some circuits, for example, a clause that merely requires arbitration for "any disputes arising hereunder" will be considered a "narrow" clause—and thus, it may be held not to encompass an allegation of fraudulent inducement. Cf. RCM Technologies, Inc. v. Brignik Technology, Inc., 137 F. Supp.2d 550 (D.N.J.2001)("Because the arbitration clause at issue here is substantially narrower than the clause in *Prima Paint,* the court declines to compel arbitration of the fraudulent inducement claims on the basis of that case"). Nor may it encompass a tort claim for misappropriation of trade secrets—even though the defendant has allegedly used trade secrets and confidential information obtained during the term of a license agreement. The omission from the arbitration clause of the words "relating to," which appear in the AAA's standard clause, may be considered "significant." See Mediterranean Enterprises, Inc. v. Ssangyong Corp., 708 F.2d 1458 (9th Cir.1983) ("arising hereunder" is intended to cover "only those [disputes] relating to the interpretation and performance of the contract itself"); Tracer Research Corp. v. National Environmental Services Co., 42 F.3d 1292 (9th Cir.1994). At the same time, a court may seize on drafting distinctions—admittedly rather "subtle"—to order arbitration of fraudulent inducement questions where the agreement mandates arbitration of disputes "arising out of" the agreement, or disputes that "shall arise or occur under" the agreement, or "all claims and disputes of whatever nature arising under this contract"! Cf. Sweet Dreams Unlimited, Inc. v. Dial–A–Mattress Int'l, Ltd., 1 F.3d 639 (7th Cir.1993); S.A. Mineracao Da Trindade–Samitri v. Utah Int'l, Inc., 745 F.2d 190 (2d Cir.1984); Genesco, Inc. v. T. Kakiuchi & Co., 815 F.2d 840 (2d Cir.1987).

7. Should the attitude of a court be different if the case to be decided by an arbitrator falls towards the "interest" side of the dispute spectrum? In such cases should a court begin with a different presumption as to arbitrability?

722 CHAPTER V ARBITRATION

Consider Bowmer v. Bowmer, 50 N.Y.2d 288, 428 N.Y.S.2d 902, 406 N.E.2d 760 (N.Y. 1980). Husband and wife entered into a 37–page separation agreement providing for payment of alimony and child support according to a complex formula. Certain matters such as adjustments to the formula in the event of changes in the tax laws or in the Government's cost of living index were expressly made arbitrable. The agreement also provided that:

> Any claim, dispute or misunderstanding arising out of or in connection with this Agreement, or any breach hereof, or any default in payment by the Husband, or any matter herein made the subject matter of arbitration, shall be arbitrated.

Five years later the husband gave notice that because of changed circumstances he would be reducing his support payments, and sought to compel arbitration of this issue. The court held that the husband's claim was not arbitrable since the arbitration clause "was not intended to encompass the dispute here":

> [What the husband] seeks, in essence, is to have the arbitrator rewrite the terms of the agreement because he now views them as onerous. This cannot be considered merely a claim arising from the contract. Instead, it requires the making of a new contract, not by the parties, but by the arbitrator. Obviously, the parties never agreed to such a procedure for it would mean that, once the agreement made provision for arbitration, the arbitrator would be completely unfettered by the terms of the contract in resolving disputes.

Compare Egol v. Egol, 118 A.D.2d 76, 503 N.Y.S.2d 726 (App. Div.), aff'd, 68 N.Y.2d 893, 508 N.Y.S.2d 935, 501 N.E.2d 584 (N.Y. 1986), where a husband and wife in a pre-divorce agreement expressly provided for arbitration of any claims for reduction in the husband's maintenance and support obligations should he "suffer a substantial, adverse and involuntary change in his financial circumstances, making his support obligations under this Agreement inequitable or a substantial hardship for him." The court granted a motion to compel arbitration: "This is not a case where the arbitrator is asked to reform the instrument. The arbitrator is called upon only to interpret it."

8. Agreements between brokerage firms and their employees commonly provide for arbitration of disputes "arising out of employment or the termination of employment." A former account executive brought suit against his employer for prima facie tort and slander, alleging that his superiors had (1) made defamatory statements to former customers and falsely informed others that his broker's license had been suspended, (2) attempted to "scrounge up" complaints from former customers concerning the handling of their investments, and (3) told fellow office workers that the plaintiff had stolen things from their desks at night. The court held that the first two claims were arbitrable, because they "involved significant aspects of the employment relationship," but that the third was not: "No customers or securities agencies are implicated, and no significant issue of [plaintiff's] job performance *qua* broker is implicated." Morgan v. Smith

C. ARBITRATION AND THE COURTS 723

Barney, Harris Upham & Co., 729 F.2d 1163 (8th Cir.1984). See also Dean Witter Reynolds, Inc. v. Ness, 677 F.Supp. 866 (D.S.C.1988) (brokerage firm caused former employee to be arrested for trespass when he repeatedly visited the office; employee's suit for false arrest, imprisonment, and intentional infliction of emotional distress held not arbitrable).

9. Mr. and Mrs. Seifert contracted with U.S. Home for the construction of a house; the contract provided that "any controversy or claim arising out of or related to this Agreement" would be submitted to arbitration. After they moved into their home, their car was left running in the garage, and the air conditioning system located in the garage picked up the carbon monoxide emissions and distributed them into the house, killing Mr. Seifert. U.S. Home moved that Mrs. Seifert's claim for negligence be referred to arbitration. Mrs. Seifert "concedes that an action for breach of contract or any of the warranties or other rights and obligations arising out of the contract would be subject to arbitration": However, the court held, "because the wrongful death action here is predicated upon a tort theory of common law negligence unrelated to the rights and obligations of the contract," the action "was not contemplated by the parties when the contract was made and should not be subject to arbitration." According to the court, this result was also "supported" by "public policy"—since referral to arbitration would "deprive [the plaintiff] of her rights to a trial by jury, due process and access to the courts." A concurring judge concluded that "the authors of these arbitration provisions need to go back to the drafting board." Seifert v. U.S. Home Corp., 750 So.2d 633 (Fla.1999).

10. A defendant refuses to participate in arbitration, asserting that he never agreed to arbitrate the dispute. Should the plaintiff first seek an order under § 4 of the FAA to "compel" arbitration? Or should he simply proceed without the defendant? The AAA Commercial Arbitration Rules permit arbitrators to proceed despite the absence of one party, although the award may not be made solely by default and the party who is present must submit evidence supporting his claim. (Rule 31).

If the defendant fails to appear, and the arbitration does proceed without him, may the defendant later resist judicial enforcement of the resulting award? As in the case of default in litigation, the defendant has certainly lost the ability to defend the claim on the merits. May he also be found to have waived the right to assert any defense of lack of agreement? Most commentators assume that a defendant who remains out of the proceeding may still at a later time challenge the existence of an agreement to arbitrate. See Martin Domke, Commercial Arbitration § 18:04 at 266 (rev. ed.); see also MCI Telecommunications Corp. v. Exalon Industries, Inc., 138 F.3d 426 (1st Cir.1998)(if there is no written agreement to arbitrate, "the actions of the arbitrator have no legal validity"; "in both the FAA and personal jurisdiction contexts, albeit for different reasons, the non-appearing party can subsequently challenge the authority of the decision-maker, but not the merits of the decision"); but cf. Ian Macneil, Richard Speidel, & Thomas Stipanowich, Federal Arbitration Law §§ 17.6, 40.1.3 (1994). This seems also to be the sense of the Revised Uniform

724 CHAPTER V ARBITRATION

Arbitration Act, which allows a court to vacate an arbitration award where "[t]here was no agreement to arbitrate, unless the person participated in the arbitration proceeding without raising the objection ... not later than the commencement of the arbitration hearing." § 23(a)(5).

However, see Comprehensive Accounting Corp. v. Rudell, 760 F.2d 138 (7th Cir.1985). The defendants in this case refused to participate in an arbitration, and later opposed confirmation of the award on the ground that they did not actually know about the arbitration clause when they signed the agreement. The court commented that this was "irrelevant," even if the defendants could make out a claim of fraud in the inducement. "[A]fter an award has been entered, § 4 [of the FAA] is no longer in play." It was "too late" for the defendants to "sit back and allow the arbitration to go forward, and only after it was all done * * * say: oh by the way, we never agreed to the arbitration clause. That is a tactic that the law of arbitration, with its commitment to speed, will not tolerate." See also Ramonas v. Kerelis, 102 Ill.App.2d 262, 243 N.E.2d 711 (Ill.App.1968) ("in refusing to appear," defendant "acted at [his] own peril," and his "defense that he did not sign the contract nor was a party to the contract was lost due to a situation of his own creation").

On the other hand, if the defendant *does* appear before the arbitrators to raise and argue the contention that there was no agreement to arbitrate the dispute, he may also incur certain risks: Might his conduct be taken as a consent to allow *the arbitrators themselves* to determine the threshold question of their own jurisdiction? E.g., Yorkaire, Inc. v. Sheet Metal Workers Int'l Ass'n, 758 F.Supp. 248 (E.D.Pa.1990), aff'd mem., 931 F.2d 53 (3d Cir.1991) ("Although [the employer] vigorously argued from the start that the panel did not have jurisdiction to resolve the substance of the Union's grievances, it did not contest the arbitration panel's authority to determine whether the grievances fell within its jurisdiction"). And if the arbitrators go on to conclude that the dispute is in fact arbitrable, will that decision benefit from the same degree of deference that is enjoyed by arbitral awards generally?

See First Options of Chicago, Inc. v. Kaplan, 514 U.S. 938 (1995). In this case the claimant brought an arbitration proceeding against the respondents and their wholly-owned investment company; the respondents—who had not personally signed any arbitration agreement—denied that the dispute was arbitrable and filed written objections to that effect with the arbitrators. The award in favor of the claimant was vacated by the Third Circuit and the Supreme Court affirmed:

> Did the parties agree to submit the arbitrability question itself to arbitration? If so, then the court's standard for reviewing the arbitrator's decision about *that* matter should not differ from the standard courts apply when they review any other matter that the parties have agreed to arbitrate. * * * But merely arguing the arbitrability issue to an arbitrator does not indicate a clear willingness to arbitrate that issue, *i.e.,* a willingness to be effectively bound by the arbitrator's decision on that point. To the contrary, insofar as the [respondents]

C. ARBITRATION AND THE COURTS

were forcefully objecting to the arbitrators deciding their dispute with [the claimant], one naturally would think that they did *not* want the arbitrators to have binding authority over them. * * * [B]ecause the [respondents] did not clearly agree to submit the question of arbitrability to arbitration, the Court of Appeals was correct in finding that the arbitrability of the * * * dispute was subject to independent review by the courts.

What other steps are open to a defendant who does not believe that he is subject to a valid agreement to arbitrate?

Note: Loss of the Right to Arbitrate through Delay or "Waiver"

A particular dispute may be conceded to be within the scope of a valid arbitration clause. However, one of the parties may resist on the ground that the other has *lost* the right to arbitrate—perhaps through delay in asserting the right, or by engaging in some action supposedly "inconsistent" with arbitration. This defense may be phrased indiscriminately in terms of "waiver," or "laches," or may be based on the other party's failure to comply with time limits or procedures specified in the contract for seeking arbitration. Is this a matter for the court or the arbitrator to decide? And why does this matter?

The cases frequently distinguish between "substantive" and "procedural arbitrability" and hold that the latter is a question for the arbitrator: "Once it is determined * * * that the parties are obligated to submit the subject matter of a dispute to arbitration, 'procedural' questions which grow out of the dispute and bear on its final disposition should be left to the arbitrator." John Wiley & Sons, Inc. v. Livingston, 376 U.S. 543, 557 (1964). In *Wiley* the employer argued that the union had failed to follow the various grievance steps required in the collective bargaining agreement as prerequisites to arbitration; the Supreme Court held that this question was itself arbitrable. The Court noted that "procedural" questions will often be intertwined with the merits of the dispute, and that reserving "procedural" issues for the court "would thus not only create the difficult task of separating related issues, but would also produce frequent duplication of effort" and delay in a final decision. See also Trafalgar Shipping Co. v. International Milling Co., 401 F.2d 568 (2d Cir.1968) (laches) ("in the often esoteric field of commercial dealings," severity of prejudice suffered through delay should be submitted to "expertise of the arbitrators").

However, where the parties' agreement lays down precise time limits within which arbitration must be initiated, a court will often take this as an invitation to make the determination of arbitrability itself, rather than leave the matter to the arbitrator. See, e.g., Virginia Carolina Tools, Inc. v. Int'l Tool Supply, Inc., 984 F.2d 113 (4th Cir.1993) (since "a broad, non-specific arbitration clause" was accompanied in the agreement by "an express termination date provision," an intention to arbitrate "the very continuation of contractual obligations * * * cannot properly be inferred"). Another example can be found in securities arbitration, where the rules of "self-regulatory organizations" like the NYSE and NASD commonly im-

726   CHAPTER V   ARBITRATION

pose a limit of six years after which no customer claim "shall be eligible for submission to arbitration." Brokerage firms will usually prefer that the *courts* decide whether this time limit has passed, while on the other hand customers will argue that this should be an issue for the *arbitrators*. (Why?) *Compare* J.E. Liss & Co. v. Levin, 201 F.3d 848 (7th Cir.2000)("A majority of courts, including ours, applying the principle that courts decide issues of arbitrability unless the parties have clearly indicated that the arbitrators are to decide them, hold that whether the six-year limit has been exceeded is for the courts rather than the arbitrators to decide") *and* Smith Barney Shearson Inc. v. Sacharow, 91 N.Y.2d 39, 666 N.Y.S.2d 990, 992–93, 689 N.E.2d 884 (N.Y. 1997)(contractual proviso "limits the subject of, entitlement to, and range of arbitrable matters" and thus "creates a substantive feature that may affect the right and obligation to arbitrate"); *with* Prudential Securities Inc. v. Laurita, 1997 WL 109438 (S.D.N.Y.)(the "principle continues to be applied in this Circuit" that "any limitations defense—whether stemming from the arbitration agreement, arbitration association rule, or state statute—is an issue to be addressed by the arbitrators").

Another common scenario goes something like this: One party who now wishes to arbitrate will have earlier taken an active part in litigation concerning the very same dispute—for example, he may have earlier filed a counterclaim, or engaged in discovery. He may then be met with the assertion that he has "waived" his right to arbitration. In such cases, courts will often pass directly on the "waiver" issue, sometimes without expressly addressing the appropriateness of their doing so. It has in fact been suggested that a claim of waiver "predicated solely upon participation in the lawsuit by the party seeking arbitration" should be decided by a court, while the issue of waiver "by other conduct" should be for the arbitrator. See The Brothers Jurewicz, Inc. v. Atari, Inc., 296 N.W.2d 422 (Minn.1980). Why should this be true? See also Bridas Sociedad Anonima Petrolera Industrial Y Comercial v. International Standard Elec. Corp., 128 Misc.2d 669, 490 N.Y.S.2d 711 (Sup.Ct.1985) ("Logic would dictate" that where a claim of waiver turns on "the degree of a party's participation in a court action," then the issue of waiver should be determined by the court and not the arbitrator). Does the final proviso of § 3 of the FAA have any bearing at all on this question?

Some state courts seem to approach this question of waiver in a fairly rigid and mechanical way, asking whether the party now seeking arbitration had earlier acted in a way that is "inconsistent" with an assertion of the right to arbitrate or had made "an election" between a judicial and an arbitral forum. E.g., Sanford Construction Co., Inc. v. Rosenblatt, 25 Ohio Misc. 99, 266 N.E.2d 267 (Ohio Mun.Ct.1970) (defendant's statement, "If you want to collect, sue us!" constituted an "express waiver" of arbitration); Lapidus v. Arlen Beach Condominium Ass'n, Inc., 394 So.2d 1102 (Fla.App.1981) ("filing an answer without asserting the right for arbitration acts as waiver"). Such cases seem to counsel that a decision whether or not to pursue arbitration under an arbitration clause should be made at the earliest possible moment. See also Texas International Commercial Arbitration and Conciliation Act, V.T.C.A., Civ.Prac. & Rem.Code § 172.052 (court shall stay judicial proceedings in favor of arbitration if a party requests a stay "not later than the time the party submits the party's first statement on the substance of the dispute").

In contrast, many *federal* cases seem to be considerably slower in finding "waiver" where a party has vacillated and participated in litigation before moving to compel arbitration. Given the "strong federal policy favoring enforcement of arbitration agreements between knowledgeable business people," a finding of waiver is not favored in federal court; the party asserting waiver is said to bear a heavy burden of proof. Knorr Brake Corp. v. Harbil, Inc., 556 F.Supp. 489 (N.D.Ill.1983). But cf. Cabinetree of Wisconsin, Inc. v. Kraftmaid Cabinetry, Inc., 50 F.3d 388 (7th Cir.1995) (Posner, J.) ("[i]n determining whether a waiver has occurred, the court is not to place its thumbs on the scales").

The majority of federal courts therefore tend to ask whether one of the parties will have been "prejudiced" if his adversary is permitted to take part in litigation and then later demand arbitration. Without such a finding of "prejudice," the mere fact that a party has delayed in calling for arbitration will not be enough to cause a waiver of his right to arbitrate. (In many cases, of course, delay in demanding arbitration will simply reflect the fact that negotiations over a settlement of the dispute are being carried on.) Nor will the fact that he has filed pleadings in the lawsuit. So, for example, a party has been allowed to seek arbitration thirteen months after a suit was filed, even though he had answered the complaint, served several interrogatories and requests for the production of documents, and participated in a pretrial conference. Walker v. J.C. Bradford & Co., 938 F.2d 575 (5th Cir.1991). See also Stifel, Nicolaus & Co. Inc. v. Freeman, 924 F.2d 157 (8th Cir.1991) (brokerage firm sued customers for outstanding balances; customers filed a counterclaim and the parties engaged in written discovery; six months after filing suit, the brokerage firm moved to compel arbitration).

Whether a party has suffered enough "prejudice" to warrant a finding of waiver is obviously an inquiry heavily dependent on the facts of the particular case. Courts will often rely on the fact that the party resisting arbitration has incurred substantial costs in preparing for trial and in defending against the litigation moves of his opponent; see, e.g., Prudential–Bache Securities, Inc. v. Stevenson, 706 F.Supp. 533 (S.D.Tex.1989) (defendants "have incurred attorneys' fees and expenses in excess of $5,000 connected with the preparation of their answer"); Fraser v. Merrill Lynch Pierce, Fenner & Smith, Inc., 817 F.2d 250 (4th Cir.1987) (the parties "participated in four status conferences, five hearings on pending motions, and two pretrial conferences"; waiver was found in light of "the extent of the moving party's trial-oriented activity" and the "substantial time and effort" expended by the plaintiff). In addition, courts often find it important that the party now demanding arbitration has earlier benefited from using judicial discovery mechanisms that are not available as of right in arbitration. See, e.g., Zwitserse Maatschappij Van Levensverzekering En Lijfrente v. ABN Int'l Capital Markets Corp., 996 F.2d 1478 (2d Cir.1993)

728 CHAPTER V ARBITRATION

(defendant "suffered prejudice because the deposition-type discovery obtained [by plaintiff] in the Netherlands would not have been available" in securities arbitration in the United States). In other cases, however, the benefits of pre-trial discovery obtained by the party seeking arbitration seem to play a smaller role: A court may even note that the party resisting arbitration and claiming waiver will *itself* derive advantages from the discovery that has already taken place. See *Stifel, Nicolaus & Co.,* supra (defendants' claim of "waiver" rejected; "the limited discovery conducted will be usable in arbitration"). On the availability of discovery in arbitration, see generally Section D.2.d. infra.

NOTES AND QUESTIONS

1. Are the state cases and statutes referred to in the text consistent with federal policy? Is a separate state standard of waiver permissible in cases falling within the ambit of the FAA? See Alan Rau, The UNCITRAL Model Law in State and Federal Courts: The Problem of Waiver, 6 Am.Rev.Int'l Arb. 223 (1995).

2. A finding of waiver is more readily made where it is the *plaintiff* in a lawsuit who later seeks to compel arbitration of the dispute. See, e.g., Christensen v. Dewor Developments, 33 Cal.3d 778, 191 Cal.Rptr. 8, 661 P.2d 1088 (Cal. 1983) (plaintiff filed complaint in order to "have some feel for what the Defendants' position would be at arbitration"). See also Note, Contractual Agreements to Arbitrate Disputes: Waiver of the Right to Compel Arbitration, 52 So.Cal.L.Rev. 1513 (1979), which advocates that a plaintiff who files suit over an arbitrable issue should be "deemed" to have waived any right to arbitration. Are there any virtues in such a mechanical rule? What of the case where a plaintiff files a complaint and then, the same day, changes his mind and makes a formal demand for arbitration? See Cavac Compania Anonima Venezolana de Administracion y Comercio v. Board for Validation of German Bonds in the U.S., 189 F.Supp. 205 (S.D.N.Y.1960).

3. A plaintiff brings a lawsuit, and the defendant successfully moves for a stay on the ground that the parties had agreed to arbitrate. So the plaintiff acquiesces, and makes a demand for arbitration. Then the defendant tries to claim that the plaintiff—by originally instituting the suit—has waived his right to arbitration. Can the defendant thereby accomplish the "stunning tour de force" of denying the plaintiff any forum at all? See 795 Fifth Ave. Corp. v. Trusthouse Forte (Pierre) Management, Inc., 131 Misc.2d 291, 499 N.Y.S.2d 857 (1986) (no).

4. A finding that the right to arbitration has been "waived" is often a value-laden judgment, comprehensible only as a response to other, unarticulated policies. An extreme example of this point is Davis v. Blue Cross of Northern California, 25 Cal.3d 418, 158 Cal.Rptr. 828, 600 P.2d 1060 (Cal. 1979). A number of insureds alleged in a class action that Blue Cross had refused to pay for hospital expenses to which they were entitled. Shortly after the filing of the complaint Blue Cross moved to submit the disputes to a "medical arbitration panel" as required by the policies. The trial court found that the arbitration clause had been "buried in an obscure provision" of the agreements and that Blue Cross, in rejecting claims, had failed to bring the arbitration procedure to its insureds' attention. The Supreme Court of California agreed with the trial court that Blue Cross had "breached its duty of good faith and fair dealing" to its insureds "by failing timely or adequately to apprise them of the availability" of arbitration and that "as a consequence, Blue Cross waived any right subsequently to compel its insureds to resort to arbitration."

Is this a case of "waiver"? How have the plaintiffs been prejudiced by Blue Cross's failure to inform them of the availability of arbitration? In the course of its opinion, the Supreme Court also noted that:

> Under hospitalization policies, in which disputes over benefits may frequently involve a simple disagreement between the insured's physician and the insurer's medical consultant as to the reasonableness of fees or the necessity for certain medical procedures, the existence of an arbitral process will often enable the insured to obtain an impartial review of the insurer's decision without the need to incur the significant expense of legal counsel; as a consequence, the reduced cost of the process may make it practicable for the insured to secure a binding resolution of disputes over smaller claims than would otherwise be financially feasible.

How does the court's finding of "waiver" respond to this rhetoric about the advantages of the arbitration process?

5. A defendant in an arbitration asserts that if the dispute had been litigated, the state's statute of limitations would have barred the underlying claim. The arbitrator finds that questions relating to the statute of limitations are within the scope of the arbitration clause, and rules in favor of the claimant. On a motion to vacate the award, what result? See NCR Corp. v. CBS Liquor Control, Inc., 874 F.Supp. 168 (S.D.Ohio 1993), aff'd, 43 F.3d 1076 (6th Cir.1995) ("the effect of a statute of limitations is to bar an action at law, not arbitration"); Hanes Corp. v. Millard, 531 F.2d 585 (D.C.Cir.1976) ("the arbitrator may be forced to decide at what point any breach might have occurred and when the [plaintiffs] did or should have acquired knowledge of the alleged breach. Such an inquiry will require considerable factual probing"). A New York statute permits a party, by application to the court, to assert the statute of limitations "as a bar to arbitration"; "the failure to assert such bar by such application shall not preclude its assertion before the arbitrators, who may, in their sole discretion, apply or not apply the bar." N.Y.C.P.L.R. § 7502(b).

4. JUDICIAL SUPERVISION AND REVIEW

For arbitration to function as an efficient process of private dispute resolution—to realize the benefits of expert decision-making with reduced cost and delay—litigation challenging the process, or aimed at upsetting the resulting award, must be minimized. One danger is exemplified by a

CHAPTER V   ARBITRATION

tongue-in-cheek comment of a lawyer from Latin America, a region where arbitration is neither familiar nor generally accepted:

> "We lawyers like arbitration. It assures us three litigations: one before, one during and one after the arbitration."[1]

In addition, arbitrators faced with heightened judicial scrutiny might ultimately come to focus less on the merits of the particular dispute, or the relationship between the parties, and more on the task of producing opinions or building a record that would enable their awards to survive later challenge.

There is thus a need to prevent a "judicialization" of the arbitral process. But at the same time, some sort of "public" supervision and control may be necessary to protect wider social interests that may be ignored or jeopardized by "private" arbitrators. The inevitable tension between these two values is a theme that figures in much of these materials.

The occasion for judicial supervision and control of the arbitral process may arise at a number of different stages. Such supervision may be exercised at the time an award made by arbitrators comes before a court for review and enforcement. Or it may be exercised at a still earlier stage— when the question is posed whether a particular dispute is at all suitable for arbitration in the first place: This is the question whether "public policy" demands that the full panoply of judicial procedure remain available to an aggrieved party, despite his earlier agreement to submit to arbitration. Even at that threshold stage, however, an inquiry into whether "public policy" forbids arbitration of the dispute must take into account the fact that any ultimate award is likely to be treated with considerable deference by a reviewing court, even with respect to matters of "law." We begin, therefore, with an overview of the critical subject of the judicial review of arbitral awards.

a. JUDICIAL REVIEW OF ARBITRAL AWARDS

By far the greatest number of the many awards rendered by arbitrators are voluntarily complied with. This seems especially true in collective bargaining cases: Recent estimates suggest that less than 1% of labor arbitration awards in the private sector are ever challenged in court.[2] However, where one party is recalcitrant, official sanctions to enforce the award may be needed. Modern arbitration statutes make available the assistance of courts in enforcing arbitration awards: See, for example, §§ 9 and 13 of the FAA. How closely will a court scrutinize an arbitration award? Under what circumstances will it decline to give the award legal effect?

---

1. Quoted in Nattier, International Commercial Arbitration in Latin America: Enforcement of Arbitral Agreements and Awards, 21 Tex.Int'l L.J. 397, 408 (1986).

2. Feuille & LeRoy, Grievance Arbitration Appeals in the Federal Courts: Facts and Figures, 45 Arb.J. 35 (Mar. 1990).

C. ARBITRATION AND THE COURTS   **731**

The conventional wisdom is that successful challenges to arbitration awards are rare. Thirty years ago one commentator could write that in "the overwhelming majority of that miniscule portion which are appealed, only an infinitesimal few have ever been vacated."[3] In more recent years, the amount of "litigious wrangling" over the enforcement of awards—and thus the number of successful challenges—has unquestionably increased, so as to make that something of an overstatement.[4] Nonetheless the essential point about judicial deference to arbitral awards still appears to be valid.[5]

Modern arbitration statutes provide only limited grounds on the basis of which a court may refuse to enforce an award. See §§ 10 and 11 of the FAA. What does it mean to say (as in § 10(d)) that an award can be overturned if the arbitrators have "exceeded their powers"? Among other things, this can often be a peg on which to hang a challenge—even after an award is rendered—to the "arbitrability" of the dispute, at least if the point has been preserved by a proper objection before the arbitrator. The question then becomes whether the arbitrator has in fact determined an issue which the parties in their agreement have empowered him to decide. See also § 11(b).

Does § 10 of the FAA have a bearing on *other* challenges to arbitration awards besides assertions that under the agreement the underlying dispute was not "arbitrable"? And are the grounds specified in the federal statute *exclusive*? Or are there other grounds on which a court can rely in refusing to enforce an award? In the materials that follow you will come across a number of variant formulations, sometimes in terms borrowed from labor arbitration cases. Do these constitute alternative grounds to vacate an award? Or do they instead amount to nothing more than dressing up the same idea in different semantic garb?

United Paperworkers International Union v. Misco, Inc.

Supreme Court of the United States, 1987.
484 U.S. 29, 108 S.Ct. 364, 98 L.Ed.2d 286.

■ JUSTICE WHITE delivered the opinion of the Court.

The issue for decision involves several aspects of when a federal court may refuse to enforce an arbitration award rendered under a collective-bargaining agreement.

---

3. Jones, Evidentiary Concepts in Labor Arbitration: Some Modern Variations on Ancient Legal Themes, 13 U.C.L.A.L.Rev. 1241, 1296 (1966).

4. See Gould, Judicial Review of Labor Arbitration Awards—Thirty Years of the *Steelworkers Trilogy* : The Aftermath of *AT & T* and *Misco*, 64 Notre Dame L.Rev. 464, 467, 474 (1989). Gould attributes this phenomenon at least in part to the decline in the number of employees represented by unions, which has "simultaneously encouraged and emboldened employers to challenge arbitration awards and unions as well."

5. While "the odds of a successful appeal have improved somewhat" in recent years, federal courts are still enforcing labor arbitration awards approximately 70% of the time. See LeRoy & Feuille, The *Steelworkers Trilogy* and Grievance Arbitration Appeals: How the Federal Courts Respond, 13 Ind.Rel. L.J. 78, 103, 117 (1991); Calvin Sharpe, Judicial Review of Labor Arbitration Awards: A View from the Bench, Proceedings, 52nd Annual Meeting, National Academy of Arbitrators 126, 142 (2000).

I

Misco, Inc. operates a paper converting plant in Monroe, Louisiana. The Company is a party to a collective-bargaining agreement with the United Paperworkers International Union, AFL–CIO, and its union local; the agreement covers the production and maintenance employees at the plant. Under the agreement, the Company or the Union may submit to arbitration any grievance that arises from the interpretation or application of its terms, and the arbitrator's decision is final and binding upon the parties. The arbitrator's authority is limited to interpretation and application of the terms contained in the agreement itself. The agreement reserves to management the right to establish, amend, and enforce "rules and regulations regulating the discipline or discharge of employees" and the procedures for imposing discipline. Such rules were to be posted and were to be in effect "until ruled on by grievance and arbitration procedures as to fairness and necessity." For about a decade, the Company's rules had listed as causes for discharge the bringing of intoxicants, narcotics, or controlled substances on to plant property or consuming any of them there, as well as reporting for work under the influence of such substances.[2] At the time of the events involved in this case, the Company was very concerned about the use of drugs at the plant, especially among employees on the night shift.

Isiah Cooper, who worked on the night shift for Misco, was one of the employees covered by the collective-bargaining agreement. He operated a slitter-rewinder machine, which uses sharp blades to cut rolling coils of paper. The arbitrator found that this machine is hazardous and had caused numerous injuries in recent years. Cooper had been reprimanded twice in a few months for deficient performance. On January 21, 1983, one day after the second reprimand, the police searched Cooper's house pursuant to a warrant, and a substantial amount of marijuana was found. Contemporaneously, a police officer was detailed to keep Cooper's car under observation at the Company's parking lot. At about 6:30 p.m., Cooper was seen walking in the parking lot during work hours with two other men. The three men entered Cooper's car momentarily, then walked to another car, a white Cutlass, and entered it. After the other two men later returned to the plant, Cooper was apprehended by police in the backseat of this car with marijuana smoke in the air and a lighted marijuana cigarette in the front-seat ashtray. The police also searched Cooper's car and found a plastic

---

2. Rule II.1 lists the following as causes for discharge:

"Bringing intoxicants, narcotics, or controlled substances into, or consuming intoxicants, narcotics or controlled substances in the plant, or on plant premises. Reporting for duty under the influence of intoxicants, narcotics, or controlled substances."

C. ARBITRATION AND THE COURTS **733**

scales case and marijuana gleanings. Cooper was arrested and charged with marijuana possession.[3]

On January 24, Cooper told the Company that he had been arrested for possession of marijuana at his home; the Company did not learn of the marijuana cigarette in the white Cutlass until January 27. It then investigated and on February 7 discharged Cooper, asserting that in the circumstances, his presence in the Cutlass violated the rule against having drugs on the plant premises.[4] Cooper filed a grievance protesting his discharge the same day, and the matter proceeded to arbitration. The Company was not aware until September 21, five days before the hearing before the arbitrator was scheduled, that marijuana had been found in Cooper's car. That fact did not become known to the Union until the hearing began. At the hearing it was stipulated that the issue was whether the Company had "just cause to discharge the Grievant under Rule II.1" and, "[i]f not, what if any should be the remedy."

The arbitrator upheld the grievance and ordered the Company to reinstate Cooper with backpay and full seniority. The arbitrator based his finding that there was not just cause for the discharge on his consideration of seven criteria.[5] In particular, the arbitrator found that the Company failed to prove that the employee had possessed or used marijuana on company property: finding Cooper in the backseat of a car and a burning cigarette in the front-seat ashtray was insufficient proof that Cooper was using or possessed marijuana on company property. The arbitrator refused to accept into evidence the fact that marijuana had been found in Cooper's car on company premises because the Company did not know of this fact when Cooper was discharged and therefore did not rely on it as a basis for the discharge.[6]

The Company filed suit in District Court, seeking to vacate the arbitration award on several grounds, one of which was that ordering reinstatement of Cooper, who had allegedly possessed marijuana on the plant premises, was contrary to public policy. The District Court agreed that the award must be set aside as contrary to public policy because it ran counter to general safety concerns that arise from the operation of dangerous machinery while under the influence of drugs, as well as to state

---

3. Cooper later pleaded guilty to that charge, which was not related to his being in a car with a lighted marijuana cigarette in it. The authorities chose not to prosecute for the latter incident.

4. The Company asserted that being in a car with a lit marijuana cigarette was a direct violation of the company rule against having an illegal substance on company property.

5. These considerations were the reasonableness of the employer's position, the notice given to the employee, the timing of the investigation undertaken, the fairness of the investigation, the evidence against the employee, the possibility of discrimination, and the relation of the degree of discipline to the nature of the offense and the employee's past record.

6. The arbitrator stated: "One of the rules in arbitration is that the Company must have its proof in hand before it takes disciplinary action against an employee. The Company does not take the disciplinary action and then spend eight months digging up supporting evidence to justify its actions. * * *"

criminal laws against drug possession. The Court of Appeals affirmed, with one judge dissenting. The court ruled that reinstatement would violate the public policy "against the operation of dangerous machinery by persons under the influence of drugs or alcohol." The arbitrator had found that Cooper was apprehended on company premises in an atmosphere of marijuana smoke in another's car and that marijuana was found in his own car on the company lot. These facts established that Cooper had violated the Company's rules and gave the company just cause to discharge him. The arbitrator did not reach this conclusion because of a "narrow focus on Cooper's procedural rights" that led him to ignore what he "knew was in fact true: that Cooper *did* bring marijuana onto his employer's premises." [The Court of Appeals also suggested that the arbitrator's "baffling view of evidence that would with ease have sustained a civil verdict and probably a criminal conviction" might in part be explained by his formal training "as an engineer and not as a lawyer." 768 F.2d 739, 741 n. 2.] * * *

Because the Courts of Appeals are divided on the question of when courts may set aside arbitration awards as contravening public policy, we granted the Union's petition for a writ of certiorari, and now reverse the judgment of the Court of Appeals.

II

The Union asserts that an arbitral award may not be set aside on public policy grounds unless the award orders conduct that violates the positive law, which is not the case here. But in the alternative, it submits that even if it is wrong in this regard, the Court of Appeals otherwise exceeded the limited authority that it had to review an arbitrator's award entered pursuant to a collective-bargaining agreement. Respondent, on the other hand, defends the public policy decision of the Court of Appeals but alternatively argues that the judgment below should be affirmed because of erroneous findings by the arbitrator. We deal first with the opposing alternative arguments.

A

Collective-bargaining agreements commonly provide grievance procedures to settle disputes between union and employer with respect to the interpretation and application of the agreement and require binding arbitration for unsettled grievances. In such cases, and this is such a case, the Court made clear almost 30 years ago that the courts play only a limited role when asked to review the decision of an arbitrator. The courts are not authorized to reconsider the merits of an award even though the parties may allege that the award rests on errors of fact or on misinterpretation of the contract. "The refusal of courts to review the merits of an arbitration award is the proper approach to arbitration under collective bargaining agreements. The federal policy of settling labor disputes by arbitration would be undermined if courts had the final say on the merits of the awards." *Steelworkers v. Enterprise Wheel & Car Corp.,* 363 U.S. 593, 596 (1960). As long as the arbitrator's award "draws its essence from the collective bargaining agreement," and is not merely "his own brand of industrial justice," the award is legitimate.

> "The function of the court is very limited when the parties have agreed to submit all questions of contract interpretation to the arbitrator. It is confined to ascertaining whether the party seeking arbitration is making a claim which on its face is governed by the contract. Whether the moving party is right or wrong is a question of contract interpretation for the arbitrator. In these circumstances the moving party should not be deprived of the arbitrator's judgment, when it was his judgment and all that it connotes that was bargained for." * * * *Steelworkers v. American Mfg. Co.*, 363 U.S. 564, 567–568 (1960).

The reasons for insulating arbitral decisions from judicial review are grounded in the federal statutes regulating labor-management relations. These statutes reflect a decided preference for private settlement of labor disputes without the intervention of government. * * * Because the parties have contracted to have disputes settled by an arbitrator chosen by them rather than by a judge, it is the arbitrator's view of the facts and of the meaning of the contract that they have agreed to accept. Courts thus do not sit to hear claims of factual or legal error by an arbitrator as an appellate court does in reviewing decisions of lower courts. To resolve disputes about the application of a collective-bargaining agreement, an arbitrator must find facts and a court may not reject those findings simply because it disagrees with them. The same is true of the arbitrator's interpretation of the contract. The arbitrator may not ignore the plain language of the contract; but the parties having authorized the arbitrator to give meaning to the language of the agreement, a court should not reject an award on the ground that the arbitrator misread the contract. So, too, where it is contemplated that the arbitrator will determine remedies for contract violations that he finds, courts have no authority to disagree with his honest judgment in that respect. If the courts were free to intervene on these grounds, the speedy resolution of grievances by private mechanisms would be greatly undermined. Furthermore, it must be remembered that grievance and arbitration procedures are part and parcel of the ongoing process of collective bargaining. It is through these processes that the supplementary rules of the plant are established. * * * [A]s long as the arbitrator is even arguably construing or applying the contract and acting within the scope of his authority, that a court is convinced he committed serious error does not suffice to overturn his decision. Of course, decisions procured by the parties through fraud or through the arbitrator's dishonesty need not be enforced. But there is nothing of that sort involved in this case.

B

The Company's position, simply put, is that the arbitrator committed grievous error in finding that the evidence was insufficient to prove that Cooper had possessed or used marijuana on company property. But the Court of Appeals, although it took a distinctly jaundiced view of the arbitrator's decision in this regard, was not free to refuse enforcement because it considered Cooper's presence in the white Cutlass, in the circumstances, to be ample proof that Rule II.1 was violated. No dishonesty is alleged; only improvident, even silly, factfinding is claimed. This is hardly sufficient basis for disregarding what the agent appointed by the parties determined to be the historical facts.

Nor was it open to the Court of Appeals to refuse to enforce the award because the arbitrator, in deciding whether there was just cause to discharge, refused to consider evidence unknown to the Company at the time Cooper was fired. The parties bargained for arbitration to settle disputes and were free to set the procedural rules for arbitrators to follow if they chose. Section VI of the agreement, entitled "Arbitration Procedure," did set some ground rules for the arbitration process. It forbade the arbitrator to consider hearsay evidence, for example, but evidentiary matters were otherwise left to the arbitrator. Here the arbitrator ruled that in determining whether Cooper had violated Rule II.1, he should not consider evidence not relied on by the employer in ordering the discharge, particularly in a case like this where there was no notice to the employee or the Union prior to the hearing that the Company would attempt to rely on after-discovered evidence. This, in effect, was a construction of what the contract required when deciding discharge cases: an arbitrator was to look only at the evidence before the employer at the time of discharge. As the arbitrator noted, this approach was consistent with the practice followed by other arbitrators.[8] And it was consistent with our observation in *John Wiley & Sons, Inc. v. Livingston*, 376 U.S. 543, 557 (1964), that when the subject matter of a dispute is arbitrable, "procedural" questions which grow out of the dispute and bear on its final disposition are to be left to the arbitrator.

Under the Arbitration Act, the federal courts are empowered to set aside arbitration awards on such grounds only when "the arbitrators were guilty of misconduct ... in refusing to hear evidence pertinent and material to the controversy." If we apply that same standard here and assume that the arbitrator erred in refusing to consider the disputed evidence, his error was not in bad faith or so gross as to amount to affirmative misconduct.[10] Finally, it is worth noting that putting aside the evidence about the marijuana found in Cooper's car during this arbitration did not

---

8. Labor arbitrators have stated that the correctness of a discharge "must stand or fall upon the reason given at the time of discharge," see, e.g., West Va. Pulp & Paper Co., 10 Lab.Arb. 117, 118 (1947), and arbitrators often, but not always, confine their considerations to the facts known to the employer at the time of the discharge.

10. Even in the very rare instances when an arbitrator's procedural aberrations rise to the level of affirmative misconduct, as a rule the court must not foreclose further proceedings by settling the merits according to its own judgment of the appropriate result, since this step would improperly substitute a judicial determination for the arbitrator's decision that the parties bargained for in the collective-bargaining agreement. Instead, the court should simply vacate the award, thus leaving open the possibility of further proceedings if they are permitted under the terms of the agreement. The court also has the authority to remand for further proceedings when this step seems appropriate. See [FAA] § 10(e).

forever foreclose the Company from using that evidence as the basis for a discharge.

Even if it were open to the Court of Appeals to have found a violation of Rule II.1 because of the marijuana found in Cooper's car, the question remains whether the court could properly set aside the award because in its view discharge was the correct remedy. Normally, an arbitrator is authorized to disagree with the sanction imposed for employee misconduct. In *Enterprise Wheel*, for example, the arbitrator reduced the discipline from discharge to a 10–day suspension. The Court of Appeals refused to enforce the award, but we reversed, explaining that though the arbitrator's decision must draw its essence from the agreement, he "is to bring his informed judgment to bear in order to reach a fair solution of a problem. *This is especially true when it comes to formulating remedies.*" The parties, of course, may limit the discretion of the arbitrator in this respect; and it may be, as the Company argues, that under the contract involved here, it was within the unreviewable discretion of management to discharge an employee once a violation of Rule II.1 was found. But the parties stipulated that the issue before the arbitrator was whether there was "just" cause for the discharge, and the arbitrator, in the course of his opinion, cryptically observed that Rule II.1 merely listed causes for discharge and did not expressly provide for immediate discharge. Before disposing of the case on the ground that Rule II.1 had been violated and discharge was therefore proper, the proper course would have been remand to the arbitrator for a definitive construction of the contract in this respect.

C

The Court of Appeals did not purport to take this course in any event. Rather, it held that the evidence of marijuana in Cooper's car required that the award be set aside because to reinstate a person who had brought drugs onto the property was contrary to the public policy "against the operation of dangerous machinery by persons under the influence of drugs or alcohol." We cannot affirm that judgment.

A court's refusal to enforce an arbitrator's award under a collective-bargaining agreement because it is contrary to public policy is a specific application of the more general doctrine, rooted in the common law, that a court may refuse to enforce contracts that violate law or public policy. *W.R. Grace & Co. v. Rubber Workers,* 461 U.S. 757, 766 (1983). That doctrine derives from the basic notion that no court will lend its aid to one who founds a cause of action upon an immoral or illegal act, and is further justified by the observation that the public's interests in confining the scope of private agreements to which it is not a party will go unrepresented unless the judiciary takes account of those interests when it considers whether to enforce such agreements. In the common law of contracts, this doctrine has served as the foundation for occasional exercises of judicial power to abrogate private agreements.

In *W.R. Grace*, we recognized that "a court may not enforce a collective-bargaining agreement that is contrary to public policy," and stated that "the question of public policy is ultimately one for resolution by the courts." We cautioned, however, that a court's refusal to enforce an arbitrator's interpretation of such contracts is limited to situations where the contract as interpreted would violate "some explicit public policy" that is "well defined and dominant, and is to be ascertained 'by reference to the laws and legal precedents and not from general considerations of supposed public interests.' " In *W.R. Grace,* we identified two important public policies that were potentially jeopardized by the arbitrator's interpretation of the contract: obedience to judicial orders and voluntary compliance with Title VII. We went on to hold that enforcement of the arbitration award in that case did not compromise either of the two public policies allegedly threatened by the award. Two points follow from our decision in *W.R. Grace.* First, a court may refuse to enforce a collective-bargaining agreement when the specific terms contained in that agreement violate public policy. Second, it is apparent that our decision in that case does not otherwise sanction a broad judicial power to set aside arbitration awards as against public policy. Although we discussed the effect of that award on two broad areas of public policy, our decision turned on our examination of whether the award created any explicit conflict with other "laws and legal precedents" rather than an assessment of "general considerations of supposed public interests." At the very least, an alleged public policy must be properly framed under the approach set out in *W.R. Grace,* and the violation of such a policy must be clearly shown if an award is not to be enforced.

As we see it, the formulation of public policy set out by the Court of Appeals did not comply with the statement that such a policy must be "ascertained 'by reference to the laws and legal precedents and not from general considerations of supposed public interests.' " The Court of Appeals made no attempt to review existing laws and legal precedents in order to demonstrate that they establish a "well defined and dominant" policy against the operation of dangerous machinery while under the influence of drugs. Although certainly such a judgment is firmly rooted in common sense, we explicitly held in *W.R. Grace* that a formulation of public policy based only on "general considerations of supposed public interests" is not the sort that permits a court to set aside an arbitration award that was entered in accordance with a valid collective-bargaining agreement.

Even if the Court of Appeals' formulation of public policy is to be accepted, no violation of that policy was clearly shown in this case. In pursuing its public policy inquiry, the Court of Appeals quite properly considered the established fact that traces of marijuana had been found in Cooper's car. Yet the assumed connection between the marijuana gleanings found in Cooper's car and Cooper's actual use of drugs in the workplace is tenuous at best and provides an insufficient basis for holding that his reinstatement would actually violate the public policy identified by the Court of Appeals "against the operation of dangerous machinery by persons under the influence of drugs or alcohol." A refusal to enforce an award must rest on more than speculation or assumption.

C. ARBITRATION AND THE COURTS

739

In any event, it was inappropriate for the Court of Appeals itself to draw the necessary inference. To conclude from the fact that marijuana had been found in Cooper's car that Cooper had ever been or would be under the influence of marijuana while he was on the job and operating dangerous machinery is an exercise in factfinding about Cooper's use of drugs and his amenability to discipline, a task that exceeds the authority of a court asked to overturn an arbitration award. The parties did not bargain for the facts to be found by a court, but by an arbitrator chosen by them who had more opportunity to observe Cooper and to be familiar with the plant and its problems. Nor does the fact that it is inquiring into a possible violation of public policy excuse a court for doing the arbitrator's task. If additional facts were to be found, the arbitrator should find them in the course of any further effort the Company might have made to discharge Cooper for having had marijuana in his car on company premises. Had the arbitrator found that Cooper had possessed drugs on the property, yet imposed discipline short of discharge because he found as a factual matter that Cooper could be trusted not to use them on the job, the Court of Appeals could not upset the award because of its own view that public policy about plant safety was threatened. In this connection it should also be noted that the award ordered Cooper to be reinstated in his old job or in an equivalent one for which he was qualified. It is by no means clear from the record that Cooper would pose a serious threat to the asserted public policy in every job for which he was qualified.[12]

The judgment of the Court of Appeals is reversed.

So ordered.

▉ JUSTICE BLACKMUN, with whom JUSTICE BRENNAN joins, concurring.

I join the Court's opinion, but write separately to underscore the narrow grounds on which its decision rests and to emphasize what it is *not* holding today. In particular, the Court does not reach the issue upon which certiorari was granted: whether a court may refuse to enforce an arbitration award rendered under a collective-bargaining agreement on public policy grounds only when the award itself violates positive law or requires unlawful conduct by the employer. The opinion takes no position on this issue. See n. 12. Nor do I understand the Court to decide, more generally, in what way, if any, a court's authority to set aside an arbitration award on public policy grounds differs from its authority, outside the collective-bargaining context, to refuse to enforce a contract on public policy grounds. Those issues are left for another day.

I agree with the Court that the judgment of the Court of Appeals must be reversed and I summarize what I understand to be the three alternative rationales for the Court's decision:

---

12. We need not address the Union's position that a court may refuse to enforce an award on public policy grounds only when the award itself violates a statute, regulation, or other manifestation of positive law, or compels conduct by the employer that would violate such a law.

740 CHAPTER V ARBITRATION

1. The Court of Appeals exceeded its authority in concluding that the company's discharge of Cooper was proper under the collective-bargaining agreement. The Court of Appeals erred in considering evidence that the arbitrator legitimately had excluded from the grievance process, in second-guessing the arbitrator's factual finding that Cooper had not violated Rule II.1, and in assessing the appropriate sanction under the agreement. Absent its overreaching, the Court of Appeals lacked any basis for disagreeing with the arbitrator's conclusion that there was not "just cause" for discharging Cooper.

2. Even if the Court of Appeals properly considered evidence of marijuana found in Cooper's car and legitimately found a Rule II.1 violation, the public policy advanced by the Court of Appeals does not support its decision to set aside the award. The reinstatement of Cooper would not contravene the alleged public policy "against the operation of dangerous machinery by persons under the influence of drugs or alcohol." The fact that an employee's car contains marijuana gleanings does not indicate that the employee uses marijuana on the job or that he operates his machine while under the influence of drugs, let alone that he will report to work in an impaired state in the future. Moreover, nothing in the record suggests that the arbitrator's award, which gives the company the option of placing Cooper in a job equivalent to his old one, would require Cooper to operate hazardous machinery.

3. The public policy formulated by the Court of Appeals may not properly support a court's refusal to enforce an otherwise valid arbitration award. In *W.R. Grace & Co. v. Rubber Workers,* 461 U.S. 757 (1983), we stated that the public policy must be founded on "laws and legal precedents." The Court of Appeals identified no law or legal precedent that demonstrated an "explicit public policy" against the operation of dangerous machinery by persons under the influence of drugs. Far from being "well defined and dominant," as *W.R. Grace* prescribed, the Court of Appeals' public policy was ascertained merely "from general considerations of supposed public interests." I do not understand the Court, by criticizing the company's public policy formulation, to suggest that proper framing of an alleged public policy under the approach set out in *W.R. Grace* would be sufficient to justify a court's refusal to enforce an arbitration award on public policy grounds. Rather, I understand the Court to hold that such compliance is merely a necessary step if an award is not to be enforced.

It is on this understanding that I join the opinion of the Court.

NOTES AND QUESTIONS

1. In Hill v. Norfolk and Western Ry. Co., 814 F.2d 1192, 1194–95 (7th Cir.1987), Judge Posner wrote that

As we have said too many times to want to repeat again, the question for decision by a federal court asked to set aside an arbitration award—whether the award is made under the Railway Labor Act, the Taft–Hartley Act, or the United States Arbitration Act—is not whether the arbitrator or arbitrators erred in interpreting the contract; it is not whether they clearly erred in interpreting the contract; it is not whether they grossly erred in interpreting the contract; it is whether they interpreted the contract. * * * A party can complain if the arbitrators don't interpret the contract—that is, if they disregard the contract and implement their own notions of what is reasonable and fair. * * * But a party will not be heard to complain merely because the arbitrators' interpretation is a misinterpretation. Granted, the grosser the apparent misinterpretation, the likelier it is that the arbitrators weren't interpreting the contract at all. But once the court is satisfied that they were interpreting the contract, judicial review is at an end, provided there is no fraud or corruption and the arbitrators haven't ordered anyone to do an illegal act.

In *Hill,* the district court had refused to disturb an award against a discharged employee. Finding that the employee's appeal was "based largely on frivolous grounds," the Seventh Circuit on its own initiative imposed sanctions on his attorney. Judge Posner remarked that "[t]his court has been plagued by groundless lawsuits seeking to overturn arbitration awards * * *. [W]e have said repeatedly that we would punish such tactics, and we mean it." Cf. Miller Brewing Co. v. Brewery Workers Local Union No. 9, 739 F.2d 1159 (7th Cir.1984) ("because there are so few grounds for attacking arbitration awards, it is easy to pronounce most such attacks utterly groundless").

2. Different arbitrators may on different occasions come to hear cases arising under the same collective bargaining agreement, and they may, on identical facts, give opposite or conflicting interpretations of the same contractual provision. In such circumstances a court may well conclude that *neither* award should be vacated, since *each* "draws its essence" from the agreement. E.g., Graphic Arts Int'l Union Local 97–B v. Haddon Craftsmen, Inc., 489 F.Supp. 1088 (M.D.Pa.1979); Consolidation Coal Co. v. United Mine Workers of America, 213 F.3d 404 (7th Cir.2000). Cf. Connecticut Light & Power Co. v. Local 420, Int'l Brotherhood of Elec. Workers, 718 F.2d 14 (2d Cir.1983) (first arbitrator had issued cease and desist order for the future; where both awards could not be implemented, the court must "select that interpretation which most nearly conforms to the intent of the parties").

3. Assume that after the Supreme Court's decision in *Misco,* the employer wishes to discharge Cooper on the ground that it *now* knows marijuana was found in his car on company premises on January 21: Would this be consistent with the arbitral award ordering that the employee be reinstated? See part "II.B." of the Supreme Court's opinion. In a similar case, an employee was discharged for sexual harassment, and the arbitrator ordered reinstatement. The employer acquiesced in the confirmed award and reinstated the employee, but then discharged him *the same day* on the basis of earlier incidents which had come to light after the original termination, but which the arbitrator had refused to consider. The union requested that the employer be held in contempt for attempting to evade the court's order enforcing the award but the district court denied the motion "because it concluded that [the employer] had complied with its order by reinstating [the employee]". The court of appeals affirmed in Chrysler Motors Corp. v. International Union, Allied Industrial Workers of America, 2 F.3d 760 (7th Cir.1993).

Compare United States Postal Service v. Nat'l Ass'n of Letter Carriers, 64 F.Supp.2d 633 (S.D.Tex.1999), in which an employee was discharged for committing workers' compensation fraud; the arbitrator, finding a "procedural defect" in the process by which the worker was terminated, ordered reinstatement. The employer then sent a second notice of termination predicated on the same misconduct and began a disciplinary process in an attempt to "cure the procedural defect." The arbitrator determined that the collective bargaining agreement precluded a "collateral attack" on the original award through a second discipline, and the court confirmed this award: The remedy sought by the employer "is analogous to a police department's illegally executing a search warrant, seizing evidence, and on seeing it suppressed, returning the evidence to the apartment, correctly executing the warrant, and attempting to reintroduce it at trial." The worker should not become "a pinata that the government strikes until it gets a 'good' result." Is this case distinguishable from *Chrysler Motors*?

Note: Arbitral Decision–Making and Legal "Rules"

Some years ago a survey of commercial arbitrators found that 80 per cent of the studied arbitrators "thought that they ought to reach their decisions within the context of the principles of substantive rules of law, but almost 90 per cent believed that they were free to ignore these rules whenever they thought that more just decisions would be reached by so doing."[1] The readiness of arbitrators to depart from legal "rules" varies, of course. It will depend in part on the presumed willingness of the parties to allow them to do so, as well as on the presence or absence of attorneys and the arbitrator's own profession and degree of expertness. For example, in the highly informal "Autoline" program administered by the Better Business Bureau, volunteer arbitrators are expressly enjoined not to try to interpret state law or even the language of the automobile manufacturer's warranty. Rather than basing a decision on the fact that a car may be "out of warranty," for example, they are told instead to be more "flexible" and to decide only on the basis of the "facts."

At the other end of the spectrum, international commercial contracts regularly contain provisions that stipulate which substantive law the arbitrator is to apply. In international transactions the choice of law is likely to affect any number of questions, from warranty obligations to prejudgment interest, as to which the various national legal systems involved may give radically different answers. Where the parties are of different nationalities they may think it fairer to insure that the transaction is governed by the law of a *third* country, unrelated to either. Another possibility is exemplified by a contract between a German and an English company, where the

---

1. Mentschikoff, Commercial Arbitration, 61 Col.L.Rev. 846, 861 (1961).

arbitrators were instructed to apply German law if the English company was the claimant, and English law if the German company was the claimant![2] However, there does exist a familiar alternative in international arbitration. The parties may sometimes expressly provide that the arbitrators shall decide "according to natural justice and equity" or "ex aequo et bono." (The comparable French phrase, rooted in civil law tradition, is that the arbitrators shall act as *amiables compositeurs*.") The rules of international arbitral institutions such as the ICC make this device available to parties who choose to give the arbitrator such authority, as do the Arbitration Rules promulgated by the United Nations Commission on International Trade Law ("UNCITRAL") for non-administered arbitrations. In what sorts of cases might the parties prefer that their arbitrators proceed on the basis of general "equitable" standards of fairness? In what sorts of cases might they prefer instead that their arbitrators apply a particular body of national law?

The extent to which arbitrators are expected to follow external legal "rules" has given rise to considerable controversy in labor relations cases. The classic statement of the dilemma usually goes like this: Assume that an industrial plant begins Sunday operations; when work crews cannot be filled with volunteers, the employer selects workers for Sunday work on a rotating basis. An employee refuses to work on Sunday for religious reasons; he is discharged and a grievance is filed which proceeds to arbitration. The collective bargaining agreement forbids discharge without "just cause." Title VII of the 1964 Civil Rights Act makes it unlawful for an employer to discriminate on the basis of religion unless he can demonstrate "that he is unable to reasonably accommodate" the employee's religious practices "without undue hardship" on the conduct of his business. How should the arbitrator proceed?

The "orthodox" position among labor arbitrators has been that the arbitrators should adhere to the agreement and "ignore the law." The arbitrator, on this view, is merely:

> the parties' officially designated "reader" of the contract. He (or she) is their joint *alter ego* for the purpose of striking whatever supplementary bargain is necessary to handle the anticipated unanticipated omissions of the initial agreement. * * * [T]he arbitrator's mandate is plain: tell the parties (and the courts) what the contract means and let them worry about the legal consequences.[3]

Finding "the law" and interpreting statutes and cases are tasks likely to be beyond the special competence of most arbitrators, whether legally trained or not—beyond, that is, the reasons for which they were chosen by the parties, and beyond the reasons supporting the presumption of arbitrability and the practice of deference to arbitral awards.[4] So the conventional view

---

2. See Kerr, International Arbitration v. Litigation, [1980] J.Bus.Law 164, 172.

3. St. Antoine, Judicial Review of Labor Arbitration Awards: A Second Look at *Enter-*

prise Wheel and its Progeny, 75 Mich.L.Rev. 1137, 1140, 1142 (1977).

4. In a 1975 survey of the members of the National Academy of Arbitrators concerning the arbitration of discrimination cases,

744   CHAPTER V ARBITRATION

is that whether an agreement is in accord with the external "law" is "irrelevant";[5] it is a question best "postponed" for later determination by the courts.[6] The fear is frequently expressed that by presuming to decide such questions themselves, arbitrators might actually be inviting closer judicial scrutiny and thus more active judicial intervention in the arbitral process—for professional arbitrators, one of the most menacing of nightmares.

There exist in the literature all sorts of nuanced variations on this "orthodox" view. An exception is usually made for situations where the parties themselves seem to "invite" the arbitrator to decide according to the law: It is, for example, increasingly common to find cases where the parties have expressly tracked the language of a statute in their agreement, or have stipulated that the award must be "consistent with applicable laws" and in such cases it is likely that they will be found to have "necessarily bargained for the arbitrator's interpretation of the law."[7] It may be, though, that this entire subject is of more academic than practical interest. The paradigm case—where both law and agreement are clear and irreconcilably in conflict—will not often arise. There is usually plenty of room to reinterpret the agreement in light of the arbitrator's understanding of the requirements of the external law, and most arbitrators can be expected to deploy adequate resourcefulness to avoid any contradiction.[8]

After an arbitral award has been handed down, the *Misco* case clearly teaches that the arbitrator should not be treated as a sort of "lower court":

only 52% of the respondents indicated that they regularly read labor advance sheets to keep abreast of current developments under Title VII; only 14% indicated that they felt confident they could accurately define basic employment-discrimination terms like "bona fide occupational qualification." (another 30% thought they could make a good "educated guess."). Only 54% of the respondents were attorneys; of the total number of employment discrimination cases heard by the respondents, both parties were represented by counsel in only 53%. Harry Edwards, Arbitration of Employment Discrimination Cases: An Empirical Study, Proceedings, 28th Annual Meeting, Nat'l Academy of Arbitrators 59 (1976).

5. Feller, Arbitration and the External Law Revisited, 37 St. Louis U.L.J. 973, 975 (1993).

6. Meltzer, Ruminations about Ideology, Law and Labor Arbitration, Proceedings, 20th Annual Meeting, Nat'l Academy of Arbitrators 1, 17 n. 40 (1967).

7. American Postal Workers Union v. United States Postal Serv., 789 F.2d 1, 6 (D.C.Cir.1986) (Edwards, J.).

See, e.g., In re GTE North Inc., 113 Lab. Arb. 665, 672 (1999)(contract contained both a non-discrimination clause and a "Conflict with Law" provision; "[f]urthermore, compliance with the ADA can be viewed * * * as a component of 'just cause,' a necessary element for discharge"; "[f]or all these reasons, this Arbitrator is going to address the Union's ADA argument"); In re Los Angeles Community College District, 112 Lab. Arb. 733, 738 (1999)(employer agreed "to comply with all federal * * * laws regarding non-discrimination"; "[I]t becomes, then, the Arbitrator's unenviable task to decide the matter, even if it presents a novel issue under the ADA not previously settled by the courts").

8. For a recent review of the controversy and a demonstration that "the debate is narrower than it first appears" see Laura Cooper, Dennis Nolan, & Richard Bales, ADR in the Workplace 153–180 (2000).

C. ARBITRATION AND THE COURTS   **745**

A court will not decline enforcement of an award merely because the arbitrator has decided the case differently from the way a trial judge would. For over a century the cases have been full of reminders to this effect:

> If an arbitrator makes a mistake either as to law or fact, it is the misfortune of the party, and there is no help for it. There is no right of appeal, and the court has no power to revise the decisions of "judges who are of the parties' own choosing."[9]

Of course, in thinking about judicial review on matters of "law" we should distinguish between mere rules of construction, which come into play in the absence of a contrary agreement, and mandatory rules. After all, most "rules" of contract or commercial law are nothing more than "gap-fillers." They supply a term where the parties have not expressly supplied one themselves; modern commercial law looks in particular to industry custom and course of dealing to furnish the "framework of common understanding controlling any general rules of law which hold only when there is no such understanding."[10] But where the parties have bargained for dispute resolution through arbitration, the method *they* have chosen to fill any gaps in the agreement is the arbitrator's interpretation. His interpretation *is* their bargain. In contrast, legal "rules" in other areas may reflect stronger and overriding governmental or societal interests. In such cases, obviously, some greater degree of arbitral deference should be expected.

In addition, the whole subject of assuring compliance with legal "rules" can often take on an air of unreality. This is particularly true in the commercial area. The obvious lesson of innumerable commercial arbitration cases is that lack of a reasoned opinion will help to insulate an award from judicial scrutiny. Consider, for example, Stroh Container Co. v. Delphi Industries, Inc., 783 F.2d 743 (8th Cir.1986). In confirming an award in this contract dispute, the court first considered whether §§ 10 and 11 of the FAA were the exclusive grounds on the basis of which an award could be vacated or modified:

> Some courts * * * have suggested that an award may be set aside if it is in "manifest disregard of the law," is completely irrational in that it fails to draw its "essence" from the agreement, or contravenes a deeply rooted public policy. * * *

> We need not decide, however, whether to adopt any of these exceptions since, under any one of them, the award must nevertheless be affirmed. * * * [N]either the award itself nor the record before us suggests that the arbitrators in any way manifestly disregarded the law in reaching their decision. In Wilko v. Swan, 346 U.S. 427, 436 (1953), the Court carefully distinguished an arbitrator's interpretation of the law, which is insulated from review, from an arbitrator's disregard of the law, which may open the door for judicial scrutiny. Further, such disregard must "be made clearly to appear," and may be found "when

---

9. Patton v. Garrett, 116 N.C. 847, 21 S.E. 679, 682–83 (1895).

10. UCC § 1–205 comment 4; see also §§ 1–102(3), (4).

arbitrators understand and correctly state the law, but proceed to disregard the same." In the case before us, the arbitrators' decision does not clearly delineate the law applied, nor expound the reasoning and analysis used. Rather, the award presents, as the district court stated, "only a cursory discussion of what the arbitrators considered to be the key points underlying the award." It therefore cannot be said that it clearly appears that the arbitrators identified applicable law and proceeded to reach a contrary position in spite of it. Nor does the absence of express reasoning by the arbitrators support the conclusion that they disregarded the law. Arbitrators are not required to elaborate their reasoning supporting an award, and to allow a court to conclude that it may substitute its own judgment for the arbitrator's whenever the arbitrator chooses not to explain the award would improperly subvert the proper functioning of the arbitral process.

See also Perini Corp. v. Greate Bay Hotel & Casino, Inc., 129 N.J. 479, 610 A.2d 364 (N.J. 1992). In this case one of the judges noted that "after four years and sixty-four days, the arbitrators simply awarded $14 million to [the plaintiff] without any explanation whatsoever other than a finding that [the defendant] had 'failed to properly perform its obligations as construction manager pursuant to the contract * * *.' There are no reasons, no findings of fact, no conclusions of law, nothing other than the foregoing. For all we know, the arbitrators concluded that the sun rises in the west, the earth is flat, and damages have nothing to do with the intentions of the parties or the foreseeability of the consequences of a breach." 129 N.J. at 534–35, 610 A.2d at 392 (Wilentz, C.J., concurring). The award was confirmed.

Alan Rau, Contracting Out of the Arbitration Act, 8 American Review of International Arbitration 225 (1997)

The parties to an international joint venture agreed to arbitration to be held under ICC Rules in San Francisco. Under the terms of their arbitration clause, the arbitration panel was instructed to issue a written award that was to include "detailed findings of fact and conclusions of law"; the federal district court for the Northern District of California could then:

> vacate, modify or correct any award (i) based upon any of the grounds referred to in the Federal Arbitration Act, (ii) where the arbitrators' findings of fact are not supported by substantial evidence, or (iii) where the arbitrators' conclusions of law are erroneous.

An award was ultimately rendered, but the district court resolutely refused to look into the arbitrators' findings of fact or conclusions of law: It found that its "options" were "limited" by the provisions of the FAA "and may not be extended by agreement of the parties." "The role of the federal courts cannot be subverted to serve private interests at the whim of contracting parties." So the court restricted its inquiry to the "permissible statutory grounds" found in § 10 of the Act, and summarily confirmed the award. The arbitrators had not "exceeded their powers." While they had

C. Arbitration and the Courts   **747**

indeed as instructed applied at least some version of California law, they were hardly required to apply California law "without error."

* * *

This [is] the celebrated case of *Lapine Technology Corp. v. Kyocera Corp.* And to no-one's particular surprise, I think, the court of appeals soon reversed, remanding "for review of the decision by use of the agreed-to standard."[4] The Ninth Circuit thereby [committed itself] to the proposition that precisely how "binding" an award is to be is a matter for the parties themselves to determine.

I must say that I have been astonished at the extent to which this issue seems to have excited the attention of the arbitration community. It might, then, not be out of place for me to say just why I think the Ninth Circuit is so clearly right. Had it not been for the strong differences of opinion that *Kyocera* has evoked, I would have thought that the case deserved to be relegated to some routine and workmanlike set of continuing legal education materials, mentioned in passing as one more minor but interesting corollary to everything that we have known for a long time.

* * *

II.   WHAT IS THE POINT OF § 10?

It seems symptomatic of a particularly rigid cast of mind to assume that where the arbitration statute allocates certain powers to a court, then—by that very fact—any *contractual re-allocation* by the parties themselves must necessarily be forbidden. Section 3 of the FAA, for example, tells us that before staying litigation, the court must be "satisfied that the issue involved in such suit or proceeding is referable to arbitration." Are we really and truly required to conclude from this that the courts have "exclusive jurisdiction" to determine whether an arbitration clause covers a particular dispute—even *though the parties themselves* may have agreed to entrust this question of "arbitrability" to the arbitrator? The Supreme Court has sensibly indicated that the answer to this question is "no"[25]— that is, that the statute's default allocation of authority *between courts and arbitrators* need not implicate in any way the power of the *parties themselves* to structure the arbitration mechanism so as to advance their own interests.

Similarly, §§ 9 and 10 of the Act direct courts to confirm awards unless certain specified grounds for *vacatur* are present; the "merits"— that is, arbitral determinations of fact and interpretations of law—are not reviewable, being presumably left to the arbitrators. Are we really and

---

4.   130 F.3d 884, 891 (9th Cir.1997).

25.   *See* First Options of Chicago, Inc. v. Kaplan, 514 U.S. 938, 943 (1995)(the question "who has the primary power to decide arbitrability" "turns upon what the parties agreed about that matter"; if the parties agreed to submit the arbitrability question to arbitration, "then the court's standard for reviewing the arbitrator's decision about that matter should not differ from the standard courts apply when they review any other matter that parties have agreed to arbitrate").

truly required to conclude from this that *the parties themselves* may not entrust to courts—rather than to the arbitrators—the final authority to decide legal and factual questions? Must we conclude [as some commentators have argued] that giving effect to such an agreement would constitute a "patent violation" of the Act? Presented with such an assertion—and with no attempt at a functional or purposive reading of the statute—the diagnosis seems justified that we are in the presence of that most common of legal ailments, "hardening of the categories."

By contrast, I have always thought that the principal purpose of § 10 of the FAA—and for that matter, of equivalent provisions found in all modern arbitration laws—is rather to insulate from parochial or intrusive judicial review awards *that the parties intended in the usual sense to be binding*. That is, § 10 serves to assure the parties to an arbitral proceeding that they need not fear an officious or meddlesome inquiry into the merits which would impair the efficacy of the arbitral process for them. But such a purpose has nothing at all, as far as I can see, to do with the situation where the parties are eager to depart from the protective rule of § 10. It is one thing to say that their awards must have legal currency in accordance with the parties' presumed wishes; it is something totally different to say that their awards *will* have this currency, by God, over the parties' expressed wishes to the contrary. I should think that such interference with private autonomy would have to be justified—and on other than paternalistic grounds.

It is in this sense then that I see the provisions of § 10, not as an imperative command of public policy, but as no more than a set of "default rules" intended to reflect the traditional historical understanding concerning the binding effect of arbitral awards. Like any default rules, these supply a ready-made stock of implied terms, allocating the burden of being explicit and chosen at least in part to mirror the "hypothetical bargain" that the parties are assumed to have intended. And so whatever we can characterize as a "default rule" may naturally be varied by an express agreement of the parties, who may stray in the direction of expanding the statutory grounds of review—or even, perhaps, in the direction of restricting them still further.

Since a default rule is no more than a rebuttable presumption—the mere beginning of the inquiry—it by definition grants the ultimate power of decisionmaking to the parties rather than to the State. * * * Now it is of course entirely a separate question whether § 10 represents the *most desirable background* rule to govern arbitral determinations of "legal" issues. The arbitration law of England, for example, adopts more or less the opposite presumption: Judicial review for errors of law is possible, at least with leave of the court, unless the parties expressly exclude it.[33] But the

---

33. *See* Arbitration Act 1996 (1996 c.23) § 69.

In the *absence* of an exclusion agreement, the right to appeal on questions of law is generally discretionary with the court. But note that under the English Arbitration Act no leave of court is necessary if all the parties agree to such an appeal. And such an "agree-

C. ARBITRATION AND THE COURTS

749

English legislation at least demonstrates that it is plausible to treat this issue as I am suggesting it should be treated—as the search for the appropriate presumption—and for the moment, the default rule of § 10 is the only default rule we have.

III. ARBITRABILITY AND COMPARATIVE ADVANTAGE

It is at least plausible to say—it is, after all, a proposition of some antiquity—that arbitration has its greatest utility in providing expert determinations of contested matters of fact (such as the "determination of the quality of a commodity or the amount of money due under a contract").[34] By contrast, the legitimacy of the arbitration process—and any comparative advantage that it may possess over litigation—may be weakest when arbitrators attempt to follow national courts in laying down disputed legal norms. In fact such a judgment once reflected our dominant view of arbitration, and presumably explains the traditional reluctance of courts in decisions like *Wilko v. Swan*,[35] or *Alexander v. Gardner–Denver*,[36] to defer to arbitrators—or even to find arbitration permissible—in cases where the decisionmaker was called upon to interpret and apply regulatory legislation.

Now of course, the law has progressed far beyond the stage where the competence of arbitrators to decide difficult "legal" questions was systematically doubted—and cases like *Wilko*, as restrictions on the arbitral process in the name of "public policy," are long dead. But might not *the parties themselves*—who are, after all, the ultimate consumers of the process—still reasonably adopt the same attitude in individual cases?

ment" for appeal may be contained in a predispute arbitration clause, or even in "rules incorporated into that clause;" *see* David St. John Sutton et al., Russell on Arbitration 428 & n.14 (21st ed. 1997). In that respect at least the English regime is not too different from what was approved by the Ninth Circuit in *Kyocera*.

34. Wilko v. Swan, 346 U.S. 427, 435 (1953). *See* also Philip G. Phillips, *Rules of Law or Laissez–Faire in Commercial Arbitration*, 47 Harv. L. Rev. 590, 599–600, 626 (1934)("the attention of business has been on arbitration as an escape from the jury method of fact determination and not as an escape from substantive law"); Paul L. Sayre, *Development of Commercial Arbitration Law*, 37 Yale L. J. 595, 615 (1928)(the "full usefulness of arbitration lies" in making it serve "as a substitute for the preliminary stages of a court trial; "arbitration works much more cheaply and quickly when the arbitrators confine themselves to their specialty, that of passing on technical questions of fact in modem business"); Julius Henry Cohen & Kenneth Dayton, *The New Federal Arbitration*

Law, 12 Va. L. Rev. 265, 281 (1926)("[n]ot all questions arising out of contracts ought to be arbitrated;" arbitration "is a remedy peculiarly suited to the disposition of the ordinary disputes between merchants as to questions of fact—quantity, quality, time of delivery, compliance with terms of payment, excuses for non-performance, and the like") * * * .

35. Wilko v. Swan, 346 U.S. 427, 437 (1953)("the protective provisions of the Securities Act require the exercise of judicial direction to fairly assure their effectiveness").

36. Alexander v. Gardner–Denver Co., 415 U.S. 36, 56–57 (1974)(employee's statutory right to trial under Title VII of the Civil Rights Act of 1964 is not foreclosed by prior submission of his claim to arbitration under arbitration clause in collective bargaining agreement; "[a]rbitral procedures, while well suited to the resolution of contractual disputes, make arbitration a comparatively inappropriate forum for the final resolution of rights created by Title VII";"the specialized competence of arbitrators pertains primarily to the law of the shop, not the law of the land"). [See p. 787 infra].

750 CHAPTER V ARBITRATION

I am at a loss to understand why parties to commercial transactions should ever be compelled to adopt one unitary model of arbitration—making judicial oversight of awards, for example, into a Procrustean bed to which the parties must adapt themselves even at the cost of amputated limbs. But that is precisely what it means to assert that once parties choose arbitration, they must necessarily accept arbitral determinations on all "legal issues." * * *

I had always assumed it to be a commonplace that parties to a contract are able—and indeed, should be encouraged—to tailor the scope of "arbitrable issues" to fit their own particular needs, circumstances, or desires. The ability to do this is in fact one of the principal selling points of the arbitration process: As the prophets of private ordering suggested long ago, arbitration is in this respect "the parties' dream."[39] The parties are free, as the Supreme Court wrote in *Volt*, "to structure their arbitration agreements as they see fit. Just as they may limit by contract the issues which they will arbitrate, so too may they specify by contract the rules under which that arbitration will be conducted." So, for example, they are free, if they think it advisable, to:

- draw a distinction between disputes over fees "due and owing" under a distributorship agreement, and disputes over alleged copyright and trademark infringement—and choose to arbitrate only the former;[41]* * *

- draw a distinction between disputes over past breaches of contract, and disputes relating to future adjustments of the contract—and choose to arbitrate only the former.

Certain well-established "rules" of arbitration law are also in essence little more than background presumptions, which the parties may vary by redefining in their contract the scope of arbitrable issues. So, for example, the parties may:

- draw a distinction between disputes over breach of contract and disputes alleging fraudulent inducement of the contract—and choose

---

39. Henry M. Hart, Jr. & Albert M. Sacks, The Legal Process: Basic Problems in the Making and Application of Law 310 (1994 ed.). [See also p. 834 infra].

41. Zenger–Miller, Inc. v. Training Team, GmbH, 757 F.Supp. 1062 (N.D.Cal. 1991); *see also* Coady v. Ashcraft & Gerel, 996 F.Supp. 95, 98, 109 (D.Mass.1998)(employment agreement provided for arbitration of "any ambiguities or questions of interpretation of this contract"; held, claim of breach of fiduciary duty is not subject to arbitration since "fiduciary duties arise out of agency law and do not depend on any interpretation of the Employment Agreement"); Tracer Re-

search Corp. v. National Environmental Services Co., 42 F.3d 1292, 1295 (9th Cir.1994)(arbitration clause covering "any controversy or claim arising out of this Agreement" refers only to disputes "relating to the interpretation and performance of the contract itself"; tort claim for misappropriation of trade secrets is not arbitrable).

Or they may draw a distinction between disputes over the terms of a charter agreement, and tort disputes arising out of a collision between the vessel and a dock; *see* Texaco, Inc. v. American Trading Transport. Co., Inc., 644 F.2d 1152 (5th Cir.1981).

C. ARBITRATION AND THE COURTS

751

to arbitrate only the former, thereby reversing the default rule of *Prima Paint*[44] * * *.

● Now, given this familiar background, is it not understandable that the parties—relying here on hoary considerations of comparative advantage—might choose to draw a distinction between "any unresolved questions of fact" and "questions of law"? If they do so, they may prefer to draft an arbitration clause by which they agree to submit only the former to arbitration—thereby entrusting factual determinations to arbitrators chosen specifically for that purpose, while *withholding* from their arbitrators the power to make ultimate determinations of "legal" issues.

Would this not, in fact, be just one more example of the unremarkable, everyday practice by which parties "agree to submit to arbitration only some of the disputes that may arise between them"? The contract in *Kyocera* might then be understood simply as an attempt to limit the scope of authority of the arbitrators and to carve out a particular class of disputes as "arbitrable": And from this point of view, the Ninth Circuit's decision becomes nothing more than a natural corollary of a half-dozen or more cases in which the Supreme Court's "presumption of arbitrability" left abundant room for an inquiry into whether the parties had agreed on anything to the contrary.

* * *

IV. CONTRACTING FOR NON–BINDING ARBITRATION

We can arrive at precisely the same result reached by the Ninth Circuit in *Kyocera* by taking a somewhat different route. While it would be unusual to do so, the parties to an agreement might wish to alter in some respects the binding effect of an arbitral award. * * * [There are cases, for example,] where commercial parties dealing at arm's length have stipulated that their arbitral award shall be completely non-binding. These are the cases where the parties may see the virtues of what is in effect an "advisory opinion" as an aid to evaluating a case for settlement purposes—although they may be unwilling to give up all notion of recourse to litigation. In particular the parties may think that a "trial run" of the case, ending in a prediction by a neutral expert, may cause the more recalcitrant among them to reassess their own partisan estimates of the likely outcome of adjudication. Another object may be for attorneys or management representatives to be able to use the opinion of a third party to "sell" a compromise settlement to reluctant clients or constituents, allowing them to withdraw without loss of face from hardened positions. In this respect "non-binding arbitration" has much in common with other formal "reality testing" devices such as "court-annexed arbitration," the "summary jury trial," the

---

44. *See* Carro v. Parade of Toys, Inc., 950 F.Supp. 449, 452 (D.P.R.1996) (agreement to arbitrate any dispute arising under this "Purchase Order" reflected "an intent to arbitrate only a limited range of disputes," those "relating to the interpretation and performance of a contract," and did not cover allegations of fraud in the inducement of the entire contract, nor claims for negligent misrepresentation or conversion). * * *

CHAPTER V ARBITRATION

"mini-trial," and fact finding in public-sector employment disputes. The utility of such non-binding evaluative processes has long been recognized, to the point that they have become commonplace and unremarkable remedies in the ADR armamentarium.

Such agreements for non-binding arbitration have been held to be within the Federal Arbitration Act for the purposes of stays or orders to compel under §§ 3 and 4. (The leading case probably remains *AMF Inc. v. Brunswick*,[71] but there are a number of more recent holdings to the same effect.)[72] However, the applicability of the FAA seems to be a question of largely theoretical interest—given the undoubted power of a court to enforce such agreements as a matter of ordinary contract law.[73] A federal court with the requisite jurisdiction over the case would be expected routinely to apply this general corpus of state law—under which compliance with the prescribed arbitration process becomes merely a precondition to litigation in accordance with the intention *of* the parties.[74] Should the process fail in its goal of inducing settlement, the court would then of course proceed to hear the case in the usual manner.

From this point *of* view, then, aren't *Kyocera* and similar cases—which honor the parties' wishes that arbitral determinations *of* "legal" issues not be binding—merely natural corollaries *of AMF Inc. v. Brunswick?* The thesis that the parries may preserve the right to reject an arbitrator's

---

71. AMF Inc. v. Brunswick Corp., 621 F.Supp. 456, 458 (E.D.N.Y.1985)(settlement agreement between competitors provided that any future dispute involving an advertised claim of "data based comparative superiority" would be submitted to the National Advertising Division of the Council of Better Business Bureaus "for the rendition of an advisory opinion"). * * *

72. *See* Wolsey, Ltd. v. Foodmaker, Inc., 144 F.3d 1205 (9th Cir. 1998)(agreement between franchiser of Jack in the Box restaurants and Hong Kong corporation established a three-step dispute resolution process, in which non-binding arbitration under AAA rules could be followed by litigation in federal court); Kelley v. Benchmark Homes, Inc., 250 Neb. 367, 550 N.W.2d 640, 642–43 (Neb. 1996)(warranty contract entered into by home buyers provided for arbitration which "shall not be legally binding, but shall be a condition precedent to the commencement of any litigation"). * * *

73. Whether an agreement for non-binding arbitration falls within the FAA can of course have practical, as well as mere "theoretical," significance should a party seek to invoke one of the other procedural provisions of the Act designed to support the

arbitration process—*e.g.*, § 5 (court appointment of arbitrator), § 6 (any application to the court to be heard as a motion). * * *

74. * * * Similar results are reached without difficulty in other cases that do not even consider it necessary to use the word "arbitration." *See, e.g.,* Haertl Wolff Parker, Inc. v. Howard S. Wright Construction Co., 1989 WL 151765 (D.Or.)(parties agreed to submit future disputes to a neutral third party "for a recommendation;" held, claim dismissed "with leave to refile without prejudice if the disputes are not resolved after referral" to the neutral; "the court cannot say that it would be futile to refer the deadlocked issues to him"); DeValk Lincoln Mercury, Inc. v. Ford Motor Co., 811 F.2d 326, 334–38 (7th Cir.1987)(agreement between automobile dealership and manufacturer provided that any claim by the dealer arising out of termination or nonrenewal "shall be appealed" to the company's Dealer Policy Board as "a condition precedent to the Dealer's right to pursue any other remedy;" the company, but not the dealer, "shall be bound by the decision of the Policy Board;" held, because "the mediation (sic) clause demands strict compliance with its requirement of appeal," summary judgment ordered for manufacturer).

"conclusions of law" should be fairly unobjectionable, should it not, once one concedes an even broader proposition—that they may preserve the right to a trial *de novo* on *all issues* in the case?

In stark contrast to this analysis, [some distinguished commentators have argued that]:

> Obtaining a resolution of a dispute ... in a speedy and efficient manner provides a compelling reason for limiting the scope of judicial review to the bare essentials needed to afford due process and to protect the state's own interests.... [I]f arbitral awards could be reviewed for errors of law or fact, arbitration would easily degenerate into a device for adding still another instance to the usual three instances of litigation in the ordinary courts.... [P]ermitting contractual modification of the scope of judicial review would undermine the public policy of encouraging arbitration. For it would inexorably cause arbitral awards to be final dispositions to a far lesser extent and thus lessen the social desirability of arbitration.[76]

But I find the argument that parties should not be permitted to alter the binding character of their awards, "because it would impair the efficacy of arbitration," to be extremely troubling. More than anything, it reminds me of the stereotypical librarian resentful of the whole practice of borrowing books—because the annoying tendency of patrons to do so disrupts the symmetry and orderly appearance of the shelves, and the comforting assurance that everything can always be found in its rightful place.

However, the arbitration process—just like the public library—exists and is designed above all to serve the interests of its users, not those of the guardians of the temple. The Supreme Court has reminded us often enough that "efficiency" is not an ultimate value in arbitration: The overriding goal of the FAA, in the eyes of the Court, is not "to promote the expeditious resolution of claims" but rather to "rigorously enforce agreements to arbitrate"—even though this admittedly "thwarts" our interest in "speedy and efficient decisionmaking." But in any event there is a more fundamental point: It is to the practice of contracting parties—and to that exclusively—that we must look to determine what under the circumstances is efficient *for them*. The quoted argument strikes me as excellent drafting advice—a sage warning to transactional attorneys that inserting into their arbitration agreements a clause of the sort involved in *Kyocera* may be

---

76. Hans Smit, *Contractual Modification of the Scope of Judicial Review of Arbitral Awards,* 8 Am. Rev. Int'l Arb. 147, 149, 150 (1997). *See also* Andreas Lowenfeld, *Can Arbitration Coexist with Judicial Review? A Critique of* LaPine v. Kyocera, ADR Currents, Sept. 1998 at pp. 1, 15 ("judicial review of the merits would inevitably prolong the process, negating the expeditiousness that is one of the important advantages of arbitration") * * *.

This has long been a familiar point. Cf. Fudickar v. Guardian Mut. Life Ins. Co., 62 N.Y. 392, 400 (1875)("If courts should assume to judge the decision of arbitrators upon the merits, the value of this method of settling controversies would be destroyed, and an award instead of being a final determination of a controversy would become but one of the steps in its progress").

754   CHAPTER V ARBITRATION

folly.[78] But would it not be just a tad dogmatic to assert that there exist no cases where the parties might ever rationally choose to make a different choice?

So in high-stakes cases I can imagine that a desire to ensure predictability in the application of legal standards, a desire to guard against a "rogue tribunal," or against the distortions of judgment that can often result from the dynamics of tripartite arbitration—may all weigh heavily in the decision to limit by contract the binding effect of an arbitral award. Parties who, through risk aversion or inadequate confidence, have ex *ante* the perspective of a "potential loser" may particularly be impelled in this direction. * * * Similarly, I find it quite plausible to assert that review of awards for "errors of law"—with all the formality and need for reasoned opinions that are likely to come in its wake—is quite likely to impair the ability of arbitrators to "fashion creative solutions"; arbitrators might shun reasonable solutions if they had to worry that courts might not be willing or able to endorse the legal bases on which they rest. Indeed I have argued elsewhere that it is precisely an arbitrator's "freedom from overbroad rules or time-honored categories" that makes possible arbitration's "flexibility in decisionmaking and a maximum attention to context." But in the absence of externalities, here too surely the proper tradeoff is for the parties themselves—who may be less enamored of clever and creative solutions than those of us who do not have to live with the practical consequences.

* * *

During oral argument before the Ninth Circuit in *Kyocera,* Judge Kozinski asked pointedly what could account for the sudden popularity of clauses in which the binding effect of awards was restricted: What, he wondered, "was happening in the middle of the 1980's that caused the parties to start drafting arbitration agreements that departed from the standard clause.... [T]here's no case law there, there's no legislation. Suddenly it starts popping up." He didn't receive much of an answer, but the question was certainly a good one.

Reasons for drafting clauses of the sort involved in *Kyocera* have always existed, of course, but in light of a number of developments the moment does indeed seem "right" for lawyers increasingly to resort to them. The blanket assumption of arbitral competence that has in recent years swept whole areas of statutory and regulatory law into arbitration has certainly contributed to a countervailing impulse—the desire to ensure

---

78. It is interesting to note, though, that among all the reasons why parties prefer to submit their disputes to arbitration rather than litigation, savings in time and in cost appear—at least in international cases—to be factors of "slight" or even "non-existent" importance, *see* Christian Bühring-Uhle, Arbitration and Mediation in International Business 137–39 (1996). This survey of practitioner attitudes also suggests that the "ab-

sence of appeals" is a somewhat "ambivalent" attribute of the arbitration process: For a large number of respondents, this was "crucial for the aim of obtaining a final decision within a reasonable time span"—although "according to some of the practitioners interviewed [the absence of appeals was] seen as a disadvantage since the possibility to correct even grave errors of the arbitral tribunal is very restricted." Id. at 137.

that awards in such cases are not too discordant with "public" jurisprudence. The growing use of custom-tailored arbitration clauses—whether intended to diminish the finality of awards or to increase formality in arbitral procedure—is surely but one manifestation of what is often described and decried as the "judicialization" or "legalization" of arbitration; it is in a sense the natural consequence of the capture of the ADR movement by lawyers intent on remaking all dispute resolution in the image of the courtroom. In international cases, this process has been attributed to an increased involvement on the part of American litigators in transnational arbitration;[142] the habits—and perceived duties—of such litigators, may, it is said, lead them "to push to enlarge the limited means of appeal and therefore expand the control of the courts over private justice."

The increasingly altered appearance of arbitration may also suggest that one of the principal messages of the ADR movement—that parties can experiment with dispute resolution, shaping and adapting different processes to meet their own particular needs—is at last beginning to percolate through the profession. On a more mundane level, the diffusion of information about particular innovations in dispute resolution will inevitably encourage, if not coerce, imitation. * * *

One can expect that it is attorneys least familiar and comfortable with the peculiar nature of arbitration who will be most tempted to tinker with the default rules that govern arbitral finality. Long-term, repeat users will by contrast have the greatest stake in the proper functioning of the system—and will be most likely to understand that combining private justice with judicial oversight of the merits represents some considerable conceptual confusion, certain over time to lessen the potential utility of arbitration to contracting parties. In this sense I am tempted to join Professor Lowenfeld in the hope that what he calls "arbitration plus" "does not catch on" generally.[148] But clearly there will be occasions when limits on the binding effect of an award may be critical to acceptance of the process: For some litigators, I imagine, arbitration will only be tolerated at all with what appears to be the added safeguard of a controlled outcome firmly grounded in "the law." In such cases, the persistent feeling that people will unfailingly make the wrong decisions if allowed to choose for themselves is a poor basis for lawmaking.

NOTES AND QUESTIONS

1. The standard of judicial review of arbitration awards "has taken on various hues and colorations in its formulations," some courts suggesting

---

142. *See* Yves Dezalay & Bryant G. Garth, Dealing in Virtue: International Commercial Arbitration and the Construction of a Transnational Legal Order 33–58 (1996)("Arbitration as Litigation"; electing arbitration, says an American practitioner, "doesn't mean that I necessarily want to give up all the trappings of full-scale litigation and what

might come with it"; "[o]ne understands the irritation of the founding fathers confronted by these newcomers who permit themselves to transform the nature of arbitration by multiplying the incidents of procedure and technical appeals").

148. Lowenfeld, supra n.76 at 17.

756 CHAPTER V ARBITRATION

that awards may be set aside if they are "arbitrary and capricious" or "completely irrational." "Although the differences in phraseology have caused a modicum of confusion, we deem them insignificant. We regard the standard of review undergirding these various formulations as identical, no matter how pleochroic their shadings and what terms of art have been employed to ensure that the arbitrator's decision relies on his interpretation of the contract as contrasted with his own beliefs of fairness and justice. However nattily wrapped, the packages are fungible." Advest, Inc. v. McCarthy, 914 F.2d 6, 9 (1st Cir.1990).

2. One California judge has advised commercial arbitrators that in the event "they feel impelled by some uncontrollable urge, literary fluency, good conscience, or mere garrulousness to express themselves about a case they have tried, the opinion should be a separate document and not part of the award itself." Loew's, Inc. v. Krug (Cal.Super.1953); *quoted in* Sherman, Analysis of Pennsylvania's Arbitration Act of 1980, 43 U.Pitts.L.Rev. 363, 397 n. 94 (1982). Or, as the AAA's Guide for Commercial Arbitrators (1985) puts it, "The obligations to the parties are better fulfilled when the award leaves no room for attack."

3. Section 20(d) of the Revised Uniform Arbitration Act permits a reviewing court to resubmit a case to the arbitrators "to clarify the award," and courts proceeding under the FAA have asserted a similar power to demand "clarification." Such power is occasionally used to determine the effect or scope of an award—to determine just what it was that the arbitrator had in fact decided. See, e.g., Diapulse Corp. of America v. Carba, Ltd., 626 F.2d 1108 (2d Cir.1980) (arbitrator's injunction against sale of competing "similar devices" was not adequately specific as to definition of devices nor as to geographical scope or duration of injunction). But such power is rarely if ever used to compel the arbitrator to explain his reasoning process.

See Sargent v. Paine Webber Jackson & Curtis, Inc., 882 F.2d 529 (D.C.Cir.1989). In this case the arbitrators, without any explanation, had awarded the plaintiffs a fraction of the amount they were claiming. The district court vacated the award and remanded to the arbitrators "for a full explanation of the manner in which damages were computed," reasoning that in order for the court to be able to engage in "meaningful judicial review" the "basis for the calculations underlying the award must be made known." However, the court of appeals reversed. It noted that "the absence of a duty to explain is presumably one of the reasons why arbitration should be faster and cheaper than an ordinary lawsuit"; the interest "in assuring that judgment be swift and economical * * * must generally prevail" over any interest "in rooting out possible error." See also Robbins v. Day, 954 F.2d 679 (11th Cir.1992) ("an arbitration award that only contains a lump sum award is presumed to be correct"; the burden is on the party seeking to overturn the award to refute "every rational basis upon which the arbitrator could have relied"); Container Technology Corp. v. J. Gadsden Pty., Ltd., 781 P.2d 119 (Colo.App.1989) (taking deposition of arbitrators is not permitted if the purpose is to inquire into their "thought processes").

4. Except in the most complex or technical cases, it is not common practice to make a record or transcript of the proceedings in commercial arbitration. See Martin Domke, Commercial Arbitration § 24:07 (rev. ed.). This of course reinforces the absence of a reasoned opinion in making the work of a reviewing court that much more problematical. See House Grain Co. v. Obst, 659 S.W.2d 903 (Tex.App.1983) (in absence of transcript, there was insufficient evidence to support trial court's finding that arbitration award was the result of "such gross mistake as would imply bad faith and failure to exercise honest judgment").

5. A common rationale for deference to arbitration is that the parties have bargained for the judgment of an arbitrator rather than a court to resolve their disputes and that this bargain, once made, should be respected. Might it follow that the scope of judicial review should be broader in arbitrations arising out of "adhesion" contracts? Consider, for example, the arbitration of uninsured motorist claims under standard automobile insurance policies. Is judicial deference due to an arbitrator's award of $500 (one-sixth of funeral expenses) to the widow of a 23–year old man with two children? Such an award was confirmed in In the Matter of the Arbitration of Torano and Motor Vehicle Accident Indemnification Corp., 15 N.Y.2d 882, 258 N.Y.S.2d 418, 206 N.E.2d 353 (N.Y. 1965). A dissenting judge noted that "[i]t is to incongruities of this sort that the critics of arbitration point when they argue that in the long run it is better to leave disposition of litigation with professional judges and not with occasional amateurs."

6. Is even greater judicial deference due to an award in an "interest" arbitration? Why should this be true? See Local 58, Int'l Brotherhood of Elec. Workers v. Southeastern Mich. Chapter, Nat'l Elec. Contractors Ass'n, Inc., 43 F.3d 1026 (6th Cir.1995) (because the arbitrator is "acting as a legislator, fashioning new contractual obligations" rather than "as a judicial officer, construing the terms of an existing agreement and applying them to a particular set of facts").

7. A number of states have enacted statutes that purport to govern international commercial arbitrations (that is, arbitrations arising out of contracts between parties of different nationalities or that envisage performance abroad). Such statutes are patterned after the "Model Law" adopted by UNCITRAL in 1985, and provide—in accordance with the general understanding in international arbitration—that the arbitral tribunal may "decide ex aequo and bono * * * if the parties have expressly authorized it to do so." See, e.g., Cal.Code Civ.Pro. § 1297.284; Tex. Int'l Commercial Arbitration and Conciliation Act, Tex.Civ.Prac. & Rem.Code § 172.251(d). What is the effect of such provisions? Are these statutes not in fact more restrictive than the general practice in American commercial arbitration? After all, isn't it true that when American arbitrators decide *ex aequo et bono,* they "do not think of themselves as doing anything special"? See W. Laurence Craig, William Park, & Jan Paulsson, International Chamber of Commerce Arbitration 110 (3rd ed. 2000); see also Rene David, Arbitration in International Trade 119, 332 (1985).

8. Imagine that you have agreed to act as arbitrator in one of the cases discussed in note 3. Will the process by which you reach a decision be different depending on whether you are obligated to write an opinion which explains and justifies the reasons for your result? In what ways? Consider the following excerpt.

Alan Rau, On Integrity in Private Judging

14 Arbitration International 115, 146–150 (1998)

It is a familiar enough proposition that an arbitrator's freedom from the need to explain or justify his award is closely linked to his lack of accountability in terms of judicial review: The naked award that is the norm in domestic commercial arbitrations can be explained as much by a desire to insulate decisions from judicial scrutiny as to any desire to avoid the delay or added expense that written opinions would entail. And this tactic of ensuring the finality of arbitration by harnessing Delphic decisions to a hard-to-rebut presumption of validity has been extremely effective. Conversely, one can expect that any attempt to impose reasoned awards on arbitrators will be motivated at least in part by the desire to expand judicial supervision of the process.

For arbitrators as for jurors, our present lack of accountability can be both liberating and intoxicating. And for arbitrators and jurors equally, decisionmaking that is so safe and easy can just as readily lead to lazy and uninformed judgment—where minds have not been concentrated nor strenuous efforts made to question initial impulses.[149] From this point of view, reasoned opinions can be seen as one means of imposing transparency on the decisionmaking process and in particular, of imposing a certain self-discipline on the decisionmakers themselves. This is the phenomenon in which the judge or arbitrator supposedly finds—at the point where it becomes necessary to turn inclination into reasoned judgment—that it simply "will not write":[150] Forced to think through the implications of his

---

149. See Christine Cooper, 'Where Are We Going with Gilmer?—Some Ruminations on the Arbitration of Discrimination Claims, 11 St Louis U. Pub. Law. Rev. 203, 219 (1992)(an arbitrator "who is not a professional arbitrator and who knows the scope of judicial review cannot be expected to view the case as seriously as a federal judge who is developing public law"); Margaret Jacobs, "Men's Club: Riding Crop and Slurs: How Wall Street Dealt With a Sex–Bias Case," Wall St J, June 9, 1994, at A 1, A8 (arbitrator in employment discrimination case explained that "[u]sually you see and hear things and you get a feeling, and the decision is based on that").

I think it would be a serious error, though, to underestimate the sobering and disciplining effects on decisionmaking that

one sees simply as a result of deliberation on a panel of three arbitrators—especially when the members of the panel are experienced attorneys and businesspeople, willing to invest some care in taking apart the elements of a dispute, and anxious to demonstrate to their colleagues that they have done so.

150. See * * * Frederick Schauer, Giving Reasons, 47 Stan. L. Rev. 633, 652 (1995); see also Rt. Hon. Lord Justice Bingham, Reasons and Reasons for Reasons: Differences Between a Court Judgment and an Arbitration Award, 4 Arb. Int'l 141, 143 (1988) ("I cannot, I hope, be the only person who has sat down to write a judgment, having formed the view that A must win, only to find in the course of composition that there are no sustainable grounds for that conclusion and that on any rational analysis B must succeed").

decision, he may in the course of explanation be surprised to find that it is not internally consistent, that it does not take account of all relevant interests, that it overlooks authority or ignores factual complexities. "[W]hen institutional designers have grounds for believing that decisions will systematically be the product of bias, self-interest, insufficient reflection, or simply excess haste, requiring decisionmakers to give reasons may counteract some of these tendencies."[151]

However, one need not be inordinately cynical to suspect that in arbitration, a requirement of reasoned awards would be somewhat less likely to affect outcomes in this way than it would be to serve merely as a challenge to an arbitrator's craftsmanship. It is hard to take issue with the proposition that a mandate to give reasons will "drive out illegitimate reasons when they are the only plausible explanation for particular outcomes"[152]—but surely in most cases we can expect the qualifying phrase to swallow up whatever possible interest inheres in the original claim. Surely an arbitrator obligated to make a reasoned award may be expected to deploy his rhetorical ability, ingenuity, creativity and imagination in articulating the narrowest, the most plausible, or the most conventional rationale for his decision—all in the interest of commanding the acquiescence of the disputing parties or a reviewing court.[153] The claim here is not that reasoned opinions must always and necessarily be products of a conscious "Houdini-like manipulation"—when they are not indeed the result of self-deception or rationalization[154]—although this will very often be the case. The point is just that even under the very best of circumstances, the process of crafting reasoned awards will not be congruent with the decision-making process; the award must be an imperfect "reconstruction" after the fact of actual decision, the product of a struggle to marshal arguments in support of the result in such a way that it will "pass without objection in the trade."

European academics and arbitrators, accustomed to reasoned awards as a matter of course, often find it paradoxical that it is only in this country—where a common law, case-based jurisprudence has become so highly developed—that we are so willing to dispense with such opinions from arbitrators. But as with most paradoxes, this observation makes

151. Schauer, supra n. 150 at 657. The CPR's "Non–Administered Arbitration Rules" provide that awards "shall state the reasoning on which the award rests unless the parties agree otherwise," Rule 13.2. In its Commentary, the drafting Committee suggested that it would be "good discipline for arbitrators to require them to spell out their reasoning. Sometimes this process gives rise to second thoughts as to the soundness of the result."

152. Schauer, supra n.150 at 657–58.

153. This of course has been a commonplace of Realist insight for some time. See, e.g., Letter from O.W. Holmes, Jr. to

Harold Laski, 19 February 1920, in 1 Holmes–Laski Letters 243 (1953) ("I always say in conference that no case can be settled by general propositions, that I will admit any general proposition you like and decide the case either way") * * *.

154. See Scott Altman, Beyond Candor, 89 Mich. L. Rev. 296, 311 (1990) ("Houdini is willing to manipulate. By manipulation, I mean intentionally ignoring what one believes to be the most convincing argument and instead offering legal arguments that one believes to be less strong, while failing to disclose one's reasons for doing so").

possible a further leap of insight. I should think that it is precisely our common law background that enables us to do this: More particularly, it is precisely because our legal education has so carefully honed the skills of deconstructing judicial opinions, and so laboriously trained us to debunk their explanatory power, that we can no longer believe in the presence of such opinions as an indispensable element of a just decision.

* * *

While reasoned opinions often do not constrain choice as much as we would like to believe, there is also a counter-proposition that may seem somewhat paradoxical—that at the same time they often constrain more than we would think desirable. The case for "naked" awards thus has an important positive as well as a defensive aspect. Here the continual dialectic between "rule-based decisionmaking" on the one hand, and "particularistic decisionmaking" or "case by case optimization" on the other—which lies at the heart of the judicial enterprise—has a particular resonance. When we talk about the arbitrator's freedom from reasoned awards, it will frequently be the case that we are really talking about his freedom from over-broad rules or time-honored categories that might otherwise appear to dictate a result he would prefer to avoid. This is, then, a freedom that makes possible an arbitrator's flexibility in decisionmaking and a maximum attention to context.

Some concrete examples may illustrate the point. Where a buyer has refused to perform under an installment sales contract, an arbitrator's decision may award damages to the seller for breach but at the same time relieve the buyer of any further performance. As a teacher of Contracts, I would find it rather difficult to rationalize this result in doctrinal terms—but it may nevertheless make some rough sense in terms of the business situation and the equities of the parties. Or again, a strong claim may be made based on fraud for the rescission of a joint venture agreement; the arbitrators may be sympathetic to the claim but feel that the plaintiff is at least in part responsible for its own dilemma and at least in part to blame for its reliance—and so they may resort to the analogy of "comparative negligence" to reduce its recovery. Here too, lawyer-arbitrators obligated to justify this result in the form of a reasoned opinion might well feel the need to do so in terms of existing contract doctrine: Should they find that they are not in fact up to the task, they would inexorably be led to apply "that most ubiquitous of principles, winner-take-all, which is more typical of a judicial forum."

It has been suggested that a major source of the common law's commitment to an "all-or-nothing bias" has been the "combative aspects of the search for reality in our courts": It is a "reflection of the egocentric dialectic of the adversary system," and of our "fighting instinct." But the prevalence of hard-fought arbitrations suggests that this may give us at best an incomplete account. Perhaps a more satisfactory explanation might be found in the mandate to our courts to rationalize results in written opinions. It is striking that by contrast to the judicial forum, arbitration shares with other processes of private settlement two major characteristics:

both a tendency to look for intermediate solutions—responsive to the uniqueness of each dispute—and the absence of any need to justify the outcome.

So a naked award in the cases I mentioned above might appear at first glance to be nothing more than further examples of unprincipled arbitral "compromise". Yet such awards do not readily fit our usual understanding of "compromise" as a response to factual or legal indeterminacy, or as the reflection of an arbitrator's insecurity of tenure, or of his inadequate energy or care. Still less do they strike us as a kind of "formless and unpredictable qadi justice." Lack of a reasoned opinion here may make possible an arbitral decisionmaking which, while departing from the judicial model, is nevertheless infused with attention to such things as commercial understanding, good business practice and notions of honorable behavior, and with practical reasoning from familiar legal norms.[164] And we should remember that private dispute settlement—which lacks any adjudicative dimension whatever—may often work in the same way. In a sense, then, we are returning here to where we began—with the premise that the process of arbitration can only be understood in terms of bargain and contract, as part of a private exercise in the planning of transactions.

Note: Judicial Review of Awards and "Public Policy"

At the end of his shift a worker suffered a nervous breakdown; he "flew into a rage," attacked other employees, and damaged company property. He was discharged and later spent 30 days in a hospital psychiatric ward. The arbitrator found that the likelihood of a recurrence was "remote" and that he was "not at fault for his outburst"; the company was ordered to reinstate him. The district court vacated the award, noting "public policy concerns regarding the safety of the workplace." The Court of Appeals reversed, E.I. DuPont de Nemours & Co. v. Grasselli Employees Ind. Ass. of East Chicago, Inc., 790 F.2d 611 (7th Cir.1986). In his concurring opinion, Judge Easterbrook wrote:

> Suppose DuPont's contract expressly excused a single psychotic tantrum, provided the problem was unlikely to recur, or suppose a contract excused a single episode of larceny from the employer. If the firm, honestly implementing its contract with the employees, reinstated the berserker or the thief (or never discharged him), no public policy would stand in the way. If the person's immediate supervisor fired him, and someone higher in the line of command reversed that decision as a result of a grievance, there would be no greater reason for review. A contract of arbitration transfers the power of this manager to the arbitrator. If the arbitrator carries out the contract, the decision should be treated the same as the management's own. Firms may place

---

164. Cf. Lisa Bernstein, Opting Out of the Legal System: Extralegal Contractual Relations in the Diamond Industry, 21 J. Leg. Stud. 115, 127 (1992)(arbitrators in the diamond industry's arbitration mechanism "explain that they decide complex cases on the basis of trade custom and usage, a little common sense, some Jewish law, and, last, common-law legal principles").

762 CHAPTER V ARBITRATION

decisionmaking authority where they please, and the Arbitration Act restricts the court to ascertaining that the arbitrator was a faithful agent of the contracting parties. * * *

[I]f because of potential liability to its workers for having an unsafe working environment no firm would adopt a clause giving a psychotic worker a second chance, an arbitrator who provides a second chance is expressing sympathy, administering home-brewed justice rather than the contract. Public policy may be a useful guide to the sorts of provisions that will not appear in contracts, and when no one will write the provisions expressly arbitrators may not infer them. If a court concludes, however, that the implication of a rule by the arbitrator is not a frolic, that a rational firm could have such a rule and apply it prospectively, then the only further role for public policy is to determine whether the rule violates positive law.

The Supreme Court seems to have adopted Judge Easterbrook's position in Eastern Associated Coal Corp. v. United Mine Workers of America, 531 U.S. 57, 121 S.Ct. 462 (2000). Here a truck driver twice tested positive for marijuana, was twice discharged, and was twice reinstated by arbitrators who found that there was no "just cause" for termination. (The second arbitrator made reinstatement conditional on suspension without pay, participation in a substance abuse program, and continued random drug testing). The employer claimed that "considerations of public policy" made the second award unenforceable, but both the lower courts and the Supreme Court disagreed. Six Justices joined Justice Breyer's opinion:

In considering this claim, we must assume that the collective-bargaining agreement itself calls for [the employee's] reinstatement. That is because both employer and union have granted to the arbitrator the authority to interpret the meaning of their contract's language, including such words as "just cause." They have "bargained for" the "arbitrator's construction" of their agreement. * * * Hence we must treat the arbitrator's award as if it represented an agreement between [the employer] and the union as to the proper meaning of the contract's words "just cause." For present purposes, the award is not distinguishable form the contractual agreement. * * * To put the question more specifically, does a contractual agreement to reinstate [the employee] with specified conditions run contrary to an explicit, well-defined, and dominant public policy, as ascertained by reference to positive law and not from general considerations of supposed public interests?

In this case, "neither Congress [in the Omnibus Transportation Employee Testing Act of 1991, 49 U.S.C. § 31306(b)(1)(A)] nor the Secretary [of Transportation] has seen fit to mandate the discharge of a worker who twice tests positive for drugs."

NOTES AND QUESTIONS

1. During an overnight layover the "Pilot in Command" of a Delta flight consumed large quantities of alcohol, and when he arrived at the airport the next morning shortly before departure, "[h]is face was very red; his eyes were glassed over; and he appeared to be very disoriented." He nevertheless flew the aircraft between Bangor, Maine and Boston. A later blood test indicated that at the time of the flight his blood alcohol level was .13. The pilot's license was suspended by the FAA, and Delta discharged him. An arbitrator, however, found that the discharge was "without just cause," since Delta had not enforced its alcohol policy "uniformly or fairly" and the pilot, after being discharged, "had pursued a rehabilitation program with effective results." Delta was ordered to reinstate him and to cooperate with him and with the FAA so that he could be relicensed. The court set aside the award: "We emphasize that we have found no state that approves of operation of an aircraft while drunk." Delta Air Lines, Inc. v. Air Line Pilots Ass'n Int'l, 861 F.2d 665 (11th Cir.1988).

An arbitrator concluded that a registered nurse had engaged in "serious substandard nursing practices"—failure to monitor the condition of a four-month old infant admitted to hospital with second-degree burns—and that her conduct had contributed to the baby's death. The arbitrator nevertheless ordered reinstatement, finding that the nurse had not "callously disregarded" the welfare of the patient, and that discharge was "too harsh" a sanction given the nurse's unblemished ten-year record. The court vacated the award: "If the recognized policy favoring optimal health care is to have practical meaning, an otherwise preventable death occasioned by negligence simply must warrant the most severe employment penalty—discharge." "This Court has found no case where reinstatement has been ordered against a public policy argument after a preventable death." Boston Medical Center v. Service Employees Int'l Union, 113 F.Supp. 2d 169 (D.Mass.2000).

Is it likely that in these cases the process of labor arbitration—so oriented towards "industrial due process" and the maintenance of good working relations between employer and union—will adequately protect the interests of society generally? How would Judge Easterbrook or Justice Breyer have voted to decide these cases?

2. Stroehmann Bakeries discharged one of its drivers for "immoral conduct while on duty" after a store clerk complained that he had sexually assaulted her when he was making a delivery. The arbitrator found that the driver had been dismissed without just cause, and the employer was ordered to reinstate him with full back pay and benefits. "Considerations referred to by the arbitrator in conjecturing on the matter" included the observation that the victim lacked a social life, had a female roommate, was "unattractive and frustrated," and that she might have fabricated the entire incident in order to "titillate herself and attract her mother's caring attention." The court vacated the award and remanded the matter for a *de novo* hearing before another arbitrator: The arbitrator's "reasoning process, language, tone, considerations, and award violate public policy." "The manner in which the award was reached could easily deter other victims," and the award also "sends a message" to the company's other employees and to the public "that complaints of sexual assault are not treated

764 CHAPTER V ARBITRATION

seriously [or] sensitively." Stroehmann Bakeries, Inc. v. Local 776 Int'l Brotherhood of Teamsters, 762 F.Supp. 1187 (M.D.Pa.1991), aff'd, 969 F.2d 1436 (3d Cir.1992). Cf. Note, Arbitral Decision–Making and Legal "Rules," supra.

3. In an effort to promote the sale of its fighter aircraft to Saudi Arabia, Northrop entered into a "marketing agreement" with Triad. In exchange for commissions on sales, Triad was to act as Northrop's exclusive agent in soliciting contracts for aircraft for the Saudi Air Force. Some of the sales were to be made through the United States Government as a result of contracts between Northrop and the Defense Department. The agreement was to be governed by California law and contained an arbitration clause.

Several years later the Saudi Arabian government issued a decree prohibiting the payment of commissions in connection with armaments contracts, and requiring that existing obligations for the payment of commissions be suspended. Northrop ceased paying commissions and the dispute was submitted to arbitrators, who awarded Triad over $31 million. The district court held that the arbitrator's award was "contrary to law and public policy." California's Civil Code provides that "performance of an obligation" is "excused" when it is "prevented * * * by the operation of law." The court interpreted the Saudi decree as applying to and indeed "formulated specifically with the Northrop–Triad agency relationship in mind." In addition, it noted that the Defense Department "wished to conform its policy precisely to that announced by Saudi Arabia" and was now requiring that arms suppliers under contract to the Department certify that their price included no costs for agent's commissions not approved by the purchasing country.

On appeal, what result? See Northrop Corp. v. Triad Int'l Marketing S.A., 811 F.2d 1265 (9th Cir.1987).

4. Party Yards borrowed $160,000 from Templeton in order to meet production costs and expenses in connection with an important contract. In addition to interest at 18% (the maximum interest rate allowed under state usury laws), Templeton was to receive a "commission" on the gross revenue of all of Party Yard products for a period ending twenty years after Templeton's death. The contract contained an arbitration clause and the lower court ordered arbitration; the court of appeals, however, found "that the trial court's reliance on *Prima Paint* was misplaced because that case is inapplicable": "A party who alleges and offers colorable evidence that a contract is illegal cannot be compelled to arbitrate the threshold issue of the existence of the agreement to arbitrate; only a court can make that determination." "A court's failure to first determine whether the contract violates Florida's usury laws could breathe life into a contract that not only violates state law, but also is criminal in nature, by use of an arbitration provision." Party Yards, Inc. v. Templeton, 751 So.2d 121 (Fla.App.2000).

Do you agree that "the separability doctrine (à la *Prima Paint*) should have insulated the arbitral clause from automatic ricochet invalidity"? World Arb. & Med. Rep., April 2000, at p. 103. See p. 696, supra. Cf.

Harbour Assurance Co. (UK) Ltd. v. Kansa General Int'l Ins. Co. Ltd., [1993] Q.B. 701, 704 (C.A. 1993)(Hoffmann, L.J.):

> [I]t is particularly necessary to have regard to the purpose and policy of the rule which invalidates the contract and to ask * * * whether the rule strikes down the arbitration clause as well. There may be cases in which the policy of the rule is such that it would be liable to be defeated by allowing the issue to be determined by a tribunal chosen by the parties. This may be especially true of *contrats d'adhésion* in which the arbitrator is in practice the choice of the dominant party. Thus, saying that arbitration clauses, because separable, are never affected by the illegality of the principal contract is as much a case of false logic as saying that they must be.

5. A "weighmaster" at a town landfill was terminated after pleading nolo contendere to the charge of larceny by embezzlement for pocketing daily landfill fees. He purportedly made the decision to enter the plea because he could not afford the legal fees he would incur by contesting the charges at trial. Because the city relied exclusively on the plea, and did not seek to independently prove the charge, an arbitrator found that the city lacked "just cause" for the termination and ordered reinstatement. The court vacated the award on the ground that it "violated the clear public policy against embezzlement," which "encompasses the policy that an employer should not be compelled to reinstate an employee who has been convicted of embezzling the employer's funds, irrespective of whether the conviction followed a trial, a guilty plea or a nolo contendere plea." The employer "is entitled to expect that he be able to trust an employee who is in a position of financial responsibility." Town of Groton v. United Steelworkers of America, 254 Conn. 35, 757 A.2d 501 (Conn. 2000).

What exactly is the "public policy" implicated here? Is the term being used in the same sense as in the foregoing cases?

6. The United Nations Convention on the Recognition and Enforcement of Foreign Arbitral Awards (the "New York Convention") has been ratified by most important commercial nations, including the United States. See Appendix G. This Convention requires participating states to enforce commercial arbitration awards, rendered in another state, with the same effect as if they were domestic awards (Art. III). There are a number of exceptions to the mandate of Art. III.

See, for example, Art. V(2)(b). American cases have narrowly confined the defense of Art. V(2)(b) to the exceptional situation "where enforcement would violate the forum country's most basic notions of morality and justice." Parsons & Whittemore Overseas Co., Inc. v. Société Générale de l'Industrie du Papier (Rakta), 508 F.2d 969, 974 (2d Cir.1974). See also Brandeis Intsel Ltd. v. Calabrian Chemicals Corp., 656 F.Supp. 160 (S.D.N.Y.1987) (defense of "manifest disregard of the law" does not rise to the level of a "public policy" violation within the meaning of Art. V).

766 CHAPTER V ARBITRATION

b. "PUBLIC POLICY" AND ARBITRABILITY

Mitsubishi Motors Corp. v. Soler Chrysler–Plymouth, Inc.

Supreme Court of the United States, 1985.
473 U.S. 614, 105 S.Ct. 3346, 87 L.Ed.2d 444.

■ JUSTICE BLACKMUN delivered the opinion of the Court.

The principal question presented by these cases is the arbitrability, pursuant to the federal Arbitration Act and the Convention on the Recognition and Enforcement of Foreign Arbitral Awards (Convention), of claims arising under the Sherman Act, 15 U.S.C. § 1 et seq., and encompassed within a valid arbitration clause in an agreement embodying an international commercial transaction.

I

Petitioner-cross-respondent Mitsubishi Motors Corporation (Mitsubishi) is a Japanese corporation which manufactures automobiles and has its principal place of business in Tokyo, Japan. Mitsubishi is the product of a joint venture between, on the one hand, Chrysler International, S.A. ("CISA"), a Swiss corporation registered in Geneva and wholly owned by Chrysler Corporation, and, on the other, Mitsubishi Heavy Industries, Inc., a Japanese corporation. The aim of the joint venture was the distribution through Chrysler dealers outside the continental United States of vehicles manufactured by Mitsubishi and bearing Chrysler and Mitsubishi trademarks. Respondent-cross-respondent Soler Chrysler–Plymouth, Inc. (Soler), is a Puerto Rico corporation with its principal place of business in Pueblo Viejo, Guaynabo, Puerto Rico.

On October 31, 1979, Soler entered into a Distributor Agreement with CISA which provided for the sale by Soler of Mitsubishi-manufactured vehicles within a designated area, including metropolitan San Juan. On the same date, CISA, Soler, and Mitsubishi entered into a Sales Procedure Agreement (Sales Agreement) which, referring to the Distributor Agreement, provided for the direct sale of Mitsubishi products to Soler and governed the terms and conditions of such sales. Paragraph VI of the Sales Agreement, labeled "Arbitration of Certain Matters," provides:

> "All disputes, controversies or differences which may arise between [Mitsubishi] and [Soler] out of or in relation to Articles I–B through V of this Agreement or for the breach thereof, shall be finally settled by arbitration in Japan in accordance with the rules and regulations of the Japan Commercial Arbitration Association."

Initially, Soler did a brisk business in Mitsubishi-manufactured vehicles. As a result of its strong performance, its minimum sales volume, specified by Mitsubishi and CISA, and agreed to by Soler, for the 1981 model year was substantially increased. In early 1981, however, the new-car market slackened. Soler ran into serious difficulties in meeting the

C. ARBITRATION AND THE COURTS **767**

expected sales volume, and by the spring of 1981 it felt itself compelled to request that Mitsubishi delay or cancel shipment of several orders. About the same time, Soler attempted to arrange for the transshipment of a quantity of its vehicles for sale in the continental United States and Latin America. Mitsubishi and CISA, however, refused permission for any such diversion, citing a variety of reasons, and no vehicles were transshipped. Attempts to work out these difficulties failed. Mitsubishi eventually withheld shipment of 966 vehicles, apparently representing orders placed for May, June, and July 1981 production, responsibility for which Soler disclaimed in February 1982.

The following month, Mitsubishi brought an action against Soler in the United States District Court for the District of Puerto Rico under the federal Arbitration Act and the Convention.[2] Mitsubishi sought an order to compel arbitration in accord with ¶ VI of the Sales Agreement. Shortly after filing the complaint, Mitsubishi filed a request for arbitration before the Japan Commercial Arbitration Association.

Soler denied the allegations and counterclaimed against both Mitsubishi and CISA. It alleged numerous breaches by Mitsubishi of the Sales Agreement, raised a pair of defamation claims, and asserted causes of action under the Sherman Act; the federal Automobile Dealers' Day in Court Act; the Puerto Rico competition statute; and the Puerto Rico Dealers' Contracts Act. In the counterclaim premised on the Sherman Act, Soler alleged that Mitsubishi and CISA had conspired to divide markets in restraint of trade. To effectuate the plan, according to Soler, Mitsubishi had refused to permit Soler to resell to buyers in North, Central, or South America vehicles it had obligated itself to purchase from Mitsubishi; had refused to ship ordered vehicles or the parts, such as heaters and defoggers, that would be necessary to permit Soler to make its vehicles suitable for resale outside Puerto Rico; and had coercively attempted to replace Soler and its other Puerto Rico distributors with a wholly owned subsidiary which would serve as the exclusive Mitsubishi distributor in Puerto Rico.

After a hearing, the District Court ordered Mitsubishi and Soler to arbitrate each of the issues raised in the complaint and in all the counterclaims save two and a portion of a third. [The Court of Appeals agreed that the arbitration clause "encompass[ed] virtually all the claims arising under the various statutes, including all those arising under the Sherman Act."[9]

---

2. The complaint alleged that Soler had failed to pay for 966 ordered vehicles; that it had failed to pay contractual "distress unit penalties," intended to reimburse Mitsubishi for storage costs and interest charges incurred because of Soler's failure to take shipment of ordered vehicles; that Soler's failure to fulfill warranty obligations threatened Mitsubishi's reputation and good will; * * * and that the Distributor and Sales Agreements had expired by their terms or, alternatively,

that Soler had surrendered its rights under the Sales Agreement.

9. As the Court of Appeals saw it, "[t]he question . . . is not whether the arbitration clause mentions antitrust or any other particular cause of action, but whether the factual allegations underlying Soler's counterclaims—and Mitsubishi's bona fide defenses to those counterclaims—are within the scope of the arbitration clause, whatever the legal labels attached to those allegations." * * *

768　CHAPTER V　ARBITRATION

It held, however, that arbitration of Soler's antitrust claims could not be compelled.]

* * *

II

At the outset, we address the contention raised in Soler's cross-petition that the arbitration clause at issue may not be read to encompass the statutory counterclaims stated in its answer to the complaint. In making this argument, Soler does not question the Court of Appeals' application of ¶ VI of the Sales Agreement to the disputes involved here as a matter of standard contract interpretation. Instead, it argues that as a matter of law a court may not construe an arbitration agreement to encompass claims arising out of statutes designed to protect a class to which the party resisting arbitration belongs "unless [that party] has expressly agreed" to arbitrate those claims, by which Soler presumably means that the arbitration clause must specifically mention the statute giving rise to the claims that a party to the clause seeks to arbitrate. Soler reasons that, because it falls within the class for whose benefit the federal and local antitrust laws and dealers' acts were passed, but the arbitration clause at issue does not mention these statutes or statutes in general, the clause cannot be read to contemplate arbitration of these statutory claims.

We do not agree, for we find no warrant in the Arbitration Act for implying in every contract within its ken a presumption against arbitration of statutory claims. * * *

[T]he first task of a court asked to compel arbitration of a dispute is to determine whether the parties agreed to arbitrate that dispute. The court is to make this determination by applying the "federal substantive law of arbitrability, applicable to any arbitration agreement within the coverage of the Act." And that body of law counsels "that * * * any doubts concerning the scope of arbitrable issues should be resolved in favor of arbitration * * *." Thus, as with any other contract, the parties' intentions control, but those intentions are generously construed as to issues of arbitrability.

There is no reason to depart from these guidelines where a party bound by an arbitration agreement raises claims founded on statutory rights. * * * Of course, courts should remain attuned to well-supported claims that the agreement to arbitrate resulted from the sort of fraud or overwhelming economic power that would provide grounds "for the revoca-

The court read the Sherman Act counterclaim to raise issues of wrongful termination of Soler's distributorship, wrongful failure to ship ordered parts and vehicles, and wrongful refusal to permit transshipment of stock to the United States and Latin America. Because the existence of just cause for termination turned on Mitsubishi's allegations that Soler had breached the Sales Agreement by, for example, failing to pay for ordered vehicles, the wrongful termination claim implicated [several] provisions within the arbitration clause [including]: Article I–D(1), which rendered a dealer's orders "firm" * * * and Article I–F, specifying payment obligations and procedures. The court therefore held the arbitration clause to cover this dispute.

* * *

C. Arbitration and the Courts

tion of any contract." [FAA, § 2]. But, absent such compelling considerations, the Act itself provides no basis for disfavoring agreements to arbitrate statutory claims by skewing the otherwise hospitable inquiry into arbitrability.

That is not to say that all controversies implicating statutory rights are suitable for arbitration. There is no reason to distort the process of contract interpretation, however, in order to ferret out the inappropriate. Just as it is the congressional policy manifested in the federal Arbitration Act that requires courts liberally to construe the scope of arbitration agreements covered by that Act, it is the congressional intention expressed in some other statute on which the courts must rely to identify any category of claims as to which agreements to arbitrate will be held unenforceable. For that reason, Soler's concern for statutorily protected classes provides no reason to color the lens through which the arbitration clause is read. By agreeing to arbitrate a statutory claim, a party does not forego the substantive rights afforded by the statute; it only submits to their resolution in an arbitral, rather than a judicial, forum. It trades the procedures and opportunity for review of the courtroom for the simplicity, informality, and expedition of arbitration. We must assume that if Congress intended the substantive protection afforded by a given statute to include protection against waiver of the right to a judicial forum, that intention will be deducible from text or legislative history. Having made the bargain to arbitrate, the party should be held to it unless Congress itself has evinced an intention to preclude a waiver of judicial remedies for the statutory rights at issue. Nothing, in the meantime, prevents a party from excluding statutory claims from the scope of an agreement to arbitrate.

In sum, the Court of Appeals correctly conducted a two-step inquiry, first determining whether the parties' agreement to arbitrate reached the statutory issues, and then, upon finding it did, considering whether legal constraints external to the parties' agreement foreclosed the arbitration of those claims. We endorse its rejection of Soler's proposed rule of arbitration-clause construction.

III

We now turn to consider whether Soler's antitrust claims are nonarbitrable even though it has agreed to arbitrate them. In holding that they are not, the Court of Appeals followed the decision of the Second Circuit in *American Safety Equipment Corp. v. J.P. Maguire & Co.*, 391 F.2d 821 (1968). Notwithstanding the absence of any explicit support for such an exception in either the Sherman Act or the federal Arbitration Act, the Second Circuit there reasoned that "the pervasive public interest in enforcement of the antitrust laws, and the nature of the claims that arise in such cases, combine to make ... antitrust claims ... inappropriate for arbitration." We find it unnecessary to assess the legitimacy of the *American Safety* doctrine as applied to agreements to arbitrate arising from domestic transactions. As in *Scherk v. Alberto–Culver Co.*, 417 U.S. 506 (1974), we conclude that concerns of international comity, respect for the

CHAPTER V ARBITRATION

capacities of foreign and transnational tribunals, and sensitivity to the need of the international commercial system for predictability in the resolution of disputes require that we enforce the parties' agreement, even assuming that a contrary result would be forthcoming in a domestic context.

* * *

[The Court in *Scherk*] Court emphasized:

"A contractual provision specifying in advance the forum in which disputes shall be litigated and the law to be applied is ... an almost indispensable precondition to achievement of the orderliness and predictability essential to any international business transaction....

"A parochial refusal by the courts of one country to enforce an international arbitration agreement would not only frustrate these purposes, but would invite unseemly and mutually destructive jockeying by the parties to secure tactical litigation advantages.... [It would] damage the fabric of international commerce and trade, and imperil the willingness and ability of businessmen to enter into international commercial agreements."

* * *

Thus, we must weigh the concerns of *American Safety* against a strong belief in the efficacy of arbitral procedures for the resolution of international commercial disputes and an equal commitment to the enforcement of freely negotiated choice-of-forum clauses.

At the outset, we confess to some skepticism of certain aspects of the *American Safety* doctrine. As distilled by the First Circuit, the doctrine comprises four ingredients. First, private parties play a pivotal role in aiding governmental enforcement of the antitrust laws by means of the private action for treble damages. Second, "the strong possibility that contracts which generate antitrust disputes may be contracts of adhesion militates against automatic forum determination by contract." Third, antitrust issues, prone to complication, require sophisticated legal and economic analysis, and thus are "ill-adapted to strengths of the arbitral process, i.e., expedition, minimal requirements of written rationale, simplicity, resort to basic concepts of common sense and simple equity." Finally, just as "issues of war and peace are too important to be vested in the generals, ... decisions as to antitrust regulation of business are too important to be lodged in arbitrators chosen from the business community—particularly those from a foreign community that has had no experience with or exposure to our law and values."

Initially, we find the second concern unjustified. The mere appearance of an antitrust dispute does not alone warrant invalidation of the selected forum on the undemonstrated assumption that the arbitration clause is tainted. A party resisting arbitration of course may attack directly the validity of the agreement to arbitrate. See *Prima Paint Corp.* Moreover, the party may attempt to make a showing that would warrant setting aside the forum-selection clause—that the agreement was "[a]ffected by fraud, undue influence, or overweening bargaining power"; that "enforcement would be unreasonable and unjust"; or that proceedings "in the contractual forum will be so gravely difficult and inconvenient that [the resisting party] will for all practical purposes be deprived of his day in court." But absent such a showing—and none was attempted here—there is no basis for assuming the forum inadequate or its selection unfair.

Next, potential complexity should not suffice to ward off arbitration. We might well have some doubt that even the courts following *American Safety* subscribe fully to the view that antitrust matters are inherently insusceptible to resolution by arbitration, as these same courts have agreed that an undertaking to arbitrate antitrust claims entered into after the dispute arises is acceptable. And the vertical restraints which most frequently give birth to antitrust claims covered by an arbitration agreement will not often occasion the monstrous proceedings that have given antitrust litigation an image of intractability. In any event, adaptability and access to expertise are hallmarks of arbitration. The anticipated subject matter of the dispute may be taken into account when the arbitrators are appointed, and arbitral rules typically provide for the participation of experts either employed by the parties or appointed by the tribunal. Moreover, it is often a judgment that streamlined proceedings and expeditious results will best serve their needs that cause parties to agree to arbitrate their disputes; it is typically a desire to keep the effort and expense required to resolve a dispute within manageable bounds that prompts them mutually to forgo access to judicial remedies. In sum, the factor of potential complexity alone does not persuade us that an arbitral tribunal could not properly handle an antitrust matter.

For similar reasons, we also reject the proposition that an arbitration panel will pose too great a danger of innate hostility to the constraints on business conduct that antitrust law imposes. International arbitrators frequently are drawn from the legal as well as the business community; where the dispute has an important legal component, the parties and the arbitral body with whose assistance they have agreed to settle their dispute can be expected to select arbitrators accordingly.[18] We decline to indulge the presumption that the parties and arbitral body conducting a proceeding will be unable or unwilling to retain competent, conscientious, and impartial arbitrators.

We are left, then, with the core of the *American Safety* doctrine—the fundamental importance to American democratic capitalism of the regime

---

18. * * * [T]he arbitration panel selected to hear the parties' claims here is composed of three Japanese lawyers, one a former law school dean, another a former judge, and the third a practicing attorney with American legal training who has written on Japanese antitrust law.

The Court of Appeals was concerned that international arbitrators would lack "experience with or exposure to our law and values."

The obstacles confronted by the arbitration panel in this case, however, should be no greater than those confronted by any judicial or arbitral tribunal required to determine foreign law. See, e.g., Fed.Rule Civ.Proc. 44.1. Moreover, while our attachment to the antitrust laws may be stronger than most, many other countries, including Japan, have similar bodies of competition law.

772   CHAPTER V   ARBITRATION

of the antitrust laws. Without doubt, the private cause of action plays a central role in enforcing this regime. As the Court of Appeals pointed out:

> "A claim under the antitrust laws is not merely a private matter. The Sherman Act is designed to promote the national interest in a competitive economy; thus, the plaintiff asserting his rights under the Act has been likened to a private attorney-general who protects the public's interest."

The treble-damages provision wielded by the private litigant is a chief tool in the antitrust enforcement scheme, posing a crucial deterrent to potential violators.

The importance of the private damages remedy, however, does not compel the conclusion that it may not be sought outside an American court. Notwithstanding its important incidental policing function, the treble-damages cause of action conferred on private parties by § 4 of the Clayton Act, and pursued by Soler here by way of its third counterclaim, seeks primarily to enable an injured competitor to gain compensation for that injury.

> "Section 4 ... is in essence a remedial provision. It provides treble damages to '[a]ny person who shall be injured in his business or property by reason of anything forbidden in the antitrust laws....' Of course, treble damages also play an important role in penalizing wrongdoers and deterring wrongdoing, as we also have frequently observed.... It nevertheless is true that the treble-damages provision, which makes awards available only to injured parties, and measures the awards by a multiple of the injury actually proved, is designed primarily as a remedy." *Brunswick Corp. v. Pueblo Bowl–O–Mat, Inc.,* 429 U.S. 477, 485–486 (1977).

* * *

There is no reason to assume at the outset of the dispute that international arbitration will not provide an adequate mechanism. To be sure, the international arbitral tribunal owes no prior allegiance to the legal norms of particular states; hence, it has no direct obligation to vindicate their statutory dictates. The tribunal, however, is bound to effectuate the intentions of the parties. Where the parties have agreed that the arbitral body is to decide a defined set of claims which includes, as in these cases, those arising from the application of American antitrust law, the tribunal therefore should be bound to decide that dispute in accord with the national law giving rise to the claim.[19] And so long as the

---

19. In addition to the clause providing for arbitration before the Japan Commercial Arbitration Association, the Sales Agreement includes a choice-of-law clause which reads: "This Agreement is made in, and will be governed by and construed in all respects according to the laws of the Swiss Confederation as if entirely performed therein." The United States raises the possibility that the arbitral panel will read this provision not simply to govern interpretation of the contract terms, but wholly to displace American law even where it otherwise would apply. Brief for United States as *Amicus Curiae* 20. The International Chamber of Commerce opines that it is "[c]onceivabl[e], although we

C. ARBITRATION AND THE COURTS

773

prospective litigant effectively may vindicate its statutory cause of action in the arbitral forum, the statute will continue to serve both its remedial and deterrent function.

Having permitted the arbitration to go forward, the national courts of the United States will have the opportunity at the award enforcement stage to ensure that the legitimate interest in the enforcement of the antitrust laws has been addressed. The Convention reserves to each signatory country the right to refuse enforcement of an award where the "recognition or enforcement of the award would be contrary to the public policy of that country." Art. V(2)(b). While the efficacy of the arbitral process requires that substantive review at the award-enforcement stage remains minimal, it would not require intrusive inquiry to ascertain that the tribunal took cognizance of the antitrust claims and actually decided them.[20]

As international trade has expanded in recent decades, so too has the use of international arbitration to resolve disputes arising in the course of that trade. The controversies that international arbitral institutions are called upon to resolve have increased in diversity as well as in complexity. Yet the potential of these tribunals for efficient disposition of legal disagreements arising from commercial relations has not yet been tested. If they are to take a central place in the international legal order, national courts will need to "shake off the old judicial hostility to arbitration," and also their customary and understandable unwillingness to cede jurisdiction of a claim arising under domestic law to a foreign or transnational tribunal. To this extent, at least, it will be necessary for national courts to subordinate domestic notions of arbitrability to the international policy favoring commercial arbitration.

Accordingly, we "require this representative of the American business community to honor its bargain," by holding this agreement to arbitrate

---

believe it unlikely, [that] the arbitrators could consider Soler's affirmative claim of anti-competitive conduct by CISA and Mitsubishi to fall within the purview of this choice-of-law provision, with the result that it would be decided under Swiss law rather than U.S. Sherman Act." Brief for International Chamber of Commerce as *Amicus Curiae* 25. At oral argument, however, counsel for Mitsubishi conceded that American law applied to the antitrust claims and represented that the claims had been submitted to the arbitration panel in Japan on that basis. The record confirms that before the decision of the Court of Appeals the arbitral panel had taken these claims under submission.

We therefore have no occasion to speculate on this matter at this stage in the proceedings, when Mitsubishi seeks to enforce the agreement to arbitrate, not to enforce an award. Nor need we consider now the effect

of an arbitral tribunal's failure to take cognizance of the statutory cause of action on the claimant's capacity to reinitiate suit in federal court. We merely note that in the event the choice-of-forum and choice-of-law clauses operated in tandem as a prospective waiver of a party's right to pursue statutory remedies for antitrust violations, we would have little hesitation in condemning the agreement as against public policy.

20. See n. 19, supra. We note, for example, that the rules of the Japan Commercial Arbitration Association provide for the taking of a "summary record" of each hearing, for the stenographic recording of the proceedings where the tribunal so orders or a party requests one, and for a statement of reasons for the award unless the parties agree otherwise. * * *

774   CHAPTER V ARBITRATION

"enforce[able] ... in accord with the explicit provisions of the Arbitration Act."

The judgment of the Court of Appeals is affirmed in part and reversed in part, and the cases are remanded for further proceedings consistent with this opinion.

■ JUSTICE STEVENS, with whom JUSTICE BRENNAN joins, and with whom JUSTICE MARSHALL joins except as to Part II, dissenting.

One element of this rather complex litigation is a claim asserted by an American dealer in Plymouth automobiles that two major automobile companies are parties to an international cartel that has restrained competition in the American market. Pursuant to an agreement that is alleged to have violated § 1 of the Sherman Act, those companies allegedly prevented the dealer from transshipping some 966 surplus vehicles from Puerto Rico to other dealers in the American market.

The petitioner denies the truth of the dealer's allegations and takes the position that the validity of the antitrust claim must be resolved by an arbitration tribunal in Tokyo, Japan. Largely because the auto manufacturers' defense to the antitrust allegation is based on provisions in the dealer's franchise agreement, the Court of Appeals concluded that the arbitration clause in that agreement encompassed the antitrust claim. * * *

* * * Because I am convinced that the Court of Appeals' construction of the arbitration clause is erroneous, and because I strongly disagree with this Court's interpretation of the relevant federal statutes, I respectfully dissent. In my opinion, (1) a fair construction of the language in the arbitration clause in the parties' contract does not encompass a claim that auto manufacturers entered into a conspiracy in violation of the antitrust laws; (2) an arbitration clause should not normally be construed to cover a statutory remedy that it does not expressly identify; (3) Congress did not intend § 2 of the Federal Arbitration Act to apply to antitrust claims; and (4) Congress did not intend the Convention on the Recognition and Enforcement of Foreign Arbitral Awards to apply to disputes that are not covered by the Federal Arbitration Act.

* * *

Until today all of our cases enforcing agreements to arbitrate under the Arbitration Act have involved contract claims. * * * [T]his is the first time the Court has considered the question whether a standard arbitration clause referring to claims arising out of or relating to a contract should be construed to cover statutory claims that have only an indirect relationship to the contract. In my opinion, neither the Congress that enacted the Arbitration Act in 1925, nor the many parties who have agreed to such standard clauses, could have anticipated the Court's answer to that question.

* * *

In view of the Court's repeated recognition of the distinction between federal statutory rights and contractual rights, together with the undisputed historical fact that arbitration has functioned almost entirely in either the area of labor disputes or in "ordinary disputes between merchants as to questions of fact," it is reasonable to assume that most lawyers and executives would not expect the language in the standard arbitration clause to cover federal statutory claims. Thus, in my opinion, both a fair respect for the importance of the interests that Congress has identified as worthy of federal statutory protection, and a fair appraisal of the most likely understanding of the parties who sign agreements containing standard arbitration clauses, support a presumption that such clauses do not apply to federal statutory claims.

* * *

It was Chief Justice Hughes who characterized the Sherman Anti–Trust Act as "a charter of freedom" that may fairly be compared to a constitutional provision. * * * More recently, the Court described the weighty public interests underlying the basic philosophy of the statute:

> "Antitrust laws in general, and the Sherman Act in particular, are the Magna Carta of free enterprise. They are important to the preservation of economic freedom and our free-enterprise system as the Bill of Rights is to the protection of our fundamental personal freedoms. And the freedoms guaranteed each and every business, no matter how small, is the freedom to compete—to assert with vigor, imagination, devotion, and ingenuity whatever economic muscle it can muster." * * * *United States v. Topco Associates, Inc.,* 405 U.S. 596, 610 (1972).

The Sherman and Clayton Acts reflect Congress' appraisal of the value of economic freedom; they guarantee the vitality of the entrepreneurial spirit. Questions arising under these Acts are among the most important in public law.

The unique public interest in the enforcement of the antitrust laws is repeatedly reflected in the special remedial scheme enacted by Congress. Since its enactment in 1890, the Sherman Act has provided for public enforcement through criminal as well as civil sanctions.

* * *

The provision for mandatory treble damages—unique in federal law when the statute was enacted—provides a special incentive to the private enforcement of the statute, as well as an especially powerful deterrent to violators. What we have described as "the public interest in vigilant enforcement of antitrust laws through the instrumentality of the private treble damage action" is buttressed by the statutory mandate that the injured party also recover costs, "including a reasonable attorney's fee." The interest in wide and effective enforcement has thus, for almost a century, been vindicated by enlisting the assistance of "private Attorneys General"; we have always attached special importance to their role because "[e]very violation of the antitrust laws is a blow to the free-enterprise system envisaged by Congress."

There are, in addition, several unusual features of the antitrust enforcement scheme that unequivocally require rejection of any thought that Congress would tolerate private arbitration of antitrust claims in lieu of the statutory remedies that it fashioned. * * * [A]n antitrust treble damage case "can only be brought in a District Court of the United States." The determination that these cases are "too important to be decided otherwise than by competent tribunals" surely cannot allow private arbitrators to assume a jurisdiction that is denied to courts of the sovereign States.

* * *

Arbitration awards are only reviewable for manifest disregard of the law, and the rudimentary procedures which make arbitration so desirable in the context of a private dispute often mean that the record is so inadequate that the arbitrator's decision is virtually unreviewable.[31] Despotic decision making of this kind is fine for parties who are willing to agree in advance to settle for a best approximation of the correct result in order to resolve quickly and inexpensively any contractual dispute that may arise in an ongoing commercial relationship. Such informality, however, is simply unacceptable when every error may have devastating consequences for important businesses in our national economy and may undermine their ability to compete in world markets.[32] Instead of "muffling a grievance in the cloakroom of arbitration," the public interest in free competitive markets would be better served by having the issues resolved "in the light of impartial public court adjudication."

* * *

In my opinion, the elected representatives of the American people would not have us dispatch an American citizen to a foreign land in search of an uncertain remedy for the violation of a public right that is protected by the Sherman Act. This is especially so when there has been no genuine bargaining over the terms of the submission, and the arbitration remedy provided has not even the most elementary guarantees of fair process. Consideration of a fully developed record by a jury, instructed in the law by a federal judge, and subject to appellate review, is a surer guide to the competitive character of a commercial practice than the practically unreviewable judgment of a private arbitrator.

31. The arbitration procedure in this case does not provide any right to evidentiary discovery or a written decision, and requires that all proceedings be closed to the public. Moreover, Japanese arbitrators do not have the power of compulsory process to secure witnesses and documents, nor do witnesses who are available testify under oath. Cf. 9 U.S.C. § 7 (arbitrators may summon witnesses to attend proceedings and seek enforcement in a district court).

32. The greatest risk, of course, is that the arbitrator will condemn business practices under the antitrust laws that are efficient in a free competitive market. In the absence of a reviewable record, a reviewing district court would not be able to undo the damage wrought. Even a Government suit or an action by a private party might not be available to set aside the award.

C. ARBITRATION AND THE COURTS 777

Unlike the Congress that enacted the Sherman Act in 1890, the Court today does not seem to appreciate the value of economic freedom. I respectfully dissent.

NOTES AND QUESTIONS

1. Consider carefully footnote 19 to the Court's opinion in *Mitsubishi*. The ICC's concession that it was "unlikely" the arbitrators would apply Swiss law in deciding Soler's antitrust claims "came as a bad surprise to many long time users of ICC arbitration," according to one commentator: One of "the very basics" of arbitration is that it functions within the limits fixed by the agreement of the parties, and "what is indeed very unlikely, to say the least, is that arbitrators would accept to apply U.S. antitrust law to claims to be ruled, according to [the] parties' clear will, by Swiss law!" Werner, A Swiss Comment on *Mitsubishi*, 3 J. of Int'l Arb. 81, 83 (1986). Cf. Lowenfeld, The *Mitsubishi* Case: Another View, 2 Arb.Int'l 178, 186 (1986) ("antitrust law is 'mandatory law,' on the same level as export controls, criminal law, or tax law, i.e., law that cannot ordinarily be avoided by party choice of law in the same way that, for instance, otherwise applicable statutes of limitations, or law governing the extent of implied warranties, or the measure of damages for breach of contract, can be avoided by the parties through a choice of law clause."). The opposing views are canvassed thoroughly in Mayer, Mandatory Rules of Law in International Arbitration, 2 Arb.Int'l 274 (1986).

2. In PPG Industries, Inc. v. Pilkington PLC, 825 F.Supp. 1465 (D.Ariz. 1993), the contract between the parties contained a clause by which "the Agreement shall be governed by the laws of England." The court compelled arbitration but warned that:

> the Court may, and certainly will, withdraw the reference to arbitration if U.S. antitrust law does not govern the substantive resolution of [the plaintiff's] claims. In addition, the Court directs that any damages determination, or arbitral award, made by the arbitrators shall be determined according to U.S. antitrust law irrespective of any conflict that may exist between those laws and the laws of England.

Similar questions have arisen in a number of recent securities fraud cases brought against Lloyd's of London, in which underwriters have suffered massive losses arising out of liability for asbestos and toxic-waste damage. Standardized contracts in such cases did not mandate arbitration, but they commonly joined an English choice-of-law clause with a choice-of-forum clause giving jurisdiction to English courts. See, e.g., Haynsworth v. The Corporation, 121 F.3d 956 (5th Cir.1997)("The view that every foreign forum's remedies must duplicate those available under American law would render all forum selection clauses worthless and would severely hinder Americans' ability to participate in international commerce"; "[t]he plaintiffs' remedies in England are adequate to protect their interests and the policies behind the statutes at issue"); Lipcon v. Underwriters at Lloyd's, London, 148 F.3d 1285 (11th Cir.1998)("the Court in *Mitsubishi* recognized

778 CHAPTER V ARBITRATION

and affirmed *Scherk's* policy of treating international commercial agreements as *sui generis*"; "[w]e will not invalidate choice clauses ... simply because the remedies available in the contractually chosen forum are less favorable than those available in the courts of the United States"); Richards v. Lloyd's of London, 135 F.3d 1289 (9th Cir.1998)("Without question this case would be easier to decide if [footnote 19] in *Mitsubishi* had not been inserted").

3. How convincing is the Supreme Court's assurance that the arbitral award, once rendered, can be effectively reviewed at the enforcement stage to "ensure that the legitimate interest in the enforcement of the antitrust laws has been addressed"? In light of the highly restricted scope of judicial review of the merits of awards, is this a realistic prospect? Will it be enough if a reviewing court is satisfied that the Japanese arbitrators merely "took cognizance of the antitrust claims and actually decided them"? Or will *Mitsubishi* encourage courts to engage in a more extensive review of the substantive issues?

4. Professor Eric Posner notes that the *Mitsubishi* case has been much criticized on the ground that "the holding of the majority and the dicta in footnote 19 contradict each other": "If the Court meant to hold that all arbitration clauses must be enforced, then international arbitration will flourish but arbitrators will not respect mandatory rules in the hope of attracting clients." If, on the other hand, the Court included footnote 19 "in order to signal that courts will review arbitration clauses in de novo trials, then courts can ensure that mandatory rules are enforced but international arbitration will lose its value." Posner argues, however, that these polar solutions are not the only ones possible: The "optimal strategy" of courts may instead be to engage in *random* de novo review of awards—a strategy that would result "in arbitrators frequently respecting mandatory rules" (since they would "fear the possibility of de novo review"), and courts refraining from *always* reviewing arbitration awards ("creating savings in congestion"). And he goes on to argue that the Court in *Mitsubishi* implemented precisely this strategy ("though perhaps not intentionally")—by creating conditions of "ambiguous threat": If parties are "not sure whether American courts will review arbitration awards or not— and if American courts occasionally do review arbitration awards—that would be a good thing." Eric A. Posner, Arbitration and the Harmonization of International Commercial Law: A Defense of *Mitsubishi,* 39 Va. J. Int'l L. 647, 651–52, 667–68 (1999).

5. Justice Blackmun's opinion claims that the Court found it "unnecessary to assess the legitimacy of the *American Safety* doctrine as applied to agreements to arbitrate arising from domestic transactions." Is this disingenuous? Can the rationale of *Mitsubishi* possibly be limited to international arbitration? Or is an antitrust claim now arbitrable even if it arises out of a purely domestic transaction? See Nghiem v. NEC Electronic, Inc., 25 F.3d 1437 (9th Cir.1994) (referring to *Mitsubshi*'s "meticulous step-by-step disembowelment of the *American Safety* doctrine"); Kotam Electronics, Inc. v. JBL Consumer Products, Inc., 93 F.3d 724 (11th Cir.1996)(holding that arbitration agreements concerning domestic antitrust claims are enforceable "in light of *Mitsubishi* and its progeny, as well as the persuasive authority from our sister circuits").

6. ILC Peripherals Leasing Corp. v. International Business Machines Corp., 458 F.Supp. 423 (1978) was a suit against IBM for monopolizing or attempting to monopolize various markets in the computer industry. The trial lasted for five months and consumed 96 trial days; the parties called 87 witnesses whose testimony filled more than 19,000 pages of transcript. After deliberating for 19 days, the jury reported itself hopeless deadlocked, and the court declared a mistrial. "Throughout the trial, the court felt that the jury was having trouble grasping the concepts that were being discussed by the expert witnesses." Only one of the jurors had even "limited technical education." "While the court was appreciative of the effort they put into deciding the case, it is understandable that people with such backgrounds would have trouble applying concepts like cross-elasticity of supply and demand, market share and market power, reverse engineering, product interface manipulation, discriminatory pricing, barriers to entry, exclusionary leasing, entrepreneurial subsidiaries, subordinated debentures, stock options, modeling, and etc." Cf. John R. Allison, Arbitration Agreements and Antitrust Claims: The Need for Enhanced Accommodation of Conflicting Public Policies, 64 N. Car. L. Rev. 219., 246 (1986)("One is led to wonder whether the rule prohibiting arbitration of antitrust claims actually contributes to the interest that a party with a weak claim has in generating confusion.").

7. Separation agreements usually contain detailed provisions relating to the children of the marriage. Where children are involved, the unraveling of the family can never be complete, and so there will be a need to lay down ground rules for all sorts of matters: custody and visitation rights, child support, and various other continuing incidents of the family relationship (such as the choice of a school or summer camp, religious training, medical treatment, or trips and vacations). With increasing frequency, agreements provide that the inevitable disputes over such matters will be settled by arbitration. Some courts deny on grounds of "public policy" that such disputes are arbitrable. See, e.g., Glauber v. Glauber, 192 A.D.2d 94, 600 N.Y.S.2d 740 (App. Div. 1993) ("when circumstances require determining which living arrangements are in the best interests of children, the courts alone must undertake the task"). Other courts enforce arbitration agreements, but with the caveat that "a special review" of the resulting award is necessary: "The courts should conduct a de novo review unless it is clear on the face of the award that the award could not adversely affect the substantial best interests of the child." Faherty v. Faherty, 97 N.J. 99, 477 A.2d 1257 (N.J. 1984); see also Miller v. Miller, 423 Pa.Super. 162, 620 A.2d 1161 (Pa.Super.1993) ("an award rendered by an arbitration panel would be subject to the supervisory power of the court in its parens patriae capacity in a proceeding to determine the best interests of the child"; if the court finds that the award is in the child's best interests, "the court may adopt the decision as its own").

780   CHAPTER V ARBITRATION

What is the justification for compelling arbitration of a domestic dispute—but at the same time treating the process as something of a rehearsal for a separate judicial inquiry, with an inevitable duplication of time and expense? Are there aspects of arbitration that make it particularly attractive as a device for resolving domestic disputes over child support and custody? Cf. Agur v. Agur, 32 A.D.2d 16, 298 N.Y.S.2d 772 (App. Div. 1969) (separation agreement provided that custody disputes would be decided by three arbitrators, including an Orthodox rabbi, versed in "Jewish religious law"; court refused to order arbitration). One court has observed that "the process of arbitration, useful when the mundane matter of the amount of support is in issue, is less so when the delicate balancing of the factors comprising the best interests of a child is the issue. The judicial process is more broadly gauged and better suited in protecting these interests." Nestel v. Nestel, 38 A.D.2d 942, 331 N.Y.S.2d 241 (App. Div. 1972). What precisely do you think this means? Do you agree?

8. A law firm's partnership agreement provided for post-retirement benefits, but also called for the forfeiture of all such benefits if a partner engaged in a competing practice of law within three years after retirement. An arbitrator found that a former partner had forfeited his entitlement to post-employment benefits under this provision. On the partner's motion to vacate, the trial court declined to review the award de novo, giving "great deference" to the arbitrator's finding of fact and legal conclusions. The Supreme Court of Connecticut, however, concluded that the arbitrator's decision "implicated a legitimate public policy—facilitating clients' access to an attorney of their choice"—a policy that was embodied in Rule 5.6 of the Rules of Professional Conduct. [See Appendix D.] In such circumstances, the court held, the trial court should have conducted a de novo review: Given that "courts have greater expertise and knowledge" in the identification and application of state public policy, "it comports with logic for the court to review the arbitrator's interpretation of an ethics rule de novo rather than to leave it to the arbitrators themselves to attempt to apply pertinent public policy." "So too is a reviewing court better suited to evaluate whether certain facts, as found by the arbitrator, comport with the specific public policy that is at issue." Nevertheless, "adher[ing] to the long-standing principle that findings of fact are ordinarily left undisturbed upon judicial review," the court noted that it would "defer to the arbitrator's interpretation of the agreements regarding the scope of the forfeiture upon competition provision." Schoonmaker v. Cummings & Lockwood, 252 Conn. 416, 747 A.2d 1017 (Conn. 2000).

9. An important tenet of American patent law is that the validity of patents must be freely challengeable, so as not to impede free competition in the exploitation of the "public domain." Invalid patents are "vicious Zombis." Aero Spark Plug Co. v. B.G. Corp., 130 F.2d 290, 299 (2d Cir.1942) (Frank, J., concurring). Patent licensees, therefore, are free to attack the patents of their licensors. Lear, Inc. v. Adkins, 395 U.S. 653 (1969). And once a patent has been successfully challenged in court, its invalidity is established not only between the litigants but as to the world generally; the owner of the patent will be estopped from claiming infringement in a later suit against a third party. Blonder–Tongue Labs., Inc. v. University of Illinois Found., 402 U.S. 313 (1971).

Given this public interest in challenging invalid patents, it was traditionally assumed that patent disputes were not arbitrable. See, e.g., Diematic Mfg. Corp. v. Packaging Industries, Inc., 381 F.Supp. 1057 (S.D.N.Y. 1974), appeal dismissed, 516 F.2d 975 (2d Cir.1975) ("Questions of patent law are not mere private matters"). In 1982, however, Congress expressly authorized the arbitration of "any dispute relating to patent validity or infringement." 35 U.S.C.A. § 294. The statute provides that the arbitration award is to be "final and binding between the parties to the arbitration," but that it "shall have no force or effect on any other person." What does this language mean? See Goldstein, Arbitration of Disputes Relating to Patent Validity or Infringement, 72 Ill.Bar.J. 350, 351 (1984) ("phrase is intended to remove the defense of collateral estoppel and permit the patentee to enforce a patent against others").

It appears that as yet the potential for arbitration in patent cases has not been widely exploited. One recent survey of practice in patent disputes suggests that corporations "overwhelmingly favor arbitration for disputes involving smaller stakes," but "only a very small percentage prefer arbitration where the risks exceed six figures." Wesley & Peterson, "Patent Arbitration," BNA ADR Rep., vol. 4 no. 2 (1990), at 30. Similar results were found in Field & Rose, Prospects for ADR in Patent Disputes: An Empirical Assessment of Attorneys' Attitudes, 32 Idea 309, 317–18 (1992). Why might this be true?

10. The Magnuson–Moss Act, 15 U.S.C. § 2301, was enacted in 1974 "to make warranties on consumer products more readily understood and enforceable": It requires sellers or manufacturers who give written warranties on consumer products to "fully and conspicuously disclose in simple and readily understood language the terms and conditions" of their warranties, and lays down federal minimum standards that must be met before a warrantor can designate a warranty as a "full" (as opposed to a "limited") warranty. Consumers may bring claims "under a written warranty [or] implied warranty" in federal court, and prevailing plaintiffs may recover reasonable attorneys' fees in addition to damages. Warrantors are also encouraged to establish "informal dispute settlement procedures" under FTC guidelines: If the "written warranty" so provides, a consumer must "initially" resort to such procedure before bringing any suit under the Act; the decision in the "procedure" is, however, admissible in any later civil action.

May a seller or a manufacturer of a mobile home rely on a pre-dispute arbitration clause to force a warranty claim into an arbitration process intended to be binding on the consumer? A number of courts have recently held that the Magnuson–Moss Act makes such arbitration clauses unenforceable when a claim is made under a written warranty: "Congress's intent [was] that any non-judicial dispute resolution procedures would be non-binding, and [that] consumers would always retain the right of final access to court"; the "informal dispute resolution procedures" may there-

782 CHAPTER V ARBITRATION

fore be a "prerequisite, but not a bar, to relief in court." See Wilson v. Waverlee Homes, Inc., 954 F.Supp. 1530 (M.D.Ala.1997)(warranty claim against manufacturer, not a signatory to arbitration agreement; held, defendant may not, by relying on the agreement between the consumer and the dealer, "do by surrogate or vicarious means what it is forbidden to do on its own behalf"); Federal Trade Commission, Final Action Concerning Review of Interpretations of Magnuson–Moss Warranty Act, 64 Fed. Reg. 19700, 19708–09 (April 22, 1999)(FTC rules "will continue to prohibit warrantors from including [clauses in their contracts] that would require consumers to submit warranty disputes to binding arbitration," although "warrantors are not precluded from offering a binding arbitration option to consumers after a warranty dispute has arisen.") *Contra,* In re American Homestar of Lancaster, Inc., 50 S.W.3d 480 (Tex.2001)("we find no clear congressional intent in the Magnuson–Moss Act to override the FAA policy favoring arbitration"). Cf. Boyd v. Homes of Legend, Inc., 981 F.Supp. 1423 (M.D.Ala.1997)(warranty claim against dealer; "it is only with respect to *written* warranties that Congress sought in the Magnuson–Moss Act to protect consumers from exploitation by more powerful manufacturers and suppliers who desired to impose the requirement that disputes be resolved by binding arbitration"; the court could discern "no contrary congressional intent regarding binding arbitration of *non-written or implied warranty* claims").

11. Plaintiff, a minor, brought suit against Cigna Healthplans for medical malpractice, and also for violation of the California Consumer Legal Remedies Act [CLRA]—claiming that Cigna had deceptively advertised the quality of medical services which would be provided under its health care plan. Alleging that the plaintiff's mother had received "substandard prenatal medical services" that caused the plaintiff to suffer severe injuries at birth, the suit asked for actual and punitive damages and for "an order enjoining [Cigna's] deceptive practices." The trial court granted the motion to compel arbitration of the medical malpractice action, but denied the motion as to the CLRA claim, and Cigna appealed. The Supreme Court of California held that the plaintiff's damage claim under CLRA was indeed "fully arbitrable," but that his claim for an injunction was not. Distinguishing *Mitsubishi,* the court held that there was an "inherent conflict" between arbitration and the injunctive relief provisions of the CLRA: The "evident purpose" of the latter was not to "resolve a private dispute" or to "compensate for an individual wrong," but instead to "prohibit and enjoin conduct injurious to the general public"; in seeking an injunction, the plaintiff was in effect here "playing the role of a private attorney general." Furthermore, arbitration would not be a "suitable forum" because of "evident institutional shortcomings": A court, unlike an arbitrator, could "retain its jurisdiction over a public injunction until it is dissolved," providing "a necessary continuity and consistency for which a series of arbitrators is an inadequate substitute"; also unlike arbitrators, courts are "publicly accountable" and thus "the most appropriate overseers of injunctive remedies explicitly designed for public protection." Broughton v. Cigna

Healthplans of California, 21 Cal.4th 1066, 90 Cal.Rptr.2d 334, 988 P.2d 67 (Cal. 1999).

Note: Investor/Broker Disputes Under the Securities Acts

The Securities Act of 1933 imposes liability for making misleading statements in the sale of a security "by means of a prospectus or oral communication."[1] The SEC's Rule 10b–5, promulgated under the Securities Exchange Act of 1934, prohibits the making of false statements or the failure to disclose material facts in connection with the sale of securities, and also makes it unlawful to engage "in any act, practice, or course of business which operates or would operate as a fraud or deceit upon any person, in connection with the purchase or sale of any security."[2] Provisions of this Rule have been used to attack a wide variety of securities practices such as "insider trading" and the "churning" of customer accounts by brokers (making numerous trades in order to increase commissions); a private cause of action for those injured by violations of the Rule has long been implied.

For many years, disputes arising under both of these statutes were thought to be not arbitrable as a matter of "public policy." The Supreme Court held in Wilko v. Swan, 346 U.S. 427 (1953), that an investor could litigate a misrepresentation claim against a brokerage firm under the Securities Act of 1933, despite the fact that the investor's agreement with the firm contained an arbitration clause. The Court noted that arbitrators must make determinations "without judicial instruction on the law" and that an award "may be made without explanation of their reasons and without a complete record of their proceedings"; it concluded that "the protective provisions of the Securities Act require the exercise of judicial direction to fairly assure their effectiveness." The statute should therefore be read as preventing a "waiver of judicial trial and review," and any agreement to arbitrate future disputes was invalid.

However, the Supreme Court—in line with its increasing tendency to presume arbitral competence even as to statutory or "public policy" matters—has recently reversed course. In Shearson/American Express, Inc. v. McMahon, 482 U.S. 220 (1987), the Court held that arbitration of claims against a broker under the Securities Exchange Act and Rule 10b–5 could be compelled where the customer had earlier signed an arbitration agreement. The Court reached this conclusion by relying heavily on *Mitsubishi*, noting that "the mistrust of arbitration that formed the basis for the *Wilko* opinion in 1953 is difficult to square with the assessment of arbitration that has prevailed since that time." The Court pointed to the fact that the SEC had specifically approved the arbitration procedures of the various stock exchanges, and has exercised its "oversight authority" to ensure that the procedures of the exchanges "adequately protect statutory rights." Nor were arbitration agreements made unenforceable by § 29(a) of the Securities Exchange Act, which prohibits any agreement by which a party

---

1. 15 U.S.C.A. §§ 77a, 77l.

2. 15 U.S.C.A. §§ 78a, 78j; 17 C.F.R. § 240.10b–5.

784 CHAPTER V ARBITRATION

undertakes "to waive compliance with any provision of [the Act]"[3]. The Court—in what has now become a familiar rhetorical move—concluded that by "agreeing to arbitrate a statutory claim, a party does not forego the substantive rights afforded by the statute; it only submits to their resolution in an arbitral, rather than a judicial, forum."

At the same time the Supreme Court held in *McMahon* that claims under the Racketeer Influenced and Corrupt Organizations Act ("RICO") were also subject to arbitration under a pre-dispute arbitration clause. "RICO" makes it unlawful to use any money derived "from a pattern of racketeering activity" in the operation of an interstate enterprise.[4] As Justice O'Connor noted in *McMahon,* the scope of RICO has in recent years been dramatically extended far beyond the activities of "the archetypal, intimidating mobster," to reach ordinary business disputes involving "respected and legitimate" enterprises.[5] The RICO statute follows the model of the antitrust laws in giving a private cause of action, including the right to attorney's fees and treble damages, to persons injured by such conduct. "Although the holding in *Mitsubishi* was limited to the international context, much of its reasoning is equally applicable here." 482 U.S. at 239.

While the *McMahon* case did not expressly overrule *Wilko v. Swan,* it did not take long for the Supreme Court to give *Wilko* a formal burial: In Rodriguez de Quijas v. Shearson/American Express, Inc., 490 U.S. 477 (1989), the Court held that claims under the Securities Act of 1933 were also arbitrable where the parties had entered into a pre-dispute arbitration agreement.

At the present time, virtually all brokerage firms require customers to sign a pre-dispute arbitration agreement as a condition for opening an account, particularly in the case of margin or option accounts. Broker-customer contracts commonly provide for arbitration under the auspices of an industry organization such as the New York Stock Exchange (NYSE) or the National Association of Securities Dealers (NASD). Of the more than 6600 arbitration cases filed with these organizations in 1997, approximately 90% were filed with the NASD and about 8% with the NYSE. Under current NASD rules, cases involving more than $50,000 are presumptively to be heard by a panel of three arbitrators, a majority of whom must be "public" arbitrators, "not from the securities industry."

These exchange-administered arbitrations have been the subject of frequent and vocal criticism for many years. See, e.g., "When Investors Bring Claims Against Brokers," New York Times, March 29, 1987, Sec. 3, pp. 1, 8 (lawyer who represents investors says, "I would rather defend a capitalist before the comrades' court than a client before an arbitration panel of the New York Stock Exchange"). Following the Supreme Court's

---

3. 15 U.S.C.A. § 78cc(a).

4. 18 U.S.C.A. § 1961.

5. "Racketeering activity" under the statute is defined as the violation of certain predicate statutes—for example, those deal-

ing with bribery and narcotics sales, but also including "mail fraud" and "fraud in the sale of securities"; a "pattern" of such activity is found when at least two such violations occur within a period of ten years.

decision in *McMahon,* the industry's arbitration rules were amended in an attempt to address some of these concerns. The definition of just who can serve as a "public" arbitrator has been clarified and tightened: Not only individuals associated with brokers and dealers, but also attorneys or accountants who have devoted 20% of their work to securities industry clients, persons who are retired from the industry, and the spouses and immediate family members of all such persons, are excluded.[6] In addition, it is now required that arbitral awards contain a "summary of the issues" and "a statement of [the] issues resolved"; the awards, along with the names of the parties—and those of the arbitrators—are to be made publicly available.[7]

One frequently-expressed concern has been that in disputes between customers and "repeat players" like brokers, the decisions of arbitrators who hope to decide a large number of cases may be affected by the desire to obtain future assignments—and an appearance of partiality toward the industry may be exacerbated by a tendency of some exchanges to call frequently on particular arbitrators.[8] Under the NYSE rules the exchange itself—rather than the parties—names the members of the arbitration panel. This was formerly the NASD's practice as well, but in 1998 the NASD moved to a system of arbitration selection similar to that of the AAA—in which the parties are provided lists of potential arbitrators, strike the names of those found to be unacceptable, and rank the remaining names in order of preference.[9] A software program will now generate names for forwarding to the parties "on a rotating basis," listing first those potential arbitrators who have participated least often in the process.[10]

A 1992 study conducted by the United States General Accounting Office could find "no indication of pro-industry bias in arbitration decisions at industry-sponsored forums." Investors were successful in about 59% of the cases in which they initiated claims against broker-dealers, and those receiving awards got an overall average of 61% of the amount they claimed.[11] More recent figures show a similar pattern.[12] Since investors

---

6. NASD Code of Arbitration Procedure, R. 10308(a)(4),(5).

7. NASD Code of Arbitration Procedure, R. 10330.

8. See U.S. General Accounting Office, Securities Arbitration: How Investors Fare 57–58 (1992) (at the Chicago Board Options Exchange, one arbitrator had decided 47% of the cases the GAO reviewed—and he decided 71% of these in favor of the broker-dealer). See also Robbins, Securities Arbitration from the Arbitrators' Perspective, 23 Rev.Sec. & Commodities Reg. 171, 175 (1990) ("One too often sees the same faces week after week at certain arbitration forums. With all due respect, arbitration should not be a supplement to social security. * * * [W]hen they sit on cases day after day, arbitrators build up an

immunity to outrageous conduct"). Arbitrators in securities cases are compensated for their services (although not handsomely—at the NASD, they receive $200 for an eight-hour day).

9. NASD Code of Arbitration Procedure, R. 10308(b),(c); NYSE Arbitration Rules R. 607(b), R. 608, R. 609 (each party has right to one peremptory challenge, and unlimited challenges for cause). See generally p. 836 infra.

10. See generally Cheryl Nichols, Arbitrator Selection at the NASD: Investor Perception of a Pro–Securities Industry Bias, 15 Ohio St. J. Disp. Res. 63, 107–112 (1999).

11. U.S. G.A.O., Securities Arbitration, supra n.8 at 35.

CHAPTER V ARBITRATION

with small monetary claims against broker-dealers often have difficulty obtaining legal representation in arbitration, around 40% of investors represent themselves in securities arbitration—and as might be expected, investors represented by counsel achieve a significantly higher recovery rate than pro se claimants.[13]

In any event the suspicion has persisted (in the words of Justice Blackmun's dissent in *McMahon*) that "[t]he uniform opposition of investors to compelled arbitration and the overwhelming support of the securities industry for the process suggest that there must be *some* truth to the investors' belief that the securities industry has an advantage in a forum under its own control."[14] Arbitration of disputes between members of a trade and "outsiders" often brings to the surface a tension between two widely-accepted values underlying the arbitration process. On the one hand, there are the often-cited advantages of expert knowledge and experience on the part of decision-makers familiar with industry practice. The task, for example, of educating a jury or even the average judge in the conventions of securities or commodities trading may be a daunting one. On the other hand, there is a need to preserve the fairness of the process by avoiding onesidedness. Even decision-makers who think of themselves as scrupulously neutral are often hard put to avoid the predispositions and preconceptions that seem to accompany technical "expertise." This is particularly true where one of the parties claims to have observed "trade standards," and the dispute seems likely to call into question long-standing practices and patterns of behavior widespread throughout an entire industry. "Expertise provides a powerful basis to determine what behavior is reasonable, economically efficient, or even economically necessary." And "[p]ressures to decide cases quickly without an intrusive investigation into

---

12. See *http://www.nasdadr.com* (customers were awarded damages in 61% of cases decided by the NASD in 1999). A GAO study published in June 2000 found that the percentage of cases favoring investors averaged around 51% in the years 1992–1996, then rose to 57% in 1998. The amount of awards made to investors as a percentage of what they had claimed declined to about 51% during those years, although an increase in the percentage of cases settled—generally 50–60% of the total cases concluded—"may have changed the mix of cases going to a final arbitration award." U.S. General Accounting Office, Securities Arbitration: Actions Needed to Address Problem of Unpaid Awards (2000). Investors claimed punitive damages in about 20% of the cases decided in 1998, and were awarded punitives in about 34% of decided cases in which such damages were requested—a significant increase from the 12% reported in 1992. The 2000 GAO report also found, however, that 49% of the awards

rendered in 1998 were not paid at all, and an additional 12% were only partially paid—although when investors complained, suspensions or the threat of suspensions by the NASD against noncomplying broker-dealers resulted in many of these awards being satisfied. Most of the unpaid awards had been rendered against broker-dealers who were no longer in business.

13. See U.S. Securities and Exchange Commission, Office of Inspector General, "Oversight of Self–Regulatory Organization Arbitration" (1999).

14. See also Nichols, supra n.10 at 129 (amended NASD rules illustrate "the difficulty, maybe the impossibility, of eliminating the perception of pro-securities industry bias in the NASD arbitrator pool when an economically dependent relationship exists between one of the parties (securities industry respondents) and the arbitrators deciding the dispute").

C. ARBITRATION AND THE COURTS **787**

motives and the like * * * may enforce the failure to challenge" long-standing practices.[15] The arbitration of broker-customer disputes illustrates the inevitable tension; how to draw the balance between these values is a persistent theme in discussions of arbitration. Cf. Section D.2.b. infra ("Arbitral Impartiality").

Note: Employment Disputes and the Statutory Rights of Employees

A large number of federal statutes have been enacted in recent years that extend protection to employees against various forms of discrimination in the workplace. Perhaps the most important of these is Title VII of the Civil Rights Act of 1964, which makes it an "unlawful employment practice" to "fail or refuse to hire or to discharge any individual, or otherwise to discriminate against any individual with respect to his compensation, terms, conditions, or privileges of employment, because of such individual's race, color, religion, sex, or national origin." 42 U.S.C. § 2000e–2(a)(1). When—if at all—may claims brought under such statutes be subject to mandatory and binding arbitration? This is a question that has been the focus of much litigation—and the cause of considerable and continuing confusion.

In Alexander v. Gardner–Denver Co., 415 U.S. 36 (1974), the Supreme Court was presented with a collective bargaining agreement protecting employees from discharge without "just cause," and also prohibiting "discrimination against any employee on account of race." After being fired, an employee claimed at an arbitration hearing that his discharge was the result of racial discrimination. The arbitrator made no explicit reference to the racial discrimination claim but found that the employee had been fired for "just cause," and denied the grievance. The employee then sued the employer, alleging that his discharge was in violation of Title VII. The district court granted the employer's motion for summary judgment, finding "that the claim of racial discrimination had been submitted to the arbitrator and resolved adversely" to the employee: Having "voluntarily elected to pursue his grievance to final arbitration under the nondiscrimination clause of the collective bargaining agreement," the employee "was bound by the arbitral decision and thereby precluded from suing his employer under Title VII." Before the Supreme Court, the employer argued that federal courts should defer to arbitral decisions on discrimination claims, at least "where (i) the claim was before the arbitrator; (ii) the collective-bargaining agreement prohibited the form of discrimination charged in the suit under Title VII; and (iii) the arbitrator has authority to rule on the claim and to fashion a remedy."

The Supreme Court, however, rejected this argument and reversed:

> The purpose and procedures of Title VII indicate that Congress intended federal courts to exercise final responsibility for enforcement of Title VII; deferral to arbitral decisions would be inconsistent with that

---

15. Garth, Privatization and the New Market for Disputes: A Framework for Analysis and a Preliminary Assessment, 12 Studies in Law, Politics and Society 367, 382 (1992).

CHAPTER V ARBITRATION

goal. * * * [The employer's] deferral rule is necessarily premised on the assumption that arbitral processes are commensurate with judicial processes and that Congress impliedly intended federal courts to defer to arbitral decisions on Title VII issues. We deem this supposition unlikely.

Gardner–Denver was followed by two other important cases, also dealing with the effects of an arbitral award under a collective bargaining agreement on the statutory rights of employees. In Barrentine v. Arkansas–Best Freight System, Inc., 450 U.S. 728 (1981), an employee had unsuccessfully submitted wage claims to arbitration; the Court held that this did not preclude a later suit, based on the same underlying facts, alleging a violation of the minimum wage provisions of the Fair Labor Standards Act.

In McDonald v. City of West Branch, 466 U.S. 284 (1984), a police officer was discharged by a city and filed a grievance pursuant to the collective bargaining agreement. Here too the arbitrator ruled against him, finding that there was "just cause" for the discharge. McDonald did not challenge the award, but later filed an action against the city under 42 U.S.C. § 1983 (imposing liability on any person who "under color of" state law deprives another "of any rights, privileges, or immunities secured by the Constitution and laws" of the United States; McDonald alleged that he had been discharged for exercising his First Amendment rights.) The court of appeals concluded that McDonald's First Amendment claims were barred by res judicata and collateral estoppel, but the Supreme Court, relying heavily on *Gardner–Denver,* reversed: While "arbitration is well suited to resolving contractual disputes," it said, it cannot in a § 1983 action "provide an adequate substitute for a judicial trial. Consequently, according preclusive effect to arbitration awards in § 1983 actions would severely undermine the protection of federal rights that the statute is designed to provide."

The Court buttressed this conclusion by pointing to a number of characteristics of arbitration. Noting first that "many arbitrators are not lawyers," the Court suggested that:

> [A]n arbitrator's expertise "pertains primarily to the law of the shop, not the law of the land." An arbitrator may not, therefore, have the expertise required to resolve the complex legal questions that arise in § 1983 actions.

> Second, because an arbitrator's authority derives solely from the contract, an arbitrator may not have the authority to enforce § 1983. As we explained in *Gardner–Denver:* "The arbitrator ... has no general authority to invoke public laws that conflict with the bargain between the parties.... If an arbitral decision is based 'solely upon the arbitrator's view of the requirements of enacted legislation,' rather than on an interpretation of the collective-bargaining agreement, the arbitrator has 'exceeded the scope of the submission,' and the award will not be enforced." * * *

Third, when, as is usually the case, the union has exclusive control over the "manner and extent to which an individual grievance is presented," there is an additional reason why arbitration is an inadequate substitute for judicial proceedings. The union's interests and those of the individual employee are not always identical or even compatible. As a result, the union may present the employee's grievance less vigorously, or make different strategic choices, than would the employee. Thus, were an arbitration award accorded preclusive effect, an employee's opportunity to be compensated for a constitutional deprivation might be lost merely because it was not in the union's interest to press his claim vigorously.

Finally, arbitral factfinding is generally not equivalent to judicial factfinding. * * * The record of the arbitration proceedings is not as complete; the usual rules of evidence do not apply; and rights and procedures common to civil trials, such as discovery, compulsory process, cross-examination, and testimony under oath, are often severely limited or unavailable.

In all three cases, however, the Court suggested that—even though an arbitral award would not preclude a later action by the employee—the award might still be admitted as evidence in the lawsuit. The weight to be given the award "must be determined in the court's discretion with regard to the facts and circumstances of each case":

Relevant factors include the existence of provisions in the collective-bargaining agreement that conform substantially with [the statute or Constitution], the degree of procedural fairness in the arbitral forum, adequacy of the record with respect to the issue [in the judicial proceeding], and the special competence of particular arbitrators. Where an arbitral determination gives full consideration to an employee's [statutory or constitutional] rights, a court may properly accord it great weight. This is especially true where the issue is solely one of fact, specifically addressed by the parties and decided by the arbitrator on the basis of an adequate record.

See, e.g., Wilmington v. J.I. Case Co., 793 F.2d 909 (8th Cir.1986) ("the arbitrator's decision [that the employee was fired for "just cause"] was simply another piece of evidence presented to the jury, and it was for the jury to decide what weight to give it"; however, the trial court properly refused to admit into evidence the text of the award, since the arbitrator's comments and findings "would either usurp the jury's role in assessing credibility [of witnesses who also testified at trial] or would be unfairly prejudicial").

Some years later, however, the relentless federal policy favoring arbitration caused the pendulum to swing in the opposite direction. Gilmer v. Interstate/Johnson Lane Corporation, 500 U.S. 20 (1991), involved an individual employee who was hired as a "Manager of Financial Services" by a brokerage house, and required to register as a securities representative with the New York Stock Exchange; NYSE rules at the time required the arbitration of any dispute "arising out of the employment or termination of

CHAPTER V ARBITRATION

employment" of registered representatives. Gilmer later brought suit against his employer alleging that he had been discharged in violation of the Age Discrimination in Employment Act of 1967 (ADEA), 290 U.S.C. § 621. The Supreme Court—relying again on *Mitsubishi,* supra p. 766, as well as on *Shearson/American Express, Inc. v. McMahon* and *Rodriguez de Quijas v. Shearson/American Express*, supra pp. 783–784, held that arbitration of the claim should be compelled. Again the Court repeated that "[b]y agreeing to arbitrate a statutory claim, a party does not forgo the substantive rights afforded by the statute; it only submits to their resolution in an arbitral, rather than a judicial, forum." Again the Court stressed that "generalized attacks" on arbitration—to the effect that the arbitration process may not adequately permit vindication of the claimant's statutory rights—rested on an unwarranted "suspicion of arbitration," and were "far out of step with our current strong endorsement of the federal statutes favoring this method of resolving disputes."

For example, while it is true that discovery permitted in arbitration is more limited than in the federal courts, the Court found it "unlikely"

> that age discrimination claims require more extensive discovery than other claims that we have found to be arbitrable, such as RICO and antitrust claims. Moreover, there has been no showing in this case that the NYSE discovery provisions, which allow for document production, information requests, depositions, and subpoenas, will prove insufficient to allow ADEA claimants such as Gilmer a fair opportunity to present their claims. Although those procedures might not be as extensive as in the federal courts, by agreeing to arbitrate, a party "trades the procedures and opportunity for review of the courtroom for the simplicity, informality, and expedition of arbitration." Indeed, an important counterweight to the reduced discovery in NYSE arbitration is that arbitrators are not bound by the rules of evidence.

Nor was the Court persuaded by the contention that "there often will be unequal bargaining power between employers and employees.":

> Mere inequality in bargaining power * * * is not a sufficient reason to hold that arbitration agreements are never enforceable in the employment context. Relationships between securities dealers and investors, for example, may involve unequal bargaining power, but we nevertheless held in *Rodriguez de Quijas* and *McMahon* that agreements to arbitrate in that context are enforceable. * * * There is no indication in this case * * * that Gilmer, an experienced businessman, was coerced or defrauded into agreeing to the arbitration clause in his registration application. As with the claimed procedural inadequacies discussed above, this claim of unequal bargaining power is best left for resolution in specific cases.

How could *Gilmer* be distinguished from earlier cases like *Alexander v. Gardner–Denver* and its progeny? Most notably, the Court pointed out, "because the arbitration in those cases occurred in the context of a collective-bargaining agreement, the claimants there were represented by their unions in the arbitration proceedings. An important concern therefore

C. Arbitration and the Courts **791**

was the tension between collective representation and individual statutory rights, a concern not applicable to the present case." Other purported distinctions seem considerably less persuasive—and more like mere make-weights. The Court also pointed out, for example, that the *Gardner–Denver* line of cases, unlike *Gilmer,* were not decided under the FAA—which "reflects a liberal federal policy favoring arbitration agreements." And it also stressed that those cases

> did not involve the issue of the enforceability of an agreement to arbitrate statutory claims. Rather, they involved the quite different issue whether arbitration of contract-based claims precluded subsequent judicial resolution of statutory claims. Since the employees there had not agreed to arbitrate their statutory claims, and the labor arbitrators were not authorized to resolve such claims, the arbitration in those cases understandably was held not to preclude subsequent statutory actions.

The relationship between *Gilmer* and *Gardner-Denver* was revisited—although inconclusively—by the Supreme Court in Wright v. Universal Maritime Service Corp., 525 U.S. 70 (1998). Here, an employee subject to a collective bargaining agreement filed suit alleging an employer's violation of the Americans with Disability Act of 1990, 42 U.S.C. § 12101. The Supreme Court acknowledged that there was "obviously some tension between these two lines of cases." The employee's contention—that "federal forum rights" could not be waived at all in union-negotiated collective bargaining agreements, even if they could be waived in individually executed contracts—"assuredly finds support in the text of *Gilmer.*" The employer, on the other hand, argued that *Gilmer* "has sufficiently undermined *Gardner-Denver*" that henceforth a union too should be able to surrender an employee's right to litigate a statutory claim. The Court found it "unnecessary to resolve" this question": For *"Gardner-Denver* at least stands for the proposition that the right to a federal judicial forum is of sufficient importance to be protected against less-than-explicit union waiver in a [collective bargaining agreement]." Matters which "go beyond the interpretation and application of contract terms"—like the meaning of a federal statute—will not be presumed to be arbitrable, but any such requirement in a collective bargaining agreement must instead be "particularly clear." And since the agreement in *Wright* could not meet such a standard, the employer's attempt to compel arbitration was denied. In *Gilmer,* by contrast—since it involved "an individual's waiver of his own rights, rather than a union's waiver of the rights of represented employees"—such a "clear and unmistakable" standard did not apply.

NOTES AND QUESTIONS

1. In 1990, Congress enacted the Older Workers Benefit Protection Act, 29 U.S.C. § 626(f), which amended the ADEA to prohibit waiver of "any right or claim" under the Act that is not "knowing and voluntary." Any such waiver must be "written in a manner calculated to be understood" by the employee; the employee must be "advised in writing to consult with an attorney" prior to signing it, and in any event there could be no waiver of "rights or claims that may arise after the date the waiver is executed." Should this amendment affect the validity of agreements providing for the arbitration of ADEA claims? *Compare* Thiele v. Merrill Lynch, Pierce, Fenner & Smith, 59 F. Supp.2d 1060 (S.D.Cal.1999)(arbitration clause "did not contain a knowing and voluntary waiver of Thiele's right to a jury trial, as required by the OWBPA, and it is therefore unenforceable with respect to his ADEA claim"), *with* Rosenberg v. Merrill Lynch, Pierce, Fenner & Smith, Inc., 170 F.3d 1 (1st Cir.1999)(to interpret the OWBPA to include "the right to a judicial forum" "would be to ignore the Supreme Court's repeated statements that arbitral and judicial fora are both able to give effect to the policies that underlie legislation").

2. The holding in *Gilmer* has been routinely applied by lower courts to other federal legislation extending rights to individual employees against job discrimination. See, e.g., Alford v. Dean Witter Reynolds, Inc., 939 F.2d 229 (5th Cir.1991) (Title VII); Koveleskie v. SBC Capital Markets, Inc., 167 F.3d 361 (7th Cir.1999)(Title VII); Bercovitch v. Baldwin School, Inc., 133 F.3d 141 (1st Cir.1998)(Americans with Disabilities Act).

See also McNulty v. Prudential–Bache Securities, Inc., 871 F.Supp. 567 (E.D.N.Y.1994) (claim under Jurors' Act, making it unlawful to discharge an employee "by reason of such employee's jury service"); Saari v. Smith Barney, Harris Upham & Co., Inc., 968 F.2d 877 (9th Cir.1992) (claim under Employee Polygraph Protection Act); Jones v. Fujitsu Network Communications, Inc., 81 F.Supp.2d 688 (N.D.Tex.1999)(claim under Family Medical Leave Act). In Williams v. Katten, Muchin & Zavis, 837 F.Supp. 1430 (N.D.Ill.1993), a claim under the Civil Rights Act of 1870 [42 U.S.C.A. § 1981, equal rights "to make and enforce contracts"] was held arbitrable; the court rejected arguments that racial discrimination is a more serious offense "morally distinguishable" from gender and age claims, and that § 1981 is more "constitutional in nature" than statutes enacted pursuant to the commerce clause such as Title VII. *But see* Nguyen v. City of Cleveland, 121 F.Supp.2d 643 (N.D.Ohio 2000)(claim under whistleblower protection provision of the False Claims Act, [31 U.S.C. § 3730(h)], is not arbitrable; "an employee who brings a claim against his employers on behalf of the federal government should not be forced by unequal bargaining power to accept a forum demanded as a condition of employment by the very party on which he informed").

3. The district court in *Alexander v. Gardner–Denver* had granted summary judgment to the employer; it feared that "[t]o hold that an employee has a right to an arbitration of a grievance which is binding on an employer but is not binding on the employee—a trial balloon for the employee, but a moon shot for the employer—would sound the death knell for arbitration clauses in labor contracts." 346 F.Supp. 1012, 1019 (D.Colo.1971). This prediction has not of course been borne out. Many collective bargaining agreements now include non-discrimination clauses and often incorporate Title VII or similar state statutes; labor arbitrators regularly decide such cases and engage in interpreting this language. See the discussion at p. 742 supra ("Arbitral Decision–Making and Legal 'Rules' "). But given the holdings in *Gardner–Denver* and *McDonald,* what incentive is there for employers to agree to submit such disputes to arbitration if employees are able to get "a second bite of the apple"?

4. Strictly speaking, *Gardner–Denver* and *McDonald* were only concerned with the preclusive effect of *a prior arbitration award* on a *later* judicial claim. However, it seems clear that an employee subject to a collective bargaining agreement may always proceed *directly* to pursue litigation under Title VII or other civil rights statutes, without first exhausting his rights under the agreement. See 2 Larson, Employment Discrimination §§ 49.14, 49.15 (1990) (since courts in Title VII actions are not bound by the results of grievance and arbitration procedures in collective bargaining agreements, requiring exhaustion would "needlessly prolong the deprivation of rights"). This option of course no longer remains open to an employee in the position of Robert Gilmer. Is it not something of a paradox that statutory rights against discrimination are apparently subject to binding arbitration only in individual employment agreements—which are so often contracts of adhesion—and not in the hard-fought and actually "dickered" collective bargaining agreements between employers and unions?

5. In the securities industry, employees like Gilmer were for many years required by NASD and NYSE rules to submit employment disputes to arbitration before industry fora, under the same procedures as customers. A 1994 study found that arbitrators in such fora were not selected on the basis of any particular "expertise" in employment or discrimination law, and that most of them were "white men, averaging 60 years of age." U.S. General Accounting Office, Employment Discrimination: How Registered Representatives Fare in Discrimination Disputes 2, 8, 12 (1994)(of the 726 arbitrators in NYSE's New York arbitrator pool, 89% were men; of the 349 arbitrators whose race could be identified, 97% were white).

Commentators predictably seized on this fact to conclude that the awards of such arbitrators must tend to disfavor minority or female complainants—indeed, the presence of at least "unconscious bias" is usually taken to be self-evident without the need for any further discussion. How, though, would you characterize the typical federal judge? See Alan Rau, On Integrity in Private Judging, 14 Arb. Int'l 115, 135–40 (1998).

A number of recent accounts of the security industry's arbitration procedures in employment discrimination cases have been highly critical and widely-publicized. One NYSE panel apparently decided against the claimant in a sexual harassment case because her supervisor's behavior "was common within the industry"; the arbitrators were unfamiliar with the current state of antidiscrimination law and, in the words of one law professor, were "10 years behind where the courts are." One article concluded that "So grim are the prospects for most women who go through the securities-industry arbitration process that lawyers say they now advise their clients not to bother with arbitration at all. Instead, they urge women

794 CHAPTER V ARBITRATION

to take modest settlements and walk away." See Jacobs, "Men's Club: Riding Crop and Slurs: How Wall Street Dealt With a Sex–Bias Case," Wall St.J., June 9, 1994 at p. A1.

Studies and articles like these have naturally prompted calls for legislation to restrict the use of arbitration in resolving employment discrimination claims. See, e.g., 11 World Arb. & Mediation Rep. 153 (June 2000)(proposed "Civil Rights Procedures Protection Act," supported by the Department of Justice, would amend the FAA to exclude from arbitration claims of unlawful discrimination in employment on the basis of race, religion, gender, age or disability). Recent amendments to the rules of both the NASD and the NYSE have eliminated any industry-wide requirement of mandatory arbitration with respect to statutory discrimination claims. (However, industry employees are still required under these rules to arbitrate any common-law claims, such as wrongful termination or infliction of emotional distress. In addition, under the new NASD rules individual brokerage firms remain free to insert pre-dispute arbitration clauses in their employment agreements should they wish to do so, thereby making mandatory the arbitration of even discrimination claims). See SEC, Release No. 34–40109, 1998 WL 339422 (F.R.); SEC, Release No. 34–40858, 1999 WL 3315 (F.R.). As part of the settlement of a class action gender-discrimination suit, Merrill Lynch has agreed to waive any contractual right to insist on arbitration with respect to all future discrimination claims brought by employees. See 66 U.S.L.W. 2697 (May 19, 1998).

6. Outside the (now much diminished) sphere of cases like *Gardner–Denver* and *McDonald,* arbitration awards can be expected to have res judicata and collateral estoppel effects on later proceedings. The Restatement of Judgments, for example, generally provides that "a valid and final award by arbitration" will have the same preclusive effects as a judgment of a court. "If the arbitration award were not treated as the equivalent of a judicial adjudication for purposes of claim preclusion, the obligation to arbitrate would be practically illusory." Restatement (Second) of Judgments, § 84 and comment b. In addition, the arbitrators' determination of a particular *issue* will prevent later relitigation of the same issue (i.e., will have "collateral estoppel" effect), at least where the proceedings possess "the elements of adjudicatory procedure"—including notice to the parties, the right to present and rebut evidence and legal argument, and "such other procedural elements as may be necessary to constitute the proceeding a sufficient means of conclusively determining the matter in question." Id. at §§ 84(3), 83(2). Under modern arbitration statutes, once an award is confirmed by a court it is given "the same force and effect" as a judgment rendered in a suit, FAA § 13. But judicial confirmation is not necessary in order for an award to have a preclusive effect barring later relitigation. See generally 4 Ian Macneil, Richard Speidel, & Thomas Stipanowich, Federal Arbitration Law § 39.6 (1994).

In some cases, however, the collateral estoppel effects of an arbitration award may be limited by the "informality" of the arbitration proceeding. For example, where there is no transcript and where the arbitrators do not write a reasoned opinion, it may often be difficult to tell just what it is that they have actually decided. See, e.g., Tamari v. Bache & Co. (Lebanon) S.A.L., 637 F.Supp. 1333 (N.D.Ill.1986). In this case a customer initiated arbitration proceedings against a brokerage firm, seeking to hold it accountable for the acts of its subsidiary, and the arbitrators denied the claim without an opinion. This was held not to preclude a later suit against the subsidiary itself, since "it is impossible to tell" the basis for the arbitrators' award. After all, the court reasoned, the arbitrators could have found *either* that the subsidiary had done nothing wrongful, *or* that the subsidiary had simply not been acting as an agent of the parent. See also Clark v. Bear Stearns & Co., Inc., 966 F.2d 1318 (9th Cir.1992) (dismissal by arbitrators of state-law claims against broker did not preclude a later suit on federal-law claims; the award did not mention the applicable law selected by the arbitrators and if they chose California law "the defendants' alleged negligence need not have been addressed by the arbitrators at all," since the common-law claim would be barred by the state's statute of limitations); Shell, Res Judicata and Collateral Estoppel Effects of Commercial Arbitration, 35 U.C.L.A. L.Rev. 623 (1988).

In addition, even a confirmed arbitration award may not be given a *nonmutual* collateral estoppel effect in the absence of some express agreement between the parties. This is the situation in which A & B arbitrate a particular dispute, and A loses. In later litigation between A & C involving some of the same issues, C argues that A should be bound by adverse findings made by the arbitrator in the earlier proceeding. The Supreme Court of California rejected that argument in Vandenberg v. Superior Court, 21 Cal.4th 815, 88 Cal.Rptr.2d 366, 982 P.2d 229 (Cal. 1999). The earlier arbitration had been between a landowner and its lessee for contamination of soil and groundwater; the court held that findings adverse to the lessee did not prevent him, in a later indemnification action against his insurers, from arguing that the discharge was "sudden and accidental" and thus not excluded from pollution coverage under the policy. The court noted that while in arbitration the parties have voluntarily traded "the safeguards and formalities of court litigation for an expeditious, sometimes roughshod means of resolving their dispute," "these same features can be serious, unexpected disadvantages if issues decided by the arbitrators are given leveraged effect in favor of strangers to the arbitration." But cf. Witkowski v. Welch, 173 F.3d 192 (3d Cir. 1999)(the arbitrator had dismissed plaintiff's claim against an investment advisor alleging that his conveyance of real property acquired with the plaintiff's retirement funds had been fraudulent and should be set aside; held, summary judgment should be granted to the transferee of the disputed property in a later action brought against him by the plaintiff; "the fraud and fraudulent conveyance issues brought against [the investment advisor and the transferee] are so inextricably intertwined with one another that the disposal of the claims against the one is necessarily fatal to the alleged claim against the other").

7. After an employee was discharged in 1989, her union filed a grievance alleging unjust termination under the collective bargaining agreement; she also filed discrimination charges with the state Commission on Human Rights and with the EEOC. Two years later, the employer and the employee agreed to be bound by an arbitration decision. A "Stipulated Arbitration Award" was later confirmed by a state court: Under it, the employee was to be reinstated and compensated for lost wages, and she was to withdraw the discrimination charges filed with state and federal agencies. The employee later filed a lawsuit alleging a series of unlawful acts—up to and including her 1989 termination—which allegedly constituted discrimination and retaliation under Title VII and a deprivation of her civil rights under 42 U.S.C. § 1983. The employer moved to dismiss. The court noted that "if the prior resolution was an arbitration award, the plaintiff may proceed with the case, even if the only act of discrimination she can prove is the 1989 termination"—for, as in *Gardner–Denver*, "the arbitration was limited to determining the plaintiff's rights under a collective bargaining agreement." On the other hand, "if the prior resolution was a settlement," the plaintiff can only recover if she can prove "discriminatory acts which occurred *after* the settlement"—for an employee "who freely settles her demand with the employer may not sue on the same cause of action later merely because she grows dissatisfied with the payment for which she settled." For purposes of the motion to dismiss, the court accepted the plaintiff's characterization of the earlier resolution as "an arbitration award," and denied the motion. Tang v. State of Rhode Island Department of Elderly Affairs, 904 F.Supp. 69 (D.R.I.1995).

Armendariz v. Foundation Health Psychcare Services, Inc.

Supreme Court of California, 2000
24 Cal.4th 83, 99 Cal.Rptr.2d 745, 6 P.3d 669.

MOSK, J.

* * *

I. STATEMENT OF FACTS AND PROCEDURAL ISSUES

Marybeth Armendariz and Dolores Olague–Rodgers (hereafter the employees) filed a complaint for wrongful termination against their former employer, Foundation Health Psychcare Services, Inc. (hereafter the employer). The complaint and certain documents filed in support of the employer's petition to compel arbitration provide us with the basic factual background of this case. In July and August of 1995, the employer hired the employees in the "Provider Relations Group" and they were later given supervisory positions with annual salaries of $38,000. On June 20, 1996, they were informed that their positions were "being eliminated" and that they were "being terminated." During their year of employment, they claim that their supervisors and coworkers engaged in sexually based harassment and discrimination. The employees alleged that they were "terminated . . . because of their perceived and/or actual sexual orientation (heterosexual)."

Both employees had filled out and signed employment application forms, which included an arbitration clause pertaining to any future claim of wrongful termination. Later, they executed a separate employment arbitration agreement, containing the same arbitration clause. The clause states in full: "I agree as a condition of my employment, that in the event my employment is terminated, and I contend that such termination was wrongful or otherwise in violation of the conditions of employment or was in violation of any express or implied condition, term or covenant of employment, whether founded in fact or in law, including but not limited to the covenant of good faith and fair dealing, or otherwise in violation of any of my rights, I and Employer agree to submit any such matter to binding arbitration * * * . I and Employer further expressly agree that in any such arbitration, my exclusive remedies for violation of the terms, conditions or covenants of employment shall be limited to a sum equal to the wages I would have earned from the date of any discharge until the date of the arbitration award. I understand that I shall not be entitled to any other remedy, at law or in equity, including but not limited to reinstatement and/or injunctive relief."

The employees' complaint against the employer alleges a cause of action for violation of the [California Fair Employment and Housing Act, Gov. Code § 12900 (FEHA)] and three additional causes of action for wrongful termination based on tort and contract theories of recovery. The complaint sought general damages, punitive damages, injunctive relief, and the recovery of attorney fees and costs of suit.

The employer countered by filing a motion for an order to compel arbitration * * *. [T]he trial court denied the motion on the ground that the arbitration provision in question was an unconscionable contract, * * * [finding] that several of the provisions of the contract are "so one-sided as to shock the conscience." * * *

After the employer filed a timely appeal, the Court of Appeal reversed. * * * We granted review.

II. DISCUSSION

A. Arbitrability of FEHA Claims

The employees urge us to adopt the conclusion of the United States Court of Appeals for the Ninth Circuit in Duffield v. Robertson Stephens & Co., 144 F.3d 1182 (9th Cir.1998) (*Duffield*), which held that the Civil Rights Act of 1991 prohibits the enforcement of mandatory employment agreements to arbitrate claims under Title VII of the Civil Rights Act of 1964, or equivalent state antidiscrimination statutes, such as the FEHA. *Duffield* involved a securities broker who sought to litigate Title VII and FEHA claims against her employer after alleged sexual discrimination and harassment, and who was subject to a mandatory arbitration agreement. The starting point for the *Duffield* court is the fact that the 1991 Act "was primarily designed to 'overrule' hostile Supreme Court decisions in order to make discrimination claims easier both to bring and to prove in federal courts...." It is against this background that the court examined section

798 CHAPTER V ARBITRATION

118 of the 1991 Act, which provides: "Where appropriate and to the extent authorized by law, the use of alternative means of dispute resolution, including ... arbitration, is encouraged to resolve disputes arising under the Acts or provisions of Federal law amended by this title." The *Duffield* court found the language "where appropriate and to the extent authorized by law" to be indicative of a congressional intent to outlaw compulsory arbitration of employee civil rights claims, despite the apparently pro-arbitration thrust of section 118. The court reasoned as follows: The term "where appropriate," must be considered in the context of the statute as a whole, which provided "for a vast strengthening of employees' rights"; " 'Where appropriate,' as used in the Act, would appear to mean where arbitration furthers the purpose and objective of the Act—by affording victims of discrimination an opportunity to present their claims in an alternative forum, a forum that they find desirable—not by forcing an unwanted forum upon them."

Likewise, the *Duffield* court explained the phrase "to the extent authorized by law" in context: "As the Supreme Court has stated, we should examine initially the statute with an eye toward determining Congress' perception of the law that it was shaping or reshaping. The overwhelming weight of the law at the time Congress drafted section 118, and it was reported out of the House Education and Labor Committee, was to the effect that compulsory agreements to arbitrate Title VII claims were unenforceable. In other words, such agreements were not 'authorized by law.' To the contrary, the law at that time prohibited employers from compelling employees to arbitrate Title VII claims pursuant to collective bargaining agreements, 'in large part' because of the Court's recognition of the critical role that Congress envisioned for the independent federal judiciary in advancing Title VII's societal goal. [citing *Alexander v. Gardner–Denver* and *McDonald v. West Branch,* supra pp. 787–789]. This reading of the statute is especially supported by the legislative history, particularly the report of the House Committee on Education and Labor (the House report), which stated of the bill that was to become the 1991 Act: 'The Committee emphasizes ... that the use of alternative dispute mechanisms is ... intended to supplement, not supplant, the remedies provided by Title VII. Thus, for example, the committee believes that any agreement to submit disputed issues to arbitration, whether in the context of collective bargaining or in an employment contract, does not preclude the affected person from seeking relief under the enforcement provisions of Title VII. This view is consistent with the Supreme Court's interpretation of Title VII in Alexander v. Gardner–Denver Co.... The Committee does not intend this section to be used to preclude rights and remedies that would otherwise be available.' H.R.Rep. No. 40(I) at 97.' "*

---

* [This House report on the 1991 Act, from which the court quotes, was dated just 19 days before the Supreme Court handed down its decision in *Gilmer.* As the Supreme Court of California goes on to point out, however, *Gilmer* had been decided by the time Congress actually passed the Act.—Eds.]

C. ARBITRATION AND THE COURTS 799

Finally, the *Duffield* court reasoned that if the 1991 Act precluded the enforcement of mandatory employment arbitration agreements with respect to Title VII claims, the employee's FEHA claims must also be exempted from mandatory arbitration. Because "parallel state anti-discrimination laws are explicitly made part of Title VII's enforcement scheme, FEHA claims are arbitrable to the same extent as Title VII claims."

As the employer points out, the Ninth Circuit stands alone in its interpretation of the 1991 Act. Aside from the fact that *Duffield* is a minority of one, we find its reasoning unpersuasive. First and foremost, it is difficult to believe that Congress would have chosen to ban mandatory employment arbitration by means of a clause that encourages the use of arbitration and has no explicit prohibitory language, when it could have simply and straightforwardly proscribed mandatory employment arbitration of Title VII claims. Second, the *Duffield* court's analysis of the phrase "to the extent authorized by law" would perhaps be credible but for the fact that, as the court acknowledged, the United States Supreme Court decided *Gilmer* shortly before the passage of the 1991 Act. *Gilmer* modified the *Gardner-Denver* decision referred to in the congressional legislative history quoted above. * * *

The *Gilmer* court did not decide whether employment contracts are generally subject to the FAA, nor definitively rule on whether Title VII claims were arbitrable. But at the very least, it was not at all clear at the time the 1991 Act was enacted that mandatory arbitration of Title VII claims (outside of the collective bargaining context) was prohibited according to judicial interpretation of Title VII, and in fact the contrary appeared to be more likely the case. The fact that the authors of the House report may have believed that section 118 of the 1991 Act was intended to incorporate a broad reading of the *Gardner-Denver* line of cases to preclude mandatory employment arbitration agreements of all types does not negate the fact that at the time Congress passed the 1991 Act, *Gilmer* was the law. Congress must be presumed to have been aware of *Gilmer* when it used the phrase "to the extent authorized by law."

Nor can the phrase "where appropriate" bear the weight given to it by the *Duffield* court. There is no reason to suppose that Congress believed mandatory arbitration agreements of civil rights claims to be inappropriate, provided that arbitration gives claimants the full opportunity to pursue such claims. Although the *Gilmer* court acknowledged that federal statutes may provide exceptions to the rule of arbitrability found in the FAA, it held that "questions of arbitrability must be addressed with healthy regard for the federal policy favoring arbitration." We cannot discern in the general phrase "where appropriate and to the extent authorized by law" a specific congressional intent to ban mandatory employment arbitration agreements.

We therefore conclude that nothing in the 1991 Act prohibits mandatory employment arbitration agreements that encompass state and federal antidiscrimination claims.

* * *

C. Arbitration of FEHA Claims

The United States Supreme Court's dictum that a party in agreeing to arbitrate a statutory claim, "does not forgo the substantive rights afforded by the statute but only submits to their resolution in an arbitral ... forum" (*Mitsubishi Motors Corp.*, 473 U.S. at p. 628) is as much prescriptive as it is descriptive. That is, it sets a standard by which arbitration agreements and practices are to be measured, and disallows forms of arbitration that in fact compel claimants to forfeit certain substantive statutory rights.

Of course, certain statutory rights can be waived. But arbitration agreements that encompass unwaivable statutory rights must be subject to particular scrutiny. This unwaivability derives from two statutes that are themselves derived from public policy. First, Civil Code section 1668 states: "All contracts which have for their object, directly or indirectly, to exempt anyone from responsibility for his own fraud, or willful injury to the person or property of another, or violation of law, whether willful or negligent, are against the policy of the law." "Agreements whose object, directly or indirectly, is to exempt [their] parties from violation of the law are against public policy and may not be enforced." Second, Civil Code section 3513 states, "Anyone may waive the advantage of a law intended solely for his benefit. But a law established for a public reason cannot be contravened by a private agreement."

There is no question that the statutory rights established by the FEHA are "for a public reason." * * * As we stated in [Rojo v. Kliger, 276 Cal. Rptr. 130, (1990)]: "The public policy against sex discrimination and sexual harassment in employment, moreover, is plainly one that inures to the benefit of the public at large rather than to a particular employer or employee. No extensive discussion is needed to establish the fundamental public interest in a workplace free from the pernicious influence of sexism. So long as it exists, we are all demeaned." It is indisputable that an employment contract that required employees to waive their rights under the FEHA to redress sexual harassment or discrimination would be contrary to public policy and unlawful.

In light of these principles, it is evident that an arbitration agreement cannot be made to serve as a vehicle for the waiver of statutory rights created by the FEHA. * * *

The employees argue that arbitration contains a number of shortcomings that will prevent the vindication of their rights under the FEHA. In determining whether arbitration is considered an adequate forum for securing an employee's rights under FEHA, we begin with the extensive discussion of this question in Cole v. Burns Intern. Security Services, 105 F.3d 1465 (*Cole*), in the context of Title VII claims. In that case, the employee, a security guard, filed Title VII claims against his former employer alleging racial discrimination and harassment. He had signed an arbitration form committing himself to arbitrate such claims.

The court began its analysis by acknowledging the difficulties inherent in arbitrating employees' statutory rights, difficulties not present in arbitrating disputes arising from employee rights under collective bargaining agreements. "The reasons for this hesitation to extend arbitral jurisprudence from the collective bargaining context are well-founded. The fundamental distinction between contractual rights, which are created, defined, and subject to modification by the same private parties participating in arbitration, and statutory rights, which are created, defined, and subject to modification only by Congress and the courts, suggests the need for a public, rather than private, mechanism of enforcement for statutory rights." Although *Gilmer* had held that statutory employment rights outside of the collective bargaining context are arbitrable, the *Cole* court recognized that *Gilmer*, both explicitly and implicitly, placed limits on the arbitration of such rights. "Obviously, *Gilmer* cannot be read as holding that an arbitration agreement is enforceable no matter what rights it waives or what burdens it imposes. Such a holding would be fundamentally at odds with our understanding of the rights accorded to persons protected by public statutes like the ADEA and Title VII. The beneficiaries of public statutes are entitled to the rights and protections provided by the law."

* * *

Based on *Gilmer*, and on the basic principle of nonwaivability of statutory civil rights in the workplace, the *Cole* court formulated five minimum requirements for the lawful arbitration of such rights pursuant to a mandatory employment arbitration agreement. Such an arbitration agreement is lawful if it "(1) provides for neutral arbitrators, (2) provides for more than minimal discovery, (3) requires a written award, (4) provides for all of the types of relief that would otherwise be available in court, and (5) does not require employees to pay either unreasonable costs or any arbitrators' fees or expenses as a condition of access to the arbitration forum. Thus, an employee who is made to use arbitration as a condition of employment effectively may vindicate [his or her] statutory cause of action in the arbitral forum."

Except for the neutral-arbitrator requirement, which we have held is essential to ensuring the integrity of the arbitration process and is not at issue in this case, the employees claim that the present arbitration agreement fails to measure up to the Cole requirements enumerated above. We consider below the validity of those requirements and whether they are met by the employer's arbitration agreement.[8]

---

8. We emphasize at the outset that our general endorsement of the *Cole* requirements occurs in the particular context of mandatory employment arbitration agreements, in order to ensure that such agreements are not used as a means of effectively curtailing an employee's FEHA rights. These requirements would generally not apply in situations in which an employer and an employee knowingly and voluntarily enter into an arbitration agreement after a dispute has arisen. In those cases, employees are free to determine what trade-offs between arbitral efficiency and formal procedural protections best safeguard their statutory rights. Absent such freely negotiated agreements, it is for

802 CHAPTER V ARBITRATION

1. Limitation of Remedies

The principle that an arbitration agreement may not limit statutorily imposed remedies such as punitive damages and attorney fees appears to be undisputed.

* * *

The employer does not contest that the damages limitation would be unlawful if applied to statutory claims, but instead contends that the limitation applies only to contract claims, pointing to the language in the penultimate sentence that refers to "my exclusive remedy for violation of the terms, conditions or covenants of employment...." Both the trial court and the Court of Appeal correctly rejected this interpretation. While the above quoted language is susceptible to the employer's interpretation, the final sentence—"I understand that I shall not be entitled to any other remedy...."—makes clear that the damages limitation was all-encompassing. We conclude this damages limitation is contrary to public policy and unlawful.

2. Adequate Discovery

The employees argue that employers typically have in their possession many of the documents relevant for bringing an employment discrimination case, as well as having in their employ many of the relevant witnesses. The denial of adequate discovery in arbitration proceedings leads to the de facto frustration of the employee's statutory rights. They cite a report by the Department of Labor's Commission on the Future of Worker–Management Relations, chaired by former Secretary of Labor John Dunlop and including employee and employer representatives, which concludes that "if private arbitration is to serve as a legitimate form of private enforcement of public employment law," it must among other things provide "a fair and simple method by which the employee can secure the necessary information to present his or her claim." (Com. on the Future of Worker–Management Relations, Reported Recommendations (1994) p. 31 (hereafter Dunlop Commission Report).)

We agree that adequate discovery is indispensable for the vindication of FEHA claims. The employer does not dispute the point, but contends that the arbitration agreement at issue in this case does provide for adequate discovery by incorporating by reference all the rules set forth in the CAA. Adequate provisions for discovery are set forth in the CAA at Code of Civil Procedure section 1283.05, subdivision (a).[10]

the courts to ensure that the arbitration forum imposed on an employee is sufficient to vindicate his or her rights under the FEHA.

10. Code of Civil Procedure section 1283.05, subdivision (a), states: "To the extent provided in Section 1283.1 depositions may be taken and discovery obtained in arbitration proceedings as follows:

(a) After the appointment of the arbitrator or arbitrators, the parties to the arbitration shall have the right to take depositions and to obtain discovery regarding the subject matter of the arbitration, and, to that end, to use and exercise all of the same rights, remedies, and procedures, and be subject to all of the same

The employees point out that the provisions of Code of Civil Procedure section 1283.05 are only "conclusively deemed to be incorporated into" an agreement to arbitrate under section 1283.1 if the dispute arises "out of . . . any injury to, or death of, a person caused by the wrongful act or neglect of another", and argue that this language does not apply to FEHA claims. They further argue that because adequate discovery is not guaranteed under the arbitration agreement, FEHA claims should not be deemed arbitrable.

We note that one Court of Appeal case has held that a FEHA sexual harassment claim is considered an "injury to . . . a person" within the meaning of Code of Civil Procedure section 1283.1, subdivision (a). * * * The scope of this provision is not before us. But even assuming that the claim in this case is not the sort of injury encompassed by section 1283.1, subdivision (a), subdivision (b) of that section permits parties to agree to incorporate section 1283.05. We infer from subdivision (b), and from the fundamentally contractual nature of arbitration itself, that parties incorporating the CAA into their arbitration agreement are also permitted to agree to something less than the full panoply of discovery provided in section 1283.05. We further infer that when parties agree to arbitrate statutory claims, they also implicitly agree, absent express language to the contrary, to such procedures as are necessary to vindicate that claim. As discussed above, it is undisputed that some discovery is often necessary for vindicating a FEHA claim. Accordingly, whether or not the employees in this case are entitled to the full range of discovery provided in Code of Civil Procedure section 1283.05, they are at least entitled to discovery sufficient to adequately arbitrate their statutory claim, including access to essential documents and witnesses, as determined by the arbitrator(s) * * *.[11]

Therefore, although the employees are correct that they are entitled to sufficient discovery as a means of vindicating their sexual discrimination claims, we hold that the employer, by agreeing to arbitrate the FEHA claim, has already impliedly consented to such discovery. Therefore, lack of discovery is not grounds for holding a FEHA claim inarbitrable.

3. Written Arbitration Award and Judicial Review

The employees argue that lack of judicial review of arbitration awards makes the vindication of FEHA rights in arbitration illusory. * * * Arbitra-

---

duties, liabilities, and obligations in the arbitration with respect to the subject matter thereof, * * * as if the subject matter of the arbitration were pending before a superior court of this state in a civil action other than a limited civil case, subject to the limitations as to depositions set forth in subdivision (e) of this section." Subdivision (e) states that depositions may only be taken with the approval of the arbitrator.

11. We recognize, of course, that a limitation on discovery is one important component of the "simplicity, informality and expedition of arbitration." (*Gilmer*, 500 U.S. at p. 31.) The arbitrator and reviewing court must balance this desirable simplicity with the requirements of the FEHA in determining the appropriate discovery, absent more specific statutory or contractual provisions.

804　　CHAPTER V　ARBITRATION

tion, they argue, cannot be an adequate means of resolving a FEHA claim if the arbitrator is essentially free to disregard the law.

* * *

We are not faced in this case with a petition to confirm an arbitration award, and therefore have no occasion to articulate precisely what standard of judicial review is "sufficient to ensure that arbitrators comply with the requirements of [a] statute." (*McMahon*, 482 U.S. at p. 232.) All we hold today is that in order for such judicial review to be successfully accomplished, an arbitrator in a FEHA case must issue a written arbitration decision that will reveal, however briefly, the essential findings and conclusions on which the award is based. While such written findings and conclusions are not required under the CAA, nothing in the present arbitration agreement precludes such written findings, and to the extent it applies to FEHA claims the agreement must be interpreted to provide for such findings. In all other respects, the employees' claim that they are unable to vindicate their FEHA rights because of inadequate judicial review of an arbitration award is premature.

4.　Employee Not to Pay Unreasonable Costs and Arbitration Fees

The employees point to the fact that the agreement is governed by Code of Civil Procedure section 1284.2, which provides that "each party to the arbitration shall pay his pro rata share of the expenses and fees of the neutral arbitrator, together with other expenses of the arbitration incurred or imposed by the neutral arbitrator." They argue that requiring them to share the often substantial costs of arbitrators and arbitration effectively prevents them from vindicating their FEHA rights.

In considering the employees' claim, we start with the extensive discussion of this issue in *Cole*. The *Cole* court held that it was unlawful to require an employee who is the subject of a mandatory employment arbitration agreement to have to pay the costs of arbitration. The issue in that case was an arbitration agreement that was to be governed by the rules of the American Arbitration Association (AAA). Under these rules, the court noted that the employee may well be obliged to pay arbitrators' fees ranging from $500 to $1,000 per day or more, a $500 filing fee, and administrative fees of $150 per day, in addition to room rental and court reporter fees. The court's reasons for requiring employer-financed arbitration are worth quoting at length:

> In *Gilmer* the Supreme Court endorsed a system of arbitration in which employees are not required to pay for the arbitrator assigned to hear their statutory claims. There is no reason to think that the Court would have approved arbitration in the absence of this arrangement. Indeed, we are unaware of any situation in American jurisprudence in which a beneficiary of a federal statute has been required to pay for the services of the judge assigned to hear her or his case. Under *Gilmer*, arbitration is supposed to be a reasonable substitute for a judicial forum. Therefore, it would undermine Congress's intent to

C. Arbitration and the Courts 805

prevent employees who are seeking to vindicate statutory rights from gaining access to a judicial forum and then require them to pay for the services of an arbitrator when they would never be required to pay for a judge in court.

There is no doubt that parties appearing in federal court may be required to assume the cost of filing fees and other administrative expenses, so any reasonable costs of this sort that accompany arbitration are not problematic. However, if an employee like Cole is required to pay arbitrators' fees ranging from $500 to $1,000 per day or more, . . . in addition to administrative and attorney's fees, is it likely that he will be able to pursue his statutory claims? We think not. * * * [I]t is unacceptable to require Cole to pay arbitrators' fees, because such fees are unlike anything that he would have to pay to pursue his statutory claims in court.

Arbitration will occur in this case only because it has been mandated by the employer as a condition of employment. Absent this requirement, the employee would be free to pursue his claims in court without having to pay for the services of a judge. In such a circumstance— where arbitration has been imposed by the employer and occurs only at the option of the employer—arbitrators' fees should be borne solely by the employer.

The Tenth and Eleventh Circuit Courts of Appeal have adopted a position on arbitration fees for statutory employment claims essentially in accord with *Cole*. In Shankle [v. B–G Maintenance Management of Colorado, Inc., 163 F.3d 1230, (10th Cir.1999)], the court estimated that the employee would have to pay between $1,875 and $5,000 in forum costs to resolve his claim. As the court stated: "Mr. Shankle could not afford such a fee, and it is unlikely other similarly situated employees could either. The Agreement thus placed Mr. Shankle between the proverbial rock and a hard place—it prohibited use of the judicial forum, where a litigant is not required to pay for a judge's services, and the prohibitive cost substantially limited use of the arbitral forum. Essentially, B–G Maintenance required Mr. Shankle to agree to mandatory arbitration as a term of continued employment, yet failed to provide an accessible forum in which he could resolve his statutory rights. Such a result clearly undermines the remedial and deterrent functions of the federal anti-discrimination laws."

* * *

[I]f it is possible that the employee will be charged substantial forum costs, it is an insufficient judicial response to hold that he or she may be able to cancel these costs at the end of the process through judicial review. Such a system still poses a significant risk that employees will have to bear large costs to vindicate their statutory right against workplace discrimination, and therefore chills the exercise of that right. Because we conclude the imposition of substantial forum fees is contrary to public policy, and is therefore grounds for invalidating or "revoking" an arbitration agreement and denying a petition to compel arbitration, * * * we hold that the cost issues should be resolved not at the judicial review stage but when a court is petitioned to compel arbitration.

Accordingly, consistent with the majority of jurisdictions to consider this issue, we conclude that when an employer imposes mandatory arbitration as a condition of employment, the arbitration agreement or arbitration process cannot generally require the employee to bear any type of expense that the employee would not be required to bear if he or she were free to bring the action in court. This rule will ensure that employees bringing FEHA claims will not be deterred by costs greater than the usual costs incurred during litigation, costs that are essentially imposed on an employee by the employer.

Three principal objections have been raised to imposing the forum costs of arbitration on the employer. The first is that such a system will compromise the neutrality of the arbitrator. As the *Cole* court recognized, however, it is not the fact that the employer may pay an arbitrator that is most likely to induce bias, but rather the fact that the employer is a "repeat player" in the arbitration system who is more likely to be a source of business for the arbitrator. Furthermore, as the *Cole* court recognized, there are sufficient institutional safeguards, such as scrutiny by the plaintiff's bar and appointing agencies like the AAA, to protect against corrupt arbitrators.

The second objection is that although employees may have large forum costs, the cost of arbitration is generally smaller than litigation, so that the employee will realize a net benefit from arbitration. Although it is true that the costs of arbitration is on average smaller than that of litigation, it is also true that amount awarded is on average smaller as well. The payment of large, fixed, forum costs, especially in the face of expected meager awards, serves as a significant deterrent to the pursuit of FEHA claims.

To be sure, it would be ideal to devise a method by which the employee is put in exactly the same position in arbitration, costwise, as he or she would be in litigation. But the factors going into that calculus refuse to admit ready quantification. Turning a motion to compel arbitration into a mini-trial on the comparative costs and benefits of arbitration and litigation for a particular employee would not only be burdensome on the trial court and the parties, but would likely yield speculative answers. Nor would there be an advantage to apportioning arbitration costs at the conclusion of the arbitration rather than at the outset. Without clearly articulated guidelines, such a post-arbitration apportionment would create a sense of risk and uncertainty among employees that could discourage the arbitration of meritorious claims.

Moreover, the above rule is fair, inasmuch as it places the cost of arbitration on the party that imposes it. Unlike the employee, the employer is in a position to perform a cost/benefit calculus and decide whether arbitration is, overall, the most economical forum. Nor would this rule necessarily present an employer with a choice between paying all the forum costs of arbitration or forgoing arbitration altogether and defending itself in court. There is a third alternative. Because this proposed rule would only apply to mandatory, predispute employment arbitration agreements, and because in many instances arbitration will be considered an efficient means of resolving a dispute both for the employer and the employee, the employer seeking to avoid both payment of all forum costs and litigation can attempt to negotiate postdispute arbitration agreements with its aggrieved employees.

The third objection to requiring the employer to shoulder most of the costs of arbitration is that it appears contrary to statute. As noted, Code of Civil Procedure section 1284.2 provides that unless the arbitration agreement provides otherwise, each party to the arbitration must pay his or her pro rata share of arbitration costs. But section 1284.2 is a default provision, and the agreement to arbitrate a statutory claim is implicitly an agreement to abide by the substantive remedial provisions of the statute. As noted, FEHA rights are unwaivable. * * * We do not believe the FEHA contemplates that employees may be compelled to resolve their antidiscrimination claims in a forum in which they must pay for what is the equivalent of the judge's time and the rental of the courtroom.

* * *

We therefore hold that a mandatory employment arbitration agreement that contains within its scope the arbitration of FEHA claims impliedly obliges the employer to pay all types of costs that are unique to arbitration. Accordingly, we interpret the arbitration agreement in the present case as providing, consistent with the above, that the employer must bear the arbitration forum costs. The absence of specific provisions on arbitration costs would therefore not be grounds for denying the enforcement of an arbitration agreement.

D. Unconscionability of the Arbitration Agreement

1. General Principles of Unconscionability

In the previous section of this opinion, we focused on the minimum requirements for the arbitration of unwaivable statutory claims. In this section, we will consider objections to arbitration that apply more generally to any type of arbitration imposed on the employee by the employer as a condition of employment, regardless of the type of claim being arbitrated. These objections fall under the rubric of "unconscionability."

We explained the judicially created doctrine of unconscionability in [*Graham v. Scissor–Tail,* see p. 704 supra]. Unconscionability analysis begins with an inquiry into whether the contract is one of adhesion. "The term [contract of adhesion] signifies a standardized contract, which, imposed and drafted by the party of superior bargaining strength, relegates to the subscribing party only the opportunity to adhere to the contract or reject it." If the contract is adhesive, the court must then determine whether "other factors are present which, under established legal rules—legislative or judicial—operate to render it [unenforceable]." "Generally speaking, there are two judicially imposed limitations on the enforcement of adhesion contracts or provisions thereof. The first is that such a contract or provision which does not fall within the reasonable expectations of the weaker or 'adhering' party will not be enforced against him. The second—a principle of equity applicable to all contracts generally—is that a contract or provision, even if consistent with the reasonable expectations of the parties, will be denied enforcement if, considered in its context, it is unduly oppressive or 'unconscionable.' " * * *

Because unconscionability is a reason for refusing to enforce contracts generally, it is also a valid reason for refusing to enforce an arbitration agreement under Code of Civil Procedure section 1281, which, as noted, provides that arbitration agreements are "valid, irrevocable, and enforceable, save upon such grounds as exist at law or in equity for the revocation of any contract." The United States Supreme Court, in interpreting the same language found in section 2 of the FAA, recognized that "generally applicable contract defenses, such as fraud, duress, or unconscionability, may be applied to invalidate arbitration agreements. . . . "

"[U]nconscionability has both a 'procedural' and a 'substantive' element," the former focusing on "oppression" or "surprise" due to unequal bargaining power, the latter on "overly harsh" or "one-sided" results. "The prevailing view is that [procedural and substantive unconscionability] must both be present in order for a court to exercise its discretion to refuse to enforce a contract or clause under the doctrine of unconscionability." But they need not be present in the same degree. "Essentially a sliding scale is invoked which disregards the regularity of the procedural process of the contract formation, that creates the terms, in proportion to the greater harshness or unreasonableness of the substantive terms themselves." In other words, the more substantively oppressive the contract term, the less evidence of procedural unconscionability is required to come to the conclusion that the term is unenforceable, and vice versa.

2. Unconscionability and Mandatory Employment Arbitration

Applying the above principles to this case, we first determine whether the arbitration agreement is adhesive. There is little dispute that it is. It was imposed on employees as a condition of employment and there was no opportunity to negotiate.

* * *

Aside from FEHA issues discussed in the previous part of this opinion, the employees contend that the agreement is substantively unconscionable because it requires only employees to arbitrate their wrongful termination claims against the employer, but does not require the employer to arbitrate claims it may have against the employees. In asserting that this lack of mutuality is unconscionable, they rely primarily on the opinion of the Court of Appeal Stirlen v. Supercuts, Inc., 60 Cal. Rptr.2d 138 (Cal.App. 1997). The employee in that case was hired as a vice president and chief financial officer; his employment contract provided for arbitration "in the event there is any dispute arising out of [the employee's] employment with the Company," including "the termination of that employment." The agreement specifically excluded certain types of disputes from the scope of arbitration, including those relating to the protection of the employer's intellectual and other property and the enforcement of a post-employment covenant not to compete, which were to be litigated in state or federal court. The employee was to waive the right to challenge the jurisdiction of such a court. The arbitration agreement further provided that the damages available would be limited to "the amount of actual damages for breach of contract, less any proper offset for mitigation of such damages." When an arbitration claim was filed, payments of any salary or benefits were to cease "without penalty to the Company," pending the outcome of the arbitration.

The *Stirlen* court concluded that the agreement was one of adhesion, even though the employee in question was a high-level executive, because of the lack of opportunity to negotiate. The court then concluded that the arbitration agreement was substantively unconscionable. * * * The employee pursuing claims against the employer had to bear not only with the inherent shortcomings of arbitration—limited discovery, limited judicial review, limited procedural protections—but also significant damage limitations imposed by the arbitration agreement. The employer, on the other hand, in pursuing its claims, was not subject to these disadvantageous limitations and had written into the agreement special advantages, such as a waiver of jurisdictional objections by the employee if sued by the employer.

The *Stirlen* court did not hold that all lack of mutuality in a contract of adhesion was invalid. "We agree a contract can provide a 'margin of safety' that provides the party with superior bargaining strength a type of extra protection for which it has a legitimate commercial need without being unconscionable. However, unless the 'business realities' that create the special need for such an advantage are explained in the contract itself, which is not the case here, it must be factually established." The *Stirlen* court found no "business reality" to justify the lack of mutuality, concluding that the terms of the arbitration clause were " 'so extreme as to appear unconscionable according to the mores and business practices of the time and place.' "

* * *

We conclude that *Stirlen* [is] correct in requiring this "modicum of bilaterality" in an arbitration agreement. Given the disadvantages that may exist for plaintiffs arbitrating disputes, it is unfairly one-sided for an employer with superior bargaining power to impose arbitration on the employee as plaintiff but not to accept such limitations when it seeks to prosecute a claim against the employee, without at least some reasonable justification for such one-sidedness based on "business realities." As has been recognized unconscionability turns not only on a "one-sided" result, but also on an absence of "justification" for it. If the arbitration system established by the employer is indeed fair, then the employer as well as the employee should be willing to submit claims to arbitration. Without reasonable justification for this lack of mutuality, arbitration appears less as a forum for neutral dispute resolution and more as a means of maximizing employer advantage. Arbitration was not intended for this purpose

The employer cites a number of cases that have held that a lack of mutuality in an arbitration agreement does not render the contract illusory as long as the employer agrees to be bound by the arbitration of employment disputes. We agree that such lack of mutuality does not render the contract illusory, i.e., lacking in mutual consideration. We conclude, rather, that in the context of an arbitration agreement imposed by the employer on the employee, such a one-sided term is unconscionable. Although parties are free to contract for asymmetrical remedies and arbitration clauses of varying scope, *Stirlen* [is] correct that the doctrine of unconscionability limits the extent to which a stronger party may, through a contract of adhesion, impose the arbitration forum on the weaker party without accepting that forum for itself.

* * *

Applying these principles to the present case, we note the arbitration agreement was limited in scope to employee claims regarding wrongful termination. Although it did not expressly authorize litigation of the employer's claims against the employee, as was the case in *Stirlen*, such was the clear implication of the agreement. Obviously, the lack of mutuality can be manifested as much by what the agreement does not provide as by what it does.

This is not to say that an arbitration clause must mandate the arbitration of all claims between employer and employee in order to avoid invalidation on grounds of unconscionability. Indeed, as the employer points out, the present arbitration agreement does not require arbitration of all conceivable claims that an employee might have against an employer, only wrongful termination claims. But an arbitration agreement imposed in an adhesive context lacks basic fairness and mutuality if it requires one contracting party, but not the other, to arbitrate all claims arising out of the same transaction or occurrence or series of transactions or occurrences. The arbitration agreement in this case lacks mutuality in this sense because it requires the arbitration of employee—but not employer—claims arising out of a wrongful termination. An employee terminated for stealing trade secrets, for example, must arbitrate his or her wrongful termination claim under the agreement while the employer has no corresponding obligation to arbitrate its trade secrets claim against the employee.

The unconscionable one-sidedness of the arbitration agreement is compounded in this case by the fact that it does not permit the full recovery of damages for employees, while placing no such restriction on the employer. Even if the limitation on FEHA damages is severed as contrary to public policy, the arbitration clause in the present case still does not permit full recovery of ordinary contract damages. The arbitration agreement specifies that damages are to be limited to the amount of back pay lost up until the time of arbitration. This provision excludes damages for prospective future earnings, so-called "front pay," a common and often substantial component of contractual damages in a wrongful termination case. The employer, on the other hand, is bound by no comparable limitation should it pursue a claim against its employees.

The employer in this case, as well as the Court of Appeal, claim the lack of mutuality was based on the realities of the employees' place in the organizational hierarchy. As the Court of Appeal stated: "We ... observe that the wording of the agreement most likely resulted from the employees' position within the organization and may reflect the fact that the parties did not foresee the possibility of any dispute arising from employment that was not initiated by the employee. Plaintiffs were lower-level supervisory employees, without the sort of access to proprietary information or control over corporate finances that might lead to an employer suit against them."

The fact that it is unlikely an employer will bring claims against a particular type of employee is not, ultimately, a justification for a unilateral arbitration agreement. It provides no reason for categorically exempting employer claims, however rare, from mandatory arbitration. Although an employer may be able, in a future case, to justify a unilateral arbitration agreement, the employer in the present case has not done so.

E. Severability of Unconscionable Provisions

The employees contend that the presence of various unconscionable provisions or provisions contrary to public policy leads to the conclusion that the arbitration agreement as a whole cannot be enforced. The employer contends that, insofar as there are unconscionable provisions, they should be severed and the rest of the agreement enforced.

Civil Code section 1670.5, subdivision (a) provides that "if the court as a matter of law finds the contract or any clause of the contract to have been unconscionable at the time it was made the court may refuse to enforce the contract, or it may enforce the remainder of the contract without the unconscionable clause, or it may so limit the application of any unconscionable clause as to avoid any unconscionable result." Comment 2 of the Legislative Committee Comment on section 1670.5, incorporating the comments from the Uniform Commercial Code, states: "Under this section the court, in its discretion, may refuse to enforce the contract as a whole if it is permeated by the unconscionability, or it may strike any single clause or group of clauses which are so tainted or which are contrary to the essential purpose of the agreement, or it may simply limit unconscionable clauses so as to avoid unconscionable results."

Thus, the statute appears to give a trial court some discretion as to whether to sever or restrict the unconscionable provision or whether to refuse to enforce the entire agreement. But it also appears to contemplate the latter course only when an agreement is "permeated" by unconscionability.

* * *

Two reasons for severing or restricting illegal terms rather than voiding the entire contract appear implicit in case law. The first is to

CHAPTER V ARBITRATION

prevent parties from gaining undeserved benefit or suffering undeserved detriment as a result of voiding the entire agreement—particularly when there has been full or partial performance of the contract. Second, more generally, the doctrine of severance attempts to conserve a contractual relationship if to do so would not be condoning an illegal scheme. The overarching inquiry is whether "the interests of justice ... would be furthered" by severance. Moreover, courts must have the capacity to cure the unlawful contract through severance or restriction of the offending clause, which, as discussed below, is not invariably the case.

* * *

In this case, two factors weigh against severance of the unlawful provisions. First, the arbitration agreement contains more than one unlawful provision; it has both an unlawful damages provision and an unconscionably unilateral arbitration clause. Such multiple defects indicate a systematic effort to impose arbitration on an employee not simply as an alternative to litigation, but as an inferior forum that works to the employer's advantage. In other words, given the multiple unlawful provisions, the trial court did not abuse its discretion in concluding that the arbitration agreement is permeated by an unlawful purpose.[13]

Second, in the case of the agreement's lack of mutuality, such permeation is indicated by the fact that there is no single provision a court can strike or restrict in order to remove the unconscionable taint from the agreement. Rather, the court would have to, in effect, reform the contract, not through severance or restriction, but by augmenting it with additional terms. * * * Code of Civil Procedure section 1281.2 authorizes the court to refuse arbitration if grounds for revocation exist, not to reform the agreement to make it lawful. Nor do courts have any such power under their inherent, limited authority to reform contracts. (See Kolani v. Gluska, 64

---

13. We need not decide whether the unlawful damages provision in this arbitration agreement, by itself, would be sufficient to warrant a court's refusal to enforce that agreement. We note, however, that in the analogous case of overly broad covenants not to compete, courts have tended to invalidate rather than restrict such covenants when it appears they were drafted in bad faith, i.e., with a knowledge of their illegality. The reason for this rule is that if such bad faith restrictive covenants are enforced, then "employers are encouraged to overreach; if the covenant is overbroad then the court will redraft it for them." This reasoning applies with equal force to arbitration agreements that limit damages to be obtained from challenging the violation of unwaivable statutory rights. An employer will not be deterred from routinely inserting such a deliberately illegal clause into the arbitration agreements it

mandates for its employees if it knows that the worst penalty for such illegality is the severance of the clause after the employee has litigated the matter. In that sense, the enforcement of a form arbitration agreement containing such a clause drafted in bad faith would be condoning, or at least not discouraging, an illegal scheme, and severance would be disfavored unless it were for some other reason in the interests of justice. The refusal to enforce such a clause is also consistent with the rule that a party may waive its right to arbitration through bad faith or willful misconduct. Because we resolve this case on other grounds, we need not decide whether the state of the law with respect to damages limitations was sufficiently clear at the time the arbitration agreement was signed to lead to the conclusion that this damages clause was drafted in bad faith.

Cal. App. 4th 402, 407–408 (1998)) [power to reform limited to instances in which parties make mistakes, not to correct illegal provisions]. Because a court is unable to cure this unconscionability through severance or restriction, and is not permitted to cure it through reformation and augmentation, it must void the entire agreement.

* * *

The approach described above is consistent with our holding in *Scissor–Tail*. In that case, we found an arbitration agreement to be unconscionable because the agreement provided for an arbitrator likely to be biased in favor of the party imposing the agreement. We nonetheless recognized that "the parties have indeed agreed to arbitrate" and that there is a "strong public policy of this state in favor of resolving disputes by arbitration." The court found a way out of this dilemma through the [California Arbitration Act,] specifically Code of Civil Procedure section 1281.6, which provides in part: "In the absence of an agreed method [for appointing an arbitrator], or if the agreed method fails or for any reason cannot be followed, or when an arbitrator appointed fails to act and his or her successor has not been appointed, the court, on petition of a party to the arbitration agreement, shall appoint the arbitrator." Citing this provision, the court stated: "We therefore conclude that upon remand the trial court should afford the parties a reasonable opportunity to agree on a suitable arbitrator and, failing such agreement, the court should on petition of either party appoint the arbitrator." Other cases, both before and after *Scissor-Tail,* have also held that the part of an arbitration clause providing for a less-than-neutral arbitration forum is severable from the rest of the clause.

Thus, in *Scissor-Tail* and the other cases cited above, the arbitration statute itself gave the court the power to reform an arbitration agreement with respect to the method of selecting arbitrators. There is no comparable provision in the arbitration statute that permits courts to reform an unconscionably one-sided agreement.

* * *

The employer also points to two cases in which unconscionably one-sided provisions in arbitration agreements were severed and the agreement enforced. [Saika v. Gold, 56 Cal. Rptr.2d 922 (Cal.App.1996)] involved an arbitration agreement with a provision that would make the arbitration nonbinding if the arbitration award were $25,000 or greater. In Beynon v. Garden Grove Medical Group [161 Cal. Rptr. 146 (Cal.App.1980)], a provision of the arbitration agreement gave one party, but not the other, the option of rejecting the arbitrator's decision. The courts in both instances concluded, in *Saika* implicitly, in *Beynon* explicitly, that the offending clause was severable from the rest of the arbitration agreement.

The provisions in these two cases are different from the one-sided arbitration provision at issue in this case in at least two important respects. First, the one-sidedness in the above two cases were confined to single provisions regarding the rights of the parties after an arbitration award was made, not a provision affecting the scope of the arbitration. As such, the unconscionability could be cured by severing the unlawful provisions. Second, in both cases, the arguments against severance were made by the party that had imposed the unconscionable provision in order to prevent enforcement of an arbitration award against them, and the failure to sever would have had the effect of accomplishing the precise unlawful purpose of that provision the invalidation of the arbitration award. As discussed, courts will generally sever illegal provisions and enforce a contract when nonenforcement will lead to an undeserved benefit or detriment to one of the parties that would not further the interests of justice. In *Beynon* and *Saika*, the interests of justice would obviously not have been furthered by nonenforcement. The same considerations are not found in the present case.

The judgment of the Court of Appeal upholding the employer's petition to compel arbitration is reversed, and the cause is remanded to the Court of Appeal with directions to affirm the judgment of the trial court.

■ BROWN, J., CONCURRING. Although I agree with most of the majority's reasoning, I write separately on the issue of apportioning arbitral costs. The majority takes the simple approach: where the employer imposes mandatory arbitration and the employee asserts a statutory claim, the employer must bear all costs "unique to arbitration." Simplicity, however, is not a proxy for correctness. * * *

In adopting the bright-line approach advocated by *Cole,* supra, the majority argues that the mere risk that an employee may have to bear certain arbitral costs necessarily "chills the exercise" of her statutory rights. Thus, arbitration is not a reasonable substitute for a court if arbitral costs, such as the arbitrator's fees, may be imposed on the employee. The majority, however, assumes too much. "Arbitration is often far more affordable to plaintiffs and defendants alike than is pursuing a claim in court." Because employees may incur fewer costs and attorney fees in arbitration than in court, the potential imposition of arbitration forum costs does not automatically render the arbitral forum more expensive than—and therefore inferior to—the judicial forum.

The majority's approach also ignores the unique circumstances of each case. Not all arbitrations are costly, and not all employees are unable to afford the unique costs of arbitration. Thus, the imposition of some arbitral costs does not deter or discourage employees from pursuing their statutory claims in every case. (See, e.g., Williams v. Cigna Financial Advisors Inc.,197 F.3d 752, 764–765 (5th Cir.1999) [compelling arbitration because the employee did not show that he was unable to pay the arbitral costs or that these costs would deter him from pursuing his claims]; McCaskill v. SCI Management Corp., 2000 WL 875396 (N.D.Ill.) [compelling arbitration because there was no evidence that the costs of arbitration would be prohibitively expensive for the employee]; Cline v. H.E. Butt Grocery Co.,79 F. Supp. 2d 730, 733 (S.D.Tex.1999) [compelling arbitration because there was no evidence that the employee would have to pay any costs or that the employee could not afford to do so].) Indeed, the uniqueness of each case makes it impossible for any court to "conclude that the payment of fees will constitute a barrier to the vindication of ... statutory rights" without knowing the exact amount the employee must pay.

Accordingly, I would reject the majority's approach and follow the approach suggested by courts in several other jurisdictions. As long as the mandatory arbitration agreement does not require the employee to front the arbitration forum costs or to pay a certain share of these costs, apportionment should be left to the arbitrator. When apportioning costs, the arbitrator should consider the magnitude of the costs unique to arbitration, the ability of the employee to pay a share of these costs, and the overall expense of the arbitration as compared to a court proceeding. Ultimately, any apportionment should ensure that the costs imposed on the employee, if known at the onset of litigation, would not have deterred her from enforcing her statutory rights or stopped her from effectively vindicating these rights.

If the employee feels that the arbitrator's apportionment of costs is unreasonable, then she can raise the issue during judicial review of the arbitration award. I believe such an approach is preferable because it accounts for the particular circumstances of each case without sacrificing the employee's statutory rights.

NOTES AND QUESTIONS

1. As the *Armendariz* case indicates, arbitration agreements are increasingly common in nonunion employment agreements outside of the securities industry. Companies like Rockwell International, Brown and Root, Borg–Warner, and Hughes Electronics are now requiring such clauses, which usually call for arbitration under the auspices of an organization like the AAA. The General Accounting office estimated in 1995 that about 10% of companies with more than 100 employees were using binding arbitration to resolve employment discrimination claims (although arbitration was not made mandatory in all cases); another 8.4% were considering instituting such a policy. Most of these arbitration policies had been implemented in the previous five years, and the number would certainly be considerably larger today. GAO, Employment Discrimination: Most Private–Sector Employers Use Alternative Dispute Resolution 6–8, 28 (July 1995).

2. Does Justice Brown have the better of the argument when he urges that the issue of costs should be postponed, until such time as a court is asked to confirm or vacate the award? This was in fact the approach of the United States Supreme Court in a recent non-employment case, Green Tree Financial Corp.-Alabama v. Randolph, 531 U.S. 79 (2000). Here a buyer of a mobile home had financed the purchase, and later brought suit against the lender alleging violations of the Truth in Lending Act, 15 U.S.C. § 1601. The Eleventh Circuit held that the arbitration clause in the agreement was unenforceable: Since the agreement was silent with respect to the payment of filing fees and arbitrator compensation, there was a risk that the plaintiff's ability to assert her statutory rights under the TILA

816 CHAPTER V ARBITRATION

would be undone by "steep" arbitration costs. The Supreme Court reversed.

The Court acknowledged the possibility that "the existence of large arbitration costs could preclude a litigant such as [the plaintiff] from effectively vindicating her federal statutory rights in the arbitral forum." However, if a party seeks to invalidate an arbitration agreement on the ground that arbitration "would be prohibitively expensive," she must "bear the burden of showing the likelihood of incurring such costs." Here, the "risk" that the plaintiff "will be saddled with prohibitive costs is too speculative to justify the invalidation of an arbitration agreement," and the agreement's silence on the subject of costs "alone is plainly insufficient to render it unenforceable." Four dissenting justices would have preferred to remand for "clarification" and "further consideration of the accessibility of the arbitral forum" to the plaintiff, rather than "leaving the issue unsettled until the end of the line," that is, until after the arbitration. They noted that under the AAA's Consumer Arbitration Rules, consumers in small-claims arbitration incur no filing fee and are required to pay only $125 of the total fees charged by the arbitrator—but stressed that "there is no reliable indication in this record that [the plaintiff's] claim will be arbitrated under any consumer-protective fee arrangement."

3. On the subject of "non-mutual" arbitration clauses—where only one of the parties to the agreement is obligated to arbitrate—compare *Stevens/Leinweber/Sullens, Inc. v. Holm Development and Management, Inc.*, supra pp. 692–698.

4. Note that the Supreme Court of California apparently assumed in *Armendariz* that it was *for a court—rather than for an arbitrator—*to determine whether the terms of the agreement were "unlawful" or "unconscionable." Cf. p. 697 supra; see also Margaret M. Harding, The Redefinition of Arbitration By Those With Superior Bargaining Power, 1999 Utah L. Rev. 857, 922–23 ("The claim that an arbitration clause is invalid because it improperly restricts statutory remedies should be distinguished from the situation where the parties in the container contract exclude certain types of damages"; "a defense to arbitration based on public policy stemming * * * from the unsuitability of the particular arbitral scheme crafted for determining the claim does indeed challenge the validity of the arbitration agreement and the arbitrability of the dispute"). Do you agree?

Assume, though, that this is indeed a question for the court: Does it follow that a judicial finding of "unconscionability" necessarily means that *the arbitration agreement as a whole* "is tainted and cannot be enforced"? See Harding, supra at 944 (courts should "penalize parties who attempt to use the arbitral process for improper means"; [w]hen a party attempts to abuse the arbitral process and gets caught, that party should completely lose the privilege—gained only by its superior economic position—of requiring the weaker party to arbitrate). Do you agree? See also Coddington Enterprises, Inc. v. Werries, 54 F.Supp.2d 935 (W.D.Mo.1999), in which an arbitration clause, in an agreement between retail grocers and their whole-

C. ARBITRATION AND THE COURTS **817**

sale supplier, provided that the arbitrators "will not award punitive, consequential or indirect damages." In the grocers' action for RICO violations, the court found the arbitration clause to be unenforceable: The quoted phrase amounts to "a limitation on the authority of arbitrators, something the parties can doubtless agree to—even if their agreement means that arbitration provides inadequate remedies and cannot be enforced." Cf. Wright v. Circuit City Stores, 82 F.Supp.2d 1279 (N.D.Ala. 2000), in which an employment agreement limited punitive damages "to the greater of the monetary awards rendered for back pay and/or front pay or $5000," and also provided that if any of the company's "Dispute Resolution Rules and Procedures" were held to be "in conflict with a mandatory provision of applicable law," it would be "modified." The employee sued for violations of Title VII and of 42 U.S.C. § 1981, but the court held that arbitration should be compelled; it relied both on the severability clause, and the employer's "good faith in devising the arbitration plan" as evidenced by the fact that employees were given an opportunity to "reject" Circuit City's arbitration proposal by opting out within 30 days following signature. The arbitration clause was, however, to be "modified * * * so that it allows for the full range of remedies that the Plaintiffs would be entitled to under § 1981."

5. Once it is clear that asserted violations of statutory rights may now be sent to arbitration, is it inevitable that a more intensive judicial scrutiny of arbitral awards will follow? See the *Mitsubishi* case, supra. One distinguished labor arbitrator has warned that "[w]hen arbitrators start interpreting statutes * * * there is no reason why their interpretations of the proper application of statutes should be given greater weight than that of the district courts. District courts' interpretations of statutes are constantly being reviewed by appellate courts." Feller, Arbitration and the External Law Revisited, 37 St. Louis U.L.J. 973, 980 (1993).

See, e.g., Halligan v. Piper Jaffray, Inc., 148 F.3d 197 (2d Cir. 1998). Although a discharged employee had presented the arbitrators with "overwhelming evidence" of age-based discrimination, "an NASD arbitration panel denied any relief in an award that 'did not contain any explanation or rationale for the result.'" The Second Circuit held that the award should be vacated: "In view of the strong evidence that Halligan was fired because of his age and the agreement of the parties that the arbitrators were correctly advised of the applicable legal principles, we are inclined to hold that they ignored the law or the evidence or both." The court stressed that in making this decision, the arbitrators' failure to explain their award "can be taken into account." If the arbitrators had given as their rationale that they had simply believed the employer's witnesses rather than the employee's, "on this record it would have been extremely hard to accept—but they did not do even that." The court disclaimed any holding that arbitrators must write reasoned awards in every case or "even in most cases"—but it observed that "where a reviewing court is inclined to find that arbitrators manifestly disregarded the law or the evidence and that an explanation, if given, would have strained credulity, the absence of explanation may

818   CHAPTER V   ARBITRATION

reinforce the reviewing court's confidence that the arbitrators engaged in manifest disregard.''

Is it possible that too great an enthusiasm for arbitration in cases that touch on individual rights may create the danger of a ''backlash'' of hostility to the process generally?

6. The theoretical notion that an arbitration award could be overturned for ''manifestly disregarding the law'' has always been in considerable tension with a view of arbitration as a ''nonlegal'' process—a model in which arbitrators are ''free to ignore'' substantive rules of law in order to ''do justice as they see it,'' see pp. 611–613, 742–744 supra. The anomaly could be ignored as long as the doctrine of ''manifest disregard'' was largely moribund—see pp. 745–746 supra and, for a very poor prophecy, Alan Rau, The New York Convention in American Courts, 7 Amer. Rev. of Int'l Arb. 213, 238 (1996)(''This will never happen in our lifetimes.''). Cases like *Halligan v. Piper Jaffray* seem, however, to represent efforts to breathe new life into the doctrine—for as disputes over statutory rights are increasingly swept into arbitration, courts naturally come under increasing pressure to ensure that these rights are being adequately addressed.

More recently, by contrast, the Seventh Circuit has attempted to put the doctrine of ''manifest disregard'' in its place—by essentially equating it with the review of awards on grounds of ''public policy,'' and suggesting that it is subject to the same limitations as ''public policy'' review. In George Watts & Son, Inc. v. Tiffany & Co., 248 F.3d 577 (7th Cir.2001), an arbitrator granted relief to a distributor under the state's ''Fair Dealership Law,'' but failed, allegedly in violation of the statute, to award attorneys' fees and costs. The court nevertheless upheld confirmation of the award: ''Manifest disregard of the law,'' according to Judge Easterbrook, means simply that ''an arbitrator may not direct the parties to violate the law.'' ''The judiciary may step in when the arbitrator has commanded the parties to violate legal norms,'' but ''judges may not deprive arbitrators of authority to reach compromise outcomes that legal norms leave within the discretion of the parties to the arbitration agreement.'' Here, the parties themselves could certainly have negotiated a settlement under which each side would bear its own fees and costs. And if there would be no legal objection to such an outcome, ''what the parties may do, the arbitrator as their mutual agent may do.'' For a similar rationale in ''public policy'' cases, see *Eastern Associated Coal Corp. v. United Mine Workers,* supra p. 762.

7. Another response to growing criticism of employment arbitration may be found in rules that have recently been approved by the AAA for the arbitration of employment disputes. These rules provide that the arbitrators must be ''experienced in the field of employment law,'' and that ''[t]he parties shall bear the same burdens of proof and * * of producing evidence as would apply if their claims * * * had been brought in court.'' The arbitrator has ''the authority to order such discovery, by way of deposition, interrogatory, document production, or otherwise,'' as he considers necessary; he may grant any relief that he deems ''just and equitable, including any remedy or relief that would have been available to the parties had the matter been heard in court." The arbitrator must also "provide the written reasons for the award unless the parties agree otherwise," and the resulting award (with the exception of the names of the parties and witnesses) "shall be publicly available, on a cost basis." AAA, National Rules for the Resolution of Employment Disputes (effective January 1, 2001), R. 7, R. 11(a), R. 22, R. 34(b), (c), (d). According to one attorney who helped draft them, by arbitrating under the new rules "you are getting something close to the type of hearing that you would have had, [in] a bench trial in state or federal court." Aquino, "Revamping Employment Arbitration," The Recorder, Aug. 4, 1994 at p. 1. Are these changes desirable?

8. Attorneys who represent management in employment matters have cautioned that there might be some dangers in using arbitration agreements: For example, arbitrators might "borrow from the experience of labor arbitrators" under collective bargaining agreements that require "just cause" for discharge, and thereby expand the rights of "at-will" employees. Piskorski & Ross, Private Arbitration as the Exclusive Means of Resolving Employment–Related Disputes, 19 Employee Relations L.J. 205, 210 (1993); see also Guidry & Huffman, Legal and Practical Aspects of Alternative Dispute Resolution in Non–Union Companies, 6 Lab.Law. 1, 25 (1990) (employer may be "hoist on its own petard"). Is this a serious risk? In PaineWebber, Inc. v. Agron, 49 F.3d 347 (8th Cir.1995), arbitrators found that a brokerage firm had "improperly fired" one of its vice-presidents. The employer objected that this award "manifestly disregarded" the state's employment-at-will doctrine, but the court disagreed. Even if a "manifest disregard of the law" standard applied, "the use of the arbitration procedure as a means of settling employment-related disputes * * * necessarily alters the employment relationship from at-will to something else—some standard of discernable cause is inherently required in this context where an arbitration panel is called on to interpret the employment relationship." If the plaintiff's employment was purely at-will, "the arbitration procedure designed to interpret that employment relationship would serve no identifiable purpose."

9. The Supreme Court in *Gilmer* was "unpersuaded" by the employee's argument that compelling arbitration would "undermine" the role of the EEOC in enforcing statutes like the Age Discrimination in Employment Act: After all, it noted, a claimant subject to an arbitration agreement "will still be able to file a charge with the EEOC, even though [he] is not able to institute a private judicial action." And in any event, the EEOC's role in combating age discrimination is not dependent on the filing of a charge by a claimant—since the agency may receive information concerning alleged violations of the Act "from any source" and has independent authority to investigate discrimination. 500 U.S. at 28.

What possibilities then are open to the EEOC if it is convinced that Gilmer's employer had been violating the ADEA? It seems generally accepted (as the Supreme Court made clear in *Gilmer* itself) that "arbitration agreements will not preclude the EEOC from bringing actions seeking class-wide and equitable relief." The EEOC, however, is also empowered to seek monetary relief, such as back pay and damages, to "make whole" aggrieved employees: May it do so on behalf of employees like Gilmer who are bound to arbitrate their own claims?

The EEOC has asserted that it is allowed to seek such an order because it would not be "standing in the shoes" of the employees, but would rather be "suing in the public interest." The Sixth Circuit agreed with the EEOC in EEOC v. Frank's Nursery & Crafts, Inc., 177 F.3d 448 (6th Cir.1999)(EEOC and the employee "are not in privity, and [they] do not possess identical causes of action or interests"; the EEOC was granted by Congress "a right to represent an interest broader than that of a particular individual"; "[t]o empower a private individual to take away this congressional mandate, by entering into arbitration agreements or other contractual arrangements, would grant that individual the ability to govern whether and when the EEOC may protect the public interest * * * against employment discrimination"). It has even been suggested that in such cases the possibility of such EEOC actions "could slow the trend towards arbitration of employment-discrimination claims * * * by providing claimants with an end-run around *Gilmer*." See Negris, "Employment ADR: Sidestepping *Gilmer*," World Arb. & Med. Rep., March 1993 at 55. Other circuits, however, have disagreed, and the Supreme Court is likely to resolve the issue shortly. See EEOC v. Waffle House, Inc., 193 F.3d 805 (4th Cir.1999), *cert. granted,* 2001 WL 285799 ("when the EEOC seeks 'make-whole' relief for [an employee], the federal policy favoring enforcement of private arbitration agreements outweighs the EEOC's right to proceed in federal court because in that circumstance, the EEOC's public interest is minimal"); see also EEOC v. Kidder, Peabody & Co., Inc., 156 F.3d 298 (2d Cir. 1998)("where an individual has freely contracted away, waived, or unsuccessfully litigated a claim, the public interest in a back pay award is minimal"). Cf. Olde Discount Corp. v. Tupman, supra pp. 667–668.

10. The obstacles faced by an employee in pursuing an employment discrimination claim—whether through the EEOC's enforcement mechanism, or through a private suit—may be considerable. To seek relief on a federal statutory claim—under Title VII, the Age Discrimination in Employment Act, or the Americans with Disability Act—an individual must first file a charge of discrimination with the EEOC. If its investigation suggests the existence of a valid claim the EEOC must attempt conciliation, and may ultimately bring suit on behalf of the individual claimant. If for any reason the agency determines not to pursue the case, it must issue a "right to sue" notice informing the individual that she is free to initiate her own court action. In *each* of the years 1998 through 2000, between 77,000 and 80,000 charges of discrimination were filed by employees, former employees, or rejected job applicants; in these years the EEOC filed 366, 439, and 291 lawsuits respectively. The average processing time for a charge is "upwards of 300 days," and in some district offices is considerably higher. In discrimination lawsuits brought by individual employees, plaintiffs tend to receive a favorable jury verdict in fewer than half of litigated cases. More to the point, though, relatively few of these suits even reach a jury—since around 60% are disposed of by pre-trial motion, virtually always in favor of the defendant. In addition, a recent study indicates that employment discrimination plaintiffs who *do* win at trial see their judgments overturned on appeal in 43.6% of cases, while verdicts in favor of the employer are reversed in fewer than 6% of cases. See U.S. Commission on Civil Rights, Overcoming the Past, Focusing on the Future (Sept. 2000); U.S. Dept. of Justice, Bureau of Justice Statistics, Special Report: Civil Rights Complaints in U.S. District Courts, 1990–1998 (Jan. 2000); Gary R. Siniscalo, "Comparative Analysis of Jury Trials in Employment Cases," in Samuel Estreicher (ed.), Proceedings, New York University 49th Annual Conference on Labor 413 (1997); "Plaintiff Wins in Bias Cases Often Overturned: Study," Chicago Tribune, July 18, 2001 at p. 4.

In these circumstances, it is hardly surprising that employees may have some difficulty enlisting an attorney willing to pursue discrimination litigation on a contingent-fee basis: "Experienced litigators across the country tell me that the good plaintiffs' attorneys will accept on the average only about one in a hundred of the discrimination claimants who seek their help. One of the Detroit area's top employment specialists was more precise. His secretary kept an actual count; he took on one out of eighty-seven persons who contacted him for possible representation." Theodore J. St. Antoine, Mandatory Arbitration of Employment Discrimination Claims: Unmitigated Evil or Blessing in Disguise?, 15 T.M. Cooley L. Rev. 1 (1998)(arbitration "may well be the most realistic hope of the ordinary claimant"); see also Samuel Estreicher, Saturns for Rickshaws: The Stakes in the Debate over Predispute Employment Arbitration Agreements, 16 Ohio St. J. Disp. Resol. 559, 563 (2001)("the people who benefit under a litigation-based system are those whose salaries are high enough to warrant the costs and risks of a law suit undertaken by competent counsel"; "the system works well for high-end claimants and most plaintiff lawyers, and not very well for average claimants").

11. Professor Jerome Cohen once remarked, in a very different context, that the worst kind of Comparative Law thinking is that which compares "*our* theory" with "*their* reality"—and, inevitably, finds the latter deficient. Might the same thing be said about some of the literature critical of employment arbitration—redolent as it is with what has been termed "litigation romanticism"? See Carrie Menkel–Meadow, Mothers and Fathers of Invention: The Intellectual Founders of ADR, 16 Ohio St. J. on Disp. Resol. 1, 20 (2000).

12. There is very little reliable evidence that allows us to compare results in arbitration with those in *litigated* employment discrimination cases. One study of AAA employment arbitrations indicated that the total amount received by all plaintiffs in arbitration was 18% of the amount they had demanded, while all plaintiffs in litigation received only 10.4%, Lewis Maltby, Private Justice: Employment Arbitration and Civil Rights, in Paul Haagen (ed)., Arbitration Now 1, 18–19 (1999). Another comparison of litigated and arbitrated cases asserts that "an employee prevails with about the same frequency in each forum." The author did note that the average recovery in cases actually litigated through trial was "significantly greater

822 CHAPTER V ARBITRATION

than in arbitration." However, plaintiffs' lawyers typically required minimum provable damages of $60,000–$65,000, and a retainer of $3,000 to $3,600, before they would even accept a case—suggesting that "only the larger cases are litigated," William Howard, Arbitrating Claims of Employment Discrimination, Disp. Resol. J., Oct.-Dec. 1995, at pp. 40, 45. *But see* David Schwartz, Enforcing Small Print to Protect Big Business: Employee an Consumer Rights Claims in an Age of Compelled Arbitration, 1997 Wisc. L. Rev. 33, 64–66(while "evidence is admittedly sketchy, it does tend to support the perception * * * that regulated defendants systematically gain an advantage * * * at the expense of plaintiffs when they arbitrate rather than litigate their disputes"); Katherine Stone, Mandatory Arbitration of Individual Employment Rights: The Yellow Dog Contract of the 1990s, 73 Denv. U.L. Rev. 1017, 1040 (1996)(while "there is no comprehensive survey data on the subject * * * there is some anecdotal data that suggests that nonunion arbitration schemes tend to generate pro-employer outcomes"). Cf. Cole v. Burns Int'l Security Services, 105 F.3d 1465, 1485 n. 17 (D.C.Cir.1997)("It is hard to know what to make of these studies without assessing the relative *merits* of the cases in the surveys").

Assume, however, for the sake of argument, that employees can indeed be expected regularly to do better before a jury than before a panel of arbitrators: What do you think of the argument that "the lower arbitration awards are really the more fair assessments of redress"—since "the preconceived anti-employer sentiment of juries results in inflated court awards for plaintiffs"? David Sherwyn et al., In Defense of Mandatory Arbitration of Employment Disputes, 2 U. Pa. J. Lab. & Employment L. 73, 142–143 (1999). Aren't we still committed to the proposition that a jury verdict is necessarily the baseline for any notion of a "correct" result? Cf. William Glaberson, "Juries, Their Powers Under Siege, Find Their Role Is Being Eroded," N.Y. Times, March 2, 2001 at pp. A1, A15 (only 1.5% of federal civil cases are resolved by juries, down from 5.4% in 1962; in a survey of federal trial judges, 27.4% said "juries should decide fewer types of cases"); Kent Syverud, ADR and the Decline of the American Civil Jury, 44 U.C.L.A. L. Rev. 1935 (1997)("Other than the trial bar and an occasional exhilarated juror, is there anyone left in America whose impression of a civil jury trial is so positive that he or she is willing to pay for one?").

13. A job applicant signed an agreement to arbitrate. The agreement was included by the employer in its application packet and was made a condition of employment; it did not, however, run between the employer and the potential employee—it was instead between the employee and "Employment Dispute Services, Inc." EDSI agreed to provide an arbitration forum in exchange for the employee's agreement to submit to arbitration any dispute with his potential employer; the employer was purportedly a third-party beneficiary of the employee's agreement to arbitrate. The employee later filed suit against the employer for violations of the Americans with Disabilities Act, and the employer filed a motion to compel arbitration. The court held that the motion should be denied. The employee had argued that EDSI would be biased in favor of the employer "because it has a financial interest in maintaining its arbitration service contracts with employers."

The court noted that it too had "serious reservations" as to whether the arbitral forum was "suitable for the resolution of statutory claims," in light of the "uncertain relationship" between the employer and EDSI: Although "the record does not clearly reflect whether EDSI, in contrast to the American Arbitration Association, operates on a non-profit basis," the court agreed that "the potential for bias exists." It did not, however, decide the case on that basis—finding an alternative rationale to make the arbitration agreement unenforceable. (Since EDSI had "unfettered discretion" to alter the arbitration rules and procedures without notice, its promise to provide an arbitration forum was "illusory" and thus "mutuality of obligation" was lacking.) Daniels v. Ryan's Family Steak Houses, Inc., 211 F.3d 306 (6th Cir.2000). See also Penn v. Ryan's Family Steakhouses, Inc., 95 F.Supp.2d 940 (N.D.Ind.2000)(since the employer is a "repeat" customer of EDSI, EDSI has an incentive to "load" its lists of arbitrators "with names that have sided with * * * any EDS customers/employers in the past"), aff'd, 269 F.3d 753 (7th Cir.2001) (but criticizing trial court for "plac[ing] too much weight on certain specifics of this system that * * * do not distinguish it from many others that have passed muster"); Geiger v. Ryan's Family Steak Houses, Inc., 134 F.Supp.2d 985 (S.D.Ind.2001)(EDSI "clearly has an incentive to maintain its contractual relationship" with the employer, while employees "have no leverage").

14. Another recent study of AAA employment arbitrations indicates that the process may give an advantage to employers who are "institutional repeat players": Employees who arbitrated with "repeat player employers"—that is, those who were in the case sample more than once—prevailed around 16% of the time, while employees arbitrating with "one-time player" employers prevailed over 70% of the time. In cases involving non-repeat player employers, employees recovered an average of 48% of their demands, while against repeat player employers they recovered only 11%. Lisa Bingham, On Repeat Players, Adhesive Contracts, and the Use of Statistics in Judicial Review of Employment Arbitration Awards, 29 McGeorge L. Rev. 223 (1998).

Where, as in AAA arbitrations, arbitrators are chosen from a panel list submitted to the parties, only the institutional repeat player is likely to develop an "institutional memory": It is only the employer, and not the employee, who is likely to have the ability and incentive to invest in information about the arbitrator's background—and to monitor his past awards. Such asymmetry may suggest the need for some incremental reform of the arbitral process—perhaps in the form of tinkering with the institutional rules that are presented to the parties for adoption. The AAA's new National Rules for the Resolution of Employment Disputes—not yet in effect at the time of the Bingham study—now require that prospective arbitrators disclose their "service as a neutral in any past or pending case involving any of the parties and/or their representatives," Rule 11(b). Is this an adequate response? Cf. Alan Rau, Integrity in Private Judging, 38 So. Tex. L. Rev. 485, 526–27 (1997)("This must be of limited utility where information about the arbitrator's awards in analogous cases—involving, for example, other employers in employment disputes, or

CHAPTER V ARBITRATION

other insurance companies, or other repeat players faced with similar issues of contract interpretation—cannot be expected to be equally available to both parties. * * * [I]t is at least conceivable that the process of arbitrator selection could be structured so as to exclude *both* parties from any participation in naming their arbitrators'').

c. LIMITATIONS ON REMEDIES IN ARBITRATION

Mastrobuono v. Shearson Lehman Hutton, Inc.

Supreme Court of the United States, 1995.
514 U.S. 52, 115 S.Ct. 1212, 131 L.Ed.2d 76.

■ JUSTICE STEVENS delivered the opinion of the Court.

New York law allows courts, but not arbitrators, to award punitive damages. In a dispute arising out of a standard-form contract that expressly provides that it "shall be governed by the laws of the State of New York," a panel of arbitrators awarded punitive damages. The District Court and Court of Appeals disallowed that award. The question presented is whether the arbitrators' award is consistent with the central purpose of the Federal Arbitration Act to ensure "that private agreements to arbitrate are enforced according to their terms." Volt Information Sciences, Inc. v. Board of Trustees of Leland Stanford Junior Univ., 489 U.S. 468, 479 (1989).

I

In 1985 petitioners, Antonio Mastrobuono, then an assistant professor of medieval literature, and his wife Diana Mastrobuono, an artist, opened a securities trading account with respondent Shearson Lehman Hutton, Inc. (Shearson), by executing Shearson's standard-form Client's Agreement. Respondent Nick DiMinico, a vice president of Shearson, managed the Mastrobuonos' account until they closed it in 1987. In 1989, petitioners filed this action in the United States District Court for the Northern District of Illinois, alleging that respondents had mishandled their account and claiming damages on a variety of state and federal law theories.

Paragraph 13 of the parties' agreement contains an arbitration provision and a choice-of-law provision. Relying on the arbitration provision and on §§ 3 and 4 of the Federal Arbitration Act (FAA), respondents filed a motion to stay the court proceedings and to compel arbitration pursuant to the rules of the National Association of Securities Dealers. The District Court granted that motion, and a panel of three arbitrators was convened. After conducting hearings in Illinois, the panel ruled in favor of petitioners.

In the arbitration proceedings, respondents argued that the arbitrators had no authority to award punitive damages. Nevertheless, the panel's award included punitive damages of $400,000, in addition to compensatory damages of $159,327. Respondents paid the compensatory portion of the award but filed a motion in the District Court to vacate the award of punitive damages. The District Court granted the motion, and the Court of Appeals for the Seventh Circuit affirmed. Both courts relied on the choice-of-law provision in Paragraph 13 of the parties' agreement, which specifies that the contract shall be governed by New York law. Because the New York Court of Appeals has decided that in New York the power to award punitive damages is limited to judicial tribunals and may not be exercised by arbitrators, Garrity v. Lyle Stuart, Inc., 353 N.E.2d 793 (N.Y.1976), the District Court and the Seventh Circuit held that the panel of arbitrators had no power to award punitive damages in this case.

We granted certiorari because the Courts of Appeals have expressed differing views on whether a contractual choice-of-law provision may preclude an arbitral award of punitive damages that otherwise would be proper. We now reverse.

II

* * *

[T]he Seventh Circuit interpreted the contract to incorporate New York law, including the *Garrity* rule that arbitrators may not award punitive damages. Petitioners ask us to hold that the FAA preempts New York's prohibition against arbitral awards of punitive damages because this state law is a vestige of the "ancient" judicial hostility to arbitration. Petitioners rely on Southland Corp. v. Keating and Perry v. Thomas, in which we held that the FAA preempted two California statutes that purported to require judicial resolution of certain disputes. In *Southland*, we explained that the FAA not only "declared a national policy favoring arbitration," but actually "withdrew the power of the states to require a judicial forum for the resolution of claims which the contracting parties agreed to resolve by arbitration."

Respondents answer that the choice-of-law provision in their contract evidences the parties' express agreement that punitive damages should not be awarded in the arbitration of any dispute arising under their contract. Thus, they claim, this case is distinguishable from *Southland* and *Perry,* in which the parties presumably desired unlimited arbitration but state law stood in their way. Regardless of whether the FAA preempts the *Garrity* decision in contracts not expressly incorporating New York law, respondents argue that the parties may themselves agree to be bound by *Garrity,* just as they may agree to forgo arbitration altogether. In other words, if the contract says "no punitive damages," that is the end of the matter, for courts are bound to interpret contracts in accordance with the expressed intentions of the parties—even if the effect of those intentions is to limit arbitration.

We have previously held that the FAA's pro-arbitration policy does not operate without regard to the wishes of the contracting parties. * * * Relying on our reasoning in *Volt* [Volt Information Sciences, Inc. v. Board of Trustees of the Leland Stanford Jr. Univ.], respondents thus argue that the parties to a contract may lawfully agree to limit the issues to be arbitrated by waiving any claim for punitive damages. On the other hand, we think our decisions in * * * *Southland* and *Perry* make clear that if

826   CHAPTER V Arbitration

contracting parties agree to include claims for punitive damages within the issues to be arbitrated, the FAA ensures that their agreement will be enforced according to its terms even if a rule of state law would otherwise exclude such claims from arbitration. Thus, the case before us comes down to what the contract has to say about the arbitrability of petitioners' claim for punitive damages.

III

Shearson's standard-form "Client Agreement," which petitioners executed, contains 18 paragraphs. The two relevant provisions of the agreement are found in Paragraph 13.[2] The first sentence of that paragraph provides, in part, that the entire agreement "shall be governed by the laws of the State of New York." The second sentence provides that "any controversy" arising out of the transactions between the parties "shall be settled by arbitration" in accordance with the rules of the National Association of Securities Dealers (NASD), or the Boards of Directors of the New York Stock Exchange and/or the American Stock Exchange. The agreement contains no express reference to claims for punitive damages. To ascertain whether Paragraph 13 expresses an intent to include or exclude such claims, we first address the impact of each of the two relevant provisions, considered separately. We then move on to the more important inquiry: the meaning of the two provisions taken together. See Restatement (Second) of Contracts § 202(2) (1979) ("A writing is interpreted as a whole").

The choice-of-law provision, when viewed in isolation, may reasonably be read as merely a substitute for the conflict-of-laws analysis that otherwise would determine what law to apply to disputes arising out of the contractual relationship. Thus, if a similar contract, without a choice-of-law provision, had been signed in New York and was to be performed in New York, presumably "the laws of the State of New York" would apply, even though the contract did not expressly so state. In such event, there would be nothing in the contract that could possibly constitute evidence of an intent to exclude punitive damages claims. Accordingly, punitive damages

---

2. Paragraph 13 of the Client's Agreement provides:

> This agreement shall inure to the benefit of your [Shearson's] successors and assigns[,] shall be binding on the undersigned, my [petitioners'] heirs, executors, administrators and assigns, and shall be governed by the laws of the State of New York. Unless unenforceable due to federal or state law, any controversy arising out of or relating to [my] accounts, to transactions with you, your officers, directors, agents and/or employees for me or to this agreement or the breach thereof, shall be settled by arbitration in accordance with the rules then in effect, of the National Association of Securities

Dealers, Inc. or the Boards of Directors of the New York Stock Exchange, Inc. and/or the American Stock Exchange Inc. as I may elect. If I do not make such election by registered mail addressed to you at your main office within 5 days after demand by you that I make such election, then you may make such election. Judgment upon any award rendered by the arbitrators may be entered in any court having jurisdiction thereof. This agreement to arbitrate does not apply to future disputes arising under certain of the federal securities laws to the extent it has been determined as a matter of law that I cannot be compelled to arbitrate such claims.

C. ARBITRATION AND THE COURTS   **827**

would be allowed because, in the absence of contractual intent to the contrary, the FAA would preempt the *Garrity* rule.

Even if the reference to "the laws of the State of New York" is more than a substitute for ordinary conflict-of-laws analysis and, as respondents urge, includes the caveat, "detached from otherwise-applicable federal law," the provision might not preclude the award of punitive damages because New York allows its courts, though not its arbitrators, to enter such awards. In other words, the provision might include only New York's substantive rights and obligations, and not the State's allocation of power between alternative tribunals. Respondents' argument is persuasive only if "New York law" means "New York decisional law, including that State's allocation of power between courts and arbitrators, notwithstanding otherwise-applicable federal law." But, as we have demonstrated, the provision need not be read so broadly. It is not, in itself, an unequivocal exclusion of punitive damages claims.[4]

The arbitration provision (the second sentence of Paragraph 13) does not improve respondents' argument. On the contrary, when read separately this clause strongly implies that an arbitral award of punitive damages is appropriate. It explicitly authorizes arbitration in accordance with NASD rules; the panel of arbitrators in fact proceeded under that set of rules. The NASD's Code of Arbitration Procedure indicates that arbitrators may award "damages and other relief." NASD Code of Arbitration Procedure ¶ 3741(e) (1993). While not a clear authorization of punitive damages, this provision appears broad enough at least to contemplate such a remedy. Moreover, as the Seventh Circuit noted, a manual provided to NASD arbitrators contains this provision:

> "B. Punitive Damages. The issue of punitive damages may arise with great frequency in arbitrations. Parties to arbitration are informed that arbitrators can consider punitive damages as a remedy."

Thus, the text of the arbitration clause itself surely does not support— indeed, it contradicts—the conclusion that the parties agreed to foreclose claims for punitive damages.[7]

---

4. The dissent makes much of the similarity between this choice-of-law clause and the one in *Volt*, which we took to incorporate a California statute allowing a court to stay arbitration pending resolution of related litigation. In *Volt*, however, we did not interpret the contract *de novo*. Instead, we deferred to the California court's construction of its own state's law. 489 U.S., at 474 ("the interpretation of private contracts is ordinarily a question of state law, which this Court does not sit to review"). In the present case, by contrast, we review a federal court's interpretation of this contract, and our interpretation accords with that of the only decision-maker

arguably entitled to deference—the arbitrator.

7. "Were we to confine our analysis to the plain language of the arbitration clause, we would have little trouble concluding that a contract clause which bound the parties to 'settle' 'all disputes' through arbitration conducted according to rules which allow any form of 'just and equitable' 'remedy of relief' was sufficiently broad to encompass the award of punitive damages. Inasmuch as agreements to arbitrate are 'generously construed,' it would seem sensible to interpret the 'all disputes' and 'any remedy or relief' phrases to indicate, at a minimum, an intention to resolve through arbitration any dis-

828   CHAPTER V ARBITRATION

Although neither the choice-of-law clause nor the arbitration clause, separately considered, expresses an intent to preclude an award of punitive damages, respondents argue that a fair reading of the entire Paragraph 13 leads to that conclusion. On this theory, even if "New York law" is ambiguous, and even if "arbitration in accordance with NASD rules" indicates that punitive damages are permissible, the juxtaposition of the two clauses suggests that the contract incorporates "New York law relating to arbitration." We disagree. At most, the choice-of-law clause introduces an ambiguity into an arbitration agreement that would otherwise allow punitive damages awards. As we pointed out in *Volt,* when a court interprets such provisions in an agreement covered by the FAA, "due regard must be given to the federal policy favoring arbitration, and ambiguities as to the scope of the arbitration clause itself resolved in favor of arbitration."

Moreover, respondents cannot overcome the common-law rule of contract interpretation that a court should construe ambiguous language against the interest of the party that drafted it. Respondents drafted an ambiguous document, and they cannot now claim the benefit of the doubt. The reason for this rule is to protect the party who did not choose the language from an unintended or unfair result.[10] That rationale is well-suited to the facts of this case. As a practical matter, it seems unlikely that petitioners were actually aware of New York's bifurcated approach to punitive damages, or that they had any idea that by signing a standard-form agreement to arbitrate disputes they might be giving up an important substantive right. In the face of such doubt, we are unwilling to impute this intent to petitioners.

Finally the respondents' reading of the two clauses violates another cardinal principle of contract construction: that a document should be read to give effect to all its provisions and to render them consistent with each other. We think the best way to harmonize the choice-of-law provision with the arbitration provision is to read "the laws of the State of New York" to encompass substantive principles that New York courts would apply, but not to include special rules limiting the authority of arbitrators. Thus, the choice-of-law provision covers the rights and duties of the parties, while the arbitration clause covers arbitration; neither sentence intrudes upon the

pute that would otherwise be settled in a court, and to allow the chosen dispute resolvers to award the same varieties and forms of damages or relief as a court would be empowered to award. Since courts are empowered to award punitive damages with respect to certain types of claims, the Raytheon–Automated arbitrators would be equally empowered." Raytheon Co. v. Automated Business Systems, Inc., 882 F.2d 6, 10 (1st Cir.1989).

10. The drafters of the Second Restatement justified the rule as follows:

Where one party chooses the terms of a contract, he is likely to provide more

carefully for the protection of his own interests than for those of the other party. He is also more likely than the other party to have reason to know of uncertainties of meaning. Indeed, he may leave meaning deliberately obscure, intending to decide at a later date what meaning to assert. In cases of doubt, therefore, so long as other factors are not decisive, there is substantial reason for preferring the meaning of the other party.

Restatement (Second) of Contracts § 206, Comment a (1979).

other. In contrast, respondents' reading sets up the two clauses in conflict with one another: one foreclosing punitive damages, the other allowing them. This interpretation is untenable.

We hold that the Court of Appeals misinterpreted the parties' agreement. The arbitral award should have been enforced as within the scope of the contract. The judgment of the Court of Appeals is, therefore, reversed.

■ JUSTICE THOMAS, dissenting.

* * *

In this case, as in *Volt,* the parties agreed to mandatory arbitration of all disputes. As in *Volt,* the contract at issue here includes a choice-of-law clause. Indeed, the language of the two clauses is functionally equivalent: whereas the choice-of-law clause in *Volt* provided that "[t]he Contract shall be governed by the law of [the State of California]," the one before us today states, in Paragraph 13 of the Client's Agreement, that "[t]his agreement . . . shall be governed by the laws of the State of New York." * * *

The majority claims that the incorporation of New York law "need not be read so broadly" as to include both substantive and procedural law, and that the choice of New York law "is not, in itself, an unequivocal exclusion of punitive damages claims." But we rejected these same arguments in *Volt,* and the *Garrity* rule is just the sort of "state rule[ ] governing the conduct of arbitration" that *Volt* requires federal courts to enforce. 489 U.S. at 476. "Just as [the parties] may limit by contract the issues which they will arbitrate, so too may they specify by contract the rules under which that arbitration will be conducted." *Id.* at 479. To be sure, the majority might be correct that *Garrity* is a rule concerning the State's allocation of power between "alternative tribunals," although *Garrity* appears to describe itself as substantive New York law.[2] Nonetheless, *Volt* makes no distinction between rules that serve only to distribute authority between courts and arbitrators (which the majority finds unenforceable) and other types of rules (which the majority finds enforceable). Indeed, the California rule in *Volt* could be considered to be one that allocates authority between arbitrators and courts, for it permits California courts to stay arbitration pending resolution of related litigation.

* * *

Thankfully, the import of the majority's decision is limited and narrow. This case amounts to nothing more than a federal court applying Illinois and New York contract law to an agreement between parties in Illinois. Much like a federal court applying a state rule of decision to a case when sitting in diversity, the majority's interpretation of the contract represents only the understanding of a single federal court regarding the requirements

---

2. The New York Court of Appeals rested its holding on the principle that punitive damages are exemplary social remedies intended to punish, rather than to compensate. Because the power to punish can rest only in the hands of the State, the Court found that private arbitrators could not wield the authority to impose such damages. *Garrity,* 353 N.E.2d, at 796–797.

CHAPTER V ARBITRATION

imposed by state law. As such, the majority's opinion has applicability only to this specific contract and to no other. But because the majority reaches an erroneous result on even this narrow question, I respectfully dissent.

NOTES AND QUESTIONS

1. Even before *Mastrobuono,* federal courts regularly asserted that under the FAA arbitrators had the power to award punitive damages. It would readily be presumed that the parties had been willing to grant such power to the arbitrators, especially where the arbitration clause was broadly phrased so as to make "all disputes" arbitrable, or to give the arbitrators power to award "any remedy or relief which is just and equitable." See Raytheon Co. v. Automated Business Systems, Inc., 882 F.2d 6 (1st Cir. 1989) (agreement to arbitrate under AAA rules); Kelley v. Michaels, 830 F.Supp. 577 (N.D.Okl.1993) (NASD Code of Arbitration; agreement to arbitrate "any dispute, claim or controversy" includes a claim for punitive damages). In such cases it would take a "clear and express exclusion" in the agreement to deprive the arbitrator of the power to award punitive damages. And if authorized by the parties' agreement, an award of punitive damages by arbitrators was not considered by these courts to be against any "public policy." "[A]n arbitrator steeped in the practice of a given trade is often better equipped than a judge not only to decide what behavior so transgresses the limits of acceptable commercial practice in that trade as to warrant a punitive award, but also to determine the amount of punitive damages needed to (1) adequately deter others in the trade from engaging in similar misconduct, and (2) punish the particular defendant in accordance with the magnitude of his misdeed." Willoughby Roofing & Supply Co., Inc. v. Kajima Int'l, Inc., 598 F.Supp. 353 (N.D.Ala. 1984), aff'd, 776 F.2d 269 (11th Cir.1985).

Can the *Mastrobuono* decision be taken as an approval of these federal cases? See note 7 to the Supreme Court's opinion.

2. As the Court notes, however, a number of states (notably New York) have taken the position that arbitrators may *not* award punitive damages. In these states, an arbitral award of punitive damages is against "public policy" even though the parties had granted the arbitrators the power to award such damages—and even though on a similar cause of action a court or jury could impose them. The leading case is Garrity v. Lyle Stuart, Inc., 40 N.Y.2d 354, 386 N.Y.S.2d 831, 353 N.E.2d 793 (N.Y. 1976), in which the court vacated an award of punitive damages to an author for his publisher's "malicious withholding of royalties":

> If arbitrators were allowed to impose punitive damages, the usefulness of arbitration would be destroyed. It would become a trap for the unwary given the eminently desirable freedom from judicial overview of law and facts. It would mean that the scope of determination by arbitrators, by the license to award punitive damages, would be both unpredictable and uncontrollable. * * *

In imposing penal sanctions in private arrangements, a tradition of the rule of law in organized society is violated. One purpose of the rule of law is to require that the use of coercion be controlled by the State. In a highly developed commercial and economic society the use of private force is not the danger, but the uncontrolled use of coercive economic sanctions in private arrangements. For centuries the power to punish has been a monopoly of the State, and not that of any private individual. The day is long past since barbaric man achieved redress by private punitive measures.

What is the practical result of the New York rule? The lower courts in *Mastrobuono* assumed that the plaintiff, merely by agreeing to arbitration, should be deemed to have "waived" any potential right to receive punitive damages at all. In other cases, however, it is apparently envisaged that the plaintiff would have to institute a separate judicial proceeding in order to assert a claim for punitive damages—at best a wasteful exercise undermining many of the advantages of arbitration. E.g., DiCrisci v. Lyndon Guaranty Bank of New York, 807 F.Supp. 947, 953 (W.D.N.Y.1992).

3. The Oregon Constitution prohibited judicial review of jury awards of punitive damages "unless the court can affirmatively say there is no evidence to support the verdict." In Honda Motor Co., Ltd. v. Oberg, 512 U.S. 415 (1994), the Supreme Court held that this violated the due process clause of the 14th Amendment:

"Punitive damages pose an acute danger of arbitrary deprivation of property. Jury instructions typically leave the jury with wide discretion in choosing amounts, and the presentation of evidence of a defendant's net worth creates the potential that juries will use their verdicts to express biases against big businesses, particularly those without strong local presences. Judicial review of the amount awarded was one of the few procedural safeguards which the common law provided against that danger."

By contrast, Oregon apparently permitted judicial review to ensure only "that there is evidence to support *some* punitive damages, not that there is evidence to support the amount actually awarded. * * * What we are concerned with is the possibility that a guilty defendant may be unjustly punished; evidence of guilt warranting some punishment is not a substitute for evidence providing at least a rational basis for the particular deprivation of property imposed by the State to deter future wrongdoing."

Is *Honda Motor Co.* at all relevant to the problems in these notes?

4. The *Volt* case in 1989 created considerable confusion as to the continuing validity of state law in cases otherwise governed by the FAA. See, e.g., Barbier v. Shearson Lehman Hutton Inc., 948 F.2d 117 (2d Cir.1991), holding that a New York choice of law clause captured that state's bar on punitive damages in arbitration: "It is apparent from the inclusion of the choice-of-law provision that the parties intended to be bound by *Garrity*, and as with any other contract, the parties' intentions control." Has the Supreme Court clarified this question? See note 4 to the Court's opinion.

828

CHAPTER V ARBITRATION

For a while, New York courts were ready to indulge in the grossest forms of wishful thinking—believing that they still remained free independently to construe choice-of-law clauses differently from the Supreme Court in *Mastrobuono,* and that, should they do so, federal courts would have to defer to their reading even where the result would be to exclude punitive damage awards. See Dean Witter Reynolds, Inc. v. Trimble, 166 Misc.2d 40, 631 N.Y.S.2d 215, 217 n. 4 (Sup. Ct. 1995)("the interpretation of contracts is a matter of state law"). This, however, failed to take very seriously that "liberal federal policy favoring arbitration agreements" which has been the subject of a relentless Supreme Court jurisprudence. In more recent cases the New York courts seem, at last, to have sensibly capitulated—and they now appear to consider themselves bound by *Mastrobuono*'s reading of choice-of-law clauses to permit arbitral awards of punitive damages. See Olde Discount Corp. v. Dartley, N.Y.L.J., Dec. 12, 1997, at pp. 26–27 (Sup. Ct.)(under the FAA, "a reference to the substantive law of a particular State, without more, is simply insufficient to bar arbitrators from considering the question of punitive damages"); Americorp Securities, Inc. v. Sager, 239 A.D.2d 115, 656 N.Y.S.2d 762 (App. Div. 1997)(petitioner's reliance on New York rule "was unjustified in light of the judicial recognition of the FAA's preemptive effect in *Mastrobuono*").

Is there, then, anything left of the opinion in *Volt*? What does it mean to say that the case can be "limited to its own facts"? See NOS Communications, Inc. v. Robertson, 936 F.Supp. 761, 765 n. 1(D.Colo.1996).

5. After *Mastrobuono,* would you expect that potential defendants will now begin to draft arbitration clauses that contain an "unequivocal exclusion of punitive damages claims"? The National Association of Securities Dealers has warned its members that attempts in customer agreements to limit the arbitrators' power to award punitive damages—either directly or "indirectly by the use of a so-called 'governing law clause' "—would violate NASD rules and could result in disciplinary action. NASD NTM no. 95–16 (1995 NASD LEXIS 28) (March 1995).

6. Strictures against arbitral "punishment" (such as those in *Garrity*) may as a practical matter turn out to be meaningless unless the arbitrator is ingenuous enough to label his award as punitive. As all first-year law students quickly learn, calculating "compensatory" damages in contract cases is hardly an exact science. In addition, arbitrators may find in particular cases that remedies other than the traditional award of damages are warranted; for example they may think it appropriate, on a theory of unjust enrichment, to require the defendant to "disgorge" the benefits he has made from breach. Cf. International Union of Operating Engineers v. Mid–Valley, Inc., 347 F.Supp. 1104 (S.D.Tex.1972). In the absence of a reasoned opinion or a transcript, it will be difficult to say that the arbitrator has in fashioning appropriate remedies gone beyond permitted "flexibility" to forbidden "punishment."

7. Staklinski was hired as an executive. His contract provided that should he become "permanently disabled" he would receive reduced compensation for the next three years, and then the contract would end. Several years later the company's Board determined that Staklinski had become permanently disabled; he disagreed with this finding and the dispute was submitted to arbitration. The arbitrator found in favor of Staklinski and ordered the corporation to reinstate him. The court confirmed the award: "The power of an arbitrator to order specific performance in an appropriate case has been recognized from early times. * * * Whether a court of equity could issue a specific performance decree in a case like this is beside the point." In the Matter of the Arbitration Between Staklinski and Pyramid Electric Co., 6 N.Y.2d 159, 188 N.Y.S.2d 541, 160 N.E.2d 78 (1959). See also Coopertex, Inc. v. Rue De Reves, Inc., 1990 WL 6548 (S.D.N.Y.) (specific performance of a contract for the sale of goods; "[w]hether or not a court would have awarded specific performance in this case is not the issue").

8. As the preceding note suggests, arbitrators are usually assumed to have broad discretion in fashioning a remedy for the particular circumstances of the case. An important recent decision is Advanced Micro Devices, Inc. v. Intel Corp., 9 Cal.4th 362, 885 P.2d 994, 36 Cal.Rptr.2d 581 (1994). AMD and Intel had entered into a contract under which each company could acquire the right to manufacture under license semiconductor products initially developed by the other. After an arbitration that lasted almost five years, an arbitrator found that Intel had "breached the implied covenant of good faith and fair dealing" under this contract. The arbitrator found that Intel's breach had prevented AMD from acquiring the right to manufacture Intel's highly successful "386" computer chip, and had also delayed AMD's efforts to independently develop its own competitive product by "reverse engineering" Intel's chip. AMD's actual damages were found to be "immeasurable." So the arbitrator gave AMD a permanent, royalty-free license to any of Intel's intellectual property that was embodied in AMD's competing chip—thereby providing AMD with "a complete and dispositive defense" against "legal harassment by Intel over AMD's alleged use of Intel intellectual property," notably in patent and copyright infringement claims that were being pressed by Intel in separate litigation. In confirming the award, the California Supreme Court rejected the proposition that arbitrators could not award a party "benefits different from those the party could have acquired through performance of the contract." The court also rejected any rule by which the remedial power of arbitrators would be limited to remedies "that a court could award on the same claim." "The choice of remedy * * * may at times call on any decision maker's flexibility, creativity and sense of fairness."

The dissenting judges protested that "the majority has greatly increased the risks and uncertainty of arbitration," and that the decision "will make businesses think twice about whether they should agree to resolve disputes by arbitration." They acknowledged that a number of reasons might contribute to granting wide remedial powers to *labor* arbitrators—such as the impossibility of reducing all aspects of a labor-management relationship to writing, and the need for "an ongoing process during the life of a collective bargaining agreement that adjusts and modifies the agreement to meet the changing conditions of the workplace." By contrast, in *commercial* arbitration the "possibility of unlimited and unpredictable

834   CHAPTER V   ARBITRATION

forms of relief is not one of the advantages that a party normally expects to receive from choosing to arbitrate." Under the majority test, the dissent wrote, "it is theoretically possible for an arbitrator to order the losing party to be placed in the stocks or the pillory, or to direct that the contractual relationship be repaired by ordering the marriage of the parties' first-born children."

See also Alan Rau, Resolving Disputes Over Attorneys' Fees: The Role of ADR, 46 S.M.U.L.Rev. 2005, 2071 (1993) (in fee dispute between attorney and client, an arbitrator awarded the attorney $356 "to be paid with no more than 12 hairstylings"; "[i]f the client was in fact a hairstylist, this is surely an efficient settlement, reducing the cost of settlement 'with the same net gain to plaintiff at a lower cost to the defendant' "); David Co. v. Jim W. Miller Construction, Inc., 444 N.W.2d 836 (Minn.1989) (developer sought monetary damages against contractor who had built defective townhouses; arbitrators fashioned an "innovative and unique remedy" ordering the builder—who was himself a real estate developer—to purchase from the plaintiff the townhouses and the land on which they were built).

D.   THE ARBITRATION PROCEEDING

"Within broad limits * * * private parties who submit an existing dispute to arbitration may write their own ticket about the terms of submission, if they can agree to a ticket. [The authors refer to an old story about a person who, in a dream, was threatened by an ominous character and who asked, tremulously, "Wh-what are you going to do now?"—only to receive the answer, "How do I know? This is *your* dream."] The arbitration of an existing dispute is the parties' dream, and they can make it what they want it to be.

The trouble is that it takes time and money to draft elaborate private laws * * *. Only in the most exceptional circumstances can a private disputant stop to negotiate and draft a complete constitution, together with a substantive and procedural code, for the governance of his private court.[1]"

It is quite common to find leading members of the ADR community willing to question whether arbitration is "really" an "ADR process" at all—who may suggest, for example, that it is somehow inappropriate to include a discussion of the arbitration process in a conference or law school course devoted primarily to "the gentler arts of reconciliation and accommodation."[2] We gather that this is true because, paradoxically, arbitration "matters"—that is, that it is merely "adjudication."[3] Nevertheless it

---

1. Henry Hart & Albert Sacks, The Legal Process 310 (1994).

2. Derek Bok, A Flawed System of Law Practice and Training, 33 J. Legal Educ. 570, 582–83 (1983).

3. See, e.g., Jean Sternlight, Is Binding Arbitration A Form of ADR?: An Argument That the Term "ADR" Has Begun to Outlive its Usefulness, 2000 J. of Disp. Resol. 97, 102 (discussing the agenda at annual conferences of the Society of Professionals in Dispute

D. The Arbitration Proceeding

should be obvious enough that what the arbitration process is in fact all about is private ordering and self-determination. "In the run-of-the-mill case, the task of planning for dispute resolution necessarily requires a high level of party participation. Choosing a dispute resolution process, designing its structure, and selecting the decisionmaker, all proceed through negotiation and agreement—and giving thought to such matters may thus make the same calls on the parties' creativity and imagination as do more openly 'empowering' ADR processes."[4]

Rather than draft their own "procedural code," however, parties to arbitration agreements commonly prefer to incorporate by reference the standard rules for the conduct of arbitration proceedings prepared by institutions like the AAA. This allows them to avoid having to reinvent the wheel through lengthy negotiation and drafting—especially at a time when there may not be much incentive for cooperation—and instead to build upon the experience of others. In the materials that follow, frequent reference will be made to the practice of the AAA and particularly to its Commercial Arbitration Rules. But it must be remembered that arbitration remains ultimately "the parties' dream." It is always necessary to consider carefully the special features of each individual transaction, with a view to adding to the pre-existing structure or adapting it in light of the parties' particular circumstances.

1. The Decision-Makers

a. SELECTION OF ARBITRATORS

Selecting the arbitrators is obviously a critical aspect of the arbitration process. After all, the ability to have a dispute decided by "judges" of one's own choosing is perhaps the most distinctive characteristic of this dispute resolution mechanism. How to provide for arbitrator selection is therefore an essential question for the parties in their planning.

The parties may, of course, simply try to agree by name on the individuals who will arbitrate their dispute. The arbitrator might, for example, be named in the original agreement. Or selection of the arbitrator might be left for later agreement on an ad hoc basis after a dispute arises. The choice of the "appropriate" arbitrator may in fact often be a function of the nature of the dispute which has arisen, or of the issues which happen to be in contention. In labor arbitration, for example, the parties may prefer lawyers as arbitrators when the issue is one of arbitrability, but may

Resolution), 103–04 ("Where is the empowerment?"), 106 ("It makes no more sense to group all these techniques together than it would to group together contracts, torts, property, UCC, etc. in a single three credit course called 'private law' "); William Howard, Arbitrating Employment Discrimination Claims: Do You Really Have To? Do You Really Want To?, 43 Drake L. Rev. 255, 279–80 (1994)(since arbitration is "nonconsensual," it "has nothing in common with the other ADR techniques beyond not being a state institution").

4. See Alan Rau, Integrity in Private Judging, 38 So. Tex. L. Rev. 485, 486 (1997).

CHAPTER V ARBITRATION

well prefer economists for wage disputes in "interest" arbitration, and industrial engineers for disputes over job evaluation.[5]

However, reliance on this method of arbitrator selection carries obvious dangers. When the arbitrator is named in advance, he may have become unwilling or unable to serve by the time a dispute later arises. This may then open up a challenge to the whole process; one party may argue that his agreement to arbitration was not unconditional but dependent on the personal choice of this "known and trusted expert," and that therefore arbitration should not proceed in his absence.[6] Such an argument will rarely be found persuasive, but in any event a means must be found to select a replacement.

On the other hand, where the agreement contemplates only that the parties will select their arbitrator *after* a dispute arises, there is an obvious potential for a recalcitrant party to drag his feet. The larger the stakes in the transaction, the more likely it is that the parties will wish to retain at least a veto over the identity of the decision-maker. Consider for example the agonizingly prolonged contract dispute between the Hunt brothers of Texas and the major oil-producing companies, a complex case arising out of various interests in Libyan oil concessions and involving sixteen parties and a welter of legal issues. The arbitration extended over a period of seven years; more than *two years* were consumed by the process of screening arbitrators, "as arbitrators proposed by one party were rejected by one or more of the other parties." The complexity of the issues in the case made the search for the requisite "arbitrators of unusual legal qualifications and broad experience in complicated transactions" particularly difficult. The court, however, made it clear that much of the delay was due to the tactics of the Hunts and their "campaign of obstruction to impede and defeat the arbitration." [7]

Under AAA rules, as soon as a demand for arbitration is made the AAA distributes to the parties a short list of potential arbitrators. It chooses these from its extensive panel of arbitrators, trying to match the names to the nature of the dispute and the industry involved. It may, for example, suggest arbitrators who have had experience in solar heating or landscape architecture if the dispute centers on practice in those trades. The parties

---

5. See Retzer and Petersen, Strategies of Arbitrator Selection, 70 Lab.Arb. 1307, 1319 (1978).

6. See Uniform Commercial Code § 2–305, Comment 4; Ballas v. Mann, 3 Misc.2d 445, 82 N.Y.S.2d 426 (Sup.Ct.1948) (was intention to arbitrate "the dominant intention, the personality of the arbitrator being an auxiliary incident rather than the essence"?). Similar questions arise when the arbitration forum agreed on by the parties declines jurisdiction over the case, see In re Salomon Inc. Shareholders' Derivative Litigation, 68 F.3d 554, 559 (2d Cir.1995) ("[b]ecause the parties had contractually agreed that only the NYSE

could arbitrate any disputes between them, [the lower court] properly declined to appoint substitute arbitrators and compel arbitration in another forum"), or is simply nonexistent, see Stinson v. America's Home Place, Inc., 108 F.Supp.2d 1278 (M.D.Ala.2000)(the "National Academy of Conciliators, the arbitrator designated in the contract for resolution of disputes, was not in existence at the time the contract was formed or at any time thereafter").

7. See Hunt v. Mobil Oil Corp., 654 F.Supp. 1487 (S.D.N.Y.1987).

may in their agreement have already specified the background or qualification of their arbitrators. In maritime arbitration, for example, it is the usual practice to stipulate that the arbitrators "shall be commercial men"—a phrase not meant to exclude women, but definitely meant to exclude lawyers.[8] Unless the parties have ruled out the possibility, however, it is customary to have at least one attorney on the list. Lawyers in fact play a dominant part in many AAA arbitrations. In 1999, for example, almost half of the names on the AAA's construction arbitration panel were attorneys—almost twice as many as the next largest professional category, engineers. And a recent survey of labor arbitrators indicates that almost 60% of them have law degrees.[9]

The information that the parties are given about a potential arbitrator is not extensive; it usually contains summary biographical information indicating the arbitrator's profession, present and past employment, education, and areas in which he claims expertise. There is no mechanism analogous to voir dire in which the parties have the opportunity to examine potential arbitrators prior to selection—although in large cases they have an obvious incentive to do some research on their own. Under AAA procedure, each party is allowed to cross off the list any names he finds unacceptable. Each then ranks the remaining names in order of preference, and from these the AAA is supposed to appoint an arbitrator "in accordance with the designated order of mutual preference." (The British refer to this method as "knocking the brains out of the panel.")[10] In the (unusual) event that every name turns out to be objectionable to one or both of the parties, the AAA may at that point simply choose another name from its panel without submitting any further lists; barring disqualification for cause, this selection is final.

Arbitration can proceed before any number of arbitrators—it is, again, "the parties' dream." But the most common pattern is to use either a single individual or three arbitrators. Under AAA rules, a single arbitrator is to be used unless the parties specify otherwise or unless the AAA "in its discretion" selects a larger number. In the year 2000, 25% of the AAA's commercial and construction cases involved claims of $75,000 or less and were administered under its "Expedited Procedures," where a single arbitrator is always used. However, in complex cases, or cases where the stakes are large, it is common to use three neutral arbitrators; current AAA policy is to prefer three arbitrators where the amount in controversy exceeds

---

8. In W.K. Webster & Co. v. American President Lines, Ltd., 32 F.3d 665 (2d Cir. 1994), the Society of Maritime Arbitrators took the position (as *amicus curiae*) that a person cannot be a "commercial man" and a practicing attorney at one and the same time. The court disagreed, however, and upheld the appointment of an attorney who "had substantial practical experience on the commercial side of the maritime industry"—it noted that the attorney had not obtained his experience *"solely* as [a] practicing" attorney.

9. Bognanno & Smith, The Demographic and Professional Characteristics of Arbitrators in North America, Proceedings, 41st Annual Meeting, Nat'l Academy of Arbitrators 266, 270 (1988).

10. Bernstein, Nudging and Shoving All Parties to a Jurisdictional Dispute Into Arbitration: The Dubious Procedure of *National Steel*, 78 Harv.L.Rev. 784, 790–91 (1965).

CHAPTER V ARBITRATION

$300,000. (The ICC's rule of thumb is that only a single arbitrator is warranted in cases involving less than $1 million). With three arbitrators, of course, far more time is consumed in selection, in scheduling the hearings, and, probably, in hearing time; the fees paid to the arbitrators are also likely to be higher.

What do parties look for in selecting arbitrators? In labor cases, where a large cadre of professional arbitrators has developed, it is often observed that parties have a strong preference for only the most experienced and active arbitrators. A recent survey submitted a sample case to a selected number of union and management representatives and asked for their preferences as to whom they wanted to hear the case: 47.6% of the management representatives and 61.5% of the union representatives chose a decision-maker whose primary occupation was as a "full-time arbitrator."[11] Some union and management representatives, in responding to another survey, indicated that they would require a potential arbitrator to have a case load of at least fifty arbitrations in one year.[12] The fact that many labor arbitration opinions are published not only helps the parties in doing "research" on potential arbitrators; it also serves to focus even greater attention on the well-known "name" arbitrators whose cases appear regularly in the reports.

This leads to a classic "Catch–22." Without experience, it is difficult for an arbitrator to be chosen to hear a labor case—and difficult therefore to develop the experience and reputation that will enable her to be chosen to hear *future* cases. One survey's estimate of the number of labor arbitrators "willing and able to practice" in 1986 was 3,669. Only 16% of these practiced full-time as arbitrators. Part-timers worked an average of four days per month as arbitrators—although 30% of them would have wanted to work full-time. And approximately 22% of the entire group did not work at all as arbitrators during the year, largely because no assignments were offered to them.[13] So "a small percentage of arbitrators do most of the business."[14]

The natural result of this selective demand is that there are often lengthy delays before the chosen arbitrator will have the time to hear and dispose of a given case; the most experienced arbitrators may not be available for a hearing within several months after being asked to serve. While this is not perhaps a long time in comparison with some crowded judicial dockets, it is still troubling for a supposedly "expeditious" dispute

---

11. See Nelson, The Selection of Arbitrators, Lab.L.J., October 1986, at 703, 711.

12. Rezler and Petersen, Strategies of Arbitrator Selection, 70 Lab.Arb. 1307, 1308 (1978).

13. Bognanno & Smith, The Demographic and Professional Characteristics of Arbitrators in North America, Proceedings, 41st Annual Meeting, Nat'l Academy of Arbitrators 266, 269, 277–79 (1988).

14. Mario Bognanno & Charles Coleman, Labor Arbitration in America: The Profession and Practice 89 (1992). See also The Chronicle (Journal of the Nat'l Academy of Arbitrators), May 1988 at p. 3 (11.9% of all active arbitrators handled 60 or more cases in 1986, representing 50.5% of the total grievance arbitration case load).

D. THE ARBITRATION PROCEEDING

resolution process—particularly in cases where an employee has been discharged, and the employer is facing potential liability for back pay.

The profession of "labor arbitrator" is made possible by the often substantial fees that arbitrators are regularly paid for their services in labor cases. According to internal reports compiled by the Federal Mediation and Conciliation Service, the average per diem fee in the year 2000 for private arbitrators on the Service's roster was $672—although individual fees could of course range considerably higher. We have already noted the possible effects of such a prospect on the decision patterns of professional arbitrators. See pp. 640–642 supra. Commercial arbitrators, in contrast, rarely hear more than a few cases a year; the supply of acceptable arbitrators here is relatively more elastic. For many years, the AAA's Commercial Arbitration Rules provided that commercial arbitrators were expected to serve without compensation for the first day of hearing— presumably as a form of public service. Under the current rules, however, arbitrators are paid beginning with the first day of hearing where a claim exceeds $10,000;[15] arbitrators may also be paid for "study time" prior to the hearing. Arbitrators are free to state their own rate of compensation, and a $2000 per diem fee has been termed not "excessively high" or "far beyond the applicable standard for such services."[16] This is in addition to the administrative fee, based on the amount of the claim, which is paid to institutions like the AAA and the ICC for their services in supervising the arbitration.

NOTES AND QUESTIONS

1. Another traditional pattern in arbitration is a "tripartite" panel, in which each party is allowed to select one arbitrator and a third, "neutral" chairman is chosen by the other two (or in the absence of agreement, by an institution like the AAA).

What effects might this kind of panel have on the decision-making process? The AAA's Commercial Arbitration Rules provide that where there is a panel of more than one arbitrator, decision is to be by *majority vote* unless the agreement provides otherwise. To the same effect is § 4 of the Uniform Arbitration Act, which has been enacted by most states. Where the party-appointed arbitrators agree on a particular result, may the neutral be led to acquiesce in what is in reality a negotiated settlement being given the prestige of an arbitral award? And where the other two arbitrators *disagree,* may the neutral be forced to trim or compromise his own views in order to obtain a majority? Consider In re Publishers' Ass'n of N.Y. and N.Y. Typographical Union, 36 Lab.Arb. 706 (1961). The neutral

---

15. AAA, Commercial Arbitration Rules, R. 53(a),(b).

16. Polin v. Kellwood Co., 103 F.Supp.2d 238, 257 n. 27 (S.D.N.Y.2000).

In California, arbitrators in patient-HMO disputes "typically charge $250 to $400 per hour," Nieto & Hosel, Arbitration in Cal-ifornia Managed Health Care Systems 2 (California Research Bureau 2000). JAMS/Endispute arbitrators charge an average of $400 per hour, although "fees of $500 or $600 per hour are not uncommon," Cole v. Burns Int'l Security Services, 105 F.3d 1465, 1480 n. 8 (D.C.Cir.1997).

840 CHAPTER V ARBITRATION

arbitrator here voted with the employer to discharge a worker but wrote, in an unusually candid opinion, that this penalty had been "forced upon" him. While he would have preferred a lesser penalty such as a disciplinary suspension, his most "patient and painstaking efforts" had convinced him that "there was no possibility whatever of an award issuing which would reflect a view intermediate to the polar position of my colleagues." He therefore saw no choice other than to join in the position which was *closest* to the one he preferred!

Would it have been possible or appropriate for the neutral in *Publishers' Association* to have acted differently? To avoid placing such a burden on the neutral, would it not be better simply to stipulate that in the absence of a majority decision the final decision is to be made by the neutral alone—or even that the function of the party-appointed arbitrators is always to be merely advisory? This is in fact commonly provided in collective bargaining agreements. And in that case, is any purpose ever served by having a tripartite board at all? Can you think of any countervailing advantages to using a tripartite board with party-named representatives? See Zack, Tripartite Panels: Asset or Hindrance in Dispute Settlement?, Proceedings, 34th Annual Meeting, Nat'l Academy of Arbitrators 273, 279 (1982) (deliberations between neutral and party-appointed arbitrators can help clarify technical issues, provide assurance that the neutral fully understands the issues and background of the case, and allow discussion and review of the possible implications of the neutral's written opinion); Lowenfeld, The Party–Appointed Arbitrator in International Controversies: Some Reflections, 30 Tex.Int'l L.J. 59, 65–67 (1995) (in international disputes a party-appointed arbitrator can help in the "translation of legal culture * * * when matters that are self-evident to lawyers from one country are puzzling to lawyers from another"; such an arbitrator also gives some "confidence that at least one member of the tribunal is listening, and listening sympathetically, to the submission of counsel").

2. Where the parties are unable to agree on an arbitrator and the proceeding is not being administered by an institution like the AAA, modern statutes empower a court to make the choice. See FAA, § 5.

A contract for the delivery of rice provided that any disputes "shall be resolved by means of the judgment of arbitrators appointed by mutual agreement. This could be in Nicaragua or the Rice Millers' Association [RMA] in the United States." When a dispute arose over the condition of the rice, the buyer made a demand for arbitration with the RMA. Under RMA rules, the RMA arbitration committee appoints the arbitrators; the panel appointed by this committee proceeded to arbitrate the dispute and awarded the buyer $1.3 million. The court vacated the award, holding that the seller was instead "entitled" to an arbitration before arbitrators chosen by mutual agreement of the parties. "The arbitration clause does not set forth how this choice of arbitrators by the parties should be conducted." The district court was therefore instructed to require that arbitration "be conducted under the standard method, where both parties choose an arbitrator and these arbitrators select a third arbitrator"; if the two party-appointed arbitrators cannot agree, then the third arbitrator would be appointed by the court under § 5 of the FAA. Cargill Rice, Inc. v. Empresa Nicaraguense Dealimentos Basicos, 25 F.3d 223 (4th Cir.1994). Does this make any sense at all?

3. Where an arbitration clause calls for "tripartite" arbitration, one of the parties may be tempted to delay or frustrate the proceedings by simply refusing to name "its" arbitrator. To deal with this problem, contracts frequently provide that should one party fail to appoint an arbitrator, "the one arbitrator nominated may act as sole arbitrator"—or alternatively, that the party who has named one arbitrator should also have the right to appoint the second arbitrator himself. Either method should speed things along considerably.

In one case, a respondent refused to arbitrate, and the claimant moved for an order under § 4 of the FAA to compel arbitration. The court denied the motion, because the arbitration clause allowed the claimant to name a second arbitrator if the respondent refused to do so. Since "the very purpose of such a self-executing mechanism in an arbitration clause is to avoid the time and expense of Federal Court motion practice," the claimant was simply not a party "aggrieved" within the meaning of § 4 by the respondent's refusal to arbitrate. Waterspring, S.A. v. Trans Marketing Houston Inc., 717 F.Supp. 181 (S.D.N.Y.1989). Do you agree with this result? Does it matter that if the respondent should later successfully challenge the existence of a binding arbitration agreement, the claimant would then find that the arbitration had turned out to be nothing more than a useless gesture?

4. Three members of a family were parties to a partnership agreement: Charles, Albert (Charles' son), and Isidore (Charles' brother). The agreement provided for arbitration in which Charles and Albert would jointly name one arbitrator, Isidore would name another, and the two arbitrators would select a third.

However, the drafting of this clause proved to be inept. There was a change of alignment in the partnership not originally contemplated; Isidore and Charles, complaining about Albert's lack of concern for the partnership, sought arbitration. Charles and Albert could not jointly agree on an arbitrator; Albert insisted that he be permitted to select an arbitrator independently since the interests of the other two parties were identical and adverse to his. On application to the court to name an arbitrator, what result? See Lipschutz v. Gutwirth, 304 N.Y. 58, 106 N.E.2d 8 (N.Y. 1952).

5. One study of party preferences in labor arbitration suggests that employers tend to prefer economists over lawyers as arbitrators, while unions on the other hand "prefer arbitrators with legal training and dislike economists." Why might this be true? The authors speculate that this result may be explained by "the fact that economists are likely to be heavily influenced by efficiency considerations, whereas lawyers are more likely to place greater emphasis on equity." Bloom & Cavanagh, An Analysis of the Selection of Arbitrators, 76 Am.Econ.Rev. 408, 418, 421 (1986).

842   CHAPTER V ARBITRATION

6. A "routine contract suit" was assigned to a magistrate judge. "Protracted efforts at settlement ensued but were unsuccessful. Then the lawyers had a brainstorm: appoint [the magistrate judge] the arbitrator of their dispute." An order, drafted by the lawyers and signed by the judge, provided that an independent auditor selected by the parties would determine the actual losses sustained, and "the Court will retain jurisdiction to act as the arbitrator * * * and shall make a decision binding upon the parties." The auditor submitted a report; the magistrate judge then held two hearings to consider the parties' objections and issued a document, captioned "judgment," calling for the defendant to pay $125,000.

The Seventh Circuit (in an opinion by Judge Posner) affirmed this "judgment"—"if that is what it is"—but seemed puzzled by just what it was that the parties and the magistrate judge had done. Had the judge issued an award as arbitrator, and then judicially confirmed his own award? If so, his order would clearly be void: "[A]rbitration is not in the job description of a federal judge"; "since 'alternative dispute resolution' is all the rage these days * * * the day may not be distant when federal judges will be recommissioned (or issued supplementary commissions) as arbitrators. But it has not arrived." However, there was an alternative characterization of what the parties had done that was "slightly more plausible": Perhaps they had simply "stipulated to an abbreviated, informal procedure for [the magistrate judge's] deciding the case in his judicial capacity. * * * [T]hey agreed that the judge would make a decision on a record consisting of the auditor's report plus the parties' objections, * * * and that they would not appeal the decision. So viewed, the procedure was not improper." By "talking the language of arbitration" the parties had essentially intended to limit judicial review of the magistrate judge's decision. DDI Seamless Cylinder Int'l, Inc. v. General Fire Extinguisher Corp., 14 F.3d 1163 (7th Cir.1994).

b. ARBITRAL IMPARTIALITY

Commonwealth Coatings Corp. v. Continental Casualty Co.

Supreme Court of the United States, 1968.
393 U.S. 145, 89 S.Ct. 337, 21 L.Ed.2d 301.

MR. JUSTICE BLACK delivered the opinion of the Court.

At issue in this case is the question whether elementary requirements of impartiality taken for granted in every judicial proceeding are suspended when the parties agree to resolve a dispute through arbitration.

[Having read this far, what do you think the answer is going to be?—Eds.]

The petitioner, Commonwealth Coatings Corp., a subcontractor, sued the sureties on the prime contractor's bond to recover money alleged to be due for a painting job. The contract for painting contained an agreement to arbitrate such controversies. Pursuant to this agreement petitioner ap-

D. THE ARBITRATION PROCEEDING 843

pointed one arbitrator, the prime contractor appointed a second, and these two together selected the third arbitrator. This third arbitrator, the supposedly neutral member of the panel, conducted a large business in Puerto Rico, in which he served as an engineering consultant for various people in connection with building construction projects. One of his regular customers in this business was the prime contractor that petitioner sued in this case. This relationship with the prime contractor was in a sense sporadic in that the arbitrator's services were used only from time to time at irregular intervals, and there had been no dealings between them for about a year immediately preceding the arbitration. Nevertheless, the prime contractor's patronage was repeated and significant, involving fees of about $12,000 over a period of four or five years, and the relationship even went so far as to include the rendering of services on the very projects involved in this lawsuit. An arbitration was held, but the facts concerning the close business connections between the third arbitrator and the prime contractor were unknown to petitioner and were never revealed to it by this arbitrator, by the prime contractor, or by anyone else until after an award had been made. Petitioner challenged the award on this ground, among others, but the District Court refused to set aside the award. The Court of Appeals affirmed.

* * * [B]oth sides here assume that [the FAA] governs this case. Section 10 sets out the conditions upon which awards can be vacated. The two courts below held, however, that § 10 could not be construed in such a way as to justify vacating the award in this case. We disagree and reverse. Section 10 does authorize vacation of an award where it was "procured by corruption, fraud, or undue means" or "[w]here there was evident partiality * * * in the arbitrators." These provisions show a desire of Congress to provide not merely for *any* arbitration but for an impartial one. It is true that petitioner does not charge before us that the third arbitrator was actually guilty of fraud or bias in deciding this case, and we have no reason, apart from the undisclosed business relationship, to suspect him of any improper motives. But neither this arbitrator nor the prime contractor gave to petitioner even an intimation of the close financial relations that had existed between them for a period of years. We have no doubt that if a litigant could show that a foreman of a jury or a judge in a court of justice had, unknown to the litigant, any such relationship, the judgment would be subject to challenge. This is shown beyond doubt by Tumey v. State of Ohio, 273 U.S. 510 (1927), where this Court held that a conviction could not stand because a small part of the judge's income consisted of court fees collected from convicted defendants. Although in *Tumey* it appeared the amount of the judge's compensation actually depended on whether he decided for one side or the other, that is too small a distinction to allow this manifest violation of the strict morality and fairness Congress would have expected on the part of the arbitrator and the other party in this case. Nor should it be at all relevant, as the Court of Appeals apparently thought it was here, that "[t]he payments received were a very small part of [the arbitrator's] income * * *." For in *Tumey* the Court held that a decision should be set aside where there is "the slightest pecuniary interest" on the

844 CHAPTER V ARBITRATION

part of the judge, and specifically rejected the State's contention that the compensation involved there was "so small that it is not to be regarded as likely to influence improperly a judicial officer in the discharge of his duty * * *." Since in the case of courts this is a *constitutional* principle, we can see no basis for refusing to find the same concept in the broad statutory language that governs arbitration proceedings and provides that an award can be set aside on the basis of "evident partiality" or the use of "undue means." It is true that arbitrators cannot sever all their ties with the business world, since they are not expected to get all their income from their work deciding cases, but we should, if anything, be even more scrupulous to safeguard the impartiality of arbitrators than judges, since the former have completely free rein to decide the law as well as the facts and are not subject to appellate review. We can perceive no way in which the effectiveness of the arbitration process will be hampered by the simple requirement that arbitrators disclose to the parties any dealings that might create an impression of possible bias.

[Justice Black then referred to the AAA rules of procedure which, "while not controlling in this case," called on an arbitrator "to disclose any circumstances likely to create a presumption of bias or which he believes might disqualify him as an impartial Arbitrator."]

[B]ased on the same principle as this Arbitration Association rule is that part of the 33d Canon of Judicial Ethics which provides:

33. Social Relations

* * * [A judge] should, however, in pending or prospective litigation before him be particularly careful to avoid such action as may reasonably tend to awaken the suspicion that his social or business relations or friendships, constitute an element in influencing his judicial conduct.

This rule of arbitration and this canon of judicial ethics rest on the premise that any tribunal permitted by law to try cases and controversies not only must be unbiased but also must avoid even the appearance of bias. We cannot believe that it was the purpose of Congress to authorize litigants to submit their cases and controversies to arbitration boards that might reasonably be thought biased against one litigant and favorable to another.

Reversed.

Mr. Justice White, with whom Mr. Justice Marshall joins, concurring.

While I am glad to join my Brother Black's opinion in this case, I desire to make these additional remarks. The Court does not decide today that arbitrators are to be held to the standards of judicial decorum of Article III judges, or indeed of any judges. It is often because they are men of affairs, not apart from but of the marketplace, that they are effective in their adjudicatory function. This does not mean the judiciary must overlook outright chicanery in giving effect to their awards; that would be an abdication of our responsibility. But it does mean that arbitrators are not automatically disqualified by a business relationship with the parties before them if both parties are informed of the relationship in advance, or if they are unaware of the facts but the relationship is trivial. I see no reason

D. The Arbitration Proceeding   845

automatically to disqualify the best informed and most capable potential arbitrators.

The arbitration process functions best when an amicable and trusting atmosphere is preserved and there is voluntary compliance with the decree, without need for judicial enforcement. This end is best served by establishing an atmosphere of frankness at the outset, through disclosure by the arbitrator of any financial transactions which he has had or is negotiating with either of the parties. In many cases the arbitrator might believe the business relationship to be so insubstantial that to make a point of revealing it would suggest he is indeed easily swayed, and perhaps a partisan of that party.* But if the law requires the disclosure, no such imputation can arise. And it is far better that the relationship be disclosed at the outset, when the parties are free to reject the arbitrator or accept him with knowledge of the relationship and continuing faith in his objectivity, than to have the relationship come to light after the arbitration, when a suspicious or disgruntled party can seize on it as a pretext for invalidating the award. The judiciary should minimize its role in arbitration as judge of the arbitrator's impartiality. That role is best consigned to the parties, who are the architects of their own arbitration process, and are far better informed of the prevailing ethical standards and reputations within their business.

Of course, an arbitrator's business relationships may be diverse indeed, involving more or less remote commercial connections with great numbers of people. He cannot be expected to provide the parties with his complete and unexpurgated business biography. But it is enough for present purposes to hold, as the Court does, that where the arbitrator has a substantial interest in a firm which has done more than trivial business with a party, that fact must be disclosed. If arbitrators err on the side of disclosure, as they should, it will not be difficult for courts to identify those undisclosed relationships which are too insubstantial to warrant vacating an award.

MR. JUSTICE FORTAS, with whom MR. JUSTICE HARLAN and MR. JUSTICE STEWART join, dissenting.

I dissent and would affirm the judgment.

The facts in this case do not lend themselves to the Court's ruling. The Court sets aside the arbitration award despite the fact that the award is unanimous and no claim is made of actual partiality, unfairness, bias, or fraud.

* * *

Both courts below held, and petitioner concedes, that the third arbitrator was innocent of any actual partiality, or bias, or improper motive. There is no suggestion of concealment as distinguished from the innocent failure to volunteer information.

---

* In fact, the District Court found—on the basis of the record and petitioner's admissions—that the arbitrator in this case was entirely fair and impartial. I do not read the majority opinion as questioning this finding in any way.

CHAPTER V ARBITRATION

The third arbitrator is a leading and respected consulting engineer who has performed services for "most of the contractors in Puerto Rico." He was well known to petitioner's counsel and they were personal friends. Petitioner's counsel candidly admitted that if he had been told about the arbitrator's prior relationship "I don't think I would have objected because I know Mr. Capacete [the arbitrator]."

Clearly, the District Judge's conclusion, affirmed by the Court of Appeals for the First Circuit, was correct, that "the arbitrators conducted fair, impartial hearings; that they reached a proper determination of the issues before them, and that plaintiff's objections represent a 'situation where the losing party to an arbitration is now clutching at straws in an attempt to avoid the results of the arbitration to which it became a party.'"

* * *

Arbitration is essentially consensual and practical. The United States Arbitration Act is obviously designed to protect the integrity of the process with a minimum of insistence upon set formulae and rules. The Court applies to this process rules applicable to judges and not to a system characterized by dealing on faith and reputation for reliability. Such formalism is not contemplated by the Act nor is it warranted in a case where no claim is made of partiality, of unfairness, or of misconduct in any degree.

NOTES AND QUESTIONS

1. Did Justice White really "join" in Justice Black's opinion? Note that the votes of Justices White and Marshall were essential to a majority in *Commonwealth Coatings*.

2. The current version of the AAA's Commercial Arbitration Rules requires "any person appointed as a neutral arbitrator" to "disclose to the AAA any circumstance likely to affect impartiality or independence, including any bias or any financial or personal interest in the result of the arbitration or any past or present relationship with the parties or their representatives." The AAA communicates this information to the parties and if any of them objects, "the AAA shall determine whether the arbitrator should be disqualified and shall inform the parties of its decision, which shall be conclusive." (Rule 19). A "Code of Ethics for Arbitrators in Commercial Disputes" has also been adopted by the AAA and by the American Bar Association. Canon II of this Code provides that "An Arbitrator should disclose any interest or relationship likely to affect impartiality or which might create an appearance of partiality or bias":

A. Persons Who Are Requested To Serve As Arbitrators Should, Before Accepting, Disclose:

(1) Any direct or indirect financial or personal interest in the outcome of the arbitration;

D. The Arbitration Proceeding 847

(2) Any existing or past financial, business, professional, family or social relationships which are likely to affect impartiality or which might reasonably create an appearance of partiality or bias. Persons requested to serve as arbitrators should disclose any such relationships which they personally have with any party or its lawyer, or with any individual whom they have been told will be a witness. They should also disclose any such relationships involving members of their families or their current employers, partners or business associates.

E. In The Event That An Arbitrator Is Requested By All Parties To Withdraw, The Arbitrator Should Do So. In The Event That An Arbitrator Is Requested To Withdraw By Less Than All Of The Parties Because Of Alleged Partiality Or Bias, The Arbitrator Should Withdraw Unless Either Of The Following Circumstances Exists:

(1) If an agreement of the parties, or arbitration rules agreed to by the parties, establishes procedures for determining challenges to arbitrators, then those procedures should be followed; or

(2) If the arbitrator, after carefully considering the matter, determines that the reason for the challenge is not substantial, and that he or she can nevertheless act and decide the case impartially and fairly, and that withdrawal would cause unfair delay or expense to another party or would be contrary to the ends of justice.

Notes to this "Canon" make clear that it is

intended to be applied realistically so that the burden of detailed disclosure does not become so great that it is impractical for persons in the business world to be arbitrators, thereby depriving parties of the services of those who might be best informed and qualified to decide particular types of cases.

3. What use can be made of the AAA Rules and Canons in a judicial proceeding to vacate an arbitral award? Judge Posner has written that:

[E]ven if the failure to disclose was a material violation of the ethical standards applicable to arbitration proceedings, it does not follow that the arbitration award may be nullified judicially. * * * The arbitration rules and code do not have the force of law. If [a party] is to get the arbitration award set aside it must bring itself within the statute * * *.

The American Arbitration Association is in competition not only with other private arbitration services but with the courts in providing—in the case of the private services, selling—an attractive form of dispute settlement. It may set its standards as high or as low as it thinks its customers want. The [FAA] has a different purpose—to make arbitration effective by putting the coercive force of the federal courts behind arbitration decrees that affect interstate commerce or are otherwise of federal concern. * * * The standards for judicial intervention are therefore narrowly drawn to assure the basic integrity of the arbitration process without meddling in it. Section 10 is full of words like corruption and misbehavior and fraud. The standards it sets are minimum ones. * * * The fact that the AAA went beyond the statutory standards in drafting its own code of ethics does not lower the threshold for judicial intervention.

Merit Ins. Co. v. Leatherby Ins. Co., 714 F.2d 673 (7th Cir.1983).

Do you agree?

4. The arbitration statutes of some states impose additional and more explicit requirements of disclosure on potential arbitrators. For example, a recent California statute provides that any potential arbitrator shall disclose the "names of any prior or pending cases involving any party to the arbitration agreement or the lawyer for a party" for whom she "served or is serving as a neutral arbitrator, and the results of each case arbitrated to conclusion * * * and the amount of monetary damages awarded, if any." The proposed appointee "shall be disqualified as a neutral arbitrator on the basis of the disclosure statement" after any of the party objects to her serving on the panel. Cal.Code Civ.Pro. § 1281.9.

5. If courts held arbitrators to the same standards of isolation and purity to which they hold Article III judges, an adverse decision might invariably become the occasion for frantic research by the losing party into possible links between his adversary and the arbitrator. The obvious dangers to the arbitral process have led courts to be unreceptive to such attempts.

In their reluctance to set aside awards on these grounds courts have also been sensitive to the need for decision-makers with extensive professional experience and knowledge, and to what Judge Posner has called the necessary "tradeoff between impartiality and expertise." *Merit Ins. Co.,* 714 F.2d at 679. A good example is presented by International Produce, Inc. v. A/S Rosshavet, 638 F.2d 548 (2d Cir.1981). This was a maritime arbitration in which the neutral arbitrator was the Vice–President of a management firm retained by owners of various commercial vessels. After the hearings had begun, this arbitrator's firm became involved in an unrelated arbitration involving another vessel. It happened that the law firms representing the parties in the second arbitration were the same firms that were handling the *International Produce* arbitration; in this second proceeding the arbitrator appeared as a non-party witness, prepared in his testimony by one of the law firms and cross-examined by the other. Although requested to withdraw, the arbitrator refused to do so, and his award was successfully challenged in district court. The Second Circuit held that the award should not have been vacated:

> It is not unusual that those who are selected as arbitrators in maritime arbitrations have had numerous prior dealings with one or more of the parties or their counsel. * * * Arbitrator Klosty aptly analogized New York's maritime-arbitration community to a busy harbor, where the wakes of the members often cross.

> The most sought-after arbitrators are those who are prominent and experienced members of the specific business community in which the dispute to be arbitrated arose. Since they are chosen precisely because of their involvement in that community, some degree of overlapping

D. THE ARBITRATION PROCEEDING 849

representation and interest inevitably results. Those chosen as arbitrators in important shipping arbitrations have typically participated in a great number of prior maritime disputes, not only as arbitrators but also as parties and witnesses. They have therefore almost inevitably come into contact with a significant proportion of the relatively few lawyers who make up the New York admiralty bar. Under these circumstances, a decision on our part to vacate arbitration awards whenever a mere appearance of bias can be made out would seriously disrupt the salutary process of settling maritime disputes through arbitration.

Of course, the alleged conflict of interest in *International Produce* was immediately known to both of the parties in the case as soon as it arose. Would the matter be different—should a higher standard be imposed—if one party is claiming that the arbitrator failed before the hearing to disclose facts about his relationship with the other?

6. A labor arbitrator issued an award sustaining a grievance by the United Mine Workers against a coal company. The employer moved to vacate the award, alleging that the arbitrator had failed to disclose that his brother was employed by the UMW. The court suggested that the standard of FAA § 10(a)(2)—which permits a court to vacate an award for "evident partiality" in the arbitrators—should also apply to awards arising out of collective bargaining agreements. "To demonstrate evident partiality under the FAA, the party seeking vacation has the burden of proving that a reasonable person would have to conclude that an arbitrator was partial to the other party to the arbitration." Under this standard, the court declined to vacate the award. Neither the arbitrator nor his brother "had any discernible interest in the outcome of the proceeding." In addition, the court stressed that the coal industry decisions that this arbitrator had made in the past underlined the absence of "evident partiality." He had served as a "coal industry arbitrator" for three years under procedures adopted by the UMW and the Bituminous Coal Operators Association; of his 66 awards, the Union had "won 30, lost 29, split 5, and settled 2 before a hearing." Consolidation Coal Co. v. Local 1643, United Mine Workers of Amer., 48 F.3d 125 (4th Cir.1995). See also pp. 640–641 supra ("Compromise Decisions").

7. There are at least some cases in which one can recognize "evident partiality" without a great deal of trouble. In one major insurance arbitration, the claimant was awarded $92 million by a "tripartite" panel. After the award was rendered—but before confirmation by a court—the losing attorneys surreptitiously made videotapes indicating that the claimant's lawyer and the panel's "neutral" arbitrator had spent several nights together in the lawyer's hotel room. "She says he spent the two nights in question in a separate room in her suite, one night because she was sick and another night because he didn't have a room of his own." (A full account appears in Schmitt, "Suite Sharing: Arbitrator's Friendship With Winning Lawyer Imperils Huge Victory," Wall St. J., Feb. 14, 1990, p. 1.)

We understand that the award was later vacated by stipulation of the parties.

8. Are party-appointed representatives on "tripartite" boards held to the same standards as other arbitrators? Section 23(a)(2) of the Revised Uniform Arbitration Act permits a court to vacate an award where there was "corruption by an arbitrator," "misconduct by an arbitrator prejudicing the rights of a party," or "evident partiality by an arbitrator *appointed as a neutral*." What do the italicized words add? The AAA/ABA "Code of Ethics for Arbitrators in Commercial Disputes" presumes that party-appointed arbitrators "should be considered non-neutrals" unless the parties have specified otherwise. Under the Code, they "may be predisposed toward the party who appointed them." With respect to Canon II concerning disclosure, the Code provides that non-neutral party-appointed arbitrators "need not include as detailed information as is expected from persons appointed as neutral arbitrators"; in addition, they "are not obliged to withdraw if requested to do so by the party who did not appoint them."

This different treatment of party-appointed arbitrators is reflected in most of the cases, which "implicitly recognize it is not necessarily unfair or unconscionable to create an effectively neutral tribunal by building in presumably offsetting biases." Tate v. Saratoga Savings & Loan Ass'n, 216 Cal.App.3d 843, 265 Cal.Rptr. 440, 445 (Cal. App. 1989). In one case an arbitrator, after being appointed, assisted the party that had named him "in preparing its case by attending and participating in meetings with [its] witnesses [and suggesting] lines or areas of testimony." The court found this conduct "not only unobjectionable, but commonplace," Sunkist Soft Drinks, Inc. v. Sunkist Growers, Inc., 10 F.3d 753 (11th Cir.1993). But for the view that this sort of behavior might constitute "overt misconduct" that exceeds even the partisanship expected of party-appointed arbitrators, see Metropolitan Property & Casualty Ins. Co. v. J.C. Penney Casualty Ins. Co., 780 F.Supp. 885 (D.Conn.1991).

Assuming that proper disclosure is made, can a party appoint a member of its Board of Directors as "its" arbitrator on a tripartite board? See In the Matter of the Arbitration between the Astoria Medical Group v. Health Ins. Plan of Greater N.Y., 11 N.Y.2d 128, 227 N.Y.S.2d 401, 182 N.E.2d 85 (N.Y. 1962) (yes; the right to appoint "one's own arbitrator" "becomes a valued right, which parties will bargain for * * * only if it involves a choice of one believed to be sympathetic to his position or favorably disposed to him"). Does it follow, then, that an individual party can *itself* sit as its own arbitrator? See Edmund E. Garrison, Inc. v. International Union of Operating Engineers, 283 F.Supp. 771 (S.D.N.Y. 1968). Can the claimant in an arbitration agree to compensate "its" arbitrator on the basis of a percentage of the award? See Aetna Casualty & Surety Co. v. Grabbert, 590 A.2d 88 (R.I.1991).

9. In international commercial arbitrations, the "tripartite" model is in fact a norm which will be surrendered only with difficulty—to many, indeed, the right to choose one member of the panel is the very essence of arbitration. And in such arbitrations the general understanding calls for a

D. THE ARBITRATION PROCEEDING   **851**

rule that is nominally different from our domestic practice: Arbitrators on international panels are expected to be both independent of the party appointing them and impartial. Apparently there is "no room for debate" that a party-appointed arbitrator may be partisan, and ICC practice, for example, is to refuse confirmation to an arbitrator where there exists a professional or financial relationship with any of the parties.

Cf. Rau, On Integrity in Private Judging, 14 Arb. Int'l 115, 230–31 (1998):

> Nevertheless it is usually conceded that without violating in any way this theoretical obligation of independence, the arbitrator may quite acceptably share the nationality, or political or economic philosophy, or "legal culture" of the party who has nominated him—and may therefore be supposed from the very beginning to be "sympathetic" to that party's contentions, or "favorably disposed" to its position. * * *

> I would think it very doubtful that this could possibly be considered an improvement over the practice in our domestic commercial arbitrations. Even in the best of circumstances an official rhetoric of "independence" and a tolerated latent "sympathy" must exist in an uneasy tension. Indeed one occasionally comes across the argument that codes of ethics mandating impartiality are useful precisely in that they give arbitrators who "wish to behave entirely impartially" some sort of "moral protection" against pressure to rule in favor of the party naming them—an argument that itself illustrates nicely the sort of dynamic that must often arise.

> When the Continental jurist writes that a party-appointed arbitrator must be impartial—but can be impartial "in his own fashion"—the echo of Cole Porter is undoubtedly inadvertent. But in such circumstances the potential for ambiguity, uncertainty and confusion seems obvious. Even the arbitrator himself may be unaware of the extent to which his identification with the party who has appointed him may be affecting his view of a given procedural or substantive issue—and what is more important, this may be appreciated still less by his two colleagues, particularly the chairman. A mythology that promotes the belief that international arbitrators can be relied on not to allow their sympathy "to override their conscience and professional judgment"— regardless of whether this is taken as empirical description or as a mere aspiration—seems calculated only to increase these dangers of self-deception and sandbagging.

> It is true of course that too visible an advocacy is likely to be simply counterproductive. Once he is perceived as little more than an agent for the party appointing him, an arbitrator may well lose all his clout with the rest of the panel and all his ability to influence the course of the proceedings. But these are counsels of prudence and discreet self-presentation, not of impartiality. In the course of discussions aimed at selecting party-appointed arbitrators in international cases, the highest praise one can give, apparently—one actually hears this said—is that the potential arbitrator "knows just how far he can go in advocacy" without losing all credibility with his colleagues. By contrast, to recog-

852 CHAPTER V ARBITRATION

nize quite openly the inevitability of partisanship once party-appointed arbitrators are used might instead * * * be "the only intellectually honest approach to the situation".

10. Westinghouse entered into a contract with the New York City Transit Authority (NYCTA) for the delivery of equipment for the New York subway system. Numerous disputes arose between the parties; NYCTA declared Westinghouse in default, and Westinghouse submitted a claim for additional compensation. Under the contract, disputes were to be submitted to the Superintendent of the NYCTA—who was an NYCTA employee and its Chief Electrical Officer; judicial review was to be limited to the question whether the Superintendent's decision was "arbitrary, capricious, or grossly erroneous to evidence bad faith." Westinghouse later challenged an adverse determination by the Superintendent, arguing that the contract "imposes a procedure for dispute resolution by a functionary inseparable from one of the parties to the dispute and, thus, fosters a predisposed adjudication process" contrary to public policy. The court, however, rejected this argument: "Westinghouse chose, with its business eyes open, to accept the terms, specifications and risk" of the contract; this was "part of the calculated business risk it undertook." Private contractors are "often economic giants in their own right," and the fact that municipalities may enjoy a "virtual monopolistic-kind of power" on their public works jobs "does not make these contracts adhesion agreements. * * * [W]here, as here, the parties are dealing at arm's length with relative equality of bargaining power, they ought to be left to themselves." The court found its conclusion buttressed by the fact that the contract "allows broader review than the usual and stricter standards" of judicial review of arbitration awards. Westinghouse Electric Corp. v. New York City Transit Authority, 82 N.Y.2d 47, 603 N.Y.S.2d 404, 623 N.E.2d 531 (N.Y. 1993). Compare Graham v. Scissor–Tail, Inc., supra p. 704. ("Contracts of Adhesion and Unconscionability").

11. The CPR Institute for Dispute Resolution has published a set of rules for "non-administered arbitration"—rules "that could be used by sophisticated users who didn't need a babysitter," see 18 Alternatives 149, 151–52 (Sept. 2000). A recent revision of these rules provides for an optional "screened" selection of party-appointed arbitrators—designed "in such a manner so that the arbitrators wouldn't know who picked them." Under the new rules, parties wishing to follow this procedure are given a copy of the CPR "Panel of Distinguished Neutrals," and each party is to designate three candidates, in order of preference, "as candidates for its party-designated arbitrator." A party may object to any appointment "on independent and impartial grounds by written and reasoned notice to CPR," which is to make a final decision with respect to any objection. "Neither CPR nor the parties shall advise or otherwise provide any information or indication to any arbitrator candidate or arbitrator as to which party selected either of the party-designated arbitrators." Rule 5.4(d).

What do you think of this solution?

D. THE ARBITRATION PROCEEDING 853

12. On occasion a losing party, claiming that the arbitrator did not decide fairly or that he proceeded in violation of the rules, will bring a suit directly against the arbitrator or the administering institution. Such claims are usually rebuffed with an invocation of "arbitral immunity." Just as with judges, it is thought that "the independence necessary for principled and fearless decision-making can best be preserved by protecting these persons from bias or intimidation caused by the fear of a lawsuit arising out of the exercise of official functions within their jurisdiction." Corey v. New York Stock Exchange, 691 F.2d 1205 (6th Cir.1982). This "federal policy" dictates that the only remedy for a disgruntled party is under § 10 and § 11 of FAA and not by means of collateral attacks on the award. A similar interest in protecting arbitrators also means that when a court *does* hear a motion under § 10 or § 11, it is unlikely to permit depositions or examination of the arbitrators themselves aimed at developing a factual basis for impeaching the award. See, e.g., Portland Gen. Elec. Co. v. U.S. Bank Trust Nat'l Ass'n, 38 F.Supp.2d 1202 (D.Or.1999)("discovery in the challenge of an arbitral award is tightly circumscribed and available only upon 'clear evidence of impropriety' ").

The Revised Uniform Arbitration Act also provides that "an arbitrator or an arbitration organization acting in such capacity is immune from civil liability to the same extent as a judge of a court of this State acting in a judicial capacity"; where a suit against an arbitrator or an arbitral institution is dismissed on the ground of immunity, the defendants are entitled to recover "reasonable attorney's fees and other reasonable expenses of litigation." § 14(a),(e).

13. Who is acting as an "arbitrator" for purposes of "arbitral immunity"? Can former New York City mayor Edward Koch, who presided over a televised episode of "The People's Court," be liable for allegedly defamatory statements made in the course of the hearing? See Kabia v. Koch, 186 Misc.2d 363, 713 N.Y.S.2d 250 (City Ct.2000)(no; this is "arbitration" under state law even though any award is to be paid by the producers of the television program and not by the losing party; "arbitrators in contractually agreed upon arbitration proceedings are absolutely immune from liability for all acts within the scope of the arbitral process").

Should immunity be extended to an architect, employed and paid by the owner of a construction project and charged with interpreting the contract documents and deciding whether the contractor has substantially performed? See Lundgren v. Freeman, 307 F.2d 104, 116–19 (9th Cir.1962) (granting immunity when architect was acting as "quasi-arbitrator"). What about an accountant who is hired by both parties to a contract for the sale of stock to determine the earnings of the company? See Wasyl, Inc. v. First Boston Corp., 813 F.2d 1579 (9th Cir.1987) (claim of breach of contract and gross negligence by defendant in appraisal of value of partnership interest; immunity granted, relying on state arbitration statute that expressly "includes * * * valuations [and] appraisals"); contra, Comins v. Sharkansky, 38 Mass.App.Ct. 37, 644 N.E.2d 646 (Mass.App.1995) (defendant-accountant "is neither an arbitrator exercising 'quasi-judicial' functions nor an

854 CHAPTER V ARBITRATION

expert rendering expert services to the court"; "[w]hile an arbitration may be less formal than court proceedings, the parties contemplate that an arbitrator will hold hearings and will take evidence in the presence of the parties"). Cf. Arenson v. Casson Beckman Rutley & Co., [1975] 3 All E.R. 901 (H.L.) (Lord Kilbrandon) ("It would be absurd if the situation were that, when an expert is asked by one customer to value a picture, he is liable in damages if he is shown to have done so negligently, but that if two customers had jointly asked him to value the same picture he would have been immune from suit").

Do the reasons justifying arbitral immunity extend to protecting an arbitrator from a lawsuit that alleges he is liable for "breach of contract" for simply failing to render any award at all? See Baar v. Tigerman, 140 Cal.App.3d 979, 189 Cal.Rptr. 834 (Cal.App.1983) (arbitrator did not meet deadline imposed for decision under AAA rules; cases granting immunity were distinguished because here the arbitrators were not "acting in a quasi-judicial capacity" and plaintiffs had not alleged "misconduct in arriving at a decision").

2. CONDUCT OF THE PROCEEDING

a. INTRODUCTION

In any discussion of arbitration it is almost mandatory to mention the supposed "informality" of the process: "Submission of disputes to arbitration always risks an accumulation of procedural and evidentiary shortcuts that would properly frustrate counsel in a formal trial."[1] However, there is not merely one form of procedure for arbitration in the United States, but an almost infinite variety:

> At one extreme, we have what is practically courtroom procedure, with carefully drawn submissions, formal procedures, emphasis upon technicalities, formal opening and closing statements, arguments as to the admissibility and relevance of evidence, qualifications of witnesses, and the burden of proof, and briefs, rebuttal briefs, and sur-rebuttal briefs. At the other extreme, we have an atmosphere which is barely distinguishable from a mediation proceeding; the issue is vague and ill-defined, everybody talks at the same time, says irrelevant things, no standards of evidence appear, and the arbitrator seems to be working chiefly at the task of securing agreement between the disputants. Between the extremes are innumerable shadings and variations.[2]

The personality and the professional background of the arbitrator, the attitudes and the relationship of the parties, the issues in contention—all will influence the way the arbitration proceeds.

We should not be surprised to find a considerable amount of procedural innovation in the practice of arbitration—stemming, first, from the un-

---

1. Forsythe Int'l, S.A. v. Gibbs Oil Co. of Texas, 915 F.2d 1017, 1022 (5th Cir.1990).

2. Stein, The Selection of Arbitrators, N.Y.U. Eighth Annual Conference on Labor 291, 293 (1955).

D. THE ARBITRATION PROCEEDING

bounded ability of the parties to "write their own ticket," and, second, from the traditionally broad discretion of arbitrators in structuring the proceedings. "Indeed, short of authorizing trial by battle or ordeal or, more doubtfully, by a panel of three monkeys, parties can stipulate to whatever procedures they want to govern the arbitration of their disputes."[3] In one large and complex antitrust dispute, for example, the parties had selected as their arbitrator a noted antitrust scholar and law professor:

Based on his reading of briefs and affidavits, [the arbitrator] advised counsel which witnesses he wanted to have at the hearing. Rather than putting on the plaintiff's case in full, followed by defendant's case in full, [the arbitrator] proceeded by topic or category of witness; and in several instances, he put corresponding witnesses for the two sides on the stand at the same time. In so doing, he was able to let both parties' witnesses respond in succession to the same question and then engage in dialogue to explore differences of opinion. Throughout the proceeding, [he] peppered counsel with questions to explore the bases for and merits of various legal theories.

This technique avoided both the rigidity of traditional direct and cross-examination, and the usual "ships-passing-in-the-night" quality of most competing expert testimony. In fact most of the questioning at the hearing was done by the arbitrator, and only "limited follow-up questioning" was conducted by counsel. In addition, the parties agreed that the arbitrator would write a reasoned opinion that "could be published because of its potential value to other parties who might be faced with similar issues."[4]

b. THE ROLE OF LAWYERS

"[E]ven in the most informal of proceedings certain minimum requirements of 'due process' must be met if the award is to be legally binding."[5] State and federal statutes governing arbitration mandate certain elements supposed to be essential to a fair hearing. Under the Revised Uniform Arbitration Act, "the parties to the arbitration proceeding are entitled to be heard, to present evidence material to the controversy and to cross-examine witnesses appearing at the hearing." § 15(d). The parties also have the right to be represented by an attorney, and any waiver of that right "before a controversy arises" subject to the arbitration agreement is ineffective. §§ 4(b)(4), 16.

Attorneys can play a useful role in arbitration. In framing and focusing the issues, and in eliciting and marshalling the evidence, the attorney can help create a more coherent and rational process. However, the use of attorneys—along with the adversarial proceedings that seem to be envi-

---

3. Baravati v. Josephthal, Lyon & Ross, Inc., 28 F.3d 704, 709 (7th Cir.1994)(Posner, C.J.).

4. Baker, Alexander, Cohan & Heike, "The First Texas–Pulse Arbitration: A Case Study," reprinted in John Murray, Alan Rau, and Edward Sherman, Dispute Resolution: Materials for Continuing Legal Education IV–136, IV–141 (NIDR 1991).

5. Smith, Merrifield & Rothschild, Collective Bargaining and Labor Arbitration 212 (1970).

CHAPTER V ARBITRATION

saged by the arbitration statutes—may be responsible for some of the vociferous complaints about the growing "legalization" of the arbitration process. These complaints seem to be heard most loudly in the self-contained enclave of labor arbitration. One observer, for example, has written:

> In the past two decades, a change in orientation of labor arbitrators and a rise in the use of attorneys as advocates have accelerated the introduction into labor arbitration of procedures that approximate those of the courts. * * *

> [The former president of the National Academy of Arbitrators has written that]

> * * * The ratio of hard fought, legalistic arbitration presentations to problem-solving presentations is increasing. I now have more long, drawn-out cases in which employers and unions present prehearing briefs, spend endless hours haggling over the language of the submitted issue, have stenographic records made of the hearings and insist upon briefs, reply briefs, and sometimes, reply briefs to the reply briefs. * * *

> Legalism adds to the complexity of arbitration, and correspondingly to the confusion of an employee. The impersonality that legalism brings to the process undermines its credibility. Employees who have been assisted in their grievances by union representatives who may have known them for years may be represented at the arbitration by attorneys whom they have seen for the first time on the day of the arbitration. When these attorneys, competent though they may be, neglect to raise questions that the grievants feel are important, which they feel would have been asked by union representatives, the grievants feel cheated.[6]

In this debate, however, as in most others, where one ends up may well depend upon one's starting point. The author of the preceding excerpt is a "Professor of Human Resource Development" in a College of Business. A lawyer, by contrast, is far more likely to be using a judicial yardstick when he evaluates arbitration. He may be struck most forcibly by the way in which the process *falls short* of the ritual trappings and judicial solemnity of the model with which he is most comfortable.

Commercial arbitrations are somewhat more likely even than labor cases to involve lawyers (acting either as arbitrators or as advocates), and to look like "loose approximations of judicial proceedings."[7] This is a tendency that may be accelerating. More than half a century ago, Lon

---

6. Raffaele, Lawyers in Labor Arbitration, 37 Arb.J. No. 3 (Sept. 1982). See also Alleyne, Delawyerizing Labor Arbitration, 50 Ohio St. L.J. 93 (1989)("creeping formalism took sway with the commonly held notion that representation by a lawyer in an adversary proceeding, even a labor arbitration hearing, enhances the possibility of a successful outcome").

7. Shell, ERISA and Other Federal Employment Statutes: When Is Commercial Arbitration an "Adequate Substitute" for the Courts?, 68 Tex.L.Rev. 509, 534 (1990).

D. THE ARBITRATION PROCEEDING

Fuller could advise advocates that the commercial arbitrator, "who will usually be a layman, * * * will be unimpressed by arguments resting upon the abstract 'rights' of the parties. The arbitrator will chiefly want to know whether the parties conducted themselves honorably and fairly and made a genuine effort to settle their differences by negotiation."[8] Given the remedial flexibility and freedom from the constraint of legal rules that typify arbitration, there remains much truth in this counsel. On the other hand, pressures by lawyers "always to guarantee as much due process as possible" may be creating subtle changes in the appearance of arbitration—and might well cause it "over time by accretion" to become almost "indistinguishable from the system you were trying to get away from."[9] When important questions of external law are routinely entrusted to arbitrators— and when the paradigm arbitration case increasingly becomes, not a dispute over the quality of goods delivered but over alleged violations of the Sherman Act or Title VII—then the attention to legal rules, and the accompanying level of procedural formality, may be expected to be much higher.

The attorney can still however expect in all forms of arbitration to encounter an environment that is noticeably different from that of litigation. Lawyers who are unfamiliar with the process may at first find it difficult to adapt themselves to the different quality of advocacy expected in arbitration, and must struggle to adjust their behavior to the different style and atmosphere of an arbitration proceeding. Such a mainstay of a litigator's life as pre-"trial" motion practice is for all practical purposes absent from arbitration. And a forensic style carefully honed for courtroom use may be totally out of place in an arbitration proceeding, where the parties and the arbitrators are all seated together around a conference-room table. In this more relaxed setting a non-theatrical, even conversational style is likely to be much more effective. A less confrontational and less argumentative approach may be hardest to pull off in the cross-examination of the opponent's witnesses—although this may be all the more important if the arbitrators are prone to identify closely with witnesses from the industry involved in the dispute.

c. EVIDENCE

The classic illustration of the relative "informality" of the arbitration process is the usual absence of the rules of evidence, which play such a dominant role in any courtroom. Under the AAA's Commercial Arbitration Rules, "[c]onformity to legal rules of evidence shall not be necessary"; "[t]he arbitrator shall determine the admissibility, relevance, and materiality of the evidence offered and may exclude evidence deemed by the arbitrator to be cumulative or irrelevant." (Rule 33). It is not unusual for evidence to be presented in the form of affidavits rather than live testimo-

---

8. Lon Fuller, Basic Contract Law 713 (1947).

9. McKeen, "Med–Mal Arbitration in California: Murky Results," Legal Times, Sept. 13, 1993, at pp. 10, 13 (quoting the general counsel for the Association for California Tort Reform).

858   CHAPTER V ARBITRATION

ny, despite the absence of any possibility for cross-examination. See Commercial Arbitration Rules, Rule 34 (but it shall be given "only such weight as the arbitrator deems it entitled to after consideration of any objection made to its admission"); Pierre v. General Accident Ins., 100 A.D.2d 705, 474 N.Y.S.2d 622 (App. Div. 1984) (widow's claim for death benefit under automobile insurance policy was denied; arbitrator accepted "an unsworn report, in the form of a letter, from respondent's expert cardiologist, who did not testify or make himself available for cross-examination").

An arbitrator is in fact more likely to get into trouble by following the rules of evidence than by ignoring them—and far more likely to get into trouble by excluding evidence than by admitting it. Section 10(a)(3) of the FAA allows a court to vacate an award where the arbitrator was "guilty of misconduct" "in refusing to hear evidence pertinent and material to the controversy." There are many cases in which an arbitrator's disregard of testimony in reliance on rules of evidence has caused his award to be vacated, on the ground that a party has been denied a "fair hearing." See, e.g., Harvey Alum. v. United Steelworkers of America, 263 F.Supp. 488 (C.D.Cal.1967). Perhaps as a consequence, the common tendency of arbitrators seems to be to admit most proffered evidence and to consider it "for whatever it may be worth." "I am prepared to listen to just about anything a party wants me to hear."[10]

A good example of how this can work in practice is provided by one lawyer's account of his service on an arbitration panel. In this construction case a contractor who had built a building for a private school submitted a substantial claim for "extras," work done but supposedly not covered by the contract price:

> In his opening statement to the panel, the lawyer for the school asserted that even without the extras, the contractor had made a profit. He then gave the arbitrators an affidavit from the school's controller. It stated that the school, which enjoyed an excellent reputation in the community, would have to raise each student's tuition at least $1,300 a year just to pay the interest on the amount sought by the contractor. The affidavit also stated that the school had granted scholarships to at least 28 students, who might have to withdraw if the contractor obtained the award he was seeking.

[Over an objection by the contractor's lawyer that the affidavit was "incompetent, irrelevant, hearsay, prejudicial, and not probative on any issue in dispute," the panel (which also included an architect and an engineer) received it in evidence. The arbitration lasted for weeks, with copious, and confusing, evidence offered on each of the contractor's claims:]

> Among the few facts which retained their persuasive power throughout the arbitration were the points the school lawyer had made at the outset. Almost every day, in private conversations over lunch or over an early evening drink, or during any one of the several recesses taken

---

10. McDermott, An Exercise in Dialectic: Should Arbitration Behave As Does Litigation?, Proceedings, 33rd Annual Meeting, Nat'l Academy of Arbitrators 1, 14 (1981).

D. THE ARBITRATION PROCEEDING   **859**

during the day, one or more of the arbitrators mentioned that the contractor had already made a profit and that granting the claim would injure the school and hurt innocent scholarship students.

The ultimate decision was in favor of the school.[11]

NOTES AND QUESTIONS

1. The lowering of barriers to the admission of evidence in arbitration is often the subject of serious criticism, particularly on the part of lawyers, who are likely to find it chaotic, sloppy—and worse. For example, one prominent attorney and arbitrator has written:

> [T]he common arbitration practice often admits costly immaterial and/or prejudicial evidence. * * * The arbitrators do that out of [a desire] to appear to be fair and * * * [t]hereby they become unfair by receiving prejudicial evidence or making parties spend effort and money responding to immaterial evidence. * * * It is fairly common knowledge that uncross-examined affidavit evidence is *extremely* unreliable. Lawyers hear a narrative, draft a preliminary affidavit proposal with many voids filled in out of their own imagination, send it to the affiant perhaps "to check and execute if it is OK." * * * The wildest hearsay upon hearsay is often pretended to be "personal knowledge." A party ought not [to] have to fight such irresponsible evidence presented by the adversary.

Arnold & Hubert, Focus Points in Arbitration Practice 51–52 (1992, unpublished), quoted in Rau & Sherman, Tradition and Innovation in International Arbitration Procedure, 30 Tex.Int'l L.J. 89, 95, 101 (1995).

In many cases such criticism is undoubtedly well-founded. In some kinds of cases, however, may criticisms of this sort overlook some of the premises of arbitration? The opportunity to present evidence that is not particularly relevant or even particularly reliable by the usual standards of the courtroom may nevertheless provide arbitrators with an insight into the "total situation" of the parties not afforded by a narrower scope of inquiry. (This may be true of the school construction arbitration discussed above.) And when the parties are engaged in a continuing relationship, such an opportunity can permit a useful "ventilation" of a grievance; as in mediation, when the parties are given a sense that they have had a full opportunity to "have their say" on points that are personally important to them, the process is legitimated and their confidence in it increased: "This is therapy evidence." Jones, Evidentiary Concepts in Labor Arbitration: Some Modern Variations on Ancient Legal Themes, 13 U.C.L.A.L.Rev. 1241, 1254 (1966). In addition, it is far from clear that generosity in admitting evidence will necessarily prolong the hearings: Laying a proper "foundation" for evidence and qualifying witnesses, making a series of

---

11. Roth, When to Ignore the Rules of Evidence in Arbitration, 9 Litigation 20 (Winter 1983).

860   CHAPTER V   ARBITRATION

witnesses personally available for the purposes of cross-examination—and resolving the inevitable attorney wranglings over admissibility—all may consume at least as much if not more time than does the present practice.

2. On the tendency of labor arbitrators to admit evidence "for what it is worth," see W. Daniel Boone, A Debate: Should Labor Arbitrators Receive Evidence "For What It's Worth"?: The Union Perspective, Proceedings, 51st Annual Meeting, Nat'l Academy of Arbitrators 89, 92 (1999):

> Within the arbitrator community in Northern California, I take this to mean, "this evidence is not worth anything, but I'll let it in anyway." I understand the arbitrator to be saying (1) the evidence is neither relevant nor probative, (2) it has no persuasive impact, (3) it will not assist in making a decision, (4) the opposing party need not respond with evidence or argument, and (5) the proponent may proceed only if a truly short amount of time is taken.

3. Although it is well known that arbitrators are not bound by "rules of evidence," it is nevertheless quite common to find lawyers objecting in arbitration to the introduction of what, in litigation, would be "inadmissible" evidence. The goal here, obviously, is not so much to keep the evidence out—as it is to emphasize its unreliability, and to reduce the weight it might have for the arbitrator.

4. In none of the statutes governing arbitration is there any mention of improperly *admitting* evidence as a form of arbitral "misconduct." Can an award ever be vacated on such grounds? It is quite common for arbitrators to hear testimony in the form of what would be "hearsay" in a court of law, and this clearly is not a ground for overturning an award. Farkas v. Receivable Financing Corp., 806 F.Supp. 84 (E.D.Va.1992). See also In the Matter of the Arbitration between Norma Brill and Muller Brothers, Inc., 40 Misc.2d 683, 243 N.Y.S.2d 905 (Sup. Ct. 1962), in which the arbitrator received in evidence a detective agency report consisting of a "dime-novel series of stories about the petitioner and her behavior, said to be gathered from her former neighbors" and "detailing specific acts of alleged avarice, malice and chicanery." The trial court, calling this "hearsay on hearsay" and "thoroughly unfair evidence," "inflammatory and prejudicial to the highest degree," vacated the award. Higher courts, however, reversed, 17 A.D.2d 804, 232 N.Y.S.2d 806 (App. Div. 1962), aff'd, 13 N.Y.2d 776, 242 N.Y.S.2d 69, 192 N.E.2d 34 (N.Y. 1963).

5. In a Better Business Bureau arbitration between General Motors and a car owner, the owner requested that GM be made to buy back the car; he had bought it second-hand, and had replaced the engine after driving it for an additional 23,000 miles. "The arbitrator awarded the owner half the cost of the second engine, or $875. The rationale was that, during mediation, the manufacturer had indicated a willingness to assume half the cost of the engine * * *." This anecdote is reported without comment in Note, Virginia's Lemon Law: The Best Treatment for Car Owner's Canker?, 19 U.Rich.L.Rev. 405, 421 (1985).

D. The Arbitration Proceeding

See Bowles Financial Group, Inc. v. Stifel, Nicolaus & Co., Inc., 22 F.3d 1010 (10th Cir.1994). In this case the attorney for the claimant had "deliberately, intentionally, affirmatively and repeatedly communicated to the arbitrators an offer of settlement" from the respondent, arguing that the settlement offer "evidenced [the respondent's] admission of liability." "Counsel also indicated he routinely submitted settlement offers to the arbitrators in the cases where he represented clients in arbitration." The arbitrators, "after receiving the settlement offer, commented they would not consider it," but they subsequently made an award to the claimant that exceeded the offer. The court held that the respondent "has not proven it was subjected to a fundamentally unfair hearing":

> Had [the claimant's] counsel done before a court of law what he did before the arbitrators, significant sanctions would have been imposed and a mistrial ordered. But however well-established may be the judicial rules of evidence, they legitimately did not apply to this arbitration.

See also Appendix C concerning the inadmissibility at trial of offers made during settlement negotiations.

6. Should the arbitrator be expected to make a decision based solely on the evidence received at the hearing? After all, one of the premises of arbitration is that the arbitrator may himself be an "expert," chosen to bring to the process his own knowledge and familiarity with the subject matter. It seems clear that an arbitrator, unlike a judge, is free to draw on this background. In one commercial dispute, for example, the arbitrators awarded the buyer money damages for non-delivery even though no evidence as to the market price of the goods had been introduced. Judge Learned Hand dismissed the seller's argument that this constituted arbitral "misconduct," remarking that if the arbitrators "were of the trade, they were justified in resorting to their personal acquaintance with its prices." When the parties have chosen arbitration, he added, "they must be content with its informalities; they may not hedge it about with those procedural limitations which it is precisely its purpose to avoid." American Almond Prods. Co. v. Consolidated Pecan Sales Co., 144 F.2d 448, 450–51 (2d Cir.1944). See also In the Matter of the Arbitration between Oinoussian Steamship Corp. of Panama and Sabre Shipping Corp., 224 F.Supp. 807 (S.D.N.Y.1963) (arbitrators allegedly relied on trade custom not mentioned at hearing; "it would be carrying coals to Newcastle to require presentation of evidence to experts in the field").

However, the arbitrator's relative freedom in supplementing the evidence introduced by the parties is hardly a license to make his own independent investigation into the facts of the dispute. Where the quality of goods is in dispute, an arbitrator who gives samples of the goods to his own salesmen for the purpose of obtaining an opinion as to "merchantability" is inviting a court to vacate his award for "misconduct.". See Stefano Berizzi Co. v. Krausz, 239 N.Y. 315, 146 N.E. 436 (N.Y. 1925) (Cardozo, J.) ("The plaintiff, knowing nothing of the evidence, had no opportunity to rebut or even to explain it."). So is the arbitrator who in attempting to fix the rental

862 CHAPTER V ARBITRATION

value of real estate asks the opinion of real estate brokers as to the value of similar property. See 290 Park Ave. v. Fergus Motors, 275 A.D. 565, 90 N.Y.S.2d 613 (App. Div. 1949).

7. The conduct of an international arbitration is naturally likely to be influenced by the legal background and nationality of the arbitrators, and particularly of the chairman. Arbitrators from civil-law jurisdictions may share the preference of judges in those systems for the submission and exchange of documentary evidence and written witness statements, de-emphasizing oral testimony. Written statements "may entirely replace oral testimony," as "the entire testimony of some witnesses and much of the testimony of others often goes unchallenged." See W. Laurence Craig, William Park, & Jan Paulsson, International Chamber of Commerce Arbitration § 24.05 (3rd ed. 2000); id. at § 26.02 (practice of taking depositions outside the presence of the arbitrators to be submitted to panel as part of documentary evidence). See also the International Bar Association's "Supplementary Rules Governing the Presentation and Reception of Evidence in International Commercial Arbitration," which contain detailed ground rules for the production of documents and witness statements. Under these rules each party would be required to provide in advance a witness statement containing "a full statement of the evidence it is desired by that party to present through the testimony of that Witness." A witness may only give oral evidence if all parties agree or if the Arbitrator himself "in his discretion" orders that oral evidence be given; the testimony of all other witnesses "shall be taken by means of his Witness Statement only." See Alan Redfern & Martin Hunter, The Law and Practice of International Commercial Arbitration 704 (2d ed. 1991).

Arbitrators with a civil-law background are also likely to share the propensity of civil-law judges to take a more active role in the development of the facts. They may themselves routinely call—and examine—witnesses, obtain the assistance of experts, or order inspections or site visits, all on their own initiative. See generally Craig et al., supra at 415–434; Lowenfeld, The Two–Way Mirror: International Arbitration as Comparative Procedure, 7 Mich. Yrbk. of Int'l Legal Studies 163 (1985); Rau & Sherman, Tradition and Innovation in International Arbitration Procedure, 30 Tex. Int'l L.J. 89 (1995).

d. DISCOVERY

Another illustration of the relative informality of arbitration is the sharply limited availability of discovery, both "pre-trial" and at the hearing itself.

A starting point is a common statutory provision such as § 7 of the Uniform Arbitration Act:

> (a) The arbitrators may issue subpoenas for the attendance of witnesses and for the production of books, records, documents and other evidence, and shall have the power to administer oaths. * * *

D. THE ARBITRATION PROCEEDING   **863**

(b) On application of a party and for use as evidence, the arbitrators may permit a deposition to be taken, in the manner and upon the terms designated by the arbitrators, of a witness who cannot be subpoenaed or is unable to attend the hearing.

See also § 7 of the FAA.

Issuance or enforcement of a subpoena is, however, rarely necessary; an informal request for information by the arbitrator at a hearing usually suffices. At least where it is a *party* who has been requested to produce evidence, he will be reluctant to antagonize the arbitrator by refusing. Most importantly, the party will be aware that should he decline to produce relevant evidence within his control, the arbitrator is likely to draw the inference that it would have been unfavorable to him.[12] And so in most cases "an informal indication that such an inference will or may be drawn is sufficient to extract the document."[13]

The provisions of § 7 leave it to the discretion of the arbitrator to decide what materials he feels he needs to resolve the dispute; a party has no "right" to the issuance of a subpoena.[14] Exercise of this discretion is likely to be limited to demands for documents that can be "described with specificity (for example, if they are internally referenced in documents put into evidence by one side").[15] It is conceivable that an arbitrator's refusal to order the production of evidence might lead to a successful challenge to the award: In one maritime case, for example, the arbitrators had refused to order the shipowner to produce the ship's logs during the proceeding; a court indicated that this could constitute a violation of § 10(a)(3) of the FAA where the charterer of the ship could "show prejudice as a result." The court noted that the ship's logs are "perhaps the most important items of documentary evidence in any maritime controversy," and failure to supply them before the hearing's end could prejudice the ability of a party "not only in cross examination of witnesses, but in the preparation of its own case."[16] Such judicial action is, however, extremely rare.

---

12. See In re U.S. Dept. of Labor and American Federation of Govt. Employees, 98 Lab.Arb. 1129 (1992) (sexual harassment case; "I draw an adverse inference against Management from its failure to produce [the supervisor alleged to have harassed the grievant] to testify at the hearing to deny that he conducted himself as grievant testified or to otherwise explain his behavior").

13. Lowenfeld, The *Mitsubishi* Case: Another View, 2 Arb.Int'l 178, 184 (1986).

14. See National Broadcasting Co., Inc. v. Bear Stearns & Co., Inc., 165 F.3d 184, 187 (2d Cir. 1999)("§ 7 explicitly confers authority only upon *arbitrators*; by necessary implication, the *parties* to an arbitration may not

employ this provision to subpoena documents or witnesses").

15. Tupman, "Discovery and Evidence in U.S. Arbitration: The Prevailing Views," 44 Arb.J. (March 1989) at pp. 27, 32. Cf. Hunt v. Mobil Oil Corp., 654 F.Supp. 1487, 1512 (S.D.N.Y.1987) (arbitrators refused to issue a "broadcast subpoena" demanding "all documents" of various kinds; such a request "is not uncommon in litigation [but] is precisely the type of production demand that is the exception rather than the rule in arbitration").

16. In the Matter of the Arbitration between Chevron Transport Corp. and Astro Vencedor Compania Naviera, S.A., 300 F.Supp. 179 (S.D.N.Y.1969).

864 CHAPTER V ARBITRATION

True "discovery" in the litigation sense—for example, interrogatories and depositions taken before "trial" for the purposes of "trial" preparation—is even more limited. Provisions such as § 7 of the Uniform Arbitration Act assume, of course, that the arbitrators have already been named. Even where the arbitration panel is in place, the power of arbitrators to order pre-hearing discovery—at least in the absence of an agreement between the parties—is uncertain. An arbitrator's authority to order the production of documents in advance of a hearing has been upheld;[17] in some other jurisdictions, however, even this authority has been denied.[18] In any event the full range of discovery provided by the Federal Rules of Civil Procedure will not be available: While the Rules apply to motions made under the FAA (for example, motions to compel arbitration or to confirm an award), it is clear that they do not apply *to the conduct of the actual proceedings* before the arbitrators.

There are, however, some state statutes that do envisage more extensive arbitral discovery. For example, the Texas version of the Uniform Arbitration Act adds to § 7 that the arbitrators "may authorize a deposition of an adverse witness for discovery or evidentiary purposes, such depositions to be taken in the manner provided by law for depositions in a civil action pending in a district court." Tex.Civ.Prac. & Rem.Code § 171.007(b). The recent Revised Uniform Arbitration Act adds that an arbitrator may "permit such discovery as the arbitrator decides is appropriate in the circumstances, taking into account the needs of the parties to the arbitration proceeding and other affected persons and the desirability of making the proceeding fair, expeditious, and cost effective." § 17(c). See also Cal.Code Civ.Pro. §§ 1283.05, 1283.1 ("right to take depositions and to obtain discovery" in arbitration of personal injury claims).

The reluctance to make pre-hearing discovery more widely available in arbitration may reflect the concern that this would be inconsistent with the goal of rapid and inexpensive dispute resolution. Looming over the debate is likely to be the specter of the "abuse" of the discovery process— "unfocused, unthoughtful, often massive, and always expensive"—which many observers blame for the delay and excessive cost characterizing complex federal litigation.[19] The fear is expressed that the use of pre-

---

17. Meadows Indemnity Co., Ltd. v. Nutmeg Ins. Co., 157 F.R.D. 42 (M.D.Tenn. 1994) (given "the sheer number of documents," it would be "quite fantastic and practically unreasonable" for the arbitrators to require a witness to bring them all to the hearing; their power to compel production of documents for the purposes of a hearing "implicitly authorizes the lesser power to compel such documents for arbitration purposes prior to a hearing"); Security Life Ins. Co. of Amer. v. Duncanson & Holt, Inc., 228 F.3d 865 (8th Cir.2000)("interest in efficiency" is "furthered by permitting a party to review

and digest relevant documentary evidence prior to the arbitration hearing").

18. North American Foreign Trading Corp. v. Rosen, 58 A.D.2d 527, 395 N.Y.S.2d 194 (App. Div. 1977) (arbitration panel "exceed[ed] its authority by directing pre-arbitration disclosure").

19. See Lundquist, In Search of Discovery Reform, 66 A.B.A.J. 1071 (1980). Cf. Mullenix, Discovery in Disarray: The Pervasive Myth of Pervasive Discovery Abuse and the Consequences for Unfounded Rulemaking, 46 Stan.L.Rev. 1393 (1994) (the notion of discovery abuse "is based on questionable social

D. THE ARBITRATION PROCEEDING 865

hearing discovery would add one further layer of complexity and "legalism" to a process which in the eyes of some observers has already come too much to resemble formal adjudication. In addition, there is a concern that judicial supervision and administration of the discovery process might interfere with the functions of the arbitrators chosen by the parties, and "preshape" the issues presented to them for decision. The point is also frequently made that by choosing arbitration, the parties have voluntarily accepted the risk that pre-hearing discovery and the other "procedural niceties which are normally associated with a formal trial" would not be available to them.[20]

The general unavailability of pre-hearing discovery in arbitration often leads parties to an arbitrable dispute to seek discovery ordered and supervised by a *court*. A fairly liberal attitude towards allowing discovery is exemplified by Bigge Crane & Rigging Co. v. Docutel Corp., 371 F.Supp. 240 (E.D.N.Y.1973). In *Bigge,* a subcontractor brought suit against a general contractor for payments due under a construction contract. The plaintiff, asserting that it had been given "no explanation" of the reasons it had not been paid for the work performed, then sought to take depositions of the defendant's employees and to obtain inspection of job records, contracts, and other documents. The defendant moved for a stay of the action under § 3 of the FAA and for an order compelling arbitration. The court granted the motion and stayed the trial pending completion of arbitration—"without prejudice," however, "to the rights of [the parties] to utilize the pretrial discovery procedures of the Federal Rules of Civil Procedure in a manner which does not delay the course of the arbitration":

> In this case there will have been considerable delay by the time the elaborate proceedings of the American Arbitration Association for the selection of arbitrators have been completed; and the arbitrators, selected for this particular case, may be under some pressure to complete their task promptly. On the other hand, discovery proceedings in the court action can go forward while the selection of arbitrators and scheduling of a hearing is under way.

> * * *

> Arbitration is not a separate proceeding independent of the courts, as was sometimes thought. The courts are brigaded with the arbitral tribunal in proceedings to compel arbitration or stay judicial trials, proceedings to enforce or quash subpoenas issued by arbitrators and proceedings to enforce or set aside arbitral awards. * * * [T]he court believes that it should exercise discretion to permit discovery in this case because (1) discovery is particularly necessary in a case where the claim is for payment for work done and virtually completed, and the nature of any defense is unknown; (2) the amounts involved are so substantial that any expense in taking depositions is relatively small; [and] (3) the action has proceeded to such a point that the taking of

science, 'cosmic anecdote,' and pervasive, media-perpetuated myths").

20. Burton v. Bush, 614 F.2d 389, 390 (4th Cir.1980).

866   CHAPTER V ARBITRATION

depositions can probably be accomplished without delaying the arbitration.

Most cases, however, are considerably more restrictive than *Bigge*. There is a tendency to require that pre-arbitration discovery be "necessary" to a party to allow him to "present a proper case to the arbitrators," or even that "extraordinary circumstances" be present, before a court may order it.[21] Cf. Deiulemar Compagnia Di Navigazione S.p.A. v. M/V Allegra, 198 F.3d 473 (4th Cir.1999). Here an agreement for a time charter specified that the vessel would maintain a guaranteed speed of 12–13 knots; the agreement also provided for arbitration in London. When the vessel reached its final destination at Baltimore, the charterer claimed that the promised performance specifications had not been met, and tried to inspect the vessel in order to gather and preserve evidence to support its claim. The owner refused, and argued that all of the information sought "could be requested through the arbitration process" in London. The trial court granted the charterer's request for discovery under Rule 27 of the Federal Rules Civil Procedure, and the Fourth Circuit affirmed: Since the ship's engine was scheduled for repair, "the circumstances and conditions extant today can never be recreated"; since the vessel was scheduled to leave the territorial waters of the United States immediately following repairs, the charterer "was in danger of losing access to any evidence of the ship's condition." "Given the time sensitive nature of [the charterer's] request and the evanescent nature of the evidence sought, we do not believe that the district court abused its discretion" in accepting the charterer's representation that it could not obtain "emergency discovery" from the London arbitrator "in time to preserve the rapidly changing condition of the ship." The sealed evidence gathered from the vessel was to be transferred to the pending arbitration in London: "The arbitrator does not have to admit the evidence; nor does he have to suppress it; that choice is left entirely to the arbitrator."

NOTES AND QUESTIONS

1. "[I]n the large, complex case, discovery is almost inevitable." Gorske, An Arbitrator Looks at Expediting the Large, Complex Case, 5 Ohio St.J.Disp.Res. 381, 394 (1990). In an increasing number of such disputes, procedures are being introduced aimed at insuring that both parties in arbitration will have available to them all the information they need for the full presentation of their cases. Experiments in this area usually arise out of some combination of arbitrator initiative and party cooperation.

In one large construction case—involving claims of almost $800 million and requiring more than 2½ years to complete—the arbitrators "proposed, and the parties agreed upon, a format similar to that used by numerous regulatory agencies whereby direct testimony and exhibits would be pre-

---

21. See In re the Application of Moock, 99 A.D.2d 1003, 473 N.Y.S.2d 793 (App. Div. 1984); International Components Corp. v. Klaiber, 54 A.D.2d 550, 387 N.Y.S.2d 253 (App. Div. 1976) ("absolutely necessary").

filed in written form two weeks before each hearing session in order to reduce hearing time and to facilitate preparation for cross-examination." Discovery depositions of each sides' witnesses "were conducted by agreement of the parties or at the suggestion of the [panel] in order to reduce the likelihood that hearing time would be used for discovery" and as "the most efficient way for each side to prepare for cross-examination." This discovery was "closely supervised" by the arbitrators, who would often pass on any objections raised by one of the parties "within hours of their submission." Gorske, supra at 383–85; see also Hedlund & Paskin, Another View of Expediting the Large, Complex Case, 6 Ohio St.J.Disp.Res. 61 (1990); Gorske, A Reply, 6 id. 77 (1990).

As such devices have become more familiar, they have also become the subject of institutional rules that attempt to create a formal framework for information exchange prior to the actual hearings. For example, the AAA has recently published its "Optional Procedures for Large, Complex Commercial Disputes." These procedures—obviously influenced by the "case-management" role of federal judges—call for a preliminary hearing shortly after the selection of the arbitrators. The preliminary hearing provides an opportunity to draw up a detailed statement of claims, damages, and defenses and "a statement of the issues asserted by each party," to stipulate to uncontested facts, to "exchange * * * those documents which each party believes may be offered at the hearing," and to identify witnesses and their expected testimony. The "Procedures" also provide:

> 5(b) Parties shall cooperate in the exchange of documents, exhibits and information within such party's control if the arbitrator(s) consider such production to be consistent with the goal of achieving a just, speedy and cost-effective resolution of a Large, Complex Commercial Case.
>
> (c) The parties may conduct such document discovery as may be agreed to by all the parties provided, however, that the arbitrator(s) may place such limitations on the conduct of such discovery as the arbitrator(s) shall deem appropriate. If the parties cannot agree on document discovery, the arbitrator(s) for good cause shown and consistent with the expedited nature of arbitration, may establish the extent of same.
>
> (d) The arbitrator(s) upon good cause shown may order the conduct of the deposition of, or the propounding of interrogatories to, such persons who may possess information determined by the arbitrator(s) to be necessary to a determination of a Large, Complex Commercial Case.

2. If depositions of adverse witnesses have not been taken prior to the hearing, attorneys may feel compelled at the hearing itself to engage in protracted cross-examination that can become "a 'fishing expedition'—in effect, a deposition with the arbitrators looking on." Stipanowich, Rethinking American Arbitration, 63 Indiana L.J. 425, 451 (1988). See also Wilkinson, "Streamlining Arbitration of the Complex Case," Disp. Res. J., Aug.-Oct. 2000 at pp. 8, 11 ("I have witnessed many cross-examinations at arbitration hearings that plod down one dead-end street after another,

868 CHAPTER V ARBITRATION

while the questioner endlessly gropes for any testimony that might be of help"). Alternatively, an arbitration proceeding may readily be adjourned or continued at the arbitrator's discretion, to allow a party to study and respond to information revealed as a result of testimony or document production—it is in this respect unlike a trial which once begun is likely to proceed more or less continuously. "If [the arbitrators] wish to allow the questioner further opportunity to investigate after receiving the answers they will do so. What more is there to an examination before trial?" Motor Vehicle Accident Indemnification Corp. v. McCabe, 19 A.D.2d 349, 243 N.Y.S.2d 495 (App. Div. 1963). See also Thomson, Arbitration Theory and Practice: A Survey of AAA Construction Arbitrators, 23 Hofstra L.Rev. 137, 147–48 (1994) (survey indicates that 51% of construction arbitrators would grant a request for a continuance during the hearing on the ground that evidence is being "seen for the first time").

3. One study suggests that there is a "striking difference" between the settlement rate of cases that are litigated and those that are arbitrated: "Only about 5 percent of court cases are fully adjudicated, compared to over 50 percent of AAA arbitration cases." Kritzer & Anderson, The Arbitration Alternative, 8 Justice System J. 6, 11 (1983). Might the lower settlement rate of cases in arbitration be attributable to the relative unavailability of discovery? Is settlement less likely in part because the parties have not been led to clarify or narrow the issues in dispute, or to focus on the relative strengths and weaknesses of their cases and that of their opponents? Stipanowich, Rethinking American Arbitration, 63 Indiana L.J. 425, 444 & n. 110 (1988). Cf. Henry H. Perritt, "And the Whole Earth Was of One Language": A Broad View of Dispute Resolution, 29 Villanova L. Rev. 1221, 1269 n.161 (1984)("The greater likelihood of an arbitration award that both parties can live with also reduces the incentives for negotiated settlement"). Or might there be other explanations as well? See, e.g., p. 889 infra.

4. May an arbitrator issue a subpoena to a *non-party* to the arbitration, directing him to appear for a pre-hearing deposition? See Integrity Ins. Co. v. American Centennial Ins. Co., 885 F.Supp. 69 (S.D.N.Y.1995) (no); see also COMSAT Corp. v. National Science Foundation, 190 F.3d 269 (4th Cir.1999)(FAA "does not authorize an arbitrator to subpoena third parties during prehearing discovery, absent a showing of special need or hardship"; in addition, if non-party recipient of a subpoena is a governmental agency, "principles of sovereign immunity" apply and the decision whether to provide documents or employee testimony "is committed to agency discretion"). What about an order to a non-party to produce documents prior to the hearing, for inspection by a party? See Integrity Ins. Co., supra, 885 F. Supp. at 73 ("Documents are only produced once, whether it is at the arbitration or prior to it. Common sense encourages the production of documents prior to the hearing so that the parties can familiarize themselves with the contents of the documents"). See also Brazell v. American Color Graphics, Inc., 2000 WL 364997 (S.D.N.Y.)(arbitrators have authority to provide for pre-hearing production of documents from third parties).

5. Are there any territorial limits to the power of arbitrators to issue subpoenas under FAA § 7? See Fed. R. Civ. P. R. 45, Appendix A infra.

D. The Arbitration Proceeding

869

Compare Amgen Inc. v. Kidney Center of Delaware County, Ltd., 879 F.Supp. 878 (N.D.Ill.1995) ("the statute is specific in stating that the arbitrator may summon any person," and so "there is no territorial limitation on that ability"), *with* Commercial Solvents Corp. v. Louisiana Liquid Fertilizer Co., 20 F.R.D. 359 (S.D.N.Y.1957) (arbitrators "could not perhaps" compel the attendance of witnesses on whom service of subpoenas could not be made within the territorial limits of Fed. R. Civ. P. R.45). Cf. In re Security Life Ins. Co. of America, 228 F.3d 865 (8th Cir.2000)("whether or not [respondent] is correct in insisting that a subpoena for witness testimony must comply with Rule 45, we do not believe an order for the production of documents requires compliance with Rule 45(b)(2)'s territorial limit. This is because the burden of producing documents need not increase appreciably with an increase in the distance those documents must travel").

In the unusual event that the arbitrator's subpoena is not honored, a petition to enforce it must under § 7 be brought before *the district court where the arbitration is to take place*—and the power of that court is undoubtedly limited, under Fed. R. Civ. P. R.45(b)(2), to enforcement within its own district or within 100 miles of the place of the hearing (*Amgen,* supra, 879 Supp. at 882: "Although the Act allows the arbitrator to subpoena anyone, it also provides that this court may enforce the arbitrator's subpoena only in the same manner that it would compel attendance before the court"). Rather than conclude that there is a gap in the law, however, the *Amgen* court "direct[ed]" the party's attorney himself to issue a subpoena under Fed. R. Civ. P. R. 45 (a)(3)(B)—with the understanding that this subpoena could then be enforced by the district court where the production of documents was to take place.

6. At an arbitration hearing the arbitrator orders the plaintiff to produce certain documents; the plaintiff refuses to comply, asserting that this material consists of the confidential communication of information to his attorney and is thus exempt from subpoena on the basis of the attorney-client privilege. The arbitrator then announces that following his usual practice, he will conclude that the evidence if produced would have been unfavorable to the plaintiff; his award is in favor of the defendant. On the plaintiff's motion to vacate the award, what result?

The California Evidence Code makes the testimonial privileges applicable in all "proceedings," a term defined to include arbitration and any other hearing "in which, pursuant to law, testimony can be compelled to be given." Cal.Evidence Code §§ 901, 910. Section 913 further provides that if a privilege is exercised not to testify or disclose information, "the trier of fact may not draw any inference therefrom as to the credibility of the witness or as to any matter at issue in the proceeding."

7. A party to a collective bargaining agreement frequently needs information to help him decide whether to carry a grievance to arbitration in the first place. For example, the agreement may state a general policy against the subcontracting of work, and provide that where equipment is moved to another plant, employees who are laid off as a result may transfer to the new location. If machinery is moved out of the plant, the union will need to

870 CHAPTER V ARBITRATION

know where it has gone and what it is being used for. See NLRB v. Acme Industrial Co., 385 U.S. 432 (1967). To obtain such information in advance of arbitration, the Union may appeal to the National Labor Relations Board. In *Acme,* the Board found that the employer's refusal to furnish information about the removed equipment was in violation of the statutory duty to "bargain in good faith" because the information was "necessary in order to enable the Union to evaluate intelligently the grievances filed." The employer was therefore ordered to furnish the information to the union prior to any arbitration hearing. The Supreme Court held that this order should be enforced; Justice Stewart wrote that:

> Far from intruding upon the preserve of the arbitrator, the Board's action was in aid of the arbitral process. Arbitration can function properly only if the grievance procedures leading to it can sift out unmeritorious claims. For if all claims originally initiated as grievances had to be processed through to arbitration, the system would be woefully overburdened. Yet, that is precisely what the respondent's restrictive view would require. It would force the union to take a grievance all the way through to arbitration without providing the opportunity to evaluate the merits of the claim. The expense of arbitration might be placed upon the union only for it to learn that the machines had been relegated to the junk heap.

Invoking the Board's enforcement machinery can, however, be a slow and cumbersome process. See Laura Cooper et al., ADR in the Workplace 226 (2000) ("a party seeking a legally-enforceable order to disclose information may have to wait for years").

8. Consider the following provision in an arbitration clause:

> In no case shall the arbitrators order or permit any party to obtain from any other party documents, testimony, or any other evidence relating in any way to a transaction or occurrence other than the specific transaction or occurrence which is the subject of the arbitration proceeding.

Such a clause, it has been suggested, can ensure that "pattern and practice discovery"—which "permits plaintiffs' lawyers to rifle through company files looking for potential new clients and discovering potentially inflammatory fact situations which are analogous to their own cases"—"can be eliminated almost entirely in arbitration." Russel Myles & Kelly Reese, Arbitration: Avoiding the Runaway Jury, 22 Am. J. Trial Advoc. 129, 140 (1999). (This article was originally presented at a seminar for insurance executives and corporate counsel).

e. INTERIM MEASURES

Teradyne, Inc. v. Mostek Corp.

United States Court of Appeals, First Circuit, 1986.
797 F.2d 43.

[Mostek manufactured and marketed semiconductor components for use in computers and telecommunications equipment. Virtually all of

D. The Arbitration Proceeding 871

Mostek's supply of laser systems and memory testers, which were essential to its manufacturing operations, were provided by Teradyne. Mostek always bought from Teradyne pursuant to the terms of a Quantity Purchase Agreement (QPA), which provided that Mostek would get price discounts on Teradyne equipment if it ordered certain minimum quantities, and that Mostek would be liable for cancellation and rescheduling charges if it cancelled an order.

[In early 1985 a dispute arose between the parties over cancellation charges claimed by Teradyne. At that time the 1984 QPA had expired; Mostek had held off entering into a QPA for 1985 because it was experiencing financial difficulties. As consideration for waiving the claimed charges, Teradyne demanded that Mostek place an order for twenty memory testers; Teradyne also supposedly "insisted" that before it would fill earlier orders placed by Mostek at the quoted prices, Mostek had to enter into a new QPA for 1985. In March 1985, Mostek did agree to enter into a QPA for 1985 and to place an order for twenty memory testers.

[Later that year, Mostek cancelled its orders; it refused to pay the cancellation charges demanded by Teradyne, assessed at 70% of the original purchase price. In September Teradyne requested arbitration, claiming approximately $3,500,000 for cancellation charges, goods and services invoiced, and incidental and consequential damages. In October Mostek's parent company announced that Mostek would cease operations; in November, substantially all of Mostek's assets were sold for approximately $71 million in cash. The proceeds of the sale were deposited in a separate bank account in Mostek's name and dedicated to the payment of the claims of its creditors. Teradyne then brought an action seeking an injunction ordering Mostek to set aside sufficient funds to satisfy a judgment pending the outcome of arbitration. The district court enjoined Mostek from disposing of or encumbering $4,000,000 of its assets and directed it to set that amount aside in an interest-bearing account to satisfy any arbitration award obtained by Teradyne.

[The First Circuit first held that the district court's "interlocutory order which has the attributes of both an attachment and an injunction" should be treated as a preliminary injunction, and was therefore appealable.

[The court then addressed Mostek's contention "that the policy of the Arbitration Act precludes the grant of preliminary injunctive relief in an arbitrable dispute."]

The Arbitration Act does not address this issue specifically and it has not previously been ruled upon by this circuit. Other circuits, however, have examined the issue in some detail. The Second, Fourth and Seventh Circuits all take the view that a court can, and should, grant a preliminary injunction in an arbitrable dispute whenever an injunction is necessary to preserve the status quo pending arbitration.

* * *

872 CHAPTER V ARBITRATION

The Fourth Circuit's examination of this issue, in Merrill Lynch, Pierce, Fenner & Smith, Inc. v. Bradley, 756 F.2d 1048 (4th Cir.1985), focused on the effect of § 3 of the Arbitration Act on the court's power to issue preliminary injunctive relief. * * * Merrill Lynch sued Bradley, a former account executive, for damages for alleged breach of contract, and sought injunctive relief to prevent Bradley from using its records and soliciting its clients. The district court granted Merrill Lynch a preliminary injunction * * * and ordered expedited arbitration, both parties having agreed that the dispute was arbitrable. Bradley appealed, claiming that the injunction was an abuse of discretion because § 3 of the Arbitration Act precluded a court from considering the merits of an arbitrable dispute. The Fourth Circuit rejected this argument, holding that nothing in § 3 abrogated the equitable power of district courts to enter preliminary injunctions to preserve the status quo pending arbitration. The court also stated that it thought its decision would further rather than frustrate the policies underlying the Arbitration Act by ensuring that the dispute resolution would be a meaningful process.

* * *

Running counter to the approach taken by the Second, Fourth and Seventh Circuits is that taken by the Eighth Circuit in Merrill Lynch, Pierce, Fenner & Smith, Inc. v. Hovey, 726 F.2d 1286 (8th Cir.1984) * * *. Hovey involved a petition by Merrill Lynch for an injunction against five former employees to prevent them from using Merrill Lynch's records and from soliciting Merrill Lynch clients. The employees counterclaimed, seeking to compel arbitration pursuant to New York Stock Exchange rules regulating dispute resolution procedures. The district court granted Merrill Lynch a preliminary injunction and refused to submit the dispute to arbitration. The employees appealed, claiming that the dispute was arbitrable. The Eighth Circuit held that the dispute was arbitrable and that issuing a preliminary injunction was, therefore, precluded by § 3 of the Arbitration Act. The court took the view that granting preliminary injunctive relief in an arbitrable dispute ran counter to the "unmistakably clear congressional purpose that the arbitration procedure, when selected by the parties to a contract, be speedy and not subject to delay and obstruction in the courts." (quoting *Prima Paint Corp.*).

* * *

[W]e are persuaded that the approach taken by the Second, Fourth and Seventh Circuits should be followed. We hold, therefore, that a district court can grant injunctive relief in an arbitrable dispute pending arbitration, provided the prerequisites for injunctive relief are satisfied. * * * We believe that the congressional desire to enforce arbitration agreements would frequently be frustrated if the courts were precluded from issuing preliminary injunctive relief to preserve the status quo pending arbitration and, ipso facto, the meaningfulness of the arbitration process. Accordingly, we hold that it was not error for the district court to issue the preliminary injunction before ruling on the arbitrability of this dispute. We next consider whether Teradyne established the prerequisites for such relief.

[The court then turned to the question whether the criteria for preliminary injunctive relief were satisfied. In the First Circuit, a court must find: "that plaintiff will suffer irreparable injury if the injunction is not granted"; "that such injury outweighs any harm which granting injunctive relief would inflict on the defendant"; and "that plaintiff has exhibited a likelihood of success on the merits."]

The district court here clearly articulated its reasons for finding that Teradyne had satisfied the prerequisites for injunctive relief. It held that Mostek's freedom to dispose of its assets created a substantial risk of irreparable harm to Teradyne, given that Mostek was in the process of winding down after selling the bulk of its assets, that it had failed to provide adequate assurances to alleviate Teradyne's concerns, and that it could at any time make itself judgment proof. Further, the court found that the affidavits submitted to it showed a likelihood that Teradyne would succeed on its contractual claims, and that the balance of hardships was in Teradyne's favor. The court dismissed Mostek's claims that the injunction would create a ripple effect whereby the creditors would rush to court seeking similar relief, noting that the injunction would have no precedential effect on other disputed claims, and that Mostek could pay undisputed claims and thereby avoid any possible ripple effect on them.

* * *

Although Mostek realized assets far exceeding Teradyne's claims when the sale of its assets occurred, the record shows that those assets were being used to pay off creditors' claims and wind down expenses in what Mostek itself described as an "orderly liquidation process." Further, the amount Mostek received for its assets was stated to be subject to a number of unspecified offsets and debits and no assurances were given that Mostek would be able to pay a Teradyne judgment.

* * * Under these circumstances, we affirm the district court's conclusion that the possible hardship to Teradyne of having a $3–4 million judgment prove worthless, outweighed the inchoate hardship to Mostek of having $4 million of its assets tied up in an interest bearing account pending judgment.

[The court then turned to the trial court's conclusion that Teradyne had a "reasonable likelihood of success on the merits." Mostek had argued that the 1985 QPA and the order for the twenty memory testers were "void for duress"; it asserted "that Teradyne took advantage of Mostek's weak financial condition and used its position, as Mostek's only source of supply, to force Mostek to sign the QPA and to place the new order."]

Mostek's allegations of undue pressure exerted on it by Teradyne are rebutted to some extent by Teradyne's account of the facts which indicates that Mostek entered the 1985 QPA voluntarily in order to obtain discounts on its 1984 orders and that it ordered the twenty memory testers of its own accord. But, even if the facts were as Mostek alleges, it is not clear that it has made out a prima facie case of economic duress.

874 CHAPTER V ARBITRATION

It is well established that not all economic pressure constitutes duress. * * * [Under Massachusetts law,] "[m]erely taking advantage of another's financial difficulty is not duress," * * * the person alleging financial difficulty must allege that it was "contributed to or caused by the one accused of coercion," and the assertion of duress "must be proved by evidence that the duress resulted from defendant's wrongful and oppressive conduct and not by plaintiff's necessities." There is no indication here that Teradyne caused or contributed to Mostek's financial difficulties. Indeed, Mostek itself concedes that its difficulties came about as a result of a downturn in the semiconductor industry. Accordingly, we see no abuse of discretion in the trial court's conclusion that Teradyne had shown a likelihood of success on the merits.

Affirmed.

NOTES AND QUESTIONS

1. Will the arbitrator be bound by the views of the First Circuit as to the "merits" of the controversy? Is he likely to be influenced by them? Might this "threaten the independence of the arbitrator's ultimate determination"? Cf. The Guinness–Harp Corp. v. Jos. Schlitz Brewing Co., 613 F.2d 468, 471 n. 1 (2d Cir.1980).

2. Provisional relief granted by an arbitrator will not, of course, always be an adequate substitute for the sort of judicial order approved in *Teradyne*. (Why not?) Nevertheless such relief, if backed by the courts, can often be an effective way of preserving the status quo pending a final decision. See, e.g., Sperry Int'l Trade, Inc. v. Government of Israel, 532 F.Supp. 901 (S.D.N.Y.1982), in which arbitrators required the parties to place the proceeds of a letter of credit in a joint escrow account, pending a later decision on the merits of the underlying claim. The district court temporarily enjoined one of the parties from taking any action to collect the proceeds and confirmed the arbitrators' order within two weeks. It rejected the argument that the order was not "final" within the meaning of § 10(a)(4) of the FAA. See also Yasuda Fire & Marine Ins. Co. of Europe, Ltd. v. Continental Casualty Co., 37 F.3d 345 (7th Cir.1994) (at preliminary hearing, arbitration panel ordered respondent to post a $2.5 million interim letter of credit "against a possible future arbitration award"; award confirmed).

3. Should the interim relief granted by a court in a case like *Teradyne* remain in effect until the award is handed down? Or should a party only be entitled to judicial preservation of the status quo until the arbitrators *themselves* can decide whether interim relief should be granted, and how it should be structured—so that the court order would "expire when the issue of preserving the status quo is presented to and considered by the arbitration panel"? The latter solution was adopted in Merrill Lynch, Pierce, Fenner & Smith, Inc. v. Dutton, 844 F.2d 726 (10th Cir.1988) (preliminary injunction preventing former employee from removing customer lists and soliciting former clients). See also Performance Unlimited, Inc. v. Questar Publishers, Inc., 52 F.3d 1373 (6th Cir.1995) (license agreement; court should issue preliminary injunction requiring licensee "to pay only that

D. THE ARBITRATION PROCEEDING   **875**

amount of royalties necessary to ensure that [licensor] is not driven out of business prior to the time the arbitration proceeds"; "once the arbitration begins, it is for the arbitrators to decide how to maintain the status quo during the pendency of the arbitration process").

4. The AAA's Commercial Arbitration Rules provide (at Rule 36) that

> The arbitrator may take whatever interim measures he or she deems necessary, including injunctive relief and measures for the protection or conservation of property and disposition of perishable goods.

In addition, the AAA has promulgated a separate set of "Optional Rules for Emergency Measures of Protection" which provides for the possibility of interim relief "prior to the constitution of the panel": If the parties have adopted these rules in their arbitration clause or by special agreement, the AAA will appoint within one business day "a single emergency arbitrator from a special AAA panel of emergency arbitrators designated to rule on emergency applications"; this arbitrator may enter an interim award if he is satisfied "that immediate and irreparable loss or damage will result in the absence of emergency relief."

5. Under the New York Convention, each contracting state is required to "recognize" written agreements to arbitrate controversies; the courts of each nation, when seized of an arbitrable matter, "shall, at the request of one of the parties, refer the parties to arbitration * * *." (Art. II(3)). Curiously enough, it has been held that this language prohibits a court "from acting in any capacity except to order arbitration"; on this view they would have no power to take any interim measures in aid of international arbitrations to which the Convention applies. Cooper v. Ateliers de la Motobecane, S.A., 57 N.Y.2d 408, 456 N.Y.S.2d 728, 442 N.E.2d 1239 (1982). In this case the New York Court of Appeals, in denying an order of attachment, wrote:

> It is open to dispute whether attachment is even necessary in the arbitration context. Arbitration, as part of the contracting process, is subject to the same implicit assumptions of good faith and honesty that permeate the entire relationship. Voluntary compliance with arbitral awards may be as high as 85%. Moreover, parties are free to include security clauses (e.g., performance bonds or creating escrow accounts) in their agreements to arbitrate.

* * *

> The essence of arbitration is resolving disputes without the interference of the judicial process and its strictures. When international trade is involved, this essence is enhanced by the desire to avoid unfamiliar foreign law.

Is this convincing? Does the language of the New York Convention require this result? Might it not be argued—given the complexity, delays, and risks inherent in international commercial disputes—that judicial intervention is *particularly* appropriate to insure that an arbitration award will ultimately be meaningful? It has been said that the United States "stands alone" among all the signatories to the New York Convention in having case law to the effect that pre-arbitration attachment is incompati-

876 CHAPTER V ARBITRATION

ble with the treaty. W. Laurence Craig, William Park & Jan Paulsson, International Chamber of Commerce Arbitration § 27.04 at 483–484 (3rd ed. 2000); see also Ebb, Flight of Assets from the Jurisdiction "In the Twinkling of a Telex": Pre–and Post–Award Conservatory Relief in International Commercial Arbitrations, 7 J.Int'l Arb. 9 (1990).

6. The California International Commercial Arbitration and Conciliation Act makes it clear that:

> It is not incompatible with an arbitration agreement for a party to request from a superior court, before or during arbitral proceedings, an interim measure of protection, or for the court to grant such a measure.

> Measures which the court may grant in connection with a pending arbitration include, but are not limited to:

> (a) An order of attachment issued to assure that the award to which applicant may be entitled is not rendered ineffectual by the dissipation of party assets.

> (b) A preliminary injunction granted in order to protect trade secrets or to conserve goods which are the subject matter of the arbitral dispute.

> The statute also authorizes the arbitral tribunal itself to "order a party to take any interim measure of protection as the arbitral tribunal may consider necessary in respect of the subject matter of the dispute," and a court may enforce such an interim award. See Cal.Code Civ.Pro. §§ 1297.91, 1297.92, 1297.93, 1297.171.

7. The Eighth Circuit continues to adhere to the restrictive view that "injunctive relief is inappropriate in a case involving arbitrable issues unless the contract terms contemplate such relief and it can be granted without addressing the merits." In Manion v. Nagin, 255 F.3d 535 (8th Cir.2001), the district court had denied the request by a dismissed employee for interim relief in aid of arbitration; the arbitration clause stipulated that the agreement to arbitrate was "without prejudice to the right of a party under applicable law to request interim relief from any court * * *." The court of appeals affirmed: "The provision allowing a party to *request* interim relief has been fulfilled since [the employee] filed a motion for a preliminary injunction and it was ruled on by the district court."

E. VARIATIONS ON A THEME

1. COMPULSORY ARBITRATION

John Allison, The Context, Properties, and Constitutionality of Nonconsensual Arbitration

1990 Journal of Dispute Resolution 1, 6, 15.

Most ADR mechanisms have been and continue to be completely voluntary. Alongside the evolution of volitional alternatives, however, we recently have witnessed the accelerating use of nonconsensual ADR mechanisms in both the private claims and administrative contexts. [The author refers to arbitration as "nonconsensual" "when its selection as a dispute resolution mechanism is driven primarily by governmental power rather than by the volition of contracting parties."] Although several forms of nonconsensual ADR have been attempted for the resolution of private disputes,[25] the most ambitious and well-known is the "court-annexed arbitration" now found in a substantial number of states and federal districts.

Several important instances of nonconsensual ADR have been adopted within the administrative-regulatory realm, as well. When a nontraditional form of conflict resolution is imposed without the full consent of the parties in the administrative arena, arbitration appears so far to be the procedure of choice. Examples include * * * commodity futures customer-broker disputes, and data compensation disputes under the federal pesticide law. Use of nonconsensual ADR will probably become much more common in this setting than in the resolution of purely private claims, because in the former case (a) a substantial degree of government coercion is already established and expected and (b) the constitutional barriers to nonconsensual ADR will be easier to surmount. Perhaps the most unusual form of nonconsensual administrative ADR to date is the data compensation arbitration program of the Federal Insecticide, Fungicide, and Rodenticide Act (FIFRA).

Note: Data Compensation Disputes Under "FIFRA"

Pesticide manufacturers are required to register their products with the Environmental Protection Agency (EPA), and must submit research and test data to the EPA concerning the product's health, safety, and environmental effects. The development of a potential commercial pesticide may require the expenditure of millions of dollars annually over a period of several years. Frequently, after one product has been registered, *another* applicant may wish to register the same or a similar product. Can the EPA consider, in support of this second application, data already in its files that had been submitted by the previous registrant? By avoiding some duplication of test data, this would presumably result in lower costs and increased competition. (Such later registrations are colloquially known as "me too" or "follow on" registrations.)

The Federal Insecticide, Fungicide, and Rodenticide Act (FIFRA) allows the EPA to consider such data (after a 10–year period of exclusive use), but "only if the applicant has made an offer to compensate the original data submitter." 7 U.S.C.A. § 136a(c)(1)(F)(ii). "In effect, the provision instituted a mandatory data-licensing scheme." See Ruckelshaus

---

25. Medical malpractice prescreening and early neutral evaluation are two examples. [See Chapter IV, and pp. 644–645 supra.—Eds.].

878 CHAPTER V ARBITRATION

v. Monsanto Co., 467 U.S. 986, 992 (1984). If the original data submitter and the second applicant fail to agree on the terms of compensation, then either may ask for binding arbitration.

The statute entrusts the arbitration program to the Federal Mediation and Conciliation Service (FMCS)—a federal agency whose primary function is to provide mediators and arbitrators to aid in the resolution of labor disputes. Since the FMCS "rarely arranges or conducts arbitration of commercial disputes," the Service has delegated its administrative functions to the AAA: The FMCS decided "to adopt and use the Commercial Arbitration Roster of the AAA as its roster and to adopt the AAA's rules of commercial arbitration as its rules of procedure for disputes arising under FIFRA." 45 Fed.Reg. 55,395 (1980). Under the statute, the award of the arbitrators is "final and conclusive," with no judicial review "except for fraud, misrepresentation, or other misconduct by one of the parties to the arbitration or the arbitrator." If the original data submitter fails to participate in an arbitration proceeding, he forfeits any right to compensation for the use of his data; if a "follow-on" applicant fails to participate, his application is denied.

A number of large firms engaged in the development and marketing of pesticides challenged this arbitration scheme, claiming that Article III of the Constitution bars Congress from requiring arbitration of disputes concerning compensation "without also affording substantial review by tenured judges of the arbitrator's decision." A unanimous Supreme Court upheld the FIFRA arbitration scheme in Thomas v. Union Carbide Agricultural Prods. Co., 473 U.S. 568 (1985).

In an earlier case, the Supreme Court had suggested that Congress could not establish Article I "legislative courts" to adjudicate "private rights" disputes. Such disputes, involving "the liability of one individual to another under the law as defined," "lie at the core of the historically recognized judicial power." Northern Pipeline Construction Co. v. Marathon Pipe Line Co., 458 U.S. 50 (1982). Justice O'Connor, writing for the Court in *Thomas*, found that the situation presented by FIFRA was different:

> [T]he right created by FIFRA is not a purely "private" right, but bears many of the characteristics of a "public" right. Use of a registrant's data to support a follow-on registration serves a public purpose as an integral part of a program safeguarding the public health. Congress has the power, under Article I, to authorize an agency administering a complex regulatory scheme to allocate costs and benefits among voluntary participants in the program without providing an Article III adjudication. It also has the power to condition issuance of registrations or licenses on compliance with agency procedures. Article III is not so inflexible that it bars Congress from shifting the task of data valuation from the agency to the interested parties.
>
> * * * Congress, without implicating Article III, could have authorized EPA to charge follow-on registrants fees to cover the cost of data and could have directly subsidized FIFRA data submitters for their contri-

butions of needed data. Instead, it selected a framework that collapses these two steps into one, and permits the parties to fix the amount of compensation, with binding arbitration to resolve intractable disputes. Removing the task of valuation from agency personnel to civilian arbitrators, selected by agreement of the parties or appointed on a case-by-case basis by an independent federal agency, surely does not diminish the likelihood of impartial decisionmaking, free from political influence.

* * *

The danger of Congress or the Executive encroaching on the Article III judicial powers is at a minimum when no unwilling defendant is subjected to judicial enforcement power as a result of the agency "adjudication." See, e.g., L. Jaffe, Judicial Control of Administrative Action 385 (1965) (historically judicial review of agency decisionmaking has been required only when it results in the use of judicial process to enforce an obligation upon an unwilling defendant).

We need not decide in this case whether a private party could initiate an action in court to enforce a FIFRA arbitration. But cf. 29 CFR pt. 1440, App. § 37(c) (1984) (under rules of American Arbitration Association, parties to arbitration are deemed to consent to entry of judgment). FIFRA contains no provision explicitly authorizing a party to invoke judicial process to compel arbitration or enforce an award. In any event, under FIFRA, the only potential object of judicial enforcement power is the follow-on registrant who explicitly consents to have his rights determined by arbitration.

* * *

Our holding is limited to the proposition that Congress, acting for a valid legislative purpose pursuant to its constitutional powers under Article I, may create a seemingly "private" right that is so closely integrated into a public regulatory scheme as to be a matter appropriate for agency resolution with limited involvement by the Article III judiciary. To hold otherwise would be to erect a rigid and formalistic restraint on the ability of Congress to adopt innovative measures such as negotiation and arbitration with respect to rights created by a regulatory scheme.

Justice Brennan, joined by Justices Marshall and Blackmun, wrote in concurrence:

Congress has decided that effectuation of the public policies of FIFRA demands not only a requirement of compensation from follow-on registrants in return for mandatory access to data but also an administrative process—mandatory negotiation followed by binding arbitration—to ensure that unresolved compensation disputes do not delay public distribution of needed products. * * * Although a compensation dispute under FIFRA ultimately involves a determination of the duty

880 CHAPTER V ARBITRATION

owed one private party by another, at its heart the dispute involves the exercise of authority by a federal government arbitrator in the course of administration of FIFRA's comprehensive regulatory scheme. As such it partakes of the character of a standard agency adjudication.

NOTES AND QUESTIONS

1. In one FIFRA case arbitrators awarded Stauffer (the original registrant) one-half of its direct testing cost for a chemical, plus a royalty on all sales of the product by PPG (the second applicant) between 1983 and 1992. PPG asked the court to vacate this award; it argued that the arbitrators were limited to compensating Stauffer for the actual cost of producing the test data and could not make an award based on the value to PPG of earlier market entry. The court granted Stauffer's motion to dismiss, concluding that "Congress intentionally left to the arbitrators the choice of what formula to use in determining compensation." PPG Industries, Inc. v. Stauffer Chemical Co., 637 F.Supp. 85 (D.D.C.1986).

FIFRA had originally provided that in the absence of an agreement between the parties as to compensation, the figure was to be determined by the EPA. However, the court noted that "[t]he EPA found this task to be beyond its means":

> Congress concluded that the EPA lacked the requisite expertise in determining compensation, and Congress and the EPA agreed that a determination of compensation did not require "active government involvement." Consequently, Congress removed all suggestion of a standard from the statute and replaced EPA with binding arbitration as the mechanism for determining what compensation was proper. It seems quite reasonable to this Court that Congress intentionally obliterated all suggestion of a standard in view of the fact that not even the EPA could identify a formula which would adequately compensate a data submitter in every case. Congress determined to leave the matter to arbitrators who had more expertise and could evaluate each case individually.

The court also rejected the argument that such "standardless delegation" to private arbitrators was an unconstitutional delegation of legislative authority:

> [T]he concern with delegation to private parties has to do with the private party's interest in the industry being regulated. See, e.g., [A.L.A. Schechter Poultry Corp. v. United States, 295 U.S. 495 (1935)] (holding unconstitutional a statute delegating power to institute penal provisions to a body comprised of members of the industry involved). The private parties involved here are not members of the pesticide industry, but rather disinterested arbitrators appointed by the FMCS, which adopted the roster of the American Arbitration Association.

Is it important in FIFRA cases to develop a body of "common law" concerning the measure of compensation, in order to provide guidance for the future conduct of registrants and later applicants? Will a series of arbitration awards be likely to provide such standards and criteria of decision? See "Data Compensation Decision Seen as Victory by Both Sides in a Lengthy FIFRA Dispute," Pesticide & Toxic Chemical News, October 8, 1998 (arbitrators added a 25% "enhancement" to respondent's share of compensable costs "to reflect [its] early entry into the market by means of citations of claimants' data"; this was "the first time since the award in [*PPG Industries*] that an arbitration award has been based on the value of early entry"). How is the "expertise" of the individual arbitrators likely to aid in resolving the disagreement in *PPG* as to the choice of the appropriate standard of compensation?

2. The Supreme Court supported its decision in *Thomas* by stressing that FIFRA "does not preclude review of the arbitration proceeding by an Article III court." The judicial review provided by the statute "preserves the appropriate exercise of the judicial function," said the Court, since it "protects against arbitrators who abuse or exceed their powers or willfully misconstrue their mandate under the governing law." 473 U.S. at 592. What does this mean?

3. The Commodity Futures Trading Commission (CFTC) is an independent agency established by Congress. The CFTC requires members of commodity exchanges like the Chicago Board of Trade (CBOT) to submit disputes with customers to arbitration if their customers request it; at CFTC insistence, this requirement is incorporated into the rules of the exchanges. Geldermann, a member of the CBOT, refused to arbitrate a customer-initiated claim, and brought suit challenging the arbitration requirement. The court held that "by virtue of its continued membership in the CBOT," Geldermann had "consented to arbitration, and thus waived any right he may have possessed to a full trial before an Article III court." The court also rejected Geldermann's claim that the mandatory arbitration scheme violated its right to a jury trial: Since "Geldermann is not entitled to an Article III forum, the Seventh Amendment is not implicated." That Geldermann "had no choice but to accept the CBOT's rules" if it were to continue in business was irrelevant. Geldermann, Inc. v. CFTC, 836 F.2d 310 (7th Cir.1987).

The statute creating the CFTC also provides an alternative "reparations procedure" by which the agency itself may hear complaints brought by aggrieved customers of commodity brokers. In one such CFTC proceeding, the broker asserted a counterclaim for the balance owed by the investor on his account—a "traditional" state-law action for debt. The investor invoked Article III to challenge the CFTC's authority to hear the counterclaim, but the Supreme Court rejected this challenge: "[I]t seems self-evident that just as Congress may encourage parties to settle a dispute out of court or resort to arbitration without impermissible incursions on the separation of powers, Congress may make available a quasi-judicial mechanism through which willing parties may, at their option, elect to resolve their differences." CFTC v. Schor, 478 U.S. 833 (1986).

882 CHAPTER V ARBITRATION

Is arbitration under FIFRA similarly limited to "willing parties"? Consider the Court's characterization in *Thomas* of the pesticide registration scheme as "voluntary," and its reliance on the fact that the follow-on registrant "explicitly consents to have his rights determined by arbitration."

4. We have already come across a number of cases in which the state has chosen to require arbitration as a dispute resolution mechanism. Recall, for example, the statutory schemes making "lemon law" arbitration under AAA auspices mandatory on automobile manufacturers at the initiative of the consumer; consider also the states in which arbitration of fee disputes is made mandatory for attorneys at the initiative of the client. See pp. 651–652 supra. There are many other instances. See, e.g., Nev.Rev.Stat. § 689A.0403 ("Each policy of health insurance must include a procedure for binding arbitration to resolve disputes concerning independent medical evaluations pursuant to the rules of the [AAA]"); N.J.Stat. § 39:6A–5 (required coverage for personal injury protection in automobile policy; all insurers "shall provide any claimant with the option of submitting a dispute * * * to binding arbitration" administered by AAA). The Amateur Sports Act of 1978 requires every amateur sports organization that wishes to be recognized as the national governing body for a particular sport to submit disputes over the rights of athletes to participate in competition— for example, disputes over alleged drug use—to arbitration; the arbitration is to be "conducted in accordance with the commercial rules of the [AAA]." See 36 U.S.C.A. §§ 371, 391(b)(3).

"Mandatory arbitration may indeed not benefit from the dynamic of self-government that often makes labor and commercial arbitration an extension of the parties' own negotiations. It may indeed lack the legitimacy of processes founded on consent, in which an arbitrator chosen and paid by the parties is charged with interpreting substantive standards laid down by them in their agreement, in accordance with procedures to which they have also consented. Mandatory arbitration is, instead, simply a form of economic or professional regulation." Alan Rau, Resolving Disputes Over Attorneys' Fees: The Role of ADR, 46 S.M.U.L.Rev. 2005, 2032–33 (1993).

5. Are there plausible claims that constitutional rights have been violated when a binding arbitration process is imposed on private parties? In GTFM, LLC v. TKN Sales, Inc., 2000 WL 364871 (S.D.N.Y.), a Minnesota distributor alleged that it had been wrongfully terminated in violation of the Minnesota Sales Representative Act, and brought suit against the manufacturer not only for violations of the Act, but also for failure to pay commissions and for breach of contract. There was no arbitration agreement between the parties—but the Act provided that a sales representative had the right to submit any such claims to "final and binding" arbitration. The court held that the MSRA's "mandatory and binding arbitration system operates to deny [the manufacturer] its right to a jury trial" guaranteed by the Seventh Amendment: Claims under the Act for wrongful termination were "analogous to actions at common law," for the Act "provides a specialized remedy for a breach of contract claim involving sales representatives and supplies additional terms to sales representative agreements regarding notice and grounds for termination."

Compare Motor Vehicle Manufacturers Ass'n of the U.S. v. New York, 75 N.Y.2d 175, 551 N.Y.S.2d 470, 550 N.E.2d 919 (N.Y. 1990), in which New York's "lemon law" arbitration statute was upheld against a claim that it deprived manufacturers of their right to a trial by jury. The statutory remedies—replacement of the vehicle or refund of the purchase price—were found analogous to claims for specific performance and restitution; since such remedies were "equitable in nature" they would not in any event "have been triable by jury under the common law." Nor did the law deprive them of their right to "have a court or public officer adjudicate their disputes" with consumers by "delegating sovereign judicial power to private arbitrators": The court reasoned that the legislature had "merely created a new limited class of disputes and provided a procedure for resolving them, much in the same way it removed automobile claims from judicial cognizance by the No–Fault Insurance Law." In addition, since "arbitrators are selected pursuant to detailed standards, the procedures they must follow are specified, the grounds for relief defined and their determinations are subject to judicial review," it followed that "the arbitration proceeding remains within the judicial domain." See also Lyeth v. Chrysler Corp., 929 F.2d 891 (2d Cir.1991) ("the compulsory alternative arbitration mechanism affords the basic procedural safeguards required by due process").

6. The Florida "lemon law" provides that an aggrieved consumer may apply for arbitration before the "New Motor Vehicle Arbitration Board"— whose members are appointed by the Attorney General—and that the consumer *must* submit to arbitration before filing a civil suit under the law. By contrast with the New York statute, either the consumer or the manufacturer in Florida is entitled to a trial de novo after completion of this "mandatory alternative dispute resolution procedure"; at such a trial the decision of the arbitration board is admissible in evidence.

In Chrysler Corp. v. Pitsirelos, 721 So.2d 710 (Fla.1998), the consumer prevailed before the arbitration board, and the trial judge instructed the jury that the board's decision was "presumed to be correct." The state supreme court held, however, that the statute should not be interpreted in this way—indeed, that such a presumption would raise serious constitutional issues, since it "would diminish the right to have the ultimate decision in a case made by a court." The board's decision should be treated "only as evidence with its weight to be determined by the fact-finder." Nevertheless the court held that the manufacturer now had the burden of persuasion in establishing why the board's decision was erroneous: To require the consumer to bear the burden of proof "as if no previous proceeding had been held" would "relegate the mandatory arbitration to simply being a procedural impediment to the consumer." Does *Pitsirelos* appear to you to be a coherent decision?

7. The state's traditional supervisory authority over the legal profession has provided strong constitutional support for any requirement that attor-

884 CHAPTER V ARBITRATION

neys submit to binding arbitration of fee disputes. See Rau, supra note 4, at 2036–40. Some courts have in addition found more fanciful justifications: Does an attorney somehow "waive" her right to a jury trial merely by engaging in the profession? See Kelley Drye & Warren v. Murray Indust., Inc., 623 F.Supp. 522 (D.N.J.1985) (New Jersey's mandatory arbitration program; "by taking advantage of the opportunity to practice law in New Jersey" the firm had "voluntarily given up its right to a trial of any kind" and had agreed to arbitration).

Note: Mandatory Arbitration in Public Employment

A number of statutes require the arbitration of "interest" disputes concerning the terms of a new collective bargaining agreement between a state or local government, and a union representing its employees. Fairly typical examples of the growing number of such statutes are Rhode Island's Fire Fighter's Arbitration Act and Policemen's Arbitration Act.[1] In recognition of "the necessity to provide some alternative method of settling disputes where employees must, as a matter of public policy, be denied the usual right to strike," the legislation requires that where a city and a union cannot reach agreement, "any and all unresolved issues" shall be submitted to arbitration. The arbitration panel is to be tripartite—one arbitrator being named by each of the parties and the third, in the absence of agreement, is selected under the rules of the AAA. The legislation attempts to enumerate the "factors" which the panel must take into account—including the "interest and welfare of the public," the "community's ability to pay," and a comparison of wage rates and employment conditions with prevailing local conditions "of skilled employees of the building trades and industry" and with police or fire departments in cities of comparable size.

It is obvious that "interest" disputes in public sector employment are intimately connected to the political process. Many public services, such as police protection and education, raise questions that are "politically, socially, or ideologically sensitive."[2] A number of such sensitive issues have in fact been held to be "non-bargainable"—despite their obvious impact on the working conditions of public employees—and thus outside the permissible scope of "interest" arbitration. Such "non-negotiable matters of governmental policy" might in public education include questions of curriculum or of class size; in police services, questions of the manpower level of the force or a civilian review board for police discipline. See, e.g., San Jose Peace Officer's Ass'n v. City of San Jose, 78 Cal.App.3d 935, 144 Cal.Rptr. 638 (Cal.App.1978) (police policy governing when officer is allowed to fire weapon; "The forum of the bargaining table with its postures, strategies, trade-offs, modifications and compromises is no place for the 'delicate balancing of different interests: the protection of society from criminals, the protection of police officers' safety, and the preservation of all human life, if possible.' ").

1. R.I.Stat. § 28–9.1–1; R.I.Stat. § 28–9.2–1.

2. Harry Wellington & Ralph K. Winter, Jr., The Unions and the Cities 23 (1971).

In a more general sense, however, the resolution of *all* disputes over the terms of public employment—even disputes over nuts and bolts issues like wages—is inescapably "political." To resolve a wage dispute by applying the "factors" set out in the Rhode Island legislation requires an accommodation of the competing interests of employees, taxpayers, and the users of public services. The arbitrator will inevitably be led to determine priorities among various public programs, the level of public services, or the need and feasibility of increased public revenue. Such exercises of judgment are necessarily political compromises. Should such issues be resolved "in an arbitrator's conference room as an alternative to facing up to vexing problems in the halls of state and local legislatures"?[3] It has been suggested in fact that "interest" arbitration of public-sector disputes may be inconsistent with the democratic premise that governmental priorities are to be fixed by elected representatives, responsible to all the competing interest groups and responsive to the play of political forces. Resolving public sector "interest" disputes, it is asserted, is not an exercise in neutral, "objective" adjudication but rather one in "legislative" policymaking:

> The size of the budget, the taxes to be levied, the purposes for which tax money is to be used, the kinds and levels of governmental services to be enjoyed, and the level of indebtedness are issues that should be decided by officials who are politically responsible to those who pay the taxes and seek the services. The notion that we can or should insulate public employee bargaining from the political process either by arbitration or with some magic formula is a delusion of reality and a denigration of democratic government.[4]

It should not be surprising, then, that the constitutionality of compulsory interest arbitration in the public sector has repeatedly been challenged. Successful challenges have been rare.[5] Nevertheless, it is clear that there are real tensions here with the values traditionally underlying the arbitration process. It seems hard to justify compulsory "interest" arbitration on the usual rationale that the process is merely an extension of the parties' own bargaining, an application of "self-government" in the workplace. In the final analysis, how does compulsory "interest" arbitration in public-sector employment differ from decisions made directly by a governmental agency? How different really is Rhode Island's compulsory arbitration statute from the Nebraska scheme—which entrusts the settlement of public-sector "interest" disputes to a state "Commission of Industrial Relations" consisting of five "judges" named for six-year terms by the Governor with the advice and consent of the legislature?[6]

---

3. Dearborn Fire Fighters Union v. City of Dearborn, 394 Mich. 229, 231 N.W.2d 226 (Mich. 1975).

4. Summers, Public Sector Bargaining: Problems of Governmental Decisionmaking, 44 U.Cinn.L.Rev. 669, 672 (1975). See also Grodin, Political Aspects of Public Sector Interest Arbitration, 64 Cal.L.Rev. 678 (1976).

5. See, e.g., Salt Lake City v. International Ass'n of Firefighters, 563 P.2d 786

(Utah 1977) (the "legislature may not surrender its legislative authority to a body wherein the public interest is subjected to the interest of a group which may be antagonistic to the public interest").

6. Neb.Rev.Stat. § 48–801; see also id. § 48–805 (the "judges" of the Commission

886 CHAPTER V ARBITRATION

Some years ago the Rhode Island Supreme Court rebuffed a constitutional attack on that state's compulsory arbitration statutes by the simple device of characterizing the arbitrators as "public officers" rather than as mere "private persons": The arbitration panel *must* be considered "an administrative or governmental agency," reasoned the court; after all, the arbitrators had been granted "a portion of the sovereign and legislative power of the government"![7] But such a semantic tour de force obviously does not resolve the problem. If the arbitrators are appointed on an ad hoc basis, with no continuing legislative or administrative oversight, there may be no real accountability to the electorate; these are "hit and run" decisionmakers.[8] If, in contrast, the arbitrators are *not* to be private decisionmakers and are instead made politically responsible, may not the neutrality of the entire process be called into question? Does the arbitrator not then become merely "an agent of government involved primarily in implementing public policy"?[9] Isn't it implicit in the very notion of an "impartial" or "neutral" arbitrator that the decision-maker is *not* to be responsive to political intervention, or to be held accountable for his decision by any constituency? Or might the personal "accountability" of private arbitrators be affected in any event by the well-known need of those in the profession to maintain their acceptability for future employment?

NOTES AND QUESTIONS

1. Is the same judicial deference traditionally accorded arbitral awards appropriate in the case of compulsory "interest" arbitration in the public sector? In many states with such statutes, the arbitration panel is in fact treated for purposes of review much like an administrative agency. A record of the proceedings and a written decision are commonly required, and courts may examine the result to see whether it is "supported by substantial credible evidence present in the record." See Hillsdale PBA Local 207 v. Borough of Hillsdale, 263 N.J.Super. 163, 622 A.2d 872 (N.J.Super. 1993).

What is it that justifies a more extensive standard of judicial review here? Is it primarily the fact that "interest" rather than grievance arbitration is involved? See Craver, The Judicial Enforcement of Public Sector Interest Arbitration, 21 B.C.L.Rev. 557, 572 (1980) (deference to arbitral determinations gives rise to the "possibility of catastrophic consequences resulting from an entirely intemperate award"). Is it the fact that public-sector arbitration is more likely to involve "governmental" decisions—so that any delegation to arbitrators necessarily calls for a closer scrutiny of their assessment of the "interest and welfare of the public"? Or might it

---

"shall not be appointed because they are representatives of either capital or labor, but * * * because of their experience and knowledge in legal, financial, labor and industrial matters").

7. City of Warwick v. Warwick Regular Firemen's Ass'n, 106 R.I. 109, 256 A.2d 206 (R.I. 1969).

8. Dearborn Fire Fighters Union v. City of Dearborn, 394 Mich. 229, 231 N.W.2d 226, 243 (1975) (Kavanagh, C.J., concurring).

9. Grodin, supra n. 4, 64 Cal.L.Rev. at 693–94.

simply be the fact that the arbitration process has been imposed on the parties and does not arise out of their consent? Cf. General Accident Ins. Co. v. Poller, 321 N.J.Super. 252, 728 A.2d 845 (1999)(in automobile insurance policy for personal injury protection, arbitration is mandatory for the carrier under state law at the election of the insured; however, "the carrier's participation in this market, circumscribed as it is by state law, is nevertheless voluntary," and so "no different standard" of judicial review from that familiar in private voluntary arbitration is warranted).

2. A "Model Termination of Employment Act" was approved by the National Conference of Commissioners on Uniform State Laws in 1991. Under this Act, an employee who has worked for the same employer for at least one year may not be fired without "good cause"—a term defined to include both the employee's misconduct and job performance, and the employer's good faith "exercise of business judgment" concerning the goals and organization of his operations and the size and composition of his work force. An employee who has been wrongfully terminated under the Act may be entitled to reinstatement or, alternatively, up to three years of severance pay, along with attorneys' fees. "[D]ecisionmaking by professional arbitrators is the preferred method of enforcing the Act"—although states that are concerned about "the possible extra expense of outside arbitrators" may instead choose hearing officers who are full-time civil service personnel, while states concerned "about possible constitutional problems" may leave enforcement in the hands of the courts. In addition to all the usual procedural grounds for overturning awards that are found in modern arbitration statutes, the arbitrator's decision may be vacated for "a prejudicial error of law." This standard of review was apparently thought necessary because "individual statutory rights are the issue, and arbitration as the enforcement method has been imposed upon, not agreed to by, the parties." Model Employment Termination Act, prefatory note, § 8 & cmt.

Note: Mandatory Arbitration and Public Regulation

Nursing homes, and care facilities for the mentally retarded, must in Texas be licensed by the Texas Department of Human Services. As the state agency responsible for their regulation, the Department is required to inspect these facilities periodically to see if they are meeting state health and safety standards; if a facility is not in compliance with the state's standards, the Department may initiate enforcement action and may seek remedies such as the suspension or revocation of a license, or "administrative penalties." (In determining the amount of such a penalty, the Department is to consider "the seriousness of the violation, including the * * * hazard or potential hazard * * * to the health or safety of the public," and "deterrence of future violations." Tex. Health & Safety Code § 242.066.)

However, a 1995 statute now permits either the Department, or the nursing home or care facility itself, to "elect binding arbitration" of any such dispute; such arbitration "is an alternative to a contested case hearing" brought by the Department seeking suspension or revocation of a license or the imposition of a penalty. The arbitrator "must be on an approved list of a nationally recognized association that performs arbitrations" or be otherwise qualified under rules promulgated by the State Office of Administrative Hearings; he may be paid up to $500 per day for his services. The arbitrator's decision may be vacated by a court if it was "arbitrary or capricious and against the weight of the evidence." Tex. Health & Safety Code §§ 242.252, 242.253, 242.254, 242.267.

The sponsor of this legislation claimed that it gives the state "a new tool to enforce the rules regulating nursing homes. If this tool is properly used, nursing homes who do not comply with basic standards of health and safety will face the quick collection of the appropriate fines and penalties." Austin American–Statesman, Dec. 20, 1995, at A14. Is this claim completely disingenuous? Is this statutory use of ADR appropriate? Is it consistent with the historical goals of alternative processes?

2. FINAL–OFFER ARBITRATION

For almost 100 years professional baseball players were bound to their teams for life by the sport's infamous "reserve clause." In consequence, most players had little choice but to accept the salary their team was willing to pay them. In recent years, however, collective bargaining between the clubs and the players' union has replaced the old "reserve clause" with a system that considerably enhances player mobility between teams. At the same time, it has introduced a novel form of "interest" arbitration to fix salaries where player and team cannot agree.

Under the collective bargaining agreement between the teams and the players' union, players who have been in the major leagues for at least six years can choose to become "free agents"; they can thus have their salaries determined through negotiation in the free market with other teams that might be interested in them.[10] Players with fewer than six years in the majors are still not free to look elsewhere, but are tied to their original team unless they are traded or released. However, those with at least *three* years service do have the right to submit the question of their salary to binding arbitration.[11]

Salary disputes are submitted to arbitration in February. The collective bargaining agreement specifies a number of criteria which the "interest" arbitrators must consider in determining salaries for the coming season— for example, the player's contribution to the team during the past season (including his "overall performance, special qualities of leadership, and public appeal"), "the length and consistency of his career contribution," and "comparative baseball salaries" (which may include salaries paid to

---

10. At least in theory. In a number of grievance arbitrations between 1987 and 1990, arbitrators found that the owners of baseball teams had been acting in concert to restrain salaries by refraining from bidding competitively on "free agents." See Andrew Zimbalist, Baseball and Billions 24–26 (1992).

11. In addition, 17% of the players with at least two, but less than three, years of experience are also eligible for salary arbitration. See generally Roger Abrams, The Money Pitch: Baseball Free Agency and Salary Arbitration (2000).

free agents). They are instructed *not* to consider salary offers made by either party prior to arbitration, salaries in other sports or occupations, or the financial situation of the player or the team. The hearing is to be private and informal. Unless extended by the arbitrators, each party is limited to one hour for an initial presentation and one-half hour for rebuttal; awards are to be handed down by the arbitrators, without explanation, within 24 hours following the hearing.

The most distinctive feature of this arbitration scheme is the limits it places on the discretion of the arbitrators. The arbitrators are not free to choose whatever salary figure they think is appropriate. Instead, the player and the club each submits a "final offer" on salary for the coming season (these "final offers" need not be the figures offered during prior negotiations). The arbitrators may then award "only one or the other of the two figures submitted."

What is the rationale behind this final-offer arbitration? As we have seen, in conventional arbitration it is often assumed that arbitrators will have a tendency to compromise and "split the difference" between the parties in an effort to maintain their future acceptability. Being aware of this, the parties at the bargaining stage are likely to hold back concessions that they would otherwise be willing to make, in order to avoid giving the game away. "If the parties view conventional arbitration as a procedure for securing compromise, bargaining tactics dictate that each party preserve a position *from* which the arbitrator can move to a compromise."[12] Indeed, the party which stakes out the *most extreme* initial position may hope to gain the most from an eventual arbitral compromise, and this is often said to have a "chilling effect" on good-faith bargaining.[13] On the other hand, the constraints imposed by "final-offer arbitration" should have the opposite effect on the parties' negotiating behavior. Where the arbitrators may not compromise, each party may fear that if its offer is perceived as extreme or "unreasonable," the arbitrators will choose the offer of the *other* party. This may impel each party to adjust his bargaining position to make it more "reasonable"—and thus more likely to be chosen—than his opponent's. There is thus set up a movement of each party towards the other, narrowing the difference between them and at best making any arbitration award unnecessary. Ideally, "final-offer arbitration" operates as a "doomsday weapon that invariably induces negotiated settlement."[14]

To some extent this dynamic can be observed in major league baseball. Typically, more than 80% of cases will settle after players have filed for arbitration and hearings have been scheduled.[15] Only a handful of cases actually go through the arbitration process—in the years between 1995 and 2001, an average of around 9 cases per year. "For most players, filing for arbitration and submitting salary proposals are stages of an ultimately

12. Chelius & Dworkin, An Economic Analysis of Final–Offer Arbitration as a Conflict Resolution Device, 24 J.Conflict Res. 293, 294 (1980).

13. See Feuille, Final Offer Arbitration and the Chilling Effect, 14 Ind.Rel. 302 (1975).

14. Id. at 307.

15. Abrams, supra n.11 at 147, 152.

CHAPTER V ARBITRATION

successful bargaining process."[16] There are, of course, many other reasons for a high settlement rate in "baseball" arbitration. An arbitration hearing at which a player sits and listens to management's presentation of his many faults and shortcomings must inevitably strain the relationship between him and the club. And if the parties settle, they "can be creative in designing a compensation package, including bonuses, for example, or a no-trade clause," or a multi-year deal;[17] the product of salary arbitration, on the other hand, is merely a standard player contract (contained in the "Uniform Player's Contract" that is made part of the collective bargaining agreement) for a single year at a defined salary.

Final-offer arbitration is also frequently used to resolve "interest" disputes in public-sector employment. In contrast to arbitration in major-league baseball, however, public-sector "interest" arbitrators are frequently charged with determining a wide range of bargainable issues in addition to salary—all going to make up the terms of employment in the new agreement. In some states, the statutory scheme calls for each party to present to the arbitrators a "package" including a position on *all* the bargainable issues not yet agreed on. The arbitrators must then choose what they consider to be the more reasonable of the two "packages." In other states, in contrast, the arbitrators are allowed to consider each issue separately and to choose between the positions of the parties on an issue-by-issue basis. This variation enables the arbitrators to develop their own compromise "package" by balancing the parties' positions on the various issues. See, e.g., Mich.Comp.Laws § 423.238 (arbitration panel shall adopt "last offer of settlement" "as to each economic issue," while disputes over "non-economic" issues are resolved by conventional arbitration).

NOTES AND QUESTIONS

1. How might the strategy and bargaining behavior of the parties differ depending on whether the final-offer arbitration is to be on an "issue-by-issue" or "package" basis?

2. It should be obvious that all forms of final-offer arbitration have the greatest impact on the party who is the more risk-averse. In determining its final offer, each party is faced with a trade-off. It must weigh the loss involved in making a particular concession (say, a reduction in salary demands) against the greater probability of having its offer chosen by the arbitrator should an award become necessary. The more risk-averse party will be likely to move further in adjusting his demand downwards, in the direction of "reasonableness," in order to reduce the chances of an unfavorable result. This is particularly likely where arbitration is on a "package" basis. There is some evidence that unions nominally "win" public-sector "interest" arbitrations more frequently than public employers, and this would seem to support the proposition that the unions are more likely than

---

16. Faurot & McAllister, Salary Arbitration and Pre–Arbitration Negotiation in Major League Baseball, 45 Ind. & Lab.Rel. Rev. 697, 701 (1992).

17. Abrams, supra n.11 at 124–25, 149.

the employer to be risk-averse. See Farber, An Analysis of Final–Offer Arbitration, 24 J.Conflict Res. 683 (1980); Bloom, Collective Bargaining, Compulsory Arbitration, and Salary Settlements in the Public Sector, 2 J.Lab.Res. 369 (1981); Schwochau & Feuille, Interest Arbitrators and Their Decision Behavior, 27 Ind.Rel. 37, 53–54 (1988) (union demands are much larger under conventional arbitration than under final offer arbitration, while offers by employers "show no significant differences").

See also Howard Raiffa, The Art and Science of Negotiation 118 (1982):

> [I]t seems that the proportion of cases going to final-offer arbitration is smaller than the proportion going to conventional arbitration. This is often cited as an advantage of final-offer arbitration. Of course, the logic is marred a bit because conventional arbitration preceded by a round of Russian roulette would still do better.

3. The concern is often expressed that final-offer arbitration on a "package" basis may lead to results that are unworkable or inequitable. Consider, for example, the dilemma of the arbitrator in an "interest" dispute between a city and a firefighter's union. The union submits a proposal on salary and benefits which the arbitrators find preferable to the city's. However, the union has also included a "zinger," in the form of a demand for mandatory manning levels at certain fire stations—an unusual proposal that the arbitrators find objectionable. (Perhaps union negotiators slipped in this demand hoping that it would be carried along by the force of their "irresistible" economic package; perhaps they were forced to include it for reasons of internal union politics.) In such circumstances, arbitrators often express frustration at being limited to choosing one package or the other. Cf. In re Monroe County, 113 Lab. Arb. 933 (1999)("If I had the authority to decide this on an issue by issue basis, I would adopt the [union's] wage proposal and the [employer's] vacation proposal. Unfortunately, I do not possess that authority. It is all or nothing").

Is it a sufficient answer to such concerns to say that the *whole point* of final-offer arbitration is to discourage actual arbitration, and that "if the case reaches the arbitrator, the parties both deserve whatever they get"? Zack, Final Offer Selection—Panacea or Pandora's Box, 19 N.Y.L.F. 567, 585 (1974). Consider the following proposal for an alternative system of final-offer arbitration by "package": Each side is to submit *three* different final offers. The arbitrator chooses one of the six packages presented to him but does not reveal his choice to the parties; instead, he merely announces *which side* has made the better offer. The *losing party* is then allowed to choose one of the three packages submitted by the winning party, and this becomes the final award. See Donn, Games Final–Offer Arbitrators Might Play, 16 Ind.Rel. 306, 312 (1977). What might be the advantages of such a system?

4. Consider this variation of final-offer arbitration: The arbitrator first draws up a proposed award without having seen the respective final offers of the parties. The final offer that was "closest" to this proposed settlement by the arbitrator then becomes the actual award binding on the parties. This is sometimes referred to as "night baseball." What are the possible advantages of this variant?

892 CHAPTER V ARBITRATION

5. Under some statutes governing public-sector employment, "interest" disputes may be submitted to a neutral "fact-finder," who after hearing evidence from the parties makes a "recommendation." The term "fact-finder" may be chosen to lend an air of precision and inevitability to the process—but the fact-finder, in issuing his recommendations, is still likely to make the same sorts of value judgments and show the same concern for the acceptability of his conclusions to the parties as is typical of the "interest" arbitrator. The fact-finder's recommendations are usually made public, in the hope that the resulting public scrutiny and pressure of "public opinion" may make it more difficult for the parties to reject them. See, e.g., Ore.Rev.Stat. § 243.722(3), (4) (fact-finder's recommendations shall be "publicized" unless parties agree to accept them or agree to submit the dispute to final and binding arbitration). In all but the most exceptional cases, however, there is room for considerable skepticism as to the extent of any public awareness of or concern for the reports of public-sector fact-finders.

In some states, fact-finding is the final prescribed stage in the resolution of public-sector "interest" disputes. In others, both mediation and then fact-finding are imposed as preliminary steps before mandatory arbitration. Such arbitration is often of the "final-offer" variety. See, e.g., N.J.Stat. § 34:13A–16 (police and fire departments). Iowa's version adds further flexibility to the process: The arbitrators are allowed to choose not only one of the parties' last offers, but also—as a third option—the recommendation of the fact-finder on "each impasse item." Iowa Code §§ 20.21, 20.22. As might be expected this recommendation usually turns out to be a compromise, an intermediate position between the positions taken by the parties. And in those cases where an award proves necessary, the arbitrators tend overwhelmingly to choose the recommendation of the fact-finder. Even in jurisdictions where this option is not given to the arbitrator, the fact-finder's recommendation will often simply be incorporated into the final offer of one of the parties; the arbitration may then become a "show cause" hearing as to why this offer should not be accepted. "For those disputes that are not going to get resolved at the bargaining table, fact-finding is where the concrete for the foundation of an arbitration award is first poured." Holden, Final Offer Arbitration in Massachusetts, 31 Arb.J. 26, 28–29 (1976).

What might be the advantages and disadvantages of combining fact-finding and arbitration in this way? Might this two-step process tend to dilute the supposed benefits of final-offer arbitration? See generally Bierman, Factfinding: Finding the Public Interest, 9 Rutgers–Camden L.J. 667 (1978).

3. "MED–ARB"

There are many different styles of arbitration. One arbitrator may see himself chiefly as a passive adjudicator, presiding over the confrontation of adversaries. At the other extreme may be found the arbitrator who intervenes actively, in an effort to help the parties reach their own mutually agreeable settlement without the need for an imposed award.

Combining the roles of mediator and adjudicator poses a unique challenge to an arbitrator's skill: "When you sit there with the parties, separately or together—listening, persuading, cajoling, looking dour or relieved—your responsibility is a heavy one. Every lift of your eyebrow can be interpreted as a signal to the parties as to how you might eventually decide an issue if agreement is not reached."[18] This style of arbitration is seen most frequently in public-sector "interest" disputes. In fact, one survey estimates that arbitrators with experience in such disputes first attempt to mediate in at least 30 to 40 percent of their cases.[19]

Frequently, the statutory procedure for the settlement of public-sector disputes encourages and even institutionalizes "med-arb." For example, Michigan's form of final-offer arbitration permits the parties to revise their offers as the hearing progresses; in addition the arbitrators, after hearing evidence, may remand the dispute to the parties for further negotiations before the ultimate "final" offers must be submitted. In the course of the hearing, the arbitrator may indicate that on a particular issue he is "leaning towards" the position of one party. It does not require much imagination to see how this may influence the settlement process, and may force an adjustment in the position taken by the *other* party. In addition, use in public-sector "interest" disputes of a tripartite panel may also encourage resort to mediation techniques. In the executive session following the hearing, the neutral arbitrator has the opportunity to consult with his "partisan" colleagues. He may be expected to make efforts to reduce the area of disagreement between them, and can certainly draw on them in order to put together a coherent package reflecting the parties' true priorities.

The New Jersey statute is even more explicit, expressly mandating that in the "interest" disputes of police and firefighters, "[t]hroughout formal arbitration proceedings [the arbitrators] may mediate or assist the parties in reaching a mutually agreeable settlement."[20] Arbitrators under this statute are often quite outspoken in inducing settlement by advising parties of the unacceptability of their positions. This is what has often been termed "mediation with a club." One arbitrator explained that "I beat up on the parties. I believe that scaring them helps them to settle their own dispute."[21]

Lon Fuller, Collective Bargaining And The Arbitrator

Proceedings, Fifteenth Annual Meeting, National Academy of Arbitrators 8, 29–33, 37–48 (1962).

There remains the difficult problem of mediation by the arbitrator, where instead of issuing an award, he undertakes to persuade the parties to

---

18. Bairstow, The Canadian Experience, Proceedings, 34th Annual Meeting, Nat'l Academy of Arbitrators 93 (1982).

19. James L. Stern et al., Final–Offer Arbitration: The Effects on Public Safety Employee Bargaining 140 (1975).

20. N.J.Stat. § 34: 13A–16f(3).

21. Weitzman & Stochaj, Attitudes of Arbitrators toward Final–Offer Arbitration in New Jersey, 35 Arb.J. 25, 30 (1980).

reach a settlement, perhaps reinforcing his persuasiveness with "the gentle threat" of a decision. Again, there is waiting a too-easy answer: "Judges do it." Of course, judges sometimes mediate or at least bring pressure on the parties for a voluntary settlement. Sometimes this is done usefully and sometimes in ways that involve an abuse of office. In any event the judiciary has evolved no uniform code with respect to this problem that the arbitrator can take over ready-made. Judicial practice varies over a wide range. If the arbitrator were to pattern his conduct after the worst practices of the bench, arbitration would be in a sad way.

Analysis of the problem as it confronts the arbitrator should begin with a recognition that mediation or conciliation—the terms being largely interchangeable—has an important role to play in the settlement of labor disputes. There is much to justify a system whereby it is a prerequisite to arbitration that an attempt first be made by a skilled mediator to bring about a voluntary settlement. This requirement has at times been imposed in a variety of contexts. Under such systems the mediator is, I believe, invariably someone other than the arbitrator. This is as it should be.

Mediation and arbitration have distinct purposes and hence distinct moralities. The morality of mediation lies in optimum settlement, a settlement in which each party gives up what he values less, in return for what he values more. The morality of arbitration lies in a decision according to the law of the contract. The procedures appropriate for mediation are those most likely to uncover that pattern of adjustment which will most nearly meet the interests of both parties. The procedures appropriate for arbitration are those which most securely guarantee each of the parties a meaningful chance to present arguments and proofs for a decision in his favor. Thus, private consultations with the parties, generally wholly improper on the part of an arbitrator, are an indispensable tool of mediation.

Not only are the appropriate procedures different in the two cases, but the facts sought by those procedures are different. There is no way to define "the essential facts" of a situation except by reference to some objective. Since the objective of reaching an optimum settlement is different from that of rendering an award according to the contract, the facts relevant in the two cases are different, or, when they seem the same, are viewed in different aspects. If a person who has mediated unsuccessfully attempts to assume the role of arbitrator, he must endeavor to view the facts of the case in a completely new light, as if he had previously known nothing about them. This is a difficult thing to do. It will be hard for him to listen to proofs and arguments with an open mind. If he fails in this attempt, the integrity of adjudication is impaired.

These are the considerations that seem to me to apply where the arbitrator attempts to mediate before hearing the case at all. This practice is quite uncommon, and would largely be confined to situations where a huge backlog of grievances seemed to demand drastic measures toward an Augean clean-up. I want now to pass to consideration of the case where the arbitrator postpones his mediative efforts until after the proofs are in and the arguments have been heard. * * *

One might ask of mediation first undertaken after the hearing is over, what is the point of it? If the parties do not like the award, they are at liberty to change it. If there is some settlement that will effect a more apt adjustment of their interests, their power to contract for that settlement is the same after, as it is before, the award is rendered. One answer would be to say that if the arbitrator undertakes mediation after the hearing but before the award, he can use "the gentle threat" of a decision to induce settlement, keeping it uncertain as to just what the decision will be. Indeed, if he has a sufficiently Machiavellian instinct, he may darkly hint that the decision will contain unpleasant surprises for both parties. Conduct of this sort would, however, be most unusual. Unless the role thus assumed were played with consummate skill, the procedure would be likely to explode in the arbitrator's face.

There is, however, a more convincing argument for mediative efforts after the hearing and before the award. This lies in the peculiar fact—itself a striking tribute to the moral force of the whole institution of adjudication—that an award tends to resist change by agreement. Once rendered it seems to have a kind of moral inertia that puts a heavy onus on the party who proposes any modification by mutual consent. Hence if there exists the possibility of a voluntary settlement that will suit both parties better than the award, the last chance to obtain it may occur after the hearing and before the award is rendered. This may in fact be an especially propitious moment for a settlement. Before the hearing it is quite usual for each of the parties to underestimate grossly the strength of his adversary's case. The hearing not uncommonly "softens up" both parties for settlement.

What, then, are the objections to an arbitrator's undertaking mediative efforts after the hearing and before rendering the award, this being often so advantageous a time for settlement? Again, the objection lies essentially in the confusion of role that results. In seeking a settlement the arbitrator turned mediator quite properly learns things that should have no bearing on his decision as an arbitrator. For example, suppose a discharge case in which the arbitrator is virtually certain that he will decide for reinstatement, though he is striving to keep his mind open until he has a chance to reflect on the case in the quiet of his study. In the course of exploring the possibilities of a settlement he learns that, contrary to the position taken by the union at the hearing, respectable elements in the union would like to see the discharge upheld. Though they concede that the employee was probably innocent of the charges made by the company, they regard him as an ambitious troublemaker the union would be well rid of. If the arbitrator fails to mediate a settlement, can he block this information out when he comes to render his award?

It is important that an arbitrator not only respect the limits of his office in fact, but that he also appear to respect them. The parties to an arbitration expect of the arbitrator that he will decide the dispute, not according to what pleases the parties, but by what accords with the contract. Yet as a mediator he must explore the parties' interests and seek to find out what would please them. He cannot be a good mediator unless

CHAPTER V ARBITRATION

he does. But if he has then to surrender his role as mediator to resume that of adjudicator, can his award ever be fully free from the suspicion that it was influenced by a desire to please one or both of the parties?

* * *

These, then, are the arguments against the arbitrator's undertaking the task of mediation. They can all be summed up in the phrase, "confusion of role." Why, then, should any arbitrator be tempted to depart from his proper role as adjudicator? In what follows I shall try to analyze the considerations that sometimes press him toward a departure from a purely judicial role.

* * *

[Fuller then discusses "polycentric" (that is, "many-centered") problems—the type of problem exemplified by the testator who in her will left a varied collection of paintings to two museums "in equal shares." See Chapter I supra at p. 24.]

[P]robably the nearest counterpart to Mrs. Timken's will is the following case: Union and management agree that the internal wage structure of the plant is out of balance—some jobs are paid too little in comparison with others, some too much. A kind of wage fund (say, equal to a general increase of five cents an hour) is set up. Out of this fund are to be allotted, in varying amounts, increases for the various jobs that will bring them into better balance. In case the parties cannot agree, the matter shall go to arbitration. Precisely because the task is polycentric, it is extremely unlikely that the parties will be able to agree on most of the jobs, leaving for arbitration only a few on which agreement proved impossible. Since in the allotment every job is pitted against every other, any tentative agreements reached as to particular jobs will have to lapse if the parties fail in the end to reach an agreement on the reorganization of the wage structure as a whole. In short, the arbitrator will usually have to start from scratch and do the whole job himself.

Confronted with such a task the arbitrator intent on preserving judicial proprieties faces a quandary much like that of a judge forced to carry out Mrs. Timken's "equal" division through adjudicative procedures. * * *

What modifications of his role will enable the arbitrator to discharge this task satisfactorily? The obvious expedient is a resort to mediation. After securing a general education in the problems involved in reordering the wage scale, the arbitrator might propose to each side in turn a tentative solution, inviting comments and criticisms. Through successive modifications a reasonably acceptable reordering of rates might be achieved, which would then be incorporated in an award. Here the dangers involved in the mediative role are probably at a minimum, precisely because the need for that role seems so obvious. Those dangers are not, however, absent. There is always the possibility that mediative efforts may meet shipwreck. Prolonged involvement in an attempt to work out a settlement agreeable to both parties obscures the arbitrator's function as a judge and makes it difficult to reassume that role. Furthermore, a considerable taint of the "rigged" award will in any event almost always attach to the final solution. The very fact that this solution must involve a compromise of interests within the union itself makes this virtually certain.

* * *

There is one general consideration that may incline the arbitrator to resolve any doubts presented by particular cases in favor of assuming a mediative role. This lies in a conviction—to be sure, not expressed in the terms I am about to employ—that all labor arbitrations involve to some extent polycentric elements. The relations within a plant form a seamless web; pluck it here, and a complex pattern of adjustments may run through the whole structure. A case involving a single individual, say a reclassification case, may set a precedent with implications unknown to the arbitrator, who cannot see how his decision may cut into a whole body of practice that is unknown to him. The arbitrator can never be sure what aspects of the case post-hearing consultations may bring to his attention that he would otherwise have missed.

That there is much truth in this observation would be foolish to deny. The integrity of the adjudicative process can never be maintained without some loss, without running some calculated risk. Any adjudicator—whether he be called judge, hearing officer, arbitrator, or umpire—who depends upon proofs and arguments adduced before him in open court, with each party confronting the other, is certain to make occasional mistakes he would not make if he could abandon the restraints of his role. The question is, how vital is that role for the maintenance of the government—in this case a system of industrial self-government—of which he is a part?

In facing that question as it arises in his practice, the arbitrator ought to divest himself, insofar as human nature permits, of any motive that might be called personal. It has been said that surgeons who have perfected some highly specialized operation tend strongly to favor a diagnosis of the patient's condition that will enable them to display their special skills. Can the arbitrator be sure he is immune from a similar desire to demonstrate virtuosity in his calling? It is well known in arbitrational circles that combining the roles of arbitrator and mediator is a tricky business. The amateur who tries it is almost certain to get in trouble. The veteran, on the other hand, takes an understandable pride in his ability to play this difficult dual role. He would be less than human if he did not seek out occasions for a display of his special talents, even to the point of discerning a need for them in situations demanding nothing more than a patient, conscientious judge, about to put a sensible meaning on the words of the contract.

* * *

Sometimes judgment on the issues here under discussion is influenced by a kind of slogan to the effect that an agreed settlement is always better than an imposed one. As applied to disputes before they have gone to

898 CHAPTER V ARBITRATION

arbitration, this slogan has some merit. When the case is in the hands of the arbitrator, however, I can see little merit in it, except in the special cases I have tried previously to analyze. After all, successful industrial self-government requires not only the capacity to reach and abide by agreements, but also the willingness to accept and conform to disliked awards. It is well that neither propensity be lost through disuse. Furthermore, there is something slightly morbid about the thought that an agreement coerced by the threat of decision is somehow more wholesome than an outright decision. It suggests a little the father who wants his children to obey him, but who, in order to still doubts that he may be too domineering, not only demands that they obey but insists that they do so with a smile. After having had his day in court, a man may with dignity bend his will to a judgment of which he disapproves. That dignity is lost if he is compelled to pretend that he agreed to it.

NOTES AND QUESTIONS

1. One arbitrator has noted that,

> [y]ou have to recognize the danger is there even by the mere overture to the arbitrator to step outside and "Let's have a look at this." It could be nothing more than one side broadly indicating, "Yes, we are ready to compromise this," and the other side saying, "Under no circumstances. We think we have a solid case." Back we go into the room, and you have to decide. It is conceivable that that conversation is going to influence the arbitrator. * * * I just don't think you can say even in the most cautious way that there won't be some prejudice.

Panel Discussion (Valtin), Proceedings, 33rd Annual Meeting, National Academy of Arbitrators 232 (1981).

Is it fair to suggest, then, that the "med-arb" process may often serve as an invitation to the parties to be candid—an invitation which only the more inexperienced or ingenuous of the two is likely to accept?

2. A recent survey of litigators indicated that the overwhelming majority preferred judges in settlement conferences to "actively offer suggestions and observations" for the settlement of the case: "They want the judge's opinions. They want the judge's suggestions. They want the perspective of the experienced neutral." See Wayne Brazil, Settling Civil Disputes 44–46 (1985). Does this affect in any way your view of Fuller's criticisms respecting arbitrators who depart from the proper "judicial role"?

3. Where in other legal cultures arbitrators routinely engage in efforts to induce a negotiated settlement, they do not seem overly troubled by Fuller's concern with respect to a possible "confusion of role." See pp. 630–631 supra. "As the Chinese put it: who better to be the arbitrator than the failed conciliator"? Kaplan, Hong Kong and the UNCITRAL Model Law, 4 Arb.Int'l 173, 176 (1988). See also Marriott, The Role of ADR in the Settlement of Commercial Disputes, 3 Asia Pacific L.Rev. 1, 15 (1994) ("the Chinese concept of * * * a rolling arbitration, whereby the arbitrator could

become a conciliator and then revert to an adjudicatory role if the search for compromise and consensus proved in vain"). Attempts by arbitrators to facilitate compromise, suggest formulas for settlement, and induce agreement are not only seen in the Far East; such activity is also apparently quite common in Northern European arbitration. See, e.g., Trappe, Conciliation in the Far East, 5 Arb.Int'l 173 (1989) (approach of "concilioarbitration," combining arbitration and mediation, "makes German practice, at least to a certain extent, similar to the Chinese"); cf. Peter, Med–Arb in International Arbitration, 8 Amer. Rev. Int'l Arb. 83 (1997)(referring to a "low-intensity form of mediation" used in Swiss and German arbitations; "there is minimal, if any, intervention in the negotiation process," and "confidential private caucusing is not commonly used.").

4. The Hong Kong Arbitration Ordinance provides expressly that the arbitrator "may act as a conciliator," and in so doing may meet with the parties "collectively or separately." Where the parties fail to reach an agreement, the arbitrators may then "resume" the arbitration process. But in such a case, how should the arbitrators treat the confidential information that they were bound to receive in the course of their earlier efforts? The Ordinance requires the arbitrator to "disclose to all other parties * * * as much of [the confidential] information as he considers is material to the arbitration proceedings." § 2B. What do you think of this solution?

5. Nine union members were laid off by their employer, but were nevertheless told to report for work the next day—to perform substantially the same duties, but in the nominal capacity of "temporary" workers. The union brought a grievance; after an initial arbitration hearing was held, "the parties invited the arbitrator to attempt mediation." However, mediation was not successful and the arbitration resumed. The arbitrator ultimately issued an award in favor of the union; in calculating the award, she relied in part on answers that the laid-off employees had given to questions in a questionnaire that the parties had developed jointly during their efforts at mediation. The employer's motion to vacate the award was denied: "None of the information that was used in calculating the award came from [the employer]," whose participation "was in no way necessary to the Union's gathering of this information from its own members." "Had the parties not developed the questionnaire jointly during mediation, the same information still would have been required during the remedy phase," and the union could have collected it alone. WWOR–TV, Inc. v. Local 209, NABET–CWA, 166 F.3d 1203 (2d Cir.1998).

6. The AAA is now offering a program it refers to as "MEDALOA"— mediation combined with last-offer arbitration. Under this program, parties mediate their dispute under the AAA's Commercial Mediation Rules; if they are unable to reach a settlement, they agree that a neutral appointed by the AAA—or the mediator himself if the parties choose—will select between their final negotiated positions, that selection being binding on them. "During the mediation phase each party has made concessions and has developed some sort of feel for the other party's concessions and views. * * * Often the offers come so close together that the arbitrator's choice is

CHAPTER V ARBITRATION

of no real importance—you get what in effect is a mediated compromise." It has even been claimed that this "little-known-little used process * * * is the process of choice in the vast majority of commercial cases." Arnold, A Vocabulary of ADR Procedures, in PLI, 1 Patent Litigation 1994 at pp. 287, 330–31.

7. Consider a process by which the arbitrator *first* hears evidence and reaches a decision in the traditional manner; an award is written and placed in a sealed envelope without having been revealed to the parties. Only *then* does she attempt to bring the parties to a consensual agreement through mediation; if she is successful in doing so, the award is simply destroyed. (This in effect is "arb-med.") What might be the advantages of such a process?

8. Some schemes of "med-arb" provide for the different functions of mediation and arbitration to be performed by different individuals. If mediation fails, the dispute is then entrusted to a separate arbitrator who has the power to make a binding award. See Iowa Code §§ 20.20–20.22; Goldberg, The Mediation of Grievances Under a Collective Bargaining Contract: An Alternative to Arbitration, 77 Nw.U.L.Rev. 270 (1982).

In some cases, however, the mediator is charged also with making a *recommendation* to the ultimate decision-maker as to how the dispute should be resolved. This is true, for example, under California's mandatory mediation scheme, where the mediator may make a recommendation to the court as to child custody and visitation matters. See Cal.Fam.Code, §§ 3170, 3183. How might the possibility of such a recommendation by the mediator affect the mediation process? See Jay Folberg & Alison Taylor, Mediation 277–78 (1984):

> The consensus among mediators appears to confirm that the trust and candor required in mediation are unlikely to exist if the participants know the mediator may be formulating an opinion or recommendation that will be communicated to a judge or tribunal. The recommendation of the mediator, particularly in a child custody and visitation case, would generally be given such great weight that the mediator, in effect, would be switching roles from decision facilitator to decision maker. The confusion and suspicion created by this crossover role taint the validity, effectiveness, and integrity of the mediation process.
>
> The participants may, in some circumstances, agree or contract for the mediator to decide the matter if they are unable to do so or to testify as to a recommendation. Using the informal, consensual process of mediation with no evidentiary or procedural rules as the basis for an imposed decision does, however, create a considerable risk that the more clever or sophisticated participant may distort or manipulate the mediation in order to influence the mediator's opinion.

4. "RENT A JUDGE"

A California statute provides that "upon the agreement of the parties," a court may "refer" a pending action to any person or persons whom the parties themselves may choose. The court may also "refer" an action where the parties had previously entered into a written contract calling for a referee to hear controversies that might arise in the future. Referees may be asked:

> to try any or all of the issues in an action or proceeding, whether of fact or of law, and to report a statement of decision thereon; [or] to ascertain a fact necessary to enable the court to determine an action or proceeding.

Cal.Code Civ.Pro. §§ 638, 640.

After hearing the case, the referees are to report their decision to the court within twenty days after the close of testimony; judgment must then be entered on the referees' decision "in the same manner as if the action had been tried by the court." Cal.Code Civ.Pro. §§ 643, 644.

Barlow F. Christensen, Private Justice: California's General Reference Procedure

1982 American Bar Foundation Research J. 79, 81–82, 103.

The statute says nothing at all about the qualifications of referees. Presumably, the parties might agree to have a case referred to almost anyone—to another lawyer, perhaps, or even to a layman. But parties using this statutory procedure are seeking judicial determination of their causes, and so references are made to retired judges selected by the parties. The reasons are obvious. A retired judge who would be acceptable to both parties would almost surely possess acknowledged judicial skills and, in many instances, expertise in the particular kind of case at issue, thus ensuring a trial that is both expeditious and fair.

The statute is also silent about the time and place of trials by referees. As a consequence, the parties and the referee are free to select the times and places that will be most convenient. This has obvious advantages with respect to such things as securing the presence of witnesses, and it means that trials can be scheduled at times that will be most advantageous to counsel. Moreover, because the procedure is most often used by parties who want to get to trial promptly, both sides know that when they do go to trial both parties will be ready, thus avoiding the continuances and postponements that are often so frustrating in the course of regular trials in courts.

Trials by referees are conducted as proper judicial trials, following the traditional rules of procedure and evidence. Transcripts are made of the proceedings, and the judgment of the referee becomes the judgment of the court. It is thus enforceable and appealable, as any other judgment would be. One lawyer who uses the reference procedure suggests that parties might agree to submit disputes to retired judges for decision independently, without any court order, but that they use the statutory procedure to preserve their rights of enforcement and appeal. * * *

902 CHAPTER V ARBITRATION

In theory, almost any kind of case might be referred to a referee for trial. The consensual portion of the statute imposes no restrictions. In practice, however, the procedure has been used primarily in technical and complex business litigation involving substantial amounts of money. The case in which the procedure was first used, for instance, was a complicated dispute between a medical billing company and two attorneys who had acquired interests in the company. Other examples have been a suit by major oil companies against a California governmental agency over air pollution control standards, a contract dispute between a nationally known television entertainer and his broadcasting company employer, and an action between a giant motor vehicle manufacturer and one of its suppliers over the quality of parts supplied.

The compensation of a retired judge appointed to try a case as a referee is also the subject of agreement between the parties, and the cost is borne equally by the parties.

NOTES AND QUESTIONS

1. A survey of private ADR firms and independent neutrals offering dispute resolution services in Los Angeles is reported in Elizabeth Rolph et al., Escaping the Courthouse: Private Alternative Dispute Resolution in Los Angeles, 1996 J. Disp. Resol. 277. According to this study, the total "private ADR caseload" in Los Angeles grew at an average rate of 15% per year between 1988 and 1993—while during that period, the *public* court caseload declined an average of about 0.5%; private ADR, however, still represented only 5% of the total dispute "caseload" filed both in private fora and in the public courts (small claims, municipal, and superior courts) combined. Claims involving amounts in controversy greater than $25,000 accounted for between 60–70% of the private caseload, as compared to only 14% of the public court caseload.

This private ADR market was dominated by arbitration (58% of disputes) and by mediation (22%): Only 5% of private forum disputes were handled in "private judging" proceedings under the California statute (including discovery matters that courts often refer to private judges even without the consent of the parties, see Cal. Code Civ. Pro. Sec. 639 (e)). About 91 former judges are now offering their services in Los Angeles as neutrals in private ADR; most of these retired from the bench following 20 years of service, and "therefore cannot be characterized as leaving the bench 'prematurely.'" Of those neutrals who were characterized as "heavy hitters"—each handling 100 or more disputes in a year—almost half came from the bench. Unsurprisingly, while attorneys tended to dominate the provision of arbitration services, "former judges provide voluntary settlement conferences and private judging much more often than do attorneys."

2. The California statute appears to be the most often-used, and is certainly the most highly-publicized, in the country. However, comparable procedures exist in some other states. In some cases, the "referee" is *required* to be a retired judge. Under the Texas statute, for example, a "special judge" must be a retired or former district, county, or appellate judge with at least four years service, who has "developed substantial experience in his area of specialty" and who each year completes five days of continuing legal education courses. Here too, however, the parties are free to select their own "special judge" and to agree with him on the fee that he is to be paid. See Texas Trial by Special Judge Act, Tex.Civ.Prac. & Rem.Code § 151.001 et seq.

3. How does the California or Texas reference procedure differ from arbitration? Are there reasons why parties might prefer to utilize the reference procedure rather than to submit an existing dispute to arbitration?

Consider the following provisions of the Texas statute:

Sec. 151.005. Rules and statutes relating to procedure and evidence in district court apply to a trial under this chapter.

Sec. 151.006. (a) A special judge shall conduct the trial in the same manner as a court trying an issue without a jury.

(b) While serving as a special judge, the judge has the powers of a district court judge except that he may not hold a person in contempt of court unless the person is a witness before him.

Sec. 151.011. The special judge's verdict must comply with the requirements for a verdict by the court. The verdict stands as a verdict of the district court. * * *

Sec. 151.013. The right to appeal is preserved. * * *

4. In response to a number of criticisms of the "rent-a-judge" system, the Judicial Council of California approved new rules in February 1993 to govern trials by privately compensated judges. What objections were these rules intended to address—and how adequately do they deal with the perceived problems?

Rule 532.1. Reference by agreement

(b) * * * The referee shall disclose as soon as practicable any facts that might be grounds for disqualification. A referee who has been privately compensated in any other proceeding in the past 18 months as a judge, referee, arbitrator, mediator, or settlement facilitator by a party, attorney, or law firm in the instant case shall disclose the number and nature of other proceedings before the first hearing. Any objection to the appointment of a person as a referee shall be in writing and shall be filed and served upon all parties and the referee.

(c) A party who has elected to use the services of a privately compensated referee * * * is deemed to have elected to proceed outside the courthouse; therefore, court facilities and court personnel shall not be used, except upon a finding by the presiding judge that the use would further the interests of justice. * * *

(d) The presiding judge or supervising judge, on request of any person or on the judge's own motion, may order that a case before a privately

904 CHAPTER V ARBITRATION

compensated referee must be heard at a site easily accessible to the public and appropriate for seating those who have made known their plan to attend hearings. * * * The order may require that notice of trial or of other proceedings be given to the requesting party directly. * * *

(e) * * * A motion to seal records in a cause before a privately compensated referee shall be served and filed and shall be heard by the presiding judge or a judge designated by the presiding judge. The moving party shall mail or deliver a copy of the motion to the referee and to any person or organization who has requested that the case take place at an appropriate hearing site.

A motion for leave to file a complaint for intervention in a cause before a privately compensated referee shall be served and filed, and shall be assigned for hearing as a law and motion matter. The party seeking intervention shall mail or deliver a copy of the motion to the referee. If intervention is allowed, the case shall be returned to the trial court docket unless all parties stipulate * * * to proceed before the referee.

See also Tex.Civ.Prac. & Rem.Code § 151.009(c) ("The state or a unit of local government may not pay any costs related to a trial under this chapter"); § 151.010 ("A trial under this chapter may not be held in a public courtroom, and a public employee may not be involved in the trial during regular working hours").

5. The following excerpts from a student-written note raise a number of objections to the California reference procedure. In light of everything that you have read in this chapter on arbitration, how do you assess these criticisms?

While the comparatively affluent can realize the cost and time savings of hiring a referee, other litigants may not. Those appearing pro se, for example, or who are represented by Legal Aid or by attorneys appearing pro bono or on a contingency fee basis, may be able to afford little or no out-of-pocket expenditure prior to entry of a judgment and hence will be unable to hire a referee. The use of referees paid by the parties, then, in effect creates two classes of litigants: wealthy litigants, who can afford the price of a referee, and poorer litigants, who cannot. The former group obtains all of the advantages of reference, while the latter must endure all the systemic disadvantages that led wealthy litigants to seek reference in the first place.

Such a system of reference is clearly unfair to the poorer litigant and may even run against the best interests of society. It would allow, in the extreme case, an utterly frivolous suit to obtain a speedy trial solely because the litigants were wealthy, while forcing a suit involving issues important to society and vital to the parties to languish for a considerable time awaiting trial. Even if the suits are similar, the bias against the poor is still striking. If, for example, the poor litigant is in court because he needs to protect a valuable property interest affected by the dispute, his interest is kept in jeopardy for a longer period of time than that of a similarly situated litigant using the referee system. The state's action in according the wealthy the privilege of using a faster form of procedure gives them an additional property right, the right to be more secure in their ownership.

* * *

A due process problem may arise when referees are privately paid, particularly if overloading in the regular court system has driven some parties to a reference procedure they otherwise might not have chosen. As early as 1215, Magna Charta declared that it was wrong for the government to sell justice or to delay or deny it to anyone. In a private reference system, the state does not sell justice, but it does sanction the payment of private adjudicators to act in its place. The ultimate product purchased by these payments is a judgment that is entered on the court rolls and enforced by state authority. To whom the payments ultimately go is not nearly so important as the fact that they are made, with the sanction of the state, in order to obtain a state-monopolized enforceable order.

Note, The California Rent–A–Judge Experiment: Constitutional and Policy Considerations of Pay–As–You–Go Courts, 94 Harv.L.Rev. 1592, 1601–02, 1607–08 (1981). Similar arguments are advanced in Note, Rent–A–Judges and the Cost of Selling Justice, 44 Duke L.J. 166 (1994) ("The rent-a-judge system is an unconstitutional, elitist institution that unfairly grants privileges to the wealthy").

CHAPTER VI

INTERNATIONAL DISPUTE RESOLUTION: CROSS–CULTURAL DIMENSIONS AND STRUCTURING APPROPRIATE PROCESSES

Since the 1970s, domestic ADR has grown and evolved into a dynamic field of study and practice that has impacted on the way lawyers in the United States represent their clients. As examined in this textbook, lawyers are using new and more sophisticated methods to resolve their clients' disputes including representing their clients in mediations, minitrials, and innovative variations of arbitration. The end of the Cold War in the early 90s opened opportunities for exporting these "made in the USA" dispute resolution methods. As international markets opened up in the former Soviet Union, China, Latin America, and elsewhere, more opportunities opened up for U.S. lawyers to represent clients outside of the United States. These new opportunities have created a glaring need for lawyers to learn how to resolve disputes between parties from different countries.

In this chapter, the materials explore how to adapt domestic ADR to the special needs of international disputes.[1] The first section on "Demystifying Cross–Cultural Dimensions" examines how cultural differences can impede international negotiations and ways to overcome the differences. The second section on "International ADR Clauses for Business Disputes" considers the ADR options for avoiding the hazards of transnational lawsuits. The section delves into the distinctive issues that arise when designing alternative private processes.

A. DEMYSTIFYING CROSS–CULTURAL DIMENSIONS

Cross-cultural differences among parties can hamper if not obstruct an international negotiation. Cross-cultural negotiators must know how to overcome differences by becoming cultural sensitive and learning practical strategies for bridging cultural gaps.

---

1. Due to limitations in space, this chapter does not examine the striking and unconventional ways that dispute resolution methods are adapted to resolve disputes for parties that are not private ones but are sovereign nations. Disputes between nations comprise a distinct field of dispute resolution with its own lessons and techniques.

906

A. Demystifying Cross-Cultural Dimensions

Most people are familiar with the concept of cross-cultural differences. We are often cited examples of cultural practices that vary from country to country, such as whether to use first names at a business meeting or take gifts to the home of a foreign host. Participants in international matters hope that their own cross-cultural faux pax do not attract the international attention and embarrassment suffered by then U.S. Ambassador to Japan, Walter Mondale, when he appeared in a kimono at a banquet in Japan. He created a stir by tucking the right side of his kimono over the left side, unintentionally using the tucking method for dressing a corpse.[2] Or with much more at risk in a delicate negotiation, then Congressman Bill Richardson unwittingly insulted Iraqi President Saddam Hussein when they met to negotiate the release of two jailed Americans. The Congressman inadvertently showed the soles of his feet to Saddam Hussein, prompting him to walk out of the room.[3]

The challenge in dealing with cross-cultural differences is to move beyond memorizing a multitude of cultural tidbits to a deeper understanding and practical application of cross-cultural insights in the rough and tumble of complex negotiations. This does not mean negotiators must become cross-cultural experts in psychology, anthropology, or sociology, but they can learn more than cultural etiquette. Negotiators must understand that both "we" and "they" may be products of different cultures and as a result "we" may not share the same values, interests, attitudes, behavior, and linguistic styles as "they."

"Even though it is very likely that the negotiators on the other side of the table view the world very differently than you do, they should always be approached with respect and with a willingness to learn. You should not try to reform the other culture at the negotiating table in hopes that they will eventually be more like yourself, for the simple reason that it will not work. On the other hand, you should not go overboard in the other direction by 'going native.' Most people tend to be suspicious of anyone imitating their gestures or behaviors. The soundest advice is to learn to understand and respect cultural differences while retaining one's own."[4]

1. Cross-Cultural Differences

a. WHAT IS CULTURE?

There is no generally accepted definition of culture. One exceptionally broad definition of culture characterizes all negotiations as "intercultural" because each person is unique. "When two individuals meet, it is an

---

2. Nicholas D. Kristof, "Monderu–San's Last Campaign", New York Times Magazine (November 5, 1995)

3. Tim Weiner, "New Star Scores Home Runs for the Democrats", New York Times (July 18, 1995)(Fortunately, the nego-

tiation resumed and the two Americans were freed from a Baghdad jail.)

4. Gary P. Ferraro, The Cultural Dimension of International Business 143 (2nd edition, 1994)

908 CHAPTER VI INTERNATIONAL DISPUTE RESOLUTION

intercultural encounter since they both have different (sometimes drastically different, if not opposite) ways to perceive, discover, create reality." [5]

Professor Geert Hofstede, a Dutch social psychologist and author of renowned studies on culture, defines culture as mental programming:

> The sources of one's mental programs lie within the social environments in which one grew up and collected one's life experiences. The programming starts within the family; it continues within the neighborhood, at school, in youth groups, at the work place, and in the living community. * * *
>
> A customary term for such mental software is *culture*. * * *
>
> In social anthropology, "culture" is a catchword for all those patterns of thinking, feeling, and acting.... Not only those activities supposed to refine the mind are included ..., but also the ordinary and menial things in life: greeting, eating, showing or not showing feelings, keeping a certain physical distance from others, making love, or maintaining body hygiene....
>
> Culture ... is always a collective phenomenon, because it is at least partly shared with people who live or lived within the same social environment, which is where it was learned. It is *the collective programming of the mind which distinguishes the members of one group or category of people from another.*
>
> Culture is learned, not inherited. It derives from one's social environment, not from one's genes. Culture should be distinguished from human nature on one side, and from an individual's personality on the other, although exactly where the borders lie between human nature and culture, and between culture and personality, is a matter of discussion among social scientists.
>
> *Human nature* is what all human beings, from the Russian professor to the Australian aborigine, have in common: it represents the universal level in one's mental software.... However, what one does with these feelings, how one expresses fear, joy, observations, and so on, is modified by culture....
>
> The *personality* of an individual, on the other hand, is her/his unique personal set of mental programs which (s)he does not share with any other human being. It is based upon traits which are partly inherited with the individual's unique set of genes and partly learned. "Learned" means: modified by the influence of collective programming (culture) *as well as* unique personal experiences.[6]

Professor Gary Ferraro, an American anthropologist, further illuminates our understanding of culture by pointing out that[7] "[A]ll cultures of the

---

5. Pierre Casse and Surinder Deol, Managing Intercultural Negotiations xiii (1985).

6. Geert Hofstede, Cultures and Organizations 4–6 (1997).

7. Gary P. Ferraro, The Cultural Dimension of International Business Ch. 2 (2nd edition, 1994); Also, see, Guy Olivier Faure and Gunnar Sjostedt, Culture and Negotiation: An Introduction in Culture and Negotia-

world—despite many differences—face a number of common problems and share a number of common features, which we call cultural universals." Cultural universals include the need to develop: an economic system for producing, distributing, and consuming essential resources for living; a system for marriage, family, and raising children; a method for educating children about the life of the society; a system of preserving social order over anarchy; and a way to explain the unexplainable as through magic, religion, witchcraft, sorcery, and astrology. These universals can be met in different ways; these different ways reflect alternative cultural approaches or differences.

b. DIFFICULTIES IN IDENTIFYING CULTURAL BEHAVIOR

It can be difficult to identify differences that are due to culture.

The other negotiator's culture cannot be simply gleaned from her nationality because her nationality is not necessarily the same as her culture. People living in the same country can follow different cultural practices. Even in the United States, with its reputation as a melting pot of immigrant cultures, many distinctive cultures flourish. The United States is more accurately a country with many cultures living together in one pot. Each culture does not merely reflect regional differences. One important work on ethnicity in the United States compiled studies of over forty American ethnic groups.[8] The studies demonstrated that the cultural values of each ethnic group is a product of multiple factors including the group's distinctive native cultural values, migration history, racist's experiences, class tensions, family life cycle stresses, and intermarriage.[9]

Difficulties in identifying cultural behavior are compounded by the likelihood that the other party is the product of more than one distinct cultural upbringing. The ethnic cultural experience of the other party may be further shaped by complementary and competing values of another clearly identifiable cultural experience. The other party also may be a member of a religious culture, corporate culture, international culture, and/or a professional culture of attorneys, economists, engineers, or other

tion 33(Edited by Guy Olivier Faure and Jeffrey Z. Rubin, 1993).

8. See, *Ethnicity and Family Therapy* 1 (Eds. Monica McGoldrick, Joe Giordano, and John K. Pearce, 2nd edition, 1996) This book examines the role of ethnicity for therapists who are designing therapeutic interventions. "Ethnicity refers to a common ancestry through which individuals have evolved shared values and customs. It is deeply tied to the family, through which it is transmitted. A group's sense of commonality is transmitted over generations by the family and reinforced by the surrounding community. Ethnicity is a powerful influence in determining identity."

Although this group of articles was written for therapists, not mediators or negotiators, the readings provide valuable insights into the type of ethnocultural factors that shape the behavior of people with whom we may be negotiating. The readings give us clues about where other people as well as ourselves might be coming from. These readings are especially helpful for domestic conflicts involving parties from different ethnic groups because the readings give special attention to the factors shaping individuals who have migrated to the United States.

9. See, *Ethnicity and Family Therapy* 10–20 (Eds. Monica McGoldrick, Joe Giordano, and John K. Pearce, 2nd edition, 1996)

professionals. Each of these other cultures consists of a community with its own norms of behavior.

For instance, the other negotiator can be influenced by her professional upbringing:

> ... one should not neglect [its] complexity.... For example, the professional culture of lawyers takes into account various elements: national differences in legal training, differences between common law and civil law traditions (the role of case law compared with the role of codified law), purely administrative experience and court experience, degree of familiarity with international law as a body of very specific rules and procedures, and relative dependence on or independence of the political authority issuing instructions. Nevertheless, despite variations within the professional culture of lawyers, who are part of different national delegations, they tend to speak a common language and are likely masters of largely identical concepts.[10]

The other negotiator may be influenced by the international culture in which she participates. The negotiator may be part of a culture that is based in the diplomatic community, business world, or a multi-country region such as the European Union. The practices of the culture are derived from the shared experience of participating and negotiating in the particular international community.

When you try to interpret another person's negotiating behavior, you may be blinded by your own cultural biases. As Jeffry Rubin and Jeswald Salacuse pointed out,[11] negotiators can operate on the mistaken assumption that:

> *"Culture is everything*. According to this view, culture has an over-determining effect on negotiation. Armed with the stereotypes that Americans are impatient and Latins are volatile, for example, negotiators think they can function more effectively. The problem with stereotypes such as these is that, even though they may contain elements of truth, the exceptions are often as or more compelling than the rule.... Clearly, factors other than culture have an effect on what transpires in negotiation–for example, the structure of issues, the personality of the parties, and the organization of the companies involved."

They also point out that negotiators can be prisoners of their own culture:

> "The ways we think about culture and conflict are informed by the culture of which we are a part. American social scientists tend to think in terms of dichotomies, continua: straight lines. Would a cultural analyst from an Asian state categorize the world in similar ways, or would a circle or spiral perhaps be a more appropriate metaphor?"

---

10. Winfried Lang, A Professional's View, 45–46, in Culture and Negotiation (Edited by Guy Olivier Gaure and Jeffrey Z. Rubin, 1993).

11. Jeffrey Z. Rubin and Jeswald W. Salacuse, Culture and International Negotiation: Lessons for Business 11 Alternatives 95–98 (July, 1993).

In short, because you view the behavior of others through your cultural biases, behavior that is the product of multiple factors, you face great difficulties when trying to identify the other side's cultural behavior.[12]

2. CULTURAL CONCEPTUAL FRAMEWORK

A cross-cultural negotiator needs a conceptual framework in which cultural characteristics can be organized and understood. Various conceptual frameworks have been developed from studies of differences among cultures, especially differences relevant to conflict resolution. Each study considers a finite number of generic cultural characteristics, characteristics that vary in number and substance from study to study. In this section, four cross-cultural studies are considered.[13] Despite the overlap in the ideas covered, it is striking how each study is organized to present a different view of culture that emphasizes different dimensions of culture.

In a landmark study on different cultural attitudes toward work, Geert Hofstede[14] identified *four* cultural dimensions that explain dominant value differences among cultures. First, does the culture follow low or high power distances? In a low power distance culture, people value power equalization and competence over seniority, while high power distance cultures value status, formality and hierarchy. Second, are the people in the culture risk avoiders or risk takers? Risk avoiders are uncomfortable in risky and ambiguous situations and prefer conformity and safe behavior. Risk takers (or low risk-avoiders) are more inclined toward new ideas and problem solving. Third, does the culture emphasize individualism or collectivism? In individualistic cultures, people value independence and individual needs over the needs of the community. Collectivist cultures recognize the interdependence among individuals, the paramount needs of the group, and value of cooperation. Fourth, does the culture tend toward particular

---

12. See, Guy Olivier Faure, Culture and Negotiation: An Introduction 5; Winfried Lang, A Professional's View in Culture and Negotiation; Victor A. Kremenyuk, A Pluralistic Viewpoint 47–50 (Edited by Guy Olivier Faure and Jeffrey Z. Rubin, 1993)

13. For other studies, see, Donald W. Hendon, Rebecca Angeles Hendon, and Paul Herbig, Cross–Cultural Business Negotiations (1996)(identified seven broad areas of cultural differences); Gary P. Ferraro, The Cultural Dimension of International Business(2nd edition, 1994)(identified three features of cross cultural differences and nine contrasting cultural values); David W. Augsburger, Conflict Mediation Across Cultures (1992)(identified nine conflict and dispute patterns);.Dean Allen Foster, Bargaining Across Borders—How to Negotiate Business Successfully Anywhere in the World 272–293 (1992, 1995); Terence Brake, Danielle Medina

Walker, and Thomas (Tim) Walker, Doing Business Internationally—The Guide to Cross–Cultural Success 36–37,44–74 (1995); David A. Victor, International Business Communication (1992) (developed a framework for conducting business communications across cultures); and Raymond Cohen, Negotiating Across Cultures—Communication Obstacles in International Diplomacy 160–161(1991) (makes ten recommendations for the low-context intercultural negotiator who is faced with a high-context opponent).

14. Geert Hofstede, Culture's Consequences (Abridged, 1980, 1984); also see Geert Hofstede, Cultures and Organizations—Software of the Mind (1997) and Dean Allen Foster, Bargaining Across Borders— How to Negotiate Business Successfully Anywhere in the World 264–272 (1992, 1995)(shows how Hofstede's work relates to international negotiations)

912 CHAPTER VI INTERNATIONAL DISPUTE RESOLUTION

gender characteristics? Societies more "masculine" value assertiveness, independence, and competitiveness, while societies more "feminine" value cooperation, nurturing, and relationships.

Glen Fisher[15] prepared a study of international negotiations for the Department of State's training programs. By applying a number of social psychological insights,[16] Fisher identified *five* considerations relevant to negotiating with persons from another culture.

First, the negotiator should collect information about how the other party views the negotiation encounter in terms of negotiating style, formalities of the setting, protocols, and who attends (title, expertise). Second, the negotiator needs to understand the other party's styles of decision-making—whether centralized and hierarchical and whether based on consensus or diffused among different agencies. Third, the negotiator should investigate the "national character" of the other negotiator's society. This means gathering information about the national self-image, specific values, implicit assumptions such as attitudes toward compromise or importance of defending principles, and styles of logic, reasoning, and persuasion. Fourth, the negotiator should be prepared to cope with cross-cultural "noise," background distractions unrelated to the substance of the negotiations. Common behavior of Americans may create cultural "noise" in a negotiation such as using a first name prematurely, forgetting titles, starting speeches with a joke or acting too egalitarian. Fifth, the negotiator should be cognizant of the limitations and opportunities for distortion of meanings when relying on interpreters and translators. Not all concepts or even words can be easily translated to other languages, and languages have built-in styles of reasoning that may be lost when translated.

Another valuable study[17] identified cultural values that make it more likely that the parties will achieve "win-win" solutions in negotiations. The authors found that negotiators are more likely to find joint gains if: (1) They value information sharing which is vital for identifying possibilities for trade-offs that might add value to each side. (2) They deal with information and issues polychronically instead of monochronically. By considering many issues or tasks at once, negotiators are more likely to find integrative solutions which call for a process of trading high priority for low

---

15. Glen Fisher, International Negotiation (1980) (the author served as Dean of the Department of State's Foreign Service Institute's School of Area Studies); also see, Glen Fisher, Mindsets–The Role of Culture and Perception in International Relations (2nd edition, 1997)

16. In the study for foreign service officers, Fisher first describes **four** normal features of communication and perception that interfere with effective communication across cultures. He explains how human minds, as *information processors*, are programmed differently by different cultural experiences;

how the mind strives for *internal consistency* which may mean rejecting inconsistent but possibly relevant information; how we *project* our own interpretations of meanings to explain what other people mean; and the tendency to unconsciously *attribute motives* based on our own experience to explain actions of others.

17. Jeanne M. Brett, Wendi Adair, Alain Lempereur, Tetsushi Okumura, Peter Shikhirev, Catherine Tinsley, and Anne Lytle "Culture and Joint Gains in Negotiation" Neg. J. 61 79–81 (January 1998).

priority issues or connecting issues in creative ways. (3) They are oriented toward an egalitarian culture instead of a hierarchical one in which the focus on status and power may distract parties from generating joint gains. (4) They are motivated by self-interest which appears to motivate parties to persistently search for joint gains.

In the following excerpt, Jeswald Salacuse identified *ten* ways that culture impacts on negotiations:[18]

Jeswald W. Salacuse,[19] Making Global Deals

58–70 (1991).

Ten Ways Culture Affects Negotiations

* * *

Some may argue that these traits are a result of personality rather than culture. Culture certainly does not determine behavior, but it does predispose persons of a given cultural group to act in certain ways in specific situations. But rather than pursue this debate, it is enough to point out that these ten traits are common in negotiating behavior and, whether they are caused by personality or culture or both, the practical negotiator must learn to deal with them.

1. Negotiating Goal: Contract or Relationship?

An initial question is whether the two sides in a negotiation have the same goal and see the deal-making process in the same light. It is possible for businesspersons from different cultures to interpret the very purpose of their negotiation differently. For many Americans, the purpose of a business negotiation, first and foremost, is to arrive at a signed contract between the parties. Americans view a signed contract as a definitive set of rights and duties that strictly binds the two sides, an attitude succinctly summed up in the declaration that "a deal is a deal."

Japanese and certain other cultural groups consider that the goal of negotiation is not a signed contract but a relationship between the two sides. Although the written contract expresses the relationship, the essence of their deal is the relationship itself. For the American, signing a contract

---

18. In a limited survey based on these ten ways, Professor Salacuse asked respondents to rate their negotiating style. The survey confirmed that "culture can influence the way in which persons perceive and approach certain key elements in the negotiating process." Jeswald W. Salacuse, "Ten Ways that Culture Affects Negotiating Style: Some Survey Results" Neg. J. 221, 237 (July 1998).

19. Jeswald Salacuse, a professor of international law at Tufts University and a member of Harvard's Program on Negotiation, drew upon his business experience in more than thirty countries when he identified seven barriers to successful negotiations that are common in international business deals but are not ordinarily relevant to domestic deals. Of these seven barriers, one was the impact of culture.

914   CHAPTER VI INTERNATIONAL DISPUTE RESOLUTION

is closing a deal; for the Japanese, signing a contract might more appropriately be called opening a relationship.

* * *

2.   Negotiating Attitude: Win/Lose or Win/Win?

Because of culture or personality, or both, businesspersons appear to approach deal making with one of two basic attitudes: that a negotiation is either a process through which both can gain (win/win) or a process through which, of necessity, one side wins and the other loses (win/lose). As you enter negotiations, it is important to know which type of negotiator is sitting across the table from you. If one side has much greater bargaining power than the other, the weaker side has a tendency to see the negotiation as a win/lose situation: every gain for the powerful side is automatically a loss for the weaker party. As one Indian executive put it, "Negotiations between the weak and the strong are like negotiations between the lamb and the lion. Invariably, the lamb gets eaten." Win/win negotiators see deal making as a collaborative and problem-solving process; win/lose negotiators view it as confrontational.

* * *

3.   Personal Style: Informal or Formal?

An executive's "style" at the negotiating table is usually characterized as formal or informal. References to style focus on the way a negotiator talks to others, uses titles, dresses, speaks, and interacts with other persons. A negotiator with a formal style insists on addressing the other team by their titles, avoids personal anecdotes, and refrains from questions touching on the private or family life of members of the other side. An informal style of negotiator tries to start the discussion on a first-name basis, quickly seeks to develop a personal, friendly relationship with the other team, and may take off his jacket and roll up his sleeves when deal making begins in earnest. Each culture has its own formalities, which have special meaning. They are another means of communication among the persons sharing that culture. For an American or an Australian, calling someone by his first name is an act of friendship and therefore a good thing. In other cultures, such as the French, Japanese, or Egyptian, the use of a first name at a first meeting is an act of disrespect and therefore a bad thing.

* * *

4.   Communication: Direct or Indirect?

Methods of communication vary among cultures. Some place emphasis on direct and simple methods of communication; others rely heavily on indirect and complex methods. The latter may use circumlocutions, figurative forms of speech, facial expressions, gestures, and other kinds of body language. In a culture that values directness, such as the German, you can expect to receive a clear and definite response to questions and proposals.

In cultures that rely on indirect communication, reaction to your proposal may be gained only by interpreting a series of signs, gestures, and seemingly indefinite comments. What you will not receive at a first meeting is a definite commitment or rejection.

* * *

5. Sensitivity to Time: High or Low?

Discussions of national negotiating styles invariably treat a particular culture's attitudes toward time. So it is said that Germans are always punctual, Mexicans are habitually late, Japanese negotiate slowly, and Americans are quick to make a deal. Commentators claim that some cultures "value" time more than others, but this may not be an accurate characterization of the situation. Rather, they value differently the amount of time devoted to and measured against the goal pursued. For Americans, the deal is a "signed contract" and "time is money," so they want to make a deal quickly. Americans therefore try to reduce formalities to a minimum and get down to business. For members of other cultures, who view the purpose of the negotiation as creating a relationship rather than simply signing a contract, there is a need to invest time in the negotiating process so that the parties can get to know one another well and determine whether they wish to embark on a long-term relationship. Aggressive attempts to shorten the negotiating time may be viewed by the other side as efforts to hide something and therefore may be a cause of distrust.

6. Emotionalism: High or Low?

Accounts of negotiating behavior of persons from other cultures almost always point to a particular group's tendency or lack thereof to act emotionally. According to the stereotype, Latin Americans show their emotions at the negotiating table, but Japanese hide their feelings. Obviously, individual personality plays a role here. There are passive Latins and hotheaded Japanese. But various cultures have different rules as to the appropriateness of displaying emotions, and these rules are usually brought to the negotiating table as well.

7. Form of Agreement: General or Specific?

Cultural factors also influence the form of agreement that parties try to make. Generally, Americans prefer very detailed contracts that attempt to anticipate all possible circumstances, no matter how unlikely. Why? Because the "deal" is the contract itself, and one must refer to the contract to determine how to handle a new situation that may arise. Other cultures, such as that of China, prefer a contract in the form of general principles rather than detailed rules. Why? Because, it is claimed, the essence of the deal is the relationship of trust that exists between the parties. If unexpected circumstances arise, the parties should look to their relationship, not the contract, to solve the problem. So in some cases, the American drive at the negotiating table to foresee all contingencies may be viewed by persons

916 CHAPTER VI INTERNATIONAL DISPUTE RESOLUTION

from another culture as evidence of lack of confidence in the stability of the underlying relationship.

Some persons argue that differences over the form of an agreement are caused more by unequal bargaining power between the parties than by culture. In a situation of unequal bargaining power, the stronger party always seeks a detailed agreement to "lock up the deal" in all its possible dimensions, while the weaker party prefers a general agreement to give it room to "wiggle out" of adverse circumstances that are almost bound to occur in the future.... According to this view, it is not culture but context that determines this negotiating trait.

* * *

8.   Building an Agreement: Bottom Up or Top Down?

Related to the form of an agreement is the question of whether negotiating a business deal is an inductive or deductive process. Does it start from agreement on general principles and proceed to specific items, or does it begin with agreement on specifics, such as price, delivery date, and product quality, the sum total of which becomes the contract? Different cultures tend to emphasize one approach over the other.

Some observers believe that the French prefer to begin with agreement on general principles, while Americans tend to seek agreement first on specifics. For Americans, negotiating a deal is basically making a whole series of compromises and tradeoffs on a long list of particulars. For the French, the essence is to agree on basic general principles that will guide and indeed determine the negotiation process afterward. The agreed-upon general principles become the framework, the skeleton, upon which the contract is built.

A further difference in negotiating style is seen in the dichotomy between the "building down" approach and the "building up" approach. In the building-down approach, the negotiator begins by presenting a maximum deal if the other side accepts all the stated conditions. In the building-up approach, one side starts by proposing a minimal deal that can be broadened and increased as the other party accepts additional conditions. According to many observers, Americans tend to favor the building-down approach, while the Japanese prefer the building-up style of negotiating a contract.

9.   Team Organization: One Leader or Group Consensus?

In any international business negotiation, it is important to know how the other side is organized, who has the authority to make commitments, and how decisions are made. Culture is one important factor that affects the way executives organize themselves to negotiate a deal. One extreme is the negotiating team with a supreme leader who has complete authority to decide all matters. Americans tend to follow this approach, described as the "John Wayne style of negotiations": one person has all the authority and plunges ahead to do a job, and to do it as quickly as possible. Other cultures, notably the Japanese and the former Soviets, stress team negotiation and consensus decision making. When you negotiate with such a team, it may not be apparent who is the leader and who has the authority to commit the side. In the first type, the negotiating team is usually small; in the second, it is often large. For example, in negotiations in China on a major deal, it would not be uncommon for the Americans to arrive at the table with three persons and for the Chinese to show up with ten. Similarly, the one-leader team is usually prepared to make commitments and decisions more quickly than a negotiating team organized on the basis of consensus . . . .

10. Risk Taking: High or Low?

Studies seem to support the idea that certain cultures try to avoid risk more than others. In any given deal, the willingness of one side to take "risks" in the negotiation process—to divulge information, to be open to new approaches, to tolerate uncertainties in a proposed course of action— can be affected by the personality of the negotiator and the context of the negotiation. Nonetheless, there are certain cultural traits to this effect. The Japanese, with their emphasis on requiring enormous amounts of information and on their intricate group decision-making process, tend to be risk adverse. Americans, by comparison, are risk takers. If you determine that the team on the other side of the table is risk adverse, focus your attention on proposing rules, mechanisms, and relationships that will reduce the apparent risks in the deal for them.

3. DEVELOPING CULTURAL SENSITIVITY

A cross-cultural negotiator must learn to recognize when cultural factors are contributing to a conflict and may be impeding the success of the negotiation. This cultural sensitivity cannot be acquired by simply memorizing facts about the other party's culture. In addition to the previously discussed difficulties in even identifying the other party's culture, a negotiator needs to know how to use cultural information. Gathering a large quantity of cultural information by itself does not prepare the negotiator to use the information in a particular negotiation with a particular person.

> The better negotiators, the more successful global businesspeople, are not those who have memorized hundreds or thousands of do's and don'ts. Rather, they are those who have developed an international feel, a global mind-set, an empathic approach toward doing business with people from other cultures. Certainly, the better international negotiators do try to learn about the people of the country they are negotiating with. And, certainly, those more experienced with one particular country will have an advantage over those less experienced in that country. But, first and foremost, the better negotiators understand the larger process of achieving effective communication with business associates whose cultural baggage is different from their own. And they know the importance of understanding cultural differences in

918 CHAPTER VI INTERNATIONAL DISPUTE RESOLUTION

order to prevent such differences from undermining their negotiations.[20]

How does an attorney develop this "international feel" or "global mind-set"? In other words, how does an attorney guard against culturally-based impasses and bridge cultural gaps?

Consider this five step approach. In the first three steps, the attorney prepares for a cross-cultural negotiation by mastering a cultural conceptual framework, learning about his own cultural upbringing, and investigating the culture of the other negotiators. The next two steps provide a guide for the attorney in the negotiation sessions. The attorney should view negotiating behavior of others with an open mind and then figure out how to bridge any differences.

These five steps will be elaborated through the use of a hypothetical. Consider how a U.S. attorney might react when she learns that the other party, an institutional client, will not be represented by someone with substantial settlement authority. Instead, the other side will be represented by a team of negotiators who will make decisions by consensus. Furthermore, all the team members will not be present in the negotiation sessions. Under these circumstances, the U.S. attorney is likely to suspect that the other side is acting in bad faith. The other side appears to be replacing the person with real settlement authority with an unwieldy team of negotiators. How might the attorney proceed?

The three preparatory steps are:

First, the attorney should learn a *conceptual framework* which can help her identify and understand cultural characteristics. The attorney must grasp the meaning of "cultural behavior" and how it is different from universal "human behavior." Cultural characteristics, as discussed in the previous section, have been isolated in numerous studies of culture, including studies of characteristics relevant to conflict resolution.[21]

The hypothetical implicates a cultural characteristic related to the process of decisionmaking. Does settlement authority reside with a leader

---

20. Dean Allen Foster, Bargaining Across Borders 5 (1992).

21. See, e.g. Geert Hofstede, Culture's Consequences (Abridged, 1980, 1984); Geert Hofstede, Cultures and Organizations—Software of the Mind (1997) and Dean Allen Foster, Bargaining Across Borders—How to Negotiate Business Successfully Anywhere in the World 264–272 (1992, 1995)(shows how Hofstede's work relates to international negotiations); Glen Fisher, International Negotiation (1980) (the author served as Dean of the Department of State's Foreign Service Institute's School of Area Studies); Glen Fisher, Mindsets–The Role of Culture and Perception in International Relations (2nd edition, 1997); Donald W. Hendon, Rebecca Angeles Hendon, and Paul Herbig, Cross–Cultural Business Negotiations(1996);Gary P. Ferraro, The Cultural Dimension of International Business (2nd edition, 1994); David W. Augsburger, Conflict Mediation Across Cultures 8–10, 26–28 (1992);Dean Allen Foster, Bargaining Across Borders—How To Negotiate Business Successfully Anywhere in the World 272–293 (1992,1995); and Terence Brake, Danielle Medina Walker, and Thomas (Tim) Walker, Doing Business Internationally—The Guide to Cross–Cultural Success 36–37,44–74 (1995).

A. Demystifying Cross-Cultural Dimensions **919**

or with a team that makes decisions based on consensus? This generic characteristic, as virtually all cultural characteristics, encompasses a continuum bound at each end with a value-based pole. At one extreme, societies can be found that are hierarchical in which decisions are made by leaders. At the other extreme, societies can be found that are collective in which decisions are made by consensus. The actual cultural practice is rarely one extreme or the other. The cultural practice usually falls somewhere between these two end poles of the continuum. As practiced in U.S. businesses, decisionmaking is predominately hierarchical, placing the practice near the leader pole but not at the pole because input and collaboration also are valued.

Second, the attorney should fill-in this conceptual framework with a deep understanding of her *own culture or cultures*.[22] An attorney is not always cognizant of the degree to which her own behavior is universal or culturally determined. Yet, it is though this personal lens that an attorney observes and assesses the negotiating behavior of others. To reduce distortions, the attorney should learn about her own cultural upbringing in order to appreciate the extent to which her view of other people's behavior may not necessarily reflect a universal view. In the hypothetical, the U.S. attorney should be aware that her view that organizations tend to be hierarchical in which decisionmaking is centralized in "leaders" is not universal organizational behavior.

Third, the attorney should strengthen her conceptual framework with an understanding of the *culture or cultures of the other negotiator(s)*. Despite the difficulties in identifying cultural behavior, the attorney should try to identify and research the culture(s) of her client, the other attorney, and the other party.[23] Furthermore, the attorney should learn as much as possible about the other negotiators as individuals, that is their personalities and ways their negotiating behavior may vary from practices of their culture(s). In the hypothetical, the research might reveal that the other side is from a society in which organizations typically make decisions based on consensus, but the research may reveal little about their individual personalities.

These first three preparatory steps are relatively easy to complete because they entail collecting mostly accessible information on cultural characteristics. The next two steps, however, are much more difficult to accomplish because they require suspending judgments and developing strategies during intense, dynamic, and fast moving negotiation sessions.

---

22. For studies of American culture, see Gary Althen, American Ways xiii, 4, 8, 9–10, 14, 17, 24–25, 136–137 (1988); Edward C. Stewart and Milton J. Bennett, American Cultural Patterns–A Cross–Cultural Perspective (1991); Alison R. Lanier (revised by Charles William Gay), Living in the U.S.A., Part I (5th edition, 1996); and Dean Engel, "Passport USA" (1997), and Dean Allen Foster, Bargaining Across Borders—How to Negotiate Business Successfully Anywhere in the World, Chpts. 3–6 (1995).

23. See Notes and Questions, Note 9 on Researching Culture.

Fourth, the attorney should learn to withhold judgments about the other side and instead view key negotiating behavior with an *open mind*. This requires considerable discipline. It is too easy to for an attorney who routinely judges negotiating behavior to prematurely judge it in a cross-cultural negotiation. In the hypothetical, the U.S. negotiator should not judge the other side's decisionmaking process as evidence of good or bad faith; instead she should view this key negotiating behavior as a difference that needs to be dealt with.

Fifth and finally, the attorney should search for ways to *bridge* the resulting gap. In doing so, the attorney should *not* assume that just because a person was brought up in a clearly identifiable culture, the person will act in accordance with its cultural norms.

Gaps might be closed by the attorney negotiating a resolution or deferring to the other side's practice. The attorney could negotiate a solution through resort to an interest-based approach, where the interests behind the practices are respected. Parties also might negotiate a compromise. In the hypothetical, instead of viewing as bad faith the other side's claim that they cannot agree to anything without a consensus, the U.S. attorney might focus on how to respect their need for consensus while still meeting her need for clients to be present with substantial settlement authority. The attorney, for example, could negotiate an arrangement in which the other side brings to the negotiation sessions all the people who must concur or at least be sure the absent people are available by telephone. Then, in the sessions, the consensus approach could be respected by giving members of the negotiating team ample time to meet privately.

As an alternative to negotiating over closure of the gap, one side may choose simply to defer to the other side's practice, especially when the other practice is not a deal-breaker or does not implicate core personal values. For instance, the U.S. attorney may defer to the other side's formal practices of carefully using titles and avoiding personal questions about family. The gap, however, can be difficult to bridge when the difference reflects engrained strategic practices, such as a conflict between a problem-solving style and haggling.

In another example applying the five steps, consider that the typical U.S. lawyer usually insists that signed business agreements cover many details and contingencies. The U.S. lawyer will likely interpret any reluctance by the other side to reduce details to writing as reluctance about the deal or a specific issue. In preparing for a cross-cultural negotiation with a Japanese lawyer, however, the U.S. lawyer should realize that his own preference for reducing everything to writing may be due to his own cultural upbringing and may not be a universal mode of behavior (step 2). The drafting of comprehensive contracts is taught in U.S. law school and reinforced in law practice. A Japanese lawyer may have been brought up differently (step 3). Instead of being concerned about the details of a written agreement, the Japanese lawyer may be more concerned about the business relationship, leaving for the written contract a general statement about the relationship and basic principles for governing the business deal.

A.   DEMYSTIFYING CROSS-CULTURAL DIMENSIONS   **921**

In the negotiations, the U.S. lawyer should view the reluctance of the Japanese lawyer to put everything in writing as ambiguous behavior to be viewed with an open mind (step 4). This difference might be investigated through a conversation in which the U.S. attorney explains why he prefers detailed contracts and then inquires why the other attorney may not. If the U.S. attorney learns that the other side believes business deals are about relationships, not contracts, the U.S attorney needs to find a way to bridge this resulting gap in practices. The attorney may close the gap by respecting the reasons for the different practices. He may negotiate a compromise in which both sides seek to cultivate a relationship of trust and then enter into a contract that may cover key obligations but not every conceivable contingency (step 5.)

NOTES AND QUESTIONS

1. What are the common characteristics identified in the four generic studies of culture in the readings? Do each of the cultural characteristics fit the definition of culture? Are any of these characteristics influenced by other factors such as genetics and personality? If differences in negotiating behavior can be due to factors other than culture, is there any value served by focusing on differences due to culture?

2. Reflect on the key features of your negotiation approach (e.g. what information you gather before meeting, how you begin a negotiation, how you respond to the other side's initiatives, what end product you are seeking, etc.) Which of your practices are universal and which are shaped by your cultural upbringing?

3. Cultural Country Studies. When investigating the cultural practices of another country, it can be useful to read country specific studies. Here are two excerpts that describe how several cultural characteristics are practiced in two particular countries, Japan and Mexico.

a.   Japan[24]

"Japanese negotiators are well-known for their indirectness and vagueness of response. This arises from a fear of offending the other party out of a concern for maintaining harmonious relations. The tendency, therefore, is to avoid extremes and steer a middle course on the various issues.

Indirectness is partly a result of the complex nature of the Japanese company decision-making process. In large, well-established Japanese companies in which no one person wields absolute power, a definite position cannot be taken on a particular issue until a consensus has been forged. Vagueness is an avenue through which the Japanese can save face in case a reversal of a position is needed at a later time. It is not a deliberate attempt to deceive the other party. The message which the Japanese negotiating

---

24. For a more comprehensive cultural study of Japan, see Rosalie L. Tung, Business Negotiations with the Japanese (1984)

team most wants to convey will be found in its non-verbal signals. In Japan this is known as *Jiaragei* and can be described as "the process of feeling another out on an issue."

A good cross-cultural negotiator will always be responsive to the mood of the negotiation and will realize that the more important the matter being discussed, the more indirect the Japanese manner of communication will be.

* * *

Possibly, the most frustrating example of vagueness is found in the Japanese reluctance to say "no" to a proposal. However, there are certain expressions, consistently used, which are intended to indicate a "no" response. It is important that these be recognized because they could otherwise be misinterpreted as evasiveness or delay tactics. Standard indicators of "no" appear in the following forms:

(A) Prolonged inactivity.

(B) A discussion of deficiencies in the proposal.

(C) A suggestion that there are better alternatives.

(D) A mere failure to draw up a proposal.

Maintaining "Face"

You should make every effort to adopt a negotiating style which will respect the Japanese concern to maintain "face." Disagreement with a proposal should not be expressed in outright rejection. To do so would be construed as a failure to treat the other party with the respect that should flow from your mutual concern for the overall business relationship. You should indicate your rejection subtly by suggesting alternative proposals. Forthright statements of positions should be avoided. Although it is important to be forceful when necessary, you should generally adopt a posture that allows the other party sufficient room to change position without losing face."

Peter H. Corne, The Complex Art of Negotiation Between Cultures

Arbitration Journal 46, 48 (December 1992)

b. Mexico

"The difference between monochronic and polychronic societies may also be illustrated through different attitudes toward deadlines. Simply speaking, U.S. Americans have been raised believing that there is great value in planning and scheduling, quick answers, and prompt solutions. A U.S. American's day is likely to be packed with appointments and deadlines. In contrast, Mexicans believe in relaxed observation of deadlines and are likely to spend more time evaluating problems before making decisions. As a result, Mexicans often view the term "deadline" as flexible and factor it in with other priorities. For example, Mexican contracts contain an implied extension for important events. In Mexican society, interruptions are routine and delays are to be expected in both business and personal life.

* * *

...Mexico exemplifies an extremely high power distance culture, and the United States is recognized as a relatively low power distance culture.

Generally, high power distance countries are more comfortable with disparity of power and hierarchies in their societies. Low power distance countries, however, question the legitimacy of different levels of power and strongly attempt to de-emphasize any stratification or inequality in their societies. Accordingly, Mexico places a high value upon hierarchies and rank within the business context. Leadership is autocratic and authoritative. It is based upon the values of age, sex, connections and expedience. Subordinates rarely, question their leaders: therefore, it is important to show proper deference and respect to the senior members of a Mexican negotiating team during a mediation.''

Julie Barker, International Mediation—A Better Alternative for the Resolution of Commercial Disputes: Guidelines for a U.S. Negotiator Involved in an International Commercial Mediation with Mexicans 19 Loyola of LA Intl & Comp. L.J. 32, 33–37, 39–43, 45–49 (1996).

4. Rubin and Salacuse have suggested ways for turning cultural differences into an opportunity for building a working relationship.

"Too often, negotiators regard culture as an obstacle to reaching agreement. Instead, try to find ways in which culture can serve as a way to build a relationship with the other side. How can these bridging opportunity be created?

First, try to show genuine interest in the culture of the other side. Asking questions about the history and customs of the country from which the other negotiator comes is not only a sign of respect and interest, but a way of gathering valuable information that can only help you be a more effective negotiator. If you have done some reading about the culture, so that your questions and comments are knowledgeable, that will help you gain the respect of the other side.

Second, look for cultural experiences that you and the other negotiator have in common. President Anwar Sadat of Egypt, when negotiating with the Sudanese, would apparently begin by observing that his mother came from Sudan. African–Americans, in dealing with African business executives, will often stress their common cultural heritage as a way of building a bridge, and Italian–Americans often use the same approach in Italy. President Jimmy Carter used religion as a shared value system binding together Sadat, Israel's Menachem Begin, and himself at Camp David in 1978. Such appeals to common experiences, history, or values can help to remind negotiators that while they may be divided over the issues between them, they are also joined in ways that transcend the current conflict.

924 CHAPTER VI INTERNATIONAL DISPUTE RESOLUTION

Third, search for a third culture that is of shared interest to both of you. For example, a Thai and an American business negotiator may discover their common love of opera in a negotiation, and that discovery may help to build a bridge between the two.

Fourth, give yourself plenty of time for what is called "pre-negotiation." The most important events in negotiation often take place *before* the parties ever come to the table. During the preliminary stages, people get to know one another, figure out what sorts of agreements will ultimately be possible and which will not, and begin developing the basis for a relationship. Follow the Japanese example: develop relationship. Among other things, this will help you learn valuable things about the people you are negotiating with. And that, in turn, will make it more likely that you will be able to get the agreement you want."

Jeffrey Z. Rubin and Jeswald W. Salacuse, "Culture and International Negotiation: Lessons for Business 11 Alternatives 95, 98–99 (July, 1993)"

5. You represent a client who needs a stable source of reliable computers for its large business customers. Your client asked you to negotiate the purchase of ten thousand computers over the next five years from a Japanese computer company. In telephone calls and emails, you have been trying to work out the details including the price per computer, firm delivery dates, and a liquidated damage clause to cover late deliveries. You are having difficulty getting direct answers from your Japanese counterpart who keeps telling you that everything will be fine and that your client will get what it needs. Your client is very concerned about these vague responses. To finalize the deal, your client decided to send you to Japan.

You know that your Japanese counterpart lived in Japan his whole live except for going to the United States for three years to earn his law degree at New York University. You also know that your Japanese counterpart has had little experience negotiating business deals with U.S. businesses.

Develop a cross-cultural negotiation strategy based on the five step approach. Use the information on the Japanese culture that is described in this Note and the Salacuse article on ten ways culture affects negotiations.

6. In his book, The Mediation Process, Christopher Moore suggested that a mediation may reach an impasse due to various causes. He points out that parties may reach an impasse because of their conflicting views of critical information (data conflicts), unequal bargaining positions (structural conflicts), or competing needs (interest conflicts). They also may be in conflict due to hostile personal relationships (relationship conflicts) or conflicting personal values (value conflicts). For each of these five sources of conflicts, Moore lists possible causes. In which of these five conflict categories might cross-cultural differences arise as a cause? See, Christopher W. Moore, The Mediation Process 60–61(2nd edition, 1996).

7. Culture also plays an important role in mediation. For articles on the subject, see Raymond Cohen "Cultural Aspects of International Mediation" in Resolving International Conflicts—The Theory and Practice of Mediation, Ch. 5, 107–128 (Jacob Bercovitch, ed., 1996) (The author identifies three cross-cultural roles of mediators: the interpreter who bridges intercultural communication gap, a buffer who protects face of adversaries, and the coordinator who synchronizes dissonant negotiating conventions.); Cynthia A. Savage, "Culture and Mediation: A Red Herring" 5 Am. U.J.Gender & Law 269 (1996)(The author recommends that instead of approaching differences in terms of racial, ethnic, or other single identifying characteristic, negotiators should recognize differences in terms of various value orientations that also can account for individual differences and effects of multiple cultures.); Selma Myers and Barbara Filner, Mediation Across Cultures 23 (1994) (The author identified five cultural issues that most significantly affect the mediation process: language, assumptions, expectations that others will conform to us, biases against the unfamiliar, and values in conflict.); and Paul B. Pederson and Fred E. Jandt, "Culturally Contextual Models for Creative Conflict Management" and "The Cultural Context of Mediation and Constructive Conflict Management" in Constructive Conflict Management—Asia–Pacific Cases 3–26, 249–275 (Fred E. Jandt and Paul B. Pederson, eds., 1996)(The authors analyze over 100 case studies of cultural components of mediations in various Asian cultures and substantive settings, including the testing of two models of constructive conflict resolution, one based on high or low context cultures and another based on separating culturally learned expectations of behavior from actual behavior.)

8. Interpreters and Translators. Cultural differences are magnified when the native language of each of the parties is different. The obvious solution of bringing in a professional interpreter or translator[25] still poses risks. Even professionals can make grave mistakes that distort communications.

Many examples of interpretation problems can be found in settings familiar to lawyers. The need for selecting qualified interpreters was conspicuously demonstrated when Secretary of State Madeleine K. Albright, who speaks fluent Czech, became frustrated with her interpreter at a news conference in Prague. She finally interrupted him with the remark "not exactly" and then served as her own interpreter.[26] Errors in translating treaties can occur, as happened when a conflict arose between two official versions of an international trade treaty, one in Spanish and the other in English. The Spanish version referred to "leyes" as a source of law which included treaties while the English version referred to "relevant statutes" which by definition did not include treaties. The conflict left unclear the authority of the adjudicatory body to rely on treaties as a source of law when resolving the dispute.[27] Even translating common

25. Interpreters translate spoken words orally from one language to another as the words are spoken to the listener(s). Translators translate contracts and other written documents into another written language. Translators have the relative luxury of more time and the opportunity to use dictionaries and other research tools.

26. R.W. Apple Jr. "Honors of a Homecoming Adorn Albright's Success" New York Times A3, col. 4 (July 15, 1997).

27. In the Matter of the Mexican Antidumping Investigation Into Imports of Cut-

CHAPTER VI INTERNATIONAL DISPUTE RESOLUTION

dispute resolution words into a foreign language may produce unintended meanings. For example, in Iran, the word "mediator" in Persian suggests that the person is a meddler and the word "compromise" evokes a negative meaning as in compromising one's integrity.[28]

We also have to recognize that certain ideas do not exist, or exist in very different form, in other languages. Glen Fisher observes:

> When a thought loses something in translation, that is probably the point to dig in and find out what it was that was lost, for it is precisely in those instances in which cultures do not have equivalent conceptions that the two sides in a discussion find themselves talking past each other. For example, there was no word for "democracy" when Japan was exposed to the West. Something had to be created out of three written characters to produce something like "peopleness" or populism. Usage may now make the gap smaller, but the communication problem presented is clear. Glen Fisher, International Negotiation 62 (1980)

In view of these risks, a negotiator should carefully select a professional interpreter or translator who is qualified for the particular negotiation. Not every bilingual person is qualified to serve in this professional capacity. These are highly skilled duties. A qualified person must possess a deep understanding of the nuances of both languages, the culture underlying both languages, the technical words and concepts relevant to the particular negotiation, and the unique demands of interpreting or translating. Because a negotiator works closely with her interpreter when interacting with the other side, the negotiator should prepare her interpreter for the substance of the negotiation and know how to skillfully work with her interpreter during the negotiation sessions.[29]

9. Researching Culture.[30] A negotiator should prepare for a cross-cultural negotiation by reading, talking to people, and visiting the other country. For example, an American preparing to negotiate a business deal in Northern China may derive valuable cultural information about that region from modern histories of China, cultural studies of the Chinese people, newspaper articles published in foreign and Chinese papers, articles in popular Chinese magazines, and accounts of negotiations with people from China. Chinese films and television shows also are worth watching. Addi-

---

to-Length Plate Products from the United States, Binational Panel No. MEX–94–1904–02 August 30, 1995 (Chapter XIX of the North American Free Trade Agreement)(adopted Spanish language version because of ample support that treaties are an important source of law and should be used).

28. See, Roger Fisher and William Ury, Getting to Yes–Negotiating Agreement Without Giving In 34 (1981)

29. See, Abramson, International Mediation Basics in Practitioner's Guide to Inter-

national Arbitration and Mediation Ch. 10.06 (Editors–Chernick, Kolkey, and Rhoades, to be published in Fall, 2001). Also see, Ileana Dominguez–Urban, "The Messenger as the Medium of Communication: The Use of Interpreters in Mediation" J.Disp. Resol. 1(1997).

30. For an excellent chapter on how to reseach cultural information, see Gary P. Ferraro, The Cultural Dimension of International Business, Ch. 6 (2nd edition, 1994).

tional insights can be learned from the policy choices made in Chinese laws and in the ways Chinese governmental institutions are organized. Most of this information can be found in libraries and on the internet.

The negotiator should contact people with knowledge and experience in the other culture. Insights can be collected from professionals who have business experience in Northern China. These professionals may be lawyers, accountants, bankers, or interpreters who live in the United States and have done deals in or have lived in Northern China. These professionals may be Chinese nationals, American–Chinese, or non-Chinese. The negotiator may even hire a cultural consultant who specializes in assisting others working in other cultures.

It is enormously valuable for a negotiator to spend time visiting the other culture, including learning its language. If this cannot be done before the negotiation, a negotiator should at least arrive early enough before a negotiation session in the foreign country to do some "in-country research." Spending time in the foreign culture means doing more than being a tourist. A negotiator should reach out to collect cultural information by meeting as many local people as possible, walking the streets, and visiting places where local people spend time, such as shops, markets, and parks. The negotiator also should visit museums, libraries and book stores and read local newspapers, some of which may be published in English.

Two useful and underutilized sources of cultural data are the U.S. Department of State and local universities. A negotiator can gather information from the U.S. Department of State, especially its country desk on China and from the American Embassy or Consulate in China, especially its commercial officers in China. Contacting local universities might turn up a department specializing in the culture or region, such as a China department or a department on Asia or Pacific Rim Countries. A university department can provide access to both valuable resource materials and resident experts.

B. INTERNATIONAL ADR CLAUSES FOR BUSINESS DISPUTES[1]

"From jets to jeans, turbines to telephones, oil to beans–globalization of commerce has increased exponentially in the more than fifty years since the last world wide war. During this time, businesses have expanded beyond national borders and markets into "multinational corporations" with international networks of suppliers, customers, employees, and shareholders. Domestic and multinational companies, together with state-owned enterprises, seek strategic advantages by creating joint ventures, alliances, and partnering relationships with foreign enterprises. British Air allies

---

1. Anyone deeply interested in this subject should read the book, Arbitration and Mediation in International Business by Christian Buhring–Uhle. This superb 1996 book is informed by the author's empirical survey of practitioners.

with American Airlines; General Motors joint ventures with Chinese state-owned enterprises; French–German–Japanese construction joint ventures build the airport and approaches in Hong Kong. . . . Business arrangements are complex; potential rewards are great, but risks are also huge. The investments required to compete effectively expose businesses to all of the uncertainties inherent in any long-term interdependent relationship plus those associated with cross-cultural, transnational matters, including possible expropriation by one's partner, submission to the jurisdiction of foreign courts, and reliance on an alien legal system.

Conflict is a natural component of long-term commercial relations. It is atypical for a large scale infrastructure project, development project, or trading relationship not to produce claims, disputes and disagreements over rights, responsibilities, powers, obligations, and monetary rewards." Eric D. Green, "International Commercial Dispute Resolution: Courts, Arbitration, and Mediation—Introduction" 15 Bost.U.Intl.L.J.175–176 (1997).[2]

When an international business conflict arises, private parties cannot count on access to a compulsory, binding international court system to resolve their dispute. There is none. While parties can resort to the national court system of one of the parties, cross-border litigation presents parties with a host of risks that can make the litigation process enormously expensive and uncertain.[3] Some of the transnational litigation risks can be reduced by parties agreeing which national court system will be used (choice of forum provision) and which law will be applied (choice of law provision). Many of these risks can be further reduced by parties designing their own private dispute resolution systems, known as alternative dispute resolution clauses or ADR clauses.

A domestic boilerplate ADR clause[4] should not be adopted wholesale for resolving an international dispute. The domestic clause should be adapted to cover the distinctive needs of resolving a dispute between parties from different countries. Some of the domestic provisions should be modified and a number of uniquely international provisions added. A few of these special provisions are recognized in boilerplate international arbitration clauses. The international clause recommended by the American Arbitration Association,[5] for instance, includes several fill-in the blank options:

2. Also, see C. Buhring–Uhle, Arbitration and Mediation in International Business, 3–17 (1996)

3. See C. Buhring–Uhle, Arbitration and Mediation in International Business, 17–37 (1996); Jack J. Cole, Jr. International Commercial Arbitration: American Principles and Practice in a Global Context ch. 1, Sections 1.8.1–1.8.2 (1997); and Lawrence Perlman and Steven C. Nelson "New Approaches to the Resolution of International Commercial Disputes" 17 Intl Lawyer 215, 218–225(1983).

4. Many domestic deals include short boilerplate clauses such as the one suggested by the American Arbitration Association: "Any controversy or claim arising out of or relating to this contract, or the breach thereof, shall be settled by arbitration administered by the American Arbitration Association under its Commercial Arbitration Rules, and judgment on the award rendered by the arbitrator(s) may be entered in any court having jurisdiction thereof ." AAA Commercial Arbitration Rules(July 1, 1996)

5. For discussion of different arbitration rules, see section E.2.

"Any controversy or claim arising out of or relating to this contract shall be determined by arbitration in accordance with the International Arbitration Rules of the American Arbitration Association."

"The parties may wish to consider adding (a) 'The number of arbitrators shall be (one or three)'; (b) 'The place of arbitration shall be (city and/or country)'; or (c)'The language(s) of the arbitration shall be ___.' "[6]

This section examines a number of issues that deserve special attention when negotiating and designing an international ADR clause.

1. DISTINCTIVE ISSUES WHEN MEDIATING INTERNATIONAL BUSINESS DISPUTES[7]

When going internationally with mediation, a number of distinctive issues arise. The section on cross-cultural differences considered two issues: how to bridge cultural gaps and the vital role of interpreters and translators. This section examines a number of other international issues.

a. BENEFITS OF INTERNATIONAL MEDIATION

Neither domestic nor international ADR clauses routinely include a provision that obligates parties to try mediation before resorting to adjudication. This underutilitization of mediation persists despite the impressive settlement record of domestic mediations[8] and despite the fact that most international organizations have promoted the use of mediations through exhortation and publication of rules.[9] International mediations may not be widely used in part because of cross-cultural confusion and because of the difficulties and costs in convening mediation sessions. Yet, a compelling case can be made for parties first trying mediation in an international business conflict.

---

6. AAA International Arbitration Rules (April 1, 1997)

7. The substance of this section was published in Abramson, International Mediation Basics in Practitioner's Guide to International Arbitration and Mediation (Editors–Chernick, Kolkey, Rhoades, to be published in Fall, 2001).

8. See e.g. Jeanne M. Brett, Zoe I. Barsness, and Stephen B. Goldberg "The Effectiveness of Mediation: An Independent Analysis of Cases Handled by Four Major Service Providers" Neg. J 259, 261(July 1996) (The overall settlement rate was 78%.) and Robert C. Meade and Philip Ferrara, Ph.D. "An Evaluation of the Alternative Dispute Resolution Program of the Commercial Division: Survey Results and Recommendations" 4–5 (July 1997) (The overall settlement rate was

close to 70% for the Alternative Dispute Resolution Program of the Commercial Division of the Supreme Court, Civil Branch, New York County, New York State.)

9. ICC offered conciliation services from its beginning in 1923, UNCITRAL in 1980, and ICSID in 1965. Interestingly, before WWII, the ICC handled more conciliations than arbitrations, but the number of conciliations dropped off after WWII while the number of arbitrations increased to the point that today most ICC cases are arbitrations with only a handful of conciliations. W. Laurence Craig, William W. Park, and Jan Paulsson, International Chamber of Commerce Arbitration 681–682 (2nd edition, 1990). Also see section D.1. on rules for mediations.

Walter G. Gans, Saving Time And Money In Cross–Border Commercial Disputes

Dispute Resolution Journal 52–54 (January 1997)

In international agreements among parties which operate under different legal systems and in different cultural and language environs, it is all the more imperative to anticipate in advance differences in business philosophies, language and cultural practices, by including in the contract provisions for dispute resolution that take these differences into account.

* * *

Neutral forum arbitration of those disputes has certainly become the method of choice insofar as binding adjudication is concerned. But it is often far more preferable to devise procedures to resolve these disputes informally—through structured negotiations, facilitation, through mediation or other non-binding modality, all with the assistance of a mutually respected neutral—before resorting to any binding process through a third-party decision maker. There are sound reasons for requiring disputants in most cross-border transactions to go through these informal procedures * * * before resorting to binding arbitration, or, in the rare case, litigation. What are some of these?

1. Cultural differences favor inclusion of informal processes. Most foreign companies (whether European, Latin American or Asian) do not favor, in the first instance, having their business disputes aired externally and decided for them by others. When it has become necessary to do so, it is often deemed a sign of failure on the part of the businessmen, who then tend to wash their hands of the matter, at which point it becomes strictly a legal matter to be handled by the lawyers.

Because it is so embedded in foreign culture, it is generally deemed not necessary—indeed, it often may be considered crass—to recite in a legal document informal and well-understood practices that business managers routinely use to resolve disputes. That's why ADR as we know it (apart from binding administered arbitration) was suspect in many quarters, at least in Europe and Japan. But with the sharp increase in all manner of transnational projects over the last several years, there is a greater understanding that the unwritten norms that pertain within a particular culture do not necessarily find acceptance in another. This is particularly the case insofar as that other culture is the United States. Accordingly, foreign-based companies are now much more prone to accept inclusion in the documents of even informal procedures that would be exhausted before resorting to the familiar binding adjudication.

* * *

2. Businessmen should control their disputes. There is now a view outside the U.S., which has been reinforced by the U.S. proponents of ADR, and that is finally taking hold in Europe and elsewhere, that dispute resolution should not be left exclusively to the lawyers. As mentioned, it is common practice abroad for foreign businessmen to resolve their disputes by themselves, informally, possibly with the assistance of a mutual friend or business acquaintance, but certainly not with the assistance of lawyers acting as such. If in the odd case that approach proved unsuccessful, then the matter migrated from a business disagreement to a legal dispute. At that stage, the business people bowed out and it became solely a legal matter leading to (hopefully) a so-called "correct" result: that is, one reached in a well-accepted court of law or arbitration. Expense at that point didn't really matter as long as the process was deemed to be fair or "correct."

We know that for the most part things have evolved differently in our culture. The trend here is for the business people to become active participants in dispute resolution, and for good reason. After all, such disputes typically arise out of a business transaction (legally formulated or not), or at least in a business setting. Why shouldn't those who are involved in the underlying business matter have an active stake in the resolution of the dispute emanating from it?

3. Legal remedies are often too draconian to resolve business impasse. Most disputes arising out of transnational transactions are business issues—what should be done if there's overcapacity? undercapacity? the need for new financing? Invocation of traditional legal remedies, as opposed to finding business solutions, is an admission that there's serious impasse and it cannot be resolved for whatever reason. Suing the other party for breach of contract or to compel dissolution or a buy-sell arrangement rarely serves the business goals as they were envisaged. Creative business solutions, on the other hand, will often resolve these problems, and the chances are better for achieving them if the respective managements recognize that dispute resolution is a management, not legal, responsibility. This can be facilitated by the lawyers who ideally would encourage management to adopt practical, cost-effective and timely solutions as opposed to proceeding immediately with costly and time-consuming adjudication. The legal advisers have the opportunity (even the duty) to counsel toward those ends, beginning at the transaction's negotiation stage, by incorporating in the contract dispute resolution processes and procedures that best facilitate a business solution. If that is not possible, then they should at least be knowledgeable and informed about modalities short of litigation that might be invoked and, finally, an arbitration procedure that makes best sense from the client's perspective.

4. High incidence of disputes has led to greater scrutiny of costs. Even in civil law countries which used to believe that the "correct" result was important regardless of expense, there is now a greater consciousness of the enormous costs attendant to adjudication in courts or even arbitration tribunals. Perhaps because of the higher incidence of international disputes, scrutiny of legal (along with other) expenses has become de regueur not only by U.S. but also by foreign companies operating in the global marketplace.

5. Traditionally high forum costs in administered arbitration. Although arbitration of international commercial disputes has become the preferred

932 CHAPTER VI INTERNATIONAL DISPUTE RESOLUTION

ADR method of last resort, the attendant forum costs can be very high. Judicial fora, despite their deficiencies for international disputes, are at least made available for the most part at government expense, whereas forum costs of arbitration are borne by the parties. Even in ad hoc arbitration the fees and expenses of the arbitrators, who are likely to be experienced counsel, can be considerable. If the parties opt for institutional arbitration, there is, of course, the added cost of the administrative fee charged by the institution, which in some cases can also be a very high amount.

---

b. Convening a Mediation Session

In the optimal mediation setting, the mediator convenes in a neutral location the clients with settlement authority, along with each of their attorneys, and the mediator. All the participants work together to resolve the dispute. By meeting in the same place, everyone gets to know each other through personal, continuous and sustained interactions in both formal meetings and during breaks.[10]

This optimal meeting arrangement can be cumbersome to schedule and costly to convene for international business disputes.[11] International disputes involve parties from different countries who are usually spread out geographically and over different time zones. The participants may have no language in common, may have to communicate with each other through interpreters, and may face other cross-cultural obstacles when trying to understand each other.

In an effort to reduce these practical obstacles to convening everyone at a single location, mediators are starting to experiment with the use of new technologies for convening sessions.[12] These new technologies, when intelligently used with face-to-face sessions, can create a cost-effective, hospitable environment for international mediations.[13]

The preferred new technology is *videoconferencing*[14] because it permits participants from different locations to hear each other, to see each other, to exchange documents, and to collaborate in editing drafts. It also is the most expensive technological option due to the combination of three significant costs. First, participants must incur the cost of either buying desktop conferencing software and hardware (video camera and speakers), establishing a large screen videoconferencing facility, or renting a videoconferencing facility. Second, participants must pay the cost of a high speed, long distance transmission connection among the participants in the videocon-

---

10. For more detail, see Chapter 3.

11. See, C. Buhring–Uhle, Arbitration and Mediation in International Business 173–174 (1996).

12. See discussion of cybermediation in Chapter 3.

13. See, Jeswald W. Salacuse, Making Global Deals, 19–21 (1991)(pros and cons of using technologies to facilitate negotiations of global deals).

14. See, Evan Rosen, Personal Videoconferencing 32–44 (1996).

ference. Third, in less technologically advanced countries, it may take some effort to secure access to videoconferencing technology.

The cost of videoconferencing has been dropping and the quality of picture improving. Still, if the most advanced technologies are not used, the video can be choppy, the screen small, facial expressions unclear, and eye contact difficult to make due to the angle of the camera. Participants who are unfamiliar with the technology or unaccustomed to appearing in front of a camera need to become comfortable with this new means of real time interaction. These difficulties can be compounded by cultural differences and no generally accepted code of etiquette for behaving during a videoconference. Nevertheless, a videoconference in which participants use the latest technologies and prepare carefully can be an effective means of meeting.

Other technological options include teleconferencing, "chat rooms", and whiteboarding. *Teleconferencing* is easily accessible through either the telephone equipment of one of the participants or a telephone operator. The obvious limitation is that the participants can not see each other. *"Chat rooms"* through the internet provides a facility that permits all the participants to converse in writing in their own "private room." Once each of the parties has signed on, participants can communicate with each other through real time messages that all the participants can observe simultaneously on their screens. It is even possible to caucus through side written communications. This option, by far the cheapest one, also encourages more precision in the exchanges because each participant must type his or her comments. However, participants lose the benefit of spontaneous exchanges as well as the benefit of hearing or seeing each other. A *whiteboard* on each participant's personal computer gives each participant the ability to see and edit simultaneously the same draft, an option that is similar to all the participants sitting around a table editing a draft agreement.

These technologies can be used in combination with face-to-face sessions, giving the participants a number of ways to meet during the course of a mediation. One scenario could be as follows: In the first session, everyone meets together in one location during which time the participants develop a working relationship with each other and the mediator. The participants become educated about the mediation process, parties present each of their "stories," parties' interests are explicated and understood, and issues are defined. Before adjourning, the participants develop an agenda and assignments for the next session. If they have developed a sufficient working relationship, participants may not need to meet in one location for the next session. Instead, they may be able to meet technologically. For the second session, they may meet through *teleconferencing* at which time each of the parties may report any information collected and further refine the issues. Then, they may agree to meet a third time through *videoconferencing*. By now, the parties may be ready to resolve some of the most contentious issues and even come to an agreement in principle. Next, a fourth session may be held in a *chat room* or on a *whiteboard* where the parties can exchange specific drafts in an effort to resolve some of the details, especially about some of the noncontroversial aspects of the settlement. Then, they may follow a *store and forward* approach in which detailed drafts are prepared and forwarded for comments, giving each party time to reflect and return comments. Finally, they may all convene again in one location to work out the final details and sign the settlement agreement.

c. SELECTING A MEDIATOR

Not all mediators are suitable for mediating international business disputes. Parties not only should select a mediator who is trained and experienced in the standard techniques of mediation, but also who is trained and experienced in dealing with disputes in which cross-cultural differences can contribute to the conflict and impede its resolution.

Furthermore, parties may have difficulty selecting a mediator that is viewed as neutral. Parties must be confident in the mediator's neutrality so that they will trust disclosing information and trust the mediator's initiatives. Even though professional mediators know to scrupulously maintain their neutrality, parties may still be skeptical of any mediator from the country of another party.

Fortunately, these concerns are not as weighty in mediations which is a nonbinding process then in arbitrations where the neutral possesses decisionmaking authority. Parties who do not trust the mediator can simply walk away from the mediation, an option that is not available in arbitrations in which parties must demonstrate prejudice as a basis for disqualifying an arbitrator.

International parties have several options for selecting a mediator that is viewed as neutral; each option offers different advantages:

(i) Parties may select a mediator from a neutral third country. The parties' attorneys can contact such organizations as the American Arbitration Association or Center for Public Resources to see if their rosters include mediators from the neutral country.

(ii) Parties may select co-mediators, with one mediator from the country of each party. This option offers the obvious advantage of a balanced team of mediators. But, it presents the risk of creating a mediation team of neutrals with different philosophies and styles who may have difficulty working together. Mediation is not like arbitration where the neutrals arrive from different countries with different legal and cultural upbringings but who have common training in working together in a highly structured setting for deliberation and decision-making. In contrast, the mediation process is much more fluid and flexible shaped by the personalities and styles of the mediators, and as result, may not proceed as smoothly with a team of mediators who are not compatible with each other. This is not to say that team mediations cannot work. There is a long history of success in the United States of using team mediations in community disputes and public

B. INTERNATIONAL ADR CLAUSES FOR BUSINESS DISPUTES

policy disputes, especially environmental disputes. But, parties should be sure that they select mediators who are comfortable working with each other.

(iii) Parties may decide that the country of the mediator is not a significant factor. Realizing that the mediator has no decisionmaking power, they may be less concerned about the country of the neutral and more concerned about her credentials and experience as a mediator. Instead, they may find it convenient and less expensive to select a mediator from the country in which the mediation is being held. This approach can be attractive when the case is in a U.S. court, for instance, and all the parties (foreign and domestic) have retained local counsel. As a compromise, parties could seek out a local mediator who is a nationality of a neutral country.

d. STYLE OF MEDIATION

In international mediations, U.S. attorneys should be careful to clarify the style of mediation[15] envisioned because distinctive and unusual variations of mediation can be occasionally encountered in the international business arena. Some foreign attorneys may expect a more structured and formal process than customarily practiced in U.S. domestic mediations.[16] The mediator, for instance, might investigate the facts and law and issue a written report containing her recommendations.[17] In another unfamiliar arrangement, each party in an international dispute may designate a mediator, then the mediators meet with each other to hammer out a resolution that is presented to the parties for their confirmation.[18] Because some of these approaches are not common in domestic mediations, parties should guard against surprises by inquiring specifically about the type of international mediation each party contemplates. This inquiry is essential in order to avoid a cross-cultural misunderstanding.

e. CONFIDENTIALITY OF MEDIATION PROCESS

One of the great benefits of mediation, its confidentiality, can be less

---

15. See Chapter 3 on styles of domestic mediators. For articles, see, S. Silbey & S. Merry, Mediator Settlement Strategies, 8 Law & Policy 7 (1986); L. Riskin, "Understanding Mediators' Orientations, Strategies, and Techniques: A Grid for the Perplexed" 1 Harv. Neg. L. Rev. 7 (1996); R. Baruch Bush & J. Folger, The Promise of Mediation: Responding to Conflict Through Empowerment and Recognition (1994).

16. See, L. Reif, Conciliation as a Mechanism for the Resolution of International Economic and Business Disputes, 14 Fordham Intl LJ 578, 582–587 (1991/92).

17. See, L. Reif, Conciliation as a Mechanism for the Resolution of International Economic and Business Disputes, 14 Fordham Intl LJ 578, 585–587 (1991/92) and Tobi

Dress, "International Commercial Mediation and Conciliation" 10 Loy. L.A. Intl. & Comp. L.J.569, 574(1988).

18. See, William Fox, Jr., International Commercial Agreements 193 (1992) and L. Reif, "Conciliation as a Mechanism for the Resolution of International Economic and Business Disputes", 14 Fordham Intl LJ 578, 632–633 (1991/92). A variation of a joint conciliation was developed by the AAA with a Chinese foreign trade organization in which each party appoints a conciliator and then the two conciliators jointly conciliate the dispute. Michael F. Hoellering, "World Trade to Arbitrate or Mediate—That Is The Question" 49 Disp.Res. J. 67, 68–69(1994).

936 CHAPTER VI INTERNATIONAL DISPUTE RESOLUTION

secure internationally than domestically[19] due to the less developed and untested laws in some countries.

f. ENFORCING SETTLEMENT AGREEMENTS

In cross-border disputes, attorneys should give special attention to how any resulting settlement agreement will be enforced. In domestic disputes, attorneys know that they can always fall back on the local U.S. court in the jurisdiction in which the agreement was signed to remedy any breaches. In cross-border enforcement actions, the local court option in a foreign country can be less reliable and take more time and expense. Attorneys need to retain local counsel in the breaching party's country and commence a lawsuit in a foreign jurisdiction with all the risks and uncertainties of transnational litigation. These burdens of cross-border enforcement can be less onerous, however, in a foreign country with a mature legal system where the client does regular business and already has local counsel.

In cross-border disputes, parties can more easily enforce a settlement agreement when it is the by-product of an arbitration proceeding. Rather then assuming the risks of enforcing a settlement agreement in a transnational lawsuit, parties can request an arbitral tribunal to incorporate the settlement agreement into an arbitration award. This option is explicitly authorized by both domestic and international arbitration rules.[20] The resulting "consent" award may be enforceable in foreign jurisdictions under the relatively reliable procedures of the New York Convention on Recognition and Enforcement of Foreign Arbitral Awards.[21]

This method of enforcement works relatively smoothly for parties who sign a settlement agreement after the arbitration proceeding has been initiated and the arbitral tribunal formed. If no tribunal has yet been constituted, however, parties have several other options for facilitating enforcement. First, parties could add to a settlement agreement a personal jurisdiction clause. Under the clause, parties would agree to submit to the personal jurisdiction of a domestic court for the purpose of enforcing a

---

19. See Chapter 3 on confidentiality.

20. See, e.g. AAA Commercial Arbitration Rules, Rule 44 (July 1, 1996); AAA International Arbitration Rules, Art. 29(1)(April 1, 1997); UNCITRAL Model Law on International Commercial Arbitration, Art. 30(1985); UNCITRAL Arbitration Rules, Art. 34 (1)(1976); and ICC Rules of Arbitration, Art. 26 (January 1, 1998).

21. For discussion of the New York convention, see Notes and Questions after subsection E.

There is no international convention for the recognition and enforcement of settlements although at least one group has proposed a "Draft of a Convention for the Enforcement of Conciliation Settlements." See, Dr. Ottoarndt Glossner, "Enforcement of Conciliation Settlements" 11 Intl. Bus. Lawyer 151 (1983). For discussion of NY Convention, see Section E, Notes and Comments.

settlement agreement. Second, parties could simply include in a settlement agreement a clause that provides that any breaches would be resolved in arbitration. This is an obvious precaution that can be too easily forgotten. The arbitration clause would give an aggrieved party access to an arbitration process that would produce an award enforceable under the New York Convention. Third, parties could initiate an arbitration proceeding for the purpose of securing a consent award. This strategy would increase the expense and time in connection with settling a dispute but may be worthwhile in order to give parties the added security offered by a consent arbitration award. However, there may be some uncertainty as to whether a consent arbitration award would be enforceable because some jurisdictions might consider this to be a sham arbitration proceeding that is "contrary to the public policy of that country."[22]

To reduce the time and costs of enforcing settlement agreements through arbitration awards, parties should consider adopting "fact-track" arbitration procedures. While these fast-track procedures were a response to the complaints about the length and expense of conventional arbitrations and have not been widely used, these new procedures can benefit parties who need a quick procedure to enforce a settlement agreement. Parties could trigger the expedited process either when the settlement agreement is signed in order to secure a "consent" award or when the settlement agreement is allegedly breached.[23]

Finally, parties can further reduce the costs and length of the arbitration proceeding by resorting to a non-administered arbitration process. Instead of contracting with an administering organization, parties can

22. New York Convention, Art. V.2.(b).

23. Expedited procedures have been adopted by several organizations. See, e.g. Commercial Arbitration and Mediation Center of the Americas, Arbitration Rules, Art. 39 (March 15, 1996); WIPO Expedited Arbitration Rules (October 1, 1994); and Stockholm Rules for Expedited Arbitrations (Arbitration Institute of the Stockholm Chamber of Commerce, July 1995). Also see, Eva Muller "Fast–Track Arbitration—Meeting the Demands of the Next Millennium," 15 J.of Intl.Arb.5(1998)(comparison of fast-track arbitration rules issued by seven institutions).

The new Commercial Arbitration and Mediation Center for the Americas, for instance, issued rules for expediting claims no greater than $50,000 although the procedures can be adopted for larger claims. The expedited procedures shorten an arbitration proceeding by relying on telephone notices, limiting the number of arbitrators and number of hearing days to one, shortening the procedure for selecting the arbitrator, and reducing the number of days for giving notice of hearing and for rendering an award. See,

Commercial Arbitration and Mediation Center of the Americas, Arbitration Rules, Art. 39 (March 15, 1996)(CAMCA is a Center created by major national dispute resolution organizations in Canada, United States, and Mexico for dealing with trade disputes in the free trade area created by NAFTA.)

It is even possible to expedite an arbitration proceeding under the regular rules of arbitration. This was accomplished in an ICC arbitration when the ICC along with the arbitrators, attorneys, and parties in a multimillion dollar dispute decided to make a concerted effort to expedite an arbitration proceeding. Through their determined effort, the arbitration took an unprecedented two months from initiation to issuance of the award, instead of what could have been 18–24 months. See, Christian Buhring–Uhle, Arbitration and Mediation in International Business 110–111 (1996)and articles written by participants in the ICC arbitration in Special Section: Fast Track Arbitration 2 Am. Rev. Int'l Arb. 137–162 (1991).

agree to self-administer the process by following the specially designed UNCITRAL Arbitration Rules or the Non–Administered International Arbitration Rules of the CPR Institute for Dispute Resolution.

g. BACK–UP ADJUDICATORY PROCESS

International mediations are not automatically backed-up by a reliable adjudicatory process. Instead of relying on the default process of transnational litigation with all of its attendant uncertainties, the attorney should add a provision that supports the settlement process with a private, binding adjudicatory process.[24] The back-up process is necessary in order to provide a means for enforcing a settlement agreement or for finally resolving the dispute.

2. INTERNATIONAL ADJUDICATORY OPTIONS

The two primary adjudicatory options for backing-up mediations are transnational litigation and arbitration. Both options have in common the designation of a neutral third party who will hear the case and issue a decision that will bind the parties and bring the conflict to closure. For international business disputes, the more widely used of these two options is arbitration[25] because it ameliorates a number of the risks and concerns that complicates transnational litigation.[26] Instead of parties contending with the gaps in transnational litigation law and any troublesome features of different national court systems, parties design a private, supranational dispute resolution process that operates separately from disparate national court systems. But, the private process does not operate independently; national court systems still perform an essential back-up function in case a party needs to enforce an agreement to arbitrate or an arbitration award.

In comparing transnational litigation with international arbitration, it has been suggested that international arbitration is not really an alternative to litigation but is simply a better way to litigate international business conflicts.

Christian Buhring–Uhle, Arbitration And Mediation In International Business

141–143 (1996)

[I]t appears that the reasons why international commercial arbitration has become the principal means of dispute resolution in international

---

24. See Section F on combining settlement options with arbitration

25. See, W. Lawrence Craig, "Some Trends and Developments in the Laws and Practice of International Commercial Arbitration" 36 Tex. Intl L.J.1,2(1995).

26. See Chapter V B. See also, Gary B. Born, International Commercial Arbitration in the United States 5–9 (1994) and Richard

H. Kreindler "Arbitration or Litigation?" ADR Issues in Transnational Disputes 79 Dispute Resolution Journal 79 (1997) (Both authors point out how the advantages of arbitration cannot be guaranteed. For example, Born notes that countries hostile toward arbitrations have enacted laws that pose obstacles to the enforcement of arbitral awards.)

business have more to do with the specific problems of litigating international disputes in national courts than with the desire to create a type of procedure that is fundamentally different from litigation.

The two considerations that stand out as the most significant advantages of international commercial arbitration, the *neutrality* of the forum and the *international enforceability* of the results clearly address two fundamental problems of transnational litigation: whether justified or not, players in international commerce do not seem to have confidence in the complete neutrality of national courts towards foreign litigants and therefore have a strong desire to avoid having to stand trial in the other side's "home court." This consideration is particularly important if one of the parties is a government or a state-owned entity because on the one hand governments are reluctant—and sometimes prevented by constitutional constraints—to submit to the jurisdiction of an another government and on the other hand private entities tend to abhor the prospect of confronting a sovereign in its own courts.

The participants in international commerce seem to be painfully aware of the deficiencies of the legal framework of transnational litigation and particularly the problems of enforcing judgments in a foreign jurisdiction:

> "If for judgments there existed a convention similar to the New York convention, 50% of the big international commercial arbitrations would be court litigation."

A consideration that was regarded as less relevant but that is clearly connected to the enforceability aspect is the degree of *voluntary compliance* with arbitral awards which, according to the ICC is very high. Although there are no data available on *why* parties comply voluntarily, it is plausible to assume that an effective enforcement mechanism operates as a strong motivation.

The next group of advantages of international arbitration that were considered significant are, again, unrelated to any search for "alternative" methods of dispute resolution. *Confidentiality* simply means that the public—and the competitors—are excluded from the proceedings but it has no bearing on what type of procedure it is that is being conducted behind closed doors. And the objective of having the dispute decided by a "judge" with *expertise* in the subject matter and of curtailing the excesses of protracted *discovery* and lengthy *appeals* have to be understood as the desire to improve the quality and effectiveness of litigation rather than to create a different type of procedure.

Finally, the objectives which are at the heart of the quest for more informal, "alternative" methods of dispute resolution, the desire to achieve a process that is *faster, less expensive* and *more amicable*, seem to have only marginal relevance for the choice of arbitration in international commerce. This may be due either to the perception that, in international arbitration, these advantages do not materialize, or that these qualities are not among the real priorities of the participants. Both reasons seem to be—at least in part—true: more than one half of the respondents denied that arbitration is less expensive and more than one third disputed the notion that it was faster or more amicable. And only about one tenth of the respondents affirmed that speed, cost savings and amicability were "highly relevant" factors for the choice of arbitration as a method of dispute resolution. As one practitioner explained:

> "...parties are often not that concerned with costs because their main preoccupation is with the outcome of the procedure; the advantage of arbitration is not to cut costs, it is a tailor-made procedure that emphasizes quality."

In sum, what international arbitration offers and what the participants expect is not an "alternative" to litigation but *a system of litigation that works in an international context* and avoids the pitfalls of transnational litigation in national courts. In the words of the Secretary General of the ICC Court of Arbitration:

> "...[the reasons that] people are driven to international commercial arbitration in large measure is not that they want a simpler form of justice but that they want a *forum in which to have confidence,* and this forum *is the main service the arbitral institutions have to offer...*"

These justifications for resorting to arbitration does not mean arbitrations are always preferable:

> "Nonetheless, sometimes *litigation can be preferable.* Where the enforcement of judgments abroad is either unnecessary (because the defendant has sufficient assets in the jurisdiction of the court that decided the case) or where it is enhanced by international agreements such as the Brussels Convention, some of the key advantages of arbitration are obsolete. Also, in certain standard types of cases accelerated procedures like summary or documents-only proceedings may offer a more efficient form of dispute resolution.... Another problem may be that in some jurisdictions arbitration agreements are interpreted to preclude interim measures of protection by the courts. And litigation may be the only solution where the assets of the defendant are located in a country that is not party to any relevant international agreement and generally does not enforce foreign arbitral awards." C. Buhring–Uhle, Arbitration and Mediation in International Business 88 (1996)

NOTES AND QUESTIONS

1. In the Gans article, which of his reasons for using settlement processes in international business disputes do you find most convincing? Can you think of other reasons for using settlement processes in international disputes? Why do you think mediations are not more widely used for resolving international business disputes?

B. INTERNATIONAL ADR CLAUSES FOR BUSINESS DISPUTES

2. At least three issues deserve special attention when you are considering using technologies for convening international mediations. (i) Effective Meeting Place. Do you think any of the technological ways of meeting will provide a satisfactory means of mediating? What factors should you weigh when deciding which of these suboptimal meeting options to use at a particular point in the mediation process? (ii) Access to Videoconferencing. In order to preserve the perception of neutrality, should the neutral use a separate facility even though it might be more convenient and less costly to share a facility with one of the parties? (iii) Security. Is the technology sufficiently secure for the type of information that will be discussed and exchanged?

3. In a dispute with a party from India that is pending in a New York federal court, how would you propose that the parties select a mediator that would be perceived as neutral to both sides?

4. What key provisions do you think should be included in an agreement to mediate an international dispute?

5. Do you find convincing the contention of Christian Buhring–Uhle that international arbitration is not an "alternative" to litigation but is "*a system of litigation that works in an international context*"? Can this same point be made about the use of domestic arbitration? If so, then what does it mean to describe a process as an alternative dispute resolution method?

3. INSTITUTIONAL OR AD HOC ADMINISTRATION OF PROCESSES[27]

A number of well-established and new international organizations are in the business of administering dispute resolution processes.[28] These organizations have their own professional staff, facilities, and procedural rules to govern dispute resolution processes. They are primarily in the arbitration business although they also serve mediations. The organizations can be sorted into two groups: ones that handle virtually any business dispute[29] and ones that specialize in handling certain types of disputes.[30]

The more complex the dispute resolution process and conflict, the more administrative tasks someone must handle, and the more appealing it is to use an independent organization .. To set up an arbitration, for instance, someone must prepare and send notices to parties, administer the procedures for selecting arbitrators, arrange the scheduling of hearings (time,

---

27. See Chapter V Section B.1. Also see, C. Buhring–Uhle, Arbitration and Mediation in International Business 45–51 (1996); William K. Slate II, "International Arbitration: Do Institutions Make a Difference?" 31 Wake Forest LR 41, 52–59 (1996).

28. See Chapter 4 regarding description of international arbitration institutions.

29. For example, there are the International Chamber of Commerce (ICC), American Arbitration Association (AAA), London Court of International Arbitration (LCIA), The Arbitration Institute of the Stockholm Chamber of Commerce, and the CPR Institute for Dispute Resolution.

30. For example, there are the International Center for the Settlement of Investment Disputes (ICSID), China International Economic and Trade Arbitration Commission (CIETAC), Commercial Arbitration and Mediation for the Americas (CAMCA), and World Intellectual Property Organization Arbitration Center (WIPO).

date, and place), and deal with any post-award enforcement issues. A reputable neutral institution has the know how to handle these administrative details, offers its time-tested rules, provides access to a list of professional and qualified neutrals, and insulates arbitrators from the parties. Moreover, an institution can offer expertise in determining whether an award meets legal requirements for enforcement in multiple jurisdictions. An arbitration process administered by a highly-regarded institution also gives its award additional credibility when a party seeks voluntary or legal enforcement. Due to these numerous benefits, many parties use an independent institution to administer their arbitrations.

Institutions can be especially attractive for administering an international dispute resolution process because the process can be more complex than administering a domestic one. Straightforward tasks of communications and scheduling become more complicated when parties and neutrals reside in different countries, speaking different languages. There also is a greater likelihood that parties will need professional translators, bilingual stenographic transcripts, and an understanding of different foreign legal requirements for enforcing settlement agreements, arbitral awards, or agreements to use a dispute resolution process.

All this convenience and support can be costly: a neutral institution charges substantial administrative fees and can take time to provide its services. As an alternative, parties can elect to self-administer a process, known as ad hoc administration. In practice, parties can find it cumbersome and at times awkward to both self-administer a process and participate in it. But, this option can be more flexible, quicker, and cost-effective, if certain critical conditions are satisfied: if parties are cooperating, if they can efficiency negotiate the administrative details to be done, and if they can proficiently handle the administrative responsibilities.[31] However, even with ad hoc administration, parties usually find it helpful to select an "appointing authority"[32] to handle the vital stage of securing the arbitrators (selection, challenges, and replacement of arbitrators .)[33]

4. ADOPTING OR ADAPTING OFF–THE–SHELF PROCEDURAL RULES

Virtually all the dispute resolution institutions offer their own procedural rules to govern arbitrations and mediations. Some institutions offer

---

31. The United Nations Commission on International Trade Law (UNCITRAL), which does not serve as an administering institution, has published helpful instructions on how to organize arbitral proceedings. " UNCITRAL Notes on Organizing Arbitral Proceedings," U.N. Doc. V.96–84935.

32. A number of established institutions are willing to serve as an appointing authority including the ICC, AAA, CPR and Stockholm Chamber of Commerce.

33. In the standard clause proposed in the CPR's Non–Administered International Arbitration Rules & Commentary, CPR suggests that a neutral organization be "designated to perform the functions specified in Rule 6 [selection of arbitrator], Rule 7.7(b) [challenges of arbitrators regarding independence or impartiality], Rule 7.8 [replacement of arbitrators], and Rule 7.9 [failure to act by arbitrators]. "(bracketed information added.)

B. International ADR Clauses for Business Disputes **943**

rules that are designed for ad hoc administrations[34] such as the rules designed by the United Nations Commission on International Trade Law [35] (UNCITRAL.) These various mediation and arbitration rules can either be adopted intact or modified to meet special needs of the parties. Of course, parties can create their own rules from scratch but this option would be an expensive route to essentially re-inventing much of what has already been devised and tested by others.

a. MEDIATION

Almost every major international dispute resolution institution has developed and published rules for mediations. The rules generally do not contain any distinctively international provisions. They cover procedures for initiating and terminating a mediation and for appointing a mediator. They address the role of the mediator, conduct of the mediation, confidentiality of the process, and matters related to payment for mediation services.

Two of these rules deserve special attention. Because cross-cultural confusion over the role of the mediator is unlikely to be eliminated by the rules, the rules may need to be modified to clarify the style of mediation that the parties envision. Even though mediation rules generally establish the confidentiality of the process, the degree of protection can vary among the rules.[36] Deficiencies can be remedied by the parties executing a supplemental confidentiality agreement.[37]

b. ARBITRATION[38]

Comprehensive arbitration rules are offered by UNCITRAL and every significant dispute resolution institution. Given the abundance of choices,

---

34. CPR also has designed rules specifically for ad hoc administration. See CRP's Non–Administered International Arbitration Rules & Commentary (1995).

35. UNCITRAL's arbitration rules, adopted by the General Assembly of the United Nations, are designed to be broadly acceptable in countries with different legal and economic systems, whether common law or civil law jurisdictions or capital-exporting or capital-importing nations.

UNCITRAL is not a dispute resolution institution. UNCITRAL was established by the General Assembly of the United Nations in 1966 to promote "the progressive harmonization and unification of the law of international trade" (G.A. Res. 2205, 21 U.N. GAOR, Annex 3, U.N. Doc. A/6396 and (Add. 1 & 2)(1966), *reprinted in* 1 Y.B. Comm'n Int'l. Trade L. 65 (1968–70), U.N. Doc. A/CN.9/SER.A/1970.)

Membership in UNCITRAL is limited to nation-states. Among its many significant

contributions, it adopted Arbitration Rules in 1976 (U.N. Doc. Sales No. E.7 v. 6 (1977)), Conciliation Rules in 1980 (U.N. Doc. A/35/17 (1980)), Model Law on International Commercial Arbitration in 1985 (U.N. Doc. A/35/17 (1980)), and updated its Notes on Organizing Arbitral Proceedings in 1996 (U.N. Doc. V.96–84935.)

36. See, e.g. ICC Rules of Optional Conciliation, Arts. 6, 10, 11 (January 1, 1988); WIPO Mediation Rules, Art. 14–17 (October 1, 1994); UNCITRAL Conciliation Rules, Art. 14 (1984); and AAA Commercial Mediation Rules, Rule 12 (January 1, 1992).

37. As noted earlier, however, an agreement cannot guarantee that the confidentiality of the process will be respected by the courts in every jurisdiction. See Section 1 on "Confidentiality of Mediation Process."

38. Procedural practices in international arbitrations changed significantly during the 1970s and 80s. International arbitrations

944   CHAPTER VI   INTERNATIONAL DISPUTE RESOLUTION

how do parties determine which set of rules to adopt in an arbitration clause?

> The nature of a contract, the type of contractual disputes likely to arise, and the sorts of interim and final remedies likely to be sought are factors which must be taken into account in selecting one of the available systems of rules. In some cases, political considerations may also play a role. For example, it has been reported that for years the People's Republic of China adamantly refused to use ICC Rules because the ICC is organized on the basis of national committees, one of which is Taiwan's. In comparing the relative advantages and disadvantages of each set of arbitral rules, the prudent lawyer must focus on the way in which each set of rules will interact with the unique components of the specific contract and the specific parties. W. Michael Reisman, W. Laurence Craig, William Park, and Jan Paulsson, International Commercial Arbitration 243 (1997)

Unfortunately, it is not unusual for parties to fail to examine the rules they are considering adopting. They just incorporate them wholesale into the ADR clause. The parties then hope that, if the rules must be used, any surprises in the pre-packaged rules will be small ones. In international deals, the risks of bigger surprises are bigger, increasing the importance of addressing critical questions before a conflict arises.

Parties should give special attention to a number of issues that can impact on the quality and substantive outcome of the arbitration process. Boilerplate international clauses usually recommend adding several other provisions.[39]

The ICC suggests a typical arbitration clause:

> All disputes arising out of or in connection with the present contract shall be finally settled under the Rules of Arbitration of the International Chamber of Commerce by one or more arbitrators appointed in accordance with the said Rules.

developed initially as an informal process cultivated in Continental Europe, primarily in Paris under the auspices of the ICC. In the civil law tradition, international arbitrators gave considerable attention to the law while giving little attention to the development and consideration of the facts. International arbitrations were dominated by Continental academics and an exclusive "club" of gentlemen (yes, all men) engaged in business affairs.

During the 1970s and 80s, procedures in international arbitrations were transformed by pressures exerted by the increased participation of Anglo–American law firms in international business deals. When the major U.S. law firms went international, they exported what they knew best; they knew how to aggressively represent their clients in adver-

sarial proceedings. U.S. lawyers were determined to employ a U.S. style litigation strategy in the arbitrations. These pressures lead to what became known as the "judicialization" of international commercial arbitrations. See, Yves Dezalay and Bryant G. Garth, Dealing in Virtue—International Commercial Arbitration and the Construction of a Transnational Legal Order chs. 3,4,5 (1996). Also see, Rau and Sherman, Tradition and Innovation in International Arbitration Procedure, 30 Tex. Int'l L.J. 89 (1995).

39. See e.g., ICC Rules of Arbitration (January 1, 1998), AAA International Arbitration Rules (April 1, 1997), CPR Non–Administered International Arbitration Rules & Commentary(1995), and UNCITRAL Arbitration Rules (1976).

The ICC further suggests that "[p]arties are reminded that it may be desirable for them to stipulate in the arbitration clause itself the law governing the contract, the number of arbitrators and the place and language of the arbitration."[40] If the parties omit adding these additional provisions, the parties are then electing to rely on the arbitrator(s) to impose them when needed, which may result in unpleasant surprises and undesirable results.

In the following article, the former Secretary General of the ICC Court of Arbitration discusses several key provisions that parties should consider when drafting an international arbitration clause.

Stephen R. Bond,* "How To Draft An Arbitration Clause"

J. of Int'l Arb. 65, 66, 72, 74–75, 76, 78 (June, 1989)

So, even businessmen who wish to deal with lawyers as little as possible have a major interest in involving an attorney in the negotiation of the dispute settlement provision, unless those businessmen wish to prove, once again, the old adage that arbitration is a procedure that has too few lawyers in the beginning (when the clause is drafted) and too many in the end (when an arbitration is actually under way).

I would like to present some thoughts as to elements which should be considered in drafting and negotiating an arbitration clause.

* * *

c. THE PLACE OF ARBITRATION

The importance of the place of arbitration cannot be overestimated. Its legislation determines the likelihood and extent of involvement of national courts in the conduct of the arbitration (either for judicial "assistance" or "interference"), the likelihood of enforceability of the arbitral award (depending on what international conventions the *situs* State is a party to), and the extent and nature of any mandatory procedural rules that you will have to adhere to in the conduct of the arbitration. (For example, in Saudi Arabia, the arbitrators must be Muslim and male.) Such factors are of far greater importance than the touristic attractions of any particular place

---

40. See ICC Publication No. 581 which contains the new ICC Rules of Arbitration that became effective on January 1, 1998.

* The author analyzed the arbitration clauses contained in the 237 arbitration cases presented in the prior year to the lCC's Court of Arbitration.

that sometimes appear to be the decisive factor in making this decision.... This mention of *situs* is, after the choice of applicable law, the element most often added to the basic ICC arbitration clause. The choice of the place of arbitration may literally determine the outcome of the case. In one ICC arbitration between a Finnish corporation and an Australian corporation. London was selected as the place of arbitration in the arbitration clause. The case involved royalty payments allegedly not made and the purported cancellation of the relevant agreement in 1976. In 1982 the licensor initiated arbitration. The arbitrator found that because the arbitration was taking place in England, the statute of limitations contained in the U.K. Limitation Act had to be applied. So, even assuming that Finnish law was applicable and Finnish law had no comparable statute of limitations, the arbitrator applied the relevant U.K. 6–year statute of limitations and barred all claims arising prior to 1976, which effectively meant all claims.

* * *

d. APPLICABLE LAW

While the choice of the law to be applied by the arbitrators to determine the substantive issues before them is not an element necessary for the validity of an arbitration clause, it is certainly desirable for the parties to agree upon the applicable law in the arbitration clause if at all possible. Failure to do so is a significant factor in increasing the time and cost of an arbitration. Moreover, the decision of the arbitral tribunal on the matter (for it is an issue to be decided by the arbitrators, even if institutional arbitration is used) may bring an unpleasant surprise to one of the parties. Finally, where an institution is to select the chairman or sole arbitrator it is, as a practical matter, far easier to appoint the best possible person when it is known in what country's law the arbitrator should be most expert.

For these reasons, the element most often added to the contract, often directly in the arbitration clause itself, is that of the law applicable to the contract.

* * *

A few points should be borne in mind in deciding upon an applicable law and I will very briefly mention them.

Firstly, it is preferable that the legal system you agree upon in fact is developed in regard to the specific issues likely to arise.

Secondly, you may wish to exclude the conflict of laws principles of the chosen law, either explicitly or by specifying the "substantive law" of the particular country concerned.

Thirdly, be sure that the law you choose considers the subject matter of the contract to be arbitrable. Copyright or patent law questions, antitrust matters, etc. are often not permitted to be resolved by arbitration, but only in the national courts.

e. Composition of the Arbitral Tribunal

The next element which should be given the most serious attention is that of the composition of the arbitral tribunal. How many arbitrators do you want? How should they be selected? Should they have any particular qualifications? No broad generalities can cover all the situations likely to arise.

* * *

f. Language of the Arbitration

Many parties may mistakenly believe that the language in which the contract is written will automatically be the language of any arbitration arising out of that contract. It is true that the ICC Rules, for example, state in Article 15(3) that the arbitrator shall give "due regard ... in particular to the language of the contract" in determining the language of the arbitration. It will, however, be for the arbitral tribunal to decide the question should the parties not have agreed on it.

As can well be imagined, simultaneous interpretation at hearings and translation of all documents into two or more languages are enormously expensive and time-consuming. If it is not possible to agree on a language in the arbitration clause then it would be desirable to try to agree either that costs for interpretation and translation are shared or else borne by the party requiring the interpretation or translation.

* * *

CONCLUSIONS

I will not end this presentation by revealing to you the all-purpose, miraculous arbitration clause, because there is probably no single clause that is appropriate in every case. You cannot escape the need, each time you negotiate an arbitration clause, to engage in a rigorous analysis of the circumstances related to the particular transaction in order to produce an arbitration clause tailored to the situation at hand. In the long run, this work will result in immeasurable savings of time and money.

NOTES AND QUESTIONS

1. When drafting an arbitration clause, there are some other provisions that deserve special attention:

a. Party–Appointed Arbitrators

In international arbitrations, parties ardently favor tripartite tribunals in which each party appoints an arbitrator and then either the party-appointed arbitrators or an appointing institution selects the chair of the tribunal. This preference for party-appointed arbitrators is surprising because it appears to violate the principles of neutrality and independence

CHAPTER VI INTERNATIONAL DISPUTE RESOLUTION

that form the foundation of judicial justice.[41] Yet, parties commonly select this procedure because:

> In arbitration, parties accept virtually non-appealable finality of the arbitrators' decision largely in exchange for the ability to participate in the selection of their tribunal rather than accept an anonymous, governmentally chosen decision maker—a judge—whose rulings may be less predictable but generally are subject to appellate review.... Party-appointed arbitrators also may be expected to play a role in selecting the third arbitrator, bringing their judgment and experience to bear on this important task. James H. Carter "Living with the Party–Appointed Arbitrator: Judicial Confusion, Ethical Codes and Practical Advice" 3 Am. Rev.153(1992)

> At least one of the persons who will decide the case will listen carefully—even sympathetically—to the presentation, and if the arbitrator is well chosen, will study the documents with care. That fact alone is likely to spur the other arbitrators to study the documents as well, whether or not they would have done so in any case. Thus the presence of a well chosen party-appointed arbitrator goes a long way toward promising (if not assuring) a fair hearing and a considered decision.

> [I]n an international case a party-appointed arbitrator serves as a translator. I do not mean just of language.... I mean rather the translation of legal culture, and not infrequently of the law itself, when matters that are self-evident to lawyers from one country are puzzling to lawyers from another. Andreas F. Lowenfeld "The Party–Appointed Arbitrator in International Controversies: Some Reflections" 30 Tex. Intl L.J.59, 65 (1995)

Must a party select an arbitrator one who is independent and impartial?[42] Party-appointed arbitrators in international arbitrations strive for greater neutrality[43] than observed in domestic arbitrations.[44] The expected

41. Alan Scott Rau "Integrity in Private Judging" 38 S. Tex. L.Rev. 485, 497–514 (1997).

42. See Chapter V D on party-appointed representatives and international commercial arbitrations.

43. See, ICC Rules of Arbitration, Arts. 7(1) and 11(1)(January 1, 1998); International Bar Association Ethics for International Arbitrators, Rule 5 (1987)(restricts communications between arbitrators and parties); UNCITRAL Arbitration Rules, Art. 10(1)(1976)(challenges to arbitrator's impartiality and independence); James H. Carter, "Rights & Obligations of the Arbitrator" 52 Disp. Res. J. 56(1997); and Stephen Bond "The Selection of ICC Arbitrators and the Requirement of Independence" 4 Arb. Intl

300 (1980)(examines the ICC rules and practices on appointment of independent arbitrators).

In the new AAA International Arbitration Rules, Article 7 states that "[n]o party or anyone acting on its behalf shall have any ex parte communication relating to the case with any arbitrator, or with any candidate for appointment as party-appointed arbitrator except to advise the candidate of the general nature of the controversy and of the anticipated proceedings and to discuss the candidate's qualifications, availability or independence in relation to the parties, or to discuss the suitability of candidates for selection as a third arbitrator where the parties or party-designated arbitrators are to participate in that selection. No party or anyone acting on its behalf shall have any ex parte communica-

B. International ADR Clauses for Business Disputes

949

degree of neutrality guides parties in how they relate to their party-appointed arbitrator. Should parties be permitted to interview candidates? What can parties discuss during an interview? What ex parte contacts, if any, can parties have with their party-appointed arbitrator during the arbitration proceeding?

b. Interim Relief

The availability of interim relief by a court in aid of arbitration—in the form, for example, of an attachment or a temporary injunction—is often quite unclear. This is discussed in Chapter V, Section D.2.e. It is important, therefore, for parties to investigate relevant arbitration rules and national laws to determine whether they can secure interim relief in court or from the arbitration panel pending the issuance of the arbitration award.

c. Currency of Awards[45]

Parties may want to resolve in what currency any awards or settlement will be paid. If the choice is among currencies that are freely convertible in international markets, parties should resolve which party will assume the foreign exchange risk. Foreign parties should determine whether the local law where the arbitration is taking place requires the foreign party to accept payments in the local currency which could be a problem if the local currency is not freely convertible. The party then must figure out whether the local government permits exchanging local currency for hard currency.

d. Waiver of Sovereign Immunity.[46]

If one of the parties is a governmental entity such as a state owned automobile manufacturer, the other party should determine whether the governmental entity has waived its immunity from lawsuits. Many countries have adopted laws that waive sovereign immunity for "commercial acts." To be safe, the non-governmental party should negotiate a waiver of sovereign immunity that would be included in the dispute resolution clause of the business contract.

2. An attorney's position on a provision may be shaped as much by her cultural upbringing and professional experience as by her strategic views of what best serves the interests of her client.

tion relating to the case with any candidate for presiding arbitrator." AAA International Arbitration Rules, Arts. 7 (April 1, 1997)(amendments to the 1993 International Arbitration Rules).

44. In domestic arbitrations, party-appointed arbitrators are sometimes described as non-neutral arbitrators or partisan arbitrators who may not observe the same rules of ethical conduct as neutral arbitrators. In the 1977 Code of Ethics for Arbitrators in Commercial Disputes, Canon VII identifies which ethical obligations a "non-neutral arbi-

trator" should observe and which obligations are not applicable. For instance, in contrast with neutral arbitrators, non-neutral party-appointed arbitrators "may be predisposed toward the party who appointed them." See, Code of Ethics for Arbitrators in Commercial Disputes, Canon VII (ABA and AAA, 1977)

45. Jeswald W. Salacuse, Making Global Deals Ch. 7 (1991)

46. See Chapter VB1 where the use of the ICSID is considered for the Paris Disneyland contract between Disney Productions and the French Government.

CHAPTER VI INTERNATIONAL DISPUTE RESOLUTION

a. Discovery

Different philosophies about discovery can shape each party's views of appropriate discovery for arbitrations. U.S. lawyers are taught in law school and in practice to engage in thorough pre-hearing discovery. Many civil law lawyers view the U.S. style of discovery as excessive and oppressive, especially the broad and liberal view of what is discoverable and the wide use of depositions. Civil lawyers are brought up to rely on restricted discovery, limited to production of relevant, critical documents. It is in this environment of competing upbringings that parties try to negotiate a compromise discovery provision with which everyone can be comfortable. In practice, discovery in arbitrations reflect a philosophy closer to civil law than common law norms.[47]

b. Punitive Damages

Parties from different parts of the United States and the World follow different views on whether arbitrators should have the power to award punitive damages. Even if parties agree to adopt rules that make it clear that the tribunal has the authority, the award still may not be enforced by a local court that views the payment of punitive damages as a violation of local public policy.

c. Awarding Costs of Arbitration

Parties may enter negotiations with a cultural preference for either the English or American Rule for determining who will pay attorney fees and other costs of the arbitration. The American rule of each party paying her own costs regardless of outcome is not the practice everywhere.[48] Many civil law jurisdictions follow the English rule of the loser paying. Parties should be aware of these competing national practices when negotiating over which practice they want arbitrators to apply.

3. International arbitration has been widely embraced due in great part to the vital opportunity to enforce domestic arbitral awards in foreign courts. In what is probably the most important treaty in the field of international dispute resolution—the New York Convention,[49] the signatory countries gave up some of their sacred sovereignty by agreeing to enforce arbitration awards issued by foreign arbitration tribunals. Over a hundred nations have ratified the New York Convention.

The key features of the New York Convention can be found in its first five articles. Article I establishes the general obligation of a state to recognize and enforce foreign arbitral awards. The Article also gives each state the option to limit this obligation to awards made in the territory of

---

47. Jack J. Coe, Jr. ,International Commercial Arbitration: American Principles and Practice in a Global Context 242–244 (1997)

48. See, Dan B. Dobbs, Dobbs Law of Remedies, Section 3.10 (Vol. 1, 2nd Edition, 1993) (description of American rule including comparison with English rule).

49. 1958 Convention on Recognition and Enforcement of Foreign Arbitral Awards 21U.S.T.2517, 330 U.N.T.S.38, T.I.A.S. No. 6997 (1959)(known as the New York Convention). See Appendix G.

another contracting state (reciprocity reservation) and to disputes that are commercial under its own national law (commercial reservation). The United States has adopted both of these reservations. Article II limits enforcement of *agreements to arbitrate* to agreements that are (1) in writing and (2) that a local court does not find to be "null and void, inoperative or incapable of being performed." When these two conditions are met, the local court will refer the parties to arbitration. Article III imposes a national treatment-type obligation; a contracting state shall not impose "substantially more onerous conditions" on enforcement of foreign awards than enforcement of domestic awards. Article IV establishes the only conditions that must be satisfied by a party who seeks *enforcement of an arbitration award.* The conditions deal with authentication and certification of the award. Article V(1) sets forth grounds for refusing recognition and enforcement of a foreign award, grounds that can be asserted by a party against whom enforcement is sought. In addition to grounds familiar in domestic arbitration laws (e.g. procedural defects and lack of arbitrability), a court can refuse recognition when the foreign award had been set aside in the foreign country. Article V(2) sets forth grounds for a local court to act on its own motion to refuse recognition and enforcement. The two grounds include are when the subject matter is "not capable of settlement by arbitration under the law" of the local country and when recognition and enforcement "would be contrary to the public policy" of the local country.

At the recent celebration of the fortieth anniversary of the New York Convention, scholars and practitioners from around the world convened for the day at the United Nations to consider what the treaty has accomplished and what should be done to improve the treaty.[50] Everyone seemed to agree that the New York Convention has been a great success. Participants still suggested several areas for improvement. Procedures for local enforcement should be more uniform among different states.[51] Article II(2) provision on only enforcing arbitration agreements in writing should recognize the validity of agreements created by modern means of contract formation.[52] A supplementary convention should be adopted to provide for foreign enforcement of provisional and conservatory relief.[53] Finally, a local court should not be barred from enforcing a foreign award because a foreign court nullified the award, especially when the reasons may be considered internationally intolerable.[54] Participants thought that these improvements could

---

50. New York Convention Day—June 10, 1998 A/CN.9/1998/INF.1 (UN, 20 May 1998).

51. Robert Briner "Philosophy and Objectives of the Convention" in New York Convention Day—June 10, 1998 A/CN.9/1998/INF.1 pp. 2–3 (UN, 20 May 1998).

52. Neil Kaplan "New Developments on Written Form" in New York Convention Day—June 10, 1998 A/CN.9/1998/INF.1 pp. 5–6 (UN, 20 May 1998).

53. V.V. Veeder "Provisional and Conservatory Measures" in New York Convention Day—June 10, 1998 A/CN.9/1998/INF.1 p. 8 (UN, 20 May 1998).

54. Jan Paulsson "Awards Set Aside at Place of Arbitration" in New York Convention Day—June 10, 1998 A/CN.9/1998/INF.1 p. 10 (UN, 20 May 1998). For a contrary view, see William W. Park, Duty and Discre-

952 CHAPTER VI INTERNATIONAL DISPUTE RESOLUTION

be implemented through adoption of a supplementary treaty or more likely through enlightened domestic law or judicial interpretations.

4. Draft a three step dispute resolution clause in which the international parties agree to first try negotiating a settlement, then to try mediation, and finally to resolve any remaining issues in binding arbitration.

5. COMBINING SETTLEMENT PROCESSES WITH ARBITRATION

In this subsection, two very different dispute resolution designs are considered. Each design incorporates a process sequence that combines arbitration with settlement processes. The term settlement processes encompasses any initiative to settle a case ranging from full-fledged mediations by independent mediators to arbitrators simply encouraging parties to settle.

a. SET–ARB–SET–ARB

Private, inventive process designs are needed more in disputes between parties from different countries than in disputes that are domestic. At least when parties fail to plan for domestic disputes, parties can fall back on their own familiar and stable public court systems. Parties may not always find their domestic systems inviting but they are more manageable than the international default process of transnational litigation with its additional risks and unfamiliarity. When parties wait until an international dispute arises to design the dispute resolution process, parties face the unwieldy obstacles of again convening attorneys and possibly their clients when relationships are strained and when they are separated by large distances, time zones, culture and language. Therefore, international parties who want to avoid the public default process should try early to design a private process.

In the following excerpt, Christian Buhring–Uhle builds on the familiar two step med-arb option[55] by recommending a more dynamic process design in which parties shift back and forth between consensus-based and adjudicatory processes until the dispute is resolved. This process sequencing can be called: Set–Arb–Set–Arb.

---

tion in International Arbitration, 93 Am. J. Int'l L. 805, 814 (1999): "Deference to good faith annulments often furthers the very same interests as enforcement of the arbitration agreement and award, holding the parties to their bargain. Just as an agreement to arbitrate in London means driving to hearings on the left side of the road, so it means that proceedings are subject to the English Arbitration Act."

55. A Med–Arb clause establishes a two step sequence in which parties agree to first use mediation and then if it is unsuccessful, they agree to resolve the dispute in arbitration. See Chapter V.E.3 and, James T. Peter, "Med–Arb in International Arbitration" 8 The Am. Rev. of Intl. Arb. 83 (1997).

Christian Buhring–Uhle, Arbitration and Mediation in International Business

371, 389–391 (1996)

[T]he guiding principle for dispute resolution process design should be to maximize the consensual element in any solution and to have third-party decisionmaking available but to limit it to the indispensable minimum.

3. BASIC ELEMENTS OF THE SYSTEM

[T]he two main elements of the proposed system for dispute resolution process design are *interest-based negotiations* and a *rights-based adjudication* procedure as a *back-up* in case no agreement is reached.[33]

The best way to achieve consensus is through negotiation. Since interests are the yardstick for commercial dispute resolution the *negotiations* should be primarily *interest-based.* There are a number of ADR techniques, most notably mediation, that can improve the effectiveness of negotiation. They should therefore be considered when structuring the negotiation element of the system.

Previous chapters have shown that arbitration is the most effective *back-up* available in international commercial disputes. Litigation, however, is also a rights-based adjudication procedure and has to be considered as an option in specific contexts where arbitration is not available or where international agreements such as the Brussels Convention have improved the legal framework for transnational litigation.

There are two intermediate steps between these two principal elements: *rights-based negotiation* as a filter to adjudication and *loop-backs* as a way to revert to interest-based negotiation.

Rights-based negotiations are an important *filter* to adjudication. Rather than incurring the costs of going through an adjudication procedure the parties try to anticipate its result in negotiations. These negotiations typically take the form of an exchange of legal arguments and a confrontation of conflicting predictions about the outcome of the back-up procedure. This form of "bargaining in the shadow of the law" characterizes conventional settlement negotiations. It can be enhanced through certain forms of predictive ADR, most notably mini-trials and related mediation structures. In practice, interest-based and rights-based negotiation are blended into one procedure which in the shadow of an impending adjudication is dominated by rights-based negotiation. However, it is important to make this distinction, mentally and through the structure of the process, in order not to loose sight of the ultimate goal of dispute resolution process design— a consensual solution that reconciles the interests of the parties on the highest possible level. Both interest-based and rights-based negotiations can be brought to their maximum effectiveness through the assistance of a

---

33. The system proposed here is inspired by Ury, Brett & Goldberg, Getting Disputes Resolved (1989) but tries to take the model suggested there one step further and to adapt it to the particularity of international commercial disputes.

954 CHAPTER VI INTERNATIONAL DISPUTE RESOLUTION

mediator but in mediation, too, it is important to distinguish problem-solving and predictive techniques in order to accomplish the two objectives of realizing the interests of the parties and having their rights respected.

A *loop back is* a structure that permits the participants of a rights-based adjudication procedure to revert to interest-based negotiation, always in line with the guiding principle to maximize consensus and to minimize third-party decisionmaking. Examples for loop backs are mediation windows in arbitration and post-award-settlements which through negotiation try to improve the result of adjudication.

How Mediation Windows Work

... [S]ettlement facilitation during an on-going arbitration in the form of low-intensity mediation efforts by the tribunal itself are a common feature of the practice of international arbitration. By contrast, a full-scale mediation as a separate procedure in the "shadow" of an on-going arbitration, and with the participation of high-level executives from the parties, is less usual though not entirely uncommon. It can be conducted by the tribunal or by a separate mediator. Such a "mediation window" does not necessarily disrupt the arbitration since there are long periods during any arbitration where no hearings are conducted and the participants simply prepare for the next step in the proceedings. Setting aside a few days for a mediation attempt—the maximum duration will be of one or two weeks—is therefore possible without causing a noticeable disruption.

b. ARB–SET–ARB

This subsection considers the opportunities for third party assistance in settling a dispute after the parties have activated the international arbitration clause and the arbitrators have been selected. This process sequencing can be called Arb–Set–Arb.

This sequencing of dispute resolution methods is already familiar to litigators. Pursuant to parties' agreement or a court order, their court case is channeled into a separate mediation process. If the case does not settle in mediation, the case is returned to court for final resolution. This process sequence is also available in international arbitrations for parties who elect to channel the case into mediation and if unsuccessful, to return the case to arbitration.

As an alternative to referring the case to a separate mediator, the arbitrators could try to settle the dispute. This can be a practical option that takes advantage of the infrequent presence of all the international participants for the arbitration and that avoids delays due to the time it would take to select a mediator and reconvene all the participants for the mediation. This is a very controversial process design because of the inherent difficulties posed by one neutral trying to serve two very different processes. Much has been written about the risks to the integrity of each process.[56]As a result, international arbitrators rarely assist in settlement efforts.[57]

International arbitrators have been known, however, to occasionally resort to settlement techniques that range from mild to intensive interventions.[58] Arbitrators may (1) suggest that parties try to negotiate a settlement of the case, (2) actively participate in settlement negotiations (at parties' request), (3) propose a settlement formula (at parties' request), (4) meet with parties separately to discuss settlement options (with parties' consent), (5) hint at possible outcome of the arbitration, and (6) render a "case evaluation" (at parties' request). The more intensive the intervention, the more controversial its use.

The next article suggest how international arbitrators may safely try to settle cases by following safeguards that are designed to preserve the impartiality of the neutrals while giving them some settlement flexibility.

Harold Abramson, Protocols For International Arbitrators Who Dare To Settle Cases

10 Am. Rev. of Intl. Arb. 1–2, 8–15 (1999)

[The author emphasizes that the protocols are designed to create a small opening through which arbitrators can try to settle cases. This excerpt lists the twelve protocols and includes explanations for three of them.]

Ideally, I think international arbitrators should stay out of the direct settlement business. I favor the optimal arrangement in which the neutral who tries settling a case is different from the neutral who decides the case.[5] This arrangement preserves the impartiality of the neutral as decisionmaker while giving the neutral as settler the maximum flexibility to do her job well.

But as a pragmatist, I worry about lost opportunities for settlement in international arbitrations. It is extremely cumbersome to convene all the parties and attorneys. The first opportunity to meet face-to-face may be the

56. See, Chapter V.E.3 on "Med–Arb" and Abramson, Protocols for International Arbitrators Who Dare to Settle Cases 10 Am. Rev. of Intl. Arb. 1, 3–5 (1999)

57. Christian Buhring–Uhle, Arbitration and Mediation in International Business 188–192,193–196,211 (1996)(Attorneys appear more receptive to settlement initiatives by arbitrators than the actual practice of international arbitrators!)

58. Christian Buhring–Uhle, Arbitration and Mediation in International Business 188–192 (1996).

5. In international arbitrations, parties may engage a "shadow mediator" who at-

tends the arbitration hearings and confers with parties and attorneys at promising moments during the arbitration proceeding such as at the beginning or end of each hearing day. See, James J. Myers "10 Techniques for Managing Arbitration Hearings" 51 Dis. Resol. J. 28 (January/March, 1996). In the CPR Non–Administered Arbitration Rules, Rule 17 explicitly authorizes the arbitration panel "to permit the Mediator to attend conferences and hearings held in connection with the arbitration." CPR Non–Administered Arbitration Rules and Commentary, Rule 17(1994).

first day of the arbitration hearings (or the night before in a foreign city while recovering from jet-lag). This may be their first real opportunity to discuss settling the case. In this paper, I consider whether these settlement discussion can be facilitated by the arbitrators.

* * *

[In this section, the author suggests a series of protocols that parties and their neutral(s) should follow]. These protocols may work best when settlement initiatives are restricted to quasi-mediations. In some limited situations, adopting these protocols may make it feasible for arbitrators to engage in real mediations.

(1) *Neutral is Trained in Both Processes*

(2) *Neutral Consents to Serve Both Roles*

(3) *Neutral as Settler Will Respect Principle of Party Self–Determination*

(4) *Clients with Settlement Authority Should Be Present*

(5) *Documents and Statements in Settlement Process are Confidential*

(6) *Neutral as Settler Will Not Evaluate Merits, Evidence or Reasonableness of Positions*

Any evaluation by the neutral as settler poses a significant risk of compromising the neutral's impartiality if she resumes the role of arbitrator. The arbitrator who offers an evaluation during the settlement process may appear to have prejudged the case when the arbitration proceeding resumes. When the neutral returns to arbitrating, the neutral also may discover that the evaluation done in the settlement process may contaminate her view of the record in the arbitration proceeding. This protocol barring evaluations directs the neutral as settler to resist slipping prematurely into an adjudicatory mindset. . . .

This restriction should not be interpreted to bar a mediator or quasi-mediator from helping the parties evaluate the case. The settler can still ask even-handed questions about the quality of evidence, credibility of witnesses, clarity of law, and likelihood of success in the arbitration proceeding. The settler can introduce to the parties the use of decision tree analysis to help the parties asses alternatives to settlement. . . .

(7) *Neutral Will Not Caucus, Unless Parties Agree to Exception*

Arbitrators turned settlers increase the risk of compromising their appearance of impartiality when they hold private meetings. The excluded party may become concerned that the neutral played one party against the other during settlement efforts. The excluded party also may become suspicious that the other party corrupted the neutral's view of the case under circumstances where the excluded party could not challenge the information. Presumably for these reasons, international practitioners have judged caucuses as the least appropriate technique for arbitrator-turned-mediator.

Barring caucuses means barring the use of a tool that many quasi-mediators and mediators consider vital for settlement efforts to be successful. Many settlers believe that private meetings create a unique and safe opportunity for neutrals to help parties vent and release anger, clarify positions and interests, and assess the acceptability of alternative settlement options. . . .

(8) *Parties Agree to Reconfigure Arbitration Panel to Suit Settlement Process*

Arbitrators can take many different pathways toward helping parties settle a case. Each pathway offers different ways for preserving the impartiality of the neutral as arbitrator while opening opportunities for settlement. Many of these pathways are built around the flexibility offered by the usual international tribunal of three arbitrators. Five configurations are considered here although other permutations can be imagined. [This excerpt describes one option.]

[W]hen a typical panel of a neutral chair with two party-appointed arbitrators is constituted, the two party-appointed arbitrators could work together as a settlement team without the participation of the chair. This arrangement would preserve the neutrality of the chair who would not be tarnished by settlement efforts.

The settlement team could serve as quasi-mediators or even full-fledged mediators. They might function like a panel in a minitrial, hearing the parties' claims and helping them settle the dispute. The settlement team of party-appointed arbitrators may even be permitted by the parties to use caucuses because the third arbitrator, the chair, remains in reserve, insulated from the settlement process (Protocol 7). The settlement team should caucus only as a team which means each party-appointed arbitrator should avoid any *ex parte* contacts with the appointing party.

If settlement efforts are unsuccessful, the chair could serve as a sole arbitrator. This option, however, may be resisted by many international attorneys who prefer their party-appointed arbitrators to participate in the deliberations. In the alternative, all three arbitrators could hear the case. The impartiality of the panel may survive because any partiality by the party-appointed arbitrators would off-set each other, leaving the chair with the neutral and decisive role in the deliberations.

(9) *Arbitrator Will Not Be Influenced by Information Revealed in Settlement Process*

(10) *Parties Agree Not to Challenge Arbitrator or Award Based on Combined Roles*

(11) *Settlement Initiatives Should Not Unduly Delay the Arbitration Proceeding*

(12) *Parties Consent to Combined Processes*

NOTES AND QUESTIONS

1. What is the difference between the use of "mediation windows" in an international arbitration and a referral to mediation in a domestic court

958 CHAPTER VI INTERNATIONAL DISPUTE RESOLUTION

proceeding? Draft a dispute resolution clause that implements the Set–Arb–Set–Arb Process.

2. Do the protocols establish sufficient safeguards to protect the impartiality of arbitrators who try to settle cases? Do the protocols that bar evaluations and caucusing disable arbitrators from engaging in meaningful efforts to settle? Are there other configurations of tripartite tribunals that can serve the twin goals of maintaining the impartiality of the arbitrators and giving them sufficient flexibility to engage in effective settlement efforts?

3. Is it easier to justify the same person serving as settler and arbitrator in domestic or international arbitrations? Who is in a better position to help parties design dispute resolution processes—mediators or arbitrators? Why is it generally acceptable for judges, but not arbitrators, to try to settle their own cases?

6. PUBLIC DISPUTE RESOLUTION SYSTEMS FOR COMMERCIAL DISPUTES

Various countries around the world have formed regional and international institutions and processes for resolving business-related disputes.[59] The disputes, however, are not business disputes that arise out of private business deals. The disputes arise under commercial treaties that establish rules of fair business behavior in the global marketplace. These commercial treaties between governments regulate many types of governmental and business policies. These treaties deal with such issues as tariffs on imports, technical standards that might create non-tariff barriers to trade, and pirating of intellectual property rights. They also prohibit governments from unfairly subsidizing exports and prohibit businesses from dumping goods at less than their costs in foreign markets. Furthermore, the treaties try to facilitate doing business in the global marketplace by establishing mechanisms for coordinating and harmonizing various business policies and technical standards of different countries.

These commercial treaties create public systems of dispute resolution for disputes that arise under them. These public systems operate separately and independently from the private justice systems established by businesses in their dispute resolution clauses. Like private systems, public systems must include several key features in order to be credible dispute resolution processes. In evaluating these public processes, consider these questions: Is the decisionmaker neutral? Does the hearing give parties a reasonable opportunity to be heard? Is the decision of the adjudicatory body transparent? Did the signatory countries agree to be bound by the decision? Are the remedies meaningful? And, is there an effective mechanism for enforcing the decision? Two other questions deserve special attention by attorneys representing private clients: What *type of disputes* falls within the jurisdiction of the adjudicatory process? And, can a *private party* either

---

59. See, Schneider, "Getting Along: The Evolution of Dispute Resolution Regimes in International Trade Organizations" 20 Mich.J.of Intl. L. 697 (1999).

B. International ADR Clauses for Business Disputes 959

initiate or participate in the public dispute resolution process? Each of these adjudicatory features can be conceived in different ways as demonstrated in the following brief descriptions of the dispute resolution processes administered by the World Trade Organization and under the North American Free Trade Agreement.

a. WORLD TRADE ORGANIZATION[60] (WTO)

The new WTO,[61] the successor to GATT, administers a unified dispute resolution process through its *Dispute Settlement Body* (DSB) which is composed of all the members of the WTO. The DSB handles disputes that may arise under a number of covered treaties.[62]

Under WTO's strict timetables, governmental parties first try to resolve any disputes through a process of informal *consultation*. If unsuccessful, the complaining country can request the DSB to convene a *panel* of three to five governmental or non-governmental individuals. The panel hears the dispute and issues a written report. The report is automatically adopted by the DSB unless rejected by consensus of the DSB's members or a party appeals the report to the *Appellate Body*. Review by the Appellate Body is limited to issues of law covered in the report and legal interpretations made by the panel. A decision of the Appellate Body is automatically adopted by the DSB, unless rejected unanimously by its members.

The terms of the report are enforced in three steps. First, the losing party must *conform* with the terms of the report within a "reasonable period of time." Second, if the losing party fails to conform, the complaining party can ask the losing party to *negotiate* mutually acceptable compensation. Third, if the parties cannot agree upon terms of compensation, the complaining party can request the DSB for authorization to *retaliate*. Retaliation does not include punitive actions; it usually consists of the complaining party suspending equivalent concessions or obligations made to the violating party. Claims of excessive retaliation are subject to review in arbitrations.

b. NAFTA[63] (NORTH AMERICAN FREE TRADE AGREEMENT)

NAFTA creates a free trade area in North America consisting of Canada, United States, and Mexico. In contrast with WTO procedures,

---

60. Final Act Embodying the Results of the Uruguay Round of Multinational Trade Negotiations, Annex 2: Understanding on Rules and Procedures Governing the Settlement of Disputes, Apr. 15, 1994, app. 1, *in The Results of the Uruguay Round of Multilateral Trade Negotiations*, 33I.L.M. 1226, 1224 ; See, Gabrielle Marceau, "NAFTA and WTO Dispute Settlement Rules—A Thematic Comparison" 31 J.of World Trade 26, 53–72(1997); Also see Ernst–Ulrich Petersmann, The GATT/WTO Dispute Resolution System:

International Law, International Organizations and Dispute Resolution (1997).

61. The treaty has been ratified by over one hundred countries.

62. The better known treaties include the General Agreement on Tariffs and Trade (GATT 1994–goods), General Agreement on Trade in Services(GATS), and Trade–Related Intellectual Property Agreement (TRIPS.)

63. North American Free Trade Agreement, Dec. 17, 1992, 32 I.L.M. 289.

960 CHAPTER VI INTERNATIONAL DISPUTE RESOLUTION

NAFTA does not offer a unified dispute resolution process. Instead, NAFTA establishes primarily two very different processes for handling disputes under the treaty. Each process is quite elaborate and intricate. This description provides only an overview of each process.

Chapter 19 of NAFTA[64] creates a binding dispute resolution process for challenging governmentally imposed antidumping and countervailing duties.[65] This process can be initiated by private parties. This process stands out as unusual because each country surrendered some domestic sovereignty to binding review by an international adjudicatory body. The process works as follows: When a local agency decides to impose an antidumping or countervailing duty on imports, the complaining foreign party can circumvent local court review by appealing the final agency decision to a NAFTA binational panel. The binational panel consists of two panelists from each country and a fifth panelist selected by agreement of the parties. The binational panel does not apply international law; it reviews the agency decision based on domestic law and in accordance with the domestic standard of review. The panel's decision on the validity of the duty is binding on the parties.

There is a limited opportunity to appeal the panel's decision to a three member Extraordinary Challenge Committee (ECC). This right to appeal can only be exercised by a NAFTA party (country, not private party.) The grounds for a challenge are limited to issues that may threaten the integrity of the binational review process such as whether a panel member is guilty of gross misconduct. Parties are barred from appealing a panel's decision to a local court.

Chapter 20 of NAFTA establishes a non-binding process for handling most other types of disputes under the treaty.[66] This process can only be initiated by governments at the federal level. Private parties are relegated to trying to convince their own government to initiate the dispute resolution process. The process consist of three stages: First, governments *consult* with each other to try to resolve the conflict. Second, the conflict can be referred to the *Free Trade Commission (FTC)*, the central institution of NAFTA which is comprised of cabinet-level representatives of each NAFTA country. The FTC can employ a variety of ADR methods in an effort to secure a negotiated resolution of the dispute. However, the FTC cannot arbitrate the dispute. Third, the dispute can be referred to a *five member panel* which will issue a report that is not binding on the parties. If the parties still do not resolve the conflict, the successful complainant can

64. NAFTA, Chapter 19. Also see Leon E. Trakman, Dispute Settlement Under The NAFTA: Manual and Source Book , Ch. 4 (1997); In the Matter of the Mexican Antidumping Investigation into Imports of Cut-to-Length Plate Products from the United States, Panel No. MEX–94–1904–02 (August 30, 1995).

65. Antidumping duties are imposed on imported goods to offset the below cost prices charged by an importing business. Countervailing duties are imposed on imported goods to offset foreign governmental subsidies that are used to reduce the price of the imported goods.

66. NAFTA, Chapter 20. Also see Leon E. Trakman, Dispute Settlement Under The NAFTA: Manual and Source Book , Ch. 1 (1997).

suspend equivalent NAFTA benefits to the nonconforming NAFTA party. This unilateral retaliation can be reviewed by a panel to determine whether the retaliation is "manifestly excessive."

NOTES AND QUESTIONS

1. Other regional treaties create public dispute resolution mechanisms for handling cross-border disputes. An important and well developed system has been established by the European Union(EU) for disputes among members of its custom union. The EU Court of Justice and Court of First Instance resolve disputes relating to the interpretation and implementation of various EU treaties. The cases can be brought by private parties, member states or an EU agency. The Court can hear cases directly or take cases referred by local courts.[67]

2. The emergence of these public dispute resolution processes may some day impact on the continued use of private international arbitration. Consider this tantalizing possibility for the future use of a public international dispute resolution processes:

> We now ask if the construction of large regional markets—the European Community, NAFTA—or detailed mechanisms for regulating international commerce—the World Trade Organization under GATT—could also disrupt the landscape and introduce new stakes and even an "international new deal." The restructuring of the international market of disputes would build on emerging institutions such as the European Court of Justice, NAFTA, GATT, and even revived and transformed antitrust regulations. These institutions and approaches offer new opportunities for business. Even if it is not at first apparent, these institutions compete with the International Chamber of Commerce and private arbitrations. At the same time, new approaches and institutions may facilitate the recomposition of this field of practice closer to the pole of the state....
>
> If this line of development continues, the field of transnational business justice will be more closely connected to states and to supranational, statelike entities than it was in the period when the ICC gained its eminence. Major business conflicts would be fought on terrain closer to the states—with the states implicated in the contests and the contestants. We cannot say at this point whether this development will take place, and whether, if so, the world constituted around the ICC and its networks will assume a secondary position.

67. The ANDEAN Common Market of several South American countries also has established a Court of Justice for resolving regional disputes. Furthermore, it has been recommended that the free trade area of ASEAN (Association of Southeast Asian Nations), known as AFTA, adopt a dispute settlement mechanism for resolving trade disputes. See, Jeffrey A. Kaplan "ASEAN's Rubicon: A Dispute Settlement Mechanism for AFTA" 14 UCLA Pac. Basin L.J. 147(1996).

Yves Dezalay and Bryant G. Garth, Dealing in Virtue—International Commercial Arbitration and the Construction of a Transnational Legal Order 312, 315 (1996)

3. What additions to the dispute resolution processes of the WTO or NAFTA would be necessary before either of the processes would be acceptable to private business parties? Are these changes likely to be acceptable to the signatory countries such as the United States?

APPENDIX A

FEDERAL RULES OF CIVIL PROCEDURE

Rule 11.

SIGNING OF PLEADINGS, MOTIONS, AND OTHER PAPERS; SANCTIONS

(a) Signature. Every pleading, written motion, and other paper shall be signed by at least one attorney of record in the attorney's individual name, or, if the party is not represented by an attorney, shall be signed by the party. Each paper shall state the signer's address and telephone number, if any. Except when otherwise specifically provided by rule or statute, pleadings need not be verified or accompanied by affidavit. An unsigned paper shall be stricken unless omission of the signature is corrected promptly after being called to the attention of the attorney or party.

(b) Representations to Court. By presenting to the court (whether by signing, filing, submitting, or later advocating) a pleading, written motion, or other paper, an attorney or unrepresented party is certifying that to the best of the person's knowledge, information, and belief, formed after an inquiry reasonable under the circumstances,—

(1) it is not being presented for any improper purpose, such as to harass or to cause unnecessary delay or needless increase in the cost of litigation;

(2) the claims, defenses, and other legal contentions therein are warranted by existing law or by a nonfrivolous argument for the extension, modification, or reversal of existing law or the establishment of new law;

(3) the allegations and other factual contentions have evidentiary support or, if specifically so identified, are likely to have evidentiary support after a reasonable opportunity for further investigation or discovery; and

(4) the denials ·of factual contentions are warranted on the evidence or, if specifically so identified, are reasonably based on a lack of information or belief.

(c) Sanctions. If, after notice and a reasonable opportunity to respond, the court determines that subdivision (b) has been violated, the court may, subject to the conditions stated below, impose an appropriate

963

sanction upon the attorneys, law firms, or parties that have violated subdivision (b) or are responsible for the violation.

(1) How Initiated.

(A) By Motion. A motion for sanctions under this rule shall be made separately from other motions or requests and shall describe the specific conduct alleged to violate subdivision (b). It shall be served as provided in Rule 5, but shall not be filed with or presented to the court unless, within 21 days after service of the motion (or such other period as the court may prescribe), the challenged paper, claim, defense, contention, allegation, or denial is not withdrawn or appropriately corrected. If warranted, the court may award to the party prevailing on the motion the reasonable expenses and attorney's fees incurred in presenting or opposing the motion. Absent exceptional circumstances, a law firm shall be held jointly responsible for violations committed by its partners, associates, and employees.

(B) On Court's Initiative. On its own initiative, the court may enter an order describing the specific conduct that appears to violate subdivision (b) and directing an attorney, law firm, or party to show cause why it has not violated subdivision (b) with respect thereto.

(2) Nature of Sanction; Limitations. A sanction imposed for violation of this rule shall be limited to what is sufficient to deter repetition of such conduct or comparable conduct by others similarly situated. Subject to the limitations in subparagraphs (A) and (B), the sanction may consist of, or include, directives of a nonmonetary nature, an order to pay a penalty into court, or, if imposed on motion and warranted for effective deterrence, an order directing payment to the movant of some or all of the reasonable attorneys' fees and other expenses incurred as a direct result of the violation.

(A) Monetary sanctions may not be awarded against a represented party for a violation of subdivision (b)(2).

(B) Monetary sanctions may not be awarded on the court's initiative unless the court issues its order to show cause before a voluntary dismissal or settlement of the claims made by or against the party which is, or whose attorneys are, to be sanctioned.

(3) Order. When imposing sanctions, the court shall describe the conduct determined to constitute a violation of this rule and explain the basis for the sanction imposed.

(d) Inapplicability to Discovery. Subdivisions (a) through (c) of this rule do not apply to disclosures and discovery requests, responses, objections, and motions that are subject to the provisions of Rules 26 through 37.

As amended 1983, 1987, 1993.

Rule 16.

PRETRIAL CONFERENCES; SCHEDULING; MANAGEMENT

(a) Pretrial Conferences; Objectives. In any action, the court may in its discretion direct the attorneys for the parties and any unrepresented parties to appear before it for a conference or conferences before trial for such purposes as

(1) expediting the disposition of the action;

(2) establishing early and continuing control so that the case will not be protracted because of lack of management;

(3) discouraging wasteful pretrial activities;

(4) improving the quality of the trial through more thorough preparation, and;

(5) facilitating the settlement of the case.

(b) Scheduling and Planning. Except in categories of actions exempted by district court rule as inappropriate, the district judge, or a magistrate judge when authorized by district court rule, shall, after receiving the report from the parties under Rule 26(f) or after consulting with the attorneys for the parties and any unrepresented parties by a scheduling conference, telephone, mail, or other suitable means, enter a scheduling order that limits the time

(1) to join other parties and to amend the pleadings;

(2) to file motions; and

(3) to complete discovery.

The scheduling order may also include

(4) modifications of the times for disclosures under Rules 26(a) and 26(e)(1) and of the extent of discovery to be permitted;

(5) the date or dates for conferences before trial, a final pretrial conference, and trial; and

(6) any other matters appropriate in the circumstances of the case.

The order shall issue as soon as practicable but in any event within 90 days after the appearance of a defendant and within 120 days after the complaint has been served on a defendant. A schedule shall not be modified except upon a showing of good cause and by leave of the district judge or, when authorized by local rule, by a magistrate judge.

(c) Subjects for Consideration at Pretrial Conferences. At any conference under this rule consideration may be given, and the court may take appropriate action, with respect to

(1) the formulation and simplification of the issues, including the elimination of frivolous claims or defenses;

(2) the necessity or desirability of amendments to the pleadings;

(3) the possibility of obtaining admissions of fact and of documents which will avoid unnecessary proof, stipulations regarding the

966 APPENDIX A

authenticity of documents, and advance rulings from the court on the admissibility of evidence;

(4) the avoidance of unnecessary proof and of cumulative evidence, and limitations or restrictions on the use of testimony under Rule 702 of the Federal Rules of Evidence;

(5) the appropriateness and timing of summary adjudication under Rule 56;

(6) the control and scheduling of discovery, including orders affecting disclosures and discovery pursuant to Rule 26 and Rules 29 through 37;

(7) the identification of witnesses and documents, the need and schedule for filing and exchanging pretrial briefs, and the date or dates for further conferences and for trial;

(8) the advisability of referring matters to a magistrate judge or master;

(9) settlement and the use of special procedures to assist in resolving the dispute when authorized by statute or local rule;

(10) the form and substance of the pretrial order;

(11) the disposition of pending motions;

(12) the need for adopting special procedures for managing potentially difficult or protracted actions that may involve complex issues, multiple parties, difficult legal questions, or unusual proof problems;

(13) an order for a separate trial pursuant to Rule 42(b) with respect to a claim, counterclaim, cross-claim, or third-party claim, or with respect to any particular issue in the case;

(14) an order directing a party or parties to present evidence early in the trial with respect to a manageable issue that could, on the evidence, be the basis for a judgment as a matter of law under Rule 50(a) or a judgment on partial findings under Rule 52(c);

(15) an order establishing a reasonable limit on the time allowed for presenting evidence; and

(16) such other matters as may facilitate the just, speedy, and inexpensive disposition of the action.

At least one of the attorneys for each party participating in any conference before trial shall have authority to enter into stipulations and to make admissions regarding all matters that the participants may reasonably anticipate may be discussed. If appropriate, the court may require that a party or its representative be present or reasonably available by telephone in order to consider possible settlement of the dispute.

(d) Final Pretrial Conference. Any final pretrial conference shall be held as close to the time of trial as reasonable under the circumstances. The participants at any such conference shall formulate a plan for trial, including a program for facilitating the admission of evidence. The conference shall be attended by at least one of the attorneys who will conduct the trial for each of the parties and by any unrepresented parties.

(e) Pretrial Orders. After any conference held pursuant to this rule, an order shall be entered reciting the action taken. This order shall control the subsequent course of the action unless modified by a subsequent order. The order following a final pretrial conference shall be modified only to prevent manifest injustice.

(f) Sanctions. If a party or party's attorney fails to obey a scheduling or pretrial order, or if no appearance is made on behalf of a party at a scheduling or pretrial conference, or if a party or party's attorney is substantially unprepared to participate in the conference, or if a party or party's attorney fails to participate in good faith, the judge, upon motion or the judge's own initiative, may make such orders with regard thereto as are just, and among others any of the orders provided in Rule 37(b)(2)(B), (C), (D).* In lieu of or in addition to any other sanction, the judge shall require the party or the attorney representing the party or both to pay the reasonable expenses incurred because of any noncompliance with this rule, including attorney's fees, unless the judge finds that the noncompliance was substantially justified or that other circumstances make an award of expenses unjust.

As amended 1983, 1987, 1993.

Rule 45.

Subpoena

(a) Form; Issuance.

(1) Every subpoena shall

(A) state the name of the court from which it is issued; and

(B) state the title of the action, the name of the court in which it is pending, and its civil action number; and

(C) command each person to whom it is directed to attend and give testimony or to produce and permit inspection and copying of designated books, documents or tangible things in the possession, custody or control of that person, or to permit inspection of premises, at a time and place therein specified; and

(D) set forth the text of subdivisions (c) and (d) of this rule.

---

* ["(B) An order refusing to allow the disobedient party to support or oppose designated claims or defenses, or prohibiting that party from introducing designated matters in evidence; (C) An order striking out pleadings or parts thereof, or staying further proceedings until the order is obeyed, or dismissing the action or proceeding or any part thereof, or rendering a judgment by default against the disobedient party; (D) In lieu of any of the foregoing orders or in addition thereto, an order treating as a contempt of court the failure to obey any orders except an order to submit to a physical or mental examination." Rule 37(b)(2).]

A command to produce evidence or to permit inspection may be joined with a command to appear at trial or hearing or at deposition, or may be issued separately.

(2) A subpoena commanding attendance at a trial or hearing shall issue from the court for the district in which the hearing or trial is to be held. A subpoena for attendance at a deposition shall issue from the court for the district designated by the notice of deposition as the district in which the deposition is to be taken. If separate from a subpoena commanding the attendance of a person, a subpoena for production or inspection shall issue from the court for the district in which the production or inspection is to be made.

(3) The clerk shall issue a subpoena, signed but otherwise in blank, to a party requesting it, who shall complete it before service. An attorney as officer of the court may also issue and sign a subpoena on behalf of

    (A) a court in which the attorney is authorized to practice; or

    (B) a court for a district in which a deposition or production is compelled by the subpoena, if the deposition or production pertains to an action pending in a court in which the attorney is authorized to practice.

(b) Service.

(1) A subpoena may be served by any person who is not a party and is not less than 18 years of age. Service of a subpoena upon a person named therein shall be made by delivering a copy thereof to such person and, if the person's attendance is commanded, by tendering to that person the fees for one day's attendance and the mileage allowed by law. When the subpoena is issued on behalf of the United States or an officer or agency thereof, fees and mileage need not be tendered. Prior notice of any commanded production of documents and things or inspection of premises before trial shall be served on each party in the manner prescribed by Rule 5(b).

(2) Subject to the provisions of clause (ii) of subparagraph (c)(3)(A) of this rule, a subpoena may be served at any place within the district of the court by which it is issued, or at any place without the district that is within 100 miles of the place of the deposition, hearing, trial, production, or inspection specified in the subpoena or at any place within the state where a state statute or rule of court permits service of a subpoena issued by a state court of general jurisdiction sitting in the place of the deposition, hearing, trial, production, or inspection specified in the subpoena. When a statute of the United States provides therefor, the court upon proper application and cause shown may authorize the service of a subpoena at any other place. A subpoena directed to a witness in a foreign country who is a national or resident of the United States shall issue under the circumstances and in the manner and be served as provided in Title *28, U.S.C. § 1783.*

(3) Proof of service when necessary shall be made by filing with the clerk of the court by which the subpoena is issued a statement of the date and manner of service and of the names of the persons served, certified by the person who made the service.

(c) Protection of Persons Subject to Subpoenas. * * *

(3) (A) On timely motion, the court by which a subpoena was issued shall quash or modify the subpoena if it

(i) fails to allow reasonable time for compliance;

(ii) requires a person who is not a party or an officer of a party to travel to a place more than 100 miles from the place where that person resides, is employed or regularly transacts business in person, except that, subject to the provisions of clause (c)(3)(B)(iii) of this rule, such a person may in order to attend trial be commanded to travel from any such place within the state in which the trial is held, or

(iii) requires disclosure of privileged or other protected matter and no exception or waiver applies, or

(iv) subjects a person to undue burden.

(B) If a subpoena

(i) requires disclosure of a trade secret or other confidential research, development, or commercial information, or

(ii) requires disclosure of an unretained expert's opinion or information not describing specific events or occurrences in dispute and resulting from the expert's study made not at the request of any party, or

(iii) requires a person who is not a party or an officer of a party to incur substantial expense to travel more than 100 miles to attend trial, the court may, to protect a person subject to or affected by the subpoena, quash or modify the subpoena or, if the party in whose behalf the subpoena is issued shows a substantial need for the testimony or material that cannot be otherwise met without undue hardship and assures that the person to whom the subpoena is addressed will be reasonably compensated, the court may order appearance or production only upon specified conditions. * * *

(e) Contempt. Failure by any person without adequate excuse to obey a subpoena served upon that person may be deemed a contempt of the court from which the subpoena issued. An adequate cause for failure to obey exists when a subpoena purports to require a non-party to attend or produce at a place not within the limits provided by clause (ii) of subparagraph (c)(3)(A).

Rule 68.

OFFER OF JUDGMENT

At any time more than 10 days before the trial begins, a party defending against a claim may serve upon the adverse party an offer to allow judgment to be taken against the defending party for the money or property or to the effect specified in the offer, with costs then accrued. If within 10 days after the service of the offer the adverse party serves written notice that the offer is accepted, either party may then file the offer and notice of acceptance together with proof of service thereof and thereupon the clerk shall enter judgment. An offer not accepted shall be deemed withdrawn and evidence thereof is not admissible except in a proceeding to determine costs. If the judgment finally obtained by the offeree is not more favorable than the offer, the offeree must pay the costs incurred after the making of the offer. The fact that an offer is made but not accepted does not preclude a subsequent offer. When the liability of one party to another has been determined by verdict or order or judgment, but the amount or extent of the liability remains to be determined by further proceedings, the party adjudged liable may make an offer of judgment, which shall have the same effect as an offer made before trial if it is served within a reasonable time not less than 10 days prior to the commencement of hearings to determine the amount or extent of liability.

As amended 1948, 1966, 1987.

APPENDIX B

FEDERAL RULES OF CRIMINAL PROCEDURE

Rule 11.

PLEAS

(e) Plea Agreement Procedure.

(1) In general. The attorney for the government and the attorney for the defendant—the defendant when acting pro se—may agree that, upon the defendant's entering a plea of guilty or nolo contendere to a charged offense, or to a lesser or related offense, the attorney for the government will:

(A) move to dismiss other charges; or

(B) recommend, or agree not to oppose the defendant's request for a particular sentence or sentencing range, or that a particular provision of the Sentencing Guidelines, or policy statement, or sentencing factor is or is not applicable to the case. Any such recommendation or request is not binding on the court; or

(C) agree that a specific sentence or sentencing range is the appropriate disposition of the case, or that a particular provision of the Sentencing Guidelines, or policy statement, or sentencing factor is or is not applicable to the case. Such a plea agreement is binding on the court once it is accepted by the court.

The court shall not participate in any discussions between the parties concerning any such plea agreement.

(2) Notice of such agreement. If a plea agreement has been reached by the parties, the court shall, on the record, require the disclosure of the agreement in open court or, on a showing of good cause, in camera, at the time the plea is offered. If the agreement is of the type specified in subdivision (e)(1)(A) or (C), the court may accept or reject the agreement, or may defer its decision as to the acceptance or rejection until there has been an opportunity to consider the presentence report. If the agreement is of the type specified in subdivision (e)(1)(B), the court shall advise the defendant that if the court does not accept the recommendation or request the defendant nevertheless has no right to withdraw the plea.

(3) Acceptance of a plea agreement. If the court accepts the plea agreement, the court shall inform the defendant that it will

APPENDIX B

embody in the judgment and sentence the disposition provided for in the plea agreement.

(4) Rejection of a plea agreement. If the court rejects the plea agreement, the court shall, on the record, inform the parties of this fact, advise the defendant personally in open court or, on a showing of good cause, in camera, that the court is not bound by the plea agreement, afford the defendant the opportunity to then withdraw the plea, and advise the defendant that if the defendant persists in a guilty plea or plea of nolo contendere the disposition of the case may be less favorable to the defendant than that contemplated by the plea agreement.

(5) Time of plea agreement procedure. Except for good cause shown, notification to the court of the existence of a plea agreement shall be given at the arraignment or at such other time, prior to trial, as may be fixed by the court.

(6) Inadmissibility of pleas, plea discussions, and related statements. Except as otherwise provided in this paragraph, evidence of the following is not, in any civil or criminal proceeding, admissible against the defendant who made the plea or was a participant in the plea discussions:

(A) a plea of guilty which was later withdrawn;

(B) a plea of nolo contendere;

(C) any statement made in the course of any proceedings under this rule regarding either of the foregoing pleas; or

(D) any statement made in the course of plea discussions with an attorney for the government which do not result in a plea of guilty or which result in a plea of guilty later withdrawn.

However, such a statement is admissible (i) in any proceeding wherein another statement made in the course of the same plea or plea discussions has been introduced and the statement ought in fairness be considered contemporaneously with it, or (ii) in a criminal proceeding for perjury or false statement if the statement was made by the defendant under oath, on the record, and in the presence of counsel.

As amended Dec. 1, 1999.

APPENDIX C

FEDERAL RULES OF EVIDENCE

Rule 408.

COMPROMISE AND OFFERS TO COMPROMISE

Evidence of (1) furnishing or offering or promising to furnish, or (2) accepting or offering or promising to accept, a valuable consideration in compromising or attempting to compromise a claim which was disputed as to either validity or amount, is not admissible to prove liability for or invalidity of the claim or its amount. Evidence of conduct or statements made in compromise negotiations is likewise not admissible. This rule does not require the exclusion of any evidence otherwise discoverable merely because it is presented in the course of compromise negotiations. This rule also does not require exclusion when the evidence is offered for another purpose, such as proving bias or prejudice of a witness, negativing a contention of undue delay, or proving an effort to obstruct a criminal investigation or prosecution.

Rule 409.

PAYMENT OF MEDICAL AND SIMILAR EXPENSES

Evidence of furnishing or offering or promising to pay medical, hospital, or similar expenses occasioned by an injury is not admissible to prove liability for the injury.

Rule 410.

INADMISSIBILITY OF PLEAS, PLEA DISCUSSIONS, AND RELATED STATEMENTS

Except as otherwise provided in this rule, evidence of the following is not, in any civil or criminal proceeding, admissible against the defendant who made the plea or was a participant in the plea discussions:

(1) a plea of guilty which was later withdrawn;

(2) a plea of nolo contendere;

(3) any statement made in the course of any proceedings under Rule 11 of the Federal Rules of Criminal Procedure or comparable state procedure regarding either of the foregoing pleas; or

(4) any statement made in the course of plea discussions with an attorney for the prosecuting authority which do not result in a plea of guilty or which result in a plea of guilty later withdrawn.

974   APPENDIX C

However, such a statement is admissible (i) in any proceeding wherein another statement made in the course of the same plea or plea discussions has been introduced and the statement ought in fairness be considered contemporaneously with it, or (ii) in a criminal proceeding for perjury or false statement if the statement was made by the defendant under oath, on the record and in the presence of counsel.

As amended 1975, 1980.

APPENDIX D

AMERICAN BAR ASSOCIATION MODEL RULES OF PROFESSIONAL CONDUCT

RULE 1.1 Competence

A lawyer shall provide competent representation to a client. Competent representation requires the legal knowledge, skill, thoroughness and preparation reasonably necessary for the representation.

RULE 1.2 Scope of Representation

(a) A lawyer shall abide by a client's decisions concerning the objectives of representation, subject to paragraphs (c), (d) and (e), and shall consult with the client as to the means by which they are to be pursued. A lawyer shall abide by a client's decision whether to accept an offer of settlement of a matter. In a criminal case, the lawyer shall abide by the client's decision, after consultation with the lawyer, as to a plea to be entered, whether to waive jury trial and whether the client will testify.

(b) A lawyer's representation of a client, including representation by appointment, does not constitute an endorsement of the client's political, economic, social or moral views or activities.

(c) A lawyer may limit the objectives of the representation if the client consents after consultation.

(d) A lawyer shall not counsel a client to engage, or assist a client, in conduct that the lawyer knows is criminal or fraudulent, but a lawyer may discuss the legal consequences of any proposed course of conduct with a client and may counsel or assist a client to make a good faith effort to determine the validity, scope, meaning or application of the law.

(e) When a lawyer knows that a client expects assistance not permitted by the rules of professional conduct or other law, the lawyer shall consult with the client regarding the relevant limitations on the lawyer's conduct.

RULE 1.6 Confidentiality of Information

(a) A lawyer shall not reveal information relating to representation of a client unless the client consents after consultation, except for disclosures that are impliedly authorized in order to carry out the representation, and except as stated in paragraph (b).

975

976 APPENDIX D

(b) A lawyer may reveal such information to the extent the lawyer reasonably believes necessary:

(1) to prevent the client from committing a criminal act that the lawyer believes is likely to result in imminent death or substantial bodily harm; or

(2) to establish a claim or defense on behalf of the lawyer in a controversy between the lawyer and the client, to establish a defense to a criminal charge or civil claim against the lawyer based upon conduct in which the client was involved, or to respond to allegations in any proceeding concerning the lawyer's representation of the client.

RULE 1.8   Conflict of Interest: Prohibited Transactions

(a) A lawyer shall not enter into a business transaction with a client or knowingly acquire an ownership, possessory, security or other pecuniary interest adverse to a client unless:

(1) the transaction and terms on which the lawyer acquires the interest are fair and reasonable to the client and are fully disclosed and transmitted in writing to the client in a manner which can be reasonably understood by the client;

(2) the client is given a reasonable opportunity to seek the advice of independent counsel in the transaction; and

(3) the client consents in writing thereto.

(b) A lawyer shall not use information relating to representation of a client to the disadvantage of the client unless the client consents after consultation, except as permitted or required by Rule 1.6 or Rule 3.3.

(c) A lawyer shall not prepare an instrument giving the lawyer or a person related to the lawyer as parent, child, sibling, or spouse any substantial gift from a client, including a testamentary gift, except where the client is related to the donee.

(d) Prior to the conclusion of representation of a client, a lawyer shall not make or negotiate an agreement giving the lawyer literary or media rights to a portrayal or account based in substantial part on information relating to the representation.

(e) A lawyer shall not provide financial assistance to a client in connection with pending or contemplated litigation, except that:

(1) a lawyer may advance court costs and expenses of litigation, the repayment of which may be contingent on the outcome of the matter; and

(2) a lawyer representing an indigent client may pay court costs and expenses of litigation on behalf of the client.

(f) A lawyer shall not accept compensation for representing a client from one other than the client unless:

(1) the client consents after consultation;

RULE 2.2 ABA MODEL RULES 977

(2) there is no interference with the lawyer's independence of professional judgment or with the client-lawyer relationship; and

(3) information relating to representation of a client is protected as required by Rule 1.6.

(g) A lawyer who represents two or more clients shall not participate in making an aggregate settlement of the claims of or against the clients, or in a criminal case an aggregated agreement as to guilty or nolo contendere pleas, unless each client consents after consultation, including disclosure of the existence and nature of all the claims or pleas involved and of the participation of each person in the settlement.

(h) A lawyer shall not make an agreement prospectively limiting the lawyer's liability to a client for malpractice unless permitted by law and the client is independently represented in making the agreement, or settle a claim for such liability with an unrepresented client or former client without first advising that person in writing that independent representation is appropriate in connection therewith.

(i) A lawyer related to another lawyer as parent, child, sibling or spouse shall not represent a client in a representation directly adverse to a person whom the lawyer knows is represented by the other lawyer except upon consent by the client after consultation regarding the relationship.

(j) A lawyer shall not acquire a proprietary interest in the cause of action or subject matter of litigation the lawyer is conducting for a client, except that the lawyer may:

(1) acquire a lien granted by law to secure the lawyer's fee or expenses; and

(2) contract with a client for a reasonable contingent fee in a civil case.

RULE 2.2 Intermediary

(a) A lawyer may act as intermediary between clients if:

(1) the lawyer consults with each client concerning the implications of the common representation, including the advantages and risks involved, and the effect on the attorney-client privileges, and obtains each client's consent to the common representation;

(2) the lawyer reasonably believes that the matter can be resolved on terms compatible with the clients' best interests, that each client will be able to make adequately informed decisions in the matter and that there is little risk of material prejudice to the interest of any of the clients if the contemplated resolution is unsuccessful; and

(3) the lawyer reasonably believes that the common representation can be undertaken impartially and without improper effect on other responsibilities the lawyer has to any of the clients.

(b) While acting as intermediary, the lawyer shall consult with each client concerning the decision to be made and the considerations relevant in making them, so that each client can make adequately informed decisions.

978 APPENDIX D

(c) A lawyer shall withdraw as intermediary if any of the clients so request, or if any of the conditions stated in paragraph (a) is no longer satisfied. Upon withdrawal, the lawyer shall not continue to represent any of the clients in the matter that was the subject of the intermediation.

RULE 3.1 Meritorious Claims and Contentions

A lawyer shall not bring or defend a proceeding, or assert or controvert an issue therein, unless there is a basis for doing so that is not frivolous, which includes a good faith argument for an extension, modification or reversal of existing law. A lawyer for the defendant in a criminal proceeding, or the respondent in a proceeding that could result in incarceration, may nevertheless so defend the proceeding as to require that every element of the case be established.

RULE 3.3 Candor Toward the Tribunal

(a) A lawyer shall not knowingly:

(1) make a false statement of material fact or law to a tribunal;

(2) fail to disclose a material fact to a tribunal when disclosure is necessary to avoid assisting a criminal or fraudulent act by the client;

(3) fail to disclose to the tribunal legal authority in the controlling jurisdiction known to the lawyer to be directly adverse to the position of the client and not disclosed by opposing counsel; or

(4) offer evidence that the lawyer knows to be false. If a lawyer has offered material evidence and comes to know of its falsity, the lawyer shall take reasonable remedial measures.

(b) The duties stated in paragraph (a) continue to the conclusion of the proceeding, and apply even if compliance requires disclosure of information otherwise protected by Rule 1.6.

(c) A lawyer may refuse to offer evidence that the lawyer reasonably believes is false.

(d) In an ex parte proceeding, a lawyer shall inform the tribunal of all material facts known to the lawyer which will enable the tribunal to make an informed decision, whether or not the facts are adverse.

RULE 3.8 Special Responsibilities of a Prosecutor

The prosecutor in a criminal case shall:

(a) refrain from prosecuting a charge that the prosecutor knows is not supported by probable cause;

* * *

(d) make timely disclosure to the defense of all evidence or information known to the prosecutor that tends to negate the guilt of the accused or mitigates the offense, and, in connection with sentencing, disclose to the defense and to the tribunal all unprivileged mitigating information known to the prosecutor, except when the prosecutor is relieved of this responsibility by a protective order of the tribunal;

RULE 8.4 ABA MODEL RULES

979

(e) exercise reasonable care to prevent investigators, law enforcement personnel, employees or other persons assisting or associated with the prosecutor in a criminal case from making an extrajudicial statement that the prosecutor would be prohibited from making under Rule 3.6.

* * *

RULE 4.1 Truthfulness in Statements to Others

In the course of representing a client a lawyer shall not knowingly:

(a) make a false statement of material fact or law to a third person; or

(b) fail to disclose a material fact to a third person when disclosure is necessary to avoid assisting a criminal or fraudulent act by a client, unless disclosure is prohibited by Rule 1.6.

RULE 4.4 Respect for Rights of Third Persons

In representing a client, a lawyer shall not use means that have no substantial purpose other than to embarrass, delay, or burden a third person, or use methods of obtaining evidence that violate the legal rights of such a person.

RULE 5.6 Restrictions on Right to Practice

A lawyer shall not participate in offering or making:

(a) a partnership or employment agreement that restricts the right of a lawyer to practice after termination of the relationship, except an agreement concerning benefits upon retirement; or

(b) an agreement in which a restriction on the lawyer's right to practice is part of the settlement of a controversy between private parties.

RULE 8.4 Misconduct

It is professional misconduct for a lawyer to:

(a) violate or attempt to violate the Rules of Professional Conduct, knowingly assist or induce another to do so, or do so through the acts of another;

(b) commit a criminal act that reflects adversely on the lawyer's honesty, trustworthiness or fitness as a lawyer in other respects;

(c) engage in conduct involving dishonesty, fraud, deceit or misrepresentation;

(d) engage in conduct that is prejudicial to the administration of justice;

(e) state or imply an ability to influence improperly a government agency or official; or

(f) knowingly assist a judge or judicial officer in conduct that is a violation of applicable rules of judicial conduct or other law.

APPENDIX E

THE STANDARDS OF CONDUCT FOR MEDIATORS

[These standards were approved in 1994 by the American Arbitration Association, SPIDR and the American Bar Association Section on Dispute Resolution.]

INTRODUCTORY NOTE

The initiative for these standards came from three professional groups: the American Arbitration Association, the American Bar Association, and the Society in Professionals in Dispute Resolution.

The purpose of this initiative was to develop a set of standards to serve as a general framework for the practice of mediation. The effort is a step in the development of the field and a tool to assist practitioners in it—a beginning, not an end. The standards are intended to apply to all types of mediation. It is recognized, however, that in some cases the application of these standards may be affected by laws or contractual agreements.

PREFACE

The standards of conduct for mediators are intended to perform three major functions: to serve as a guide for the conduct of mediators; to inform the mediating parties; and to promote public confidence in mediation as a process for resolving disputes. The standards draw on existing codes of conduct for mediators and take into account issue and problems that have surfaced in mediation practice. They are offered in the hope that they will serve an educational function and to provide assistance to individuals, organization, and institutions involved in mediation.

Mediation in a process in which an impartial third party—a mediator— facilitates the resolution of a dispute by promoting voluntary agreement (or "self-determination") by the parties to a dispute. A mediator facilitate communications, promotes understanding, focuses the parties on their interests, and seeks creative problem solving to enable the parties to reach their own agreement. These standards give meaning to this definition of mediation.

I. SELF-DETERMINATION:

A MEDIATOR SHALL RECOGNIZE THAT MEDIATION IS BASED ON THE PRINCIPLE OF SELF-DETERMINATION BY THE PARTIES

Self-determination is the fundamental principle of mediation. It requires that the mediation process rely upon the ability of the parties to reach a voluntary, uncoerced agreement. Any party may withdraw from mediation at any time.

Comments:

The mediator may provide information about the process, raise issues, and help parties explore options. The primary role of the mediator is to facilitate a voluntary resolution of a dispute. Parties shall be given the opportunity to consider all proposed options.

A mediator cannot personally ensure that each party has made a fully informed choice to reach a particular agreement, but it is a good practice for the mediator to make the parties aware of the importance of consulting other professionals, where appropriate, to help them make informed decisions.

II. IMPARTIALITY:

A MEDIATOR SHALL CONDUCT THE MEDIATION IN AN IMPARTIAL MANNER

The concept of mediator impartiality is central to the mediation process. A mediator shall mediate only those matters in which she or he remain impartial and evenhanded. If at any time the mediator is unable to conduct the process in an impartial manner, the mediator is obligated to withdraw.

Comments:

A mediator shall avoid conduct that gives the appearance of partiality toward one of the parties. The quality of the mediation process is enhanced when the parties have confidence in the impartiality of the mediator.

When mediators are appointed by a court or institution, the appointing agency shall make reasonable efforts to ensure that mediators serve impartiality.

A mediator should guard against partiality or prejudice based on the parties' personal characteristics, background or performance at the mediation.

III. CONFLICTS OF INTEREST:

A MEDIATOR SHALL DISCLOSE ALL ACTUAL AND POTENTIAL CONFLICTS OF INTEREST REASONABLY KNOWN TO THE MEDIATOR

AFTER DISCLOSURE, THE MEDIATOR SHALL DECLINE TO MEDIATE UNLESS ALL PARTIES CHOOSE TO RETAIN THE MEDIATOR

THE NEED TO PROTECT AGAINST CONFLICTS OF INTEREST ALSO GOVERNS CONDUCT THAT OCCURS DURING AND AFTER THE MEDIATION

A conflict of interest is a dealing or a relationship that might create an impression of possible bias. The basic approach to questions of conflict of interest is consistent with the concept of self-determination. The mediator has a responsibility to disclose all actual and potential conflicts that are reasonably known to the mediator and could reasonably be seen as raining a question about impartiality. If all parties agree to mediate after being informed of conflicts, the mediator may proceed with the mediation. If, however, the conflict of interest casts serious doubt on the integrity of the process, the mediator shall decline to proceed.

A mediator must avoid the appearance of conflict of interest both during and after the mediation. Without the consent of all parties, a mediator shall not subsequently establish a professional relationship with one of the parties in a related matter, or in an unrelated matter under circumstances which would raise legitimate questions about the integrity of the mediation process.

Comments:

A mediator shall avoid conflicts of interests in recommending the services of other professionals. A mediator may make reference to professional referral services of associations which maintain rosters of qualified professionals.

Potential conflicts of interest may arise between administrators of mediation programs and mediators and there may be strong pressures on the mediator to settle a particular case or cases. The mediator's commitment must be to the parties and the process. Pressure from outside of the mediation process should never influence the mediator to coerce parties to settle.

IV. COMPETENCE:

A MEDIATOR SHALL MEDIATE ONLY WHEN THE MEDIATOR HAS THE NECESSARY QUALIFICATIONS TO SATISFY THE REASONABLE EXPECTATIONS OF THE PARTIES

Any person may be selected as a mediator, provided that the parties are satisfied with the mediator's qualifications. Training and experience in mediation, however, are often necessary for effective mediation. A person who offers herself or himself as available to serve as a mediator gives parties and the public the expectation that she or he has the competency to mediate effectively. In court-connected or other forms of mandated mediation, it is essential that mediators assigned to the parties have the requisite training and experience.

Comments:

Mediators should have available for the parties information regarding their relevant training, education and experience.

The requirements of appearing on a list of mediators must be made public and available to interested persons.

When mediators are appointed by a court of institution, the appointing agency shall make reasonable efforts to ensure that each mediator is qualified for the particular mediation.

V. Confidentiality:

A Mediator Shall Maintain the Reasonable Expectations of the Parties With Regard to Confidentiality

The reasonable expectations of the parties with regard to confidentiality shall be met by the mediator. The parties' expectations of confidentiality depend on the circumstances of the mediation and any agreements they may make. A mediator shall not disclose any matter that a party expects to be confidential unless given permission by all parties or unless required by law or other public policy.

Comments:

The parties make their own rules with respect to confidentiality, or accepted practice of an individual mediator or institution may dictate a particular set of expectations. Since the parties expectations' regarding confidentiality are important, the mediator should discuss these expectations with the parties.

If the mediator holds private sessions with a party, the nature of these sessions with regard to confidentiality should be discussed prior to undertaking such sessions.

In order to protect the integrity of the mediation, a mediator should avoid communicating information about how the parties acted in the mediation process, the merits of the case, or settlement offers. The mediator may report, if required, whether parties appeared at a scheduled mediation.

Where the parties have agreed that all or a portion of the information disclosed during a mediation is confidential, the parties' agreement should be respected by the mediator.

Confidentiality should not be construed to limit or prohibit the effective monitoring, research, or evaluation of mediation programs by responsible persons. Under appropriate circumstances, researchers may be permitted to obtain access to statistical data and, with the permission of the parties, to individual case files, observations of live mediations, and interviews with participants.

VI. Quality of the Process:

A Mediator Shall Conduct the Mediation Fairly, Diligently, and in a Manner Consistent with the Principle of Self Determination by the Parties

A mediator shall work to ensure a quality process and to encourage mutual respect among the parties. A quality process requires a commitment by the mediator to diligence and procedural fairness. There should be adequate opportunity for each party in mediation to participate in the discussions. The parties decide when and under what conditions they will reach an agreement or terminate a mediation.

984 APPENDIX E

Comments:

A mediator may agree to mediate only when he or she is prepared to commit the attention essential to an effective mediation.

Mediator should only accept cases when they can satisfy the reasonable expectations of the parties concerning the timing of the process. A mediator should not allow a mediation to be unduly delayed by the parties or their representatives.

The presence or absence of persons at a mediation depends on the agreement of the parties and mediator. The parties and mediator may agree that others may be excluded from particular sessions or from the entire mediation process.

The primary purpose of a mediator is to facilitate the parties' voluntary agreement. This role differs substantially from other professional-client relationships. Mixing the role of mediator and the role of a professional advising a client is problematic, and mediators must strive to distinguish between the roles. A mediator should therefore refrain from providing professional advice. Where appropriate, a mediator should recommend that parties seek outside professional advice, or consider resolving their dispute through arbitration, counselling, neutral evaluation, or other processes. A mediator who undertakes, at the request of the parties, an additional dispute resolution role in the same matter assumes increased responsibilities and obligations that may be governed by the standards of the other professions.

A mediator shall withdraw from a mediation when incapable of serving or when unable to remain impartial.

A mediator shall withdraw from the mediation or postpone a session if the mediation is being used to further illegal conduct, or if a party is unable to participate due to drug, alcohol, or other physical or mental incapacity.

Mediators should not permit their behavior in the mediation process to be guided by a desire for a high settlement rate.

VII. Advertising and Solicitation:

A Mediator Shall Be Truthful in Advertising and Solicitation for Mediation

Advertising or any other communication with the public concerning services offered or regarding the education, training, and expertise of a mediator should be truthful. Mediators shall refrain from promises and guarantees of results.

Comments:

It is imperative that communication with the public educate and instill confidence in the process.

In an advertisement or other communication to the public, a mediator may make reference to meeting state, national, or private organization qualifications only if the entity referred to has a procedure for qualifying mediators and the mediator has been duly granted the requisite status.

VIII. Fees:

A Mediator Shall Fully Disclose and Explain the Basis of Compensation, Fees and Charges to the Parties

The parties should be provided sufficient information about fees at the outset of a mediation to determine if they wish to retain the services of a mediator. If a mediator charges fees, the fees shall be reasonable considering, among other things, the mediation service, the type and complexity of the matter, the expertise of the mediator, the time required, and the rates customary in the community. The better practice in reaching an understanding about fees is to set down the arrangements in a written agreement.

Comments:

A mediator who withdraws from a mediation should return any unearned fee to the parties.

A mediator should not enter into a fees agreement which is contingent upon the result of the mediation or amount of the settlement.

Co-mediators who share a fee should hold to standards of reasonableness in determining the allocation of fees.

A mediator should not accept a fee for referral of a matter to another mediator or to any other person.

IX. Obligations to Mediation Process

Mediators have a duty to improve the practice of mediation.

Comments:

Mediators are regarded as knowledgeable in the process of mediation. They have an obligation to use their knowledge to held educate the public about mediation; to make mediation accessible to those who would like to use it; to correct abuses; and to improve their professional skills and abilities.

*

Appendix F

Federal Arbitration Act
9 U.S.C. § 1 (1925)

CHAPTER 1. GENERAL PROVISIONS

§ 1. "Maritime Transactions," and "Commerce" Defined; Exceptions to Operation of Title

"Maritime transactions," as herein defined, means charter parties, bills of lading of water carriers, agreements relating to wharfage, supplies furnished vessels or repairs of vessels, collisions, or any other matters in foreign commerce which, if the subject of controversy, would be embraced within admiralty jurisdiction; "commerce," as herein defined, means commerce among the several States or with foreign nations, or in any Territory of the United States or in the District of Columbia, or between any such Territory and another, or between any such Territory and any State or foreign nation, or between the District of Columbia and any State or Territory or foreign nation, but nothing herein contained shall apply to contracts of employment of seamen, railroad employees, or any other class of workers engaged in foreign or interstate commerce.

§ 2. Validity, Irrevocability, and Enforcement of Agreements to Arbitrate

A written provision in any maritime transaction or a contract evidencing a transaction involving commerce to settle by arbitration a controversy thereafter arising out of such contract or transaction, or the refusal to perform the whole or any part thereof, or an agreement in writing to submit to arbitration an existing controversy arising out of such a contract, transaction, or refusal, shall be valid, irrevocable, and enforceable, save upon such grounds as exist at law or in equity for the revocation of any contract.

§ 3. Stay of Proceedings Where Issue Therein Referable to Arbitration

If any suit or proceeding be brought in any of the courts of the United States upon any issue referable to arbitration under an agreement in writing for such arbitration, the court in which such suit is pending, upon being satisfied that the issue involved in such suit or proceeding is referable to arbitration under such an agreement, shall on application of one of the parties stay the trial of the action until such arbitration has been had in

APPENDIX F

accordance with the terms of the agreement, providing the applicant for the stay is not in default in proceeding with such arbitration.

§ 4. Failure to Arbitrate Under Agreement; Petition to United States Court Having Jurisdiction for Order to Compel Arbitration; Notice and Service Thereof; Hearing and Determination

A party aggrieved by the alleged failure, neglect, or refusal of another to arbitrate under a written agreement for arbitration may petition any United States district court which, save for such agreement, would have jurisdiction under Title 28, in a civil action or in admiralty of the subject matter of a suit arising out of the controversy between the parties, for an order directing that such arbitration proceed in the manner provided for in such agreement. Five days' notice in writing of such application shall be served upon the party in default. Service thereof shall be made in the manner provided by the Federal Rules of Civil Procedure. The court shall hear the parties, and upon being satisfied that the making of the agreement for arbitration or the failure to comply therewith is not in issue, the court shall make an order directing the parties to proceed to arbitration in accordance with the terms of the agreement. The hearing and proceedings, under such agreement, shall be within the district in which the petition for an order directing such arbitration is filed. If the making of the arbitration agreement or the failure, neglect, or refusal to perform the same be in issue, the court shall proceed summarily to the trial thereof. If no jury trial be demanded by the party alleged to be in default, or in the matter in dispute is within admiralty jurisdiction, the court shall hear and determine such issue. Where such an issue is raised, the party alleged to be in default may, except in cases of admiralty, on or before the return day of the notice of application, demand a jury trial of such issue, and upon such demand the court shall make an order referring the issue or issues to a jury in the manner provided by the Federal Rules of Civil Procedure, or may specially a jury for that purpose. If the jury find that no agreement in writing bitration was made or that there is no default in proceeding thereun- proceeding shall be dismissed. If the jury find that an agreement ation was made in writing and that there is a default in proceed- der, the court shall make an order summarily directing the oceed with the arbitration in accordance with the terms

nt of Arbitrators or Umpire

nent provision be made for a method of naming or or or arbitrators or an umpire, such method shall be od be provided therein, or if a method be provided all fail to avail himself of such method, or if for ll be a lapse in the naming of an arbitrator or lling a vacancy, then upon the application of the court shall designate and appoint an mpire, as the case may require, who shall act under the said agreement with the same force and effect as if he or they had been specifically named therein; and unless otherwise provided in the agreement the arbitration shall be by a single arbitrator.

§ 6. Application Heard as Motion

Any application to the court hereunder shall be made and heard in the manner provided by law for making and hearing of motions, except as otherwise herein expressly provided.

§ 7. Witnesses Before Arbitrators; Fees; Compelling Attendance

The arbitrators selected either as prescribed in this title or otherwise, or a majority of them, may summon in writing any person to attend before them or any of them as a witness and in a proper case to bring with him or them any book, record, document, or paper which may be deemed material as evidence in the case. The fees for such attendance shall be the same as the fees of witnesses before masters of the United States Courts. Said summons shall issue in the name of the arbitrator or arbitrators, or a majority of them, and shall be signed by the arbitrators, or a majority of them, and shall be directed to the said person and shall be served in all the same manner as subpoenas to appear and testify before the court; if any person or persons so summoned to testify shall refuse or neglect to obey said summons, upon petition the United States court in and for the district in which such arbitrators or a majority of them, are sitting may compel the attendance of such person or persons before said arbitrator or arbitrators, or punish said person or persons for contempt in the same manner provided on February 12, 1925, for securing the attendance of witnesses or their punishment for neglect or refusal to attend in the courts of the United States.

§ 8. Proceedings Begun by Libel in Admiralty and Seizure of Vessel or Property

If the basis of jurisdiction be a cause of action otherwise justiciable in admiralty, then, notwithstanding anything herein to the contrary, the party claiming to be aggrieved may begin his proceeding hereunder by libel and seizure of the vessel or other property of the other party according to the usual course of admiralty proceedings, and the court shall then have jurisdiction to direct the parties to proceed with the arbitration and shall retain jurisdiction to enter its decree upon the award.

§ 9. Award of Arbitrators; Confirmation; Jurisdiction; Procedure

If the parties in their agreement have agreed that a judgment of the court shall be entered upon the award made pursuant to the arbitration, and shall specify the court, then at any time within one year after the award is made any party to the arbitration may apply to the court so specified for an order confirming the award, and thereupon the court must grant such an order unless the award is vacated, modified, or corrected as prescribed in sections 10 and 11 of this title. If no court is specified in the agreement of the parties, then such application may be made to the United

990 APPENDIX F

States court in and for the district within which such award was made. Notice of the application shall be served upon the adverse party, and thereupon the court shall have jurisdiction of such party as though he had appeared generally in the proceeding. If the adverse party is a resident of the district within which the award was made, such service shall be made upon the adverse party or his attorney as prescribed by law for service of notice of motion in an action in the same court.

§ 10. Same; Vacation; Grounds; Rehearing

(a) In any of the following cases the United States court in and for the district wherein the award was made may make an order vacating the award upon the application of any party to the arbitration?

(1) Where the award was procured by corruption, fraud, or undue means.

(2) Where there was evident partiality or corruption in the arbitrators, or either of them.

(3) Where the arbitrators were guilty of misconduct in refusing to postpone the hearing, upon sufficient cause shown, or in refusing to hear evidence pertinent and material to the controversy; or of any other misbehavior by which the rights of any party have been prejudiced.

(4) Where the arbitrators exceeded their powers, or so imperfectly executed them that a mutual, final, and definite award upon the subject matter submitted was not made.

(5) Where an award is vacated and the time within which the agreement required the award to be made has not expired the court may, in its discretion, direct a rehearing by the arbitrators.

(b) The United States district court for the district wherein an award was made that was issued pursuant to section 580 of title 5 may make an order vacating the award upon the application of a person, other than a party to the arbitration, who is adversely affected or aggrieved by the award, if the use of arbitration or the award is clearly inconsistent with the factors set forth in section 572 of title 5.

§ 11. Same; Modification or Correction; Grounds; Order

In either of the following cases the United States court in and for the district wherein the award was made may make an order modifying or correcting the award upon the application of any party to the arbitration?

(a) Where there was an evident material miscalculation of figures or an evident material mistake in the description of any person, thing, or property referred to in the award.

(b) Where the arbitrators have awarded upon a matter not submitted to them, unless it is a matter not affecting the merits of the decision upon the matter submitted.

§ 15   FEDERAL ARBITRATION ACT   **991**

(c) Where the award is imperfect in matter of form not affecting the merits of the controversy.

The order may modify and correct the award, so as to effect the intent thereof and promote justice between the parties.

§ 12.   Notice of Motions to Vacate or Modify; Service; Stay of Proceedings

Notice of a motion to vacate, modify, or correct an award must be served upon the adverse party or his attorney within three months after the award is filed or delivered. If the adverse party is a resident of the district within which the award was made, such service shall be made upon the adverse party or his attorney as prescribed by law for service of notice of motion in an action in the same court. If the adverse party shall be a nonresident then the notice of the application shall be served by the marshal of any district within which the adverse party may be found in like manner as other process of the court. For the purposes of the motion any judge who might make an order to stay the proceedings in an action brought in the same court may make an order, to be served with the notice of motion, staying the proceedings of the adverse party to enforce the award.

§ 13.   Papers Filed with Order on Motions; Judgment; Docketing; Force and Effect; Enforcement

The party moving for an order confirming, modifying, or correcting an award shall, at the time such order is filed with the clerk for the entry of judgment thereon, also file the following papers with the clerk:

(a) The agreement: the selection or appointment, if any, of an additional arbitrator or umpire; and each written extension of the time, if any, within which to make the award.

(b) The award.

(c) Each notice, affidavit, or other paper used upon an application to confirm, modify, or correct the award, and a copy of each order of the court upon such an application.

The judgment shall be docketed as if it was rendered in an action.

The judgment so entered shall have the same force and effect, in all respects, as, and be subject to all the provisions of law relating to, a judgment in an action; and it may be enforced as if it had been rendered in an action in the court in which it is entered.

§ 14.   Contracts Not Affected

This title shall not apply to contracts made prior to January 1, 1926.

§ 15.   Inapplicability of the Act of State Doctrine

Enforcement of arbitral agreements, confirmation of arbitral awards, and execution upon judgments based on orders confirming such awards shall not be refused on the basis of the Act of State doctrine.

§ 16. Appeals

(a) An appeal may be taken from?

(1) an order?

(A) refusing a stay of any action under section 3 of this title,

(B) denying a petition under section 4 of this title to order arbitration to proceed,

(C) denying an application under section 206 of this title to compel arbitration,

(D) confirming or denying confirmation of an award or partial award, or

(E) modifying, correcting, or vacating an award;

(2) an interlocutory order granting, continuing, or modifying an injunction against an arbitration that is subject to this title; or

(3) a final decision with respect to an arbitration that is subject to this title.

(b) Except as otherwise provided in section 1292(b) of title 28, an appeal may not be taken from an interlocutory order?

(1) granting a stay of any action under section 3 of this title;

(2) directing arbitration to proceed under section 4 of this title;

(3) compelling arbitration under section 206 of this title; or

(4) refusing to enjoin an arbitration that is subject to this title.

CHAPTER 2. CONVENTION ON THE RECOGNITION AND ENFORCEMENT OF FOREIGN ARBITRAL AWARDS

§ 201. Enforcement of Convention

The Convention on the Recognition and Enforcement of Foreign Arbitral Awards of June 10, 1958, shall be enforced in United States courts in accordance with this chapter.

§ 202. Agreement or Award Falling Under the Convention

An arbitration agreement or arbitral award arising out of a legal relationship, whether contractual or not, which is considered as commercial, including a transaction, contract, or agreement described in section 2 of this title, falls under the Convention. An agreement or award arising out of such relationship which is entirely between citizens of the United States shall be deemed not to fall under the Convention unless that relationship involves property located abroad, envisages performance or enforcement abroad, or has some other reasonable relation with one or more foreign states. For the purpose of this section a corporation is a citizen of the United States if it is incorporated or has its principal place of business in the United States.

§ 203. Jurisdiction; Amount in Controversy

An action or proceeding falling under the Convention shall be deemed to arise under the laws and treaties of the United States. The district courts of the United States (including the courts enumerated in section 460 of title 28) shall have original jurisdiction over such an action or proceeding, regardless of the amount in controversy.

§ 204. Venue

An action or proceeding over which the district courts have jurisdiction pursuant to section 203 of this title may be brought in any such court in which save for the arbitration agreement an action or proceeding with respect to the controversy between the parties could be brought, or in such court for the district and division which embraces the place designated in the agreement as the place of arbitration if such place is within the United States.

§ 205. Removal of Cases From State Courts

Where the subject matter of an action or proceeding pending in a State court relates to an arbitration agreement or award falling under the Convention, the defendant or the defendants may, at any time before the trial thereof, remove such action or proceeding to the district court of the United States for the district and division embracing the place where the action or proceeding is pending. The procedure for removal of causes otherwise provided by law shall apply, except that the ground for removal provided in this section need not appear on the face of the complaint but may be shown in the petition for removal. For the purposes of Chapter 1 of this title any action or proceeding removed under this section shall be deemed to have been brought in the district court to which it is removed.

§ 206. Order to Compel Arbitration; Appointment of Arbitrators

A court having jurisdiction under this chapter may direct that arbitration be held in accordance with the agreement at any place therein provided for, whether that place is within or without the United States. Such court may also appoint arbitrators in accordance with the provisions of the agreement.

§ 207. Award of Arbitrators; Confirmation; Jurisdiction; Proceeding

Within three years after an arbitral award falling under the Convention is made, any party to the arbitration may apply to any court having jurisdiction under this chapter for an order confirming the award as against any other party to the arbitration. The court shall confirm the award unless it finds one of the grounds for refusal or deferral of recognition or enforcement of the award specified in the said Convention.

§ 208. Chapter 1; Residual Applications

Chapter 1 applies to actions and proceedings brought under this chapter to the extent that chapter is not in conflict with this chapter or the Convention as ratified by the United States.

CHAPTER 3. INTER–AMERICAN CONVENTION ON INTERNATIONAL COMMERCIAL ARBITRATION

§ 301. Enforcement of Convention

The Inter–American Convention on International Commercial Arbitration of January 30, 1975, shall be enforced in United States courts in accordance with this chapter.

§ 302. Incorporation by Reference

Sections 202, 203, 204, 205, and 207 of this title shall apply to this chapter as if specifically set forth herein, except that for the purposes of this chapter "the Convention" shall mean the Inter–American Convention.

§ 303. Order to Compel Arbitration; Appointment of Arbitrators; Locale

(a) A court having jurisdiction under this chapter may direct that arbitration be held in accordance with the agreement at any place therein provided for, whether that place is within or without the United States. The court may also appoint arbitrators in accordance with the provisions of the agreement.

(b) In the event the agreement does not make provision for the place of arbitration or the appointment of arbitrators, the court shall direct that the arbitration shall be held and the arbitrators be appointed in accordance with Article 3 of the Inter–American Convention.

§ 304. Recognition and Enforcement of Foreign Arbitral Decisions and Awards; Reciprocity

Arbitral decision or awards made in the territory of a foreign State shall, on the basis of reciprocity, be recognized and enforced under this chapter only if that State has ratified or acceded to the Inter–American Convention.

§ 305. Relationship Between the Inter–American Convention and the Convention on the Recognition and Enforcement of Foreign Arbitral Awards of June 10, 1958

When the requirements for application of both the Inter–American Convention and the Convention on the Recognition and Enforcement of Foreign Arbitral Awards of June 10, 1958, are met, determination as to which Convention applies shall, unless otherwise expressly agreed, be made as follows:

(1) If a majority of the parties to the arbitration agreement are citizens of a State or States that have ratified or acceded to the Inter–American Convention and are member States of the Organization of American States, the Inter–American Convention shall apply.

(2) In all other cases the Convention on the Recognition and Enforcement of Foreign Arbitral Awards of June 10, 1958, shall apply.

§ 306. Applicable Rules of Inter–American Commercial Arbitration Commission

(a) For the purposes of this chapter the rules of procedure of the Inter–American Commercial Arbitration Commission referred to in Article 3 of the Inter–American Convention shall, subject to subsection (b) of this section, be those rules as promulgated by the Commission on July 1, 1988.

(b) In the event the rules of procedure of the Inter–American Commercial Arbitration Commission are modified or amended in accordance with the procedures for amendment of the rules of that Commission, the Secretary of State, by regulation in accordance with section 553 of title 5, consistent with the aims and purposes of this Convention, may prescribe that such modifications or amendments shall be effective for purposes of this chapter.

§ 307. Chapter 1; Residual Application

Chapter 1 applies to actions and proceedings brought under this chapter to the extent chapter 1 is not in conflict with this chapter or the Inter–American Convention as ratified by the United States.

APPENDIX G

UNITED NATIONS CONVENTION ON THE RECOGNITION AND ENFORCEMENT OF FOREIGN ARBITRAL AWARDS

[The New York Convention]

June 10, 1958

Article I

1. This Convention shall apply to the recognition and enforcement of arbitral awards made in the territory of a State other than the State where the recognition and enforcement of such awards are sought, and arising out of differences between persons, whether physical or legal. It shall also apply to arbitral awards not considered as domestic awards in the State where their recognition and enforcement are sought.

2. The term "arbitral awards" shall include not only awards made by arbitrators appointed for each case but also those made by permanent arbitral bodies to which the parties have submitted.

3. When signing, ratifying or acceding to this Convention, or notifying extension under article X hereof, any State may on the basis of reciprocity declare that it will apply the Convention to the recognition and enforcement of awards made only in the territory of another Contracting State. It may also declare that it will apply the Convention only to differences arising out of legal relationships whether contractual or not, which are considered as commercial under the national law of the State making such declaration.

Article II

1. Each Contracting State shall recognize an agreement in writing under which the parties undertake to submit to arbitration all or any differences which have arisen or which may arise between them in respect of a defined legal relationship, whether contractual or not, concerning a subject matter capable of settlement by arbitration.

New York Convention

997

2. The term "agreement in writing" shall include an arbitral clause in a contract or an arbitration agreement, signed by the parties or contained in an exchange of letters or telegrams.

3. The court of a Contracting State, when seized of an action in a matter in respect of which the parties have made an agreement within the meaning of this article, shall, at the request of one of the parties, refer the parties to arbitration, unless it finds that the said agreement is null and void, inoperative or incapable of being performed.

Article III

Each Contracting State shall recognize arbitral awards as binding and enforce them in accordance with the rules of procedure of the territory where the award is relied upon, under the conditions laid down in the following articles. There shall not be imposed substantially more onerous conditions or higher fees or charges on the recognition or enforcement of arbitral awards to which this Convention applies than are imposed on the recognition or enforcement of domestic arbitral awards.

Article IV

1. To obtain the recognition and enforcement mentioned in the preceding article, the party applying for recognition and enforcement shall, at the time of the application, supply:

(a) the duly authenticated original award or a duly certified copy thereof;

(b) the original agreement referred to in article II or a duly certified copy thereof.

2. If the said award or agreement is not made in an official language of the country in which the award is relied upon, the party applying for recognition and enforcement of the award shall produce a translation of these documents into such language. The translation shall be certified by an official or sworn translator or by a diplomatic or consular agent.

Article V

1. Recognition and enforcement of the award may be refused, at the request of the party against whom it is invoked, only if that party furnishes to the competent authority where the recognition and enforcement is sought, proof that:

(a) the parties to the agreement referred to in article II were, under the law applicable to them, under some incapacity, or the said agreement is not valid under the law to which the parties have subjected it or, failing any indication thereon, under the law of the country where the award was made; or

(b) the party against whom the award is invoked was not given proper notice of the appointment of the arbitrator or of the arbitration proceedings or was otherwise unable to present his case; or

(c) the award deals with a difference not contemplated by or not falling within the terms of the submission to arbitration, or it contains decisions on matters beyond the scope of the submission to arbitration, provided that, if the decisions on matters submitted to arbitration can be separated from those not so submitted, that part of the award which contains decisions on matters submitted to arbitration may be recognized and enforced; or

(d) the composition of the arbitral authority or the arbitral procedure was not in accordance with the agreement of the parties, or, failing such agreement, was not in accordance with the law of the country where the arbitration took place; or

(e) the award has not yet become binding on the parties, or has been set aside or suspended by a competent authority of the country in which, or under the law of which, that award was made.

2. Recognition and enforcement of an arbitral award may also be refused if the competent authority in the country where recognition and enforcement is sought finds that:

(a) the subject matter of the difference is not capable of settlement by arbitration under the law of that country; or

(b) the recognition or enforcement of the award would be contrary to the public policy of that country.

Article VI

If an application for the setting aside or suspension of the award has been made to a competent authority referred to in Article V paragraph (1)(e), the authority before which the award is sought to be relied upon may, if it considers it proper, adjourn the decision on the enforcement of the award and may also, on the application of the party claiming enforcement of the award, order the other party to give suitable security.

Article VII

1. The provisions of the present Convention shall not affect the validity of multilateral or bilateral agreements concerning the recognition and enforcement of arbitral awards entered into by the Contracting States nor deprive any interested party of any right he may have to avail himself of an arbitral award in the manner and to the extent allowed by the law or the treaties of the country where such award is sought to be relied upon.

2. The Geneva Protocol on Arbitration Clauses of 1923 and the Geneva Convention on the Execution of Foreign Arbitral Awards of 1927 shall cease to have effect between Contracting States on their becoming bound and to the extent that they become bound, by this Convention.

Article VIII

1. This Convention shall be open until 31 December 1958 for signature on behalf of any Member of the United Nations and also on behalf of any other State which is or hereafter becomes a member of any specialized

agency of the United Nations, or which is or hereafter becomes a party to the Statute of the International Court of Justice, or any other State to which an invitation has been addressed by the General Assembly of the United Nations.

2. This Convention shall be ratified and the instrument of ratification shall be deposited with the Secretary?General of the United Nations.

Article IX

1. This Convention shall be open for accession to all States referred to in article VIII.

2. Accession shall be effected by the deposit of an instrument of accession with the Secretary?General of the United Nations.

Article X

1. Any State may, at the time of signature, ratification or accession, declare that this Convention shall extend to all or any of the territories for the international relations of which it is responsible. Such a declaration shall take effect when the Convention enters into force for the State concerned.

2. At any time thereafter any such extension shall be made by notification addressed to the Secretary?General of the United Nations and shall take effect as from the ninetieth day after the day of receipt by the Secretary?General of the United Nations of this notification, or as from the date of entry into force of the Convention for the State concerned, whichever is the later.

3. With respect to those territories to which this Convention is not extended at the time of signature, ratification or accession, each State concerned shall consider the possibility of taking the necessary steps in order to extend the application of this Convention to such territories, subject, where necessary for constitutional reasons, to the consent of the Governments of such territories.

Article XI

1. In the case of a federal or non-unitary State, the following provisions shall apply:

(a) With respect to those articles of this Convention that come within the legislative jurisdiction of the federal authority, the obligations of the federal Government shall to this extent be the same as those of Contracting States which are not federal States;

(b) With respect to those articles of this Convention that come within the legislative jurisdiction of constituent states or provinces which are not, under the constitutional system of the federation, bound to take legislative action, the federal Government shall bring such articles with a favourable recommendation to the notice of the appropriate authorities of constituent states or provinces at the earliest possible moment;

(c) A federal State party to this Convention shall, at the request of any other Contracting State transmitted through the Secretary?General of the United Nations, supply a statement of the law and practice of the federation and its constituent units in regard to any particular provision of this Convention, showing the extent to which effect has been given to that provision by legislative or other action.

Article XII

1. This Convention shall come into force on the ninetieth day following the date of deposit of the third instrument of ratification or accession.

2. For each State ratifying or acceding to this Convention after the deposit of the third instrument of ratification or accession, this Convention shall enter into force on the ninetieth day after deposit by such State of its instrument of ratification or accession.

Article XIII

1. Any Contracting State may denounce this Convention by a written notification to the Secretary?General of the United Nations. Denunciation shall take effect one year after the date of receipt of the notification by the Secretary–General.

2. Any State which has made a declaration or notification under article X may, at any time thereafter, by notification to the Secretary–General of the United Nations, declare that this Convention shall cease to extend to the territory concerned one year after the date of the receipt of the notification by the Secretary–General.

3. This Convention shall continue to be applicable to arbitral awards in respect of which recognition or enforcement proceedings have been instituted before the denunciation takes effect.

Article XIV

A Contracting State shall not be entitled to avail itself of the present Convention against other Contracting States except to the extent that it is itself bound to apply the Convention.

Article XV

The Secretary–General of the United Nations shall notify the States contemplated in article VIII of the following:

(a) Signature and ratifications in accordance with article VIII;

(b) Accessions in accordance with article IX;

(c) Declarations and notifications under articles I, X and XI;

(d) The date upon which this Convention enters into force in accordance with article XII;

(e) Denunciations and notifications in accordance with article XIII.

Article XVI

1. This Convention, of which the Chinese, English, French, Russian and Spanish texts shall be equally authentic, shall be deposited in the archives of the United Nations.

2. The Secretary–General of the United Nations shall transmit a certified copy of this Convention to the States contemplated in article VIII.

Note:

The United States became a party to the New York Convention in 1970. As of December 15, 1999, 124 nations—including most major commercial states—had ratified the Convention. (In addition, Pakistan had signed but not yet ratified the Convention.) At the present time, Brazil and Taiwan are perhaps the only states of any commercial importance that have not yet acceded to the Convention.

The United States ratified the Convention with the reservation that it would be applied, "on the basis of reciprocity, to the recognition and enforcement of only those awards made in the territory of another Contracting State." A total of 68 contracting states have ratified with this reservation of "reciprocity"—those that have ratified *without* making this reservation have the obligation to enforce *all* foreign awards, wherever rendered. See art. I(3). The United States also ratified the Convention with the reservation that it would be applied "only to differences arising out of legal relationships, whether contractual or not, which are considered as commercial under the national law of the United States." See art. I (3); FAA sec. 202. A total of 40 states have ratified with this reservation.

APPENDIX H

INTER–AMERICAN CONVENTION ON INTERNATIONAL COMMERCIAL ARBITRATION

[The Panama Convention]

January 30, 1975

PREAMBLE

The Governments of the Member States of the Organization of American States, desirous of concluding a convention on international commercial arbitration, have agreed as follows:

Article 1

An agreement in which the parties undertake to submit to arbitral decision any differences that may arise or have arisen between them with respect to a commercial transaction is valid. The agreement shall be set forth in an instrument signed by the parties, or in the form of an exchange of letters, telegrams, or telex communications.

Article 2

Arbitrators shall be appointed in the manner agreed upon by the parties. Their appointment may be delegated to a third party, whether a natural or juridical person. Arbitrators may be nationals or foreigners.

Article 3

In the absence of an express agreement between the parties, the arbitration shall be conducted in accordance with the rules of procedure of the Inter–American Commercial Arbitration Commission.

Article 4

An arbitral decision or award that is not appealable under the applicable law or procedural rules shall have the force of a final judicial judgment. Its execution or recognition may be ordered in the same manner as that of decisions handed down by national or foreign ordinary courts, in accordance with the procedural laws of the country where it is to be executed and the provisions of international treaties.

Article 5

1. The recognition and execution of the decision may be refused, at the request of the party against which it is made, only if such party is able to prove to the competent authority of the State in which recognition and execution are requested:

a. That the parties to the agreement were subject to some incapacity under the applicable law or that the agreement is not valid under the law to which the parties have submitted it , or, if such law is not specified under the law of the State in which the decision was made; or

b. That the party against which the arbitral decision has been made was not duly notified of the appointment of the arbitrator or of the arbitration procedure to be followed, or was unable, for any other reason, to present his defense; or

c. That the decision concerns a dispute not envisaged in the agreement between the parties to submit to arbitration; nevertheless, if the provisions of the decision that refer to issues submitted to arbitration can be separated from those not submitted to arbitration, the former may be recognized and executed; or

d. That the constitution of the arbitral tribunal or the arbitration procedure has not been carried out in accordance with the terms of the agreement signed by the parties or, in the absence of such agreement, that the constitution of the arbitral tribunal or the arbitration procedure has not been carried out in accordance with the law of the State where the arbitration took place; or

e. That the decision is not yet binding on the parties or has been annulled or suspended by competent authority of the State in which, or according to the law of which, the decision has been made.

2. The recognition and execution of an arbitral decision may also be refused if the competent authority of the State in which the recognition and execution is requested finds:

a. That the subject of the dispute cannot be settled by arbitration under the law of the State; or

b. That the recognition or execution of the decision would be contrary to the public policy ("ordre public") of that State.

Article 6

If the competent authority mentioned in Article 5.1.e has been requested to annul or suspend the arbitral decision, the authority before which such decision is invoked may, if it deems it appropriate, postpone a decision on the execution of the arbitral decision and, at the request of the party requesting execution, may also instruct the other party to provide appropriate guaranties.

1004 APPENDIX H

Article 7

This Convention shall be open for signature by the Member States of the Organization of American States.

Article 8

This Convention is subject to ratification. The instruments of ratification shall be deposited with the General Secretariat of the Organization of American States.

Article 9

This Convention shall remain open for accession by any other State. The instruments of accession shall be deposited with the General Secretariat of the Organization of American States.

Article 10

This Convention shall enter into force on the thirtieth day following the date of deposit of the second instrument of ratification.

For each State ratifying or acceding to the Convention after the deposit of the second instrument of ratification, the Convention shall enter into force on the thirtieth day after deposit by such State of its instrument of ratification or accession.

Article 11

If a State Party has two or more territorial units in which different systems of law apply in relation to the matters dealt with in this Convention, it may, at the time of signature, ratification or accession, declare that this Convention shall extend to all its territorial units or only to one or more of them.

Such declaration may be modified by subsequent declarations, which shall expressly indicate the territorial unit or units to which the Convention applies. Such subsequent declarations shall be transmitted to the General Secretariat of the Organization of American States, and shall become effective thirty days after the date of their receipt.

Article 12

This Convention shall remain in force indefinitely, but any of the States Parties may denounce it. The instrument of denunciation shall be deposited with the General Secretariat of the Organization of American States. After one year from the date of deposit of the instrument of denunciation, the Convention shall no longer be in effect for the denouncing State, but shall remain in effect for the other States Parties.

Article 13

The original instrument of this Convention, the English, French, Portuguese and Spanish texts of which are equally authentic, shall be deposited with the General Secretariat of the Organization of American

States. The Secretariat shall notify the Member States of the Organization of American States and the States that have acceded to the Convention of the signatures, deposits of instruments or ratification, accession, and denunciation as well as of reservations, if any. It shall also transmit the declarations referred to in Article 11 of this Convention.

Note:

As of December 15, 1999, 17 nations had ratified the Panama Convention. (In addition, the Dominican Republic and Nicaragua had signed but not yet ratified the Convention). Of these states, four—Brazil, the Dominican Republic, Honduras, and Nicaragua—were not parties to the New York Convention.

The United States became a party to the Panama Convention effective October 27, 1990. In ratifying the Convention, the Government of the United States made the following reservations:

"1. Unless there is an express agreement among the parties to an arbitration agreement to the contrary, where the requirements for application of both the Inter–American Convention on International Commercial Arbitration and the Convention on the Recognition and Enforcement of Foreign Arbitral Awards are met, if a majority of such parties are citizens of a state or states that have ratified or acceded to the Inter–American Convention and are member states of the Organization of American States, the Inter–American Convention shall apply. In all other cases, the Convention on the Recognition and Enforcement of Foreign Arbitral Awards shall apply.

"2. The United States of America will apply the rules of procedure of the Inter–American Commercial Arbitration Commission which are in effect on the date that the United States of America deposits its instrument of ratification, unless the United States of America makes a later official determination to adopt and apply subsequent amendments to such rules.

"3. The United States of America will apply the Convention, on the basis of reciprocity, to the recognition and enforcement of only those awards made in the territory of another Contracting State."

*

FURTHER REFERENCES

In addition to the principal selections throughout this book, there are other sources that may be useful to the reader for reference. These books and articles are listed by chapter.

Chapter I

Books:

Abel, Richard L. (ed.), The Politics of Informal Justice: The American Experience (2 vols. 1982).

Brunet, Edward, & Charles B. Craver, Alternative Dispute Resolution: The Advocate's Perspective (1997).

Carbonneau, Thomas E., Alternative Dispute Resolution: Melting the Lances and Dismounting the Steeds (1989).

Dauer, Edward A., Manual of Dispute Resolution (1994).

Ellickson, Robert C., Order Without Law: How Neighbors Settle Disputes (1991).

Galanter, Marc, & Joel Rogers, The Transformation of American Business Disputing?. Some Preliminary Observations (Disputes Processing Research Program 1991).

Goldberg, Stephen B., Frank E.A. Sander, & Nancy H. Rogers, Dispute Resolution: Negotiation, Mediation and Other Processes (3d ed. 1999).

Kheel, Theodore W., The Keys to Conflict Resolution: Proven Methods of Settling Disputes Voluntarily (1999).

Lieberman, Jethro K., The Litigious Society (1981).

Olson, Walter, The Litigation Explosion (1991).

Riskin, Leonard L. & James E. Westbrook, Dispute Resolution and Lawyers (2d ed. 1998).

Roth, Bette J., Randall W. Wulff & Charles A. Cooper, The Alternative Dispute Resolution Practice Guide (1993).

Singer, Linda R., Settling Disputes: Conflict Resolution in Business, Families, and the Legal System (2d ed. 1994).

Stone, Katherine, Private Justice: The Law of Alternative Dispute Resolution (2000).

Trachte–Huber, E. Wendy & Stephen K. Huber, Alternative Dispute Resolution: Strategies for Law and Business (1996).

1007

CHAPTER I FURTHER REFERENCES

Ware, Stephen J., Alternative Dispute Resolution (2001).

Wilkinson, John H. (ed.), Donovan Leisure Newton & Irvine ADR Practice Book (1990).

Articles:

Bordone, Robert C., Electronic Online Dispute Resolution: A Systems Approach—Potential, Problems, and a Proposal, 3 Harv. Negotiation L. Rev. 175 (Spring 1998).

Baruch Bush, Robert A., Dispute Resolution Alternatives and the Goals of Civil Justice: Jurisdictional Principles for Process Choice, 1984 Wis. L.Rev. 893.

Brunet, Edward, Questioning the Quality of Alternate Dispute Resolution, 62 Tul.L.Rev. 1 (1987).

Cochran, Robert F., Jr., ADR, the ABA, and Client Control: A Proposal that the Model Rules Require Lawyers to Present ADR Options to Clients, 41 S. Tex. L. Rev. 183 (Winter 1999).

Dauer, Edward A., Justice Irrelevant: Speculations on the Causes of ADR, 74 So. Cal. L. Rev. 83 (2000).

Delgado, Richard, Chris Dunn, Pamela Brown, Helena Lee & David Hubbert, Fairness and Formality: Minimizing the Risk of Prejudice in Alternative Dispute Resolution, 1985 Wis.L.Rev. 1359.

Edwards, Harry T., Alternative Dispute Resolution: Panacea or Anathema?, 99 Harv.L.Rev. 668 (1986).

Frey, Martin A., Representing Clients Effectively in an ADR Environment, 33 Tulsa L.J. 443 (Fall 1997).

Galanter, Marc, Why the "Haves" Come Out Ahead: Speculations or, the Limits of Legal Change, 9 Law & Soc'y Rev. 95 (1974).

———, Reading the Landscape of Disputes: What We Know And Don't Know (And Think We Know) About Our Allegedly Contentious and Litigious Society, 31 UCLA L.Rev. 4 (1983).

———, Justice in Many Rooms: Courts, Private Ordering, and Indigenous Law, 19 J. Pluralism & Unofficial L. 1 (1981).

——— & Mia Cahill, Most Cases Settle: Judicial Promotion and Regulation of Settlements?, 46 Stan.L.Rev. 1339 (1994).

Garth, Bryant G., Privatization and the New Market for Disputes: A Framework for Analysis and a Preliminary Assessment, 12 Stud. Law Pol. & Soc'y 367 (1992).

Kupfer Schneider, Andrea, Building a Pedagogy of Problem–Solving: Learning to Choose Among ADR Processes, 5 Harv. Negotiation L. Rev. 113 (Spring 2000).

Lind, E. Allen, Robert Maccoun, Patricia Ebener, William Felstiner, Deborah Hensler, Judith Resnik, & Tom Tyler, In the Eye of the Beholder:

Tort Litigants' Evaluations of Their Experiences in the Civil Justice System, 24 Law & Soc'y Rev. 953 (1990).

Menkel–Meadow, Carrie, Pursuing Settlement in an Adversary Culture: A Tale of Innovation Co–Opted or "the Law of ADR", 19 Fla.St.U.L.Rev. 1 (1991).

___, What Will We Do When Adjudication Ends? A Brief Intellectual History of ADR, 44 UCLA L. Rev. 1613 (August 1997).

Picker, Bennett G., New Roles: Problem Solving ADR: New Challenges, New Roles, and New Opportunities, 72 Temple L. Rev. 833 (Winter 1999).

Polythress, Norman G., Procedural Preferences, Perceptions of Fairness and Compliance with Outcomes: A Study of Alternatives to the Standard Adversary Trial Procedure, 18 Law & Hum. Behav. 361(1994).

Resnik, Judith, Many Doors? Closing Doors? Alternative Dispute Resolution and Adjudication, 10 Ohio St.J. on Disp. Res. 211 (1995).

Sander, Frank E.A., Varieties of Dispute Processing, 70 F.R.D. 111 (1976).

___, Fitting the Forum to the Fuss: A User–Friendly Guide to Selecting an ADR Procedure, 10 Negotiation J. 49 (1994).

Shavell, Steven, Alternative Dispute Resolution: An Economic Analysis, 24 J. Leg. Stud. 1 (1995).

Special Edition: Alternative Dispute Resolution and Procedural Justice, 46 S.M.U.L.Rev. (1993)

Stempel, Jeffrey W., Reflections on Judicial ADR and the Multi–Door Courthouse at Twenty: Fait Accompli, Failed Overture, or Fledgling Adulthood?, 11 Ohio St. J. on Disp. Res. 297 (1996).

Sternlight, Jean R., Is Binding Arbitration a Form of ADR?: An Argument That the Term "ADR" Has Begun to Outlive its Usefulness, 2000 J. Disp. Resol. 97 (2000).

Stipanowich, Thomas J., The Multi–Door Contract and Other Possibilities, 13 Ohio St. J. on Disp. Res. 303 (1998).

Symposium Issue, Quality of Dispute Resolution, 66 Denv. U.L.Rev. No. 3(1989).

Symposium, The Lawyer's Duties and Responsibilities in Dispute Resolution, 38 South Texas Law Review No. 2 (1997).

Symposium, Dispute Resolution in the Law School Curriculum: Opportunities and Challenges, 50 Fla. L. Rev. No. 5 (1998).

Symposium, ADR and the Professional Responsibility of Lawyers, 28 Fordham Urban L.J. No. 4 (2001).

Wangerin, Paul T., The Political and Economic Roots of the "Adversary System" of Justice and Alternative Dispute Resolution, 9 Ohio St.J. on Disp. Res. 203 (1994).

1010 CHAPTER I FURTHER REFERENCES

Ware, Stephen J. & Sarah Rudolph Cole, Introduction: ADR in Cyberspace, 15 Ohio St. J. on Disp. Res. 589 (2000).

Chapter II

Books:

Arrow, Kenneth J. (ed.), Barriers to Conflict Resolution (1995).

Axelrod, Robert M., The Evolution of Cooperation (1984).

Bazerman, Max H., & Roy J. Lewicki, Negotiating in Organizations (1983).

___, & Margaret A. Neale, Negotiating Rationally (1991).

Brams, Steven J., & Alan D. Taylor, The Win–Win Solution: Guaranteeing Fair Shares to Everybody (1999).

___, & Alan D. Taylor, Fair Division: From Cake–Cutting to Dispute Resolution (1996).

Brazil, Wayne D., Effective Approaches to Settlement: A Handbook for Lawyers and Judges (1988).

Breslin, J. William, & Jeffrey Z. Rubin (eds.), Negotiation Theory and Practice (1991).

Cialdini, Robert B., Influence: Science and Practice (3d ed. 1993).

Cloke, Kenneth, & Joan Goldsmith, Resolving Personal and Organizational Conflict: Stories of Transformation and Forgiveness (2000).

Dixit, Avinash K., & Barry J. Nalebuff, Thinking Strategically: The Competitive Edge in Business, Politics, and Everyday Life (1991).

Fisher, Roger, & William J. Ury, with Bruce Patton, Getting to Yes (2d ed. 1991).

Freund, James C., Smart Negotiating: How to Make Good Deals in the Real World (1992).

Goleman, Daniel, Emotional Intelligence (1995).

Hammond, John S., Ralph L. Keeney, & Howard Raiffa, Smart Choices: A Practical Guide to Making Better Decisions (1999).

Heifitz, Ron, Leadership Without Easy Answers (1994)

Isaacs, William, Dialogue and the Art of Thinking Together (1999)

Kahneman, Daniel, Paul Slovic, & Amos Tversky, Judgment under Uncertainty: Heuristics and biases (1982).

Kritzer, Herbert M., Let's Make a Deal: Understanding the Negotiation Process in Ordinary Litigation (1991).

Kolb, Deborah M., & Judith Williams, The Shadow Negotiation: How Women Can Master the Hidden Agendas That Determine Bargaining Success (2000).

Lax, David, & James K. Sebenius, The Manager as Negotiator (1986).

Lewicki, Roy J., David M. Saunders, & John W. Minton, Negotiation (3d ed. 1999).

Mnookin, Robert, Scott Peppet, & Andrew Tulumello, Beyond Winning:

Creating Value in Negotiating Deals and Disputes (2000)

___, & Lawrence E. Susskind (eds.), Negotiating on Behalf of Others (1999).

Nelken, Melissa L., Understanding Negotiation (2001).

Raiffa, Howard, The Art and Science of Negotiation (1982).

Rogers, Carl, On Becoming a Person (1961).

Schelling, Thomas C., Strategies of Conflict (1960).

Schon, Donald, The Reflective Practitioner (1987)

Stone, Douglas, Bruce Patton, & Sheila Heen, Difficult Conversations: How to Discuss What Matters Most (1999).

Ury, William L., Getting Past No: Negotiating With Difficult People (1991).

Walton, Richard E., Joel E. Cutcher–Gershenfeld, & Robert B. McKersie, Strategic Negotiations: A Theory of Change in Labor–Management Relations (1994).

Articles:

Gross, Samuel R., & Kent D. Syverud, Getting to No: A Study of Settlement Negotiations and the Selection of Cases for Trial, 90 Mich. L.Rev. 319 (1991).

Guernsey, Thomas F., Truthfulness in Negotiation, 17 Univ. Rich. L.Rev. 99 (1982).

Korobkin, Russell, & Chris Guthrie, Psychological Barriers to Litigation Settlement: An Experimental Approach, 93 Mich. L.Rev. 107 (1994).

Menkel–Meadow, Carrie, Toward Another View of Legal Negotiation: The Structure of Problem Solving, 31 UCLA L.Rev. 754 (1984).

Mnookin, Robert H., & Ronald J. Gilson, Disputing Through Agents: Cooperation and Conflict Between Lawyers in Litigation, 94 Colum.L.Rev. 509 (1994).

Murray, John S., Understanding Competing Theories of Negotiation, 2 Negotiation J. 179 (1986).

Perschbacher, Rex R., Regulating Lawyers' Negotiations, 27 Ariz.L.Rev. 75 (1985).

Peters, Geoffrey M., The Use of Lies in Negotiation, 48 Ohio St.L.J. 1 (1987).

Watson, Carol, Gender versus Power as a Predictor of Negotiation Behavior and Outcome, 10 Negotiation J. 117 (1994).

Wetlaufer, Gerald B., The Ethics of Lying in Negotiation, 76 Iowa L.Rev. 1219 (1990).

1012   CHAPTER II   FURTHER REFERENCES

White, James J., Machiavelli and the Bar: Ethical Limitations on Lying in Negotiation, 1980 Am.Bar.Found. Research J. 926.

Chapter III

Websites:

www.mediate.com (Mosten–Mediation)

www.natcm.org (National Assoc. of Community Mediation)

www.fmcs.gov (Federal Mediation and Conciliation Service).

Books:

Alfini, James, & Eric Galton (eds.), ADR Personalities and Practice Tips (ABA Section on Litigation., 1998).

Baruch Bush, Robert, The Dilemmas of Mediation Practice (1992).

___ & Joseph Folger, The Promise of Mediation (1994).

Bühring-Uhle, Christian, Arbitration and Mediation in International Business (1996).

Cooley, John, Mediation Advocacy (1996)

___, The Mediator's Handbook (2000).

Folberg, Jay, & Alison Taylor, Mediation: A Comprehensive Guide to Resolving Conflicts Without Litigation (1994).

Galton, Eric, Representing Clients in Mediation (1994).

___ & Kimberlee Kovach, Representing Clients in Mediation (1994).

Haynes, John, The Fundamentals of Family Mediation (1994).

Henry, James, & Lethro K. Lieberman, The Manager's Guide to Resolving Legal Disputes (1985).

Moore, Christopher, The Mediation Process: Practical Strategies for Resolving Conflict (1996).

Picker, Bennett, Mediation Practice Guide: A Handbook for Resolving Business Disputes (1998).

Rogers, Nancy & Craig McEwen, Mediation: Law, Policy, Practice (2d ed. 1994).

Rothman, John D., A Lawyer's Practical Guide to Mediation (1995).

Susskind, Lawrence, Sarah McKearnan, & Jennifer Thomas Larmer (eds.), The Consensus Building Handbook: A Comprehensive Guide to Reaching Agreement (1999).

Van Winkle, John, Mediation—The Path Back for the Lost Lawyer (2001).

Articles:

Adler, Peter S., *Lawyer & Nonlawyer Mediations*, 33 Nat'l Inst. Disp. Resol. 45 (1997).

Alfini, James J., *Trashing, Bashing, and Hashing It Out: Is This the End of "Good Mediation"?*, 19 Fla. State U. L. Rev. 47 (1991).

Brett, Jeanne M., Zoe I. Barsness, & Stephen Goldberg, *The Effectiveness of Mediation: An Independent Analysis of Cases Handled by Four Major Service Providers*, NEGO. J. 259 (1996).

Cobb, Sarah & Janet Rifkin, Practice and Paradox: Deconstructing Neutrality in Mediation, 16 Law & Social Inquiry 35 (1991).

Cooley, John W., *A Classical Approach to Mediation—Part I: Classical Rhetoric and the Art of Persuasion in Mediation*, 19 U. Dayton L. Rev. 83 (1993).

Dougherty, Judy K., & Josefina M. Rendon, *Models, Styles and the Process of Family Mediation*, Alternative Resolutions 22 (June 2001).

Hermann, Jean, *The Dangers of ADR :A Three–Tiered System of Justice*, 3 J. of Contemp. Legal Issues 117 (1990).

Kovach, Kimberlee K., *New Wine Requires New Wineskins: Transforming Lawyer Ethics for Effective Representation in a Non–Adversarial Approach to Problem Solving: Mediation*, 28 Fordham Urban L. J. 935 (2001).

___ & Lela P. Love, *Mapping Mediation: The Risks of Riskin's Grid*, 3 Harv. Negotiation L. Rev. 71 (1998).

McEwen, Craig, & Thomas Milburn, *Explaining a Paradox of Mediation*, 9 Negotiation J. 23 (1993).

Menkel–Meadow, Carrie, *Lawyer Negotiations: Theories and realities— What We Learn from Mediation*, 56 Mod. L. Rev. 361 (May 1993).

Nolan–Haley, Jacqueline M., *Lawyers, Clients, and Mediation*, 73 Notre Dame L. Rev. 1369 (1998).

Shannon, Brian D., *Confidentiality of Texas Mediations: Ruminations on Some Thorny Problems*, 32 Texas Tech L. Rev. 77 (2000).

Sherman, Edward F., *Confidentiality in ADR Proceedings: Policy Issues Arising from the Texas Experience*, 38 South Tex. L. Rev. 541 (1997).

Stulberg, Joseph B., *Facilitative Versus Evaluative Mediator Orientations: Piercing the "Grid" Lock*, 24 Florida State U. L. Rev. 985, 991–995 (1997).

Special Edition: Alternative Dispute Resolution and Procedural Justice, 46 S.M.U.L. Rev. (1993).

Susskind, Lawrence, Mediated Negotiation in the Public Sector, in Negotiation Theory and Practice 401 (J. William Breslin & Jeffrey Z. Rubin, eds, 1991)

Symposium: Dispute Resolution Ethics, Dispute Resolution Magazine (Spring 2001).

Symposium: Standards of Professional Conduct in Alternative Dispute Resolution, 1995 J. of Dis. Resol. 95.

1014 CHAPTER III FURTHER REFERENCES

Weckstein, Donald T., *In Praise of Party Empowerment—And of Mediator Activism*, 33 Willamette L. Rev. 501 (1997).

Chapter IV

Books:

Bergman, Edward J. & John G. Bickerman, Court–Annexed Mediation: Critical Perspectives on Selected State and Federal Programs (2001).

Niemic, Robert, Donna Stienstra, & Randall Ravitz, Guide to Judicial Management of Cases in ADR (2001).

Plapinger, Elizabeth, & Donna Stienstra, Source Book on Federal District Court ADR and Settlement Procedures (Federal Judicial Center 1996).

Articles:

Bernstein, Lisa, *Understanding the Limits of Court–Connected ADR: A Critique of Federal Court–Annexed Arbitration Programs*, 141 U. Pa. L. Rev. 2169 (1993).

Fitzgibbon, Susan A., *Appellate Settlement Conference Programs: A Case Study*, 1993 J. OF Disp. Resol. 57 (March 22, 1993).

Ganzfried, Jerrold J., *Bringing Business Judgment to Business Litigation: Mediation and Settlement in the Federal Courts of Appeals*, 65 Geo. Wash. L. Rev. 531 (1997).

Hogan, Michael, *Judicial Settlement Conferences: Empowering the Parties to Decide through Negotiation*, 27 Willamette L. Rev. 429 (1991).

Katz, Lucy V., Compulsory Alternative Dispute Resolution and Voluntarism: Two–Headed Monster or Two Sides of the Coin?, 1993 J. Disp. Resol. 1 (1993).

Moberly, Robert B., Ethical Standards for Court–Appointed Mediators and Florida's Mandatory Mediation Experiment, 21 Fla. St. U.L. Rev. 701 (1994).

Shaw, Margaret, *Election, Training, and Qualifications of Neutrals* (National Symposium on Court Connected Dispute Resolution, State Justice Institute, Oct. 15–16, 1993).

Sherman, Edward F., Court–Mandated Alternative Dispute Resolution: What Form of Participation Should be Required?, 46 SMU L. Rev. 2079 (1993).

——, A Process Model and Agenda for Civil Justice Reform in the States, 46 Stan. L. Rev. 1553 (1994).

Streeter–Schaefer, Holley A., *A Look at Court Mandated Civil Mediation*, 49 Drake L. Rev. 367 (2001).

Woodley, Ann E., *Strengthening the Summary Jury Trial: A Proposal to Increase its Effectiveness and Encourage Uniformity in its Use*, 12 Ohio St. J. on Disp. Resol. 541 (1997).

Chapter V

Websites:

www. adr.org (American Arbitration Association)

www.naarb.org (National Academy of Arbitrators)

www.arbitrators.org (Chartered Institute)

www.lcia-arbitration.com (LCIA)

www.jamsadr.com (JAMS)

www.iccwbo.org (ICC)

www.cpradr.org (CPR Institute of Dispute Resolution)

www.asser.nl (T.M.C. Asser Institute)

Books:

Born, Gary, International Commercial Arbitration in the United States (1994).

_____, International Arbitration and Forum Selection Agreements: Planning, Drafting, and Enforcing (1999).

Bühring-Uhle, Christian, Arbitration and Mediation in International Business: Designing Procedures for Effective Conflict Management (1996).

Carbonneau, Tom, Cases and Materials on Commercial Arbitration (1997).

Cooper, Laura J., Dennis R. Nolan, & Richard A. Bales, ADR in the Workplace (2000).

Craig, W. Laurence, William W. Park & Jan Paulsson, International Chamber of Commerce Arbitration (3d ed. 2000).

_____, Craig, Park, & Paulsson's Annotated Guide to the 1998 ICC Arbitration Rules: with Commentary (1998).

Dezalay, Yves & Bryant G. Garth, Dealing in Virtue: International Commercial Arbitration and the Construction of a Transnational Legal Order (1996).

Derains, Yves & Eric A. Schwartz, A Guide to the New ICC Rules of Arbitration (1998).

Domke, Martin, Commercial Arbitration (Rev. ed.).

Elkouri, Frank, & Edna A. Elkouri, How Arbitration Works (5th ed. 1997) (labor arbitration).

Fox, William F., Jr., International Commercial Agreements: A Primer on Drafting, Negotiating, and Resolving Disputes (3d ed. 1998).

Fouchard, Philippe, Emmanuel Gaillard, & Berthold Goldman, International Commercial Arbitration (1999).

Frommel, Stefan N. & Barry A. K. Rider (eds.), Conflicting Legal Cultures in Commercial Arbitration: Old Issues and New Trends (1999).

Haagen, Paul, Arbitration Now: Opportunities for Fairness, Process Renewal and Invigoration (1999).

Hill, Marvin F. Jr., & Sinicropi, Anthony V., Remedies in Arbitration, (2d ed. 1991) (labor arbitration).

Lookofsky, Joseph, M., Transnational Litigation and Commercial Arbitration: A Comparative Analysis of American, European and International Law (1992).

Macneil, Ian R., American Arbitration Law: Reformation, Nationalization, Internationalization (1992).

⸺, Richard E. Speidel, & Thomas J. Stipanowich, Federal Arbitration Law: Agreements, Awards, and Remedies Under the Federal Arbitration Act (1994).

Redfern, Alan, & Martin Hunter, Law and Practice of International Commercial Arbitration (3d ed. 1999).

Reisman, W. Michael, W. Lawrence Craig, William Park & Jan Paulsson, International Commercial Arbitration (1997).

Samuel, Adam, Jurisdictional Problems in International Commercial Arbitration (1989).

Schoonhoven, Ray J. (ed.), Fairweather's Practice and Procedure in Labor Arbitration (3d ed. 1991).

Várady, Tibor, John J. Barceló, III, & Arthur T. von Mehren, International Commercial Arbitration (1999).

Zack, Arnold M. (ed.), Arbitration in Practice (1984) (labor arbitration).

⸺, Grievance Arbitration: Issues on the Merits in Discipline, Discharge, and Contract Interpretation (1989).

Zimny, Max, William F. Dolson, & Christopher A. Barreca, Labor Arbitration: A Practical Guide For Advocates (ABA 1990).

Articles:

Allison, John R., The Context, Properties and Constitutionality of Non-Consensual Arbitration, 1990 J.Disp.Resol. 1 (1990).

Bruff, Harold H., Public Programs, Private Deciders: The Constitutionality of Arbitration in Federal Programs, 67 Tex. L.Rev. 441 (1989).

Brunet, Edward, Arbitration and Constitutional Rights, 71 N.C.L.Rev. 81(1992).

⸺, Replacing Folklore Arbitration with a Contract Model of Arbitration, 74 Tulane L.Rev. 39 (1999).

Carbonneau, Thomas E., Arbitral Justice: The Demise of Due Process in American Law, 70 Tul. L. Rev. 1945 (1996).

Carrington, Paul D. & Paul H. Haagen, Contract and Jurisdiction, 1996 Sup. Ct. Rev. 331 (1997).

Cole, Sarah Rudolph, Managerial Litigants? The Overlooked Problem of Party Autonomy in Dispute Resolution, 51 Hastings L.J. 1199 (2000).

Dezalay, Yves, & Bryant Garth, Merchants of Law as Moral Entrepreneurs: Constructing International Justice from the Competition for Transnational Business Disputes, 29 Law & Scooby Rev. 27 (1995).

Drahozal, Christopher R., Privatizing Civil Justice: Commercial Arbitration and the Civil Justice System, 9 Kan. J.L. & Pub. Pol'y 578 (2000).

___, Commercial Norms, Commercial Codes, and International Commercial Arbitration, 33 Vanderbilt J. of Transnational L. 79 (2000).

___, "Unfair" Arbitration Clauses, 2001 U. of Illinois L. Rev. 695.

Getman, Julius G., Labor Arbitration and Dispute Resolution, 88 Yale L.J. 916 (1979).

Heilbron, David M., The Arbitration Clause, the Preliminary Conference, and the Big Case, 45 Arb.J. 38 (1990).

Hill, Marvin F., Jr., Interest Criteria in Fact–Finding and Arbitration: Evidentiary and Substantive Considerations, 74 Marq.L.Rev. 399 (1991).

Kerr, Justice, International Arbitration vs. Litigation, J.Bus.L. 164 (May, 1980).

Mehtschikoff, Soia, Commercial Arbitration, 61 Colum. L.Rev. 846 (1961).

___, The Significance of Arbitration–A Preliminary Inquiry, 17 Law & Contemp.Probs. 698 (1952).

Morgan, Edward M., Contract Theory and the Sources of Rights: An Approach to the Arbitrability Question, 60 S.Cal. L.Rev. 1059 (1987).

Park, William W., Duty and Discretion in International Arbitration, 93 Am. J. Int'l L. 805 (1999).

___, Arbitration's Discontents: Of Elephants and Pornography, 17 Arb. Int'l 263 (2001).

Peter, James T., Med–Arb in International Arbitration, 8 Amer. Rev. Int'l Arb. 83 (1997).

Rau, Alan Scott, Resolving Disputes Over Attorneys' Fees: The Role of ADR, 46 SMU L.Rev. 2005 (1993).

___, The UNCITRAL Model Law in State and Federal Courts: The Case of "Waiver," 6 Am. Rev. Int'l Arb. 223 (1995).

___, The New York Convention in American Courts, 7 Am. Rev. Int'l Arb. 213 (1996).

___, "The Arbitrability Question Itself," 10 Am. Rev. of Int'l Arb. 287 (1999).

Speidel, Richard E., Arbitration of Statutory Rights Under the Federal Arbitration Act: The Case for Reform, 4 Ohio St.J. on Disp.Res. 157(1989).

CHAPTER V FURTHER REFERENCES

Sternlight, Jean R., As Mandatory Binding Arbitration Meets the Class Action, Will the Class Action Survive?, 42 William & Mary L. Rev. 1 (2000).

——, Rethinking the Constitutionality of the Supreme Court's Preference for Binding Arbitration: A Fresh Assessment of Jury Trial, Separation of Powers, and Due Process Concerns, 72 Tulane L. Rev. 1 (1997).

——, Mandatory Binding Arbitration and the Demise of the Seventh Amendment Right to a Jury Trial, 16 Ohio St. J. on Disp. Res. 669 (2001).

Stipanowich, Thomas J., Rethinking American Arbitration, 63 Ind.L.J. 425(1988).

——, Punitive Damages and the Consumerization of Arbitration, 92 Northwestern U. L. Rev. 1 (1997).

Symposium on International Commercial Arbitration, 30 Tex. Int'l. L.J. No. 1 (Winter 1995).

Symposium, Commercial Arbitration: A Discussion of Recent Developments and Trends, 31 Wake Forest L. Rev. No. 1 (1996).

Chapter VI

Books:

Carroll, Eileen, and Mackie, Karl, International Mediation—The Art of Business Diplomacy (2000).

Chew, Pat K., (ed.), The Conflict and Culture Reader (2001).

Fisher, Glen, International Negotiation: A Cross–Cultural Perspective (1980).

Fisher, Roger, Andrea Kupfer Schneider, & Elizabeth Borgwardt, Coping with International Conflict: A Systematic Approach to Influence in International Negotiation (1997).

Plant, David W., Resolving International Intellectual Property Disputes (ICC, 1999).

Articles:

Carter, James H., "Litigating in Foreign Territory: Arbitration Alternatives and Enforcement Issues" (National Institute, Doing Business Worldwide, American Bar Association Center for Continuing Legal Education, February 8–10, 1998).

Epstein, Judd, "The Use of Comparative Law in Commercial International Arbitration and Commercial Mediation" 75 Tul. L.R. 913 (2001).

Schneider, Andrea K., "Getting Along: The Evolution of Dispute Resolution Regimes in International Trade Organizations" 20 Mich. J. Intl. L. 697 (1999).

Von Mehren, Robert B. "An International Arbitrator's Point of View" 10 Am. Rev. Int'l Arb. 203 (1999).

INDEX

References are to pages

AAA, see American Arbitration Association

ABA, see American Bar Association

ADJUDICATION
See also Courts; Litigation
International options, 938–940
Limits of, 15–33, 617–618
Litigation, distinguished from, 15
Private adjudication, 15, 599–620, 901–905
Public values in, 33–40

ADMINISTRATIVE DISPUTE RESOLU-TION ACT OF 1990, 336

ADVERSARY MODEL, 1–4, 11–12, 49–77, 854–857
Problem solving model, distinguished from, 126–130, 358–370

AGENCY COSTS, 377–380

AGENT ORANGE LITIGATION, 300–304

AGREEMENT
To arbitrate, see Arbitration
International ADR clauses, 927–958
Joint defense, 228
Mary Carter, 228–229, 295–296
To mediate, see Mediation
Zone of possible agreement, 81–83

ALTERNATIVE DISPUTE RESOLU-TION
ADR Act of 1998, 47–48
"Movement", 44–49, 329–337

AMERICAN ARBITRATION ASSOCIA-TION (AAA), 611, 622, 624–628, 631, 642–644, 672, 720–723, 834–839, 847, 850, 867, 875, 899
AAA standard clause for commercial con-tracts, 720, 928–929
International arbitration clause, 928–929, 948–949

AMERICAN BAR ASSOCIATION (ABA)
Model Code of Professional Responsibility, 210, 217–218, 455
Model Rules of Professional Conduct, 210–217, 222–224, 227, 234–235, 455, 457, 459–460, 652, 780, 975–979

AMERICAN BAR ASSOCIATION (ABA)
—Cont'd
Standards of Practice for Lawyer–Mediators in Family Disputes, 457, 460, 510–511
Standards of Conduct for Mediators, 533, 535–539

APPELLATE ADR, see Court-annexed ADR Processes

ARBITRATION
Generally, 597–905
Agreement to arbitrate, 674–682, 684–730
Adhesion contracts, and unconscionabili-ty, 47, 642–653, 697–711, 757, 796–824
AAA standard clause for commercial con-tracts, 720, 928–929
"Separability," 690–699, 721, 764, 816
And state contract law, 653–654, 684–690
United Nations Convention on Contracts for the International Sale of Goods and, 688
Arbitrability, 712–730, 766–796
"Procedural arbitrability," 725
Arbitrator,
Caseloads, 837–838
Disclosure of relations with party, 842–848
Expertise, 601–602, 834–839, 861–862
Fees, 838–839
Immunity, 853–854
Impartiality, 704, 842–854
Lawyer as arbitrator, 837, 841, 855–857
Selection of, 834–842
Attorney-client disputes, 602–603, 651–653, 883–884
Automobile warranty disputes, 650–651, 882–883
Baseball contracts, 888–890
and class actions, 643, 656–660, 682–684, 710–711
Commercial arbitration, 620–633, 839, 846–850
Complex disputes, 866–867
Compromise decisions, 640–641, 849
Compulsory arbitration, 876–888
In administrative actions, 876–884
In public employment disputes, 884–888
In public regulation, 887–888
Consolidation, see Multi-party disputes

1019

ARBITRATION—Cont'd

Consumer disputes, see generally Adhesion contracts

Court-annexed arbitration, see Court-annexed ADR Processes

Discovery in, 862–870

Employment disputes, 669–670, 722–723, 787–796, 832–833, 887–888
And public policy, 761–764, 787–794

Evidence, 857–862
Privileges, 869–870

Failure to appear at arbitration, effect of, 723–725

Final-offer arbitration, 888–892
Mediation and, 899–900

Frequent uses of, 620–653

"Interest" and "rights" arbitration, 613–620, 721–722, 757, 884–887, 888–893

Interim relief, 870–876

International commercial arbitration, 626–633, 742–743, 757, 765, 766–778, 850–852, 862, 875–876, 938–962
Arbitration clauses, 944–950
Choice of law, 946
Combine with settlement options, 952–958
Institutional or ad hoc administration, 942–942
Party-appointed arbitrators, 842–854, 947–949
Place of arbitration, 945–946
Rules, 942–950
Protocols, 954–957

Judicial supervision and review, 729–834
Awards, judicial review of, 730–766, 778, 824–834, 886–887

Labor arbitration, 601–602, 619–620, 633–639, 718–719, 743, 762–763, 791–796, 838–842, 849, 869–870, 884–893

Lawyers, role of, 855–857

Legal rules, 611–613, 742–761

Med-arb, 892–900, 952–958

Medical malpractice arbitration, 556, 644–653, 699–707

Multi-party disputes, 670–684

Non-binding arbitration, 751–754

and Olympic games, 632–633

Patent disputes, 780–781

Preemption of state law, 655–684

Privileges, 869–870

Procedure, 834–876

Public policy, 613, 670, 745, 761–824

Punitive damages in, 816–817, 824–834

Res judicata and collateral estoppel, 787–795

Securities disputes, 783–787, 824–830

Waiver of the right to, 725–729

Written opinions, 599–600, 611–612, 633, 755–761

ATTORNEYS, see Lawyers

BARGAINING

See also Negotiation

BARGAINING—Cont'd

"Bargaining in the shadow of the law," 363, 388

BEST ALTERNATIVE TO A NEGOTIATED AGREEMENT (BATNA), 81–83, 100–105

BOULWARISM, 136, 209

BURGER, WARREN, 33, 44–47

CENTER FOR PUBLIC RESOURCES (CPR), 333, 388, 563, 584, 852, 938, 941–944, 955

CHILD CUSTODY, 29–30, 779–780

CHINA INTERNATIONAL ECONOMIC AND TRADE ARBITRATION COMMISSION (CIETAC), 630–631, 898–899

CIVIL JUSTICE REFORM ACT OF 1990, 577–578, 579, 585

CIVIL LITIGATION RESEARCH PROJECT (CLRP), 12–15

COLLECTIVE BARGAINING, see Arbitration, Labor arbitration

CONFERENCE

Pre-trial, 548–549, 570, 583

Settlement, 297–326

Obligation to attend, 311–326

CONFIDENTIALITY

See also specific ADR processes; Rule 408, Federal Rules of Evidence

Generally, 279–288, 461–514

Contractual agreements of, 510–514

In arbitration, 604

In International mediation, 935–936

In mediation, State statutory approaches, 481–510
Judicially created, 457–481

In negotiation, 279–288

In summary jury trials, 570–571

CONSENT DECREES, 254–260

CONSUMER DISPUTES, see Disputes

COOPERATION, EVOLUTION OF, 145–153

COOPERATIVE APPROACH, see also Problem–Solving

COURT-ANNEXED ADR PROCESSES

See also Conference, Settlement

Generally, 296–326, 545–546

Appellate ADR, 595–596

Court-annexed arbitration, 550–559, 644–645
Cases referred, 554
Discovery, 555
Evidence, rules of, 555
Powers of arbitrators, 555

INDEX 1021

COURT-ANNEXED ADR PROCESSES
—Cont'd
Court-annexed arbitration—Cont'd
Sanctions for failure to participate, 555–557
Satisfaction rate in, 552–554, 558–559
Selection of arbitrators, 554–555
Settlement rate, 557–559
Early neutral evaluation, 549–550
Judicial settlement conference, 548–549
Mediation, 547–548
Mini-trial
Generally, 559–564
Confidentiality, 563
Discovery limitation, 560–561
Neutral advisor, 559–560
Procedural formality, 545–546
Settlement promotion, relation to, 333
Summary jury trial, 564–578
Confidentiality, 570–571
Description, 565–568
Mandatory participation, 572–578
Settlement rate, 569
Summarization technique, 568–570
Summoning jurors, 571

COURT-ANNEXED ARBITRATION, see Court-annexed ADR Processes, Court-annexed arbitration

COURTS
See also Adjudication; Litigation
"Court-ness," 22–32
Rabbinical courts, 606–611
Role of, 5–11, 26–32

CREATING VALUE, see also Negotiation, creating value

CULTURE
See also Negotiation, cultural aspects
Conceptual framework, 911–917
Cultural characteristics, 911–917
Cultural sensitivity, 917–921
Cultural country studies, Japan and Mexico, 921–923
Definition, 907–909
Difficulties in identifying, 909–911
Impact of culture on arbitration clauses, 949–950
International mediation, 929
Interpreters and translators, 925–926
Researching culture, 926–927

DAMAGES
Prejudgment interest, 108
Present value, 108

DISCOVERY
In arbitration, 862–870
In court-annexed arbitration, 555

DISCOVERY—Cont'd
In international arbitration, 950
In mediation, 465
In negotiation, 288–296

DISPUTES
See also Arbitration, Mediation
Community, 332–333
Consumer, arbitration of, 642–653, 706–710, 781–782, 882–883
Discrimination, 8–9, 787–824
Family law, 330–331
Incidence of, 2–11
Labor, 329–330, 633–642, 718, 762–763, 787–791, 838–839, 849, 884–886
Narrowing by lawyers, 97–99
Public policy, 335–336

DISTRIBUTIVE/INTEGRATIVE BARGAINING, see Negotiation

DIVORCE MEDIATION, 330–331, 406–414, 440–442
See also Disputes, Family law; Mediation, Family law disputes

EARLY NEUTRAL EVALUATION, see Court-annexed ADR Processes, Early neutral evaluation

EMOTION, see Negotiation, Emotion

EMPATHY, 180–182, 185–189

ETHICAL ISSUES
Alternatives to existing Model Rules of Professional Conduct, 229–236
In arbitration, 842–854
In mediation, 532–544
In negotiation, current professional obligations, 156–157, 210–229

EVIDENTIARY EXCLUSION, see Confidentiality; Rule 408, Federal Rules of Evidence; Arbitration, Evidence

EXPECTED VALUE, see Litigation, Analysis

FAMILY LAW DISPUTES, see Child Custody; Disputes; Mediation

FEDERAL ARBITRATION ACT (FAA), 655–670, 674–684, 687–688, 696, 718, 730–731, 746–756, 842–846, 862–863

FEDERAL INSECTICIDE, FUNGICIDE, AND RODENTICIDE ACT (FIFRA), 877–881

FEDERAL MEDIATION AND CONCILIATION SERVICE (FMCS), 329, 476–477

FEE-SHIFTING, 270–279

1022 INDEX

FISHER, ROGER, 81, 109–110, 118–119, 125, 126–128, 133–134, 184–185, 243–244, 334

FISS, OWEN, 33–40, 44–48, 68

FREUND, JAMES G., 387–400

FULLER, LON, 22–26, 31–32, 68–69, 338, 376, 601–602, 618, 893–898

GOOD FAITH, see Negotiation, Good faith

ICC (INTERNATIONAL CHAMBER OF COMMERCE), 627–628, 633, 709, 777, 838, 851, 929, 939, 944–945,

ICSID (INTERNATIONAL CENTER FOR THE SETTLEMENT OF INVESTMENT DISPUTES), 629–630, 633

INFORMATION, see Discovery; Mediation; Mini-trial, Exchange of information; Negotiation, Information

INTEGRATIVE BARGAINING, see Negotiation, Distributive/integrative bargaining

INTER-AMERICAN CONVENTION ON INTERNATIONAL COMMERCIAL ARBITRATION, 629, 1002–1005

INTERNATIONAL ARBITRATION, see Arbitration, International commercial

INTERNATIONAL MEDIATION, see Mediation, International disputes

JOINT DEFENSE AGREEMENTS, 228

JUDICIAL ARBITRATION & MEDIATION SERVICES, INC. (JAMS), 625, 643

JUDICIAL REVIEW, see Arbitration, Judicial supervision and review

LAWYERS
Arbitration, 603–604, 625, 837, 855–857
Choice of process, 5–7, 49–77
Ethics, 210–245
Fees, 55–68
Malpractice, 245–254
Mediation, 431–461
Negotiation, 97–102, 153–157
Sanctions for improper conduct, 260–270
Skills, 855–857

LISTENING, 180–189

LITIGATION
See also Adjudication; Courts
Adjudication, distinguished from, 15
Analysis, 100–109
Cross-border litigation, 928, 936, 938–940, 952–953
Dimensions of, 11–15
International adjudicatory options, 938–940
Judicial process,
Case for, 33–44

LITIGATION—Cont'd
Limits of, 15–33
Lincoln on, 15–16
In public law disputes, 32–33, 39–40

MED-ARB, 630–631, 892–900
International settlement and arbitration, 952–958

MEDIATION
Generally, 327–544
Agreement,
Compliance rates, 372–375
Settlement agreements, enforceability of, 514–532
To mediate, 370–371
Brainstorming, 360–361
Caucus (private position), 348, 444–451
Classical model, 337–375
Information gathering, 347–358
Introductory remarks of mediator, 340–345
Problem identification, 349–358
Problem solving, 358–370
Statement of problem by parties, 345–347
Writing of agreement, 370–377
Community disputes, 330–333
Dispute Resolution Centers (DRC), 330–333, 515
Conciliation, distinguished from, 527–528, 529–530
Confidentiality, 461–514
Contractual agreement, 510–514
Discovery limitations, 465
Evidentiary exclusion for compromise discussions (Rule 408), 463–466
Judicially-created privilege, 467–481
Statutory privilege, 481–510
Cooperative problem solving, 334
Court-annexed, 547–548
Cybermediation, 337
Discovery, 334–335
Empowering process, 423–431
Evaluative mediation, 335, 415–422
Facilitative, 335, 337–340, 415–422
Fairness of settlements, 382–383, 406–407
Family law disputes, 330–331
Feminist critique, 406–414
Grievance mediation, see Disputes, Labor
History of, 327–337
Impasse, 451
International Disputes, 929–938
Combined with arbitration, 952–958
Convening problems, 932–934
Confidentiality, 935–936
Enforcing settlement agreements, 936–938
Institutional or ad hoc administration, 941–942
Rules, 942–943
Selecting a mediator, 934–935
Style of mediation, 935
Labor disputes, 329–330
Federal Mediation and Conciliation Service (FMCS), see separate entry
Grievance mediation, 330

MEDIATION—Cont'd
Law, role of, 362–370
Lawyers, role of, 431–461
  Attorney as mediator, 452–461
  Duty to advise concerning ADR, 431–433
  Mediation representation, 436–451
  Post-mediation representation, 452–461
  Pre-mediation advice and preparation, 433–436
Mandatory mediation, 315–326, 333, 411, 547, 555–557, 572–578
Med-arb, see Med–Arb
Mediator
  Credentials and licensing, 532–534
  Generating options, 358–362
  Immunity, 539–544
  Lawyer-mediators, 432–461
  Liability, 539–544
  Role of, 375–431
  Strategies, 349–362, 375–406
  Styles, approaches and orientation, 349–370, 380–402, 414–431
Neighborhood justice centers, 332, 516
Power imbalances, 405–414
Privilege, see Mediation, Confidentiality
Professional conduct regulation, 532–544
Sources of, 327–337
Transformative mediation, 423–431
Ventilation, 346
Voluntariness of, 370–376

MEDICAL MALPRACTICE
Arbitration of, 644–650, 699–706
Negotiation example, 80–86

MINI-TRIAL, see Court-annexed ADR Processes, mini-trial

MISREPRESENTATION, 142–144, 202–229

NEGOTIATION
  See also Best Alternative to Negotiated Agreement; Settlement
  Generally, 78–326
Anchoring effects, 123, 158–160
Availability heuristic, 159–160
Computer-assisted, 124–125, 133
Confidentiality, 279–288
Contingent contracts, 91–93
Creating value, 83–96
Cultural aspects, 189–201
Detecting lies, 241–242
Distributive/integrative bargaining, 81–86
Efficiency, 84
Emotion, 173–178
Empathy, 180–182, 185–189

NEGOTIATION—Cont'd
Endowment effects, 169–170
Expected value analysis, 102–103
Fairness and norms, 133–142, 215–217
First offer problem, 119–125
Fixed pie bias, 132–133
Focal points, 137
Fraud, 202–210
Gender, 189–201
Good faith, 206–209, 232–234
Information, the role of, 96–109
Interests, 88–89, 97–100, 126–130
Malpractice, 245–254
Misrepresentation, 142–144, 202–229, 242–245
Multiple issues, 83–86
Non-disclosure, 213–215, 217–222
Overconfidence, 162–164, 170–171
Positional bargaining, 109–119
Post-settlement settlement, 130–131
Problem solving, 126–142, 153–157
Race in, 189–201
Reactive devaluation, 167–168, 171–173
Reservation value, 81
Risk preferences, 90, 104, 106–107
Strategy, 109–157
Style, 179–189
Tactics,
  Commitment, 114–118
  Competitive, 110–114, 117–118
Two tables approach, 131
Ultimatum games, 135, 140–141

NEW YORK CONVENTION ON INTERNATIONAL COMMERCIAL ARBITRATION, see United Nations Convention on the Recognition and Enforcement of Foreign Arbitral Awards

NORTH AMERICAN FREE TRADE AGREEMENT (NAFTA), 958–962

OPEN MEETINGS AND RECORDS ACTS, effect on confidentiality, 491–492

"POLYCENTRICITY," 22–26, 31–32, 617–618, 896–897

PREJUDGMENT INTEREST, 108

PRISONERS' DILEMMA, 145–153

PRIVATE ORDERING, 18–20, 601–602, 834–835

PROFESSIONAL CONDUCT, MODEL RULES OF, see American Bar Association

INDEX

PSYCHOLOGY
See also Negotiation
Generally, 157–173
Anchoring effects, 123, 158–160
Availability heuristic, 159–160
Endowment effects, 169–170
Fixed pie bias, 132–133
Overconfidence, 162–164, 170–171
Prospect theory, 164–166, 169
"Psychological price tag" of litigation practice, 20–22
Reactive devaluation, 167–168, 171–173

PUBLIC POLICY DISPUTES
Generally, 335–336

PUBLIC VALUES
In adjudication, 33–44
In arbitration, 612–613, 742–745, 761–765, 777–783, 787–822, 830–831, 884–886
PUT CASE, 387–399

RELATIONS, CONTINUING, 74–75, 145–153, 330–331, 601, 605, 621–626

"RENT–A–JUDGE," 643, 900–905

RISK, see Negotiation, risk preferences

RULE 11, FEDERAL RULES OF CIVIL PROCEDURE, 260–270, 963–964

RULE 11(e), FEDERAL RULES OF CRIMINAL PROCEDURE, 971

RULE 16, FEDERAL RULES OF CIVIL PROCEDURE, 48, 296–297, 965–967

RULE 26, FEDERAL RULES OF CIVIL PROCEDURE, 288–296, 465

RULE 45, FEDERAL RULES OF CIVIL PROCEDURE, 868–869, 967–969

RULE 68, FEDERAL RULES OF CIVIL PROCEDURE, 270–279, 969–970

RULE 81, FEDERAL RULES OF CIVIL PROCEDURE, 682–683

RULE 408, FEDERAL RULES OF EVIDENCE, 279–288, 463–466, 473, 485–486, 494, 860–861, 973

RULE 409, FEDERAL RULES OF EVIDENCE, 973

RULE 410, FEDERAL RULES OF EVIDENCE, 973–974

RULE 501, FEDERAL RULES OF EVIDENCE, 467

SETTLEMENT
See also Best Alternative to Negotiated Agreement; Mediation; Negotiation

SETTLEMENT—Cont'd
Court-annexed settlement processes, see Court-annexed ADR Processes
Judicial promotion of, 296–326
Stability of, 254–259

"SHADOW OF THE LAW", see Bargaining

SUMMARY JURY TRIAL, see Court-annexed ADR Processes, summary jury trial

SUMMARIZATION TECHNIQUE, see Court-annexed ADR Processes, Summary jury trial

SYSTEMS DESIGN, 336

UNIFORM MEDIATION ACT, 483, 493, 535

UNITED NATIONS CONVENTION ON THE RECOGNITION AND ENFORCEMENT OF FOREIGN ARBITRAL AWARDS, 626–627, 629, 765, 766–777, 875–876, 950–952, 996–1001

UNITED STATES ARBITRATION ACT, see Federal Arbitration Act

VETERANS ADMINISTRATION (VA), 55–69

WORLD TRADE ORGANIZATION (WTO), 958–959, 961–962

ZERO-SUM BARGAINING, see Negotiation

†